MᶜDOUGALL'S
ETYMOLOGICAL
AND
BIOGRAPHICAL
DICTIONARY

WITH
AIDS TO
PRONUNCIATION
AND
NUMEROUS
APPENDICES

MᶜDOUGALL'S
EDUCATIONAL
COY LTD
30 ROYAL TERRACE, EDINBURGH

FOREWORD.

This Dictionary, while of necessarily restricted size, is nevertheless sufficiently comprehensive for the requirements of the general reader.

The Dictionary is pronouncing as well as etymological, and great pains have been taken to make it as accurate in pronunciation, etymology, and in meaning as possible. For this purpose the New English Dictionary has been taken as a guide, although other standard authorities have also been consulted.

Up-to-date additions to vocabulary and scientific terms now mingling in the main stream of our language have been included, while many interesting and useful appendices have been added, notably biographical sections on Artists, Composers, Scientists, Explorers, and English Authors.

In short, the general purpose kept in view has been to make the book as concise and clear, yet comprehensive, accurate, and instructive, as possible.

The following points should be noted :—

1. When a word may be used as more than one part of speech, the meanings applicable to one of these are separated from those applicable to another by a semicolon. *E.g.*, **As-sent'**, agree to ; act of agreeing to.

2. Letters *without influence* on the pronunciation of words liable to be wrongly spoken by virtue of their insertion are printed in italics, as in **Beau'ty**. But letters which, though not themselves sounded, influence the pronunciation of other letters, as **gh** in **Right**, **e** in **Case**, are not so marked.

3. Common combinations of letters anomalously sounded as **tion** in **Mo'tion**, etc., are not specially marked.

4. Less common anomalies are noted, as **Be-lov′ed** $(o = \breve{u})$; **Ra′ti-o** $(t = sh)$; **Lieu-ten′ant** $(ieu = ef)$; **Pae′an** $(ae = ee)$; **Gimp** $(g \text{ hard})$; **Cam′bric** $(a = ai)$.

5. Quite anomalous pronunciations are given more fully in brackets after the word, as **Corps** $(core)$; **Cha-grin′** $(sha\text{-}green')$; **Ae′gis** $(ee'jis)$.

6. Indications of the pronunciation of vowels are to be understood thus :—ai (like a in mate); $\breve{a}$ (like a in fat); ah (like a in father); aw (like aw in law); ee (like ee in seen); $\breve{e}$ (like e in get); $\breve{i}$ (like i in pin); $\bar{i}$ (like i in mine); $\breve{o}$ (like o in dot); $\bar{o}$ (like o in hole); oo (like oo in poor); ow (like ow in now); $\breve{u}$ (like u in nut); $\bar{u}$ (like u in pure).

7. In certain cases where new words are formed by prefixes, some such words are given in lists without meanings.

8. Etymology is given in square brackets after the word. This, as a rule, helps to clarify and fix the meaning which follows. Where advisable long vowels in Latin and Greek are marked thus : *habēre, oidē*.

CONTENTS.

KEY TO ABBREVIATIONS.

abbr., abbrev., abbreviation
acc., accusative
adj., adjective
A.F., Anglo-French
A.Norm., Anglo-Norman
Amer.-Ind., American-Indian
Ang., Anglian
app., apparently
Arab., Arabic
arch., archaic
Ary., Aryan
assim., assimilate, assimilated
Assyr., Assyrian
aug., augmentative

Boh., Bohemian
Braz., Brazilian
Bret., Breton

c., L. *circa*=about
cc., centuries
cf., compare
Chin., Chinese
cogn., cognate
coll., collectively
colloq., colloquial
com., common
comb., combined, combination, etc.
comp., compound
compar., comparative
conn., connected
contr., contraction
Corn., Cornish
corr., corruption

Dan., Danish
deriv., derivative
dial., dialectic
dim., diminutive
Du., Dutch
dub., dubious

E., Eng., } English
eccl., ecclesiastical
Egypt., Egyptian
erron., erroneously
esp., especially
etym., etymology
exc., except

F., French
fam., familiar
fem., feminine
fl., flourished
fr., from
freq., frequent., } frequentative
Fl., Flem., } Flemish

Fries., Frisian

Gael., Gaelic
gen., genitive
geol., geological
G., Ger., } (modern) German
Gk., Greek
Goth., Gothic

Heb., Hebrew
Hind., { Hindi, Hindustani
hist., history
Hung., Hungarian

Icel., Icelandic
imit., imitative
imper., imperative
Ind., India, Indian
inf., infinitive
interj., interjection
intr., intransitive
Ir., Irish
It., Italian

Jap., Japanese

L., Latin
L.G., Low German
late L., } late Latin
L.L.,
low L., low Latin
lit., literal, -ly

masc., masculine
milit., military
M.beforeDan., Du., E., F., L., etc., } middle or mediæval
M.H.G., Middle High German
mod., modern
modif., modification

n., noun
neg., negative
N., north, northern
N.B., *nota bene* (note well)
N.F., Norman-French
neut., neuter
Norm., Norman
Northumb., Northumbrian
Norw., Norwegian

o., old
O.E., Old English
O.H.G., Old High German
O.N., Old Norse
O.N.F., Old Norman-French
obs., obsol., } obsolete
orig., origin, -ally

p.p., past participle
part., participle
per., person
perh., perhaps
Pers., Persian
Peruv., Peruvian
pl., plural
Pol., Polish
Polynes., Polynesian
pop., popular
Port., Portuguese
poss., possibly
pr. p., present participle
prec., preceding
pres., present
prob., probably
pron., pronunciation
Prov., Provençal
prov., provincial

q.v., Latin *quod vide*= which see

redup., reduplicate
rel., related
R. and Rom., Roman, Romance

Russ., Russian

Scand., Scandinavian
Sc., Scot., } Scottish
Serv., Servian
sing., singular
Skr., Sanskrit
Sp., Span., } Spanish
S.A.Du., South African-Dutch
suf., suffix
sup., supine
superl., superlative
Swed., Swedish

Teut., Teutonic
tr., transitive
Turk., Turkish
transl., translation

uncert., uncertain
ult., ultimately
U.S.A., United States of America

usu., usual, -ly

var., variant, various
vb., verb
voc., vocative

W., Welsh
w., with
? origin unknown or obscure

Note.—An asterisk (*) preceding a word denotes that while no record of such a form remains that form is assumed to have existed.

ETYMOLOGICAL
AND BIOGRAPHICAL DICTIONARY

A

A-back′ [a-, on, and Back], backward, by surprise.

Ab′a-cus [L. abacus; Gk. abax (abac-os), tablet], calculating frame with balls on wires.

A-baft′ [a-, on, be, by; O.E. æftan, behind], towards the stern, behind.

A-ban′don [O.F. abandoner, to let go; à bandon, at liberty], to leave, give up wholly. Aban′doned, Aban′donment.

A-base′ [O.F. abaissier, to lower; Late L. ad, to, bassus, thick, short], to bring low.

A-bash′ [O.F. esbaïr, to astound], to make ashamed.

A-bate′ [L. ad, to, batuere, to beat], to become less, to lessen. Abate′ment.

A-bat-toir′ (a-ba-twarr′) [F.], public slaughter-house.

Ab′bey [O.F. abaïe], a convent or monastery.

Ab′bot, fem. Ab′bess [Syriac Abbā, father], the head of an abbey. [shorten.

Ab-bre′vi-ate [L. ad, to, brevis, short], to Ab-bre′vi-a′tion, shortening.

Ab′di-cate [L. ab, from, dicāre, to declare], to resign (high office). Abdica′tion.

Ab-do′men [L. abdōmen], lower part of the body or trunk. Abdom′inal.

Ab-duct′ [L. ab, from, ducěre (p.p. ductus), to lead], kidnap; take away by force or fraud. Abduc′tion.

A-bed′ [a-, on or in, and Bed], in bed.

Ab-er-ra′tion [L. ab, away, errāre (p.p. er-rātus), to wander], a wandering, delusion.

A-bet′ [O.F. à, to, and beter, to bait (a bear), to hound on], to help (to do wrong).

A-bet′ter, or A-bet′tor, one who abets.

A-bey′ance [O.F. abeance, waiting], state of being held over.

Ab-hor′ [L. ab, from, horrēre, to dread], to dislike greatly.

Ab-hor′rence, great dislike. Abhor′rent.

A-bide′ [O.E. abidan, to wait], to dwell, to wait for, suffer.

A-bil′i-ty, power to do, cleverness.

Ab′ject [L. ab, from, jacere (p.p. in compounds -jectus), to throw], degraded, mean-spirited. Abjec′tion.

Ab-jure′ [L. ab, from, jurāre, to swear], to swear to give up, to renounce.

Ab′lat-ive [L. ab, from, lātus, p.p. of ferre, to carry], case in Latin which expresses agent, instrument, source.

A-blaze′ [a-, on, and Blaze], in a blaze.

A′ble [L. habilis, handy, skilful], having power, clever.

Ab-lu′tion [L. ab, from, luere, to wash], bodily washing.

Ab′ne-gate [L. ab, from, negāre (p.p. negātus), to deny], to deny, to reject. Abnega′tion.

Ab-nor′mal [L. ab, from, norma, a rule], not according to rule, unusual. Abnor′mally.

A-board′ [a-, on, and Board], on a ship or boat.

A-bode′ [see Abide], place where one lives.

A-bol′ish [L. abolescere, to be growing out of use, to be doing away with], to do away with.

A-bo-li′tion, act of abolishing.

A-bom′i-na-ble [L. ab, from, ōmen, an omen], very hateful.

A-bom′i-nate, dislike extremely.

A-bom-i-na′tion, great dislike, hateful thing.

Ab-o-ri′gi-nal, earliest in a country.

Ab-o-ri′gi-nes [L. ab, from, orīgo (orīgǐn-is), beginning], first natives of a country.

A-bor′tive [L. ab, away, orīrī (p.p. ortus), to begin], coming to nothing. Abor′tion.

A-bound′ [L. abundāre, overflow, ab, away, unda, a wave], be or have in plenty.

A-bout′ [O.E. onbūtan, on-, on, be, by, and útan, outward], round the outside, near (in number, etc.), in connexion with.

A-bove′ [O.E. a-, on, be, by, ufan, upward], overhead, higher than.

A-brade′ [L. ab, from, rādere (p.p. rāsus), to scrape], rub off (a piece of skin, etc.).

A-bra′sion (si=zh), a rubbing off.

A-breast′ [a-, on, and Breast], side by side.

A-bridge′ [O.F. abregier, abreger; L. abbrevi-āre, to shorten, fr. ad, to, brevis, short], A-bridg′ment, shortened form. [shorten.

A-broad′ [a-, on, and Broad], in foreign lands.

Ab′ro-gate [L. ab, away, rogāre (p.p. rogātus), to ask, propose a law], cancel, repeal.

Ab-rupt′ [L. ab, off, rumpere (p.p. ruptus), to break], as if broken off, steep, sudden.

Abs′cess [L. abs, away, cēdere (sup. cessum), to go], gathering of matter in the body.

Ab-scond′ [L. abs, away, and condere, to hide], depart secretly to escape responsibility.

Ab′sence, state of being away.

Ab′sent [L. absens (absentis), pr.p. of abesse, to be away; ab, away, esse, to be], away, not present.

Ab-sent′, take or keep (oneself) away.

Ab-sen-tee′, one who is absent.

Ab′so-lute [L. ab, from, and solvěre (p.p. solūtus), to loosen], without limit or control,

A *

1

Ab-so-lu′tion, a setting free from sin.

Ab-solve′ [see Absolute], pronounce free from.

Ab-sorb′ [L. *ab*, from, *sorbēre*, to suck], suck up, engage wholly.

Ab-sorp′tion, act of absorbing ; state of being absorbed.

Ab-sorb′ent, sucking up ; that which sucks up.   [from.

Ab-stain′ [L. *abs*, from, *tenēre*, to hold], keep

Ab-sten′tion, act of keeping from.

Ab-stain′er, one who keeps from alcohol.

Ab-ste′mi-ous [L. *abs*, from, and *temētum*, strong drink], sparing in food and drink.

Ab′sti-nence, practice or state of abstaining.

Ab-stract′ [L. *abs*, away, *trahere*(p.p. *tractus*), to draw], withdraw, summarize.

Ab′stract, apart from objects; abridgment.

Ab-strac′tion, taking away, absence of mind.

Ab-struse′ [L. *abs*, away, *trūdere* (p.p. *trūsus*), to thrust], hard to understand.

Ab-surd′ [L. *ab*, utterly, *surdus*, deaf, stupid], against reason.   **Absurd′ly, Absurd′ity.**

A-bun′dance [see Abound], plenty.

A-buse′ (*s=z*) [L. *ab*, away, *ūti* (p.p. *ūsus*), to use], use wrongly, treat badly.

A-buse′, bad treatment, insulting words.

A-bu′sive, full of abuse.

A-but′ [O.F. *abouter*, to place end to end, *abuter*, to touch with one end (*à*, to, *bout*, *but*, an end), border upon. **Abut′ting, Abut′ment.**

A-byss′ [Gk. *abyssos*, bottomless ; *a*, without, *byssos*, depth], great chasm or depth.

Abys′mal, bottomless.

A-ca′ci-a (*a-kai′shi-a*) [Gk. *acācia*, perh. fr. *acē*, a point], class of trees of Mimosa tribe.

A-cad′e-my [Gk. *Acadēmeia*, a grove where Plato taught], school, society for advancement of science or art. **Academ′ic, Academ′ical.**

Ac-cede′ [L. *ad*, to, *cēdere* (sup. *cessum*), to go], agree, consent.

Ac-cel′er-ate [L. *ad*, to, *celer*, swift], hasten.

Ac′cent [L. *ad*, to, *canere* (p.p. *cantus*), to sing], tone of voice, stress on a syllable.

Ac-cent′, mark with accent, to stress.   [tion.

Ac-cen′tu-ate, bring out clearly. **Accentua′-**

Ac-cept′ [L. *ad*, to, and *capēre* (p.p. *captus*)—in compounds, *-ceptus*), to take], take what is offered.

Ac-cep′ta-ble, pleasing.   [ness.

Ac-cep′tance, act of accepting, acceptable-

Ac-cep-ta′tion, usual meaning of a word.

Ac-cess′ (or **Ac′cess**) [see Accede], approach, increase.

Ac-ces′sa-ry, Ac-ces′so-ry (or **Ac′-**), secondary ; helper (in wrong).

Ac-ces′si-ble, easy of approach.   [crease.

Ac-ces′sion (*ak-sesh′on*), a coming to, in-

Ac′ci-dence [see Accident], part of grammar which treats of inflections of words.

Ac′ci-dent [L. *accidere*, fall upon ; *ad*, to, *cādēre*, fall], unexpected event, mishap.

Ac-ci-den′tal, by chance.

Ac-claim′ [L. *ad*, to, *clāmāre*, to shout], cry out, shout, hail as.

Ac-cla-ma′tion, shouts of approval.

Ac-cli′ma-tize, Ac′clim-ate (American) [F. *à*, to, *climat*, climate], accustom to a climate.   [slope.

Ac-cliv′i-ty [L. *ad*, to, *clīvus*, a slope], upward

Ac-col-ade′ [L. *ad*, to, *collum*, neck], sign of bestowal of knighthood, as stroke on shoulder with flat of sword, kiss, etc.

Ac-com′mo-date [L. *ad*, to, *commodus*, fit], suit, furnish with something needed, lodge.

Ac-com-mo-da′tion, that which supplies a want, lodging, loan.

Ac-com′pa-ni-ment, that which accompanies.

Ac-com′pan-ist, one who accompanies a singer on an instrument.

Ac-com′pa-ny (*o=u*) [F. *accompagner*, to attend ; see Company], go with.

Ac-com′plice (*ice=iss*) [for *a complice* ; F. *complice* ; L. *com-*, with, *plicāre*, to fold], partner in crime.

Ac-com′plish [L. *ad*, to, *com-*, together, *plēre*, to fill], perform, complete.

Ac-com′plish-ment, performance, part of education meant to polish or perfect.

Ac-cord′ [L. *ad*, to, *cor* (*cordis*), the heart], agreement ; agree.   **Accord′ance.**

Ac-cord′ing-ly, because of that, therefore.

Ac-cor′di-on [It. and L.L. *accordāre*, to accord, attune], small, keyed musical instrument.

Ac-cost′ [Late L. *accostāre*, to come beside; L. *ad*, to, and *costa*, a rib, a side], speak to, address.

Ac-count′ [L. *ad*, to, *computāre*, to calculate; see Compute], a reckoning, story of events, give a reason.

Ac-count′a-ble, answerable.

Ac-count′ant, one who examines accounts.

Ac-cou′tre-ments (*ou=oo*) [M.F. *accoustrer*, to dress], military dress and arms.

Ac-cred′it [L. *ad*, to, *crēdere*, to entrust], give letters of authority.

Ac-cre′tion [L. *ad*, to, *crescere* (p.p. *crētus*), to grow], a growth to.

Ac-crue′, [L. *ad*, to, *crescere*, to grow], be added as increase.

Ac-cu′mu-late [L. *ad*, to, fr. *cumulare*, to heap up, *cumulus*, a heap], heap up, gather. **Accumula′tion.**

Ac′cu-ra-cy, exactness, correctness.

Ac′cu-rate [L. *ad*, to, *cūra*, care], correct.

Ac-curs′ed [O.E. *a-* (intensive), and *cursian*, to curse], cursed, doomed.

Ac-cu-sa′tion, act of accusing, that of which one is accused, charge.

Ac-cu′sa-tive, a noun case (in English denoting the object).

Ac-cuse′ (*s=z*) [L. *ad*, to, *causa*, a cause (lawsuit)], charge with an offence.

Ac-cus′tom [O.F. *acostumer* ; L. *ad*, to, *con-suetūdo* (*-tūdinis*), custom], make used to.

Ace [L. *as*, unity], the one on dice and cards.

A-cerb′i-ty [L. *acerbus*, bitter], sourness, bitterness.   [vinegar.

A-cet′ic [L. *acetum*, vinegar], relating to

A-cet′y-lene [see Acetic], colourless gas, burning with bright flame.

Ache (*ake*) [O.E. *œce*, a pain], be in pain.

A-chieve' [F. *achever*; *à* (L. *ad*), to, *chef* (L. *caput*), a head, *venir* (L. *venīre*), to come], get by effort, bring to an end. **Achieve'-ment.**

A'cid [L. *acidus*, sour], sour, sour substance.

A-cid'i-ty, sourness.

A-cid'u-late [L. *acidulus*, dim. of *acidus*, sour], make slightly sour. **Acidula'tion.**

Ac-*k*nowl'edge (ŏ) [*a*, on, and **Knowledge**], to own knowledge of, confess, reward.

Ac-know'ledg-ment, act of acknowledging.

Ac'me [Gk. *acmē*, a point], highest point.

A'co-lyte [Gk. *acolouthos*, an attendant], one who attends or waits upon a priest.

Ac'o-nite [Gk. *aconiton*, monkshood], poisonous herb, monkshood.

A'corn [O.E. *æcern* (orig. fruit of the field); *æcer*, field], fruit of the oak. [sounds.

A-cous'tics [Gk. *acouein*, to hear], science of

Ac-quaint' [L. *ad*, to, *cognoscere* (p.p. *cognitus*), to know], make (one) know.

Ac-quaint'ance, knowledge, person whom one knows. **Acquaint'anceship.**

Ac-qui-es'ce [L. *ad*, to, *quiescere*, to rest], accept or consent silently. **Acquies'cence.**

Ac-quire' [L. *acquīrere* (p.p. *acquīsītus*); *ad*, to, *quærere*, to seek], get as one's own.

Ac-quire'ment, thing acquired.

Ac-qui-si'tion [L. *acquisitio*; see **Acquire**], acquirement.

Ac-quis'i-tive (*s*=*z*), eager to acquire.

Ac-quit' [L. *ad*, to, *quies* (*quiētis*), rest], set free from a charge, conduct oneself.

Ac-quit'-tal, a setting free from a charge.

A'cre (*cre*=*ker*) [O.E. *æcer*, a field. Cf. L. *ager*, a field], 4840 square yards of land.

A'cre-age, whole number of acres.

Ac'rid [L. *ācer* (*āc-ris*), bitter, sharp], harsh and bitter.

Ac'ri-mo-ny [L. *ācrimōnia*; *ācer*, sharp], bitterness of temper. **Acrimon'ious.**

Ac'ro-bat [Gk. *acrobatos*, walking on tiptoe, *acros*, topmost; *bainein*, to go], ropedancer, tumbler. **Acrobat'ic.**

A-crop'o-lis [Gk. *acros*, topmost, *polis*, a city], fortress in a Greek city.

A-cross' [*a*-, on, and **Cross**], in form of a cross, from side to side, on the other side (of).

A-cros'tic [Gk. *acrostichos*; *acros*, topmost, first, *stichos*, a row], verse or other composition in which initial, and sometimes middle and final, letters of the lines form a word. [done.

Act [L. *agere* (p.p. *actus*), to do], do, thing

Ac'tion, deed, battle, suit (at law).

Ac'tive [see **Act**], quick, brisk, that acts.

Ac-tiv'i-ty, state of being active.

Ac'tor, fem. Ac'-tress, stage-player.

Ac'tu-al [F. *actuel*; L. *actus*, done], real.

Ac'tu-a-ry [L. *actuārius*; *agere* (p.p. *actus*), to do], registrar or clerk, one who calculates probabilities for an insurance company, etc. **Actua'rial.**

Ac'tu-ate [see **Act**], move or rouse to action.

A-cu'men [L. *acūmen*; *acuere*, to sharpen], sharp insight.

A-cute' [L. *acūtus* (p.p. of *acuĕre*, to sharpen)], sharp.

Ad'age [L. *adāgium*; *ad*, to, *āgium*, a saying], old saying, proverb.

Ad'a-mant [Gk. *adamas*, a very hard stone], very hard substance. **Adaman'tine.**

A-dapt' [L. *ad*, to, *aptus*, fit], to fit, make suitable.

A-dap-ta'tion [see **Adapt**], act of adapting, adapted form.

Add [L. *ad*, to, *dare*, to put], join one thing to another.

Ad-den'dum [L. gerundive of *addere*, to put], thing to be added. [serpent.

Add'er [O.E. *neædre*, a snake], poisonous

Ad-dict' [L. *ad*, to, and *dīcere* (p.p. *dictus*), to say], give (oneself) up to, as a habit.

Ad-di'tion, adding things together, something added on.

Ad-di'tion-al, added on. [added.

Ad'dle [O.E. *adela*, mud], become rotten, muddle; rotten, vain.

Ad-dress' [F. *adresser*; *à*, to, *dresser*, to dress, to direct], speak or write to; a speech, name of a place where a person lives.

Ad-duce' [L. *ad*, to, *dūcere*, to lead], bring forward.

A-dept' (or Ad'ept) [L. *ad*, to, *aptus*, fit], well-skilled; one well-skilled. [sufficient.

Ad'e-quate [L. *ad*, to, *æquus*, equal], equal to,

Ad-here' [L. *ad*, to, and *hærēre* (p.p. *hæsus*), to stick], stick to.

Ad-he'rence, state of adhering.

Ad-he'rent, sticking; follower. [he'sive.

Ad-he'sion (*si*=*zh*), state of adhering. **Ad-**

Ad-hib'it [L. *ad*, to, and *habēre* (p.p. *habitus*), to have, hold], put on, apply, affix.

A-dieu' [F. *à*, to, *Dieu*, God], farewell.

Ad'i-pose [L. *adeps* (*adi-pis*), fat], fatty.

Ad-ja'cent [L. *ad*, to, *jacēre* (pr.p. *jacens*), to lie], close to.

Ad'jec-tive [L. *adjectīvus*; *ad*, to, *jacēre*, to throw], a word added to a noun to qualify or limit it. **Adjectiv'al.**

Ad-join' [L. *ad*, to, *jungere*, to join], join to, lie next to.

Ad-journ' [L. *ad*, to; Late L. *jurnus*, a day, from L. *diurnus*, daily], put off to another time.

Ad-judge' [O.F. *ajuger*; see **Adjud'icate**], award or decide by judging.

Ad-ju'di-cate [L. *ad*, to, and *judicāre* (p.p. *judicātus*), to judge; *judex*, a judge], sit in judgment, give sentence. **Adjudica'tion.**

Ad'junct [L. *ad*, to, *junctus* (p.p. of *jungere*), to join], person or thing joined to another.

Ad-jure' [L. *ad*, to, *jurāre*, to swear], charge on oath or solemnly.

Ad-just' [F. *adjuster*; now *ajuster*; L. *ad*, to, *juxta*, near], put right, adapt. **Adjust'-ment.**

Ad'ju-tant [L. *adjutāre*, to assist; *ad*, to, *juvāre*, to help], officer who assists a commanding officer; kind of large stork.

Ad-min'is-ter [L. *ad*, to, *minister*, a servant], manage, supply.

Ad-min-is-tra'tion, management, government, the Government.

Ad-min'is-tra-tor, manager, one authorized to manage. **Admin'istrative.**

Ad'mi-ra-ble [L. *admirabilis*; see **Admire**], worthy of admiration.

Ad'mi-ral [O.F. *amiral*; Arab. *amīr-al-(bahr)*, commander of the (sea)], commander of a fleet.

Ad'mi-ral-ty, government department in charge of naval affairs.

Ad-mi-ra'tion, wondering delight.

Ad-mire' [L. *ad*, at, *mīrāri*, to wonder], regard with wonder and delight.

Ad-mis'si-ble, that can be admitted.

Ad-mis'sion, act of admitting, something admitted.

Ad-mit' [L. *ad*, to, *mittere* (p.p. *missus*), to send], allow to enter, grant as true.

Ad-mit'tance, being admitted, permission to enter.

Ad-mix'-ture [*ad*, to, and **Mixture**], a mixing.

Ad-mon'ish [L. *ad*, to, *monēre*, to warn], warn, reprove.

Ad-mo-ni'tion, warning, reproof.

Ad-mon'i-to-ry, warning, reproving.

A-do' (*o=oo*) [Scan. *a*, sign of the infinitive, and **Do**], stir, fuss.

A-do-les'cence [L. *adolescere*, to grow up (pr.p. *adolescens*)], youth, the age after childhood. **Adoles'cent.**

A-dopt' [L. *ad*, to, *optāre*, to choose], take for one's own (especially the child of another).

A-do-ra'tion, worship, deep admiration.

A-dore' [L. *ad*, to, *ōrāre*, to pray; *ōs* (gen. *ōris*), mouth], to worship, love extremely.

A-dorn' [L. *ad*, to, *ornāre*, to adorn], beautify (with dress, etc.).

A-drift' [*a-*, on, and **Drift**], floating away without control. [skilful.

A-droit' [F. *à*, to, *droit*, right], clever-handed.

Ad-u-la'tion [L. *adulāri* (p.p. *adulātus*), to flatter], too much praise.

A-dult' [L. *adultus* (p.p. of *adolescere*), to grow up], grown-up person.

A-dul'ter-ate [L. *adulterāre* (p.p. *adulterātus*), to corrupt], mix with something of less value. **Adultera'tion.**

Ad'um-brate [L. *ad*, to, *umbra*, shade], represent in outline, foreshadow.

Ad-vance' [O.F. *avancer*, to go forward; L. *ab*, from, *ante*, before], go or put forward; progress; loan of money.

Ad-van'tage [F. *avantage*, see **Advance**], something in a person's favour.

Ad-van-ta'geous, of advantage, profitable.

Ad'vent [L. *ad*, to, *venīre* (sup. *ventum*), to come], arrival, the four weeks before Christmas.

Ad-ven-ti'tious [L. *adventīcius*; see **Advent**], added casually from without.

Ad-ven'ture [L. *adventūrus*, about to happen; *ad*, to, *venīre*, to come], bold undertaking.

Ad-ven'tu-rous, ready for adventure.

Ad'verb [L. *ad*, to, *verbum*, a word], a word that modifies a verb, adjective, etc. or other adverb. **Adverb'ial.**

Ad'ver-sa-ry, one opposed to another.

Ad'verse [O.F. *avers*; L. *adversus*; see **Advert**], acting against, contrary. **Ad-ver'sative.**

Ad-ver'si-ty, state of misfortune.

Ad-vert' [L. *ad*, to, *vertere* (p.p. *versus*), to turn], turn to.

Ad'ver-tise (*s=z*) [see **Advert**], give public notice. **Advertis'er.**

Ad-ver'tise-ment, public notice.

Ad-vice' [O.F. *avis*, notice; see **Advise**], opinion to be followed.

Ad-vi'sa-ble, proper to be done. **Advis-abil'ity.**

Ad-vise' (*s=z*) [L. *ad*, to, *vidēre* (p.p. *vīsus*), to see], give advice, inform of. **Advis'edly.**

Ad'vo-ca-cy, pleading for, defence.

Ad'vo-cate [L. *ad*, to, *vocāre* (p.p. *vocātus*), to call], one who pleads for another, barrister (in Scotland); uphold.

Adze [O.E. *adesa*, an axe], kind of axe.

Ae'gis (*eéjis*) [Gk. *aigis*], protection.

Æ'on (*eéon*) [Gk. *aiōn*, age], an age of the universe, immeasurable period. [gas.

A'ër-ate [L. *aēr*, air], charge (a liquid) with

A-ë'ri-al [L. *aërius*, fr. *aēr*; Gk. *aēr*, air], belonging to the air; wire for receiving broadcast matter.

A'e-rie, A'e-ry [O.F. *aire*; M.L. *aeria, aerea*, perhaps fr. L. *area*, level ground], nest of a bird of prey.

A'er-o-drome [Gk. *aēr*, air, *dromos*, a course], place for flying machines starting and alighting.

A'er-o-gram [Gk. *aēr*, air, *gramma*, writing], message sent by wireless telegraphy. Cf. **Telegram.**

A'er-o-graph [Gk. *aēr*, air, *graphein*, to write], to send a wireless message. Cf. **Telegraph.**

A'ër-o-lite [Gk. *aēr*, air, *lithos*, a stone], stone which has fallen to earth from outer space.

A'er-o-naut [Gk. *aēr*, air, *nautēs*, a sailor], one who uses a flying machine.

A'er-o-plane [Gk. *aēr*, air; L. *plānus*, flat], flying-machine heavier than air and supported by one or more plane surfaces.

Aes-thet'ics (*aes=ees*) [Gk. *aisthanesthai*, to perceive; *aistheticos*, perceptive], science of the beautiful. **Aesthet'ic.**

A-far' [*a-*, on, and **Far**], at a distance.

Af-fa-bi'li-ty, pleasantness in conversation.

Af'fa-ble [L. *affābalis*, easily spoken to; *ad*, to, *fāri*, to speak], easy to speak to.

Af-fair' [F. *à faire*, to do], business.

Af-fect' [L. *affectāre*, to aim at; *ad*, to, *facere*, to do], act upon, pretend.

Af-fec-ta'tion, unreal display, pretence.

Af-fec'tion, love; diseased state. **Affec'-tionate.**

Af-fi'ance [L. *ad*, to, *fīdes*, faith], promise in marriage.

Af-fi-da'vit [Late L. *affidāvit*, 3rd pers. sing. perfect tense of *affīdāre*, to pledge; L. *ad*, to, *fīdes*, faith], written statement on oath.

Af-fil'i-ate [L. *ad*, to, *fīlius*, a son], connect with a society, etc. **Affilia'tion.**

Af-fin'i-ty [L. *affīnis*, near], close connection.

Af-firm′ [L. *ad*, to, *firmus*, strong], declare as true. **Affirma′tion.**

Af-fir′ma-tive, that which affirms.

Af-fix′ [L. *ad*, to, *figere* (p.p. *fixus*), to fix], fasten to. **Affix′ture.**

Af′fix, addition to the end of a word.

Af-fla′tus [L. *ad*, to, *flāre* (p.p. *flātus*), to blow], inspiration.

Af-flict′ [L. *affligere* (p.p. *afflictus*), to dash], give trouble or pain to.

Af-flic′tion, state of pain or grief.

Af′flu-ence [see **Affluent**], wealth.

Af′flu-ent [L. *ad*, to, *fluere* (pr.p. *fluens, -entis*), to flow], rich; river that flows into another.

Af-ford′ [O.E. *geforthian*, to further], supply, bear (an expense).

Af-for-es-ta′tion [L. *ad*, to, *foresta*, a forest], turning into forest land.

Af-fray′ [O.F. *effrei*; L.L. *ex*, out of: *fridus* (Teut. *fridhu*), peace], fighting in public.

Af-fright′ [O.E. *a-*, intensive, *fyrhtan*, to terrify], frighten; fright.

Af-front′ (*o=u*) [L. *ad*, to, *frons* (*front-is*), forehead], insult openly; an insult.

A-flame′ [*a-*, in, and **Flame**], in flames.

A-float′ [*a-*, on, and **Float**], borne on the water or air; current.

A-foot′ [*a-*, on, and **Foot**], on foot, going on.

A-fore′ [*a-*, on, and **Fore**], in front.

A-fore′said, said or named before.

A-fraid′ [orig. *affrayed*, p.p. of obs. *affray*, to fight], full of fear.

A-fresh′ [*a-*, on, of, and **Fresh**], over again, anew.

Af-ri-kan′der [perh. S. African Du. *Afri-kaander*, fr. Du. *Afrikaner*, an African], South African born of European (esp. Dutch) parents.

Aft [O.E. *æftan*, behind], towards the stern, abaft.

Af′ter [O.E. *æfter* (comparative of *af*, off)], behind, in pursuit of.

Aft′er-math [**After** and *math* (O.E. *mæth*), mowing], second crop.

Aft-er-noon′, between noon and evening.

A-gain′ [O.E. *ongeán*, *ongœng*; *on*, in, *gagn*, opposite], once more, back, moreover, besides.

A-gainst′ [O.E. *ongeán*, again, against], contrary to, facing.

Ag′ate [It. *agata*; Gk. *achatēs* (so named because found near the river Achates in Sicily)], kind of quartz.

Age [O.F. *aage*, age; L. *ætas*, period], period of time, time a person, animal, or thing has lived or existed; grow old.

A′ged, old. [action.

A′gen-cy [see **Agent**], office of an agent,

A-gen′da [L. neut. pl. of gerundive of *agere*, to do], things to be done, notes of matters to be discussed at a meeting.

A′gent [L. *agere* (pr.p. *agens, -entis*), to do], one who acts for another, active power.

Ag-glom-er-a′tion [L. *ad*, to, *glomus* (*glomer-is*), a heap], mass, heap.

Ag-glu′tin-ate [L. *ad*, to, *glūten* (*glūtin-is*), glue], fasten together (as with glue).

Ag′gran-dize [F. *agrandir*; L. *ad*, to, *grandis*, large], make great, enlarge.

Ag′gra-vate [L. *ad*, to, *gravis*, heavy], make worse, provoke. **Aggrava′tion.**

Ag′gre-gate [L. *ad*, to, *grex* (*greg-is*), a flock], sum, mass, the whole. **Aggrega′tion.**

Ag-gres′sion [L. *ad*, to, *gradī* (p.p. *gressus*), to step], unjust attack, first act in a quarrel.

Ag-gres′sive, of the nature of an attack, quarrelsome.

Ag-gres′sor, one who makes the first attack.

Ag-grieve′ [L. *ad*, to, *gravis*, heavy], to pain, vex.

A-ghast′ [O.E. *a-* (intensive), *gǣstan*, to terrify], showing signs of terror.

A′gile [L. *agere*, to do], quick and easy in motion, nimble. **A-gil′i-ty,** nimbleness.

A′gi-tate [L. *agitāre* (p.p. *agitātus*), freq. of *agere*, to do], set in motion, disturb.

A′gi-ta′tion, feeling of disturbance.

A′gi-ta′tor, one who stirs up others.

A-glow′, [*a-*, on, in, and **Glow**], in a glow.

Ag-nos′tic [Gr. *a*, not, *gignoscein*, to learn, to know], one who believes that nothing is known, or likely to be known, of the existence of a God. **Agnos′ticism.**

A-go′ [shortened from *agone*, p.p. of obs. verb *ago*, to go forth], gone-by, past.

A-gog′ [etym. doubtful], expectant.

Ag′o-nize, put or be in great pain.

Ag′o-ny [L. and Gk. *agōnia*, a contest], intense feeling, very great pain.

A-gra′ri-an [L. *agrārius*; *ager*, a field], relating to land. [consent.

A-gree′ [L. *ad*, to, *gratus*, pleasing], be at one,

A-gree′a-ble, pleasant, ready to agree.

A-gree′ment, state of being at one with, a bargain.

Ag′ri-cul′ture [L. *ager*, a field, *colere* (p.p. *cultus*), to till], art of cultivating the ground, farming. **Agricul′tural.** [ground.

A-ground′ [*a-*, on, and **Ground**], on the

A′gue [O.F.; L. *acūtus*, sharp], fever that comes and goes with cold and hot stages.

A-head′ [*a-*, on, and **Head**], in front.

Aid [O.F. *aider*; L. *ad*, to, *juvāre* (p.p. *jutus*), to help], help. [a general.

Aide-de-camp′ (F.), military officer attending

Ai′gret or Ai′grette [F. *aigrette*, egret, a kind of heron; see **Egret**], white heron, ornament of feathers or gems.

Ail [O.E. *eglan*, to pain], be ill.

Aim [Prov. *esmer*, fr. L. *æstimāre*, to esteem, aim at], direct or point at: point which is meant to be hit, object.

Air [Gk. *aēr*, air], invisible fluid round the earth, tune, manner; expose to open air.

Air′craft, airships and aeroplanes. **Anti-aircraft**, against air attack.

Air-pocket, part of atmosphere in which an aeroplane suddenly drops, probably due to the fact that the air here is more rarefied.

Air′y, open to the air, gay. [church.

Aisle [O.F. *ele*; L. *ala*, a wing], side of a

A-jar′ [O.E. *a char*, *on char*, on the turn; O.E. *cyrr*, a turn], partly open. [hip.

A-kim′bo [?], with elbow out and hand on

A-kin' [a-, of, and Kin], related.

Al'a-bast-er [Gk. *alabastros*; said to be from *Alabastron*, a town in Egypt], kind of limestone or marble. [readiness.

A-lac'ri-ty [L. *alacer*, brisk, lively], cheerful

A-larm' [It. *all' arme!* to arms l], give notice of danger; sudden fear, warning.

A-larm'ist, one who raises alarms on slight grounds.

A-lar'um, alarm signal.

A-las' [O.F. *ha la'*, *ha*, ah, *las*, *lasse*, wretched; L. *lassus*, weary], interjection expressing grief.

Alb [Late L. *alba* (*tunica*), white (tunic); L. *albus*, white], long white vestment worn by priests.

Al'ba-tross [Sp. and Port. *alcatruz*; Arab. *alqādūs*, pelican,= bucket. *N.B.*— The pelican carries water in its pouch], large sea-bird.

Al-bi'no (*i*=*ee* or *ī*) [Port. *albino*; L. *albus*, white], person or animal with unusually white skin and hair and pink eyes.

Al'bum [L. *album*, a tablet, neut. of *albus*, white], blank book for cuttings, etc.

Al-bu'men [L. *albumen*, fr. *albus*, white], white of an egg, a constituent of same and of animals and plants. Albu'minous.

Al'che-my (*ch*=*k*) [Arab. *al*, the, *kīmīā*, chemistry; fr. Gk. *chemia*, native name for Egypt], so-called science which aimed at turning other metals into gold. Al'chemist.

Al'co-hol [Arab. *al*, the, *koh'l*, a powder for painting the eyelids], pure spirit.

Alcoran (*al'kor-ahn*, *al-kor-ahn'*) [Arab. *al-qoran*, the reading], Koran, sacred book of the Mohammedans.

Al'cove [Arab. *al*, the, *qobbah*, a vault], recess.

Al'der [O.E. *alor*, *aler*, *alr*], kind of tree related to birch.

Al'der-man [O.E. *aldor*, *ealdor*, a chief or elder, and Man], magistrate in a borough or county.

Ale [O.E. *alu*], kind of beer.

Al-em'bic [Arab. *al*, the, and *ambīq*, a still], a vessel for distilling.

A-lert' [L. *ad illam erectam*, to that erect one], watchful, lively.

Al-ex-an'drine [fr. French poem on Alexander the Great], iambic line of six feet.

Al'ge-bra [Arab. *al*, the, *jabr*, setting, reduction of fractions to integers, algebra], calculation by means of symbols.

A'li-as [L. *aliās*, otherwise; *alius*, another], otherwise; assumed name.

Al'ib-i [L. *alibi*, elsewhere], the plea that when an alleged act was done, one was elsewhere.

Al'ien (*a*=*ai*) [L. *aliēnus*, strange; *alius*, another], foreign; foreigner.

Al'ien-ate, give over to another, estrange.

A-light' [O.E. *á*, of, off, *lihtan*, to make light, adj. *liht*, light], get down. [up.

A-light' [O.E. *a*, on, and Light (n.)], lighted

A-lign', A-line' [L. *ad*, to, *līnea*, a line], lay in a line, bring into line.

A-like' [O.E. *gelic* (adj.), *gelice* (adv.), *ge-*, together, *lic*, like; also O.N. *álíkr* (adj.), *álíka* (adv.), *á*, on, *lík*, like], like, the same.

Al'i-ment [L. *alimentum*, food; *alere*, to nourish], food, means of support.

Al'i-quot [L. *aliquot*, some; *alius*, other, and *quot*, how many], (in division) exact (part).

A-live' [*a*, on, M.E. *live*, O.E. *life* (dative of *lif*, life)], in life.

Al'ka-li [Arab. *al*, the, *qaliy*, ashes abounding in soda], substance such as soda or potash that neutralizes acids. Al'kaline, Al'kaloid.

All (*awl*) [O.E. *eal*, pl. *ealle*], whole; entire number of; utterly.

Al-lay' [*a*-, on, and Lay], make quiet, make less severe.

Al-le-ga'tion, that which is alleged.

Al-lege' [L. *ad*, to, *legāre* (p.p. *legātus*), to dispatch], bring forward positively.

Al-le'giance [O.F. *ligeance*, homage], duty or faithfulness to rulers.

Al'le-go-ry [Gk. *allos*, other, *agoreuein*, to speak; *agora*, a place of assembly], speech about one thing in the image of another.

Al-le'vi-ate [L. *ad*, to, *levāre* (p.p. *levātus*), to lift], lighten or lessen. Allevia'tion.

Al'ley [F. *aller*; O.F. *aler*, to go], narrow walk or passage.

Al-li'ance [see Ally], union.

Al'li-ga-tor [Sp. *el lagarto*; L. *lacerta*, the lizard], American crocodile.

Al-lit-er-a'tion [L. *ad*, to, *litera*, a letter], repetition of a sound at the beginning of three or more words or syllables at short intervals.

Al'lo-cate [L. *allocāre* (p.p. *allocātus*), fr. *ad*, to, *locus*, a place], give each his place or share.

Al-lop'a-thy [Gk. *allos*, other, *pathos*, suffering], ordinary system of medicine; curing by inducing another action of the body of a different kind.

Al-lot' [O.F. *à*, to, *loter*, divide by lot], give each his share or lot. Allot'ment.

Al-low' [O.F. *alouer*; L. *ad*, to, *locāre*, to place], let one have or do, grant.

Al-low'ance, stated quantity or sum.

Al-loy' [L. *alligāre*, to bind together; see Ally], baser metal mixed with a finer; mix with base metal.

All'spice (*awl*), Jamaica pepper, which is said to combine the flavours of several spices.

Al-lude' [L. *ad*, to, *lūdere* (p.p. *lūsus*), to play], refer to indirectly.

Al-lure' [O.F. *à leurre*, to the lure], draw by something pleasant.

Al-lu'sion (*si*=*zh*), slight reference.

Al-lu'vi-um [L. *ad*, to, *luēre*, to wash], soil laid down by water. Allu'vial.

Al-ly' [L. *ad*, to, *ligāre*, to bind], unite by treaty; one who is on the same side.

Al'ma-nac [M.L. *almanach*. Etym. unknown], book or table with a list of days, weeks, etc.

Al-migh'ty [O.E. *ælmeahtig*], all-powerful.

Alm'ond [O.F. *almande*; L. *amygdala*; Gk. *amygdalē*], kind of nut.

Al'mon-er (*al=ah*), one who distributes alms.

Al'most, nearly.

Alms (*ahmz*) [Gk. *eleēmosynē*, pity ; Gk. *eleos*, pity], gifts to the poor.

Al'oe [L. *aloē* ; Gk. *aloē*], class of plants of many kinds.

A-loft' [O.N. *á*, on, *lopt*, air], on high.

A-lone' [M.E. *al oon*, all one], by oneself.

A-long' [O.E. *andlang* ; *and-*, against, *lang*, long], by the length.

A-loof' [for *on loof*; see **Luff**], at a distance.

A-loud' [*a-*, on, and **Loud**), loudly.

Al-pac'a [Span. ; (Arab. *al*, the, *paco*, the Peruvian name for the animal)], animal of Peru.

Al'pha-bet [Gk. *alpha*, *bēta*, the first two letters of the alphabet], letters of a language in order. **Alphabet'ic.** [time.

Al-read'y [**All** and **Ready**], before this or that

Al'so [**All** and **So**], likewise, besides. [ings.

Al'tar [L. *altus*, high], raised place for offer-

Al'ter [L. *alter*, other], to change.

Al-ter-a'tion, change.

Al-ter-ca'tion [L. *altercāri* (p.p. *altercātus*), to dispute ; *alter*, other], exchange of angry words.

Al-ter'nate [L. *alternāre* (p.p. *alternātus*), to do things by turns ; *alter*, other], by turns.

Al'ter-nate (of two things), to occur or arrange time about.

Al-ter'na-tive, choice of two things.

Al-though' [**All** and **Though**], even if, notwithstanding that.

Al'ti-tude [L. *altus*, high], height.

Al'to [Ital. *alto* ; L. *altus*, high], part sung by lowest female voice ; highest male voice.

Al-to-geth'er, as a whole, with none left out.

Al'-tru-ism [through Ital. *altrui*, others ; L. *alteri huic*, to this other], regard for others. **Altruis'tic.**

Al-u-min'i-um [L. *alūmen*, alum], bluish white metal. [for ever.

Al'ways (*al=awl*) [**All** and **Way**], at all times,

A-mal'gam [Gk. *malagma*, an emollient, *malacos*, soft], mixture of a metal with mercury. **Amalgama'tion.**

A-mal'ga-mate, mix or blend well.

A-man-u-en'sis (plur. *-ses*) [L. *ā manū*, by the hand], writer to dictation.

A-mass' [L. *ad*, to, *massa*, a mass], collect into a mass, to pile.

A-ma-teur' [L. *amāre* (p.p. *amātus*), to love], one who studies or practises an art merely for the love of it.

Am'a-tor-y, pertaining to lovers. [greatly.

A-maze' [*a-*, on, and **Maze**], bewilder, surprise

A-maze'ment [see **Amaze**], great surprise.

Am'a-zon [Gk. *Amazōn*, one of a warlike race of women in Scythia], female warrior.

Am-bas'sa-dor [L. *ambactus*, of Celtic or German origin], one sent to represent a sovereign or state in a foreign country.

Am'ber [Arab. *'anbar*, ambergris], fossil resin.

An.'ber-gris [F. *ambre gris*, grey amber], fragrant waxy substance.

Am-bi-dex'trous [L. *ambi*, both sides, *dexter*, right-handed], using both hands alike.

Am'bi-ent [*ambi*, about, *īre*, to go], surrounding.

Am'bi-gu'i-ty, doubtfulness of meaning.

Am-big'u-ous [L. *ambiguus*, doubtful; *amb-*, both ways, *agere*, to drive], that can be taken in two ways.

Ambit [see **Ambient**], scope, compass.

Am-bi'tion [L. *ambi*, about, *īre* (sup. *ītum*), to go], desire of power or high place.

Am-bi'tious, actuated by ambition.

Am'ble [L. *ambulāre*, to walk], gait of a horse in which both legs on the same side are lifted together.

Am-bro'si-a [Gk. *ambrosia*, fem. of *ambrosios*, immortal], fabled food of the gods.

Am'bu-lance [L. *ambulāre*, to go], movable field hospital.

Am-bus-cade', **Am'bush** [L. *in*, in; Late L. *boscum*, a bush], a lying in wait.

A-me'lio-rate [L. *ad*, to, *melior*, better], make or grow better.

A-me'lio-ra'tion, improvement.

A-men' [Heb. *āmēn*, truly, verily], so let it be.

A-me'na-ble [L. *ad*, to; L. *mināre*, to threaten (F. *amener*, to bring)], willing to yield, answerable.

A-mend' [L. *e* or *ex*, from, *menda*, a fault], make better, alter, correct.

A-mend'ment, change for the better. [etc.

A-mends', something to make up for loss,

A-men'i-ty [L. *amœnus*, pleasant; *amāre*, to love], pleasantness.

A-merce' [O.F. *à*, at, *merci*, mercy], to fine.

Am'e-thyst [Gk. *amethystos*, fr. *a*, not, *methystos*, drunken. The stone was supposed to prevent drunkenness], violet-coloured stone. [of temper.

A'mi-a-bi'li-ty [L. *amāre*, to love], sweetness

A'mi-a-ble, lovable.

Am'i-ca-ble [L. *amīcus*, a friend, fr. *amāre*, to love], friendly.

A-mid', **A-midst'** [O.E. *on middan*, in the middle], in the middle (of).

A-miss' [*a-*, on, and **Miss**], wrong.

Am'i-ty [F. *amitié*, fr. L. *amīcus*, a friend], friendship.

A-mok', same as **A-muck'**.

Am-mo'ni-a [fr. L. *sal-ammōniacum*, rock-salt, said to have been first prepared near the temple of Jupiter Ammon in Lydia], spirit of hartshorn, colourless alkaline gas.

Am-mu-ni'tion [F. (l')*amunition*, corruption of *la munition* ; see **Munition**], materials for loading firearms.

Am'nes-ty [L. and Gk. *amnēstia*, forgetfulness ; Gk. *a-*, not, *mnēstos*, remembered], general pardon.

A-mong', **A-mongst'** [*o=u*) [O.E. *on*, in, *gemang*, an assemblage, a crowd], mixed with ; (to divide) in portions to.

Am'or-ous [L. *amor*, love], loving, fond.

A-mor'phous [Gk. *a-*, not, *morphē*, shape], shapeless.

A-mount' [O.F. *amonter* ; L. *ad*, to, *montem*, acc. of *mons*, a mountain], mount up to ; whole sum.

Am-père [name of a French electrician], unit of electric current.

Am′per-sand [corr. of '*and per se and*'. L. *per se*, by itself], the contraction for *and*, written &.

Am-phib′i-ous [Gk. *amphi*, both, *bios*, life], living both on land and in water.

Am-phi-the′a-tre [Gk. *amphi*, on both sides, *theatrōn*, a theatre], building with rows of seats above an open space.

Am′ple [L. *amplus*, large, spacious], large, more than enough. **Am′ply.**

Am′pli-fy, enlarge, enhance. **Amplifica′tion.**

Am′-pli-tude, breadth, wide range.

Am′pu-tate [L. *ambi*, about, *putāre* (p.p. *putātus*), to lop], cut off (a limb).

A-muck′ [Malay, *amoq*, rushing frantically], recklessly. ("To run *amuck*," used of Malays running frantically and striking or killing any whom they meet.)

Am′u-let [L. *amulētum*. Etym. doubtful], something worn as a charm.

A-muse′ (*s=z*) [O.F. *amuser*, to gaze at, muse; see **Muse**], occupy in a pleasant way.

A-muse′ment, that which amuses.

An-ach′ro-nism (*ch=k, s=z*) [Gk. *ana-*, up, back, *chronos*, time], a misplacing in time. **Anachronis′tic.**

An-a-col-u′thon [Gk. *an-*, not, *akolouthein*, to follow], sentences or words lacking grammatical sequence.

An-æ′mi-a (*æ=ee*) [Gk. *an-*, not, *haima*, blood], bloodlessness. **Anæ′mic.**

An′æs-thet′ic [Gk. *anaisthētos*, insensible; *an-*, not, *aisthēsis*, sensation], that which produces a state in which pain is not felt.

An′a-gram [Gk. *ana*, up, *gramma*, a letter of the alphabet], word formed from another by changing the order of the letters.

A-nal′o-gous, like. **A′alogue.**

A-nal′o-gy [Gk. *ana*, upon, and *logos*, a word, statement], likeness.

A-na-lyse′ (*s=z*), to separate into parts.

A-nal′y-sis [Gk. *ana*, back, and *lyein*, to loosen], separation into first parts.

An′ar-chy (*ch=k*) [Gk. *an-*, negative prefix, *archos*, a ruler], lawlessness.

A-nath′e-ma [Gk. *anathema*, a thing devoted to evil or accursed; *ana*, up, *tithenai*, to put], a curse. **Ana′thematize.**

A-nat′o-my [Gk. *ana*, up, *temnein*, to cut], science of bodily structure. **Anat′omist.** **Anatom′ical.**

An′ces-tor [L. *ante*, before, *cedēre* (sup. *cessum*), to go], forefather. **An′cestry.** **Ances′tral.**

An′chor [L. *ancora*; Gk. *agcyra*, a bent hook, anchor], an iron that holds a ship fast. **An′chorage.**

An′cho-rite [Gk. *ana*, back, *chōrein*, to withdraw], religious hermit.

An-cho′vy [Sp. *anchova*; perh. Basque *antzua*, dry], small fish.

An′cient (*a=ai*) [Late L. *antiānus*, old, *ante*, before], very old, of long ago.

An′cil-la-ry [L. *ancillārius*; *ancilla*, a handmaid], subordinate.

And [O.E. *and*, against, *end*, and], conjunction connecting words, clauses, etc.

An′ec-dote [Gk. *anecdota*, things unpublished; *an-*, not, *ek*, out, *dotos*, given], short story.

A-nem′o-ne [Gk. *anemos*, wind], "windflower."

A′ner-oid [Gk. *a-*, not, *nēros*, wet], kind of barometer made without liquid.

A-new′ [*a-*, of, and **New**] over again.

An′gel [Gk. *aggelos*, a messenger], messenger of God. **Angel′ic.**

An-gel′i-ca [M.L. (*herba*) *angelica*, angelic plant], a plant used in medicine and cooking; candied root of this plant.

An′ger (*g* hard) [O.N. *angr*, grief; cf. Dan. *anger*; Swed. *ånger*, regret], strong displeasure, rage.

An′gle [L. *angulus*, a corner], corner.

An′gle [O.E. *angul*, a fish-hook], to fish with hook and line.

An′gry [see **Anger**], feeling or showing anger.

An′guish (*u=w*) [L. *angere*, to choke], great pain.

An′gu-lar, having an angle or angles.

An′i-line [Arab. *annil*, fr. *al*, the, and Sanscrit, *nīlī*, indigo plant], oily fluid from which dyes are made.

An′i-mad-vert′ [L. *animus*, mind, *ad*, to, *vertere*, to turn], pass judgment, to censure.

An′i-mal [L. *animal*, fr. *anima*, breath, life], living body which moves of itself.

An-i-mal′cule [L. *animalculum*, dim. of *animal*], microscopic animal.

An′i-mate [L. *animāre* (p.p. *animātus*); *anima*, life], put life into; living. **Anima′tion.**

An′i-mos′i-ty [L. *animōsitas*; fr. *animus*, mind], hatred leading to opposition.

An′i-mus [L. *animus*, mind, temper], temper.

An′ise [L. *anīsum*; Gk. *anison*, anise], plant bearing spicy seeds.

An′kle [O.E. *anclēow*], joint between foot and leg.

An′na, **A′na** [Hind. *ana*, sixteenth part], Indian coin, sixteenth part of a rupee.

An′nal-ist, writer of annals.

An′nals [L. *annus*, a year], history that follows the order of time.

An-neal′ [O.E. *an*, on, *ælan*, to burn; partly also from O.F. *neeler*, to enamel; Late L. *nigellāre*, to blacken, *niger*, black], make glass, etc., less brittle by cooling slowly from great heat.

An-nex′ [L. *ad*, to, *nectere* (p.p. *nexus*), to bind], join on. **Annexa′tion.**

An-ni′hil-ate [L. *ad*, to, *nihil*, nothing], reduce to nothing.

An-ni-ver′sa-ry [L. *annus*, a year, *versus* (p.p. of *vertere*, to turn)], yearly return of a date.

An′no-tate [L. *ad*, to, *notāre* (p.p. *notātus*), to mark], make notes on.

An-nounce′ [L. *ad*, to, *nuntius*, a messenger], make known. **Announce′ment.**

An-noy′ [L. *in odiō*, in hatred], go on disturbing, vex.

An-noy′ance, vexation, that which annoys.

An'nu-al [L. *annus*, a year], yearly; yearly magazine. [yearly.

An-nu'i-ty [L. *annus*, a year], sum payable

An-nul' [L. *ad*, to, *nullus*, none], bring to nothing, do away with. [ring.

An'nu-lar [L. *annulus*, a ring], forming a

An-nun-ci-a'tion [see **Announce**], announcement.

An'o-dyne [Gk. *an-*, not, *odynē*, pain], medicine that lessens pain.

A-noint' [M.E. *anoint* (obs. p.p.); L. *in*, in, *ungere* (p.p. *unctus*), to anoint], rub with oil, pour oil upon.

An-om'a-lous [Gk. *an-*, not, and *homalos*, even], irregular, deviating from rule.

A-nom'a-ly, departure from common rule.

A-non' [O.E. *on*, on, in, *ān*, one], soon, at once. [without name.

A-non'y-mous [Gk. *an-*, not, *onoma*, a name],

An'swer [O.E. *and-*, against; *swerian*, to swear], speak or write in return; that which is said in reply.

An'swer-a-ble, responsible. [insect.

Ant [O.E. *ǣmete*, an emmet, ant], small

An-tag'o-nism, opposition, strife.

An-tag'o-nist [Gk. *anti*, against, *agōn*, a contest], one who is opposed, a foe.

Ant-arc'tic [Gk. *anti*, opposite to, *arcticos*, Arctic], connected with the South Polar region.

Ante, see Latin Prefixes.

An-te-ce'dent [L. *ante*, before, *cēdere*, to go], going before; that which goes before, esp. noun to which relative pronoun refers.

An'te-cham-ber [L. *ante*, before, and **Chamber**], outer chamber.

An'te-date' [L. *ante*, before, and **Date**], to date before the true time.

An-te-di-lu'vi-an [L. *ante*, before, *diluvium*, deluge], before the flood.

An'te-lope [Gk. *antholops*. Etym. uncertain], deer-like animal.

An'te-me-rid'i-an [L. *ante*, before, *meridiem* (acc. of *meridies*), noon], before noon.

An-ten'nae [L. plur. of *antenna*, the yard of a sail], feelers of insects, etc.; raised apparatus for sending out or receiving electric waves in wireless telegraphy.

An-te'ri-or [L. *anterior*, former; *ante*, before], before in time or place.

An'te-room. See **Antechamber**.

An'them [Gk. *antiphōna*; *anti*, over against, *phōnē*, sound], prose selection (esp. from the Scriptures) set to music and sung in parts.

An'ther [Gk. *anthēra*, flowery; *anthos*, a young bud], tip of the stamen of a flower.

An-thol'o-gy [Gk. *anthos*, a flower, *legein*, to cull], collection of short poems or passages from prose literature. [coal.

An'thra-cite [Gk. *anthrax*, coal], kind of hard

An'thrax [Gk. *anthrax*, a carbuncle], a cattle disease, also affecting man.

An-thro-pol'o-gy [Gk. *anthrōpos*, a man, *logos*, reason, discourse], whole science of man.

Anti, see Greek Prefixes.

An'tic [It. *antico*; L. *antiquus*, old], grotesque; a caper, clown.

An-ti'ci-pate [L. *ante*, before, *capere*, to take], be before in doing; foresee.

An-ti-cli'max [Gk. *anti*, reverse of, and **Climax**], addition of some particular that weakens the climax.

An'ti-clin'al [Gk. *anti*, against, *klinein*, to lean], ridge in which strata lean against each other and from which they slope down in opposite directions.

An'ti-dote [Gk. *anti*, against, *dotos*, given], remedy against poison.

An'ti-mo-ny [M.L. *antimonium*, orig. unknown], bluish-white metal.

An-tip'a-thy [Gk. *anti*, against, *pathein*, to suffer], feeling against, dislike.

An'ti-phon [Late L. *antiphōna*, an anthem; see **Anthem**], anthem or part of anthem sung responsively.

An-tip'o-des [Gk. *anti*, against, *pous* (*pod-os*), a foot], exact opposites, the opposite side of the earth.

An'ti-qua-ry [L. *antiquārius*; *antiquus*, ancient], one who studies far back history from old remains. **Antiquar'ian**.

An'ti-qua'ted, grown old, old-fashioned.

An-tique' (*an-teek'*) [L. *antiquus*, old, *ante*, before], ancient; object of ancient art.

An-tiq'ui-ty, ancientness, ancient times.

An'ti-sep'tic [Gk. *anti*, against, *septicos*, putrifying; *septos*, rotten], preventing corruption.

An-tith'e-sis [Gk. *anti*, against, *tithenai*, to place], opposition, contrast.

An'ti-type [Gk. *anti*, against (corresponding to), and **Type**], that which a type represents.

Ant'ler [O.F. *antoillier*; L. *ante*, before, *oculus*, the eye], branch of a horn of stag, etc.

An'vil [O.E. *onfilti*. Etym. uncertain], blacksmith's iron block.

Anx-i'e-ty (*x=gz*), uneasiness of mind.

Anx'ious [L. *anxius*; *angere*, to choke], troubled, desirous. [some, every.

An'y (*a=ē*) [O.E. *ǣnig*, fr. *ān*, one], one,

A-pace' [*a-*, on, and **Pace**], quickly.

A-part' [F. *à part*; L. *ad partem*, to one part], aside, to pieces. [room.

A-part'ment [F. *appartement*; see **Apart**],

Ap'a-thy [Gk. *apatheia*; *a-*, not, *pathos*, suffering], want of feeling. **Ap'a-thet'ic**.

Ape [O.E. *apa*], kind of monkey; imitate like an ape.

A-per'i-ent [L. *aperīre* (pr.p. *aperiens, -entis*), to open], laxative medicine. [opening.

Ap'er-ture [L. *aperīre* (p.p. *apertus*), to open],

A'pex [L. *apex*, summit], top.

A-pha'si-a [Gk. *a-*, not, *phasis*, speech], loss of speech due to brain disease.

A-phe'li-on [Gk. *ap-* (*apo*), from, *helios*, the sun], point furthest from the sun of a planet's orbit.

Aph'o-rism [Gk. *aphorismos*; *apo*, off, *horos*, a boundary], short, pithy statement of a general truth. **Aphorist'ic**.

A'pi-a-ry [L. *apiārium*; *apis*, a bee], place where bees are kept. [by itself.

A-piece' [*a*, the indef. art., and **Piece**], each

A-plomb' [F. *à*, to, *plomb*, plummet], self-possession.

A-poc'a-lypse [Gk. *apocalypsis*, a revelation], Book of Revelation. **Apocalypt'ic.**

A-poc'ry-pha [Gk. *apocrypha*, neut. pl. of *apocryphos*, hidden], certain writings received by some, but not by all, as part of the Bible. **Apoc'ryphal.**

Ap'o-gee (*g*=*j*) [Gk. *apo*, from, *gē*, the earth], point in moon's orbit farthest from the earth.

A-pol'o-gize, make an apology. [fable.

Ap'o-logue [Gk. *apo*, off, *logos*, speech], moral

A-pol'o-gy [L. and Gk. *apologia*, fr. *apo*, off, and *logos*, speech], excuse, expression of regret. **Apologet'ic.** [religion.

A-pol-o-get'ics, defence of the Scriptures or of

Ap'oph-thegm [Gk. *apo*, off, *phtheggesthai*, to utter], short aphorism.

Ap'o-plex-y [Gk. *apo*, off, *plēssein*, to strike], sudden loss of sense and motion due to pressure on the brain.

A-pos'ta-sy [Gk. *apo*, off, *stasis*, a standing], abandonment of faith, betrayal.

A-pos'tle [Gk. *apo*, off, *stellein*, to send], one sent forth (especially one of the twelve disciples whom Jesus sent forth to preach, or their immediate successors).

A-pos'tro-phe [Gk. *apo*, away, *strophē*, a turning], a turning away in speech to address persons present or absent, a mark (') of contraction. **Apos'trophize.**

A-poth'e-ca-ry [Gk. *apothēkē*, storehouse ; *apo*, away, and *tithenai*, to put], druggist.

Ap'o-thegm, see **Apophthegm.**

A-poth-e-o'sis [Gk. *apo*, away, *theos*, a god], deification, regarded as a god.

Ap-pal' [perh. L. *ad*, to, *pallidus*, pale], overcome with fear.

Ap'pan-age, Ap'an-age [O.F. *apaner*, supply with bread ; L. *ad*, to, *panis*, bread], provision for younger children of kings, perquisite, dependency, attribute.

Ap-pa-ra'tus [L. *apparātus* (p.p. of *apparāre*), to prepare for: *ad*, for, *parāre*, to prepare], instrument, means of doing something.

Ap-par'el [O.F. *apareiller*, to dress ; L. *ad*, to, *par*, equal], dress : to clothe.

Ap-pa'rent [see **Appear**], easily seen.

Ap-pa-ri'tion, appearance, ghost.

Ap-peal' [O.F. *apeler*, to call ; L. *ad*, to, *pellere*, to drive], call, refer to : act of appealing, right of appealing.

Ap-pear' [L. *ad*, to, *parēre*, to come in sight], be or come in sight.

Ap-pear'ance, act of appearing, looks.

Ap-pease' (*s*=*z*) [O.F. *apaisier* ; L. *ad*, to, *pax* (*pacis*), peace], to calm.

Ap-pel'lant, one who appeals.

Ap'pel-la'tion, name. [add.

Ap-pend' [L. *ad*, to, *pendere*, to hang], hang to,

Ap-pend'age, something appended to.

Ap-pend'ix, part added to a book, small part attached to the surface of a bodily organ.

Ap-per-tain' [L. *ad*, to, *pertinēre*, to belong], belong.

Ap'pe-tite [O.F. *appetit* ; L. *ad*, to, *petēre* (p.p. *petītus*), to seek], desire or relish for food.

Ap'pe-tize [see **Appetite**], whet the appetite.

Ap-plaud' [L. *ad*, to, *plaudere* (p.p. *plausus*), to clap (hands)], express approval loudly.

Ap-plause' (*s*=*z*), act of applauding.

Ap'ple [O.E. *æppel*], a fruit, pupil of the eye.

Ap-pli'ance, act of applying, thing applied.

Ap-pli-ca'tion, appliance, industry, request.

Ap-ply' [O.F. *aplier* ; L. *applicāre* ; *ad*, to, *plicāre*, to fold, twine], put to use, fix closely, make request.

Ap-point' [O.F. *apointer* ; *à point*, to the point], fix, name for.

Ap-point'ment, office, act of appointing.

Ap-por'tion [O.F. *apportionner* ; *à*, to, *portion-ner*, to portion out], divide out.

Ap'po-site [L. *ad*, to, *pōnere* (p.p. *positus*), to put], suitable, pat.

Ap-po-si'tion, state of being close together or side by side, especially of two nouns referring to the same thing.

Ap-praise' (*s*=*z*) [L. *ad*, to, *pretium*, a price], set a value on.

Ap-pre'ci-a-ble (*ci*=*sh*), noticeable.

Ap-pre'ci-ate [L. *ad*, to, *pretium*, price], to value, estimate justly, rise in value.

Ap-pre-ci-a'tion, just estimate of worth, increase in value.

Ap'pre-hend' [L. *ad*, to, *prehendere* (p.p. *pre-hensus*), to grasp], take hold of, arrest, understand.

Ap-pre-hen'sion, a seizing, arrest, understanding, fear.

Ap-pre-hen'sive, in dread of harm.

Ap-pren'tice (*ice*=*iss*) [O.F. *apprentis* ; Late L. *apprenditus* (used as p.p. of *apprendere*, to learn) ; short for *apprehendere*], one bound to a master to learn a trade.

Ap-prise' [F. *appris*, fem. *apprise* (p.p. of *apprendre*), to learn], give notice.

Ap-proach' [O.F. *aprochier* ; L. *ad*, to, *prope*, near], come near : act of drawing near, path to a building.

Ap-pro-ba'tion [see **Approve**], act of approving, good opinion.

Ap-pro'pri-ate [L. *ad*, to, *proprius*, one's own], take to one's self : suitable.

Ap-prov'al (*o*=*oo*), good opinion.

Ap-prove' (*o*=*oo*) [O.F. *aprover* ; L. *ad*, to, *probāre*, to test], prove, think well of, confirm.

Ap-prox'i-mate [L. *ad*, to, *proximus*, next], come near to : near.

Ap-pur'te-nance [see **Appertain**], something belonging to another thing.

A'pri-cot (*a*=*ai*) [formerly also *apricock*. Span. *albar*(*i*)*coque* ; Arab. *al burquq* ; Gk. *praicocion* ; L. *præcoquus*, early ripe], a stone fruit.

A'pril [L. *aperīre*, to open], the fourth month of the year (Rom. second).

A'pron [formerly *napron*. O.F. *naperon*, dim. of *nape*, a table-cloth ; L. *mappa*, a cloth], article of dress worn in front.

Apse [Gk. *hapsis*, a felloe of a wheel, a curve, an arch], recess at the east end of a church.

Apt [L. *apere* (p.p. *aptus*), to fit, to join together], fit, quick to learn, liable.

Apt'i-tude, fitness, readiness in learning.

Apt'ness, fitness.

A-qua'ri-um [L. *aquārium*, a water-vessel ; *aqua*, water], tank or pond for keeping aquatic plants and animals.

A-quat'ic [L. *aqua*, water], living in water.

Aq'ue-duct [L. *aqua*, water, *ducere* (p.p. *ductus*), to lead], bridge, pipe, open channel or tunnel made to convey water.

A'que-ous, watery, made by water.

Aq'ui-line [L. *aquila*, an eagle], like an eagle, hooked.

Ar'a-ble [L. *arāre*, to plough], fit for ploughing.

Ar'bit-er, Ar-bi-tra'tor [L. *arbiter*, a judge], one chosen to judge.

Ar'bi-tra-ry, following one's own will.

Ar'bit-rate, hear and decide.

Ar-bi-tra'tion, settlement by arbitrators.

Ar-bo-re'tum [L. *arbor*, a tree], place for growing trees.

Ar-bor-i-cul'ture [L. *arbor* (*arboris*), a tree, *cultura*, culture], cultivation of trees.

Ar'bour, Arbor [Orig. (*h*)*erber* ; O.F. (*h*)*erbier*, a grass lawn ; *herba*, grass, herb. Form of the word due to confusion with *arbor*, a tree], shelter covered with branches, etc.

Arc [L. *arcus*, a bow], part of a circle.

Ar-cade' [Ital. *arcata* ; L. *arcus*, a bow], arched walk.

Arch [O.F. *arche* ; L. *arca*, a chest, confused with L. *arcus*, a bow], curved structure over an open space ; to span.

Arch [from Gk. prefix *arch-*, *archi-*, chief], chief, roguish.

Ar-chæ-ol'o-gy [Gk. *archē*, beginning, *logos*, discourse], study of remains of long-past times.

Ar-cha'-ic, old.

Ar'cha-ism [Gk. *archaios*, old], a word or expression no longer commonly in use.

Arch'an'gel [Gk. *archi-*, chief, *aggelos*, a messenger], chief angel.

Arch'bish'op [Gk. *archi-*, chief, *episcopos*, a bishop], chief bishop.

Arch'er [L. *arcārius* ; *arcus*, a bow], one who shoots with a bow.

Ar'che-type (*ch*=*k*) [Gk. *archē*, beginning, and *typos*, a type], original model.

Ar'chi-pel'a-go (*ch*=*k*) [Gk. *archi-*, chief, *pelagos*, sea], sea dotted with many islands.

Ar'chi-tect (*ch*=*k*) [Gk. *archi-*, chief, *tectōn*, a builder], one who plans buildings.

Ar'chi-tec'ture (*ch*=*k*), art of building.

Ar'chives (*ch*=*k*) [Gk. *archeion*, a public building ; *archē*, government], records, place where records are kept.

Arc'tic [Gk. *arctos*, a bear], relating to the region round the North Pole.

Ar'dent [L. *ardēre*, to burn], hot, fiery.

Ar'dour [L. *ardēre*, to burn], warmth, zeal.

Ar'du-ous [L. *arduus*, steep], hard, difficult.

A're-a [L. *area*, an open space], surface, sunken front courtyard.

A-re'na [L. *arēna*, sand], sand-covered area in an amphitheatre, place of public contest.

Ar'gent [F. *argent* ; L. *argentum*, silver], silver (colour), esp. in heraldry.

Ar-gil-la'ceous [L. *argilla*, clay, esp. white clay ; Gk. *argēs*, white], of clay.

Ar'gon [Gk. *a-*, not, *ergon*, work, neut. of *argos*, idle], a gas, inert constituent of atmosphere.

Ar'gue [L. *arguere*, to make clear], give reasons for or against.

Ar'gu-ment, reason for or against.

Ar'gu-men'ta-tive, consisting of or given to argument.

Ar'id [L. *aridus*, dry], dry, parched.

A-right' [*a*, on, and **Right**], rightly.

A-rise' (*s*=*z*) [O.E. *a-*, intensive prefix, *risan*, to rise], get up.

Ar'is-toc'ra-cy [Gk. *aristos*, best, *cratia*, rule], the nobility, government by the nobility.

A-ris'to-crat, one of a ruling class, a noble.

A-rith'me-tic [Gk. *arithmos*, number], science of numbers.

Ark [O.E. *arc*, prob. fr. L. *arca*, a box], chest, Noah's chest-like ship.

Arm [O.E. *earm*, cogn. with L. *armus*, the shoulder], limb from shoulder to hand, anything like an arm.

Arm [L. *armāre*, to furnish with arms ; *arma*, arms], take up or furnish with arms (usu. pl.), weapon.

Ar-ma-dil'lo [Sp. *armadillo*, dim. of *armado*, armed one], S. American burrowing animal with a hard shell.

Ar'ma-ment [L. *armamentum* ; see **Arms**], force armed for war.

Ar'mis-tice (*ice*=*iss*) (L. *arma*, arms, *stāre*, to stand], stop for a time in fighting.

Ar'mour [L. *armātūra* ; *arma*, arms], arms for protecting. **Armo'rial.**

Ar'mour-er, maker of arms, one in charge of arms.

Ar'mour-y, place where arms are kept.

Arm'pit [**Arm** and **Pit**], hollow between shoulder and arm.

Arms [L. *arma*, arms], weapons, devices borne on shields and banners by families, kingdoms, etc.

Ar'my [F. *armée* ; L. *armāre*, to arm], body of men armed for war.

A-ro'ma [Gk. *arōma*, a spice], agreeable smell, fragrance.

A-ro-mat'ic, fragrant, spicy.

A-round' [*a-*, on, and **Round**], on every side, about.

A-rouse' [*a* (intensive), and **Rouse**], stir up.

Ar-raign' [O.F. *araisnier* ; *à*, to, *raison* (L. *ratio*), reason], to call to the bar of a court to answer to a charge, accuse.

Ar-range' [O.F. *à*, to, *rangier*, to range], put in order. **Arrange'ment.**

Ar'rant [variant of **Errant**], thorough (in a bad sense).

Ar'ras [F. *Arras*, a town in Artois famed for tapestry], tapestry.

Ar-ray' [O.F. *areyer* ; L. *ad*, to, and L.G. *rēde*, ready], order of battle, dress ; draw up in order, dress.

Ar-rears' [L. *ad*, to, *retro*, behind], that which remains unpaid.

Ar-rest' [L. *ad*, to, *restāre*, to stay], to stop, seize by authority of law ; act of arresting, seizure.

Ar-ri'val, coming to a place.

Ar-rive' [L. *ad*, to, *rīpa*, a bank, shore], come, reach.

Ar'ro-gant, proud and insolent.

Ar'ro-gate [L. *ad*, to, *rogāre* (p.p. *rogātus*), to ask], claim unduly or proudly.

Ar'row [O.E. *earh*, *arwe*], pointed weapon to be shot from a bow.

Ar'row-root [so named because used as an antidote against poisoned arrows], plant yielding starch used as food.

Ar'sen-al [Ital. *arsenale* ; Arab. *dār*, a house, *al*, the, *çinā'ah*, construction], place for warlike stores.

Ar'sen-ic [Arab. *azzernikh* ; *al*, the, *zernīkh*, orpiment, yellow arsenic], mineral poison.

Ar'son [L. *ardēre* (p.p. *arsus*), to burn], wilful setting on fire.

Art [L. *ars* (*artis*), art], skill in doing some special work well, painting and sculpture, cunning.

Ar'te-ry [L. and Gk. *artēria*, the windpipe], vessel which conveys blood from the heart.

Ar-te'si-an [F. *Artois*, town in France, L. *Artesium*], kind of deep well bored into the earth.

Art'ful, cunning.

Ar'ti-choke [Ital. *articiocco* ; Arab. *al kharshūf*], a thistle-like plant.

Ar'ti-cle [L. *articulus*, dim. of *artus*, a joint], distinct portion, particular one, part of speech (in grammar).

Ar-tic'u-late [see **Article**], jointed, distinctly uttered ; to joint, speak distinctly.

Ar-tic'u-la'tion, connection by joints, utterance of distinct sounds.

Ar'ti-fice (*ice=iss*) [L. *ars* (*art-is*), art, *facere*, to make], skill, cunning.

Ar-tif'i-cer, mechanic, one whose work requires special skill.

Ar-ti-fi'cial, made by art, not natural.

Ar-til'ler-y [O.F. *artillerie*, fr. *artiller*, a maker of artillery ; L. *ars* (*art-is*), art], cannon, soldiers who manage the cannon.

Ar'ti-san [L. *artītus*, skilled, *ars* (*art-is*), art], handicraftsman.

Art'ist, one who practises a fine art.

Ar-tis'tic, following the rules of art.

Art'less, without art, simple.

As [contr. of **Also**, O.E. *allswá*], in the same degree, though, which, while.

As-bes'tos [Gk. *a-*, not, *sbestos*, quenchable], fibrous mineral which does not burn.

As-cend' [L. *ad*, to, *scandere* (p.p. *scansus*), to climb], go up, climb.

As-cend'an-cy, or **As-cend'en-cy**, control.

As-cen'sion, rising.

As-cent', rise, act of climbing.

As-cer-tain' [L. *ad*, to, *cernere*, to decide], find out, make sure.

As-cet'ic [Gk. adj. *ascēticos*, from noun *ascētēs*, one given to exercise, an athlete], extremely self-denying ; one who practises rigid self-denial.

A-scribe' [L. *ad*, to, *scrībere*, to write], refer to a person or cause.

A-sep'tic [Gk. *a-*, not, *sēpticos*, decaying], not liable to decay.

Ash [O.E. *æsc*], kind of tree.

Ash (usu. pl.) [O.E. *asce*, ashes], remains of what is burned.

A-shamed' [O.E. *a-*, very, *scamian*, to shame], full of shame.

Ash'lar [L. *axilla*, dim. of *axis*, an axis, a board], masonry consisting of square hewn stones.

As'i-nine [L. *asinus*, an ass], of or like an ass.

Ask [O.E *áscian*, *acsian*], to question, call for an answer.

A-skance' [?], with a side glance, sideways.

A-skew' [?], twisted to one side.

Asp [Gk. *aspis*], small poisonous serpent.

As-par'a-gus [Gk. *asparagos*. Etym. doubtful. Earlier *sparrow-grass*], garden vegetable.

As'pect [L. *aspicere* (p.p. *aspectus*), to look at ; *ad*, to, *specere*, to look], look. [poplar.

Asp'en, Asp [O.E *æspe*, *æps*], trembling

As-per'i-ty [L. *asper*, rough], harshness.

As-per'sion [L. *aspergere* (p.p. *aspersus*), to besprinkle], slander, evil report.

As'phalt (*ph=f*) [Gk. *asphaltos*, asphalt (an Eastern word], mineral pitch.

As'pho-del (*ph=f*) [Gk. *asphodelos*], plant of the lily kind. [suffocate.

As-phyx'i-ate [Gk. *a-*, not, *sphyxis*, pulse],

As'pic [Etym. dub.], savoury meat-jelly.

As'pir-ant (*or* **As-pi'rant**) [see **Aspire**], one who aspires, candidate.

As'pi-rate, breathing sound, sound of *h*.

As-pi-ra'tion, desire, drawing of breath.

As-pire' [L. *ad*, to, *spirāre*, to breathe], to aim at higher things.

Ass [O.E. *assa*], animal of horse family with long ears.

As'sa-gai, As'se-gai [Arab. *azzaghayah* ; *al*, the, and a Berber word *zaghayah*], slender spear.

As-sail' [L. *ad*, to, *salīre*, to leap], attack.

As-sail'ant, one who attacks.

As-sas'sin [Arab. *hashshash*, *hashishiyy*, eater of hashish, the dried leaves of a kind of hemp], one who tries to kill treacherously.

As-sas'sin-ate, kill by secret assault.

As-sault' [L. *ad*, to, *salīre* (p.p. *saltus*), to leap], violent attack ; to attack.

As-say' [same as **Essay**], try (the purity of metal or ore).

As-sem'blage, As-sem'bly, company.

As-sem'ble [O.F. *asembler* ; Late L. *assimulāre*, to bring together ; *ad*, to, *simul*, together], come or bring together.

As-sent' [L. *ad*, to, *sentīre*, to feel, to perceive], agree to ; act of agreeing to.

As-sert' [L. *ad*, to, *serere* (p.p. *sertus*), to join], say that anything is so. [asserted.

As-ser'tion, act of asserting, or that which is

As-sess' [L. *assidēre* (p.p. *assessus*), to sit near], fix the value of. **Assess'or**.

As'sets [O.F. *asez*, enough ; L. *ad*, to, *satis*, enough], property (of a bankrupt or of a deceased person).

As-sev′er-ate [L. *ad*, to, *sevērus*, earnest], assert seriously.

As-si-du′i-ty, constant attention, diligence.

As-sid′u-ous [L. *assiduus*, fr. *assidēre*, to sit near], diligent, unwearied.

As-sign′ (*sign=sine*) [L. *ad*, to, *signum*, a mark], mark out, make over.

As′sig-na′tion, appointment to meet.

As-sim′i-late [L. *ad*, to, *similis*, like], make like, absorb.

As-sist′ [L. *ad*, to, *sistere*, to place], to help.

As-sist′ance, help.

As-sist′ant, helper.

As-si′zes [O.F. *asise*, assembly of judges, a tax ; L. *ad*, to, *sedēre* (p.p. *sessus*), to sit], sessions of the judges in English and Irish county towns.

As-so′ci-ate (*c=sh*) [L. *ad*, to, *socius*, a companion], keep company ; companion.

As-so′ci-a′tion, union.

As-soil′zie (*assoil′yi*) [cf. arch. *assoil*, to absolve from sin, 3rd pers. sing. pres. indic. of O.F. *assoudre* ; L. *ab*, from, *solvere*, to loosen]. Scottish law term meaning to acquit.

As′so-nance [L. *ad*, to, *sonus*, sound], resemblance of sound ; rhyming of vowels of corresponding syllables and not of the consonants.

As-sort′ [L. *ad*, to, *sors* (*sort-is*), lot], arrange, sort, classify.

As-suage′ (*u=w*) [L. *ad*, to, *suāvis*, sweet], soften, calm.

As-sume′ [L. *ad*, to, *sūmere* (p.p. *sumptus*), to take], take upon oneself, take for granted.

As-sump′tion, act of assuming, a thing assumed.

As-su′rance (*ss=sh*), positive statement, confidence, impudence, insurance.

As-sure′ [L. *ad*, to, *sēcūrus*, safe], say with certainty.

As′ter [Gk. *astēr*, a star], kind of flower.

As′ter-isk [Gk. *astēriskos*, a little star], star-shaped mark (*).

A-stern′ [*a-*, in, at, and **Stern**], in or at the stern. [planet.

As′ter-oid [Gk. *astēr*, a star, *eidos*, form], small

As*th*′**ma** [Gk. *asthma*, fr. *azein*, to breathe hard], disease which causes shortness of breath.

A-stir′ [*a-*, on, and **Stir**], in active motion.

As-ton′ish [L. *ex*, out, *tonāre*, to thunder], surprise greatly.

As-tound′ [see **Astonish**], stun with surprise.

As′tral [L. *astralis* ; *astrum*, a star], pertaining to the stars, starlike. [way.

A-stray′ [*a-*, on, and **Stray**], out of the right

A-stride′ [*a-*, on, and **Stride**], with legs apart.

A-strin′gen-cy [see **Astringent**], power of contracting.

A-strin′gent [L. *ad*, to, *stringere*, to draw tight], substance that produces contraction ; contracting.

As-trol′o-gy [Gk. *astron*, a star, *logos*, a discourse], study of the stars for the purpose of foretelling events.

As-tron′o-mer [Gk. *astron*, a star, *nomos*, a law], student of astronomy.

As-tron′o-my, the science of the stars.

As-tute′ [L. *astūtus*, crafty], shrewd.

A-sun′der [*a-*, on, and **Sunder**], apart, in two.

A-sy′lum [Gk. *asylon* ; *a-*, not, *sylē*, a right of seizure], place of refuge and protection (esp. for lunatics).

At′av-ism [L. *atavus*, great-grandfather's grandfather], resemblance to remote ancestors, reversion to original type in plants and animals. **Atavis′tic**.

A′the-ism [Gk. *a-*, not, *theos*, God], belief that there is no God.

Ath′lete [Gk. *athlētēs*, a combatant], one who excels in physical exercises.

Ath-let′ic, of or connected with athletes.

A-thwart′ [*a-*, on, and **Thwart**], across.

At′las [Gk. *Atlas*, a demi-god, who carried the world on his shoulders], book of maps.

At′mos-phere [Gk. *atmos*, vapour, *sphaira*, a sphere], whole mass of air. **Atmospher′ic**.

A-toll′ [Maldive *atollon*, *atoll*], ring-shaped coral island.

At′om (Gk. *atomos*, indivisible ; *a-*, not, *temnein*, to cut), the smallest particle in which matter actually exists.

A-tone′ [At and One], set at one, make up for.

A-tone′ment, a setting at one, amends.

A-tro′cious [*ci=zh*] [L. *atrox* (*atrōc-is*), cruel], extremely wicked.

A-tro′ci-ty (*ŏ*), cruel wickedness.

At′ro-phy [Gk. *atrophia* ; *a-*, not, and *trophē*, food], a wasting away.

At-tach′ [L. *ad*, to, and the root of **Tack**], bind, fasten.

At-tach′ment, act of attaching, affection.

At-tack′ [a doublet of **Attach**], fall upon ; onset.

At-tain′ [L. *ad*, to, *tangere*, to touch], reach by effort.

At-tain′der [see **Attain**], loss of civil rights in consequence of sentence of death, etc.

At′tar [Arab. *'utur*, perfume ; fr. *'atara*, to breathe perfume], fragrant oil obtained from roses. [trial.

At-tempt′ [L. *ad*, to, *tentāre*, to try], try ;

At-tend′ [L. *ad*, to, *tendere* (p.p. *tentus*), to stretch], give heed to, be present at, wait.

At-tend′ance, waiting, presence. [with.

At-tend′ant, one who attends ; going along

At-ten′tion, act of giving heed to. [thin.

At-ten′u-ate [L. *ad*, to, *tenuis*, thin], become

At-test′ [L. *ad*, to, *testis*, a witness], bear witness to. **Attesta′tion**.

At′tic [from the Attic order of architecture ; Gk. *Atticos*, Attic], room just below the roof.

At-tire′ [O.F. *atirer*, to adorn ; *a*, to, *tire*, *tiere*, a row], to dress ; dress. [posture.

At′ti-tude [L. *aptitudo*, aptitude ; *aptus*, fit],

At′ti-tu′di-nize, strike attitudes.

At-tor′ney (*o=ŭ* as in **Turn**) [L. *ad*, to, *tornāre*, to turn], in English law, any person authorised to act for another, lawyer.

At-tract′ [L. *ad*, to, *trahere* (p.p. *tractus*), to draw], draw to.

At-trac′tion, power of drawing to, that which attracts.

At-trac′tive, having the power of attracting.

At-trib′ute [L. *ad*, to, *tribuere* (p.p. *tributus*), to assign], refer, as an effect to a cause.

At′tri-bute [see **Attribute** (vb.)], quality which belongs to.

At-tri′tion [L. *atterere* (p.p. *attrītus*), to rub away], a rubbing away, friction.

At-tune′ [L. *ad*, to, and **Tune**], put in tune.

Au′burn [L. *alburnus*, whitish], reddish brown (used of *hair*).

Auc′tion [L. *augēre* (p.p. *auctus*), to increase], public sale to highest bidder.

Auc-tion-eer′, one who sells by auction.

Au-da′cious [L. *audax* (*audāc-is*), bold], bold.

Au-da′ci-ty, boldness. [heard.

Au′di-ble [L. *audīre*, to hear], that can be

Au′di-ence [L. *audīre*, to hear], a hearing, assembly of hearers.

Au′dit [L. *audīre*, to hear], examine and adjust accounts; an examination of accounts.

Au′di-tor, one who audits accounts.

Au′ger [O.E. *nafugár*, an auger; *nafu*, a nave, *gár*, a piercer], tool for boring holes.

Aught [O.E. *áht*, *áwiht*, fr. *á*, ever, and *wiht*, wight, whit], anything.

Aug-ment′ [L. *augmentāre*, to enlarge, fr. *augēre*, to increase], make or grow larger.

Aug-men-ta′tion, increase.

Au′gur [L. *augur*, a soothsayer, perh. fr. *avis*, a bird, and *garrire*, to talk], one who foretold the future from observation of birds; forebode.

Au′gu-ry, omen, sign of the future. [noble.

Au′gust [L. *augustus*, venerable], majestic,

Au′gust [L. *Augustus* (*mensis*), (month) of August, named after *Augustus* Cæsar], eighth month of the year (Rom. sixth).

Auk [cogn. with Swed. *alka*; Dan. *alke*; O.N. *álka*, an auk], Arctic sea-bird.

Aunt [L. *amita*, a father's sister], sister of father or mother.

Au′re-ole [L. *aureola*, golden; *aurum*, gold], halo, circle of rays of light.

Au-ric′u-lar [L. *auricula*, the lobe of the ear, double dim. of *auris*, the ear], told in the ear. [gold-bearing.

Au-rif′er-ous [L. *aurum*, gold, *ferre*, to bear],

Au′rist [L. *auris*, the ear], ear-doctor.

Au-ro′ra Bo-re-a′lis [L. *aurōra*, dawn, *borealis*, northern], northern lights.

Aus-cul-ta′tion [L. *auscultāre* (p.p. *auscultātus*), to listen], examination of health by listening to the sounds of the chest, etc.

Aus′pi-ces [L. *auspicium*, watching of birds for omens; *avis*, a bird, *specere*, to look into], omens, patronage.

Aus-pi′cious (*pĭ*) [see **Auspices**], giving promise of success. [severe.

Aus-tere′ [Gk. *austēros*, harsh; *auein*, to dry],

Aus-ter′i-ty, plainness, severity.

Aus′tral [L. *Australis*, southern; *Auster*, south wind], southern.

Au-then′tic [Gk. *authentēs*, one who does a thing himself], genuine.

Au-then′ti-cate [M.L. *authenticāre*; see **Authentic**], prove authentic.

Au-then-ti′ci-ty (*i* short), genuineness.

Au′thor [L. *auctor*, an originator, *augēre* (p.p. *auctus*), to increase], one who creates, a writer of books. [manding.

Au-thor′i-ta-tive, having authority, com-

Au-thor′i-ty [see **Author**], right to command or to act, a person in power, book or person referred to in support of a statement.

Au′thor-ize, give a right to act.

Au′to-bi-og′ra-phy [Gk. *autos*, self, *bios*, life, *graphein*, to write], history of a life written by the subject of it.

Au′to-bus (short for **automobile omnibus**), motor-bus.

An′to-crat [Gk. *autos*, self, *cratos*, might], uncontrolled ruler.

Au′to-graph [Gk. *autos*, self, *graphein*, to write], one's own handwriting, signature.

Au-to-mat′ic [see **Automaton**], self-acting.

Au-tom′a-ton (pl. *-ta*) [Gk. *automatos*, self-moving; *autos*, self, *-matos*, moving], machine which is or appears to be self-acting.

Au-to-mo-bile′ (*i=ee*) [F. fr. Gk. *autos*, self; L. *movēre*, to move, moving], motor-car.

Au-ton′o-my [Gk. *autos*, self, *nomos*, law], self-government.

Au′tumn [L. *autumnus*, *auctumnus*, perh. from *augēre* (p.p. *auctus*), to increase], third season of the year.

Au-tum′nal, of or peculiar to autumn.

Aux-il′ia-ry [L. *auxilium*, help], helping, a helper; (pl.) foreign troops employed in war.

A-vail′ [prob. fr. F. *valoir*, to be worth; L. *valēre*, to be strong], be of use or advantage; use, advantage.

A-vail′a-ble, that can be got or used for.

Av′a-lanche [F. *à val*, to the valley], sliding mass of snow or ice.

Av′a-rice (*ice=iss*) [L. *avārus*, greedy], greed of gain.

Av′a-ri′cious (*ci=sh*), greedy of gain.

Avaunt [F. *avant*, forward], begone !

A-venge′ [O.F *avengier*; L. *ad*, to, *vindicāre*, to avenge], take satisfaction for a wrong.

Av′e-nue [L. *ad*, to, *venīre*, to come], way of approach, walk bordered by trees, broad street.

A-ver′ [F. *avérer*; L. *ad*, to, and *vērus*, true], assert. [quantities.

Av′er-age [?], mean of unequal sums or

A-verse′, disinclined, unwilling.

A-ver′sion, dislike.

A-vert′ [L. *a* (*ab*), away, and *vertere*, to turn], turn from.

A′vi-a-ry (*A=ai*) [L. *avis*, a bird], place for keeping birds.

A-vi-a′tion (*A=ai*) [L. *avis*, a bird], act or art of travelling in flying-machines or airships, etc.

A′vi-a-tor (*A=ai*), one who directs a flying-machine, airship, etc. [eagerness.

A-vid′i-ty [L. *avidus*, greedy], greediness,

A-vo-ca′tion [L. *a* (*ab*), away, *vocāre* (p.p. *vocātus*), to call], hobby (improperly used for **Vocation**).

A-void' [O.F. *es* (L. *ex*), out, *vuide*, void], keep clear of.

Av'oir-du-pois' (*s*=*z*) [F. *avoir du pois*, to have weight], British standard system of weights.

A-vouch' [O.F. *avochier*; L. *advocāre*; see **Vouch**], affirm, call upon as defender.

A-vow' [L. *ad*, to, *vovēre*, to vow], declare openly. **Avow'al.** [wait for.

A-wait' [O.N.F. *awaitier*, cogn. with **Wait**],

A-wake' [O.E. *awœcnan*; see **Wake**], rouse ; not sleeping.

A-wa'ken [see **Waken**], awake, arouse.

A-ward' [A.F. *awarder*; O.F. *es* (L. *ex*), out, *guarder*, to guard], adjudge, assign after consideration ; final decision of judges.

A-ware' [O.E. *gewœr*], on guard, conscious of.

A-way' [O.E. *on weg*, on way], to or at a distance, without ceasing, without delay.

Awe [O.E. *ege*, awe], reverence mingled with fear.

Aw'ful, filling with awe, dreadful.

Awk'ward [perh. fr. O.N. *afug*, turned the wrong way], clumsy.

Awl [O.E. *œl*], pointed tool for boring holes in leather or wood.

Awn'ing [perh. fr. F. *auvent*, etym. dub.], canvas roof.

A-wry' [*a-*, on, and **Wry**], turned or twisted to one side.

Axe [O.E. *œx* ; akin to Gk. *axinē* and perh. L. *ascia*], tool for hewing timber, etc.

Ax'il-la-ry [L. *axilla*, the armpit], pertaining to the armpit.

Ax'i-om [Gk. *axiōma* ; *axioein*, to approve], self-evident truth. **Axioma'tic.**

Ax'is [L. *axis*, an axis, a pivot], imaginary line on which a body revolves or about which parts are arranged.

Ax'le [Icel. *öxull*, axis, dim. of form found in L. *axis*, a pivot], pin or spindle on which a wheel revolves.

Ax'le-tree [**Axle** and **Tree**], bar or beam connecting the opposite wheels of a carriage.

Ay, Aye (=*i*) [perh. variant of **Yea**], yes.

A'yah (*Ay*=*i*) [Port. *aia*, a nurse, governess], native Indian nurse or lady's maid.

Aye (*ai*) [O.N. *ei*, *ey*, cogn. with L. *aevum*, an age], ever, always.

A-za'le-a (*za*=*zai*) [Gk. *azalea*, fem. of *azaleos*, dry], kind of flowering shrub.

A'zure (or **Az'ure**) (*z*=*zh*) [O.F. *azur* ; M.L. *azura* ; Arab. *al*, the, *lazward*, fr. Pers. *lazhward*, an azure-coloured stone named from the mines of Lajward], sky-blue.

B

Bab'ble [imit. of a baby's "*ba-ba*"], utter unmeaning words ; senseless talk, murmur.

Ba'bel [fr. the tower described in Gen. xi.], confusion of sounds, din.

Ba'boo, Ba'bu [Hindu *babu*], Hindu title like Mr, native Indian clerk who writes English.

Bab-oon' [?], large ape.

Bac-cha-na'li-an [L. *Bacchanālis*, a worshipper of *Bacchus*], given to drunken revels.

Bach'e-lor [L. *baccalārius*, a farm-servant], unmarried man, one who has taken the lowest degree in arts, etc.

Ba-cil'lus (pl. -**li**) [L.L. dim. of L. *baculus*, a stick], microscopic rod-shaped organism, disease-germ.

Back [O.E. *baec*], hinder part of the body in man, upper part in beasts ; in the rear, to the place from which one came ; to support, bet on, move backward.

Back'bi'ter, one who speaks spitefully of an absent person.

Back'gam'mon [**Back** and M.E. *gamen*, a game], game of chance played with draughts and dice.

Back'ground, ground or space behind, part of picture, etc., that sets off things in front.

Back'hand', Back-hand'ed, with the hand turned backward, indirect.

Back-slide', fall back into sin.

Back'ward, directed to the rear, dull, behindhand.

Ba'con [O.F. *bacon*, fr. O.H.G. *bacho*], cured back and sides of a pig.

Bac-te'ri-um (pl. **Bac-te'ri-a**) [Gk. *bactērion*, dim. of *bactron*, a stick], microscopic vegetable organism.

Bad [M.E. *badde*, perh. O.E. *bœddel*], worthless, of poor quality, wicked.

Badge [M.E. etym. dub.], thing worn as a distinctive mark.

Bad'ger [Modern E., perh. fr. **Badge**], burrowing animal ; to worry.

Bad'in-age (*age*=*ahzh*) [F. *badiner*, to jest], banter, light jocularity.

Bad'min-ton [name of country seat of Duke of Beaufort in Gloucester], kind of lawntennis played with shuttlecocks, a summer drink.

Baf'fle [?], check, defeat.

Bag [O.N. *baggi* ; cf. O. Swed. *bagge*, a pack], sack or pouch ; put in a bag ; capture, swell like a bag.

Bag'a-telle' [It. *bagatella*, a trifle, dim. perh. of *baga*, a chest], trifle, game resembling billiards. [luggage.

Bag'gage [O.F. *bagage* ; *bague*, a bundle],

Bag'pipe, musical wind-instrument.

Bail [L. *bajulāre*, to carry a burden], security for the appearance of a prisoner, to get out of custody on bail, to procure release by giving bail.

Bail [L.L. *bacula*, dim. of *bacca*, *baca*, a water vessel], throw water out of a boat.

Bail [O.F. perh. fr. L. *baculum*, a stick], cross-pieces over stumps at cricket.

Bail'ie [see **Bailiff**], town magistrate in Scotland.

Bail'iff [Late L. *bājulīvus*, a custodian], sheriff's deputy, overseer of an estate.

Bait [O.N. *beita*, to cause to bite], something on a hook to attract fish ; furnish with bait, torment for sport.

Baize [mistake for *bayes*, pl. fem. of F. *bai*, L. *badius*, chestnut-coloured], coarse woollen cloth. [heat.

Bake [O.E. *bacan*], cook or harden in dry

Bake'house, place for baking.

Ba'ker, one who bakes.

Ba'ker-y, bake-house.

Bal'ance [L. *bilanx* (*bilanc-is*), having two scales ; *bi* (*bis*), twice, *lanx*, plate, scale of a balance], pair of scales, equality of weight, etc., excess on either side of an account ; poise, weigh, make an entry necessary to equalize accounts.

Bal'co-ny [It. *balcone*, a stage ; O.H.G. *balcho*, a beam], gallery in front of a window.

Bald (*a=aw*) [Gael. and Irish *bal*, a spot, orig. a white spot], without hair on the head, bare. [nonsense.

Bal'der-dash [Du. *balderen*, to roar (?)],

Bal'dric (*a=aw*) [O.F. *baudrei*, cf. M.H.G. *balderich*, perh. fr. *balteus*, belt ; L. *baltes*], warrior's belt slung from one shoulder to opposite hip.

Bale [O.F. *bale*, fr. It. *balla*, *palla*, fr. O.H.G. *balla*, *palla*, or Gk. *palla*, ball], large package of goods.

Bale [O.E. *balu*, evil], misery.

Bale [see Bail[2]], throw out water.

Bale'ful, hurtful, woeful.

Balk, Baulk (*bawk*) [O.E. *balca*, a ridge], ridge of land left unploughed, great beam ; baffle, hinder.

Ball[1] [M.E. *bal*; O.N. *böllr*], round mass.

Ball[2] [Late L. *ballāre*, to dance], assembly for dancing.

Bal'lad [Provençal *balada*, a dancing-song], short narrative poem.

Bal'last [perh. O. Swed. and O. Dan. *barlast*, a bare load, mere weight], any heavy substance put into the hold to keep a ship steady.

Bal-loon' [augment. form of It. *balla*. See Ball[1]], ball filled with gas.

Bal'lot [It. *ballotta*, dim. of *balla*, a ball. See Ball[1]], secret voting by use of balls, tickets, or papers ; vote by ballot.

Balm (*al=ah*) [L. *balsamum*, balsam], fragrant herb, anything soothing.

Balmy (*al=ah*), fragrant, mild.

Bal'sam (*al=awl*) [L. *balsamum*], fragrant resin, annual garden plant.

Bal'us-ter [It. *balausta* ; Gk. *balaustion*, the flower of the wild pomegranate], pillar supporting a protecting rail.

Bal'us-trade, row of balusters topped by a rail edging a balcony or staircase.

Bam-boo' [Malay *bambū*], giant grass with a woody stem.

Bam-boo'zle [?], deceive by confusing.

Ban [O.E. *bannan*, to summon], a curse ; put under a curse.

Ban'al [F. *banal*], commonplace, stupid.

Ba-na'na [Sp. *banana*, from native name in Guinea], palm-like plant, also its fruit.

Band[1] [O. Teut. *bindan*, to bind ; through O.N. *band* ; F. *bande*], a tie, strap.

Band[2] [F. *bande* ; L.L. *bandum*, banner, from Teut. as Band[1]], a company ; unite in a band.

Band'age [see Band[1]], strip of material used for binding ; cover with a bandage.

Ban-da'na [Hindu *bāndhnū*, a method of dyeing by tying the cloth so as to prevent some parts from receiving the dye], coloured spotted handkerchief.

Band'box [see Band[1]], light box for bands, etc.

Ban'dit (pl. **Ban'dits** or **Ban-dit'ti**) [It. *bandito*, pl. *banditi* ; M.L. *bannīre*, to proclaim], brigand.

Ban'dog [earlier *band-dog*, see Band[1]], chained dog, mastiff.

Ban-do-leer', Ban-do-lier' [It. *bandoliera* ; *banda*, a band], shoulder-belt with cartridge-loops.

Ban'dy [F. *bander*, to bandy, at tennis], toss to and fro, exchange.

Ban'dy [perh. from *bandy*, a curved stick for striking a ball in an old game called *bandy*], bent.

Bane [O.E. *bana*, murder, ban], poison, cause of ruin.

Bang (?) [cf. O.N. *banga* ; Dan. *banke*, to beat ; O. Swed. *bång* ; Icel. *bang*, a hammering], to thump ; heavy blow.

Ban'gle [Hindu *bangri*, a bracelet], ring for the arm or ankle.

Ban'ian, Ban'yan [Port. *banyan* ; Sanskrit *banij*, a merchant. The tree was used as a market-place for merchants], Indian fig-tree.

Ban'ish [O.F. *banir* (pr.p. *banissant*) ; Low L. *bannīre*, to proclaim], drive away.

Ban'ish-ment, forced absence, exile.

Ban'is-ter [corrupt. of Baluster], baluster.

Ban'jo [Negro corrupt. of earlier *bandore* ; Gk. *pandoura*, a musical instrument with three strings], stringed musical instrument.

Bank[1] [M.E. *banke* (of Teut. origin)], mound, side of a river, etc.

Bank[2] [F. *banque* ; It. *banca*], place for depositing and lending money ; put in a bank.

Bank'rupt [Bank[2] and L. *rumpere* (p.p. *ruptus*), to break], one who cannot pay his debts ; unable to pay debts.

Bank'rupt-cy, state of being bankrupt.

Ban'ner [Low L. *bandāria*, a banner ; probably allied to Band[2]], flag.

Banns [pl. of variant of Ban], proclamation of marriage.

Ban'quet [F., dim. of *banc*, a bench], feast.

Ban'tam [from *Bantam* in Java], kind of small fowl, soldier under normal minimum height.

Ban'ter [?], jest about ; raillery.

Bap'tism, washing with water as a sacrament.

Bap-tize' [Gk. *baptein*, to dip], administer baptism.

Bap'tist, one who baptizes (esp. of John the B.), one who approves of adult baptism only.

Bap'tis-ter-y or **-try,** building or part of a building where baptisms take place.

Bar [Late L. *barra*, a bar], long piece, hindrance, bank at a river's mouth, line across the staff in music, enclosure in court of justice, profession of barrister, counter where liquors are sold ; close by a bar, hinder.

Barb [L. *barba*, a beard], point that curves backward in an arrow, fish-hook, etc.

Barb [from *Barbary*], breed of horse from Barbary.

Bar-ba′ri-an [see **Barbarous**], a savage.

Bar-bar′ic [see **Barbarous**], like or belonging to barbarous peoples.

Bar′ba-rism, state of savagery.

Bar-bar′i-ty, cruelty.

Bar′bar-ous [Gk. *barbaros*, foreign, perh. imit. of strange sounds of a foreign language], savage, uncivilized, cruel. [-dresser.

Bar′ber [L. *barba*, a beard], hair-cutter and

Bar′bi-can [F. *barbacane*, perh. fr. Arab.-Pers. *bab-khanah*, a gatehouse], projecting watch-tower over a gate.

Bard [W. *bardd* ; Gael. and Irish *bàrd*, a poet], minstrel, poet.

Bare [O.E. *bœr*], uncovered.

Barely, scarcely.

Bar′gain [O.F. *bargaigner* ; Late L. *bar-cāniāre*, to bargain], agreement, cheap purchase ; make a bargain.

Barge [O.F., prob. same as **Bark**[3]], elegantly-fitted rowing-boat, flat-bottomed freight-boat.

Bar′i-tone [It. *baritono* ; Gk. *barys*, heavy, *tonos*, tone], voice between bass and tenor.

Bark[1] [Swed. and Dan. *bark* ; O.N. *börkr*], rind of a tree.

Bark[2] [O.E. *beorcan*], short, loud sound made by a dog ; to utter barks.

Bark,[3] **Barque** [F. *barque* ; fr. It., Sp. or Port. *barca*, fr. L. *barca*, a ship's boat], three-masted vessel(fore and main square-rigged).

Bar′ley [O.E. *bœrlic* ; *bere*, barley, and *lic*, like], kind of grain.

Barm [O.E. *beorma*], yeast.

Barn [O.E. *bere*, barley, *œrn*, a place for storing], building for storing grain, etc.

Bar′na-cle [O.F. *bernaque*. Etym: doubtful], shell-fish adhering to ships, etc.

Bar′na-cle (usu. pl.) [M.E. *bernak* ; O.F. *bernac*], hinged instrument placed on nose of a horse to keep it quiet ; spectacles.

Ba-rom′e-ter [Gk. *baros*, weight, *metron*, a measure], instrument for measuring the weight of the atmosphere.

Bar′on [M.E. and O.F. *barun* ; Late L. *baro*, (*barōn-is*), a man], peer of the lowest rank.

Bar′on-ess [O.F. *barnesse* ; see **Baron**], fem. of baron.

Bar′on-et [dim. of **Baron**], hereditary title of honour below baron ; *Sir* prefixed to name and *Bart.* added.

Bar′on-et-cy, rank of a baronet.

Ba-ro′ni-al, relating to a baron or barony.

Bar′o-ny, domain or rank of a baron.

Ba-rouche′ (*ouche*=*oosh*) [It. *baroccio*, orig. a two-wheeled car ; L. *birotus*, two-wheeled], kind of four-wheeled carriage.

Bar′racks [It. *baracca*, a soldiers' tent], building to lodge soldiers.

Bar′rage [F. *barre*, a bar], obstruction put in a river to increase depth of water, artificial cloud of smoke raised to cover an attack.

Bar′rel [perh. from L.L. *barra*, a bar], a round wooden vessel made of bars or staves and bound with hoops; metallic tube.

Bar′ren [?], producing nothing.

Bar-ri-cade′ [Sp. *barricada*, a barricade; *barrica*, a barrel], quickly-built barrier; defend by a barricade.

Bar′ri-er [L.L. *barra*, a bar], anything which hinders approach.

Bar′ris-ter [L.L. *barra*, bar], pleader at the English or Irish bar.

Bar′row [O.E. *beran*, to bear], small hand- or one-wheel carriage.

Bar′row [O.E. *beorg*, a mountain], large mound over a grave.

Bar′ter [O.F. *barat*, cheating], exchange of goods ; trade by barter.

Ba′salt [L. *basaltes*, from an African word], an igneous rock.

Base[1] [L. *basis* ; Gk. *basis*, a step, a base], groundwork ; found on.

Base[2] [L.L. *bassus*, short, low], vile, low.

Base′ball, American kind of cricket.

Base′ment [see **Base**[1]], ground-floor.

Bash′ful [for Abash+*ful*], shy.

Bas′il (*s*=*z*) [O.F. *basile* ; Gk. *basilicos*, royal], sweet herb.

Bas′i-lisk (*bas*=*baz*) [Gk. *basiliscos*, a kinglet ; also a lizard, from a spot, like a crown, on the head], kind of lizard.

Ba′sin [perh. from Late L. *bacca*, a water-vessel], hollow circular dish, land drained by a river.

Ba′sis [L. and Gk. *basis*], foundation, pedestal.

Bask [O.N. *batha sik*, to bathe oneself], lie in warmth.

Bas′ket [?], a vessel of wickerwork.

Bass [O.E. *bœrs*, a perch ; *byrst*, a bristle], kind of fish.

Bass [corrupt. of **Bast**], inner bark of the lime, thick mat.

Bass (*a*=*ai*) [It. *basso* ; see **Base**[2]], lowest part in music, deepest male voice.

Bass-re-lief′, Bas-re-lief′ [see **Base**[2] and **Relief**], sculpture.

Bas-si-net′ [F. dim. of *bassin*, basin], hooded cot or perambulator.

Bas-soon′ [perh. F. *bas son*, deep sound], double-reed instrument.

Bast [O.E. *bœst*], inner bark of the lime-tree. [fat.

Baste [?], beat, moisten roasting meat with

Baste [O.F. *bastir*. Etym. doubtful], sew with long stitches.

Bas-ti-na′do [Sp. *bastonada*, a beating, *baston*, a stick], Eastern punishment by blows on the feet with a stick.

Bas′ti-on [It. *bastione*, L.L. *bastire*, to build], projecting part of a fortification.

Bat [Scand. ; cf. Dan. *aften-bakke*, evening-bat], flying animal with a body like a mouse.

Bat [O.F. *batte*, club, *battre*, to strike], flat club for games. [one time.

Batch [O.E. *bacan*, to bake], bread baked at

Bate [short for **Abate**], abate.

Bath [O.E. *bœth*, orig. a warm place], plunge in water, a place for bathing. [water.

Bathe [O.E. *bathian*], cover the body with

Ba'thos [Gk. *bathos* depth], absurd descent from elevated to common place in speech or writing.

Bat'man [F. *bât*, pack-saddle], officer's servant, man in charge of pack-horse.

Bat'on [F., etym. dub.], staff of office, truncheon.

Bat-tal'i-on [It. *battaglione*, a battalion ; *battaglia*, a battle], body of foot-soldiers which is divided into companies.

Bat'ten [another spelling of **Baton**], narrow strip of timber, fasten with battens.

Bat'ten [O.N. *batna*, to grow better], grow fat (at expense of another).

Bat'ter [frequent. of obs. vb. *bat*], mixture of flour, water, eggs, etc., beaten together], beat with force.

Bat'ter-y [F. *batterie*, fr: *battre*, to strike], section of guns, company of artillery, apparatus for producing electricity.

Bat'tle [Late L. *battuālis*, fighting ; *battuere*, to beat], general fight.

Bat'tle-dore [perh. Prov. *batedor*, fr. *batre*, to beat, and suffix *dor* (*tor*)], light bat.

Bat'tle-ment [O.F. *batailler*, to fortify, fr. *bataille*, a turret], notched parapet.

Batt'ue [F. *battre*, to beat], kind of hunt in which game are driven to the slaughter by *beaters*.

Bau'ble, Baw'ble [O.F. *babel*, a child's toy], showy toy, trifle.

Bawl [M.L. *baulāre*, to bark], cry loudly.

Bay [Late L. *baia*, a harbour], inlet of the sea, space added to a room by a projecting window.

Bay [L. *bāca*, a berry], kind of shrub.

Bay [O.F. *bayer*, to yelp], bark at, barking. At bay, forced to face round.

Bay [F. *bai* ; L. *badius*, bay-co'oured], reddish brown.

Bay'o-net [perh. fr. *Bayonne*, in France], small spear or pike fixed at the end of a musket.

Ba-zaar', Ba-zar' [Pers. *bāzār*, a market], Eastern market, shop for fancy goods, fancy fair.

Beach [?], shore.

Bea'con (*ea=ee*) [O.E. *béacn*, a beacon], signal-fire.

Bead [orig. a prayer ; O.E. *gebed*, a prayer], little ball pierced for stringing.

Bea'dle (*ea=ee*) [O.E. *bydel* ; *béodan*, to bid], inferior parish officer, court crier, caretaker of a church (in Scotland), university mace-bearer. Also **Be'dell.**

Bea'gle (*ea=ee*) [perh. F. *béqueule* from *béer*, to gape, *gueule*, throat], small hunting-dog.

Beak [Late L. *beccus* ; of Gaulish origin], bill of a bird, projection at prow of ancient warship.

Beak'er [perh. fr. Gk. *bikos*, a wine-vessel], large drinking-cup.

Beam [O.E. *béam*], long piece of timber, ray.

Bean [O.E. *béan*], plant of which the seed is in pods, the seed.

Bear (*bair*) [O.E. *beran*, to bear], hold up, carry, bring forth. [animal.

Bear [O.E. *bera*], heavy, thick-furred wild

Beard (*ea=ee*) [O.E. *beard*, cf. Ger. *bart*], hair on the chin.

Bear'ing, carriage, relation.

Beast [L. *bestia*, a beast], four-footed animal.

Beat [O.E. *béatan*], to strike repeatedly, to overcome ; stroke, course frequently gone over.

Be-a-tif'ic [L. *beātus*, blessed, *facere*, to make], making happy, very happy.

Be-at'i-tude [L. *beātus*, blessed], bliss, (pl.) the blessings in the Sermon on the Mount.

Beau (*bō*) (pl. **Beaux**) [F. *beau*, beautiful], dandy, lover.

Beau'te-ous, Beau'ti-ful, having beauty.

Beau'ti-fy, make beautiful.

Beau'ty [O.F. *bealte*, *beaute* ; L. *bellus*, beautiful], that which is pleasing to look at, hear, or think about, loveliness.

Bea'ver [O.E. *beofor*], aquatic animal, its fur, kind of hat.

Bea'ver [M.E. *baviere* ; O.F. *bavière*, bib], lower part of a helmet.

Be-calm' (*al=ah*) [O.E. *be-*, causative, and F. *calme* ; Gk. *cauma*, heat], make calm.

Be-cause' (*s=z*) [By and Cause], by or for the cause.

Beck [same as **Beckon**], sign, nod, etc.

Beck [O.N. *bekkr*], small brook.

Beck'on [O.E. *biecnan*, to make signs], make a sign.

Be-come' [O.E. *becuman*, to arrive ; pref. *be-* and **Come**], come to be, suit.

Bed [O.E. *bed*, *bedd*, cf. Ger. *bett*], thing to sleep on, bottom of a stream, layer of rock.

Bed'ding, mattress and bed-clothes, etc.

Bed'lam [corrupt. of Bethlehem Asylum in London], madhouse. **Bed'lamite.**

Bed-ou-in' (*i=ee*) [Arab. *badawin*, pl. of *badawiy*, dweller in the desert], an Arab of the desert.

Bed'rid-den [O.E. *bedreda* ; *bed*, a bed, and *rida*, a rider], confined to bed.

Bed'stead [O.E. *bed*, a bed, *stede*, a stand], frame to hold a bed.

Bee [O.E. *béo*], honey-storing insect.

Beech [O.E. *bóece*, *béce*, both from an older form *bóc*], tree with a smooth bark.

Beef [F. *bœuf* ; L. *bōs* (*bov-is*, an ox], flesh of an ox or cow.

Beef'eat'er, yeoman of the guard. [hops.

Beer [O.E. *béor*], drink made of malt and

Beet [L. *bēta*, beet], plant with a thick root.

Bee'tle [1] [O.E. *bietel* ; O. Teut. *bautan*, to beat], wooden mallet.

Bee'tle [2] [O.E. *bitula*, biter, *bítan*, to bite], insect with an outer pair of sheath-like wings.

Bee'tle [perh. from **Beetle** [3]], overhang.

Beeves [see **Beef**], cattle.

Be-fall′ [pref. *be-* and **Fall**], happen to.

Be-fit′ting [pref. *be-* and **Fit**], suitable.

Be-friend′ [pref. *be-* and **Friend**], act as a friend to.

Beg [see **Beggar**], ask earnestly, to ask in charity.

Beg′gar [perh.=**Beg Hard**. The *Beghards*, or *Beguins*, were religious devotees in the thirteenth century], one who begs.

Beg′gar-ly, mean.

Be-gin′ [O.E. *beginnan*, fr. pref. *be-* and *ginnan*, to begin], take rise, do the first part.

Be-gin′ning, first act or part. [away!

Be-gone′ [O.E. pref. *be-* and *gan*, to go], go

Be-guile′ [O.E. pref. *be-* and *wil*, a wile], deceive by guile, while away.

Be′gum [Pers. *begum*, a lady of highest rank], Indian Mohammedan princess.

Be-half′ [O.E. *be-*, by, *healf*, side], interest, support. [oneself.

Be-have′ [O.E. *be-*, by, and **Have**], conduct

Be-ha′viour, manner of behaving.

Be-head′ [O.E. *be-*, from, and **Head**], cut the head off.

Be-hest′ [O.E. pref. *be-* and *hæs*, a command], command.

Be-hind′ [O.E. *be-* and *hindan*, at the back], in or to the back of, too late.

Be-hold′ [O.E. *be-* and *haldan*, to hold], look at.

Be-hold′en, indebted.

Be-hoof′ [O.E. *bihóf*], profit.

Be-la′bour [*be-* and **Labour**], beat soundly.

Be-la′ted [p.p. of obsolete *belate*; see **Late**], too late.

Be-lay′ [O.E. *be-* and *lecgan*, to lay], fasten a rope by winding round a pin.

Belch [O.E. *bealcian*, to utter], eject violently from within.

Be-lea′guer [*ea=ee*] [Dutch *be*, round, and *leger*, a camp], besiege.

Bel′fry [O.F. *berfrei*, *belfroi*; M.H.G. *bercorit*, a watch-tower; *bergen*, to protect; O.H.G. *fridu*, peace], bell-tower.

Be-lie′ [O.E. *be-*, by, *léogan*, to lie], give a false notion of.

Be-lief′, that which is held to be true.

Be-lieve′ [O.E. pref. *be-*+*geléfan*, to believe], hold to be true, trust.

Be-lit′tle [*be-* and **Little**], speak slightingly of.

Bell [O.E. *bellé*, a bell, perh. fr. *bellan*, to roar], metal vessel which rings when struck, cup of a flower.

Belle [F. fem. of *beau* (L. *bella*, fem. of *bellus*), beautiful], woman of great beauty.

Bel′li-cose [L. *bellum*, war], warlike.

Bel-li′ger-ent [L. *bellum*, war; *gerere*, to carry on (war)], carrying on war; nation at war.

Bel′low [?], roar as a bull; a roar.

Bel′lows [earlier *belg*, a bag; northern form *belu*, *belw*], instrument for producing a current of air.

Bel′ly [O.E. *bœlg*, a bag, a skin for holding things], lower front of the body.

Be-long′ [*be-* intensive, obs. *long*, to belong], be the property of, be a native of.

Be-lov′ed (*o=ŭ*) [*be-* intensive, and **Loved**], greatly loved. [place.

Be-low′ [*be-*, by, and **Low**], under, lower in

Belt [L. *balteus*, a belt], encircling band.

Be-moan′ [O.E. *be* and *mǽnan*, to moan], lament.

Bench [O.E. *benc*, bench, table. Doublet of **Bank**], long seat, judge's seat.

Bend [O.E. *bendan*, orig. to string a bow], move or be moved out of a straight line; yield; a curve.

Be-neath′ [O.E. *beneothan*], under.

Ben′e-dic′tion [L. *bene*, well, *dicere* (p.p. *dictus*), to say, to tell], blessing.

Ben′e-fac′tion [L. *bene*, well, *facere* (p.p. *factus*), to do, to make], good deed, alms.

Ben′e-fac′tor (fem. Ben′e-fac′tress), one who confers a benefit.

Ben′e-fice (*ice=iss*) [L. *beneficium*, well-doing, a kindness], church living.

Be-nef′i-cence [L. *bene*, well, and *facere*, to do], active kindness.

Be-nef′i-cent, doing or producing good.

Ben-e-fi′cial (*ci=sh*), conferring benefit.

Ben-e-fi′ci-a-ry, one who derives an income from a trust estate.

Ben′e-fit [L. *bene*, well, *facere* (p.p. *factus*), to do], something productive of good.

Be-nev′o-lence [L. *bene*, well, *volens* (pr.p. of *velle*), to wish], will to do good.

Be-night′ed [pref. *be-* and **Night**], overtaken by darkness, ignorant. [kind.

Be-nign′ (*ign=ine*), Be-nig′nant [L. *běnignus*], graciousness.

Be-nig′ni-ty, graciousness.

Ben′i-son [O.F. *beneison*; L. *benedictio*; see **Benediction**], blessing.

Bent [from **Bend**], tendency of the mind.

Bent [O.E. *beonet*], kind of grass. [feeling.

Be-numb′ [pref. *be-* and **Numb**], take away

Ben′zene, Ben′zine (*ine=een*) [ult. from Arab. *lubān jāwī*, frankincense of Java], an inflammable fluid which removes grease-stains.

Be-queath′ (*th=the* in **Breathe**) [O.E. *be-* and *cwethan*, to say], leave by will.

Be-quest′ [see **Bequeath**], legacy. [deprive.

Be-reave′ [O.E. *be-* and *réafian*, to strip off],

Ber′ry [Teut. cf. Ger. *beere*], small fruit.

Berth [prob. fr. verb **Bear**], sleeping-place in a ship, situation; moor (a ship) in harbour, etc.

Ber′yl [Gk. *bēryllos*, beryl], precious stone.

Be-seech′ [pref. *be-*; M.E. *secen*, *sechen*, to seek], ask urgently.

Be-set′ [*be-* and **Set**], set upon on all sides, assail.

Be-sides′ [O.E. *be sidan*, by the side], over and above.

Be-siege′ [*be-* and **Siege**], lay siege to, beset.

Be-smear′ [*be-* and **Smear**], smear over.

Be′som [*s=z*] [O.E. *besema*], brush of twigs.

Be-sot′ted [*be-* causative) and **Sot**], made sottish, or stupid. [hand.

Be-speak′ [*be-* and **Speak**], speak for before-

Best [O.E. *betst*, *betest*, best], *adj*. superl. of **Good**; good in the highest degree; *adv*. superl. of **Well**.

Bes'ti-al [L. *bestia*, a beast], belonging to a beast, vile. [brisk action.

Be-stir' [*be-* (causative) and **Stir**], put into

Be-stow' [*be-* (causative) and **Stow**], place, give. [over.

Be-strew' [*be-* (causative) and **Strew**], scatter

Be-stride' [pref. *be-* and **Stride**], stand over with legs astride.

Bet [short for **Abet**], that which is staked to be lost or won on any uncertain result; make a bet.

Be-take' [*be-* and **Take**], (with a reflexive pronoun), go.

Be-tide' [pref. *be-* and **Tide**], happen.

Be-times' [equal to *by time*], in good time, early. [foreshow.

Be-to'ken [*be* and **Token**], show by a sign;

Be-tray' [pref. *be-*; O.F. *traïr*; L. *trādere*, to deliver up], be faithless to, disclose.

Be-troth' [M.E. *be-* and *treuthe*, truth], engage to marry.

Be-tro'thal, engagement for a marriage.

Bet'ter [O.E. *betera*], more good; improve.

Bet'ter or Bet'tor, one who bets.

Be-tween' [O.E. *be*, by, and *twēone*, double], see **Betwixt**.

Be-twixt' [O.E. *betwix*, extended from *betwih*, between], in the space which separates, shared by two.

Bev'el [?], tool for setting off angles; sloping edge; to slant. [a drink.

Bev'er-age [O.F. *beivre*; L. *bibere*, to drink],

Bev'y [perh. O.F. *bevee*, a drink; *beivre*, to drink], company, a flock of certain birds.

Be-wail' [*be-* and **Wail**], to lament.

Be-ware' [*be-* and **Ware**], take care.

Be-wil'der [*be-* and obsolete E. *wildern*, a wilderness], confuse, perplex.

Be-witch' [*be-* and **Witch**], affect by witchcraft, charm.

Bey [Turk. *bey*, a lord], Turkish governor.

Be-yond' [O.E. *be*, by, *geond*, across; *geon*, yon], on the farther side, past.

Bi'as [?] inclination in one direction.

Bib [L.*bibere*, to drink], cloth under the chin.

Bi'ble [Gk. *biblia*, a collection of writings, *biblos*, papyrus bark], book of sacred writings, Old and New Testaments.

Bib'li-cal, pertaining to the Bible.

Bib-li-og'ra-phy [Gk. *biblos*, book, *graphein*, to write], history and description of books and MSS. [drink.

Bib'u-lous [L. *bibere*, to drink], inclined to

Bi'ceps [L. *biceps*, two-headed; *bis*, twice, *caput*, the head], muscle of the upper-arm.

Bick'er [perh. freq. of obs. *bike*, to pierce], angry dispute.

Bi'cy-cle [L.*bi*(*s*), twice; Gk. *cyclos*, a circle], two-wheeled velocipede.

Bid [O.E. *béodan*, to offer, command], to offer, command, invite; offer of a price.

Bi-en'ni-al [*bi-*, *bis*, twice, *annus*, a year], once in two years.

Bier (*ie*=*ee*) [O.E. *beran*, to carry], portable frame on which a corpse is placed.

Bi'fur-ca-ted [L. *bi*(*s*), twice, *furca*, a fork], two-pronged. **Bifurca'tion.**

Big'a-my [L. *bi*(*s*), twice; Gk. *gamos*, marriage], having two wives or two husbands at once. [bay.

Bight [O.E. *byht*, from *búgan*, to bend], bend,

Big'ot [F. *bigot*. Orig. unknown], one who unreasonably condemns those who differ from him. [party.

Big'o-try, obstinate devotion to creed or

Bil'ber-ry [*cf.* Dan. *böllebœr*], bluish fruit, whortleberry.

Bile [L. *bilis*], fluid secreted by the liver.

Bilge [a variant of **Bulge**], part of a ship on each side of the keel, foulness which gathers there.

Bi-lin'gual [L. *bis*, two, *lingua*, tongue], having two languages.

Bil'i-ous, having too much bile.

Bill[1] [O.E. *bile*], beak; stroke bill with bill.

Bill[2] [O.E. *bil*], pruning-hook.

Bill[3] [L. *bulla*, a seal], formal written statement, draft of proposed Act of Parliament, account, placard.

Bil'let [dim. of **Bill**[3]], ticket given to soldiers to tell them where to lodge; to quarter soldiers.

Bil'let [F. *billette*, *billot*, dim. of *bille*, a log], stick of wood.

Bil'liards [F. *billard*, a cue, dim. of *bille*, a log, stick], game played on a cloth-covered table with cue and balls.

Bil'lion [L. *bi*(*s*), twice, and **Million**], a million millions (English system), a thousand millions (French and American systems).

Bil'low [O.N. *bylgja*], great wave.

Bi-met'al-ism [L. *bi*(*s*), twice, and **Metal**], system of money in which gold and silver have a fixed relative value.

Bin [O.E. *binn*, a manger], enclosed place for corn, wine, etc.

Bi'na-ry [L. *bini*, two together], made up of two things or parts.

Bind (*i* long) [O.E. *bindan*], to tie, cover (a book); to edge with a band.

Bind'ing, anything that binds.

Bind'weed, kinds of convolvulus.

Bin'na-cle [earlier *bittacle*; L. *habitāculum*, a little dwelling], case for a ship's compass.

Bin-oc'u-lar [L. *bini*, two by two, *oculus*, the eye], telescope for two eyes.

Bi-no'mi-al [Late L. *binōmias*, having two names, *bi-*, twice, and *nomen*, a name], of two names.

Bi-og'ra-phy [Gk. *bios*, life, *graphein*, to write], written story of a life.

Bi-ol'o-gy [Gk. *bios*, life, *logos*, a discourse], science of plant and animal life.

Bi'ped [L. *bi*(*s*), twice, *pēs* (*ped-is*), a foot], two-footed animal.

Bi'plane [L. *bis*, two, and **Plane**], kind of aeroplane with two planes.

Birch [O.E. *bere*, *bierce*], tree with white bark, bundle of birch twigs used for flogging.

Bird [O.E. *brid*], feathered flying animal.

Bi-ret'ta [Late L. *birēttum*, from *birrus*, silk or wool cape, prob. Gk. *pyrrhos*, flame-coloured], square cap worn by R.C. clergy.

Birth [prob. O.N. *byrthr*], coming into life.

Bis'cuit [L. *bis*, twice, *coquere* (p.p: *coctus*), to cook], hard flat cake of unraised bread.

Bi-sect' [L. *bi(s)*, twice, *secāre* (p.p. *sectus*), to cut], cut into two equal parts.

Bish'op [Gk. *episcopos*; *epi*, upon, and *scopos*, a watcher], clergyman of high rank.

Bish'op-ric [Gk. *episcopos*, an overseer, and O.E. *rice*, realm], district which a bishop oversees, his office.

Bis'muth [Ger. *bismuth*, now *wismut*. Orig. unknown], brittle crystalline metal.

Bi'son [L. *bison*; cf. O.H.G. *wisunt*], animal of the wild ox kind.

Bis-sex'tile [L. *bissextus* (fr. *bis*, twice, *sextus*, sixth), the extra day which was inserted in the Julian calendar every fourth year after 24th February, the *sixth* day before the calends, *i.e.* the first day of March, according to the Roman method of reckoning, both 1st March and 24th February being included], leap (year).

Bit [O.E. *bitan*, to bite], small piece, mouth-piece of a bridle.

Bitch [O.E. *bicce*], female dog.

Bite [O.E. *bitan*], seize with the teeth; the act of seizing with the teeth, morsel.

Bit'ter [O.E. *biter*, prob. from *bitan*, to bite], tasting like wormwood.

Bit'tern [O.F. *butor*, prob. named from its cry], bird of the wading kind.

Bit'ters, infusion of bitter herbs.   [pitch.

Bi-tu'men, Bit'u-men [L. *bitūmen*], mineral

Bi'valve [L. *bi(s)*, twice, and **Valve**], shelled animal of which the shell consists of two plates hinged.

Biv'ou-ac (*ou*=*oo*) [F. *bivouac*. Perh. fr. Ger. *bei*, by, and *Wacht*, watch], encampment without tents.

Bi-zarre' [F. *bizarre*; cf. Sp. *bizarro*, brave; perh. fr. Basque *bizarra*, a beard], odd, grotesque.   [secret.

Blab [M.E. *blaberen*, to babble; imit.], tell a

Black [O.E. *blœc*, *blac*], colourless from the absence of all light, very dark.

Black'a-moor [Black and **Moor**], negro, very dark person.

Black-ball', vote against by putting a black ball into a ballot-box.

Black'ber-ry, fruit of the bramble.

Black'bird, black singing-bird.

Black'cock, male of the black grouse. (The female is called the **Grey hen**.)

Black'en, make black.

Black'guard [Black and **Guard**. The name was given to kitchen menials], scoundrel.

Black'ing, preparation for making things black.

Black-lead', mineral (not lead) used for making writing pencils, etc.

Black'mail' [Black and obs. *mail*, rent], extort money by threats.

Black'smith, smith who works in iron.

Black'thorn, sloe-tree.   [fluid or air.

Blad'der [O.E. *blādre*], thin bag containing

Blade [O.E. *blœd*, a leaf], leaf (especially of grass), cutting part of an instrument, flat part of an oar.

Blae'ber-ry (Scot.) [*blae*, livid, and **Berry**], whortleberry, bilberry.

Blain [O.E. *blegen*, a boil], inflammatory swelling.

Blame'able, Bla'ma-ble, Blame'wor-thy, worthy of blame.

Blame [Gk. *blasphēmein*, to speak ill], find fault with; disapproval, fault.

Blanch [F. *blanc*, fem. *blanche*, white], whiten, skin almonds.

Blanc-mange (*bla-manzh*) [F. *blanc*, white, *manger*, to eat], shaped preparation of milk and corn-flour, or the like.

Bland [L. *blandus*, mild], mild, smooth and soothing.

Blan'dish-ments [L. *blandīrī*, to flatter; *blandus*, mild], flattery, caresses.

Blank [F. *blanc*, white], white, free from marks, unrhymed (verse); empty space.

Blan'ket [O.F. *blanquette*; dim. of *blanc*, white], cover, usually of wool, and having a nap, used in bed-clothing.

Blare [perh. imit.], harsh noise of a trumpet.

Blar'ney [fr. the *Blarney* stone in a castle near Cork. He who kisses it has the gift of saying pleasant things], smooth, wheedling talk.

Blas-pheme' [Gk. *blasphēmein*, to speak ill], speak wickedly of sacred things. **Blas'-phemous.**

Blas'phem-y, speaking evil of God.

Blast [O.E. *blǣst*], strong gust, sound made by blowing a wind-instrument, a rending by explosion; injure by lightning.

Bla'tant (*a*=*ai*) [prob. imitative. Cf. Ger. *platzen*, to crash], noisy, vulgarly assertive.

Blaze [O.E. *blœse*, a flame], flame; glow with flame.

Blaze [O.N. *blesi*, a white mark on a horse], to mark trees (and so a path) by stripping bark.

Bla'zon (*a*=*ai*) [F. *blason*, a shield, etym. dub.], coat of arms, description of a coat of arms; make public.

Bleach [O.E. *blǣcan*, to whiten], whiten.

Bleak [O.E. *blǣc*, shining, pale], open and desolate, dreary.

Blear [?], dim with water or rheum.

Bleat [O.E. *blǣtan*], cry of a sheep; give the cry of a sheep.

Bleed [O.E. *blēdan*, from *blōd*, blood], emit blood, take blood from.

Blem'ish [O.F. *blemir* (pr.p. *blemissant*), to wound, to make pale], flaw, stain; to mar.

Blench [O.E. *blencan*, to deceive], draw back from lack of courage.

Blend [O.N. *blanda*; cf. Dan. *blande*, to blend], mix or mingle together; mixture of one thing with another.

Bless [O.E. *blētsian*, *blœdsian*. Perh. from O. Teut. *blōdom*, blood, consecrate by sacrifice], make happy, call down a blessing on.

Bless'ing, means of happiness, uttered wish for happiness to another.

Blight [etym. dub.], mildew; prevent the growth of, affect with blight.

Blind (1) [O.E. *blind*, common Teut.], unable to see; make blind.

Blind'fold [O.E. *blind*, and *fellen*, to strike], having the eyes covered.

Blind'ers, Blink'ers [see **Blind** and **Blink**], flaps to keep a horse from seeing sideways.

Blind'worm, lizard with small eyes.

Blink [M.E. *blenken*, to shine], twinkle with the eye, shirk; glimpse, gleam.

Bliss [O.E. *bliss*, contr. from *bliths*, happiness], great happiness.

Blis'ter [perh. O.N. *blasa*, to blow], raised part of the outer skin with watery fluid below, plaster which raises a blister; raise a blister.

Blithe, Blithe'some [O.E. *bliths*, happiness], gay, joyous.

Bliz'zard [modern word. Cf. **Blow, Blast**], fierce gale with fine snow.

Bloat'ed [M.E. *blout*, soft, cogn. with O.N. *blautr*, soaked], swollen beyond the natural size.

Bloat'er [O.N. *blautr*, soaked. Cf. Swed. *blötfisk*, soaked fish], herring smoked and half-dried.

Block [F. *bloc*, perh. fr. O.H.G. *bloh*, a block], heavy piece of wood or stone, number of houses built touching each other, obstruction, mould on which hats are shaped; obstruct, shape on.

Block-ade' [from **Block**], shutting up of a place by an enemy's forces to prevent access to it or egress from it, to shut up.

Block'head, stupid person.

Block'house, wood or iron house for defence.

Blonde, Blond [F. *blond, blonde*, fair], fair; a fair person.

Blood (*oo = ŭ*) [O.E. *blód*], red fluid in animals.

Bloom [O.N. *blóm*, a flower], flower, powdery coating on certain fruits, fresh beauty; to blossom.

Blos'som [O.E. *blóstm*, prob. cogn. with **Bloom**], flower; to put forth blossoms.

Blot [cf. O.N. *blettr*], stain, to stain.

Blotch [variant of **Blot**], large irregular spot.

Blot'ting-pa'per, unsized paper to dry up ink.

Blouse (*s = z*) [F. *blouse*, a loose outer garment], loose over-garment, loose bodice.

Blow [etym. dub.], stroke.

Blow [O.E. *blówan*], to flower.

Blow [O.E. *bláwan*], move as air, drive by wind, sound by the breath, puff up.

Blow'y, windy.

Blub'ber [M.E. *blober*, a bubble; imit.], fat of whales; weep noisily.

Blud'geon [?], stick with a heavy end; strike again and again with such.

Blue [O.F. *bleu*, ultimately Teut.], colour.

Bluff [cf. M. Dutch *blaf*, flat, broad], frank and hearty; high, steep bank.

Blun'der [prob. O.N. *blanda*, to mix. Allied to **Blend**], great mistake; make great mistakes.

Blun'der-buss [perversion of Du. *donderbus*, thunder gun], ancient short wide-bore gun which could hold a great many balls.

Blunt [?], dull of edge, abrupt.

Blur [perh. fr. **Blear**], stain; make dim.

Blurt [imit.], utter suddenly.

Blush [M.E. *blusche*; O.E. *ablisian*], sudden reddening of the face; to redden with shame.

Blus'ter [prob. aug. of **Blast**], fitful noise, boasting; do or utter with noisy violence.

Bo'a [etym. dub.], large crushing snake, long round fur for the neck. **Boa-constric'tor.**

Boar [O.E. *bár*], male of swine.

Board [O.E. *bord*, board], piece of timber sawn thin, table, daily food, council; lay with boards, supply with or obtain meals for pay.

Board [short for *aborde*, from F. *à* (L. *ad*), to, and *bord*, edge, side of a ship], enter (a ship) by force.

Board'er, one who has meals, or meals and lodgings, for pay.

Boast [?], talk big; speech of self-approval.

Boat [O.E. *bát*], small open vessel.

Boat'swain (pron. and sometimes spelt **bo's'n**), ship's officer who has charge of the boats, sails, etc. [down.

Bob [perh. imit.], pendant; jerk up and

Bob'bin [F. *bobine*. Orig. unknown], small cylinder for thread.

Bode [O.E. *bodian*, to announce], foreshow.

Bod'ice (*ice = iss*) [corrupt. of " *bodies* "], upper part of a dress.

Bod'i-ly, of or in the body, entirely.

Bod'kin [?], implement for piercing holes, tape needle.

Bod'y [O.E. *bodig*], person, material part, main part, many spoken of as one.

Bo'er [Du. *boer*, a peasant], Dutch colonist (originally a farmer) of S. Africa.

Bog [Ir. and Gael. *bog*, soft], wet, spongy ground.

Bo'gey, Bo'gy, Bo'gle [?], goblin, bugbear.

Bog'gy, marshy.

Bo'gie (*g* hard) [?], four-wheeled truck supporting a locomotive, etc.

Bo'gus [U.S. word. Orig. doubtful], sham.

Bo-hea' (*ea = ee*) [Chin. *Wui*, name of district], kind of tea.

Boil [L. *bullíre*, to boil; *bulla*, a bubble], be made to bubble by heat.

Boil [O.E. *býl*, a boil, swelling], hard, painful swelling of the skin.

Boil'er, vessel for boiling. [stormy.

Bois'ter-ous [M.E. *boistous*, noisy], noisy,

Bold [O.E. *bald*], brave, forward.

Bole [O.N. *bolr*, trunk or stem of a tree], stem of a tree.

Boll (*ō*) [same as **Bowl**; O.E. *bolla*], pod.

Boll [?], old Scottish measure.

Bol'ster (*ō*) [O.E. *bolster*; Teut. *bul*, to puff up], long pillow; hold up.

Bolt [?], short arrow, strong pin of iron, sliding catch, sudden departure; swallow without chewing, fasten with a bolt, to dart. [sift.

Bolt [O.F. *bulter*; It. *bura*, coarse cloth],

Bo'lus [Gk. *bólos*, a clod], large pill.

Bomb [Gk. *bómbos*, a humming noise], iron shell filled with explosives.

Bom-bard' [E. *bombard*, a great gun; see Bomb], attack with shot and shell. **Bombard'ment.**

Bom-bar-dier', lowest non-commissioned officer in the British artillery.

Bom'bast [Late L. *bombax* (gen. *bombac-is*), cotton (hence padding); Gk. *bombyx*, silk cotton], high-sounding talk.

Bon'bon [F. *bon*, good], sweetmeat.

Bond [see Band 1], anything that binds, writing which binds to pay money, mortgage.

Bond'age [O.E. *bónda*, a husbandman; O.N. *bóndi*, a husbandman, *bua*, to till], state of being bound, slavery. [duties.

Bond'ed, locked up, pending payment of **Bond'man, Bonds'man**, slave.

Bone [O.E. *bán*], hard material of the skeleton of an animal; take the bones from. [air.

Bon'fire [Bone and Fire], large fire in the open

Bon'net [O.F. *bonet*. Orig. unknown], covering for the head.

Bon'ny [perh. F. *bon, bonne*, L. *bonus*, good], beautiful (*Scots*); stout, strong (*Shakespeare*).

Bon'spiel [?], great curling match.

Bo'nus [L. *bonus*, good], extra payment.

Bo'ny, full of bones, having prominent bones.

Boo'by [prob. Span. *bobo*, a blockhead, perh. from L. *balbus*, stammering], dunce.

Book [O.E. *bóc*, a book], sheets of paper bound together, whole or part of a literary work; enter in a book, pay a fare for travel.

Book'keep'er, one who keeps accounts.

Boom [Du. form of Beam], spar to extend the bottom of a sail, chain or line of spars to bar the mouth of a river or harbour.

Boom [imit.], hollow roar, rapid growth in market value.

Boom'er-ang [the Australian name], wooden missile used in Australia. [favour.

Boon [O.N. *bón*, a petition], good gift;

Boon [F. *bón*; L. *bonus*, good], bounteous, jolly.

Boor (Du. *boer*, a peasant; A. or O.E. *gebúr*, a dweller], clown, rude person.

Boot [O.F. *bote*. Orig. unknown], cover for the foot and lower part of the leg.

Boot [O.E. *bót*, profit], to profit.

Booth [M.E. *bothe*; cf. Da. and Sw. *bod*, fr. East Norse, *bóa*, to dwell], shed of boughs or boards.

Boot'jack [Boot and Jack (familiar form of John)], instrument for pulling off boots.

Boots, hotel servant who cleans boots, etc.

Boot'tree, mould to shape boots.

Boot'y [perh. F. *butin*, booty; O.N. *býti*, exchange, booty], plunder.

Bo-ra'cic (*cic = sic*), **Bo'ric**, relating to borax.

Bo'rax [Arab. *bauraq*; prob. fr. Pers. *búrah*, borax], crystalline salt.

Bor'der [Low L. *bordáre*, to edge; Teut. *bord*, side], edge, boundary; come near, touch at the boundaries, put a border to.

Bore [O.E. *borian*], pierce, weary by dulness; tool for boring, hollow inside a gun, a tiresome person. **Bore'dom.**

Bore [perh. fr. O.N. *bára*, a wave], high tidal flood at some river-mouths.

Bo're-as [Gk. *boreas*, the north wind], north wind.

Bor'ough (*búr'o*) [O.E. *burh, burg*, a fort, perh. fr. Teut. *bergan*, to protect], town with a town council, town that sends a member to Parliament. [loan.

Bor'row [O.E. *borh, borg*, a pledge], take as a

Bosk'y [It. *boschetto*, dim. of *bosco*, a wood], woody or bushy.

Bos'om (*os = ooz*) [O.E. *bósm*], breast.

Boss [M.E. and O.F. *boce*; It. *bozza*, a swelling], knob, stud.

Bo-tan'ic, Bo-tan'ic-al, relating to the study of plants.

Bot'an-ize, search for plants for study.

Bot'an-y [Gk. *botanē*, a plant], science of plants.

Botch [?], spoiled work; to spoil.

Both'er [?], annoy; feel anxious; one who or that which bothers.

Bot'tle [Late L. *buticula*, double dim. of *butis*, a cask], narrow-mouthed vessel for liquor; put into bottles.

Bot'tom [O.E. *botm*], lowest part, ground under water.

Bou'doir (*boodwahr*) [F.], lady's private room.

Bough [O.E. *bóg, bóh*, an arm, *bugan*, to bend], a branch.

Boul'der [?], large mass of rock.

Bounce [M.E. *bunsen*, to thump, prob. imit. of sound], spring suddenly, to bound, to boast; sudden leap, empty boasting.

Bound 1 [O.F. *bodne*; Late L. *butina*, a limit], to limit; a limit.

Bound 2 [F. *bondir*, perh. fr. L. *bombitáre*, to resound], move by leaps; a leap.

Bound 3 [O.N. *búa*, to till, to prepare], ready to start, on the way.

Bound'a-ry, bounding line.

Boun'te-ous, free in giving, generous.

Boun'ti-ful, free in giving, plentiful.

Boun'ty [L. *bonus*, good], generosity, sum granted to encourage some industry, or to induce men to enter the army or navy.

Bou-quet' (*boo-kai'* or *boo'kai*) [F., fr. It. *boschetto*, a little wood], bunch of flowers; perfume of wine. [goal.

Bourn, Bourne (*boorn*) [F. *borne*], boundary,

Bout [etym. dub.], set-to at anything, a turn.

Bo'vine [L. *bos* (*bōv-is*), an ox], ox-like.

Bow [O.E. *búgan*, to bend], to bend; a bending of the head or body, stem and forepart of a ship.

Bow [O.E. *boga*, a bow; *búgan*, to bend], a curve, weapon to shoot arrows, rod used in playing a stringed instrument, knot with loops. [intestines.

Bow'els [L.L. *botellus*, a sausage, an intestine],

Bow'er [O.E. *búr*, a chamber], arbour.

Bow'er [see Bow], anchor at the bow.

Bow'ie-knife [From Col. J. *Bowie*, and Knife], American hunting-knife.

Bowl [O.E. *bolla*, orig. a round seed-vessel], hollow vessel.

Bowl [F. *boule*; L. *bulla*, a bubble, ball],

wooden ball; (pl.) the game played with such balls; deliver a ball at cricket, roll as bowls.

Bow'line [Bow and Line], rope used to keep the weather edge of the square sails tight forward.

Bow'sprit [see Bow. Sprit from O.E. *spréot*, a pole], spar projecting over the bows.

Box [L. *buxus*; cf. Gk. *puxos*, the box-tree; *puxis*, a box], small shrub, case of firm material, partitioned-off space in a theatre, driver's seat; rehearse the points (of a compass) in right order.

Box [?], blow on the ear, fight with fists.

Boy [cf. E. Fris. *boi*, young gentleman], male child; native labourer in India, etc.

Boy'cott [fr. the treatment given to Capt. *Boycott* in Mayo, 1880], combine with others to have no dealings with some person.

Boy'hood, state or time of being a boy.

Boy'ish, like or natural to a boy.

Brace [O.F. *brace*, the two arms; L. *brachium* (pl. *brachia*), the arm], that which holds tightly, a couple; (pl.) trouser-straps; give vigour, tighten; printer's mark ({).

Brace'let [O.F. dim. of *bracel*, an armlet; L. *brachium*, an arm], arm-band.

Brach'i-al (*ch=k*) [L. *brachiālis*; *brachium*, an arm], belonging to the arm.

Brack'en, Brake [M.E. *braken*; cf. Swed. *bräken*, fern], kind of large fern.

Brack'et [formerly *bragget*; L. *braccæ*, breeches], ornamental projection from a wall, one of two characters to enclose words, etc.; place within brackets.

Brack'ish [Du. *brak*, briny, brackish], saltish.

Brad [O.N. *broddr*, a spike], thin nail with no head, but a slight projection at the top on one side.

Brad'awl, small boring-tool.

Brag [etym. dub.], boast; card game.

Brag'gart, boaster. Braggado'cio (*cio=shio*), boasting.

Brah'man, Brah'min [Sanscrit *brāhmana*, a holy man; *brahmaṇ*, prayer], Hindu of the priestly caste.

Braid [O.E. *bregdan*, to move to and fro], narrow woven fabric, plait; to plait, ornament with braid.

Brain [O.E. *brægen*], grey nerve cells and white nerve fibres in the skull, the thinking part; dash out brains. Brain'less.

Brake [perh. fr. root of Break], contrivance for checking a wheel's motion; wagonette.

Brake [cf. M.L.G. *brake*, stumps of broken trees, cogn. with Break], thicket.

Bram'ble [O.E. *brembel*; *brēmel*, dim. of O. Teut. word cogn. with *brōm*, broom], blackberry, the blackberry shrub.

Bran [O.F. *bren*], broken husk of grain.

Branch [Late L. *branca*, a paw], shoot from the main stem; to spread in branches.

Brand [O. Teut. *brinnan*, to burn], partly-burnt stick; mark made with a hot iron, make a distinctive mark as with a hot iron.

Bran'dish [F. *brandir* (p.p. *brandissant*)], wave or flourish.

Bran'dy [formerly *brand-wine*; Du. *brande-wijn*, burnt (*i.e.* distilled) wine], strong liquor distilled from wine.

Bra'sier, Bra'zier [F. *brasier*, fr. *braise*, hot coal], worker in brass, pan for holding burning coals.

Brass [O.E. *bræs*], alloy of copper and zinc.

Brat [?], child (so called in contempt).

Bra-va'do [Span. *bravada*], mere show of boldness.

Brave [F. *brave*, etym. dub.], stout-hearted, bold, gay; defy.

Bra'ver-y, courage, finery.

Brawl [?], noisy quarrel; quarrel noisily.

Brawn [O.F. *braon*; fr. West. Ger. *brādan*, to roast], muscle, boar's flesh, preparation of pig's head and ox feet.

Brawn'y, muscular.

Brax'y [?], Scots name for disease of sheep, diseased mutton.

Bray [F. *braire*; cf. Gael. *bragh*, an explosion], the cry of an ass; give the cry of an ass.

Bray [O.F. *breier*], pound small.

Bra'zen, made of or like brass, shameless; behave shamelessly.

Bra'zier (see Bra'sier).

Breach [O.E. *brecan*, to break], act of breaking, gap. [flour.

Bread [O.E. *bréad*], a food made of baked

Bread'fruit, tree of the Pacific Islands.

Breadth [see Broad], distance from side to side.

Break (*ea=ai*) [O.E. *brecan*, to break], to part, snap, burst; an opening, points scored continuously in billiards.

Break'er, wave broken into foam. [day.

Break'fast [Break and Fast], first meal in the

Break'wa-ter, barrier to break the force of waves.

Breast [O.E. *bréost*], part of the body below the neck; oppose manfully.

Breast'plate, armour for the breast.

Breath [O.E. *bréth*], air drawn into and given out by the lungs. [out.

Breathe, draw air into the lungs and give it

Breech [O.E. *bréc* (pl.), fr. O. Teut. *brōks*, loin and thigh garment], hinder part of a gun-barrel; (pl.) trousers.

Breed [O.E. *brédan*, to produce], race, kind; raise, as any kind of stock.

Breeze [earlier *brize*, fr. O. Span. *briza*, N.E. wind], light wind.

Breve [var. of Brief], the longest note in music: in old Church music it was the *shorter* of the two notes used.

Brev'et [L. *brevis*, short], commission giving an officer rank above his pay.

Bre'vi-a-ry [L. *brevis*, short], book containing the ordinary daily services of the R.C. Church.

Brev'i-ty [L. *brevis*, short], shortness.

Brew [O.E. *bréowan*], make malt liquor, amount brewed at once, quality of liquor so made.

Brew′er-y, building where beer is brewed.

Bri′ar, Bri′er [?], prickly shrub.

Bribe [perh. O.F. *bribe*, bread given to a beggar. Orig. unknown], gift to influence a decision ; give a bribe.

Bri′ber-y, giving or taking of bribes.

Brick [prob. F. *brique*, a brick, a fragment, cognate with **Break**], block of burnt clay.

Brick′bat, piece of a brick.

Bri′dal [formerly *bride-ale*, a bride-feast], of or connected with a bride or a marriage ; marriage, marriage feast.

Bride (O.E. *brýd*], woman newly married or about to be married.

Bride′groom [for *bridegoom* ; O.E. *brýd*, bride, and *guma*, a man], man newly married or about to be married.

Bridge [O.E. *brycg*], structure over a river, chasm, etc. ; to erect such.

Bridge [?], game at cards.

Bri′dle [O.E. *brídel*, earlier *brigdel* ; *bregdan*, to pull], headgear with which a horse is governed ; put a bridle on, check, put on a lofty manner or show that offence is taken.

Brief [L. *brevis*, short], short ; written instructions on which barristers advocate causes.

Brig [short for **Brigantine**], square-rigged two-masted vessel.

Bri-gade′ [It. *brigata*, a troop, *brigare*, to strive], force of two or more regiments.

Brig′and [prob. It. *brigante*, orig. pr.p. of *brigare*, to strive], one of a band of robbers.

Brig′an-tine (*ine=een*) [It. *brigantino*, a pirate-ship ; *brigante*, a robber], vessel with the mainmast of a schooner and the foremast of a brig.

Bright [O.E. *beorht*], shining, brilliant, lively.

Bril′lian-cy, great brightness.

Bril′liant [F. *brillant*, pr.p. of *briller*, to shine ; orig. to sparkle, like a beryl ; L. *beryllus*, a beryl], very bright ; diamond cut in a particular way.

Brim [M.E. *brimme*], upper edge, rim of a hat ; fill, be full.

Brim′stone [M.E. *brennen*, to burn, *stoon*, stone], sulphur in sticks or rolls.

Brin′dle, Brin′dled [earlier *brinded*, perh. cogn. with **Brand**], spotted or streaked.

Brine [O.E. *brýne*], salt water.

Bring [O.E. *bringan*], cause to come, to carry.

Brink [M.E., prob. fr. Scand., cf. Dan. *brink*, a descent], edge of a steep place or water.

Bri′ny, of or pertaining to brine.

Bri-*quette′*, **Bri′quet** (*q=k*) [F. dim. of *brique*, brick], block of coal-dust and pitch.

Brisk [W. *brisg*, quick-footed, or fr. **Brusque**], active, lively, quick.

Bris′ket [etym. dub., cf. F. *brechet*], part of the breast of an animal next the ribs.

Bris′tle [dim. of O.E. *byrst*, a bristle], strong hair on the back of a hog ; stand stiff like bristles, show defiance.

Bris′tly, set with bristles, rough.   [broken.

Brit′tle [O.E. *bréotan*, to break], easily

Broach [F. *broche*, It. *brocca*, a spit], a spit ; pierce as with a spit, open up or begin.

Broad (*brawd*) [O.E. *brád*], wide.

Broad′cast, cast in all directions, used specifically in sending information by wireless telephony.

Broad′catch, to receive information by wireless telephony.

Broad′side, discharge of all the guns on one side of a ship.

Broad′sword [O.E. *brád*, broad, and **Sword**], sword with broad blade.

Bro-cade′ [Sp. *brocado*, It. *broccato*. See **Broach**], kind of figured silk.

Broc′co-li [It. pl. of *broccolo*, a sprout, dim. of *brocco*, a stalk], kind of cauliflower.

Brogue [?], Irish pronunciation of English.

Brogue [Gael. and Ir. *brog*, shoe], coarse kind of shoe of untanned hide.

Broil [F. *brouiller*, to confuse], noisy quarrel.

Broil [etym. dub., perh. F. *brûler*, to burn], cook meat on a gridiron or on the coals.

Bro′ker [A.-F. *brocour*, fr. prob. L. *broccátor*, one who broaches], agent or middleman.

Bron′chi-al (*ch=k*) [Gk. *brogchia*, bronchial tubes], relating to the tubes branching from the windpipe.

Bron-chi′tis (*ch=k*), inflammation of bronchial tubes.

Bronze [It. *bronzo* ; L. (*æs*) *Brundusīnum*, (brass) of Brindisi], alloy of copper and tin.

Brooch (*oo=ō*) [F. *broche*, a spit, a point. See **Broach**], ornamental pin.

Brood [O.E. *bród*], birds hatched at one time ; sit on eggs, think anxiously.

Brook [O.E. *bróc*, stream], small stream.

Brook′let.   [bear.

Brook, (O.E. *brúcan*, to use, to enjoy], to

Broom [O.E. *bróm*], shrub with yellow flowers, besom.

Broth [O.E. *bréowan*, to brew], liquid in which flesh, vegetables, etc., have been boiled.

Broth′er (*o=ŭ*) [O.E. *bróthor*], son of the same parents as another person.

Broth′er-hood, state of being brothers, a religious association.

Broth′er-ly, like a brother.

Brough′am (*oom* or *oo-am*) [named after the first Lord *Brougham*], closed one-horse carriage.

Brow [O.E. *brú*], ridge over the eye, forehead, edge or projecting upper part of a steep place.   [manners.

Brow′beat, bear down by looks and

Brown [O.E. *brún*], dark colour.

Brown′ie, good-natured goblin ; Girl Guide under eleven years.

Browse (*s=z*) [F *brouster*], feed on as pasture.

Bruise (*s=z*) [O.E. *brysan*, to crush ; influenced by A.F *brusier*, to break], hurt as with blows, crush ; hurt from a blow or knock.

Bruit (*ui=oo*) [F. *bruit*, noise], report.

Bru-nette′ [F. fem. of *brunet*, brownish ; dim. of *brun*, brown], woman of dark complexion.

Brunt [?], utmost violence of an onset

B

Brush [O.F. *broce, brosse*, brushwood, *broce, broisse*, a brush], underwood, thicket, instrument of bristles, etc., for taking off dust, laying on colour, etc., tail of a fox, slight encounter ; apply a brush.

Brush'wood, thicket. [abrupt.

Brusque [F. *brusque*; It. *brusco*], sharp, sour,

Bru'tal [L. *brutus*, stupid], like a brute, very coarse, cruel.

Bru-tal'i-ty, quality of being brutal.

Brute [L. *brutus*, stupid], lower animal, brutal person.

Bru'tish, coarse and stupid.

Bry'on-y [L. and Gk. *bryonia*], kind of climbing plant.

Bub'ble [imit. orig.], round film of liquid filled with air or gas ; rise in bubbles.

Buc-ca-neer' [F. *boucan*, wooden frame used for broiling. *Boucan* is of Brazilian origin], pirate.

Buck [O.E. *buc, bucca*], male of fallow deer and antelopes.

Buck'et [O.F. *buket*, a tub, a pail, or O.E. *buc*, a pitcher], vessel for holding water.

Buck'le [F. *boucle* ; L. *buccula*, cheek-strap of a helmet, dim. of *bucca*, the cheek], instrument for fastening a strap or band ; fasten with a buckle. [shield.

Buck'ler [O.F. *boucler*, a shield. See **Buckle**],

Buck'ram [O.F. *boquerant*. Orig. uncertain], coarse linen or cotton cloth stiffened with size.

Buck'-tooth', projecting tooth.

Buck'wheat' [O.E. *bóc*, beech, *hwǽte*, wheat], cereal plant. [rustic.

Bu-col'ic [Gk. *bucolicos, bous*, an ox], pastoral,

Bud [?], first shoot of a plant ; put forth buds.

Budge [F. *bouger*, to stir ; perh. L. *bullíre*, to boil], stir.

Bud'get [F. *bougette*, dim. of *bouge*, a leather bag ; L. *bulga*, a bag], contents of a bag ; annual financial statement made by the Chancellor of the Exchequer.

Buff [F. *buffle*, a buffalo], oil-dressed leather, military coat, a dull light yellow.

Buf'fa-lo [Port. *búfalo*, L. *búfalus* ; Gk. *boubalos*, an antelope], large kind of ox ; American bison.

Buf'fer [obs. vb. *buff*, prob. imit. of sound made by striking soft body], apparatus to deaden the jar of collision.

Buf'fet (*boo'fai*) [F. *buffet*. Orig. unknown], sideboard, counter for refreshments, a restaurant.

Buf'fet [O.F., dim. of *buffe*, a blow, esp. on the cheek], a blow ; deal blows.

Buf-foon' [F. *buffon* ; It. *buffone*, a jester, *buffa*, a jest], jester.

Buf-foon'er-y, conduct as of a buffoon.

Bug [?], name applied to various insects.

Bug'bear [Etym. dub.], cause of needless fear.

Bug'gy [?], kind of gig or carriage.

Bu'gle [short for *bugle-horn* ; O.F. *bugle*, a young bull ; L. *buculus*, dim. of *bós*, an ox], copper wind-instrument, a hunter's horn.

Bu'gle [?], long glass bead.

Bu'gloss [Gk. *bouglossos*, lit. ox-tongue], kind of weed.

Buhl, Boule (*uh=oo* ; *ou=oo*) [fr. A. C. *Boule*, a cabinetmaker of Louis XIV's time], sort of inlaying of brass scrolls, etc., in wood.

Build [M.E. *bulden*, O.E. *bold*, a house], raise on a foundation ; general figure.

Bulb (Gk. *bolbos*, an onion], onion-like root.

Bul'bul (*u=oo*) [Pers. *bulbul*], Eastern song-thrush.

Bulge [L. *bulga*, a bag], swell out ; irregular swelling.

Bulk [O.N. *bulki*, a heap], size, largest portion.

Bulk'head [O.N. *balkr*, partition ; O.E. *héafod*, head], partition in a ship.

Bulk'y, of great size.

Bull (*u=oo*) [O.E. *bule-* (in compounds), perh. connected with **Bellow**], male of cattle, etc.

Bull [L. *bulla*, a bubble, knob, leaden seal], papal document with a seal.

Bull [perh. O.F. *boul*, trickery], absurd, self-contradictory expression.

Bull'dog, kind of dog formerly used for bull-baiting.

Bul'let [F. *boulette*, dim. of *boule*, a ball ; L. *bulla*, a knob], missile to be discharged from a small firearm.

Bul'le-tin [It. *bullettino*, a ticket, double dim. of *bulla*, a knob, a seal], brief written statement of recent news.

Bull'finch, a singing-bird.

Bull'ion [Late L. *bullio*, a boiling ; *bullíre*, to bubble up], uncoined gold or silver in masses.

Bull'ock [O.E. *bulluc*], ox.

Bull's'-eye, thick glass lens on a lantern, centre of a target.

Bull'y [oldest meaning, dear one ; perh. fr. Du. *boel*, a lover], overbearing fellow ; act as a bully.

Bul'rush [?], kind of large rush.

Bul'wark [cf. Du. *bolwerk*. Perh. **Bole** and **Work**], strong projecting outwork for the defence of the rampart, or main work, side protection of a deck.

Bum'ble-bee' [imit. orig. and **Bee**], large kind of bee which makes a humming noise.

Bump [imit. orig.], a thump, swelling ; strike violently against anything. [brim.

Bump'er [ff. **Bump**], glass filled to the

Bump'kin [perh. Du. *boomken*, dim. of *boom*, a tree], heavy country fellow. [forward.

Bump'tious [fr. **Bump**], conceited and

Bun [perh. O.F. *bugne*, a swelling], small raised cake.

Bunch [?], number of things growing or fastened together.

Bun'dle [perh. cogn. with O.E. *bindan*, to bind], number of things bound together ; tie in a bundle. [bung.

Bung [?], stopper for a cask ; stop as with a

Bun'ga-low [Hind. *bangla*, belonging to Bengal], house of one story with a verandah.

Bun′gle [imit. orig. Cf. **Bang**], clumsy performance ; to act, make, or mend clumsily.

Bun′ion [Perh. It. *bugnone*, swelling], inflamed swelling on the first joint of the great toe.

Bunk [?], one of a series of beds in tiers.

Bunk′er [?], coal-bin, sandy hollow on a golf course.

Bunt′ing [?], kind of bird.

Bunt′ing [perh. M.E. *bonten*, to sift], thin woollen stuff for flags.

Buoy [M.Du. *boei* ; O.F. *boie* ; L. *boia*, a fetter], floating mark in harbours or channels ; keep from sinking. [heart.

Buoy′an-cy, floating power ; lightness of

Buoy′ant, tending to float ; light-hearted.

Bur, Burr [E., cf. Dan. *borre*], prickly flowerhead. **Burr**, guttural pronunciation of *r*.

Bur′den [O.E. *byrthen*], load ; load heavily.

Bur′den [F. *bourdon* ; Late L. *burdo*, a drone], refrain of a song.

Bur′den-some (*some*=*sum*), oppressive.

Bur′dock [**Bur** and **Dock**], kind of coarse herb.

Bu′reau (*eau*=*ō*) [O.F. *burel*, reddish coarse woollen cloth ; L. *burrus*, red], writing-table with drawers, office for transacting business.

Bureau′-cracy [**Bureau** and Gk. *kratein*, to rule], government by officials of various ranks and grades. **Bur′eaucrat, Bureau-crat′ic.**

Bur′gess, Bur′gher [O.F. *burgeis* ; Du. *burger*, a citizen], inhabitant of a borough, freeman or citizen. [(Scottish).

Burgh (*bŭr′o*) [see **Borough**], borough

Bur′gla-ry [Low L. *burgulāre*, to break into a house], house-breaking.

Bur′go-mas′ter [Du. *burg*, a borough, *meester*, master], chief magistrate in Holland or Belgium.

Bur′i-al (*u*=*ĕ*) [O.E. *byrgels*, a tomb ; *byrgan*, to bury], act of burying.

Bu′rin [F. *burin* ; perh. O.H.G. *bora*], an engraver's tool.

Burke [fr. the criminal *Burke*, who smothered people], smother, avoid.

Bur-lesque′ (*que*=*k*) [It. *burlesco* ; *burla*, mockery], style of speaking, acting, or writing, which caricatures ; turn into ridicule.

Bur′ly [M.E. *borlich*, fr. prob. O.E. *bŭrlic*, handsome ; *bŭr*, a bower], stout and strong.

Burn [O E. *brinnan* (intrans.), *bœrnan* (trans.), to burn], hurt caused by fire ; consume with or be on fire. [brook.

Burn [Teut., cf. Du. *born*], Scots word for

Burn′er, that which gives out flame.

Bur′nish [O.F. *burnir*, to polish ; cogn. with **Brown**], cause to shine, polish ; effect of burnishing, gloss.

Bur′row [perh. varied spelling of **Borough**], hole in the ground made by certain animals ; make a burrow.

Bur′sar [M.L. *bursārius*, a purse-bearer ; *bursa*, a purse], treasurer of a college or monastery, holder of a bursary. [school.

Bur′sa-ry, scholarship at a university or

Burst [O.E. *berstan*, to burst], fly apart, break open ; sudden breaking forth.

Bur′y (*u*=*ĕ*) [O.E. *byrgan*, to bury], to cover out of sight.

Bus′by [?], a military headdress of fur.

Bush (*u*=*oo*) [M.E. *busk*, O.N. *buskr*], shrub, an unsettled place abounding in trees and shrubs.

Bush′el [Late L. *buscellus*, a small box], a dry measure for grain, fruit, etc.

Bus′i-ness (*us*=*iz*), regular occupation, buying and selling, affair.

Busk [O.N. *búa*, to prepare ; *sik*, oneself], to dress oneself.

Bust [F. *buste* ; It. *busto*], sculpture representing the head, shoulders, and breast ; chest.

Bus′tard [L. *avis tarda*, a slow bird], large swift-running bird.

Bus′tle [perh. var. of obs. *buskle*, fr. obs. *busk*, prepare], great stir.

Bus′y (*us*=*iz*) [O.E. *bisig*], hard at work (habitually, or for the time) ; keep busy.

Bus′y-bod′y, meddling person.

But [O.E. *be-útan*, without], except, only, if not, otherwise, on the contrary.

Butch′er (*u*=*oo*) [O.F. *bochier*, fr. *boc*, a goat], one who slaughters, one who sells flesh for food ; to slaughter.

Butch′er-y, cruel slaughter.

But′ler [O.F. *bouteillier*, cogn. with **Bottle**], man-servant who has charge of wines, plate, etc.

Butt[1] [cf. Dan. *but*, Du. *bot*, stumpy], thick end.

Butt[2] [F. *but*, a mark], mark to be shot at.

Butt[3] [O.F. *boter*, *buter*, to thrust], thrust given by the head.

Butt[4] [Late L. *buttis*, cask], large cask.

But′ter [O.E. *butere* ; L. *bŭtyrum* ; Gk. *boutyron*], fatty substance obtained from cream or milk by churning.

But′ter-fly [probably so named from the colour of a yellow species], beautiful winged insect.

But′ter-milk, milk that remains after the butter has been separated.

But′ter-y [O.F. *boterie*, cogn. with **Butler**, **Bottle**], place for provisions in colleges, etc.

But′ton [O.F. *boton*, a bud, a button ; *boter*, to push out], knob ; fasten with buttons.

But′tress [O.F. *bouterez*, *bouteret*, a prop], projection to give support to a wall ; to prop.

Bux′om [M.E. *buhsum*, orig. obliging ; O.E. *búgan*, to bend], stout and rosy.

Buy (O.E. *byegan*, to buy), get for a price.

Buzz [imit.], hum as bees ; humming sound.

Buz′zard [O.F. *busard* ; L. *buteo*, a sparrow-hawk], kind of hawk.

By [O E. *bi*, *bi*, *be*], near, along, through.

By-and-by [O.E. *bi*, by], later on.

By′law, Bye′-law [prob. O.E. *bý*, O.N. *byr*, a town, and **Law**], town-law.

By′play, action carried on aside.

Byre [O.E. *býre*, perh. cogn. with **Bower**], cow-house.

By'stand-er, looker-on.

By-the-bye (or by), in passing.

By'way, path aside from the main road.

By'word, common saying.

C

Cab, Cab-ri-o-let' (*et*=*ai*) [*Cab* is short for F. *cabriolet*; F. *cabriole*; It. *capriola*, a goat's leap; L. *caper*, a goat], carriage for hire.

Ca-bal' [Heb. *qabbālāh*, mysterious doctrine, tradition], small intriguing party.

Cab-a-lis'tic, having a mysterious meaning.

Cab'bage [formerly *cabbage-cole*, head-vegetable, fr. F. *caboche*, head, L. *caput*, head], vegetable with a head of leaves.

Cab'in [Late L. *capanna*, a hut], hut, room in a ship.

Cab'i-net [F. dim. of *cabin*, a cabin], small room; the body of ministers who carry on the government; case with drawers.

Ca'ble [perh. Late L. *capulum*, *caplum*, a halter; L. *capere*, to take], large rope or chain; send a cablegram.

Ca'ble-gram [Cable and Gk. *gramma*, a letter], message sent by a submarine telegraphic cable.

Ca-boose' [cf. Du. *kabuis*], cooking-room on board ship.

Cab-ri-o-let [see Cab].

Ca-ca'o (-*cai'o*) [Sp. *cacao*; Mex. *cacauatl*, the cacao-tree], tree from the seed of which cocoa and chocolate are prepared.

Cache (*cash*) [F. *cacher*, to hide], store of concealed provisions, etc.

Cach'in-na'tion (*ch*=*k*) [L. *cachinnāre* (p.p. *cachinnātus*), to laugh], immoderate laughter.

Cac'kle [imit.], cry of a hen or goose; make the cry of a hen or goose.

Ca-coph'on-y [Gk. *cacos*, bad, *phōnē*, sound], harsh sound. Cacoph'onous.

Cac'tus [Gk. *cactos*], plant with clusters of prickles instead of leaves. [like.

Ca-dav'er-ous [L. *cadāver*, a corpse], corpse-

Cad'dice, Cad'dis [?], grub of a May-fly.

Cad'die [F. *cadet*, the younger], golfer's attendant.

Cad'dy [Malay *kāti*, a weight equal to 1¼ lb.], small box for tea.

Ca'dence [L. *cadere*, to fall], fall of the voice; close of a phrase in music.

Ca-det' [F. *cadet*, orig. a younger son], younger son of a noble house; student at a military or naval school.

Cadge [perh. var. of Catch], go about peddling.

Ca'di (*kah* or *kai*) [Arab. *qādī*, a judge], judge.

Cad'mi-um [Gk. *cadmia* (*gē*), Cadmean (earth)], white metal.

Cad-u'cous [L. *cadūcus*, falling; *cadere*, to fall], falling off.

Ca'fé [F. *café*, coffee, coffee-house], coffee-house, restaurant.

Caf'fe-ine [F. *caféine*], a vegetable alkaloid found in the leaves and seeds of the coffee and tea plants.

Cæ-su'ra (*si-zūra*) [L. *cædere* (p.p. *cæsus*), to cut], pause in a verse.

Caf'tan [Turk. *qaftan*, a dress], long under-tunic with girdle.

Cage [L. *cavus*, hollow], inclosure of open-work for birds or beasts; confine as in a cage.

Cairn [Gael. Ir., and W. *carn*, a rock, a pile of stones], artificial heap of stones.

Cairn-gorm' [Scot. mountain *Cairngorm*; Gael. *carn*, rock; *gorm*, blue], brown or yellow rock-crystal.

Cai'tiff [O. Norm. F. *caitif*, a captive, a wretch; L. *captīvus*, captive], mean scoundrel.

Ca-jole' [?], persuade by flattery.

Ca-jo'ler-y, flattery.

Cake [perh. O.N. *kaka*; cf. Dan. *kage*], sweetened loaf or piece of bread with or without currants, etc.; flat solid mass of matter; form into a hard mass.

Cal'a-bash [Span. *calabaça*; perh. fr. Pers. *kharbuz*, a melon], large gourd, utensil made from it.

Ca-lam'i-ty [L. *calamitas*, a misfortune], great misfortune.

Cal-ash' [F. *calèche*; cf. Pol. *kolaska*], small hooded carriage.

Cal-ca're-ous, Cal-ca'ri-ous (*c*=*k*) [L. *calx* (*calc-is*), lime], made of or containing lime.

Cal'ce-o-la'ri-a (*c*=*s*) [L. *calceolus*, dim. of *calceus*, a shoe], slipper-like flower.

Cal'cine (*c*=*s*) [M.L. *calcināre*, to reduce to lime; *calx*, lime], reduce to powder by heat.

Cal'cu-late [L. *calculāre* (p.p. *calculātus*), to reckon by means of pebbles], reckon up.

Cal-cu-la'tion, act or result of calculating.

Cal'cu-lus [L. *calculus*, a pebble], stone in any part of the body; a method of calculating in mathematics.

Cal'dron, Caul'dron [L. *caldārium*, a hot bath; *calidus*, hot], large kettle or boiler.

Cal'en-dar [L. *calendæ*, calends], register of the year with its divisions.

Cal'en-der [Gk. *cylindros*, a roller], pressing-machine composed of rollers; to smooth between rollers.

Cal'ends [L. *calendæ*; *calāre*, to proclaim], first day of month in Roman calendar.

Cal'en-ture [Sp. *calentura*; L. *calēre*, to be hot], tropical fever on board ship.

Calf (*al*=*ah*) [Teut., cf. Ger. *kalb*], young of the cow.

Calf [O.N. *kálfi*, calf of the leg; etym. doubtful], fleshy hinder part of the leg.

Cal'i-bre, Cal'i-ber [F. and Span. *calibre*, perh. Arab. *qālib*, a form], diameter of the bore of a firearm; capacity of mind.

Cal'i-co [fr. *Calicut* in India], cotton cloth.

Ca'lif, Ca'liph, Kha'lif [Arab. *khalīfah*, successor], title borne by the successors of Mohammed. Cal'iphate.

Cal-(l)i-pers [perh. fr. Calibre], compasses for measuring diameters.

Calk (*al=aw*), **Caulk** [L. *calcāre*, to tread, press down], stop the seams of a ship with tarred oakum.

Call [O.N. *kalla*], to name, summon, cry aloud, make a short visit ; a cry, summons, short visit.

Cal-lig′ra-phy [Gk. *callos*, beauty ; *graphein*, to write], art of beautiful writing.

Call′ing, business.

Cal-lis-then′ics [Gk. *callos*, beauty ; *sthenos*, strength], exercises to give grace of movement. [skin.

Cal-los′i-ty [see **Callous**), hard swelling on

Cal′lous [L. *callōsus*, thick-skinned], hard, unfeeling.

Cal′low [O.E. *calu*; perh. L. *calvus*, bald], without feathers, inexperienced.

Calm (*al=ah*) [Late L. and Gk. *cauma*, heat], quiet, still ; peace, stillness ; quieten.

Cal′o-mel [Gk. *calos*, fair ; *melas*, black], preparation of mercury.

Ca-lor′ic [L. *calor*, heat], heat ; of or pertaining to heat.

Cal-o-rif′ic [L. *calor*, heat, and *facere*, to make], heating.

Cal-o-ri′me-ter, instrument for measuring specific heat.

Cal′u-met [Gk. *calamos*, a reed], " peacepipe " of the North American Indians.

Ca-lum′ni-ate [L. *calumniāri* (p.p. *calumniātus*), to make a false charge)], accuse falsely.

Cal′um-ny [L. *calumnia*, calumny ; *calvi*, to deceive], slander. **Calum′nious.**

Ca′lyx, Cal′yx [L. and Gk. *calyx*, covering of a bud], flower-cup.

Cam′bric (*a=ai*) [fr. *Cambrai* in Flanders], fine, thin linen.

Cam′el [Gk. *camēlos* ; cf. Heb. *gāmāl*, camel], large humped animal of West Asia and North Africa.

Ca-mel′li-a [fr. the botanist, G. J. *Kamel*], evergreen shrub with glossy leaves and beautiful flowers.

Cam-el′o-pard [see **Camel** and **Pard**], giraffe.

Cam′e-o [It. *camēo*], stone or shell cut in relief. [instrument.

Cam′er-a [L. *camera*, a vault], photographing

Cam′i-sole [Sp. *camisola*, fr. *camisa*, chemise], formerly a loose sleeved jacket, now a sleeveless bodice.

Cam′let [F. *camelot* ; perh. Arab. *khaml*, nap], fabric of hair, or of wool mixed with silk, cotton, or linen.

Cam′o-mile, Cham′o-mile [Gk. *chamaimēlon*, earth-apple], fragrant plant whose flowers are used for medicine.

Cam-ou-flage′ (*ou=oo, ge=zh*) [F. *camoufler*, to disguise], disguise, partic. in war, conduct intended to deceive.

Camp [It. *campo* ; L. *campus*, a field], ground on which tents are erected, collection of tents, or the people who occupy the tents ; prepare a camp, lodge in a camp.

Cam-paign′ [It. *campagna*, open country, a campaign ; L. *campus*, a field], time an army keeps the field. **Campaign′er.**

Cam-pa-ni′le (*-nee′lai*) [It. *campāna*, a bell], bell-tower, usually detached from the church. **C**

Cam-pan′u-la [M.L. *campanula*, dim. of L. *campāna*, a bell], plant with bell-shaped flower.

Cam′phor [Low L. *camphora* ; Arab. *kāfūr*, camphor ; Malay, *kāpūr*, chalk], tough, white, fragrant gum. **Cam′phorated.**

Can [O.E. *canne*], vessel for holding liquids ; put in sealed cans.

Can [O.E. *can*, 1st per. sing. pres. of *cunnan*, to know], be able (followed by an infinitive without *to*).

Ca-nal′ [L. *canālis*, a channel, a trench], artificial channel filled with water ; duct of the body.

Ca-nard′ [F. *canard*, a duck], made-up sensational story.

Ca-na′ry [fr. the *Canary* Islands], yellow singing-bird ; wine made in the Canary Islands.

Can′cel [Low L. *cancellāre*, to cancel a deed by drawing lines across it ; L. *cancelli*, lattice work, crossed lines], mark out by cross lines, set aside. **Cancella′tion.**

Can′cer [L. *cancer*, a crab], dangerous growth in the body. **Can′cerous.**

Can-de-la′brum (*-lai′*) (pl. -bra) [L. *candēla*, a candle], branched candlestick.

Can′did [L. *candidus*, white], frank and fair, outspoken.

Can′di-date [L. *candidātus*, white-robed ; *candidus*, white], one who offers himself or is put forward by others for a vacant post. **Can′didature.**

Can′dle [L. *candēla*, a candle ; *candēre*, to glow], cylinder of tallow or wax round a wick used for lighting.

Can′dour [L. *candor*, brightness, whiteness], frankness and sincerity.

Can′dy [F. *(sucre)-candi*, (sugar)-candy ; Arab, *qāndi*, made of sugar], sweetmeat ; make sugar crystals of or in, crust with sugar.

Can′dy-tuft (*Candia*, obs. name for Crete) [and **Tuft**], plant with flowers in flat tufts.

Cane [O.F., L. and Gk. *canna*, a reed], stem of a reed or small palm, light walking-stick ; beat with a cane.

Ca-nine′, Can′ine [L. *canis*, a dog], relating to or like a dog.

Can′is-ter [Gk. *canastron*, a basket ; *canna*, a reed], small box for tea, etc., kind of caseshot in a case fitting the cannon.

Can′ker [see **Cancer**], corroding ulcer, anything which corrodes ; eat away as a canker.

Can′nel (coal) [perh. fr. **Candle**], coal which burns with a clear flame and is used in making gas.

Can′ni-bal [Sp. *Canibales*, var. of *Caribal*, a Carib native of W. Ind. islands], human man-eater.

Can′non [F. *canon* ; cf. It. *cannone*, a cannon, orig. a great tube ; L. *canna*, a reed], great gun.

Can-non-ade′, attack with cannon.

Ca-noe' (*oe*=*oo*) [Sp. and Haytian *canoa*], light boat moved by paddles.

Can'on [Gk. *canōn*, a rod, a rule; *canna*, a cane], a law, general rule or standard; cathedral dignitary; the books received as genuine Holy Scriptures; kind of musical composition.

Ca'ñon, Can'yon [Sp. *cañon*, a tube; L. *canna*, a cane], deep river-ravine.

Ca-non'ic-al, of or pertaining to a canon; (pl.) clerical dress.

Can'on-ize, put in the catalogue of saints.

Can'on-ry, office of a canon.

Can'o-py [Gk. *cōnōpeion*, a mosquito curtain; *cōnōps*, a mosquito], covering projecting over a bed, etc., or carried on poles over an exalted person, sacred image, etc.

Cant[1] [perh. Gk. *canthos*, corner of the eye], tilt to one side.

Cant[2] [prob. L. *cantāre*, freq. of *canere*, to sing], talk with a pretence of piety, hypocritical speech.

Can-tan'ker-ous [perh. M.E. *contak*, contention], ill-natured and fault-finding.

Can-ta'ta [It. *cantāre*, to sing], somewhat dramatic musical composition with choruses, solos, etc.

Can-teen' [F. *cantine*; It. *cantina*, a cellar], place for buying provisions in a garrison, soldier's water-vessel.

Can'ter [short for *Canterbury* gallop (pilgrims' easy pace)], easy gallop; move in a canter.

Can'ti-cles [L. *canticulum*, dim. of *canticum*, a song; *canere*, to sing], Song of Solomon.

Can'ti-lē-ver [Cant[1] and Lever], projecting bracket to support balcony, etc. [poem.

Can'to [It. *canto*, song], division of a long poem.

Can'ton, Can-ton' [O.F. *canton*, a corner. See Cant[1]], state in Switzerland, division of territory.

Can-ton'ment (*-ton* or *-toon*) [see Canton], buildings assigned to troops for temporary quarters, permanent military station in India.

Can'vas [L. and Gk. *cannabis*, hemp], sailcloth, cloth prepared to receive painting in oil.

Can'vas-back [named from ashy white colour of its back], American wild duck.

Can'vass [orig. to toss in a sheet. See **Canvas**], examine thoroughly, solicit votes; solicitation of votes.

Can'yon [see Cañon].

Caout'chouc (*kow'-chook*) [Caribbean *cahuchu*], india-rubber.

Cap [Late L. *cappa*, a cap], covering for the head, top piece; put a cap on, outdo.

Ca'pa-ble (*cai'-*) [L. *capere*, to hold], of sufficient size, strength, etc.

Ca-pa'cious [L. *capax* (*capāc-is*), able to hold; *capere*, to hold], able to contain much.

Ca-pa'ci-ty, power of receiving or containing, outward condition, position.

Ca-par'i-son [Sp. *caparazon*; M.L. *caparo*, a cowl; *cāpa*, a cape], ornamental trappings; to deck with such.

Cape [F. *cap*, Rom. *capo*, a headland; L. *caput*, the head], piece of land jutting into the sea. [for the shoulders.

Cape [F. fr. Span. *capa* or It. *cappa*] covering

Ca'per [L. *caper*, a goat], skip about; frolicsome leap, prank.

Ca'per [L. and Gk. *capparis*, the caper plant, also its fruit], pickled flower-buds of the caper-bush.

Cap-er-cail'zie [Gael. *capullcoille*, great cock (lit. horse) of the wood; *capull*, horse, *coill*, wood], wood-grouse.

Ca-pil'la-ry, Cap'ill-a-ry [L. *capillus*, hair], like a hair; one of the minute vessels which connect the arteries and the veins.

Cap'i-tal [L. *caput* (*capit-is*), the head], first-rate, punishable with death.

Cap'i-tal [L. *capitellum*, head of a pillar; *caput*, the head], uppermost part of a column], chief city, means with which business is carried on, a large letter.

Cap'i-tal-ist, one who has large investments.

Cap-i-ta'tion [L. *caput*, the head], numbering by heads.

Cap'i-tol [L. *Capitōlium*, temple of Jupiter at Rome; *caput*, the head], temple of ancient Rome; U.S. Congress House.

Ca-pit'u-late [Late L. *capitulāre* (p.p. *capitulātus*), to divide under headings; *caput*, the head], surrender on certain terms.

Ca-price' (*ice*=*eess*) [F. *caprice*; It. *capriccio*, a whim; It. *capro*, a goat], whim. [able.

Ca-pri'cious (*ici*=*ish*) whimsical, change-

Cap'si-cum [perh. L. *capsa*, a case], kind of plant with hot capsules and seed.

Cap-size' [perh. fr. Sp. *capuzar*, to sink (a ship), by the head], overturn.

Cap'stan [F. or Port. *cabestan*; L. *capistrāre* (*capistrum*, a halter, *capere*, to hold)], upright machine which is turned so as to wind a cable on it.

Cap'sule [L. *capsula*, dim. of *capsa*, a case], kind of seed-vessel, gum envelope for medicine.

Cap'tain [Late L. *capitāneus*, a chief; L. *caput*, the head], company or troop commander, commander of a ship.

Cap'tain-cy, rank or commission of captain.

Cap'tious (*ti*=*sh*) [L. *capere* (p.p. *captus*), to take], ready to find fault.

Cap'ti-vate [L. *captivāre* (p.p. *captivātus*), to take captive], enslave, charm.

Cap'tive [L. *capere* (p.p. *captus*), to take], taken prisoner; one taken in war, one held in bondage. [bondage.

Cap-tiv'i-ty, state of being a prisoner,

Cap'tor, one who takes a prize or a captive.

Cap'ture, take by force or surprise; act of capturing, thing captured.

Car [L. *carrus*, a car; Bret. *karr*, a chariot], vehicle on wheels, the cage or box hanging from a balloon.

Car'a-cole [Sp. *caracol*, a snail, a winding staircase], half-turn of a horseman.

Ca-rafe' [Sp. *garrafa*, a vessel to cool wines in; Arab. *gharafa*, to draw water], glass water-bottle.

Car′a-mel [Sp. *caramelo*], burnt sugar, a cube of confectionery.

Car′at [Arab. *qirāt*, a weight of 4 grs.], weight for precious stones ; word used to indicate the fineness of gold, pure gold being of 24 carats.

Car-a-van′, Car′a-van [Pers. *kārwān*], company of merchants travelling together ; house on wheels.

Car-a-van′se-rai (*ai*=*ī*) [Pers. *kārwānsarāy*], kind of unfurnished inn where caravans rest at night.

Car′a-way [M.L. *carui* ; cf. Arab. *al*, the, *karawiyā*, caraway], plant with aromatic seeds. [rifle.

Car′bine, Car′a-bine [orig. uncertain], short **Car-bin-eer′, Car-a-bin-eer′**, soldier armed with a, carbine.

Car-bol′ic [L. *carbo*, coal ; -*ol*, suf. in chemistry from termination of Alcohol], acid obtained from coal-tar.

Car′bon [L. *carbo* (*carbōn-is*), coal], substance which occurs pure in blacklead and in the diamond. [carbon.

Car-bon′ic, of, pertaining to, or containing

Car-bon-if′er-ous [L. *carbo*, coal, *ferre*, to carry], containing carbon.

Car′bun-cle [L. *carbunculus*, small coal], red gem ; kind of tumour. [carbon.

Car-bu-ret′ted [see Carbon], combined with

Car′cass, Car′case [F. *carcasse*, a dead body], body ; kind of fire-ball from gun.

Card[1] [Gk. *chartēs*, a papyrus leaf], piece of pasteboard (blank, written on, or marked).

Card[2] [F. *carde*, a teasel-head ; L. *carduus*, a thistle], instrument for combing wool, etc. ; to comb with a card.

Card′board, pasteboard for making cards, etc.

Car′di-ac [Gk. *cardia*, the heart], pertaining to the heart.

Car′di-gan [fr. an Earl of *Cardigan*], knitted woollen waistcoat.

Car′di-nal [L. *cardo* (*cardin-is*), a hinge], chief ; one of the Roman Catholic clergy who rank next to the pope.

Care [O.E. *caru*], anxiety, charge, heed ; have interest or regard.

Ca-reen′ [L. *carīna*, a keel], heave (said of a ship) or lean to one side.

Ca-reer′ [Late L. *carrāria via*, a road for cars ; L. *carrus*, a car], running, course through life ; run rapidly.

Care′ful, full of care, taking care. [touch.

Ca-ress′ [L. *carus*, dear], fondle ; fondling

Ca′ret [L. *caret*=it needs, there is wanting], mark (^) to show the place of something omitted.

Car′go [Sp. *cargo*, freight ; Late L. *carricāre*, to load a car], goods carried by a ship.

Car-i-bou′ (*ou*=*oo*) [Canadian F. *caribou*], N. American reindeer.

Car-i-ca-ture′ [It. *caricatura* ; *caricāre*, to load], picture or description in which peculiarities are exaggerated ; represent with absurd exaggeration. **Caricatur′ist**.

Ca′ri-es (*a*=*ai*) [L. *cariēs*, rottenness], decay of bone or teeth.

Car′il-lon (*lon*=*yon*) [F. from Low L. *quadrilion*(-*em*), a quaternary], an air played on bells.

Cark′ing [O.N.F. *carkier*, L.L. *carricāre*, to load. See **Cargo**], vexatious.

Car′mine [Sp. *carmin* ; Arab. *qirmizī*, crimson, *qirmazi*, cochineal], crimson.

Car′nage [L. *caro* (*carn-is*), flesh], slaughter.

Car′nal [L. *caro* (*carn-is*), flesh], fleshly.

Car-na′tion [L. *carnātio* (*carnātiōn-is*), fleshiness], rosy pink.

Car-na′tion [earlier *coronation* (prob. original name), *cornation*], double-flowering variety of the clove-pink.

Car-ne′li-an, Cor-ne′li-an [formerly *cornaline*. F. *corneline*, etym. dub.], flesh-red stone.

Car′ni-val [It. *carnevale*, the three days before Lent ; L. *carnem levāre*, to put away meat], festival in the week before Lent ; merry-making.

Car-niv′o-rous [L. *caro* (*carn-is*), flesh, *vorāre*, to devour], flesh-eating.

Car′ol [O.F *carole*, a chorus dance. Etym. doubtful], song of joy ; sing joyfully.

Ca-rot′id [Gk. *carōtides*, the two great arteries of the neck ; *caros*, stupor], one of the two great arteries of the neck.

Ca-rous′al (*s*=*z*), a jovial feast.

Ca-rouse′ [Ger. *gar aus*, right out, used of emptying a drinking vessel], take part in a drunken revel.

Carp [O.F. *carpe*], fresh-water fish.

Carp [O.N. *karpa*, to boast], find fault ill-naturedly.

Car′pen-ter [L.L. *carpentum*, a carriage], worker in timber for building. **Car′pentry**.

Car′pet [O.F *carpite* or It. *carpita* ; L. *carpere*, to pluck], woven covering for a floor.

Car′pet-knight, one made a knight through court favour ; effeminate person.

Car′riage [O.N.F. *cariage* ; *carier*, to carry], vehicle for conveying persons ; price of carrying, bearing. [porter.

Car′ri-er, one who or that which carries, a

Car′ri-on [O.N.F. *caroine*, perh. fr. L. *caro* (*carn-is*), flesh], corrupt flesh.

Car-ron-ade′ [fr. *Carron* in Stirlingshire], short kind of ship′s gun. [food.

Car′rot [Gk. *carōton*, a carrot], root used for

Car′ry [L. *carrus*, a car], bear or convey.

Cart [prob. O.N. *kartr*, a cart], wheeled carriage for loads. [gristle.

Car′ti-lage [L. *cartilāgo* (*cartilāgin-is*), gristle],

Car′ti-la′gi-nous, gristly.

Car-tog′raph-y [F. *carte*, chart ; Gk. *graphein*, to draw], map-drawing.

Car-toon′ [F *carton* or It. *cartone*, a large paper ; L. *carta*, a card], full-sized design to be copied ; political caricature.

Car′tridge [It. *cartoccio*, a roll of paper ; Late L. *carta*, paper], complete charge for a firearm contained in a case.

Carve [O.E. *ceorfan*, to carve], cut patterns on wood or other material, cut up meat.

Carv′er, one who carves, carving-knife.

Ca-ry-at′ids, Ca-ry-at′id-es [Gk. *Caryatides*,

women of Caryae, priestesses of Diana], figures of women, serving as columns to support entablatures.

Cas-cade' [It. *cascāre*, to fall], waterfall.

Case [L. *capsa*, a case, fr. *capere*, to hold], box or covering.

Case [L. *cadere* (p.p. *casus*), to fall], state of things; action at law; relation of a noun or pronoun to some other word.

Case'har-den, to harden, as iron, by turning surface into steel. Hence, to become callous. **Case-hardened.** [hinges.

Case'ment [see **Case**], window-sash on

Ca'se-ous [L. *caseus*, cheese], of or like cheese.

Cash [orig. a money-box; F. *casse*, now *caisse*, a case], money, ready money; give or receive money for.

Cash'ew (*ew*=*oo*) [F. *acajou*; Braz. *acajoba*], W. and E. Indian tree, with kidney-shaped fruit. [dismiss.

Cash-ier', one who has charge of money; to

Cash'mere [fr. *Cashmere* in India], fine woollen stuff.

Cask [Sp. *casco*, a skull, a cask], vessel of staves bound with hoops.

Ca-si'no (*si*=*see*) [It. dim. of *casa*, a house], public room for dancing, singing or gaming.

Cas'ket [dim. of **Cask**], small box for jewels.

Casque [F.], helmet.

Cas-sa'va [Haytian *casabbi*, *casávi*, Mandioc], plant from which tapioca is made.

Cas'ser-ole [F.], earthenware vessel in which food is cooked and served.

Cas'sock [perh. It. *casacca*, an outer coat], loose robe worn by clergymen. [bird.

Cas'so-wa-ry [Malay *kasuārī*], ostrich-like

Cast [O.N. and Swed. *kasta*; cf.Dan. *kaste*, to throw], throw, reckon, form into a shape; a throw, slight squint, object shaped in a mould.

Cas'ta-nets [Sp. *castañetas*; L. *castānea*, a chestnut], two pieces of wood struck together in time with dancing.

Cast'a-way, one who is shipwrecked.

Caste [Port. *casta*, a race, pure breed; perh. L. *castus*, pure], distinct class of society in India.

Cas'tel-lan [L. *castellānus*], keeper of a castle.

Cas'tel-la-ted, built with turrets like a castle.

Cast'er, Cast'or [fr. an obsolete sense of *cast*, meaning to turn], little wheel on furniture; a cruet.

Cas'ti-gate [L. *castigāre* (p.p. *castigātus*), to chasten], punish, expose faults. **Castiga'tion.**

Cast'ing, mass of metal cast in a mould.

Cas'tle [L. *castellum*, dim. of *castrum*, a fort], fortified house.

Cas'tor oil [?], an oil pressed from seeds.

Cas'u-al (*s*=*zh* or *z*) [L. *cāsus*, chance], chance.

Cas'u-al-ty, accident.

Cas'u-ist [F. *casuiste*; L. *cāsus*, case], one who is given to casuistry, quibbler.

Cas'u-ist-ry, reasoning (often false) in regard to right and wrong.

Cat [L. *catta*], a common domestic animal.

Cat'a-clysm [Gk. *cata*, down, *klysein*, to wash], deluge; social upheaval.

Cat'a-combs (pl.) (*ŏ*) [?], underground cemetery.

Cat'a-falque [Ital. *catafalco*. Orig. unknown], temporary structure used as a stand for the coffin of some great person before burial.

Cat-a-lec'tic [Gk. *cata*, down, *lēgein*, to stop], wanting a syllable at the end of a line of poetry.

Cat'a-lep-sy [Gk. *cata*, down, *lēpsis*, seizure], sudden fixedness of the body with lack of power to move. **Catalep'tic.**

Cat'a-logue [Gk. *cata*, down, *legein*, to choose], list of names, etc.

Cat-a-mar-an' [Tamil, *katta-maram*, tied logs], kind of raft.

Cat'a-plasm [Gk. *cata*, down, *plasmein*, to mould], poultice.

Cat'a-pult [Gk. *cata*, down, *pallein*, to hurl], forked stick with an elastic band for throwing stones.

Cat'a-ract [Gk. *cata*, down, *rhēgnymi*, to break], large waterfall; disease of the eye.

Ca-tarrh' [Gk. *cata*, down, *rheein*, to flow], flow of mucus from the nose, etc.

Ca-tas'tro-phe [Gk. *cata*, down, *strophē*, a turning], great misfortune, turning-point or climax of a tragedy.

Catch [O.N.F. *cachier*, to hunt; L. *capere* (p.p. *captus*), to take], lay hold of, come up with; that which is caught; humorous round in music.

Catch'up, Cat'sup (also **Ket'chup**) [perh. Chin. *kôe-chiap*, brine of pickled fish], sauce made from mushrooms.

Cat'e-chise (*ch*=*k*) [Gk. *cata*, down, *ēchein*, to sound], examine by asking questions.

Cat'e-chism, book of instruction by questions and answers. **Cat'echist.**

Cat-e-chu'men [see **Catechise**], young member of the Church who is receiving instruction before taking the Lord's Supper.

Cat'e-go-ry [Gk. *cata*, down, against, *agora*, an assembly], class or order.

Ca'ter (*a*=*ai*) [M.E. *cater* (short for *acater*), a caterer; O.F. *acat*, a buying], supply provisions. **Ca'terer.**

Cat'er-an (*a*=*ă*) [Gael. *ceathairne*, peasantry], Highland cattle-lifter.

Cat'er-pil-lar [O.F. *chatepelose*; *chate* (fem. of *chat*, cat), and *pelose*, hairy], wormlike grub of butterflies and moths. [cat.

Cat'er-waul [Cat and *waul*, imit.], cry like a

Cat'gut, intestines (not cat's) made into strings for musical instruments.

Cath-ar'tic [Gk. *catharticos*; *cathairein*, to cleanse], purgative.

Ca-the'dral [Gk. *cathedra*, a seat; *cata*, down, and *hedra*, a chair], church with a bishop's throne; an important church of architectural beauty.

Cath'o-lic [Gk. *cata*, throughout, *holos*, the whole], universal, broad in sympathy, member of the Catholic Church.

Ca-thol'i-cism, adherence to the Catholic Church, broad-mindedness.

Ca-tho-li'ci-ty, freedom from prejudice.

Cat′kin [Du. *katteken*, kitten; also catkin of willow, hazel, etc.], blossom of the willow, etc.

Cat-o′-nine-tails, a whip with nine lashes.

Cat′s-paw [from the fable of the monkey which used the paws of the cat to draw nuts from the fire], dupe or tool of another, slight breeze.

Cat′sup [see Catchup].

Cat′tle [O.N.F. *catel*; L. *capitāle*, property], animals of the ox kind.

Cau′cus [U.S. word, perh. from Algonkin *kaw-kaw-asu*, a counsellor], private meeting of politicians to choose candidates, etc.

Cau′dal [L. *cauda*, a tail], pertaining to a tail.

Cau′dle [L. *calidus*, hot], warm drink for sick persons.

Cau′li-flow′er [F. *chou flori*, fr. L. *caulis*, a stem, *florēre*, to flourish, assim: to L. *caulis* and E. *flower*], kind of cabbage with a curd-like head.

Caulk [see Calk].

Caul′dron [see Caldron].

Cause (*s*=*z*) [L. *causa*, a cause], that which produces a result; a suit in court; bring about.

Cause′way [O.N.F. *caucie*; Late L. *calciāta* (*via*), trodden (way), and **Way**], raised and paved pathway.

Caus′tic [Gk. *causticos*, burning], burning, corroding, cutting and severe; substance which corrodes.

Cau′ter-ize [Gk. *cautērion*, a branding-iron], burn with a caustic or hot iron.

Cau′tion [L. *cavēre* (p.p. *cautus*), to beware], provident care, warning; to warn.

Cau′tious, full of caution.

Cav-al-cade′ [F. fr. Port. *cavalcada*; L. *caballus*, a horse], procession on horseback.

Cav-a-lier′ (*ie*=*ee*) [It. *cavaliere*, a cavalier; L. *caballus*, a horse], knight, gallant; offhand.

Cav′al-ry [It. *cavalleria*, cavalry; L. *caballus*, a horse], body of mounted troops.

Cave [L. *cavus*, hollow], hollow place in the earth.

Ca′ve-at [L. *caveat*=let him beware], a warning, caution.

Cav′ern [L. *caverna*, cavern, *cavus*, hollow], large cave.

Ca-vi-ar′, Ca-vi-are′ [?], salted roes of the sturgeon; unpalatable.   [trifles.

Cav′il [L. *cavilla*, mockery], find fault for

Cav′i-ty [L. *cavus*, hollow], hollow.

Caw [imit.], cry of a crow; make the cry of a crow.

Cay′man, Cai′man [prob. Carib. *acáyouman*], American alligator.

Cay-enne′ [Braz. *kyýnha*, assim. to *Cayenne*, capital of French Guiana], strong kind of pepper.   [leave off.

Cease [L. *cēdere* (sup. *cessum*), to go, to yield],

Ce′dar [Gk. *cedros*, a cedar], evergreen tree.

Cede [L. *cēdere*, to go, to yield], give up or yield.

Ce-dil′la [It. *zediglia*, dim. of *zēta*, Gk. letter ʃ], mark under c (ç) before *a*, *o*, or *u* to show that it is to be sounded like *s*.

Ceil′ing [L. *cœlum*, heaven], roof of a room.

Cel′an-dine [Gk. *chelidonion*, swallow-wort; *chelidōn*, a swallow], plant with yellow flowers.

Cel′e-brate [L. *celeber*, frequented], honour by tokens of respect, to perform with proper ceremonies. **Cel′e-bra-ted**, famous.

Cel-e-bra′tion, act or time of celebrating.

Ce-leb′ri-ty, fame; famous person.

Ce-ler′i-ty [L. *celer*, swift], swiftness.

Cel′er-y [F. *céleri*; L. and Gk. *selinon*, parsley], vegetable.

Ce-les′ti-al [L. *cœlum*, heaven], heavenly.

Cel′i-ba-cy [L. *cœlebs* (*cœlib-is*), unmarried], unmarried state. **Cel′ibate.**

Cell [L. *cella*, a small room], small room in a prison, convent, etc., smallest element of living structure.

Cell′ar [see Cell], room under a house.

Cel′lu-lar [L. *cellula*, dim. of *cella*, a cell], made up of cells.

Cel′lu-loid [L. *cellula*, dim. of *cella*, a cell], substance made of gun-cotton and camphor.

Celt (or **Kelt**) [L. *Celta*], ancient inhabitant of Western Europe.

Celt [founded on *celte* in the Vulgate, Job xix. 24, and rendered "with a chisel"], a primitive chisel.

Ce-ment′ [L. *cœmentum*, chippings of stone, *cœdere*, to cut], substance which joins two bodies; join firmly.

Cem′e-ter-y [Gk. *coimētērion*, a sleeping-place], burial-place.

Cen′o-taph [Gk. *cenos*, empty, *taphos*, a tomb], monument in honour of a person who is buried elsewhere.

Cen′ser [O.F. *censier*, fr. *encensier*; L. *incensum*, incense; *incendere*, to kindle], vessel to contain incense.

Cen′sor [L. *censēre*, to tax, to give an opinion], officer who examines books, etc.; permit or forbid publication.

Cen-so′ri-ous, fault-finding.

Cen′sure, blame; to blame.   [the people.

Cen′sus [L. *censēre*, to rate], numbering of

Cent [L. *centum*, a hundred], hundred; American coin worth ₁₀₀th part of a dollar.

Cen′taur [Gk.], a being half-man half-horse.

Cen-te-na′ri-an, one who has lived one hundred years.

Cen′te-na-ry (or **Cen-te′-**) [L. *centenarius*, *centēni*, a hundred each], anniversary or commemoration of an event at the end of a hundred years.

Cen-ten′ni-al [L. *centum*, a hundred, *annus*, a year], happening every hundred years, after a hundred years.

Cen′ti-grade [L. *centum*, a hundred, *gradus*, a step], divided into 100 degrees (of Celsius's thermometer, with freezing-point 0° and boiling-point 100°).

Cen′ti-me-tre [L. *centum*, a hundred; Gk. *metron*, a measure], the 100th of a metre, about ·39 inch.

Cen′ti-pede [L. *centum*, a hundred, *pes* (*ped-is*), a foot], worm-like animal with many feet.

B *

Cen'tral [L. *centrum*, a centre], belonging to, in, or near the centre.

Cen'tral-ize, gather into or about a centre.

Cen'tre [Gk. *centron*, a spike], middle point ; collect to a point.

Cen-trif'u-gal [L. *centrum*, a centre, *fugere*, to flee], tending or causing to fly from the centre.

Cen-trip'e-tal [L. *centrum*, a centre, *petere*, to seek], tending or causing to approach the centre.

Cen'tu-ple (u=oo) [L. *centum*, a hundred, *plicāre*, to fold], hundredfold.

Cen-tu'ri-on [see Century], Roman commander of about a hundred foot-soldiers.

Cen'tu-ry [L. *centuria*, number of one hundred], hundred years ; in Roman history a company of soldiers, orig. a hundred.

Ce-ram'io [Gk. *ceramos*, potter's earth], of or pertaining to pottery.

Ce're-al [L. *Ceres*, the goddess of corn], grain ; relating to grain.

Cer'e-bral [L. *cerebrum*, the brain], of or pertaining to the brain.

Cere'cloth, Cere'ment (*seer'ment*) [L. *cera*, wax], waxed cloth in which to wrap a dead body ; (pl.) grave-clothes.

Çer-e-mo'ni-al, relating to ceremony ; system of ceremonies.

Cer'e-mo'ni-ous, observant of forms.

Cer'e-mo-ny [L. *cærimonia*, a rite], outward form, religious or otherwise.

Cer'tain [L. *certus*, sure, orig. p.p. of *cernere*, to discriminate], sure, fixed on, not specially named.

Cer'tain-ty, state of being certain, truth.

Cer-tif'i-cate [L. *certus*, sure, *facere*, to make], written statement of facts.

Cer'ti-fy [F. *certifier* ; L. *certificāre*, to make sure], assure. [certainty.

Cer'ti-tude [L. *certitūdo* ; *certus*, sure].

Ce-ru'le-an [L. *cœruleus* (for *cœluleus*), blue, *cœlum*, sky], sky-blue.

Cer'vi-cal [L. *cervix* (*cervic-is*), the neck], of or pertaining to the neck.

Ces-sa'tion [L. *cessāre* (p.p. *cessātus*), to stop], stoppage.

Ces'sion [L. *cēdere* (sup. *cessum*), to yield], a giving up to others.

Cess'pool [origin uncertain, perhaps Celt. *soss*, filth, or It. *cesso*, privy], pool in which filthy water collects.

Ce-ta'ce-an (c=sh) [Gk. *cētos*, a whale], of the order of aquatic mammals, including whales.

Chafe [O.F. *chaufer*, to warm], warm or fret by rubbing ; fret.

Cha'fer [O.E. *cefer*], kind of beetle.

Chaff [O.E. *ceaf*], husks of corn ; banter.

Chaf'fer [O.E. *cēap*, a bargain, and *faru*, a journey], to bargain. [bird.

Chaf'finch (Chaff and Finch), kind of songbird.

Cha-grin' (*sha-green'*) [F. *chagrin*, melancholy], vexation.

Chain [L. *catēna*, a chain], line of links fitted together ; fasten with a chain.

Chair [L. and Gk. *cathedra*, a throne, a raised seat ; O.F. *chaère*], seat with a back for one person.

Chair'man, one who presides at a meeting.

Chaise (*shaiz*) [F. *chaise*, O.F. *chaère*, a chair], kind of light carriage.

Chal-ced'o-ny [Gk. *chalcēdōn*], whitish quartz.

Chal dron [O.F *chauderon*, as Caldron], coalmeasure of 36 bushels.

Chal'ice (*ice=iss*) [L. *calix* (*calic-is*), a cup], drinking-cup.

Chalk (*al=aw*) [L. *calx* (*calc-is*), lime], earthy limestone, similar preparation for writing ; to mark with same.

Chal'lenge [O.F *chalenge* ; L. *calumnia*, false accusation], summons to fight ; call to fight ; call to answer. Chal'lenger.

Cha-lyb'e-ate [Gk. *chaybos*, steel, named from the *Chalybes* of Pontus, who made steel], (water) containing iron or steel.

Cham'ber (*a=ai*) [F. *chambre*: L. *camera*, a room, a vault], room, hall, assembly.

Cham'ber-lain (*a=ai*) [O.F., fr. Teut. (cf. O.H.G. *chamarling*, fr. L. *camera*, a room], high officer of a court.

Cha-me'le-on [Gk. *chamai*, on the ground, *leōn*, lion], kind of lizard which changes colour.

Cham'ois (*sham'wah*) [F. *chamois*], small kind of antelope ; (*shammy*) soft leather.

Cham'o-mile [see Camomile].

Champ [prob. imit.], bite the bit (as a horse).

Cham-pagne' (*ch=sh*) [fr. the province of *Champagne*, in France], wine of France.

Cham-paign' (*ch=sh*) [O.F. *champaigne* ; L. *campus*, a plain], flat, open country.

Cham'pi-on [L.L. *campio* (*campiōn-is*), a combatant ; *campus*, a field], one who fights for a person or cause ; one who is victorious over all.

Chance [O.F. *cheance* ; Late L. *cadentia*, a falling, chance ; L. *cadere*, to fall], accident, opportunity ; to risk.

Chan'cel [L.L. *cancellus*, a chancel, a screen ; L. *cancelli* (pl.), a grating], that part of a church where the altar is placed.

Chan'cel-lor [L. *cancellārius*, orig. an officer who stood near the *cancelli* round the judgment seat], title given to many officers of state ; president of a court.

Chan'cer-y [for *chancelry* ; Late L. *cancellāria*, the record-room of the cancellarius], division of the English or Irish High Court of Justice.

Chan-de-lier' (*ch=sh*, *ie=ee*) [F. *chandelier* ; a candle-holder ; L. *candēla*, a candle], hanging frame with branches for lights.

Chan'dler [L. *candēla*, a candle], maker or seller of candles ; dealer in general.

Change [O.F. *changer* ; L. *cambīre*, to exchange], become or make different ; act of changing ; small money.

Change'a-ble, given to change.

Chan'nel [L. *canālis*, a channel], watercourse, narrow sea.

Chant [F. *chanter* ; L. *cantāre*, to sing], short tune to accompany prose psalms ; sing, especially as a chant.

Chant'er [see **Chant**], finger-pipe in a bag-pipe.

Chant'i-cleer [name of the cock in O.F. beast-epic of Reynard the Fox], a cock.

Cha'os (a=ai) [Gk. *chaos*], boundless confusion.

Cha-ot'ic [see **Chaos**], confused.

Chap [M.E. *chappen*, cf. M.Du. *cappen*], crack in slits ; cleft, jaw.

Chap'el [Late L. *cappella*, orig. a shrine where the *cappa* or cloak of St. Martin was kept], place of worship, compartment of a cathedral.

Chap'er-on (*ch=sh*) [F. *chaperon*, a protector, orig. a kind of hood ; *chape*, a hooded cloak], matron who acts as protector to a young lady in public ; to attend as chaperon.

Chap'lain [see **Chapel**], clergyman to the court, to troops, etc. **Chap'laincy.**

Chap'let [O.F. *chapelet*, a head-dress ; *chape*, a cloak], wreath for the head. [pedlar.

Chap'man [O.E. *céap*, barter, and **Man**],

Chap'ter [F. *chapitre* ; L. *capitulum* (dim. of *caput*, the head), division of a book, clergymen belonging to a cathedral. [work.

Char[1] [O.E. *cerran*, to turn], to do a turn of

Char[2] [?], to roast, burn, scorch.

Char'ac-ter [Gk. *character*, a stamped mark], letter or figure ; the sum of a person's qualities ; a person in a book or play ; peculiar person. [tinctive.

Char-ac-ter-is'tic, part of a character ; dis-

Char'ac-ter-ize, point out the character of, be a mark of.

Cha-rade' (*ch=sh*) [Prov. *charrada*, a long talk], syllable-puzzle.

Char'coal, charred wood.

Charge [F. *charger*, to load ; L. *carricāre*, to load a cart ; *carrus*, a car], keeping, load, cost, command, accusation, sudden attack ; to load, put a price on, command, accuse, attack.

Char'ger, large dish ; war-horse.

Char'i-ot [O.F., augment. of *char*, a car ; L. *carrus*, a car], in ancient times a kind of carriage used in war, races, etc.

Char-i-ot-eer', driver of a chariot.

Char'i-ta-ble, free in giving to the poor, kind, connected with charity.

Char'i-ty [L. *cārus*, dear], good-will, alms, charitable institution.

Char'la-tan (*ch=sh*) [It. *ciarlatano*, a mountebank ; *ciarlare*, to prattle], quack.

Char'lock [O.E. *cerlic*], wild mustard.

Charm [F. *charme* ; L. *carmen*, a song], that which pleases greatly, magical words, thing worn for good luck ; please greatly.

Char'nel-house [O.F. *charnel*, a cemetery ; L. *carnālis*, carnal], place for bones of the dead.

Chart [L. *charta*, paper], marine map, table of facts.

Char'ter [L. *charta*, a paper], formal writing bestowing rights, etc. ; hire by charter.

Char'wo-man [see **Char**[1]], woman house-worker hired for single days. [careful.

Cha'ry [O.E. *cearig*, full of care], cautious,

Chase [O.F. *chacier*, to pursue ; see **Catch**], pursuit ; to hunt.

Chase [F. *châsse*, a case], frame for types.

Chase [short for *enchase* ; F. *en châsse*, in a case], engrave metal.

Chasm [L. and Gk. *chasma*], deep gap.

Chaste [L. *castus*, chaste], pure, refined.

Chas'ten, afflict with a good purpose.

Chas-tise' (*s=z*) [O.F. *chastier* ; L. *castigāre* ; see **Chaste**], punish.

Chas'tise-ment, punishment.

Chat [imit.], talk at ease ; familiar talk.

Chateau' (*sha-tō*) [F.], a castle.

Chat'e-laine (*shat-*) [F. *chastel*, castle], female castellan or castle-keeper ; ornamental appendage at lady's belt.

Chat'tels [O.F. *chatel* ; *catel*, property], property or goods.

Chat'ter [see **Chat**], talk idly ; make a noise like a magpie.

Chat'ty, given to light talk.

Chauf-feur' (*shō-fer'*) [F. *chauffeur,* fr. *chauffer,* to make hot], driver of motor-car.

Chau'vin-ism (*chau=shō*) [F. *Chauvin,* devoted soldier of Napoleon], exaggerated patriotism ; Jingoism. **Chau'vinist.**

Cheap [O.E. *céap*, price], at a low price.

Cheat [short for *escheat* ; O.F. *eschete*, rent], to deceive ; a swindler.

Check[1] [O.F. *eschec*, check, fr. Pers. *shah*, the shah], to stop, hinder, make sure by comparison ; a stop, token.

Check[2] [same as *checker,* or *chequer* ; O.F. *eschekier*, a chess-board], pattern of squares or one of the squares.

Check'ered (see **Chequered**).

Check-mate' [Arab. *shah matā,* the king is dead], complete check of king in chess ; final defeat. [eye.

Cheek [O.E. *céce*], side of the face below the

Cheep [imit.], chirp like a young bird.

Cheer [O.F. *chere* ; Late L. *cara*, the face], state of mind, shout of applause ; make glad.

Cheer'ful, Cheer'y, full of good spirits.

Cheese [L. *cāseus*, cheese], pressed curd of milk.

Chee'tah [Hind. *chita* ; Skrt. *chitraka,* spotted], the hunting leopard in India.

Chef (*ch=sh*) [F. *chef*, head, fr. L. *caput*], head cook of a large establishment.

Chem'i-cal (*ch=k*) [see **Chemist**], relating to chemistry.

Chem-ise' (*shem-eez'*) [F. *chemise* ; Late L. *camisia*, a shirt], undergarment worn by women.

Chem'ist (*ch=k*) [short for **Alchemist**; see **Alchemy**], one skilled in chemistry, maker or seller of chemicals or drugs.

Chem'is-try, science which treats of the properties of elementary substances and their laws of combination, etc.

Che-nille' (*ille=eel*) [F. lit. a caterpillar)], tufted cord, of silk or worsted, used in ladies' dresses.

Cheque [variant of **Check**[2]], money order on a banker.

Cheq′uered, Check′ered, marked in squares; varying from light to dark, etc.

Cher′ish [F. *cher* ; L. *carus*, dear], treat with tenderness.

Che-root′ [*ch=sh* or *tsh*] [Tamil, *shuruttu*, a roll], kind of cigar.

Cher′ry [Gk. *cerasos*, a cherry-tree, perh. fr. *Cerasos*, in Pontus], kind of stone-fruit.

Cher′ub, pl. **Cher′ubs** and **Cher′u-bim** [Heb. *k′rub* (pl. *k′rubim*)], winged creature with human face.

Cher-u′bic, angelic.

Chess [O.F. *eschec*, a check, lit. a king ; Pers. *shah*, a king], game for two persons with 32 pieces on a board with 64 squares.

Chest [Gk. *cistē*, a chest, a box], large box; part of the body.

Chest′nut [Gk. *castanea*, perh. fr. *Castanea*, in Pontus], kind of tree, its fruit.

Chev-a-lier′ (*ch=sh*) [F. *cheval*, a horse], knight.

Chev′ron (*ch=sh*) [F. *chevron*, a rafter], bent bar like inverted V, bar on sleeve of an N.C.O.

Chew [O.E. *céowan*], bruise with the teeth.

Chi-bouk′ (*ou=oo*) [Turk. *chibūk*, tube, pipe], Turkish pipe.

Chi-ca′ner-y (*ch=sh*) [F. *chicaner*, to wrangle, originally to dispute in the game of mall or chicane], trickery. **Chicane′**.

Chick, Chick′en [O.E. *cicen*], young fowl.

Chic′o-ry [Gk. *cichora*], plant of which the root is ground and mixed with coffee.

Chide [O.E. *cidan*], reprove.

Chief [O.F. *chef*, the head], principal, leader.

Chief′tain, a chief, head of a clan.

Chif-fon-ier′ (*ch=sh*, *ier=eer*) [F. *chiffonier*, a rag-picker, a cupboard; *chiffon*, augmentative of *chiffe*, a rag], movable cupboard.

Chil′blain [O.E. *cele*, coldness, *blegen*, to blow], swelling on hands, feet or ears caused by cold.   [daughter.

Child [O.E. *cild*], young person, son or

Chill [O.E. *cele*], coldness ; grow or make cold.

Chill′y, somewhat cold.

Chime [M.E. *chymbe*, orig. a cymbal; Gk. *cymbalon*, a cymbal], set of bells in tune, the sound of bells ; to sound (said of bells).

Chi-me′ra (*ch=k*) [Gk. *chimaira*, a she-goat, also a monster with a goat's body], monster in fable; vain fancy.

Chi-mer′ic-al, wildly imagined.

Chim′ney [L. *caminus*, an oven], funnel for escape of smoke.

Chim-pan′zee or **Chim′pan-zee** [African name, *tsimpanzee*], African ape.

Chin [O.E. *cin*], lower end of the face.

Chi′na [fr. *China*, first country of origin], fine earthenware.

Chin-chil′la [Sp. dim. of *chinche*, a bug], small South American animal with soft fur.

Chin′cough (*ough=off*) [for **Chink-Cough**], whooping-cough.

Chine [1] [O.F. *eschine*, the back-bone, perh. O.G.H. *seina*, a splinter], backbone, part of the backbone of an animal.

Chine [2] [O.E. *cinu*], ravine, ridge.

Chink [etym. dub., perh. fr. *Chine* [2]), narrow opening.

Chintz [for *chints*, pl. of *chint* ; Hind. *chint*, spotted cotton cloth], glazed printed calico.

Chip [dim. of *chop*], cut small pieces off ; small piece cut off ; fine straw-plait.

Chi′ro-man-cy (*ch=k*, *ī*) [Gk. *cheir*, the hand, *manteia*, prophecy], palmistry.

Chi-rop′o-dist (*ch=k*) [Gk. *cheir*, the hand, *pous* (*pod-os*), the foot], one who doctors hands and feet.

Chirp, Chi′rrup [imit.], noise of young birds or crickets.

Chis′el (*s=z*) [Late L. *cīsellum*, a cutting instrument; *cædere* (p.p. *cæsus*), to cut], small cutting tool.

Chiv′al-rous (*ch=sh*), pertaining to chivalry, brave and courteous.

Chiv′al-ry (*ch=sh*) [O.F. *chevalerie*, fr. L. *caballārius*, a cavalier], knighthood, ideal knightly conduct.

Chlor′ine (*ine=een*) [Gk. *chlōros*, green], gas of greenish colour used in bleaching.

Chlo′ro-form [Gk. *chlōros*, green ; L. *formīca*, an ant], liquid used to produce insensibility.   [full.

Chock′full [perh. O.N.F. *choque*, a log], quite

Choc′o-late [Mex. *chocolatl*, chocolate], paste made from the seeds of the cacao-tree, drink made from this.

Choice [O.F. *chois*, choice], act of choosing, thing chosen ; select.

Choir (*quire*) [Gk. *choros*, a dance, a troop of dancers or singers], company of singers, part of a church.

Choke [O.E. *acéocian*, to choke], block up, stop the windpipe.

Chol′er (*ŏ*) [Gk. *cholē*, bile], bile, anger.

Chol′er-a (*ŏ*) [Gk. *cholera*, cholera, *cholē*, bile], dangerous disease.

Chol′er-ic, passionate.

Choose [O.E. *céosan*], take by preference, select.

Chop [a later form of **Chap**], cut by strokes of a sharp instrument ; piece of meat chopped off ; (pl.) jaws.

Chop′sticks, two small sticks used by Chinese to convey food to the mouth.

Cho′ral (*ŏ*), belonging to a choir.

Chord [Gk. *chordē*; same word as **Cord**], string of a musical instrument, three (rarely two) or more notes sounded together.

Chore [U.S. See **Char**], job, small piece of work.

Chor′is-ter, one of a choir.

Cho′rus [see **Choir**], band of singers, vocal part-music for a number of voices.

Chough (*chuff*) [E.], red-legged crow.

Chrism [Gk. *chrisma*], consecrated oil.

Chris′ten [L. *Christus*, Christ ; Gk. *christos*, anointed], baptize and name.

Chris′ten-dom, whole body of Christians.

Chris′tian, one who professes to follow Christ.

Chris-ti-an′i-ty, religion of Christians.

Christ′mas [*Christ* and *Mass*], yearly festival in memory of the birth of Christ.

Chro-mat'ic [Gk. *chrōma*, colour], relating to colour; in music proceeding by semitones.

Chron'ic [Gk. *chronos*, time], lasting a long time, habitual.

Chron'i-cle [Gk. *chronica*, annals], record of events in order of time; to record.

Chro-nol'o-gy [Gk. *chronos*, time; *logos*, a discourse], science of time.

Chron-o-lo'gi-cal (*lŏ*), in order of time.

Chro-nom'e-ter [Gk. *chronos*, time; *metron*, measure], very exact clock or watch.

Chrys'a-lis [Gk. *chrysos*, gold], stage of insect life between the caterpillar and the butterfly.

Chrys-an'the-mum [Gk. *chrysos*, gold, *anthemon*, a flower], flower of early winter.

Chub [?], kind of fresh-water fish.

Chubb [fr. *Chubb*, a London locksmith], kind of lock. [umbrella.

Chub'by [fr. **Chub**], full-cheeked; short

Chuck [formerly *chock*; perh. F. *choquer*, to give a shock], pat gently (under the chin), toss.

Chuc'kle [imit.], low, broken laugh; to laugh with restraint.

Chum [?], room-mate, close friend; to be very intimate with.

Church [Gk. *cyriakon* (perh. *dōma*), the Lord's (house); *kyrios*, a lord], all Christians, body of Christian worshippers, building for such worship.

Church'yard, graveyard round a church.

Churl [O.E. *ceorl*, a man], rustic, rude fellow.

Churl'ish, rude and ungracious.

Churn [O.E. *cyrin*], butter-making machine; stir, or beat milk or cream to make butter.

Chute (*shoot*) [F. *chute*, fall], downward slide with or without water. [relish.

Chut'ney [Hind. *chatni*], kind of hot Indian

Chyle (*ch=k*) [Gk. *chylos*, juice], milky fluid formed from food in the intestines.

Chyme (*ch=k*) [Gk. *chymos*, juice], food reduced to pulp in the stomach.

Cic'a-trice, Ci-ca'trix (*cic=cik*) [L. *cicātrix* (*cicātric-is*), a scar], scar over a healed wound.

Ci-ce-ro'ne (*cice=tshǐshǐ* or *si-se*) [It. *cicerone*, fr. L. *Cicero*, a Roman orator], guide.

Ci'der [Gk. *sicera*, strong drink], drink made from apples.

Ci-gar' [Sp. *cigarro*], roll of tobacco leaves.

Cig'a-rette' [F. dim. of Cigar], cut tobacco rolled in paper.

Cin-cho'na (*cho=ko*) [Sp. place-name *Chinchon*. The Countess of C. was cured by cinchona, A.D. 1638], tree which yields quinine. [belt.

Cinc'ture [L. *cingere* (p.p. *cinctus*), to gird],

Cin'der [O.E. *sinder*], partly-burned coal.

Cin'e-ma [see Cinematograph], a theatre where pictures are shown.

Cin-e-mat'o-graph [Gk. *cinein*, to move, *graphein*, to describe], a motion picture.

Cin'er-ar-y [L. *cinerārius*, fr. *cinis* (*cineris*), ashes], relating to ashes.

Cin'na-mon [Heb. *qinnamon*, said to be of Malay origin], aromatic bark.

Ci'pher [Arab. *sifr*, zero (orig. *empty*)], figure 0, any Arabic numeral, person of no importance, monogram, secret writing; do sums.

Cir'cle [L. *circulus*, round, dim. of *circus*, a ring], curve without ends, surface within the curve; move around.

Cir'cuit (*cuit=kit*) [L. *circum*, round, *īre* (sup. *itum*), to go], act of moving round, regular round in discharge of duty.

Cir-cu'it-ous, roundabout.

Cir'cu-lar, round; paper for circulation.

Cir'cu-late, go round as in a circle, spread.

Cir-cum-am'bi-ent [L. *circum*, round, *ambī*, about; *īre*, to go], surrounding.

Cir-cum'fer-ence [L. *circum*, round, *ferre*, to bear, to carry], curve which encloses a circle, etc.

Cir'cum-flex [L. *circum*, round, *flectere* (p.p. *flexus*), to bend], accent marked thus (^ (or ^ in Greek)).

Cir-cum-ja'cent [L. *circum*, round, *jacēre* (pr.p. *jacens* (*-entis*)), to lie], lying round.

Cir-cum-lo-cu'tion [L. *circum*, round about, *loqui* (p.p. *locūtus*), to speak], round-about language.

Cir-cum-nav'i-gate [L. *circum*, round, *navigāre*, to navigate; *navis*, a ship], sail round.

Cir'cum-scribe [L. *circum*, round, *scrībere*, to write], draw line round, limit.

Cir'cum-spect [L. *circum*, round, *specere* (p.p. *spectus*), to look], cautious, prudent.

Cir'cum-stance [L. *circum*, round, *stāre* (pr.p. *stans*), to stand], something relating to a main fact, detail; (pl.) state of affairs.

Cir-cum-stan'tial (*ti=sh*), consisting in circumstances, detailed.

Cir-cum-val-la'tion [L. *circum*, round, *vallum*, a wall], act of surrounding with a wall.

Cir-cum-vent' [L. *circum*, round, *venīre* (sup. *ventum*), to come], deceive, outwit.

Cir-cum-vo-lu'tion [L. *circum*, round, *volvēre* (p.p. *volūtus*), to roll], rolling round.

Cir'cus [L. *circus*, a circle], circular inclosure for feats of horsemanship, etc.

Cir'rus, (pl.) **Cir'ri** [L. *cirrus*, a curl], light, fleecy cloud. [coffin.

Cist [L. *cista*; Gk. *cistē*, a chest], prehistoric

Cis'tern [L. *cisterna*, cistern; *cista*, a box], tank for water.

Cit'a-del [It. *cittadella*, dim. of *cittade*, a city], fortress in or near a city.

Ci-ta'tion, summons, quotation.

Cite [L. *citāre* (p.p. *citātus*), to call], call to appear, quote.

Cith'ern, cith'er, cith'ern [L. *cithera*], musical instrument like the guitar.

Cit'i-zen, one who lives in a city, a townsman, a freeman. [lemon.

Cit'ron [It. *citrone*; L. *citrus*], large kind of

Cit'y [O.F. *cité*; L. *civitās*, a city], town of superior rank to others.

Civ'et [Arab. *zabad*, civet], perfume taken from the civet-cat (called also the civet).

Civ'ic [L. *civis*, a citizen], relating to a city or a citizen.

Civ'il [L. *civis*, a citizen], relating to a city or a state, within the state ; polite.

Ci-vil'ian, one whose pursuits are those of civil, not military, life.

Ci-vil'i-ty, politeness.

Civ'i-li-za'tion, state of being civilized ; usages of civilized life.

Civ'i-lize [L. *civis*, a citizen], instruct in the manners of civil life.

Clack [imit.], sharp sound as by striking ; clatter of voices ; to chatter ; make sharp sound.

Claim [L. *clamāre*, to call out], to demand as a right ; demand as of right, thing demanded, an allotment.

Claim'ant [L. *clamāre* (pr.p. *clamans -antis*), to call out], one who claims.

Clair-voy'ance [F. *clair*, clear, *voyant*, seeing], alleged power of seeing things not present to the senses. **Clairvoy'ant.**

Clam [see **Clamp**], bivalve shellfish.

Cla'mant [see **Claimant**], crying out, urgent.

Clam'ber [perh. fr. **Climb**], climb with hands and feet.

Clam'my [perh. fr. O.E. *clám*, clay], damp and sticky.

Clam'or-ous, noisy.

Clam'our [L. *clamor*, noise], great noise.

Clamp [perh. O.E. *clam*], piece of wood or metal used to hold things together ; fasten with a clamp ; tread heavily.

Clan [Gael. *clann*], number of families bearing the same surname, under a chief.

Clan-des'tine [L. *clandestīnus*, close], secret.

Clang, Clang'our [L. *clangere*, to resound ; *clangor*, a loud noise], ringing sound.

Clank [perh. fr. **Clang**, but cf. Du. *klank*, a ringing], sound such as a chain makes.

Clan'nish, caring almost exclusively for family connections.

Clap [cf. O.N. and Swed. *klappa*, to clap], strike together, pat ; noise made by striking together, a pat.

Clap'per, tongue of a bell.   [words.

Clap'trap [**Clap** and **Trap**], empty, imposing

Clar'et [O.F. *clairet*, dim. of *clair* (L. *clarus*), clear], French red wine.

Clar'i-fy [L. *clarus*, clear, *facere*, to make], make clear. **Clarifica'tion.**

Clar'i-net, Clar-i-o-net' [dim. of **Clarion**], reed wind instrument.

Clar'i-on [O.F. *claron*, a clear-sounding horn ; L. *clarus*, clear], kind of trumpet.

Clar'i-ty [L. *clarus*, clear], clearness.

Clash [imit.], noisy dashing together.

Clasp [E., etym. dub.], catch for holding together ; grasp ; fasten together ; embrace.

Class [L. *classis*, a class, an assembly], rank or order, number of scholars taught together ; put in a class.

Clas'sic [L. *classicus*, of the first class], book or author of the first rank.

Clas'sic-al, of or relating to Greek and Roman, also to modern authors and works of the first rank.

Clas'si-fi-ca'tion [L. *classis*, a class ; *facere*, to make], formation into classes.

Clas'si-fy [L. *classis*, a class, *facere*, to make], put into classes.

Clat'ter [imit.], make rattling sounds.

Clause (*s=z*) [L. *claudere* (p.p. *clausus*), to shut], part of a sentence, section of a document.

Claus'tral [see **Cloister**], like a cloister.

Clav'i-cle [L. *clavicula*, dim. of *clavis*, a key], collar-bone.

Claw [O.E. *clawu*], sharp, hooked nail ; grasp, clutch, tear.

Clay [O.E. *clég*], stiff kind of earth.

Clay'more [Gael. *claidheamh mòr*, a great sword], old Highland two-edged long-sword.

Clean [O.E. *clǽne*], free from dirt ; make clean.

Clean'ly, clean in habits. **Clean'liness.**

Cleanse (*s=z*) [O.E. *clǽnsian*], to clean.

Clear [L. *clarus*, clear], free from dimness, plain ; make clear, free from, leap over, gain.

Clear'ance, a clearing away.

Clear'sto-ry, Clere'sto-ry, upper wall with row of windows in the nave of a church.

Cleav'age [see **Cleave** 2], act of splitting.

Cleave 1 [O.E. *clifian*, *clīfan*, to adhere], cling.

Cleave 2 [O.E. *clēofan*], to split.

Cleav'er, butcher's axe.

Cleek [Scot. cogn. with M.E. *cleche*, to clutch], large hook used in fishing ; iron-headed golf-club.

Clef [F. *clef* ; L. *clavis*, a key], in music a character which fixes pitch.

Cleft [see **Cleave** 2], split.

Cleg [O.N. *kleggi*, cleg], horsefly.

Clem'a-tis [Gk. *clēmatis*], kind of climbing plant.   [ness.

Clem'en-cy [L. *clemens* (-*entis*), mild], mild-

Clem'ent, mild.

Clench [see **Clinch**].

Clere'stor-y [see **Clearstory**].

Cler'gy [O.F. *clergie* ; L. *clēricus*, a clerk], body of men set apart for the service of God.

Cler'gy-man, ordained minister, especially of churches of Rome and England.

Cler'ic-al [see **Clergy**], relating to the clergy or to a clerk.

Clerk (*e=a*) [L. *clēricus*, a clerk], one who keeps records or accounts. **Clerk'ship.**

Clev'er [etym. dub. ; cf. M.E. *cliver*, ready to seize], able, skilful.

Clew [O.E. *cliwen*], ball of thread, thread which guides, that which gives a hint towards finding out.

Click [imit.], small, sharp sound.

Cli'ent [L. *cliens* (-*entis*), orig. a hearer (pr.p. of *cluere*, to hear)], one for whom a professional man (esp. lawyer) acts. **Cli'entele.**

Cliff [O.E., cf. Du. *clif*], high, steep rock.

Cli-mac'ter-ic [Gk. *climaktēr*, step of a ladder], critical period in human life.

Cli′mate [Gk. *clima*, a slope, climate], conditions of a place in regard to heat and cold, moisture, etc.

Cli′max [Gk. *climax*, a ladder], steady increase in impressiveness, highest point.

Climb (*clīme*) [E.], to climb, go up.

Clime [Gk. *clima*, climate], climate, region.

Clinch, Clench [O.E. *clenc(e)an*, cogn. with **Cling**], hold fast, close tightly, make conclusive.

Cling [O.E. *clingan*, to dry up, to shrink], hold closely together.

Clin′ic [Gk. *clinē*, a bed], teaching medicine or surgery beside sick-bed in hospital. **Clin′ic-al.**

Clink [imit. word], sharp, tinkling sound.

Clink′er [Du. *klinker*, fr. *klinken*, to clink], hard cinder, hard yellow brick.

Clip [prob. O.N. *clippa*; cf. Dan. *klippe*, to clip], cut with shears.

Clip′per [see **Clip**], fast sailing-ship.

Clique (*cleek*) [F *clique*, a gang, a noisy set], narrow set of people.

Cloak [Late L. *cloca*, a bell, a horseman's cape shaped like a bell], loose outer garment, a covering; hide, disguise.

Clock [M. Du. *clocke*, a bell], machine which measures time. [stocking.

Clock [?], pattern worked on one side of a

Clod [var. of **Clot**], lump of clay or turf.

Clod′hop-per, coarse country fellow.

Clog [?], hindrance; wooden shoe.

Clois′ter [L. *claustrum*, lit. an enclosure; *claudere* (p.p. *clausus*), to shut], monastery or nunnery, covered passage round walls. **Clois′tral.**

Close [L. *claudere* (p.p. *clausus*), to shut], shut tight, near, dense, stifling; inclosed place near neighbourhood of cathedral.

Close (*s=z*), to shut, to end, come together; the end.

Clos′et (*s=z*) [dim. of F. *clos*, an enclosed place], small room.

Clo′sure (*s=z*) [L. *clausura*, from *claudere*, to shut], stoppage of a debate.

Clot [E.], mass of curdled soft matter.

Cloth [O.E. *clāth*], woven material.

Clothe [E.], put on dress. [clothes.

Clo′thi-er [orig. *clother*], dealer in men's

Clo′thing, Clothes, dress.

Cloud [O.E. *clūd*, a round mass; cogn. with **Clod**], visible mass of vapour. **Cloud′y.**

Clout [O.E. *clūt*], piece of cloth, patch; blow.

Clove [F. *clou*; L. *clāvus*, a nail], bud of a tree used as spice.

Clo′ver [O.E. *clāfre*], plant of which the leaves are divided in three.

Clown [prob. cogn. with **Clot**; cf. Icel. *klunni*, a boorish fellow], country fellow, rude person; jester.

Clown′ish [see **Clown**], rude and awkward.

Cloy [earlier *accloy*, fr. O.F. *encloyer*, to nail; L. *clāvus*, a nail], weary by over sweetness, etc.

Club [perh. O.N. *klubba*, a club], heavy stick, association for a special purpose; join together, beat with heavy stick.

Cluck [imit. cry of a hen], make the cry of a hen.

Clue, same as **Clew.**

Clump [allied to **Club**], lump, cluster.

Clum′sy (*s=z*) [M.E. *clomsen*, to be stiff with cold; cf. Swed. *klummsen*, benumbed], without grace. **Clum′siness.**

Clus′ter [O.E. *clyster*], bunch, group.

Clutch [O.E. *clyccean*], to grasp.

Coach [said to be from Hung. *kosci*, a coach, named from village of *Kocs*], large four-wheeled carriage; a special tutor.

Co-ad′ju-tor [L. *co-*, together, *adjūtor*, a helper], fellow-worker.

Co-ag′u-late [L. *coagulum*, rennet; *co-*, together, *agere*, to drive], curdle.

Coal [O.E. *col*], mineral used for fuel.

Co-a-lesce′ [L. *co-*, together, *alescere* (sup. *alitum*), to grow], unite. **Coales′cent.**

Co-a-li′tion [see **Coalesce**], union of persons, parties, or states.

Coarse [formerly *course*, fr. *in course*, denoting anything ordinary], rough, rude.

Coast [L. *costa*, a rib], land next the sea; sail along a coast or from port to port.

Coast′er, vessel that trades between ports along a coast.

Coat [O.F. *cote*, a coat; cf. O.H.G. *chozza*, a coarse mantle], upper outer garment.

Coat′ing, layer.

Coax [formerly *cokes*, vb. from noun *cokes*, a simpleton], persuade by soft words and ways.

Cob [?], stout, short-legged horse.

Co′balt [Ger. *kobalt*, prob. fr. *kobold*, a goblin of the mines), reddish-gray metal; blue obtained from the metal.

Cob′ble [?], rounded stone; mend clumsily; mend shoes.

Cob′le, Cob′ble [cf. Welsh *ceubal*, a boat], flat-bottomed fishing-boat.

Co′bra [Port. *cobra*, also *cobra de capello*, a hooded snake; L. *colubra*, a snake], poisonous Indian snake.

Cob′web [M.E. *coppe*, a spider, and **Web**], net of a spider.

Coch′i-neal [Sp. *cochinilla*; L. *coccinum*, scarlet robe, *coccum*, a berry], scarlet dye-stuff consisting of the dried bodies of a certain species of insect.

Cock [imit. from the bird's cry], male bird, tap for liquor; hammer of a firearm; set erect.

Cock-ade′ [F. *cocarde*, deriv. of *coq*, a cock, perh. from the cock's comb], knot of ribbon or rosette of leather.

Cock-a-too′ [Malay *kakatúa*, so named from the bird's cry], kind of parrot.

Cock′a-trice [L. *cōcātrix*, fr. *calcātrix*, a treader], fabulous monster.

Cock′cha-fer, large beetle, May bug.

Cock′er [perh. fr. obs. vb. *cock*, in same sense], pamper; dog of the spaniel kind.

Cock′le [Gk. *cogchylion*, dim. of *cogchē*, a mussel], small bivalve shellfish.

Cock′le [O.E. *coccul*; perh. fr. L. dim. of *coccum*, berry], weed that grows among corn.

Cock′ney [M.E. *cokenay*, a foolish person; from *coken*, gen. pl. of *cok*, a cock, and *ay*, *ey*, an egg], Londoner.

Cock′pit, part of a warship kept for the wounded during action.

Cock′roach [Sp. *cucaracha*, a wood-louse], "blackbeetle."

Co′coa [corr. of **Cacao**], beverage prepared from the ground seeds of the cacao-tree.

Co′coa-nut, Co′co-nut, Co′ker-nut [Port. and Sp. *coco*, a bugbear, applied to the nut because of grotesque face at foot of it], nut of a palm.

Co-coon′ [F. *cocon*, a cocoon, dim. of *coque*, a shell], silken sheath spun by the grubs of some insects.

Cod [?], sea-fish.

Cod′dle [perh. for **Caudle**], pamper, fondle.

Code [L. *cōdex* (*cōdic-is*), earlier *caudex*, a tree-trunk, tablet], system of laws or rules.

Cod′i-cil (*cil*=*sil*) [L. *cōdicillus*, dim. of *codex*; see **Code**], clause added to a will.

Co′di-fy [L. *cōdex*, and *facere*, to make; see **Code**], put into the form of a code.

Cod′lin, Cod′ling [perh. Irish *cueirt*, an apple], kind of cooking apple.

Cod′ling, young cod.

Co-ef-fi′cient (*ci*=*sh*) [L. *co-*, together; see **Efficient**], joint agent; in algebra the number prefixed to another quantity.

Co-erce′ [L. *coercēre*, to force, fr. *co-*, together, and *arcēre*, to shut up], to force.

Co-er′cion, force.

Co-e′val [L. *co-*, together, *ævum*, an age], of same age.

Cof′fee [Turk. *qahveh*; Arab. *qahweh*], beverage infused from seeds.

Cof′fer [Gk. *cophinos*, a basket], chest, esp. money-chest.   [body.

Cof′fin [doublet of **Coffer**], case for a dead

Cog [cf. Sw. *kugge*, Norw. *kug*], tooth of a wheel.

Co′gent [L. *cōgere* (pr.p. *cōgens*, *-entis*), to compel], forcible, compelling. **Co′gency.**

Cŏ′gi-tate [L. *co-*, together, *agitāre*, to agitate], think.

Cognac (*con′yac*) [fr. town *Cognac*, in Charente], kind of brandy.

Cog′nate [L. *co-*, together, *gnātus* (old form of *nātus*, p.p. of *nas-ci*, to be born)], related to, akin.

Cog-ni′tion [L. *cognitus* (p.p. of *cognoscere*, to know)], action or faculty of knowing.

Cog′ni-zance [O.F. *conoissant* (pr.p. of *conoitre*, to know)], knowledge, notice, badge.

Cog-no′men [L. *co-*, together, *nomen* (altered to *gnōmen*), a name], surname.

Co-here′ [L. *co-*, together, *hærēre* (sup. *hæsum*), to stick], stick together.

Co-he′rence, Co-he′ren-cy, union of parts.

Co-he′rent [L. *co-*, together, *hærens* (*-entis*), pr.p of *hærēre*, to stick], hanging well together.

Co-he′sion (*si*=*zh*), a sticking together.

Co-he′sive (*s*=*z*), sticking together.

Co′hort [L. *cohors* (*cohort-is*)], body of Roman soldiers.

Coif [O.F. *coife*, perh. fr. M.H.G. *kupfe*], close-fitting cap. **Coiff′ure.**

Coign [old form of **Coin** (q.v.)], corner, wedge.

Coil [perh. F. *cueillir*, to collect; see **Collect**], series of rings into which a rope, etc., is wound; wind in a coil.

Coin [L. *cuneus*, a wedge], piece of stamped metal used as money; make metal into money; invent (words, etc.).   [word.

Coin′age, coins of a country, invention, coined

Co-in-cide′ [L. *co-*, together, *incidĕre*, to fall upon], fall in with, agree.   [chance).

Co-in′ci-dence, agreement (usually by **Co-in′ci-dent**, occurring together.

Coin′er, maker of false coin.

Coir [Malay. *kayar*, cord], coco-nut fibre.

Coke [?], coal from which gas has been driven out by heating.

Col′an-der, Cul′len-der [perh. fr. L. *cōlāre* (pr.p. *cōlans*), to strain, *cōlum*, a sieve], strainer.

Cold [O.E. *cald*], of low temperature, absence of heat; disease caused by chill.

Col-e-op′ter-a [Gk. *coleon*, a sheath, *pteron*, a wing], order of insects having outer hard wings over true wings.

Cole′wort [L. *caulis*, a stalk; O.E. *wyrt*, a plant], kind of cabbage.

Col′ic [Gk. *colicos*, suffering in the colon], painful affection of the intestines.

Col-lab′o-ra-tor [L. *con-*, together, *labōrāre* (p.p. *labōrātus*), to labour], associate in work. **Collabora′tion.**

Col-lapse′ [L. *con-*, together, *lābī* (p.p. *lapsus*), to slip], fall together; a falling in.

Col′lar [L. *collum*, the neck], neck-band.

Col-late′ [L. *con-*, together, *latus* (p.p. of *ferre*), to bring], compare critically.

Col-lat′er-al [L. *con-*, together, *latus* (*later-is*), a side], side by side, parallel, indirect.

Col-la′tion, comparison; light repast.

Col′league [L. *collēga*, a partner in office; L. *con-*, together, *legere*, to choose], associate in office.

Col-lect′ [L. *con-*, together, *legere* (p.p. *lectus*), to gather], gather together.

Col′lect [sea-vb. **Collect**], short comprehensive prayer in a liturgy.

Col-lec′ted, calm, cool, self-possessed.

Col-lec′tion, process of collecting, that which is collected.

Col-lec′tive, formed by collecting.

Col-lect′or, one who collects.

Col′lege [L. *collēgium*, an association of colleagues; see **Colleague**], society of persons joined together generally for learned pursuits; the building set apart for these pursuits.

Col-le′gi-ate, pertaining to a college.

Col-lide′ [L. *con-*, together, and *lædere*, to strike], strike together.

Col′lie, Col′ly [perh. same as *coaly*, coal-coloured], shepherd's dog.

Col′lier [M.E. *colier*; see **Coal**], coal-miner, a coal-ship.

Col-li′sion (*si*=*zh*) [see **Collide**], violent meeting, a clashing.

Col-lo-ca′tion [L. *con-*, together, *locāre* (p.p. *locātus*), to place], placing together.

Col-lo′di-on [Gk. *colla*, glue], solution of gun-cotton in ether.

Col′lop [?], slice of meat.

Col-lo′qui-al, used in familiar conversation.

Col′lo-quy [L. *con-*, together, *loquī*, to speak], conversation.

Col-lu′sion (*si*=*zh*) [L. *con-*, together, *lūdere* (p.p. *lūsus*), to play], secret agreement to deceive. [punctuation (:).

Co′lon [Gk. *colon*, a limb, a clause], mark of

Co′lon [Gk. *cōlon*], part of the intestines.

Colonel (*kur′nel*) [corrected from earlier *coronel*; It. *colonello*, dim. of It. *colonna*, a column], officer commanding a regiment.

Co-lo′ni-al, pertaining to a colony; inhabitant of a colony.

Col′o-nist, inhabitant of a colony.

Col′o-nize, establish a colony in.

Col-on-nade′ [F. *colonne*, a column], range of columns.

Col′o-ny [L. *colōnia*, a colony, *colōnus*, a husbandman; *colere*, to till], settlement in another land which is subject to the parent state.

Co-los′sal [Gk. *colossos*, a large statue], huge.

Col′our (*col*=*cŭl*) [L. *color* (*colŏr-is*)], property of light which makes things look different, as red, green, etc.; to paint, misrepresent.

Col′por-teur [F. *col*, the neck, *porter*, to carry], hawker of tracts and books.

Colt [?], young horse.

Col′ter, Coul′ter (*ō*) [L. *culter*, a coulter, a knife], fore-iron of a plough.

Col′um-bine [L. *columba*, a dove], flower with beaklike spurs; chief lady in a harlequinade.

Col′umn [L. *columna*, a pillar], pillar; body of troops several ranks in depth; perpendicular section of a page or line of figures.

Col′za (F. fr. Low Ger. *cōlsât*, cole-seed], cabbage of which the seeds yield oil used for lamps.

Co′ma [Gk. *cōma* (*cōmat-os*), a deep sleep], deep sleep of disease.

Co′ma-tose (*s*=*z*), as in coma, drowsy.

Comb (*ō*) [O.E. *camb*, a comb, crest], toothed instrument for the hair; crest of a cock; waxen framework in which bees store honey.

Com′bat [L. *con-*, together, *battere*, *batuere*, to fight], fight; fight with.

Com′bat-ant, one engaged in combat.

Com′bat-ive, fond of combat.

Com′bi-na′tion, act of combining, union.

Com-bine′ [L. *con-*, together, *bīnus*, two-fold], unite, join forces.

Com-bus′ti-ble, easily set on fire; something which is easily set on fire.

Com-bust′ion (*tion*=*tyun*) [L. *con-*, together, and *ūrere*, to burn (*b* inserted)], state of burning. [comedy.

Co-me′di-an [see **Comedy**], an actor in

Com′e-dy [Gk. *cōmos*, a banquet, *aoidos*, a singer], play of a happy nature.

Come′ly (*cum′*) [O.E. *cymlic*, beautiful], good-looking.

Co-mes′ti-ble [Late L. *comestibilis*; L. *comedere*, to eat up], an eatable.

Com′et [Gk. *comētēs*, long-haired, *comē*, hair], heavenly body with a tail of light.

Com′fit (*com*=*cum*) [O.F. *confit*; L. *con-*, together, *facere*, to make], sweetmeat.

Com′fort (*com*=*cum*) [L. *con-*, together, *fortis*, strong], console and cheer; consolation, quiet enjoyment, something which gives enjoyment or ease.

Com′fort-er (*com*=*cum*), one who, or that which, comforts; a woollen scarf.

Com′ic, Com′ic-al [see **Comedy**], relating to comedy, causing mirth.

Com′i-ty [L. *cōmis*, friendly, courteous], courtesy.

Com′ma [Gk. *comma*, that which is struck, a clause, a comma], mark of punctuation (,).

Com-mand′ [L. *con-*, together, *mandāre*, to entrust to, to command], to order, be leader of; order, leadership, control.

Com-man-dant′, commanding officer of a place or body of troops.

Com-man-deer′ [S. Af. Du. *kommanderen*; see **Command**], force into military service, seize for military purposes.

Com-mand′er, high officer in the navy.

Com-mand′ment, order, especially one of those given to Moses on Mount Sinai.

Com-mem′o-rate [L. *com*=*cum*, together, *memor*, mindful], call to remembrance by a special observance. **Commemora′tion.**

Com-mence′ [L. *con-*, together, *initiāre*, to begin; see **Initiate**], begin. **Commence′-ment.**

Com-mend′ [L. *commendāre*; see **Command**], entrust, praise.

Com-mend′a-to-ry, containing praise.

Com-men′su-rate [L. *con-*, with, *mensūra*, a measure], equal in measure. **Commen′-surable.**

Com′ment [L. *con-*, together, *mens* (*ment-is*) mind], remark, criticism. **Com′mentator.**

Com-ment′, make remarks on. [book.

Com′men-tary, series of comments on a

Com′merce [L. *con-*, with, *merx* (*merc-is*), merchandise], trade, especially on a large scale.

Com-mer′cial (*ci*=*sh*), relating to commerce.

Com-min-a′tion [F. *commination*; L. *comminātio*; *com-*, intensive, and *minārī*, to threaten], a threatening denunciation.

Com-mis′er-ate [*s*=*z*] [L. *con-*, with, *miser*, wretched], to pity. **Commisera′tion.**

Com-mis-sa′ri-at (*sa*=*sai*), department which furnishes provisions, as for an army; supply of provisions.

Com′mis-sa-ry [see **Commit**], one to whom some duty or office is committed.

Com-mis′sion [see **Commit**], act of doing, charge, written warrant or certificate of rank, allowance to an agent, company joined in the performance of a duty.

Com-mis′sion-er, person who has a commission to fill some office.

Com-mit′ [L. *com-* (*cum*), with, *mittere* (p.p. *missus*), to send], give in trust, do, bind (oneself) by some act or word.

Com-mit′tee (*ee=i*) [F. *commis*, p.p. of *commettre*; see **Commit**], body of persons to whom some affair is committed.

Com-mode′ [see **Commodious**], chest of drawers; bedroom convenience.

Com-mo′di-ous [L. *commodus*, fit, fr. *cum-*, with, and *modus*, a measure], roomy and convenient.

Com-mod′i-ty [L. *cum*, with, *modus*, a measure], movable bought and sold.

Com′mo-dore [formerly *commandore*; see **Command**], commander of a squadron.

Com′mon [L. *commūnis*, *cum*, with, *mūnis*, ready to serve], shared by more than one, general, ordinary; open piece of ground which is public property; (pl.) the mass of the people, lower House of Parliament, food. **Com′moner.**

Com′mon-al-ty, common people.

Com′mon-ly, usually.

Com′mon-place, ordinary; ordinary, uninteresting remark.

Com′mon-wealth, a state, the body politic.

Com-mo′tion [L. *com* (intensive), *movēre* (p.p. *mōtus*), to move], disturbed movement.

Com-mune′ [O.F. *comuner*; see **Common**], converse together.

Com′mune [F. *commune*], municipality in France.

Com-mu′ni-cant [L. *commūnis*, common], one who partakes of the Lord's Supper.

Com-mu′ni-cate, make known, impart.

Com-mu′ni-ca′tion, that which is imparted.

Com-mu′ni-ca-tive, ready to impart.

Com-mu′nion, intercourse, the Lord's Supper.

Com′mu-nism, the theory or condition of holding wealth in common.

Com-mu′ni-ty [L. *commūnis*, common], common possession, a society, whole people (with *the*).

Com-mute′ [L. *cum*, with, *mutāre*, to change], exchange, put something less in place of something greater.

Com-pact′ [L. *com* (*cum*), together, *pangēre* (p.p. *pactus*), to fasten], close.

Com′pact [L. *com-*, together, *pacisci* (p.p. *pactus*), to make a bargain], agreement.

Com-pan′ion, one who is in company with another.

Com′pa-ny (*com=cum*) [O.F. *compaignie*; L. *con-*, together, *pānis*, bread], society, people associating for trade, etc., subdivision of a regiment, crew.

Com-par′a-tive, estimated by comparison.

Com-pare′ [L. *comparāre*, to adjust, *cum*, with, *par*, equal], examine things so as to decide their comparative value, liken.

Com-par′i-son, act of comparing.

Com-part′ment [L. *con-*, together, *partīre*, to share, to part], division of a closed space.

Com′pass (*o=u*) [L. *cum*, with, *passus*, a pace, a track], extent, bounds, magnetised needle balanced so as to show north, south, etc.; (pl.) an instrument for drawing circles; surround, go about.

Com-pas′sion [L. *cum*, with, and *passio*, suffering], sorrowing with another, pity.

Com-pat′i-ble [L. *cum*, with, *pati*, to endure], capable of existing in harmony, consistent.

Com-pa′tri-ot [L. *cum*, with, *patriōta*, patriot], one of the same country.

Com-peer′ [L. *con-*, together, *par*, equal], an equal, companion.

Com-pel′ [L. *con-*, together, *pellere* (p.p. *pulsus*), to drive], to force. [hensive.

Com-pen′di-ous [see **Compendium**], compre-

Com-pen′di-um [L. *con-*, together, *pendere*, to weigh], condensed summary.

Com′pen-sate [L. *con-* (*cum*), together, *pensāre* (p.p. *pensatus*), to weigh], make up for, reward.

Com-pen-sa′tion, reward, amends.

Com-pete′ [L. *con-*, together, *petere*, to seek], strive for the same thing or reward as another.

Com′pe-ten-cy, fitness, sufficiency.

Com′pe-tent [F. *compétent*, orig. pr.p. of *competer*, to be sufficient for], fit.

Com-pe-ti′tion, trying to gain what another is trying to gain at the same time.

Com-pet′i-tor, one who competes.

Com-pi-la′tion, act of compiling, work compiled.

Com-pile′ [L. *compīlāre*, to plunder, *cum*, with, *pīlāre*, to rob], compose a book by taking material from other books.

Com-pla′cence, Com-pla′cen-cy (*a=ai*) [L. *cum*, with, *plăcere* (pr.p. *placens*), to please], calm contentment.

Com-plain′ [L. *cum*, with, *plangere*, to bewail], express pain, blame, etc.

Com-plain′ant, one who makes complaint.

Com-plaint′, expression of grief, fault-finding, illness. [please.

Com-plai′sant [see **Complacence**], desirous to

Com′ple-ment [L. *con-*, together, *plēre*, to fill], what fills up or completes.

Com-ple-ment′, fill up or complete.

Com-plete′ [L. *complētus*, *cum*, with, and *plēre*, to fill], finished, whole; make complete, finish.

Com-ple′tion, act of completing.

Com′plex [L. *con-*, together, *plectere* (p.p. *plexus*), to plait], of many parts, intricate.

Com-plex′ion [see **Complex**], aspect, colour of the skin, especially of the face.

Com-plex′i-ty, state of being complex.

Com-pli′ance, a yielding, consent.

Com′pli-cate [L. *con-*, together, *plicāre* (p.p. *plicātus*), to fold], mix up, entangle.

Com′pli-ment [doublet of **Complement**], expression of admiration or civility.

Com-pli-ment′, pay a compliment.

Com′pline [M.E. *cumplie*: O.F. *conplie*; L. *complēta* (*hora*); see **Complete**], in R.C. Church the last service of the day.

Com-ply′ [It. *complire*; L. *complēre*, to fill up], yield to.

Com-po′nent [L. con-, together, pŏnere (pr.p. ponens, -entis), to put], helping to form, composing ; one of the composing parts.

Com-port′ [L.con-, together, portāre, to carry], accord (with), conduct (oneself).

Com-pose′ (s=z) [L. con-, together, and F. poser, to put], form by uniting, write books or music, to calm, set up printer's types.

Com-po′ser, author (esp. of music).

Com′pos-ite [L. con-, together, pŏnere (p.p. positus), to put], made up of distinct parts.

Com-po-si′tion [see Compound³], act of composing, thing composed, agreement whereby payment of part of debt is taken for whole.

Com-pos′i-tor [see Compound³], one who sets types.

Com′post [see Compound³], mixture, especially for fertilizing land.

Com-po′sure (s=zh) [see Compose], calmness.

Com′pound¹ (adj.), composed of parts ; that which is formed by union or mixture.

Com′pound² [perh. Malay, kampong], in India the enclosure containing a house, outbuildings, etc.

Com-pound′³ [L. com=cum), together, pŏnere (p.p. positus), to put], form by combining, come to terms.

Com-pre-hend′ [L. con-, together, prehendere (p.p. prehensus), to seize], understand, include. **Com-pre-hen′sion**, understanding.

Com-press′ [L. con-, together, pressāre, frequent. of premere, to press], press together, condense. **Com-pres′sion**.

Com-prise′ (s=z) [F. compris, p.p. of comprendre, to comprehend ; see Comprehend], include.

Com′pro-mise (s=z) [F. compromis, orig. p.p. of compromettre ; L. con-, together, and promittere, to promise], settlement of a dispute by each side yielding something ; yield on each side.

Com-pul′sion [see Compel], force.

Com-pul′so-ry, compelling, obligatory.

Com-punc′tion [L. cum, with, pungere (p.p. punctus), to prick], a pricking of conscience, slight remorse. **Compunc′tious.**

Com-pu-ta′tion, calculation.

Com-pute′ [L. con-, together, putāre (p.p. putātus), to reckon], calculate.

Com′rade (com=cum) [Sp. camarada ; Sp. camara, L. camera, a chamber], companion, mate.   [peruse.

Con [O.E. cunnan, to know], to study,

Con-cat-e-na′tion [L. con-, together, catēna, a chain], chain.   [hollow.

Con′cave [L. con-, with, căvus, hollow],

Con-ceal′ [L. con-, intensive, cēlāre, to hide], hide.   [place.

Con-ceal′ment, act of concealing, a hiding

Con-cede′ [L. con-, together, cēdere (sup. cessum), to yield], yield, grant.

Con-ceit′ [see Conceive], quaint fancy, vanity.

Con-ceive′ [O.F. conceveir ; L. con-, together, capere, to take], form in the mind, think.

Con′cen-trate [L. con-, together, centrum, a centre], bring towards the same centre, fix (the attention).

Con-cen′tric [L. con-, together, and Centre], having the same centre.

Con-cep′tion [see Conceive], idea, notion.

Con-cern′ [L. con-, with, cernere, to sift, to decree], relate to ; affair, care.

Con-cert′ [It. poss. fr. L. con-, together, certare, to struggle], plan together.

Con′cert, musical entertainment, agreement.

Con-cer′to [It.], musical composition for solo instrument with orchestral accompaniment.

Con-cer-ti′na (i=ee), musical instrument.

Con-ces′sion [see Concede], yielding, thing yielded.   [shell.

Conch (ch=k) [Gk. cogchē, a shell], large sea-

Con-cil′i-ate [L. conciliāre (p.p. conciliātus), to conciliate ; concilium, a council], win over, make friendly. **Concilia′tion.**

Con-cil′i-a-to-ry, tending to conciliate.

Con-cise′ [L. concisus (p.p. of concīdere), to cut up], saying much in few words.

Con′clave [L. con-, together, clāvis, a key], assembly of cardinals to choose a pope, secret meeting.

Con-clude′ [L. con-, together, claudere (p.p. clausus), to shut], end, infer.

Con-clu′sion (si=zh), end, inference.

Con-clu′sive (s=z), bringing to a conclusion.

Con-coct′ [L. con-, together, coquere (p.p. coctus), to cook], prepare from raw materials, as food ; plan.

Con-com′i-tant [L. con-, together ; comitāri (pr.p. comitans, -antis), to accompany], accompanying.

Con′cord [L. con-, together, cor (cord-is), the heart], agreement.

Con-cord′ance, agreement, index of the chief words of a book, esp. the Bible.

Con-cor′dat [L. concorditas ; see Concord], agreement, esp. between the pope and a government.

Con′course [L. con-, together, currere (sup. cursum), to run], a running together, assembly.

Con′crete [L. con-, together, crescere (p.p. crētus), to grow], existing in material form ; mixture of lime, sand, and water with broken stones, etc.

Con-cre′tion, union of particles in a mass.

Con-cur′ [L. con-, together, currere, to run], unite, agree.

Con-cur′rence [see Concur], agreement.

Con-cus′sion [L. concutere (p.p. concussus), to shake together], shock due to collision.

Con-demn [L. con-, intensive, and damnāre, to condemn], pronounce judgment against.

Con-dem-na′tion, state of being condemned, blame, sentence.

Con-dense′ [L. con-, together, densus, thick], make or become more close.

Con-de-scend′ [L. con-, with, dēscendere, to descend ; see Descend], stoop, make a show of stooping to inferiors.

Con-de-scen′sion, act of condescending.

Con-dign' (*dign=dine*) [L. *con-* (intensive), and *dignus*, worthy], deserved, adequate.

Con'di-ment [L. *condīre*, to pickle], seasoning.

Con-di'tion [L. *con-*, together, *dicere* (p.p. *dictus*), to say], state, term of a contract, etc.

Con-dole' [L. *con-*, with, *dolēre*, to grieve], grieve in sympathy.

Con-do'lence, sympathy in sorrow.

Con-done' [L. *con-* (intensive), *dōnāre*, to give], pardon, pass over.

Con'dor [Sp. *condor*; Peruv. *cuntur*], South American vulture.

Con-duce' [L. *con-*, together, *ducere* (p.p. *ductus*) to lead], tend to.

Con-du'cive, tending, contributive.

Con'duct [see **Conduce**], behaviour, guidance.

Con-duct', to lead.

Con-duct'or, leader, thing or material that transmits heat or electricity.

Con'duit (*duit=dit*) [F. *conduit*; see **Conduce**], pipe or channel to convey water.

Cone [Gk. *cōnos*, a cone], solid having a circular base and tapering to a point.

Con-fab'u-late [L. *con-*, together, *fābula*, a tale], talk together.

Con-fec'tion [L. *con-*, together, *facere*, to put], sweetmeat.

Con-fed'er-a-cy [see **Confederate**], league, conspiracy.

Con-fed'er-ate [L. *con-*, together, *fœdus* (*fœder-is*), a treaty], leagued together; member of a league; join in a league.

Con-fed-er-a'tion, league of states.

Con-fer' [L. *con-*, together, *ferre*, to bring], bestow, consult together.

Con'fer-ence, a meeting for discussion.

Con-fess' [L. *confitēri* (p.p. *confessus*); *con-* (intensive), and *fatēri*, to acknowledge], own, make confession.

Con-fes'sion, acknowledgment of sins, declaration of belief.

Con-fes'sion-al, recess where a priest hears confession.   [friend.

Con-fi-dant', fem. **Con-fi-dante'**, confidential

Con-fide' [L. *con-* (intensive), *fīdere*, to trust], trust (in), trust (to).

Con'fi-dence, firm trust, private matters imparted.

Con'fi-dent, assured, sure, trustful.

Con-fi-den'tial (*ti=sh*), treated with trust.

Con-fig-u-ra'tion [L. *con-* (intensive), *figūrāre* (p.p. *figūrātus*), to fashion], form.

Con-fine' [L. *con-*, with, *finis*, a boundary], limit, shut up.

Con'fine (usually pl.), limit, border.

Con-fine'ment, restraint within bounds.

Con-firm' [L. *con-* (intensive), *firmāre* (p.p. *firmātus*), to strengthen, *firmus*, strong], make sure.

Con-fir-ma'tion, proof, rite administered in certain churches.

Con'fis-cate [L. *con-*, together, *fiscus*, a purse], seize property as forfeited.

Con-fla-gra'tion [L. *con-*, together, *flāgrāre*, to burn], general burning.

Con'flict, struggle.

Con-flict' [L. *con-*, together, *flīgere* (p.p. *flictus*), to strike], struggle, be contradictory.

Con'flu-ence, Con'flux [L. *con-*, together, *fluere* (p.p. *fluxus*), to flow], flowing together.

Con-form' [L. *con-*, together, *formāre* (p.p. *formātus*), to form], make like, be in agreement.

Con-form'a-ble, corresponding in form, etc.

Con-for-ma'tion, shape.

Con-for'mi-ty, resemblance, compliance.

Con-found' [L. *con-*, together, *fundere* (p.p. *fūsus*), to pour], confuse, dismay.

Con'frère [L. *con-*, together, F. *frère*, brother], an associate.

Con-front' (*ont=unt*) [L. *con-*, together, *frons* (*front-is*), the face], stand or bring face to face.

Con-fuse' [*s=z*] [see **Confound**], mix so as to cause disorder.

Con-fu'sion, disorder, shame.

Con-fute' [L. *con-*, together, *fūtāre*, probably from same root as *fundere*, to pour], disprove completely.   **Confuta'tion**.

Con-geal' [L. *con-*, together, *gelāre*, to freeze; *gelu*, frost], freeze, solidify by cooling, etc.

Con-ge'ner or **Con'ge-ner** [L. *con-*, together, *genus* (*gener-is*), kind], person or animal of the same kind.

Con-ge'ni-al [L. *con-*, together, and **Genial**], partaking of the same nature, suited.

Con-gen'ital [L. *con-*, with, *genitus*, born], belonging to from birth.   [sea-eel.

Con'ger (*g* hard) [L. *conger*; Gk. *goggros*],

Con-ge'ri-es [L. *con-*, together, *gerere*, to carry], heap.

Con-ges'tion [L. *con-*, together, *gerere* (p.p. *gestus*), to carry], over-crowding, over-fulness of blood-vessels.

Con-glom'er-ate [L. *con-*, together, *glomus* (*glomer-is*), a ball], gathered into a mass; gravel bound together by a cement; gather into a ball or mass. **Conglomera'tion**.

Con-grat'u-late [L. *con-* (intensive), *grātulāri*, to wish joy; *grātus*, pleasing] express joyful sympathy.   **Congratula'tion**.

Con'gre-gate [L. *con-*, together, *grex* (*greg-is*), a flock], come together.   [worship.

Con-gre-ga'tion, assembly, especially for

Con-gre-ga'tion-al-ist, one who holds that each congregation is a separate church.

Con'gress [L. *congredī* (p.p. *congressus*), to meet together; *con-*, together, *gradī*, to walk], assembly to consider special affairs, legislature of the U.S.A.   **Congres'sional**.

Con'gru-ous [L. *congruus*; *con-*, together, *gruere*, to suit], fitting, conformable.

Con'ic, Con'ic-al [Gk. *cōnicos*; *cōnos*, a cone], of or pertaining to a cone.

Co-nif'er-ous [**Cone**, and L. *ferre*, to bear], bearing cones.

Con-jec'ture [L. *con-*, together, *jacere* (p.p. *jactus*), to throw], to guess; a guess.

Con-join' [L. *con-*, together, *jungere*, to join], join together.

Con-joint', united, held in common.

Con'ju-gal [L. *con-*, together, *jugum*, a yoke], belonging to marriage.

Con'ju-gate [L. *con-*, together, *jugum*, a yoke], give the inflections, or parts, of a verb. **Conjuga'tion.**

Con-junc'tion [see Conjoin], joining together, joining word.

Con-junc'ture, combination of events, crisis.

Con-jure' [L. *con-*, together, *jurāre*, to swear], call upon solemnly.

Con'jure (*o=ŭ*), use a conjurer's tricks.

Con'jur-er, -or, one who practises sleight of hand.

Con-nect' [L. *con-*, together, *nectere* (p.p. *nexus*), to bind], to join.

Con-nex'ion, Con-nec'tion, act of connecting, the state of being connected.

Con'ning-tower [see Con and Tower], pilot-house of a war-ship.

Con-ni'vance, intentional oversight of an act or fault.

Con-nive' [L. *connivēre*, to overlook; *con-*, together, *nictāre*, to wink], wink at.

Con-nois-seur' [F. fr. L. *cognoscere*, to become acquainted with], critical judge.

Con'note [L. *con-*, together, *notāre*, to mark], to denote, designate, imply, include. **Connota'tion.**

Con-nu'bi-al [L. *con-*, with, *nūbere*, to marry], of or relating to marriage.

Con'quer [O.F *conquerre*; L. *conquīrere* (p.p. *conquīsītus*), to seek after, conquer; *con-*, with, *quærere*, to seek], overcome.

Con'quest, act of overcoming by force, that which is conquered.

Con-san-guin'i-ty [L. *con-*, together, *sanguis* (*sanguin-is*), blood], blood relationship. **Consanguin'eous.**

Con'science (*sci=sh*) [L. *con-*, with, *scīre* (pr.p. *sciens, -entis*), to know], faculty which judges self.

Con-sci-en'tious, governed by conscience.

Con'scious [L. *conscius*; *con-*, with, *scīre*, to know], aware, sensible, felt.

Con-scrip'tion [L. *con-*, together, *scrībere* (p.p. *scriptus*), to write], compulsory enrolment for military or naval service. **Con'script.**

Con'se-crate [L. *con-*, with, *sacer*, holy], set apart as sacred.

Con-sec'u-tive [L. *con-*, with, *sequī* (p.p. *secūtus*), to follow], in regular succession.

Con-sen'sus [see Consent], general agreement.

Con-sent' [L. *con-*, with, *sentīre* (p.p. *sensus*), to feel], agreement; express willingness.

Con'se-quence [L. *con-*, with, *sequī* (pr.p. *sequens, -entis*), to follow], result, importance. **Con'sequent.**

Con-se-quen'tial (*ti=sh*), self-important.

Con-ser-va'tion, a keeping entire.

Con-ser'va-tive, one who wishes to keep customs, etc., as they are; slow to change.

Con-ser'va-to-ry, plant-house.

Con-serve' [L. *con-*, together, *servāre* (p.p. *servātus*), to keep], keep from harm; preserved fruit.

Con-sid'er [L. *con-*, together, *sīdus* (*sīder-is*), a star], give thought to.

Con-sid'er-a-ble, noteworthy, large.

Con-sid'er-ate, thoughtful.

Con-sid-er-a'tion, careful thought, importance, a reward.

Con-sign' (*sign=sine*) [L. *con-*, together, *signare*, to sign], deliver, intrust.

Con-sign'ment, act of consigning, thing consigned.

Con-sist' [L. *con-*, together, *sistere*, to stop], be made up (of).

Con-sist'ence, Con-sist'en-cy, degree of firmness, harmony of conduct.

Con-sist'ent (see Consist), uniform, not contradictory.

Con-sis'to-ry [see Consist], church court.

Con-so-la'tion, comfort in trouble.

Con-sol'a-to-ry, of a consoling nature.

Con-sole' [L. *con-*, with, *sōlāri*, to comfort], to comfort in trouble. **Consol'able.**

Con'sole [F., etym. dub.], a bracket in architecture, frame containing manuals and stops of an organ.

Con-sol'i-date [L. *con-*, together, *solidāre*, to make solid, *solidus*, solid], make firm.

Con'sols [abbrev. for Consolidated Annuities], Government securities of Great Britain, consolidated into a single stock in 1751.

Con'so-nant [L. *con-*, together, *sonāre*, to sound], letter of alphabet which can only be sounded when combined with a vowel sound, agreeing.

Con'son-ance, Con'son-an-cy, agreement, harmony, unison.

Con'sort [L. *consors* (*consort-is*), a sharer, *con-*, with, *sors* (*sort-is*), lot], husband or wife; one of two ships.

Con-sort', join in company with.

Con-spic'u-ous [L. *con-* (intensive) and *spicere*, to see], easy to be seen.

Con-spir'a-cy, a plot.

Con-spire' [L. *con-*, together, *spirāre*, to breathe], plot together.

Con'stable [O.F. *conestable*; L.L. *comes stabuli*, count of the stable], officer of the peace.

Con-stab'u-la-ry, body of constables.

Con'stan-cy, fixedness, steadiness.

Con'stant [L. *con-*, together, *stāre* (pr.p. *stans, stantis*), to stand], unchanging.

Con-stel-la'tion [L. *con-*, together, *stella*, a star], group of stars.

Con-ster-na'tion [L. *con-*, together, *sternere*, to strew], dismay.

Con-sti-pa'tion [L. *con-*, together, *stipāre*, to pack], irregular and insufficient action of the bowels. **Con'stipated.**

Con-stit'u-en-cy, body of voters.

Con-stit'u-ent, something which helps to make up a whole, one of those who elect a representative; making up a whole.

Con'stit-ute [L. *con-*, together, *statuere*, to set up], make up.

Con-stit-u'tion, state of being, the frame of government.

Con-strain' [L. *con-*, together, *stringere* (p.p. *strictus*), to draw tight], to force, hold tightly.

Con-straint', force that cannot be resisted.

Con-stric'tion [see Constrain], compressing or drawing together, a tightening or limiting.

Con-struct' [L. con-, together, struere (p.p. structus), to pile], build, to draw or form geometrically.

Con-struc'tion, building, meaning.

Con-struct'or, one who constructs.

Con-strue, Con-strue' [see Construct], show the arrangement in another language, explain, translate.

Con-sue-tu'-din-ar-y (sue=swe) [L. consuetūdo, custom], customary.

Con'sul [L. consul. Etym. doubtful], one of the two chief magistrates of the Roman republic; one who lives in a foreign land to look after the interests (especially commercial) of his own country.

Con-sult' [L. consultāre (p.p. consultātus), to consult. Etym. doubtful], ask advice.

Con-sul-ta tion, act of consulting, a meeting to consider something.

Con-sume [L. con-, together, sūmere (p.p. sumptus), to take up], to waste, eat up.

Con-sum mate [L. con-, together, summāre (p.p summātus), to sum], perfect. Con-summa'tion.

Con'sum-mate, to perfect, complete.

Con-sump'tion [see Consume], wasting illness, a using up.

Con'tact [L. con-, together, tangere (p.p. tactus), to touch], touch.

Con-ta'gion [L. con-, together, tangere, to touch], communication of disease by contact, infection. Conta'gious.

Con-tain' [L. con-, together, tenēre, to hold], hold within limits.

Con-tam'in-ate [L. contamen, contagion, con-, together, tangere, to touch], defile.

Con-temn' [L. con- (intensive), temnere (p.p. temptus), to despise], scorn.

Con'tem-plate [L. con-, together, templum, a temple, an open place for observation], to view, to purpose. Contem'plative.

Con-tem-pla'tion, deep thought, design.

Con-tem-po-ra'ne-ous [L. con-, with, tempus (tempor-is), time], at the same time.

Con-tem'po-ra-ry, living or happening at the same time.

Con-tempt' [see Contemn], scorn.

Con-tempt'i-ble, worthy of scorn.

Con-temp'tu-ous, scornful.

Con-tend' [L. con- (intensive), tendere (p.p. tentus), to strive], strive in opposition.

Con-tent' [see Contain], satisfied, satisfy.

Con-ten'tion [see Contend], strife.

Con-ten'tious, fond of strife.

Con-tent'ment [see Content], satisfaction.

Con-test [see Contest (vb.)], dispute, strife.

Con-test' [L. con-, together, testis, a witness], dispute, contend for. Con-test'ant.

Con'text [L. con-, together, texere (p.p. textus), to weave], parts which go before or come after a passage in a book, etc.

Con-ti-gu'i-ty, nearness.

Con-tig'u-ous [L. con-, together, tangere (p.p. tactus), to touch], touching, adjoining.

Con'tin-ence [see Contain], self-restraint, moderation, purity.

Con'ti-nent [see Contain], one of the large divisions of the earth, mainland of Europe.

Con-tin'gen-cy, event which may occur.

Con-tin'gent [L. contingens (-entis), con-, together, tangere, to touch], dependent on something, future; chance, proportion of troops for a joint expedition.

Con-tin'u-al, without stop.

Con-tin'u-ance, going on.

Con-tin-u-a'tion, carrying on, that which carries on.

Con-tin'ue [L. con-, together, tenēre, to hold], prolong, to last.

Con-tin'u-ous, without break.

Con-tort' [L. con-, together, torquēre (p.p. tortus), to twist], twist out of shape.

Con-tor'tion, a twisting out of shape.

Con'tour (ou=oo) [L. con-, together, and tornāre, to turn in a lathe], outline.

Con'tra-band [Sp. contrabanda; It. contrabando; L. contra, against; Late L. bandum, a ban], prohibited goods.

Con-tract' [L. con-, together, trahere (p.p. tractus), to draw], draw together.

Con'tract, agreement.

Con-tract'or, undertaker of a contract.

Con-tra-dict' [L. contra, against, dicere (p.p. dictus), to say], oppose in words.

Con-tra-dic'to-ry, saying the contrary.

Con-tra-dis-tinc'tion [L. contra, against, and Distinction], distinction by contrast.

Con-tral'to [It. contra, opposite to, alto, high], deepest voice in boys and in women.

Con-tra-ri'e-ty, opposition.

Con'tra-ry [L. contra, against], opposite, opposed.   [parison.

Con'trast, something very different; com-

Con-trast' [L. contra, against, stāre, to stand], compare by showing difference.

Con-tra-vene' [L. contra, against, venīre, to come], set aside, thwart. Contraven'tion.

Con-trib'ute [L. con-, together, tribuere, to bestow], give in common with others, help to bring about.

Con-tri-bu'tion, that which is contributed.

Con'trite [L. con-, together, and terere (p.p. tritus), to rub], humbly penitent.

Con-tri'tion, sorrow for sin.

Con-tri'vance, plan, device.

Con-trive' [O.F. controver, to find out; L. con-, together, and O.F. trover, to find], invent, plan.

Con-trol' [short for contre-roll. O.F. contre-rolle, copy of a roll; L. contra, against, rotulus, a roll], check; to rule, keep in check.

Con'tro-ver-sy [L. contra, against, vertere (p.p. versus), to turn], dispute. Controver'sial.

Con-tu-ma'cious [L. contumax (contumāc-is), perh. from con-, and tumēre, to swell], stubborn, obstinately rebellious.

Con'tu-ma-cy, obstinate disobedience.

Con-tu-me'li-ous, insolent.

Con'tume-ly [L. contumēlia, perh. allied to Contumacy], scornful insolence.

Con-tu'sion [L. con-, with, tundere (p.p. tusus), to strike], bruise.

Co-nun'drum [?], kind of riddle.

Con-va-les'cence [L. con-, together, valère, to be strong], recovery after illness. Convales'cent.

Con-vene' [L. con-, together, venire, to come], meet, call together.

Con-ve'nience, ease, suitable time.

Con-ve'nient [see Convene], fit, timely.

Con'vent [L. conventus, an assembly; conventus (orig. p.p. of convenire, to come together], monastery or nunnery.

Con-ven'ti-cle [L. conventiculum, dim. of conventus, an assembly], secret religious meeting.

Con-ven'tion [see Convent], assembly; recognised custom. [formal.

Con-ven'tion-al, depending on convention;

Con-verge' [L. con-, together, vergere, to bend], tend to one point.

Con'ver-sant [see Converse], familiar with.

Con-ver-sa'tion, sustained talk.

Con-verse' [L. con-, with, and versāri, to dwell], to talk together. [gether.

Con'verse (n.) [see Converse (vb.)], talk to-

Con'verse [L. con-, wholly, vertere (pp. versus), to turn], contrary. [etc.

Con-ver'sion [see Convert], change of views,

Con'vert, one who is converted.

Con-vert' [L. con-, together, vertere (p.p. versus), to turn], change or turn from one course or belief to another.

Con'vex [L. con-, together, vehere (p.p. vectus), to bring], rounded like the outside of a sphere.

Con-vey' [L. con-, with, via, a way], carry.

Con-vey'ance, carriage ; transfer of property.

Con-vey-an-cer, one who draws up deeds for transferring property. Convey'ancing.

Con-vict' [see Convince], pronounce guilty.

Con'vict, criminal who has been sentenced to penal servitude. Convic'tion.

Con-vince' [L. con-, wholly, vincere (p.p. victus), to conquer], overcome by argument, to satisfy by proof.

Con-viv'i-al [L. con-, together, and vivere, to live], relating to a feast, festive. Con-vivial'ity.

Con-vo-ca'tion, act of calling together, an assembly.

Con-voke' [L. con-, together, vocāre (p.p. vocātus), to call], call together.

Con-vo-lu'tion [L. con-, together, volvere (p.p. volūtus), to roll], twisted winding or coil.

Con-vol'vu-lus [L. convolvulus; see Convolution], climbing plant. [protection.

Con'voy [same as Convey], accompany for

Con'voy, an escort, ships escorted by others.

Con-vulse' [L. con-, with, vellere (p.p. vulsus), to pull], shake violently.

Con-vul'sion, violent twitching, disturbance.

Co'ny, Con'ey [?], a rabbit.

Cook [L. coquus, a cook, coquere, to cook], one who prepares food ; prepare, as food by boiling, etc. ; falsify (accounts).

Cook'er-y, ar of preparing food.

Cool [O.E. cól], somewhat cold ; make or become colder.

Coo'ly, Coo'lie [Hind. qulī, a labourer], Indian or Chinese hired labourer.

Coomb, Combe (koom), [O.E. cumb], small wooded valley.

Coop [L. cūpa, a tub], box with a grating for poultry : shut up in a small space. [etc.

Coo'per [see Coop], one who makes barrels.

Co-op'er-ate [L. co-, with, and operāri, to work], act together. Co-opera'tion.

Co-or'di-nate [L. co-, with, ordināre (p.p. ordinātus), to order], equal in rank or order. Co-ordina'tion.

Coot [M.E. cote, etym. dub.], wading bird.

Co'pal [Sp. copal ; Mex. copalli, incense], resin used in making varnish.

Cope [1] [M.L. cāpa, a cap], semicircular cloak worn by priests in processions, etc.

Cope [2] [O.F. coper, to strike ; Late L. colpus ; L. colaphos, a blow], contend with, face difficulties.

Cope'stone [Cope [1] and Stone], top stone.

Co'pi-ous [L. cōpia, plenty], plentiful.

Cop'per [L. cuprum (for Cuprium æs, Cyprian brass) reddish-brown metal.

Cop'per-as [M.L. cuprōsa, adj. from cuprum, copper], sulphate of iron.

Cop'pice (ice=iss), Copse [O.F. copeiz, cop-pice ; L. colpāre, to cut with a blow], wood of low growth.

Cop'ra (prob. Malayalam, koppara, coco-nut), dried kernel of coco-nut. [join.

Cop'u-la-tive [L. cōpula, a band], serving to

Cop'y [L. copia, plenty], imitation ; single book, MS. to be set up in type ; imitate.

Cop'y-right, the sole right to publish.

Co-quette' (-ket) [F. coquette, fem. of coquet, a little cock], flirt. Jo'quetry.

Cor'al [Gk. corallion], hard substance built up in the sea by small animals.

Cord [L. chorda, cord ; Gk. chordē, the string of a musical instrument], thick string.

Cord'age, ropes used in the rigging of a ship.

Cor'di-al [L. cor (cord-is), the heart], hearty; strengthening beverage.

Cor-di-al'i-ty, heartiness.

Cor'don [see Cord], ribbon worn as a badge of honour, line of sentries.

Cor-du-roy' [F. corde du roi, king's cord], ribbed cotton, or any thick-ribbed stuff.

Cord'wain-er [O.F. cordoan, Cordovan leather], shoemaker (now only as one of a guild).

Core [?], heart of a thing.

Co-ri-an'der [Gk. coriannon], plant, also its aromatic seed.

Cork [Span. corche, cork ; L. cortex (cortic-is), bark], bark of a kind of oak; stopper made of cork ; stop with a cork.

Cor'mo-rant [F. cormoran, from L. corvus marinus, a marine crow], dark kind of sea-bird.

Corn [1] [E.], grain used for food ; preserve with salt.

Corn [2] [L. cornu, a horn], horny growth on the foot.

Corn′crake [Corn [1] and **Crake** (imit.)], bird (the Landrail).

Cor′ne-a [L. *cornea*, fem. of *corneus*, horny; *cornu*, a horn], transparent cover of the eyeball.

Cor′ner [L. *cornu*, a horn], point where two streets, walls, etc., meet.

Cor′ner-stone, stone at corner of two walls, uniting them; principal stone.

Cor′net [F. *cornet*, *cornette*, dim. of *corne*, a horn], kind of trumpet.

Cor′nice (*ce*=*ss*) [F. *cornice*, *corniche*; It. *cornice*; etym. dub.], top moulding of a room, etc.

Cor-nu-co′pi-a [L. *cornu*, a horn, *copia*, plenty], horn of plenty.

Cor-ol′la [L. *corolla*, dim. of *corōna*, a crown], inner whorl of leaves forming the envelope of a flower.

Cor′ol-la-ry, Cor-ol′la-ry [see **Corolla**], inference from something stated.

Cor′o-nach [Gael. *corronach*], dirge.

Cor-o-na′tion [L. *corōna*, a crown], the act of crowning.

Cor′o-ner (also obs. *Crowner*) [L. *corōna*, a crown], officer who enquires into the causes of sudden or violent death.

Cor′o-net [dim. of O.F. *corone*, a crown], crown worn by noblemen.   [bodily.

Cor′po-ral [1] [L. *corpus* (*corpor-is*), the body],

Cor′po-ral [2] [see **Corporal** [1]], non-commissioned officer.

Cor-po-ra′tion [L. *corpus* (*corpor-is*), the body], society acting as one person.

Cor-po′re-al [L. *corpus*, the body], having a body.

Corps (*core*) [F. *corps*; L. *corpus*, the body], body of soldiers.

Corpse [O.F. *cors*; L. *corpus*, the body], dead body.

Cor′pu-lent [L. *corpus*, the body], very stout. **Cor′pulence**.

Cor′pus-cle, Cor-pus′cule [L. *corpusculum*, dim. of *corpus*], minute particle; animal cell. **Corpus′cular**.

Cor-ral′ [Sp. *corro*, a circle, *correr toros*, hold a bull-fight; L. *currere*, to run], pen for horses, etc.

Cor-rect′ [L. *corrigere* (p.p. *correctus*), to correct, *con-*, together, *regere*, to rule], right; make right; punish. **Correc′tion**.

Cor-re-la′tion [fr. L. *con-*, together, and **Relate**], mutual relation.

Cor-re-spond′ [fr. L. *con-*, together, and **Respond**], answer one to another, hold intercourse by letter.   [letter.

Cor-re-spond′ent, one who communicates by

Cor′ri-dor [It. *corridore*, corridor, *correre* (L. *currere*), to run], passage-way from room to room.

Cor-rob′o-rate [L. *con-*, wholly, *rōbur* (*rōbor-is*), strength], confirm.

Cor-rode′ [L. *con-*, wholly, *rōdere* (p.p. *rōsus*), to gnaw], eat or wear away.

Cor-ro′sion (*si*=*zh*), eating away as by rust.

Cor′ru-gate [L. *con-*, wholly, *rugāre* (p.p. *rugātus*), to wrinkle], to wrinkle, furrow.

Cor-rupt′ [L. *con-*, wholly, *rumpere* (p.p. *ruptus*), to break], unsound; make putrid, infect with badness, bribe.

Cor-rupt′i-ble, that can decay, capable of being bribed. **Corruptibil′ity**.

Cor′sair [M.L. *cursārius*, a pirate; L. *cursus*, a course], pirate.

Corse. See **Corpse**.

Corse′let, Cors′let [double dim. of O.F. *cors*, the body], armour for the body.

Cor′set [dim. of O.F. *cors*, the body], stays.

Cor′tex [L. *cortex* (*corticis*)], bark, outer covering.

Cor-us-ca′tion [L. *coruscāre* (pp. *coruscātus*), to glitter], a flashing.

Cos-met′ic (*s*=*z*) [Gk. *cosmein*, to adorn, *cosmos*, order], preparation for the skin.

Cos-mog′o-ny (*s*=*z*) [Gk. *cosmos*, the world, *gon*, root of *gignesthai*, to be born], theory of the origin of the world.

Cos-mo-pol′i-tan [Gk. *cosmos*, the world; *politēs*, a citizen], free from local prejudice; citizen of the world.

Cost [L. *con-*, together, *stare*, to stand], amount paid or charged; be bought for, or necessitate spending of.

Cos′tard [?], large apple.

Cos′ter-mon′ger, Costard and **Monger**. **Monger** [fr. O.E. *mangere*, a dealer], hawker of fruit, etc.

Cos′tive (O.F. *costivé*; L. *constipāre*, *con-*, together, *stipāre*, to press], constipated.

Cost′ly, dear, expensive.

Cos′tume (doublet of **Custom**], mode of dress, set of outer garments.

Co′sy, Co′zy [?], snug; wadded cover for a teapot.

Cot [1] [Θ.E. *cot*], a small house.

Cot [2] [Hind. *khat*, a bedstead], swinging bed, small bed.

Cote [see **Cot** [1]], sheepfold.

Co′te-rie [O.F. *coterie*, an association of cottars; *cotier*, a cottar], exclusive set of persons.

Cot′tage [Cot [1] and F. suffix -*age*], small house.

Cot′ta-ger, one who lives in a cottage.

Cot′tar, Cot′ter, Cot′ti-er [see **Cot** [1]], cottager.

Cot′ton [F. and O.Sp. *coton*; Arab. *qutun*], down which grows on the seeds of a plant, cloth made from it.

Cot-y-le′-don [Gk. *cotylē*, a cup], seed-leaf.

Couch [F. *coucher*, to place; L. *collocāre*, to place], place for rest or sleep; lie down, to fix (a spear) in rest.

Couch′ant [pr.p. of F. *coucher*, to lie down], lying down.

Cou′gar (*ou*=*oo*) [F. *couguar*, from native name], large American puma.

Cough (*ough*=*off*) [O.E. *cohhetan*, to make a noise. Imit.], convulsive expulsion of air from the lungs, sound of this; expel air from the lungs noisily.

Coul′ter [L. *culter*, a knife], iron blade in front of a ploughshare.

Coun′cil [L. *con-*, together, *calāre*, to summon], assembly to consult or administer.

Coun′cil-lor, member of a council.

Coun'sel [L. *consilium*, deliberation; *con-sulere*, to consult], advice; barrister; advise.

Coun'sel-lor, one who advises.

Count [O.F. *conte*, also *comte*; L. *comes* (*comit-is*), a companion], continental title equal to earl.

Count [O.F. *cunter*, *conter*; L. *computāre*, to compute], to number, rely upon.

Coun'te-nance [L. *continēre*, to contain], face; approve openly.

Count'er, one who counts; piece of ivory, etc., used in games; narrow shop-table.

Count'er [F. *contre*; L. *contra*, against], opposite; act contrary to.

Coun-ter-act', act in opposition to.

Coun-ter-bal'ance, oppose with equal weight.

Coun'ter-feit [O.F. *contrefait*, p.p. of *contrefaire*, to imitate; L. *contra*, against; *facere*, to make], imitate, forge; made in imitation; copy made to deceive.

Coun'ter-foil [Counter and L. *folium*, a leaf], part of a document which is kept as a check.

Coun-ter-mand' [L. *contra*, against, and *mandāre*, to command], recall an order.

Coun'ter-pane [M.F. *contrepointer*, to quilt], bedcover.

Coun'ter-part [Counter and L. *pars* (*part-is*), a part], corresponding part, duplicate.

Coun'ter-point [O.F. *contrepoint*; M.L. *contropunctum*; L. *contra*, against, *pungere* (pp. *punctus*), to prick], art of combining melodies.

Coun'ter-sign (*sign=sine*) [F. *contre*, over against, *signer*, to sign], second signature to a document, watchword; sign a document already signed.

Count'ess [O.F. *contesse*, Late L. *comitissa*. See Count], wife of an earl or a count.

Count'less, that cannot be numbered.

Coun'try [O.F. *cuntrée*, Late L. *contrāta*, land lying opposite; *contra*, against], large tract of land, kingdom or state; places away from town.

Coun'ty [L. *comitātus*, from *comes* (*comit-is*), a count], one of the sub-divisions of Great Britain and Ireland, or of one of the U.S.A.

Coup'le [L. *cōpula*, a link], pair; link together.

Coup'let [F. dim. of Couple], pair of consecutive lines of verse (esp. when rhyming).

Coup'ling, pairing; connecting parts in machinery, etc.

Cou'pon (*ou=oo*) [F. *coupon*, a coupon, a piece cut off; *couper*, to cut], detachable ticket.

Cour'age [L. *cor*, the heart], bravery.

Cou'ra-geous (*ou=oo*), brave.

Cou'ri-er (*ou=oo*) [L. *currere*, to run], express messenger; travelling attendant who makes arrangements.

Course (*ou=ō* usually) [L. *currere* (p.p. *cursus*), to run], way, passage, ground run over, succession, part of a meal, channel, ship's path, series of lectures, etc.

Cours'er, swift horse. [greyhounds.

Cours'ing, pursuit of running game with

Court [L. *cohors* (*cohort-is*), a court, also a cohort], space with buildings round it, residence or retinue of a sovereign, place where judges try cases; woo.

Cour'te-ous [O.F. *corteis*; see Court], of court-like manners, polite. [ness.

Cour'te-sy [O.F. *cortesie*; see Court], polite-

Court'ier, one who attends at court.

Court'ship, wooing.

Cous'in (*s=z*) [L. *con-*, together; *sobrīnus*, belonging to a sister], son or daughter of an uncle or aunt.

Cove [O.E. *cofa*], small inlet. [agreement.

Cov'e-nant (*o=ŭ*) [see Convene], mutual

Cov'er (*o=ŭ*) [O.F. *cuvrir*, to cover; L. *co-*, wholly, *operīre*, to shut], that which is laid or set over, that which conceals; lay or spread over; include, provide for.

Cov'er-let (*o=ŭ*) [perh. O.F. *covre-lit*, bedcover], bedspread.

Cov'ert (*o=ŭ*) [O.F. *cuvert*, p.p. of *cuvrir*, to cover], hidden; shelter; thicket.

Cov'et (*o=ŭ*) [O.F. *cuveitier*, to covet; L. *cupidus*, greedy], desire possession of.

Cov'et-ous (*o=ŭ*), very eager to obtain, especially money. **Cov'etousness.**

Cov'ey (*o=ŭ*) [O.F. *covée*, fr. *couver*, to hatch], flock of game birds.

Cow [O.E. *cú*], female of bovine animal.

Cow [perh. O.N *kúga*; cf. Dan. *kue*, to suppress], crush with fear.

Cow'ard [L. *cauda*, a tail, and *-ard*], faint-hearted, fearing person. **Cow'ardliness.**

Cow'ard-ice (*ice=iss*), want of courage.

Cow'er [etym. dub., cf. Icel. and Swed. *kúra*; Dan. *kure*, to sleep, to lie quiet], shrink down through fear.

Cowl [L. *cuculla*, a cowl], monk's hood; hood-like covering over a chimney.

Cow'rie, Cow'ry [Hind. *kaurī*], small shell.

Cow'slip [O.E. *cú-slyppe*, prob. *cú*, a cow, *slyppe*, slimy substance (i.e. dung)], spring flower.

Cox'comb [fr. cap worn by professional fools: see Cock and Comb], fop.

Cox'swain (also pron. *coksn*) [O.F. *coque*, kind of boat, and Swain], steersman of a boat and commander of its crew.

Coy [F. *coi*, quiet, still], shy.

Coy-ot'e (or *yōt*) [Mex. *coyotl*], prairie-wolf.

Coz'en (*o=ŭ*) [F. *cousiner*, to claim kinship with interested motives], cheat.

Crab [O.E. *crabba*, a crab], sea-animal with a strong claw.

Crab [?], small sour apple.

Crab'bed [see Crab], crossgrained, sour.

Crack [imit.], narrow break; short, sharp sound; break partially, snap; first-rate.

Crack'er, small firework; thin biscuit.

Crac'kle [dim. and freq. of Crack], make small cracking sounds.

Cra'dle [?], rocking bed for a baby.

Craft [O.E. *craeft*, strength], skill, cunning; a trade; vessel, vessels collectively. **Craft'i-ness.**

Crag [W. *craig*; Gael. and Ir. *creag*, a rock], ragged rock, point of rock.

Cram [O.E. *crammian*, fr. *crimman*, to insert], thrust in ; fill to overflowing.

Cramp [O.F. *crampe* ; fr. same root as Cram], sudden, painful drawing together of muscles ; keep from free action.

Cran'ber-ry [Low G. *krönbere*], sour red berry.

Crane [O.E. *cran*], wading bird ; machine for lifting weights ; stretch forward with head and neck. [brain-case.

Cra'ni-um [L. *cranium* ; Gk. *cranion*, a skull],

Crank [perh. fr. O.E. *crincan* (past, *cranc*), to sink in a heap], lever on a shaft which changes to-and-fro motion into circular motion, or vice versa, faddist. [opening.

Cran'ny [prob. F. *cran*, etym. dub.], narrow

Crape [F. *crêpe* ; L. *crispus*, curled], thin crimped stuff.

Crap'ul-ous, Crap'ul-ent [L. *crapula*, intoxication], sick through intemperance.

Crash [imit.], sound of things breaking ; break in pieces with a harsh noise.

Crash [?], coarse linen.

Crass [L. *crassus*, coarse], coarse, dense.

Crate [prob. L. *cratis*, a hurdle], large hamper of wickerwork.

Cra'ter [Gk. *cratēr*, a mixing bowl], mouth of a volcano.

Cra-vat' [F. *cravate*, fr. Ger. *Krabate*, Croatian], neckcloth.

Crave [O.E. *crafian*], ask eagerly.

Cra'ven [?], coward ; cowardly.

Craw'fish, Cray'fish [M.E. and O.F. *crevice*; O.H.G. *crebig*, a crab], fresh-water animal with a shell.

Crawl [prob. Norse; cf. Dan. *kravle*, to crawl], draw one's body along the ground, creep.

Cray'on [F. *crayonner*, to draw with crayons, *craie*, chalk], chalk drawing-pencil.

Craze [Swed. *krasa* ; Dan. *krase*, to crackle], strong fancy.

Cra'zy, disordered in mind, shaky.

Creak [prob. imit.], make a grating sound.

Cream [F. *crème* ; L. *chrisma*, consecrated oil], richer part of milk ; take cream off.

Crease (*se=ss*) [?], mark made by folding ; mark by folding or crushing.

Cre-ate' [L. *creāre* (p.p. *creātus*), to create], bring into being. Creat'ive. [created.

Cre-a'tion, act of creating ; that which is

Cre-a'tor, the one who creates ; God.

Crea'ture, anything created, a living being.

Cre'dence [L. *credere*, to believe], belief.

Cre-den'tial (*ti=sh*), that which gives a claim to credit.

Cred'i-ble, worthy of belief. Credibil'ity.

Cred'it [L. *credere* (p.p. *creditus*), to believe], belief ; trust given or received ; honour ; believe, attribute.

Cred'it-a-ble, deserving or bringing credit.

Cred'it-or, one to whom debt is due.

Cred'u-lous [L. *credulus*, credulous, *credere*, to believe],very ready to believe. Credul'ity.

Creed [L. *credo*, I believe (the first word in the old Latin Creed)], summary of beliefs.

Creek [etym. dub., M.E. *crike*], small bay.

Creel [etym. dub., Scot.], osier basket.

Creep [O.E. *créopan*], move slowly as a worm, or on hands and knees as a child.

Creep'er, plant that clings like ivy.

Crem-a'tion [L. *cremāre* (p.p. *cremātus*), to burn], burning of the dead. Cremator'ium.

Cren-a'ted [It. *crena*, a notch, etym. dub.], with toothed edge.

Cre'o-sote, Cre'a-sote [Gk. *creas*, flesh ; *sozein*, to preserve], wood-tar oil.

Crep-i-ta'tion [L. *crepitāre* (p.p. *crepitātus*), freq. of *crepāre*, to creak], crackling sound.

Cre'pon (or Cre-pon') [F.], stuff similar to crape, but finer.

Cres'cent [L. *cresco* (pr.p. *crescens*, *-entis*), to grow], new moon, anything in the shape of the new moon.

Cress [O.E. *cresse*], plant with edible leaves.

Crest [O.F. *creste* ; L. *crista*, a tuft], comb or tuft; heraldic figure originally on the top of a helmet.

Crest'fall-en, with hanging head, dispirited.

Cre-ta'ceous (*ce=sh*) [L. *crēta*, chalk], chalky.

Cre'tin-ism [F. *crétin*, deformed idiot, fr. L. *Christianus*, Christian in modern Rom. sense, "barely human "], diseased state, goitre, idiocy. Cre'tinous.

Cre-tonne' [F.], thick printed cotton cloth.

Cre-vasse' [see Crevice], fissure in a glacier.

Crev'ice (*ice=iss*) [O.F. *crevace*, a rift ; L. *crepāre*, to crack], small opening caused by a crack.

Crew (*ew=oo*) [O.F. *creue*, increase ; L. *crescere*, to grow], petty officers and seamen of a ship. [embroidery.

Crew'el (*ew=oo*) [?], twisted yarn used for

Crib [O.E. *crib*],rack or manger; stall for oxen; a child's bed ; to steal from an author.

Crib'bage [fr. same root as Crib], game of cards.

Crick [perh. allied to Crack], cramp of the neck or back.

Crick'et [O.F. *criquet*, connected with *criquer*, to creak], a chirping insect.

Crick'et [O.F. *criquet*, a game with a stick and a ball], open-air game with bat and ball.

Cri'er [see Cry], one who makes proclamations.

Crime [L. *crimen* (*crimin-is*), an accusation, a fault ; allied to *cernere*, to decide], great sin.

Crim'in-al, pertaining to crime ; one guilty of crime. Criminal'ity.

Crimp [causative deriv. of Cramp], crisp, wavy ; give a wavy look to.

Crimp [?], agent who decoys men to be sailors or soldiers.

Crim'son (*s=z*) [Sp. *carmesi* ; Arab. *qirmazī*, crimson ; Arab. *qirmiz*, the cochineal insect], deep red.

Cringe [O.E. *cringan*, curl up], bend like a slave, fawn.

Crin'kle [freq. form of O.E. *crincan*, to sink in a heap], form with short turns; wrinkle

Crin'o-line [L. *crinis*, hair, *linum*, flax], hooped skirt.

Crip'ple [O.E. *crypel*], to lame, hinder; one who limps or cannot walk.

Cri'sis (pl. Cri'ses) [Gk. *crisis*, a decision], decisive moment, the turning-point.

Crisp [L. *crispus*, curled], brittle, firm and fresh, brisk. **Crisp'ness.**

Cri-te'ri-on [Gk. *critērion*, a test, *critēs*, a judge], standard of judging.

Crit'ic [Gk. *critēs*, a judge], one skilled in judging merit. [crisis.

Crit'ic-al, inclined to judge; pertaining to a

Crit'i-cise (*s=z*), give an opinion as to what is good and what is bad in.

Crit'i-cism, critical opinion.

Crit-ique' (*ique=eek*) [F.], criticism in form of essay or review.

Croak [imit.], make a hoarse sound.

Cro'chet (*chet=shay*) [F. *crochet*, dim. of *croc*, a hook], threadwork with a hooked needle.

Crock [O.E. *croc*], earthen vessel.

Crock [perh. cogn. with **Crack**, cf. Norw. *krake*, a poor beast], an old ewe or an old broken-down horse. [ware.

Crock'er-y [fr. obs. *crocker*, a potter], earthen-

Croc'o-dile [L. *crocodīlus*; Gk. *crocodeilos*, a lizard, a crocodile], large river-reptile.

Cro'cus [L. *crocus*; Gk. *crocos*, crocus], bulb and its flower.

Croft [etym. dub., cf. Du. *kroft*, high dry land], small farm.

Crom'lech (*ch=k*) [W. *crom*, bent, *llech*, a flat stone], old monument of upright stones with another stone across the top.

Crone (perh. fr. Picard, *carone*, carrion], old woman.

Cro'ny [?], familiar friend.

Crook [perh. fr. O.N. *krókr*, a hook], bend; shepherd's staff; bishop's staff.

Croon [Scottish till 19th cent.], low singing or murmur.

Crop [O.E. *crop*], first stomach of a bird; produce of a field; cut short.

Cro'quet (*quet=kay*) [perh. North F. dial.; same as **Crochet**], game with hoops and balls.

Cro'sier, Cro'zier [O.F. *crocier*, fr. M.L. *cruciarius*, confused with F. *croisier*, a cross-bearer], bishop's pastoral staff or crook.

Cross [ult. fr. L. *crux* (*cruc-is*), a cross], two pieces of wood, etc., laid across each other; great trouble; ill-humoured; mark with a cross, go to the other side.

Cross'-bow, bow fastened to wooden stock and worked by a mechanism.

Cross'-ex-am'ine, examine a witness on the other side. [head.

Cross'trees, pieces of timber across a mast-

Crotch'et [F. *crochet*, dim. of *croc*, a hook. *N.B.*—The hooked time-note called a quaver was *crochet* in French], time-note, whim.

Crouch, bend low.

Croup [1] (*ou=oo*) [F. *croupe*; see **Crop**], place behind the saddle on a horse.

Croup [2] [imit. Cf. O.E. *krópan*, to cry out], disease of the windpipe and larynx.

Crou-pier' (*ou=oo*, *ier=eer*) [F. *croupier*, orig. rider on a *croupe*], assistant chairman at lower end of dinner-table, collector of money at a gaming table.

Crow [O.E. *cráwe*], black bird; make the sound of a cock; boast.

Crow'bar, bar of iron used as a lever.

Crowd [O.E. *crúdan*, to push], many persons or things close together; press in numbers.

Crown [L. *corōna*, a wreath, allied to Gk. *corōnos*, curved], top of anything, especially the head; royal headdress; coin worth five shillings; put a crown on.

Cru'cial (*c=sh*) [L. *crux* (*cruc-is*), a cross], relating to a cross; severe.

Cru'ci-ble [Late L. *crucibulum*, a melting-pot, a night-lamp; perh. fr. *crux*, a cross], melting-pot.

Cru'ci-fix [L. *crux* (*cruc-is*), a cross; *fīgere* (p.p. *fixus*), to fix], cross with the figure of Christ on it.

Cru-ci-fix'ion, death on the cross.

Cru'ci-form, cross-shaped. [cross.

Cru'ci-fy [see **Crucifix**], put to death on a

Crude [L. *crūdus*, raw], raw, unfinished.

Cru'di-ty, crude state; thing in a crude state.

Cru'el [L. *crūdēlis*, cruel; allied to *crudus*, raw], pleased to hurt.

Cru'el-ty, pleasure in hurting; act of giving unnecessary pain.

Cru'et [dim. of O.F. *cruie*, a pot], small glass bottle for vinegar, oil, etc.

Cruise [Du. *kruisen*, to cruise; ult. fr. L. *crux*, a cross], voyage to and fro; sail to and fro.

Cruis'er [see **Cruise**], warship adapted for cruising. [bread, etc.).

Crumb [O.E. *cruma*], small fragment (of

Crum'ble [orig. a dim. of **Crumb**], break into small pieces.

Crum'pet [?], cake of flour, egg, milk, etc., baked on an iron plate.

Crum'ple [freq. of obsol. *crump*, to curl up], wrinkle by crushing.

Crunch [imit.], crush noisily with the teeth.

Crup'per [see **Crop** and **Croup** [1]], leather loop from a saddle, placed under a horse's tail.

Cru-sade' [F. *croisade*; Sp. *cruzada*, a crusade; L. *crux* (*cruc-is*), a cross], a "war of the Cross," war against some great evil. **Crusad'er.**

Cruse [etym. dub., cf. Du. *kroes*], cup, bottle for water or oil, etc.

Crush [O.F. *croissir*, to crash], press together, break or bruise. [ing.

Crust [L. *crusta*, a crust], hard outer cover-

Crus-ta'ce-a (*ce=sh*) [neut. pl. of Mod. L. *crustaceus*, crust-like], class of animals with shells. **Crusta'cean.**

Crust'y, having a crust; rough-mannered.

Crutch [O.E. *cryce*], staff or support for cripples.

Cry [F. *crier*; L. *quirītāre*, to cry; orig. to ask the aid of the Rom. citizens (Quirites)], loud vocal sound; utter a loud sound of fear, joy, weeping, etc.

Crypt [Gk. *cryptos*, hidden], a vault, a hidden cave, vault under a church.

Cryp'tic, hidden, secret.

Cryp-to'gra-phy [see **Crypt** and Gk. *graphein*, to write], art of writing in secret characters. **Cryp'togram.**

Crys′tal [Gk. *crystallos*, ice, crystal], transparent quartz, superior kind of glass, regular form which a substance takes on becoming solid. **Cry′stalline.**

Crys′tal-lize, form into crystals.

Cub [?], young wild animal (bear, lion, etc.).

Cube [Gk. *cubos*, a cube, a die], solid with six equal square sides, product of a number twice multiplied by itself.

Cu′bic, cube-shaped, of three dimensions.

Cu′bi-cle [L. *cubiculum*, fr. *cubāre*, to lie down], division with one bed in a dormitory.

Cu′bit [L. *cubitus*, an elbow], measure of about 18 inches.

Cu′ckoo [F. *coucou*; imit.], bird so named from its cry.

Cu′cum-ber [F. *cocombre*; L. *cucumis* (*cucumer-is*), a cucumber], creeping plant with long fruit.

Cud [O.E. *cwidu*], food of a cow, etc., chewed a second time.

Cud′gel [O.E. *cycgel*], short thick stick; beat with same.

Cue [perh. fr. L. *quando*, when], last word of an actor's speech, catchword.

Cue [O.F. *cue*, cue, fr. L. *cauda*, a tail], rod used in billiards, pigtail.

Cuff [?], lower part of a sleeve.

Cuff [?] [cf. Swed. *kuffa*, to push], slap.

Cui-rass′ (*cui=cwi*) [L. *coriāceus*, leathern; *corium*, leather], breastplate and backplate fastened together.

Cui-rass-ier′ (*ie=ee*), horse-soldier wearing a cuirass.

Cu′li-na-ry [L. *culīna*, a kitchen], relating to the kitchen or to cooking.

Cull [O.F. *cuillir*, to collect; see **Collect**], pick out and gather.

Cul′len-der [see **Colander**].

Cul′mi-nate [L. *culmen* (*culmin-is*), the top], reach the highest point.

Cul′pa-ble [L. *culpa*, a fault], worthy of blame. **Culpabil′ity.**

Cul′prit [abbrev. of **Culpable**, and O.F. *prist*, or *prest*, ready], guilty person.

Cult [L. *colere* (p.p. *cultus*), to till, to worship], system of belief and worship. [till.

Cul′ti-vate [see **Cult**], bestow labour on, to **Cul′ture**, tillage, mental and moral training.

Cul′vert [?], arched underground channel.

Cum′ber [Late L. *cumbrus*, a heap, a barrier], burden, hinder. **Cum′bersome.**

Cu′mu-la-tive [see **Cumulus**], increasing by additions.

Cu′mu-lus [L. *cumulus*, a heap], heaped cloud.

Cu′ne-ate [L. *cuneus*, a wedge], wedge-shaped. [sly.

Cun′ning [O.E. *cunnan*, to know], skilful,

Cup [perh. O.F. *cope*; L.L. *cuppa*], small drinking-vessel; draw blood into a cupping glass.

Cup′board (*kub′urd*), closet with shelves.

Cu-pid′i-ty [L. *cupidus*, greedy], greed for wealth.

Cu′po-la [It. *cupola*, a dome; L. *cūpula*, a small cask; *cūpa*, a cask], rounded roof.

Cu′pre-ous [L. *cuprum*, copper], of or like copper.

Cur [M.E. *kur-dogge*], inferior dog, surly ill-bred fellow.

Cu′rate [see **Cure**], assistant clergyman.

Cu-ra′tor [L. *curāre* (p.p. *curātus*), to cure], one who has care of a museum, etc.

Curb[1] [F. *courber*; L. *curvāre*, to bend], chain or strap attached to the bit of a bridle; check.

Curb,[2] **Kerb** [F. *courbe*; same orig. as **Curb**[1]], stone set along an edge. **Curb′stone.**

Curd [perh. fr. O.E. *crūdan*, to press together], thickened part of milk.

Cur′dle, change into curd.

Cure [L. *cūra*, care], healing, care of souls; make well, salt and dry.

Cur′few [O.F. *couvrir*, to cover; *feu*, fire], evening bell. [thing.

Cu′ri-o [abbrev. of **Curiosity**], curious, rare

Cu-ri-os′i-ty, rare thing; desire to know.

Cu′ri-ous [L. *curiosus*, full of care, *cura*, care], eager for knowledge, prying, strange.

Curl [fr. obs. *crull*, *croll*, curly; cf. Du. *krullen*, to curl], ringlet; bend into rings.

Cur′lew [O.F. *courlieus*; imit.], wading bird with curved bill.

Cur′ling, sport with smooth stones on ice.

Cur′rant [F. (*raisins de*) *Corinthe*, raisins of *Corinth*], small dried seedless grape, berry with acid juice.

Cur′ren-cy [see **Current**], that which is in circulation, money in use, time during which a thing is current. [passing.

Cur′rent [L. *currere*, to run], a stream; now

Cur′ri-cle [L. *curriculum*, course or race-chariot; *currere*, to run], two-wheeled carriage.

Cur-ric′u-lum [see **Curricle**], course of study.

Cur′ry [Tamil, *kari*, sauce], mixed Indian spice; prepare with curry.

Cur′ry [O.F. *correier*, orig. to prepare], dress leather; comb (a horse); seek (favour) by flattery.

Curse [?], prayer for evil; cause of great evil; invoke evil.

Cur′sive [L. *currere*, to run], running (writing in MS.).

Cur′so-ry [L. *cursor*, a runner; *currere*, to run], hasty. [courtesy.

Curt [L. *curtus*, short], short; without

Cur-tail′ [L. *curtus*, short], cut short.

Cur′tain [L. *cortīna*, a curtain, orig. a small yard; *cōrs* (*cort-is*), a court], hanging screen of cloth, etc.

Curt′sy, -sey [same word as **Courtesy**], bending of the knees to show respect.

Cur′va-ture, a bending or curve.

Curve [L. *curvāre* (p.p. *curvātus*, to bend)], a bending without angles; bend.

Cush′at [(?), Scot. dial.], wood-pigeon.

Cush′ion (*u=oo*) [O.F. *coissin*, a cushion], stuffed bag for ease and support; to support with this.

Cusp [L. *cuspis*, a point], apex, pointed end.

Cus′pi-dor [Port. *cuspir*; L. *conspuere*, to spit], a spittoon.

Cus'tard [L. *crusta*, a crust], mixture of milk and eggs baked or boiled.

Cus'to-dy [L. *custos* (*custōd-is*), a guardian], keeping charge. **Custod'ian.**

Cus'tom [L. *consuētudo* (*consuētudin-is*), custom; *con-* together, *suescere* (p.p. *suētus*), to be accustomed], habit; general usage; business support; (pl.) the tax on imports. **Cus'tom-a-ry** fixed by custom. **Cus'tom-er,** regular purchaser.

Cut [(?), cf. M. Swed. *kotta*, to cut], wound with an edged instrument; divide or gash with a knife, etc.

Cu-ta'ne-ous [L. *cutis*, the skin], of or relating to the skin.

Cute [colloquial, corruption of Acute], sharp.

Cu'ti-cle [L. *cuticula*, dim. of *cutis*, the skin], outer skin.

Cut'lass [F. *coutelas*, aug. of *couteau*, a knife], broad curved sword.

Cut'ler-y [O.F. *coutel*, a knife], general name for small cutting instruments, as knives.

Cut'let [F. *côtelette*, double dim. of *côte* (L. *costa*), a rib], small cut of meat, especially veal or mutton.

Cut'ter [see Cut], yacht with one mast.

Cut'tle-fish [O.E. *cudele*], sea-animal which throws out an inky fluid.

Cy'cle [Gk. *cyclos*, a circle, a cycle], round in which certain events are regularly repeated, an age, bicycle or a tricycle; ride on a cycle. **Cy'clic.**

Cy'clone [Gk. *cyclos*, a circle], system of winds round centre of low pressure, circular storm.

Cyg'net [L. *cygnus*, a swan], young swan.

Cyl'in-der [Gk. *cylindros*, a roller], circular-ended body like a roller. **Cylin'drical.**

Cym'bals [Gk. *cymbalon*, a cymbal, from *cymbē*, a cup], pair of musical brass or brezon instruments.

Cyn'ic [Gk. *cynicos*, dog-like, a Cynic, from *cyōn*, *cynos*, a dog], disbeliever in human worth. **Cyn'icism.**

Cyn'o-sure [L. *cynosura*, the tail of the Lesser Bear, fr. Gk. *cyōn*, a dog, and *oura*, a tail], centre of attraction.

Cy'press [Gk. *cyparissos*, a cypress], kind of cone-bearing tree.

Czar, Tsar, Tzar [*zar* or *tsar*) [Russ. *tsare*, a king; L. *Cæsar*], Emperor (of Russia).

Czar'e-witch (*tsar'i-vitsh*) [Russ. *tsarivitsh*], son of a Czar.

Cza-ri'na (*i=ee*) [from *Czar*, with It. suffix *ina*], Empress of Russia.

D

Dab [?], strike gently, peck; slight blow, fish.

Dab'ble [frequent. of Dab], move undecidedly in water; dip slightly into anything.

Dab'chick [Dab perh. cogn. with **Dip** and **Chick**], water-bird noted for diving.

Dace [sometimes called *dare* and *dart* from its swiftness; O.F. *darz*], fresh-water fish.

Da-coit' [Hind. *dākāit*, fr. *daka*, gang-robbery], member of a robber-band in India and Burma.

Dac'tyl [Gk. *dactylos*, a finger], tri-syllabic foot (– ᴗ ᴗ).

Da'do [It. *dado*, die or square part in middle of a pedestal], cube of a pedestal above the base, lower part of a room-wall coloured or panelled differently from higher part.

Daf'fo-dil [L. *asphodelus*; Gk. *asphodelos*, a kind of lily], bulb and its yellow flower.

Dag'ger [F. *dague*, a dagger; orig. unknown], short sword, stabbing knife.

Da-guerr'eo-type [F. *daguerréotype*, fr. *Daguerre*, name of inventor], early photographic process, portrait produced by the process.

Dah'lia (*ah=ai*) [fr. Swedish botanist *Dahl*], autumn flower. [boat.

Da-ha-bee'yah [Arab. *dahabīya*], large Nile

Dai'ly, belonging to each day.

Dain'ty [O.F. *dainté*, dainty; L. *dignitas* (*dignitat-is*), dignity], choice morsel; elegant, fastidious.

Dai'ry [fr. obs. *dey*, O.E. *dǣge*, a maid-servant, cogn. with O.E. *dáh*, dough], place where milk is kept.

Da'is [O.F. *deis* fr. L.L. *discus*, table], raised floor at upper end of a dining-hall, raised seat with canopy.

Dai'sy [O.E. *dæges éage*, the eye of day], common flower with yellow disk and white or pinkish petals which close at night.

Dale [O.E. *dœl*], low place between hills; valley.

Dal'li-ance, caressing, trifling.

Dal'ly [O.F. *dalier*, to chat], to trifle, delay.

Dam [same as Dame], mother (usually of animals).

Dam [common Teut., cf. Du. *dam*; Ger. *damm*], bank to confine water; confine water thus.

Dam'age [O.F. *damage*, damage; L. *damnāre* (p.p. *damnātus*), to condemn], hurt.

Dam'ask [It. *Damasco*; L. *Damascus*], figured silk, linen, or steel.

Dame [O.F. *dame*; L. *domina*, a lady], mistress of a house, noble lady.

Damn [L. *damnāre*, to condemn], condemn, curse.

Damp [cf. Du. and Dan. *damp*, Ger. *dampf*, vapour], moisture, moist; to wet, make dull.

Damp'er, something that damps or depresses, movable plate in a chimney, something depressing.

Dam'sel [M.L. *domnicella*, double dim. of L. *domina*, a lady], young woman.

Dam'son [L. *Damascenum* (*prunum*), plum of Damascus], small plum.

Dance [O.F. *danser*; perh. O.H.G. *dansōn*, to drag along], measured stepping or springing to music; step or spring to music, skip about.

Dan'de-li-on [F. *dent de lion*, lion's tooth], plant with yellow flowers.

Dan′dle [prob. imit.; cf. It. *dandolare*, to dandle, *dandola*, a doll], dance (a child) on the knee.

Dan′druff, Dan′driff [ending perh. Yorksh. *hurf*, fr. Icel. *hrufa*, scab], scurf on the head.

Dan′dy [origin unknown. Note that *Dandy* is a form of *Andrew*], one who is fond of finery in dress.

Dan′ger (*a=ai*), [O.F.*dangier*, absolute power; L. *dominium*, power, *dominus*, a lord], exposure to harm, risk, peril.

Dan′gle [etym. dub., cf. Dan. *dangle* ; Swed. *dangla*, to swing about], hang loose, swing.

Dank [cf. Swed. *dank*, marshy ground], damp.

Dap′per [cf. Du. *dapper*, brave], little and active; trim.

Dap′ple [perh. Icel. *depill*, a spot], spotted.

Dare [O.E. *durran*, to dare; *ic dearr*, I dare], have boldness to, defy.

Da′ring, boldness; bold, adventurous.

Dark [O.E. *deorc*], lacking light, black or of a deep colour.

Dar′ling [O.E. *déorling*, dim. of *déor*, dear], little dear; dearly loved; favourite.

Darn [O.E. *dern*, secret, hidden], fill in holes with yarn or thread.

Dar′nel [cf. Walloon, *darnelle*], kind of weed among corn.

Dart [O.F. *darz*, a dart; cf. Dace], pointed weapon for throwing, sudden rush; throw or fly as a dart.

Dash [perh. imit.], sudden rush; throw or come against with great force; punctuation mark.

Dash′board, splash-board.

Dash′ing, bold and showy.

Das′tard [perh. fr. Dazed], coward.

Da′ta (pl.) [L. *dare*, to give (p.p. *datus*)], facts given or admitted.

Date [Gk. *dactylos*, a date, a finger], fruit of the date-palm.

Date [F. *date* ; L. *dare* (p.p. *datus*), to give], given point of time ; mark the time of.

Da′tive [L. *dare* (p.p. *datus*), to give], grammatical case denoting remoter object.

Daub [O.F *dauber* ; L. *dealbāre*, to plaster, *de*, down, very, *albus*, white], smear, paint coarsely.

Daugh′ter [O.E. *dohtor*], female child.

Daunt, [O.F *danter* ; L. *domitāre*, to tame], check by fear. **Daunt′less.**

Dau′phin [family name of several lords of *Dauphiné*, who had three dolphins for their crest; L. *delphinus*, a dolphin], formerly the title of the eldest son of the king of France.

Dav′it [formerly *david*, as if from proper name], crane for hoisting anchor, one of a pair of cranes for lowering boat.

Daw [imit. of noise made by the bird], bird of the crow kind.

Daw′dle [?], waste time, walk idly.

Dawn [Swed. and Dan. *dagning*, dawning ; O.E. *dagian*, to become day], break of day ; grow light. [24 hours.

Day [O.E. *dœg*], time from sunrise to sunset,

Daze [M.E. *dasen*, to stupefy. Cf. O.N. *dasask*, to be bewildered], stupefy with too much light, a blow, etc.

Daz′zle [frequent. of Daze], overpower by light.

Dea′con [Gk. *diaconos*, a servant, a deacon], office-bearer in a church.

Dead [O.E. *déad*], without life.

Dead′en, make as dead, lessen force.

Dead′lock, complete stoppage of action.

Dead′ly, that may cause death, like death.

Deaf [O.E. *déaf*], unable to hear.

Deal [cf. Du. *deel*, a plank], plank.

Deal [O.E. *dǽl*], quantity ; distribute, do business, behave; business transaction. **Deal′er.**

Dean [F. *doyen* ; L. *decānus*, one placed over ten soldiers or ten monks ; *decem*, ten], one who presides over the other clergy in cathedrals or collegiate churches.

Dear [O.E. *déore*], beloved, high-priced.

Dearth [fr. Dear], scarcity.

Death [O.E. *déath*], passing from life.

De-bar′ [O.F. *desbarer* ; L. *de*, off, and **Bar**], shut off.

De-base′ [*dē*, down, and **Base**], lower.

De-bate′ [L. *dē*, down; Rom. *battere*, to fight], argument ; argue for and against. **Debat′able.**

De-bauch′ [F.*débaucher*, entice from a master; perh. *de*, from, *bauche*, a workshop], excess in eating and drinking; deprave, vitiate. **Debauch′ery.**

De-ben′ture [L. *dēbentur*, (they) are due], deed which is security for a loan.

De-bil′i-ty [L. *dēbilis*, weak], weakness. **Debil′itate.**

Deb′it [L. *debitum*, debt], left-hand side of account in which entries of sums due are entered.

De′bon-air′ [F. *de bon air*, of good appearance], elegant, courteous, gay.

De-bouch′ [F. *de-* [L. *dis*) away, *bouche*, mouth], issue from wood, etc., into open ground. **Debouch′ment.**

De′bris [*deb′ree*) [F. *débris*, fragments; *de-*, down, *briser*, to break], fragments, ruins.

Debt [O.F. *dette*, L. *debēre*, to owe (p.p. *debitum*), whence mistaken letter *b*], that which is owing.

Debt′or, one who owes.

Dec′ade [Gk. *decas* (*decados*), decade, *deca*, ten], period of ten years.

Dec′a-dence [L. *dē*, down, *cadere*, to fall], falling away, a growing worse.

Dec′a-gon [Gk. *deca*, ten ; *gōnia*, a corner], ten-sided plane figure.

Dec′a-logue [Gk. *deca*, ten ; *logos*, a speech], the ten commandments.

De-camp′ [L. *dis-*, away ; *campus*, a field], move away.

De-cant′ [L. *dē*, from ; *canthus*, the lip of a cup], pour from one vessel to another.

De-can′ter, ornamental bottle for decanted wine, etc.

De-cap′i-tate [L. *dē*, down, *caput* (*capit-is*), the head], cut off the head of.

De-cay' [O.F. *decair*, to decay ; L. *dē*, down, *cadere*, to fall], gradual loss of strength, corruption ; waste away.

De-cease' [F. *décès*; L. *dē*, from and *cēdere* (sup. *cessum*, to go], death.

De-ceit', wilful misleading, trickery.

De-ceive' [O.F. *deceveir*, to deceive ; L. *dē*, away, *capere* (p.p. *captus*), to take], mislead, cheat.

De'cen-cy, propriety.

De-cen'ni-al [L. *decem*, ten, and *annus*, a year], belonging to ten years.

De'cent [L. *decēre* (pr.p. *decens, -entis*), to be fitting], suitable in behaviour, modest, respectable.   [deceived.

De-cep'tion, deceiving or state of being

De-cide' [L. *dē*, down, *cœdere* (p.p. *cœsus*), to cut], make up one's mind, settle.

De-ci'ded, firm and clear.

De-cid'u-ous [L. *dē*, down, *cadere*, to fall], falling off at certain seasons like leaves.

De'ci-mal (*e* short) [L. *decima*, a tithe ; *decem*, ten], number expressed by tens ; numbered by tens.

De'ci-mate [L. *decimāre* (p.p. *decimātūs*), to take the tenth man ; *decem*, ten], take the tenth part of, kill every tenth man, destroy in large numbers.

De-ci'pher [F. *déchiffrer* ; see **Cipher**], make out (puzzling or bad writing).

De-cis'ion (*si*=*zh*), judgment, firmness.

De-ci'sive (*s*=*z*), final.

Deck [prob. M.Du. *deken*, to cover; cogn. with **Thatch**], platform from side to side of a ship ; to cover, adorn.

De-claim' [L. *dē*, down, fully, *clāmāre*, to cry], make a formal speech.

Dec-la-ma'tion, set speech in public.

Dec-lam'a-tor-y, declaiming, esp. noisily.

Dec-la-ra'tion, distinct statement, act of declaring publicly.

De-clar'a-tor-y, making clear or manifest.

De-clare' [L. *dēclārāre* (p.p. *dēclārātus*), to declare; *dē*, fully, *clārus*, clear], make known by speech.

De-clen'sion [see **Decline**], downward tendency, case changes in the forms of nouns, etc.

Dec-li-na'tion, bending downward, variation of magnetic needle from true north.

De-clin'a-ture, refusal.

De-cline' [F. *décliner* ; L. *dēclīnāre* (p.p. *dēclīnātus*); *dē*, from, and *-clīnāre* (only in compound words), to lean], falling off, consumption ; bend down, fall away, refuse.

Dec-liv'i-ty [L. *dē*, down, *clīvus*, a slope], downward slope.

De-coc'tion [L. *dē*, down, *coquere*, to cook], extract got by boiling.

De-com-pose' (*s*=*z*), [L. *dē*, and **Compose**], separate into original elements, decay.

Dec'o-rate [L. *decus* (*decor-is*), ornament], adorn, beautify. **Dec'orative**.

Dec-o-ra'tion, that which adorns, a badge of honour to be worn.

De-co'rous, Dec'orous [L. *decus* (*decor-is*), ornament, *decēre*, to be fit], seemly, proper.

De-co'rum, propriety of conduct.

De-coy' [earlier *coy*, Du. *kooi*, decoy ; L. *cavea*, a cage], anything meant to lead into a snare ; lead into danger by a lure.

De'crease, De-crease', a growing less.

De-crease' [L. *dēcrescere* (p.p. *dēcrētus*), *dē*, down, *crescere*, to grow], grow less, make less.

De-cree' [O.F. *decrē* ; L. *dē*, away, *cernere* (p.p. *crētus*), to distinguish], order or law ; determine by decree.

De-crep'it [L. *dē*, away, *crepāre* (p.p. *crepitus*), to crackle], broken down with age. **De-crep'itude**.

De-cry' [L. *dē*, down (here meaning reversal), and **Cry**], cry down, under-value in speech.

Ded'i-cate [L. *dē*, down, *dicāre*, to proclaim], set apart for sacred use. **Ded'icatory**.

Ded-i-ca'tion, a setting apart, address to some one at the beginning of a book.

De-duce' [L. *dē*, down, *ducere* (p.p. *ductus*), to lead], derive or draw from. **Deduc'tion**.

De-duct' [see **Deduce**], take away or subtract.

Deed [O.E. *dǣd*], that which is done, sealed paper containing the terms of a transfer or bargain.   [opinion.

Deem [O.E. *dēman*, to judge], to judge, be of

Deem'ster, the name given to each of the two justices of the Isle of Man.

Deep [O.E. *dīop, dēop*], far down, far to the back, thorough ; a deep part of the ocean, the ocean.

Deer [O.E. *dēor*, a wild animal], swift animal with horns.

De-face' [obs. F. *defacer* ; L. *dē*, down, and *faciēs*, a face], injure the surface.

De-fal-ca'tion [L. *dē*, away, *falx* (*falc-is*), a sickle], abstraction of trust-money.

De-fame' [L. *diffāmāre* (p.p. *diffāmātus*), to spread a bad report ; *dis-*, apart, *fama*, a report], slander, speak evil of. **Defama'tion.** **Defam'atory**.

De-fault' [O.F. *default* ; L. *dis-*, apart, and **Fault**], to fail through neglect of duty ; to fail to appear in court when called on. **Default'er**.

De-feat' [O.F. *defeit* (p.p. of *desfaire*), to make void], an overthrow ; conquer, make ineffectual.

De-fect' [L. *dēficere* (p.p. *dēfectus*), to undo; *dē*, away, and *facere*, to make], want, fault. **Defec'tive**.

De-fec'tion, falling away, abandonment.

De-fence', protection, answer to a charge.

De-fend' [L. *dēfendere* (p.p. *dēfensus*), *dē*, down, and *fendere* (only in compound words), to strike], to guard, uphold.

De-fend'ant, the one who opposes a charge.

De-fen'si-ble, capable of being defended.

De-fen'sive, in a state of defence.

De-fer' [1] [L. *differre*, to delay; *dis-*, apart, *ferre*, to bear], put off.

De-fer' [2] [L. *dēferre*, to bring down; *de-*, down, *ferre*, to bring], yield to another.

Def'er-ence [see **Defer** [2]], a yielding of one's opinion, respect.

Def′er-en′tial (*ti=sh*), showing deference.

De-fi′ance, challenge, contempt of opposition or danger.

De-fi′cien-cy (*ci=sh*), shortcoming.

De-fi′cient [L. *dēficere* (pr.p. *dēficiens*, *-entis*), to be wanting, to fail], wanting.

Def′i-cit [L. *dēficit*, it fails, fr. *deficere*, to fail], deficiency in amount.

De-file′ [O.E. *fȳlan*, to make foul], make foul.

De′file [L. *dis-*, apart, *filum*, a thread], narrow pass ; **De-file′, De′file**, march in a line.

De-fine′ [L. *dē*, down, *finīre* (p.p. *finītus*), to finish], fix the bounds of, to explain, make clear in outline.

Def′i-nite, exact. **Def′initeness**.

Def-i-ni′tion, description of a thing by its properties, exact explanation, clearness of outline. [final.

De-fin′i-tive, defining or limiting, positive,

De-flate′ [L. *dē*, down, *flāre*, to blow], to release the air from (anything inflated). **Defla′tion**.

De-flec′tion, De-flex′ion [L. *dē*, down, and *flectere* (p.p. *flexus*), to bend], a turning aside.

De-formed′ [L. *dēformis*, ugly ; *dē*, away, *forma*, shape, beauty], misshapen.

De-for′mi-ty, unnatural shape.

De-fraud′ [L. *dē*, away, *fraus* (*fraud-is*), fraud], to cheat.

De-fray′ [F. *défrayer*, fr. *frai* (pl. *frais*), expenses], pay.

Deft [O.E. *ge-dæfte*, meek, *dæftan*, to prepare], clever, neat-handed.

De-funct′ [L. *dē*, fully, *fungī* (p.p. *functus*), to perform], dead.

De-fy′ [O.F. *defier*, to defy ; L. *dis-*, apart, *fidere*, to trust], challenge, dare.

De-gen′er-ate [L. *dē*, down, *genus* (*gener-is*), race], be or grow worse than one's kind or than one was formerly. **Degen′eracy**.

De-glu-ti′tion [L. *dē*, down, *glūtīre* (p.p. *glūtītus*), to swallow], swallowing.

De-grade′ [L. *dē*, from, *gradus*, a step], to reduce to lower rank. **Degrada′tion**.

De-gree′ [L. *dē*, down, *gradus*, a step], a step, rank, extent, 360th part of a circle, unit of angular measurement, division on a scientific instrument, university distinction.

De′i-fy [L. *deus*, God, *facere*, to make], make a god of. **Deifica′tion**.

Deign (*dane*) [L. *dignāre*, to deem worthy], think worthy, stoop.

De′ism, belief in the existence of a God but not in revelation. **De′ist**.

De′i-ty [L. *deus*, god], God.

De-jec′tion [L. *dē*, down, *jacere* (p.p. *jectus*), to throw], lowness of spirits. **Deject′ed**.

De-lay′ [O.F. *delaier*, perh. from L. *dīlātāre*, to put off], putting off, stop ; put off, hinder. [delightful.

De-lec′ta-ble [L. *dēlectāre*, to delight],

Del′e-gate [L. *dē*, away, *lēgāre* (p.p. *lēgātus*), to depute], one chosen to act for others ; send as a representative, entrust to.

Del-e-ga′tion, body of delegates.

De-lete′ [L. *dēlēre* (p.p. *dēlētus*), to destroy], blot out. **Dele′tion**.

Del-e-tō′ri-ous [Gk. *dēlētērios*, harmful, *dēle-esthai*, injure], hurtful.

Delf, Delft [fr. *Delft*, formerly *Delf*, in Holland], coarse glazed earthenware.

De-lib′or-ate [L. *dē*, thoroughly, *librāre*, to weigh], carefully considered, slow ; discuss, weigh in the mind.

De-lib-er-a′tion, careful thought, discussion.

Del′i-ca-cy, fineness, frailty, a dainty.

Del′i-cate [L. *dēlicātus*, luxurious, prob. allied to *dēliciæ*], fine, frail.

De-li′cious (*ici=ish*) [L. *dēliciæ*, delights], very pleasing.

De-light′ [O.F. *delitier* ; L. *dēlectāre*, to delight], joy ; please greatly, joy in.

De-lin′e-ate [L. *dē*, down, *lineāre*, to mark out, *linea*, a line], to outline, sketch.

De-lin′quen-cy, omission of duty, fault.

De-lin′quent [L. *dēlinquere* (pr.p. *dēlinquens*, *-entis*), to fail; *dē*, away, *linquere*, to leave], one who fails in duty, culprit.

De-lir′i-um [L. *dē*, from, *līra*, a furrow], a wandering of the mind.

De-li′ver [F. *délivrer* ; L. *dē*, from, *līberāre*, to free], set free, give up, utter.

De-liv′er-ance, setting free.

De-liv′er-y, setting free, giving over, utterance.

Dell [O.E. *dæl*], dale, deep natural hollow.

Del′ta [Gk. *delta* △, the fourth letter of the alphabet], tract occupied by the mouths of a river.

De-lude′ [L. *dē*, down, *lūdere* (p.p. *lusus*), to play], lead from truth, deceive.

Del′uge [F. *déluge* ; L. *dīluvium* ; *dis-*, apart, *luere* to wash], flood. [ledge.

De-lu′sion, false opinion from want of knowledge.

Delve [O.E. *delfan*], dig.

Dem′a-gogue [Gk. *dēmos*, the people, *agōgos*, leading], noisy leader of the people.

De-mand′ [L. *dē*, away, *mandāre*, to order], claim, an asking for with authority ; claim as a right.

De-mar-ca′tion [L. *dē*, down, and Span. *marcar*, to mark], marking a limit.

De-mean′[1] [O.F. *demener*, to conduct ; L. *dē*, down ; F. *mener*, to lead], behave.

De-mean′[2] [L. *dē*, down, and **Mean**], debase, lower in dignity.

De-mean′our [earlier *demenure* ; see **De-mean**[1]], behaviour, bearing.

De-ment′ed [L. *dē*, from, *mens* (*ment-is*), mind], mad.

De-mer′it [L. *dē*, fully, *merērī* (p.p. *meritus*), to deserve], that which deserves blame.

De-mesne′ (*esne=ain*), **Do-main′** [see **Domain**], house and land round it kept for the owner's use.

Dem′i-god [F. *demi* ; L. *dīmidius*, half, and **God**], hero who was half a god.

De-mise′ (*s=z*) [O.F. *demise* (p.p. of *desmettre*, to dismiss) ; L. *dēmittere* (p.p. *dēmissus*, to dismiss], transfer of property, death. **Demis′sion**.

De-mo′bi-lize [L. *dē*, down, and **Mobilize**], bring back (an army) to peace footing.

De-moc'ra-cy [formerly *democraty*; Gk. *dēmos*, the people; *cratein*, to rule], government by the people.

Dem'o-crat, one who believes in government by the people.

De-mol'ish [L. *dēmōlīrī*; *dē*, down, *mŏels*, a heap], destroy.

De-mo-li'tion, destruction.

De'mon [Gk. *daimon*, a deity, a spirit], spirit, especially of evil.

De-mo'ni-ac [see **Demon**], one possessed by a demon.

Dem'on-strate [L. *dē*, down, *monstrāre* (p.p. *monstrātus*), to show], show, prove.

Dem-on-stra'tion, exhibition, proof.

De-mon'stra-tive, showing clearly; apt to make a show of feeling.

Dem'on-stra-tor, one who proves, a teacher of practical work.

De-mor'al-ize [F. *démoraliser*; see **Moral**], undermine the morals, discipline, or courage.

De-mur' [L. *demorārī*, to tarry; *dē*, fully, *morārī*, to delay], raise objections, make difficulties, take exception to.

De-mure' [O.F. *meur*, mature; L. *dē*, very, *mātūrus*, ripe], grave, affectedly modest.

Den [O.E. *denn*], cave or hollow.

De-ni'al, refusal, contradiction.

Den'i-zen [A.F. *deinzein*, fr. *deinz*, within; L. *dē intus*, from within], dweller in a country, town, etc., foreigner admitted to rights of a native.

De-nom'i-nate [L *dē*, down, fully, *nomināre* (p.p. *nominātus*), to name], to name.

De-nom-i-na'tion, a name, sect.

De-nom'i-na-tor, one who, or that, which gives a name ; lower number of a fraction.

De-note' [F.'*dénoter*; L. *dē*, down, *notāre*, to mark], point out, mean.

De-noue'ment (*ment=mong*) [F. *dénouer*, to untie], unravelling plot or mystery of drama or romance, climax.

De-nounce' [L. *dēnuntiāre* (p.p. *denuntiātus*); *dē*, down, *nuntiāre*, to tell], condemn openly.

Dense [L. *densus*, thick], thick, stupid.

Den'si-ty, thickness, closeness.

Dent [variant of **Dint**; O.E. *dynt*, a blow], hollow made by a blow or by pressure; to make a hollow thus.   [teeth.

Den'tal [L. *dens* (*dent-is*), a tooth], of the

Den'ti-frice (*ice=iss*) [L. *dens* (*dent-is*), a tooth; *fricāre*, to rub], tooth wash or powder.

Den'tist, tooth surgeon.   **Den'tistry**.

De-nude' [L. *dē-*, fully, *nudāre*, to make bare; *nudus*, naked], make bare.

De-nun-ci-a'tion, open accusation.

De-ny' [F. *dénier*, to deny; L. *dē*, fully, *negāre*, to deny], declare untrue, refuse.

De-part' [L. *dis-*, away, from, *partīre*, to part], go away.

De-part'ment, separate division.

De-par'ture, a going away.

De-pend' [L. *dē*, down, *pendēre*, to hang], hang down, rely for support (on), trust.

De-pend'ant, one who depends on another, hanger-on.   [ing.

De-pend'ence, De-pend'ance, state of depend-

De-pend'ent, hanging down, not self-supporting, under another state. (As a *noun*, same as **Dependant**.)

De-pict' [L. *dē*, fully, and *pingere* (p.p. *pictus*), to paint], paint, describe.

De-plete' [L. *dē*, away, and *plēre* (p.p. *plētus*), to fill], empty, exhaust.   **Deple'tion**.

De-plore' [L. *dē*, fully, *plōrāre*, to cry], express grief for, regret.   **Deplor'able**.

De-ploy' [F. *déployer*, fr. L. *dis-*, apart, and *plicāre*, to fold], spread out so as to extend the front (of troops).

De-po'nent [L. *dēpōnere*, to lay down, fr. *dē*, down, and *pŏnere* (p.p. *pŏnens*, -*entis*), to place], one who testifies under oath. Of verbs (Gk. and Lat.), originally reflexive with passive form but active in meaning, wrongly regarded as having *laid aside* their passive meaning. **Depone'** (vb.).

De-pop'u-late [L. *dē*, down, *populāre*, to populate; *populus*, the people], deprive of inhabitants.

De-port' [L. *dē*, down, *portāre*, to carry], carry away, expel, exile, behave (oneself).

De-port'ment, behaviour, bearing.

De-pose' (*s=z*) [F. *de*, from, *poser*, to place], remove from office; bear witness.

De-pos'it [L. *dē*, down, *pōnere* (p.p. *positus*), to place], that which is laid down or placed, something given as security; lay down.

De-pos'i-ta-ry, one with whom anything is left in trust.

De-po-si'tion, laying down, written testimony, setting aside a king, etc.

De-pos'i-to-ry, place where things are placed for safe keeping.

Dep'ot [F. *dépôt*; L. *dēpositum*, a thing laid down; see **Deposit**], storing-place for goods, railway plant, tram-cars, etc.

De-prave' [L. *dē*, fully, *pravus*, crooked], make bad, corrupt.

De-prav'i-ty, badness of character.

Dep're-cate [L. *dē*, away, and *precārī* (p.p. *precātus*), to pray], plead against, express disapproval.

De-pre'ci-ate (*c=sh*) [L. *dēpretiāre* (p.p. *dēpretiātus*), fr. *dē*, down, and *pretium*, price], fall in value, under-value. **De-precia'tion. Depre'ciatory**.

Dep-re-da'tion [L. *dē*, fully, and *prædārī* (p.p. *prædātus*), to plunder], a robbing, inroad.

De-press' [L. *dē*, down, and *premere* (p.p. *pressus*), to press], press down, cause to sink, sadden. **Depres'sion**.

Dep-ri-va'tion, a taking away, loss.

De-prive' [L. *dē*, fully, *privāre* (p.p. *prīvātus*), to deprive], take away. **Depriva'tion**.

Depth [see **Deep**], measurement downward from the top or backward from the front.

Dep-u-ta'tion, persons deputed.

De-pute' [L. *dē*, down, *putāre*, to cut off], appoint to act in place of others.

Dep'u-ty, one appointed to act for others.

De-range′ [F. *déranger*; L. *dis-*, apart; F. *rang*, rank], put out of order.

Der′e-lict [L. *dē*, from, *relinquere* (p.p. *relictus*), to leave], forsaken (esp. of a ship).

Der-e-lic′tion, a forsaking, neglect.

De-ride′ [L. *dē*, down, *rīdēre* (p.p. *rīsus*), to laugh], laugh at, mock. [mockery.

De-ris′ion (*isi=izh*), scornful laughter.

Der-i-va′tion, act of tracing origin, the origin. Deriv′a-tive.

De-rive′ [L. *dērivāre*, to drain off water, fr. *rivus*, a stream], receive as from a source.

Der′o-gate [L. *dē*, away, and *rogāre* (p.p. *rogātus*), to ask], take away, lessen. Deroga′tion.

De-rog′a-to-ry, tending to lessen.

Der′rick [Du. *Dierryk*, surname of noted hangman at Tyburn], machine for hoisting or moving heavy weights. (Originally hangman, and then the gallows.)

Der′vish [Pers. *darvesh*, poor], Mohammedan monk professing poverty.

Des-cant′ [M L. *discantus*, kind of singing; *dis-*, apart, *cantāre*, to sing], make remarks freely.

De-scend′ [L. *dē*, down, *scandere*, to climb], go or come down.

De-scend′ant, offspring (to any generation).

De-scent′, a coming down.

De-scribe′ [L. *dē*, down, and *scrībere* (p.p. *scriptus*), to write], mark out, give an account of. **Descrip′tive.**

De-scrip′tion, sketch in words.

De-scry′ [O.F. *descrire*, short form of *descrivre*, to describe], catch sight of.

Des′e-crate [L. *dēsecrāre* (p.p. *dēsecrātus*), to desecrate, fr. *sacer*, sacred], insult, misuse (something sacred). **Desecra′tion.**

Des′ert [1] [L. *dēsertum*, a wilderness; see **Desert** [2]], vast waste of land.

De-sert′ [2] [L. *dēserere*, to forsake; *dē*, away, and *serere* (p.p. *sertus*), to join], forsake.

De-sert′er [see **Desert** [2]], run-away (soldier).

De-serts′ [O.F. *desert*; see **Deserve**], that which is deserved. [worthy of.

De-serve′ [L. *dē*, fully, *servīre*, to serve], be

Des′ic-cate [L. *dē*, away, *siccāre* (p.p. *siccātus*), to make quite dry], dry, dry up.

De-sid′er-ate [L. *dēsiderāre*; see **Desire**], long for intensely, miss. **Desidera′tum.**

De-sign′ (*sign=zine*) [L. *dē*, down, *signāre* (p.p. *signātus*), to mark], plan; to plan.

Des-ig-na′tion, a pointing out, name.

De-si′ra-ble (*s=z*), to be wished for.

De-sire′ [O.F. *desirer*; L. *dēsiderāre*, to long for], wish; long for.

De-si′rous, eagerly wishing.

De-sist′ (*si=zi*) [L. *dē*, away, *sistere*, to put], leave off.

Desk [L. *discus*, a desk], a writing or reading table or case.

Des′o-late [L. *dē*, fully, and *sōlāre* (p.p. *sōlātus*), to make lonely; *sōlus*, alone], laid waste; lonely.

De-spair′ [L. *dē*, from, and *spērāre* (p.p. *spērātus*), to hope], hopelessness; lose hope.

Des′per-ate, without hope, beyond hope.

Des′pi-ca-ble [see **Despise**], deserving to be despised.

De-spise′ (*s=z*) [L. *dēspicere* (p.p. *dēspectus*); *dē*, down, *specere*, to look], look down upon, scorn.

De-spite′ [O.F. *despit*; see **Despise**], ill-will; in spite of. [rob.

De-spoil′ [L. *dē*, fully, *spoliāre*, to strip], strip,

De-spond′ [L. *dē*, away, *spondēre*, to promise], be cast down.

De-spond′en-cy, lowness of spirits.

Des′pot [Gk. *despotēs*, a master], unlimited ruler, tyrant. **Des′potism.**

Des-pot′ic, having unlimited power.

Des′quam-ate [L. *dē*, off, *squāma*, a scale], come off in scales.

Des-sert′ [F. *desservir*, to clear the table; L. *dis-*, away, and *servīre*, to serve], fruits, etc., after dinner.

Des-ti-na′tion, place to which person or thing is going to or sent.

Des′tine [L. *dēstināre* (p.p. *dēstinātus*), to destine], to design, mark out, determine beforehand.

Des′ti-ny, fate, fixed order.

Des′ti-tute [L. *dēstituere* (p.p. *dēstitutūs*), to leave alone; *dē*, away, and *statuere*, to place], absolutely without means or friends. **Destitu′tion.**

De-stroy′ [L. *dē*, down, and *struere* (p.p. *structus*), to build], pull down or break up, put an end to.

De-stroy′er, torpedo-boat.

De-struc′tion, act of destroying, ruin.

Des′ue-tude (*ue=wē*) [L. *dēsuescere* (p.p. *dēsuētus*), to grow out of use], disuse.

Des′ul-to-ry [L. *dēsultor*, a circus-rider; *dē*, down, and *salīre* (p.p. *saltus*), to leap], disconnected, aimless.

De-tach′ [F. *détacher*; F. *de*, from; Rom. *tacca*, a nail], separate.

De-tach′ment, separation, small body of troops detached for some duty.

De′tail [F. *détail*; *détailler*, to cut into pieces], small particular.

De-tail′ [F. *de*, from, *tailler*, to cut; see **Tailor**], tell off in particulars.

De-tain′ [L. *dē*, down, *tenēre* (p.p. *tentus*), to hold], keep back.

De-tect′ [L. *dē*, away, *tegere* (p.p. *tectus*), to cover], find out.

De-tec′tive, one whose business is to trace wrongdoing to the doer.

De-ten′tion [see **Detain**], a keeping back.

De-ter′ [L. *dē*, from, *terrēre*, to frighten], hinder. [become worse.

De-te′ri-o-rate [L. *dēterior*, worse], make or

De-ter-mi-na′tion, ending, fixed purpose.

De-ter′mine [L. *dē*, down, *termināre* (p.p. *terminātus*), to bound, *terminus*, a boundary], set bounds to, decide, resolve.

De-ter′rent [L. *dēterrens* (*-entis*), pr.p. of *dēterrēre*, to deter], that which prevents; such as to prevent.

De-test′ [L. *dē*, down, *testārī*, to witness], hate. **Detesta′tion.**

De-throne' [L. *dis-*, apart, *thronus* (Gk. *thronos*), a chair], remove from a throne.

Det-o-na'tion [L. *dē*, from, and *tonāre* (p.p. *tonātus*) to thunder], explosion with a report. **Det'onator.**

De-tour' (*ou=oo*) [F. *détourner*, to turn aside; see **Turn**], a turning from a course.

De-tract' [L. *dē*, away, and *trahere* (p.p. *tractus*), to draw], take away credit from, to decry.

Det'ri-ment [L. *dē*, down, *terere* (p.p. *trītus*), to rub], injury, damage.

De-tri'tus [see **Detriment**], gathering of fragments worn off rocks.

Deuce [perh. F. *deux*, two (the deuce or two at dice being the worst throw], an evil spirit, demon, devil.

Dev-as-ta'tion [L. *dē*, down, *vastāre* (p.p. *vastātus*), to waste], a laying waste.

De-vel'op [F. *développer*, etym. dub.; cf. It. *viluppo*, wrapping], unfold, lay open by degrees. **Devel'opment.**

De'vi-ate [L. *dēviāre* (p.p.*dēviātus*), to deviate; *dē*, from, *via*, a way], go out of the way.

De-vice' [Late L. *divisum*, *divīsa*, a division; L. *dīvidĕre*, to divide], scheme, contrivance, emblem.

Dev'il [Gk. *diabolos*, a slanderer, a devil; *diaballein*, to slander, *dia*, through, *ballein*, to throw], evil spirit, tormentor; season highly and broil. [indirect.

De'vi-ous [L. *dē*, from, *via*, a way], winding.

De-vise' (*s=z*) [see **Device**], to plan.

De-void' [short p.p. of obs. *devoid*, fr. O.F. *devuidier*, to empty], not in possession of.

De-volve' [L. *dē*, down, *volvere*, to roll], pass on, hand over. **Devolu'tion.**

De-vote' [L. *dē*, fully, *vovēre* (p.p. *vōtus*), to vow], vow to, give oneself up to.

Dev-o-tee', one wholly given up to.

De-vo'tion, act of worship, great love.

De-vour' [L. *dē*, down, fully, *vorāre*, to swallow], eat up greedily, consume.

De-vout' [O.F. *devot*, devoted; see **Devote**], given to devotion.

Dew [O.E. *dēaw*], moisture from the air condensed by cool bodies on their surfaces.

Dew'lap [perh. from **Dew**, and O.E. *læppa*, a lobe], the hanging skin under an ox's neck.

Dex-ter'i-ty [L. *dexter*, on the right-hand side], skill.

Di-a-be'tes [Gk. *dia*, through, *bainein*, to go], disease marked by excessive discharge from the bladder. [devilish.

Di-a-bol'i-cal [Gk. *diabolos*, the devil],

Di-ac'on-ate [L. *diāconus*, a deacon], office of a deacon, deacons.

Di'a-dem [Gk. *diadema*, a fillet; *dia*, apart, *deein*, to bind], crown.

Di-ær'e-sis (*æ=ē*) [Gk. *dia*, apart, *hairein*, to take], mark ('') over a vowel to show that it is to be separately pronounced.

Di-ag-nose' [Gk. *dia*, between, *gnōsis*, enquiry], know from symptoms. **Diagnos'is.**

Di-ag'o-nal [Gk. *dia*, through, *gōnia*, an angle], straight line between opposite angles of a figure; oblique.

Di'a-gram [Gk. *dia*, through, *gramma*, a letter], simple drawing to illustrate a statement or help in proving a proposition.

Di'al [L. *diālis*, relating to a day; *dies*, a day], instrument on which the time is shown by a shadow, clock face.

Di'a-lect [Gk. *dialectos*, speech, dialect; Gk. *dia*, between, *legein*, to speak], local form of speech. [discussion.

Di-a-lec'tic (often in pl.) [see **Dialect**], logical

Di'a-logue [Gk. *dia*, across, *legein*, to discourse], conversation between two or more persons.

Di-am'e-ter [Gk. *dia*, through, *metron*, a measure], straight line through the centre.

Di'a-mond [M.E. and O.F. *diamant*, doublet of **Adamant**], precious stone.

Di-a-pa'son [Gk. *dia*, through, *pas* (gen. pl. *pasōn*), all], whole range of tones in the musical scale, burst of harmony, compass of a voice or instrument, two chief foundation stops in an organ.

Di'a-per [Gk. *diaspros*, pure white, *dia*, wholly, *aspros*, white], figured linen.

Di-aph'a-nous [Gk. *dia*, through, *phanein*, to show], allowing light to pass through.

Di'a-phragm [Gk. *dia*, through, *phragma*, a fence], muscle which separates the chest from the abdomen.

Di-ar-rhe'a, Di-ar-rhœ'a [Gk. *dia*, through, *rhein*, to flow], persistent looseness of the bowels.

Di'a-ry [L. *diārium*, a daily allowance; *dies*, a day], daily record.

Di-a-ton'ic [Gk. *dia*, through, *tonos*, a tone], proceeding by intervals of the natural scale.

Di'a-tribe [Gk. *dia*, through, *tribein*, to rub], long abusive speech.

Dice, *pl.* of **Die** [see **Die** [1]], cubes of ivory used in gaming.

Dick'ey, Dick'y [etym. doubtful], driver's seat, seat behind a carriage, detached shirt-front.

Dic'tate [L. *dictāre* (p.p. *dictātus*), freq. of *dicere*, to say], authoritative direction, injunction. (Usually pl., as *dictates* of conscience or reason); **Dic-tate',** tell what to write or say.

Dic-ta'tion, that which is dictated, overbearing conduct.

Dic'tion [L. *dicere* (p.p. *dictus*), to say], choice of words in writing or speech.

Dic'tion-ar-y, book of words arranged alphabetically with their meanings.

Dic'tum [(pl. dicta, dictums) [L. *dictum*, thing said], saying, formal pronouncement.

Di-dac'tic [Gk. *didascein*, to teach], teaching, teaching moral lessons.

Die [1] [O.F. *de*, pl. *dez*; L. *dare* (p.p. *datus*), to give], small cube.

Die [2] [M.E. *deghen*, perh. fr. O.N. *deyja*, to die], pass from life.

Di'et [1] [Gk. *diaita*, mode of life, diet], food, special food chosen for a patient, give special food to.

Di'et [2] [M.L. *diēta*, assembly, day's work, perh. from **Diet** [1]], assembly of the estates.

Dif'fer [L. *dif- (dis-)*, apart, *ferre*, to carry], be unlike, disagree.

Dif'fer-ence, unlikeness, measure of unlikeness, disagreement, remainder left after subtraction. [the difference.

Dif-fer-en'ti-ate (*ti=sh*) [see **Differ**], mark

Dif'fi-cult, hard to do or to make.

Dif'fi-cul-ty [L. *dis-*, negative, and *facilis*, easy], state of being difficult, difficult thing, (pl.) money trouble.

Dif'fi-dent [L. *dis-*, apart, *fīdere* (pr.p. *fīdens*, *-entis*), to trust], distrustful, modest. **Dif'fidence**.

Dif-fuse' (*s=z*) [L. *dis-*, apart, *fundere* (p.p. *fusus*), to pour], pour out and spread.

Dif-fuse' (*se=ss*), covering much ground, wordy. **Diffu'sion**.

Dig [perh. from F. *diguer*, to make a dike, *digue*, a dike], work with a spade.

Di'gest [L. *dis-*, apart, *gerere* (p.p. *gestus*), to carry], summary.

Di-gest', prepare food in its passage through the body for nourishing the body, classify, summarize.

Di'git [L. *digitus*, a finger], finger or toe, one of the ten symbols of number (0-9).

Dig'ni-fy [L. *dignus*, worthy, *facere*, to make], mark with honour. [honour.

Dig'ni-ta-ry, one who has a position of

Dig'ni-ty [L. *dignus*, worthy], stately bearing, high honour.

Di-gress' [L. *dīgredī* (p.p. *dīgressus*), to go aside, *dī-*, apart, *gradī*, to go], turn aside.

Dike, Dyke [O.E. *dīc*], channel made by digging, embankment, wall.

Di-lap-i-da'tion [L. *dī-*, apart, *lapis* (*lapid-is*), a stone], partial or complete ruin.

Di'-late' [L. *dīlātāre*, to dilate, *dī-*, apart, *lātus*, broad], expand, enlarge.

Dil'a-to-ry [L. *dīlātus*, p.p. of *differre*, to detain], given to delay.

Di-lem'ma [Gk. *di-*, twice, *lemma*, an assumption], difficult position involving choice between two evils.

Dil-et-tan'te (pl. **-ti**=*tee*) [It. *dilettante*, from *dilettare* (L. *dēlectāre*), to delight], a lover of the fine arts, usu. a trifler.

Dil'i-gence, steady application, public conveyance in France, etc.

Dil'i-gent [L. *dīligere* (pr.p. *dīligens*, *-entis*), to love, to select, *dis-*, apart, *legere*, to choose], industrious.

Di-lute' [L. *dis-*, apart, *luere*, to wash], weaken by adding water, etc. **Dilu'tion**.

Dim [O.E. *dim*], not bright, indistinct.

Dime [O.F. *disme*, from L. *decima*, fem. of *decimus*, tenth], silver coin (10 cents) of the U.S.A.

Di-men'sion [L. *dis-*, from, *metīrī* (p.p. *mensus*), to measure], measure in a single direction (length, breadth, or height).

Di-min'-ish [coined from L. *di-*, apart, and arch. E. *minish*, to lessen, in imitation of L. *dīminuere*], make or become less.

Dim-i-nu'tion, making or becoming less.

Di-min'u-tive, very small; a word formed from another to express a little one of its kind.

Dim'i-ty [Gk. *di-*, double, *mitos*, a thread], cotton fabric with raised pattern.

Dim'ple [perh. cogn. with Ger. *tümpel*, a pool], slight depression.

Din [O.E. *dyne*, cf. O.N. *dynr*], loud confused noise. [dinner.

Dine [L.L. *dis-*, apart, *jējūnāre*, to fast], take

Ding'hy, Ding'y (*g* hard) [Bengali *dengi*, a small boat], small extra boat of a ship.

Din'gle [?], small dell.

Din'go [native name, formerly *teingo*], wild dog of Australia.

Din'gy [E. orig. soiled with dung, dungy], dark, soiled-looking. **Din'giness**.

Din'ner [see **Dine**], chief meal of the day.

Dint [O.E. *dynt*], hollow made by a blow; dint of, by force of, by means of.

Di'o-cese [Gk. *di- (dia)*, through, and *oikos*, a house], district over which a bishop has authority. **Dio'cesan** (*o* short).

Di-op'trics [Gk. *dioptra*, an optical instrument for taking heights, etc.], science of the refraction of light.

Di-o-ram'a [Gk. *dia-*, through, *horama*, a sight], show of pictures seen from a distance through a large opening.

Dip [O.E. *dyppan*], put into and take out of a liquid quickly; act of dipping, slope.

Diph-the'ri-a [Gk. *diphthera*, leather (the membrane)], dangerous disease of the throat.

Diph'thong [formerly *dipthong*. Gk. *di-*, double, and *phthoggos*, sound], union of two vowel sounds.

Di-plo'ma [Gk. *diploos*, double, probably from folded paper], writing conferring some power or honour.

Di-plo'ma-cy [see **Diploma**], art of conducting the intercourse of nations, tact.

Dip-so-man'i-a [Gk. *dipsa*, thirst, *mania*, madness], mad thirst for alcohol. **Dipso-ma'niac**.

Dire [L. *dīrus*, fearful], dreadful, dismal.

Di-rect' [L. *dī- (dis-)*, apart, *regere* (p.p. *rectus*), to rule], straight; point out the way, govern, address (a letter). **Direc'tion**.

Di-rect'or, one who directs, one of a number who manage the affairs of a company.

Di-rect'or-y, containing directions; book with names of inhabitants of a district, etc.

Di-rect'or-ate, body of directors.

Dirge [short for *dīrige* (imper. of *dīrigere*, to direct), first word of an anthem in the Office for the Dead], funeral hymn.

Dir'i-gi-ble [L. *dīrigere*, to direct], that can be guided; balloon that can be steered.

Dirk [earlier *dork*. Perh. from Du. *dolk*, a dagger], dagger.

Dirt [M.E. *drit*; prob. O.N. *drit*, dirt], any foul substance.

Dis-a-bil'i-ty, want of power, something that disqualifies.

Dis-a'ble [L. *dis-*, to imply reversal, and **Able**], to unfit.

Dis-a-buse' (*use=uze*) [L. *dis-*, to imply reversal, and **Abuse**], set free from mistakes.

Dis-ad-van'tage [L. *dis-*, to imply reversal, and **Advantage**], something unfavourable. **Disadvanta'geous.**

Dis-af-fec'tion [L. *dis-*, to imply reversal, and **Affection**], unfriendliness, discontent.

Dis-a-gree' [L. *dis-*, to imply reversal, and **Agree**], differ.

Dis-a-gree'a-ble, unpleasant.

Dis-a-gree'ment, difference, quarrel.

Dis-al-low' [L. *dis-*, to imply reversal, and **Allow**], refuse to allow, reject.

Dis-ap-pear' [L. *dis-*, to imply reversal, and **Appear**], go out of sight. **Disappear'ance.**

Dis-ap-point' [L. *dis-*, to imply reversal, and **Appoint**], defeat expectation.

Dis-ap-pro-ba'tion [L. *dis-*, to imply reversal, and **Approbation**], disapproval.

Dis-ap-prove' (*ove=oov*) [L. *dis-*, to imply reversal, and **Approve**], regard or speak of unfavourably. **Disapprov'al.**

Dis-arm' [L. *dis-*, to imply reversal, and **Arm**], take away weapons or arms from.

Dis-ar-range' [L. *dis-*, to imply reversal, and **Arrange**], put out of order.

Dis-ar-ray' [L. *dis-*, to imply reversal, and **Array**], disorder, undress.

Dis-as'ter [L. *dis-* (with the sense, bad), and *astrum*, a star], great misfortune. **Disas'trous.**

Dis-a-vow' [L. *dis-*, to imply reversal, and **Avow**], refuse to own.

Dis-band' [L. *dis-*, to imply reversal, and **Band**], break up and scatter.

Dis-be-lieve' [L. *dis-*, to imply reversal, and **Believe**], hold not to be true.

Dis-burse' [O.F. *desbourser*; L. *dis-*, away; L.L. *bursa*, a purse], give out money. **Disburse'ment.**

Disc, Disk [Gk. *discos*, a plate, a quoit], flat round plate, anything resembling this, apparently flat surface of sun, moon, etc., any round luminous flat surface.

Dis-card' [L. *dis-*, away, and **Card**[1]], cast off as useless, dismiss.

Dis-cern' [L. *dis-*, apart, *cernere* (p.p. *crētus*), to separate], see clearly, distinguish. **Discern'ible.**

Dis-charge' [L. *dis-*, to imply reversal, and **Charge**], unload, fire off, give forth, perform, dismiss, pay; firing off, performance, flow, unloading, dismissal, payment.

Dis-ci'ple [L. *discipulus*, a disciple; *discere*, to learn], learner, follower.

Dis'cip-line, training, punishment, or correction and training.

Dis-claim' [L. *dis-*, to imply reversal, and **Claim**], give up or deny claim to.

Dis-claim'er, disavowal.

Dis-close' (*s=z*) [L. *dis-*, apart, and *claudere* (p.p. *clausus*), to close], make known, reveal.

Dis-clos'ure (*s=z*), revelation, thing disclosed.

Dis-col'our [L. *dis-*, to imply reversal, and **Colour**], change the colour of, stain. **Discol'ouration.**

Dis-com'fit [O.F. *desconfit* (p.p. of *desconfire*), to discomfit; L. *dis-*, apart, and *conficere*, to preserve], defeat, foil. **Discom'fiture.**

Dis-com'fort (*com=cum*) [L. *dis-*, to imply the reverse, and **Comfort**], want of comfort, uneasiness.

Dis'com-pose' (*s=z*) [L. *dis-*, to imply reversal, and **Compose**], disturb. **Discompos'ure.**

Dis'con-cert' [L. *dis-*, to imply reversal, and **Concert**], throw into confusion.

Dis-con-nect'ed [L. *dis-*, to imply reversal, and **Connect**], without connection.

Dis-con'so-late [L. *dis-*, apart, and *consōlāri* (p.p. *consōlātus*), to console], dispirited, comfortless.

Dis'con-tent' [L. *dis-*, to imply reversal, and **Content**], dissatisfaction.

Dis-con-tin'ue [L. *dis-*, to imply reversal, and **Continue**], leave off. **Discontin'uance.**

Dis'cord [L. *dis-*, apart, and *cor* (*cord-is*), the heart], disagreement, want of musical harmony. **Discor'dant.**

Dis'count[1], something taken off an account.

Dis-count'[2] [L. *dis-*, away, and **Count**], lend money, abating discount, leave out of account.

Dis-coun'te-nance [L. *dis-*, to imply reversal, and **Countenance**], show no favour to.

Dis-cour'age [L. *dis-*, apart, and **Courage**], dishearten, check.

Dis'course, Dis-course' [F. *discours*; L. *dis-*, apart, *currere*, to run], speech, lecture, sermon, etc. [subject.

Dis-course', speak or write at length on a

Dis-cour'te-ous [L. *dis-*, to imply reversal, and **Courteous**], impolite.

Dis-cov'er (*o=ŭ*) [L. *dis-*, apart, and **Cover**], make known, find out.

Dis-cred'it [L. *dis-*, to imply reversal, and **Credit**], disbelief, dishonour; refuse belief to, disgrace.

Dis-creet' [see **Discern**], wise and cautious.

Dis-crep'an-cy [L. *dis-*, apart, *crepāre* (pr.p. *crepans*, *-antis*), to make a noise, to crackle], want of agreement, difference. **Discrep'ant.**

Dis-cre'tion (*è*) [see **Discreet**], wise conduct, prudence, freedom of choice.

Dis-crim'i-nate [L. *discrimināre* (p.p. *discrimīnātus*), to discriminate, from *dis-cernere*, to discern], note differences in or between, distinguish; noting differences exactly, discerning.

Dis-crim-i-na'tion, nicety in noting differences.

Dis-cur'sive [see **Discourse**], rambling.

Dis-cuss' [L. *discutere* (p.p. *discussus*), to shake asunder; *dis-*, apart, *quatere*, to shake], examine by argument, debate.

Dis-dain' [L. *dē*, down, *dignāre*, to think worthy], scorn, look upon with scorn.

Dis-ease' [L. *dis-*, to imply reversal, and **Ease**], illness.

Dis-em-bark' [L. *dis-*, to imply reversal, and **Embark**], to go or put ashore.

Dis-em-bod'ied [L. *dis-*, to imply reversal, and **Embody**], without a body.

Dis-en-chant' [L. *dis-*, to imply reversal, and **Enchant**], to free from enchantment.

Dis-en-gage' [L. *dis-*, to imply reversal, and **Engage**], to free from.

Dis-es-tab'lish [L. *dis-*, to imply reversal, and **Establish**], unsettle, break connection (as of Church with State).

Dis-fa'vour [L. *dis-*, to imply reversal, and **Favour**], disapproval; withhold favour from, discountenance.

Dis-fig'ure [L. *dis-*, negative, and **Figure**], mar form or beauty. **Disfigura'tion, Dis-fig'urement.**

Dis-fran'chise [L. *dis-*, to imply reversal (of **Enfranchise**), and **Franchise**], take away the rights of citizenship.

Dis-gorge' [O.F. *des-*(L. *dis-*), away, and *gorge*, the throat], throw out from the throat, give up what has been wrongfully gained.

Dis-grace' [L. *dis-*, apart, *gratia*, grace], shame; bring shame to.

Dis-guise' (*ise*=*ize*) [L. *dis-*, apart, and **Guise**], dress worn for concealment; conceal by unusual dress or false appearance.

Dis-gust' [L. *dis-*, apart, *gustāre*, to taste], distaste, strong dislike; produce distaste.

Dish [L. *discus*, a plate], broad vessel to hold meat, food in a dish; put on a dish for table.

Dis-*h*ab-ille', Des-*h*ab-ille' (*ille*=*eel*) [F. *déshabillé*, undress; *habiller*, to clothe], careless dress.

Dis-heart'en [L. *dis-*, to imply reversal, and **Hearten**], lessen courage and hope.

Dishev'el (*e* short) [obs. F. *descheveler* (now *décheveler*), *des* (L. *dis-*), apart, *chevel* (now *cheveu*), L. *capillus*, hair)], to loosen the hair. **Dishev'elled**, in loose disorder.

Dis-*h*on'est-y [L. *dis-*, to imply reversal, and **Honesty**], lack of honesty, fraud.

Dis-*h*on'our [L. *dis-*, to imply reversal, and **Honour**], shame; treat as unworthy, bring shame on.

Dis-il-lu'sion, Dis-il-lu'sion-ize (*si*=*zh*) [L. *dis-*, to imply reversal, and **Illusion**], to free from false but pleasant beliefs. **Dis-illu'sionment.**

Dis-in-cli-na'tion [L. *dis-*, to imply reversal, and **Inclination**], unwillingness.

Dis-in-fect' [L. *dis-*, to imply reversal, and **Infect**], cleanse from infection.

Dis-in-gen'u-ous [L. *dis-*, to imply reversal, and **Ingenuous**], wanting in candour, insincere, having hidden motives.

Dis-in-her'it [L. *dis-*, to imply reversal, and **Inherit**], cut off from inheriting.

Dis-in'te-grate [L. *dis-*, to imply reversal; *integrāre* (p.p. *integrātus*), to make whole; *integer*, whole], break up or cause to fall into pieces. **Disintegra'tion.**

Dis-in-ter' [L. *dis-*, to imply reversal, and **Inter**], bring out as from a grave or hiding-place.

Dis-in'ter-est-ed, free from selfish motive.

Dis-joint'ed [L. *dis-*, to imply reversal, and **Jointed**], separated at the joints, unconnected.

Dis-junc'tion [L. *dis-*, to imply reversal, and **Junction**], separation.

Dis-like' [L. *dis-*, to imply reversal, and **Like**[2]], want of liking, strong feeling against; have a feeling against.

Dis'lo-cate [L. *dis-*, apart, and *locāre* (p.p. *locātus*), to put in place], put out of joint.

Dis-lodge' [L. *dis-*, to imply reversal, and **Lodge**], drive from position, remove.

Dis-loy'al [L. *dis-*, to imply reversal, and **Loyal**], not true (to one's king, etc.). **Disloy'alty.** [and sad.

Dis'mal (*s*=*z*) [L. *dies mali*, bad days], dull

Dis-man'tle [O.F. *des-* (L. *dis-*), apart; *manteller*, to cloak], strip (of furniture, cannon, etc.).

Dis-may' (L. *dis-*, to imply reversal; O.H.G. *magan*, to be able], disabling terror; deprive of vigour through fear.

Dis-mem'ber [L. *dis-*, to imply reversal, and **Member**], take limb from limb. **Dismem'-berment.**

Dis-miss' [L. *dis-*, apart, and *mittere* (p.p. *missus*), to send], send away. **Dismiss'al.**

Dis-mount' [L. *dis-*, to imply reversal, and **Mount**], get down (as from a horse).

Dis-o-be'di-ence [L. *dis-*, to imply reversal, and **Obedience**], refusal to obey.

Dis-o-bli'ging [L. *dis-*, to imply reversal, and **Obliging**], unwilling to help or do kind things.

Dis-or'der [L. *dis-*, to imply reversal, and **Order**], upset, put out of order; confusion, illness.

Dis-or'gan-ize [L. *dis-*, to imply reversal, and **Organize**], throw into disorder.

Dis-own' [L. *dis-*, to imply reversal, and **Own**] refuse to own.

Dis-par'age [O.F. *des-*, apart, *parage*, equality; L. *par*, equal], undervalue, speak slightingly of. **Dispar'agement.**

Dis-par'i-ty [L. *dis-*, apart, and F. *parité*, equality; L. *par*, equal], inequality. **Dis'-parate.**

Dis-pas'sion-ate [L. *dis-*, to imply reversal, and **Passionate**], without passion, cool.

Dis-patch', Des-patch' [Sp. *despachar*, to dispatch; L. *dis-*, away, *pangere* (p.p. *pactus*), to fasten], send away, perform; a sending away, performance, speed, official letter.

Dis-pel' [L. *dis-*, apart, *pellere*, to drive], drive away.

Dis-pen'sa-ry, place where medicines are prepared and given out.

Dis-pen-sa'tion, dealing out, that which is dealt out, exemption from penalty or duty.

Dis-pense' [L. *dis-*, apart, *pendere* (p.p. *pensus*), to weigh], give out, make up (medicine), do without (followed by *with*).

Dis-perse' [L. *dispergere* (p.p. *dispersus*), to disperse; *dis-*, apart, *spargere*, to scatter], scatter. **Disper'sal.**

Dis-pir'it-ed [L. *dis-*, to imply reversal, and **Spirited**], discouraged.

Dis-place' [L. *dis-*, apart, and **Place**], put out of place, take the place of. **Displace'ment.**

Dis-play' [O.F. *desployer*, to unfold; L. *dis-*, apart, *plicāre*, to fold], make a show; a show.

Dis-please' (s=z) [L. dis-, to imply reversal, and **Please**], offend.

Dis-port' (oneself) [L. dis-, away, portāre, to carry], sport, play.

Dis-po'sal (s=z), arrangement, getting rid of, control, management.

Dis-pose' [O.F .dis-, apart, poser, to place], set in order, bestow, part with.

Dis-po-si'tion [L. dis-, apart, pōnere (p.p. positus), to place], arrangement, temperament.

Dis-pos-sess' [L. dis-, to imply reversal, and **Possess**], put out of possession.

Dis'pro-por'tion [L. dis-, apart, and **Proportion**], want of proportion. **Dispropor'-tionate.**

Dis-prove' (ove=oov) [L. dis-, to imply reversal, and **Prove**], prove to be false.

Dis'pu-tant, one who engages in a dispute.

Dis-pute' [L. dis-, apart, putāre, to think], argue against, discuss, call in question; debate, quarrel. **Disputa'tion.**

Dis-qual'i-fy (a=aw) [L. dis-, to imply reversal, and **Qualify**], make unfit, pronounce unfit.

Dis-qui'et [L. dis-, to imply reversal, and **Quiet**], uneasiness.

Dis'qui-si'tion [L. disquīrere (p.p. disquīsītus), to examine; dis-, apart, quærere, to seek], formal inquiry into or discussion of a subject.

Dis-re-gard' [L. dis-, to imply reversal, and **Regard**], pay no heed to, neglect.

Dis-rel'ish [L. dis-, to imply reversal, and **Relish**], distaste.

Dis-re-pair' [L. dis-, implying reversal, and **Repair**], bad condition from want of repairs.

Dis-rep'u-ta-ble [L. dis-, to imply reversal, and **Reputable**], of bad repute, low.

Dis-re-spect' [L. dis-, to imply reversal, and **Respect**], want of respect, discourtesy.

Dis-robe' [L. dis-, to imply reversal, and **Robe**], undress.

Dis-rup'tion [L. dis-, apart, rumpere (p.p. ruptus), to break], a breaking asunder. **Disrup'tive.**

Dis-sat'is-fy [L. dis-, to imply reversal, and **Satisfy**], fail to satisfy.

Dis-sect' [L. dis-, apart, secāre (p.p. sectus), to cut], cut into separate parts. **Dissec'tion.**

Dis-sem'ble [L. dis-, away, simulāre, to pretend], hide under false seeming.

Dis-sem'in-ate [L. dis-, apart, semināre, to sow; semen, seed], spread, scatter.

Dis-sen'sion, disagreement, strife.

Dis-sent' [L. dis-, apart, sentīre, to feel], disagreement; differ in opinion.

Dis-sent'er, one who dissents, esp. from the doctrines of an established church.

Dis-sen'tient (ti=sh), declaring dissent; one who expresses disagreement.

Dis-ser-ta'tion [L. dissertāre (p.p. dissertātus), to debate; dis-, apart, and serere, to join], argumentative discourse.

Dis-sev'er [O.F. dessevrer; L. dis-, asunder, and **Sever**], sever, divide.   [disagreeing.

Dis'sid-ent [L. dis-, apart, sedēre, to sit],

Dis-sim'i-lar [L. dis-, implying reversal, and similis, like], unlike.

Dis-sim'u-late [L. dis-, to imply reversal, and **Simulate**], put on a false appearance, pretend not to feel or have. **Dissimula'-tion.**

Dis-si-pa'tion [L. dissipāre (p.p. dissipātus), to disperse; dis-, apart, and L. sipāre, to throw], scattering, wasteful spending, frivolous amusement, intemperance.

Dis-so'ci-ate (c=sh) [L. dis-, apart, and sociāre, to associate; socius, a companion], separate, disconnect.   [conduct.

Dis'so-lute [see **Dissolve**], loose in morals and

Dis-so-lu'tion, act of dissolving, death.

Dis-solve' [L. dis-, apart, and solvere (p.p. solūtus), to loosen], separate into parts, break up, melt in liquid (as salt in water), liquefy, disappear.

Dis'son-ance [L. dis-, apart, and sonāre, to sound], discord. **Dis'sonant.**

Dis-suade' (u=w) [L. dis-, apart, and suadēre, to persuade], advise against.

Dis'taff [O.E. distæf, distaff; Low G. diesse, a bunch of flax on a distaff; O.E. stæf, a staff], staff from which wool or flax is drawn in spinning by hand.

Dis'tance [L. dī- (for dis-), apart, and stāre (pr.p. stans), to stand], space between two places, state of being far away; leave behind (as in a race).

Dis-taste' [L. dis-, to imply reversal, and **Taste**], dislike.

Dis-tem'per [L. dis-, apart, temperāre, to regulate], disease of dogs, preparation of paint tempered with weak size.

Dis-tend' [L. dis-, apart, tendere, to stretch], stretch from within. **Disten'tion.**

Dis'tich [Gk. di- (dis-), double, and stichos, a line], two lines of verse, couplet.

Dis-til' [L. dis-, apart, and stillāre, to drop], fall in drops, turn to vapour by heat and condense by cold.

Dis-til'ler-y, works where distilling of alcoholic spirits is carried on.

Dis-tinct' [see **Distinguish**], marked, different.

Dis-tinc'tion, difference, eminence, honour.

Dis-tin'guish [L. dis-, apart, and stinguere (p.p. stinctus), to extinguish], mark off, see differences, to honour.

Dis-tort' [L. dis-, apart, and torquēre (p.p. tortus), to twist], twist out of shape.

Dis-tract' [L. dis-, apart, and trahere (p.p. tractus), to draw], draw away (the mind, etc.). **Distrac'tion.**

Dis-train' [L. dī- (for dis), apart, and stringere (p.p. strictus), to draw tight], seize (goods) for debt. **Distraint'.**

Dis-tress' [O.F. destrece; see **Distrain**], misery, distraining; cause pain.

Dis-trib'ute [L. dis-, apart, and tribuere (p.p. tribūtus), to assign], divide among several. **Distrib'utive.**

Dis'trict [M.L. districtus, jurisdiction, from distringere; see **Distrain**], defined portion of a state, town, etc., tract of land of undefined extent.

Dis-trust' [L., *dis-* to imply reversal, and Trust], want of trust ; have no trust in.

Dis-turb' [L. *dis-*, apart, and *turbāre*, to disorder ; *turba*, a crowd], throw into disorder, take away calmness, interrupt.

Dis-turb'ance, disquiet, tumult.

Dis-u'nion [L. *dis-*, to imply reversal, and Union], lack of, or end of, union.

Dis-use' (*s* sharp) [L. *dis-*, to imply reversal, and Use], cessation of use.

Dis-use' (*s*=*z*), cease to use.

Di-syl'la-ble, Dis-syl'la-ble [Gk. *dī-* (for *dis-*), twice, *syllabē*, a syllable], word of two syllables. Disyllab'ic. [digging.

Ditch [O.E. *dīc*], long, narrow hole made by

Dith'y-ramb [Gk. *dithyrambos*, hymn in honour of Bacchus], poem written in wild, enthusiastic strains.

Dit'to [It. *ditto*, *detto*, that which has been said ; L. *dīcere* (p.p. *dictus*), to say], same as aforesaid.

Dit'ty [O.F. *dité*, ditty ; L. *dictātum*, neut. of *dictātus*, p.p. of *dictāre*, to dictate], little poem to be sung.

Di-ur'nal [L. *diurnālis*, daily ; *diēs*, a day], relating to the daytime, daily.

Di-va-ga'tion [L. *dī-* (for *dis-*), apart, *vagāri* (p.p. *vagātus*), to wander], wandering about.

Div-an' [Pers. *dēvān*, a tribunal ; Arab. *dīvān*, a tribunal, a royal court], council of state (in some Eastern countries), fixed low sofa.

Dive [O.E. *dȳfan*, to immerse], plunge head foremost.

Di-verge' [L. *dī-* (for *dis-*), apart, and Verge], extend or go from the same point in different directions. Diver'gence.

Di'vers [L. *dī-* (for *dis-*), apart, and *vertere* (p.p. *versus*), to turn], several, various.

Div-erse', Di-verse' [see Divers], different.

Di-ver'si-fy [L. *dīversus*, diverse, *facere*, to make ; see Divers], give variety to.

Di-ver'sion, act of turning from, amusement.

Di-ver'si-ty, variety.

Di-vert' [L. *dī-* (for *dis-*), apart, *vertere* (p.p. *versus*), to turn], turn aside, amuse.

Di-vest' [L. *dī-* (for *dis-*), apart, and *vestīre*, to clothe], strip, deprive.

Di-vide' [L. *dīvidere* (p.p. *dīvīsus*), to divide, part asunder, give in shares.

Div'i-dend, number to be divided, share of a sum divided (debts, profits, etc.) that falls to each person.

Div-i-na'tion, foreseeing of events.

Di-vine' [L. *dīvīnus* ; allied to *dīvus*, *deus*, god], of or belonging to God, godlike ; foretell, guess, detect.

Di-vin'i-ty, nature of God ; a god ; science which treats of God.

Di-vis'i-ble (*s*=*z*), that can be divided.

Di-vis'ion (*si*=*zh*), act of dividing, state of being divided ; body of soldiers.

Di-vorce' [L. *dīvortere*, same as *dīvertere* ; see Divert], separation by law of husband and wife ; put away.

Di-vulge' [L. *dī-* (for *dis-*), apart, and *vulgāre*, to publish ; *vulgus*, the people], disclose, tell (a secret).

Diz'zy [O.E. *dysig*, stupid], having a whirling feeling in the head. Diz'ziness. [cheat.

Do (*o*=*oo*) [O.E. *dón*, to do], perform, act,

Do'cile [L. *docēre*, to teach], easily taught. Docil'ity.

Dock [1] [O.E. *docce*], weed.

Dock [2] [Flem. *dok*, a rabbit-hutch], enclosure for an accused person in court.

Dock [3] [Du. *docke*, a harbour], basin for shipping, closed siding at railway station.

Dock [4] [Icel. *dockr*, a stumpy tail], cut short.

Dock'et [perh. allied to Dock [4]], label or endorsement containing a summary of a document.

Doc'tor [L. *doctor*, a teacher ; *docēre*, to teach], highest university title of honour for the learned, physician ; treat medically, tamper with.

Doc'trine [L. *doctrīna*, learning ; see Doctor], that which is taught, principle of faith.

Doc-trin-aire', one who holds a theory and attempts to apply it without considering suitability of circumstances.

Doc'u-ment [L. *docēre*, to teach], original or official paper. [trick.

Dodge [?], avoid by starting aside ; cunning

Doe [O.E. *dá*, perh. fr. L. *dāma*, a deer], female deer.

Doff [short for *do off*], take off.

Dog [O.E. *docga*], domestic animal of many kinds ; follow closely.

Doge (*dōj*) [It. *doge*, form of *doce*, a duke ; L. *dux* (*duc-is*), a leader], chief magistrate in the republics of Venice and Genoa.

Dog'ged, obstinately determined.

Dog'ger-el [?], loose, irregular, trivial verse.

Dog'ma [Gk. *dogma*, an opinion], that which is held as undoubtedly true.

Dog-mat'ic, asserting positively. Dog'matism. [napkin.

Doi'ly, Doyley [fr. name of inventor], small

Doit [Du. *duit*], very small sum or coin.

Dole [1] [O.E. *dál*, variant of Deal], that which is dealt out, alms.

Dole [2] [L. *dolēre*, to grieve], grief.

Dole'ful, sorrowful.

Doll [fr. *Doll*, for Dorothy], toy man, woman, or child.

Dol'lar [Du. *daler* ; Ger. *thaler* (short for *Joachimsthaler*, made from silver found in *Joachimsthal*, Joachimsdale], coin of the U.S.A. and other countries.

Dol'man [Turk. *dolaman*], kind of robe open in front.

Dol'men [F., perh. fr. Corn. *doll*, a hole ; *men*, stone], two upright stones with a third across them.

Dol'o-mite [F. geologist, *Dolomieu*], kind of rock found in the Tyrol.

Dol'or-ous [see Dole [2]], sorrowful.

Dol'phin [earlier *delphin* ; Gk. *delphis*, a dolphin], small kind of whale.

Dolt (*ō*) [perh. fr. Dull], blockhead.

Do-main' [L. *dominicus*, belonging to a lord ; *dominus*, a lord], territory governed, estate.

Dome [It. *duomo*, a cathedral; L. *domus*, a house], arched roof like a half-sphere.

Do-mes′tic [L. *domus*, a house], belonging to or fond of home, tame.

Do-mes′ti-cate, accustom to home life, tame.

Dom-es-ti′ci-ty, home life. [residence.

Dom′i-cile [L. *domus*, a house], place of

Dom′i-nant [L. *dominans* (*-antis*), pr.p. of *domināri*, to rule], ruling, fifth tone of the musical scale. **Domina′tion**.

Dom′i-nate [L. *domināri* (p.p. *dominātus*), to rule, *dominus*, a lord], to rule.

Dom-i-neer′ [Du. *domineren*; L. *domināri*, to rule], rule insolently.

Dom′in-ie [fr. vocative ot L. *dominus*, a master], Scots name for schoolmaster.

Do-min′ion [L. *dominus*, a lord], power of governing, country which is governed.

Dom′i-no [F. *domino*, perh. fr. L. *dominus*, a lord], kind of mask, dotted piece of ivory used in a game.

Don [short for *do on*], put on.

Don [Sp. *don*; L. *dominus*, a lord], Spanish title. [gift.

Do-na′tion [L. *dōnāre* (p.p. *dōnātus*), to give],

Don′jon [old spelling of **Dungeon**], chief tower of a castle.

Don′key [perh. fr. **Dun**,[2] with double dim.], ass.

Do′nor [L. *dōnāre*, to give], giver.

Doom [O.E. *dōm*], sentence by a judge, fate; condemn.

Door (*oo*=*ō*) [O.E. *duru*], entrance way, frame of boards in an entrance.

Dope [Du. *doop*, sauce], stupefying drink; to drug (slang).

Dor′ic [dialect of ancient Greece, Gk. *Dorikos*], an order of architecture; rustic, simple.

Dor′mant [O.F. *dormant*, pr.p. of *dormir*, to sleep], sleeping, unexercised (of a right), lying inactive.

Dor′mer [L. *dormīre*, to sleep], upright window in a sloping roof.

Dor′mi-to-ry [L. *dormīre*, to sleep], sleeping-room for several. [back.

Dor′mouse [perh. fr. F. *dormir*, to sleep, and **Mouse**], mouse-like animal which sleeps through the winter.

Dor′sal [L. *dorsum*, the back], on or near the back.

Do′ry [also *John Dory*. *Dory* probably from F. *dorée*, fem. p.p. of *dorer*, to gild], kind of fish.

Dose (*s*=*ss*) [Gk. *dosis*, a giving, *didonai*, to give], quantity of medicine to be taken at one time; give medicine to.

Dot [O.E. *dott*, head of a boil], small point as made with a pen.

Do′tage [fr. **Dote**], childishness of old age.

Do′tard, one whose mind is weakened by age.

Dote [cf. M. Du. *doten*], be foolishly fond.

Doub′le [L. *duplus*, double; *duo*, two, and *-plus*, allied to *plēnus*, full], twofold; fold in two, multiply by two, turn in running.

Doub′let [see **Double**], close-fitting garment for men, one of two words of same origin but different in sense.

Doub-loon′ [Sp. *doblon*; *doblo*, double; see **Double**], Sp. gold coin, double of a pistole.

Doubt [O.F. *doute* (n.) *douter* (vb.); allied to L. *dubius*, doubtful], unsettled state of belief; be unresolved, question the truth of.

Dou-ceur′ (*ou*=*oo*) [F. *douceur*, sweetness], gratuity, tip.

Douche (*oosh*) [F. *douche*; It. *doccia*, a water-pipe], jet of water applied to the body.

Dough (*doh*) [O.E. *dáh*], paste of bread.

Dough′ty [O.E. *dohtig*; *dugan*, to be worth], strong and brave. **Dough′tiness**.

Dove (*ove*=*ŭv*) [perh. cogn. with O.E. *dúfan*, to plunge into], kind of pigeon.

Dove′cot or **-cote** (*ove*=*ŭv*), house for pigeons.

Dove′tail (*o*=*ŭ*), kind of interlocking joint; to join by such.

Dow′a-ger [O.F. *douagere*, dowager; *douage*, an endowment], titled widow who has been succeeded in her title.

Dow′dy [obs. *dowd*, a slut], shabby, lacking in smartness.

Dow′er [O.F. *douaire*, dower; L. *dōtāre*, to endow], provision for a widow on a husband's death. **Dow′erless**.

Dow′las [fr. *Doulas*, in Brittany], kind of coarse linen.

Down [O.N. *dún*, down], outgrowth of fine hair, etc., from animals and plants.

Down (mostly in pl.) [O.E. *dún*, a hill; cf. Irish *dún*, Gael. *dun*, W. *din*, a hill-fort], hillock of sand, wavy grassy upland.

Down [corruption of *adown*; O.E. *of dúne*, of the hill], from higher to lower.

Down′right, plain, absolute.

Dow′ry [fr. O.F. as **Dower**], bride's portion on her marriage.

Dox-ol′o-gy [Gk. *doxa*, glory, *legein*, to speak], short hymn or prayer of praise to God.

Doze [cf. Dan. *döse*, to make dull; O.N. *dúsa*, to doze], sleep lightly, be half-asleep.

Doz′en (*o*=*ŭ*) [O.F. *dozeine*; L. *duodecim*, twelve], set of twelve.

Drab [F. *drap*, cloth], colour between gray and brown.

Drachm, **Dram** [L. *drachma*; Gk. *drachme* (used both as weight and coin); Gk. *drassesthai*, to grasp], small weight.

Dra-con′i-an [Gk. legislator, *Dracōn*], harsh, cruel.

Draff [M.E. *draf*], dregs, dregs of malt after brewing.

Draft [see **Draught**], written order for payment of money, soldiers detached from an army.

Drag [perh. variant of **Draw**], draw slowly along; retarding contrivance fixed to a wheel in going downhill.

Drag′gle [see **Drag**], hang trailing in mud, etc., lag in the rear.

Drag′o-man [F. *dragoman*; O. Arab. *tar-gumān*, dragoman], an interpreter.

Drag′on [Gk. *dracōn*, dragon], winged monster in fable. [soldier.

Dra-goon′ [F. *dragon*, carbine], cavalry

C *

Drain [O.E. *dréahnian*, cogn. with **Dry**], draw off or flow off by degrees; channel for drawing off.

Drake [cf. Ger. dial. *draak*], male of the duck.

Dram [see **Drachm**], drachm, as much spirits as is drunk at once.

Dram'a [Gk. *drama*; *draein*, to do], literary composition for acting. **Dra-mat'ic, Dram'atize.**

Drape [F. *drap*, cloth], cover with or arrange folds of cloth.

Dra'per, one who sells cloth. **Dra'pery.**

Dras'tic [Gk. *drasticos*, fr. *draein*, to draw], severe, violent.

Draught (*draft*) [M.E. *draht*; O.E. *dragan*, to draw], act of drawing or pulling, liquor drunk at once, sketch, depth to which a floating ship sinks, current of air, (pl.) game on a checkered board. **Draughts'-man, Draught'iness.**

Draw [O.E. *dragan*], pull out or along, sketch.

Draw'back, hindrance, excise duty paid back.

Draw'bridge, bridge which can be raised or turned aside.

Draw'er, box in a case from which it may be drawn.

Draw'ing-room [contracted from *with-drawing*-room], room to which company *withdraws* from the dining-room.

Drawl (freq. of **Draw**], speak in a slow dragging way.

Dray [O.E. *drœge*, fr. *dragan*, to draw], strong low cart.

Dread [M.E. *dreden*, *draeden*], fear; to fear.

Dread'nought (*ough=aw*), kind of large modern battleship.

Dream [cf. Ger. *traum*], vision in sleep; have dreams.

Drear'y (*ea=ee*) [O.E. *dréorig*, sad; *dréor*, gore], cheerless. **Drea'riness.**

Dredge [O.E. *dragan*, to draw], drag (from the bottom of the sea, etc.).

Dredge [fr. obs. *dredge*, sweetmeat; O.F. *dragée*], sprinkle flour, etc.

Dregs [cf. Icel. *dregg*, pl. *dreggjar*, dregs], grounds.

Drench [O.E. *drencan*, causative of *drincan*, to drink], wet thoroughly.

Dress [O.F. *dresser*, fr. L. *dīrigere* (p.p. *directus*), to direct], clothes, a gown; clothe, prepare for use, treat (wounds) with bandages, etc.

Dress'er, hospital assistant who dresses wounds.

Dress'er [O.F. *dresseur*; *dresser*, to dress], low cupboard for dishes, etc.

Drib'ble [freq. of *drib*, obs. form of **Drip**], fall, or let fall, in drops.

Drift [O.E. *drífan*, to drive], be driven (as) by wind or water; that which is driven, general meaning.

Drill [1] [Du. *drillen*, to pierce, to train soldiers], boring tool, regular exercise for training, furrow; to bore, exercise regularly.

Drill [2] [earlier *drilling*; Ger. *drillich*; L. *trilix*, fr. *tri-*, three, and *licium*, a thread; linen fabric.

Drink [O.E. *drincan*], liquid to be swallowed; swallow liquid.

Drip [O.E. *dryppan*], fall in drops.

Drive [O.E. *drífan*], force, rush, convey in a carriage; journey in a carriage, driving road.

Driv'el [O.E. *dreflian*], slaver, talk weak nonsense.

Driv'er, wooden-headed golf-club for driving long distances.

Driz'zle [O.E. *dréosan*, to drip], rain in very fine drops.

Droll (*ō*) [F. *drôle*, a waggish fellow; etym. doubtful], queer, comic. **Droll'ery** (*ō*).

Drom'e-da-ry [L. *dromas*; L.L. *dromedārius*; Gk. *dromas*, a runner], a swift camel of the Arabian breed, usually one-humped.

Drone [O.E. *dran*, *drœn*], male bee, lazy person, part of a bagpipe, monotonous utterance; make deep monotonous sounds.

Droop [O.N. *drūpa*], to sink or hang down.

Drop [O.E. *dropa*], liquid globule, sudden descent; pour in drops, let fall, have done with (a person).

Drop'sy [formerly *ydropsie*; Gk. *hydrōps*, fr. *hydōr*, water], unnatural collection of water in any part of the body.

Drosh'ky, Dros'ky [Russ. *drozhki*, dim. of *drogi*, a waggon], Russian low four-wheeled carriage, German cab.

Dross [O.E. *drós*], waste from metals in smelting, refuse.

Drought [O.E. *drúgad*, fr. *drýge*, dry], dryness.

Drove [see **Drive**], animals driven in a body.

Drown [perh. fr. *drunken*, pp. of **Drink**; cf. M. Dan. *drukne*, to drown; O.N. *drukna*, to sink, to be drowned], drench, perish or cause to perish in water.

Drow'sy (*s=z*) [prob. cogn. with O.E. *drusian*, to be sluggish], sleepy.

Drub'bing [perh. fr. Arab. *darb*, a beating with a stick], sound beating.

Drudge [perh. cogn. with O.E. *dréogan*, to work, to endure], one who does hard, tiresome work; work as a drudge. **Drud'gery.**

Drug [F. *drogue*, a drug; etym. dub.], substance used as a medicine.

Drug'get [F. *droguet*; etym. doubtful], coarse woollen cloth.

Drug'gist, one who buys and sells drugs.

Drum [cf. Du. *trom*; imit.], musical instrument, small cylindrical box, part of the ear.

Drunk'ard [E.], one who takes too much strong drink. **Drunk'enness.**

Drupe [L. *drūpa*; Gk. *dryppa*, an over-ripe olive], stone-fruit.

Dry [O.E. *drýge*], having little or no moisture; free or become free from moisture.

Dry'ad [Gk. *dryas* (*dryad-os*), a dryad; *drys*, a tree], wood-nymph.

Dry'salt-er, dealer in dyes, chemicals, etc.

Du'al [L. *duālis*, dual; *duo*, two], consisting of two, twofold. **Du'alism.**

Dub [?], confer knighthood on, entitle.

Dub'bin, Dub'bing [fr. **Dub**], grease for leather.

Du'bi-ous [L. *dubiōsus, dubius*, dubious; *duo*, two], uncertain. **Dubi'ety.**

Du'cal, of or connected with a duke.

Duc'at [It. *ducato*, a ducat, a duchy, fr. L.L. *ducātus* (duchy of Apulia)], coin, either of gold or silver (no longer in use).

Duch'ess [F. *duchesse*; Late L. *ducissa*; see **Duke**], wife of a duke, female sovereign of a duchy.

Duch'y [O.F. *duché*; Late L. *ducātus*; see **Duke**], dominion of a duke.

Duck [O.E. *duce*], water-fowl.

Duck [Du. *doeck*, canvas], kind of coarse cloth.

Duck [M.E. *d(o)uke*], lower the head suddenly.

Duct [L. *ducere* (p.p. *ductus*), to lead], tube for conveying liquid, canal in body.

Duc'tile [L. *ducere* (p.p. *ductus*), to lead], easily led, that can be drawn out. **Duc'til'ity.**

Dud [a war-word], a shell that has not exploded, ineffective person.

Dud'geon [?], anger, displeasure.

Due [O.F. *deü*, fem. *deüe* (p.p. of *devoir*), to owe], owing; that which is owing.

Du'el [F. fr. L. *duellum* (old form of *bellum*, war), *duo*, two], fight with weapons between two.

Du-en'na [Sp. fr. *dueña*, fr. L. *domina*, mistress], chief lady-in-waiting on the Queen of Spain, elderly woman in charge of the girls of a Spanish family, chaperon.

Du-et' [Ital. *duetto*, dim. of *duo*, a duet; L. *duo*, two], musical composition for two performers.

Duf'fel, Duf'fle [fr. *Duffel* in Brabant], coarse woollen cloth.

Dug-out [see **Dig**], canoe made by hollowing tree-trunk; underground shelter from fire of the enemy.

Duke [F. *duc*; L. *dux* (*duc-is*) a leader], in Britain one of the highest order of nobility, in some countries a reigning sovereign. **Duke'dom.**

Dul'cet [L. *dulcis*, sweet], sweet to the ear.

Dul'ci-mer [L. *dulce melos*, sweet sound], stringed musical instrument.

Dull [M.E., cf. O.E. *dol*, mad], stupid, blunt, not clear; make or become dull.

Dulse (*se=ss*) [Irish and Gael. *duileasg*], seaweed that may be eaten.

Du'ly, as it (anything) ought to be, at the proper time.

Dumb [O.E. *dumb*], not able to speak, silent.

Dumb'bells, double-headed weights used in gymnastics.

Dum-found', Dumb-found', Dum-found'er [fr. **Dumb** and **Confound**], strike dumb with astonishment.

Dum'my [fr. **Dumb**], dumb person; sham article.

Dump [cf. Dan. *dumpe*; Norw. *dumpa*, to fall plump], throw down, unload; heap.

Dumps [?], low spirits.

Dump'ling [double dim. of prov. E. *dump*, a lump], pudding of suet paste.

Dump'y [?], short and stout.

Dun[1] [perh. allied to **Din**], press for payment; one who duns.

Dun[2] [O.E. *dun*; cf. Irish and Gael. *donn*; W. *dwn*], greyish brown.

Dunce [fr. John *Duns* Scotus], one slow at learning.

Dune [O.Du. *düne*; akin to O.E. *dún*, a down], sandhill on the sea-coast.

Dun'geon [F. *donjon*; Late L. *domnio*, a dungeon-tower], place of confinement usually underground.

Du-o-de'ci-mo (*é*) [L. *duodecimus*, twelfth], book-size with each leaf the twelfth of a printing-sheet.

Du'o-logue [Gk. *duo*, two, *logos*, speech], conversation between two.

Dupe [perh. F. *dupe*, a hoopoe (a S. European bird)], one who is cheated; impose on.

Du'pli-cate [L. *duplicāre* (p.p. *duplicātus*), to double; *duplex*, twofold], double; that which is exactly like something else; make a copy of.

Du-pli'ci-ty [L. *duo*, two, *plicāre*, to fold], double conduct, acting deceitfully.

Dur'a-ble [L. *durus*, hard], lasting. **Dura-bil'ity.**

Du'rance [F. *durance*, duration; *durer*, to last], imprisonment.

Du-ra'tion [L. *dūrāre* (p.p. *dūrātus*), to last], time of lasting.

Dur'bar [Pers. and Hind. *darbar*, a court], state reception in India.

Du-resse', Du-ress' [obs. F. *duresse*; L. *durus*, hard], imprisonment, hardship.

Dusk [M.E. *dosc*, fr. O.E. *dox*, cf. Norw. *dusk*, mist], twilight.

Dusk'y, partially dark, dark-coloured.

Dust [O.E. *dúst*], powdered earth, etc.; sprinkle with dust or powder, remove dust.

Du'teous [see **Due**], obedient.

Du'ti-a-ble, liable to customs duty.

Du'ty [see **Due**], what one ought to do, respect, tax.

Dwarf [O.E. *dweorh*], one much below the common size; make small, make to appear small.

Dwell [O.E. *dwellan*, to lead astray, *dwelian*, to delay, to dwell], live in a place, continue; (with *on*), treat at length in speech or writing.

Dwell'ing, house for living in.

Dwin'dle [obs. *dwine*; O.E. *dwinan*], become less.

Dye [O.E. *déag*], colouring matter; to colour.

Dy-nam'ics [Gk. *dynamicos*, powerful, *dynamis*, power], science of matter and force. [explosive.

Dyn'a-mite [Gk. *dynamis*, power], powerful

Dy'na-mo [Gk. *dynamis*, power], machine for producing electric currents.

Dyn'as-ty [Gk. *dynasteia*, lordship], race of sovereigns of the same family. **Dynas'tic.**

Dys'en-te-ry [Gk. *dys-*, bad, and *entera*, bowels], disease of the intestines.

Dys-pep'si-a [Gk. *dys-*, bad, and *peptein*, to cook], indigestion. **Dyspep'tic.**

E

Each [O.E. *ǽlc*, each (short for *ǽghwile*, aye-like, ever like)], every (one) taken separately.

Ea'ger (*g* hard), [F. *aigre*; L. *acris*, sharp], keen, impatiently desirous.

Ea'gle [O.F. *aigle*; L. *aquila*, eagle], large bird of prey.

Ea'gre [?], large tidal wave. [corn.

Ear [O.E. *éare*], organ of hearing; spike as of

Earl [O.E. *eorl*; cf. O.N. *jarl*], third title of nobility in Great Britain and Ireland.

Ear'ly [O.E. *árlíce*, early; *ar*, positive of *ǽr*, ere, *líc*, like], in good time or season, near the first, forward, not late.

Earn [O.E. *ge-earnian*], deserve or receive as wages. [seriousness.

Ear'nest [O.E. *eornust*], warmly eager;

Ear'nest [M.E. *ernes*, *erles*, *arles*; L. *arrha*, a pledge], a pledge.

Earth [O.E. *eorthe*], world, land, soil; to connect with the earth (wireless term).

Earth'en-ware, ware made of clay.

Earth'quake, shaking of the earth.

Ear'wig [O.E. *éarwicga*, fr. *éare*, ear, *wicga*, an earwig], kind of insect.

Ease (*s=z*) [O.F. *aise*; orig. unknown], freedom from pain, trouble, or constraint; to relieve, to relax. **Ease'ment**.

Ea'sel (*s=z*) [Du. *ezel*, an ass, also an easel], framework to hold a canvas upright.

East [O.E. *éastan*, *éast*], the quarter where the sun rises.

East'er [O.E. *éastre*, perh. fr. O.E. *Eostre*, the goddess of dawn or spring, in whose honour a yearly festival was held in April], time of year when Christ's resurrection is commemorated.

Ea'sy, comfortable, not difficult.

Eat [O.E. *etan*], take food; wear away.

Eaves [O.E. *efes*], overhanging edges of a roof.

Eaves'drop-per, secret listener.

Ebb [O.E. *ebba*], flowing back (of the tide, etc.), flow back.

Eb'o-ny [L. *hebeninus*; Gk. *ebeninos*, ebon], hard, black wood.

Eb-ul-li'tion [L. *ē*, out, *bullīre* (p.p. *bullītus*), to boil], a boiling up, outburst. **Ebul'lient**.

Ec-cen'tric [Gk. *ec*, out of, *centron*, centre], having the axis out from the centre, odd. **Eccentric'ity**.

Ec-cle'si-as'tic [Gk. *ecclesia*, an assembly, a church], clergyman or priest.

Ec-cle'si-as'tic-al, relating to church.

Ech'e-lon (*ch=sh*) [F. *échelon*; *échelle*, L. *scala*, a ladder], formation of troops in parallel divisions, each with its front clear of that in advance.

Ech-id'na (*ch=k*) [Gk. *echidna*, a viper], Australian animal like a hedgehog.

Ech'o [Gk. *ēchē*, sound], reflected sound; resound. [success.

É-clat' (*ai-kla'*) [F. *éclat*], brilliancy of

Ec-lec'tic [Gk. *eclecticos*; *ec*, out, and *legein*, to choose], selecting from various systems.

E-clipse' [Gk. *ec*, out, *leipein*, to leave], cutting off of the light of one of the heavenly bodies by some other body, loss of light; darken, throw into the shade, surpass.

E-clip'tic [see Eclipse], seeming path of the sun round the earth.

Ec'logue [Gk. *eclegein*, to select; see Eclectic], pastoral poem in which shepherds talk together.

E-con-om'ics (*ε=ee*) [see Economy], science dealing with the production and distribution of wealth.

E-con'o-my [Gk. *oicos*, a house, *nemein*, to manage], household management, orderly management, thrift. **Econom'ical**, **Econ'-omist**, **Econ'omize**.

Ec'sta-sy [Gk. *ec*, out, *stasis*, a standing], state of being beside oneself, excess of joy, fear, etc. **Ecstat'ic**.

Ec-u-men'ic-al, **Œc-u-men'ic-al** [Gk. *oicumenicos*, universal, *oicos*, a house], general, representing the Christian world.

Ec'ze-ma [Gk. *ek*, out, *zeein*, to bo'l], inflammation of the skin.

Ed'dy [?], small whirlpool.

Edge [O.E. *ecg*], cutting part of a knife, etc., border; move sideways. **Edg'ing**.

Ed'i-ble [L. *edere*, to eat], eatable.

E'dict [L. *ē*, out, *dicere* (p.p. *dictus*), to speak], public command by a supreme authority.

Ed'i-fice (*ice=iss*) [F. *édifice*; see Edify], a building.

Ed'i-fy [L. *œdēs*, a building, *facere*, to make], instruct and improve. **Edifica'tion**.

Ed'it [fr. noun Editor; L. *ē*, out, *dare*, to give], revise for publication. [time.

E-di'tion, copies of a work published at one

Ed'it-or, one who edits, one who conducts a newspaper or magazine. [editor.

Ed-it-o'ri-al, of an editor; article by an

Ed'u-cate [L. *educāre*, to rear, related to *edu-cēre*], train and instruct. **Educa'tion(al)ist**.

E-duce' [L. *ē*, out, *ducere*, to lead], draw out.

Eel [O.E. *ǽl*], long, worm-like fish.

Ee'ry, **Ee'rie** [M.E. *eri*, etym. doubtful], superstitiously fearful, weird.

Ef-face' [L. *ex*, out, *facies*, the face], rub or blot from a surface.

Ef-fect' [L. *ex*, out, *facere*, to make], that which springs from a cause, result, impression made, (pl.) goods; bring about.

Ef-fec'tive, producing an effect.

Ef-fec'tu-al, having the effect desired.

Ef-fem'in-ate [L. *ex*, thoroughly, *femina*, a woman], womanish. **Effem'inacy**.

Ef-fer-ves'ce [L. *ex*, out, *fervēre*, to boil], boil, bubble. **Efferves'cence**.

Ef-fete' [L. *effetus*, worn out by breeding], exhausted, worn out.

Ef-fi-ca-cy [see Effect], power to produce an effect. **Effica'cious**.

Ef-fi'cient (*ci=sh*) [see Effect], capable.

Ef'fi-gy [L. *effigiēs*; *ex*, out, *fingere*, to form], imitative figure.

Ef-flor-es'cence [L. *ex*, out, *florescere* (from *flos*, *floris*, a flower), to flourish], bursting into flower.

Ef´flu-ence [L. *effluere* (pr.p. *effluens*); *ex*, out, *fluere*, to flow], a flowing out.

Ef-flu´vi-um, (pl.) **-vi-a** [L. *ex*, out, *fluere*, to flow], that which flows out from a body invisibly, smell. [do.

Ef´fort [L. *ex*, out, *fortis*, strong], trying to

Ef-front´er-y (*o=ŭ*) [F. *effonterie*; L. *ex*, out, *frons* (*frontis*), the forehead], impudent boldness.

Ef-ful´gence [L. *effulgēre* (pr.p. *effulgens*), to shine forth; *ex*, out, *fulgēre*, to shine], shining brightness. **Efful´gent.**

Ef-fu´sion (*si=zh*) [L. *ex*, out, *fundere* (p.p. *fusus*, to pour], pouring out, literary production (spoken of with contempt).

Ef-fu´sive (*s=z*), gushing.

Eft [O.E. *efeta*, an eft], newt.

Egg [O.E. *ǣg*; cf. O.N. *egg*; Swed. *ägg*; Dan. *æg*, egg], germ, etc., laid by birds, fish, reptiles, insects, etc.

Egg [O.N. *eggja*, to goad], urge on.

Eg´lan-tine [O.F. *aiglent*; cf. L. *aculeus*, a prickle, dim. of *acus*, a needle], sweet-brier.

Eg´o-ism [F. *égoisme*, fr. L. *ego*, I], too great love of self. **Eg´oist.**

Eg´o-tism [L. *ego*, I], speaking too often of self. **Eg´otist.**

E-gre´gious [L. *ē*, out, *grex* (*greg-is*), a flock], notable (in a bad sense).

E´gress [L. *ēgredi* (p.p. *ēgressus*), to go out; *ē*, out, and *gradi*, to go], going out.

Eg´ret (or *e´gret*) [var. of **Aigrette**; O.H.G. *heigir*, a heron], kind of heron.

E-gypt-ol´o-gy, the study of the remains of ancient Egyptian civilization.

Ei´der [Swed. *ejder*; Icel. *æthar*, eider], northern sea-duck. **Ei´der-down.**

Eighth [O.E. *ahta*, eight], next in order after the seventh. **Eighteen.**

Eis-tedd´fod (*ei=ai*) [W. *eisteddfa*, to sit], congress of bards, Welsh musical festival.

E-jac´u-late [L. *ē*, out, *jaculum*, a dart; *jacere*, to throw], exclaim suddenly.

E-ject´ [L. *ējicere* (p.p. *ējectus*), *ē*, out, *jacere*, to throw], cast out. **Ejec´tion.**

Eke [O.E. *ēcan*], add to.

Eke [O.E. *ēac*, cf. Ger. *auch*], also.

E-lab´o-rate [L. *ē*, out, *laborāre*, to work], produce or improve on with labour; highly wrought. [lope.

E´land [Du. *eland*, an elk], S. African antelope.

E-lapse´ [L. *ē*, out, *lābī* (p.p. *lapsus*), to glide], slip away (as time).

E-las´tic [Gk. *elasticos*, propulsive, fr. *elaunein*, to drive], springing back, able to go back quickly to a former state; cord or string containing rubber. [bound.

E-las-ti´ci-ty, springiness, tendency to re-

E-la´tion [L. *efferre* (p.p. *ēlātus*), to lift up; *ē*, out, and *ferre*, to carry], raised spirits.

El´bow [O.E. *elboga*, *elnboga*, fr. *eln*, an arm, an ell, and *boga*, a bow], bend of the arm.

Eld [O.E. *eldo*, fr. *ald*, old], (archaic, poetic), old age, the olden time.

El´der [O.E. *eldra*, fr. *ald*, old], older; one who is older, office-bearer in some churches.

El´der [O.E. *ellærn*], tree with dark berries.

E-lect´ [L. *ē*, out, *legere* (p.p. *lectus*), to choose], choose; one of the chosen.

E-lec´tion, choice, right of choosing.

E-lec´tric, **E-lec´tri-cal** [Gk. *electron*, amber], caused by or containing electricity.

E-lec-tri´ci-ty, natural force which exhibits itself by attraction, repulsion, etc.

E-lec´tri-fy, cause electricity to pass through, to thrill.

E-lec-tro-cu´tion, killing by electricity.

E-lec´tron [Gk. *electron*, electron, amber], supposed to be the smallest component of matter, consisting of, or associated with, a charge of negative electricity.

E-lec´tu-ar-y [Late L. *electuārium*; perh. fr. Gk. *ecleichein*, to lick out], medicinal powder mixed with honey or syrup.

El-ee-mos´y-na-ry [Late L. *eleēmosyna*, alms], relating to alms.

El´e-gance [L. *ēlegans* (*ēlegantis*); tasteful; *ē*, out, and *legere*, to choose], beauty produced by art and good taste.

El´e-gy [Gk. *elegos*, a lament], song of mourning, a serious, sorrowful poem. **Elegi´ac.**

El´e-ment [L. *elementum*, a first principle], simple component of anything, (pl.) air, earth, water, and fire. **Elemen´tal.**

El-e-men´ta-ry, consisting of a single element, simple, primary.

El´e-phant [L. and Gk. *elephas*, an elephant], large animal of Asia and Africa. **Elephan´tine.**

El´e-vate [L. *ē*, out, *levāre*, to lighten; *levis*, light], raise. **Eleva´tion.**

El´e-va´tor, a lift.

E-lev´en [O.E. *endleofon*], one more than ten.

Elf, (pl.) **Elves** [O.E. *ælf*], fairy, tricky little person. **El´fin**, **El´fish.**

E-li´cit [L. *ēlicere* (p.p. *ēlicitus*); *ē*, out, *lacere*, to entice], draw out.

E-lide´ [L. *ēlīdere* (p.p. *ēlīsus*), to strike out; *ē*, out, *lædere*, to dash], drop out a vowel or syllable. **Elis´ion.**

El´i-gi-ble [L. *ēligere*, to choose out; see **Elect**], that may be chosen. **El´igibil´ity.**

E-lim´i-nate [L. *ēlimināre* (p.p. *ēlimīnātus*); *ē*, out, *limen* (*limin-is*), a threshold], throw out, cause to disappear. **Elim´ina´tion.**

É-lite´ (*ai-leet´*) [F.], select people in society.

E-lix´ir [Arab. *al iksīr*, the philosopher's stone; perh. fr. Gk. *xērion*, dry powder], preparation by which it was sought to change metals into gold, a drug or essence supposed to have the property of prolonging life.

Elk [O.E. *elch*, *alke*, an elk], large deer.

Ell [O.E. *eln*, a cubit; cogn. with L. *ulna*, a cubit, an elbow], measure; English ell is 45 inches.

El-lipse´ [Gk. *elleipsis*; *el-* (*en*), in, *leipein*, to leave], oval figure.

El-lip´sis, omission.

El-lip´tic-al, oval, having part omitted.

Elm [O.E. *elm*], timber tree.

El-o-cu´tion [L. *ē*, out, *loqui* (p.p. *locūtus*), to speak], art of managing the voice in public speaking.

E'long-ate [L. $\check{e}$, out, *longāre*, to lengthen; *longus*, long], lengthen. **Elonga'tion.**

E-lope' [A.F. *aloper*, perh. fr. M.E. *aleapen*, to run away], run away secretly.

El'o-quence [L. *ēloquī* (pr.p. *ēloquens*), to speak out; $\check{e}$, out, *loquī*, to speak], powerful persuasive speaking. **El'oquent.**

E-lu'ci-date [Late L. *ēlucidāre* (p.p. *ēlucidātus*); $\check{e}$, out, *lucidus*, clear], make clear, illustrate. **Elucida'tion.**

E-lude' [L. $\check{e}$, out, and *lūdere* (p.p. *lūsus*), to play], avoid or escape slyly.

E-lu'sive ($s=z$), escaping the grasp.

E-lys'ium [Gk. *elysion*, short for *Elysion pedion*, the Elysian plain], a paradise of the ancient Greeks, very happy place. **Elys'ian.**

E-ma'ci-a'tion [L. *ēmaciāre* (p.p. *emaciātus*); $\check{e}$, very, *macies*, leanness], great leanness.

Em'a-nate [L. $\check{e}$, out, *manāre* (p.p. *manātus*), to flow], flow or proceed from.

E-man'ci-pate [L. $\check{e}$, out, *mancipāre*, to transfer property; *manus*, the hand, and *capere*, to take], set free. **Eman'cipa'tor.**

E-mas'cu-late [L. $\check{e}$, from, *masculus*, male], weaken.

Em-, en- (in); see Appendix, Latin Prefixes.

Em-balm' (*al=ah*) [O.F. *em-*, in, F. *baume*, balm], preserve by use of spices, etc. **Embalm'ment.**

Em-bank'ment [O.F. *em-*, in; see **Bank**], a great wall of earth or stones, to retain water, etc.

Em-bar'go [Sp. *embargo*, a stoppage of ships; *em-*, in, *barra*, a bar], government order to forbid ships to sail, suspension of commerce.

Em-bark' [F. *embarquer*; L.L. *imbarcare*, *em=im-* (in-), in, *barca*, a bark], go or put on board.

Em-bar'rass [F. *embarrasser*, cogn. with **Bar**], hinder, make uncomfortable. **Embarr'assment.**

Em'bas-sy [O.F. *ambassée*; L. *ambactia*, an office], ambassador and those with him, his residence, his office.

Em-bed' [see **Bed**], to fix firmly in surrounding mass.

Em-bel'lish [O.F. *em-*, in, and *bel*, beautiful], to ornament.

Em'bers (O.E. *ǣmerge*, an ember], smouldering remains of a fire.

Em-bez'zle [O.F. *em-*, in, *besillier*, to maltreat], take by fraud for one's own use.

Em-bit'ter [*em-*, in, and **Bitter**], make bitter.

Em-bla'zon-ry [*em-*, in, and **Blazon**], heraldic decoration.

Em'blem [Gk. *em-*, in, on, *ballein*, to throw], visible sign of an idea. **Emblemat'ic.**

Em-bod'y [*em-*, in, and **Body**], to give form to an idea, to unite into one body.

Em-bold'en [*em-*, in, and **Bold**], to make bold.

Em-boss' [*em-*, in, and **Boss**], produce a raised pattern by blows or pressure.

Em-brace' [*em-*, in, and **Brace**], to clasp in the arms, to include, to accept; folding in the arms.

Em-bra'sure ($s=z$) [*em-*, in, M.F. *braser*, to slant aside], an opening widening from within for cannon in defence works.

Em-bro-ca'tion [Gk. *embrochē*, a lotion; *-em*, in, *brechein*, to wet], a liquid for rubbing a diseased part.

Em-broi'der [*em-*, in, F. *broder*, etc., orig. to work on the edge (*bord*), to decorate with needlework. **Embroi'dery.** [strife.

Em-broil' [*em-*, in; see **Broil**], to mix in

Em'bry-o [Gk. *embryon*, *em-*, in, and *bryein*, to swell], germ, young in early stage. **Embryon'ic.**

E-men-da'tion [L. *ēmendāre* (p.p. *ēmendātus*), remove errors from; $\check{e}$, from, *menda*, a fault], removal of errors from a book, etc.

Em'er-ald [Gk. *smaragdos*, an emerald], a green precious stone.

E-merge' [L. $\check{e}$, out, and *mergere* (p.p. *mersus*), to dip], to rise out of, to come forth. **Emerg'ence.**

E-mer'gen-cy, unexpected state of things, pressing need for action or decision.

Em'e-ry [F. *émeri(l)*; Gk. *smēris*, emery], a hard mineral in grains, used for polishing.

E-met'ic [Gk. *emeein*, to vomit], a medicine which causes vomiting.

Em'i-grant [L. *emigrans* (*-antis*), pr.p. of *ēmigrāre*, to emigrate], one who leaves a country to settle in another.

Em'i-grate [L. $\check{e}$, out, *migrāre* (p.p. *migrātus*), to wander], leave a country to settle in another. **Emigra'tion.**

Em'i-nence [L. *ēminēre* (pr.p. *ēminens*), to project; $\check{e}$, out; *minēre*, to project], high place.

Em'i-nent-ly, in a high degree.

Em-ir' (*ir=eer*) [Arab. *amīr*, a prince], Arab or Saracen prince or governor.

Em'is-sa-ry [see **Emit**], secret agent.

E-mit' [L. $\check{e}$, out, *mittere* (p.p. *missus*), to send], send out. **Emis'sion.**

Em'met [doublet of **Ant**], ant.

E-mol'lient [L. *ēmollīre* (pr.p. *ēmolliens*, *-entis*), to soften; $\check{e}$, very, *mollis*, soft], something laid on to soften or soothe; softening.

E-mol'u-ment [L. $\check{e}$, out, *molere*, to grind, or *mōlīri*, to work], profits arising from office or work.

E-mo'tion [L. $\check{e}$, out, *movēre* (p.p. *mōtus*), to move], moving of the mind, feeling.

Em-pan'el [O.F. *em-*, in, see **Panel**], to enrol (jury).

Em'per-or [L. *imperātor*, to command; *im-*, in, *parāre*, to make ready], sovereign of an empire.

Em'pha-sis [Gk. *emphasis*; *em-*, in, *phainein*, to show], stress laid on words.

Em-phat'ic, laying stress, forcible.

Em'pire [L. *imperium*, command], dominion usually of many different parts, absolute control.

Em-pir'ic [Gk. *empeiricos*; *em-*, in, *peira*, a trial], one who relies merely on experience, quack; relying on experience. **Empir'icism. Empir'ical.**

Em-place′ment [*em-*, in, and **Place**], act of placing, platform for guns.

Em-ploy′ [F. *employer*; L. *im-* (*in*), in, *plicare*, to fold], use, have in service.

Em-ploy′ee, Em-ploy-ee′, one employed by another.

Em-po′ri-um [Gk. *emporion*; *em-*, in, *poros*, a way], place of trade. [ity to.

Em-pow′er [*em-*, in, and **Power**], give author-

Em′press [O.F. *emperesse*; see **Emperor**], wife of an emperor.

Emp′ty [O.E. *œmtig*, *œmetig*, at leisure; *œmta*, *œmetta*, leisure], containing nothing.

Em-pyr-e′an [Gk. *empyros*, exposed to fire; *em-*, in, *pyr*, fire], the wide sky, whole extent of cosmic space. **Empyr′eal.**

E′mu [perh. fr. Port. *ema*, an ostrich], large Australian ostrich-like bird.

Em′u-late [L. *œmulāri* (p.p. *œmulātus*), to try to equal], try to equal or excel. **Emula′tion.** [equal or excel.

Em′u-lous [L. *œmulus*, emulous], eager to

E-mul′sion [L. *ē*, out, *mulgēre* (p.p. *mulsus*), to milk], oily substance mixed with water by means of gum, etc. [able to do.

En-a′ble [pref. *en*, causal, and **Able**], make

En-act′ [pref. *en*, in, and **Act**], make into law, act the part of. **Enact′ment.**

En-am′el [O.F. *esmail*; M.L. *smaltum*, enamel; Teut. orig. cogn. with **Smelt**], glassy substance used as a coating, hard covering of teeth.

En-am′our [O.F. *en amour*, in love; L. *in*, in, *amor*, love], inflame with love, charm.

En-cage′ [*en-*, in, and **Cage**], shut up in a cage.

En-camp′ [*en-*, in, and **Camp**], pitch tents for a camp. **Encamp′ment.** [chains.

En-chain′ [*en-*, in, and **Chain**], hold as with

En-chant′ [F. *enchanter*; L. *in*, in, and *canere* (p.p. *cantus*), to sing], charm greatly.

En-cir′cle [*en-*, in, and **Circle**], form a circle about.

En-clave′ [L. *in*, in ; *clavis*, a key], territory surrounded by foreign territories.

En-close′, [*en-*, in, and **Close**], inclose. **Enclo′sure.**

En-co′mi-um [Gk. *egcōmion*, a song of praise; *en-*, in, and *cōmos*, revelry], high praise. [surround.

En-com′pass (*o=ŭ*) [*en-*, in, and **Compass**],

En′core (nearly *ang′core*) [F. *encore*, still, again; perh. fr. L. (*in*) *hanc horam*, to this hour], call for repetition.

En-coun′ter [L. *in*, in ; *contra*, against], meet; a meeting; fight.

En-cour′age [*en-*, in, and **Courage**], give courage to. **Encour′agement.**

En-croach′ [O.F. *encrochier*; F. *en*, in, *croc*, a hook], intrude on.

En-cum′ber [*en-*, in, on, and **Cumber**], load, hinder. **Encum′brance.**

En-cy-clo-pæ′di-a (*œ=ee*) [Gk. *egcyclios paideia*, all-round instruction; *cyclos*, a circle, *paideia*, instruction], work treating of all branches of knowledge. **Encyclo-pæ′dic.**

End [O.E. *ende*], limit, extreme point; to stop.

En-dan′ger [*en-*, in, and **Danger**], bring into danger.

En-dear′ [*en-*, in, and **Dear**], render dear.

En-dea′vour [*en-*, in, F. *devoir*, duty], try.

En-dem′ic [Gk. *en-*, in, *dēmos*, a people], regularly present (said of disease).

En′dive [F. *endive*; L. *intibus*, endive], kind of chicory used for salad.

En-dorse′ [O.F. *endosser*; *en-*, in, and *dos* (L. *dorsum*), the back], write on the back of, to approve. **Endorse′ment.**

En-dow′ [*en-*, in, and F. *douer*; L. *in*, in, *dotāre*, to give a dowry; *dare*, to give], make provision for, to gift. **Endow′ment.**

En-due′ [O.F. *enduire*; L. *in*, in, and *ducere*, to lead], clothe or invest with.

En-dur′ance, power of holding out.

En-dure′ [O.F. *endurer*, *en-* (L. *in*), in, *durer* (L. *durāre*), to last], to last, bear up under.

En′e-my [L. *inimīcus*, unfriendly; *in*, not, *amīcus*, a friend], one who is against another.

En-er-get′ic, having energy, vigorous.

En′er-gy [Gk. *energeia*; *en-*, in, *ergon*, work], force, power of work. **En′ergize.**

En′er-vate [L. *ēnervāre* (p.p. *ēnervātus*); *ē*, out of, *nervus*, nerve], deprive of nerve or strength.

En-fee′ble [*en-* (causal) and **Feeble**], weaken.

En-fi-lade′ [F. *enfiler*, to string; *en-*, in, and *fil* (L. *filum*), a thread], artillery fire that sweeps line of troops from end to end.

En-force′ [*en-*, in, and **Force**], compel, put in force.

En-fran′chise [*en-*, in, and **Franchise**], set free, give a vote to. **Enfran′chisement.**

En-gage′ [F. *engager*; *en-*, in, and **Gage**, a pledge], bind by a promise, occupy, bring troops into battle. **Engage′ment.**

En-ga′ging, attractive.

En-gen′der [F. *engendrer*; L. *in*, in, *generāre*, to breed], sow the seeds of, bring about.

En′gine [L. *ingenium*, skill, also an invention], compound machine driven by steam, gas, air, etc.

En-gi-neer′ [L.L. *ingeniator*; see **Engine**], one who plans or constructs engines, heavy machinery, railways, bridges, etc., one in charge of an engine; contrive, guide and carry through. [texture of.

En-grain′ [*en-*, in, and **Grain**], work into the

En-graft′ [*en-*, in, and **Graft**], to subject to the process of grafting.

En-grave′ [*en-*, in, and **Grave** 2], cut with a graving instrument.

En-gra′ving, print taken from an engraved plate or block.

En-gross′ [A.F. *engrosser*, to write large; L. *grossus*, thick], take up completely, write (a deed) in full for signature.

En-gulf′ (*en-*, in, and **Gulf**], swallow up as in a gulf.

En-hance′ [O.F. *enhaucer*; L. *in*, in ; Late L. *altiāre*, to lift], increase.

En-ig'ma [Gk. *ainigma*; *ainos*, a fable], puzzle, something difficult of explanation. **Enigmat'ical.**

En-join' [F. *enjoindre*; L. *in*, in, *jungere*, to join], lay upon as a command.

En-joy' [O.F. *enjoier*; *en*, in, *joie*, joy], take pleasure in.

En-kin'dle [*en-*, in or on, and **Kindle**], set on fire.

En-large' [*en-*, in or on, and **Large**], make larger. **Enlarge'ment.**   [to.

En-light'en [*en-*, in, and **Lighten**[1]], give light

En-list' [*en-*, in, and **List**[1]], enroll, engage for military or other service.   [to.

En-li'ven [*en-*, in; see **Life**], to give more life

En'mi-ty [L. *in-*, not, *amīcus*, a friend], strong feeling against.

En-no'ble [*en-*, in, and **Noble**], to make noble.

En'nui (nearly *ang-nwee*) [F. *ennui*; L. *in ōdiō*, in disgust: see **Annoy**], a weary, listless feeling.   [crime.

E-nor'mi-ty, state of being abnormal; a great

E-nor'mous [L. *enormis*; *ē*, out of, *norma*, rule], huge.

E-nough' (*ough=uff*) [O.E. *genóg*; *genĕah*, it suffices], sufficient.

En-quire' (see **Inquire**). **Enqui'ry.**

En-rage' [O.F. *enrager*; *en-*, in, and **Rage**], to put into a rage.

En-rap'ture [*en-*, in, and **Rapture**], to carry away with delight.

En-rich' [*en-*, in, and **Rich**], to make rich.

En-rol', En-roll' [*en-*, in, and **Roll**], to enter in a list or on rolls.

En-sconce' [*en-*, in, and **Sconce**], to place snugly or securely.

En-shrine' [*en-*, in, and **Shrine**], to enclose in a shrine, to preserve as sacred.

En'sign (*sign=sine*) [L. *in*, on, *signum*, a mark], a flag, formerly an infantry officer.

En'sil-age [Sp. *ensilar*, to store underground; *silo*, a pit for storing], storing of green fodder underground, fodder thus preserved.

En-slave' [*en-*, in, and **Slave**], to bring into slavery. **Enslave'ment.**   [trap.

En-snare' [*en-*, in, and **Snare**], to catch in a

En-sue' [L. *insequī*; *in*, on, and *sequī*, to follow], to follow.

En-sure' (*s=sh*) [*en-*, in, and **Sure**], make sure, make safe against.

En-tab'la-ture [It. *intavolatura*; *in*, on, *tavola*, a table], part of a building which lies on the columns.

En-tail' [F. *en-*, in, *tailler* (L.L. *taleāre*), to cut], to fix descent of an estate, to settle on a line of descendants, to impose (inconvenience, expense, etc.) upon.   [tangled.

En-tan'gle [*en-*, in, and **Tangle**], to make

En'ter [L. *intrāre*, to enter; *intra*, within], to come or go in.

En-ter'ic [Gk. *enteron*, intestine], relating to the intestines; *enteric fever*, typhoid fever.

En'ter-prise (*s=z*) [O.F. *entreprise*, fem. p.p. of *entreprendre*, to undertake; L. *inter*, between, *prehendere*, to lay hold of], an undertaking.

En-ter-tain' [L. *inter*, among, *tenĕre*, to hold], to receive as a guest, to amuse, to admit for consideration. **Entertain'ment.**

En-thrall', En-thral' [*en-*, in, and **Thrall**], to enslave, to captivate. **Enthral'ment.**

En-throne' [*en-*, on, and **Throne**], to put on the throne.

En-thu'si-asm [Gk. *en-*, in, *theos*, a god], great zeal. **Enthu'siast.**

En-tice' [*en-*, in, L. *titio*, a firebrand], to draw on by tempting. **Entice'ment.**

En-tire' [L. *integer*, entire], whole. **Entire'ty.**

En-ti'tle [*en-*, in, and **Title**], to give a claim to, to give a title to (a book, etc.).

En'ti-ty [L. *ens* (*ent-is*), pr.p. of *esse*, to be], being, something that has a real existence, as a personality, a nation.

En-tomb' (*entoom'*) [*en-*, in, and **Tomb**], to put in a tomb, to bury.

En-to-mol'o-gy [Gk. *entomon*, an insect; *en-*, in, *temnein*, to cut; *logos*, a discourse], the science which treats of insects.

En'trails [Late L. *intrālia*; L. *interānea*; from *inter*, within], intestines.

En-trance' [*en-*, in, and **Trance**], to overwhelm with delight.

En'trance [see **Enter**], a way in, a going in.

En-trap' [*en-*, in, and **Trap**], to catch as in a trap.   [**Entreat'y.**

En-treat' [*en-*, in, and **Treat**], to ask earnestly.

En'try [see **Enter**], a going in, a passage in, a note written in a book.

En-trust' [*en-*, in, and **Trust**], charge (person) with, give (duty) to.

En-twine' [*en-*, in, and **Twine**], to twine or twist together.

E-nu'mer-ate [L. *ē*, out, and *numerāre* (p.p. *numerātus*), to number; *numerus*, a number], to count, to specify.

E-nun'ci-ate [L. *ē*, out, and *nuntiāre* (p.p. *nuntiātus*), to tell; *nuntius*, a messenger], to state clearly, to pronounce.

En-vel'op [O.F. *en-*, in; *voluper*, to wrap], wrap in.

En'vel-ope, cover of a letter, a covering.

En-ven'om [*en-*, in, and **Venom**], poison.

En'vi-ous, full of grudging ill-will.

En-vi'rons [F. *environ*, round about], surrounding places, neighbourhood. **Envi'ronment.**

En-vis'age [F. *envisager*, to face; L. *in-*, in, *vidēre*, to see], to face, contemplate.

En'voy [F. *en voie*, on the way; L. *via*, a way], messenger.

En'vy [L. *invidia*; *in*, on, *vidēre*, to see], discontent at the good of others, longing for advantages enjoyed by another. **En'viable, En'vious.**

Ep-au-let', Ep-au-lette' [F. *épaulette*, dim. of *épaule*, the shoulder; L. *spatula*, a shoulder-blade], (military) shoulder-ornament or badge.

E-phem'er-al [Gk. *ephēmeros*, lasting a day; *epi*, upon, *hēmera*, a day], short-lived, lasting a day.

E'phod [Heb. fr. *aphad* to put on], Jewish, priestly garment.

Ep'ic [Gk. *epos*, a word], poem about a great event written in a grand style. **Ep'ical.**

Ep'i-cure [from Gk. name *Epicouros*], follower of Epicurus, one who loves dainties. **Epicure'an.**

Ep-i-dem'ic [Gk. *epidēmos*, general ; *epi*, upon, *dēmos*, the people], disease which spreads widely in a place for a time, but is not generally present there.

Ep-i-der'mis [Gk.*epi*, upon,*derma*,the skin], outer skin, cuticle.

Ep'i-gram [Gk. *epi*, upon, *gramma*, a writing], very short poem containing a witticism, pointed saying. **Ep'igrammat'ic.**

Ep'i-lep-sy [Gk. *epilēpsia* ; *epi*, upon, *lambanein*, to seize], disease accompanied by fits. **Epilep'tic.**

Ep'i-logue [Gk. *epilogos* ; *epi*, upon, and *logos*, a speech], short speech at the end of a play, concluding part of a literary work.

E-piph'an-y [Gk. *epi*, upon, *phainein*, to show], manifestation of Christ to the Wise Men of the East.

E-pis'co-pal [Gk. *episcopos*, a bishop], relating to bishops.

E-pis'cop-a-cy, system of Church government through bishops. **Epis'copa'lian.**

Ep'i-sode [Gk. *epi*, upon, *eisodos*, entry (*eis*, into, *hodos*, a way)], incident in a story or life. **Episod'ical.**

E-pis'tle [Gk. *epistolē* ; *epi*, upon, *stellein*, to send], letter.

E-pis'to-la-ry, relating to letters.

Ep'i-taph [Gk. *epi*, upon, *taphos*, a tomb], writing on a tombstone.

Ep'i-thet [Gk. *epi*, upon, *tithenai*, to place], adjective expressing a characteristic quality.

E-pit'o-me [Gk. *epi*, upon, *temnein*, to cut], summary of a subject.

E'poch (*ch*=*k*) [Gk. *ep-* (*epi*), upon, *echein*, to hold], point of time or a period marked by some great event.

E'qua-ble [L. *æquābilis*, equable ; *æquus*, equal], not changeable, even-tempered.

E'qual [L. *æquālis*, *æquus*, equal], same in quantity, value, etc. ; person equal to another ; be equal, etc. **Equal'ity, E'qualize.**

E'qua-nim'i-ty [L. *æquus*, equal, *animus*, the mind], calmness of mind or temper.

E-qua'tion [L. *æquātio*, an equalising; *æquus*, equal], equality expressed by symbols.

E-qua'tor [L. *æquus*, equal], great circle of the earth half-way between the poles. **Equato'rial.**

Eq'uer-ry, Eq'ue-ry [F. *écurie* ; M.L. *scuria* ; O.H.G. *scûr*, a shed], officer of the royal household under the Master of the Horse.

E-ques'tri-an [L. *equester* (adj.); *eques*, a horseman ; *equus*, a horse], horseman ; relating to horses or riders.

E-qui-lat'er-al [L. *æquus*, equal, *latus* (*later-is*), a side], having equal sides.

E-qui-lib'ri-um [L. *æquus*, equal, *libra*, a balance], balance. [like a horse.

Eq'uine [L. *equīnus* ; *equus*, a horse], of or

E'qui-noc'tial, relating to equinox.

E'qui-nox [L. *æquus*, equal, *nox* (*noct-is*), night], one of the two times in the year when day and night are equal.

E-quip' [F. *équiper*, to equip ; O.N. *skipa*, to set in order, fr. *skip*, a ship], fit out. **Equip'ment.** [etc.

Eq'ui-page, carriage with horses, servants,

E'qui-poise [L. *æquus*, equal; O.F. *peser*; L. *pendere*, to weigh], state of equal balance.

Eq'ui-ty [L. *æquus*, equal], justice, fairness. **Eq'uitable.**

E-quiv'a-lent [L. *æquus*, equal, *valēre*, to be worth], equal in value, etc. **Equiv'alence.**

E-quiv'o-cal [Late L. *æquivocus* ; see Equivocate], of double meaning, questionable, open to suspicion.

E-quiv'o-cate [L. *æquus*, equal, *vocāre*, to call], to express oneself in terms that may have different meanings so as to mislead. **Equiv'oca'tion.**

E'ra [L.L. *æra*, an era, orig. number expressed in figures (pl. of L. *æs*, money)], period of time.

E-rad'i-cate [L. *ē*, out, *radicāre*, to root ; *radix* (*radic-is*), a root], root out.

E-rase' (*s*=*z*) [L. *ē*, out, *rādere* (p.p. *rāsus*), to scrape], rub or scrape out. **Era'sure.**

Er-as'ti-an [fr. *Erastus*, German philosopher], subjecting the Church to the State.

Ere (*air*) [O.E. *ǽr*], before.

E-rect' [L. *ē*, out, *regere* (p.p. *rectus*), to make straight, to rule], upright ; to build.

E-rec'tion, anything built.

Er'got [O.F. *argot*, cock's spur], diseased seed of rye used as medicine.

Er'mine [O.F. perh. fr. L. *Armenius mūs*, Armenian mouse], animal of the weasel kind whose fur becomes white in winter.

E-ro'sion (*si*=*zh*) [L. *ē*, out, *rōdere* (p.p. *rōsus*), to gnaw], an eating away.

Er-ot'ic [Gk. *erōs*, love], concerning love.

Err [L. *errāre*, to wander], go astray, make mistakes in judgment or conduct.

Er'rand [O.E. *ǽrend*], message.

Er'rant [L. *errans* (*-antis*), pr.p. of *errāre* ; see Err], roving, erring. **Er'rantry.**

Er-rat'ic [L. *errāticus* ; see Err], wandering, queer.

Er-ra'tum, (pl.) **Er-ra'ta** [L. neut. of p.p. of *errāre*, to err], mistake in writing or printing. [wrong.

Er-ro'ne-ous [L. *errōneus*, wandering],

Er'ror, [see Err], mistake. [Gaelic.

Erse (*s*=*ss*) [O. Scot. for Irish], Highland

E-ruc-ta'tion [L. *ē*, out, *ructāre* (p.p. *ructātus*), to belch], belching.

Er-u-di'tion [L. *ērudīre* (p.p. *ērudītus*), to teach ; *ē*, from, *rudis*, rude], learning. **Er'udite.**

E-rup'tion [L. *ē*, from, *rumpere* (p.p. *rup-tus*), to break], a breaking out. **Erup'tive.**

Er-y-sip'e-las [perh. fr. root of Gk. *erythros*, red, and *pella*, skin], disease of the skin.

Es-ca-pade' [Sp. *escapada* ; see **Escape**], mischievous adventure.

Es-cape' [L. *ex cappa*, out of one's cape], get free from, run away ; flight, getting away, means of getting away.

Es-carp'ment [F. *escarpe*, a scarp], steep side of a ridge sloping gently on the other side.

Esch-a-to'logy (*sch = sk*) [Gk. *eschatos*, last, *logos*, discourse], doctrine of death and future life.

Es-cheat' [O.F. *eschete* ; L. *ex*, out, *cadere*, to fall], lapsing of property to Crown or lord of the manor ; confiscate.

Es-chew' [O.F. *eschiver*, to shun], shun, abstain from.

Es'cort [It. *scorta*, a guide ; L. *ex*, out, entirely, *corrigere*, to correct], guard or body of persons in attendance.

Es-cort', accompany, attend.

Es-cri-toire' (*toire=twarr*) [F., now *écritoire* ; L.L. *scriptorium* ; L. *scrībere* (p.p. *scriptus*), to write], writing desk with drawers.

Es'cu-lent [L. *ēsca*, food], eatable ; something eatable.

Es-cutch'eon, Scut'cheon, Scutch'eon (*tcheon =tshn*) [Late L. *scūtio*, extension of L. *scūtum*, a shield], shield on which arms are painted.

Es'kim-o (pl. **Eskimoes**), **Es-qui-mau'** (pl. **Esquimaux**), a race inhabiting Greenland, Labrador, and neighbouring Arctic regions.

Es-o-ter'ic [Gk. *esōtericos*, inner ; *esō*, within], (religion, etc.) relating to the inner or spiritual meaning of a religion or teaching.

Es-pal'ier (*i=y*) [It. *spalliera* ; *spalla*, a shoulder], lattice-work on which fruit trees, etc., are trained, a tree so trained.

Es-par'to [Sp. *esparto* ; Gk. *sparton*, rope of the plant *spartos*], kind of grass.

Es-pe'cial (*eci=esh*) [L. *speciālis*, of a special kind ; L. *speciēs*, a kind], chief, uncommon, belonging to a particular person or thing.

Es'pi-o-nage [F. *espionnage* ; *espion*, a spy ; see **Espy**], the practice or employment of spies, secret watching.

Es-pla-nade' [L. *explanāre* : to level, *planus*, flat], level place for walks or drives, level space beside a castle.

Es-pouse' (*s=z*) [L. *sponsāre*, to betroth ; *spondēre* (p.p. *sponsus*), to promise], marry.

Es-py' [O.F. *espier* ; O.H.G. *spehōn*, to spy], catch sight of. **Espi'al**.

Es'quire [L. *scutārius*, a shield-bearer ; *scūtum*, a shield], formerly an attendant of a knight, now a title of courtesy.

Es'say [O.F. *essai*, a trial ; L. *exagium*, weighing ; *ex*, out, *agere*, to move], attempt, short composition.

Es-say', try.

Es'sence [L. *esse*, to be], real being, liquid extract.

Es-sene' (*ene=een*) [Gk. *Essēnos*. Etym. dub.], member of a Jewish sect of the time of Christ that held mystical beliefs and lived in religious communities.

Es-sen'tial (*ti=sh*), necessary, belonging to a thing by virtue of its essence.

Es-tab'lish [L. *stabilis*, firm], fix firmly.

Es-tab'lish-ment, settlement, place of residence or business with the people employed in it.

Es-tate' [L. *status*, a state], state, property, esp. in land.

Es-teem' [L. *æstimāre* (p.p. *æstimātus*), to esteem], to value ; high opinion.

Es'ti-mate [see **Esteem**], put a value on.

Es-trange' [L. *extraneāre*, to make strange ; see **Strange**], turn away affection. **Estrange'ment**.

Es'tu-a-ry [L. *æstus*, the tide], wide river-mouth.

Etch [Du. *etsen* ; Ger. *ätzen*, to etch, orig. " to make to eat "], engrave by means of acid. **Etch'ing**.

E-ter'nal [L. *æternus*, lasting for an age ; *ævum*, an age], endless in time. **E-ter'ni-ty**, endless time.

E'ther [Gk. *aithēr*, upper air ; *aitnein*, to glow], something thinner than air supposed to permeate space, a liquid used to render unconscious. [airy.

E-the're-al [see **Ether**], heavenly, light and **Eth'ic, Eth'ic-al** [Gk. *ethos*, custom], moral.

Eth-nol'o-gy [Gk. *ethnos*, a nation ; *logos*, discourse], science which treats of the races of mankind. **Ethnolog'ical**.

E'ti-o-late [F. *étioler* ; Norman *étieuler*, grow into stalk ; L. *stipula*, straw], blanch (plants) by excluding light.

Et'i-quette [F. *étiquette*, a label, a ticket], rules of personal behaviour observed in social intercourse.

Et-y-mol'o-gy [Gk. *etymos*, true, *logos*, discourse], origin or derivation of words.

Eu-ca-lyp'tus [Gk. *eu*, well, *calyptos*, covered], gum-tree.

Eu'cha-rist [Gk. *eu*, well, *charis*, grace, favour], Lord's Supper.

Eu-gen'ics [Gk. *eu*, well, *genes*, born], science of breeding fine offspring. [praise.

Eu'lo-gy [Gk. *eu*, well, *logos*, discourse], **Eu'phe-mism** [Gk. *eu*, well, *phēmē*, speaking], mild name for something unpleasant.

Eu'pho-ny [Gk. *eu*, well, *phōnē*, the voice], pleasing sound. **Eupho'nious**.

Eu'phu-ism [from Lyly's book *Euphues*], affectation in writing. **Eu'phuist**.

Eur-a'sian [Europe, Asia, and *-an*], of mixed European and Asiatic parentage.

Eu-re'ka [1st pers., sing., perf., of Gk. *heuriscein*, to find], an exclamation of triumph.

Eu-than-a'si-a [Gk. *euthanasia* ; *eu*, well, and *thanein*, to die], easy death. [empty.

E-vac'u-ate [L. *ē*, out, *vacuus*, empty], make **E-vade'** [L. *ē*, out, *vadere* (sup. *vāsum*), to go], avoid cleverly.

Ev-a-nes'cent [L. *ē*, away, *vānescere*, to vanish], vanishing. **Evanes'cence**.

E-van-gel'ic-al [Gk. *eu*, well, *aggelein*, to bring news ; *aggelos*, a messenger ; see **Angel**], according to the Gospel.

E-van'gel-ist, travelling preacher.

E-vap'o-rate [L. *ē*, out, *vapor*, vapour], pass off in vapour. **Evapora'tion**.

E-va'sion (si=zh) [see **Evade**], avoidance (as of a direct answer).

Eve [short for even, poetical for **Evening**], evening or day before. [by two.

E'ven [O.E. efen], level, just, still, divisible

E'ven-ing [O.E. æfnung], close of the day.

E-vent' [L. ē, out, venīre (sup. ventum), to come], that which happens.

E-ven'tu-al-ly [F. éventuel, finally resulting; see **Event**], in the end.

E-ven-tu-al'i-ty, possible event.

Ev'er [O.E. æfre], always, at any time.

Ev'er-green, always green; a plant that has green leaves throughout the year.

Ev-er-last'ing, lasting for ever; a flower that is little changed by drying.

Ev'er-y [O.E. æfre, ever; ǽlc, each], each, all.

E-vict' [L. ē, out, vincere (p.p. victus), to conquer], cast out, dispossess. [belief.

Ev'i-dence [see **Evident**], proof, ground of

Ev'i-dent [L. ē, out, vidēre, to see], plain, clear.

E'vil [O.E. yfel, bad], bad; badness, harm.

E-vince' [L. ē, out, vincere, to conquer], show clearly.

E-vis'cer-ate (sc=ss) [L. ēviscerāre (p.p. ēviscerātus); ē, out, viscera, bowels], to remove the internal organs, to gut.

E-voke' [L. ē, out, vocāre, to call], call forth.

Ev-o-lu'tion [see **Evolve**], development, unfolding, a prescribed movement of troops or ships.

E-volve' [L. ē, out, volvere (p.p. volūtus), to roll], unfold, develop.

Ewe (yoo) [O.E. eown], female of the sheep.

Ew'er (yoo'er) [O.F. aiguiere; L. aqua, water], large wide-mouthed jug.

Ex-a'cer-bate (c=s) [L. ex, out, acerbus, bitter], make more bitter. **Exacerba'tion.**

Ex-act' [L. exigere (p.p. exactus), to drive out; ex, out, and agere, to drive], correct; to demand, force payment of.

Ex-ac'tion, severe demand.

Ex-ag'ger-ate [L. ex, out, agger, a heap], enlarge beyond the truth.

Ex-alt' [L. ex, out, altus, high], raise high. **Exalta'tion.**

Ex-am-i-na'tion [see **Examine**], careful search or inquiry.

Ex-am'ine [L. exāmen, for exagmen, the tongue of a balance; as **Exact**], search into, test.

Ex-am'ple [L. exemplum, a sample; eximere (p.p. exemptus), to take out; see **Exempt**], one of a class of like things, something to be copied.

Ex-as'per-ate [L. ex, out, very, asper, rough], irritate greatly. **Exaspera'tion.**

Ex'ca-vate [L. ex, out, cavus, hollow], hollow out. **Excava'tion.**

Ex-ceed' [L. ex, out, cēdere (sup. cessum), to go], go beyond.

Ex-cel' [L. excellere, to excel; ex, out, celsus, high], go beyond in a good sense.

Ex'cel-lence, very great merit.

Ex-cept' [L. excipere (p.p. exceptus), to take out; ex, out, capere, to take], leave out; leaving out; unless.

Ex-cep'tion, that which is distinct from others of its kind, objection.

Ex-cep'tion-a-ble, open to objection.

Ex-cep'tion-al, not ordinary.

Ex'cerpt [L. excerpere (p.p. excerptus); ex, out, and carpere, to pluck], a selected passage.

Ex-cess' [see **Exceed**], undue amount, amount by which one exceeds another.

Ex-cess'ive, overmuch.

Ex-change' [O.F. eschange (n.), pref. es- (L. ex), out; see **Change**], give one thing for another; act of exchanging, a building where merchants transact business.

Ex-cheq'uer [O.F. eschequier; M.L. scaccārium, a chess-board; see **Check**], division of the High Court of Justice, public treasury.

Ex-cise' (s=z) [prob. M. Du. excijs; Late L. accensus, a payment; L. ad, to, census, a tax], tax on home goods.

Ex-cise' [L. excidere (p.p. excīsus), to excise; ex, from, cœdere, to cut], cut out.

Ex-ci'sion (si=zh), a cutting off or out.

Ex-cite' [L. excitāre, freq. of excīēre, to set in motion; ex, out, and ciēre, to set in motion], call forth, stir up. **Excit'abil'ity, Excite'ment.**

Ex-claim' [L. ex, out, clamāre (p.p. clamātus), to call], call out.

Ex-cla-ma'tion, a calling out.

Ex-clude' [L. exclūdere (p.p. exclūsus); ex, out, claudere, to shut], shut out.

Ex-clu'sion, act of shutting out.

Ex-clu'sive, shutting out, select.

Ex-cog'it-ate [L. ex, out, and **Cogitate**], to think out, contrive.

Ex-com-mu'ni-cate [L. ex, out; see **Communicate**], put out of communion.

Ex-co'ri-ate [L. ex, out, corium, skin], strip or wear the skin off.

Ex-cres'cence [L. ex, out, crescere, to grow], abnormal outgrowth. **Excres'cent.**

Ex-crete' [L. excernere (p.p. excrētus); ex, out, and cernere, to sift], expel waste matter from system. **Excre'tion.**

Ex-cru'ci-ate (c=sh) [L. ex, out, exceedingly, cruciāre, to torment; crux (crucis), a cross], to torture.

Ex'cul-pate [L. ex, from, culpa, fault], clear from blame.

Ex-cur'sion [L. ex, out, currere (sup. cursum), to run], pleasure trip, ramble.

Ex-cur'sive, rambling.

Ex-cuse' (s=z) [L. ex, from, causa, a cause], pardon, regard with indulgence.

Ex-cuse' (s=ss) [see **Excuse** (vb.)], plea for being excused.

Ex'e-cra-ble [see **Execrate**], detestable.

Ex'e-crate [L. ex, out, sacrāre, to consecrate; sacer, sacred], curse. **Execra'tion.**

Ex'e-cute [L. exsequī (p.p. execūtus), to execute; ex, out, sequī, to follow], carry out, put to death.

Ex-e-cu'tion, carrying out, skill in playing musical instrument, seizure of goods from a debtor, infliction of capital punishment.

Ex-ec′u-tive, carrying into effect; the persons who administer government.

Ex-ec′u-tor, fem. **Ex-ec′u-trix**, one who sees to the carrying out of a will.

Ex-e-ge′sis [Gk. *ex*, out, *hēgeisthai*, to lead], exposition of Scripture.

Ex-em′pla-ry (Ex′em-pla-ry) [see **Example**], fit to be an example, very good.

Ex-em′pli-fy [**Example**, and L. *facere*, to make], illustrate by example.

Ex-empt′ [L. *eximere* (p.p. *exemptus*), to take out; *ex*, out, *emere*, to take], not liable; to free from service, etc. **Exemp′tion**.

Ex′er-cise (*s*=*z*) [L. *exercēre* (p.p. *exercitus*), to drive on; *ex*, out, *arcēre*, to enclose], use, practice, bodily activity, lesson for practice; put in action.

Ex-ert′ [L. *exserere* (p.p. *exertus*, or *exsertus*); *ex*, out, and *serere*, to put], put forth, as strength. **Exer′tion**.

Ex′e-unt [3rd pers., plur., pres. of L. *exīre*, to go out], stage-direction meaning "They go out."

Ex-ha-la′tion, breath, vapour.

Ex-hale′ [L. *ex*, out, *hālāre*, to breathe], breathe out.

Ex-haust′ [L. *ex*, out, *haurīre* (p.p. *haustus*), to draw], draw off wholly, tire out; exit of steam from cylinder after stroke of piston. **Exhaust′ion**.

Ex-haust′ive, serving to exhaust, complete.

Ex-hib′it [L. *exhibere* (p.p. *exhibitus*), to exhibit; *ex*, out, *habēre*, to have], to display.

Ex-hi-bi′tion, show, place where goods, etc., are displayed on a large scale, money allowance for a student at a university.

Ex-hil′a-rate [L. *ex*, out, and *hilaris*, cheerful], make merry. **Exhilara′tion**.

Ex-hort′ [L. *ex*, out, *hortāri* (p.p. *hortātus*), to encourage], advise or warn.

Ex′hor-ta′tion, advice, discourse of advice.

Ex-hume′ [L. *ex*, out, *humus*, the ground], dig from a grave, unearth, bring to light.

Ex′i-gen-cy [L. *exigere* (pr.p. *exigens, -entis*), to exact], pressing necessity.

Ex-ig′u-ous [L. *exiguus*, fr. *ex*, out, *agere*, to drive], scanty, small.

Ex′ile [O.F. *exil*; L. *exsul*, an exile. Etym. doubtful], banish; banishment; one who has to live away from his country.

Ex-ist′ [L. *ex*, out, and *sistere*, to set; *stāre*, to stand], have real being. **Exist′ence**.

Ex′it [L. *exit*, "he goes out"; *ex*, out, and *īre*, to go], way out, departure.

Ex′o-dus [Gk. *exodos*; *ex*, out, *hodos*, a way], a going out.

Ex-on′er-ate [L. *ex*, away, and *onerāre*, to burden; *onus*, a burden], free from blame.

Ex-or′bi-tant [L. *exorbitāre* (pr.p. *exorbitans, -antis*), go out of a wheel-track; *ex*, out, and *orbita*, a wheel-track], very excessive.

Ex′or-cise (*s*=*z*) [Gk. *exorcizein*; Gk. *ex*, away, and *horcos*, an oath], cast out (evil spirits). **Ex′orcism**.

Ex-ot′ic [Gk. *exō*, outside], foreign; foreign plant.

Ex-o-ter′ic [Gk. *exōterō*, compar. of *exō*, outward], (doctrines, etc.) comprehensible to outsiders.

Ex-pand′ [L. *ex*, out, *pandere* (p.p. *pansus*), to lie open], open wide, spread.

Ex-panse′, wide extent.

Ex-pan′sion, spreading out. **Expan′sive**.

Ex-pa′ti-ate (*ti=shi*) [L. *ex*, out, and *spatiāri*, to roam; *spatium*, space], enlarge in speaking or writing. **Expatia′tion**.

Ex-pa′tri-ate (*pa=pai*) [L. *ex*, from, and *patria*, native land], send (a person) away from his country. **Expatria′tion**.

Ex-pect′ [L. *ex*, out, *spectāre*, to look], look for, look forward to.

Ex-pec-ta′tion, state of looking forward, that which is looked for. **Expec′tancy**.

Ex-pec′to-rate [L. *ex*, from, *pectus* (*pector-is*), the breast], spit. **Expectora′tion**.

Ex-pe′di-en-cy, fitness, advisability.

Ex-pe′di-ent [L. *expediens* (*-ientis*), pr.p. of *expedīre*, to expedite], fitting, advisable; suitable means for an end, shift.

Ex′pe-dite [L. *ex*, out, *pes* (*ped-is*), the foot], hasten. [journey.

Ex-pe-di′tion, speed, warlike enterprise,

Ex-pe-di′tious, quick.

Ex-pel′ [L. *ex*, out, *pellere* (p.p. *pulsus*), to drive], drive out.

Ex-pend′ [L. *ex*, out, *pendere* (p.p. *pensus*), to weigh], spend.

Ex-pend′i-ture [L. *penditus*, an irreg. p.p. of *pendere*; see **Expend**], that which is spent, spending.

Ex-pense′, outlay, cost.

Ex-pen′sive, costly, dear.

Ex-pe′ri-ence [L. *experīrī* (pr.p. *experiens*); *ex*, out, and obs. vb. *perīrī*, to go through], what one has lived through, practical wisdom; have trial of.

Ex-per′i-ment [as **Experience**], trial.

Ex-pert′ [L. *expertus*, p.p. of *experīrī*; see **Experience**], clever, skilful.

Ex′pert, one who is specially skilled, an authority.

Ex′pi-ate [L. *ex*, out, *piāre* (p.p. *piātus*), to seek to appease; *pius*, pious], atone for. **Expia′tion**.

Ex-pire′ [L. *ex*, out, *spirāre*, to breathe], breathe out, die. **Expira′tion**.

Ex-pi′ry, end.

Ex-plain′ [L. *ex*, out, *planāre* (p.p. *planātus*, to flatten; *planus*, flat], make plain, account for. **Explan′atory**.

Ex-pla-na′tion, making plain, meaning.

Ex′ple-tive [L. *ex*, out, *plēre* (p.p. *plētus*), to fill], serving to fill up; oath.

Ex′pli-ca-ble [L. *explicāre*, to unfold; *ex*, out, *plicāre*, to fold], that can be explained.

Ex-pli′cit (*i* short) [L. *explicitus*, p.p. of *explicāre*, to unfold], plainly stated.

Ex-plode′ [L. *explōdere* (p.p. *explōsus*), to explode; *ex*, out, *plodere*, *plaudere*, to clap hands], burst with violence and noise.

Ex-ploit′ [O.F. *esploit*; L. *explicitum*, neut. of *explicitus*; see **Explicit**], venturesome deed; get the value out of.

Ex-plore' [L. *ex*, out, *plorāre*, to make to flow], search through or into. **Explor'er.**

Ex-plo'sion (*si=zh*), noisy bursting out.

Ex-po'nent [L. *exponens* (*-entis*), pr.p. *ex-pōnere*, to expound], one who expounds, an index (in algebra).

Ex-port' [L. *ex*, away, *portāre*, to carry], send goods out of a country.

Ex'port, something exported.

Ex-pose' (*s=z*) [L. *ex*, out, F. *poser*, to place], set out to public view, lay open or bare.

Ex-po-si'tion [see Expound], exhibition, full explanation. **Expo'sure.**

Ex-pos'tu-late [L. *ex*, out, *postulāre*, to ask], reason with a person against his actions, remonstrate. **Expostula'tion.**

Ex-pound' [L. *ex*, out, *pōnere* (p.p. *positus*], to place], explain.

Ex-press' [L. *ex*, out, *premere* (p.p. *pressus*), to press], press out, set forth in words; clear, intended for a special purpose, sent off with special speed.

Ex-pres'sion, utterance, form of words, revelation of feeling, etc. **Expres'sive.**

Ex-press'ly, on purpose.

Ex-pro'pri-ate [L. *ex*, from, *proprius*, one's own], put out of possession.

Ex-pul'sion [see Expel], driving or forcing out.

Ex-punge' [L. *ex*, out, *pungere*, to prick], wipe out.

Ex'pur-gate, **Ex-pur'gate** [L. *ex*, from, *purgāre*, to purify], cleanse or purify.

Ex'qui-site (*s=z*) [L. *exquīrere* (p.p. *exquīsītus*), to seek out; *ex*, out, and *quærere*, to seek], choice, delicate, keen.

Ex'tant, Ex-tant' [L. *exstāre* (pr.p. *exstans, -antis*), to stand out; *ex*, out, and *stāre*, to stand], still existing.

Ex-tem-po-ra'ne-ous, Ex-tem'po-ra-ry, Ex-tem'po-re [L. *ex tempore*, at the moment; *ex*, from, *tempus* (abl. *tempore*), time], arising from the occasion, without study.

Ex-tem'po-rize, make or utter offhand.

Ex-tend' [L. *ex*, out, *tendere* (p.p. *tentus* or *tensus*), to stretch], stretch out.

Ex-ten'sion, a stretching out, enlargement.

Ex-ten'sive, very large.

Ex-tent', size, space occupied.

Ex-ten'u-ate [L. *ex*, out, *tenuis*, thin], make a partial excuse for. **Extenua'tion.**

Ex-te'ri-or [L. *exterus*, compar. of *exterior*, outside], outward; the outside.

Ex-ter'mi-nate [L. *ex*, out, *terminus*, a boundary], root out, destroy. [outside.

Ex-ter'nal [L. *externus*, outward], outward,

Ex-tinct', no longer burning, obsolete.

Ex-tinc'tion, a putting out of light, life, etc.

Ex-tin'guish [L. *extinguere* (p.p. *extinctus*); *ex*, out, *stinguere*, to quench], put out, as a light. **Extin'guisher.**

Ex-tir-pate [L. *extirpāre* (p.p. *extirpātus*), to root out; *ex*, out, *stirps*, a stem], root out.

Ex-tol' [L. *ex*, out, *tollere*, to lift], praise, glorify.

Ex-tort' [L. *ex*, out, *torquēre* (p.p. *tortus*), to twist], wrench from, exact by force. **Extor'tion.**

Ex'tra [L. *extra*, beyond], beyond what is due or usual. F

Ex-tract' [L. *ex*, out, *trahere* (p.p. *tractus*), to draw], draw out or forth.

Ex'tract, quotation, essence.

Ex-trac'tion, drawing out, family descent.

Ex-tra-di'tion [L. *ex*, out, and **Tradition**], surrender to a foreign country of a person accused of a crime. **Ex'tradite.**

Ex-tra'ne-ous [L. *extraneus*, from *extra*, outside], without or beyond a thing, not essential.

Ex-tror'di-na-ry, Ex-tra-or'di-na-ry, beyond ordinary.

Ex-trav'a-gant [L. *extra*, beyond, *vagāri* (pr.p. *vagans, -antis*), to wander], going beyond bounds, wasteful, immoderate in spending. **Extrav'agance.**

Ex-treme' [L. *extrēmus*, superl. of *exterus*, outward], utmost, outermost; utmost point or limit.

Ex-trem'i-ty, end, utmost need.

Ex'tri-cate [L. *ex*, out, *tricœ*, impediments], disentangle, set free. **Extrica'tion.**

Ex-trude' [L. *ex*, out, *trūdere*, to thrust], thrust out. **Extru'sion.** [flowing.

Ex-u'ber-ant [L. *ex*, out, *ūber*, fertile], over-

Ex-ude' [L. *ex*, out, *sūdāre* (p.p. *sudātus*), to sweat], sweat out, ooze.

Ex-ult' [L. *exsultare*; *ex*, out, and *saltare*, freq. of *salīre*, to leap], rejoice greatly, triumph. **Exulta'tion.**

Ey'as (*ey=ī*) [for *nyas*. F. *niais*, a nestling; L. *nīdus*, a nest], young hawk taken from the nest. [to watch.

Eye (*ī*) [O.E. *éage*, etym. dub.], organ of sight;

Eye'let [M.E. *oilet*; F. *œillet*, dim. of *œil*; L. *oculus*, the eye], small hole to receive a cord.

Eye'sore, something offensive to the sight.

Eye'tooth, upper tooth under the eye.

Ey'rie, Ey'ry (*ey=ī*) [see **Aerie**], nest of a bird of prey.

F

Fa'ble [L. *fabula*, a story], story usually with animals for characters. **Fab'ulist.**

Fab'ric [L. *fabrica*, a workshop; *faber*, a workman], structure, cloth.

Fab'ri-cate, to frame, make up (a lie, etc.). **Fabrica'tion.**

Fab'u-lous, told in fable, incredible.

Fa-çade' [pop. L. *facia*; L. *faciēs*, the face], front of a building.

Face [L. *facies*, the face], front surface, front of a head; meet in front, meet bravely.

Fa'cet (*ă*) [F. *facette*, dim. of *face*, face], small plane surface, a side of many-faced body.

Fa-ce'tious (*ti=sh*) [L. *facētus*, witty], witty, jocular.

Fa'cial (*ci=sh*), of or relating to the face.

Fa'cile (*ă*) [L. *facilis*, easy; *facere*, to do], easy, easily persuaded.

Fa-cil'i-tate, make less difficult.

Fa-cil'i-ty, ease, advantage.

Fac-sim′i-le [L. *fac simile*, make thou like; *fac*, imper. of *facere*, to make, *simile*, neut. of *similis*, like], exact copy.

Fact [L. *facere* (p.p. *factus*), to do], thing done (*e.g.* before the fact), a truth known by observation.

Fac′tion [L. *factus*, done; see **Fact**], party working for selfish ends.

Fac-ti′tious (*iti=ish*) [L. *factus*, made], not natural, sham.

Fac′tit-ive, verb of making, thinking, calling, which takes object and complement (*he thought her mad*).

Fac′tor [L. *factor*, a doer; *factus*, done], agent, number which multiplied by another or others produces a given number, circumstance which helps to produce a result. **Factor′ial.**

Fac′to-ry, building where goods are made, merchant company's trading station.

Fac-to′tum [L. *fac totum*, do all (see **Facsimile**)], one employed for all work.

Fac′ul-ty [L. *facultas* (=*facilitas*, facility), *facilis*, easy], mental power, department of a university, members of a profession.

Fad [?], craze, foolish hobby.

Fad′dist, one who indulges in fads.

Fade [O.F. *fade*, dull, perh. fr. L. *vapidus*, stale], grow dim, lose freshness.

Fag [perh. corrupt. of **Flag** [4]], grow weary, use as a drudge; schoolboy who drudges for another.

Fag′got, Fag′ot [F. *fagot*]. Of doubtful origin], bundle of sticks.

Fahr′en-heit (*ei=ī*) [name of Prussian inventor], thermometer with freezing-point 32°, and boiling-point 212°.

Fail [L. *fallere*, to deceive], fall short or away, become bankrupt. **Fail′ing.**

Fail′ure, a falling short or away, want of success, bankruptcy.

Fain [O.E. *fægen*, glad], glad.

Faint [O.F. *feint*, orig. p.p. of *feindre*, to feign], weak, dim, inclined to swoon; a swoon; to become senseless.

Fair [O.E. *fæger*, fair], pleasing to the eye, light complexioned, just. [market.

Fair [L. *féria*, a holiday, later, a fair].

Fair′ry [O.F. *faerie*, enchantment; *fae*, a fay], small supernatural being in human form.

Faith [O.F. *feid*, faith, fr. L. *fidēs*, faith], belief, trust.

Faith′ful, constant in affection, trustworthy.

Fa-kir′, Fa-quir′ (*ir=eer, qu=k*) [Arab. *faqīr*, a poor man], Oriental religious beggar.

Fal′chion (*a=aw; ch=sh*) [L. *falx* (*falc-is*), a sickle], short curved sword.

Fal′con (**Fa′lcon**) (*a=aw*) [L.L. *falco*, falcon, perh. fr. *falx*, a sickle], bird of prey. **Fal′coner.**

Fall (*a=aw*) [O.E. *feallan*, cf. L. *fallere*, to deceive], come down suddenly, drop; act of falling.

Fal-la′cious (*ci=sh*), deceptive.

Fal′la-cy [L. *fallax* (*fallāc-is*), deceitful; *fallere*, to deceive], deception, error founded on false reasoning.

Fal′li-ble [L.L. *fallibilis*; *fallere*, to deceive], liable to err.

Fal′low [M.E. *falwe*, ploughed land], left unsown after ploughing.

Fal′low (O.E. *falu*, perh. cogn. with L. *pallidus*, pale], light brown or red (of deer).

False (*a=aw*) [O.E. *fals*; L. *fallere* (p.p. *falsus*), to deceive], not true.

False′hood, lie.

Fal′si-fy [F. *falsifier*, to falsify; see **False**], make (a statement, account, etc.) false. **Falsifica′tion.**

Fal′si-ty, falseness.

Fal′ter (*a=aw*) [etym. dub.], hesitate, speak brokenly, stumble. [reputation.

Fame [L. *fāma*, report], public report, good

Fa-mil′iar [L. *familiāris*; see **Family**], closely acquainted, well known, unceremonious; spirit in attendance. **Familia′rity.**

Fam′i-ly [L. *familia*, household; *famulus*, a servant], household, children and parents, children of the same parents, line of ancestors. [of food.

Fam′ine [L. *famēs*, hunger], general scarcity

Fam′ish [L. *famēs*, hunger], starve.

Fa′mous, widely known and talked of.

Fan [L. *vannus*, a fan], instrument for producing a current of air; blow air on with a fan.

Fan-at′ic [L. *fānum*, a temple], wildly zealous person (esp. in religion). **Fanat′icism.**

Fan′cy [short for **Fantasy**], light effort of imagination, whim; imagine, like; extravagant, ornamental.

Fane [L. *fānum*, a temple], temple.

Fan′fare [F. *fanfare*. Prob. imit.], flourish of trumpets.

Fang [O.E. *fang*], tusk, long pointed tooth.

Fan-tas′i-a [It., see **Fantasy**], a fanciful musical composition, not governed by ordinary rules.

Fan-tas′tic, whimsical, odd.

Fan′ta-sy, Phan′ta-sy [Gk. *phantāsia*, fantasy; *phantasein*, to display], fancy, a creation of the imagination. [distance.

Far [O.E. *feor*, far], distant, at a great

Farce [L. *farcīre*, to stuff], comedy with broad humour.

Far′ci-cal, absurd.

Fare [O.E. *faran*, to go], go, be in any state good or bad, to feed; price for a journey, food.

Fare-well′ (lit. go well), good-bye.

Far-i-na′ceous (*ce=sh*) [L. *farīna*, flour, meal; *far*, corn], made of or yielding meal or flour.

Farm [F. *ferme*, farm; Late L. *firma*, fixed payment; *firmus*, strong], land leased for tillage or pasture; lease for rent, till.

Far-ra′go (*ra=rah* or *rai*) [L. *farrago*, mixed fodder; *far*, corn], mixture, medley.

Far′ri-er [O.F. *ferrier*; L. *ferrum*, iron], one who shoes or doctors horses.

Far′row [O.E. *fearh*, a pig], litter of pigs; produce pigs.

Far'ther [see **Far**; *th* euphonic], comp. of far, more distant. **Far'thest.**

Far'thing [O.E. *féorthing*, dim. of O.E. *féortha*, fourth], the fourth of a penny.

Far'thin-gale [O.F. *verdugale*; Sp. *verdugado*; Sp. *verdugo*, a rod], old-fashioned hooped petticoat.

Fas'ci-nate [L. *fascinum*, a spell], to charm, deprive of power to escape or resist.

Fash'ion [L. *factio*, a making; *facere*, to make], make or form, prevailing mode, esp. of dress; to form. **Fash'ionable.**

Fast [O.E. *fǽstan*, to fast], keep from food; abstinence from food.

Fast [O.E. *fǽste*], quick, firm.

Fast'en [O.E. *fǽstnian*], make fast, fix firmly.

Fas-tid'i-ous [L. *fastidiōsus*, fr. *fastidium*, loathing], over-nice, hard to please.

Fast'ness, firmness, a stronghold or fort.

Fat [O.E. *fǽtt*], oily animal substance; fleshy, oily.

Fa'tal, decreed by fate, deadly.

Fa-tal'i-ty, occurrence causing death.

Fate [L. *fāri* (p.p. *fātus*), to speak], lot, course of life which cannot be escaped.

Fa'ther [O.E. *fœder*], a male parent. [wife.

Fa'ther-in-law', father of one's husband or

Fath'om [O.E. *fœthm*, length reached by the arms extended, an embrace], measure of six feet; try the depth of, comprehend.

Fa-tigue' (*fa-teeg'*) [L. *fatigāre*, to weary], weariness; to tire.

Fat'ten, make or grow fat.

Fat'ty, containing fat.

Fat'u-ous [L. *fatuus*, silly], foolish. **Fatu'ity.**

Fau'cal [L. *fauces*, the throat], of the throat.

Fault [formerly *faute*; O.F. *faute*; L. *fallere*, to deceive], a want, moral failing, (geol.) dislocation of strata. **Fau'ltless.** [and a tail.

Faun [L. *Faunus*], rural demigod with horns

Fau'na [Mod. L. *Fauna*, the sister of *Faunus*; see **Faun**], animals of a given place or time.

Fa'vour [L. *favor* (n.), fr. vb. *favēre*, favour], goodwill, countenance; to countenance, be partial to. [geous.

Fa'vour-a-ble, kindly disposed, advanta-

Fa'vour'ite, one regarded with great love or esteem; preferred, chosen.

Fawn [O.F. *faon*, a fawn], young deer; light yellowish brown.

Fawn [O.E. *fahnian*, to rejoice; see **Fain**], court favour by cringing.

Fay [O.F. *fae*, a fairy; L. *fata*, pl. of *fatum*, fate], fairy.

Fe-al'ty [L. *fidēlis*, faithful; *fidēs*, faith], faithfulness to one's lord.

Fear [O.E. *fǽr*, cf. Ger. *gefahr*, danger], painful uneasiness felt on approach of danger; feel fear.

Fear'ful, full of fear, causing fear.

Fea'si-ble (*s=z*) [F. *faire* (pr.p. *faisant*); L. *facere*, to do], capable of being done. **Feasibil'ity.**

Feast [L. *festa*, pl. of *festum*, a festival], holiday, meal with much, or many kinds of, food; provide with or partake of rich provisions.

Feat [O.F. *fait*; L. *facere* (p.p. *factus*), to do], striking act of strength, skill, etc.

Feath'er [O.E. *fether*], what grows on the skin of a bird; furnish with feathers, turn (the flat of an oar) to surface of water.

Fea'ture [L. *factūra*, fut. part. fem. of *facere*, to make], distinctive part of a thing, esp. of the face.

Feb'ri-fuge [L. *febris*, fever, *fugāre*, to drive away], medicine to lessen fever.

Fe'brile or **Feb'rile** [L. *febris*, fever], relating to fever.

Feb'ru-ar-y [L. *Februarius* (*mensis*), (month) of *februa* (pl. of *februum*, purification), a festival of purification held on the 15th of this month], second month of the year (Rom. twelfth).

Feck'less [Scot., perh. for **Effectless**], feeble, ineffective. [ness.

Fe-cun'di-ty [L. *fecundus*, fruitful], fruitful-

Fed'er-al [L. *fœdus* (*fœder-is*), a treaty], relating to a league.

Fed-er-a'tion [see **Federal**], a banding together of states, etc.

Fee [O.F. *fiu*, *fé*, *fief*; M.L. *feodum*, a fee, a *fœer*], payment for service, inherited estate.

Fee'ble [L. *flebilis*, doleful, weak; *flēre*, to weep], weak. **Fee'bleness.**

Feed [O.E. *fēdan*], give food to, supply.

Feel [O.E. *fēlan*], touch, have a sense of.

Feel'er, sense organ of some animals.

Feel'ing, touch, sensation, sentiment.

Feign (*ei=ai*) [O.F. *feindre* (pr.p. *feignant*); L. *fingere*, to feign], pretend.

Feint (*ei=ai*) [F. p.p. of *feindre*, to feign], pretence.

Feld'spar, Fel'spar [corrupt. fr. Ger. *feldspath*; *feld*, a field, and *spat*, spar], mineral found in granite, etc.

Fe-li'ci-ta'tion (*i* short) [see **Felicity**], a wishing of happiness. [ness.

Fe-li'ci-ty [L. *felix* (*felīc-is*), happy], happi-

Fe'line [L. *fēles*, a cat], relating to or like a cat.

Fell [O.F. *fel*; Late. L. *fello*, a felon], cruel.

Fell [2] [O.E. *fell*, cogn. with L. *pellis*, a hide], skin with the wool or hair on.

Fell [3] [O.N. *fiall*], barren hill.

Fell [4] [causative of **Fall**], knock down.

Fel'loe, Fel'ly [O.E. *felg*, a felloe], one of the curved pieces of the rim of a wheel.

Fel'low [O.E. *féolaga*, one who lays down money in partnership. See **Fee** and **Lay**], companion, mate, man (familiarly), scholar in a college who holds a fellowship, member.

Fel'low-ship, companionship, dignity or income for a college fellow.

Fel'on [L.L. *fello* (*fellonis*), felon; see **Fell** [1]], criminal. **Felo'nious.**

Felt [O.E. *felt*, cf. Du. *vilt*], fabric wrought by rolling and pressure.

Fel-uc'ca [It. *feluca*; perh. fr. Arab. *fulk*, a ship], small Mediterranean coasting ship.

Fe'male [L. *fēmella*, dim. of *fēmina*, a woman], of the sex to which a woman belongs.

Fem′i‑nine [L. *fēmina*, a woman], relating to woman. **Feminin′ity**.

Fe′mur [L. *femur*, thigh], thigh‑bone.

Fen [O.E. *fen*, cf. Du. *ven*], marsh.

Fence [short for **Defence**], enclosure, esp. of wood; practise fighting with the sword.

Fend [short for **Defend**], keep off, resist.

Fend′er [short for **Defender**], metal frame round a fire, bars of wood, etc., to prevent barges, etc., touching.

Fen′nel [L. *fœniculum*, fennel, double dim. of *fœnum*, hay], aromatic plant.

Feoff (*ĕ*), see **Fief**.

Fer‑ment′, cause or undergo fermentation.

Fer′ment [L. *fermentum*, leaven; *fervēre*, to boil], agitation, that which causes fermentation. [tion.

Fer‑men‑ta′tion, action of yeast, etc., agita‑

Fern [O.E. *fearn*], kind of plant, usually flowerless, often producing feathery fronds or leaves.

Fe‑ro′cious (*ci=sh*) [L. *ferox* (*ferōc‑is*), cruel], fierce, wild. **Fero′city**. [iron.

Fer′re‑ous [L. *ferrum*, iron], of or containing

Fer′ret [O.F. *furet*, dim. of *furon*, fr. L.L. *furo* (*furōnis*), a robber], animal of the weasel kind; search out.

Fer‑ru′gi‑nous [L. *ferrūgo* (*ferrūgin‑is*), rust], containing iron or iron‑rust.

Fer′rule [O.F. *virelle*; L. *viriola*, a little bracelet]; metal ring round a stick, etc., to strengthen it.

Fer′ry [O.E. *ferian*, to convey across; *faran*, to go], part of a narrow water which is crossed in a boat; take over in a boat.

Fer′tile, **Fer′tile** [L. *ferre*, to bear], fruitful.

Fer′ti‑lize, make fertile.

Fer′ule [formerly *ferula*; L. *ferula*, giant fennel (its stalks were used to punish schoolboys), a rod], flat piece of wood used for punishment, esp. on the hand.

Fer′ven‑cy, warmth, ardour.

Fer′vent [L. *fervēre* (pr.p. *fervens, ‑entis*), to boil], hot, glowing, intense.

Fer′vid [L. *fervēre*, to boil], very hot, fervent.

Fer′vour, heat, great zeal.

Fes′tal [L. *festum*, a feast], relating to a feast or holiday.

Fes′ter [O.F. *festre*; L. *fistula*, an ulcer], be inflamed and suppurate. [celebration.

Fes′ti‑val [see **Festive**], time of feasting or

Fes′tive [L. *festīvus*; *festum*, a feast], gay.

Fes‑tiv′i‑ty, social joy, gaiety.

Fes‑toon′ [It. *festone*, perh. fr. L. *festum*, a feast], wreath hanging in a curve; adorn with, hang in, festoons.

Fetch [O.E. *fecc(e)an*], go and bring.

Fet′id, **Fe′tid** [L. *fetidus*, fetid; *fetēre*, to stink], having a bad smell.

Fet′ish, **Fet′ich** [Port. *feitico*, charm; L. *factīcius*, artificial; *facere*, to make], object of worship by savages, any object unduly reverenced.

Fet′lock [M.E. *fytlok*], tuft of hair about a horse's hoof, place where it grows.

Fet′ter [O.E. *feter*, a shackle for the foot; *fōt*, foot], foot‑shackle; put chains on, to bind.

Fet′tle [O.E. *fetel*, a bond], condition, state (cf. *in good fettle*).

Feu [variant of **Fee**], in Scotland a piece of ground granted in perpetuity for which rent called *feu‑duty* is paid. [enmity.

Feud [M.E. and O.F. *fede*], long‑continued

Feud [as **Fee**], fief.

Feu′dal, held of an overlord. **Feu′dalism**.

Fe′ver [L. *febris*, fever], disease characterised by high temperature. **Fe′verish**.

Few [O.E. *fēawe*], not many, small number.

Fez [Turk. *fes*, perh. from *Fez*, town in Morocco], felt or cloth cap with a tassel.

Fi‑as′co [It. *fiasco*, a bottle], complete failure.

Fi′at [L. *fiat*, let it be done, 3rd pers. sing. pres. subj. of *fieri*, fr. *facere*, to do], decree, order.

Fib [perh. fr. obs. *fible‑fable*, nonsense; see **Fable**], a lie; tell a lie.

Fi′bre [L. *fibra*, a thread], fine thread or threadlike substance. **Fi′brous**.

Fic′kle [O.E. *ficol*], changeable. **Fic′kleness**.

Fic′tion [L. *fingere* (p.p. *fictus*), to feign], story, made‑up tale.

Fic‑ti′tious (*t* short, *ti=sh*), not genuine.

Fid′dle [perh. fr. Late L. *vitula*, a viol], violin.

Fi‑del′i‑ty [L. *fidēlis*, faithful; *fidēs*, faith], faithfulness.

Fidg′et [dim. of obs. *fidge*, to move up and down], move uneasily; (n. pl.) restless movements.

Fid‑u′cia‑ry (*cia=sha*) [L. *fidūcia*, trust], held or given in trust; trustee.

Fief (*ie=ee*) [O.F. *fief*, formerly *fiu*; see **Feu**], land held of a superior on condition of military service.

Field [O.E. *feld*], piece of land enclosed for tillage, open space; stand out in the field to stop and return the ball in cricket.

Field′fare [M.E. *feldefare*], small thrush.

Field‑mar′shal, army officer of the highest rank.

Fiend [O.E. *fēond*, an enemy], one who is very wicked, devil. **Fiend′ish**. [wild.

Fierce [L. *ferus*, wild], furious, violent and

Fi′er‑y, containing or like fire, hot.

Fife [F. *fifre*, or Ger. *pfeife*, a pipe], small flute with one key.

Fif‑teen′ [see **Five** and **Ten**], number indicating sum of five and ten.

Fif′ty [**Five** and suf. *‑ty*, tens], number indicating five tens.

Fig [F. *figue*; L. *ficus*, fig], fruit of a tree with large leaves. [struggle.

Fight [O.E. *feohtan*], strive against an enemy;

Fig′ment [L. *fingere*, to feign], something feigned or imagined.

Fig′ur‑a‑tive, containing a figure of speech, representing by resemblance, not literal.

Fig′ure [L. *figūra*, figure; *fingere*, to fashion], shape, symbol representing a number, fanciful form of speech; make an image of, calculate the amount of; appear as.

Fig′ure‑head′, figure on the prow of a ship, head of a body but without influence.

Fil′a‑ment [L. *filum*, thread; *filāre*, to spin], thread

Fil'bert [dial. F. *noix de filbert*, a nut ripe about St Philbert's Day, August 22], hazel-nut.

Filch (*ch*=*tsh*) [etym. dub.], steal.

File [L. *fīlāre*, to spin; *fīlum*, a thread], row of soldiers one behind another, wire on which papers are strung; march in file, place in order for future reference.

File [O.E. *féol*], tool, cut or smooth with a file.

Fil'i-al [L. *fīlius*, a son; *fīlia*, a daughter], dutiful as son or daughter.

Fil'i-bust-er [Du. *vrijbuiter*; *vrij*, free, *buit*, booty], freebooter.

Fil'i-gree [It. *filigrana*; L. *filum*, a thread; *grānum*, grain], fine jewel work of threads and beads, usually of gold and silver. [of.

Fill [O.E. *fyllan*], make full, occupy the whole

Fil'let [F. *filet* dim. of *fil*, a thread; L. *filum*, a thread], band, lean boneless piece of meat.

Fil'lip [another form of **Flip**], jerk of the finger, something to rouse.

Fil'ly [perh. O.N. *fylja*; allied to *foli*, a foal], young mare.

Film [O.E. *filmen*, a membrane; *fel*, skin], thin skin, coating of isinglass on a photographic plate, or used instead of plate, series of pictures in a cinematograph. **Film'y.**

Fil'ter [F. *filtre*; Low L. *filtrum*, a filter; see **Felt**], strainer; purify by putting through a filter.

Filth [O.E. *fylth*], foul matter, dirt.

Fin [O.E. *finn*], limb of a fish.

Fi'nal [L. *finis*, the end], last.

Fi-nance' (ī or ĭ) [O.F. *finer*, to pay a debt], public money, money matters. **Finan'cier, Finan'cial.**

Finch [O.E. *finc*], small singing bird.

Find [O.E. *findan*], meet with, come upon after search.

Fine [F. *fin*; Rom. *fino*, perh. fr. Rom. *finito*, finished], delicate, noble.

Fine [M.E. and O.F. *fin*, settlement of dispute; L. *finis*, the end], sum paid as a penalty; impose a fine.

Fi'ner-y [see **Fine**], showy clothes.

Fin-esse' [F. *finesse*; see **Fine**], fine contrivance, artfulness.

Fin'ger [O.E. *finger*, perh. cogn. with **Five**], limb of the hand; to handle.

Fin'ic-al [perh. fr. **Fine**], too particular.

Fin'ish [L. *finīre*, to end], to end, perfect; end, perfection due to labour.

Fi'nite [L. *finīre* (p.p. *finītus*), to finish], having a limit.

Fin'nan [perh. fr. River *Findhorn*], kind of cured haddock.

Fiord, Fjord (*fyord*) [Norw. *fjord*; Dan. *fiord, fjord*], long inlet of sea between high cliffs.

Fir [O.E. *furh*; cf. O.N. and Swed. *fura*; Dan. *fyr*, fir], cone-bearing tree.

Fire [O.E. *fyr*], that which burns; set fire to.

Fire'brand, piece of burning wood; one who kindles strife. [mines.

Fire'damp, explosive gas found in coal

Fire'fly, a luminous winged beetle.

Fire'i-rons, shovel, poker, and tongs.

Fire'works, contrivances to produce a show of light, coloured fire, etc.

Fir'kin [M.E. *ferdekyn*, prob. from Du. *vierde*, fourth, and suf. *kin* (a dimin.)], an old measure containing 9 gallons, a small cask.

Firm [L. *firmus*, firm], fixed, solid. **Firm'ness.**

Firm [Sp. *firma*; L. *firmāre*, to confirm; *firmus*, firm], commercial house.

Fir'ma-ment [L. *firmus*, firm], the sky.

Fir'man [Pers. *ferman*], Oriental ruler's mandate.

First [O.E. *fyrst*], before all others.

First'ling (usu. pl.), first result or fruit, first born of season.

Firth, Frith [Scot. word, from Scand.-O.N. *fjörthr*; Dan. *fiord*; Swed. *fjärd*], an arm of the sea, estuary.

Fis'cal [L. *fiscus*, a purse], relating to the public treasury.

Fish [O.E. *fisc*, cogn. with L. *piscis*], a water animal that breathes by gills; to try to catch fish.

Fish'er-y, a place for catching fish, the business of fishing.

Fish'mon-ger (*o*=ŭ) [O.E. *fisc*, fish, *mangere*, a merchant; L. *mango*, dealer], a dealer in fish.

Fis'sile [L. *fissus*, cleft], that can be split.

Fis'sure (*ss*=*sh*) [L. *findere* (p.p. *fissus*), to cleave], a cleft.

Fist [O.E. *fýst*], a closed hand.

Fist'i-cuffs, fighting with the fists. [on.

Fit [?], suited, competent, able; make fit, try

Fit [O.E. *fitt*, a struggle], sudden seizure implying loss of consciousness.

Five [O.E. *fíf*], one more than four. [settle.

Fix [L. *figere* (p.p. *fixus*), to fix], fasten,

Fix'it-y, state of being fixed.

Fix'ture, that which is fixed.

Fizz [imit.], hissing sound. [tonish.

Flab'ber-gast [?], dumbfound, greatly as-

Flab'by [weakened form of *flappy*; see **Flap**], loose and soft.

Flac'cid [L. *flaccidus, flaccus*, limp], flabby, soft and weak.

Flag [perh. imit. of sound made; etym. dub.], strip of cloth at the end of a staff.

Flag [etym. dub., cf. Du. *flag*], aquatic plant.

Flag [earlier meaning a sod, perh. fr. O.N. *flag*, a place whence sod has been cut], flat stone. [lose vigour.

Flag [perh. from noticing flag droop], droop,

Fla-gel-la'tion [L. *flagellum*, a scourge], whipping, scourging.

Fla-geo-let', Flag'eo-let (*geo*=*jo*) [F., dim. of O.F. *flajol*, etym. dub.], wind instrument like flute.

Fla-gi'tious (*ti*=*sh*, *g* soft) [L. *flāgitium*, a crime], shamefully wicked.

Flag'on [M.E. *flacon*; O.F. *flacon*; see **Flask**], large vessel for liquor, large bottle.

Fla'grant [L. *flagrāre* (pr.p. *flagrans, -antis*), to burn], glaring, very wicked. **Fla'grancy.**

Flail [O.E. *fligel*; L. *flagellum*, a whip], hand-threshing instrument.

Flake [etym. dub., cf. Norw. *flak*, a slice], scale or layer, feathery particle.

Flam'beau (*eau=ō*) [dim. of O.F. *flambe*, a flame], torch.

Flam-boy'ant [pr.p. of F. *flamboyer*, fr. *flambe*, a flame], floridly decorated, gorgeously coloured.

Flame [L. *flamma*, a flame], stream of light and heat; to blaze.

Fla-min'go [Port. *flamengo*, perh. fr. Rom. *flama*, flame], long-legged wading-bird with scarlet plumage. [rim.

Flange [perh. O.F. *flanche*, a flank], projecting

Flank [F. *flanc*. Etym. doubtful], side.

Flan'nel [W. *gwlanen*, from *gwlân*, wool], loosely spun woollen cloth.

Flap [imit.], broad, loose hanging piece, a beating of wings; move as do wings.

Flare [?], burn with an unsteady broad light.

Flash [prob. imit.], a burst of light; break forth suddenly as light.

Flash'y, showy.

Flask [cf. It. *fiasco*, Ger. *flasche*, perh. fr. L. *vasculum*, small vessel], narrow-necked vessel of glass or metal.

Flat [O.N *flatr*; cf. Swed. *flat*; Dan. *flad*], even, dull; a plain, storey of a building, character in music (♭).

Flat'ter [perh. fr. O.F. *flater*, to smooth], praise insincerely. **Flat'tery**.

Flat'u-lent [L. *flāre* (p.p. *flātus*), to blow], windy. **Flat'ulence**.

Flaunt [?], make a bold show of.

Flau'tist (*au=aw*) [It. *flauto*, a flute], player on the flute.

Fla'-vour (*a=ai*) [O.F. *flaur*, smell; perh. fr. L. *fragrāre*, to be fragrant], marked taste; to season.

Flaw [perh. O.N. *flaga*, a flaw, a flake; see Flake], imperfection. **Flaw'less**.

Flax [O.E. *fleax*], plant of which the fibre is used for linen.

Flax'en, made of flax, light straw-colour.

Flay [O.E. *flēan*], to skin.

Flea [O.E. *fléah*], leaping insect infesting larger animals.

Fleck [fr. or cogn. with O.N. *flekkr*, a spot], spot or streak.

Fledge [M.E. *fledge*, ready to fly], furnish with feathers for flight. **Fledg'(e)ling**.

Flee [O.E. *fléon*], run away from.

Fleece [O.E. *fléos*], sheep's coat of wool; strip the fleece off, plunder.

Fleer [cf. Norw. *flira*, to grin], jeer.

Fleet[1] [O.E. *flēotan*, to fly], swift; fly swiftly.

Fleet[2] [O.E. *flēot*, a ship, shipping], number of ships under one command.

Flesh [O.E. *flǣsc*], muscle and fat.

Flex'i-ble, easily bent. **Flexibil'ity**.

Flex'ion [L. *flectere* (p.p. *flexus*), to bend], a bending.

Flex'or, muscle which bends a part.

Flick [imit.], light blow; strike lightly.

Flick'er [O.E. *flicorian* imit.], waver unsteadily.

Flight [O.E. *flyht* (O. Teut. *fleugan*, fly)], act of flying.

Flight'y, changeable, giddy. **Flight'iness**.

Flim'sy (*s=z*) [prob. imit., suggested by Film], weak and unsubstantial. **Flim'siness**.

Finch (*ch=sh*) [O.F. *flenchir*. Origin unknown], draw back, shrink.

Fling [cf. O.N. *flengja*], throw; a throw, kick.

Flint [O.E. perh. cogn. with Gk. *plinthos*, a stone], very hard kind of stone.

Flip [imit.], put in motion by a light jerk or touch; light jerk (especially of the fingers).

Flip'pant [perh. fr. Flip], light or irreverent in speech. **Flip'pancy**.

Flip'per, broad flat limb used for swimming.

Flirt [imit.], dart about lightly, play at courtship; one who plays at courtship. **Flirta'tion**.

Flit [O.N. *flytja*, cogn. with Fleet[1]], fly or move lightly, remove.

Flitch [O.E. *flicce*], side of bacon.

Float [O.E. *flotian*], rest or move on water or in air, form company; raft, cork used in angling.

Float-a'tion, Flot-a'tion, starting of a business enterprise.

Flock [O.E. *flocc*, perh. cogn. with Folk], company of sheep or birds; gather in companies.

Flock [prob. O.F. *floc*; L. *floccus*, lock of wool], stuffing of wool and cut cloth.

Floe [perh. Norse *flo*, layer], flat mass of floating ice.

Flog [perh. fr. L. *flagellāre*, to whip], beat with a rod or whip.

Flood (*oo=ŭ*) [O.E. *flōd*], great flow of water, overflow; to overflow.

Floor (*oo=ō*) [O.E. *flōr*], lower surface of a room or building, storey of a building.

Flop [var. of Flap], flap, fall clumsily.

Flo'ra [L. *Flora*, the goddess of flowers; *flos* (*flōr-is*), a flower], plants of a locality or period.

Flo'ral, made of flowers.

Flor-es'cence [L. *florescere*, fr. *flos*, *flōris*, a flower], flowering time or state.

Flor'id, flowery, red.

Flor'in [It. *florino*, dim. of *fiore*, a flower; L. *flos* (*flōr-is*), a flower, the original Florentine coin having the figure of a lily stamped upon it], coin.

Flor'ist [L. *flos* (*flōr-is*), a flower], seller of flowers. [silk.

Floss [perh. O.F. *flosche*, down], untwisted

Flo-til'la [Sp. *flotilla*, dim. of *flota*, a fleet], small fleet, fleet of small vessels.

Flot'sam [A.-F. *floteson*, flotsam; O.F *floter*, to float], floating goods from a wreck.

Flounce[1] [cf. Norw. *flunsa*, to plunge], spring or turn with a jerk.

Flounce[2] [earlier *frounce*; O.F. *froncir*, to wrinkle], ornamental strip on a dress.

Floun'der [O.F. *flondre*; cf. Norw. *flundra*; Dan. *flynder*, a flounder], flat fish.

Floun'der [imit., perh. suggested by Flounce[1] and Flood], fling about awkwardly.

Flour [short for Flower (of wheat)], meal ground to powder.

Flour′ish [L. *florēre*, to flourish; *flos* (*flŏr-is*), a flower], thrive, brandish; ornament of flowing curves, a waving motion, fanfare of trumpets.

Flout [perh. var. of **Flute**], mock. [ing.

Flow [O.E. *flówan*], move as water; a stream-

Flow′er [L. *flos* (*flŏr-is*), a flower], blossom; to blossom. **Flow′ery.**

Fluc′tu-ate [L. *fluctus*, a wave], move as a wave, waver. **Fluctua′tion.**

Flue [perh. cogn. with **Flow**], pipe or passage for conveying flame and hot gases.

Flu′en-cy [L. *fluere*, to flow], flowing speech.

Fluf′fy [orig. uncertain], soft and downy.

Flu′id [L. *fluidus*, flowing; *fluere*, to flow], body whose particles move among themselves, *i.e.* a liquid or a gas; moving easily, not stable. **Fluid′ity.**

Fluke [O.E. *flóc*, cogn. with Ger. *flach*, flat], a flounder.

Fluke [?], accidental success.

Flum′mer-y [W. *llymru*, sour oatmeal boiled], light food, trash.

Flun′key [perh. F. *flanquer*, to run by the side of; see **Flank**], liveried servant.

Flur′ry [imit.], excitement and hurry, gust or squall, sudden rush of birds; to bewilder, confuse.

Flush[1] [perh. imit., influenced by **Flash**], to flood, blush; sudden rush or flow.

Flush[2] [prob. fr. **Flush**[1]], full to overflowing, level.

Flush[3] [perh. imit., cf. **Fly**, **Rush**], fly away, start a bird or flock of birds.

Flus′ter [Icel. *flaustra* (vb.), *flaustr* (n.)], confuse; agitation.

Flute [O.F. *flaüte*, *fleüte*. Of uncertain origin], musical wind instrument, channel (as in a column or ruffle); play flute, make grooves in.

Flut′y, flute-like, soft and clear.

Flut′ter [O.E. *flotorian*, to float about], flap the wings without flying; confused motion. [rivers.

Flu′vi-al [L. *fluvius*, a river], belonging to

Flux [L. *fluere* (p.p. *fluxus*), to flow], flowing, constant change.

Fly [O.E. *fléogan*, to fly; *fléoge*, *flýge*, a fly], winged insect, light carriage; move with wings, flee from.

Fly′leaf, blank leaf at the beginning or end of a book.

Fly′wheel, large wheel to equalise the movement in machinery or accumulate power.

Foal [O.E. *fola*], young of a mare.

Foam [O.E. *fám*], froth; to froth. **Foam′y.**

Fob [?], watch pocket.

Fob [cf. Du. *foppen*, to cheat], cheat, take in, impose upon.

Fo′cus [L. *focus*, a hearth], central point, one of two points in an ellipse, etc.; to converge, adjust. **Fo′cal.**

Fod′der [O.E. *fódor*], food for cattle.

Foe [O.E. *fáh*, hostile], enemy, one who is against another. [rank grass.

Fog [orig. unknown], mist near the ground,

Fo′gy, Fo′gey [perh. fr. **Fog**], dull old fellow.

Foi′ble [O.F. *foible*; F. *faible*, weak], a weak point in character.

Foil [perh. from obs. *foin*, a thrust; O.F. *foine*, a fish-spear], blunt weapon used in fencing.

Foil [L. *folium*, a leaf], thin sheet metal, background.

Foil [O.F. *fouler*, to full cloth, to trample], defeat, outwit.

Foist [Du. *vuisten*, to take in the hand; *vuist*, fist], impose.

Fold [O.E. *fealdan*, to fold], part doubled over; double over.

Fold [O.E. *fald*], enclosure for sheep, a flock.

Fo′li-age [F. *feuillage*; L. *folium*, a leaf], leafage. **Fol′iate**, leaflike, having leaves.

Fo′li-o [from L. *in folio*, in leaf], sheet of paper once folded, book of the largest kind, page number.

Folk (*ol*=*ō*) [O.E. *folc*], people. [after.

Fol′low [O.E. *folgian*, to follow], come or go

Fol′ly [O.F. *fol*, foolish], foolishness.

Fo-ment′ [L.L. *fomentāre*, to foment; L. *fovēre*, to warm], apply warmth and moisture, encourage. **Fomenta′tion.**

Fond [M.E. *fond* or *fonned*, p.p. of obs. *fon*, to become insipid], foolish, loving.

Fon′dle [see **Fond**], to caress.

Font [L. *fons* (*font-is*), a fountain], vessel which holds water for baptism.

Food [O.E. *fóda*], what is fed upon.

Fool [L. *follis*, a wind-bag, in Late L. a fool], silly person, jester; to cheat.

Fool [prob. fr. **Fool**], juice of crushed fruit mixed with cream, etc.

Fool′har′dy [O.F. *fol hardi*], foolishly bold.

Fools′cap [fr. water-mark on it; see **Fool** and **Cap**], size of paper about 16×13 inches.

Foot [O.E. *fót*], lowest part of the leg, lowest part or base, measure of 12 inches, measure in poetry; to tread.

Foot′ing, ground for the feet, position.

Foot′lights, lights in front of a stage.

Foot′man, man-servant.

Foot′print, mark left by a foot.

Foo′zle [cf. Ger. *fuseln*, to work badly or slowly], to play badly at golf, to spoil.

Fop [?], vain, overdressed man.

For′age [O.F. *fourrage*, fodder; Rom. *fodro*], search for food; food for horses.

For′ay [Rom. *fodro*; see **Forage**], a raid; pillage.

For-bear′ [O.E. *for-*, implying abstention, and **Bear**], cease from proceeding, be patient.

For-bid′ [O.E. *for-*, implying prohibition, and **Bid**], command not to, prohibit.

For-bid′ding, repelling approach.

Force [Late L. *fortia*, strength; L. *fortis*, strong], active power, constraint, body of troops; compel. **Force′ful.**

Force [Dan. *fos*; Swed. and O.N. *fors*], waterfall.

Force′meat [obs. *force*, corruption of *farce*; see **Farce** and **Meat**], meat chopped and seasoned.

For′ceps [L. *forceps*], pair of pincers.

For′ci-ble, full of force, done by force.

Ford [cogn. with **Fare**], shallow place in a river where it may be crossed by wading; wade across. **Ford'able.**

Fore [O.E. *fore*], in front; the forward part.

Fore-bode' [O.E. *fore-*, in advance, *bodian*, to announce], foretell, be a sign of, have a presentiment of (misfortune). **Forebod'ing.**

Fore-cast' [O.E. *fore-*, in advance; O.N. *kasta*, to throw], foresee; **Fore'cast**, foresight of consequences, prophecy based on present indications, esp. regarding weather.

Forecas'tle (*fo'csl*), forward part of a ship.

Fore-close' (*s=z*) [L. *foris*, outside, *claudere* (p.p. *clausus*), to close], stop, shut out, deprive a person of the right of redeeming a mortgage. **Foreclo'sure.**

Fore'father, ancestor.

Fore-go', better **For-go'** [O.E. *forgán*, to pass over; *for-*, from, *gán*, to go], give up, let go.

Fore'ground, part of a scene which is represented as nearest to the spectator, most prominent position.

Fore'head, part of face above the eyebrows.

For'eign [L. *foris*, outside], belonging to another country, strange. **For'eigner.**

Fore'land, cape, headland.

Fore'man, chief man, overseer.

Fore'most [O.E. *formest*], first in time or place.

Fore'noon, early part of the day, before 12 o'clock.

Fo-ren'sic [L. *forensis*, relating to the forum; see **Forum**], relating to courts of law or public discussion. [water marks.

Fore'shore, shore between high- and low-

Fore-short'en [*fore-*, in front, and **Shorten**], draw (an object) so as to represent apparent shortening due to perspective.

Fore'sight, foreseeing, looking ahead.

For'est [M.L. *forestis*, open hunting-ground; L. *foris*, out of doors], large wood or woodland district. **For'estry.**

Fore-stall' (*-stawl*) [O.E. *foresteall*, ambush; *fore-*, in front, *steall*, a station], take in advance, get ahead of. [beforehand.

Fore-tell' [*fore-*, in advance, and **Tell**], tell

Fore'word [*fore-*, in advance, and **Word**], preface.

For'feit [O.F. *forfait* (p.p. of *forfaire*), to trespass; L. *foris*, out of doors; *facere*, to do], lose the right to by a fault; a fine.

For'feit-ure, loss inflicted as a penalty. [off.

For-fend' [pref. *for-*, from, and **Fend**], keep

For-gath'er [pref. *for-*, in the presence of, and **Gather**], assemble, meet with accidentally.

Forge [O.F. *forge*; L. *fabrica*, a workshop; place where iron is heated and hammered; form by hammering, imitate another's handwriting dishonestly. **For'gery.**

Forge [?], advance against difficulty (in "forge ahead ").

For-get' [O.E. *forgietan*; *for-*, from, and **Get**], let go from the memory. **Forget'ful.**

For-give' [O.E. *forgiefan*; *for-*, from, and **Give**], pardon. **Forgive'ness.**

Fork [L. *furca*, a fork], pronged instrument; to divide into branches; point where division takes place.

For-lorn' [O.E. *forloren* (p.p. of *forléosan*), to lose utterly; *for-* (with intensive meaning), and **Lose**], forsaken, almost hopeless.

Form [L. *forma*, shape], shape, fixed way of proceeding, a bench, the bed of a hare; (also **Forme**), a body of type for printing at one impression; to shape.

For'mal, in proper form, stiff. **Formal'ity.**

For'mal-ism, too strict adherence to forms.

For-ma'tion, act of forming or shaping, thing formed.

For'mer [back-formation, fr. O.E. *formest*, foremost], the first-mentioned of two, earlier. [fear.

For'mi-da-ble [L. *formidáre*, to fear], causing

For'mu-la (*pl.-as*, *-æ*) [L. *formula*, dim. of *forma*, a form], set form.

For'mu-late, express in a formula.

For-ni-ca'tion [L.L. *fornicationem*, impurity], sexual immorality.

For-sake' [O.E. *forsacan*; *for-*, implying abstention, and *sacan*, to contend], leave entirely.

For-sooth' [O.E. *forsóth*, for a truth], in truth (used in contempt).

For-swear' [O.E. *forswerian*, to forswear; *for-*, from, and **Swear**], swear to give up, swear falsely.

Fort [F. *fort*; L. *fortis*, strong], strong place, small fortified place. [point.

Forte [F. *fort* (fem. *forte*, strong], one's strong

Forth [cogn. with **Fore**], out, forward.

Forth'com'ing, about to appear.

Forth-with', immediately.

For-ti-fi-ca'tion [F., fr. L. *fortificationem*, strengthening], act of fortifying; works set up to defend.

For'ti-fy [F. *fortifier*; L. *fortis*, strong, *facere*, to make], strengthen, secure by forts or batteries.

For'ti-tude [L. *fortis*, strong], strength of mind, enduring courage.

Fort'night [O.E. *féowertíne niht*, fourteen nights], two weeks.

For'tress [L. *fortis*, strong], large and permanent fortification.

For-tu'i-tous [L. *fors* (*fort-is*), chance], happening by chance.

For'tu-nate, having good fortune, lucky.

For'tune [L. *fortuna*, allied to *fors*, chance], chance, luck, lot in life, riches.

For'ty [O.E. *féowertig*], ten times four.

Fo'rum [L. *forum*, market-place], market-place (esp. of Rome).

For'ward [O.E. *foreweard*], near the fore part, onward, advanced, bold; help onward.

Fosse, **Foss** [L. *fossa*, a ditch], ditch, moat.

Fos'sil [L. *fodere* (p.p. *fossus*), to dig], remains of an animal or plant embedded in rocks. **Fos'silize.**

Fos'ter [O.E. *fostór*], to feed, to cherish.

Fos'ter-child, child reared by persons not its parents.

Foul [O.E. *fúl*], dirty, impure, stormy; to collide with.

Found [1] [L. *fundáre*, to found; *fundus*, the bottom], to lay the groundwork.

Found [L. *fundere*, to pour, to cast metals], set to work in molten metal.

Foun-da'tion, groundwork, an endowment, an endowed charity or institution.

Found'er [O.F. *fondrer*, to plunge to the bottom], go to the bottom, fall in ruins.

Found'er [see **Found**], one who establishes or sets up.

Found'er [see **Found**], one who founds or casts metal.

Found'ling [fr. **Find** and *-ling*], deserted infant of unknown parents.

Found'ry, a building where metals are cast.

Fount, Foun'tain [L. *fons* (*font-is*) ; Late L. *fontana*, a fountain], a spring, a jet of water, the basin in which such a jet rises, source. [three.

Four (*ou=ō*) [O.E. *féower*], one more than

Fowl [O.E. *fugel*, a bird], bird (rare except in *wildfowl*), a barndoor bird.

Fox [O.E. *fox*, a fox], sly animal with a bushy tail. **Fox'y. Fox'iness.**

Fox'glove [O.E. *foxes glófa*, fox's glove], a tall flower. [turbance.

Fra-cas' [F. *fracas* ; It. *fracasso*, uproar], dis-

Frac'tion [L. *frangere* (p.p. *fractus*), to break], part; the act of breaking. **Frac'tional.**

Frac'tious (*ti=sh*), snappish, cross.

Frac'ture, a break ; to break.

Fra'gile [L. *frangere*, to break], easily broken, delicate. **Fragil'ity.**

Frag'ment [L. *frangere*, to break], a piece broken off, a small portion. **Frag'mentary.**

Fra'grant [L. *fragrans* (*-antis*), pr.p. of *frāgrāre*, to smell sweet], sweet of smell.

Frail [O.F. *frayel*], basket made of rushes, used chiefly for containing figs, raisins, etc.

Frail [L. *fragilis*, fragile], weak. **Frail'ty.**

Frame [O.E. *framian*, to be profitable; *fram*, forward], to plan, to construct by fitting parts together, to put in a frame; a form, an open structure for holding something.

Franc [perh. fr. L. *Francorum Rex*, king of the Franks, legend on an early coin], a French coin (normal value about 9½d.).

Fran'chise [O.F. *franchise*; *franchir* (pr.p. *franchissant*), to free], the right to vote.

Frank [O.F. *franc*; Low L. *francus*, free ; O.H.G. *frank*, a Frank], free, outspoken ; the sign denoting that a letter is to go free of postage; to put such a sign on.

Frank'in-cense [O.F. *franc encens*, pure incense; see **Frank** and **Incense**], a fragrant gum.

Frank'lin [see **Frank**, perh. suf. *-ling*], old English freeholder.

Fran'tic [Gk. *phreneticos*, mad; see **Frenzy**], mad, raving, furious.

Fra-ter'nal [L. *frater*, a brother], brotherly.

Fra-ter'ni-ty [L. *frater*, a brother], a brotherhood, brotherliness. **Frat'ernize.**

Frat'ri-cide [L. *frater*, brother, *cædere*, to kill], killing one's brother or sister, one who kills brother or sister.

Fraud [L. *fraus* (*fraud-is*), fraud], deception with a view to gain.

Fraud'u-lent, dishonest, unfair.

Fraught [p.p. of obsolete *fraught*, to lade a ship; see **Freight**], laden.

Fray [F. *frayer* ; L. *fricāre*, to rub], wear by rubbing.

Fray [for **Affray**], a fight.

Freak [etym. dub., cf. *frician*, to move briskly], sudden turn of the mind, whim, playful trick, a monstrosity.

Frec'kle [O.N. *freknur* ; Swed. *fräkne*, freckles], brownish spot on the skin.

Free [O.E. *fréo*], not held in or held down by the will of others, without charge, clear from, set at liberty.

Free'boot-er [Du. *vrijbuiter*; see **Free** and **Booty**], robber.

Free'hand, drawn without guiding instruments.

Free'dom, state of being free.

Free'hold, property held free of duty except to the king.

Free'man, one who has the franchise.

Free-ma'son, member of a secret brotherhood. **Free-ma'sonry.**

Free'stone, fine-grained sandstone or limestone that can be cut or sawn easily.

Freeze [O.E. *fréosan*], turn or be turned from liquid to solid by cold, chill.

Freight (*ei=ai*) [prob. M.Du. *vracht* or *vrecht*], cargo; sum paid to a shipowner for carriage of goods. **Freight'age.**

Fren'zy, Phren'zy [O.F. *frenesie* ; L.L. *phrenesis* ; Gk. *phrenetikos*, frantic], wild excitement, madness.

Fre'quent [L. *frequens* (*-entis*), crowded ; allied to *farcīre*, to cram], happening often. **Fre'quency.**

Fre-quent , visit often.

Fre-quent'-a-tive [see **Frequent**], expressing frequent repetition of an action.

Fres'co [It. *fresco*, fresh, cool], kind of painting on fresh plaster.

Fresh [O.E. *fersc*, and O.F. *freis* (fem. *fresche*), fresh], new, brisk, unfaded, not salt.

Fresh'man, a newcomer, esp. a student in his first year at a university. [worry,

Fret [O.E. *fretan*], wear by rubbing, to vex,

Fret [perh. O.F. *frete*, ferrule], bar on fingerboard of stringed instrument.

Fret'work [perh. fr. O.F. *frete*, trellis-work], ornamental open work. [crumbled.

Fri'a-ble [L. *friāre*, to crumble], easily

Fri'ar [L. *frater* (*frat-ris*), a brother], brother of a religious order, esp. a begging order.

Fric'tion [L. *fricāre* (p.p. *frictus*), to rub], rubbing.

Fri'day [O.E. *frigedæg*, day of the goddess *Frig*], sixth day of the week.

Friend [O.E. *fréond*], one who has affection for another, a well-wisher. **Friend'ship.**

Frieze [allied to Ital. *fregio*, a fringe; L. *Phrygium opus*, Phrygian work], ornamental band at the top of a wall.

Frieze [F. *frise*, frieze; F. *friser*, to curl], tufted woollen cloth.

Frig'ate [F. *frégate* ; It. *fregata*, etym. dub.], war-vessel. (Formerly a particular class of war-ship.)

Fright [O.E. *fryhto*], sudden fear. **Fright'ful.**

Fri'gid (*frĭj'ĭd*) [L. *frigēre*, to be cold ; *frĭgus*, cold], very cold, stiff and formal. **Fri-gid'ity.** [edging.

Frill [origin uncertain], a ruffle ; crimped

Fringe [O.F. *frenge* ; L. *fĭmbria*, fringe], edging of threads, border.

Frip'per-y [O.F. *frepe*, frayed out fringe ; old clothes ; perh. fr. L. *fĭbra*, a fibre], cheap finery.

Fris-eur' [F.], hairdresser.

Frisk [O.F. *frisque*, perh. cogn. with **Fresh**], skip or dance about in play.

Fri-till'ar-y [L. *fritillus*, dice-box], plant of the lily kind.

Frit'ter [perh. fr. *fitters*, fragments, fr. obs. *fitter*, to break in pieces ; cf. L. *fractūra*, a fracture], fragment ; to waste piecemeal.

Frit'ter [F. *friture* ; L. *frigere* (p.p. *frictus*), to fry], kind of fried batter cake.

Fri-vol'i-ty [L. *frivolus*, rubbed away, silly ; *friāre, fricāre*, to rub], trifling act or habit. **Friv'olous.**

Friz'zle [F. *friser*, to curl], form into small curls ; crisp.

Fro [O.N. *frá*, from], away.

Frock [Low L. *froccus* ; *floccus*, a monk's frock], gown, shirtlike outer garment.

Frog [O.E. *frogga*], leaping amphibious animal.

Frog [?], attachment to waist-belt to support bayonet, sword ; military coat-fastening. **Frogged.**

Frol'ic [Du. *vrolijk* ; cf. Ger. *fröhlich*, merry], prank, sportive mirth. **Frol'icsome.**

From [O.E. *fram*], away, forth (from . . . to=between . . . and).

Frond [L. *frons* (*frond-is*), a leaf], leaf of a fern, palm-leaf.

Front (*o=ŭ*) [L. *frons* (*front-is*), the forehead], fore or facing part.

Front'age, extent of facing part.

Front'ier (*-ŏn-*) [L. *frons* (*front-is*), front], border of a country.

Fron'tis-piece (*o=ŭ*) [L. *frons* (*front-is*), front, *specere*, to see], illustration at the beginning of a book.

Front'let, band worn on forehead.

Frost [see **Freeze**], condition of the air below freezing-point.

Froth [perh. O.N. *frotha* ; cf. O.E. *á-fréothan*, to froth], collection of bubbles. **Froth'y.**

Frou'zy, Frow'zy [?], musty, slovenly.

Fro'ward [E.], ungovernable, wayward.

Frown [O.F. *froignier*, to frown ; cf. Swed. dial. *fryna* ; Norw. *fröyna*, to make a wry face], a wrinkling of the brow in displeasure ; put on a stern look.

Fruc'ti-fy [L. *fructus*, fruit ; *facere* (p.p. *factus*), to make], to bear fruit ; to make fruitful. **Fructifica'tion.**

Fru'gal [L. *frugālis* ; *frugi*, frugal, *frugi* (orig. dat. of *frux*, fruit)], sparing, not wasteful. **Frugal'ity.**

Fruit [L. *fructus*, fruit ; *frui* (p.p. *fructus*), to enjoy], part of a plant which contains the seed, produce.

Fru-i'tion [L. *fruitionem*, from *frui*, to enjoy], attainment of an object, enjoyment, pleasure arising from possession.

Fru'men-ty, Fur'me-ty [L. *frumentum*, corn], hulled wheat boiled in milk and seasoned with sugar, cinnamon, etc.

Frus'trate [L. *frustra*, in vain], bring to nothing, balk.

Fry [F. *frire*, to fry ; L. *frigere* ; Gk. *phrygein*, to parch], cook over a fire in boiling fat.

Fry [O.N. *frió*, seed], spawn of fishes.

Fuch'si-a [*fū'shi-a*] [fr. *Fuchs*, a German botanist], plant with drooping flowers.

Fudge [?], humbug.

Fu'el [Late L. *focālia*, pl. of *focale*, fuel ; L. *focus*, a hearth], matter used for burning.

Fu'gi-tive [L. *fugere* (p.p. *fugitus*), to flee], one who flees from pursuit ; fleeing, fleeting.

Fu'gle-man [Ger. *flügel*, wing, *mann*, man], soldier formerly placed in front as example while drilling.

Fugue (*fūg*), [L. *fuga*, flight, *fugere*, to flee], musical composition in which parts seem to pursue each other.

Ful'crum, (pl.) **Fulcra** [L. *fulcīre*, to prop], prop on which a lever moves.

Ful-fil' [O.E. *fullfyllan*, fr. *full*, full, *fyllan*, to fall], bring to pass, satisfy the requirements of.

Ful-ig'in-ous (*g=j*) [L. *fūlĭgo*, soot], sooty.

Full (*u=oo*) [O.E. *full*, full], filled up, able to contain no more ; complete measure.

Full [O.F. *fuler*, to full, to trample on], cleanse and thicken cloth.

Ful'mi-nate [L. *fulmen* (*fulmin-is*), lightning], to thunder, condemn strongly, an explosive substance. **Fulmina'tion.**

Ful'some (*u=oo*) [**Full** and suf. *-some*], offensive from excess (of praise).

Fum'ble [perh. fr. O.E. *folm*, the palm of the hand], feel or grope about.

Fume [O.F. *fum* ; L. *fumus*, smoke], smoke, vapour, rage ; rise up as vapour, to rage.

Fu'mi-gate [L. *fumus*, smoke], apply fumes to (esp. in order to disinfect). **Fumiga'tion.**

Fu'mi-tor-y [O.F. *fumeterre* ; L. *fūmus terræ*, earth-smoke], a herb.

Fun [perh. fr. obs. *fon*, to hoax ; etym. doubtful], sport, merriment.

Fu-nam'bu-list [L. *fūnis*, a rope, *ambulāre*, to walk], a rope-walker.

Func'tion [L. *fungi* (p.p. *functus*), to perform], vital process, duty of a position. **Func'-tional.**

Func'tion-a-ry, an official. [capital.

Fund [L. *fundus*, bottom], store, stock or

Fun-da-men'tal [L. *fundamentum*, foundation ; *fundāre*, to found], at the foundation.

Fu'ner-al [L. *fūnus* (*fūner-is*), a funeral], burial ; pertaining to a burial or cremation.

Fu-ne're-al, suiting a funeral, gloomy.

Fun′gus, (pl.) **Fungi** [L. *fungus*; perh. cogn. with Gk. *sphoggos*, a sponge], spongy plant of which the mushroom is one. **Fun′gous**.

Fun-i′cul-ar [L. *funiculus*, fr. *funis*, cord], kind of railway worked by cable.

Funk [?], fear, panic.

Fun′nel [L. *infundibulum*, a funnel; *in*, in, *fundere*, to pour], inverted hollow cone with a pipe below, shaft of a chimney.

Fun′ny, droll, amusing.

Fur [O.F. *forrer*, fr. Rom. *foderare*, to sheathe or line], fine, soft hair on a skin, dressed skins for clothing, matter on the tongue, deposit from boiled hard water.

Fur′be-low [corr. of *falbala*, a flounce, etym. unknown], flounce, (pl.) showy accessories to dress.

Fur′bish [O.F. *forbir*; O.H.G. *forban*, to polish], rub or scour to brightness.

Fur′cate [L. *furca*, a fork], form a fork; forked or branched.

Fu′ri-ous [see **Fury**], raging.

Furl [formerly *furdle*, fr. *fardel*, a burden], roll up, wrap round.

Fur′long [O.E. *furh*, a furrow, *lang*, long], measure of 220 yards. Originally the length of the furrow in the common field.

Fur′lough [Du. *verlof*, furlough; see **Leave**], leave of absence.

Fur′nace [L. *fornax* (*fornāc-is*), a furnace, *fornus*, an oven], large enclosed fireplace.

Fur′nish [O.F. *furnir*, to furnish, fr. Rom. *fornire*, fr. Teut., cf. O.H.G. *frummen*, to provide, to furnish], provide, equip.

Fur′ni-ture, that with which anything is furnished, movable articles in a house.

Fur′ri-er, dealer in furs.

Fur′row [O.E. *furh*], trench made by a plough.

Fur′ther [O.E. *furthor* (adv.), *furthra* (adj.), *fyrthrian* (vb.)], at or to a greater distance; help forward.   [sly.

Fur′tive [L. *furtivus*, furtive; *fur*, a thief],

Fu′ry [L. *furia*, fury; *furere*, to rage], violence, rage; violent woman.

Furze [O.E. *fyrs*, etym. dub.], prickly evergreen shrub, gorse, whin.

Fuse (*s=z*) [L. *fundere* (p.p. *fūsus*), to pour], melt, blend into one.

Fuse, **Fuze** [It. *fuso*, a spindle, a fuse; L. *fusus*, a spindle], tube filled with combustible matter used in blasting, etc.

Fu-see′, light musket or firelock.

Fu′si-ble (*s=z*), that can be melted or fused.

Fu-sil-lade′ (*s=z*) [F. *fusiller*, to shoot; *fusil*, a musket], simultaneous discharge of firearms.

Fu′sion (*si=zh*), act of melting together, blending as though by melting so as to form one whole.

Fuss [prob. imit.], ado about trifles.

Fus′tian [O.F. *fustaigne*; M.L. *fustāneus*, perh. fr. *Fostat*, a suburb of Cairo], shortnapped twilled heavy cotton; bombastic, worthless.

Fus′ty [O.F. *fust*, a cask; L. *fustis*, a cudgel], mouldy.

Fu′tile [L. *fūtilis*, that easily pours out, leaky, therefore untrustworthy], useless. **Futil′ity**.   **G**

Fu′ture [L. *futūrus*, about to be], that is to be or come.

Fu-tu′ri-ty, time to come.

Fuzz [perh. imit. of *blowing*], fine, loose fibres or particles.

G

Gab′ble [imit.], rapid talk without meaning.

Gab′er-dine (*ine=een*) [Sp. *gabardina*, perh. M.H.G. *wallevart*, pilgrimage], loose gown, esp. worn by Jews.

Ga′ble [O.F. *gable*; O.N. *gafl*, a gable], upper triangular part of a wall.

Ga′by [?], simpleton.

Gad [perh. fr. obs. *gadling*, O.E. *gaedling*, a companion (*gaed*, fellowship)], walk about without purpose.

Gad′fly [fr. obs. *gad*, O.N. *gaddr*, a spike], fly that molests cattle.

Gag [perh. imit. of choking sound], something thrust into the mouth to hinder speaking.

Gage[1] [fr. Sir W. *Gage*, c. 1725], a kind of plum.

Gage[2] [O.F. *guage*; O.E. *wed*, a pledge], pledge, challenge.

Gai′e-ty, liveliness, glee, showiness.

Gain [O.F. *gain*; F. *gagne*; ult. O.H.G. *weide*, pasture], profit, benefit; get by striving, win.   [contradict.

Gain-say′ [O.N. *gegn*, against, and **Say**],

Gait [var. of **Gate**[1]], walk.

Gai′ter [F. *guêtre*, gaiter; orig. doubtful], covering for leg below knee or for instep.

Ga′la [It. *gala*, finery], show, festivity.

Gal′ax-y [Gk. *gala*, milk], cluster of stars, Milky Way, brilliant gathering.

Gale [of doubtful origin; cf. Dan. *gal*, furious], strong wind.

Gall[1] (*gawl*) [O.E. *gealla*, perh. allied to **Yellow**], bile.

Gall[2] (*gawl*) [O.E. *gealla*, sore on a horse; perh. fr. **Gall**[1]], swelling; hurt the skin by rubbing, harass.

Gall[3] (*gawl*) [F. *galle*; L. *galla*], oak-apple.

Gal′lant [F. *galant*, pr.p. of O.F. *galer*, to rejoice; perh. fr. O.H.G. *wallōn*, to wander], noble in bearing, chivalrous; fine gentleman.

Gal-lant′, polite to ladies.

Gal′lan-try, bravery, politeness to ladies.

Gal′leon (*eon=yon*) [Sp. *galeon*, a galleon], large ship, usu. Spanish.

Gal′le-ry [F. *galerie*, gallery; orig. unknown], long passage connecting rooms, long narrow platform outside a building, projecting platform within a building supported by brackets or columns, building in which works of art are exhibited.

Gal′ley [O.F. *galie*; M.L. *galea*, galley; orig. doubtful], long row-boat sometimes with sail, cookroom of a ship.

Gal′li-na′ceous (*ce*=*sh*) [L. *gallina*, a hen; *gallus*, a cock], pertaining to poultry, pheasants, etc.

Gall′nut, growth produced by an insect on the leaf of an oak.

Gal′lon [O.N.F. *galon*, a gallon, orig. "a large bowl "], measure of four quarts.

Gal-loon′ [F. *galonner*, to tie the hair with ribbons], kind of ribbon or braid for binding.

Gal′lop [F. *galoper* (vb.), prob. earlier *waloper*, etym. dub.], go at a gallop; mode of running by a horse in leaps, ride at this pace.

Gal′lows [O.E. *galga*], frame for the hanging of criminals.

Ga-loche′, Ga-losh′, Gol-osh′ [F. *galoche*, perh. late L. *galopus*, a wooden shoe], overshoe (usually of india-rubber).

Gal′op [see **Gallop**], lively dance.

Gal-ore′ [fr. Ir. *go leór*, to sufficiency], in abundance.

Gal′van-ism [fr. *Galvani*, of Bologna, discoverer, 1792], branch of electricity. **Gal-vanize′**.

Gam′ble [O.E. *gamenian*, to play at games; *gamen*, sport], play for a stake.

Gam-boge′ [Mod. L. *gambogium*, fr. *Cambodia* in Annam], yellow gum-resin.

Gam′bol [It. *gambata*, a kick; *gamba*, a leg], play about, frisk.

Game [O.E. *gamen*, sport], sport, contest for amusement, certain animals hunted (hares, grouse, etc.); gamble; spirited. **Gam′y**.

Game′ster, one who gambles.

Gam′in [F. *gamin*], neglected city-boy.

Gam′mon [O.F. *gambe*, a leg], lower end of a flitch of bacon.

Gam′mon [as **Game**], humbug.

Gam′ut [M.L. *gamma ut*, *gamma*, being Gk. letter *g*, last note of musical scale, and *ut*, the old name for first note of scale], musical scale, whole series of tones used by musicians, range of tones produced by voice or instrument.

Gan′der [O.E. *gan(d)ra*], male of a goose.

Gang [O.E. *gang*, a going; *gangan*, to go], number going in company.

Gan′gli-on [Gk. *gagglion*, a tumour near tendons, also the complex nerve-centres], a collection of grey matter in the cerebrospinal system, forming a nerve-centre.

Gan′grene [L. *gangroena*; Gk. *gaggraina*, an eating sore], death of a part of the body. **Gan′grenous**. [planks.

Gang′way [O.E. *gangweg*], passage, esp. of

Gan′net [O.E. *ganot*], the Solan goose.

Gaol (*jail*), **Jail** [O.N.F. *gaiole*, O.F. *jaiole*, fr. Rom. dim. of *cavea*, a cave], jail, prison. **Gaol′er**, **Jail′er**, **Jail′or**.

Gap [O.N. and Swed. *gap*, a gap; *gapa*, to gape], opening, breach.

Gape [see **Gap**], open wide, yawn.

Gar′age (or *gar-ah′*) [F. *garage*; *garer*, to shunt], place for housing motor-cars.

Garb [It. *garbo*, elegance, fr. Teut.; cf. O.H.G. *garawi*, preparation], dress. [matter.

Gar′bage [perh. O.F. *garbe*, a handful], refuse

Gar′ble [ult. fr. Arab. *gharbala*, to sift], misquote unfairly, misrepresent words.

Gar′den [O.N.F. *gardin*. Cogn. with **Yard**], piece of ground where flowers, vegetables, etc., are cultivated. **Gar′dener**.

Gar-gan′tu-an [*Gargantua*, giant in Rabelais], enormous, gigantic.

Gar′gle [O.F. *gargouille*, the throat, a gargoyle], throat-wash which is moved about by the breath; use a gargle. [spout.

Gar′goyle [see **Gargle**], projecting water-

Ga′rish (*a*=*ai*) [perh. fr. obs. *gaure*, to stare, etym. dub.], showy, dazzling. [wreath.

Gar′land [O.F. *garlande*. Etym. doubtful].

Gar′lic [O.E. *gárléac*; *gár*, a spear, and *léac*, a leek], plant with a bulbous root.

Gar′ment [O.F. *garniment*; *garnir*, to protect], article of clothing.

Gar′ner [O.F. *gerner*, L. *granarium*, a granary], store of grain; to store.

Gar′net [O.F. *grenat*, M.L. *granatum*, pomegranate], precious stone, red in colour.

Gar′nish [O.F. *garnir*, to protect. Cogn. with **Warn**], to ornament.

Gar′ni-ture, embellishment, dress.

Gar′ret [O.F. *garite*, a watch-tower; *garir*, to preserve], room just below the roof.

Gar′ri-son [O.F. *garison*, defence; *garir*, to defend], troops in a fortified place.

Gar-rotte′ [Sp. *garrote*, stick used in twisting cord in strangling], strangle, rob after half-strangling.

Gar′ru-lous [L. *garrire*, to chatter], talkative and tiresome. **Garru′lity**.

Gar′ter [O.F. *gartier*, garter; *garet*, the ham of the leg], band to hold up a stocking, highest order of knighthood in Britain.

Gas [word invented by a Dutchman fr. Gk. *chaos*, chaos], aeriform fluid.

Gas-e-lier′ (*gass-e-leer′*) [formed as **Chandelier**, with **Gas**], hanging frame for gas-burners.

Gas-con-ade′ [fr. *Gascony*], boasting.

Ga′se-ous (*a*=*ai*), in the form of gas.

Gash [formerly *garse*; O.F. *garser*, to pierce with a lancet], deep, long cut; make a gash.

Gas-om′e-ter, tank for holding gas.

Gasp [O.N. *geispa*, to yawn], open the mouth wide, catch breath; catching of the breath.

Gas′tric [Gk. *gastér*, the stomach], pertaining to the stomach.

Gas-tron′-o-my [Gk. *gastér*, stomach; *nomos*, law], art of good eating. **Gastronom′ic**.

Gate[1] [O.N. and Swed. *gata*, a street], a passage-way.

Gate[2] [O.E. *geat*], suspended framework which closes a passage.

Gath′er [O.E. *gaderian*], bring or come together, to pluck.

Gath′er-ing, crowd, assembly.

Gaud′y [L. *gaudium*, joy; *gaudēre*, to rejoice], vulgarly showy. **Gaud′iness**.

Gauge [O.N.F. *gauger*, to gage; *gauge*, a gage], measure contents, estimate; apparatus for measuring a special force or dimension, distance between rails.

Gaunt [?], lean.

Gaunt'let [F. *gantelet*, double dim. of *gant*, a glove], iron glove, glove covering the wrist. [parent stuff.

Gauze [F. *gaze*, perh. fr. *Gaza*], a thin, trans-

Gawk'y [?], awkward.

Gay [O.F. *gai*, gay; perh. O.H.G. *wâhi*, beautiful], merry, bright.

Gaze [Swed. dial. *gasa*, to stare at], look fixedly ; eager look.

Ga-zelle' [Arab. *ghazâl*, gazelle], graceful kind of antelope.

Ga-zette' [It. *gazzetta*, a gazette, also a coin less than a farthing], newspaper ; publish officially, as a case of bankruptcy.

Gaz-et-teer', geographical dictionary.

Gaz'o-gene [F. *gazogène* ; E. *gas*, and Gk. *genēs*, producing], small apparatus for making aerated waters.

Gear (*g* hard) [prob. O.N. *gervi*, ready], clothing, goods, harness, toothed wheels working on one another ; put gear on.

Gei'sha (*ei=ai*) [Jap. *geisha*], Japanese dancing-girl.

Gel'a-tine (*ine=ine* or *een*), **Gel'a-tin** [It. *gelatina*, gelatine ; L. *gelāre* (p.p. *gelātus*), to freeze], chief component of jellies. **Gela'tinous.**

Geld (*g* hard) [O.N. *gelda*], deprive of generative power, make animal unfit to bear offspring.

Geld'ing, gelded horse or other animal.

Gel'id (*g* soft) [L. *gelidus*, cold ; *gelu*, frost], very cold, frozen.

Gem [L. *gemma*, a bud, a gem], precious stone ; adorn as with gems.

Gen'der [L. *genus* (*gener-is*), kind], grammatical distinction roughly corresponding to sex.

Ge-ne-a'lo-gy [Gk. *genea*, race, *logia*, an account], history of descent, pedigree. **Genealog'ical.**

Gen'er-al [L. *genus* (*gener-is*), kind, race], not limited or special, common ; military officer of high rank. **General'ity.**

Gen'er-al-ize, form or state a general view.

Gen'er-ate [L. *generāre* (p.p. *generātus*), fr. *genus*, race], cause to be, produce. **Gen'erator.**

Gen-er-a'tion, single succession in natural descent, an age.

Ge-ner'ic [L. *genus* (*gener-is*), kind], relating to a genus or kind.

Gen'er-ous [L. *generōsus*, well-born, generous ; *genus*, race], noble, free in giving.

Gen'e-sis [Gk. *genesis*, source], origin, manner of formation. **Genet'ic.**

Ge'ni-al [L. *geniālis*, genial, fr. *genius*], kindly and cheerful. **Genial'ity.**

Gen'i-tive [L. *genitīvus* (*casus*, case)], grammatical case to denote possessor.

Ge'ni-us [L. *genius*, genius ; *gignere* (p.p. *genitus*), to beget], protecting spirit, distinguishing character, one who has great intellectual powers, esp. creative.

Gen-teel' [L. *gentilis*, belonging to the same *gens* or clan], elegant and stylish (used ironically).

Gen'tian (*ti=sh*, or *ti*) [L. *gentiāna*, fr. *Gentius*, an Illyrian king], mountain plant.

Gen'tile [F. *gentil* ; L. *gentilis*, gentle], one who is not a Jew.

Gen'tile [O.F. *gentil* ; see **Genteel**], well-born, mild, quiet.

Gen'tle-man, man of good breeding.

Gen'try [O.F. *genterise*, *gentilise*, rank ; see **Genteel**],people of gentle birth and breeding.

Gen'u-flec'tion, Gen'u-flex'ion [L. *genu*, the knee, *flectere* (p.p. *flexus*), to bend], a bending of the knees.

Gen'u-ine [L. *genuīnus*, genuine, of the true genus], real.

Ge'nus [L. *genus* (*gener-is*), race, kind], group of species, a kind.

Ge-og'ra-phy [Gk. *gē*, the earth, *graphia*, a description, fr. *graphein*, to write], science pertaining to description of the earth. **Geograph'ical.**

Ge-ol'o-gy [Gk. *gē*, the earth, *logos*, discourse], science pertaining to structure and mineral constitution of the earth. **Geolog'ical.**

Ge-om'e-try [Gk. *gē*, the earth, *metron*, a measure], science which treats of the properties and relations of magnitude in space as lines, surfaces, and solids. **Geomet'rical.**

Geor'gic [Gk. *georgicos*, relating to husbandry; Gk. *gē*, the earth, and *ergon*, a work], poem on agriculture.

Ge-ra'ni-um [Gk. *geranion*, geranium; *geranos*, a crane], plant with showy flowers, crane's-bill.

Germ [L. *germen* (*germin-is*), a sprout, a germ], that from which anything springs.

Ger'man [L. *germānus*, German, allied to **Germ**], nearly related.

Ger-man'der [M.L. *germandra* ; Late Gk. *khamandrua* ; Gk. *khamai*, on the ground, *drus*, oak], large class of herbs.

Ger-mane' [variant of **German**], akin, appropriate.

Ger'mi-nate, to sprout, bud. **Germina'tion.**

Ger-ry-man'der [fr. *Gerry*, governor of Massachusetts; cf. **Salamander**], to manipulate an election unfairly.

Ger'und [L. *gerundus*, that which is to be done, a verbal adj. fr. *gerere*, to carry on], part of a verb which partakes also of the character of a noun. **Gerun'dial.**

Ger'und'ive [Late L. *gerundivus*], verbal adjective from stem of gerund, meaning *deserving or requiring to be (done, etc.).*

Ges-tic'u-late [L. *gesticulus*, dim. of *gestus*, a gesture], make gestures.

Ges'ture [L. *gerere* (p.p. *gestus*), to perform, to bring], motion expressive of feeling.

Get [O.N. *geta*, to get], obtain, procure, learn, become.

Gew'gaw [orig. unknown], showy trifle.

Gey'ser (*g* hard, *ey=ai* or *ī*) [Icel. *Geysir*, a particular geyser; *geysa*, to gush], an eruptive hot spring. [shocking.

Ghast'ly [O.E. *gœstan*, to terrify], deathlike,

Gher'kin (*gh* hard) [Du. *gurkje*. Etym. doubtful], small cucumber.

Ghet'to (*gh* hard) [It. *ghetto*. Origin doubtful], Jews' quarters in a city.

Ghost (*ō*) [O.E. *gást*, prob. cogn. with O.N. *geisa*, rage], spirit appearing after death.

Ghoul (*ou*=*oo*) [Arab. *ghul*, a demon of the woods ; *ghawl*, attacking suddenly], demon that devours bodies.

Gi'ant, *fem.* Gi'ant-ess [L. *gigas* (*gigant-is*) ; Gk. *gigas*, giant], huge person.　　[talk.

Gib'ber-ish (*g* hard) [perh. imit.], unmeaning

Gib'bet (*g* soft) [O.F. *gibet*, a gibbet ; *gibet*, a large stick, dim. of *gibe*, a club], gallows on which the bodies of criminals were hanged in chains.

Gib'bon (*g* hard) [?], kind of long-armed ape.

Gib'bous (*g* hard) [L. *gibbus*, a hump], swelling, convex.

Gibe [imit. Cf. O.N. *geipa*, to talk nonsense], to scoff ; expression of scorn.

Gib'lets (*g* soft) [O.F. *gibelet*, a stew], heart, gizzard, etc., of a fowl.

Gid'dy (*g* hard) [O.E. *gydig*, insane], lightheaded, dizzy.

Gift (*g* hard) [O.E. *gift*], anything given, a special talent, *hence* Gifted, very able.

Gig (*g* hard) [?], light two-wheeled carriage ; long row-boat.　　[great size.

Gi-gan'tic (second *g* hard) [see Giant], of

Gig'gle (*g* hard) [imit.], laugh in a silly way ; laugh with short catches.　　[gold.

Gild (*g* hard) [O.E. (*be*)*gyldan*], overlay with

Gill [1] (*g* hard) [etym. dub., cf. Swed. *gäl*], organ for breathing in water.

Gill [2] (*g* hard) [O.N. *gil*, a ravine], ravine.

Gill [O.F. *gille* ; M.L. *gillo*], fourth of a pint.

Gil'lie (*g* hard) [Gael. *gille*, *giolla* ; Irish, *giolla*, a lad], Highland attendant on sportsmen.

Gil'ly-flow'er (*g* soft) [O.F. *girofle*; Gk. *caryophyllon*, a clove-tree; *caryon*, a nut, *phyllon*, a leaf], plant with a scent of cloves.

Gilt (*g* hard), gilding, imitation of gold.

Gim'crack (*g* soft) [earlier *gibecrack*, perh. fr. O.F. *giber*, to shake, and Crack], toy.

Gim'let (*g* hard) [O.F. *guimbelet*, a gimlet ; cf. Low G. *wemel*, a boring-tool], small tool for boring holes.

Gimp (*g* hard) [F. *guimpe*, a nun's wimple], kind of trimming.

Gin [short for *geneva* ; O.F. *genevre* ; L. *juniperus*, juniper], distilled spirit.

Gin [short for O.F. *engin*, a contrivance ; see Engine], trap.

Gin'ger [Gk. *ziggiberis* ; Skr. *çrngavera*, ginger], a plant which has a spicy root.

Gin'ger-ly [perh. O.F. *gensor*, comp. of *gent*, fine, orig. well-born ; L. *genitus*, born], cautiously, fastidiously.

Ging'ham (*g* hard) [F. *guingan*; Malay *gingang*, orig. striped], kind of cotton cloth.

Gipsy [see Gypsy].

Gi-raffe' [ult. fr. Arab. *zarifah*], long-necked African animal.

Gird (*g* hard) [O.E. *gyrdan*], put a belt round the waist.

Gird [?], mock, gibe (at).　　[or band.

Gir'dle (*g* hard) [O.E. *gyrdan*, to gird], belt

Gir'dle [var. of Griddle], iron plate for baking cakes.

Girl (*gerl*, *g* hard) [E.], female child.

Girth (*g* hard) [O.N. *georth*, girth], measurement round a saddle-band, saddle-band.

Gist (*g* soft) [O.F. *gist*, 3rd per. sing. of *gésir*, to lie ; L. *jacēre*, to lie], main part, pith.

Give (*g* hard) [O.E. *giefan*, to give], bestow, yield.

Giz'zard (*g* hard) [O.F. *g*(*u*)*iser*, gizzard ; perh. L. *gigěria*, cooked entrails of poultry], second stomach of a bird.

Gla'cial (*ci*=*sh*) [L. *glaciēs*, ice], pertaining to ice, cold.

Gla'cier (*ci*=*sh*), Glä'cier [F. *glacier* ; *glace*, ice], stream of ice formed by accumulated snow on high ground.

Glad [O.E. *glæd*], happy, joyful, pleased.

Glad'den, make joyful or glad.

Glade [prob. an opening for light, fr. O.E. *glad*, bright], opening in a wood.

Glad'i-ā-tor (*ā*=*ai*) [L. *gladius*, a sword], among the Romans one who fought for the public entertainment.

Glad-i-o'lus [L., dim. of *gladius*, a sword], plant with spike of bright flowers and sword-shaped leaves.

Glair [F. *glaire* ; L. *clāra*, fem. of *clārus*, clear], white of egg.

Gla'mour [corrup. of Grammar], charm, deceptive haze.

Glance [perh. a nasalised form of O.F. *glaichier*, to glide], quick look ; give a quick look, dart aside, flash.

Gland [L. *glans* (*gland-is*), an acorn], organ of secretion in the body. Glan'dular.

Glan'ders [O.F. *glandres*, fr. L. *glans*, an acorn], disease of horses.

Glare [M.E. *glaren*], emit a dazzling light, stare fiercely ; dazzling light, angry stare.

Glass [O.E. *glæs*], hard substance which transmits light, drinking vessel of glass, mirror.

Glau'cous [Gk. *glaucos*], greyish blue, covered with fine bloom (as grapes).

Glaze [M.E. *glasen*], furnish with glass, cover with a thin glassy coating ; glassy coating.

Gla'zier (*zi*=*zh*), one who sets glass.

Gleam [O.E. *glœm*], shine ; stream of light.

Glean [O.F. *glener*, to glean ; etym. dub.], gather after a reaper.

Glebe [L. *glēba*, soil], land held by a parish clergyman or minister.

Glee [O.E. *gliw*, *glēo*], merriment ; unaccompanied part song.

Glen [Gael. and Ir. *gleann* ; W. *glyn*, glen], narrow valley.

Glib [perh. imit.], fluent, smooth and flippant.

Glide [O.E. *glidan*], move gently and smoothly.

Glim'mer [cogn. with Gleam], shine faintly ; faint unsteady light.

Glimpse [M.E. *glymsen*, cogn. with Gleam], short, hurried view.

Glint [earlier *glent*, cogn. with Ger. *glänzen*, to sparkle], to sparkle, flash.

Glis′ten [O.E. *glisnian*], sparkle. [lustre.

Glit′ter [prob. O.N. *glitra*], to sparkle; showy

Gloat [cf. Ger. *glotzen*, to stare], gaze with wicked pleasure. [ball.

Globe [L. *globus*, a ball], body shaped like a

Glob-ose′, Glob′u-lar [L. *globus*, a ball, dim. *globulus*, a little ball], like a globe.

Glob′ule [L. *globulus*, a little ball], tiny globe.

Gloom [perh. M.E. *gloume*, to frown], deep shade, heaviness of spirit. **Gloom′y**.

Glo-ri-fi-ca′tion [L. *glōria*, glory; *facere*, to make], giving of glory to. **Glor′ify**.

Glo′ry [L. *glōria*, glory], praise and honour, splendour; exult.

Gloss[1] [Icel. *glossi*, a blaze], brightness on a smooth surface; give a surface brightness, make plausible. **Gloss′y**.

Gloss[2] [O.F. *glose*; L. and Gk. *glōssa*, obscure or foreign word], explanatory note.

Glos′sa-ry [L. *glossārium*; see **Gloss**[2]]; collection of explanations of words in a book.

Glot′tis [Gk. *glottis*, glottis; *glōtta*, var. of *glōssa*, tongue], opening at upper part of windpipe. [hand.

Glove (*ove=uv*) [O.E. *glóf*], covering for the

Glow [O.E. *glówan*], shine with intense heat, be flushed; white or red heat.

Glower (rhymes with **Our**) [?], look frowningly.

Glow′worm, phosphorescent wingless beetle.

Gloze [see **Gloss**[2]], explain away, extenuate, flatter, wheedle.

Glu-cose′ [Gk. *glukus*, sweet], grape sugar.

Glue [Late L. *glūs* (*glūt-is*), glue], impure gelatine; join as with glue.

Glum [see **Gloom**], sullen.

Glut [L. *glutīre*, to swallow], over-supply.

Glu′ti-nous, like glue.

Glut′ton [L.L. *glūto* - (*glūton-is*), glutton; *glutīre*, to swallow], one who eats too much, animal allied to the badger. **Glut′tonous**.

Gly′cer-ine (*y=i*) [Gk. *glyceros*, sweet], sweet oily fluid. [knotty.

Gnarled [obs. form *knurled* (*knurl*, knob)],

Gnash [imit.], strike (the teeth) together.

Gnat [O.E. *gnæt*], blood-sucking fly.

Gnaw [O.E. *gnagan*], eat away by biting.

Gneiss (*nice*) [O.H.G. *gneistan*, to sparkle], kind of crystalline rock.

Gnome [Gk. *gnōmē*, intelligence], goblin of the mines.

Gno′mon [Gk. *gnōmōn*, an interpreter], style or pin of a sun-dial.

Gnu [Hottentot word], kind of antelope, also known as wildebeest (Du. name).

Go [O.E. *gán*], move about, move away, take a course.

Goad [O.E. *gád*], spiked stick for urging cattle; urge on as with a goad.

Goal [?], place at which a race is to end.

Goat [O.E. *gát*], horned cud-chewing animal.

Gob′bet [O.F. *gobet*, a gobbet; dim. of *gobe*, a mouthful], lump, mouthful.

Gob′ble [perh. fr. O.F. *gober*, to devour], swallow greedily; (imit.) make a noise like a turkey.

Gob′let [F. *gobelet*, dim. of O.F. *gobel*, a cup], drinking-cup without a handle.

Gob′lin [F. *gobelin*, a goblin, perh. Gk. *kobalos*, a rogue], mischievous sprite.

God [O.E. *god*, perh. Ary. *gheu*, invoke or sacrifice], being who rules the universe.

God′fa′ther, and **God′mo′ther**, persons who become sponsors for a child at baptism.

God′head [M.E. *godhed*, **God** and -*head*, quality], divine nature.

God′ly, pious, obedient to God's commands.

God′send, unexpected piece of good fortune.

Gof′fer, Gof′er, Goph′er, Gauf′fer [F. *gaufre*, honeycomb; *gaufrer*, to stamp with a patterned tool], crimp with heated irons.

Gog′gle [?], full and rolling; (n. pl.) kind of spectacles.

Goi′tre (*tre=ter*) [L. *guttur*, throat], enlargement of gland in throat. **Goit′rous**.

Gold [E. Allied to **Yellow**], one of the most precious metals.

Gold′finch, beautiful singing-bird.

Gold′smith, worker in gold.

Golf [perh. Du. *kolf*, a club], game played with clubs and a ball.

Gon′do-la [It. *gondola*, etym. dub.], Venetian boat with high ends. **Gondolier′**.

Gon′fal-on [It. *gonfalone*; O.H.G. *gundfano*, battle-flag], kind of banner hung from cross-bar.

Gong [Malay *gŏng* or *gŭng*], flat-rimmed metal instrument which is struck with a mallet.

Good [O.E. *gód*], virtuous, kind, satisfactory.

Good-bye′ [contraction of "*God be with you*"], farewell.

Good′ly, pleasant, comely, large.

Goods, wares.

Goose [O.E. *gós*], web-footed bird larger than a duck; tailor's smoothing iron.

Goose′ber-ry, fruit of a prickly shrub.

Gore [O.E. *gár*, a spear], wound with horns.

Gore [O.E. *gor*, dirt], thick blood.

Gore [O.E. *gára*, a projecting piece of land, allied to *gár*, a spear], wedge-shaped piece of cloth sewn in.

Gorge [O.E., perh. fr. Late L. *gorga*, throat, variant of L. *gurgēs*, a whirlpool], throat, narrow passage between mountains; fill up to the throat.

Gor′geous [perh. O.F. *gorgias*, finely dressed; cf. O.F. *gorgias*, ruff for the neck, and F. *gorge*, throat], splendid and showy.

Gor′gon [Gk. *Gorgō*, fr. *gorgos*, terrible], one of the three snake-haired women whose looks turned the beholder into stone, ugly person. [Africa.

Go-ril′la [O. African, *gorilla*], large ape of W.

Gorse [O.E. *gorst*], furze or whin.

Gos′hawk [see **Goose** and **Hawk**], large short-winged hawk. [goose.

Gos′ling [*s=z*] [**Goose** and dim. suf.], young

Gos′pel [O.E. *gód*, good, *spel*, a story], good news, one of the four Bible narratives of the life of Jesus Christ.

Gos′sa-mer [perh. **Goose** and **Summer**], filmy substance like cobweb.

Gos'sip [O.E. *godsibb*, related in God, that is by religious obligation], sponsor, God-parent, idle talk, tattler ; tell idle tales.

Goth'ic [L. *Gothicus*, from *Gothi*, the Goths], belonging to the Goths, not classical ; style of architecture of 12th to 16th centuries, marked by pointed arches.

Gouge (*ou=ow*) [F. *gouge* ; Low L. *gubia*, a gouge], chisel with a hollow blade ; scoop as with a gouge.

Gourd (*ou=oo*) [F. *gourde* ; L. *cucurbita*, a gourd], plant of the cucumber kind, cup made from a gourd rind.

Gour'mand (*ou=oo*), **Gor'mand** [origin unknown ; F. *gourmand*], glutton. **Gor'mandize.**

Gour'met (*et=ai*) [F. *gourmet*], critical judge of table delicacies.

Gout [L. *gutta*, a drop], disease in which there is usually inflammation of the joints.

Gov'ern (*o=ŭ*) [O.F. *governer* ; L. *gubernāre* ; Gk. *cybernan*, to steer, to govern], rule.

Gov'er-ness (*o=ŭ*), female teacher, esp. in a family.

Gov'ern-ment (*o=ŭ*) ; rule, the ruling power, a state. [controls.

Gov'er-nor (*gov=gŭv*), one who governs or

Gown [O.F. *goune* ; M.L. *gunna*, fur garment], loose upper garment, dress. [grasp.

Grab [perh. modif. of **Grip**], snatch ; sudden

Grace [L. *grātia*, favour *grātus*, pleasing], favour, quality which wins favour, beauty of ease, title of a duke or archbishop ; adorn, do credit to.

Grace'ful, displaying grace, easy and beautiful. **Grace'less.** [ness.

Gra'cious (*ci=sh*), disposed to show kind-

Gra-da'tion, progress step by step, arrangement in grades. [gradient.

Grade [L. *gradus*, a step], step or degree,

Gra'di-ent [L. *gradī* (pr.p. *gradiens, -entis*), to walk], rate of graded ascent or descent in a road or railway.

Grad'u-al, by degrees.

Grad'u-ate, mark with degrees, take a degree at a university. **Gradua'tion.**

Graft [earlier *graff* ; Gk. *graphion*, a stylus, *graphein*, to write], a cutting of one tree inserted into part of another so as to bring about union.

Grain [L. *grānum*, a grain], corn, hard particle, small weight.

Gram (or **Gramme**) [Gk. *gramma*, a letter, a small weight], small weight.

Gram-i-niv'o-rous [L. *gramen* (*gramin-is*), grass, *vorāre*, to devour], feeding on grass.

Gram'ma-logue [Gk. *gramma*, a letter, *logos*, discourse], word represented in shorthand by a single sign.

Gram'mar [O.F. *gramaire* ; Gk. *grammatikē* (*technē*), (art) of letters], science which treats of parts of speech.

Gram-ma'ri-an [Gk. *gramma*, a letter], one versed in grammar.

Gram-mat'ic-al, of grammar, conforming to rules of grammar.

Gram'o-phone [Gk. *gramma*, a letter, *phōnē*, sound], instrument for reproducing sounds.

Gram'pus [formerly *graundepose*, prob. fr. O.F. *grapois* ; L. *crassus piscis*, fat fish], animal of the whale kind.

Gran'a-ry [L. *grānum*, grain], place for storing grain.

Grand [L. *grandis*, great], great, splendid.

Grand'child, son's or daughter's child. [man.

Gran-dee' [Sp. *grande*, grand], Spanish noble-

Gran'deur, greatness, splendour.

Grand'fa'ther, **Grand'sire**, parent's father.

Gran-dil'o-quence [see **Grand** and **Eloquence**], lofty speaking. **Grandil'oquent.**

Gran'di-ose' [It. *grandioso* ; see **Grand**], impressive, affecting grandeur.

Grange [M.L. *grānea*, a barn ; L. *granum*, corn], farm with the buildings, etc.

Gran'ite [It. *granito*, granite, orig. p.p. of *granire*, to reduce to grains], granular crystalline rock.

Grant [O.F. *greanter*, to grant ; L. *credere* (p.p. *crēdens, -entis*), to believe], give, yield by request ; thing granted.

Gran'u-lar [see **Grain**], consisting of grains.

Grape [O.F. *grape*, a bunch of grapes, orig. a hook], fruit of the vine.

Grape'shot, small balls put several together to scatter on being fired from cannon.

Graph [Gk. *graphein*, to write], diagram to express a system of connection.

Graph'ic [Gk. *graphein*, to write], pictorial, vividly descriptive. **Graph'ically.**

Graph'ite [Ger. *graphit*, fr. Gk. *graphein*, to write], plumbago or black lead.

Grap'nel [dim. of O.F. *grapin*, a grapnel ; O.F. *grape*, a hook], small anchor with four or five hooks.

Grap'ple [properly to seize with a **Grapnel**], seize, fight as wrestlers. **Grap'pling-iron.**

Grasp [cogn. with **Grope**], seize and hold ; seizure of the hand, power of seizing and holding.

Grasp'ing, greedy of gain.

Grass [O.E. *græs*], grain-yielding plant, herbage. [family.

Grass'hop-per, green insect of the locust

Grate [O.F. *grater*, to grate ; cf. Ger. *kratzen*, to scratch], rub with something rough, sound harshly.

Grate [M.L. *grāta, crāta* ; L. *crātis*, hurdle], framework of bars.

Grate'ful [L. *grātus*, pleasing, and **Full**], pleasing, thankful.

Gra'ter, utensil for grating.

Grat'i-fy [L. *grātus*, pleasing, *facere*, to make], please, satisfy. **Gratifica'tion.**

Gra'tis [L. *grātis*, freely, contracted from *grātiis*, abl. pl. of *gratiā*, favour], for nothing. [ness.

Grat'i-tude [L. *grātus*, pleasing], thankful-

Grat-u'i-tous [L. *grātus*, pleasing], granted without pay, uncalled for.

Grat-u'i-ty, free gift.

Grave[1] [L. *gravis*, heavy], weighty, serious.

Grave[2] [see **Engrave**], carve or cut on a hard substance.

Grave[3] [perh. O.F. *grave*, shore], clean (the bottom of a ship). [place.

Grave[4] [O.E. *græf*, *grafan*, to dig], burial-

Grav'el [O.F. *gravelle*, dim. of *grave*, gravel ; Celtic origin ; cf. W. *gro*, pebbles], small pebbles.

Gra'ver, engraving tool.

Grav'i-tate [L. *gravitāre*, to gravitate, *gravis*, heavy], tend to move towards a centre.

Grav-i-ta'tion, attractive force in matter.

Grav'i-ty, weight, seriousness. [cooking.

Gra'vy [etym. dub.], juice from meat in

Gray or **Grey** [O.E. *grǽg*], colour between white and black.

Gray'ling [see **Gray**], silver-grey fresh-water fish, kind of butterfly. [grass.

Graze [O.E. *græs*, grass], feed on growing

Graze [?], touch lightly in passing.

Gra'zier (*zi*=*zh*), one who feeds cattle for market.

Grease (*se*=*ss*) [L. *crassus*, fat], soft fat ; (*se*=*z*), smear with grease. [mighty.

Great (*ea*=*ai*) [O.E. *gréat*], large, important,

Greaves [O.F. *greves*, from *greve*, the shin], armour for the shins.

Grebe [F. *grèbe*, etym. dub.], almost tailless diving bird. [etc.).

Greed [E.], unworthy longing (for gain, food,

Greed'y [O.E. *grǽdig*], gluttonous, eager for possessions, covetous. [of grass.

Green [O.E. *gréne*, cogn. with **Grow**], colour

Green'back, American bank-note.

Green-gage [see **Gage**[1]], kind of plum.

Green'gro-cer, retailer of vegetables.

Green'horn, one easily imposed on.

Green'house, glass-house for rearing plants.

Greet [O.E. *grétan*], salute, welcome.

Gre-ga'ri-ous [L. *grex* (*greg-is*), a flock], living in flocks, fond of company.

Gre-nade' [Sp. *granada*, a pomegranate ; L. *granātus*, full of seeds], small shell thrown by hand.

Gren-a-dier' [see **Grenade**], originally a soldier who threw grenades, now a soldier of the foot-guards. [swiftness.

Grey'hound, slender, graceful dog of great

Grid'dle [also *girdle* ; prob. fr. O.F. *gredil* ; perh. fr. L. *crāticula*, a gridiron, dim. of *crātis*, a hurdle], iron plate for cooking cakes.

Grid'iron [earlier *gredire* ; see **Griddle**], grated utensil for broiling.

Grief [L. *gravis*, heavy], sorrow.

Grie'vance, cause of complaint.

Grieve [L. *gravāre*, to grieve, *gravis*, heavy], mourn, cause grief to. **Griev'ous**.

Grif'fin, Grif'fon [Gk. *gryps*, a griffin], creature half lion, half eagle.

Grig [?], small eel ; a cricket.

Grill [F. *gril*, a gridiron, *griller*, to broil], a gridiron ; cook on a gridiron.

Grilse [?], young salmon.

Grim [E. ; cf. Ger. *grimm*], fierce and stern.

Gri-mace' [F. *grimace*, origin uncertain], distortion of the face ; make wry face.

Grime [cf. Flem. *grijm*], sooty particles engrained in the skin or other surface. **Grim'y**.

Grin [O.E. *grennian*], show the teeth ; broad smile.

Grind [E. ; cf. Du. *grenden*], crush as in a mill, sharpen by friction ; monotonous labour, esp. hard study.

Grind'stone, revolving disk of stone for grinding, sharpening or polishing.

Grip [cogn. with **Gripe**], to grasp ; a firm hold.

Gripe [O.E. *grīpan*], to clutch ; (*n. pl.*) pains in the bowels.

Gris'ly [*s*=*z*) [O.E. *grislic*], horrible.

Grist [O.E. *grist*], corn for grinding, malt crushed for brewing.

Gris'tle [O.E. *gristle*], tough elastic tissue.

Grit [O.E. *gréot*, pebbles], sand, coarse part of meal, pluck.

Griz'zly [fr. obs. *grizzle*, grey], greyish.

Groan [O.E. *gránian*], deep, mournful sound expressing pain or grief.

Groat [M.Du. *groot*; orig. meaning great in the sense " thick "], old coin equal to fourpence.

Groats [cogn. with O.E. *grot*, a fragment], grain, chiefly oats, hulled, or hulled and crushed.

Gro'cer [formerly *grosser* ; O.F. *grossier*, a wholesale dealer ; see **Gross**], dealer in tea, sugar, etc. **Gro'cery**.

Grog [short for *grogram*, from " Old Grog," nickname of Admiral Vernon, who wore grogram trousers], spirits and cold water.

Grog'ram [formerly *grogran* ; F. *gros grain*, coarse grain], stuff of silk and mohair.

Groin [earlier *grynde* ; cf. O.E. *grynde*, an abyss], line between thigh and abdomen, projecting curve formed by the inter section of vaults.

Groom [perh. shortened from O.F. *gromet*, a lad, a servant], man who has charge of horses.

Grooms'man, attendant on a bridegroom.

Groove [Du. *groeve*, groove, *graven*, to dig], long hollow cut, rut.

Grope [O.E. *grápian*, to seize], feel one's way.

Gross [F. *gros* (fem. *grosse*), L.L. *grossus*, big], coarse ; twelve dozen.

Gro-tesque' (*que*=*k*) [F. *grotesque* ; It. *grottesca*, painted work on the walls of grottoes], wildly formed, fantastic.

Grot'to [It. *grotta*, a cave, cogn. with **Crypt**], cave, natural or artificial.

Ground [O.E. *grund*, earth, land ; basis ; (*pl.*) dregs ; give a foundation ; run aground.

Ground'sel [also *groundswell* ; O.E. *gundæswelgiæ*, swallower of pus, *gund*, pus], weed with small yellow flowers.

Group (*ou*=*oo*) It. *gruppo*, a group, allied to **Crop**], cluster, assemblage ; arrange in groups.

Grouse (*se*=*ss*) [?], reddish game-bird.

Grouse (*se*=*ss*) [etym. doubtful], to grumble.

Grove [O.E. *gráf*, perh. a lane cut through a wood], small wood.

Grov'el (*ŏ*) [backward formation from *Grovelling*, face downwards, an adv. taken as pr.p. fr. O.N. *á grúfu*, on one's face], lie prone or crawl, be abject.

Grow (ō) [O.E. *grówan*], exist as a living plant, increase in size.   [angrily.

Growl [perh. imit.], grumble, murmur

Growth (ō), growing, increase.

Grub [perh. cogn. with **Grave** 2], larva of some beetles; dig.

Grudge [O.F. *groucier*, *groucher*; M.L. *groussâre*, to murmur], envy, give reluctantly; ill-will, feeling of reluctance in giving.   [water or milk.

Gru'el [L. *grūtum*, meal], meal boiled in

Grue'some (*some*=*sŭm*) [obs. *grue*, to shudder, with suf. *some*], horrible.

Gruff (cf. Ger. *grob*], rough in manner.

Grum'ble [cf. F. *grommeler*; Ger. *grummeln*, to grumble], mutter with discontent.

Grunt [O.E. *grunettan*, imit.], make a noise like a pig.

Gua'no [*u*=*w*] [Sp. *guano*; Peruv. *huanu*, dung], excrement of sea-birds, chiefly of Peru, used as manure.

Guar-an-tee' [formerly *garanté*, person that gives security; cogn. with F. *garantir*, to warrant], surety; pledge oneself for.

Guard [F. *garder*, to watch], keep watch over; one who or that which protects, a watch, a train conductor.

Guard'i-an, keeper, protector; watching.

Gua'va (*u*=*w*) [Sp. and W. Ind. *guayaba*], fruit of the E. and W. Indies.

Gud'geon [F. *goujon*; L. *gobio*, gudgeon], small freshwater fish, credulous person.

Guel'der-rose [from *Guelders* in Prussia], plant with clusters of white flowers like snowballs.

Guer'don [O.F. *guerdon*; M.L. *widerdōnum*; O.H.G. *widarlón*, *wider*, back, and *lōn*, loan, assim. to L. *dōnum*, a gift], reward.

Gue-ril'la, **Guer-ril'la** [Sp. *guerrilla*, dim. of *guerra*, war], pertaining to irregular, independent warfare; man taking part in such warfare.

Guess [M.E. *gessen*; cogn. with Get], rapidly formed unproved belief; to make a guess.

Guest [O.E. *geist*; cf. O.N. *gestr*; Dan. *giest*; Swed. *gäst*, a guest], one who is entertained at the house of another.

Guf-faw' [imit.], loud laugh.

Gui'dance, direction, leading.

Guide [F. *guider*; prob. fr. Teut. root; allied to **Wit**], lead, direct; one who guides.

Guild, **Gild** [O.E. *gild*, guild, payment], association of men of the same class.

Guile [O.F. *guile*; prob. **Wile** is a doublet], deceit, wile.

Guil'le-mot [perh. from F. *Guillaume*, William], kind of diving-bird.

Guil'lo-tine (*ine*=*een*) [from F. inventor, *Guillotin*], instrument for beheading; behead by the guillotine.

Guilt [O.E. *gylt*, fr. *gildan*, to pay], offence against right, criminality.

Guin'ea [from Port. *Guiné* (in Africa)], old coin which was worth 21s.

Guise (*s*=*z*) [F. *guise*; cogn. with O.H.G. *wîsa*, a way], fashion, dress, cloak.

Gui-tar' [L. and Gk. *cithara*, a lyre], stringed musical instrument.

Gulf [Late Gk. *colphos*, a gulf, Gk. *colpos*, the bosom], arm of the sea, abyss.

Gull 1 [perh. W. *gŵylan*; cf. Corn. *gullan*; Bret. *gwelan*, a gull], sea-bird.

Gull 2 [perh. from *gull*, to delude, through *gull*, to gorge, cram], dupe; cheat, deceive.

Gull'et [O.F. *goulet*, dim. of O.F. *goule*, the throat; L. *gula*, throat], neck-passage for food.

Gull'i-ble [see Gull 2], easily cheated.

Gul'ly [L. *gula*, throat], deep channel worn by water.

Gulp [imit.], swallow in large mouthfuls.

Gum [O.E. *góma*], flesh containing roots of teeth.

Gum [Gk. *commi*, gum], sticky juice from trees; join or cover with gum.   [sense.

Gump'tion [Scot.; etym. dub.], common-sense.

Gun [?], firearm. **Gun'nery**.

Gun'pow-der, explosive mixture of saltpetre, charcoal, and sulphur.

Gun'wale (*gunnel*) [see **Gun** and **Wale**], upper edge of a vessel's side.

Gur'gle [Ital. *gorgogliare*, to gurgle, *gorgo*, a whirlpool, imit.], make a bubbling noise.

Gush [M.E. *gosshe*; perh. imit.], rush copiously; rapid outpouring.

Gus'set [F. *gousset*, dim. of *gousse*, a pod, a husk], triangular piece of material inserted into a garment.   [wind.

Gust [O.N. *gustr*, a gust], sudden blast of

Gus'to [It. *gusto*; L. *gustus*, taste], keen relish.

Gut [O.E. *gut*, (pl.) *guttas*, orig. a channel], intestine; remove the interior.

Gut-ta-per'cha [Malay *getah*, gum, *percha*, name of tree], dried milky juice of some trees.

Gut'ter [O.F. *gutiere*, gutter; L. *gutta*, a drop], eaves channel, roadside channel; to furrow with streams; (of a candle) to melt away, through the tallow or wax pouring down.

Gut'tur-al [L. *guttur*, the throat], sound formed in the throat.   [or chain.

Guy [O.F. *guier*, to guide], steadying rope

Guy [orig. used of an effigy of *Guy* Fawkes], queerly dressed person.

Guz'zle [perh. O.F. *gosiller*, to vomit; F. *gosier*, the throat], drink greedily.

Gym-na'si-um [*g*=*j*] [Gk. *gymnasion*, gymnasium, *gymnos*, naked], a place for athletic exercises, (on the Continent) preparatory school for the university.

Gym-nas'tics (*g*=*j*), athletic exercises. **Gym'nast**.

Gyp'sum (*g*=*j*) [L. *gypsum*; Gk. *gypsos*, chalk], mineral of which alabaster is one variety.

Gyp'sy, **Gip'sy** (*g*=*j*) [earlier *gypcyan*, short for Egyptian, because the gypsies were supposed (wrongly) to come from Egypt], one of a well-known wandering race.

Gy'rate (*g*=*j*) [Gk. *gyros*, a ring], move spirally, revolve. **Gyra'tion**.

Gyves (*g*=*j*) [?], fetters, esp. for the legs.

H

Hab'er-dash-er [A.F. *hapertas*, the name of a fabric], dealer in smallwares.

Hab'er-geon (*ge=j*) [F. *haubergeon*; see **Hauberk**], sleeveless coat of mail.

Ha-bil'i-ment [O.F. *habiller*, to clothe; L. *habilis*, fit, *habēre*, to have], article of clothing.

Hab'it [L. *habēre* (p.p. *habitus*), to have], custom, practice, dress.

Hab'it-a-ble [L. *habitāre* (p.p. *habitātus*), to dwell, freq. of *habēre*, to have], that can be lived in.

Hab-i-ta'tion, occupancy, dwelling-place.

Hab-it'u-al, formed by habit, usual.

Ha-bit'u-ate [L. *habituāre* (p.p. *habituātus*), from *habitus*], accustom.

Habitué (*a-bi-too-ai*) [F. p.p. of *habituer*], habitual visitor, frequenter.

Hack [M.E. *hacken*], to cut irregularly.

Hack [short for **Hackney**], horse for hire, worn-out horse.

Hack'ney [O.F. *haquenée*, an ambling horse], horse for ordinary riding, coach for hire; make commonplace. **Hack'neyed.**

Had'dock [?], sea-fish allied to the cod.

Ha'des (*haydees*) [Gk. *Hadēs*], name of the god of the lower world, his kingdom, the realm of departed spirits.

Hæm'a-tite (*hæm=hem*), see **Hem'atite.**

Hæm'or-rhage (*hæm=hem*), see **Hem'orrhage.**

Haft [O.E. *hæft(e)*, cogn. with **Heave**], a handle (of a knife, sickle, etc.).

Hag [?], ugly old woman, bog, dry spot in bog.

Hag'gard [cf. F. *hagard*, wild], wasted and hollow-eyed; untamed hawk.

Hag'gis [?], sheep's heart, etc., chopped and seasoned, and boiled in sheep's stomach-bag.

Hag'gle [freq. of North E., *hag*, to cut], to dispute in bargaining; cut clumsily.

Hail [O.N. *heill*, sound], call to, salute; a call, exclamation of salutation.

Hail [O.E. *hægl*, hail], frozen rain; fall as frozen rain.

Hair [O.E. *hǽr*,*hér*], fine thread-like outgrowth from the skin, mass of such outgrowths.

Hake [?], fish of the cod family.

Hal'berd [M.H.G. *helmbarde*, from *helm*, helmet, and *barta*, broad axe], ancient long-handled weapon.

Hal'cy-on (*c* soft) [L. *halcyon*, a kingfisher], kingfisher; calm, happy.

Hale[1] [O.E. *hál*, whole], sound, healthy.

Hale[2] [O.F. *haler*; O.H.G. *halôn*, to haul], to drag forcibly.

Half [O.E. *healf*. Com. Teut. oldest sense "side"], one of two equal parts; (n. pl.) Halves. [penny.

Half'pen-ny, Ha'pen-ny, coin worth half a

Hal'i-but [M.E. *hali*, holy; *butt*, a plaice], large flat fish.

Hall (*a=aw*) [O.E. *heall*], large public room, entrance room, manor-house.

Hall-mark, stamp (orig. used at Goldsmiths' Hall only) for marking assayed gold or silver.

Hal-le-lu'jah' (*j=y*) [Heb. *hallelǎ*, praise ye, *jāh*, Jehovah], praise Jehovah!

Hal-loa', Hal-loo' [imit.], call to attract attention.

Hal'low [O.E. *hálig*, holy], make holy.

Hal-lu'ci-na'tion [L. *hallūcinārī* (p.p. *halā-cinātus*), to wander in mind], wandering of the mind, delusion.

Ha'lo [Gk. *halōs*, a round threshing-floor], circle of light.

Halt (*a=aw*) [Ger. *halt* (in *halt machen*), stop, hold], to stop; a stop.

Halt [O.E. *halt*], to limp; lame.

Halt'er(*a=aw*)[O.E.*hœltre*], strap for leading or tying a horse.

Halve [M.E. *halfen*], cut into two equal parts.

Hal'yard, Hall'iard [M.E. *halier*, that which hales or hauls], rope or tackle for hoisting or lowering yards, etc.

Ham [O.E. *hamm*, thigh], part of the leg at the back of the knee, extends also to the back of the thigh, thigh of an animal, esp. of a hog salted and dried.

Ham'a-dry'ad [L. *Hamādryas*; Gk. *hama-dryas*, from *hama*, together with, and *drys*, tree], wood-nymph said to live and die with the tree she inhabited.

Ham'let [dim. of O.F. *hamel*, a hamlet, dim. of Teut. *ham*, home], small village.

Ham'mer [O.E. *hamer*], tool for driving nails, etc., part of a gunlock; to pound, beat out. [coach-box.

Ham'mer-cloth [?], cloth which covers a

Ham'mock [Sp. *hamaca*, a Caribbean word], swinging bed.

Ham'per [O.F. *hanapier*, orig. a vessel to keep cups in, *hanap*, a cup], large basket.

Ham'per [?], encumber, impede.

Ham'ster [Ger. *hamster*], rat-like animal with cheek-pouches.

Ham'string, one of the tendons at the back of the knee; cut the hamstrings.

Hand [O.E. *hand*], arm below the wrist, pointer on a dial, measure of 4 inches; give, pass.

Hand'cuff, put fetters on the wrists.

Hand'i-cap [from "hand i' cap," "hand in the cap," a way of drawing lots], allowance in a race; place at a disadvantage.

Hand'i-craft, trade requiring work by the hand.

Hand'ker-chief, small square of linen, etc.

Han'dle [O.E. *handlian*], use or hold with the hand, manage; part of a vessel, etc., to be grasped by the hand.

Hand'sel [O.N. *handsal*, conclusion of a bargain by shaking hands; Dan. *handsel*, earnest-money], payment, gift, etc., which is the first of a series, or pledge of what is to follow; to give such payment to, to be the first to use.

Hand'some (*some=sum*) [orig. meaning dexterous, O.E. *hand*, and suf. *-some*], good-looking, generous.

Hand´y, ready to the hand, skilful.

Hang [O.E. *hangian*], fasten without support from below.

Han´gar [F.], aeroplane-shed.

Hang´dog, sneaking, ashamed. [belt.

Hang´er [from **Hang**], short sword hung from

Hank [cf. O.N. *honk*, a hank; Swed. *hank*, a string; Dan. *hank*, a handle], coil or loop of yarn.

Han´ker [?], to long. **Han´kering**.

Han´som [from J. A. *Hansom*, its inventor], two-wheeled covered cab for two.

Hap [O.N. *happ*, chance], chance, luck.

Hap´haz´ard, chance, random.

Hap´less, unlucky.

Hap´ly, by chance.

Hap´pen, come by chance, occur.

Hap´py [see **Hap**], lucky, contented, apt.

Ha-rangue´ [M.L. *harenga*; Ital. *aringa*, a harangue; cf. It. *aringo*, an arena], noisy or disputatious address; address by a harangue.

Har´ass [F. *harasser*, perh. from O.F. *harer*, to set a dog on], weary, worry, vex.

Har´bin-ger [O.H.G. *heriberga*, a camp, lodging; see **Harbour**], forerunner, messenger.

Har´bour [M.E. *here*, army, *beorg*, shelter], shelter, haven for ships, to shelter, cherish (thoughts).

Hard [O.E. *heard*], unyielding to touch, firm, harsh, not easy to bear.

Har´di-hood [see **Hardy**], boldness. [bear.

Hard´ship [see **Hard**], that which is hard to

Hard´ware, ware made of metal.

Hard´y [F. *hardi*, orig. p.p. of *hardir*, to harden], bold, strong.

Hare [O.E. *hara*], gnawing animal (rodent) which moves by leaps.

Hare´lip, lip with a fissure.

Ha´rem [Arab. *haram*, prohibited], women's apartments in Mohammedan house, its occupants.

Har´i-cot [F., etym. dub.], kind of bean, a stew of meat with beans, etc.

Hark [M.E. *herkien*], listen.

Har´le-quin [It. *arlecchino*, harlequin; etym. doubtful], masked performer with a wand in a pantomime. **Har-le-quin-ade´**.

Har´lot [O.F. *harlot*, knave], immoral woman.

Harm [O.E. *hearm*], injure; injury, damage. **Harm´lessness**.

Har-mo´ni-ous, in concord, free from dissent.

Har-mo´ni-um [F.; see **Harmony**], musical instrument like a small organ.

Har´mo-ny [Gk. *harmonia*, harmony; *harmos*, a joining], just adaptation of parts, concord, agreement. **Harmon´ic, Har´monize**.

Har´ness [O.F. *harneis*, armour], armour; equipment of a horse for drawing; equip with harness.

Harp [O.E. *hearpe*], upright stringed instrument, played with the fingers; to play this, dwell tediously (on).

Har-poon´ [F. *harpe*, a dog's claw, a clamp; Gk. *harpē*, a sickle], spear with rope attached for throwing at whales.

Harp´si-chord [see **Harp** and **Chord**], keyboard instrument.

Har´py [Gk. *harpyiai*, lit. snatchers; Gk. *harpazein*, to snatch], fabulous winged monster.

Har´ri-dan [?.], vixenish haggard old woman.

Har´ri-er [perh. from **Hare**], dog for hunting hares.

Har´row [M.E. *harwe*], toothed agricultural implement; to draw a harrow over; distress greatly.

Har´ry [O.E. *hergian*, to harry, *here*, an army], to plunder, lay waste, harass.

Harsh [cf. Dan. *harsk*, Swed. *härsk*, rancid], rough and disagreeable.

Hart [O.E. *heort*], stag or male deer.

Harts´horn, substance originally obtained from the horns of the hart, aqueous solution of ammonia.

Har´vest [O.E. *hærfest*, autumn, orig. "crop"], ingathering of crops, season of gathering.

Hash [F. *hacher*, to hack], chop small; that which is hashed, new mixture of old matter. [end.

Hasp [O.E. *hæpse*], clasp which is fast at one

Has´sock [O.E. *hassuc*, a tuft of grass], stuffed cushion or footstool.

Haste [O.F. *haste*, haste; O.E. *hæst*, violence], speed; to hurry.

Ha´sten, make haste, hurry.

Hat [O.E. *hæt*], outdoor head-covering.

Hatch [M.E. *hacchen*], produce young from eggs, plot.

Hatch [O.E. *hæc, hec*], lower part of divided door, trap-door covering hatchway, hatchway.

Hatch [F. *hacher*, to hack], shade, usually by parallel lines.

Hatch´et [F. *hachette*, dim. of *hache*, an axe], small axe.

Hatch´ment [corr. of **Achievement**; see **Achieve**], arms of a deceased person on a panel.

Hatch´way, opening in a ship's deck.

Hate (O.E. *hete*), have a great dislike to, wish ill to; intense dislike.

Ha´tred [O.E. *hete*, hate; *ræden*, condition], intense dislike, ill-will.

Hau´berk [O.H.G. *halsberg*; *hals*, neck, and *bergan*, to cover], coat of mail.

Haugh´ty [F. *haut*; L. *altus*, high], proud and disdainful. **Haugh´ti-ness**.

Haul [var. of **Hale** [2]], to drag; draught.

Haunch (*au=aw* or *ah*) [O.F. *hanche*, haunch, cf. O.H.G. *ancha*, the leg], part between ribs and thigh, (of meat) leg and loin.

Haunt [F. *hanter*, to haunt], resort to frequently, visit as a ghost; a resort.

Haut´boy (*ho´boi*), **O´boe** (*o´boi*) [F. *hautbois*, *haut*, high, and *bois*, wood], wooden wind instrument of high pitch.

Have [O.E. *habban*], possess; also used as an auxiliary.

Ha´ven [O.E. *hæfen*], place of anchorage, shelter.

Hav´er-sack [Ger. *habersack*; *haber, hafer*, oats, *sack*, a sack], soldier's case for provisions.

Hav'oc [A.F. *havok*; O.F. *havot*, plunder], wide destruction.

Haw [O.E. *haga*, a hedge], fruit of the hawthorn.   [prey.

Hawk [O.E. *habuc*, *heafoc*, a hawk], bird of

Hawk [from **Hawker**], carry about for sale.

Hawk [imit.], clear the throat noisily.

Haw'ker [M.L.G. *hoker*; Du. *heuker*, a hawker], one who hawks goods.

Haws'er [O.F. *haucier*; Late L. *altiāre*, to lift; L. *altus*, high], large rope or small cable.

Haw'thorn [see **Haw**], thorny shrub or small tree with red or white flowers.

Hay [O.E. *hieg*], grass cut and dried.

Haz'ard [O.F. *hasard*; Sp. *azar*, hazard; perh. of Arab. orig.], danger, risk, bad ground in golf; to risk. **Haz'ardous.**

Haze [?], light vapour or smoke, dimness. **Ha'zy.**

Ha'zel [O.E. *hœsel*], small tree with an edible nut; light brown.

Head [O.E. *héafod*], seat of the brain, top, principal source, crisis; to lead, get before.   [title.

Head'ing, that which stands at the head,

Head'land, cape.

Head'long [from **Head**, and adverb suf. -*ling*], head foremost, without delay.

Head'strong, obstinate, ungovernable.

Head'way, progress.

Head'y, rash, violent.

Heal [O.E. *hǽlan*], make sound, cure.

Health [O.E. *hǽlth*], state of being sound. **Health'y.**

Heap [O.E. *héap*], pile or mass; to pile.

Hear [O.E. *hieran*], perceive sound.

Heark'en (see **Hark**), listen.

Hear'say, report, gossip.

Hearse [F. *herse*; L. *hirpex* (*hirpic-is*), a harrow], carriage for the dead.

Heart [O.E. *heorte*], organ which keeps up circulation of blood, seat of affections, courage.

Heart'en [see **Heart**], to encourage.

Hearth [O.E. *heorth*], floor of a fireplace.

Heart'y, earnest, warm, eager. **Heart'less.**

Heat [O.E. *hǽtu*], high temperature, warmth, single course in a race, etc.; make hot. **Heat'edly.**

Heath [O.E. *hǽdh*], small flowering shrub, place overgrown with shrubs.

Heath'en [O.E. *hǽdhen*, lit. a dweller on a heath], one whose religion is neither Christian, Jewish, nor Mohammedan.

Heath'er [?], common heath.

Heave [O.E. *hebban*], lift, cast; rising or swell, a throw.

Heav'en [O.E. *hefen*, later *heofone*; etym. doubtful], abode of the blest, sky.

Heav'y [O.E. *hefig*], of great weight.

Heb-dom'a-dal [Gk. *hebdomas*, a week; *hepta*, seven], weekly.

Hec'a-tomb [Gk. *hecaton*, a hundred; *bous*, an ox], sacrifice of many victims.

Hec'tic [Gk. *hexis*, habit of body; *echein*, to hold], consumptive, morbidly flushed.

D *

Hec'tor [Gk. *Hector*, the hero of Troy], to bully.

Hedge [O.E. *hecg*], row of bushes closely set to form a boundary; enclose with a hedge, to secure against loss by betting on both sides, avoid committing oneself.

Hedge'hog, spiny animal.

He'don-ism [Gk. *hēdonē*, pleasure], doctrine that pleasure is the chief good. **He'donist.**

Heed [O.E. *hédan*], to mind; notice, attention.   [side.

Heel [O.E. *hieldan*, to incline], lean to one

Heel [O.E. *héla*, also *hóh*, heel], hind part of the foot.

Hef'ty [Colloq., see **Heave**], weighty, strong.

He'gem-on-y (*g=j*) [Gk. *hēgemōn*, a leader], leadership, esp. of one State over others.

Heif'er [O.E. *heahfore*], young cow.

Height (*eigh=ī*), [O.E. *hiehto*], condition of being high, distance above.

Hei'nous (*ei=ai*) [F. *haineux*, odious, *haine*, hatred; cf. Goth. *hatjan*, to hate], hateful, very wicked. **Hein'ousness.**

Heir, *fem.* Heir'ess (*ei=ai*) [Late L. *hēres*, an heir], one who succeeds or will succeed to property.

Heir'loom [see **Heir** and **Loom** [1]], article that has been in a family for a long time.

He'li-o-graph [Gk. *hēlios*, the sun; *graphein*, to write], sun telegraph, apparatus for photographing the sun.

He'li-o-trope [Gk. *hēlios*, the sun, *tropos*, a turn], plant whose flowers and leaves turn to the sun, shade of purple of the flowers.

Hell [O.E. *hel*, *hell*], state of misery, Hades, abode of the dead.

Helm [1] [O.E. *helm*], helmet.

Helm [2] [O.E. *helma*], steering implement.

Hel'met [dim. of **Helm** [1]], armour for the head.

Hel'ot [fr. *Helos*, Laconian town], serf in ancient Sparta.   [aid.

Help [O.E. *helpan*], assist, prevent, remedy;

Help'mate [suggested by *help meet* (Gen. ii. 18); see **Help** and **Mate**], helpful companion.

Hel'ter-skel'ter [imit.], in confusion.   [etc.

Helve [O.E. *hielfe*], handle of an axe, hatchet,

Hem [O.E. *hem*], edge of cloth doubled over and sewn, edge; sew a folded edge.

Hem [imit.], slight cough to call attention.

Hem'a-tite, Hæm'a-tite [Gk. *haimatītēs*, fr. *haima*, blood], an iron ore.

Hem'i-sphere [Gk. *hemi*, half, *sphaira*, a sphere], half a sphere, half of the terrestrial sphere. **Hemispher'ical.**

Hem'i-stich (*ch=k*) [Gk. *hemi*, half, *stichos*, verse], half a line of verse.

Hem'lock [O.E. *hymlic(e)*], poisonous plant.

Hem'or-rhage, Hæm'or-rhage (*œ=ē*) [Gk. *haima*, blood, *rhēgnumi*, to break], discharge of blood.

Hemp [O.E. *hænep*, *hœnep*. Cogn. with L. and Gk. *cannabis*, hemp], plant of the nettle family, also the fibre of the plant. **Hemp'en.**

Hen [O.E. *henn*], female fowl.

Hence [M.E. *hennes*], from here; therefore.

Hench'man [O E. *hengest*, a horse, and **Man**], attendant, follower.

Hen'na [Arab. *henna'*, henna], shrub grown in the East, dye made from its leaves and shoots.

Hep-at'ic [Gk. *hēpaticos*; *hēpar*, the liver], relating to the liver.

Hep'ta-gon [Gk. *hepta*, seven, *gōnia*, an angle], plane figure with seven sides. **Hepta'-gonal.**

Hep'tar-chy (*ch=k*) [Gk. *hepta*, seven, *archein*, to rule], seven states of early England : government by seven rulers.

Her'ald [O.F. *heraut*; origin doubtful], officer who proclaimed war, etc.; announce beforehand. **Heral'dic.**

Her'ald-ry, art of recording genealogies and blazoning arms.

Herb [L. *herba*, grass], plant whose stem is not woody.

Her-ba'ceous, pertaining to herbs.

Herb'al-ist, one who has a knowledge of herbs, dealer in herbs.

Her-ba'ri-um, collection of dried plants.

Her-biv'o-rous [L. *herba*, grass, *vorāre*, to devour], herb-eating.

Her-cu'le-an [L. *Herculeus*, of or relating to *Hercules*], having or requiring great strength.

Herd [O.E. *heord*], number of large animals together ; go in a herd, tend (cattle, etc.).

Here [O.E. *hēr*], in this place.

Here-af'ter, time after this.

Here-by', by this.

Her-ed'i-ta-ry, passing from an ancestor to an heir or heirs.

Her-ed'i-ty [L. *hēres*, an heir], transmission of tendencies from ancestors to descendants.

Her'e-sy [Gk. *hairesis*, choice, sect, *hairein*, to choose], opinion contrary to that which is generally held.

Her'e-tic, one who holds to a heresy or heresies. **Heret'ical.**

Her'it-age, portion by birth. **Her'itable.**

Her-met'ic-al-ly [M.L. *hermēticus*, relating to alchemy ; *Hermēs*, Gk. name for *Mercury*], tightly (closed) by fusion or welding.

Her'mit [Gk. *erēmia*, a desert], one who lives in solitude. **Her'mitage.**

He'ro, *fem.* **Her'o-ine** [L. and Gk. *hērōs*, fem. *hērōinē*], very brave person, principal person in a story, etc. **Her'oism.**

Her-o'ic, pertaining to or worthy of a hero.

Her'on [O.F *hairon* ; O.H.G. *heiger*, a heron], long-necked, long-legged wading-bird.

Her'ring [O.E. *hǣring*], northern sea-fish.

Hes'i-tate [*s=z*] [L. *hæsitāre* (sup. *hæsitātum*), freq. of *hærēre*, to stick], be uncertain, to waver. **Hesita'tion.**

Hest, see **Behest.**

Het'er-o-dox [Gk. *heteros*, other, *doxa*, opinion], (opinions) contrary to an accepted standard. **Het'erodoxy.**

Het-er-o-ge'ne-ous [Gk. *heteros*, other, *genos*, kind], differing in kind, composed of diverse elements.

Heur-is'tic [Gk. *heuriscein*, to find], serving to discover.

Hew [O.E. *hēawan*], cut or shape with a sharp instrument.

Hex'a-gon [Gk. *hex*, six, *gōnia*, an angle], plane figure of six angles and six sides.

Hex-am'e-ter [Gk. *hex*, six, *metron*, a measure], verse of six feet. [spirits.

Hey'day (*ey=ai*) [?], time of vigour, high

Hi-a'tus (*hī-ai'tus*) [L. *hiāre* (p.p *hiātus*), to gape], gap.

Hi'ber-nate [L. *hibernus*, wintry], to winter, pass the winter in a torpid state. **Hiberna'tion.**

Hic'cup, Hic'cough (*cough=cup*) [earlier *hicket*, imit.], spasmodic drawing in of breath.

Hick'o-ry [Virginian *pohickery*], North American nut-bearing tree.

Hide [1] [O.E. *hȳd*], skin of a large animal.

Hide [2] [O.E. *hȳdan*], withdraw or put out of sight, keep secret.

Hid'e-ous [O.F. *hidos*, hideous ; *hisde*, fear], frightful, very ugly.

Hie (*ī*) [O.E. *hīgian*, to strive after], hasten.

Hi'er-ar'chy (*ch=k*) [Gk. *hieros*, sacred, *archein*, to rule], orders of angels, body of priests, etc.

Hi'er-o-glyph, Hi'er-o-glyph'ic [Gk. *hieros*, sacred, *glyphein*, to engrave], character in picture writing, as of the ancient Egyptians.

Hig'gle [form of **Haggle**], chaffer, haggle.

High [O.E. *hēah*], tall, above other things.

High'way, main road.

High'way-man, robber on the public road.

Hi-la'ri-ous [L. *hilaris*, cheerful], mirthful, boisterously merry. **Hilar'ity.**

Hill [O.E. *hyll*], low mountain, large heap.

Hil'lock [dim. of **Hill**], small hill.

Hilt [O.E. *hilt*], handle of a sword, etc.

Hind [1] (*ī*) [O.E. *hind*], female of the stag.

Hind [2] (*ī*) [M.E. *hīne*, prob. fr. *hīna*, gen. pl. of *hīgan*, servants], a farm servant, a rustic.

Hind [3] (*ī*) [perh. fr. O.E. *hinder* or *behindan*, behind], at the back.

Hind'er (*ī*) [see **Hind** [3]], in the rear.

Hin'der (*ĭ*) [O.E. *hindrian*], keep back.

Hind'most (*ī*) [see **Hind** [3]], furthest behind.

Hin'drance, act of hindering, that which hinders.

Hinge [M.E. *heng*], hook or joint to turn on ; stand or turn as on a hinge.

Hint [prob. fr. obs. *hent*, to lay hold of], slight mention or suggestion ; refer slightly.

Hip [O.E. *hype*], projecting part of the thigh.

Hip [O.E. *hēope*], fruit of the rose. [spirits.

Hip [shortened from **Hypochondria**], low

Hip'po-drome [Gk. *hippos*, a horse, *dromos*, a course], course for horses and chariots.

Hip'po-pot'a-mus [Gk. *hippos*, a horse, *potamos*, a river], large river animal with thick hide.

Hire [O.E. *hȳr*], wages, pay for temporary use ; procure for temporary use at a price. **Hire'ling.**

Hir'sute [L. *hirsūtus*, bristly], hairy.

Hiss [imit.], prolonged sound like that of *s*; make a sound like that of *s*.

His-tor'ic, celebrated in history.

His-tor'ic-al, of or relating to history.

His'to-ry [Gk. *historia*, learning by enquiry, information; *histōr*, learned], record, particularly of events affecting nations.

His-tri-on'ic [L. *histrio* (*histriōn-is*), a player], theatrical.

Hit [O.E. *hyttan*; cf. Dan. *hitte*; Swed. *hitta*, to come upon], a striking against, stroke of success; strike, come upon.

Hitch [?], sudden stop, pull up, knot; to hook, jerk.

Hith'er [O.E. *hider*], to this place.

Hith'er-to, up to this time.

Hive [O.E. *hȳf*], structure in which bees live; gather (bees) into a hive, store, live together like bees.

Hoar [O.E. *hár*], white or grayish.

Hoard [O.E. *hord*], a store, hidden supply; lay up in store.

Hoard'ing [O.F. *hourd*, a scaffold, or Du. *horde*, a hurdle], high fence of boards.

Hoarse [O.E. *hás*; M.E. *hōrs*], rough and husky.

Hoar'y [see **Hoar**], white or gray with age.

Hoax [short for *hocus*, to cheat], deceptive trick or story.

Hob [?], iron shelf at the side of a grate.

Hob'ble [prob. cogn. with Du. *hobbelen*, to rock], walk lamely, tie the legs; uneven gait, rope, etc.; to hobble a horse.

Hob'by [O.F. *hobin*, *hobi*, perh. variant of **Robin**], rocking horse, constantly recurring subject of talk, favourite pursuit.

Hob-gob'lin [*hob* (for *Robin*) and **Goblin**], ghost or spectre, mischievous fairy.

Hob'nail, short, broad-headed nail.

Hob'nob [earlier *hab nab*, O.E. *habban*, to have, *nabban*, not to have], associate familiarly.

Hock¹, Hough (*hŏk*) [O.E. *hŏh*, the heel], part in animals corresponding to the ankle in man.

Hock² [from place-name *Hochheim*], German white wine.

Hock'ey [?], game played with hooked sticks and a ball.

Hod [O.F. *hotte*, a basket], tray with a handle for mortar, etc.

Hoe [F. *houe*; O.H.G. *houwâ*, a hoe, *houwan*, to hew], tool to dig up weeds; break the ground, etc., with a hoe.

Hog [?], swine.

Hogs'head, measure of 52½ gallons, large cask.

Hoist [formerly *hoise*; cf. O.Du. *hyssen*, to hoist], a lift; raise, esp. by tackle.

Hold [for **Hole**], interior of a ship below the deck.

Hold [O.E. *haldan*], grasp; to grasp, keep fast.

Hold'ing, farm held of another.

Hole [O.E. *hol*], opening through a thing, pit.

Hol'i-day [O.E. *hálig dæg*; see **Holy, Day**], day for a public festival, day of freedom from work.

Ho'li-ness, state of being holy.

Hol'land [from province of Northern Netherlands, now *Holland*], kind of linen.

Hol'lands [Du. *hollandsch genever*, Holland gin], gin.

Hol'low [M.E. *holg, holu*; O.E. *holh*], having an empty space within; unfilled space, depression.

Hol'ly [O.E. *hole(g)n*], evergreen shrub.

Hol'ly-hock [**Holy**, and obs. *hock*, mallow (O.E. *hoc*)], tall plant with large flowers.

Holm (*hōm*) [O.N. *holmr*, an islet], islet in a river, low flat land.

Hol'o-caust [Gk. *holos*, whole, *caiein*, to burn], burnt sacrifice, great massacre.

Hol'o-graph [Gk. *holos*, whole, *graphein*, to write], document wholly in the writing of the person signing it.

Hol'ster (*ō* long) [Du. *holster*, a holster], pistol-case on a saddle.

Ho'ly [O.E. *hálig*, holy; *hál*, whole], sacred, spiritually whole. **Ho'lily**.

Hom'age [O.F. *ommage*, homage; L. *homo*, a man], reverential submission, respect.

Home [O.E. *hám*], dwelling-place, native place.

Home'ly, plain, unpretending.

Home'spun, spun at home; cloth made of yarn spun at home.

Home'stead [**Home** and O.E. *stede*, a place], house, esp. farm-house and the buildings connected with it.

Hom'i-cide [L. *homo*, a man, *cœdere*, to kill], killing of man by man, a murderer. **Homicid'al**.

Hom'i-ly [Gk. *homilos*, a crowd, *homou*, together, *ilē*, a crowd], sermon. **Homilet'ic**.

Hom'i-ny [Amer. Indian, *auhuminea*, parched corn], crushed maize boiled with water or milk.

Ho-mœ-op'a-thy (*œ=ĭ*) [Gk. *homoios*, like, *pathos*, suffering], art of curing by drugs which would produce in healthy persons symptoms like the disease. **Homœopath'ic**.

Ho-mo-ge'ne-ous [Gk. *homos*, same; *genos*, kind], of the same kind. **Homogene'ity**.

Ho-mol'o-gate [Gk. *homos*, the same, *logos*, a word, *legein*, to say], approve, confirm.

Hom'o-nym [Gk. *homos*, same, *onoma*, name], word of same sound as another but different meaning.

Hone [O.E. *hán*, a stone], whetstone.

Hon'es-ty [L. *honestus*, honest], uprightness, sincerity; a plant.

Hon'ey (*o=ŭ*) [O.E. *hunig*], sweet substance produced by bees.

Hon'ey-comb, wax cells made by bees.

Hon'ey-moon, holiday after marriage.

Hon'ey-suc-kle, climbing shrub.

Hon-o-ra'ri-um [L. *honorārius*, honorary], voluntary fee for professional service.

Hon'or-a-ry, conferred as an honour, serving without pay.

Hon'our [O.F. *honur*; L. *honor*, honour], great respect, nobility of mind.

Hood [O.E. *hŏd*], covering for head or head and shoulders.

Hood′man-blind, blind-man's buff.

Hood′wink [Hood and Wink], blind by covering the eyes, deceive.

Hoof [O.E. *hóf*], horny end or large nail on the feet of some animals.

Hook [O.E. *hóc*], bent piece of metal, etc., for catching.

Hook′ah [Arab. *huqqah*, hookah], long pipe so arranged that the smoke passes through water.

Hool′i-gan [from the Irish name *Houlihan*], street rough. **Hool′iganism.**

Hoop [1] [O.E. *hóp*], circular band of wood, etc.

Hoop [2] [F. *houper*, imit.], call out "Hoop!" shout.

Hoot [M.E. *huten*, prob. imit.], owl-cry, shout of contempt.

Hop [1] [O.E. *hoppian*], a leap on one foot; move by leaps.

Hop [2] [M.Du. *hoppe*, hop], climbing plant.

Hope [O.E. *hopa*], belief in future good; expect good.

Hop′per [see Hop [1]], grain-funnel in a mill.

Horde (*ō*) [Turk. *orda*, a camp; Tatar, *ūrdū*, a royal camp, a horde], wandering tribe, gang.

Hore′hound, Hoar′hound [O.E. *hár*, hoar, *húne*, name of a plant], bitter herb.

Ho-ri′zon [Gk. *horizōn*, fr. *horos*, a boundary], line formed by the apparent meeting of earth and sky.

Hor-i-zon′tal, parallel to the horizon, level.

Horn [O.E. *horn*], hard growth on the heads of certain animals, musical wind instrument.

Horn-blende′ [Ger. *horn*, horn, *blenden*, to dazzle], dark green or black mineral.

Hor′net [O.E. *hyrnet*(*u*)], large kind of wasp.

Horn′pipe, lively air, dance.

Ho-rol′o-gy [Gk. *hōra*, an hour, *logia*, discourse], science treating of the construction of clocks, etc.

Hor′o-scope [Gk. *hōra*, an hour, *scopein*, to observe], diagram showing the position of the planets at a particular moment, esp. the instant of a person's birth.

Hor′ri-ble, rousing horror, terrible.

Hor′rid [L. *horridus*, *horrēre*, to bristle, to dread], fitted to rouse horror, offensive.

Hor′ri-fy [L. *horror*, horror, *facere*, to make], shock, fill with horror.

Hor′ror [L. *horrēre*, to bristle, to dread], feeling of dread and detestation.

Horse [O.E. *hors*], four-footed, hoofed animal with mane and tail.

Horse-chest′nut, kind of tree and its fruit.

Horse′man-ship, art of riding.

Horse′play, rude play.

Horse′rad′ish, plant with a pungent root.

Hor′ta-tive [L. *hortāri* (p.p. *hortātus*), to exhort], giving advice. **Hor′tatory.**

Hor′ti-cul′ture [L. *hortus*, a garden, *cultūra*, cultivation], gardening. [pipe.

Hose [*s*=*z*] [O.E. *hosa*], stockings, flexible

Ho′sier (*s*=*z*), dealer in stockings, etc.

Hos′pice (*ce*=*ss*) [L. *hospes* (*hospit-is*), a host], shelter for travellers, esp. one maintained by monks.

Hos′pi-ta-ble [L. *hospes* (*hospit-is*), a host and **Able**], kind to guests and strangers.

Hos′pi-tal [M.L. *hospitāle*, place for guests; see Hospice], building for treating the sick.

Host (*ō*) [L. *hospes* (*hospitis*), a host], one who entertains guests, innkeeper; *fem.* **Host′ess.**

Host (*ō*) [O.F. *host*; L. *hostis*, an enemy], army, multitude.

Host (*ō*) [L. *hostia*, a victim in a sacrifice], sacramental bread (in the R.C. Church).

Hos′tage (*ō*) [L. *obses* (*obsid-is*), a hostage], person given as a pledge.

Hos′tel (*ō*) [O.F. *hostel*; M.L. *hospitāle*, a place for guests], inn; residence for students, etc.

Hos′tile (*ō*) [L. *hostis*, an enemy], warlike, opposed, unfriendly. **Hostil′ity.**

Hos′tler, Ost′ler [see Hostel], horse-tender at an inn.

Hotch′potch [F. *hochepot*; *hocher*, to shake, and *pot*, pot], mingled mass, dish of varied ingredients.

Ho-tel′ [O.F. *hostel*], inn of the better class.

Hough [see Hock [1]].

Hound [O.E. *hund*], dog, esp. for hunting; urge on.

Hour [L. and Gk. *hōra*, an hour], twenty-fourth part of a day, time of day.

House [O.E. *hús*, a house], building to live in, family; (*se*=*z*) receive or place in a house.

House′hold, those who dwell in the same house. [rooms.

House′maid, servant who takes care of the

House′wife, manageress of affairs of a house; (pron. *huz′if*), case for things used in sewing.

Hov′el (*o*=*ō* or *ŭ*) [?], mean house.

Hov′er (*o*=*ō* or *ŭ*) [?], flutter over, hang about.

How′dah [Pers. *haudah*; Arab. *haudaj*, a litter], seat on an elephant's back.

How-ev′er, in whatever way, in any case.

How-it′zer [Ger. *haubitze*, fr. Boh. *houfnice*, catapult], short gun for high angle firing of shells at low velocities.

Howl [M.E. *houlen*], cry as of a dog or wolf; utter such a cry.

Hoy [prob. M.Du. *hoei*, *heude*], small coasting vessel. [girl.

Hoy′den, Hoi′den [etym. dub.], rude, bold

Hub [?], central cylindrical part of a wheel.

Hub′bub [Ir. orig., cf. Gael. *ubub*, a war cry], great noise.

Huck′a-back [?], coarse figured linen.

Huck′ster [cf. M.Du. *hucker*; Low G. *hóker*, huckster; M.Du. *hucken*, to stoop], hawker.

Hud′dle [?], crowd together, put confusedly.

Hue [O.E. *hiw*], shade of colour.

Hue [O.F. *hu*, a cry; *huer*, to shout], shouting (as in "hue and cry").

Huff [imit. sound of blowing], puff, storm at, bully; fit of petulance.

Hug [?], close embrace; clasp closely.

Huge [O.F. *ahuge*; etym. doubtful], very large.

Hug′ger-mug′ger [?], secrecy, confusion; secret, confused.

Hulk [O.E. *hulc*, perh. fr. Gk. *holkas*, a towed ship], body of an old disused vessel, anything bulky.

Hulk'ing [see **Hulk**], clumsy.

Hull[1] [O.E. *hulu*, cover], outer covering, husk; to remove hull, shell or husk.

Hull[2] [etym. dub., perh. **Hull**[1]], body of a ship.

Hul-lo', see **Halloa**.

Hum [imit.], low sound as of bees; make a sound as of bees, sing with closed mouth.

Hu'man [L. *humānus*, human; L. *homo* (*homin-is*), a man], belonging to or having the qualities of man.

Hu-mane' [see **Human**], kind.   [ta'rian.

Hu-man'i-ty, mankind, kindness. **Humani-**

Hum'ble [L. *humus*, the ground], lowly, modest; to lower.

Hum'bug [?], deceiver; impose on.

Hum'drum, commonplace, tiresome.

Hu'mer-al [L. *humerus*, the shoulder], relating to the shoulder.   [ity.

Hu'mid [L. *humidus*, moist], moist. **Humid'-**

Hu-mil'i-ate [see **Humble**], to humble, depress the dignity of. **Humilia'tion.**

Hu-mil'i-ty, lowliness of mind.

Hum'mock [?], rounded knoll.

Hu'mour or **Hu'mour** [L. *hūmor*, moisture], fluid of animal or plant, state of mind, caprice, playful fancy; gratify, indulge. **Hu'morous.**

Hump [Du. *homp*, a lump], protuberance, swelling.

Hunch [?], hump, thick piece. **Hunch'back.**

Hun'dred [O.E. *hund*, hundred+-*red*=Goth. -*rath*, number], number denoting ten times ten.

Hun'dred-weight (*ei*=*ai*), weight of 112 lbs.

Hun'ger [O.E. *hungor*], craving for food; have an eager desire. **Hun'gry.**

Hunt [O.E. *hunta*, a hunter], a chase; to chase, pursue.

Hur'dle [O.E. *hyrdel*], movable frame of twigs or bars.

Hurl [prob. imit.], throw with force.

Hur-ra', **Hur-rah'** [earlier *huzza*, imit. origin], cry of joy or triumph.   [storm.

Hur'ri-cane [Sp. and Carib. *huracan*], violent

Hur'ry [imit. origin; cf. dial. Swed. *hurra*, to whirl], haste; make haste.

Hurt [O.F. *hurter*, to dash against], a wound, pain; to wound, to pain.   [swiftly.

Hur'tle [see **Hurt**], strike (against), hurl

Hus'band (*s*=*z*) [O.E. *hûsbonda*, master of house; *hûs*, a house, *bónda*, freeholder, fr. O.N. *búa*, to dwell], married man; manage frugally.

Hus'band-man, tiller of the ground.

Hus'band-ry, thrift.

Hush [imit.], stillness; make or be quiet.

Husk [?], outer covering as of fruits, etc.

Hus'ky, hoarse, rough in tone.

Hus'ky [prob. contraction of Eskimo], Eskimo, Eskimo language, Eskimo dog.

Hus-sar' (*s*=*z*) [Hung. *huszar*, a freebooter, later a light horseman; O.Serv. *husar*, a freebooter], light-cavalry trooper.

Hus'tings [O.N. *hústhing*, a house-meeting], formerly a platform for the candidates at a parliamentary election.

Hus'tle [Du. *husselen*, freq. of M.Du. *hutsen*, to shake], push or crowd, jostle.

Hut [F. *hutte*; Ger. *hütte*, a hut, perh. allied to **Hide**[2]], small house, poor cottage.

Hutch [M.E. and F. *huche*; M.L. *hûtica*, a hutch], box or the like for rabbits.

Huz-za' [imit.], shout of joy.

Hy'a-cinth [earlier *jacynth*; Gk. *Hyacinthos*, a youth killed by Apollo], bulbous plant with flowers in spikes, a precious stone.

Hy'brid [L. *hibrida*, *hybrida*, hybrid], offspring of two species.

Hy-dran'gea (*gea*=*ja*) [Gk. *hydōr*, water, *aggos*, a vessel], kind of shrub with flowers in large clusters.

Hy'drant [Gk. *hydōr*, water], pipe to which hose can be attached for discharging water.

Hy-drau'lics [Gk. *hydōr*, water, *aulos*, a pipe], branch of science which treats of fluids in motion.

Hy'dro-gen [Gk. *hydōr*, water, *gennaein*, to generate], elementary gas.

Hy-drog'raph-y [Gk. *hydōr*, water, *graphia*, description, fr. *graphein*, to write], geography of the waters of the globe.

Hy-drop'a-thy [Gk. *hydōr*, water, *pathos*, endurance], water cure. **Hydropath'ic.**

Hy-dro-pho'bi-a [Gk. *hydōr*, water, *phobos*, fear], dread of water, disease caused by the bite of a mad dog.

Hy'dro-plane [Gk. *hydōr*, water; see **Plane**], aeroplane which can rest on and rise from water.

Hy-dro-stat'ics [Gk. *hydōr*, water; see **Static**], science which treats of fluids at rest.

Hy-e'na [L. *hyœna*; Gk. *hyaina*, hyena; Gk. *hys*, a pig], flesh-eating quadruped.

Hy'giene [Gk. *Hygieia*, the goddess of health, *hygiēs*, healthy], laws of health.

Hy'gi-en'ic, relating to health.

Hy-me-ne'al [Gk. *Hymēn*, the god of marriage], relating to marriage.

Hymn [Gk. *hymnos*, a song, a hymn], song of praise, esp. religious.

Hym'nal, collection of hymns. **Hymnol'ogy.**

Hy-per'bo-le [Gk. *hyper*, beyond, and *ballein*, to throw], exaggeration. **Hyperbol'ical.**

Hy-per-bor'ean [Gk. *hyper*, beyond, *Boreas*, north wind], (inhabitant) of the extreme north.

Hy'per-crit'ic-al [Gk. *hyper*, beyond, and *criticos*, critical], over-critical.

Hy'phen [Gk. *hyphen*, together; *hypo*, under, and *hen*, one], sign [-] of connection. **Hyphena'ted.**

Hyp'no-tism [Gk. *hypnos*, sleep], sleep-like state artificially produced. **Hypnot'ic.**

Hyp-o-chon'dri-a [Gk. *hypo*, under, and *chondros*, cartilage of the breastbone], morbid depression without real cause. **Hypochon'driac.**

Hyp-oc'ri-sy [Gk. *hypocrisis*, lit. acting a part; *hypo*, under, and *crinein*, to decide], pretence of goodness.

Hyp'o-crite, pretender to goodness.

Hy-po-der'mic [Gk. *hypo*, under, *derma*, skin], introduced under the skin.

Hy-pot'en-use [Gk. *hypo*, under, *teinein*, to stretch], side of a right-angled triangle opposite the right angle.

Hyp'o-thec [L. *hypothēca*; Gk. *hypothēcē*; *hypo*, under, and *tithenai*, to place], legal security over property of a debtor.

Hy-poth'e-sis (pl. **Hypoth'eses**) [Gk. *hypo*, under, and *thesis*, a placing], supposition, esp. as a basis for reasoning. [plant.

Hys'sop [Gk. *hyssōpos*, hyssop], aromatic

Hys-te'ri-a, Hys-ter'ics (*Hys*=*hiss*) [Gk. *hystericos*, relating to hysteria, perh. from *hysteros*, latter, lower], disease in which nervous control is lost. **Hyster'ical.**

I

I-am'bus, I-amb [Gk. *iambos*, an iambic foot, a lampoon], poetic foot of two syllables (◡ –).

I'bex [L. *ibex*, an ibex], kind of wild goat.

I'bis [L. and Gk. *ibis*, an ibis], a large wading bird.

Ice [O.E. *is*], frozen water. **I'cy, I'cily.**

Ice'berg [Du. *ijs*, ice, *berg*, a mountain], large mass of ice in the sea.

Ich-neu'mon (*ch*=*k*) [Gk. *ichneumon*; *ichneuein*, to track], weasel-like animal that destroys crocodiles' eggs. [gods.

I'chor (*ch*=*k*) [Gk. *ichōr*], fluid in veins of

I'ci-cle [O.E. *is-gical*, *ises gical*; *is*, ice, *gical*, a small piece of ice], hanging mass of ice.

I'con [Gk. *eicōn*, an image], image, statue; in Eastern Church, painting or mosaic of saint.

I-con'o-clast [Gk. *eicōn*, an image, *clastēs*, a breaker], an image-breaker.

I-de'a [Gk. *idea*, form, kind; *idein*, to see], notion.

I-de'al, mental, visionary, perfect; a mental conception regarded as perfection.

I-de'al-ize, attribute ideal qualities to.

I-den'tic-al, the very same.

I-den'ti-fy, consider as the same, prove to be the same, associate inseparably (with).

I-den'ti-ty [L. *idem*, the same], state of being the same. [becility.

Id'i-o-cy [see **Idiot**], extreme mental im-

Id'i-om [Gk. *idiōma*, idiom, *idios*, one's own], expression peculiar to a language.

Id-i-o-syn'cra-sy [Gk. *idios*, own, *syn-*, together, *crasis*, a blending], peculiarity.

Id'i-ot [Gk. *idiōtēs*, a private person, fr. *idios*, own], one lacking in common intelligence. [idle.

I'dle [O.E. *idel*], useless, unemployed; be

I'dol [Gk. *eidōlon*, an image, *eidos*, form], image of a god. **Idol'ater.**

I'dyll, I'dyl [Gk. *eidyllion*, an idyl, *eidos*, form], short poem describing simple, picturesque, usu. rustic scene.

I-dyl'lic, belonging to idyls.

Ig'ne-ous [L. *ignis*, fire], produced by fire.

Ig-nite' [L. *ignis*, fire], set on fire. **Igni'tion.**

Ig-no'ble [L. *in-* (=*i*), not, *nobilis* (*gnobilis*), noble], not noble, mean.

Ig'no-mi-ny [L. *in-* (=*i*), not, *gnōmen* (old form of *nōmen*), a name], disgrace. **Igno-min'ious.**

Ig-nor-a'mus [L.=we do not know], ignorant person.

Ig-nore' [L. *in-*, not, and *gnoscere* (old form of *noscere*), to know], take no notice of.

Il-, used for **In-** before *l*, is a prefix of negation, as in **Il-le'gal, Il-le'gi-ble, Il-le-git'im-ate, Il-lim'it-a-ble, Il-lo'gic-al.**

Ilk [O.E. *ilca*, same; Sc. *that ilk*=*the same*], the same. [injury.

Ill [O.N. *illr*, ill], bad, in bad health; harm,

Il-li'cit (*i*) [L. *in-*, not, *licēre* (p.p. *licitus*), to be allowed], not allowed.

Il-lit'er-ate [L. *in-*, not, *literātus*, able to read, *littera*, a letter], ignorant of letters or books. **Illit'eracy.**

Ill'ness, sickness.

Il-log'ical [*Il-*, L. *in-*, not, and **Logic**], contrary to logic or sound reasoning.

Il-lume', Il-lu'mine, Il-lu'min-ate [L. *in*, in, *lumen* (*lumin-is*), light], throw light on, light up. **Illumina'tion.**

Il-lu'sion [*si*=*zh*] [L. *in*, upon, *lūdere* (p.p. *lūsus*), to play], false show, deception.

Il-lu'sive, Il-lu'so-ry, deceptive.

Il'lus-trate [L. *in*, upon, *lustrāre*, to shine], make clear by examples, adorn and make clear by pictures. **Illustra'tion.**

Il-lus'tri-ous, distinguished, famous.

Im, used for **In** before *b*, *m*, *p*, is a prefix of negation in the following words: **Im-ma-te'ri-al, Im-ma-ture', Im-meas'u-ra-ble** (*s*=*z*), **Im-mo'bile, Im-mod'er-ate, Im-mod'est, Im-mor'al, Im-mor'tal, Im-mu'ta-ble, Im-pal'pa-ble, Im-par'tial** (*ti*=*sh*), **Im-pas'sa-ble, Im-pa'tience, Im-pec'ca-ble, Im-pen'et-ra-ble, Im-pen'i-tent, Im-per-cep'ti-ble, Im-per'fect, Im-per'ish-a-ble, Im-per'me-a-ble, Im-per'so-nal, Im-per-turb'a-ble, Im-per'vi-ous, Im-pi'e-ty, Im'pi-ous, Im-plac'a-ble, Im-po-lite', Impol'i-tic, Im-pon'der-able, Im-pos'si-ble, Im'po-tent, Im-prac'tic-a-ble, Im-prob'able, Im-prop'er, Im-pro-pri'e-ty, Im-prov'i-dent, Im-pure'.**

Im'age [L. *imāgo* (*imāgin-is*), an image], a likeness, statue, idol

Im-a'gin-a-ry, existing only in fancy.

Im-a'gi-na'tion, power of the mind to form images or concepts.

Im-a'gine, form a mental image of.

Im'be-cile [L. *imbēcillus*, feeble], feeble-minded; one who is feeble-minded. **Imbecil'ity.**

Im-bed' [L. *in*, in, and **Bed**], lay as in a bed.

Im-bibe' [L. *in*, in, *bibere*, to drink], drink in.

Im-bro'glio (*io=yo*) [It. *imbroglio*; *in*, in, *broglio*, a broil], perplexing state of affairs.

Imbrue [O.F. *embrewer*, to moisten; L. *in*, in, *bibere*, to drink], soak, drench.

Im-bue [L. *in*, in, *bibere*, to drink], tinge deeply, dye, inspire (with).

Im'i-tate [L. *imitāri* (p.p. *imitātus*), to imitate], copy, follow as a model.

Im-mac'u-late [L. *in-*, not, *macula*, a spot], spotless, blameless.

Im'ma-nent [L. *in*, in, *manēre* (pr.p. *manens*, *-entis*), to remain], inherent, indwelling. **Im'manence.**

Im-me'di-ate [M.L. *in-*, not, *mediāre* (p.p. *mediātus*), to be in the middle; L. *medius*, the middle], without delay, close.

Im-me-mo'ri-al [L. *in-*, not, and **Memorial**], beyond memory, very ancient.

Im-mense' [L. *in-*, not, *metīri* (p.p. *mensus*), to measure], immeasurable, vast, huge. **Immen'sity.**

Im-merse' [L. *in*, in, *mergere* (p.p. *mersus*), to plunge], plunge into a fluid, engage deeply. **Immer'sion.**

Im'mi-grant [L. *in*, in, *migrāre*, to wander], one who comes into a country.

Im'mi-nent [L. *in*, on, *minēre* (pr.p. *minens*, *-entis*), to project], about to happen, impending.

Im'mo-late [L. *immolāre* (p.p. *immolātus*), to sprinkle with sacrificial meal, to sacrifice; *in*, on, *mola*, meal], to sacrifice. **Immola'tion.**

Im-mune' [L. *in-*, not, *munus*, service], free (from). **Immun'ity.**

Im-mure' [L. *in*, in, *mūrus*, a wall], imprison.

Imp [O.E. *impa*, a graft], little devil, mischievous child. **Imp'ish.**

Im'pact [see **Impinge**], forcible contact.

Im-pair' [L. *impejorāre*, to make worse, *in* (intensive), *pejor*, worse], make worse, injure, weaken. [stake.

Im-pale' [L. *in*, on, *pālus*, a stake], fix on a

Im-part' [L. *in*, to, and *pars* (*part-is*), a part], give, share.

Im-pas'se [F.], blind alley, deadlock.

Im-pas'sioned [L. *in*, in; see **Passion**], full of passion or feeling. [moved.

Im-pas'sive [L. *in-*, not; see **Passive**], un-

Im-peach' [O.F. *empecher*, to hinder; L. *in*, on, *pedica*, a fetter, *pēs* (*ped-is*), the foot], accuse (esp. of treason), call in question. **Impeach'ment.**

Im'pe-cu'ni-ous [L. *in-*, not, *pecūniōsus*, rich, *pecūnia*, money, *pecu*, cattle], without money. [hinder.

Im-pede' [L. *in*, in, *pēs* (*ped-is*), the foot], **Im-ped'i-ment,** hindrance.

Im-pel' [L. *in*, on, *pellere* (p.p. *pulsus*), to drive], drive, urge.

Im-pend' [L. *in*, on, *pendēre*, to hang], hang over, threaten.

Im-per'a-tive [L. *imperāre* (sup. *imperātum*), to command], commanding, obligatory.

Im-pe'ri-al [L. *imperiālis*, imperial, *imperium*, dominion], relating to an empire or an emperor, suitable to supreme authority.

Im-per'il [L. *in*, in; see **Peril**], endanger.

Im-pe'ri-ous [L. *imperiōsus*, imperious, *imperium*, command], commanding, haughty.

Im-per'son-ate [L. *in*, in; see **Personate**], pretend to be, play the part of. **Imperson a'tion.**

Im-pert'in-ent [L. *in-*, not; see **Pertinent**], not to the point, insolent.

Im-pet'u-ous [see **Impetus**], rushing with force, hasty. **Impetuos'ity.**

Im'pe-tus [L. *in*, on, *petere*, to seek], force of something moving.

Im-pinge' (*ge=je*) [L. *impingere* (p.p. *impactus*); *in*, on, *pangere*, to fasten], to strike against, encroach upon. [deeply.

Im-plant' [L. *in*, in; see **Plant**], to plant, fix

Im'ple-ment [L. *implēre*, to execute; *in*, in, *plēre*, to fill], tool; to fulfil, complete.

Im'pli-cate [L. *in*, in, *plicāre* (p.p. *plicātus*), to fold], imply, entangle, involve.

Im'pli-ca'tion, something understood though not expressed.

Im-plic'it (*i* short) [L. *implicitus*, old p.p. of *implicāre*; see **Implicate**], implied, complete, unquestioning. [entreat.

Im-plore' [L. *in*, on, *plorāre*, to weep], beg,

Im-ply' [L. *in-*, in, and **Ply**], include by inference, signify.

Im'port, thing imported, meaning.

Im-port' [L. *in*, in, *portāre*, to bring], bring in from abroad, signify. **Importa'tion.**

Im-por'tant [L. *importans* (*importantis*), prp. of *importāre*; see **Import**], weighty, of consequence. [urgent.

Im-por'tu-nate [see **Importune**], tiresomely

Im-por-tune' [L. *importūnus*, troublesome, orig. hard of access, from *in-*, not, and *portus*, a harbour], urge repeatedly. **Importun'ity.**

Im-pose' (*s=z*) [F. *imposer*; L. *in*, on; F. *poser*, to lay], lay (on), deceive.

Im-po'sing, impressive.

Im-po-si'tion, a laying on, a school punishment, deception.

Im'post (*ō*) [L. *impōnere* (p.p. *impositus*), to impose], tax or duty.

Im-pos'tor (*ō*) [L. *impostus*, laid on], deceiver, pretender. **Impos'ture.**

Im-pound' [L. *in*, in; see **Pound** [2]], confine in a pen, hold in the custody of a court.

Im-pov'er-ish [O.F. *em* (L. *in*), in; O.F. *povre*, (L. *pauper*), poor], make poor.

Im-pre-ca'tion [L. *in*, upon, *precāri* (p.p. *precātus*), to pray], curse.

Im-preg'na-ble [L. *in-*, not, *prehendere*, to seize], impossible of capture.

Im-preg'nate [L. *impregnāre* (p.p. *impregnātus*); see **Pregnant**], infuse, imbue.

Im-press' [L. *impressāre*, freq. of *imprimere*, to press upon; *in*, on, *premere*, to press], press in or upon, fix in the mind, compel to enter public service. [mark.

Im'press, mark made by pressure, distinctive

Im-pres'sion, stamp, effect, edition.

Im-pres'sion-ism, fashion in painting or writing that gives general effect without much detail.

Im-press'ive, weighty (conduct), effective.

Im-prim-a'tur (a=ai) [L.=let it be printed], official sanction to print, stamp.

Im-print' [L. in, on; see Print], to stamp, impress.

Im'print, impression, printer's or publisher's name, with date and place, etc., on a title-page.

Im-pris'on (s=z) [L. in, in; see Prison], put or keep in prison. Impris'onment.

Im-promp'tu [F. impromptu; L. in promptu, in readiness], offhand, unstudied.

Im-prove' (ove=oov) [A.F. emprover; em, in, and O.F. prou, profit], make or become better.

Im-pro-vise' (s=z) [It. improvvisāre, to improvise; L. in-, not, pro, before, vidēre (p.p. vīsus), to see], compose, invent, etc., on the spur of the moment. Improvisa'tion.

Im'pu-dent [L. impudens (-entis), in-, not, pudēre, to be ashamed], bold and shameless. Im'pudence.

Im-pugn' (pugn=pune) [L. in-, against, pugnāre, to fight], call in question. Im-pugn'ment.

Im'pulse [L. impulsus, urged on], force communicated, sudden feeling. Impul'sive.

Im-pu'ni-ty [L. in-, not, pœna, punishment], freedom from harm or punishment.

Im-pu-ta'tion, charge, attribution.

Im-pute' [L. in, in, putāre (p.p. putātus), to reckon], ascribe.

In- is a Latin prefix of negation which is used to form nouns and adjectives, when it means not, absence of. Among these are : In-a-bil'i-ty, In-ac-ces'si-ble, In-ac'cu-ra-cy, In-ac'cu-rate, In-ac'tion, In-ac'tive, In-ad'e-qua-cy, In-ad-mis'si-ble, In-ad-vi'sa-ble, In-ap'pli-ca-ble, In-ap'po-site, In-ap-pre'ci-a-ble, In-ap-pro'pri-ate, In-apt'i-tude, In-ar-tic'u-late, In-at-ten'-tion, In-at-ten'tive, In-au'di-ble, In-aus-pi'cious, In-cal'cu-la-ble, In-ca'pa-ble, In-ca-pa'ci-ty, In-cau'tious, In-cer'ti-tude, In-ci-vil'i-ty, In-clem'ent, In-cog'ni-zant, In-co-he'rent, In-com-men'su-rate, In-com-mu'ni-ca-ble, In-com-mu'ta-ble, In-com'pa-ra-ble, In-com-pat'i-ble, In-com'pe-tent, In-com-plete', In-com-pre-hen'si-ble, In-com-press'i-ble, In-con-ceiv'a-ble, In-con-clu'sive, In-con'gru-ous, In-con'se-quent, In-con-sid'er-a-ble, In-con-sid'er-ate, In-con-sist'ent, In-con-so'la-ble, In-con'so-nant, In-con-spic'u-ous, In-con'stant, In-con-test'a-ble, In-con-tro-vert'i-ble, In-con-ve'ni-ent, In-con-vert'i-ble, In-cor-po're-al, In-cor-rect', In-cor-rupt'i-ble, In-cred'i-ble, In-cred'u-lous, In-cu'ra-ble, In-cu'ri-ous, In-de'cent, In-de-ci'sion (s=z), In-de-cli'na-ble, In-de-co'rous or In-dec'o-rous, In-de-co'rum, In-de-fen'si-ble, In-del'i-ble, In-de-pend'ent, In-de-scri'ba-ble, In-de-struct'i-ble, In-de-ter'mi-na-ble, In-di-rect', In-dis-cern'i-ble, In-dis-creet', In-dis-cre'tion (ĕ), In-dis-crim'in-ate, In-dis-pen'sa-ble, In-dis'pu-ta-ble, In-dis'so-lu-ble or

In-dis-sol'u-ble, In-dis-tinct', In-dis-tin'-guish-a-ble, In-di-vis'i-ble, In-ef-fec'tive, In-ef-fec'tu-al, In-ef-fi-ca'cious, In-ef'fi-ca-cy, In-ef-fi'cient, In-el'e-gant, In-el'i-gi-ble, In-e-qual'i-ty, In-eq'ui-ta-ble, In-e-rad'i-ca-ble, In-es'ti-ma-ble, In-ex-act', In-ex-cu'sa-ble, In-ex-haust'i-ble, In-ex-pe'di-ent, In-ex-pen'sive, In-ex-pe'ri-ence, In-ex-pert', In-ex'pi-a-ble, In-ex'pli-ca-ble, In-ex-press'i-ble, In-ex-press'ive, In-ex'tri-ca-ble, In-fal'li-ble, In-fe-li'ci-tous, In-fi-nite, In-flex'i-ble, In-form'al, In-fre'quent, In-glo'ri-ous, In-grat'i-tude, In-har-mo'ni-ous, In-hos'pi-ta'ble, In-im'i-ta-ble, In-ju-di'cious, In-jus'tice, In-nox'ious, In-nu'mer-a-ble, In-o'dor-ous, In-of-fen'sive, In-op'er-a-tive, In-op'por-tune, In-sa-lu'bri-ous, In-sal'u-ta-ry, In-sane', In-san'i-ty, In-se-cure', In-sen'si-ble, In-sep'a-ra-ble, In-sin-cere', In-so-bri'e-ty, In-sol'u-ble, In-sol'vent, In-suf'fer-a-ble, In-suf-fi'cient, In-sup-port'a-ble, In-sur-mount'a-ble, In-tan'gi-ble, In-tem'per-ance, In-tem'per-ate, In-tol'er-a-ble, In-tol'er-ant, In-tract'a-ble, In-tran'si-tive, In-u-til'i-ty, In'val-id, In-val'id (not valid), In-va'ri-a-ble, In-ver'te-brate, In-vis'i-ble (s=z), In-vol'un-ta-ry, In-vul'ner-a-ble.

In-ad-vert'ent [L. in-, not, and obs. E. advertent; see Advert], unintentional.

In-al'ien-a-ble (al=ail) [L. in-, not; see Alien], that cannot be transferred.

In-ane' [L. inānis, empty, vain], empty, without intelligence.   [lifeless.

In-an'i-mate [L. in-, not; see Animate], In-an-i'tion [see Inane], exhaustion from lack of food.

In-an'i-ty, mental emptiness.

In-as-much' [orig. three words], since.

In-au'gu-rate [L. in, in, and Augur], cause to begin with ceremony, introduce.

In'born [L. in, in, and Born, p.p. of Bear], implanted by nature.

In'ca [Peruv. inca], ancient Peruvian monarch, one of Peruvian royal race.

In-can-des'cent [L. incandescere (pr.p. incandescens, -entis), to glow ; candēre, to glow, to be white], white or glowing with heat.

In-can-ta'tion [L. in, in, upon, cantāre, freq. of canere, to sing], form of words for enchantment.

In-ca-pa'ci-tate [L. in-, not, capax, able to hold, capere, to hold], disable, make unfit.

In-car'cer-ate [L. in, in, carcer, a prison], imprison. Incarcera'tion.

In-car'nate [L. in, in, caro (carn-is), flesh], embodied in flesh. Incarna'tion.

In-cen'di-a-ry [L. incendium, a conflagration], fire-raiser.

In-cense' [L. incendere (p.p. incensus), to set on fire], enkindle, enrage.

In'cense [L. incensum, that which is burnt], perfume from burning spices or gums.

In-cen'tive [L. incentivus, striking up a tune; in, in, and canere, to sing], motive, spur.

In-cep'tion [L. incipere (p.p. inceptus), to begin; in, upon, capere, to hold], beginning.

In-ces′sant [L. *in-*, not, *cessāre* (pr.p. *cessans, -antis*), to cease, freq. of *cēdere*, to yield], unceasing, without stop.

In′cest [L. *incestus*, fr. *in*, not, *castus*, pure], sexual intercourse between near kindred. In-ces′tuous.

Inch (*ch=sh*) [L. *uncia*, a twelfth], measure of length, twelfth part of a foot.

Inch [Gael. *innis*, an island], island.

In′cho-ate (*ch=k*) [L. *inchoāre*, (p.p. *in-choātus*), to begin], just begun, unde-veloped.

In′ci-dent [L. *incidere* (pr.p. *incidens, -entis*), to fall upon ; *in*, on, *cadere*, to fall], naturally attaching (to), liable to happen ; event, occurrence.

In-ci-dent′al, coming without design.

In-cin′er-ate [L. *in*, in, *cinis* (*ciner-is*), ashes], burn to ashes. Incin′erator.

In-cip′i-ent [L. *incipiens* (*-entis*), pr.p. of *incipere* ; see Inception], beginning to be.

In-ci′sion (*si=zh*) [L. *incidere* (p.p. *incīsus*), to cut into ; *in*, in, *cædere*, to cut], a cut into.

In-ci′sive (*s=z*), cutting, sharp.

In-ci′sor (*s=z*), front cutting tooth.

In-cite′ [L. *in*, in, *citāre*, to rouse], rouse.

In-cline′ [L. *in*, in, *clināre*, to bend], slope, bend, be disposed to. Inclina′tion.

In′cline, In-cline′, a slope.

In-close′, En-close′ [O.F. *enclore* (p.p. *enclos*), L. *inclūdere* (p.p. *inclūsus*) ; *in*, in, *claudere*, to shut], shut in. Inclos′ure.

In-clude′ [L. *inclūdere*, to shut in], contain, comprise.

In-clu′sive (*s=z*), taking in all within the stated limit. Inclu′sion.

In-cog′ni-to [It. *incognito*, unknown ; L. *in-*, not, *cognitus*, known], in disguise, under an assumed name.

In′come [In and Come], revenue, salary, annual receipts.

In-com-mode′ [L. *in*, not, *commodus*, fit], give inconvenience to.

In-con-gru′it-y [L. *in-*, not, *congruus*, suit-able], inharmonious mixture.

In-cor′po-rate [L. *in*, in, *corpus* (*corpor-is*), the body], embodied ; unite in one body.

In-cor′ri-gi-ble [L. *in-*, not, *corrigere*, to correct], not capable of being corrected.

In-crease′ [L. *in*, in, *crescere*, to grow], grow or make larger.

In′crease, enlargement, addition.   [increase.

In′cre-ment [L. *incrēmentum*, an increase], In-crim′i-nate [M.L. *incrimināre* (p.p. *in-criminātus*) ; see Crime], charge with crime, involve in accusation. Incrim′ina-tory.

In-crus-ta′tion [L. *in*, in, *crusta*, a crust], hard coating on or in.

In-cu-ba′tion [L. *in*, on, *cubāre* (sup. *cubātum*), to lie], a sitting on (eggs) for hatching.

In′cu-ba-tor, apparatus for hatching.

In′cu-bus [L.L. *incubus*, a nightmare ; L. *in*, on, and *cubāre*, to lie], oppressive burden.

In′cul-cate, In-cul′cate [L. *inculcāre* (p.p. *in-culcātus*), to inculcate ; *in*, in, and *calcāre*,

to tread], urge on the mind, teach. In-culca′tion.

In-cul′pate [L. *in*, in, and *culpāre*, (p.p. *culpātus*), to blame], show to be in fault.

In-cum′bent [L. *incumbere* (pr.p. *incumbens, -entis*), to rest on ; *in*, on, and *cumbere*, to lie], lying, resting ; holder of a church living. Incum′bency.

In-cur′ [L. *in*, in, *currere* (sup. *cursum*), to run], become liable or subject to (p.p. Incurrcd).

In-cur′sion, inroad.

In-debt′ed [O.F. *endette* (p.p. of *endetter*) ; L. *in*, in ; see Debt], under obligation, owing.

In-deed′, truly, in fact.

In-de-fat′i-ga-ble [L. *in-*, not, *de*, from, *fatigāre*, to tire], tireless.

In-de-fea′si-ble [L. *in-* not, *de*, from ; see Feasible], not to be made void.

In-dem′ni-fy [L. *indemnis*, unharmed ; *in-*, not, and *damnum*, loss, *facere*, to make], make compensation.

In-dem′ni-ty, security, compensation.

In-dent′ [L. *in*, in, *dens* (*dent-is*), a tooth], to notch, press in. Indenta′tion.

In-den′ture [see Indent], deed containing a mutual agreement.

In′dex [L. *index* (pl. *indices*); *in*, in, to, *dicāre* (p.p. *dicātus*), to declare], that which points out, reference-table in a book, the figure denoting the power of a quantity (in this sense pl. In′di-ces).

In′di-a-rub′ber, elastic gum.

In′di-cate [see Index], point out, show.

In-dict′ (*ict=īte*) [*in*, in, *dīcere* (p.p. *dictus*), to say], accuse.

In-dict′ment (*ict=īte*), formal accusation.

In-dif′fer-ent [L. *in*, not, *differens*, different], unconcerned, not very good. Indif′ference.

In-di′gen-ous [O.L. *indu*, within, *genitus*, born], native.

In′di-gent [L. *indigēre* (pr.p. *indigens, -entis*), to be in want ; *in*, in, *egēre*, to need], needy, poor. In′digence.

In-di-gest′ion [L. *in-*, not, *digestio*, digestion], failure of the proper changes which food should undergo in the body.

In-dig′nant [L. *indignāri* (pr.p. *indignans, -antis*), to deem unworthy ; *in-*, not, and *dignus*, worthy], wrathful.

In-dig′ni-ty [L. *in-*, not, *dignus*, worthy], insult, slight.

In′di-go [Sp. *indico* ; L. *indicum*, neut. of *Indicus*, Indian], deep blue ; blue dyestuff.

In-dis-po-si′tion [L. *in-*, not, *dispositio*, a setting in order], disinclination, illness.

In-dite′ [L. *indictāre*, to point out], com-pose, write.

In-di-vid′u-al [L. *in*, in, and *dividuus*, divisible], single, characteristic ; person.

In-doc′tri-nate [L. *in*, in, *doctrīna*, doctrine], to instruct in the principles of.

In′do-lent [Late L. *indolens* (*-entis*) ; *in*, not, *dolēre*, to grieve], inactive, lazy. In′-dolence.

In-dom′i-ta-ble [L. *in-*, not, *domitāre*, to subdue], that cannot be subdued.

In-dorse' [see **Endorse**], write on the back of, sanction.

In-du'bi-ta-ble [L. *in-*, not, *dubitabilis*, doubtful; see **Doubt**], that cannot be doubted.

In-duce' [L. *in*, in, *ducere* (p.p. *ductus*) to lead], lead on by persuasion, bring on.

In-duce'ment, motive.

In-duc'tion, introduction, inference from the known to the unknown, electric or magnetic effect of one body on another.

In-due', **En-due'** [L. *induere;* to put on clothes], clothe, supply with.

In-dulge' [L. *indulgēre*, to indulge ; origin unknown], give free course to, humour.

In-dul'gent, yielding, forbearing.

In'du-rate [L. *in*, in, *durus*, hard], harden.

In-dus'tri-al, pertaining to manufactures, etc.

In-dus'tri-ous, regularly occupied, busy.

In'dus-try [L. *industria ;* etym. doubtful], diligence, manufacture, trade.

In-e'bri-ate [L. *in*, in, *ēbrius*, drunken], drunken ; drunkard ; make drunk. **In-ebri'ety.**

In-ef'fa-ble [L. *in-*, not (*ef- = ex*, out), *fāri*, to speak], unspeakable.

In-ept' [L. *in-*, not, *aptus*, fit], unfit, foolish. **In-ept'it-ude.** [sluggish.

In-ert' [L. *in-*, not, *ars (art-is)*, skill], inactive,

In-er'ti-a (*t=sh*) [see **Inert**], want of energy, lifelessness.

In-ev'it-a-ble [L. *in-*, not, *evitāre*, to avoid], unavoidable.

In-ex'o-ra-ble [L. *in-*, not, *exōrābilis*, that can be moved by entreaty ; *ex*, out, greatly, and *ōrāre*, to pray], unyielding.

In-ex-pug'na-ble [L. *in-*, not, *expugnāre*, to storm], incapable of being taken.

In'fa-mous, of very bad report, base.

In'fa-my [L. *in-*, not, *fāma*, fame], disgrace.

In'fan-cy, earliest period of human life.

In'fant [L. *in-*, not, *fāri* (pr.p. *fans, fantis*), to speak], young babe ; (in English law) a person under 21 years of age.

In-fan'te, prince ; **In-fan'ta** [see **Infant**], princess, in Spain and Portugal.

In-fan'ti-cide [L. *infans*, infant, *cœdere*, to kill], murder of an infant.

In'fan-tile, **In'fan-tine**, childish.

In'fan-try [It. *infanteria*, infantry, *infante*, youth, foot-soldier ; see **Infant**], foot soldiers.

In-fat'u-ate [L. *in*, in, *fatuus*, foolish], make foolish. **Infatua'tion.**

In-fect' [L. *inficere* (p.p. *infectus*), to infect ; *in*, in, *facere*, to make], to taint, communicate, esp. disease. **Infec'tion.**

In-fer' [L. *in*, in, *ferre*, to bring], conclude from facts.

In'fer-ence, that which is inferred.

In-fe'ri-or [L. *inferior*, comp. of *inferus*, low], lower in place, value, etc.

In-fer'nal [L. *infernus*, extended from *inferus*, low, nether], relating to the lower regions.

In-fest' [L. *infestus*, hostile], to frequent and annoy. [unbeliever.

In'fi-del [L. *in*, not, *fidēlis*, faithful], an **In-fi-del'i-ty**, unbelief, treachery.

In-fil'trate [L. *in*, in ; F. *filtrer*, to strain through], filter into or through.

In-fin-ite [L. *in-*, not, *fīnītus*, finished], endless. **Infin'itude.** [small.

In-fin-i-tes'i-mal [dim. of **Infinite**], very

In-fin-i-tive [L. *in-*, not, *fīnītus*, bounded], not limited by person or number.

In-fin'i-ty, unlimited by time or space.

In-firm' [L. *in-*, not, *firmus*, strong], not firm or sound, weak.

In-firm'a-ry [M.L. *infirmāria*], hospital.

In-firm'i-ty, weakness, disease.

In-flame' [L. *inflammāre* (p.p. *inflammātus*), to inflame ; *in*, in, *flamma*, a flame], set on fire, grow hot.

In-flam'ma-ble, easily kindled.

In-flam-ma'tion, a swelling with redness, heat, and pain.

In-flam'ma-to-ry, relating to inflammation, fitted to kindle.

In-flate' [L. *in*, in, *flāre* (p.p. *flātus*), to blow], swell with air or gas. **Infla'tion.**

In-flect' [L. *in*, in, *flectere*, to bend], to bend ; modulate (as the voice) ; vary (as a noun or verb). **Inflec'tion.**

In-flict' [L. *in*, in, *fligere* (p.p. *flictus*), to dash], cause to bear.

In-flic'tion, act of inflicting, that which is inflicted (as punishment, etc.).

In-flo-res'cence [L. *inflorescere* (pr.p. *inflorescens*), come into flower ; *in*, in, *flos* (*flōr-is*), a flower], a flowering.

In'flu-ence [L. *influere* (pr.p. *influens, -entis*), to flow into ; *in*, into, *fluere*, to flow], power to affect, effect of such power ; affect.

In-flu-en'tial (*ti=sh*), possessing influence.

In-flu-en'za [It. *influenza*, influence ; doublet of **Influence**], epidemic catarrh.

In'flux [L. *in*, in, *fluere* (sup. *fluxum*), to flow], a flowing in.

In-form' [L. *informāre* (p.p. *informātus*) ; *in*, into, *forma*, form], give life to, make known to.

In-form'ant, one who gives information.

In-for-ma'tion, communicated knowledge. **Inform'ative.**

In-frac'tion [L. *in*, in, *frangere* (p.p. *fractus*), to break], act of breaking, breach.

In-fringe' [L. *infringere* ; *in*, into, *frangere*, to break], break, encroach. **Infringe'ment.**

In-fu'ri-ate [L. *in*, in, *furiāre* (p.p. *furiātus*), to madden ; *furia*, rage], enrage.

In-fuse' [L. *in*, in, *fundere* (p.p. *fūsus*), to pour], pour in, instil. **Infu'sion.**

In-ge'ni-ous [L. *ingenium*, cleverness], skilful, inventive. **Ingenu'ity.**

In-gen'u-ous [L. *ingenuus*, in-born ; *in*, in, *genitus*, born], frank, artless, noble. **Ingen'uousness.**

In'got [O.E. *in*, in, and *goten*, poured ; *geótan*, to pour], mass of metal cast in a mould.

In-grain' [orig. two words], work into texture, stain.

In'grate [L. *in-*, not, *grātus*, pleasing], ungrateful ; ungrateful person.

In-gra'ti-ate (*t=sh*) [L. *in*, in, *grātia*, favour], bring into or gain favour.

In-gre'di-ent [L. *in*, in, *grădi*, to go], part of a mixture. [entrance.

In'gress [L. *ingrēdi* (p.p. *ingressus*), to enter],

In-hab'it-ant [L. *inhabitāre* (pr.p. *inhabitans*, *-antis*), to dwell in; *in*, in, and *habitāre*, to dwell], dweller in.

In-ha-la'tion [see Inhale], act of inhaling; that which is inhaled.

In-hale' [L. *in*, in, *hālāre* (p.p. *hālātus*), to breathe], breathe or draw into the lungs.

In-he'rent [L. *inhærēre* (pr.p. *inhærens*, *-entis*), to stick in; *in*, in, and *hærēre*, to stick], naturally pertaining to, inborn.

In-her'it [L. *in*, in, *hēres*, an heir], take as heir. [descent.

In-her'it-ance, possession which passes by

In-hib'it [L. *inhibēre* (p.p. *inhibitus*), to inhibit; *in*, in, *habēre*, to have], check, forbid. Inhibi'tion.

In-hu'man [L. *in-*, not, *humānus*, human], cruel. In-hu-man'ity.

In-hume' [L. *in*, in, *humus*, the ground], bury. [unfriendly.

In-im'i-cal [L. *in-*, not, *amīcus*, a friend],

In-iq'ui-ty [L. *in-*, not, *æquus*, just, equal], wickedness, injustice.

In-i'ti-al (*ti=sh*) [L. *initium*, a beginning; *in*, in, and *īre* (p.p. *ītus*), to go], beginning; first letter of a name.

In-i'ti-ate (*ti=sh*), set afoot, acquaint with the beginnings; one who has been admitted into some society or instructed in some secret knowledge.

In-i-ti-a'tion (*ti=sh*), introduction, mode of entrance.

In-i'ti-a-tive (*ti=sh*), introductory step.

In-ject' [L. *injicere* (p.p. *injectus*), to inject; *in*, into, and *jacere*, to throw], throw in, force in. Injec'tion.

In-junc'tion [L. *injungere* (p.p. *injunctus*), to enjoin; see Enjoin], a command, urgent advice, legal order.

In'jure [see Injury], to hurt. Injur'ious.

In'ju-ry [L. *injuria*; *in-*, not, and *jūs* (*jūr-is*), right, law], damage, hurt.

Ink [O.F. *enque*; Late L. *encaustum*, purple-red ink; Gk. *egcaustos*, burnt in; *en*, in, *caiein*, to burn], black or coloured fluid for writing.

Ink'ling [?], slight notion, hint.

In'land, away from the sea, not foreign.

In-lay', lay within, insert.

In'let, entrance, bay.

In'mate, one who dwells with others in a house, etc.

In'most [O.E. *innemest*, double superl. of *inne*, in], furthest from the outside.

Inn [O.E. *inn*, in (adv.); O.N. *inne*, *inni*], lodging-house for travellers.

In-nate', In'nate [L. *in*, in, *natus*, p.p. of *nasci*, to be born], inborn.

In'ner [O.E. *innera*, compar. of *inne*], lying more within, spiritual.

In-ner'vate (L. *in*, in, *nervus*, nerve], to supply with nerve-force, stimulate.

In'nings [from In], one side's, or one player's, turn at the bat (cricket).

In'no-cent [L. *in-*, not, *nocēre* (pr.p. *nocens*, *-entis*), to hurt], harmless, guiltless. In'-nocence.

In-noc'u-ous [L. *in-*, not, *nocuus*, harmful], harmless. Innoc'uousness.

In'no-vate [L. *innovāre* (p.p. *innovātus*), to make new; *in*, in, *novus*, new], introduce something new. Innova'tion.

In-nu-en'do [L. *innuendo*, by intimating; *in*, at, and *nuere*, to nod], indirect hint (usually injurious).

In-oc'u-late [L. *in*, in, *oculus*, an eye, a bud], communicate mild form of disease as a safeguard by inserting infectious matter in the blood. Inocula'tion.

In-or'di-nate [L. *in-*, not, *ordinātus*, ordered], excessive.

In-or-gan'ic, without the organs or organized structure peculiar to living beings, not found in organized bodies.

In'quest [O.F. *enquiste*, fr. L. *inquīrere*, inquire], legal inquiry.

In-quire', En-quire' [L. *inquīrere* (p.p. *inquīsitus*), to inquire; *in*, in, *quærere*, to seek], ask, (with *into*) to examine. Inquir'y.

In-qui-si'tion [L. *inquīsītus*, inquired; see Inquest], search, examination.

In-quis'i-tive (*s=z*) [L. *inquīsītus*, inquired], inquiring, prying.

In-quis-i-to'ri-al, searching and unfriendly.

In'road, invasion.

In-san'it-ary [L. *in*, not, and Sanitary], hurtful to health.

In-sa'tia-ble, In-sa'ti-ate (*ti=sh*) [L. *in-*, not, *satiāre*, to satiate], incapable of being satisfied.

In-scribe' [L. *in*, in, *scribere* (p.p. *scriptus*), to write], write or engrave, draw a figure within another, enroll. [dedication.

In-scrip'tion, something written or engraved,

In-scru'ta-ble [L. *in-*, not, *scrutāri*, to search], unsearchable, incomprehensible.

In'sect [L. *in*, into, *secāre* (p.p. *sectus*), to cut], small animal with body almost divided into three.

In-sec-tiv'o-rous [L. *insectum*, insect; *vorāre*, to devour], insect-eating.

In-sen'sate [L. *in-*, not, *sensus*, feeling], lacking sense, stupid, unfeeling.

In-sert' [L. *in*, in, and *serere* (p.p. *sertus*), to join], set within, put in. Inser'tion.

In-set', to insert.

In'set, something extra inserted.

In-sid'i-ous [L. *insidēre*, to lie in wait; *in*, in, and *sedēre*, to sit], lying in wait, stealthy.

In'sight, power of seeing deeply into.

In-sig'ni-a [L. *insignia*, neut. pl. of *insignis*, remarkable; *in*, upon, *signum*, a mark], marks of office, etc.

In-sig-nif'i-cant [L. *in-*, not; see Significant], unimportant, small.

In-sin'u-ate [L. *in*, in, *sinus*, a bend], introduce subtly, hint indirectly.

In-sip'id [L. *in-*, not, *sapidus*, of a good taste], tasteless, uninteresting. In-sipid'ity.

In-sist′ [L. *in*, on, *sistere*, to set, to stand], take a stand, urge persistently. **Insis′-tence.**

In′so-lent [L. *in-*, not, *solēre* (pr.p. *solens*, *-entis*), to be accustomed], overbearing, impudent. **In′solence.**

In-som′ni-a [L. *in-*, not, *somnus*, sleep], sleeplessness.

In-spect′ [L. *inspicere* (p.p. *inspectus*), to inspect; *in*, into, and *specere*, to look], look into, examine officially. **Inspec′tion.**

In-spire′ [L. *in*, into, *spīrare*, to breathe], breathe in or into, influence with a feeling, idea, etc. **Inspira′tion.**

In-spir′it, encourage.

In-spis′sate, In′spis-sate [L. *inspissāre* (p.p. *inspissātus*); *in*, in, and *spissus*, thick], thicken.

In-stab-i′li-ty [L. *in*, not, *stabilis*, stable], want of firmness.

In-stall′ (*all=awl*) [L. *in*, in, *stallum*, a stall], place, invest with office.

In-stal-la′tion, act of installing.

In-stal′ment, installation, part payment.

In′stance [see **Instant**], urgency, case, example. **In′stancy.**

In′stant [L. *instāre* (pr.p. *instans*, *-antis*), to be at hand; *in*, in, *stāre*, to stand], immediate; moment; of the present month.

In-stan-ta′ne-ous, done in an instant.

In-step′ [?], arched portion of a human foot.

In′sti-gate [L. *instigāre* (p.p. *instigātus*), to goad on], urge, set on. **Instiga′tion.**

In-stil′ [L. *in*, in, *stillāre*, to drop], pour in, impart gradually. **Instil′ment.**

In′stinct [L. *instinguere* (p.p. *instinctus*), to goad on; *in*, on, *stinguere*, to prick], natural inward impulse.

In-stinct′, urged from within, alive.

In′sti-tute [L. *instituere* (p.p. *institūtus*); *in*, in, *statuere*, to place], set up, begin; institution, principle.

In-sti-tu′tion, foundation, fixed custom, established society, building occupied by such a society.

In-struct′ [L. *in*, in, *struere* (p.p. *structus*), to build], teach, inform. **Instruc′tion.**

In′stru-ment [L. *instrumentum*; as **Instruct**], tool, contrivance, agent. **Instrument′al.**

In-sub-or′di-nate [L. *in-*, not; see **Sub-ordinate**], disobedient. **Insubordina′tion.**

In′su-lar [L. *insula*, an island], pertaining to an island, narrow. **Insular′ity.**

In′su-late [L. *insula*, an island], place in a detached situation, prevent passage of heat or electricity from. **Insula′tor.**

In-sult′ [L. *insultāre*, freq. of *insilire*, to leap upon; *in*, on, *salire*, to leap], treat with contempt, abuse.

In′sult, affront, indignity.

In-su′per-a-ble [L. *in-*, not, *superāre*, to overcome; *super*, over], that cannot be overcome.

In-su′rance (*s=sh*) [O.F. *en*, in, *seūr*, sure], securing against loss, sum for which life or property is insured.

In-sur′gent [L. *in*, on, *surgere* (p.p. *surrectus*), to rise], rebel.

In-sur-rec′tion [see **Insurgent**], a rising against authority.

In-tact′ [L. *in*, in, *tangere* (p.p. *tactus*), to touch], entire, unimpaired.

In′te-ger [L. *integer*, whole; *in-*, not, *tangere*, to touch], whole number.

In′te-gral, whole, necessary to completeness.

In-teg′ri-ty, entireness, uprightness.

In-teg′u-ment [L. *in*, in, *tegere*, to cover], a covering, esp. the skin.

In-tel′lect [L. *inter*, between, *legere* (p.p. *lectus*), to choose], capacity for higher knowledge, power of thought. **Intellec′tual.**

In-tel′li-gence [L. *intelligere*, to choose between], understanding, notice, news.

In-tel′li-gi-ble, capable of being understood.

In-tend′ [L. *in*, in, *tendere* (p.p. *tentus* or *tensus*), to stretch], to purpose, mean.

In-tense′ [L. *intensus*, stretched out], strained, close, extreme in degree. **Inten′sive.**

In-ten′si-fy [L. *intensus*, stretched out, *facere*, to make], make more intense.

In-tent′, In-ten′tion, purpose, meaning.

In-tent′, bent, fixed closely.

In-ter′ [L. *in*, in, *terra*, the earth], bury.

In-ter-act′ [L. *inter*, between, *actus*, done], act upon each other.

In′ter-act, short dramatic piece between others, time between acts of a play.

In-ter′ca-late [L. *inter*, among, *calāre* (p.p. *calātus*), to proclaim], insert among others. **Intercala′tion.**

In-ter-cede′ [L. *inter*, between, *cedere* (p.p. *cessus*), to go], go between, plead (for).

In-ter-cept′ [L. *intercipere* (p.p. *interceptus*); *inter*, between, *capere*, to take], seize by the way, hinder. **Intercep′tion.**

In-ter-ces′sion, act of interceding, prayer.

In-ter-change′ [L. *inter*, between; O.F. *changier*, to change], exchange, alternate.

In′ter-change (noun).

In-ter-com-mu-ni-ca′tion [L. *inter*, between, *commūnicātus*, communicated], mutual communication.

In′ter-course [L. *inter*, between, *cursus*, a running], commerce, fellowship.

In-ter-dict′, forbid. **In′ter-dict** [L. *inter*, between, *dicere* (p.p. *dictus*), to say], prohibition, esp. in Scots law and R.C. Church. **Interdic′tion.**

In′ter-est [L. *interest*=it matters; *inter*, between, and *est*, 3rd pers. sing. pres. indic. of *esse*, to be], engage attention, concern, advantage, profit on a loan.

In-ter-fe′rence [L. *inter*, between, *ferīre*, to strike], clashing, meddling.

In′ter-im [L. *inter*, between, suf. *-im*], meantime; temporary.

In-te′ri-or [L. comp. of *interus*, within; *inter*, between], inside, inland part of a country.

In-ter-ject′ [L. *interjicere* (p.p. *interjectus*), to interject; *inter*, between, *jacere*, to throw], throw in between, esp. words. **Interjec′tion.**

In-ter-lace' [L. *inter*, between ; O.F. *las*, a noose, snare], unite as by lacing together.

In-ter-lard' [L. *inter*, between, *lardum*, lard], introduce between, mix.

In-ter-leave' [L. *inter*, between ; O.E. *léaf*, a leaf], insert (blank) leaves in a book.

In-ter-line' [L. *inter*, between, *linea*, a line], write between written lines. **Interlin'ear.**

In-ter-loc'u-tor [L. *inter*, between, *loqui* (p.p. *locūtus*), to speak], questioner, one who takes part in a dialogue, (Scots law) decree which is not final.

In-ter-lo'per [L. *inter*, between ; Du. *looper*, a runner], intruder.

In'ter-lude [L. *inter*, between, *ludus*, a play], entertainment or interval between acts or between plays, short passage played between the verses of a hymn, time between of a different character.

In-ter-mar'ry [L. *inter*, between ; see **Marry**], give and take in marriage between families, tribes, etc. **Intermar'riage.**

In-ter-me'di-ate [L. *inter*, between, *medius*, the middle], between two extremes. **Interme'diary.**

In-ter'ment, burial.

In-ter-mez'zo (*zz*=*dz*) [It.], short movement connecting main divisions of large musical work, short performance between acts of drama or opera.

In-ter'mi-na-ble [L. *in-*, not, and **Terminate**], endless.

In-ter-min'gle [L. *inter*, between ; see **Mingle**], mix together.

In-ter-mis'sion [L. *inter*, between, *mittere* (p.p. *missus*), to send], pause.

In-ter-mit'tent, ceasing at intervals.

In-tern' [see **Internal**], to confine to one locality.

In-ter'nal [L. *internus*, inward], inward, interior.

In-ter-na'tion-al [L. *inter*, between ; see **National**], between or among nations.

In-ter-ne'cine (*ne*=*nee*) [L. *inter*, between, *necāre*, to kill], mutually destructive.

In-ter-pel'late [L. *inter*, between, *pellere*, to drive], to interrupt order of day by demanding explanation (in French parliament).

In-ter'po-late [L. *interpolāre* (p.p. *interpolātus*) ; *inter*, between, and *polīre*, conn. with *polīre*, to polish], insert new or foreign matter.

In-ter-pose' (*s*=*z*) [L. *inter*, between, and F. *poser*, to put], insert (between), step in between, mediate.

In-ter'pret [L. *inter*, between, and root corresp. to Skr. *prath*, to spread abroad], explain, translate. **Interpreta'tion, Inter'preter.**

In-ter-reg'num [L. *inter*, between, *regnum*, a reign], time between reigns.

In-ter'ro-gate [L. *inter*, between, *rogāre* (p.p. *rogātus*), to ask], question.

In-ter-rupt' [L. *inter*, between, *rumpere* (p.p. *ruptus*), to break], break into or between, stop for a time. **Interrup'tion.**

In-ter-sect' [L. *inter*, between, *secāre*, to cut], cross.

In-ter-sperse' [L. *interspergere* (p.p. *interspersus*), to intersperse ; *inter*, between, and *spargere*, to scatter], set here and there among.

In-ter-stel'lar [L. *inter*, between, *stella*, a star], between the stars.

In-ter'stice (*ice*=*iss*) [L. *inter*, between, *sistere*, to stand], narrow chink. **Intersti'tial.**

In-ter-twine' [L. *inter*, between ; see **Twine**], twine or twist together.

In'ter-val [L. *intervallum*, lit. space between rampart and the soldiers' tents ; *inter*, between, and *vallum*, a rampart], time or space between, difference of pitch between two sounds in music.

In-ter-vene' [L. *inter*, between, *venīre*, to come], come in between, occur in the meanwhile. **Interven'tion.**

In'ter-view [L. *inter*, between ; see **View**], formal meeting, conference ; have an interview. **In'terviewer.**

In-tes'tate [L. *in*, not, and *testātus*, p.p. of *testari*, to make a will], without a will.

In-tes'tine [L. *intus*, within], internal ; (with *s*, n.pl.), lower part of alimentary canal. **Intes'tinal** or **Intesti'nal.**

In'ti-mate [L. *intimus*, superl. of *intus*, within], familiar, near ; to state. **In'timacy.**

In-tim'i-date [L. *in*, in, *timidus*, timid], make timid or fearful. **Intimida'tion.**

In'ton-ate, In-tone' [L. *in*, *tonum*, in tone], recite in a singing voice, chant. **Intona'tion,** chanting, modulation of the voice.

In-tox'i-cate [M.L. *in*, in, *toxicum*, poison ; Gk. *toxicon*, poison for arrows ; *toxon*, a bow], make drunk, excite greatly.

In-tract'a-ble [L. *in-*, not ; see **Tractable**], not docile, refractory.

In-tra-mu'ral [L. *intra*, within, *murus*, a wall], within the walls.

In-trans'i-gent [L. *in-*, not, *transigere* (pr.p. *transigens*, *-entis*), to transact ; see **Transact**], uncompromising. **Intrans'igence.**

In-trench' [L. *in*, in, and **Trench**], surround with a trench.

In-trep'id [L. *in-*, not, *trepidus*, alarmed], fearless, bold. **Intrepid'ity.**

In'tri-cate [L. *intricāre* (p.p. *intricātus*), to perplex ; *in*, in, *tricæ*, hindrances], entangled, hard to follow. **In'tricacy.**

In-trigue' (*in-treeg'*) [as **Intricate**], to plot ; a secret plot.

In-trin'sic [L. *intrinsecus*, intrinsic ; *intra*, within, and *secus*, following], inward, essential, real.

In-tro-duce' [L. *intro-*, within, *ducere* (p.p. *ductus*), to lead], lead or bring in, put in, begin, cause to be acquainted. **Introduc'tion.**

In-tro-spec'tion [L. *intro-*, within, *specere*, to look], looking into one's own mind. **Introspect'ive.**

In-trude' [L. *in*, into, and *trūdere* (p.p. *trūsus*), to thrust], thrust oneself in, encroach. **Intru'sion.**

In-tu-i′tion [L. *intuēri* (p.p. *intuitus*), to look upon; *in*, on, and *tuēri*, to watch], direct perception, flash of insight.

In-tu′i-tive, knowing without reasoning.

In′un-date [L. *in*, on, *unda*, a wave], overflow, flood. **Inunda′tion.**

In-ure′, Enure [F. *en*, in; O.F. *eure*, F. *œuvre*, work], to accustom, harden.

In-vade′ [L. *in*, into, *vādere* (p.p. *vāsus*), to go], go in, esp. in a hostile way.

In′val-id [L. *in*, not, *validus*, strong], weak and ill; one who is weak and ill; treat as an invalid.

In-val′id, not valid. See **Valid**.

In-val′i-date, render of no effect.

In-val′u-a-ble, priceless, of inestimable worth.

In-va′sion (*s=z*), forcible entrance. [words.

In-vec′tive [see **Inveigh**], abusive; abuse in

In-veigh′ (*ei=ai*) [L. *in*, in, *vehere* (p.p. *vectus*), to carry], to rail, criticise harshly.

In-vei′gle (*ei=ee* or *ai*) [F. *aveugler*, to blind; Late L. *aboculus*, blind; *ab*, away, and *oculus*, an eye], lead astray as if blind, entice, entrap. **Invei′gle-ment.**

In-vent′ [L. *in*, upon, *venīre* (sup. *ventum*), to come], contrive, originate. **Inven′tion.**

In′ven-to-ry [see **Invent**], list of goods with their worth.

In′verse [L. *inversus*, p.p. of *invertere*, to turn], turned upside down, opposite in effect.

In-vert′ [L. *in*, on, *vertere*, to turn], turn upside down, reverse position of. **Inver′sion.**

In-vest′ [L. *in*, on, *vestīre*, to clothe], clothe, besiege, lay out money in business to obtain profit or interest. **Invest′ment.**

In-ves′ti-gate [L. *in*, in, *vestigāre*, to track], search into. **Investiga′tion.**

In-vest′i-ture [see **Invest**], ceremony of clothing or robing, putting in possession (of an office).

In-vest′ment, act of besieging, laying out of money for profit, money invested.

In-vet′er-ate [L. *in*, in, *vetus* (*veter-is*), old], deep-rooted, habitual. **Invet′eracy.**

In-vid′i-ous [L. *invidia*, envy; *in*, on, and *vidēre*, to see], likely to produce ill-will.

In-vig′or-ate [L. *in*, in, *vigor*, vigour], strengthen, fill with new life.

In-vin′ci-ble [L. *in-*, not, *vincere*, to conquer], unconquerable. **Invincibil′ity.**

In-vi′o-la-ble [L. *in-*, not, *violāre*, to violate], not capable of being broken, sacred.

In-vi′o-late [L. *in-*, not; see **Violate**], uninjured, unbroken.

In-vite′ [F. *inviter*; L. *invītāre*, to invite], bid, ask to an entertainment, etc.

In-vo-ca′tion [see **Invoke**], act of invoking, prayer.

In′voice [O.F. *envoy*, a sending; see **Envoy**], written account of goods sent with prices; send such an account.

In-voke′ [L. *in*, on, *vocāre* (p.p. *vocātus*), to call], call on for aid, summon.

In-vo-lu′tion [see **Involve**], complication, process of raising a quantity to any power.

In-volve′ [L. *in*, in, and *volvere* (p.p. *volūtus*), to roll], complicate, imply.

In′ward [O.E. *innanweard*], placed within, towards the inside.

I′o-dine (*ine=ine* or *in*) [Gk. *iodēs*, violet-like; *ion*, a violet, and *eidos*, form], element obtained from ashes of seaweed and natural brines.

I-o′ta [Gk. *iōta*, letter corresponding to *i*], smallest Greek letter, particle.

Ip-e-cac-u-an′ha [Port. *ipecacuanha*; Braz. *ipekaaguene*, lit. small plant causing sickness], medicine obtained from a root.

Ir-, used for **In-** before *r*, is a prefix of negation in the following words: **Ir-ra′tion-al, Ir-re-con-ci′la-ble, Ir-re-duc′i-ble, Ir-re′frag-a-ble, Ir-re-fu′ta-ble** (or **Ir-ref′-u-ta-ble**), **Ir-reg′u-lar, Ir-rel′e-vant, Ir-re-li′gious, Ir-re-me′di-a-ble, Ir-rep′ar-a-ble, Ir-re-press′i-ble, Ir-re-proach′a-ble, Ir-re-sist′i-ble, Ir-res′o-lute, Ir-re-spec′tive, Ir-re-spon′si-ble, Ir-re-triev′a-ble, Ir-rev′-er-ent, Ir-re-vers′i-ble.**

I-ras′ci-ble (*c=s*) [L. *irasci* (p.p. *īrātus*), to grow angry; *īra*, anger], easily made angry.

I-rate′ [L. *īra*, anger], angry.

Ire [L. *īra*, anger], anger.

Ir-i-des′cent (*c=s*) [see **Iris**], having colours like the rainbow. **Irides′cence.**

I′ris [Gk. *iris* (*iridos*), the rainbow], the coloured part of the eye, flag-flower.

Irk′some (*some=sum*) [M.E. *irken*, etym. dub.], wearisome and vexatious.

I′ron [O.E. *īren*], metal, flat smoothing utensil made of iron, various tools and implements made of iron, (pl.) chains; smooth with a flatiron.

I-ron′ic-al [see **Irony**], expressive of or given to irony. [ware.

I′ron-mon′ger (*mong=mung*), dealer in hard-

I′ron-y [Gk. *eiron*, a dissembler], speech which conveys a meaning opposite to that of the words.

Ir-ra′di-ate [L. *in*, on, and **Radiate**], shed rays of light on. **Irradia′tion.**

Ir-rev′o-ca-ble [L. *in-*, not; see **Revoke**], that cannot be recalled.

Ir′ri-gate [L. *in*, in, *rigāre* (p.p. *rigātus*), to wet], to water. **Irriga′tion.**

Ir′ri-ta-ble, easily made angry.

Ir′ri-tate [L. *irrītāre* (p.p. *irrītātus*), perh. fr. *irrīre*, to snarl], provoke, inflame.

Ir-rup′tion [L. *in*, in, *rumpere* (p.p. *ruptus*), to break], a bursting in.

I′sin-glass (*s=z*) [M. Du. *huyzenblas*, fr. *huys*, sturgeon, and *blœse*, bladder], kind of gelatin obtained from certain fishes.

Is′land [O.E. *igland*, an island, *ig* later confused with O.F. *isle*], piece of land, smaller than a continent, surrounded by water. [island.

Isle [O.F. *isle*; L. *insula*, an island], an

Is′let [F. *islette*, dim. of *isle*], small island.

I′so-bar [Gk. *isos*, equal, *baros*, weight], line on a map connecting places of equal barometric pressure.

I'so-late [It. *isolato*, detached; *isola*, an island], place alone, detach. **Isola'tion.**

I-sos'cel-es [Gk. *isos*, equal, *scelos*, a leg], (of a triangle) having two sides equal.

I'so-therm [Gk. *isos*, equal, *thermos*, heat], line on a map connecting places with the same temperature.

Is'sue [O.F. *issue*, fem. of *issu*, p.p. of *issir*, to go out; L. *ex*, out, *ire*, to go], a going or sending out, that which is sent out, off-spring, result; go out, result.

Isth'mus [Gk. *isthmos*, an isthmus], a connecting neck of land.

I-tal'ics [L. *Italicus*; Gk. *Italicos*, Italian], letters in slant type. **Ital'icize.**

Itch [O.E. *giccan* to itch], irritation in the skin, disease of the skin; feel an itch.

I'tem [L. *item*, likewise], article, separate particular, entry in an account.

It'er-ate (L. *iterare*, fr. *iterum*, again], repeat. **Itera'tion.**

I-tin'er-ant [L. *iter* (*itiner-is*), a journey], wandering, not settled.

I-tin'er-a-ry, account of roads and routes, plan of travel.

I'vo-ry [L. *ebur* (*ebor-is*), ivory], substance of an elephant's tusk.

I'vy [O.E. *ifig*], evergreen climbing plant.

J

Jab'ber [prob. imit.], talk quickly and indistinctly.

Ja'cinth (*a=ă* or=*ai*) [Gk. *hyacinthos*, a jacinth, a hyacinth], kind of gem.

Jack[1] [perh. fr. F. *Jacques*, James, perh. connected with John], contrivance for turning a spit, a contrivance for raising a weight.

Jack[2] [perh. fr. name *Jack*], ship's flag, esp. one flown from bow of ship.

Jack'al (-*awl*) [Turk. *chakāl*; Pers. *shaghal*, a jackal], wild animal of the dog kind.

Jack'a-napes [Jack[1] and Ape], pert fellow.

Jack'daw [Jack[1] and Daw], kind of small crow.

Jack'et [O.F. *jaquette*, dim. of *jaque*, a coat of mail], short coat.

Jac-o-be'an [L. *Jacobus*, James], of the reign of James I.

Jac'o-bite, adherent of James II after his abdication, or of his son.

Jade[1] [Span. *ŷada*, the flank, *piedra de ŷada*, stone of the side (because it is said to cure a pain in the side)], an ornamental stone.

Jade[2] [?], poor horse, (contemptuously for) a woman.

Ja'ded [fr. Jade[2]], worn out with work.

Jag [?], notch.

Ja'guar (-*gwar* or -*guar*) [Braz. *yagoar*], American animal like a leopard.

Jail [see Gaol].

Jal'ap [Mex. fr. *Jalapa* or *Xalapa*, in Mexico], medicine made from a Mexican plant.

Jam [perh. fr. Jamb], a crush; to crush; fruit boiled with sugar (perhaps in sense of crushing or bruising).

Jamb [F. *jambe*; Folk L. *gamba*, a leg], side-post of a door, fireplace, etc.

Jan'gle [O.F. *jangler*; imit.], sound harshly; discordant sound.

Jan'i-tor [L. *janua*, a door], doorkeeper, keeper of a building.

Jan'u-ar-y [L. *Januarius* (*mensis*), (month) of Janus, guardian of doors and gates, a god represented with faces on front and back of head], first month of the year (Rom. eleventh).

Ja-pan' [fr. *Japan*, the country], coat with hard brilliant varnish.

Jar [F. *jarre*; Arab. *jarrah*, a jar], an earthenware vessel.

Jar [O.E. *georran*, to creak; imit.], harsh sound; to sound harshly, to quarrel.

Jar'gon [O.F. *garjon*, jargon, twittering of birds. Etym. doubtful], unintelligible talk, cant language.

Jar-go-nelle' [F. *jargonelle*, kind of pear; *jargon*, a yellow diamond], early ripening variety of pear.

Jas'mine, Jes'sa-mine [Arab. *yās(a)mīn*; Pers. *yāsmīn*, jasmine], climbing shrub.

Jas'per [L. and Gk. *iaspis*, jasper], opaque quartz, usually red, yellow or brown.

Jaun'dice (*au=aw* or *a*, *ice=iss*) [F. *jaune*; L. *galbus*, yellow], disease in which the skin, etc., become yellow.

Jaunt (*au=aw* or *a*) [?], short excursion; make such an excursion.

Jaun'ty (*au=aw* or *a*) [earlier *janty*, var. of *jantyl*, old spelling of *gentle*; F. *gentil*], gay and easy, airy.

Jave'lin [F. *javeline*, a javelin, perh. of Celtic origin], light spear.

Jaw [M.E. *jowe*, perh. from earlier *chowe*], bone in which the teeth are fixed.

Jay [O.F. *jay*, perh. fr. O.H.G. *gâhi*, quick], crested bird of the crow family, given to chattering. [envious.

Jeal'ous [L. *zēlus*, zeal], zealous, suspicious,

Jean [perh. fr. M.L. *Janua*, Genoa], twilled cotton cloth.

Jeer [?], mock, to scoff; bitter jest.

Je-ho'vah (orig. Jahveh or Yahweh), Hebrew name for God, the Almighty.

Je-june' [L. *jejunus*, fasting], scanty, unsatisfying to the mind.

Jel'ly [L. *gelāre*, to freeze], meat or juice of fruit boiled to a gelatinous condition.

Jem'my [fam. form of *James*], short crowbar.

Jen'net [Sp. *ginete*, a nag, orig. a light horseman], small Spanish horse.

Jen'ny [fam. form of *Janet*], machine for spinning.

Jeop'ard-y [O.F. *jeu parti*; Late L. *jocus partītus*, a divided game], danger.

Jer-bo'a [Arab. *yarbū*, flesh of loins, jerboa], small rodent, animal of African deserts, with long hind legs.

Jer-e-mi'ad [F. *Jérémiade*, fr. *Jeremiah*], lamentation.

Jerk [perh. imit.], give a quick pull or twist; short pull or spring.

Jerk [Peruv. *charqui*, slice of dried beef], cure (beef) by slicing and drying in sun.

Jer′kin [?], close-fitting jacket for men (16th and 17th centuries). [(building).

Jer′ry [perh. from *Jeremiah*], unsubstantial

Jess [O.F. *ges*, a short thong, fr. L. *jacere* (p.p. *jactus*), to throw, cast], strap round a hawk's leg.

Jer′sey (*s*=*z*) [fr. *Jersey*, one of the Channel Islands], kind of knitted jacket.

Jest [O.F. *geste*, a romance ; L. *gerere* (p.p. *gestus*), to carry on], a joke ; to joke, sport.

Jes′u-it [Mod. L. *Jesuita*, fr. *Society of Jesus*], member of Society of Jesus founded by Ignatius Loyola in 1533.

Jes-u-it′ic-al, dissembling, equivocating. **Jes′uitism**.

Jet [Gk. *gagātes*, jet, fr. *Gagas*, a town in Asia Minor], black fossil wood.

Jet [F. *jeter* ; L. *jactāre*, freq. of *jacere*, to throw], a spouting ; to spurt in streams.

Jet′sam or **Jet′son** [A.F. *getteson*, a casting ; L. *jactāre*, to throw ; see **Jet**], cargo thrown overboard to lighten a ship.

Jet′ti-son [as **Jetsam**], throw overboard to lighten a ship.

Jet′ty [O.F. *jetee* ; see **Jet**], small pier.

Jew′el [O.F. *joel*, jewel ; perh. conn. w. L.L. *jocālia*, jewels ; L. *jocāri*, to play], precious stone, ornament containing gems.

Jew′el-ler-y, Jew′el-ry, jewels collectively.

Jib [origin uncertain, perh. from Dan. *gibbe*, to shift a sail from side to side], triangular sail from foremast to bowsprit.

Jig [origin uncertain, perh. from O.F. *gigue* ; M.H.G. *gige*, a fiddle], lively dance.

Jilt [formerly *jillet*, dim. of *jill*, a flirt. Fr. name *Jill*], cast off a lover ; one who jilts.

Jin, Jinn [Arab. *jinn*, demons ; pl. of *jinnī*], genius or demon.

Jin′gle [imit.], sound with a sharp tinkle ; sharp rattle or tinkle.

Jin′go [fr. conjurer's gibberish], blustering patriot, so-called from a music-hall ditty (" by jingo ").

Jiu-jit′su, Ju-jut′su [Jap.], Japanese art of wrestling.

Job [?], piece of work, corrupt dealing ; do chance work, deal in stocks.   [rider.

Jock′ey [fr. *Jock*, Sc. for *Jack*], professional

Jo-cose′ (*s*=*z*) [L. *jocus*, a jest], given to jokes, merry.

Joc′u-lar [L. *joculus*, dim. of *jocus*, a jest], joking, given to jokes. **Jocular′ity**.

Joc′und (*ŏ* or *ō*) [L. *jocundus*, pleasant], merry.

Jog [?], move by small jerks, push with the elbow ; a shake, push.

Join [O.F. *joindre* ; L. *jungere* (p.p. *junctus*), to join], put or come together.

Join′er [see **Join**], one who makes doors, windows, etc.

Joint [O.F. *joint*, p.p. of *joindre*, to join], a joining, hinge, large piece of meat for roasting ; shared.

Joint′ure, property settled on a wife to be hers after her husband dies.

Joist [O.F. *giste*, a bed, a joist ; L. *jacēre*, to lie], timber to which floor-boards or ceiling-laths are fastened.

Joke [L. *jocus*, a jest], something witty or sportive ; banter, jest.

Jol′ly [origin uncertain, perh. from O.N. *jōl*, a great feast], full of life and mirth.

Jol′ly-boat [origin uncertain, perh. from Port. *galeota* ; O.F. *galiote*, a small galley], ship's boat of medium size.

Jolt (*ō*) [?], shake with jerks.

Jong [Tibetan], fortified Tibetan camp.

Jon′quil [F. *jonquille* ; Sp. *junquillo*, a jonquil ; L. *juncus*, a rush], bulb and its flower.   [Chinese idol.

Joss [perh. Port. *deos* ; L. *deus*, a god], **Jos′tle** [freq. form of M.E. *jousten*, to tilt], push out of the way, to elbow.

Jot [Gk. *iōta*, the letter i], very small quantity, whit ; to note hastily.

Jour′nal [F. *journal* ; L. *diurnālis*, daily], diary, magazine.

Jour′ney [F. *journée*, orig. a day's work], travel some distance ; distance travelled in a given time.

Jour′ney-man, one who has learned a trade.

Joust (*ou*=*ŭ* or *oo*) [O.F. *jouster*, to tilt ; L. *juxta*, near], tilting match.

Jo′vi-al [L. *jovialis*, pertaining to Jupiter. *Jupiter* (*Jov-is*)], jolly, gleeful. **Jovia′lity**.

Jowl [O.E. *ceafl*, jaw], cheek, jaw.

Joy [O.F. *joie, joye* ; L. *gaudium*, joy], gladness, delight.

Ju′bi-lant [L. *jubilāre* (pr.p. *jubilans, -antis*), to rejoice ; *jūbilum*, a shout of joy], triumphant, rejoicing. **Ju′bilation**.

Ju′bi-lee [Heb. *yōbel*, orig. ram, hence ram's horn, used as trumpet to proclaim the jubilee year], general joy, fiftieth anniversary.

Judge [L. *jūdex* (*jūdic-is*), a judge], one who decides ; decide, pass sentence.

Judg′ment, Judge′ment, decision, award, intelligence.

Ju′di-ca-ture [see **Judge**], courts of justice, judges collectively, administration of justice.

Ju-di′cial (*ci*=*sh*), pertaining to courts of justice, impartial.

Ju-di′cious, having sound judgment, wise.

Jug [?], earthenware vessel ; cook in a jug or jar placed in boiling water.

Jug′gle [O.F. *jogler*, to juggle ; L. *joculāri*, to jest], play tricks by sleight of hand.

Jug′u-lar [L. *jugulum*, the collar-bone, dim. of *jugum*, a yoke], pertaining to the throat.

Juice [L. *jūs*, broth, juice], sap of fruit and vegetables, fluid of meat. **Jui′cy**.

Ju′jube (Gk. *zizyphon* med. L. *jujuba* ; F. *jujube*], berry of a plant, gelatinous sweet.

Ju′ly [O.F. *Jule* : L. *Julius* (*mensis*), (month) of Julius, named after Caius *Julius Cæsar*], seventh month of the year (Rom. fifth).

Jum′ble [freq. form of **Jump**], to mix up ; collection without order, a mix up.

Jump [perh. imit.], to spring, leap ; a leap.

Jump′er [?], loose outer jacket worn by sailors, kind of loose blouse.

Junc′tion [L. *junctus*, joined], joining, point of union.

Junc′ture [L. *junctus*, joined], joining line or point, crisis.

June [F. *juin*; L. *Junius*], sixth month of the year (Rom. fourth).

Jun′gle [Hind. *jangal*, waste land], thicket of trees, weeds, etc.

Ju′nior [L. *junior*, comp. of *juvenis*, young], younger, lower in position. **Junior′ity.**

Ju′ni-per [L. *jūniperus*, juniper], evergreen shrub or tree. [vessel.

Junk [Port. *junco* ; Malay *adjong*], a Chinese

Junk [?], hard salt beef, old rope cut in pieces.

Jun′ker (*yoongker*) [Ger. *jung*, young, Herr, gentleman], young Prussian noble.

Jun′ket [It. *giuncata*, a cream-cheese served on rushes ; L. *juncus*, a rush], dish of curdled milk, feast.

Jun′ta, Jun′to [Sp. *junto* ; L. *junctus*, united], secret council, faction.

Ju-rid′ic-al [L. *jūs* (*jūr-is*), law, *dicāre*, to proclaim], legal.

Ju-ris-dic′tion [L. *jūs* (*jūr-is*), law, *dictus*, said], power to make, declare, or apply the law.

Ju-ris-pru′dence [L. *jūs* (*jūr-is*), law, *prudens*, prudent ; *prōvidēre*, to foresee], principles of law. [law.

Ju′rist [L. *jūs* (*jūr-is*), law], one versed in

Ju′ror, Ju′ry-man, member of a jury.

Ju′ry [L. *jurāre*, to swear], body of citizens sworn to consider evidence submitted to them and to give a verdict.

Jur′y-mast [?], temporary mast in place of broken one.

Just [L. *justus*, right (adj.), *jūs*, right (n.)], fair, upright ; exactly, by a small space of time.

Just′ice (*ice=iss*), fairness, law, a judge.

Jus-ti′ci-a-ry (*c=sh*), administrator of justice.

Jus′ti-fy [L. *justus*, just, *facere*, to make], prove to be just, clear from blame, defend as being right. **Justifica′tion.**

Jut [var. of Jet²], shoot out, project.

Ju′ve-nile [L. *juvenis*, young], youthful ; young person. **Juvenil′ity.**

Jux-ta-po-si′tion [L. *juxta*, near ; see Position], nearness in place.

K

Kai′ser (*s=z*) [Ger. *Kaiser*, ult. fr. L. *Cæsar*], emperor (esp. of Germany).

Kale, or **Kail** [Northern form of Cole ; L. *caulis*, a stem, a cabbage], kind of cabbage.

Ka-lei′do-scope [Gk. *kalos*, beautiful ; *eidos*, form, *scopein*, to see], tube with a shifting arrangement of coloured pieces of glass.

Kan-ga-roo′ [perh. Australian], Australian leaping, pouched animal. [Africa.

Kar-roo′ [of Hottentot orig.], tableland in

Kau′ri (*au=ow*) [Maori word], New Zealand pine. [canoe.

Kay′ak (*ay=ī*) [Eskimo word], light Arctic

Kedge [?], drag a ship forward by help of a small anchor called a kedge-anchor.

Ked′ger-ee [Hind. *khichri*], dish of fish, rice, eggs, etc.

Keel [O.N. *kjölr* ; Dan. *kjøl* ; Swed. *köl*, a keel], bottom timber or combination of iron plates of a ship from stem to stern.

Keen [O.E. *cēne* ; cf. Ger. *kühn*], sharp, cutting.

Keep [Late O.E. *cēpan*, of unknown origin], hold, preserve ; support, maintenance, strongest part of a castle.

Keep′er, one who has custody of, ring which keeps another on the finger.

Keep′sake, gift kept for the sake of someone.

Keg [earlier *cag*. Cf. O.N. *kaggi* ; Swed. and Norw. *kagge*, a keg], small cask.

Kelp [?], large seaweeds burnt for their ashes, the ashes. [knowledge.

Ken [O.E. *cennan*, to know], range of sight or

Ken′nel [F. *chenil*, a kennel ; L. *canis*, a dog], house for dogs, a pack of hounds.

Ken′nel [earlier *cannel*, fr. O.F. *canel*, channel], gutter.

Kerb′stone, same as Curb′stone.

Ker′chief [O.F. *couvrechief*, *covrir*, to cover, *chef*, the head], square of cloth for wearing.

Kern, Kerne [Ir. *ceithern*], light-armed Irish foot soldier of olden times.

Ker′nel [O.E. *cyrnel*, dim. of *corn*, a grain], contents of a nut-shell. [leum.

Ker′o-sene [Gk. *kēros*, wax], purified petro-

Ker′sey-mere [corruption of *Cassimere*, var. of *Cashmere*], thin twilled woollen cloth.

Kes′trel [O.F. *cresserelle*, a kestrel. Etym. doubtful], small hawk.

Ketch′up [perh. fr. Chin. *kôe-chiap* or *kê-tsiap*, brine of pickled fish], kind of sauce.

Ket′tle [L. *catillus*, a small bowl], metal vessel for boiling water, etc.

Key [O.E. *cǣg*], lock-opener, a book of solutions, one of the levers by which some stringed instruments are played, scale in which a piece of music is written.

Key′board, set of keys in organ, piano, etc.

Key′stone, top stone of an arch.

Kha′ki [Urdu (Pers.) *khak*, dust], yellowish-brown cloth.

Kham′sin [Arab. *khamsun*, fifty], hot wind for about fifty days in March, April, and May.

Khan [Pers. *khan*, a lord, a prince], eastern sovereign or nobleman.

Khe-dive′ (*i=ee*) [Pers. *khediv*, a great prince], viceroy of Egypt.

Kick [?], strike out with the foot ; blow with the foot.

Kick′shaws [F. *quelque chose*, something], fancy dish.

Kid [Dan. and Swed. *kid* ; O.N. *kith*, a kid], young goat.

Kid′nap [Kid and obs. *nap* (*Nab*), to seize], steal (a human being). [abdomen.

Kid′ney [?], one of two large glands in the

Kill [?], destroy animate bodies.

Kiln [L. *culina*, a kitchen], large stove or oven.

Kil'o, short for Kil'o-gram [Gk. *khilioi*, a thousand, *gramma*, a weight], 1000 grams.

Kil'o-me'tre (or -ter) [Gk. *khilioi*, a thousand, *metron*, a measure], 1000 metres.

Kilt [Dan. *kilte*, to tuck up], plaited skirt worn by Scottish Highlanders; tuck up.

Kim-o'no [Jap.], Japanese robe with loose sleeves. [man.

Kin [O.E. *cyn(n)*], relatives. **Kin'ship, Kins'-**

Kind (*i*) [O.E. *gecynde*], ready to do good; race, nature, sort.

Kind'er-gar'ten (*i*) [Ger. *kindergarten*, children's garden], kind of school for infants.

Kin'dle (*i*) [O.N. *kynda*, to inflame, *kyndill*, a torch], set on fire, light.

Kind'ly (*i*), kind, helpful, mild.

Kin'dred (*i*) [O.E. *cyn(n)*, kin, *ræden*, condition], relatives, relationship.

Kine [O.E. *cú*, a cow], cows.

Kin-e-mat'ics [Gk. *kinēma*, motion], science of motion without reference to force.

Kin-et'ics [Gk. *kinētikos* (adj.), *kinein*, to move], science of the relations between force and the motions of bodies.

King [O.E. *cyning*, king, same root as **Kin**], ruler of an independent state.

King'dom, country ruled by a king or queen.

King'fish-er, fish-catching bird.

Kink [Swed., Norw., and Du. *kink*], twist in a rope.

Ki-osk' (*i*) [Turk. *kiushk*], small pavilion.

Kip'per [orig. uncertain], name given to male salmon at spawning time, fish (esp. herring) split open, salted, and dried or smoked.

Kir'tle [O.E. *cyrtel*, perh. fr. L. *curtus*], skirt, man's tunic or long coat, woman's gown.

Kiss [O.E. *coss*; cf. Ger. *kuss*], salute with the lips; a salute with the lips.

Kit [M.Du. *kitte*, a tub, a wooden bowl], kind of tub, outfit.

Kit'chen [L. *coquina*, a kitchen, *coquere*, to cook], cookroom.

Kite [O.E. *cýta*], bird of the falcon family, toy for flying.

Kith [O.E. *cýth*, fr. *cúth*, known], kindred. **Kith and Kin**, friends and relations.

Kit'ten [O.F. *chitoun*, obs. var. of F. *chaton*, fr. *chat*, L. *catus*, cat, a kitten], young cat.

Klep-to-ma'ni-a [Gk. *kleptēs*, a thief, *mania*, madness], mania for theft.

Kloof [S. Afr. Dutch], a mountain cleft.

Knack [?], aptness at doing something.

Knap [Du. *knappen*, to snap, to crack, to eat; imit.], strike smartly; sharp blow.

Knap'sack, soldier's travelling-case. [rogue.

Knave [O.E. *cnafa*; cf. Ger. *knabe*, a boy],

Knead (*need*) [O.E. *cnedan*], work (dough) into a mass with the knuckles.

Knee [O.E. *cnéow*, *cnéo*; Du. and Ger. *knie*; cf. L. *genu*], joint below the thigh.

Kneel [M.E. *cneolen*; O.E. *cnéowlian*, fr. *cnéow*, knee], rest on the knees.

Knell [O.E. *cnyll* (n.), *cnyllan* (vb.); cf. M.H.G. *erknellen*], sound of a funeral bell; **toll as a bell**.

Knick'er-bock-ers [*Knickerbocker*, pen-name of Washington Irving], kind of short breeches.

Knick'knack [redupl. of knack, in obs. sense of "trinket"], trifle, toy.

Knife [Late O.E. *cníf*; Du. *knijf*; Ger. *kneif*], instrument with a cutting blade.

Knight [O.E. *cniht*, a boy, a servant], formerly one raised to a certain military rank, now one who has the title of "Sir" (non-hereditary); to create a knight. **Knight'hood**.

Knit [O.E. *cnyttan*, fr. *cnotta*, a knot], tie, form a fabric by looping.

Knob [equivalent to M.L.G. *knobbe*, knob, knot, etc.; Fl. *knobbe* (n.), lump], lump, ornament or handle like a projecting lump.

Knock [Late O.E. *cnocian*; cf. O.N. *knoka*; prob. imit.], strike; a rap.

Knock'er, kind of hammer on a door.

Knoll (*ō*) [O.F. *cnoll*, hill-top; cf. Du. *knol*, clod, ball], mound, small hill.

Knoll (*ō*) [var. of **Knell**], to toll.

Knot [O.E. *cnotta*; Du. *knot*], a tie, knob, group, nautical mile (6080 ft.), central part of a difficulty.

Knot'ty, full of knots, difficult.

Knout [Russ. *knut*, a whip], scourge formerly used in Russia.

Know [O.E. *(ge)cnáwan*; L. and Gk. *gnō*; com. Teut. and Aryan], be aware of, perceive.

Knowl'edge (*ŏ*) [M.E. *knaulage*], that which is or may be known.

Knuc'kle [M.E. *knokel*; M.Du. *knōkel*; perh. dim. of M.Du. *knoke*, a bone], finger-joint, knee-joint of a quadruped; (with down) yield.

Ko'dak [a trade name], kind of hand camera.

Ko'peck, Co'peck [Rus. *kopeika*, a kopeck], small Russian coin.

Ko-ran' [Arab. *qurān*, recitation], Mohammedan Scriptures.

Ko'sher [Heb. *kasher*, right], (food, etc.) fulfilling requirements of Jewish law.

Kou'miss (*ou*=*oo*) [Tartar *kumiz*], fermented mare's milk.

Kraal (*aa*=*ah*) [Du. *kraal*, an Af. village; Port. *curral*, an enclosure], S. African village, hut.

Ku'dos [Gk.], slang word for glory, renown.

Kvass [Russ. *kvas*], Russian rye-beer.

L

Laa'ger (*aa*=*ah*) [S. Af. Du.], S. African camp.

La'bel [O.F. *label*, *lambel*; etym. doubtful], written slip of paper, etc., attached to something. [lips.

La'bi-al, [L. *labium*, a lip], pertaining to the

Lab'or-a-to-ry [L. *labor* (*labōr-is*), toil], workroom of a scientific worker, esp. chemist.

La'bour [L. *labor* (*labōr-is*), toil], work, toil; to toil. **Labor'ious**.

La-bur'num [L. *laburnum*], tree with yellow blossoms.

Lab'y-rinth [Gk. *labyrinthos*, a maze], series of winding passages. **Labyrin'thine**.

Lac [Hind. *lākh*; Skr. *lākshā*, lac], coloured resin. [(rupees).

Lac [Hind. *lākh*; Skr. *laksha*], 100,000

Lace [O.F. *laz*, *las*; L. *laqueus*, a noose, a snare], cord for fastening (boots, etc.), open-work fabric of fine threads; fasten with a lace.

La'cer-ate [L. *lacerāre* (p.p. *lacerātus*), to lacerate, *lacer*, torn], to tear, mangle, harrow. [tears.

Lach'ry-mal [L. *laçrima*, a tear], of or for

Lach'ry-mose (*s = z*) [L. *lacrima*, a tear], tearful. [want.

Lack [Early M.E. *lac*; M.L.G. *lak*], want; to

Lack-a-dais'ic-al [Archaic, *lackaday*, fr. *Alack !*], languishing, affected, lacking energy.

Lack'ey, Lac'quey [F. *laquais*; etym. doubtful], footman.

La-con'ic, La-con'ic-al [Gk. *Lacōn*, a Spartan], saying much in few words.

Lac'quer (*cq = k*) [F. *lacre*, sealing-wax; Port. *lacca*, gumlac], varnish containing lac.

La-crosse' [F. *la*, the, *crosse*, a hooked stick], N. American game like hockey, but in which the ball is driven and caught with a long-handled racket called a *crosse*.

Lac'te-al [L. *lac* (*lact-is*), milk], pertaining to or like milk.

Lac'tic [L. *lac* (*lact-is*), milk], pertaining to milk. **Lactif'erous**.

Lac-un'a (*pl. -æ* or *-as*) [L. *lacus*, lake], blank, hiatus, cavity. [lakes.

La-cus'trine [L. *lacus*, a lake], pertaining to

Lad [M.E. *ladde*, orig. obscure], boy, youth.

Lad'der [O.E. *hlǣd(d)er*], framework of steps.

Lade [O.E. *hladan*], to load.

La'dle [O.E. *hlǣdel*, fr. *hladan*], cuplike spoon with a long handle; transfer liquid from or to a vessel by a ladle. **La'dleful**.

La'dy [O.E. *hlǣfdīge*, a lady; *hlāf*, a loaf, and perh. *dīgan*, to knead], well-bred woman; title. **La'dylike**.

La'dy-bird, small spotted beetle.

Lag [?], to slacken pace, fall behind. [slow.

Lag'gard, one who falls behind; falling behind,

La-goon' [It. and Sp. *laguna*; L. *lacūna*, extension of *lacus*, a lake] shallow salt lake near the sea, enclosed water of atoll.

Lair [O.E. *leger*, bed, camp; cogn. with **Lie**[2]], bed of a wild animal.

Laird [Sc. form of *lord*], Scottish landowner.

La'i-ty [F. *lai*, secular; Gk. *laicos*, belonging to the people], people as distinct from the clergy.

Lake [L. *lacus*, a lake], inland body of water.

Lake [F. *laque*; see **Lac**[1]], crimson paint, orig. made from lac.

La'ma [Tib. *blama*, priest], Buddhist priest of Tibet.

Lamb [E.], young of a sheep.

Lam'bent [L. *lambere* (pr.p. *lambens*, *-entis*), to lick], touching lightly, playing over.

Lame [O.E. *lama*; cf. O.N. *lame*], crippled, limping; make lame. [L

La-ment' [L. *lāmentum*, a lament, *lāmentāri*, to lament], mourn; a mournful cry. **Lamenta'tion, La'mentable**.

Lam'in-a (*pl. -æ*) [L. *lāmina*], thin plate of metal, etc.

Lamp [Gk. *lampas*, a lamp; *lampein*, to shine], contrivance for supplying artificial light.

Lam-poon' [F. *lampon*, perh. from *lampons*, let us drink], written abusive satire; write such against.

Lam'prey [Late L. *lamprēda*, perh. from *lambere*, to lick, and *petra*, rock], eel-like fish which attach themselves to stones by a sucker.

Lance [L. *lancea*, a lance], weapon with a long shaft and a steel head; open with a lancet. **Lan'cer**.

Lan'ce-o-late [L. *lanceolatus*, dim. of *lancea*, lance], shaped like a spear-head, tapering to each end.

Lan'cet [O.F. *lancette*, dim. of *lance*, a lance], sharp surgical instrument. [shore.

Land [O.E. *land*], ground, country; go on

Lan'dau (*au = aw*) [fr. *Landau* in Bavaria], carriage with a top which can be opened and thrown back.

Land'ing, place to land on, level place at the top of a flight of stairs.

Land'lord, *fem.* **Land'la-dy**, one who has tenants, inn-keeper.

Land'rail [**Land** and **Rail**[2]], bird (same as **Corncrake**).

Land'scape [Du. *landschap*, *land*, land, and *-schap* = E. suf. *-ship*], land scenery, picture of land scenery.

Lane [E.], narrow passageway, bye-way.

Lan'guage (*u = w*) [L. *lingua*, tongue], speech.

Lan'guid (*u = w*) [L. *languidus*, fr. *languēre*, to languish], lacking energy, spiritless.

Lan'guish (*u = w*) [L. *languēre*, to languish], grow weak, droop.

Lan'guor (*u = w*) [O.F. *languor*, fr. L. *languor*], weakness and weariness. **Lan'guorous**.

Lan-if'er-ous [L. *lāna*, wool, *ferre*, to bear], wool-bearing.

Lank [O.E. *hlanc*; perh. cogn. w. Ger. *lenken*, to bend], slender and thin. **Lank'y**.

Lan'tern [Gk. *lampter*, a torch], portable case for a light.

Lan'yard [formerly *lannier*; F. *lanière*, a thong of leather], short rope used in a ship.

Lap[1] [O.E. *lappa*, rag], a flap, lobe of the ear, sitting body from waist to knees with its covering garments.

Lap[2] [M.E. *lappen*, *wlappen*, to wrap, prob. fr. *lappa*], infold, lie over.

Lap[3] [O.E. *lapian*, allied to L. *lambere*, to lick], lick up, to beat upon with a rippling sound. [coat.

La-pel' [see **Lap**[1]], turned back part of a

Lap'i-da-ry [L. *lapis* (*lapid-is*), a stone], one who cuts precious stones.

Lap'pet [see **Lap**[1]], small decorative fold.

Lapse [L. *labi* (p.p. *lapsus*), to slip], slip, a falling, a passing away ; slip away, fail in duty.

Lap'wing [O.E. *hléapan*, to leap, *winc*, to waver], bird of the plover family, peewit.

Lar'board [?], left-hand side of a ship looking forward (now obsolete), port (see **Port**[5]).

Lar'ce-ny [L. *latrocinium*, robbery, *latro*, a robber], theft of personal goods.

Larch [L. *larix* (*laric-is*), a larch], kind of cone-bearing tree.

Lard [L. *lardum*, lard ; cf. Gk. *larinos*, fat], internal fat of swine ; smear with lard.

Lard'er [see **Lard**], room or box for keeping food.

Large [L. *largus*, large], of great size.

Lark [O.E. *láferce* ; cf. Ger. *lerche*], kind of small singing-bird.

Lar'va (*pl.* **larvae**) [L. *larva*, a ghost, a mask], insect in the grub state.

Lar'ynx [Gk. *larygx* (*larygg-os*), a larynx], organ of the voice. **Laryngi'tis.**

Las-ci'vi-ous (*c=s*) [L.L. *lasciviosus*, fr. *lascivius*, sportful], lustful, wanton.

Lash [?], thong, stroke with a whip ; strike as with a lash.

Las'si-tude [L. *lassus*, tired], weariness.

Las'so [Sp. *lazo* ; L. *laqueus*, a noose], rope with a noose for throwing ; catch thus.

Last [O.E. *latost*, superl. of *læt*, late], hindmost, most recent, extreme, etc.

Last [O.E. *læstan*, fulfil], continue, endure.

Last [O.E. *læst*, footstep ; *lǽst*, boot], shoe-block.

Latch [perh. O.F. *lache*, from *lachier* (*lacier*), see **Lace**], catch which holds a closed door.

Latch'et [O.F. *lachet*, dim. of *laz*, a noose], shoestring.

Late [O.E. *læt* ; cogn. w. L. *lassus*, weary], behind in time, far on in the day, week, etc., not long past, deceased, recent.

La'tent [L. *latēre* (pr.p. *latens*, *-entis*), to be hidden], hidden, not yet roused.

Lat'er-al [L. *latus* (*later-is*), the side], of or pertaining to the side.

Lath [O.E. *lætt*], thin strip of wood, esp. nailed to rafters or floor-beams to support plaster.

Lathe (*a=ai*) [O.N. *láth* ; Dan. *drejelad*, a turning lathe], machine for turning or shaping wood.

Lath'er [O.E. *léathor*, washing-soda ; cogn. with L. *lavere*], froth of soap and water, foam of sweat ; cover with lather.

Lat-in'it-y [L. *Latinus*, fr. *Latium*], quality of the Latin style. **La'tinize.**

Lat'i-tude [L. *latus*, broad], breadth, freedom from restraint, distance north or south of the equator.

Lat-i-tud-in-a'ri-an, of broad views, esp. in regard to religion.

Lat-rine' (*ine=een*) [L. *latrina*, *lavatrina*, fr. *lavare*, to wash], military water-closet.

Lat'ter [O.E. *lætra*, compar. of *læt*, late], later, second, recent.

Lat'tice (*ice=iss*) [O.F. *lattis* ; F. *latte*, a lath], network of crossing laths.

Laud'a-ble [L. *laudāre*, to praise, and **Able**], praiseworthy.

Laud'a-num [etym. dub., perh. fr. L. *lādānum*, a gum-resin, or fr. L. *laudare*, to praise], tincture of opium.

Laugh (*ugh=f*) [O.E. *hlæhhan*, prob. imit.], make the noise which sudden merriment causes ; act of laughing.

Laugh'ter, act of laughing.

Launch (*au=aw* or *a*) [O.F. *lancier*, to hurl, to fling ; L. *lanceāre*, to wield a lance], let fly, set afloat ; setting afloat of a new ship.

Launch [Sp. *lancha*, a pinnace, perh. of Malay orig.], man-of-war's largest boat, large electric or steam boat.

Laun'dry (*au=aw* or *a*) [O.F. *lavendiere*, a washer-woman ; L. *lavāre*, to wash], place for washing and ironing.

Lau're-ate [L. *laurea*, a laurel], decked with laurel. **Poet Laureate**, special poet of the British sovereign. **Laurea'tion.**

Lau'rel [L. *laurus*, a laurel-tree], evergreen shrub.

La'va [It. *lava*, lava ; L. *lavāre*, to wash], melted rock ejected by a volcano.

Lav'a-tor-y [L. *lavār* (p.p. *lavātus*), to wash], place for washing.

Lave [L. *lavāre*, to wash], wash, bathe.

Lav'en-der [M.L. *lavendula*, lavender], aromatic plant, pale greyish blue.

Lav'ish [from obsolete *lave*, to pour out], over-abundant ; give profusely, squander.

Law [O.N. *lag*, a stratum, order ; see **Lie**[2]], general principle deduced by observation or experiment, rule fixed by the state or other authoritative body.

Lawn [O.F. *launde*, a grassy plain ; cogn. with **Land**], smooth grassy space.

Lawn [perh. from *Laon* in France], fine linen.

Law'yer, one trained in a knowledge of laws.

Lax [L. *laxus*, loose], loose, slack.

Lax'a-tive [L. *laxativus*, fr. *laxare*, cogn. with *languere*, to languish], tending to loosen the bowels.

Lay[1] [Gk. *laicos*, lay, *laos*, the people], pertaining to the laity.

Lay[2] [O.F. *lai* ; cf. Ir. *lavi*, a song], song.

Lay[3] [O.E. *lecgan* ; cf. Ger. *legen*], put or set down, produce eggs.

Lay'er [see **Lay**[3]], bed, one thickness.

Lay'man, one of the laity.

Laz'ar [from name *Lazarus*], leper.

Laz-ar-et'to, hospital, esp. for lepers, ship or building for quarantine, ship's storeroom.

La'zy [?], not inclined to work, idle.

La'zy-tongs [**Lazy** and **Tongs**], contrivance of zigzag levers with scissor-like handles that can be extended to seize distant objects.

Lea [O.E. *léah*, a tract of land], grassy field, stretch of open ground.

Lead [O.E. *léad*], heavy metal. **Lead'en.**

Lead [O.E. *lǽdan* ; rel. to O.E. *lithan*, to travel], guide, go first ; direction.

Lead'er, first horse in team ; article expressing editorial opinion. **Leaderette'.**

Leaf [E.], outgrowth, usually green, from a stem, one of the folds (each containing two pages) which compose a book, a folio.

League [It. *lega*, league ; L. *ligāre*, to bind], alliance.

League [Late L. *leuga*, *leuca* ; perh. Gaulish], three miles.

Leak [perh. O.N. *leka*, to drip], accidental opening by which fluid enters or escapes.

Leal [L. *legalis*], loyal, honest.

Lean [O.E. *hlǽne*], thin ; flesh without fat.

Lean [O.E. *hleonian*, *hlīnian* ; cogn. with Gk. *klīnein*, climax, and L. *clīnāre*, decline], bend, rest for support.

Leap [O.E. *hlēapan*], to jump ; a jump.

Leap'-year, year of 366 days.

Learn [O.E. *leornian*], gain knowledge.

Lease (*s=ss*) [F. *laisser*, to let; L. *laxus*, loose], contract between landlord and tenant; let for a term of years. **Lease'hold.**

Leash [O.F. *lesse*, *laisse*, perh. fr. L.L. *laxa*, a leash], thong or cord for holding a dog or a hawk ; set of three (hounds, hares, etc.).

Least [O.E. *lǽst*, superl.], smallest, slightest.

Leath'er [O.E. *lether*], skin of an animal dressed for use.

Leave [O.E. *léaf*, cogn. w. *love*, *lief*], permission, parting.

Leave [O.E. *lǽfan* ; O. Teut. *laib*, *leiban*, to remain, cogn. w. *lave*, remainder], go away from, let stay, give up.

Leav'en [L. *levāmen*, leaven, *levāre*, to raise], portion of fermenting dough, yeast; cause to ferment, infect.

Lech'er-y (*ch=tsh*) [O.F. *lechier*, to live in debauchery], debauchery. **Lech'erous.**

Lec'tern [L. *legere* (p.p. *lectus*), to read], church reading-desk.

Lec'ture [L. *legere* (p.p. *lectus*), to read], discourse, lengthy reproof; read or deliver a lecture.

Ledge [perh. M.E. form of *legge* ; see **Lay** [3]], shelf, ridge.

Led'ger [perh. M.E. *liggen*, after Du. *legger*, fr. *leggen*, to lay], book containing a summary of accounts.

Lee [O.E. *hléo* ; O.N. *hlé*, shelter], sheltered side.

Lee [F. *lie*], in *pl.*, the sediment of wine, etc.

Leech [O.E. *lœce*, a healer], blood-sucking worm, doctor. **Leech'craft.**

Leek [O.E. *léac*], plant of the onion family.

Leer [O.E. *hléor*, the cheek], distorted expression.

Lees [earlier *lee* ; F. *lie* (sing.) ; Late L. *lia* (pl. *liæ*), lees], dregs.

Leet [perh. O.F. *eslite*, *eslete*, election], list of candidates for office.

Lee'ward, towards the sheltered side.

Leg'a-cy [L. *legāre* (p.p. *legātus*), to appoint], gift by will.

Le'gal [L. *lex* (*leg-is*), law], according to law. **Le'galize.**

Leg'ate [O.F. *legat* ; L. *legāre* (p.p. *legātus*), to appoint], ambassador from the Pope.

Leg-a-tee', one to whom a legacy is left.

Le-ga'tion, embassy, residence of an ambassador.

Legend (*lĕj'end*) [L. *legere* (fut. pass. part. *legendus*), to read], wonderful story of the past. **Leg'endary.**

Le'gi-ble (*é*) [L. *legere*, to read], capable of being read. **Legibil'ity.**

Le'gion [L. *legio* (*legiōn-is*), a legion ; *legere*, to choose], military force, multitude. **Leg'ionary.**

Leg'is-late (*g* soft), make or enact laws.

Leg'is-la-tor [L. *lēgis-lator* ; *lex* (*leg-is*), a law; *lator*, a proposer, from *latus* (used as agent-noun to *ferre*, to carry), a lawgiver.

Leg'is-la-ture (*g* soft), body that makes laws.

Le-git'i-mate [L. *legitimus*, lawful, *lex* (*leg-is*), a law], lawful. **Legit'imacy.**

Le-gu'mi-nous [L. *legumen* (*legumin-is*), a pod], pod-bearing, like pulse.

Leisure (*lezh'ur* or *leezh'ur*) [L. *licēre*, to be allowed], freedom from work, spare time.

Lem'ming [Norw. *lemende*, *lemming*], small Arctic animal of the rat kind.

Lem'on [F. *limon* : Pers. *limun*, a lemon], sour pulpy fruit.

Lem-on-ade', lemon drink.

Le'mur (*é* or *ee*) [L. *lemur*, a ghost], kind of nocturnal animals, allied to monkeys, but with fox-like faces.

Lend [O.E. *lǽnan*, fr. *lǽn*], allow use of on condition of return.

Length [O.E. *lengthu*, conn. with *lang*, long], extent from end to end.

Length'en, make longer.

Le'ni-ent [L. *lēnis*, soft], mild, not severe. **Len'ience.**

Lens [L. *lens*, a lentil], piece of curved glass by which objects are seen magnified or diminished.

Lent [O.E. *lencten*, the spring], time of fasting before Easter from Ash-Wednesday to Easter-Eve.

Len'til [L. *lenticula* (double dim. of *lens*, a lentil)], pea-like plant, also its seed.

Le'o-nine [L. *leo* (*leōn-is*), a lion], like a lion.

Leop'ard [Gk. *leopardos*, a leopard, *leon*, a lion, *pardos*, a pard], spotted wild animal.

Lep'er [L. and Gk. *lepra*, leprosy ; Gk. *lepos*, a scale], person afflicted with leprosy.

Lep-i-dop'ter-a [Gk. *lepis*, a scale, *pteron*, a wing], order of insects with scale-covered wings.

Lep'ro-sy, contagious skin-disease.

Le'sion (*si=zh*) [L. *lœsio* (*lœsiōn-is*), a lesion, *lædere* (p.p. *lœsus*), to hurt], a hurt, injury.

Less [E.], smaller.

Les-see', holder of a lease.

Less'en, make less.

Les'son [L. *legere* (*lectio*, a reading), to read], portion to be read or learned.

Lest [O.E. phrase, *thý lǽs the*, " whereby less." In M.E. *thý* was dropped, and *lǽs the* changed to *les te*], for fear that.

Let [O.E. *lǽtan*; Teut. root *lǣt*; cogn. with Late and L. *lassus*, weary], allow, lease.

Let [O.E. *lettan* (conn. with *lǽt*, late)], hinder.

Le'thal [L. *lethum*, death], causing death.

Leth'ar-gy [Gk. *lēthargos*, forgetful, *lēthe*, oblivion], morbid drowsiness, state of inaction. **Lethar'gic.**

Let'ter [L. *littera*, a letter], mark or symbol representing a sound, a written message, (*pl.*) learning.

Let'ter-press, print.

Let'tuce (*uce=iss*) [L. *lactūca*, a lettuce ; *lac* (*lact-is*), milk], plant used in salads.

Lev'ee (*ee=ĭ*) [F. *lever*, L. *levāre*, to rise], morning reception, reception for men held by the British sovereign.

Lev'el [O.F. *livel*; L. *libella* (dim. of *libra*, a balance), a level], even, even surface, equal elevation ; make flat, point (a gun).

Le'ver [L. *levāre*, to raise], bar used to raise weights. **Lev'erage.** [hare.

Lev'er-et [L. *lepus* (*lepor-is*), a hare], young

Le-vi'a-than [Heb. *livyāthān*, a leviathan], sea-monster, anything large of its kind.

Lev-i-ta'tion, rising (by lightness).

Lev'i-ty [L. *levis*, light], relative lightness, flightiness. [collect.

Lev'y [F. *lever*, L. *levāre*, to raise], raise,

Lewd [O.E. *læwede*, orig. ignorant, lay (adj.)], indecent, vicious.

Lex'i-con [Gk. *lexicon*; *lexis*, a word], dictionary. **Lexicog'raphy.**

Li'a-ble [F. *lier*, L. *ligāre*, to bind, and **Able**], bound in law, answerable.

Li-ai'son (nearly *lee-aiz-ōng*) [L. *ligāre*, to bind], connection, bond of union.

Li'ar, one who tells lies.

Li'as [O.F. *liois*, lias], blue limestone rock.

Li-ba'tion [L. *libāre* (p.p. *libātus*), to pour forth], drink-offering to the gods.

Li'bel [L. *libellus* (dim. of *liber*), a book], malicious publication ; defame. **Li'bellous.**

Lib'er-al [L. *liber*, free], free, generous ; one in favour of great political freedom.

Lib'er-ate [L. *liber*, free], to set free.

Lib'er-tine [L. *libertinus*, fr. *liber*, free], licentious ; one who is a slave to his desires.

Lib'er-ty [L. *liber*, free], freedom, permission.

Li-bra'ri-an, one in charge of a library.

Li'bra-ry [L. *liber*, a book], collection of books, building or room for books.

Li-bret'to [Ital. dim. of *libro* (L. *liber*), a book], book of words of an opera.

Li'cense, Li'cence [L. *licēre*, to be lawful], permission, document granting permission, excess of liberty. **Li'cense**, grant permission. **Licensee'.**

Li-cen'ti-ate (*t=sh*), one who has a licence to exercise a profession. [vicious.

Li-cen'tious (*tious=shus*), abusing freedom,

Li'chen (*liken* or *litchen*) [L. *lichēn*; Gk. *leichēn*, a lichen], flowerless plant growing on rocks and stems of trees.

Lick [O.E. *liccian*, to lick], pass the tongue over, to lap.

Lid [O.E. *hlid*, a lid], movable cover.

Lie [1] [O.E. *léogan*, to tell a lie ; *lyge*, a lie], untruth ; utter falsehood.

Lie [2] [O.E. *licgan*], general direction ; rest stretched out, be situated.

Lief [O.E. *léof*, dear], willingly.

Liege [O.F. *lige*, *liege*, leal, free ; M.H.G. *ledic*, *lidic*, free], sovereign, loyal ; sovereign, a subject.

Li'en (*i=ī* or *ee*) [F. *lien*; L. *ligāmen*, a tie, from *ligāre*, to bind], security over goods for a debt.

Lieu-ten'ant (*ieu=ef*) [F. *lieutenant*; L. *locum tenens*, holding the place (of another)], officer below a captain in the army, below commander in the navy.

Life [O.E. and O.N. *lif*], external and internal activities of an animal or plant, union of soul and body, time during which the union lasts, energy.

Lift [O.N. *lypta*, to lift, *lopt*, air ; Dan. *löfte* ; Swed. *lyfta*, to lift], raise ; a hoist.

Lig'a-ment [L. *ligāre*, to bind], band, fibrous tissue which unites bones.

Lig'a-ture [L. *ligāre*, to bind], bandage, string for tying blood-vessels.

Light [1] [O.E. *léoht* ; cf. Du. and Ger. *licht* ; Gk. *leukos*, white ; L. *lux*, light, all fr. Aryan root, *leuk*], natural agent which renders objects visible to the eye, opposite of darkness ; put fire to.

Light [2] [O.E. *léoht* ; cf. Du. *licht* ; Ger. *leicht* ; Gk. *elaphros*, light, and *elakhus*, small], not heavy. **Light'some.**

Light [3] [O.E. *lihtan*, to alight, to make light, as **Light** [2]], descend, come on by chance.

Light'en [1] [fr. **Light** [1]], to flash, grow lighter.

Light'en [2] [fr. **Light** [2]], make less heavy.

Light'er [fr. **Light** [3]], barge used in loading and unloading ships. [seamen.

Light'house, tower with a light to guide

Light'ning, electric discharge from clouds.

Lig'ne-ous [L. *lignum*, wood], woody, made of wood.

Lig'nite [L. *lignum*, wood], fossil wood, brown coal.

Like [1] [M.E. *lich*, fr. O.E. *gelic* (cf. Ger. *gleich*), fr. O. Teut. *galiko*, *ga*, with, *liko*, body], similar.

Like [2] [O.E. *lician*, to like], to be pleased with. **Like'able.**

Like'ly, probable, promising. **Like'lihood.**

Like'ness, resemblance, portrait. [also.

Like'wise [for "in like wise"], in like manner,

Li'king, attraction toward, pleasure, love.

Li'lac [Sp. *lilac*, a lilac ; Pers. *lilak*, var. of *nilak*, bluish, *nil*, blue], bluish ; shrub with bluish or white flowers.

Lil-li-pu'tian (*t=sh*) [*Lilliput* in *Gulliver's Travels*], very small, pigmy.

Lilt [Norw. *lilla*, to sing in a high tone], spirited rhythm, cheerful tune.

Lil'y [L. *lilium* ; Gk. *leirion*, a lily], bulbous plant, also its flower. [wing.

Limb [O.E. *lim* ; cf. O.N. *limr*], leg, arm, or

Lim'ber [F. *limon*, a shaft], harnessing part of a gun-carriage ; attach this part to gun.

Lim'ber [?], flexible.

Lime [1] [F. *lime*, Pers. *limūn*, a kind of citron], fruit like a small lemon.

Lime[2] [var. of *lind*; see **Linden**], linden-tree.

Lime[3] [O.E. *lim*, adhesive substance; cf. Ger. *leim*; cogn. with L. *limus*, mud], white earth (calcium oxide), viscous substance for catching birds.

Lim′er-ick [?], five-lined nonsense verse.

Lim′it [L. *limes* (*limit-is*, a limit), edge, bound; restrict.

Lim-i-ta′tion, act of limiting, that which limits.

Limn [fr. obs. *lumine*, to illuminate (MSS.), fr. O.F. *luminer*; L. *lumen* (*-inis*), light; see **Illuminate**], draw or paint.

Limp [cogn. with M.H.G. *limphin*], walk lamely; a lame walk.

Limp [?], lacking stiffness.

Lim′pet [Late L. *lampreda*, a lamprey], shell-fish that sticks to rocks.

Lim′pid [L. *limpidus*, clear], clear.

Linch′-pin [obs. *Linch* in same sense; O.E. *lynis*; cf. Ger. *lünse*; and **Pin**], pin passed through axle-end to keep wheel on.

Lin′den [orig. an adj. fr. O.E. *lind*, a linden-tree], kind of tree with fragrant flowers.

Line [L. *linea*, a line; *linum*, flax], rope, long marking of the pen, etc., row, series of ancestors, course; cover the inside, form a line.

Lin′e-age [see **Line**], race, descent.

Lin′e-al, **Lin′e-ar**, pertaining to lines or length.

Lin′e-a-ment [L. *linea*, a line], feature.

Lin′en [O.E. *linen*, formerly an adj. fr. *lin*, flax], thread or cloth made of flax.

Li′ner, ship belonging to a passenger line.

Ling [cogn. with **Long**[1]], food fish.

Ling [O.N. and Dan. *lyng*, heather], heather.

Lin′ger [O.E. *lengan*, to prolong, *lang*, long], delay, loiter.

Lin′gual (*u=w*) [L. *lingua*, the tongue), of or pertaining to the tongue.

Lin′guist (*u=w*) [L. *lingua*, the tongue], one skilled in languages. **Linguist′ic.**

Lin′i-ment [L. *linire*, to smear], ointment of the consistency of oil.

Li′ning, inside covering.

Link [O.N. *hlenkr*, bend of body; Dan. *lænke*; Swed. *länk*, a link], ring of a chain, tie; to join.

Link [?], torch.

Links [O.E. *hlinc*], stretch of undulating sandy ground near the sea; ground on which golf is played.

Lin′net [O.F. *linette*, named from feeding on hemp-seed; *lin*, flax], kind of singing-bird.

Lin-o′le-um [L. *linum*, flax; *oleum*, oil], canvas treated with linseed oil and ground cork.

Lin′o-type (ⓣ) [*line of type*], machine for producing stereotyped lines of words.

Lin′seed [O.E. *lin*, flax, and **Seed**], seed of flax.

Lin′sey-wool′sey [perh. O.E. *lin*, linen + obs. *say*, silk, and **Wool**], coarse material of wool and cotton, orig. wool and linen.

Lint [perh. fr. F. *linette*, linseed], linen scraped into a soft substance.

Lin′tel [Late L. *lintellus*, *limitellus*, dim. of L. *limes*, a boundary], horizontal timber or stone spanning a doorway, etc.

Li′on [L. *leo* (*leōnis*); Gk. *leōn*], large beast of prey, celebrated person. **Li′on-ess.**

Li′on-ize, to treat a person as a celebrity, to make a 'lion' of.

Lip [O.E. *lippa*; cogn. with L. *labium*], fleshy border of the mouth, edge.

Liq′ue-fy [L. *liquidus*, liquid, *facere*, to make], make or become liquid. **Liquefac′tion.**

Liq′uid [L. *liquidus* (adj.), *liquēre*, to be liquid], flowing, not solid; a fluid.

Liq′uid-ate (L. *liquidus*, liquid], to discharge, to pay off.

Liq′uor [L. *liquor*, liquor, *liquēre*, to be liquid], a liquid, esp. containing alcohol.

Liq′uor-ice, **Lic′o-rice** (*ice=iss*) [Gk. *glykyrrhiza*, liquorice, *glycos*, sweet, *rhiza*, a root], the thickened juice of a root.

Lisp [O.E. *wlisp*, lisping, imit.; cf. Du. *lispen*], to pronounce *s* and *z* as *th*.

Lis′som, **Lis′some** [contr. of *lithesome*; see **Lithe**], flexible.

List[1] [O.E. *liste*; O.F. *liste*], an edge of cloth.

List[2] [O.E. *hlyst*, hearing; *hlystan*, to listen], to listen.

List[3] [O.E. *lystan*, to desire], please.

List[4] [F. *liste*, fr. Teut.], a catalogue; to set down in a list.

List[5] [?], to incline to one side (a ship).

Lis′ten [O. Northumb. *lyma*, fr. Teut. root *hlus*; O.E. *hlosnian*; cogn. with **List**[2]], to give ear.

Lis′ten-ing post, position in front of an army where sentries have to try to find out enemy movements by hearing.

List′less [**L̥st**[3] and **Less**], spiritless, languid.

Lists, enclosure set apart for contests.

Lit′a-ny [Gk. *litaneia*, a prayer], prayer with responses.

Lit′er-al [L. *littera*, a letter], according to the letter, verbally exact.   [literature.

Lit′er-a-ry [L. *littera*, a letter], pertaining to

Lit′er-ate, able to read and write.

Lit′er-a-ture, collective writings.

Lithe [O.E. *lithe*, gentle, soft; cogn. with L. *lentus*, slow, fr. Teut. root *len*], easily bent, flexible, supple.

Lith′o-graph [Gk. *lithos*, a stone, *graphein*, to write], a print from a design on stone.

Lit′i-gate [L. *lis* (*lit-is*), strife], to go to law.

Li-ti′gious, fond of going to law. **Lit′igant.**

Lit′mus [Du. *lakmoes*; *lak*, lac, and *moes*, pulp], kind of blue dye.

Li′tre (*lee′ter*) [F. *litre*], unit of capacity in metric system; about 1¾ pint.

Lit′ter [O.F. *litiere*; L. *lectus*, a bed], a bed in a frame for carrying, bedding for animals, the young family of a quadruped, confusion of things.

Lit′tle [O.E. *lytel*, prob. fr. root of *lútan*, to bow down; see **Lout**], small.

Lit′to-ral [L. *litus* (*litor-is*), the shore], pertaining to the shore; the shore.

Lit′ur-gy [Gk. *leitourgia*, public service; *leitos*, public, *ergon*, work], a form for public worship. **Litur′gical.**

Live [O.E. *libban*, fr. Teut. root *lib*], have life, pass life, dwell.

Live (*i*), full of life, flaming, charged with electricity.

Live′li-hood [O.E. *líf*, life, *lád*, a course], means of living.

Live′long, entire, from beginning to end.

Live′ly [O.E. *líflic*, lit. life-like], full of life, brisk.

Liv′er [O.E. *lifer*], gland which secretes bile.

Liv′er-y [F. *livrée*, orig. fem. p.p. of *livrer*, to deliver; L. *liberāre*, to deliver], uniform dress of service.

Liv′id [L. *lividus*, livid], black and blue, of a lead colour.

Liv′ing, manner of life, means of living, benefice of a clergyman.

Liz′ard [O.F. *lesard*; L. *lacertus*, a lizard], a species of reptiles.

Lla′ma [Peruv. *llama*, llama], S. American animal related to the camel.

Lla′no [Sp. *llano* (L. *planus*, flat], extensive treeless plain (in America).

Loach [F. *loche*, a loach], kind of fish.

Load [O.E. *lád*, a way, course, carriage], burden, cargo; lay a load on, charge, as a gun.   [Polestar.

Load′star, Lode′star, guiding star, esp. the

Load′stone, Lode′stone, piece of magnetic iron ore.

Loaf [O.E. *hláf*], piece of bread baked separately, conical mass of sugar.

Loaf [?], lounge or loiter about.

Loaf′er, a lazy lounger.   [of soil.

Loam [O.E. *lám*, cogn. with **Lime** 3], rich kind

Loan [O.N. *lán*; Dan. *laan*; Swed. *lǎn*, a loan], that which is lent.

Loath, Loth [O.E. *láth*, hateful], unwilling.

Loathe [O.E. *láthian*], to hate, abhor.

Loath′some (*some=sum*), disgusting.

Lob′by [M.L. *lobium*, *lobia*, a gallery, a covered way; cf. **Lodge**], passage between rooms, waiting-room.

Lobe [Gk. *lobos*, a lobe], rounded projection.

Lob′ster [O.E. *loppestre*, corruption of L. *locusta* (1) a lobster, (2) a locust], marine shellfish.   [place.

Lo′cal [L. *locus*, a place], pertaining to a

Lo-cal′i-ty, geographical situation, place. **Loc′alize.**   [position.

Lo-cate′ [L. *locus*, a place], place, set in a

Loch (*ch* guttural) [Gael. and Ir. *loch*, a lake], lake, arm of the sea (Scotland).

Lock 1 [O.E. *loc*], tress of hair.

Lock 2 [O.E. *loc*, a fastening, *lúcan*, to shut], fastening (of a door, etc.), works to permit of passing between different levels of a canal, mechanism for exploding the charge of a gun; make fast, link together.

Lock′er [see **Lock** 2], compartment, esp. in a ship, that closes with a lock.

Lock′et [orig. a fastening; F. *loquet*, a latch, dim. of O.F. *loc*, a lock], small ornamental pendant case.

Lo-co-mo′tion [L. *locus*, a place; *movēre* (p.p. *mōtus*), to move], moving about.

Lo-co-mo′tive [L. *locus*, a place, *movēre* (p.p. *mōtus*, to move), engine that moves from place to place; not stationary.

Lo′cust [L. *locusta*, a lobster, a locust], insect allied to the grasshopper, tree bearing pods.

Lo-cu′tion [L. *loqui* (p.p. *locūtus*), to speak], speech, mode of expression.   [metal.

Lode [O.E. *lád*, a way], water-course, vein of

Lodge [O.F. *loge*; M.L. *lobia*, a lobby], small house, meeting-room of a brotherhood, the brotherhood itself; to shelter, stop or rest in.   [tion.

Lodge′ment, Lodg′ment, foothold, accumula-

Lodg′er, occupant of hired rooms.

Loft [O.N. *lopt*, air, sky; an upper room; Dan. and Swed. *loft*, a garret], space between roof and ceiling of uppermost storey, gallery, etc., in a church, room over a stable.

Loft′y, high, proud.

Log [late M.E. *logge*. Etym. doubtful], piece of unhewn timber, instrument for measuring a ship's speed, log-book or journal for entering all happenings espec. on ship.

Log′a-rithm [Gk. *logos*, a word, reckoning, *arithmos*, number], one of a class of auxiliary numbers used to abridge calculation. **Logarith′mic.**   [to quarrel.

Log′ger-heads [see **Log** and **Head**], (to be at),

Lo′gic (*δ*) [Gk. *logicē* (fem. of *logicos*), reasonable, *logos*, a word), science of exact reasoning. **Logi′cian.**

Lo-go-ma-chy (*ch=k*) [Gk. *logos*, word, *machia*, fighting], dispute about words.

Log′wood, dark red wood used by dyers.

Loin [O.F. *loigne*; L. *lumbus*, loin], lower part of the back between ribs and hip-bone.

Loi′ter [M.Du. *loteren*, to wag about, to delay], linger, saunter.

Loll [prob. imit.; cf. M.Du. *lollen*, to sleep, and **Lull**], lie at ease, hang (tongue) from the mouth.

Lol′li-pop [?], sugar confection.

Lone′ly [fr. *lone*, short for **Alone**], solitary, unfrequented.

Long 1 [O.E. *lang*, com. Teut; cogn. with L. *longus*], drawn out in a line, far-reaching.

Long 2 [O.E. *langian*, to crave], to desire eagerly.

Lon-gev′i-ty (*g=j*) [L. *longævitas*; *longus*, long, *ævum*, an age], length of life.

Lon′gi-tude (*g=j*) [L. *longus*, long], length, distance east or west measured by meridians. **Longitud′inal.**

Look [O.E. *lócian*, to look], a sight, glance, expression of face; direct the eyes to, seem.

Look′ing-glass, mirror.

Loom 1 [M.E. *lome*, fr. O.E. *gelóma*, tool, *ge* (*y*), and *lóma*; cf. *andloman*, apparatus], frame for weaving.

Loom 2 [cf. E. Frs. *lōmen*, to move slowly; M.H.G. *luomen*, to be weary; etym. doubtful], appear enlarged as a distant object.

Loon [O.N. *lómr*; Dan. *lom*, a loon], bird.

Loon [?], fellow.

Loop [perh. O.N. *hlaup*, a leap; cf. Swed. *löpknut*, running knot)], noose, doubling of string, etc.; form into a loop, fasten with a loop.

Loop'hole [perh. conn. with M.Du. *lûpen*, to lie in wait, and **Hole**], small opening, esp. for musketry.

Loose (*se*=*ss*) [O.E. *léas*; O.N. *lauss*, loose], unbound, slack; make loose.

Loos'en, make loose.

Loot [Hind. *lut*], plunder.

Lop [?], cut off.

Lop-sid'ed [**Lop**, of doubtful origin, and **Side**], of unequal sides.

Lo-qua'cious (*ci*=*sh*) [L. *loqui*, to speak], talkative. **Loquac'ity**.

Lord [O.E. *hláford*, lit. loaf-keeper], master, a titled nobleman, God, a title of Christ.

Lord'ly, proud.   [power.

Lord'ship, title given to a lord or a judge,

Lore [O.E. *lár* (cf. Ger. *lehre*), fr. Teut. root *lais*; cogn. with **Learn**], learning, knowledge.

Lorg-nette' (*lorn-yet*) [F.], pair of eyeglasses usually held by long handle, opera-glass.

Lorn [M.E. *loren*, p.p. of *lésen*; O.E. *léosan*, to lose], desolate, lost.

Lor'ry [?], long vehicle (for goods) without sides.

Lose (*looz*) [O.E. *losian*, to perish, fr. *los*, dissolution], cease to have, to part with unintentionally.

Loss [perh. back-formation, fr. *lost*, p.p. of **Lose**], act of losing, that which is lost.

Lot [O.E. *hlot*], fate, anything used to settle a question by chance, share.

Lo'tion [L. *lavāre* (p.p. *lotus*), to wash], a wash for wound or complexion.

Lot'ter-y [It. *lotteria*, a lottery; see **Lot**], distribution of prizes by lot.

Lo'tus [Gk. *lōtos*, a lotus], water lily of Egypt and Asia, tree with a sweet fruit said to produce forgetfulness.

Loud [O.E. *hlud*, com. West Germanic], making a strong sound, noisy, flashy.

Lough (pron. as **Loch**) [Ir. *loch*], lake or arm of the sea (in Ireland).

Lounge (*lownj*) [?], idle gait, kind of sofa; to stand, sit, or recline in a lazy way.

Louse (*lowss*) [O.E. *lús*, com. Teut.], wingless insect infesting animals.

Lout [O.E. *lútan*, to stoop], clownish fellow; bend, bow.

Love (*lŭv*) [O.E. *lufu*], strong liking; feel strong liking. **Lov'able**.

Love'ly, beautiful, lovable.

Low [O.E. *hlówan*; cogn. with L. *clamare*], to moo, call.

Low [O.N. *lágr*, cogn. with **Lie²**], not high, not loud, mean, near the ground.

Low [O.E. *hláw*], hill.

Low'er (comp. of low), let down, bring down.

Low'er, Lour [M.E. *louren*, to frown], be gloomy and threatening.

Low'ly, low in rank, humble.

Loy'al [F. *loyal*; L. *legālis*; see **Legal**], faithful to law, true to a person. **Loy'alty**.

Lo'zenge [O.F. *losenge*; perh. fr. O.F. *lauze*, a flat stone], figure with 4 equal sides having 2 acute and 2 obtuse angles, a flat sweet.

Lub'ber [perh. cogn. with **Lob**], big clumsy fellow, esp. sailor.

Lu'bri-cate [L. *lubricus*, slippery], make smooth or slippery, apply oil. **Lu'bricant**.

Luc'ent [L. *lūcentem*, pres. p. of *lūcēre*, to shine], shining, luminous.

Lu'cid [L. *lucēre*, to shine], bright, clear, sane. **Lucid'ity**.

Lu'ci-fer [L. *lūx* (*lūc-is*), light, *ferre*, to bring], the morning star, the planet Venus when she appears before sunrise, match ignited by friction.   [fortune.

Luck [L.G. *luk*, short for *geluk*], chance,

Lu'cra-tive [L. *lūcrum*, gain], yielding gain.

Lu'cre (*cre*=*ker*) [L. *lūcrum*, gain], gain.

Lu-cu-bra'tion [L. *lūcūbrāre* (p.p. *lucubrātus*), to work by lamp-light, *lūx* (*lūc-is*), light], study by night, elaborate literary work.   [absurd.

Lu'di-crous [L. *lūdere*, to play], laughable,

Luff [M.E. *lof*, a contrivance for altering a ship's course], turn a ship's head toward the wind.

Lug [Swed. and Norw. *lugga*, to pull by the hair, *lugg*, a forelock], drag along.

Lug'gage [see **Lug**], traveller's trunks, etc.

Lug'ger [perh. fr. **Lugsail**], small ship with lugsails.

Lug'sail [perh. fr. vb. **Lug** and **Sail**], square sail bent upon a yard that hangs obliquely to the mast.

Lu-gu'bri-ous [L. *lugēre*, to mourn], mournful (used lightly).

Luke'warm [**Luke**, perh. fr. O.E. *＊hléow*, and **Warm**], moderately warm, cool.

Lull [E., imit.; cf. **Loll**], to calm; calm interval during storm.

Lull'a-by (*y*=*ī*) [**Lull** and **By** (as in "Bye-Bye")], cradle song.

Lum-ba'go [L. *lumbus*, loin], rheumatism in the loins.   [loins.

Lum'bar [L. *lumbus*, loin], relating to the

Lum'ber [perh. room of the *Lombard*-broker (pawnbroker)], bulky useless things, timber sawed or split into beams, joists, etc.

Lum'ber [M.E. *lomere*; perh. fr. *lame*], move in a clumsy, noisy way.

Lu'mi-na-ry [L. *lūmen* (*lūmin-is*), light], body that gives light.

Lu'mi-nous [L. *lūmen* (*lūmin-is*), light], shining clear. **Luminos'ity**.

Lump [Swed. dial and Norw. *lump*, a block; Swed. *lumpen*, rags], irregular mass.

Lu'na-cy, madness.   [moon.

Lu'nar [L. *lūna*, the moon], relating to the

Lu'na-tic [L. *lūna*, the moon], insane; insane person.

Lunch, Lunch'eon [perh. connected with **Lump**], light meal between breakfast and dinner.

E

Lung [O.E. *lungen*, fr. Teut. root, *lung* ; cogn. with **Light**,² of little weight], one of the organs of breathing.

Lunge [earlier *longe* ; F. *allonger*, to lengthen ; L. *ad*, to, *longus*, long], sudden thrust.

Lu′pine [L. *lupus*, a wolf], flowering plant.

Lu′pus [L. *lupus*, a wolf], disease of the skin.

Lurch [?], sudden roll as of a ship ; roll or sway suddenly.

Lurch [F. *lourche*, game like backgammon], old game. *Leave in the lurch*, leave in difficulties.

Lure [O.F. *leurre*, *loerre* ; perh. fr. Teut. ; cf. Ger. *luder*, a bait], contrivance to recall hawks, enticement ; entice.

Lu′rid [L. *lūridus*, lurid], pale yellow, ghastly pale, like red glare showing amid darkness as flame through smoke, sensational.

Lurk [?], lie in wait.

Lus′cious (*sci*=*sh*) [?], delicious, excessively sweet.

Lush [?], luxuriant, succulent.

Lust [O.E. *lust*, pleasure, delight], (formerly) pleasure, inclination ; (now) sexual or passionate desire.

Lus-tra′tion [L. *lustrāre* (p.p. *lustrātus*), to purify], purification.

Lus′tre [F. *lustre* ; It. *lustro*, lustre ; L. *lustrāre*, to shine], brightness, brilliancy.

Lus′trum [L. *lustrum*, expiatory sacrifice, period of five years], period of five years.

Lust′y [O.E. *lust*, pleasure], vigorous, robust.

Lute [F. *lut*, Port. *alaude* ; Arab. *al*, the, *ūd*, wood], stringed instrument now out of use.

Lux-u′ri-ant [L. *luxuriantem*, pr. p. of *luxuriare*, to grow rank, fr. *luxuria*, luxury], abundant in growth. **Luxu′riance.**

Lux-u′ri-ate [see **Luxuriant**], indulge with delight.

Lux-u′ri-ous [O.F. *luxurius* ; fr. L. *luxuriosus*], pertaining to luxury.

Lux′u-ry [L. *luxus*, excess], free indulgence, desirable thing that can be done without.

Lydd′ite [from *Lydd* in Kent, where it was first tested + suff. *ite* of scientific terms], high explosive used in making shells.

Lye [O.E. *léag* ; O.N. *laug*, bath ; perh. cogn. with **Lather**], mixture of vegetable ashes and water for washing.

Lymph [L. *lympha*, water], colourless animal fluid.

Lym-phat′ic [L. *lymphaticus* ; see **Lymph**], sluggish.

Lynch [?], to put to death by mob-law without a legal trial. Orig. used in U.S.A.

Lynx [L. and Gk. *lynx*, a lynx ; allied to Gk. *leukos*, bright], animal of the cat kind noted for sharpness of sight.

Lyre [L. and Gk. *lyra*, a lyre], kind of harp now out of use.

Lyr′ic (*y*=*ĭ*) [Gk. *lyricos*, lyric ; see **Lyre**], kind of poem fitted for singing, poem expressing poet's own thoughts and feelings. **Lyr′ical.**

M

Mac-ad′am-ize [fr. inventor, J. L. *Macadam*], form a road of layers of broken stones, decreasing in size towards the surface, mixed with earth, and rolled.

Mac-a-ro′ni [It. *maccaroni*], wheaten paste in the form of pipes.

Mac-a-ron′ic [fr. It. *maccaroni*], kind of burlesque verse, containing Latin or other foreign words, but with a mixture of words from the writer's mother tongue with endings like those of the foreign language employed.

Mac-a-roon′ [F. *macaron*, same as **Macaroni**], sweet almond biscuit.

Ma-caw′ [Port. and Braz. *macao*], large parrot.

Mace [F. *macis*, mace, etym. doubtful], dried covering of the nutmeg, used as a spice.

Mace [O.F. *mace*, perh. allied to L. *matcola*, a mallet], staff with a metal head, official's staff of office.

Ma′cer-ate [L. *macerāre* (p.p. *macerātus*, to steep], soften by steeping, cause to waste by fasting. **Macera′tion.**

Mach-i-a-vel′li-an (*Machiavelli*, a Florentine statesman), unscrupulous, full of duplicity.

Mach′i-na′tion [L. *machināri* (p.p. *machinātus*), to contrive ; see **Machine**], artful design or plot.

Ma-chine′ (*ma-sheen′*) [Gk. *mechanĕ*, a machine, *mechos*, a contrivance], construction of combined moving parts, vehicle.

Ma-chin′er-y, machines in general, working parts of a machine.

Mack′er-el [O.F. *makerel*, etym. doubtful], mottled oceanic fish.

Mack′in-tosh [fr. C. *Mackintosh*, the patentee], waterproof coat.

Mac′ro-cosm [Gk. *macros*, great, *cosmos*, world], great world, universe.

Mad [O.E. *gemǽd*, p.p. of *gemǽden*, to make mad], disordered in mind, furious.

Ma′dam [F. *madame*, i.e. *ma dame*, my lady], complimentary title to a lady.

Mad′cap, person of wild behaviour.

Mad′den, make mad, enrage.

Mad′der [O.E. *mœdere* ; cf. Swed. *madra* ; Norw. *modra*], plant used in dyeing.

Ma-don′na [It. *ma*=*mia*, my, and *donna*, lady ; fr. L. *domina*], the Virgin Mary.

Mad′re-pore [It. *madrepora* ; *madre*, mother, and *poro* (perh. fr. Gk. *pōros*), friable stone], kind of perforate coral.

Mad′ri-gal [It. *madrigale*, a pastoral song], quaint little love poem, unaccompanied song in several parts.

Mael′strom [Du. *malen*, to grind, *stroom*, a stream], great whirlpool.

Mag-a-zine′ (*ine*=*een*) [Arab. *makhāzin*, pl. of *makhzan*, a storehouse], storehouse, periodical publication, chamber for cartridge in rifle.

Ma-gen′ta [fr. *Magenta*, in Italy], bluish-red colour obtained from coal-tar.

Mag′got [Welsh *maceiad*, a maggot, *magiad*, breeding], grub of a fly, whim.

Ma′gic [F. *magique*, fr. L. *magicus*; Gk. *magicos*], pretended art of doing wonders by supernatural means.

Ma-gis-te′ri-al, pertaining to a magistrate, authoritative, overbearing.

Ma′gis-trate [L. *magister*, a master], public civil officer.

Mag-nan′i-mous [L. *magnus*, great; *animus*, the mind], great-minded, noble. **Magna-nim′ity.**

Mag′nate [L. *magnus*, great], person of rank or distinction.

Mag-ne′si-a [Gk. *magnēsios*, belonging to *Magnesia*, in Thessaly], white earthy substance. [metal.

Mag-ne′si-um [see **Magnesia**], silver-white

Mag′net [Gk. (*lithos*) *magnētos*, magnesian (stone)], lodestone, kind of iron ore which attracts iron, piece of iron or steel so treated as to have the characteristic property of lodestone. **Mag′netize.**

Mag′net-ism, natural force of attraction.

Mag-nif′i-cent [see **Magnify**], splendid.

Mag′ni-fy [L. *magnus*, great, *facere*, to do], make great, enlarge in appearance.

Mag-nil′o-quent [L. *magnus*, great, *loqui*, to speak], pompous in speech. **Magnil′o-quence.** [ness.

Mag′ni-tude [L. *magnus*, great], size, great-

Mag-nol′i-a [fr. *Magnol*, botanist], kind of large tree with beautiful foliage and flowers.

Mag′pie [*Mag*, short for F. *Margot*; see **Pie**[1]], long-tailed, noisy bird.

Mah′di [Arab. *mahdīy*, the guided one, fr. pref. *ma* and *hadā*, to guide], among Mohammedans, the last *imam* or leader of the faithful.

Ma-hog′a-ny [?], furniture wood.

Maid, Maid′en [O.E. *mœgden*], young unmarried woman.

Mail [F. *maille*, mail; L. *macula*, a spot, a mesh], chain-armour.

Mail [O.F. *male*, O.H.G. *malha*, a wallet], post-bags, letters, etc.; to post.

Maim [O.F. *mahaignier*, to maim; etym. doubtful], to cripple, disable.

Main[1] [O.E. *mœgen*, strength], strength, ocean, principal pipe.

Main[2] [partly O.E. *mœgen*, partly O.N. *megn*, strong], principal, chief.

Main′land [**Main**[2] and **Land**], principal land, continent.

Main-tain′ [L. *manu tenēre*, to hold in the hand], keep up, assert. [ance.

Main′te-nance, means of support, continu-

Maize [Sp. *maiz*, of Cuban origin], Indian corn.

Maj′es-ty [L. *majestas*, majesty; allied to *major*], exalted dignity, title of emperors, kings and queens.

Ma-jol′i-ca [perh. fr. *Majorca*, formerly *Majolica*], kind of pottery.

Ma′jor [L. *major*, comp. of *magnus*, great], greater; field officer of lowest rank, officer ranking next below a lieutenant-colonel and above a captain.

Ma-jor′i-ty, greater number, full age, office of major.

Make [O.E. *macian*; cf. Du. *maken*; Ger. *machen*], cause to exist, to form, compel; structure, form.

Make′shift, expedient for the time.

Mal′a-chite (*ch*=*k*) [Gk. *malachē*, a stone resembling in colour leaf of mallow], green mineral.

Mal-a-droit′ [F. *mal*, bad, *adroit*, skilful], unskilful, clumsy.

Mal′a-dy [L. *male habitus*, out of condition; *male*, badly, and *habitus*, p.p. of *habēre*, to have], illness.

Mal′a-pert [O.F. *mal*, badly; *apert*, open], saucy, impudent.

Mal-a-pro-pos′ [F. *mal*, ill, *à*, to, *propos*, purpose], unsuitable, unseasonable.

Mal′a-prop-ism [fr. *Mrs Malaprop*, in Sheridan's "Rivals"], ludicrous misuse of a word.

Ma-la′ri-a [It. *malaria*, for *mala aria*, bad air], unhealthy exhalation from marshes, fever caused by mosquito bites.

Mal′con-tent [F. *mal*, ill, *content*, content], discontented person.

Male [O.F. *masle*; L. *masculus*, male], one of the sex to which a man belongs.

Mal-e-dic′tion [L. *male*, evilly, *dicere* (p.p. *dictus*), to say], curse.

Mal′e-fac-tor [L. *male*, ill; *facere* (p.p. *factus*), to do], evil-doer, criminal.

Ma-lev′o-lent [L. *male*, ill, *velle* (pr.p. *volens*, -*entis*), to wish], wishing evil, spiteful. **Malev′olence.**

Mal-for-ma′tion [L. *male*, ill, *forma*, formation], wrong formation, deformity.

Mal′ice (*ice*=*iss*) [L. *malus*, bad], ill-will.

Ma-lign′ (*ma-line′*) [L. *malignus* (adj.), *malus*, bad, *gignere*, to produce], evil, unfavourable; to slander.

Ma-lig′nant, spiteful, infectious, virulent.

Ma-lig′ni-ty, malice, deadly quality.

Ma-lin′ger [F. *malingre*, sickly; etym. doubtful], pretend illness or inability.

Mall[1] (*a*=*aw*) [F. *mail*; L. *malleus*, a hammer], wooden hammer, mallet.

Mall[2] [fr. the *Mall* (pron. *mell*) in London, where the game of pall-mall (pr. *pell mell*) was played; see **Mall**[1]], public walk.

Mal′lard [O.F. *malart*], a wild drake.

Mal′le-a-ble [L. *malleus*, a hammer], capable of being hammered out, pliable.

Mal′let [F. *maillet*, dim. of F. *mail*], hammer, usu. of wood.

Mal′low [L. *malva*, a mallow; per. cogn. with Gk. *malachos*, soft], plant with soft leaves.

Mal-nu-tri′tion [F. *mal*, badly, and **Nutrition**], insufficient nutrition.

Mal-o′dor-ous [F. *mal*, badly, and **Odorous**], evil-smelling.

Mal-prac′tice [F. *mal*, badly, and **Practice**], wrong-doing.

Malt (*a=aw*) [O.E. *mealt*; M.H.G. *malt*, soft], barley steeped in water and dried.

Mal-treat' [F. *mal*, badly, and **Treat**], treat ill.

Malt'ster, one who makes malt.

Mal-ver-sa'tion [F. *malverser*, fr. L. *male*, badly, *versari*, to behave], corrupt administration of public or trust money.

Mam-ma' [repetition of *ma*, a syllable instinctively used by children], mother.

Mam'mal [L. *mammalia*, animals that suckle their young; *mamma*, the breast], animal that suckles its young.

Mam'mon [Gk. *mamōnas*, fr. Aramaic *mamon*, riches], riches, the god of riches.

Mam'moth [Rus. *mammot*, a mammoth], huge extinct elephant.

Man [com. Teut.; O.E. *man(n)*; cogn. with Skr. *manu*, man; L. *mens*, mind], human being, male person; furnish with men.

Man'a-cle [L. *manicula*, a little hand; *manus*, the hand], handcuff; to handcuff.

Man'age [orig. a noun; It. *maneggio*, a handling; L. *manus*, the hand], to direct, control. **Man'ageable.**

Man'age-ment, direction; governing body.

Man'da-rin [Port. *mandarim*; Malay and Hind. *mantrī*, a counsellor; Skr. *man*, to think], Chinese public officer or nobleman.

Man'dat-or-y, conveying a command, or authority.

Man'date [L. *manus*, the hand, *dare* (p.p. *datus*), to give], authoritative command.

Man'di-ble [L. *mandere*, to chew], jaw, esp. lower jaw.

Man'do-lin, Man'do-line [It. *mandola*, var. of *pandora*, kind of guitar], guitar with rounded body.

Man'drake [Gk. *mandragoras*, a mandrake], narcotic plant.

Man'drel [?], axis to which turners fix their work.

Man'drill [**Man** and W. Afr. *drill*, a baboon], large baboon.

Mane [O.E. *manu*, fr. O. Teut. *manâ*, neck], long hair on the neck of the horse, etc.

Man'fu-lly, courageously.

Man-ga-nese' (*s=z*) [corruption of **Magnesia**], metallic chemical element.

Mange [O.F. *manjue*; F. *manger*, itch; L. *manducāre*, to eat], skin disease of horses, dogs, and cattle. **Mang'y.**

Man'gel- (or **Man'gold-**) **wur'zel** [Ger. *mangold*, beet; *wurzel*, root], large beet.

Man'ger (*a=ai*) [F. *mangeoire*, *manger*, to eat], open box or trough for fodder.

Man'gle [A.F. *mahangler*, freq. form of *mahaignier*, to maim], cut and bruise, spoil by gross blunders.

Man'gle [Du. *mangel* (n.); Gk. *magganon*, an engine of war], machine with rollers for smoothing linen, etc.; put through a mangle.

Man'go [Port. *manga*; Tamil *mankāy*; man-fruit], Indian fruit-bearing tree.

Man'grove [?], tropical tree growing in mud on the seashore.

Man'hood, state of being a man.

Ma'ni-a (*ma=mai*) [L. and Gk. *mania*, madness], violent mental derangement, great enthusiasm. **Mani'acal.**

Ma'niac, mad person.

Man'i-cure [L. *manus*, the hand; *cura*, care], one who undertakes care of the hand, esp. nails; to care for the hand.

Man'i-fest [L. *manus*, the hand, and perh. obs. *festus*, struck], open, apparent; show plainly; list of cargo.

Man-i-fes-ta'tion, display. [tion.

Man-i-fes'to [It. *manifesto*], public declara-

Man'i-fold [Com. Teut.; O.E. *manigfeald*], various, numerous.

Man'i-kin [Du. *manneken*, dim. of **Man**], little man, dwarf, artist's lay figure.

Man'i-oc [Tupi *mandioca*], cassava-plant.

Ma-nip'u-late [L. *manipulus*, a handful; *manus*, the hand, and *plēre*, to fill], handle skilfully, manage fraudulently. **Manipula'tion.**

Man-kind', human race.

Man'ly, having qualities becoming to a man. **Man'liness.**

Man'na [L. and Gk. *manna*; Heb. *mān*, manna], sweet ooze from a kind of ash-tree, heavenly food.

Man'ner [Late L. *man(u)āria*, manner; L. *manus*, the hand], way of doing, habitual style.

Man'ner-ism, trick of manner.

Man'nish, masculine, bold.

Ma-nœu'vre [L. *manu*, with the hand, and *opus* (*oper-is*), work], adroit proceeding, military or naval movement; manage with art, perform manœuvres.

Man'-of-war', warship.

Man'or [L. *manēre*, to remain], feudal division of land. **Manor'ial.**

Manse [L. *manēre* (sup. *mansum*), to remain], minister's house (in Scotland).

Man'sion [L. *manēre* (sup. *mansum*), to dwell], large dwelling-house.

Man'slaugh-ter, criminal but unintentional homicide.

Man'sue-tude [L. *mansuetus*, p.p. of *mansuescere*, to tame], gentleness.

Man'tel, Man'tel-piece [var. of **Mantle** and **Piece**], shelf above a fireplace and its supports.

Man-til'la [Sp. dim. of *manta*, a mantle], Spanish lady's veil.

Man'tle [L. *mantellum*, a cloak], cloak, a conical network round a gas-jet; to cloak, overspread.

Man'u-al [L. *manus*, the hand], done or made by the hand; handbook.

Man-u-fac'to-ry [L. *manu*, by hand, *facere*, to make], building where things are made.

Man-u-fac'ture, anything made by hand or by machinery; work raw materials into form for use.

Man-u-mis'sion [L. *manu*, by hand; see **Mission**], freeing (a slave). **Manumit'.**

Ma-nure' [formerly to work with the hand; contraction of **Manœuvre**], land fertilizer; apply manure to.

Man'u-script [L. *manu*, by hand, *scribere* (p.p. *scriptus*), to write], paper written with the hand.

Man'y (*a=ĕ*) [O.E., *manig*, many], numerous ; large number.

Map [L. *mappa*, a napkin, *mappa mundi*, map of the world], representation of the surface of the earth or part of it ; make a map of.

Ma'ple [O.E. *mapeltréow*, maple-tree], tree.

Mar [O.E. *merran*, to obstruct], disfigure, spoil.

Mar'a-bou, Mar'a-bout (*ou, out=oo*) [Arab. *murābit*, hermit], W. African stork, N. African hermit.

Ma-raud' [F. *marauder*, *maraud*, a rogue], make an incursion for plunder. Maraud'er.

Mar'ble [L. *marmor*, marble], compact lime-stone, little hard ball used in a game ; stain like marble.

March [1] [L. *Martius* (*mensis*), month of Mars], third month of the year (Rom. first).

March [2] [F. *marcher*; doubtful origin], walk with regular steps ; measured walk of troops, piece of music for marching to.

March [3] [O.E. *mearc*, a boundary ; doublet of Mark], border country, boundary.

Mar'chion-ess (*ch=sh*) [Low L. *marchiŏnissa*, *marchio*, a prefect of the Marches ; see March [3]], wife of a marquis.

Mar-co'ni-gram [from It. name *Marconi*, and Gk. *gramma*, a letter], message by wireless telegraphy.

Mare [O.E. *mere*], female of the horse.

Mar'ga-rine (*ine=in* or *een*) [a misapplication of the chemical term "margaric acid "], imitation of butter.

Mar'gin [L. *margo* (*margin-is*), cogn. with Mark [2]], border, edge. Mar'ginal.

Mar'grave [Du. *markgraaf*; *mark*, boundary, and *graaf*, a count], lord of the marches.

Mar'guer-ite (*ite=eet*) [Gk. *margarites*, fr. *margaron*, a pearl], ox-eye daisy.

Mar'i-gold [Mary and Gold], plant with yellow blossoms.

Marine (*ma-reen'*) [L. *marinus*, marine, *marē*, the sea], pertaining to the sea ; soldier serving on a ship.

Mar'in-er, sailor.

Mar-i-o-nette' [F. Marionnette (fr. *Marion*, dim. of *Marie*, Mary), puppet moved by strings.

Mar'i-tal [L. *maritus*, a husband], of marriage, of a husband.

Mar'i-time [L. *maritimus*, maritime, *mare*, the sea], connected with the sea.

Mar'jo-ram [M.L. *majorana*, marjoram], mint-like plant.

Mark [1] [O.E. *marc*, a weight], standard coin of Germany.

Mark [2] [O.E. *mearc*], sign, impression, object aimed at ; to note, make marks on. [land.

Mark [3] [O.E. *mearc*, a boundary], border

Mar'ket [L. *mercāri* (p.p. *mercātus*), to trade], trading place, rate of buying and selling. Mar'ketable.

Marks'man, one who shoots well.

Marl [O.F. *marle*; Late L. *margila*, dim. of *marga*, marl], mixture of clay, lime, and sand.

Mar'line-spike [Du. *marlijn*, a cord of two strands ; *marren*, to bind, *lijn*, a line ; see Spike], short tool for opening the strands of a rope.

Mar'ma-lade [Port. *marmelo*, a quince ; Gk. *meli*, honey, *mēlon*, an apple], preserve, esp. of oranges. [marble.

Mar-mor'e-al [L. *marmoreus*], of or like

Mar'mo-set [?], small monkey.

Ma-roon' [1] [F. *marron*, fugitive ; corruption of Sp. *cimarron*, wild], in the W. Indies a fugitive negro slave.

Ma-roon' [2] [F. *marron*; It. *marrone*, a chestnut], dull red.

Ma-roon' [3] [see Maroon [1]], put ashore on a desolate island.

Marque (letters of) [F. *marque*; M.L. *marcāre*, to seize as a pledge], licence to a privateer.

Mar-quee' (*qu=k*) [for *marquess*, E. spelling of F. *marquise*, orig. a marchioness's tent], large field tent.

Mar'quet-ry, Mar'quet-erie (*qu=k*) [F. *marqueter*, to variegate], inlaid work.

Mar'quis, Mar'quess [O.F. *marhis*; Low L. *marchenses*, a prefect of the Marches ; see March [2]], title of nobility next that of duke.

Mar'riage [F. *mariage*, marriage ; L. *maritus*, a husband], legal union of husband and wife. Mar'riageable.

Mar'row [O.E. *mearg*], substance in the hollow of a bone.

Mar'ry [L. *maritāre*, to marry, *maritus*, a husband], wed.

Marsh [O.E. *mersc* (M.L. *mariscus*); fr. O. Teut. *mari*, sea], tract of soft wet land. Marsh'y.

Mar'shal [O.F. *mareschal*: O.H.G. *marah-scalh*, a marshal ; *marah*, a horse, and *scalh*, a servant], officer of the highest rank ; dispose in order.

Mar-su'pi-al [Gk. *marsypion*, dim. of *marsipos*, a bag], pouched animal.

Mart [contraction of Market], market.

Mar-tel'lo (tower) [It. *Martello*, a hammer ; the watchman gave alarm by striking a bell with a hammer], small circular fort.

Mar'ten [O.F. *martre*; cf. O.E. *mearth*, a martin], animal of the weasel kind.

Mar'tial (*ti=sh*) [L. *Mars* (*Mart-is*), the god of war], warlike.

Mar'tin [F. *martin*, from name *Martin*], house swallow.

Mar-ti-net' [from *Martinet*, an officer in Louis XIV.'s time], strict disciplinarian.

Mar'tin-mas, Feast of St Martin, 11th November.

Mar'tyr [Gk. *martys*, a witness], one who suffers for conscience' sake, great sufferer. Mar'tyrdom.

Mar'vel [L. *mīrāri*, to wonder at], a wonder ; to wonder.

Mar'vel-*lous*, wonderful, miraculous.

Mar'zip-an [?], paste made of pounded almonds, sugar, etc.

Mas′cot [F. *Mascotte*], luck-bringer.

Mas′cu-line [L. *masculīnus*, masculine, *mas*, a male], of the male sex, strong.

Mash [perh. cogn. with **Mix**], soft pulpy mass ; make pulpy.

Mask [F. *masque*, fr. Sp. *máscara*, a mask ; etym. dub.], face-cover for disguise ; to disguise, to conceal.

Ma′son [O.F. *masson* ; Low L. *macio*, a mason], stoneworker, freemason.

Ma′son-ry, stonework.

Masque (*que=k*) [F. ; see **Mask**], allegorical or symbolical drama of 17th cent. in which actors (amateurs) wore masks.

Mas-quer-ade′ (*qu=k*) [Sp. *mascarada* ; see **Mask**], assembly of masked persons, pretentious show ; to frolic in disguise.

Mass [1] [L. *massa* ; Gk. *maza*, a barley cake], body of matter, bulk.

Mass [2] [Folk L. *messa* ; Late L. *missa*, Mass, L. *mittere* (p.p. *missus*), to send], Lord's Supper, usu. in the R.C. Church.

Mas′sa-cre [F. *massacre*, etym. doubtful], slaughter of many ; to slaughter many.

Mas-sage′ (*age=ahzh*) [perh. from Port. *amassar*, to knead ; *massa*, dough], a rubbing or kneading of the body ; to treat thus.

Mas′seur (*fem.* **Mas′seuse**) [F.], one who practises massage.

Mas′sive [F. *massif* (fem. *massive*) ; see **Mass** [1]], large and heavy. **Mas′sy**.

Mast [Com. Teut. ; O.E. *mæst*], upright spar on a ship.

Mast [O.E.*mæst*], fruit of beech, etc., esp. as food for swine.

Mas′ter [O.F.*maistre* ; L. *magister*, a master], one who controls ; gain command of. **Mas′terful**.

Mas′ter-ly, having superior skill.

Mas′ter-piece, a work done with extraordinary skill.

Mas′ter-y, command, supremacy.

Mas′tic [Gk. *mastichē*, a kind of gum], kind of gum resin. [ca′tion.

Mas′ti-cate [perh. fr. **Mastic**], chew. **Masti-**

Mas′tiff [Late L. *mansuetinus*, from L. *mansuetus*, tame], kind of large dog.

Mas′to-don [Gk. *mastos*, breast, *odous*, tooth], extinct kind of elephant.

Mat [L. *matta*, a mat], article of interwoven rushes, etc., used for different purposes ; tangle.

Mat′a-dor [Sp. fr. L. *mactare*, to kill], man appointed to kill bull in bull-fight.

Match [O.F. *mesche* ; perh. from Late L. *myxa*, a wick], splint tipped to strike light.

Match [O.E. *gemœcca*, a comrade, a spouse; allied to *macian*, to make], equal marriage, suitable combination, contest ; to mate, be equal, oppose as equal.

Mate [Low G. *mate*, a mate], associate, ship's officer ; to match, marry.

Mate [O.F. *mat* in *eschec mat*, checkmate], checkmate (in chess).

Ma-te′ri-al [L. *mātēria*, matter], consisting of matter, not spiritual, important ; substance. **Mate′rialize**,

Ma-ter′nal [L. *maternus*, motherly, *mater*, a mother], motherly. [hood.

Ma-ter′ni-ty [L. *mater*, a mother], mother-

Math-e-mat′ics [Gk. *mathēma*, something learned], science of magnitude and numbers. **Mathemati′cian**.

Mat′ins, **Mat′tins** [L. *Matūta*, the goddess of dawn], morning prayers in Church of England.

Mat′i-née (*é=ai*) [F. *matinēe*, *matin*, morning], entertainment in the daytime.

Mat′ri-cide [L. *māter* (*mātr-is*), a mother, *cœdere*, to kill], murder or murderer of a mother.

Ma-tric′u-late [L.*mātricula*, a register], admit to or enter a university by enrolling in a register. **Matricula′tion**.

Mat′ri-mo-ny [L. *māter* (*mātr-is*), a mother], marriage. **Matrimon′ial**.

Ma′tron (*a=ai*) [L. *mātrona*, matron, *māter*, a mother], married woman, housekeeper of an institution. **Ma′tronly**.

Mat′ted, covered with a mat, tangled.

Mat′ter [L. *mātēria*, matter], substance, subject, pus ; be important.

Mat′ting, mats in general, matwork.

Mat′tock [O.E. *mattuc*, etym. dub.], tool for digging and grubbing.

Mat′tress [O.F.*materas*, a mattress ; Arab. *al-matrah*, a place where anything is thrown], bed stuffed with hair, etc., and quilted or otherwise fastened, wire frame on which mattress is placed.

Ma-ture′ [L. *mātūrus*, ripe], ripe ; ripen. **Matur′ity**. [morning.

Mat-u-ti′nal [see **Matins**], relating to the

Maud′lin [O.F. name *Madelaine*, Magdalen], somewhat drunk, weakly sentimental.

Man′gre (*re=er*) [O.F. *malgré*, *maugré* ; from *mal*, ill, and *gré*, will], in spite of.

Maul [L. *malleus*, a hammer], wooden hammer ; beat and bruise.

Maul′-stick [Ger. *malerstock* ; *maler*, a painter, and *stock*, a stick], stick used as a rest by painters.

Maun′der [?], talk in a rambling manner.

Mau-so-le′um [Gk. *mausōleion*, orig. tomb of *Mausōlos*, a king of Caria], magnificent tomb.

Mauve (*au=aw* or *ō*) [L. *malva*, a mallow], delicate purple. [thrush.

Ma′vis (*a=ai*) [F. *mauvis*, a mavis], song-

Maw [Com. Teut. ; O.E. *maga*], stomach.

Mawk′ish [O.N. *mathkr* ; Dan. *madike*, a maggot], of faint sickly flavour, weakly sentimental.

Max-il′la-ry [L. *maxilla*, the jaw-bone], relating to the jaw-bone.

Max′im [L. *maxima* (adj., fem.), greatest], rule or precept.

Max′im [fr. Sir H. *Maxim*, inventor], single-barrelled machine-gun.

Max′i-mum [L. *neut.* of *maximus*, greatest], greatest degree or quantity.

May [F. *mai* ; L. *maius*, etym. doubtful], the fifth month (Rom. third), hawthorn plant and blossoms.

May'or [F. *maire*, mayor ; L. *major*, greater], chief magistrate of a city or borough.

May'or-al-ty, mayor's period of office.

Maze [?], network of paths, bewilderment.

Mead [O.E. *mæd*], meadow.

Mead [Com. Teut. ; O.E. *meodu*], fermented drink of honey and water.

Mead'ow [O.E. *mædwe*, dative of *mæd*, a mead], tract of low land under grass.

Mea'gre [F. *maigre* ; L. *macer*, lean], thin, scanty. [repast.

Meal [O.E. *mæl*, a stated time, a meal].

Meal [O.E. *melo*, meal ; Teut. *malan*, to grind; cogn. with L. *mola*, mill], grain (usu. exc. wheat) ground to powder.

Meal'ies [Cape Du. *milje*, from Port. *milho*, millet], name for maize in S. Africa.

Mean[1] [O.E. *mænan*], intend, signify.

Mean[2] [O.F. *meien* ; L. *mediānus*, mean, *medius*, middle], middle point or part, middle ; intermediate in size, quality, time, etc.

Mean[3] [O.E. *gemǽne*, common], low, stingy.

Means [see **Mean**[2]], agency, income.

Me-an'der [L. *Mœander* ; Gk. *Maiandros*, river in Phrygia], wind and turn.

Mea'sles (*s=z*) [M.E. *maseles* ; cf. O.H.G. *masala*, a spot], feverish disease with a rash.

Mea'sure (*eas=ēzh*) [F. *mesure*, measure ; L. *metiri* (p.p. *mensus*), to measure], standard, extent or quantity, means to an end, grouping of beats in music, stately dance ; ascertain extent, etc., by a rule or standard. **Meas'urement**.

Meat [O.E. *mete*], animal flesh used as food.

Me-chan'ic (*ch=k*) [Gk. *mēchanē*, a machine], artisan.

Me-chan'ic-al, pertaining to machinery, done as if by a machine, pertaining to mechanics.

Me-chan'ics, science which treats of the action of forces on bodies.

Mech'an-ism, structure of a machine.

Med'al [F. *médaille*, medal ; L. *metallum*, metal], coin-like piece of metal with a device to commemorate an event, etc.

Me-dal'lion [F. *médaillon* ; see **Medal**], large medal, circular decoration.

Med'al-ist, Med'al-list, one skilled in medals, one who has gained a medal.

Med'dle [O.F. *medler, mesler*, to mix ; L. *miscēre*, to mix], interfere improperly.

Me-di-æ'val, Me-di-e'val (*æ* and *e=ee*) [L. *medius*, the middle, *œvum*, an age], pertaining to the Middle Ages

Me'di-al, in the middle, average.

Me'di-a-tor [L. *medius*, the middle], one who intercedes.

Med'ic-al [L. *medicus*, a physician], relating to the curing of disease.

Me-dic'a-ment [L. *medicus*, a physician] healing application.

Med'i-cine [L. *medicīna*, medicine, *medicus*, a physician], science of health preservation and restoration, remedy, drug. **Medic'inal**.

Me'di-o-cre (*ō*) [L. *medius*, the middle], middling, ordinary. **Medioc'rity**.

Med'i-tate [L. *meditāri* (p.p. *meditatus*), to meditate], think seriously, plan. **Medita'-tion**.

Me'di-um [L. *medium*, neut. of *medius*, middle], middle place or degree, means, transmission, person supposed to be in communication with spirits.

Med'lar [O.F. *medler* ; Gk. *mespilon*, a medlar], tree and its apple-like fruit.

Med'ley [O.F. *medlee*, p.p. of *medler*, to mix], mixture, jumble.

Me-dul'la-ry [L. *medulla*, marrow], consisting of or like marrow.

Meed [O.F. *mēd* ; cogn. with Gk. *misthos* ; Skr. *mīdhá*, prize, reward], reward. [ing.

Meek [O.N. *miúkr*, meek, soft], gentle, yield-

Meer'schaum [Ger. *meerschaum* ; *meer*, sea, *schaum*, foam], white claylike mineral.

Meet [O.E., *mētan*, to meet], to come up to, to assemble, to agree ; an assembling of huntsmen. [(adj.).

Meet [M.E. *mēte*, prob. fr. O.E. *gemǽte*], fit

Meg-al-ith'ic [Gk. *megas*, great, *lithos*, stone], constructed of large stones.

Meg-al-o-ma'ni-a [Gk. *megas* (fem. *megate*), great, and **Mania**], insanity of egoism, passion for big things.

Meg'a-phone [Gk. *megas*, great, and *phōnē*, sound, voice], instrument for carrying sound to a great distance.

Me'grim [F. *migraine* ; Gk. *hemikrānia*, megrim ; *hemi*, half, *cranion*, a skull], kind of sick headache, whim, (*pl.*) low spirits.

Mel'an-chol-y (*ŏ, ch=k*) [Gk. *melas*, black, *cholē*, bile], depression of spirits. **Melan-cho'lia**. [fight.

Mê'lée (*mailai*) [F. ; see **Medley**], confused

Mel-lif'lu-ous [L. *mel* (*mell-is*), honey, *fluere*, to flow], flowing sweetly. **Melli'fluence**.

Mel'low [perh. O.E. *melo*, dat. of *melu*, meal], soft ; soften.

Mel'o-dra-ma, Mel-o-dra'ma [Gk. *melos*, a song, *drama*, a drama], kind of sensational play. **Melodrama'tic**.

Mel'o-dy [Gk. *melos*, a song ; *ōde*, a song, ode], sounds in agreeable succession, tune. **Melo'dious**.

Mel'on [Gk. *melon*, an apple], large fruit of the cucumber kind.

Melt [O.E. *meltan* (intr.), *mieltan* (tr.) ; cf. O.N. *melta*, to digest], turn from solid to liquid.

Mem'ber [L. *membrum*, a limb], limb, part of a whole, one of a church or society.

Mem'brane [L. *membrāna*, a skin], thin tissue.

Me-men'to [L. *mementō*, imper. of *meminisse*, to remember], token to awaken memory.

Mem'oir [F. *mémoire*, memory ; L. *memor*, mindful], account of events as they are remembered by the writer, biography.

Mem'or-a-ble [L. *memor*, mindful], worthy to be remembered. **Memorabil'ity**.

Mem-o-ran'dum (*pl.* **-da, -dums**) [L. *memorare*, to bring to mind], note to help memory.

Me-mo'ri-al, something to preserve remembrance, petition or written representation.

Mem'o-ry [L. *memor*, mindful], faculty which retains previous knowledge. **Mem'orize.**

Men'ace [L. *minax* (*mināc-is*), threatening, projecting], threat; threaten.

Men-a'ger-ie [F. *ménagerie*, menagerie, *ménage*, a household], wild beast show.

Mend [short for **Amend**], repair, improve.

Men-da'cious (*ci=sh*) [L. *mendax* (*mendāc-is*), false], lying. **Menda'city.**

Men'di-cant [L. *mendicus*, a beggar], beggar.

Me'ni-al [O.F. *mesnie*, a household], disparaging name for a domestic servant; servile.

Men-su-ra'tion [L. *mensūra*, a measure], process of measuring. **Men'surable.**

Men'tal [L. *mens* (*ment-is*), the mind], relating to the mind. **Mental'ity.**

Men'thol [L. *mentha*, mint, *oleum*, oil], crystalline drug.

Men'tion [L. *mentio* (*mentiōn-is*), mention], speak shortly of; a notice.

Men'tor [Gk. *Mentor*, the adviser of *Telemachus*], wise adviser.

Men'u [F. *menu*, a menu; L. *minutus*, small], bill of fare.

Me-phit'ic [L. *mephītis*, a poisonous stench], poisonous, offensive to the smell. [trade.

Mer'can-tile [see **Merchant**], having to do with

Mer'ce-na-ry [L. *mercēs* (*mercēd-is*), a reward], paid, hired, greedy of gain; soldier hired into foreign service.

Mer'cer [L. *merx* (*merc-is*), merchandise], dealer in textiles.

Mer'cer-ize [fr. J. *Mercer*, patentee], prepare cotton for dyeing by treating with chemicals.

Mer'chan-dise (*s=z*) [see **Merchant**], objects of commerce, goods.

Mer'chant [L. *mercāri* (pr.p. *mercans*, *-antis*), to trade], one who trades on a large scale.

Mer'chant-man, trading vessel.

Mer'ci-ful, full of mercy, tender.

Mer-cu'ri-al, sprightly and changeable.

Mer'cu-ry [L. *Mercurius*, the god of traffic], quicksilver, a liquid metal.

Mer'cy [L. *merces*, a reward], willingness to spare or to help.

Mere [1] [O.F.; cogn. with L. *mare*, fr. O. Teut. *mari*, sea], lake. [more.

Mere [2] [L. *merus*, unmixed], such and no

Mer'e-tri'cious (*ici=ish*) [L. *meretrīcius*; *meretri*, to earn], gaudy, tawdry.

Merge [L. *mergere*, to dip], sink, absorb.

Me-rid'i-an [L. *merīdiēs*, noon; *medius*, the middle, *dies*, a day], mid-day, an imaginary circle passing through the poles of a globe.

Me-ri'no (*i=ee*) [Sp. *merino*, roving from pasture to pasture; L. *mājōrīnus*, of a larger kind; *major*, greater], kind of sheep with fine wool, stuff made from the wool.

Mer'it [L. *merēri* (p.p. *meritus*), to deserve], desert, esp. in a good sense; deserve.

Mer-i-to'ri-ous, deserving reward or honour.

Mer'maid [**Mere** [1] and **Maid**], imaginary creature half woman, half fish.

Mer'ri-ment, gaiety with laughter.

Mer'ry [O.E. *myr(i)ge*, prob. fr. O. Teut. *murgjo*, short], joyous, gay and noisy.

Mer'ry-thought, forked bone of a fowl's breast.

Mesh [cogn. with O.E. *max*, net; etym. dub.], space between threads of a net; to engage (of teeth of a wheel).

Mes'mer-ism [fr. F. A. *Mesmer*, an Austrian doctor], doctrine of extraordinary control of one will over another.

Mess [O.F. *mes*, mess; L. *mīttere* (p.p. *missus*, to send), food for one meal, number of persons who eat together, muddle; take meals.

Mes'sage [F. *message*, message; L. *mīttere* (p.p. *missus*), to send], sent notice or communication.

Mes'sen-ger [F. *messager*; see **Message**], one who bears a message.

Mess'mate, one of the same mess.

Mes'suage (*u=w*) [A.F. *mesuage*, a manorhouse; L. *mansio*, a mansion], house with out-buildings.

Met'al [Gk. *metallon*, a mine], hard fusible substance, broken stone for roads; to put stone on road.

Met-al'lic, pertaining to or like metal.

Met'al-lur-gy, Met-al'lur-gy [Gk. *metallon*, metal; *ergon*, work], art of working metals.

Met-a-mor'phic [see **Metamor'phosis**], subject to change of structure.

Met-a-mor'pho-sis [Gk. *meta*, change, *morphē*, form], change of form.

Met'a-phor [Gk. *meta*, change, *pherein*, to bear], figure of speech by which one thing is put for another which it resembles. **Metaphor'ical.**

Met'a-phrase [Gk. *metaphrasis*; *meta*, change, and *phrasis*, phrase], word for word translation.

Met-a-phys'ics (*s=z*) [Gk. *meta ta physica*, after the physics; see **Physics**], science of abstract being, mental philosophy. **Metaphys'ical.**

Mete [Com. Teut.; O.E. *metan*], to measure.

Me-tem-psy-cho'sis (*ch=k*) [Gk. *meta*, change, *em* (*en*), in, *psychē*, the soul], transmigration of souls.

Me'te-or [Gk. *meteoros*, soaring in air; *meta*, among, and *aeirein*, to raise], aerolite, shooting star.

Me-te-or'ic, brilliant and transient.

Me'te-or-ite, fallen meteor.

Me-te-or-ol'o-gy [**Meteor** and Gk. *logos*, discourse], science which treats of atmospheric phenomena, esp. as regards weather and climate. [instrument.

Me'ter [O.E. *metan*, to measure], measuring

Meth'od [Gk. *meta*, after, *hodos*, a way], regular way, manner, order. **Meth'odize.**

Me-thod'ic-al, orderly.

Meth'o-dist [see **Method**], person belonging to one of the religious bodies founded by the Wesleys and Whitefield.

Meth'yl [Gk. *methu*, wine, and *hylē*, wood], base of wood-spirit, etc.

Meth'y-late, mix with methyl, as methylated spirit.

Me-ti'cul-ous [L. *meticulosus*, fr. *metus*, fear], over-scrupulous about minute details.

Me-ton'y-my [Gk. *meta*, change, *onoma*, a name], figure by which a part or attribute of a thing is put for the whole.

Me'tre [Gk. *metron*, a measure], rhythm, measure, measure of length=39·37 inches.

Met'ric, pertaining to the decimal system of measures.

Met'ric-al, composed in metre or verse.

Met'ro-nome [**Metre** and Gk. *nomos*, law], instrument to measure time in music.

Me-trop'o-lis [Gk. *mēter*, a mother, *polis*, a city], chief city. **Metropol'itan**.

Met'tle [var. of **Metal**], spirit.

Mew [O.E. *mœw*; cf. Ger. *mōwe*], gull.

Mew [F. *mue*, a cage for hawks], inclosure, stables; to shut up.

Mew [imit.], cry as a cat.

Mez'zo-so-pra'no (*zz=dz*) [It. *mezzo*, half, and **Soprano**], voice of compass between contralto and soprano, part for such a voice, singer possessing such a voice.

Mez'zo-tint (*zz=dz*) [It. *mezzo*, half; *tinto*, tint], kind of engraving in which lights and half-lights are produced by scraping a roughened surface.

Mi-as'ma [Gk. *miasma*, a stain, *mianein*, to stain], infected air, malaria.

Mi'ca [L. *mīca*, a crumb], mineral composed of scales.

Mi'crobe [Gk. *micros*, small; *bios*, life], tiny organism, a germ.

Mi'cro-cosm [Gk. *micros*, small, *cosmos*, world], man viewed as an epitome of the universe, miniature representation.

Mi'cro-scope [Gk. *micros*, small; *scopein*, to see], instrument through which we see minute objects enlarged.

Mi-cro-scop'ic, very minute.

Mid'dle [O.E. *middel*, *midd*, middle, and *dǣl*, part], part equally distant from the extremities.

Mid'dling, of middle rank, state, etc.

Midge [O.E. *mycg*], small gnat-like fly.

Mid'night [**Mid** and **Night**], twelve o'clock at night.

Mid'riff [O.E. *midd*, middle, *hrif*, the belly], diaphragm (q.v.). [officer.

Mid'ship-man [*mid* for *amid*], junior naval

Midst [O.E. *midd*, middle], middle; in the middle of.

Mid'wife [O.E. *midd*, and **Wife**], woman who assists other women in childbirth. **Midwif'ery**.

Mien (*ie=ee*) [F. *mine*, expression, etym. doubtful], aspect, air, bearing.

Might [O.E. *miht*, fr. O. Teut. root, *mag*, to be able], force, power. **Might'y**.

Mignonette (*min-yon-et'*) [F. *mignonette*, dim. of *mignon*, darling], fragrant plant.

Mi-graine', see **Megrim** (first sense).

Mi'grate [L. *migrāre* (p.p. *migrātus*), to wander], remove to another region. **Migra'tion**.

Mi'grant, **Mi'gra-to-ry**, removing regularly.

Mi-ka'do [Jap. *mi*, august; *kado*, door], sovereign of Japan.

Milch [as **Milk**], giving milk. **Milch-cow**.

Mild [Com. Teut.; O.E. *milde*], gentle, soft, kind.

Mil'dew [O.E. *meledéaw*; *mele*, honey, *déaw*, dew], whitish fungus growth; cover with mildew.

Mile [L. *mille*, a thousand whence *mille* (pl. *millia*), *passuum*, a thousand paces, a Roman mile], measure of distance (in Britain=1760 yards).

Mile'age, **Mil'age**, distance in miles, expense at fixed rate per mile.

Mil'foil [L. *mille*, a thousand, *folium*, a leaf], plant with finely dissected leaves, yarrow.

Mil'i-tant, engaged in warfare (literal or figurative), fighting.

Mil'i-ta-ry [L. *mīles* (*mīlit-is*), a soldier], relating to soldiers; soldiers. **Mil'i-tarism**.

Mil'i-tate [L. *mīles* (*mīlit-is*), a soldier], make war, fight, be an influence (against).

Mi-li'tia (*ti=sh*) [see **Militate**], (formerly) soldiers not organised permanently in peace, a citizen army.

Milk [Com. Teut.; O. Mercian, *milc*; O.N. *miolk*], white fluid from cow, goat, etc.; draw milk from.

Milk'sop, man or youth lacking in natural spirit.

Mill [Late L. *molīna*, extended fr. *mola*, a mill], machine for grinding, building containing machinery; grind, stamp, shape, as metal, by a rotary cutter.

Mill [L. *mille*, a thousand], thousandth part of a dollar (U.S.). [pasteboard.

Mill'board [**Mill** and **Board**], kind of stout

Mill'dam, dam to raise water high enough to turn a mill.

Mil-len'ni-um [L. *mille*, a thousand; *annus*, a year], thousand years, Christ's reign on earth, ideal state of society. **Millen'nial**.

Mill'er, one who keeps or works in a flourmill.

Mil'let [F. *millet*, dim. of *mil*; L. *milium*, millet], kind of grain native of India.

Mil'li-ard [L. *mille*, thousand], thousand millions.

Mil'li-ner [fr. *Milan* in Italy], one who makes and trims women's hats. **Mil'linery**.

Mil'lion (*io=yo*) [F. fr. L. *mille*, a thousand +augment. suff.], thousand thousand.

Mil'lion-aire' [F.], owner of a million pounds, dollars, francs, etc., very rich man.

Mime [Gk. *mimos*, a mime], ancient drama marked by mimicry, actor in such a drama. **Mimet'ic**.

Mim'ic [Gk. *mimos*, an actor], imitative; one who imitates for sport; imitate for sport. **Mim'icry**.

Mi-mo'sa (*s=z*) [fr. **Mime**, and suf. *-osa=ose*, fr. L. *osus*, abounding in], kind of podded plant.

Min'ar-et [Arab. *manārat*; from root of *nār*, fire], tall turret near a mosque.

E *

Min′a-to-ry [L. *mināri* (p.p. *minātus*), to threaten], threatening.

Mince [Late L. *minutia*, a small piece], chop fine, walk or talk primly ; minced meat, etc. **Min′cingly.**

Mind [O.E. *gemynd* ; M.E. *mynd*, fr. O. Teut. root, *men*, *man*, to think ; cogn. with L. *mens*, mind ; Gk. *menos*, rage], that in man which feels, reasons, and judges, inclination, memory ; to heed.

Mine [F. *mine*; etym. doubtful], pit from which ores, coal, etc., are dug, a hollow for explosives ; dig a mine. [substance.

Min′er-al [M.L. *minera*, a mine], inorganic

Min-er-al′o-gy, science of minerals.

Min′gle [M.E. *mengel*, fr. O.E. *mengan*, to mix], mix.

Min′i-a-ture [It. *miniatura*, miniature ; L. *miniare* (p.p. *miniato*) to colour with red lead ; L. *minium*, red lead], very small ; very small portrait.

Min′im [L. *minimus*, smallest], small liquid measure, time note in music.

Min′i-mize, make the least of.

Min′i-mum [L. neut. of *minimus*, least], least quantity possible.

Min′ion (*io=yo*) [F. *mignon*, a darling], favourite, fawning dependent or agent.

Min′is-ter [L. *minister*, a servant], servant, agent, clergyman, government member ; serve, contribute.

Min-is-te′ri-al, official, priestly.

Min-is-tra′tion, service.

Min′is-try, service, office of a minister, ministers of state as a body.

Mink [cf. Swed. *menk*, mink], animal of the weasel kind.

Min′now [O.E. *myne*, a minnow], small fish.

Mi′nor [L. *minor*, less], less ; one under 21 years of age.

Mi-nor′i-ty (*mǐ* or *mī*) [see Minor], the state of being under age, smaller number.

Min′ster [O.E. *mynster*, minister ; see **Monastery**], great church (esp. of a monastery).

Min′strel [O.F. *menestral*, a minstrel ; Late L. *ministeriālis*, a servant ; see **Minister**], singer and harper, poet. **Min′strelsy.**

Mint [O.E. *minte* ; L. *menta* ; Gk. *minthe*, mint], fragrant plant.

Mint [O.E. *mynet*, a mint ;. L. *monēta*, money], coining place ; make (coin).

Min′u-end [L. *minuere*, to lessen], number from which another is to be subtracted.

Min′u-et [F. *menuet*, dim. of F. *menu*, small], slow graceful dance.

Mi′nus [L. *minus*, neut. of *minor*, less], symbol (−), indicating subtraction ; less, excepting.

Min′ute[1] (*ute=ĭt*) [L. *minūta*, fem. of *minūtus*, small], 60 seconds, a record, memorandum ; make a record.

Mi-nute′ [2] (ĭ or ī) [L. *minūtus*, orig. p.p. of *minuere*, to lessen], very small.

Mi-nu′ti-a (*pl.* **Minutiæ**) (*t=sh*) [see **Minute** [2]], very small particular.

Minx [?], pert girl.

Mir′a-cle [L. *miraculum*, miracle ; *mirārī*, to wonder at, *mirus*, wonderful], a wonder, supernatural event. **Mirac′ulous.**

Mi-rage′ (*age=äzh*) [F. *mirage*, mirage ; *mirer*, to be reflected ; L. *mirāri*, to wonder at], optical illusion due to refraction.

Mire [O.N. *mýrr*, mire], deep mud.

Mir′ror [L. *mirāri*, to wonder at, to behold], looking-glass ; reflect.

Mirth [O.E. *myr(i)gth*, cogn. with **Merry**], joy and laughter. **Mirth′ful.**

Mis as a prefix, meaning wrong, unfavourable, before nouns, and wrongly, badly, before verbs, is used in the following words :—**Mis-ap-ply′**, **Mis-ap-pre-hend′**, **Mis-ap-pro′pri-ate**, **Mis-be-have′**, **Mis-be-lief′**, **Mis′be-lieve′**, **Mis-cal′cu-late**, **Mis-call′**, **Mis-chance′**, **Mis-con-ceive′**, **Mis-con-cep′tion**, **Mis-con′duct**, **Mis-con-struc′-tion**, **Mis-con-strue′**, **Mis-deed′**, **Mis-di-rect′**, **Mis-em-ploy′**, **Mis-for′tune**, **Mis-guide′**, **Mis-han′dle**, **Mis-hap′**, **Mis-in-form′**, **Mis-in-ter′pret**, **Mis-judge′**, **Mis-lead′**, **Mis-man′-age**, **Mis-name′**, **Mis-place′**, **Mis-print′**, **Mis-pro-nounce′**, **Mis-rep-re-sent′**, **Mis-rule′**, **Mis-sha′pen**, **Mis-spell′**, **Mis-spend′**, **Mis-state′**, **Mis-un-der-stand′**, **Mis-use′**.

Mis-ad-ven′ture [*mis-*, unfavourable, and **Adventure**], accident, misfortune.

Mis′an-thrope [Gk. *misein*, to hate, *anthropos*, man], hater of mankind. **Misan′thropy.**

Mis-car′ry [*mis-*, wrongly, and **Carry**], fail of effect. **Miscar′riage.**

Mis-cel-la′ne-ous [L. *miscellus*, mixed, *miscēre*, to mix], mixed.

Mis-cel′la-ny, collection of various kinds of compositions.

Mis′chief [*mis-*, bad, and **Chief**], harm, trouble caused by folly or perversity.

Mis′chiev-ous, harmful, fond of mischief.

Mis′cre-ant [*mis-*, wrongly, L. *crēdere* (pr.p. *crēdens*, -*entis*), to believe], unscrupulous scoundrel.

Mis-de-mean′our [*mis-*, wrong ; see **De-meanour**], evil conduct, fault. **Misde-mean′ant.**

Mi′ser (*s=z*) [L. *miser*, wretched], mean person who hoards money.

Mis′er-y (*s=z*) [L. *miser*, wretched], great unhappiness. **Mis′erable.**

Mis-giv′ing [pref. *mis-*, unfavourable ; see **Give**], doubt, distrust.

Mis-hap′ [*mis-*, unfavourable ; O.N. *happ*, luck], unlucky accident.

Mis-lay′ [*mis-*, wrongly ; see **Lay**], lay on a place not remembered.

Mis-no′mer [*mis-*, wrongly, L. *nomen*, a name], inappropriate name.

Mis-og′a-mist [Gk. *misein*, to hate, *gamos*, marriage], hater of marriage.

Mis-og′y-nist (*g=j*) [Gk. *misein*, to hate, *gynē*, a woman], woman-hater.

Mis-print′ [*mis-*, wrong, and **Print**], mistake in printing.

Mis-pri′sion (*sion=zhn*) [pref. *mis-*, wrongly ; see **Prize**], culpable neglect regarding the crime or intended crime of another.

Miss [contr. of *mistress*], title of an unmarried woman.

Miss [O.E. *missan*, to miss], failure to hit, to get, etc.; fail of getting, reaching, etc., feel the want of.

Mis'sal [Late L. *missale*, a mass-book; *missa*, mass], mass-book.

Mis'sile [L. *mittere* (p.p. *missus*), to send], weapon for throwing; capable of being thrown.

Mis'sion [L. *mittere* (p.p. *missus*), to send], errand, persons sent, station of missionaries.

Mis'sion-a-ry, one sent to spread religion.

Mis'sive [L. *mittere* (p.p. *missus*), to send], writing containing a message, official letter.

Mist [O.E. *mist*; perh. fr. O.T. *mihstoz*], visible watery vapour. **Mist'y**.

Mis-take' [*mis-*, wrongly; see **Take**], take in a wrong sense, misjudge; a blunder.

Mis'ter [see **Master**], title of courtesy (contracted to Mr) prefixed to surname of a man.

Mis'tle-toe [O.E. *mistiltán, mistil*, mistletoe, *tán*, a twig], parasitic plant.

Mis'tress [O.F. *maistresse*; see **Master**], woman having power, title of courtesy (contracted to Mrs) to a married woman.

Mis-trust' [*mis-*, unfavourable; see **Trust**], suspicion; to doubt.

Mite [M.Du. *mijt*, mite, a very small coin, a bit cut off], anything very small, small coin now out of use, small insect in cheese.

Mit'i-gate [L. *mitigāre* (p.p. *mitigātus*), to mitigate, *mitis*, mild], soften, lessen.

Mi'tre [Gk. *mitra*, a girdle, a turban], kind of cap worn by bishops.

Mit'ten, Mitt [F. *mitaine*, mitten; etym. doubtful], covering for the hand.

Mix [L. *mixtus*, p.p. of *miscēre*, to mix], unite or blend into one.

Mix'ture, that which results from mixing.

Miz'en, Miz'zen [It. *mezzana*, mizen; L. *medius*, middle], hindmost, nearest the stern.

*M*ne-mon'ics [Gk. *mnēmōn*, mindful], system of rules to assist the memory.

Moan [perh. cogn. with O.E. *mǽnan*, to intend; etym. dub.], make a dull sound of pain; low long painful sound.

Moat [O.F. *mote*, a mound, a trench; etym. doubtful], trench round a castle.

Mob [contr. of L. *mobile vulgus*, an easily moved crowd], disorderly crowd; attack in a crowd.

Mo'bile [L. *mobilis*, mobile, *movere*, to move], movable, easily moved, changing in expression. **Mobil'ity**.

Mo'bil-ize [see **Mobile**], put (troops) in a state of readiness for war. **Mobiliza'tion**.

Moc'ca-sin [N. Amer. Ind., *mockasin*], American Indian shoe of soft leather.

Mock [O.F. *mocquer*, to mock; etym. doubtful], mimic in sport, disappoint.

Mod (Gael.), assembly, meeting.

Mode [L. *modus*, measure, manner], manner, fashion. **Mod'ish**.

Mod'el [It. *modello*, model; L. *modulus*, dim. of *modus*, a measure], pattern, copy; shape from a plastic material; perfect of its kind.

Mod'er-ate [L. *moderāri* (p.p. *moderātus*), to moderate, *modus*, a measure], within bounds, not extreme; keep within bounds, lessen. **Modera'tion**.

Mod'er-a-tor, presiding officer or clergyman, esp. in Presbyterian church courts.

Mod'ern [L. *modernus*, modern, *modo*, just now], relating to the present or recent times. **Mod'ernize**.

Mod'est [L. *modestus*, modest, *modus*, a measure], not bold or self-assertive. **Mod'esty**.

Mod'i-cum [L. *modicus*, moderate; *modus*, a measure], small quantity.

Mod'i-fy [L. *modus*, a measure, *facere*, to make], change somewhat, tone down. **Modifica'tion**.

Mod'u-late [L. *modulus*, dim. of *modus*, a measure], vary in a musical manner, pass from one key to another. **Modula'tion**.

Mo'hair [Arab. *mukhayyar*, a coarse haircloth], fabric made from the hair of the Angora goat.

Mo-ham'med-an [fr. Arab. *Muhammad*, founder of Moslem religion], belonging to Mohammed or to his religion.

Moi'e-ty [F. *moitié*, a half; L. *medius*, the middle], half, small part.

Moil [O.F. *moillier*, to moisten, paddle in mud; L. *mollis*, soft], drudge (*toil* and *m.*).

Moire (*mwahr*) [perh. conn. with **Mohair**], kind of silk with watered appearance.

Moist [O.F. *moiste*; etym. dub.], damp. **Mois'ten**.

Mois'ture, that which makes damp.

Mo'lar [L. *mola*, a millstone], grinding.

Mo-las'ses [Port. *melaço*, molasses; L. *mellāceus*, made with honey, *mel*, honey], treacle.

Mole [O.E. *mál*], dark spot on the skin.

Mole [M.E. *mulle, molle*; cf. M. Du. *mol*], burrowing animal. [masonry.

Mole [L. *mōlēs*, a heap], breakwater of

Mol'e-cule [formerly *molecula*; dim. of L. *mōlēs*, a heap], minute particle of matter.

Mo-lest' [L. *molestus*, troublesome], annoy, harass. **Molesta'tion**.

Mol'li-fy [L. *mollis*, soft, *facere*, to make], soften. **Mollifica'tion**.

Mol'lusc, Mol'lusk [L. *mollusca*, a soft kind of nut, *mollis*, soft], one of a large class of hard-shelled animals with soft bodies.

Molt'en (*ō*) [old p.p. of **Melt**], melted, made of metal that has been melted.

Mo'ment [L. *movēre*, to move], point of time, force, importance. **Mo'mently**.

Mo'men-ta-ry, lasting a very short time.

Mo-men'tous [see **Moment**], very important, weighty.

Mo-men'tum [doublet of **Moment**], force of a moving body.

Mon'ad [Gk. *monas* (*monad-os*), a monad; *monos*, alone], unit, ultimate unit of being.

Mon′arch (*ch*=*k*) [Gk. *monos*, alone, *archein*, to rule], sole chief ruler. **Monar′chical.**

Mon′arch-y, state under a monarch, system in which the chief ruler is a monarch.

Mon′as-ter-y [Gk. *monastērion* ; *monazein*, to live alone ; *monos*, alone], house for monks.

Mo-nas′tic [Gk. *monastikos*, living alone ; *monos*, alone], relating to monks or monasteries. **Monas′ticism.**

Mon′day [O.E. *monandæg*, day of the moon], second day of the week.

Mon′e-ta-ry, relating to money.

Mon′ey (*o*=*ŭ*) [L. *monēta*, a mint, money], stamped metal used as a medium of exchange, wealth. ● **Mon′eyed.**

Mon′ger (*o*=*ŭ*) [L. *mango*, a dealer], dealer.

Mon′goose, Mun′goose [Marathi, *mangus*], animal common in India, able to kill venomous snakes.

Mon′grel [*o*=*ŭ*] [perh. fr. root *meng*, *mang*, *mong* (see **Mingle**), and *rel*, dim. suf. showing contempt], anything of mixed breed.

Mo-ni′tion [L. *monēre* (p.p. *monitus*), to warn], a warning. **Mon′itory.**

Mon′i-tor, one who warns or gives advice, senior pupil in a school having special duties, war vessel.

Monk (*o*=*ŭ*) [Gk. *monachos*, solitary, *monos*, alone], one of a community of men living in a monastery. [*man.*

Mon′key (*o*=*ŭ*) [?], animal closely allied to **Monks′hood,** poisonous plant, aconite.

Mon′o-chrome (*ch*=*k*) [Gk. *monos*, alone, *chroma*, colour], painting executed in different tints of one colour.

Mon′o-cle [Gk. *monos*, sole ; L. *oculus*, an eye], single eyeglass.

Mon′od-y [Gk. *monos*, alone, *aoid*, song], ode bewailing some one's death.

Mo-nog′a-my [Gk. *monos*, sole, *gamos*, marriage], marriage with one person. **Mono′gamous.**

Mon′o-gram [Gk. *monos*, sole ; *gramma*, a letter], character composed of two or more letters interwoven.

Mon′o-graph [Gk. *monos*, alone, *graphein*, to write], treatise on a limited subject.

Mon′o-lith [Gk. *monos*, alone, *lithos*, a stone], single large stone esp. shaped into a pillar.

Mon′o-logue [Gk. *monos*, alone, *logos*, speech], uninterrupted speech in company or alone by one person.

Mon-o-ma′ni-a [Gk. *monos*, alone, *mania*, madness], mental derangement on one subject.

Mon-o-met′al-lism [Gk. *monos*, alone, and **Metal**], system of currency based on one metal.

Mon′o-plane [Gk. *monos*, alone, and **Plane**], aeroplane with one plane.

Mon-op′o-lize, engross the whole of.

Mon-op′o-ly [Gk. *monos*, alone, *poleein*, to sell], exclusive right or possession.

Mon-o-syl′la-ble [Gk. *monos*, alone, *syllabē*, a syllable], word of one syllable.

Mon-o-the′ism [Gk. *monos*, alone, *theos*, God], belief in one god. **Monotheis′tic.**

Mon′o-tone [Gk. *monos*, single, *tonos*, tone], single unvaried tone. **Mono′tonous.**

Mon-ot′o-ny, irksome sameness.

Mon-soon′ [Malay *mūsim* ; Arab. *mausim*, a season], seasonal winds of eastern tropics.

Mon′ster, Mon-stros′i-ty [L. *monstrum*, a portent, *monēre*, to warn], something of unnatural size, shape, or quality.

Mon′strous, unnatural in size, appearance, etc., horrible.

Month (*o*=*ŭ*) [Com. Teut. ; O.E. *mónath*; cogn. with **Moon**], one of twelve divisions of the year.

Mon′u-ment [L. *monēre*, to remind], something which stands or remains as a memorial. **Monument′al.**

Mood [Com. Teut. ; O.E. *mōd* ; cf. Ger. *mut*], state of mind, manner of expressing action or being as positive, possible, etc.

Mood′y, subject to varying moods, gloomy.

Moon [Com. Teut. ; O.E. *mōna* ; cogn. with Gk. *men*, L. *mensis*, month], body which revolves round the earth or other member of the solar system ; move listlessly.

Moor [O.E. *mór* ; O.N. *mœr-r*], waste land with patches of heath.

Moor [M. Du. *māren*, to moor], fix or secure as a vessel.

Moor [F. *more*, fr. L. *maurus* ; Gk. *mauros*, a native of ancient Mauretania in N. Africa], one of a Mohammedan people of N.W. Africa. [*moored.*

Moor′ings, anchor, etc., by which a ship is

Moose [N. Amer. Ind. *moos*, moose], American elk.

Moot [O.E. *mótian*, to discuss, *mót*, a meeting], propose for discussion ; open to argument, undecided.

Mop [L. *mappa*, a napkin], quantity of yarn on a handle ; rub or wipe as with a mop.

Mope [?], be dull and spiritless.

Mo-raine′ [F. *moraine*, a moraine ; cf. Bavarian *mur*, sand and broken stones], deposit of earth, etc., from a glacier.

Mor′al [L. *mōs* (*mōr-is*), a custom], relating to right and wrong ; inner meaning ; (*pl.*) general conduct. **Mor′alist.**

Mor-ale′ [F.], attitude regarding discipline, danger, etc.

Mo-ral′i-ty, doctrine of moral duties, virtue.

Mor′al-ize, draw moral lessons.

Mo-rass′ [M.Du. *marasch*, a marsh], marsh.

Mor′bid [L. *morbus*, disease, *mori*, to die], diseased. **Morbid′ity.**

Mor′dant [L. *mordēre*, to bite], biting, caustic ; a fixing substance used in dyeing.

Mo-reen′ [?], a strong woollen or woollen and cotton material.

Mor-gan-at′ic [perh. fr. M.L. *morganaticum*, morning-gift], (marriage) between prince and woman of lower rank, whose children cannot succeed their father.

Mor′i-bund [L. *mori*, to die], dying.

Morn, Morn′ing [Com. Teut. ; O.E. *morgen*], first part of the day.

Mo-roc′co [fr. *Morocco*, in W. Africa], kind of fine leather.

Mo-rose′ [L. *mōs* (*mōris*), manner], sullen, ill-humoured. **Morose′ness.**

Mor′phi-a, Mor′phine [Gk. *Morpheūs*, the god of sleep], drug obtained from opium.

Mor-phol′o-gy [Gk. *morphē*, form, *logos*, discourse], study of forms of living organisms, or of words.

Mor′ris, Mor′rice [Sp. *Morisco*, Moorish], rustic dance.

Mor′row [M.E. *morwe*, *moru*, fr. *morwen*, morn], the next following day.

Morse [fr. inventor, *Morse*], telegraphic and signalling code or alphabet.

Mor′sel [L. *mordēre* (p.p. *morsus*), to bite], little piece, bite of food.

Mor′tal [L. *mors* (*mort-is*), death], subject to death, deadly ; one who is subject to death, human being.

Mor-tal′i-ty, state of being mortal, death-rate.

Mor′tar [L. *mortārium*, a mortar], vessel in which substances are pounded, short cannon for firing shell at a high angle, cement of lime and sand.

Mort′gage [O.F. *mortgage*, lit. dead pledge, fr. *mort*, dead, *gage*, a pledge], contract pledging property as security for debt.

Mor-ti-fi-ca′tion, death of part of a body, humiliation, vexation, (in Scots law) land given for religious, charitable, or public uses.

Mor′ti-fy [L. *mors* (*mort-is*), death, *facere*, to make], deaden, humble.

Mor′tise [F. *mortaise*; etym. doubtful], hole in a piece of timber cut to receive the end of another part.

Mor′tu-ar-y [L. *mortuarius*, *mortuus*, dead], building in which dead bodies are kept for a time.

Mo-sa′ic [M.L. *mosaicus*, mosaic ; Late Gk. *mouseios*, belonging to the Muses, *Mousa*, a Muse], inlaid work of marble, etc., in patterns.

Mos′lem (*s=z*) [Arab. *muslim*, a Mohammedan, *musallim*, one who acquiesces, *islām*, submission to the will of God], Mohammedan.

Mosque (*q=k*) [Arab. *masgid*, *masjid*, a temple, *sagada*, to worship], Mohammedan house of prayer.

Mos-qui′to (*qui=kee*) [Sp. *mosquito*, dim. of *mosca* (L. *musca*), a fly], stinging gnat.

Moss [O.E. *mos*, bog], flowerless plant, bog.

Mote [O.E. *mot*, perh. cogn. with Du. *mot*, dust from turf], small particle.

Mo-tet′ [F. dim. of *mot*], a sacred musical composition of several movements.

Moth [O.E. *moththe*], nocturnal insect.

Moth′er (*o=ŭ*) [Com. Teut.; O.E. *mōdor*], a female parent.

Moth′er-hood (*oth=ŭth*), state of being a mother.

Mother of pearl, smooth iridescent substance forming inner lining of certain shells.

Moth′er-in-law (*oth=ŭth*), husband's or wife's mother.

Mo′tion [L. *movēre* (p.p. *mōtus*), to move], movement, formal proposal; to make a gesture with the hand.

Mo′tive [L. *movēre* (p.p. *mōtus*), to move], that which incites to action, leading theme in work of art.

Mot′ley [?], consisting of different colours.

Mo′tor [L. *movēre* (p.p. *mōtus*), to move], source of moving power, as steam, electricity, etc., carriage moved by such power.

Mot′tled [?], spotted with different colours.

Mot′to [It. *motto*, a motto ; L. *muttum*, a murmur], short expression of a leading thought, maxim adopted as rule of conduct.

Mould [1] [O.E. *molde*, soil], soft fine earth.

Mould [2] [M.E. *muwle*, to grow mouldy], fungus growth.

Mould [3] [L. *modulus*, a mould], shape; to shape. [dust.

Mould′er [perh. fr. Mould [1]], crumble into

Mould′ing, plane or curved narrow surface used for decoration in cornices, etc.

Mould′y, overgrown with mould, musty.

Moult [L. *mutāre*, to change], cast feathers.

Mound [?], raised bank, hillock.

Mount [L. *mons* (*mont-is*), a hill], mountain, that upon which a drawing, etc., is set, horse; climb, raise into position, put (picture) in a mount, fit (on metal).

Moun′tain [L. *mons* (*mont-is*), a mountain], large hill. **Moun′tainous.**

Moun-tain-eer′, one who lives among mountains, mountain climber.

Mount′e-bank [It. *montambanco*, *montāre*, to mount, *in*, on, and *banco*, a bench], quack, boastful pretender.

Mourn (*ou=ō*) [Com. Teut.; O.E. *murnan*], grieve. **Mourn′ful.**

Mourn′ing, sorrow, dress to indicate sorrow.

Mouse [Com. Teut.; O.E. *mūs*], small gnawing animal.

Mous-tache′ [F. *moustache* ; It. *mostaccio*; Gk. *mustax*, a moustache], thick hair on the upper lip.

Mouth [Com. Teut.; O.E. *mūth*], opening between the lips, opening affording entrance or exit.

Mouth (*th* as in *the*), utter with an affectedly big voice.

Move [L. *movēre*, to move], change place or posture, excite, propose; movement. **Mov′able.** [down.

Mow [O.E. *māwan*, past tense *mēow*], cut

Mow [O.E. *mūga*], stack; place in a barn where hay is heaped.

Mu′ci-lage [L. *mūcus*, slime], gummy liquid. **Mu′cous,** slimy.

Mu′cus [L. *mūcus*, mucus of the nose], sticky substance secreted by mucous membrane.

Mud [M.E. *mode*, *mudde*], moist earth.

Mud′dle [from Mud], mix confusedly, render stupid; confusion.

Mu-ez′zin [Arab. *mu′adhdhin*, a public crier; *adhan*, a call to prayer], crier of the Mohammedan hours of prayer.

Muff [perh. Walloon *mouffe*, short form of F. *moufle*], cover usually of fur for the hands.

Muff [?], awkward or effeminate person.

Muf'fin [?], light spongy cake.

Muf'fle [O.F. *mofle*, *moufle*, a mitten, muff; Med. L. *muffula*, a muff], wrap up, deaden. **Muff'ler.**

Muf'ti [Arab. *muftī*, part. of *afta*, to decide a point of law], Mohammedan priest; plain clothes as distingusihed from uniform.

Mug [Swed. *mugg*; Norw. *mugga*, *mugge*, a mug], cylindrical drinking-cup.

Mug'gy [O.N. *mugga*, drizzling mist], warm and damp.

Mu-lat'to [Sp. *mulato*, a young mule, a mulatto], offspring of a white person and a negro.

Mul'ber-ry [O.H.G. *mûlberi*; L. *morum*, mulberry, and *beri*, berry], tree of which the leaves feed silkworms; its fruit.

Mulch (*mŭltsh*) [M.E. *molsh*], mixture of wet straw, leaves, and earth spread on ground to protect roots of newly-planted trees, etc.

Mulct [L. *mulcta*, *multa*, a fine], a fine; to fine.

Mule [L. *mūlus*, a mule], cross between a horse and an ass. **Mul'ish.**

Mull [perh. Gael. *maol*], promontory.

Mull [?], heat, sweeten and add spices to.

Mul'lah [Pers., Turk., and Hind. *mulla*; Arab. *maula*, a mullah], Mohammedan priest or theologian.

Mul'let [F. *mulet*, dim. fr. L. *mullus*, the red mullet], name of two kinds of fishes.

Mul'li-ga-taw'ny [Tamil *milagu-tannir*, lit. pepper-water], E. Indian curry soup.

Mul'lion [corruption of *munnion*; F. *moignon*, a stump], upright division between the lights of windows.

Mul-ti-fa'ri-ous [L. *multus*, many, *fārī*, to speak], of many kinds.

Mul'ti-form [L. *multus*, many, *forma*, form], having many forms.

Mul'ti-ple [L. *multiplex*, manifold; see **Multiply**], quantity containing another quantity an exact number of times.

Mul-ti-pli-cand', number to be multiplied.

Mul-ti-pli-ca'tion, process of multiplying.

Mul-ti-pli'ci-ty (ĭ), state of being many.

Mul'ti-ply [F. *multiplier*, to multiply; L. *multus* (mult-ĭ), many, *plicare* (p.p. *plicatus*), to fold], increase in number, add (a number) to itself a certain number of times.

Mul'ti-tude [L. *multitūdo* (*multitūdin-is*), multitude; *multus*, many], great many persons or things.

Mul-ti-tu'di-nous, consisting of a multitude.

Mum [imit.], silence! silent; to act in dumb show. [closed lips.

Mum'ble [M.E. *momele*], speak with partly

Mum'mer [O.F. *momer*, to mum], one who makes sport in disguise. **Mum'mery.**

Mum'my [Arab. *mūmiya*, a mummy, fr. *mūm*, wax], dead body embalmed. **Mum'mify.**

Mump [emphatic form of *mum*], to sulk.

Mumps [see **Mump**], inflammation of the salivary glands.

Munch (*ch=sh*) [prob. imit.], chew energetically. [earthly.

Mun'dane [L. *mundus*, the world], worldly,

Mu-ni'ci-pal [L. *municeps* (*mūnicip-is*), a free citizen; *munia*, official duties, *capere*, to take], pertaining to a city. **Municipal'ity.**

Mu-nif'i-cent [L. *munificus*, bountiful, *munus*, a gift, *facere*, to make], very generous. **Munif'icence.**

Mu-ni'tion [L. *mūnitio*, a defending, *munīre*, to defend], military stores.

Mu'ral L. *mūrus*, a wall], pertaining to a wall.

Mur'der [O.E. *morðhor*; cf. Goth. *maurthr*; cogn. with L. *mori*, to die], wilful killing of a human being; kill wilfully. **Mur'derous.**

Murk'y [O.N. *myrkr*; Dan. and Swed. *mörk*, dark, murky], dark, gloomy. **Murk'iness.**

Mur'mur [L. *murmurāre*, to murmur, imit.], low continued sound, complaint; utter a murmur.

Mur'rain [F. *morine*, perh. fr. L. *morī*, to die], plague among cattle.

Mus-cad-el', **Mus-cat-el'**, **Mus'ca-dine** [ult. fr. L. *muscus*, musk], strong wines from musk-flavoured kinds of grape.

Mus'cle [L. *musculus*, dim. of *mūs*, a mouse], fleshy part of the body which by its contraction produces motion.

Mus'cu-lar, pertaining to a muscle, strong.

Muse [1] [O.F. *muse*, the mouth, a muzzle; see **Muzzle**], think closely, meditate.

Muse [2] [L. *mūsa*; Gk. *mousa*], one of nine goddesses of the arts.

Mu-se'um (*s=z*) [Gk. *mouseion*, a temple of the Muses], place where scientific, natural, or other curiosities are kept.

Mush'room [F. *mousseron*, extended from *mousse*, moss], edible fungus.

Mu'sic [Gk. *mousikē*, music; see **Muse** [2]], the fine art which deals with the harmonious combination of sounds or tones, beautiful sound, melody. **Mus'ical.**

Mu-si'cian (*ci=sh*), one skilled in music.

Musk [L. *muscus*; Late Gk. *moschos*, musk], strong scent, kind of plant.

Mus'ket [It. *moschetto*, orig. a kind of hawk], hand-gun. **Musketeer'.**

Mus'lin (*s=z*) [It. *mussolina*, fr. *Mosul* in Mesopotamia], thin cotton cloth.

Mus'sel [O.E. *muscle*, fr. L.L. *muscula*], bivalve shell-fish. [mented.

Must [L. *mustus*, new], new wine unfer-

Must [O.E. *môste*, past of *môt*, may], be obliged (to).

Mus'tang [Sp. *mestengo*; perh. fr. *mesta*, a company of graziers], wild horse of the prairies.

Mus'tard [O.F. *mostarde*, mustard; L. *mustum*, must], plant with pungent seeds.

Mus'ter [O.F. *mostrer*; F. *montrer*, fr. L. *monstrāre*, to show], assembling of troops, gathering; assemble, as troops for parade.

Mus'ty [?], spoiled by age, mouldy.

Mu′ta-bil′i-ty, liability to change

Mu′ta-ble [L. *mūtāre*, to change], changeable.

Mu-ta′tion [L. *mūtāre* (p.p *mutātus*), to change], change.

Mute [L. *mūtus*, dumb], silent, dumb ; dumb person; paid attendant at a funeral.

Mu′ti-late [L. *mutilus*, maimed], maim, hack.

Mu-ti-neer′ [F. *mutin*, rebellious, ult. fr. L. *movēre*, to move], one guilty of mutiny

Mu′ti-ny [(old verb *mutine*); see **Mutineer**], a rising against authority ; revolt. **Mut′inous.**

Mut′ter [prob. imit.], utter indistinctly and in low tones.

Mut′ton [O. . *moton* ; Low L. *multo*, a sheep], flesh of a sheep used as food.

Mu′tu-al (L. *mutuus*, mutual, *mutāre*, to change], interchanged, joint, reciprocal.

Muz′zle [O.F. *musel*, muzzle ; orig. doubtful], the part of an animal's head which includes the nose and mouth, covering for the muzzle ; bind the mouth of.

My-op′i-a (ŏ) [Gk. *myo*, shut, *ops*, the eye], short-sightedness.

Myr′i-ad [Gk. *myrias* (*myriad-os*), 10,000 ; *myrios*, numberless], ten thousand, great number.

Myr′mi-don [Gk. *Myrmidones*, a warlike people of Thessaly who followed Achilles to Troy], follower or servant (often in a bad sense).

Myr*r***h** [Gk. *myrra*, myrrh ; Arab. *murr*, bitter, myrrh], aromatic gum resin.

Myr′tle [L. *myrtus* ; Gk. *myrtos*], evergreen shrub.

Mys-te′ri-ous, full of mystery.

Mys′ter-y [Gk. *mystes*, one who is initiated ; *myein*, to initiate], something unknown or concealed or that cannot be explained.

Mys′tic [Gk. *mysticos*, a mystic], one who seeks by contemplation or complete self-surrender to attain union with God.

Mys′tic-al, belonging to the spiritual or hidden side of things.

Mys′ti-cism, doctrine of the Mystics, who held that they had direct intercourse with God.

Mys′ti-fy [Gk. *mysticos*, mystic, and F. *-fier*, for L. *facere*, to make], make obscure, puzzle. **Mystifica′tion.**

Myth [Gk. *mythos*, a fable], wonder story of a god, hero, etc.; fictitious person or thing.

Myth′ic-al, described in a myth, imaginary.

Myth-ol′o-gy [Gk. *mythos*, a fable, *logos*, a discourse], science of myths; body of myths. **Mytholog′ical.**

N

Na′bob (more correctly *Nawab′*) [Urdu *nawāb*, or *nawwāb*], a nabob], Mohammedan governor of a province under the Mogul empire, wealthy Anglo-Indian.

Na′cre (*nai-ker*) [Sp. and Port. *nacar*, nacre], mother-of-pearl.

Na′dir (*a=ai*) [Arab. *nadīr*, short for *nadīr es-semt*, from *nadīr*, corresponding to, and *essemt*, the zenith], point in the heavens opposite the zenith, lowest point. **N**

Nag [?], small horse.

Nag [obs. Icel. *nagga*, to complain ; Swed. and Norw. *nagga*, to peck], find fault constantly.

Nai′ad (*ai=ī*) [Gk. *naias* (*naiad-os*), a naiad ; *naein*, to flow], water nymph.

Nail [O.E. *nœgel* ; O.N. *nagl*], horny plate on a finger or a toe, pointed piece of metal with a head ; to fasten with nails.

Nain′sook [Urdu *nainsukh*, nainsook, *nain*, eye, and *sukh*, pleasure], thick kind of muslin.

Naïve (*na-eev*) [F. *naïf* (fem. *naïve*), naïve ; L. *nātīvus*, native], ingenuous, artless. **Naïv′ety.**

Na′ked [O.E. *nacod*, *nœcad*], uncovered, bare.

Nam′by-pam′by [fr. name of pastoral poet, *Ambrose Philips*], insipidly pretty, weak and sentimental.

Name [O.E. *nama*; cogn. with L. *nomen* ; Gk. *onoma*], that by which a person or thing is called, a title ; to call. **Name′ly.**

Name′sake, one called after another, or having the same name as another.

Nan-keen′ [fr. *Nankin* in China], thick yellow cotton cloth.

Nap [O.E. *knappian*], short sleep ; to take a short sleep.

Nap [M.Du. *noppe*, allied to O.E. *knoppian*, to pluck], the woolly surface of cloth, pile.

Nape [?], back part of the neck.

Na′per-y [O.F. *naperie* ; see **Napkin**], table linen, linen in general.

Naph′tha [L. and Gk. *naphtha*, naphtha], inflammable distillation of mineral oil and coal-tar. **Naph′thaline.**

Nap′kin [Late L. *nappa*, for *mappa*, a cloth ; suf. *-kin*], little towel for wiping lips or fingers.

Nar-cis′sus (pl. -**ssuses** or -**ssi**) [Gk. *narcissos*, a narcissus, named from its *narcotic* properties], bulbous flowering plant.

Nar-cot′ic [Gk. *narcoticos*, benumbing, *narcĕ*, numbness], sleeping drug ; inducing sleep. [balsam.

Nard [Gk. *nardos*; oriental origin], aromatic

Nar′ghil-e [Pers. *nargileh*, *nargil*, a coco-nut], Eastern pipe in which the smoke is passed through water.

Nar-rate′ [L. *narrāre* (p.p. *narrātus*), to narrate], tell, as a story. [story.

Nar-ra′tion, Nar′ra-tive [L. *narrātio*], account,

Nar′row [O.E. *nearu*; cf. Du. *naar*, dismal], of little breadth ; to become or make less broad.

Nar′whal [perh. fr. O.N. *náhvalr* ; *nár*, corpse, and *hvalr*, whale], kind of whale with straight horn(s) developed from one or both teeth.

Na′sal (*s=z*) [L. *nāsus*, nose], pertaining to the nose. **Nas′alize.**

Nas′cent [L. *nascī* (pr.p. *nascens*, *-entis*), to be born], beginning to exist or grow.

Nas-tur'ti-um (*ti=shi*) [L. *nasturtium*; *nāsus*, nose, and *torquēre*, to twist], Indian cress.

Nas'ty [etym. doubtful; cf. dial. Swed. *naskug*, nasty, dirty], foul, offensive, unpleasant. **Nas'tiness.**

Na'tal (*nai*) [L. *nātus*, born], of or pertaining to one's birth.

Nat-a'tion [L. *natāre*, to swim], swimming.

Na'tion (*nai*) [L. *nascī* (p.p. *nātus*), to be born], body of inhabitants of a country. **Na'tionalize.**

Na-tion-al'i-ty (*nā*), national character.

Na'tive (*nai*) [L. *nātus*, born], pertaining to place of birth, in-born; one who is born in a place.

Na-tiv'i-ty, birth, horoscope.

Nat'ron [F. and Sp. natron; Arab. natrun; Gk. *nitron*; see **Nitre**], native carbonate of soda.

Nat'ty [?], spruce, trim, daintily tidy.

Nat'u-ral, fixed by nature, not artificial; an idiot, a character in music.

Nat'u-ral-ist, student of natural history.

Nat'u-ral-ize, admit to rights of a native.

Na'ture [L. *nātūra*, nature, *natus*, born], existing order of things, quality of mind or character.

Nau_ght_ [O.E. *nâwiht*, *nâht*, naught; *ná*, not, *wiht*, whit], nothing. [**ness.**

Nau_gh_**'ty** [fr. **Naught**], perverse. **Naught'i-**

Nau'se-a [Gk. *nausia*, sea-sickness, *naus*, a ship], feeling of sickness. **Nau'seate, Nau'seous.**

Nau'tic-al [Gk. *nautēs*, a sailor, *naus*, a ship], pertaining to seamen or ships.

Nau'ti-lus [Gk. *nautilos*, a sailor, a nautilus], kind of shell-fish. [**navy.**

Na'val [L. *nāvis*, ship], having to do with the

Nave [Com. Teut.; O.E. *nafu*], block in the centre of a wheel.

Nave [L. *nāvis*, ship], main part of a church.

Na'vel [Com. Teut.; O.E. *nafela*], depression in centre of abdomen, centre of anything.

Nav'i-gate [L. *nāvigāre* (p.p. *nāvigātus*), to navigate; *nāvis*, ship], pass over in ships, steer. **Naviga'tion.**

Nav'i-ga-tor, one skilled in seamanship, explorer of the seas, one employed in work of excavating and constructing canals, etc.

Nav'vy [abbr. of **Navigator**], labourer on excavations (for railways, canals, etc.).

Na'vy [O.F. *navie*, navy; L. *nāvis*, ship], warships of a nation, a fleet.

Na-wab', see **Nabob.**

Nay [O.N. and Dan. *nei*; cogn. with **No**], no.

Naze [E.], ness, headland. [lowest tides].

Neap [O.E. *nép* (*népflôd*)], low (applied to the

Near [orig. comp. of *ná*=O.E. *néah*, nigh], to or at a short distance.

Near-sight'ed, short-sighted.

Neat [OE. *néat*], cattle.

Neat [F. *net* (fem. *nette*), neat; L. *nitidus*, shining, *nitēre*, to shine], trim, free from admixture.

Neb [O.E. *nebb*], nose, beak.

Neb'u-la [L. *nebula*, mist], a patch of light made by a cluster of distant stars or distant gaseous matter. **Neb'ular.**

Neb'u-lous, cloudy, hazy.

Ne'ces-sa-ry [L. *necesse*, to be needful], such as must be.

Ne-ces'si-tous, needy.

Ne-ces'si-ty [L. *necesse*, to be needful], need, that which is necessary. **Neces'sitate.**

Neck [O.E. *hnecca*], slender connecting part.

Neck'lace, ornamental neckband.

Nec'ro-man-cy [Gk. *necromanteia*, necromancy, *necros*, corpse, *manteia*, prophetic power], sorcery. **Necroman'tic.**

Ne-crop'o-lis [Gk. *necros*, corpse, *polis*, city], cemetery.

Nec'tar [L. and Gk. *nectar*, nectar], drink of the gods, honey of flowers.

Nec'tar-ine [orig. adj. from *nectar*], smooth-skinned peach.

Need [Com. Teut.; O.E. *nied*], state that requires supply or relief; be in want of.

Need'le [O.E. *nædl*; cf. Ger. *nähen*, to sew; prob. cogn. with L. *nēre*, to spin], pointed instrument, esp. with eye to receive thread for sewing, magnetised steel bar in mariner's compass.

Needs, of necessity.

Need'y, in want.

Ne-fa'ri-ous [L. *nefās*, that which is wrong; *nē*, not and *fās*, law], wicked. [denial.

Ne-ga'tion [L. *negāre* (p.p. *negātus*), to deny],

Neg'a-tive, denying, not positive; denial, a word used in denial, in photography a picture on glass in which dark appears light and light dark; to counteract, reject.

Neg-lect' [L. *neglegere* (p.p. *neglectus*), *neg-*, not, *legere*, to gather], omit, slight; want of care or attention.

Neg'li-gence [see **Neglect**], lack of diligence or care. **Neg'ligible.**

Ne-go'ti-ate, Ne-go'ci-ate (*t=c=sh*) [L. *negotium*, business; *neg-*, not, *otium*, ease], bargain or trade, conduct communications.

Ne-go-ti-a'tion, transaction of business between nations or traders, a treaty.

Ne'gro, fem. **Ne'gress** [Sp. *negro*; L. *niger*, black], person of the African or black race. **Ne'groid.**

Ne'gus [fr. Colonel *Negus*], mixture of wine, hot water, sugar, and spice.

Neigh (*nay*) [O.E. *hnægan*, imit.], make the cry of a horse; the cry of a horse.

Neigh'bour [O.E. *néah*, near, *búr*, or *gebúr*, a husbandman], one who lives near another.

Neigh'bour-hood, state of being near, district round about.

Nei'ther (*ei=ee* or *ī*) [M.E. *neyther*], (with nor) not the one or the other.

Nem'es-is [Gk. *nemesis*, nemesis, *nemein*, to distribute], goddess of vengeance, just retribution.

Ne-o-lith'ic [Gk. *nēos*, new; *lithos*, a stone], belonging to the later Stone Age.

Ne-o'log-ism, Ne-ol'o-gy [F. fr. Gk. *neos*, new, *logos*, word], coining or use of new words

Ne′o-phyte [Gk. *nēos*, new, *phyein*, to grow], a new convert.

Ne-pen′the [Gk. *nē*, not, *penthos*, grief], a drug producing forgetfulness.

Neph′ew (*ph=v*) [L. *nepos* (*nepōt-is*), nephew, grandson], the son of brother or sister.

Nep′o-tism [see **Nephew**], patronage to relations.

Ner′e-id (*neer-ē-id*) [Gk. *Nērēis*, daughter of sea-god Nereus], sea-nymph.

Nerve [L. *nervus*, perh. allied to Gk. *neuron*, a sinew], fibre or a bundle of fibres connected with the brain which transmits feeling, resolution, courage; give vigour.

Ner′vous, relating to the nerves, weak nerved; (old meaning) sinewy.

Ne′science (*sci=sh*) [L. *nescīre* (pr.p. *nesciens*, *-entis*), not to know; *nē*, not, *scīre*, to know], ignorance.

Ness [O.E. *næs*; O.N. *nes*], cape.

Nest [O.E.; cogn. with L. *nidus*], structure made by a bird to lay eggs in; build a nest.

Nes′tle [O.E. *nestlian*], to lie close and snug.

Nest′ling, bird too young to leave the nest.

Net [1] [Com. Teut.; O.E. *net(t)*], fabric of interwoven twine or the like, forming meshes.

Net [2] [F. *net*, pure], free from all charges.

Neth′er [O.E. *neothera*, nether], lower.

Net′tle [Com. Teut.; O.E. *netele*], stinging plant; irritate.

Neu-ral′gi-a [Gk. *neuron*, nerve; *algos*, pain], intermittent nervous pain.

Neur-as-the′ni-a [Gk. *neuron*, nerve, *asthenes*, weak], nervous debility.

Neu-rot′ic [Gk. *neuron*, nerve], suffering from disordered nerves.

Neu′ter [L. *neuter*, neither, *nē*, not, *uter*, either], neither active nor passive, neither masculine nor feminine.

Neu′tral [L. *neutralis*, neutral; see **Neuter**], indifferent, on neither side. **Neutral′ity**.

Neu′tral-ize, render neutral, counterbalance.

Nev-er-the-less′ [O.E. *nē*, not, *æfre*, ever; *læssa*, less], not the less, yet, notwithstanding.

New [Com. Teut.; O.E. *nīwe*], first made, invented, etc., fresh, additional, modern.

New-fan′gled [M.E. *newefangel*, *newe*, new, and *fangel*, prob. fr. O.E. *fangol*, inclined to take], fond of novelty, new-fashioned.

News [transl. of F. *nouvelles*, news, pl. of O.F. *novel*, new], tidings.

News′pa-per, public print with news, etc.

Newt [for *an ewt*; O.E. *efeta*, a lizard], lizard-like aquatic animal, eft.

Nib [var. of **Neb**], a point, esp. of a pen.

Nib′ble [freq. of **Nip**], bite by little at a time; small bite.

Nice [O.F. *nice*, orig. ignorant; L. *nescius*, ignorant], dainty, particular, pleasing.

Ni′ce-ty, delicacy of feeling, a minute distinction, extreme precision.

Niche (*che=tsh*) [It. *nicchia*, a niche, *nicchio*, a sea-shell], recess in a wall.

Nick [?], notch, exact point; to notch.

Nick′el [Ger. *nickel*, nickel], silver-white metal.

Nick′nack [var. of **Knick-knack**], trifle, trinket.

Nick′name [for *an ekename*; **Eke** and **Name**], name given in sport.

Nic′o-tine (*ine=een*) [from *Nicot*, who first sent tobacco into France], alkaloid in tobacco.

Niece [F. *nièce*, niece; L. *neptis*, granddaughter, niece], daughter of one's brother or sister. [ness.

Nig′gard-ly [?], miserly, stingy. **Nig′gardli-**

Nig′gle [perh. fr. Nor. *nigla*], trifle with work, go too much into detail.

Nigh [O.E. *néah*], near.

Night [Com. Teut.; O.E. *niht*], time from sunset to sunrise.

Night′in-gale [O.E. *nihtegale*, *niht*, night, *galan*, to sing], bird that sings at night.

Night′mare [O.E. *niht*, night, *mœre*, an incubus], condition in sleep accompanied by oppressive dreams.

Night′shade, plant with poisonous berries.

Nig′rit-ude [L. *nigritudo*], blackness.

Ni′hil-ist [L. *nihil*, nothing], Russian revolutionary.

Nim′ble [O.E. *numol*, fr. *niman*, to take], quick and light. [halo.

Nim′bus [L. *nimbus*, a cloud], rain-cloud,

Nin′com-poop [?], senseless person.

Nine [O.E. *nigon*; cf. L. *novem*], one more than eight. [and ten.

Nine′teen [**Nine** and *-teen*, ten], sum of nine

Nine′ty [**Nine** and *-ty*, tens], nine times ten.

Nip [M.E. *nippen*, for *knippen*; cf. Du. *knijpen*, to pinch], pinch, blast as by frost.

Nip′pers, small pincers.

Nip′ple [?], teat.

Nir-va′na (*va=vah*) [Skr.], Buddhist state of beatitude, calm.

Nit [O.E. *hnitu*], egg of a louse.

Ni′trate, a salt formed by combination with nitric acid.

Ni′tre [Gk. *nitron*, nitre], saltpetre.

Ni′tro-gen [**Nitre** and Gk. *genna-ein*, to generate], elementary gas. **Nitro′genous**.

No-bil′i-ty, quality of being noble, collective body of nobles.

No′ble [L. *nobilis*, noble, fr. (*g*)*no*, (*g*)*noscere*, to know], of exalted rank, exalted in character, grand; person of rank.

Noc-tur′nal [L. *nox* (*noct-is*), night], pertaining to night.

Noc′turne, a dreamy piece of music, night-scene (in painting).

Nod, [?], bend the head; quick downward or forward motion of the head.

Node [L. *nōdus*, a knot], knot, knob. **No′dal**.

Nod′ule, small knot or knob.

Noise [O.F. *noise*, *nose*, a debate, noise; etym. doubtful], loud, unmusical sound, din; spread by rumour.

Noi′some (*some=sum*) [fr. obs. *noy*, for **Annoy**], hurtful, unwholesome.

No′mad [Gk. *nomas* (*nomad-os*), nomad; *nomos*, a pasture, *nemein*, to assign], one of a wandering tribe.

No-mad'ic, moving from place to place.

No'men-cla-ture [L. *nōmen*, name, *calāre*, to call], system of names.

Nom'i-nal [L. *nōmen* (*nomin-is*), a name], existing in name only.

Nom'i-nate [L. *nōmināre* (p.p. *nōminātus*), to nominate, *nōmen*, a name], name, propose by name. **Nomina'tion.**

Nom'i-na-tive, naming (said of the subject).

Nom-i-nee' [L *nōmen* (*nōmin-is*), a name], one proposed for election. [age].

Non'age [L. *non-*, not ; see Age], minority (in

Non-a-ge-na'ri-an [L. *nonageni*, ninety each ; *nonaginta*, ninety], person ninety years old, or between ninety and a hundred.

Nonce [for "(the) nonce"=then once], one single occasion.

Non'cha-lant (*ch*=*sh*) [O.F. *nonchaloir* (pr.p. *nonchalant*), to be careless ; *non-*, not, *chaloir* (L. *calēre*), to glow], indifferent. **Non'chalance.**

Non-con-form'ist [L. *non-*, not ; see **Conform**], one who does not conform to an established church.

Non'de-script [L. *non-*, not ; see **Describe**], person or thing not easily described ; hard to describe.

Non-en'ti-ty [L. *non-*, not ; see **Entity**], non-existence, person of no account.

None'such, Non'such [*none* (or "*not one*"), and **Such**], person or thing without equal.

Non-par-eil' [F.], matchless ; peerless person or thing, very small size of type.

Non'plus [L. *non-*, not, *plus*, more], to puzzle.

Non'sense [L. *non-*, not ; see **Sense**], that which has no sense, absurdity. **Non-sen'sical.**

Non'suit [A.F. *nonsute*], stoppage of a suit by a judge.

Noo'dle [?], blockhead.

Nook [?], corner, secluded place.

Noon [L. *nōna* (*hōra*), ninth (hour), orig. 3 p.m.], midday.

Noose (*se*=*ss* or *z*) [Gascon, *nus*, noose ; L. *nōdus*, knot], running knot or loop.

Norm [L. *norma*, carpenter's square], pattern, rule, standard.

Nor'mal [L. *normālis*, fr. *norma*, a rule], according to a rule or standard, usual.

North [Com. Teut. ; O.E. *north*], point of the horizon directly opposite the midday sun.

North'er-ly, towards the north, from the north (in speaking of wind).

Nose (*s*=*z*) [O.E. *nosu* ; cf. **Ness**], organ of smell, used also in speaking and breathing ; smell out.

Nose'gay, bunch of fragrant flowers.

Nos-tal'gi-a (*g*=*j*) [Gk. *nostos*, return home, *algos*, pain], homesickness.

Nos'tril [O.E. *nosthyrl* ; *nosu*, nose, and *thyrel*, perforation], opening in nose admitting air.

Nos'trum [L. neut. of *noster*, our], quack medicine.

No'ta-ble, noticeable, worthy of notice ; person of distinction. **Notabil'ity.**

No'ta-ry [see **Note**], public officer who witnesses and certifies formal documents.

No-ta'tion [see **Note**], any system of characters.

Notch [O.F. *oche* ; F. *hoche*, a notch ; with an (n) prefixed, a (n)oche], hollow cut into anything ; cut or make nicks.

Note [L. *nota*, a mark ; *notāre* (p.p. *notātus*), to note], mark, short written remark, short letter ; remark, to record in writing.

No'thing (*o*=*ŭ*) [No and **Thing**], not anything.

No'tice [L. *noscere* (p.p. *nōtus*], to know], note, warning, regard ; remark, make comments on. **Notice'able.**

No'ti-fi-a-ble, (of diseases) that must be notified to authorities.

No'ti-fy [L. *notificare*, to give notice, *nōtus*, known, *facere* (p.p. *factus*), to make], give notice. **Notifica'tion.**

No'tion [see **Notice**], an idea, inclination.

No-to'ri-ous [L. *noscere* (p.p. *nōtus*), to know], noted, esp. in a bad sense. **Notori'ety.**

Not-with-stand'ing, in spite of.

Noun [O.F. *nun* ; F. *nom* ; L. *nōmen*, a name], word used as a name (in grammar].

Nour'ish [L. *nātrīre*, to nourish], to feed and cause to grow. **Nour'ishment.**

Nov'el [L. *novellus*, dim. of *novus*, new], new ; a fictitious tale. **Novelette'.**

Nov'el-ist, a writer of novels.

Nov'el-ty, newness, a new thing.

Nov-em'ber [L. *novem*, nine], eleventh month (Roman ninth).

Nov'ice (*ice*=*iss*) [L. *novicius*, novice, *novus*, new], a beginner, candidate for admission into a religious order.

No-vi'ci-ate, No-vi'ti-ate (*t*=*sh*) [see **Novice**], state of being a novice, time of instruction for a novice.

No'wise [No and **Ways**], in no way.

Nox'ious (*nok'shus*) [L. *noxius*, hurtful, *noxa*, hurt], hurtful, corrupting.

Noz'zle [dim. of **Nose**], snout, projecting vent.

Nu'cle-us [L. *nucleus*, dim. of *nux* (*nūc-is*), nut], kernel, a central mass.

Nude [L. *nūdus*, naked], naked. **Nud'ity.**

Nudge [?], touch gently as with the elbow.

Nu'ga-to-ry [L. *nūgæ*, trifles], trifling.

Nug'get [?], lump, esp. of precious metal.

Nui'sance [F. *nuire* (pr.p. *nuisant*) ; L. *nocēre*, to hurt], something offensive or annoying.

Null [L. *nullus*, none ; *nē*, not, *ullus*, any], void, useless.

Nul'lah [Hind. *nala*], water-course.

Nul'li-fy [L. *nullus*, none, *facere*, to make, make void, cancel. **Nul'lity.**

Numb [earlier *num*, p.p. of archaic O.E. *niman*, to take], without feeling ; to deaden.

Num'ber [F. *nombre* ; L. *numerus*, number], that which can be counted, a unit or aggregate of units, many ; count, amount to. [number.

Nu'mer-al, figure or symbol to express a

Nu-mer-a'tion, the act of numbering.

Nu'mer-a-tor, one who numbers, the figure above the line in a vulgar fraction.

Nu-mer′ic-al, Nu′mer-al, denoting number.

Nu′mer-ous, of great number.

Nu-mis-mat′ics [Gk. *nomisma* (*numismat-os*), current coin, *nomos*, custom], study of coins and medals. **Numis′matist.**

Num′skull [see **Numb**], dolt, blockhead.

Nun [Late L. *nonna*, fem. of *nonnus*, monk], woman set apart for a religious life, who lives in a convent.

Nun′ci-o (*c=sh*) [It. *nuncio* ; L. *nuntius*, a messenger], pope's ambassador at a foreign court.

Nun′ne-ry, house for nuns.

Nup′tial (*ti=sh*) [L. *nuptiæ* (pl.), a wedding, *nūbĕre* (p.p. *nuptus*), to marry], connected with marriage.

Nup′tials, marriage.

Nurse [L. *nūtrix* (*nūtrīc-is*), a nurse], one who has the care of young children or sick people ; nourish, take care of.

Nurs′er-y, room for children, place for young plants.

Nur′ture [L. *nūtrīre* (p.p. *nūtrītus*), to nourish], nourishment, upbringing ; nourish, bring up.

Nut [Com. Teut.; O.E. *hnutu*], fruit with kernel in a hard covering, small perforated metal block for screwing on a bolt, etc.

Nut′meg [F. *noix muscade* ; Med. L. *nux muscāta*, musky nut], aromatic seed of an East Indian tree.

Nu′tri-ment [see **Nurture**], food.   [ing.

Nu-tri′tion [see **Nurture**], process of nourish-

Nu-tri′tious (*ti=sh*), **Nu′tri-tive,** nourishing.

Nymph [Gk. *nymphē*, a nymph], elemental female being of the sea, streams or woods, graceful young girl.

O

Oaf [var. of obs. *auf*, fr. O.N. *álfr*, elf], deformed or idiot child, lout.

Oak [Com. Teut. ; O.E. *ác*], kind of tree with strong wood.

Oak′um [O.E. *ácumba*, tow, *á-*, out, and *cemban*, to comb], material got by untwisting and picking old rope.   [ing.

Oar [O.E. and O.N. *ár*], implement for row-

O-a′sis, O′a-sis, (*pl.*) **Oases** [L. and Gk. *oasis* ; of Egypt. orig.], fertile spot in a desert.

Oath [Com. Teut. ; O.E. *ath*], declaration made in the name of God, profane exclamation.   [grain.

Oats [O.E. *áte*; etym. doubtful], kind of

Ob′du-rate [L. *ob*, against, *durus*, hard], hardhearted, stubbornly wicked. **Ob′duracy.**

O-be′di-ence, act of obeying.

O-bei′sance (*ei=a*) [see **Obey**], expression of respect, bow.

Ob′e-lisk [Gk. *obeliscos*, dim. of *obelos*, a spit], four-sided upright pillar terminating with a pyramid.

O-bese′ [L. *ob*, away, *edere* (p.p. *ēsus*), to eat], fat.

O-be′si-ty (*e=ee*), excessive fatness.

O-bey′ (*ey=ai*) [L. *obēdīre*, towards; *ob-* towards, *audīre*, to hear], comply with the orders of, yield.

Ob-fus′cate [L. *obfuscāre* (p.p. *obfuscātus*); *ob*, near, *fuscus*, brown], darken, bewilder.

O-bit′u-a-ry [L. *obitus*, death ; *ob*, against, *īre* (p.p. *ĭtus*), to go], pertaining to a death ; notice of a person deceased.

Ob-ject′ [L. *objectāre*, freq. of *objicere*, to cast towards, *ob*, against, *jacere*, to throw], oppose in words.

Ob′ject, anything set before the sight or the mind, person exciting pity, that toward which an action is directed, word, etc., denoting it.

Ob-jec′tion, adverse reason.

Ob-jec′tive, pertaining to an object ; aim.

Ob-jur-ga′tion [L. *ob*, against, *jurgāre*, to chide], strong reproof, scolding.

Ob-late′ [L. *ob*, towards, *lātus*, borne], flattened at the poles.

Ob-la′tion [L. *oblatus*, offered up], offering.

Ob-li-ga′tion, binding agreement, promise, etc., state of indebtedness.

Ob′li-ga-to-ry, binding as a duty.

O-blige′ [L. *ob*, near, *ligāre*, to bind], do a favour to, to compel.

Ob-lique′ (*ique=eek*) [L. *obliquus, oblīcus*, slanting], slanting.

Ob-liq′ui-ty (*qu=kw*), deviation from a right line ; moral perversity.

Ob-lit′er-ate [L. *ob*, over, *littera*, a letter], blot out. **Oblitera′tion.**

Ob-liv′i-on [L. *oblivisci*, to forget], forgetfulness. **Obliv′ious.**

Ob′long [L. *ob*, over, *longus*, long], rectangular and long ; rectangle which is longer than it is broad.

Ob′lo-quy [L. *ob*, against, *loquī*, to speak], reproach, slander.

Ob-nox′ious (*xious=kshus*) [L. *ob*, against, *noxius*, hurtful], offensive, odious.

O′boe (*oe=oi*) [It. *oboe* ; F. *hautbois*], wooden wind instrument (same as **Hautboy**).

Ob-scene′ [L. *obscēnus*, repulsive : etym. doubtful], indecent, impure. **Obscen′ity.**

Ob-scur′ant, Ob-scur-ant′ist, one who opposes the progress of intellectual enlightenment.

Ob-scure′ [L. *obscūrus* ; *ob*, over, *scurus*, covered], shaded, darkened, dim ; darken, make dim. **Obscur′ity.**

Ob-sec-ra′tion [L. *obsecratio*, fr. *ob* and *sacer*, sacred], earnest entreaty.

Ob′se-quies (*-sĕ-*) [L. *ob*, near, *sequī*, to follow], funeral rites.

Ob-se′qui-ous (*e=ee*) [L. *obsequium*, compliance ; *ob*, near, *sequī*, to follow], cringing.

Ob-serv′ance (*s=z*), heeding with care, performance, custom.

Ob-serv′ant (*s=z*), taking notice, attentive.

Ob-ser-va′tion (*s=z*), act or faculty of observing, view, remark.

Ob-serv′a-to-ry (*s=z*), building for astronomical observation.

Ob-serve′ (*s=z*) [L. *observāre*, to observe; *ob*, over, *servāre*, to keep], notice, comply with, remark.

Ob-sess' [L. *obsidēre* (p.p. *obsessus*), to besiege ; *ob*, over, *sedēre*, to sit], beset or possess. **Obsess'ion.**

Ob-sid'ian [L. *obsidianus*, correctly *obsianus*], dark-coloured, clear volcanic rock—called after *Obsius*, its discoverer.

Ob'so-lete [L. *obsolēre* (p.p. *obsolētus*), to decay ; *ob*, against, *solēre*, to be wont], no longer in use. **Obsoles'cent.**

Ob'sta-cle [L. *obstāculum*, obstacle ; *ob*, against, *stāre*, to stand], hindrance.

Ob'sti-nate [L. *obstināre* (p.p. *obstinātus*), to persist ; *ob*, over, and *stāre*, to stand], stubborn, persistent. **Ob'stinacy.**

Ob-strep'er-ous [L. *ob*, against, *strepere*, to make a noise], clamorous, disorderly.

Ob-struct' [L. *ob*, in the way of, *struere* (p.p. *structus*), to build], block up, be in the way of. **Obstruc'tion.**

Ob-tain' [L. *ob*, near, *tenēre*, to hold], get hold of, procure, be prevalent, exist.

Ob-trude' [L. *ob*, against, and *trūdere* (p.p. *trusus*), to thrust], thrust into or upon. **Obtru'sion.**

Ob-tuse' (*s* sharp) [L. *ob*, against, *tundere* (p.p. *tusus*), to beat], blunt, dull, greater than a right angle.

Ob'verse [L. *ob*, towards, and *vertere* (p.p. *versus*), to turn], answering as counterpart to something else ; side of a coin which has the principal image on it ; counterpart of a fact.

Ob'vi-ate [L. *obviāre* (p.p. *obviātus*), to obviate ; *ob*, against, and *via*, way], make unnecessary. [apparent.

Ob'vi-ous [L. *ob*, against, *via*, way], easily seen,

Oc-ca'sion (*si=zh*) [L. *oc-* (*ob*), at, *cadere* (p.p. *cāsus*), to fall], opportunity, timely chance, need ; to cause.

Oc-ca'sion-al, occurring at times.

Oc'ci-dent (*cc=ks*) [L. *occidere* (pr.p. *occidens*, *-entis*), to fall down ; *ob*, and *cadere*, to fall], west. **Occiden'tal.**

Oc'ci-put (*cc=ks*) [L. *occiput* ; *ob*, against, *caput*, head], back part of the skull.

Oc-cult' [L. *occulere* (p.p. *occultus*), to conceal, *ob*, against, *cēlāre*, to hide], secret, concealed. **Occult'ism.**

Oc'cu-pan-cy, possession, time of possession.

Oc'cu-pant, one in possession.

Oc-cu-pa'tion, possession, employment.

Oc'cu-py [L. *occupāre*, to occupy ; *ob*, against, *capere*, to seize], take possession of, hold and use, fill and o..ver, employ.

Oc-cur' [L. *ob*, against, *currere*, to run], happen, come to the mind.

Oc-cur'rence, event.

O'cean (*ce=sh*) [Gk. *ōceanos*, great stream encircling the earth], sea, one of the great areas of the sea. **Ocean'ic.**

O'chre (*ōker*) [Gk. *ōchra*, yellow ochre ; *ōchros*, yellow], yellow or red pigment.

Oc'ta-gon [Gk. *octō*, eight, *gōnia*, an angle], eight-sided figure. **Octa'gonal.**

Oc-ta-hed'ron [Gk. *octo*, eight, *hedra*, a base], solid figure contained by eight plane faces usu. triangles. **Octahed'ral.**

Oc'tave [L. *octava*, fem. of *octavus*, eighth ; *octo*, eight], in music an interval of five tones and two semitones, the eight days beginning with the day of a festival, eight-lined stanza.

Oc-ta'vo (*a=ai*) [see **Octave**], size of book or page given by folding sheet into 8 leaves. (Abbr. 8vo.)

Oc-to'ber [L. *October* ; *octo*, eight], tenth month (Roman eighth).

Oc-to-ge-na'ri-an [L. *octōgēnī*, eighty each, *octōginta*, eighty], person 80 years old.

Oc'to-pus [Gk. *octō*, eight, *pous*, foot], eight-armed cuttle-fish.

Oc'troi (*-trwah*) [F. *octroi*, octroi ; O.F. *otroier* ; L. *auctōrizāre*, to authorize], tax levied in some foreign towns on articles of food brought in.

Oc'u-lar [L. *oculus*, the eye], pertaining to or seen by the eye.

Oc'u-list [L. *oculus*, the eye], eye-doctor.

Odd [O.N. *oddi*, triangle, odd number], unmatched, remaining over, not exactly divisible by 2, queer. **Odd'ments.**

Odd'i-ty, singularity, queerness. [ability.

Odds, inequality, difference, balance of, prob-

Ode [Gk. *ōidē* (for *-aoidē*), a song], lyric poem in exalted style.

O'di-um [L. *odium*, hatred ; *ōdī*, to hate], hatred. **O'dious.** [fragrant.

O-dor-if'er-ous [Odour and L. *ferre*, to carry], **O'dor-ous**, fragrant. [fragrance.

O'dour [L. *odor* (*odōr-is*), odour], smell,

Œc-u-men'i-cal (*œ==ee*) [Gk. *oikoumenikos*, fr. *hē oikumenē*, the inhabited earth], of or representing the whole Christian world.

Off [emph. form of *of*], from or away.

Of'fal [=off-fall], entrails of an animal, waste, refuse.

Of-fence' [see **Offend**], crime, injury, affront, displeasure.

Of-fend' [L. *ob*, against. *fendere* (p.p. *fensus*), to strike], affront, pain, sin.

Of-fen'sive, displeasing, insulting, attacking.

Of'fer [O.E. *offrian* ; L. *offerre*, to offer ; *ob*, near, *ferre*, to bring], hold out for acceptance, propose, sacrifice, present itself.

Of'fer-ing, that which is offered, sacrifice.

Of'fer-to-ry, offerings in church.

Off-hand', ready, instant, extempore.

Of'fice [L. *officium*, office ; *ob*, towards, *facere*, to do], duty, charge or trust, function, place of business, religious rite.

Of'fi-cer, one who fills an office, one who holds a commission in army or navy.

Of-fi'cial (*ci=sh*), pertaining to an office or trust ; one who fills a public post.

Of-fi'ci-ate (*c=sh*), act in an official capacity, conduct a public service.

Of-fi'ci-nal (*fic=fiss*) [L. *officīna* (contr. of *opificīna*), a workshop], kept in stock by apothecaries.

Of-fi'cious (*ci—sh*), meddling. [shore.

Off'ing [see **Off**], the sea some distance from

Off'scour-ing, refuse.

Off'set, shoot, set-off, foil, compensation.

Off'spring, child or children, descendants.

Oft, Of′ten [E.], many times.

O′gle [Du. *oogen* ; L.G. *oegeln*, to ogle], look at with amorous glances.

O′gre [?], fabulous man-devouring giant.

Ohm [fr. G. S. *Ohm*, German physicist], unit of electrical resistance.

Oil [O.F. *oile* ; L. *oleum*, oil ; *olea*, olive-tree], fluid which does not mix with water ; treat over with oil.

Oil′cake, cake of seeds from which oil has been pressed.

Oint′ment [L. *ungere*, to anoint], soft oily substance. [animal.

O-ka′pi [Native name], Central African

O-le-a′gi-nous [L. *oleāginus* ; see Oil], oily.

O-le-an′der [M.L. ; etym. doubtful], an evergreen shrub, the rose-bay tree.

O′le-o-graph [L. *oleum*, oil ; Gk. *graphein*, to draw], picture printed in oils.

Ol-fac′to-ry [L. *olēre*, to smell, *facere*, to make], pertaining to smell.

Ol′i-gar-chy (*ch=k*) [Gk. *oligos*, few, *archein*, to rule], government by a few. **Oli-gar′chical.**

Ol′ive [L. *olīva*, olive], tree with greyish-green fruit yielding oil.

O-lym′pi-an [fr. *Olympia*, town in Ancient Greece], of Olympus, celestial, condescending ; dweller in Olympus, one of the Greek gods. **Olym′pic**, ref. to games in honour of Zeus, held at intervals of four years (revived at Athens in 1896).

Om′e-let [O.F. *alemette* ; *alemelle* (corrupt. of *la lemelle*), a thin plate ; L. *lāmella*, dim. of *lāmina*, a plate], dish of eggs beaten up, seasoned, and fried in boiling butter.

O′men [L. *ōmen* (*omin-is*), an omen], warning token, foreboding.

Om′i-nous, foreshowing evil. [out.

O-mis′sion, act of omitting, something left

O-mit′ [L. *ob*, by, *mittere* (p.p. *missus*), to send], leave out, leave undone. **Omit′ted.**

Om′ni-bus [L. *omnibus*, for all (dat. pl. of *omnis*, all], public conveyance.

Om-nip′o-tent [L. *omnis*, all, *potens*, powerful], all-powerful.

Om-ni-pres′ent [L. *omnis*, all, *præsens*, present], present everywhere.

Om-nis′cient (*sci=ch*) [L. *omnis*, all, *scientia*, knowledge], knowing all things.

Om-niv′o-rous [L. *omnis*, all *vorāre*, to devour], eating food of every kind.

On′a-ger (*ŏn′ai-jer*) [Gk. *onos*, ass, *agrios*, wild], kind of wild ass.

Once [M.E. *ânes*, gen. of *ân*, one], one time only, at some past time. [some.

On′er-ous [L. *onus* (*oner-is*), burden], burden-

On′ion (*ŭnyŭn*) [F. *oignon* ; L. *ūnio* (*ūniōnis*), a large onion], bulb with a strong flavour.

On′ly (*ō*) [O.E. *ânlíc*, lit. one-like], one, sole ; merely, solely.

On′o-mat-o-pœ′ia (*-peeya*) [Gk. *onoma* (*ono-matos*), a name ; *poiein*, to make], formation of words in imitation of natural sounds.

On′set, attack. [attack.

On′slaught [O.E. *on*, on, *sleaht*, a stroke],

O′nus [L. *onus*, a burden], burden, some duty.

On′ward, further on, advancing.

On′yx [L. and Gk. *onyx*, nail, onyx], precious stone used for cameos.

O′o-lite [Gk. *ōion*, egg, *lithos*, stone], granular variety of limestone.

Ooze [O.E. *wáse*, soft mud, *wôs*, moisture, juice], soft mud ; flow gently, leak slowly.

O-pa′ci-ty [see Opaque], want of transparency.

O′pal [L. *opalus*, an opal], gem with a peculiar play of colours. **O′paline.**

O-paque′ (*ō-paik′*) [L. *opācus*, dark, obscure], not transparent, obscure. **Opac′ity.**

O′pen [E.], not shut, free, frank ; unclose, disclose, begin.

Op′er-a [It. *opera*, a work, a musical play ; L. *opus* (*oper-is*), work], drama which is sung to the accompaniment of an orchestra.

Op′er-a bouffe (*boof*), a farcical opera.

Op-er-et′ta [dim. of Opera], short, light opera.

Op′er-ate [L. *operārī* (p.p. *operātus*), operate, *opus* (*oper-is*), work], act, exert influence, perform a work, treat surgically.

Op-er-at′ic, pertaining to or like an opera.

Op-er-a′tion, working, performance, a surgical process on the body.

Op′er-a-tive, active, in force ; one who operates a machine.

Oph-id′i-an [Gk. *ophidion*, dim. of *ophis*, a snake], relating to reptiles, including snakes.

Oph-thal′mi-a [Gk. *ophthalmos*, eye], inflammation of the eye. **Ophthal′mic.**

O′pi-ate, medicine that contains opium.

O-pine′ [L. *opināri*, to opine], suppose, express or hold opinion.

O-pin′ion [see Opine], belief stronger than an impression, estimation. **Opin′ionated.**

O-pin′ion-a-tive, stiff in opinion.

O′pi-um [Gk. *opion*, poppy-juice (dim. of *opos*, sap)], dried juice of the seed-vessels of the white poppy. [animal.

O-pos′sum [Amer.-Ind.], kind of pouched

Op-po′nent [L. *ob*, against, *pōnere*, to place], one who opposes, adversary.

Op′por-tune [L. *opportūnus* ; fr. *ob*, against, and *portus*, harbour], timely, seasonable.

Op-pose′ (*s=z*) [F. *opposer* ; L. *ob*, against ; F. *poser*, to place], place over against, act against.

Op′po-site [L. *ob*, against, *positus*, placed], facing, contrary ; that which is opposed or contrary.

Op-po-si′tion, resistance, party out of power in parliament.

Op-press′ [L. *ob*, against, *premere* (p.p. *pressus*), to press], overload, harass. **Oppres′sion.** [reproachful.

Op-pro′bri-ous [see Opprobrium], abusive,

Op-pro′bri-um [L. *opprobrium* ; *ob*, against, *probrum*, disgraceful act], disgrace, abuse.

Op-pugn′ (*ugn=ūne*) [L. *ob*, against, *pug-nāre*, to fight], resist, call in question.

Op′ta-tive, Op-ta′tive [L. *optāre*, to choose], expressing wish.

Op′tic, Op′tic-al, pertaining to sight.

Op-ti′cian (*ici=ish*), one who makes or deals in optical instruments.

Op'tics [Gk. *opticos*, relating to sight, *opsomai*, I shall see], science of light and vision.

Op'ti-mism [L. *optimus*, best], belief· that everything is for the best, extreme hopefulness. **Optimis'tic.**

Op'tion [L. *optāre*, to choose], power of choosing, choice. **Op'tional.**

Op'u-lent [L. *opulentus*, wealthy, *ops*, wealth], wealthy, rich. **Op'ulence.**

Or'a-cle, [L. *ōrāculum*, oracle, *orāre*, to pray, to speak], answer of a deity, place where the answer was given, uncommonly wise person.

O-rac'u-lar, wise like an oracle.

O'ral [L. *ōs* (*ōr-is*), mouth], pertaining to the mouth, spoken.

Or'ange [Arab. *nāranj*, an orange], tree with a juicy fruit. **O'rangery.**

O-rang'-ou-tang' [Malay, *ōrang-ūtan*; *ōrang*, man, *ūtan*, woods], East Indian ape.

O-ra'tion [L. *orare* (p.p. *ōrātus*), to speak], elaborate public speech. [speaker.

Or'a-tor [L. *ōrāre*, to speak], eloquent

Or-a-to'ri-o [It. *oratorio* (orig. musical service at an oratory)], sacred story set to music.

Or'a-to-ry [L. *ōratōrium*, place of prayer, *ōrāre*, to pray], chapel for prayer, the art of effective public speaking.

Orb [L. *orbis*, a circle], sphere, esp. one of the celestial spheres.

Or'bit [L. *orbita*, a track, *orbis*, a ring], curved path of a heavenly body, an eye-socket.

Or'chard [O.E. *ortgeard*, orchard ; L. *hortus*, garden, and O.E. *geard*, yard], garden of fruit-trees.

Or'ches-tra (*ch*=*k*) [Gk. *orchestra*, orchestra, *orchesthai*, I dance], part of a theatre where the band sits, the band itself. **Orchestra'- tion.**

Or'chid, Or'chis (*ch*=*k*) [Gk. *orchis*, an orchis], plant with a lipped flower.

Or-dain' [L. *ordināre*, to ordain ; L. *ordo*, order], decree, set apart for office.

Or'deal [Com. Teut. ; O.E. *ordál*, *ordél*], old form of test to determine guilt, severe trial.

Or'der [L. *ordo* (*ordĭn-is*), class, arrangement, usage, public quiet, command, direction, (*pl.*) office in the church ; arrange, command, give an order for.

Or'der-ly, in good order ; soldier who carries messages for a superior officer, attendant in a hospital.

Or'di-nal, number denoting order.

Or'di-nance [see **Ordain**], established law or rule, religious observance. [usual.

Or'di-na-ry [see **Order**], according to order,

Or-di-na'tion, act of setting apart.

Ord'nance [var. of **Ordinance**], heavy weapons of war, artillery.

Or'dure [O.F. *ord*, foul ; L. *horridus*, rough, horrid], dung, obscenity.

Ore [O.E. *ár*, brass ; conn. with O.E. *óra*, ore], mineral containing metal from the mine.

Or'gan [Gk. *organon*, an implement, *ergon*, work], means, part which performs a function, keyed wind instrument.

Or-gan'ic, pertaining to an organ or its functions.

Or'gan-ism, body with organic life.

Or-gan-i-za'tion, act of organizing, that which is organized.

Or'gan-ize, put into working order.

Or'gy (*g*=*j*) [formerly pl. only, L. and Gk. *orgia*, orgies, allied to Gk. *ergon*, work], drunken revel, carouse.

O'ri-el [O.F. *oriol*, a porch, corridor ; etym. doubtful], bay window.

O-ri-en'tal [L. *orīrī* (pr.p. *oriens, -entis*), to rise], eastern.

O-ri-en-ta'tion [see **Oriental**], determination of the east in taking bearings.

Or'i-fice (*ice*=*iss*) [L. *orificium* ; *ōs* (*ōr-is*), mouth, *facere*, to make], mouth, opening.

Or'i-gin [L. *orīgo* (*origin-is*), origin ; *orīrī*, to rise], beginning, source.

O-ri'gi-nal, first in order, not copied, inventive ; first-hand work, not a copy.

O-ri-gi-nal'i-ty, power of suggesting new thoughts, etc.

O-ri'gin-ate, cause to be. **Origina'tor.**

O'ri-ole [F. *oriol* ; L. *aureolus*, golden], kind of bird with bright plumage.

Or'i-son [O.F. *orison* ; L. *ōrātio*, a prayer ; see **Oration**], a prayer.

Or'mo-lu [F. *or moulu*, ground gold], a fine brass of a golden colour.

Or'na-ment [L. *ornāre*, to adorn], decoration ; adorn. **Ornamenta'tion.** [decorated.

Or-nate' [L. *ornāre* (p.p. *ornātus*), to adorn],

Or-ni-thol'o-gy [Gk. *ornis* (*ornith-os*), a bird ; *logos*, discourse], science which treats of birds.

Or-nith-o-rhyn'cus [Gk. *ornis*, bird, *rhyncos*, snout], Australian duck-bill.

O-ro'gra-phy [Gk. *oros*, mountain, *graphein*, to describe], science of mountains.

Or'phan [Gk. *orphanos*, destitute], child whose father and mother are dead. **Or'phanage.**

Or'ris [perh. corruption of **Iris**], kind of iris.

Or'tho-dox [Gk. *orthos*, right, *doxa*, opinion], (opinions) commonly accepted, esp. on religious doctrine. **Or'thodoxy.**

Or-tho'ë-py [Gk. *orthos*, right, *epos*, a word], correct pronunciation.

Or-tho'gra-phy [Gk. *orthos*, right, *graphein*, to write], spelling. **Orthograph'ical.**

Os'cil-late [L. *oscillāre* (p.p. *oscillātus*), to swing], swing, vary between limits. **Oscilla'tion.**

Os'cu-late [L. *osculārī* (p.p. *osculātus*), to kiss, *osculum*, little mouth], kiss. **Oscu-la'tion.**

O'sier (*si*=*zh* or *zi*) [F. *osier* ; etym. doubtful], name for several kinds of willow.

Os'prey [L. *ossifragus*, osprey ; *os* (*oss-is*), bone, *frangere*, to break], fishhawk.

Os'se-ous [L. *osseus* ; *os* (*oss-is*), bone], bony, like bone.

Os'si-fy [L. *os*, bone, *facere*, to make], to form into bone, to harden. **Ossifica'tion.**

Os-ten'si-ble [L. *ostendere* (p.p. *ostensus*), to show], shown, apparent.

Os-ten-ta′tion [L. *ostentāre* (p.p. *ostentātus*), freq. of *ostendere*, to show], unnecessary show. **Ostenta′tious.**

Os-te-o′lo-gy [Gk. *osteon*, bone, *-logia*, branch of knowledge], science which treats of bones.

Ost′ler [earlier *hostler*; O.F. *hostel*, an inn], stableman at an inn.

Os′tra-cism [Gk. *ostracon*, a potsherd, voting-tablet], banishment by popular vote, exclusion. **Os′tracize.**

Os′trich [L. *avis strūthio*, ostrich-bird; Gk. *strouthion*, ostrich], large running bird.

Oth′er-wise (*s=z*) [O.E. *on othre wisan*], differently, under other conditions.

O-ti-ose′ (*t=sh*) [L. *ōtium*, ease], at ease, idle.

Ot′ter [Com. Teut.; O.E. *otr*], aquatic animal which lives on fish.

Ot′to-man [from Turkish *Othman*, or *Osman*], stuffed seat without a back.

Ought (*awt*) [O.E. *āhte*, past of *agan*, to owe], be bound in duty.

Ounce [L. *uncia*, ounce, inch], twelfth part of a pound troy, sixteenth part of a pound.

Oust [O.F. *oster*, to take away; etym. doubtful], turn out, remove.

Out [Com. Teut.; O.E. *ūt*], not in, away from.

Out′cast, one driven from home or country.

Out′come, result.

Out′crop, edges of strata as they appear at the surface.

Out-do′, surpass.

Out′fit, things required for an equipment.

Out-flank′, get beyond the flank of.

Out-grow′, grow away from.

Out′growth, an offshoot.

Out′ing, an airing, an excursion.

Out-land′ish, foreign, strange.

Out′law, one who has forfeited the protection of the law; to declare an outlaw.

Out′lay, a laying out or spending.

Out′let, a passage out, a vent.

Out′line, a line round the outside, summary; sketch out.

Out-live′, live beyond.

Out′look, watch, view, prospect.

Out′rage [L. *ultra*, beyond, and suf. *-age*], gross injury; to subject to violent injury.

Out-ra′geous, furious, atrocious.

Out′ri-der, mounted servant attending a carriage.

Out-right′, completely.

Out′set, setting out, beginning.

Out-shine′, excel in splendour.

Out-side′, that which is without, the utmost.

Out′skirt, outer edge, border.

Out′span, unyoke oxen from a wagon.

Out-spo′ken, speaking or spoken freely.

Out-stand′ing, prominent, not paid.

Out-strip′ [Out and Strip (with obs. meaning, to run fast)], outrun, leave behind.

Out-vote′, defeat by votes.

Out′ward [O.E. *ūt*, and *weard*], on or directed toward the outside.

Out-wit′, surpass in cleverness.

Out′work, outer fortification.

Ou′zel, Ou′sel (*ou=oo*) [O.E., *ōsle*, an ouzel], name given to blackbird and other thrushes.

O′val, O′vate [L. *ōvum*, egg], egg-shaped.

O′va-ry [L. *ōvum*, egg], seed-vessel.

O-va′tion [L. *ovāre* (past. part. *ovātus*), to shout], lesser triumph among the Romans, triumphant reception.

Ov′en (*o=ŭ*) [Com. Teut.; O.E. *ofn*], structure which may be heated for baking, etc.

O′ver [Com. Teut.; O.E. *ofer*], above, across, too much, outward and downward; number of balls bowled in cricket.

O′ver-act′, perform to excess.

O′ver-all, loose protective outer garment.

O′ver-awe′, restrain by awe. [balance.

O′ver-bal′ance, outweigh, cause to lose

O′ver-bear′ing, domineering.

O′ver-board′, over the side of a ship.

O′ver-cast′, cloud over, sew coarsely over a raw edge.

O′ver-charge′, charge too much, fill too full.

O′ver-come′, conquer.

O′ver-do, do too much, cook too much.

O′ver-draw′, to draw upon a bank in excess of one's credit, exaggerate.

O′ver-due, delayed beyond the proper time.

O′ver-flow′, to flood, abound.

O′ver-flow′, overflowing, that which overflows.

O′ver-grow′, grow beyond, cover with growth.

O′ver-haul′, drag over, turn over for examination.

O′ver-hear′, hear by accident.

O′ver-land, by or across land.

O′ver-look′, view from above, supervise, examine, omit.

O′ver-pow′er, exceed in power, subdue.

O′ver-rate′, value too highly.

O′ver-reach′, deceive, outwit, stretch too far.

O′ver-ride′, ride beyond, supersede.

O′ver-rule′, rule over, decide against.

O′ver-run′, spread over, go beyond.

O′ver-seer′, superintendent.

O′ver-shad′ow, throw a shade over, darken.

O′ver-sight′, watchful care, omission.

O′ver-state′, exaggerate.

O′vert′ [O.F. *ovrir* (p.p. *overt*), to open], open to view, manifest.

O′ver-take′, to come up with.

O′ver-throw′, to upset, defeat.

O′ver-throw′, defeat, ruin.

O′ver-time, extra working time.

O′ver-top′, tower above.

O′ver-ture [O.F. *overture*, an opening, *overt*, opened], offer, opening orchestral piece.

O′ver-turn′, upset, destroy.

O′ver-ween′ing, unduly confident.

O-ver-whelm′ [Over and M.E. *whelmen*, perh. from O.E. *ahwylfan*, to overturn], cover as by a great wave.

O′vi-form [L. *ovum* (*ov-ī*), egg, *forma*, shape], egg-shaped.

O′vine [L. *ōvis*, a sheep], relating to sheep.

O-vi′par-ous [L. *ovum*, egg, *parere*, to bring forth], producing young by means of eggs.

Owe [O.E. *āgan*, to own], be indebted.

Owl [O.E. *üle*, an owl], nightbird. **Owl'et.**

Own [see **Owe**], possess, acknowledge; belonging to (after a possessive).

Ox, (*pl.*) **Oxen** [Com. Teut.; O.E. *oxa*], horned cattle.

Ox-al'ic [L. and Gk. *oxalis*, sorrel], derived from wood-sorrel.

Ox'ide [Gk. *oxy*- (comb. form of *oxys*, sharp], and *-ide* (comb. form of *eidos*, like], compound of oxygen with another element. **Ox'idize.**

Ox'y-gen [Gk. *oxys*, sharp, *genos*, birth], invisible gas which is essential to life.

Oy'ster [Gk. *ostreon*, an oyster], bivalve shellfish.

O-zone' [Gk. *ozein*, to smell], gas with a peculiar odour. form of oxygen.

P

Pab'u-lum [L. *pābulum*, food, *pascere*, to feed], food, nourishment for animals and plants, (in man) for the mind.

Pace [L. *passus*, a step, *pandere* (p.p. *passus*), to stretch], step, rate of walking; walk with regular steps, set the pace for.

Pach-y-der'ma-tous (*ch=k*) [Gk. *pachys*, thick, *derma* (*dermat-os*), skin], thick-skinned. [tion.

Pa-cif'ic, peacemaking, calm. **Pacifica'-**

Pa'ci-fy [F. *pacifier*; L. *pax* (*pāc-is*), peace, *facere*, to make], make peaceful, soothe.

Pack [M.E. *packe, pakke*, cogn. with early M. Flem., M.Du. *pac*, a pack], bundle, set of cards, set of hounds, wolves, etc., mass of floating ice; press into close order, put in a case, etc., go off.

Pack'age, parcel. [boat.

Pack'et [dim. of **Pack**], small package, mail-

Pact [L. *pacisci* (p.p. *pactus*), to agree], agreement, compact.

Pad [?], small cushion; to stuff.

Pad [Du. *pad*, a path], highwayman, an easy-paced horse; to travel on foot.

Pad'ding [?], material used in stuffing.

Pad'dle [?], dabble in water, propel with a paddle; short broad-bladed oar.

Pad'dock [corruption of M.E. *parrok*, fr. O.E. *pearroc*], small inclosure for pasture.

Pad'lock [perh. fr. Prov. E. *pad*, a pannier; see **Lock**], portable lock; fasten with a padlock.

Pæ'an (*ae=ee*) [Gk. *paian, paion*, hymn to Apollo, under name of *Paian*], song of triumph.

Pa'gan (*Pa=pai*) [L. *pāgus*, village, district], heathen. **Pa'ganism.** [boy.

Page [Late L. *pagius*, a servant], serving-

Page [L. *pāgina*, a page, *pangere*, to fasten], one side of leaf of a book; mark or number the pages of.

Pa'geant (*ă* or *ai*) [perh. L. *pāgina*, page], spectacle, show. **Pa'geantry.**

Pa-gin-a'tion [L. *pāgina*, page], act of paging, page number.

Pa-go'da [Port. *pagode*; perh. fr. Pers. *but-kadah*, an idol-temple], Hindu or Buddhist temple.

Pail [etym. dub.; cf. O.E. *pægel*, gill; O.F. *paelle*, frying-pan; L. *patella*, dim. of *patina*, pan], vessel for holding liquids.

Pain [L. *pœna*, punishment, pain], suffering, an ache; (*pl.*) trouble taken; cause suffering.

Paint [F. *peindre* (p.p. *peint*); L. *pingere*, to paint], colour, make a picture in colours; substance used in colouring.

Paint'er, one who paints.

Paint'er [perh. M.E. *panter*, a noose], rope to fasten a boat.

Pair [L. *paria*, neut. pl. of *par*, equal], two of a kind, two voters on opposite sides who agree not to vote; join in pairs.

Pal'ace [L. *palātium*, palace of Augustus, on the *Palatine* Hill, Rome], official residence (of a sovereign, bishop, etc.).

Pal'a-din [It. *paladino*, orig. a knight of the palace; see **Palatine**], knight errant, a peer of Charlemagne's Court.

Pal-ae-on-tol'o-gy [Gk. *palaios*, old, *onto-*, comb. form of part. of *einai*, be, *logos*, discourse], science of fossils.

Pal-an-quin', -keen' [Port. *palanquim*, palanquin; Hind. *palang*, a bed], covered litter carried by men, used in the East.

Pal'a-ta-ble, pleasant to the taste.

Pal'ate [L. *palātum*, a palate], roof of the mouth, taste.

Pa-la'tial (*ti=sh*), like a palace.

Pal'a-tine [L. *Palātinus*, name of a hill in Rome; a palace], with royal privileges (applied to special territories and their rulers).

Pa-la'ver [Port. *palavra*, a word; see **Parable**], talk, esp. idle talk, flattery, a conference; talk idly, flatter.

Pale [L. *pallidus*, pale], lacking colour, not bright; lose colour. **Pale'ly.**

Pale [F. *pal*; L. *pālus*, a stake], stake, boundary, particular territory or district.

Pal'ette [It. *paletta*, dim. of *pala*, spade; L. *pāla*, spade], thin tablet on which an artist mixes his colours.

Pal'frey (*ā*) [Gk. *para*, extra; L. *verēdus*, post-horse], small saddle-horse.

Pal'imp-sest [Gk. *palimpsestos*, scraped again; *palin*, again, *psaein*, to rub], MS. which has been twice written on, the first writing being erased.

Pa'ling, fence of pales.

Pal-i-sade' [F. *palissade*; see **Pale**], fence of sharp stakes.

Pall [*a=aw*) [L. *pallium*, a cloak], mantle, cloth thrown over a coffin. [insipid.

Pall [contraction of Appal], become dull or

Pal-la'di-um (*lai*) [Gk. *palladion*], image of Pallas on which safety of Troy was held to depend, safeguard.

Pall'et [F. *paillet*, fr. *paille*; L. *palea*, straw], bed of straw.

Pall'et [doublet of **Palette**], tool used by potters.

Pal-liasse′, Pail-lasse′ (*păl-yăs′*) [F. *paillase*, from *paille*, straw ; see **Pallet** 1], under-bed of straw.

Pal′li-ate [L. *palliāre* (p.p. *palliātus*), to cloak ; see **Pall** 1], excuse, relieve for the time. **Pallia′tive.**

Pal′lid [L. *pallidus*, pale], pale.

Pal′lor [L. *pallēre*, to be pale], paleness.

Palm 1 (*al*=*ah*) [L. *palma*, a palm], inner part of the hand between wrist and fingers. **Pal′mate.**

Palm 2 [L. *palma*, a palm-tree], kind of tree, branch or leaf of the tree.

Palm 3 [fr. **Palm** 1], pass off by trickery.

Pal′mis-try, fortune-telling from the palm of the hand.

Pal′my, bearing palms, flourishing.

Pal′pa-ble [L. *palpāre*, to touch lightly], perceptible by the touch, plain.

Pal′pi-tate [L. *palpitāre* (p.p. *palpitātus*), to throb], beat rapidly, throb. **Palpita′tion.**

Pal′sy (*pawlzy*) [as **Paralysis**], paralysis.

Pal′ter (*a*=*aw*) [fr. root of **Paltry**], act deceit-fully, trifle with.

Pal′try (*a*=*aw*) [old noun *palter*, rags ; Swed. *paltor* ; Dan. *pialter*, rags], worth-less, trifling.

Pam′pas [Peruv. *bamba*, a plain], vast plains of S. America.

Pam′per [freq. fr. Low G. *pampen*, to cram], indulge to excess.

Pam′phlet [perh. fr. *Pamphilet* ; L. love-poem of 12th c.], small unbound treatise. **Pamphleteer′.**

Pan [O.E. *panne*], shallow vessel, part of a flintlock, natural basin, upper part of skull (brainpan) ; separate, as gold from sand, by washing in a pan.

Pan-a-ce′a [Gk. *panaceia*, a panacea ; *pan*, all, *acos*, remedy], remedy for all diseases.

Pan-a′da [Sp. *panada* ; L. *panis*, bread], bread boiled and flavoured.

Pan′cre-as [Gk. *pan*, all, *creas*, flesh], gland near stomach discharging digestive fluid, sweetbread.

Pan-de-mo′ni-um [Gk. *pan*, all, *daimon*, demon], home of all the demons, uproar.

Pan′der [fr. Gk. name *Pandaros*], minister to evil wishes.

Pane [L. *pannus*, a cloth], glass in a division of a window.

Pa-ne-gyr′ic (*gyr*=*jĭr*) [Gk. *panēgyricos*, fit for a full assembly, festive ; *pan*, all, and *egyris*, related to *agora*, assembly], discourse in praise of some one.

Pan′el [M.L. *pannellus*, dim. of *pannus*, see **Pane**], division in a door, ceiling, etc., a slab on which a picture is painted, jury roll, the jury.

Pang [?], sharp extreme pain.

Pan′ic [Gk. *panicos*, pertaining to the god *Pan*], sudden overpowering terror.

Pan′ni-er [L. *pānārium*, bread-basket, *pānis*, bread], basket (used commonly in pairs).

Pan′o-ply [Gk. *panoplia* ; *pan*, all, *hopla*, arms], suit of armour.

Pan-o-ra′ma [Gk. *pan*, all, *horama*, view], unbroken view, extensive picture exhibited by unrolling. **Panora′mic.**

Pan′sy (*s*=*z*) [F. *pensée*, thought ; fr. L. *pensāre*, to ponder], flower of the violet kind.

Pant [O.F. *pantaisier*, to pant, perh. fr. Late L. *phantasiāre*, to have nightmare], breathe in a laboured manner, gasp, long ; quick breathing, a gasp.

Pan-ta-loon′ [It. *pantalone*, a buffoon, from *Pantaleone*, a common Venetian name], buffoon in pantomime, (*pl.*) trousers.

Pan′the-ism [Gk. *pan*, all, *theos*, god], doc-trine that the universe is God. **Pan′theis′tic.**

Pan′the-on [Gk. *pan*, all, *theos*, god], temple dedicated to all the gods.

Pan′ther [Gk. *panthēr*, a panther], large variety of leopard.

Pan′to-mime [Gk. *pan*, all, *mimos*, actor, imitator], acting in dumb show, Christmas theatrical spectacle. **Pantomim′ic.**

Pan′try [Late L. *pānētāria*, bread-shop ; L. *panis*, bread], room for provisions, plate, etc.

Pap 1 [imit. of sound made by infants in feeding], soft food, pulp.

Pap 2 [same as **Pap** 1], nipple, teat.   [pope.

Pa′pa-cy [L. *pāpa*, father, pope], office of the

Pa′pal [L. *pāpa*, father, pope], pertaining to the pope. **Pa′pist.**

Pa-pav′er-ous [L. *papāver*, poppy], pertain-ing to the poppy.

Pa′per [L. *papyrus*, papyrus], substance of fibrous material made in thin sheets, a periodical, a writing ; cover with paper.

Pa-pil-i-on-a′ceous (*ce*=*sh*) [L. *papilio* (*pa-piliōn-is*), butterfly], with corolla like a butterfly.

Pa-poose′ [Amer.-Ind. *papoose*], a N. Ameri-can Indian baby.

Pa-py′rus [Gk. *papyros*, papyrus], rush-like plant, also paper made from it, on which the ancient Egyptians and others wrote.

Par [L. *pār*, equal], equality (esp. of actual and nominal value).

Par′a-ble [Gk. *parabolē* ; *para*, beside, *ballein*, to throw], figurative story with a moral. **Parabol′ical.**

Par-a′bo-la [as **Parable**], plane curve formed by intersection of cone with plane parallel to its side.

Par′a-chute (*chute*=*shoot*) [F. *parachute*; *para-* (It. *parāre*, to ward off), and F. *chute*, fall], umbrella-shaped contrivance for descending from a balloon or airship. **Par′achutist.**

Par′a-clete [F. fr. Gk. *para*, beside, *kletos* (fr. *kaleō*, call)], advocate, title of the Holy Ghost.

Pa-rade′ [F. *parade* ; L. *parāre*, to prepare], show, procession, military review, drill-ground, public walk ; show off, marshal.

Par′a-di̇ɡm [Gk. *paradeigma* ; *para*, beside, *deiknymi*, to show], example (esp. of the inflections of a verb or noun). **Para-digma′tic.**

Par′a-dise [Gk. *paradeisos*; O.Pers. *pairi-daeza*, a park], Garden of Eden, Heaven, perfectly happy place or state. **Para-dis′ical.**

Par′a-dos [Gk. *para*, beside, L. *dorsum*, back], parapet behind trench, etc.

Par′a-dox Gk. *para*, beside, *doxa*, opinion], opinion contrary to received belief, apparently self-contradictory statement. **Paradox′ical.**

Par′af-fin, Par′af-fine [L. *parum*, little; *affinis*, having affinity], white waxy substance distilled from coal-tar, etc.

Par′a-gon [It. *paragone*, paragon; etym. doubtful], model of excellence.

Par′a-graph [Gk. *para*, beside, *graphein*, to write], section of a writing or chapter; divide into such sections.

Par-a-keet′, Par-o-quet′ (*qu=k*) [O.F. *paroquet*, perh. fr. It. *parrochetto*], small parrot.

Par′al-lel [Gk. *para*, beside, *allēlos*, one another], equally distant in all parts, like; line equally distant in all parts from another, similarity, comparison; show to be similar, find something similar to.

Par′al-lel-ism, correspondence of successive passages, esp. in Hebrew poetry.

Par-al-lel′o-gram [**Parallel**, and Gk. *gramma*, a line], four-sided figure whose opposite sides are parallel.

Pa-ral′y-sis [Gk. *para*, beside, *lyein*, to loosen], loss of power of motion.

Par-a-lyt′ic [see **Paralysis**], pertaining to paralysis; one affected with paralysis.

Par′a-lyse, Par′a-lyze, affect with paralysis, render ineffective.

Par′a-mount [O.F. *par amont*; *par*, by, *amont*, above; L. *per*, by, *ad montem*, to the hill], supreme.

Par′a-pet [It. *parare*, guard, and *petto*, breast], low wall at the edge of a balcony, roof, etc., or along the sides of a bridge.

Par-a-pher-na′li-a [Gk. *parapherna*, property of a bride; *para*, beside, and *phernē*, dower], appendages, equipments.

Par′a-phrase [Gk. *para*, beside, *phrasein*, to tell], statement in another form; restate in other language.

Par′a-site [Gk. *para*, beside, *sitos*, food], plant or animal that lives on another, hanger-on, a toady. [sunshade.

Par′a-sol [It. *parare*, to ward off, *sol*, sun],

Par′boil [formerly meant "to boil thoroughly"; L. *per*, through, *bullīre*, to boil], boil partly.

Par′cel [F. *parcelle*; L. *particula*, a small part], portion, packet; divide by parts, make up into a package.

Parch [?], scorch, become hot and dry.

Parch′ment [F. *parchemin*; L. *pergamēna* (*charta*—paper) of *Pergamum*, where parchment was invented], skin prepared for writing on.

Pard [Gk. *pardos*], leopard.

Par′don [L. *per*, fully, *donāre*, to give], forgive; forgiveness, remission of a penalty. **Par′donable.**

Pare [L. *parāre*, to prepare], cut off outside part, lessen, trim.

Par-e-gor′ic [Gk. *parēgoricos*, soothing; *para*, beside, *agora*, assembly], flavoured tincture of opium.

Pa′rent [L. *parens* (*parent-is*), parent], father or mother. **Pa′rentage.**

Pa-ren′the-sis (*pl.* -ses) [Gk. *para*, beside, *en*, in, *thesis*, a placing], inserted word, clause, sentence usually between brackets ( ). **Parenthet′ical.**

Pa′ri-ah [Tamil *paraiyan*, drummer, *parai*, drum], low-grade Hindu, outcast.

Pa-ri′e-tal [L. *pariēs* (*pariet-is*), a wall], pertaining to a division of the body, etc.

Par′ish [Gk. *paroicia*, an ecclesiastical district; *para*, near, *oikos*, house], district assigned to a priest or parson, subdivision of a county. **Parish′ioner.**

Par′i-ty [L. *par*, equal], equality, close correspondence.

Park [M.E. fr. O.F. *parc*], piece of ground laid out for public recreation, or attached to a mansion, stance for motor-cars.

Par′lance [F. *parler*; L. *parabolāre*, to speak], discourse, talk.

Par′ley [F. *parler*, L. *parabolāre*, to speak], discussion of terms; confer on terms.

Par′lia-ment [O.F. *parlement*, a parleying court], national legislative assembly. **Parliamen′tary.** [sitting-room.

Par′lour [O.F. *parloir*; F. *parler*, to speak],

Par′lous [for *perilous*], perilous.

Pa-ro′chi-al (*ch=k*), [Late L. *parochiālis*; see **Parish**], pertaining to a parish, narrow, limited.

Par′o-dy [Gk. *para*, beside, and *oidē*, an ode], burlesque imitation of a literary composition; to burlesque.

Pa-role′ [F. *parole*, a word; L. *parabola*, a parable], word of honour.

Par-ot′id [Gk. *parōtis*; *para*, beside, and *ous* (*ōtis*), ear], near the ear.

Par′ox-ysm [Gk. *para*, beside, *oxynein*, to sharpen], sudden and violent emotion, or attack of illness.

Par′quet-ry (*qu=k*) [F. *parqueterie*; *parquet*, a compartment, dim. of *parc*, a park], inlaid woodwork.

Par′ra-keet′, Par′ro-quet′ [see **Parakeet**].

Par′ri-cide [L. *parricīda*, murder of a relative; etym. doubtful], murderer or murder of a father.

Par′rot [F. *Perrot*, *Pierrot*, little Peter, etym. uncertain], bird which can imitate words.

Par′ry [L. *parāre*, to prepare], ward off, turn aside. [grammatically.

Parse [L. *pars*, a part], describe words

Par′see [Pers. *Pārsī*, a Persian], descendant of Persians (Zoroastrians) who took refuge in India from Mohammedan persecutio.. in 7th and 8th centuries.

Par′si-mo-ny [L. *parcere*, to spare], extreme frugality, miserliness. **Parsimo′nious.**

Pars′ley [Gk. *petroselinon*, parsley; fr. Gk. *petra*, rock, *selinon*, parsley], branching herb.

Pars′nip [M.E. *passenep*; L. *pastināca*, parsnip, perh. from *pastināre*, to dig up], plant with an edible root.

Par′son [M.E. and O.F. *persone*, parson, L. *persōna*, a person], clergyman.

Par′son-age, clergyman's house.

Part [L. *pars* (*part-is*), a part], something less than a whole, a side (in conflict), character in a play, music for one voice; divide, separate.

Par-take′, to share.

Par-terre′ [F. *par terre*, on or over the ground], level part of garden occupied by flower-beds, part of ground-floor of a theatre.

Par′thian, of *Parthia*, an ancient kingdom of W. Asia. Parthian horsemen used to shoot missiles backwards while in flight, hence the expressions *P. shot, glance*, etc.

Par′ti-al (*t=sh*) [L. *pars* (*part-is*), a part], not complete, unduly favourable.

Par-ti-al′ity (*t=sh*), inclination to favour, special taste or liking.

Par-ti′ci-pant, Par-ti′ci-pa-tor, partaker.

Par-ti′ci-pate [L. *participāre* (p.p. *participātus*); *pars* (*part-is*), a part, *capere*, to take], share in. **Participa′tion.**

Par′ti-ci-ple [see **Participate**], part of speech partaking of the nature of both verb and adjective.

Par′ti-cle [L. *particula*, double dim. of *pars* (*part-is*), a part], very small part.

Par′ti (or **Par′ty-**) col′oured, variegated.

Par-tic′u-lar [see **Particle**], belonging to one only, exact, fastidious; (*n.pl.*) details. **Particular′ity, Partic′ularize.**

Part′ing, dividing, given when departing; division, leave-taking.

Par′ti-san (*s=z*), **Par′ti-zan** (also pronounced **Par-ti-zan′**) [It. *partigiano*, a partisan; L. *pars* (*part-is*), a part], devoted, esp. unreasoning, adherent to a party. **Par′tisan-ship.**

Par′ti-san, Par′ti-zan [M.F. *pertuisane*; It. *partigiana*], long-handled spear.

Par-ti′tion [see **Part**], division, distribution.

Par′ti-tive, denoting part of a whole.

Part′ly, in part.

Part′ner [corruption of M.E. *parcener*; O.F. *parcener*, a partner; L. *pars* (*part-is*), a part], sharer, associate.

Part′ner-ship, joint possession, a firm.

Par′tridge [M.E. *pertrich*; L. and Gk. *perdix*, a partridge], kind of game-bird.

Par-tur-i′tion [L. *parturitio*, fr. *parere*, to bear], child-birth. **Partur′ient.**

Par′ty [F. *partie*; L. *partīre*, to divide], number of persons united in opinion or action, social gathering, participator.

Par′ve-nu [F. *parvenu*, p.p. of *parvenir*, to arrive], upstart.

Pas′chal (*ch=k*) [Heb. *pesakh*, a passing over], pertaining to the Passover.

Pash′a, Pach′a [Turk. fr. Pers. *bāshā, bādshāh*, a pasha; *pād*, protecting, and *shāh*, king], Turkish governor of a province, or military commander.

Pas-quin-ade′ [It. *Pasquino*, statue in Rome, on which lampoons were fixed], lampoon, satire.

Pass [Late L. *passāre*, to pass; L. *passus*, a step], to go by, take place, be accepted as adequate, thrust; passage-way, thrust, state of things, permission to pass.

Pass′a-ble, that can be passed, fairly good.

Pas′sage, transit, fare for voyage, corridor, entrance-hall, small part of writing or discourse, etc., encounter.

Pas′sen-ger [M.E. and F. *passager*, fr. *passage*], traveller by train, boat, etc.

Pas′sion [L. *patī* (p.p. *passus*), to suffer], sufferings of Jesus Christ on the Cross, overmastering emotion.

Pas′sion-ate, quick-tempered, vehement.

Pas′sive [see **Passion**], not active, unresisting. **Passiv′ity.**

Pass′-key, private key, key for opening several locks.

Pass′port [F. *passer*, to pass; L. *portus*, a harbour], permission to pass.

Past [p.p. of **Pass**], bygone, preceding, last (week, month, etc.); by, beyond; aside.

Paste [Late L. *pasta*, paste; Gk. *pasta*, pl.], barley-porridge, soft composition as of moistened flour; fasten or stick up with paste.

Paste′board, stiff substance made of sheets of paper pasted together.

Pas′tel [It. *pastello*, dim. of *pasta*, paste]; dry paste made from paints and gum-water, used for crayons.

Pas′tern [O.F. *pasturon*, pastern, perh. *pasture*, tether, pasture], part of horse's foot between fetlock and hoof.   [play.

Pas′time [from **Pass** and **Time**], amusement,

Pas′tor [L. *pastor*, shepherd, fr. *pascere* (p.p. *pastus*), to feed], minister, priest (spiritual guide or shepherd).

Pas′tor-al, relating to pastors, relating to rural life; poem dealing with shepherd life or country life, letter from a bishop to clergy or people.

Pas′tor-ate, office of a pastor.   [etc.

Pas′try (*a=ai*) [prob. fr. **Paste**], crust of tarts,

Pas′ture [L. *pascere* (p.p. *pastus*), to feed], herbage for cattle, grazing ground. **Pas′turage.**   [pie.

Pas′ty (*a=ai*) like paste in colour, etc.; meat

Pat [prob. imit.], strike gently with the hand; light, quick stroke, small mass shaped by pats; exactly suitable.

Patch [?], small piece of anything used to repair; mend with pieces.

Pat′chou-li, Pat-chou′li (*chou=shoo*) [perh. Tamil *pachchai*, green, and *ilai*, leaf], perfume from Indian plant.

Pate [?], head.

Pa′tent [L. *patēre* (pr.p. *patens*, -*entis*), to lie open), evident, (letters) open to public perusal, varnished (leather); exclusive right secured by official authority. **Patentee′.**

Pa-ter′nal [L. *pater*, a father], relating to a father, fatherly.

Pa-ter'ni-ty, fatherhood.

Pa'ter-nos'ter [L. *pater,* father, *noster,* our], Lord's Prayer.

Path [O.E. *pœth*], trodden way.

Pa-thet'ic[Gk. *pathēticos* ; see **Pathos**], rousing tender feelings.

Pa-thol'o-gy [Gk. *pathos,* suffering, *logos,* discourse], science which treats of diseases. **Patholog'ical.**

Pa'thos [Gk. *pathos,* suffering], quality which touches the feelings.

Pa'tient (*ti*=*sh*) [L. *pati* (pr.p. *patiens, -entis*), to suffer], long-suffering ; one who is under medical treatment.

Patois (*pat'va*) [F. *patois,* country talk ; etym. uncertain], provincial form of speech, dialect.

Pa'tri-arch (*ch*=*k*) [Gk. *patriarchēs* ; Gk. *patria,* a clan ; *archein,* to rule], ancestor of a tribe of Israel, venerable old man, dignitary (R.C. and Greek Churches). **Patriar'chal.**

Pa-tri'cian (*ci*=*sh*) [L. *patricius,* noble ; *pater* (*patr-is*), a father], one of the original Roman nobility, one of high birth ; noble.

Pat'ri-mo-ny [L. *patrimōnium,* patrimony ; *pater,* a father], inheritance from one's father.

Pa'tri-ot [Gk. *patriotēs,* a fellow-country-man ; *pater,* a father], one who loves his country. **Pa'triotism.**

Pat-ris'tic [L. *pater,* father], referring to the ancient fathers of the Church.

Pat-rol' [F. *patrouille* (n.) ; *patrouiller* (vb.), lit. to paddle with the feet ; O.F. *pate,* a paw], go the rounds ; going of the rounds by a guard, also the guard, detachment of troops sent to reconnoitre.

Pa'tron (*a*=*ai*), fem. **Pa'tron-ess** [L. *patrōnus,* patron; *pater* (*patr-is*), a father], one who protects or countenances, furtherer, guardian saint.

Pat'ron-age, special countenance, the right of nominating to public office.

Pat'ron-ize, act as patron of, treat con-descendingly.

Pat-ro-nym'ic [Gk. *pater,* father, *onoma,* a name], name derived from that of an ancestor.

Pat'ten [formerly *paten* ; F. *patin,* a patten], sole of wood worn under ordinary shoe.

Pat'ter [fr. *Pater* in Paternoster], mechanical repetition ; talk glibly, rapidly.

Pat'ter [freq. of *pat*], strike as raindrops ; quick succession of light sounds.

Pat'tern [M.E. *patron* ; see **Patron**], that which is to be copied ; model.

Pat'ty [F. *pâte,* pasty ; Late L. *pasta,* paste], little pie. [scarcity.

Pau'ci-ty (*c* soft) [L. *paucus,* few], fewness.

Paunch [L. *pantex* (*pantic-is*), a paunch], abdomen.

Pau'per [L. *pauper,* poor], dependent poor person. **Pau'perism, Pau'perize.**

Pause (*s*=*z*) [Gk. *pausis,* pause ; *pauein,* to pause], stop, break in speaking or reading, short period of inaction or silence ; cease, delay.

Pave [L. *pavīre,* to strike, to ram], lay with stones, etc.

Pave'ment, paved footway at side of road.

Pa-vil'ion [F. *pavillon,* a tent ; L. *pāpilio* (*pāpiliōn-is*), a butterfly], large tent, light ornamental building.

Paw [O.F. *poe,* a paw, perh. from imit. root], foot of a quadruped having claws ; strike or touch with paw.

Paw'ky [?], sly, arch.

Pawn [O.F. *paon, peon,* a pawn ; Med. L. *pedo* (*pedōn-is*), a foot-soldier ; L. *pes* (*ped-is*), a foot], piece in chess.

Pawn [O.F. *pan,* prob. fr. Du. *pand,* a pledge], state of being pledged, security given for a debt, etc. ; to pledge.

Pawn'brok-er, money - lender on pledged articles.

Pay [O.F. *paier* ; L. *pācāre,* to appease, to pay a debt ; *pax* (*pāc-is*), peace], make due return for, discharge, as a debt ; salary or wages.

Pay'ment, that which is paid.

Pea [formerly *pease* ; O.E. *pisa* ; L. *pīsum* ; Gk. *pisos,* a pea], seed in a pod.

Peace [O.F. *pais* ; L. *pax* (*pāc-is*), peace], state of quiet, freedom from war or civil disorder, treaty ending a war.

Peace'a-ble, in the spirit of peace.

Peach [L. *persicum* (*malum*), lit. Persian apple], delicious juicy fruit.

Pea'cock [O.E. *péa, páva* ; L. *pāvo,* peacock ; see **Cock**], bird with gorgeous feathers.

Pea'-jack-et [Du. *pij, pije,* coarse woollen coat ; see **Jacket**], sailor's woollen overcoat.

Peak [variant of **Pike**], point, pointed top.

Peak [?], look sickly. **Peak'y.**

Peal [perh. short for *appeal*], loud sound or succession of sounds, changes rung on a set of bells ; give out loud sounds.

Pea'nut, ground-nut.

Pear (*ea*=*ai*) [L. *pirum,* a pear], tree, also its tapering fruit.

Pearl [F. *perle* ; of unknown origin], gem formed in shell of oyster, etc.

Peas'ant (*s*=*z*) [L. *pāgensis,* belonging to a district ; *pāgus,* a district], countryman, rustic. **Peas'antry.** [plants.

Peat [?], substance formed of decomposed

Peb'ble [?], small round stone, agate, etc., kind of rock-crystal used for lenses.

Pec'ca-ble [L. *peccāre,* to sin], liable to sin.

Pec-ca-dil'lo [Sp. *pecadillo,* dim. of *pecado,* a sin], petty fault or crime.

Pec'cant [L. *peccāre,* to sin], sinning.

Pec'ca-ry [Carib. *pakira*], Central and S. American hog-like quadruped.

Peck [M.E. and O.F. *pek*; etym. doubtful], fourth part of a bushel.

Peck [perh. variant of **Pick**], quick, sharp stroke with a beak, etc. ; strike with the beak, bite.

Pec'to-ral [L. *pectus* (*pector-is*), the breast], pertaining to the breast.

Pec'u-late [L. *pecūlāri* (p.p. *pecūlātus*), to appropriate to one's own use ; see **Peculiar**], embezzle. **Pec'ulation.**

Pe-cu′l-iar (*i=y*) [L. *pecūliāris*, one's own ; *pecūlium*, private property], one's own, singular.   **Peculiar′ity.**

Pe-cu′ni-a-ry [L. *pecūnia*, property, money ; O.L. *pecu*, cattle], relating to money.

Ped′a-gogue [Gk. *pais* (*paid-os*), a boy, *agōgos*, leading], teacher of children.   **Pedagog′ic** (*gi=ji*).

Ped′al, Pe′dal [L. *pes* (*ped-is*), the foot], relating to the foot or to feet.

Ped′al, lever worked by the feet.

Ped′ant [It. *pedante* ; cogn. with *pedagogue*], one who displays learning needlessly.   **Ped′antry.**

Pe-dan′tic, fond of showing off learning.

Ped′dling [see **Pedlar**], hawking ; petty.

Ped′es-tal [It. *piedestallo*, a footstall (threshold) of a door ; L. *pes* (*ped-is*), a foot ; see **Stall**], base of a column, statue, etc.

Pe-des′tri-an [L. *pedester* (*pedestr-is*) ; *pes* (*ped-is*), a foot], on foot ; walker.

Ped′i-gree [earlier *pedegru* ; F. *pié* (*pied*) *de grue*, crane's foot ; L. *pes* (*ped-is*), foot ; *grus*, a crane], line of ancestors, descent.

Ped′i-ment [earlier *peremint* ; origin doubtful], triangular decoration over a door, etc.

Ped′lar [perh. from Sc. *pedder* ; *ped*, basket ; etym. doubtful], hawker.   [tower.

Peel [O.F. *pel*, *pal* ; L. *pālus*, a stake], small

Peel [L. *pāla*, a fire-shovel], baker's spade.

Peel [L. *pilāre*, to plunder], rind of fruit ; strip or pare off rind, bark, etc.   [chirp.

Peep [variant of **Pipe**], cry as a chicken,

Peep [?], look forth from hiding, sly look.

Peer [1] [?], look narrowly.

Peer [2] [O.F. *per*, *peer* ; L. *par*, equal], an equal, nobleman.   [nobility.

Peer′age [see **Peer** 2], the rank of a peer, the

Peer′less, matchless.

Pee′vish [?], fretful.

Peg [perh. fr. L.G. ; cf. Du. *peg*], small wooden or metal pin or bolt ; fasten with pegs, work diligently, mark out with pegs.

Pek′oe [Chin. *pekho* ; *pek*, white, and *ho*, down], superior kind of black tea.

Pelf [O.F. *pelfre*, booty ; etym. doubtful], money, gain.

Pel′i-can [Gk. *pelecān*, pelican ; *pelecas*, wood-pecker ; *pelecus*, axe], water-bird with a pouched bill.

Pe-lisse′ (*pĕ-leess′*) [L. *pelliceus*, made of skins ; *pellis*, skin], long mantle, outer garment for children.

Pel′let [M.L. *pelota*, dim. of *pila*, a ball]. little ball.

Pel′li-cle [L. *pellicula*, dim. of *pellis*, skin], thin skin, film.

Pell-mell [F. *pêle-mêle* ; F. *pelle*, a fire-shovel, *mêler*, to mix], in utter confusion.

Pel-lu′cid [L. *per*, through, and *lucēre*, to shine], clear.

Pelt [O.F. *pel* ; L. *pellis*, skin ; etym. doubtful], skin with the hair on.

Pelt [?], a downpour ; strike with many missiles.

Pel′vis [L. *pelvis*, basin], basin-shaped cavity formed by haunch-bones.

Pem′mi-can [N. Amer. Ind. *pimecan*], compressed dried meat mixed with melted fat.

Pen [L. *penna*, a feather], instrument for writing with ink ; write.

Pen [O.E. *penn* ; etym. dub.], small enclosure ; shut in.

Pe′nal [L. *pœna*, punishment], pertaining to punishment.   **Pen′alize.**

Pen′al-ty, punishment, suffering due to error or fault.

Pen′ance [see **Penitence**], punishment imposed (or self-imposed) for sin.

Pen′cil [L. *pēnicillum*, dim. of *pēniculus*, a brush, double dim. of *pēnis*, a tail], instrument for drawing or writing, small brush used by artists.   [ornament.

Pend′ant [L. *pendēre*, to hang], hanging

Pend′ent, hanging.

Pend′ing, undecided ; during.

Pen′du-lous [L. *pendulus*; *pendēre*, to hang], hanging loosely, wavering.

Pen′du-lum [L. neut. of *pendulus*, hanging], body so suspended as to swing freely to and fro.

Pen′e-trate [L. *penetrāre* (p.p. *penetrātus*), to penetrate ; cogn. with *penitus*, interior], enter into, pierce.   **Penetra′tion.**

Pen′guin (*u=w*) [?], Southern sea-bird.

Pen-in′su-la [L. *pēne*, almost ; *insula*, an island], piece of land nearly surrounded by water.   **Penin′sular.**   [fault.

Pen′i-tence (see **Penitent**), sorrow for sin or

Pen′i-tent [L. *pœnitēre* (pr.p. *pœnitens*, -*entis*), to repent ; *pœna*, punishment], sorry for fault ; one who repents.

Pen-i-ten′tial (*ti=sh*), expressing penitence.

Pen-i-ten′tia-ry (*ti=sh*), prison, house of correction.

Pen′man-ship, manner of writing.

Pen′nant [O.F. *pennon*, a flag ; L. *penna*, a feather], long narrow flag at the masthead.

Pen′non [see **Pennant**], pennant, flag borne by a mediæval knight on his lance, military ensign of lancer regiments.

Pen′ny [O.E. *pening*, *penig* ; cf. Ger. *pfennig*], bronze coin worth $\frac{1}{12}$ shilling.

Pen′ny-roy′al [formerly *pulial royal* ; O.F. *poliol*, thyme ; L. *pulegium réal*, penny-royal], kind of mint.   [grains.

Pen′ny-weight (*ei=ai*), troy weight of 24

Pen-o′lo-gy (*l=ll*) [Gk. *poinē*, fine, *logos*, discourse], study of prevention and punishment of wrong-doing.

Pen′sile [L. *pendēre* (p.p. *pensus*), to hang], hanging.

Pen′sion [L. *pendere* (p.p. *pensus*), to weigh, to pay], stated allowance for past service, etc.

Pen′sive [F. *pensif*, fem. *pensive* ; L. *pensāre*, freq. of *pendere*, to weigh], thoughtful, sad.

Pen′ta-gon [Gk. *penta*, five ; *gōnia*, an angle], plane figure having five angles.   **Penta′gonal.**

Pen-tam′e-ter [Gk. *penta*, five, *metron*, a measure], verse of five feet.

Pen′ta-teuch [Gk. *penta*, five, *teuchos*, a tool, a book], first five books of the Bible.

Pen'te-cost [Gk. *pentēcostē*, fiftieth], Jewish feast on the 50th day after the Passover.

Pent'house [formerly *pentice*; O.F. *apentis*; L. *appendicium*, appendage; *ad*, to, *pendēre*, to hang], sloping roof or shed attached to wall of main building.

Pen-ul'ti-mate [L. *pœne*, almost; *ultimus*, last], last but one.

Pen-um'bra [L. *paene*, almost, *umbra*, shadow], partial shadow surrounding total shadow, esp. round shadow of moon or earth during an eclipse.

Pen'u-ry [L. *pēnūria*; Gk. *peina*, hunger], want, extreme poverty. **Penu'rious.**

Pe'o-ny [Gk. *paiōnia*, peony, fr. *Paiōn*, physician of the gods], plant with showy flowers.

Peo'ple [L. *populus*, the people], persons, a nation, kindred; fill with people.

Pep'per [L. *piper*; Gk. *peperi*, pepper], pungent seasoning. **Pep'pery.**

Pep'per-mint, aromatic plant.

Pep'sin [Gk. *pepsis*, digestion; *pep*, to cook], property in gastric juice converting proteids into peptones.

Pep'tic [Gk. *pepticos*; *pepsis*, digestion], relating to or promoting digestion.

Per-ad-ven'ture [L. *per*, through; see Adventure], by chance.

Per-am'bu-late [L. *per*, through, *ambulāre* (p.p. *ambulātus*), to walk], walk through or over.

Per-am'bu-la-tor, child's carriage.

Per-ceive' [L. *percipere*, to perceive; *per*, thoroughly, and *capere*, to seize], understand, discern.

Per-cent'age, [L. *per*, by, *centum*, a hundred], rate on a hundred.

Per-cept'i-ble, capable of being perceived.

Per-cep'tion, seeing-power, discernment.

Perch [Gk. *percē*, a perch], fresh-water fish.

Perch [L. *pertica*, a pole], a pole (measure), roost; occupy or sit on as a perch.

Per-chance' [L. *per*, by; see **Chance**], perhaps.

Per'co-late [L. *per*, through, *colāre* (p.p. *colātus*), to filter], pass through interstices, to filter. **Per'colator.**

Per-cus'sion [L. *percutere* (p.p. *percussus*), to strike; *per*, through, and *quatere*, to shake], forcible striking together.

Per-di'tion [L. *perdere* (p.p. *perditus*), to lose], utter destruction, ruin.

Per'e-gri-nate [L. *peregrināri* (p.p. *peregrinātus*), to travel; *per*, through, *ager*, a field], travel, wander. **Peregrina'tion.**

Per'emp-to-ry [L. *peremptorius*, destructive; *per* thoroughly, *emere*, to take], decided, dictatorial. **Per'emptoriness.**

Per-en'ni-al [L. *perennis*; *per*, through, and *annus*, a year], lasting, perpetual; plant lasting several years.

Per'fect [O.F. *parfit* (adj.); L. *perficere* (p.p. *perfectus*), to complete; *per*, thoroughly, *facere*, to make], complete, faultless; finish, make perfect. **Perfec'tibility.**

Per-fec'tion, completion, entire excellence.

Per-fer'vid [L. *per*, and **Fervid**], very fervid.

Per'fi-dy [L. *perfidia*, perfidy; *per*, away, *fides*, faith], treachery, faithlessness. **Perfid'ious.**

Per'fo-rate [L. *per*, through, *forāre* (p.p. *forātus*), to bore], make holes through. **Perfora'tion.** necessity.

Per-force' [O.F. *par force*, by force], of

Per-form' [O.F. *parfournir*, to perform; L. *per*, thoroughly, and O.F. *fournir*, to furnish], carry through, to do, act in a play.

Per-form'ance, anything carried through.

Per-fume' [L. *per*, thoroughly, *fumāre*, to smoke], to scent. **Per'fume**, a scent.

Per-func'to-ry [L. *perfungī* (p.p. *perfunctus*), to perform; *per*, thoroughly, *fungi*, to perform], done merely from a sense of duty, without real interest.

Per'go-la [It. *pergola*, L. *pergula*, projecting roof], walk covered by trellis-work over which plants are trained.

Per-haps' [L. *per*, by; O.N. *happ*, chance], by chance, it may be.

Pe'ri [Pers. *pāri*], a good genie or fairy of Persian mythology, originally evil.

Per'i-gee (*g=j*) [Gk. *peri-*, round, *gē*, the earth], point in moon's or planet's orbit nearest the earth.

Per-i-he'li-on [Gk. *peri-*, round, *hēlios*, the sun], point in its orbit at which a planet is nearest the sun.

Per'il [L. *perīculum*, danger, L. *perīrī*, to try], danger. **Per'ilous.**

Per-im'e-ter [Gk. *peri-*, round, *metron*, a measure], boundary of a figure.

Pe'ri-od [Gk. *peri-*, round, *hodos*, a way], time, date, duration, end, complete sentence, point marking end of this.

Pe-ri-od'ic [see **Period**], recurring at stated times.

Pe-ri-od'ic-al, periodic; publication which appears at regular intervals.

Per-i-pa-tet'ic [Gk. *peripatēticos*, given to walking about, *peri-*, about, *patein*, to walk], walking from place to place on business.

Pe-riph'er-y [Gk. *peri-*, around, *pherein*, to carry], circumference, external boundary or surface.

Pe-riph'ra-sis (*pl.* -ses) [Gk. *peri-*, around, *phrasein*, to declare], roundabout statement. **Periphras'tic.**

Per'i-scope [Gk. *peri-*, round, and **Scope**], instrument enabling a person to see objects not on his own level or within his vision: used particularly in the steering of submarines while under water.

Per'ish [L. *perīre*, to perish; *per*, through, *īre*, to go], be destroyed, waste away. **Per'ishable.**

Per'i-style [Gk. *peri-*, around, *stulos*, pillar], columns around a temple, court, etc.; space thus surrounded.

Per-i-ton-e'um [Gk. *peri-*, around, *teinein*, to stretch], membrane lining abdominal cavity.

Per-i-ton-i´tis, inflammation of peritoneum or part of it.

Per´i-wig [earlier *perwyke*; see **Peruke**], head-dress of false hair.

Per-i-win´kle[1] [a corrupt form due to confusion with **Periwinkle**[2]; the better name is **Winkle**], kind of bivalve edible mollusc.

Per-i-win´kle[2] [O.E. *pervince*; L. *per*, through, *vincīre*, to bind], trailing plant with beautiful flowers.

Per´jure [L. *per*, through, *jurāre*, to swear], forswear, deliberately utter falsehood while on oath.

Per´ju-ry, crime of forswearing.

Perk, Perk´y [?], smart, jaunty.

Per´ma-nent [L. *per*, through, and *manēre* (pr.p. *manens*, *-entis*), to remain], lasting, durable. **Per´manence.**

Per´me-a-ble, penetrable.

Per´me-ate [L. *permeāre* (p.p. *permeātus*), *per*, through, *meāre*, to pass], pass through, to spread through. **Permea´tion.**

Per-mis´si-ble, allowable.

Per-mis´sion, leave, consent.

Per-mis´sive, giving permission.

Per-mit´ [L. *per*, through, *mittere* (p.p. *missus*], to send], allow.

Per´mit, a written permission.

Per-mu-ta´tion [L. *per*, thoroughly, *mūtāre* (p.p. *mūtātus*), to change], interchange of form and order.

Per-ni´cious (*ci*=*sh*) [L. *perniciēs*, ruin; *per*, thoroughly, *nex* (*nec-is*), death by violence], hurtful, deadly.

Per-o-ra´tion [L. *per*, through, *ōrāre* (p.p. *orātus*), to speak], conclusion, usu. rhetorical, or summing up of an oration.

Per-pen-dic´u-lar [L. *perpendiculum*, a plumb-line; *per*, thoroughly, *pendere*, to hang], upright, at right angles to a given line or surface. **Perpendicular´ity.**

Per´pe-trate [L. *perpetrāre* (p.p. *perpetrātus*); *per*, thoroughly, *patrāre*, to accomplish], perform, commit (a wrong, blunder, etc.). **Per´petrator.**

Per-pet´u-al [L. *perpetuālis*; perh. fr. *per*, through, and *petere*, to seek], never-ceasing. [tion.

Per-pet´u-ate, make perpetual. **Perpetua´-**

Per-pe-tu´i-ty, endless time.

Per-plex´ [L. *per*, thoroughly, *plectere* (p.p. *plexus*), to weave], entangle, embarrass, puzzle. **Perplex´ingly.**

Per-plex´i-ty, embarrassment, bewilderment.

Per´qui-site [L. *perquīrere* (p.p. *perquīsītus*), to seek thoroughly for; *per*, thoroughly, *quærere*, to seek], something over and above ordinary wages, gratuity.

Per´ry [F. *poire*; L. *pirum*, a pear], drink made from fermented juice of pears.

Per´se-cute [L. *per*, thoroughly, *sequī* (p.p. *secūtus*), to follow], pursue with unjust treatment, to annoy. **Persecu´tion.**

Per-se-ve´rance, continuous diligence.

Per-se-vere´ [L. *persevērāre*, to persevere; *per*, thoroughly, *sevērus*, earnest], continue steadily.

Per´sif-lage (*age*=*ahzh*) [F. fr. L. *per*, through, *sibilare*, to whistle], banter, light raillery.

Per-sist´ [L. *per*, through, *sistere*, to stand], stand firm, continue steadily. **Persis´tence.**

Per-sist´ent, inclined to persist, lasting.

Per´son [L. *persōna*, an actor's mask, a character in a play, a person], human being, body.

Per´son-a-ble, of good appearance.

Per´son-age, distinguished person.

Per´son-al, relating to a particular person, own, private.

Per-son-al´i-ty, that which constitutes a person, remark on the appearance or conduct of a person.

Per´son-al-ly, in person, as regards oneself.

Per´son-al-ty, personal property.

Per´son-ate, act the part of. **Persona´tion.**

Per-son´i-fy [F. *personnifier*; L. *persōna*, person, *facere*, to make], represent as a person. **Personifica´tion.** [staff.

Per-son-nel´ [F.], body of persons engaged,

Per-spec´tive [L. *per*, through, *spicere* (p.p. *spectus*), to look], art of drawing objects on a plane surface so that they appear to have their actual relative positions, size, etc.; view.

Per-spi-ca´ci-ty [L. *perspicax* (*perspicāc-is*), sharp-sighted; *per*, through, and *spicere*, to look], sharpness of sight or intelligence. **Perspica´cious.** [thought.

Per-spi-cu´i-ty, clearness of expression or

Per-spic´u-ous [L. *perspicuus*; *per*, through, and *spicere*, to look], easily understood, clear.

Per-spi-ra´tion, sweat.

Per-spire´ [L. *per*, through, *spīrāre*, to breathe], to sweat.

Per-suade´ [L. *per*, thoroughly, *suādēre* (p.p. *suāsus*), to advise], prevail on, win over.

Per-sua´sion, that which persuades, creed.

Per-sua´sive, tending to persuade.

Pert [shortened from *apert*; L. *aperīre* (p.p. *apertus*), to open], impertinent, saucy.

Per-tain´ [L. *per*, thoroughly, *tenēre*, to hold], belong.

Per-ti-na´ci-ty [L. *pertinax* (*pertinācit-is*), tenacious; *per*, thoroughly, *tenēre*, to hold], obstinacy, persistence. **Pertina´cious.**

Per´ti-nent [L. *pertinens* (*pertinentis*), pr.p. of *pertinēre*; see **Pertain**], to the point. **Per´tinence.**

Per-turb´ [L. *per*, thoroughly, *turbāre*, to disturb], distrust, disquiet.

Per-uke´ (*ook*), **Per-ruque´** [It. *perruca*, *paruca*; perh. from L. *pilus*, hair], a wig.

Pe-ru´sal, the act of reading, examination.

Pe-ruse´ [L. *per*, thoroughly, and **Use**], read carefully.

Per-vade´ [L. *per*, through, *vādere*, to go], pass or spread through. **Perva´sive.**

Per-verse´, contrary, obstinate in wrong.

Per-ver´sion, change to something worse, falsification.

Per-ver´si-ty, wrong-headedness.

Per-vert´ [L. *per*, thoroughly, *vertere* (p.p. *versus*), to turn], lead astray, misapply.

Per´vert, one who has turned to error.

Per'vi-ous [L. *per*, through, *via*, way], porous, admitting passage.

Pes'si-mism [L. *pessimus*, worst], belief that all things tend to evil, hopeless view. **Pessimis'tic.**

Pest [L. *pestis*, plague], plague, mischievous person or thing. [sistently.

Pes'ter [L. *pastörium*, tether], annoy per-

Pes-tif'er-ous [L. *pestis*, plague, *ferre*, to bring], very unhealthy.

Pes'ti-lence, fatal epidemic disease.

Pes'ti-lent, Pes-ti-len'tial (*tial=shal*) [L. *pestis*, plague], deadly, troublesome.

Pes'tle [L. *pinsere* (p.p. *pistus*), to pound], implement for pounding. [indulge.

Pet [?], fondling, fit of peevishness; fondle,

Pet'al [Gk. *petalon*, a leaf], flower-leaf.

Pe-tard' [F. *pétard*, a petard; L. *pēdere*, to break wind], case containing powder used to blow in gates, doors, etc.

Pe-ti'tion [L. *petere* (p.p. *petitus*), to seek], prayer, a request; make a formal request.

Pet'rel [perh. fr. St *Peter*, the bird seeming to walk on the sea], long-winged sea-bird.

Pet'ri-fy [Gk. *petra*, rock, and L. *facere*, to make], turn into or become stone. **Petri-fa'ction.**

Pet'rol [from **Petroleum**], refined petroleum.

Pe-tro'le-um [L. *petra*, rock, *oleum*, oil], rock oil.

Pet'ti-coat, under-skirt.

Pet'ti-fog'ger [Petty and *fogger* (of doubtful origin)], lawyer who deals in petty cases, tricky attorney.

Pet'tish, peevish, capricious.

Pet'ti-toes [?], pig's feet as food.

Pet'ty [F. *petit*, small], little, trifling.

Pet'u-lant [L. *petulans* (*petulant-is*), petulant, fr. *petere*, to seek], irritable, ill-humoured. **Pet'ulance.**

Pe-tun'i-a [F. *Petun*], plant of tobacco family with beautiful flowers.

Pew [O.F. *puie*, an open railed gallery; Gk. *podion*, a balcony], fixed seat in a church.

Pe'wit, Pee'wit [imit.], lapwing.

Pew'ter [O.F. *peutre*; Sp. *peltre*; etym. doubtful], alloy of tin and lead.

Phae'ton [Gk. *Phaethon*, son of *Helios*, famous for his unlucky attempt to drive the sun-chariot], open four-wheeled carriage of light build.

Phal-an'ger [Gk. *phalaggion*, spider's web; see **Phalanx**], Australian pouched animal that lives in trees.

Phal'anx, Pha'lanx (*pl.* -anxes or -anges) [L. *phalanx*; Gk. *phalagx*, phalanx], body of troops in close array.

Phan'tasm [Gk. *phantazein*, to display, *phainein*, to show], phantom, illusion.

Phan-tas-ma-go'ri-a [**Phantasm** and Gk. *agora*, an assembly], a shifting scene of real or imagined figures.

Phan'tom [O.F. *fantosme*; see **Phantasm**], airy spirit, spectre.

Pha-ris-a'ic [Gk. fr. Heb. *parush*, separated], belonging to the Pharisees, self-righteous, hypocritical. **Pharisa'ism.**

Pha'ris-ee, one of ancient Jewish sect, which strictly adhered to law, with pretensions to sanctity, self-righteous person.

Phar-ma-ceu'tic, Phar-ma-ceu'tic-al (*c=s* or *k*) [Gk. *pharmaceuticos*; see **Pharmacy**], pertaining to pharmacy.

Phar'ma-co-pœ'ia [*æ=ee*] [Gk. *pharmacon*, a drug; *poiein*, to make], list of drugs.

Phar'ma-cy [Gk. *pharmaceia, pharmacon*, a drug], preparation and dispensing of medicine.

Pha'ros [Gk. *Pharos*, name of island off Alexandria on which famous lighthouse stood], lighthouse.

Phar'ynx [Gk. *pharygx*, the pharynx], cavity behind the nose, mouth, and above the larynx.

Phase [Gk. *phasis*, appearance, *phaos*, light], appearance or aspect, esp. in a cycle of changes.

Pheas'ant (*s=z*) [Gk. *phasianos* (bird) of the river *Phasis*], beautiful game-bird.

Phen-a'cet-in [Gk. *phanein*, to show], drug used in treating headaches, neuralgia, etc.

Phe-nom'e-non (*pl.* -ena) [Gk. *phainein*, to show], appearance, something strange or unaccountable. **Phenom'enal.**

Phi'al [Gk. *phialē*, a broad flat bowl], small bottle or glass vessel.

Phil-an'der [Gk. *philandros*, fond of men], to flirt, coquet.

Phil-an-throp'ic, loving mankind.

Phil-an'thro-py [Gk. *philos*, loving, and *anthröpos*, man], readiness to do good to mankind. **Philan'thropist.**

Phil-at'e-ly [Gk. *philos*, loving, *ateleia*, freedom from tax; *a-*, not, and *telos*, tax], stamp-collecting. **Philat'elist.**

Phil-har-mon'ic [Gk. *philein*, to love, *harmonicos*, harmonic], loving music.

Phi-lip'pic [orig. the orations of Demosthenes against Philip of Macedon; Gk. *Philippos*, Philip], violent attack in words.

Phil'is-tine, Phil'is-tine [Gk. *Philistinos*, fr. Assyr. *Palastu, Pilistu*], enemy of ancient Jews, uncultured person. **Phil'istinism.**

Phi-lol'o-gy [Gk. *philos*, loving, *lögos*, discourse], science of language. **Philo-log'ical.**

Phi-los'o-pher, one who philosophizes, one versed in philosophy.

Phil-o-soph'ic, Phil-o-soph'ic-al, pertaining to philosophy, calm.

Phi-los'o-phy [Gk. *philos*, loving, *sophia*, wisdom, *sophos*, wise], knowledge of general principles, system for conduct of life, calmness. **Philos'ophize.**

Phil'tre, Philter [*tre=ter*] [Gk. *philtron*; *philos*, dear], love-potion.

Phle-bot'o-my [Gk. *phleps* (*phleb-os*), a vein, *tomos*, a cutting], blood-letting.

Phlegm [Gk. *phlegma*; *phlegein*, to burn], semi-liquid substance in air-passages, etc., sluggishness, indifference, dullness.

Phleg-mat'ic, abounding in phlegm, dull.

Phlox [Gk. *phlox*, a plant, lit. flame], plant with showy flowers.

Phœ'nix, Phe'nix (*oe=ee*) [Gk. *phoinix*, phœnix, Phœnician, purple-red], mythical bird of brilliant plumage that burned itself on a funeral pile, and rose renewed from its own ashes.

Pho-net'ic [Gk. *phōnē*, sound], representing the sounds of speech.

Pho-net'ics, the science of vocal sounds.

Phon'ic [Gk. *phōnē*, sound], pertaining to sound.

Pho'no-graph [Gk. *phōnē*, sound ; *graphein*, to write], instrument for recording and reproducing speech, song, etc.

Pho-nog'ra-phy [Gk. *phōnē*, sound, *graphein*, to write], system of phonetic shorthand.

Phos'phate [Gk. *phōs*, light ; see **Phosphorus**], salt of phosphoric acid.

Phos-phor-es'cence [see **Phosphorus** and suf. *-esce*], shining in the dark after being exposed to strong light. **Phosphores'cent.**

Phos-phor'ic, resembling or containing phosphorus.

Phos'phor-us [Gk. *phōsphoros*, light-bringing ; *phōs*, light, *pherein*, to bring), substance that absorbs sunlight and shines in the dark.

Pho'to-graph [Gk. *phōs* (*phōt-os*), light ; *graphein*, to draw], picture obtained by the action of light on sensitized surfaces ; take a photograph.

Pho-to-grav-ure', picture produced from photographic negative transferred to metal plate and etched in. [graphs.

Pho-tog'ra-phy, art of producing photo-

Phrase (*s=z*) [Gk. *phrasis*, a phrase, *phrazein*, to tell], short expression ; express in words.

Phra-se-ol'o-gy [Gk. *phrasis*, a phrase, *logos*, discourse], manner of expression.

Phre-nol'o-gy [Gk. *phrēn*, mind, *logos*, discourse], study or theory based on the belief that mental development may be ascertained from the shape of the skull. **Phrenolog'ical.**

Phthi'sis [Gk. *phthisis*, consumption ; *phthinein*, to decay], consumption of the lungs. **Phthis'ical.**

Phyl-ac'ter-y [Gk. *phylactērion*, a safeguard ; *phylassein*, to guard], small leather box containing slip of parchment inscribed with Hebrew texts, worn by Jews as a charm.

Phys'ic (*s=z*) [Gk. *physis*, nature], science of medicine, medicine. **Phy'sicist.**

Phys'ic-al, relating to the body, material.

Phy-si'cian (*ci=sh*), one skilled in healing.

Phys'ics, science of natural forces.

Phys-i-og'no-my [Gk. *physis*, nature, *gnomōn*, a judge], face with respect to expression of character, art of judging character from the features.

Phys-i-og'raph-y [Gk. *physis*, nature, *graphia*, fr. *graphein*, to write], description of nature, physical geography.

Phys-i-ol'o-gy [Gk. *physis*, nature, *logos*, discourse], science which treats of the functions of living organisms. **Physiolog'ical.**

Phy-sique' (*ique=eek*) [F. *physique* ; see **Physic**], physical structure.

Pi, Gk. letter p (π), used as symbol of ratio of circumference to diameter (3·14159).

Pi-ac'u-lar [L. *piāre*, to propitiate], expiatory.

Pi'an-ist (*Pi=pee*), player on piano.

Pi-an'o (*pl.* -os), **Pi-an'o-for'te** [It. *piano*, soft, *forte*, strong, loud], musical instrument producing tones by means of hammers and strings. [player.

Pi-an-o'la [trade name], mechanical piano-

Pi-az'za (*zz=dz*) [It *piazza* ; L. *platea*, a broad way], an open square, portico.

Pi'broch (*pee-broch—ch* as in *loch*) [Gael. *piobaireachd* ; *piobair*, a piper ;. *piob*, a pipe], piece of bagpipe music.

Pic-a-dor' [Sp. *picador* ; *picar*, to prick], horseman with lance in a bull-fight.

Pic-ar-esque' (*que=k*) [Sp. *picaro*, rogue], (fiction) dealing with rogues.

Pic'can-in-ny [Port. *pequeno*, little, small], a child, esp. a negro baby. [flute.

Pic'co-lo [It. *piccolo*, small], small, shrill

Pice [Hind. *paisa*], East Indian copper coin, fourth part of an anna.

Pick [etym. doubtful], peck at, open (a lock) as by a wire, pull apart, gather, choose ; sharp-pointed tool, choicest portion.

Pick'ax, Pick'axe, sharp-pointed tool to break the ground.

Pick'et [F. *piquet*, a pointed stick, dim. of *pic*, a pike], stake sharpened or pointed, military outpost, party on watch in a strike.

Pic'kle [?], preserve in salt or in vinegar ; solution for preserving thus, (*pl.*) pickled vegetables, a plight, mischievous child.

Pic'nic [?], excursion including a meal out of doors.

Pick'pock-et, one who steals from pockets.

Pic-to'ri-al, pertaining to pictures, graphic.

Pic'ture [L. *pingere* (p.p. *pictus*), to paint], representation of anything by painting, drawing, etc. ; represent.

Pic-tu-resque' (*q=k*) [It. *pittoresco* ; L. *pictura*, a picture], forming a picture.

Pie [L. *pica*], magpie.

Pie [perh. same origin as **Pie**], meat or fruit under pastry baked.

Pie [see **Pie**], type confusedly mixed.

Pie [Hind. *pa'i*, quarter], Ind. copper coin, twelfth part of an anna.

Pie'bald, having patches of various colours.

Piece [O.F. *piece* ; etym. doubtful], definite part, literary or artistic work, coin ; patch, unite.

Piece'meal, piece by piece.

Piece'work, work paid by the piece.

Pied [L. *pica*, a magpie], variegated.

Pier (*ie=ee*) [O.F. *piere*, a stone ; L. and Gk. *petra*, rock], bridge-supports, structure of stone, iron, or wood extending into sea or river forming protection to harbour, landing-place or promenade.

Pierce [O.F. *percier*, to pierce ; etym. doubtful], thrust into, bore.

Pi-er-rot', Pi-er-rette' [dim. of F. *Pierre*, Peter], seaside or itinerant entertainer in special costume.

F

Pi-e-tis'tic, Pi-e-tis'tic-al, affectedly religious.

Pi'e-ty [L. *pietas*, piety ; *pius*, devout], devotion to the service of God, dutiful affection.

Pig [M.E. *pigge* ; etym. doubtful], domestic animal. [furnace.

Pig-i'ron, oblong mass of iron from smelting.

Pi'geon (*ĭ*) [O.F. *pijon* ; L. *pīpio*, a chirper ; *pīpīre*, to chirp], dove.

Pi'geon-hole, hole for passage of pigeons or in nesting-place, compartment in writing-table, etc., for documents.

Pig'ger-y, place where swine are kept.

Pig'ment [L. *pingere*, to paint], colouring matter.

Pig'my, Pyg'my [Gk. *pygmaioi*, fabulous dwarfs ; *pygmē*, a fist], dwarf.

Pike [etym. doubtful], long shafted weapon with a steel head, large fresh-water fish.

Pil-as'ter [It. *pilastro* ; L. *pila*, a pillar], rectangular pillar usually attached to a wall.

Pil'chard [orig. obscure], small food-fish.

Pile [L. *pilus*, hair], nap on velvet, etc.

Pile [L. *pilum*, a javelin], large stake.

Pile [L. *pila*, a pillar], heap, large building ; heap up.

Pile [L. *pila*, a ball], kind of tumour.

Pil'fer [O.F. *pelfre*, plunder], take by petty theft.

Pil'grim [L. *peregrīnus*, a stranger ; *peregrē*, from abroad], wayfarer, wanderer, esp. one who visits sacred place out of religious devotion. **Pil'grimage**.

Pill [L. *pilula*, dim. of *pila*, a ball], small ball of medicine.

Pil'lage [F. *piller*, perh. fr. L. *pīlāre*, to plunder], plunder.

Pil'lar [L. *pila*, pillar], firm upright support, column.

Pil'lion [ult. fr. L. *pellis*, skin], cushion behind a saddle.

Pil'lo-ry [O.F. *pellari* ; etym. doubtful], frame having holes for the head and hands of an offender. [rest.

Pil'low [L. *pulvīnus*, a pillow], soft head-

Pi'lot [It. *pilota*, *pedota*, a pilot ; perh. fr. Gk. *pēdon*, oar, (pl.) a rudder], one who conducts vessels into or out of port ; direct the course of. **Pil'otage**.

Pim'per-nel [O.F. *pimprenele* ; etym. doubtful], small flower found in corn-fields, etc.

Pim'ple [?], raised skin-spot.

Pin [L. *pinna*, a wing, a point], piece of metal or wood used to support or fasten ; fasten with a pin. [child.

Pin'a-fore [see **Pin** and **Afore**], apron for a

Pin'cers. Pinch'ers, instrument for gripping things, drawing nails, etc.

Pinch [N.F. *pincher* ; F. *pincer* (vb.) ; etym. doubtful], squeeze, cramp, nip ; a nip, as much as can be taken between finger and thumb, time of stress.

Pinch'beck [fr. name of inventor, C. *Pinchbeck*], alloy of copper and zinc, resembling gold ; sham.

Pine [L. *pœna*, punishment], wear away.

Pine [L. *pinus*, a pine], cone-bearing tree.

Pi'ne-al [L. *pinea*, a pine-cone], like a pine cone (used of part of brain).

Pine'ap-ple, tropical plant, also its fruit.

Pin'fold [O.E. *pund*, enclosure, *fald*, fold], place for stray cattle.

Pin'ion [O.F. *pignon* ; L. *penna*, feather], wing ; bind the wings or the arms.

Pink [?], plant with fragrant flowers, pale rose-colour, anything supremely excellent ; of a light rose-colour.

Pink [perh. variant of **Pick**], pierce with holes, scallop, stab. [vessel.

Pin'nace [perh. L. *pīnus*, a pine], small

Pin'na-cle [L. *pinnāculum*, double dim. of *pinna*, a wing], lofty peak, spire.

Pin'nate [L. *pinnātus*, feathered ; *penna*, feather], furnished with wings or fins, with leaves on each side of common leaf-stalk.

Pint (*ĭ*) [M.E. *pynte* ; F. *pinte* ; etym. doubtful], half a quart.

Pi-o-neer' [O.F. *peonier* ; *peon*, foot-soldier], military artisan who prepares the road for an army, early settler in a new country ; go before and prepare.

Pi'ous [L. *pius*, pious], religious, devout.

Pip [1] [short for **Pippin**], seed as of an apple.

Pip [2] [M.F. *pepie* ; L. *pituita*, rheum, also the pip], disease of poultry.

Pipe [Late L. *pīpa*, a pipe ; L. *pipāre*, to chirp], wind instrument, tube, tube and bowl for smoking, butt ; play on a pipe.

Pipe'clay, fine white plastic clay.

Pip-ette' [dim. of **Pipe**], tube used in chemistry.

Pip'kin [?], small earthen pot. [kinds.

Pip'pin [perh. fr. **Pip** [1]], apple of various

Piqu'ant (*iqu=eek*) [pr.p. of F. vb. *piquer*, to prick], giving zest, sharp, pungent.

Pique (*peek*) [M.F. *picque*, *pique* ; same word as *pike*], wounded pride ; offend, sting, goad, arouse (curiosity).

Pi-quet', **Piq'uet** [F. *piquet* ; etym. doubtful], card-game.

Pi'ra-cy (*ĭ*), act or crime of a pirate.

Pi'rate [Gk. *peiratēs*, one who attempts, a pirate ; *peiraein*, to attempt], robber on the high seas ; infringe the law of copyright. **Pirat'ical**.

Pir-ou-ette' (*ou=oo*) [F. *pirouette*, dim. of Guernsey word *piroue*, a little wheel], whirl on the toes.

Pis-ca-to'ri-al, **Pis'ca-to-ry** [L. *piscător*, fisher ; *piscis*, fish], relating to fishes or fishing.

Pis'mire [obs. *mire*, ant], ant.

Pis-ta'chio (*-shio* or *-sho*) [Sp. *pistacho* ; Gk. *pistācion*, a pistachio-nut], nut with kernel of greenish colour.

Pis'til [L. *pistillum*, a small pestle], seed-vessel of a flower.

Pis'tol [It. *pistolese*, (dagger) made at *Pistola*, now *Pistoia*, town near Florence], small firearm.

Pis'ton [It. *pistone*, piston ; *pestone*, pestle], disk or short cylinder fitting into hollow cylinder and driven up and down or backwards and forwards in it.

Pit [L. *puteus*, a well], hollow, a coal-mine, part of the floor of a theatre ; mark with hollows, set forward in a contest, put into pit for storage.

Pitch [L. *pix (pic-is)*, pitch], black substance obtained from boiled tar. **Pit'chy.**

Pitch [M.E. *pichen*, to throw ; etym. doubtful], throw, place between and about wickets, cast, encamp, of a ship, to plunge with the head into the sea ; degree of tone in music.

Pitch'er [L. *bicārium*, wine-vessel ; see Beaker], vessel for liquids.

Pitch'fork, large fork to pitch hay, etc. ; to throw with this or in like manner.

Pit'e-ous [Late L. *pietōsus*, merciful ; L. *pius*, devout], mournful, showing pity.

Pit'fall, concealed pit to catch animals or men.

Pith [O.E. *pitha*], spongy substance in stems, marrow, vigour.

Pith'y, having nervous energy ; terse.

Pit'tance [O.F. *pitance*, pittance, also pity], small allowance.

Pit'y [doublet of Piety], tenderness to the weak and suffering, mercy ; to have or show feeling for. **Pit'iful, Pit'iable.**

Piv'ot [F. *pivot*, pivot ; etym. doubtful], shaft or pin on which something turns, central point. **Piv'otal.**

Pix'y, Pix'ie [?], fairy.

Pla'ca-ble, Plac'a-ble [L. *plācāre*, to pacify], ready to be pacified.

Plac'ard, Plac-ard' [F. *plaquer*, to rough-cast ; Du. *plakken*, to glue], poster ; to post placards.

Pla'cate, Pla-cate' [L. *placāre* (p.p. *placātus*), to appease], pacify.

Place [F. *place* ; Gk. *plateia (hodos)*, a broad (way)], position, site, rank, room ; put, set.   [**Placid'ity.**

Pla'cid [L. *placēre*, to please], peaceful.

Pla'gia-rize (*ag=aij*) [L. *plagiārius*, kidnapper ; *plagiāre*, to ensnare], steal from the writings of another. **Pla'giarism.**

Plague [L. *plāga* ; Gk. *plēge*, a blow, *plessein*, to strike], torment, deadly contagious disease ; vex, torment. **Pla'guy.**   [fish.

Plaice [O.F. *plaïs* ; L. *platessa*, a plaice], flat

Plaid, Plaïd [Gael. *plaide*, Ir. *ploid*, plaid ; *peall*, a skin], long wrap of woollen cloth, usually with tartan pattern, outer article of Highland costume, cloth of which this is usu. made.

Plain [L. *plānus*, plain], flat, evident, unornamented, simple, blunt ; level land.

Plaint [L. *plangere* (p.p. *planctus*), to bewail], complaint, lamentation.   [suit.

Plain'tiff [see Plaint], complainant in a law-

Plain'tive, complaining, sad.

Plait, Plaït, Pleat [L. *plicāre* (p.p. *plicātus*), to fold], flat fold ; to fold, braid.

Plan [L. *plānus*, flat ; *planāre*, to plane], drawing, diagram, map, scheme ; to draught, scheme.

Plane [Gk. *platanos*, a plane ; *plātus*, wide], spreading tree.

Plane [L. *ptāna*, fem. of *plānus*, flat], smoothing tool, flat surface ; level ; make smooth.

Plan'et [Gk. *planētēs, planēs*, a wanderer], body which revolves round the sun or other centre. **Plan'etary.**

Plan'gent [L. *plangere*, to beat the breast], loud-sounding.

Plank [L. *planca*, a flat board, perh. fr. Gk. *plax [plac-os]*, a flat plate], length of sawn timber.

Plant [L. *planta*, a plant, a shoot], organism of the vegetable kingdom, whole machinery used in an industry ; put in as seed, settle.

Plan'tain [L. *plantāgo*, a plantain, perhaps from root *planta*, sole of the foot], herb with broad leaves.

Plan'tain (Sp. *pla(n)tano*], tree with banana-like fruit.

Plan-ta'tion, place planted with trees, etc., original settlement, colonization.

Plant'i-grade [L. *planta*, sole of the foot, *gradī*, to walk], walking on the soles of the feet.

Plash [perh. imit.], puddle, splash ; to splash.

Plas'ter [Gk. *emplastron*, plaster ; *en*, on, *plassein*, to mould], adhesive application, mixture of lime, water, and sand, stucco ; cover with plaster.

Plas'tic [Gk. *plasticos* ; *plassein*, to mould], capable of being moulded. **Plas'ticine.**

Plate [O.F. *plate*, fem. of *plat*, broad ; perh. fr. Gk. *platus*, broad], sheet of metal, vessels of gold and silver, shallow round vessel of pottery, etc., cast of a page of type for printing from ; overlay with gold or silver.

Pla-teau' (*eau=ō*) [F. *plateau*, for O.F. *platel*, dim. of *plat*, a plate], tableland.

Plat'form [F. *plateforme*, fr. *plat*, flat, and *forme*, form], raised level surface formed with planks, etc., principles on which a body of persons unite.

Plat'i-num [Sp. *platina*, dim of *plata*, silver], valuable tin-white metal.

Plat'i-tude [F. *platitude* ; *plat*, flat], flat, commonplace truism.

Plat-oon' [F. *peloton*, small ball], half-company of foot-soldiers.   [plate.

Plat'ter [O.F. *plater* ; *plat*, a plate], large

Plau'dit [formerly *plaudite* ; L. *plaudite*, 2nd pers. pl. imper. of *plaudere*, to applaud], (usu. *pl.*) expression of applause.

Plau'si-ble (*s=z*) [L. *plaudere* (p.p. *plausus*), to applaud], apparently right, fair-spoken.

Play [O.E. *plegean, plegian*], to sport, act, perform (on) ; sport, game, practice, piece for acting. **Play'ful.**

Plea [O.F. *plait, plaid*, a plea ; L. *placēre*, to please], excuse, that which is pleaded.

Plead [O.F. *plaidier*, to plead ; *plaid*, a plea], urge reasons for or against.

Pleas'ant (*s=z*) [O.F. *plaisant*, pr.p. of *plaisir*, to please], pleasing, agreeable.

Pleas'ant-ry, cheerfulness, joke.

Please (*s=z*) [O.F. *plaisir* ; L. *placēre*, to please], make glad, gratify.

Plea′sur-a-ble (*sur=zher*), pleasant.

Pleas′ure [E. spelling of F. *plaisir*], enjoyment, joy, will.

Ple-be′ian [L. *plebeius*, fr. *plebs*, the common people], common; one of the common people.

Pleb′i-scite [L. *plebs* (*plebis*), the common people], direct vote of the people.

Pledge [O.F. *plege*, security, perh. fr. M.L. *plevire*, *plebire*, to warrant], solemn promise, thing in pawn, surety, toast; give as security, engage, to toast.

Ple′na-ry [L. *plēnus*, full], full, entire.

Plen-i-po-ten′ti-a-ry (*ti=sh*) [L. *plēnus*, full; *potens* (*-entis*), powerful], ambassador with full power.

Plen′i-tude [L. *plēnus*, full], abundance.

Plen′te-ous, **Plen′ti-ful** [L. *plēnus*, full], having or yielding plenty.

Plen′ty [L. *plēnus*, full], fullness, abundance.

Ple′o-nasm [Gk. *pleonasmos*, fr. *pleonazein*, to be superfluous; *pleon*, more], use of more words than are necessary, an unnecessary word. **Pleonas′tic**.

Pleth′o-ra [Gk. *plēthōre*, fullness; *plēthēs*, full], over-fullness.

Pleu′ri-sy [Gk. *pleura*, a rib, side], inflammation of the membrane which covers the lungs.

Pli′a-ble, **Pli′ant** [F. *plier*, to bend; fr. L. *plicāre*, to fold], easily bent, yielding. **Pliabil′ity**, **Pli′ancy**.

Pli′ers, pincers. [pledge.

Plight [O.E. *plihtan*, fr. *pliht*, danger], to

Plight [M.E. *plit*, doublet of Plait], condition (usu. evil).

Plinth [Gk. *plinthos*, a brick, a plinth], square slab below a column.

Plod [perh. imit.], to toil, trudge. **Plod′der**.

Plot [?], small piece of ground.

Plot [?], secret plan, combination; to plan, scheme.

Plough [Late O.E. *plôh*], implement for breaking the soil; turn up with the plough.

Plough′share [Plough and O.E. *scear*, a ploughshare], part of a plough which cuts the soil at the bottom of a furrow.

Plov′er (*o=ŭ*) [O.F. *plovier*, plover; L. *pluvārius*, rainy], wading bird.

Pluck [O.E. *ploccian*, *pluccian*], pull, strip off; internal organs of an animal used as food, courage.

Pluck′y, full of courage.

Plug [M. Du. *plugge*, a peg, bung], stopper, cake of pressed tobacco; to stop up with a plug.

Plum [L. *prūnum*, a plum], stone-fruit or its tree, raisin.

Plu′mage (*u=oo*) [F. *plume*; L. *plūma*, a feather], feathers of a bird.

Plumb [L. *plumbum*, lead], weight of lead attached to a line; perpendicular; sound with a plumb.

Plum-ba′go [L. *plumbāgo*, plumbago; *plumbum*, lead], black lead, graphite.

Plumb′er (*ŭ*) [L. *plumbum*, lead], one who works in lead.

Plume [L. *plūma*, a feather], feather or group of feathers; to pride. **Plu′my**.

Plum′met [O.F. *plommet*, dim. of *plomb*, lead], sounding lead, a plumb.

Plump [Du. *plomp*, blunt], full, rounded.

Plump [prob. imit.], drop suddenly, give all one's votes to one candidate; directly. **Plum′per**.

Plun′der [Ger. *plündern*, to plunder; *plunder*, baggage, trash], rob; robbery, spoil.

Plunge [Late L. *plumbicāre*, to heave the lead; L. *plumbum*, lead], thrust into fluid, dive, rush heavily on; a dive.

Plu′ral [L. *plus* (*plūr-is*), more], relating to more than one.

Plu-ral′i-ty, state of being plural, two or more, majority, holding of two or more offices.

Plus [L.], more, extra, in addition.

Plush [F. *pluche*, shortened from *peluche*, plush; L. *pilus*, hair], cloth with an open pile.

Plu-toc′ra-cy [Gk. *ploutos*, wealth, *cratein*, to rule], power or rule of wealth. **Plu′tocrat**.

Plu′vi-al, **Plu′vi-ous** [L. *pluvia*, rain], rainy, caused by rain.

Ply [short form for **Apply**], work at, press, go back and forth.

Ply [F. *pli*, fold; L. *plicāre*, to fold], fold, twist.

Pneu-mat′ic [Gk. *pneuma* (*pneumat-os*), air], pertaining to, worked by, or filled with air.

Pneu-mo′ni-a [Gk. *pneumon*, a lung], inflammation of the lungs. **Pneumon′ic**.

Poach [¹] [O.F. *pochier*, to poach; F. *poche*, a pocket], cook eggs by breaking into boiling water.

Poach [²] [perh. as **Poach** ¹], to rob of game.

Pock [O.E. *poc*], a pustule.

Pock′et [A. Norm. *pokete*, dim. of O.N.F. *poke*=F. *poche*, a pocket], pouch; put in the pocket.

Po-co-cur-an′te [It., caring little], indifferent.

Pod [?], seed-vessel of the pea, etc.; bear pods, strip of pods.

Pod-a′gra, **Pod′a-gra** [Gk. *pous*, *podos*, foot, *agra*, catching], gout.

Pod′gy [?; see also **Pudgy**], fat and short.

Po′em [L. *poēma*, a poem; Gk. *poiein*, to make], composition in verse.

Po′e-sy [Gk. *poēsis*, a composition, a poem], poetical skill, poetry.

Po′et, fem. **Po′et-ess** [Gk. *poiētēs*, a poet, *poiein*, to make], one who makes poetry.

Poet-as′ter [Poet and L. suf. *-aster*, sham], would-be poet, paltry poet.

Po′et-ry [O.F. *poetrie*], rhythmical composition, imaginative language. **Poet′ic**.

Poign′ant [F. *poignant*, pr.p. of *poindre*, to prick; L. *pungere*, to prick], sharp, keen.

Point [L. *pungere* (p.p. *punctus*), to prick], sharp end, dot, prominent feature, (*pl.*) movable guiding-rails; give a point to, aim, indicate.

Point-blank, (of shot) fired horizontally, plain, unqualified.

Point′er, that which points, rod for pointing, dog that points at game, (plur.) two stars in Great Bear, straight line through which points nearly to pole-star.

Poise (*s=z*) [O.F. *poiser*, *peser*, to weigh ; *pois*, weight ; L. *pendere* (p.p. *pensus*), to weigh], weight, balance ; to balance.

Poi′son (*s=z*) [L. *pōtio*, a draught], something which taints or kills ; put poison into, kill with poison.

Poke¹ [Icel. *poki* ; M.Du. *poke*, a bag], sack.

Poke² [M.E. and Du. *poken*, *pukken*, to poke], a thrust ; to thrust.

Po′ker¹ [from Poke²], bar for stirring a fire.

Po′ker² [?], card game.

Po′ky [from Poke²], confined and shabby.

Po′lar [see Pole²], pertaining to one of the poles.

Po-lar′i-ty, quality of a body in virtue of which it exhibits opposite powers in opposite directions. **Pol′arize.**

Pol′der [Du. *polder*, a polder], low land reclaimed from the sea.

Pole¹ [L. *pālus*, a stake], long slender piece of wood, measure of 5½ yards. [an axis.

Pole² [L. *polus* ; Gk. *polos*, a pivot], end of

Pol′e-ax(e) [from Pole¹], battle-axe, halbert, butcher's axe with hammer at back.

Pole′cat [?], kind of weasel.

Pol-em′ic, Pol-em′ic-al [Gk. *polemos*, war], controversial ; controversial argument, one who engages in such an argument.

Pol-ice′ (*ice = eess*) [F. *police*, orig. civil government ; L. *politia* ; Gk. *politeia*, polity], men responsible for public order ; keep order.

Pol′i-cy¹ [Gk. *politeia*, polity, citizenship ; *polis*, a city], system of management, prudence.

Pol′i-cy² [F. *police*, bill of lading, etc. Etym. doubtful], written contract of insurance.

Pol′ish [L. *polīre* (p.p. *polītus*), to polish], make glossy, esp. by rubbing ; gloss, anything used to produce gloss, refinement.

Po-lite′ [see Polish], refined, well-bred.

Pol′i-tic [Gk. *politicos* ; *politeia*, citizenship], political, wise, artful.

Po-lit′ic-al, pertaining to civil government.

Pol-i-ti′cian (*ci = sh*), one devoted to politics.

Pol′i-tics, science of government. [ment.

Pol′i-ty [see Policy¹], structure of govern-

Pol′ka [F. and Ger. *polka*], dance of Bohemian origin.

Poll [M.E. and obs. Du. *polle*, top of head], head, casting of votes ; receive or give (votes).

Pol′lard [see Poll], tree with its crown cut off. [flowers.

Pol′len [L. *pollen*, *pollis*, fine flour], dust of

Pol-lute′ [L. *polluere* (p.p. *pollūtus*), to pollute ; *pro*, forth, *luere*, to wash], make foul. **Pollu′tion.**

Po′lo [native name in valley of Indus], kind of hockey played on horseback.

Pol-o′ny [perh. from *Bologna*], kind of pork sausage.

Pol-troon′ [It. *poltrone*, a poltroon ; *poltro*, a bed], coward.

Pol-y-an′thus [Gk. *polys*, many, *anthos*, flower], kind of primrose.

Pol′y-chrome [Gk. *polys*, many, *chrōma*, colour], decorated in many colours, picture or statue of many colours. **Polychroma′tic.**

Po-lyg′a-my [Gk. *polys*, many, *gamos*, marriage], state of having more wives than one. **Polyg′amous.**

Pol′y-glot [Gk. *polys*, many, *glotta*, a tongue], in or speaking several languages.

Pol′y-gon [Gk. *polys*, many, *gōnia*, an angle], plane figure of many angles. **Poly′gonal.**

Pol-y-he′dron [Gk. *polys*, many, *hedra*, a base], many-sided solid.

Pol′yp, Pol′ype [as Polypus], tubular animal with tentacles round the mouth.

Pol′y-pus [Gk. *polypous*, cuttle-fish, *polys*, many, *pous*, a foot], kind of tumour.

Pol-y-syl′la-ble [Gk. *polys*, many, and **Syllable**], word of many syllables.

Pol-y-tech′nic [Gk. *polys*, many, *technē*, art], relating to many arts ; school where many arts are taught.

Pol′y-the-ism [Gk. *polys*, many, and **Theism**], belief in many gods. **Polytheis′tic.**

Po-ma′ceous (*ce = sh*) [L. *pōmum*, an apple], like an apple or a pear.

Po-made′, Pom-ade′, Po-ma′tum [F. *pommade* ; It. *pomada*, *pomata*, pomade ; It. *pomo*, L. *pōmum*, an apple], perfumed ointment.

Pome′gran-ate [O.F. *pome grenate*, a pomegranate ; L. *pōmum*, apple, *grānātum*, full of seeds], fruit with many seeds and acid pulp.

Pom′mel (*o = ŭ*) [Late L. *pomellum*, dim. of L. *pōmum*, an apple], knob of a saddle-bow, knob on a sword-hilt ; beat with fists.

Pomp [Gk. *pompē*, pomp, procession], show of magnificence, pride. **Pompos′ity.**

Pomp′ous, stately, pretentious.

Pond [variant of Pound²], small lake.

Pon′der [L. *ponderāre*, to weigh ; *pondus* (*ponder-is*), weight], to weigh in the mind, think over. **Pon′derable**, having appreciable weight.

Pon′der-ous, heavy.

Pon′iard (*i = y*) [F. *poignard*, fr. *poing*, the fist ; L. *pugnus*], kind of dagger.

Pon′tiff [L. *pontifex*, member of principal college of priests in Rome ; *pons* (*pont-is*), bridge, and *facere*, to make], high priest, pope. **Pontif′ical.**

Pon-tif′i-cate, high priesthood, popedom.

Pon-toon′ [L. *ponto* (*pontōn-is*), a pontoon ; *pons* (*pont-is*), a bridge], hollow cylinder used as a support of a temporary bridge, flat-bottomed boat.

Po′ny [perh. from O.F. *poulenet*, dim. of *poulain*, a foal ; L. *pullus*, foal], small horse.

Pood′le [Ger. *pudel* ; allied to Low Ger. *pudeln*, to waddle], kind of pet dog.

Pool [O.E. *pól*], body of still water.

Pool [perh. fr. F. *poule*, hen, stakes at the game having been eggs], game on a billiard-table, the stakes at cards ; make a common interest of.

Poop [L. *puppis*, hinder part of a ship], stern of a ship, highest deck in the aftmost part of a ship.

Poor [M.E. and O.F. *povre*; L. *pauper*, poor], wanting in riches or goods, needy.

Poor'ly, somewhat ill.

Pop [imit.], quick explosive sound ; make a sharp quick sound, dart.

Pope [L. *pāpa*, pope, father; Gk. *pappas*, father], head of the R.C. Church.

Pop'gun, tube and rammer for pellets.

Pop'in-jay [O.F. *papingay*, a parrot], green woodpecker, parrot. [tree.

Pop'lar [L. *pŏpulus*, a poplar], tall kind of

Pop'lin [F. *popeline*, poplin, from the *Papal* town of Avignon], fabric of silk and worsted. [opium.

Pop'py [L. *papăver*, a poppy], plant yielding

Pop'u-lace [It. *popolaccio*, populace ; *popolo*, people], common people.

Pop'u-lar [L. *populus*, the people], of the people, liked by the people. **Pop'ularize.**

Pop-u-lar'i-ty, favour with the people.

Pop'u-late [L. *populus*, people], to people.

Pop-u-la'tion [see **Populate**], all the people of a place.

Pop'u-lous [L. *populus*, the people], abounding in people.

Por'ce-lain (*ŏ*) [F. *porcelaine*, the Venus-shell, porcelain; It. *porcellana*, porcelain, *porcella*, dim. of *porco*; L. *porcus*, a pig], fine earthenware, china.

Porch (*ŏ*) [L. *porticus*, a porch], covered entrance to a doorway.

Por'cine (*sine*) [L. *porcus*, a pig], pertaining to swine.

Por'cu-pine [O.F. *porc espin*; L. *porcus*, pig, *spīna*, thorn], long-quilled animal.

Pore[1] [Gk. *poros*, a passage, pore], minute opening, esp. in the skin.

Pore[2] [M.E. *puren*, etym. doubtful], gaze steadily in reading.

Pork [L. *porcus*, a pig], flesh of swine.

Po'rous [see **Pore**[1]], full of pores.

Por'phy-ry [L. and Gk. *porphyrītes*, porphyry; Gk. *porphyros*, purple], fine-grained rock with crystals through it.

Por'poise (*oise*=*ŭs*) [O.F. *porpeis*, a porpoise; L. *porcus*, a pig, *piscis*, a fish], small animal of the whale kind.

Por'ridge [another form of **Pottage**], meal boiled in water or in milk.

Por'rin-ger [earlier *potager* ; see **Pottage**], bowl or cup for porridge. [Oporto.

Port[1] [from *Oporto*, in Portugal], wine of

Port[2] [L. *portus*, a harbour], a harbour.

Port[3] [L. *porta*, a gate], a gate, gateway.

Port[4] [F. *porter*; L. *portāre*, to carry], demeanour.

Port[5] [etym. doubtful; perh. fr. **Port**[2]], left side of a ship, larboard (q.v.); on the left side of a ship; put or turn to the left side of a ship.

Port'a-ble [L. *portāre*, to carry], capable of being carried. **Portabil'ity.**

Port'age [from **Port**[4]], carrying, place where boat must be carried between lakes or over rapids.

Por'tal [see **Port**[3]], door or gate.

Port-cul'lis [L. *porta*, a door, *cōlāre* (p.p. *cōlātus*), to glide, slide], grating sliding in grooves at the side of a gateway.

Porte [F. (in full, *la Sublime Porte*); L. *porta*, a gate], the Turkish government.

Por-tend' [L. *prŏ*, forth, *tendere* (p.p. *tentus*), to stretch], foreshow.

Por'tent [see **Portend**], omen, sign.

Por-tent'ous, foreshowing, ominous.

Por'ter [see **Port**[3]], doorkeeper.

Por'ter [L. *portāre*, to carry], carrier.

Por'ter [L. *portāre*, to carry], kind of beer.

Port-fo'li-o [It. *portafoglio*; *porta*, imper. of *portāre*, to carry, and *foglio*, a leaf], portable case for papers, etc.

Port'hole [**Port**[3] and **Hole**], opening in a ship's side.

Por'ti-co [It. *portico*; L. *porticus*, a porch], colonnade, porch.

Portière (*portyĕr*) [L. *porta*, a gate], a door curtain.

Por'tion [L. *portio*, portion, cogn. with L. *pars*, a part], part, share; distribute.

Port'ly [see **Port**[4]], imposing, bulky.

Port-man'teau (*eau*=*ō*) [F. *portemanteau*; *porter*, to carry, *manteau*, a cloak], travelling-case.

Por'trait [see **Portray**], picture of a person.

Por-tray' [O.F. *pourtraire*, to portray; L. *prŏ*, forth, *trahere*, to draw], make a likeness, describe.

Pose (*s*=*z*) [F. *pose* (n.), *poser* (vb.), pose; Late L. *pausāre*, to pause], attitude, esp. one taken for effect; strike an attitude, assume a character.

Po-seur' [F.], an affected person.

Pose [M.E. *apposen*, *opposen*, to question; see **Oppose**], to puzzle.

Pos'er, a puzzling question.

Po-si'tion [L. *pōnere* (p.p. *positus*), to place], place, attitude.

Pos'i-tive [L. *pōnere* (p.p. *positus*), to place], real, actual, decisive, certain.

Pos'i-tiv-ism, philosophical system of A. Comte, based on matters of fact and experience only. **Pos'itivist.**

Pos'se [L. *posse*, to be able], strong force, company.

Pos-sess' [L. *possidēre* (p.p. *possessus*), to possess; *potis*, able, *sedēre*, to sit], have and hold, to own. [frenzy.

Pos-ses'sion, ownership, thing possessed,

Pos-sess'or, owner.

Pos'set [M.E. *poshote*, etym. doubtful], hot milk curdled by adding wine.

Pos-si-bil'i-ty, thing that may be, power of happening.

Pos'si-ble [L. *possibilis*, possible, *posse*, to be able], able to happen, capable of being done. [placard.

Post[1] [L. *postis*, a post], upright timber; to

Post² [L. *pōnere* (p.p. *positus*), to place], station, system for carrying letters; put in the post-office, carry (an account) from journal to ledger, inform, travel with relays of horses, hasten. [post.

Post'age [see **Post²**], price for conveyance by

Post'al, relating to posts or postage.

Post'er [see **Post¹**], bill to be posted.

Pos-te'ri-or [L. *posterior*, comp. of *posterus*, coming after; *post*, after], later in time, behind.

Pos-ter'i-ty [as **Posterior**], succeeding generations, descendants.

Pos'tern [O.F. *posterle, posterne*, a back door; L. *posterus*, behind], small door or gate.

Post'hu-mous [L. *postumus*, a superl. form of *post*, behind], occurring after one's death, born after father's death, (work) published after author's death.

Pos-til'ion, Pos-til'lion (*io=yo*)[It. *postiglione*, a postilion; *posta*, a post; see **Post²**], rider of the near (*i.e.* left) horse of a pair, or the near leading horse of four, drawing a coach.

Post'mark, post-office mark on a letter.

Post-me-rid'i-an [L. *post*, after, *merīdiānus*, adj. from *merīdiēs*, noon], after noon.

Post-mor'tem [L. *post*, after, *mors* (acc. *mortem*), death], after death.

Post-o'bit [L. *post*, after, *obitus*, death], taking effect after death; bond of this nature.

Post-pone' [L. *post*, after *pōnere*, to put], put off. **Postpone'ment**.

Post-pran'di-al [L. *post*, after, *prandium*, dinner], after dinner.

Post'script [L. *post*, after, *scribere* (p.p. *scriptus*, to write], addition to a finished letter.

Pos'tu-lant [see **Postulate**], candidate, esp. for admission to religious order.

Pos'tu-late [L. *postulāri* (p.p. *postulātus*), to demand], assume without proof; thing taken for granted.

Pos'ture [L. *pōnere* (p.p. *positus*), to put], position of the body, attitude; assume attitudes.

Po'sy [short for **Poesy**], bunch of flowers, brief sentiment esp. in a ring.

Pot [O.E. *pott*; perh. cogn. with L. *potus*, drinking], metallic or earthenware vessel; put in pots.

Pot'ash, Pot-ass', alkaline substance.

Po-tas'si-um [see **Pot** and **Ash**], metal, basis of potash.

Po-ta'tion [L. *pōtāre* (p.p. *pōtātus*), to drink], a drink, drinking.

Po-ta'to [Sp. *patata*; Haytian, *batata*], plant and its edible tuber.

Po-teen', Po-theen' [Ir. *poitin*, little pot], Irish whisky.

Po'tent [L. *posse* (pr.p. *potens, -entis*), to be able], powerful. **Po'tency**.

Po'ten-tate, one who possesses great power.

Po-ten'tial (*ti=sh*), possible but not actual.

Poth'er [?], bustle.

Po'tion [L. *pōtio*, a potion; *pōtus*, drunken], draught, dose.

Pot'latch, Pot'lache [Amer. Ind.], feast given at election of N. Amer. chief by candidate.

Pot'sherd [**Pot**, and O.E. *sceard*, a fragment], fragment of a broken pot.

Pot'tage [F. *potage*; *pot*, a pot], thick soup or porridge.

Pot'ter [O.E. *pottere*], one who makes earthenware.

Pot'ter [O.E. *potian*, etym. dub.], do something in a purposeless way.

Pouch [O.F. *poche*; see **Pocket**], small bag; to pocket.

Poult [F. *poulet*, dim. of *poule*, a hen], young chicken, partridge, etc. **Poul'terer**.

Poul'tice (*ice=iss*) [L. *puls* (*pult-is*), pap], thick pap used to apply to the skin; apply a poultice.

Poul'try [see **Poult**], barnyard fowls.

Pounce [orig. a term in hawking; a hawk's claws were *pounces*. Etym. doubtful], fall on and seize.

Pounce [F. *ponce*, pumice], fine powder for spreading on unsized paper.

Pound¹ [O.E. *pūnian*], to beat.

Pound² [O.E. *pund*, enclosure], enclosure for strayed cattle.

Pound³ [O.E. *pund*, pound; L. *pondo*, by weight], 16 ozs. avoir., 12 ozs. troy, 20 shillings.

Pound'age, payment of so much per pound weight, or per pound sterling.

Pour (*pore*) [M.E. *pouren*; etym. doubtful], send forth or flow in a stream.

Pour'par-ler (*poor'parlai*) [F.], informal discussion before negotiations.

Pout [O.E. *pūta*], thrust out the lips; sulky thrusting out of the lips.

Pout'er [see **Pout**], kind of pigeon that inflates its breast.

Pov'er-ty [O.F. *povertē*; L. *pauper*, poor], state of being poor, need.

Pow'der [L. *pulvis* (*pulver-is*), dust], fine dust; reduce to powder, sprinkle with powder.

Pow'er [Late L. *potēre*; L. *posse*, to be able], ability, might, a government, product from the multiplication of a number by itself any number of times. **Pow'erful**.

Pox [see **Pock**], disease characterized by pustules.

Prac'ti-ca-ble, capable of being done with available means. **Prac'ticabil'ity**.

Prac'ti-cal [Gk. *practicos*; *prassein*, to do], having to do with practice, useful in practice, practising, inclined to act and not theorize, virtual. **Practical'ity**.

Prac'tice (*ice=iss*), habit, systematic exercise, action as distinct from theory, professional work.

Prac'tise (*ise=iss*) [Late L. *practicāre*], to do, perform, pursue as a profession, exercise in an art, etc.

Prac-ti'tion-er [formerly *practician*; see **Practise**], one who practises law or medicine.

Prag-mat'ic, Prag-mat'ic-al [Gk. *pragmaticos*, skilled in business ; *pragma*, a deed, *prassein*, to do], pertaining to public business, dogmatic, meddlesome.

Prag'mat-ist, philosopher who estimates truth by its value for the practical affairs of life.

Prai'rie [L. *pratum*, a meadow], treeless tract of level or rolling land.

Praise (*s=z*) [L. *pretium*, price], speak highly of, glorify ; approval, honour, joyful homage. **Praise'ful.**

Prance [?], spring or bound as a horse.

Prank [cf. obs. E. adj. *prank* ; cogn. with Du. *pronk*, show], to dress, adorn.

Prank [?], sportive act, trick.

Prate [E. imit.], talk foolishly.

Prat'tle [freq. form of Prate], talk like a child ; childish talk.

Prawn [etym. doubtful], large shrimp-like shell-fish.

Pray [L. *precāri*, to pray], make earnest request, address God. **Prayer'ful.**

Prayer (*prair*), request, expression of worship.

Pray'er, one who prays.

*Pre-, see Appendix, Latin prefixes.

Preach [O.F. *precher*, to preach ; L. *præ*, before, *dicāre*, to proclaim], deliver a sermon.

Preach'i-fy, preach or moralize tediously.

Pre-am'ble [L. *præ*, before, *ambulāre*, to walk], introduction or preface.

Preb'en-da-ry [L. *præbēre*, to grant, *præ*, before, *habēre*, to have], clergyman attached to a cathedral or collegiate church.

Pre-ca'ri-ous [L. *precārius*, obtained by prayer ; *prex* (*prec-is*), prayer], very uncertain, dangerous. **Precar'iousness.**

Pre-cau'tion [*pre-* and **Caution**], care or caution beforehand. **Precau'tionary.**

Pre-cede' [L. *præ*, before, *cedere*, to go], go before. **Preces'sion**, going before.

Pre-ce'dent, going before.

Prec'e-dent (*c=s*) [see **Precede**], a previous case taken as a rule.

Pre-cen'tor [L. *præ*, before, *cantor*, a singer ; *canere*, to sing], leader of a choir.

Pre'cept [L. *præcipere* (p.p. *præceptus*), to instruct ; *præ*, before, *capere*, to take], commandment, injunction.

Pre-cep'tor, one who makes rules, a teacher.

Pre'cinct [L. *præ*, · before, *cingere* (p.p. *cinctus*), to gird], limit ; (*pl.*) a district within boundaries.

Preci'ous (*eci=esh*) [L. *pretium*, price], of great price, costly ; affectedly refined.

Pre-ci-os'ity, affected refinement.

Prec'i-pice (*ice=iss*) [see **Precipitate**], very steep cliff.

Pre-cip'i-tate [L. *præceps* (*præcipit-is*), *præ*, before, and *caput* (*capit-is*), head], rash ; substance separated from a solution ; throw headlong, hasten occurrence of.

Pre-cip-i-ta'tion, rushing down, rash haste.

Pre-cip'i-tous, steep.

Pre'cis (*cis=see*) [F.], summary.

Pre-cise' [L. *præcīdere* (p.p. *præcīsus*), to cut off ; *præ*, before, *cædere*, to cut], exact, formal. **Preci'sion.**

Pre-clude' [L. *præ*, before, *claudere* (p.p. *clausus*), to shut], shut out, prevent.

Pre-co'ci-ty (*ŏ*) [L. *præcox* (*præcoc-is*] ; *præ*, before, and *coquere*, to cook], untimely ripeness, forwardness. **Preco'cious.**

Pre-cog-ni'tion [L. *præ*, before, *cognoscere* (p.p. *cognitus*), to find out], knowledge beforehand, preliminary examination of witnesses, esp. to discover whether there is ground for trial.

Pre-con-ceive' [*pre-* (L. *præ*) and **Conceive**], form a previous notion of.

Pre-con-cert' [*pre-* (L. *præ*) and **Concert**], arrange beforehand.

Pre-cur'sor [L. *præ*, before, *currere* (p.p. *cursus*), to run], forerunner, a messenger.

Pred'a-to-ry [L. *præda*, plunder], plundering, living on prey. [than.

Pre-de-cease' [*pre-* and **Decease**], die sooner

Pre-de-ces'sor [L. *præ*, before, *dēcessor*, one who goes from an office ; *dē*, from, *cedere*, to go], one who precedes.

Pre-des'ti-nate, Pre-des'tine [*pre-* and **Destine**], determine beforehand.

Pre-dic'a-ment [see **Predicate**], trying position, plight.

Pred'i-cate [L. *præ*, before, *dicāre* (p.p. *dicātus*), to tell], affirm ; affirmation, (in grammar) that which is said about the subject. **Predica'tion.**

Pre-dict' [L. *præ*, before, *dīcere* (p.p. *dictus*), to say], foretell. **Predic'tion.**

Pre-di-lec'tion [L. *præ*, before, *diligere* (p.p. *dilectus*), to choose], partiality (for).

Pre-dis-pose' (*s=z*) [*pre-* and **Dispose**], to render liable, subject, or inclined beforehand.

Pre-dom'inant [*pre-* and **Dominant**], ruling, prevailing. **Predom'inance.**

Pre-dom'i-nate [*pre-* and **Dominate**], surpass in power, be chief element. [others.

Pre-em'in-ent [*pre-* and **Eminent**], surpassing

Pre-emp'tion [L. *præ*, before, *emere* (p.p. *emptus*), to buy], act or right of buying before others.

Preen [perh. variant of **Prune**], dress (feathers) with the beak.

Pref'ace [L. *præ*, before, *fāri* (p.p. *fātus*) to speak], introduction ; introduce.

Pref'a-to-ry [see **Preface**], of the nature of a preface.

Pre'fect [L. *præficere* (p.p. *præfectus*), to set over ; *præ*, before, *facere*, to make], Roman governor, head of a French department, monitor.

Pre'fect-ure, period of office as a prefect, district ruled, official residence.

Pre-fer' [L. *præ*, before, *ferre*, to carry], set above, put forward, like better, choose rather.

Pref'er-ence, setting of one before another, power of choosing.

---

* pre-=L. *præ*, before.

Pref-er-en'tial (*ti*=*sh*), giving or having a preference.

Pre-fer'ment, promotion.

Pre-fix' [*pre-* and **Fix**], add as introduction.

Pre'fix, letters placed before a word.

Preg'nant [L. *prægnans* (*-antis*); *præ*, before, *nasci*, to be born], with child, full of consequence or meaning.

Pre-hen'sile [L. *prehendere* (p.p. *prehensus*), to lay hold of; *præ*, before, and *handere*, to grasp], having the power of grasping.

Pre-his-tor'ic [*pre-* and **Historic**], belonging to a time before written history.

Pre-judge' [*pre-* and **Judge**], **Pre-ju'di-cate** [L. *præ*, before, *judicāre*, to judge], judge before hearing. **Prejudica'tion.**

Prej'u-dice (*ice*=*iss*) [L. *præ*, before, *judex* (*judic-is*), a judge], prejudgment, bias, harm; give an unreasonable bent to, injure.

Pre-ju-di'cial (*ci*=*sh*), biassed, injurious.

Prel'a-cy, office of a prelate, prelates collectively.

Prel'ate [L. *prælātus*, set above, used as p.p. of *præferre*; see **Prefer**], clergyman of a superior order. **Prelat'ical.**

Pre-lect' [L. *præ*, before, *legere* (p.p. *lectus*), to read], read publicly, lecture. **Pre-lec'tion.**

Pre-lim'i-na-ry [L. *præ*, before, *līmen* (*līminis*), threshold], introductory; something introductory or preparatory.

Prel'ude or **Pre'lude** [L. *præ*, before, *lūdere*, to play], introductory movement of a musical work, preliminary performance; to introduce, foreshadow.

Prem'a-ture [L. *præ*, before, *maturus*, ripe], too early, untimely.

Pre-med-i-ta'tion [*pre-* and **Medita'tion**], forethought.

Prem'ier (*prem-yer* or *preem-yer*) [F. *premier*; L. *primus*, first], first; first minister of state.

Prem'ise, **Prem'iss** [L. *præ*, before, *mittere* (p.p. *missus*), to send], supposition, (*pl.*) what has just been said, building or part of one and its adjuncts.

Pre-mise' (*s*=*z*), lay down first propositions.

Pre'mi-um [L. *premium*, from *præ*, before, and *emere*, to take], reward, payment for insurance, addition to nominal value.

Pren'tice (*ice*=*iss*), short for **Ap-pren'tice.**

Pre-mon'i-to-ry [L. *præ*, before, *monēre* (p.p. *monitus*), to warn], giving previous warning.

Pre-oc'cu-py [*pre-* and **Occupy**], occupy before another, to engross. [prepared.

Prep-a-ra'tion, a making ready, that which is

Pre-par'a-tive, **Pre-par'a-to-ry** [see **Prepare**], making ready.

Pre-pare' [L. *præ*, before, *parāre* (p.p. *parātus*), to prepare], make ready, study beforehand, compound (medicine).

Pre-pense' [A.F. *purpense*; *pur-* (L. *prō*), forth; *penser*, to think], intentional.

Pre-pon'der-ate [L. *præ*, before, *ponderāre* (p.p. *ponderātus*), to weigh], outweigh, exceed in power, etc. **Prepon'derance.**

Prep-o-si'tion [L. *præ*, before, *pōnere* (p.p. *positus*), to put], particle governing the objective case. [favourably.

Pre-pos-sess' [L. *pre-* and **Possess**], bias, esp.

Pre-pos-sess'ing, attractive. **Prepossses'sion.**

Pre-pos'ter-ous [L. *præ*, before, *posterus*, later], utterly absurd.

Pre-rog'a-tive [L. *præ*, before, and *rogāre* (p.p. *rogātus*), to ask], exclusive privilege, esp. of a monarch.

Pres'age [L. *præ*, before, *sāgīre*, to observe], omen, sign.

Pre-sage', foretell.

Pres-by-te'ri-an [see **Presbytery**], (church) governed by elders; one who belongs to the Presbyterian Church.

Pres'by-ter-y [Gk. *presbyteros*, elder], church court consisting of ministers and elders, district from which these are drawn, residence of R.C. priest.

Pre'sci-ence (*sc*=*sh*) [L. *præ*, before, *scientia*, knowledge], foresight.

Pre-scribe' [L. *præ*, before, *scrībere* (p.p. *scriptus*), to write], give directions, indicate remedies.

Pre-scrip'tion, direction, medical recipe, right of use through custom.

Pres'ence, state of being present, noble company, personal appearance.

Pres'ent [L. *præsens* (*-entis*), present; *præ*, before, *esse*, to be], at hand, now existing, not delayed; gift, time now passing.

Pre-sent' [see **Present** (adj.)], introduce, give, aim.

Presen'table, of decent appearance.

Pres-en-ta'tion, a setting forth, gift.

Pre-sen'ti-ment [*pre-* and **Sentiment**], a feeling that something (esp. evil) is going to happen.

Pres'ent-ly, at once, before long.

Pre-sent'ment [see **Pre-sent'**], statement, portrait, theatrical representation.

Pres-er-va'tion, keeping safe.

Pre-serve' [L. *præ*, before, *servāre*, to keep], keep; fruit preserved, place in which game is kept for private sport.

Pre-side' [L. *præsidēre*, to preside; *præ*, before, *sedēre*, to sit], direct as chief, watch over.

Pres'i-dent, one who presides, esp. the head of a republic.

Pre-sid'i-al, **Pre-sid'i-a-ry**, pertaining to, serving as or having a garrison.

Press [L. *premere* (p.p. *pressus*), to press], bear upon, squeeze, urge; a machine for stamping or squeezing, newspapers generally, crowd, urgency, cupboard.

Press [O.F. *prester*, to lend; L. *præ*, forth, *stāre*, to stand], force into service.

Press'gang, body of men empowered to force men into the navy.

Pres'sure, squeezing, crushing, urgency.

Pres'ti-di-gi-ta'tion [L. *præstō*, ready, *digitus*, finger], sleight of hand.

Pres-tige' (*pres-teezh'* or *pres'tij*) [L. *præstigium*, illusion; *præ*, before, and *stringere*, to bind], influence from past success.

Pres'to [L. *præsto*, ready], quickly (conjurer's word).

Pre-sume' [L. *præ*, before, *sümere* (p.p. *sumptus*), to take], take for granted, take liberties. [conduct.

Pre-sump'tion, probability, over-confident

Pre-sump'tive, based on probability.

Pre-sump'tu-ous, over-confident, insolent.

Pre-sup-pose' [*pre-* and **Suppose**], suppose beforehand, imply.

Pre-tence', claim, false show, excuse.

Pre-tend' [L. *præ*, before, *tendere* (p.p. *tentus*, later *tensus*), to stretch], claim, make believe. **Preten'tious.**

Pre-ten'sion (*si=sh*) [see **Pretend**], act of laying claim, a claim.

Pret'er-it(e) [O.F. *preterit*; L. *præterire* (p.p. *præteritus*), to pass by]; *præter*, beyond, and *ïre*, to go], grammatical past tense.

Pre-ter-mit' [L. *prætermittere*, from *præter*, beyond, and *mittere*, to send], omit, leave off. **Pretermis'sion.**

Pre-ter-nat'u-ral [L. *præter*, beyond, and *naturalis*, natural], beyond what is natural.

Pre'text [L. *præ*, before, *texere* (p.p. *textus*), to weave], pretended reason or motive.

Pret'ti-ness (*et=ĭt*), beauty of a trivial kind.

Pret'ty (*e=ĭ*) [O.E. *prættig*], daintily beautiful; moderately.

Pre-vail' [L. *præ*, before, *valēre*, to be strong], overcome, be in force, be in general use.

Prev'a-lent [L. *prævalens* (-*entis*), pr.p. of *prævalere*; see **Prevail**], widespread, generally received. **Pre'valence.**

Pre-var'icate [L. *prævāricāri* (p.p. *prævaricātus*), to prevaricate; *præ*, before, *vāricus*, straddling], shift from direct truth.

Pre-vent' [L. *præ*, before, and *venïre* (p.p. *ventus*), to come], hinder, stop. **Preven'tion.**

Pre'vi-ous [L. *præ*, before, *via*, way], happening before, former.

Prey [O.F. *preie*; L. *præda*, prey], spoil, that which is seized by animals for food; (with *upon*) take as prey.

Price [O.F. *pris*, *preis*; L. *pretium*, price], money value, worth; to ask price of, put price on.

Prick [O.E. *prica*], sharp slender tool, puncture, sharp pain; pierce slightly, erect into a point. [**Prick'ly.**

Prick'le [O.E. *pricel*], small prick, thorn.

Pride [O.E. *prÿte*; of French origin], high self-esteem, loftiness, the best; (reflexive vb.) be proud of.

Priest [Gk. *presbyteros*, elder], one who officiates at the altar, clergyman.

Prig [?], affectedly superior person. **Prig'gish.**

Prim [17th century cant], formal, precise.

Pri'mal, Pri'ma-ry, first, original.

Pri'mate [Late L. *primās* (*primāt-is*), a chief man; L. *primus*, first], archbishop. **Prim'acy.**

Prime [L. *primus*, first], first, chief; first part, best part, full strength; apply powder to a gun), instruct beforehand.

Prim'er, Pri'mer [L. *primus*, first], elementary reader or textbook.

Pri-me'val, Prim-æ'val (*ae=ee*) [L. *primus*, first, *ævum*, an age], belonging to the first ages.

Pri'm-ing [see **Prime**], gunpowder in pan of fire-arm.

Prim'i-tive [L. *primus*, first], ancient, original, old-fashioned.

Pri-mo-gen'i-ture [L. *primus*, first, *gignere* (p.p. *genitus*), to be born], system by which the eldest son succeeds to a father's real estate.

Pri-mo-gen'i-tor, earliest ancestor, ancestor.

Pri-mor'di-al [L. *primus*, first, *ordïri*, to begin], first in order, fundamental, primeval.

Prim'rose [L. *prima rosa*, first rose; L. *primus*, first], early-flowering plant.

Prince [L. *princeps* (*princip-ĭs*), first, a chief; *primus*, first; *capere*, to take], sovereign, son of a king or emperor, title of high rank.

Prin'cess [see **Prince**], daughter of king or emperor, wife of a prince.

Prin'ci-pal, chief; leader, chief person concerned, sum lent at interest.

Prin-ci-pal'i-ty, state ruled by a prince.

Prin'ci-ple [L. *principium*, a beginning; see **Prince**], general truth, settled rule.

Prink [cogn. with **Prank**], dress oneself up, to trim feathers.

Print [O.F. *priente* (n.), *preindre* (p.p. *preint*), to press], to stamp, strike off impressions from type; an impression, esp. from type, publication, printed cloth.

Pri'or [L. *prior*, former; used as comp. of superl. *primus*, first], former; head of (a religious house).

Pri-or'i-ty, precedence.

Pri'or-y, monastery or nunnery governed by a prior.

Prise. Same as Prize.[3]

Prism (*s=z*) [Gk. *prisma* (*prismat-os*), a prism, lit. a piece sawn off; Gk. *prizein*, to saw], solid with two opposite faces connected by parallelograms, esp. triangular prism of glass used for analysing light.

Pris-mat'ic, prism-shaped, many-coloured like light analysed by a prism.

Pris'on (*s=z*) [L. *prensio*, a seizing; *prehendere* (p.p. *prehensus*), to seize], place of confinement or restraint. **Pris'oner.**

Pris'tine [L. *pristinus*, ancient, allied to *primus*, first], ancient, as at first.

Pri'thee (*ĭ*), I pray thee.

Pri'vate [L. *privātus*, orig. p.p. of *privāre*, to deprive], peculiar to oneself, secret; ordinary soldier. **Priv'acy.**

Pri-va-teer', private ship with a commission to make war on an enemy.

Pri-va'tion, taking away, destitution, need.

Priv'et [orig. obscure], ornamental evergreen shrub.

Priv'i-lege [L. *privus*, private, single, *lex* (*lēg-is*), law], peculiar benefit or right; give privilege to.

Priv'y, private, privately knowing; latrine.

Prize[1] [F. *prise*, capture; L. *prehendere* (p.p. *prehensus*), to seize], something captured.

Prize[2] [L. *pretium*, price, value], reward; value highly.

Prize,[3] **Prise** (*s=z*) [F. *prise*, a grasp; L. *prehendere*, to seize], force by leverage; leverage.

Pro'a [Malay *prāhu, prāu*, a proa], Malay boat.

Prob-a-bil'i-ty, likelihood.

Prob'a-ble [L. *probāre*, to prove], likely, believable.

Pro'bate [L. *probāre* (p.p. *probātus*), to prove], official proof of a will.

Pro-ba'tion [see Probate], trial, system of releasing first offenders under friendly supervision. **Proba'tionary.**

Pro-ba'tion-er, person on probation.

Probe [L. *probāre*, to prove], surgeon's instrument; examine with a probe, search to the bottom.

Prob'i-ty [L. *probus*, good], uprightness.

Prob'lem [Gk. *problēma* (*problēmat-os*); *pro*, forward, *ballein*, to throw], matter stated for proof, doubtful or difficult case, something to be done.

Prob-lem-at'ic, not shown in fact, doubtful.

Pro-bos'cis (*boscis=bossis*) [Gk. *pro*, in front, and *boscein*, to feed], snout, a trunk.

Pro-ce'dure, manner of proceeding, conduct.

Pro-ceed' [L. *prō*, before, and *cēdere* (sup. *cessum*), to go], go on.

Pro-ceed'ing, action, (pl.) legal action, account of learned society's doings.

Pro'ceeds, yield, sum from a sale, etc.

Pro'cess, progress, course, proceeding.

Pro-ces'sion, advancing train of persons.

Pro-claim' [L. *prō*, forth, *clamāre* (p.p. *clamātus*), to call], publish, declare.

Pro-cla-ma'tion, general notice, publication.

Pro-cliv'i-ty [L. *prō*, forward, *clīvus*, a slope], inclination, tendency.

Pro-cras'ti-nate [L. *prō*, forward, *crās*, to-morrow], put off. **Procrastina'tion.**

Proc'tor [shortened form of Procurator], one who acts for another, a disciplinary, esp. in a university.

Pro-cum'bent [L. *prō*, forward, *cumbere*, to recline], lying on the face.　　[another.

Proc'u-ra-tor [see Procure], one who acts for

Pro-cure' [L. *prō*, forth, and *curāre* (p.p. *curātus*), take care of], to gain, get, contrive. **Procur'able.**

Prod [?], pricking instrument as a goad, a prick; to prick, goad.

Prod'i-gal [L. *prōdigus*, lavish; *prō*, forth, and *agere*, to do], waster; extravagant. **Prodigal'ity.**

Pro-di'gious (*gi=j*), amazing, huge.

Prod'i-gy [L. *prōdigium*, a token, fr. *prō*, forth, and *agium*, a saying], marvel.

Pro-duce' [L. *prō*, forth, and *dūcere* (p.p. *ductus*), to lead], bring forth, show, extend in length.

Prod'uce, that which is produced.

Prod'uct, outcome.

Pro-duc'tion, act of producing, work.

Pro-duc'tive, Pro-duc-tiv'i-ty.　　[preface.

Pro'em [Gk. *prō*, before, *oimos*, a way],

Prof-a-na'tion, irreverent treatment (of sacred things).

Pro-fane' [L. *prō*, before, *fānum*, a temple], not sacred, unholy; treat with irreverence.

Pro-fan'i-ty, profane language.

Pro-fess' [L. *profitēri* (p.p. *professus*), to profess; *prō*, forth, and *fatēri*, to speak], declare openly, lay claim.

Pro-fes'sion, declaration, calling.

Pro-fes'sion-al, of a profession; (in sport), playing for a wage.

Pro-fess'or, one who avows belief, public teacher, esp. in a university.

Prof'fer [L. *prō*, forth, *ferre*, to bring], offer for acceptance.

Pro-fi'cient (*ci=sh*) [L. *pro*, forward, *facere*, to make], well-skilled. **Profi'ciency,** skill.

Pro'file [It. *profilo*, profile; L. *pro*, before, *filum*, a thread], outline, side face.

Prof'it [L. *prōficere* (p.p. *prōfictus*), to profit; *prō*, before, *facere*, to make], gain; to gain, to benefit.

Prof-it-eer' (war word), one who exacts excessive profit; to take too much profit.

Prof'it-a-ble, yielding gain, useful.

Prof'li-gate [L. *prōflīgāre* (p.p. *prōflīgātus*), to dash down; *prō*, forward, *flīgere*, to dash], wicked, recklessly extravagant; wicked person. **Prof'ligacy.**

Pro-found' [L. *prō*, forward, *fundus*, bottom], deep, learned, intense.

Pro-fun'di-ty, depth.

Pro-fuse' (*-fyooss*) [L. *profūsus* (p.p. of *profundere*), to pour forth], pouring forth with fullness.

Pro-fu'sion, abundance, lavish supply.

Pro-gen'i-tor [L. *prō*, before, *gignere* (p.p. *genitus*), to beget], forefather.

Pro-gen'i-ture, begetting of offspring.

Prog'e-ny (*ŏ, g=j*), children.

Prog'nath-ous [Gk. *pro*, before, *gnathos*, jaw], with projecting jaws.

Prog-nos'ti-cate [Gk. *prognosticon*, omen; *prō*, before, *gignoscein*, to know], foretell from signs, prophesy. **Prognostica'tion.**

Pro'gramme [Gk. *prō*, before, *gramma*, a writing], plan of proceedings.

Pro'gress or **Prog'ress** [L. *prōgredī* (p.p. *prōgressus*), to advance; *prō*, forward, *gradī*, to walk], moving forward, advance.

Pro-gress', go on, advance.

Pro-gres'sive, moving forward, advancing, favouring progress.

Pro-hib'it [L. *prohibēre* (p.p. *prohibitus*), to prohibit; *prō*, before, *habēre*, to have], forbid.

Pro-hi-bi'tion, a forbidding.

Pro-hib'it-ive, Pro-hib'it-o-ry, tending to forbid or exclude.

Proj'ect, plan.

Pro-ject' [L. *projicere* (p.p. *projectus*), to project; *prō*, before, *jacere*, to throw], cast forward, to plan.

Pro-jec'tile, a missile. [plan.

Pro-jec'tion, jutting out, part jutting out, a

Pro'late [L. *prolātus*; *prō*, forward, and *lātus*, carried], lengthened in the direction of the polar axis, widespread.

Pro-le-ta'ri-an [L. *prōlētārius*, one who served the State by having children ; *prōles*, offspring], belonging to the commonalty.

Pro-lif'ic [M.L. *prōlificus*; perh. fr. *prōles*, offspring, and *facere*, to make], fruitful.

Pro'lix or Pro-lix' [L. *prō*, forth, *liquēre*, to flow], long, tedious.

Pro'logue [Gk. *prō*, before, *logos*, speech], preface to a poem, play, etc.

Pro'-log-uize, write or speak a prologue.

Pro-long', lengthen, draw out.

Pro'lon-gate [L. *prō*, before, *longus*, long], extend in space or in time.

Prom-e-nade' [F. *promener*, to walk ; L. *prō*, forward, *mināre*, to drive], public walk ; to walk for pleasure.

Prom'i-nent [L. *prō*, forward ; *minēre* (pr.p. *minens*, -*entis*), to project], jutting, outstanding, eminent. Prom'inence.

Pro-mis'cu-ous [L. *prō*, forward, *miscēre*, to mix], mingled, indiscriminate. Promiscu'ity.

Prom'ise [L. *prō*, forward, and *mittere* (p.p. *missus*), to send], assurance given to do or give something ; engage to do, etc.

Prom'is-ing, likely to turn out well, full of promise.

Prom'is-so-ry, containing a promise (esp. promise to pay).

Prom'on-to-ry [perh. fr. L. *prōminēre*, to jut out], high cape.

Pro-mote' [L. *prō*, forward, *movēre* (p.p. *mōtus*), to move], forward, raise.

Pro-mo'tion, advance, preferment.

Prompt [L. *prōmere* (p.p. *promptus*), to bring forward ; *prō*, forward, and *emere*, to take], ready and quick ; move to action, suggest.

Prompt'er, one who reminds an actor of his next words.

Prompt'i-tude, quickness and readiness.

Prom'ul-gate [L. *promulgāre* (p.p. *promulgātus*), to publish. Orig. unknown], make known by declaration. Promulga'tion.

Prone [L. *prōnus*, prone], inclined, prostrate.

Prong [?], tine or sharp point of a fork.

Pro-nom'in-al, of the nature of a pronoun.

Pro'noun [L. *prō*, for, *nōmen*, a name], word used instead of a noun.

Pro-nounce' [L. *prō*, forth, *nuntiāre* (p.p. *nuntiātus*), to tell!], speak out, deliver.

Pro-nounce'ment, considered declaration or opinion.

Pro-nun-ci-a'tion, mode of utterance.

Proof [L. *probāre*, to test], test, evidence, trial impression from type ; of tried strength, etc.

Prop [?], to support ; that which supports.

Prop-a-gan'da [It. fr. Mod. L. *Congregatio de propaganda fide*, society (in Rome) for the propagation of the faith], plan for spreading principles.

Prop-a-gan'dist, one who spreads principles.

Prop'a-gate [L. *prōpāgāre* (p.p. *prōpāgātus*); *prō*, before, and perh. *pangere*, to fasten], multiply, spread. Propaga'tion.

Pro-pel' [L. *prō*, forward, *pellere* (p.p. *pulsus*), to drive], drive forward.

Pro-pel'ler, screw for propelling a steamship, airship or aeroplane.

Pro-pen'si-ty [L. *prō*, forward, *pendēre* (p.p. *pensus*), to hang], natural inclination, tendency.

Prop'er [L. *proprius*, one's own], own, fit, handsome, rightly so-called.

Prop'er-ty [L. *proprietas*, property, propriety; *proprius*, one's own], peculiar quality, ownership, thing owned, (*pl.*) stage requisites.

Proph'e-cy (*y*=ĭ), a foretelling, preaching.

Proph'e-sy (*y*=ī) [see Prophet], foretell, preach.

Proph'et [Gk. *prophetēs*, a prophet ; *prō*, before, and *phanai*, to speak], one who speaks in the name of God, foreteller, one inspired to foretell. Prophet'ic.

Pro-phyl-ac'tic [Gk. *pro*, before, *phulassein*, to keep guard], tending to prevent disease.

Pro-pin'qui-ty [L. *propinquus* (adj.), near, *prope* (adv.), near], nearness, close kinship.

Pro-pi'ti-ate (*t*=*sh*) [see Propitious], render favourable, appease. Propitia'tion.

Pro-pi'tious (*t*=*sh*) [L. *prō*, forward, *petere*, to seek], favourable.

Pro-pi'ti-a-tor-y, likely or meant to appease.

Pro-por'tion [L. *prō*, before, *portio* (*portiōn-is*), portion], comparative relation, comparative part, share, (*pl.*) dimensions ; make proportionate.

Pro-por'tion-al, Pro-por'tion-ate, having a due proportion, in suitable degree.

Pro-por'tion-ate, make proportional.

Pro-po'sal, that which is proposed, an offer.

Pro-pose' [L. *prō*, before ; F. *poser*, to place], offer, to purpose.

Prop-o-si'tion [L. *prō*, forth, *pōnere* (p.p. *positus*), to put], something offered for discussion or acceptance.

Pro-pound' [formerly *propoune* ; L. *prō*, forth, *pōnere*, to put], offer for consideration.

Pro-pri'e-ta-ry, considered as property, in private ownership.

Pro-pri'e-tor (fem. -tress or -trix), owner.

Pro-pri'e-ty [L. *proprietas*, propriety, property ; *proprius*, one's own], quality of being proper, fitness. [forward.

Pro-pul'sion [see Propel], act of driving

Pro-rogue' [L. *prō*, forth, *rogāre*, to ask], adjourn without dissolving members, delay. Proroga'tion.

Pro-sa'ic [M.L. *prosaicus* ; see Prose], unpoetical, dull.

Pro-scribe' [L. *prō*, forth, *scrībere* (p.p. *scriptus*), to write], outlaw, prohibit.

Pro-scrip'tion, outlawry, complete rejection.

Prose (*s*=*z*) [L. *prōsa* (*orātio*), direct speech; *prōsa*, fem. of *prōsus*, earlier *prōrsus*, short for *prōversus* ; *prō*, forward, and *vertere* (p.p. *versus*), to turn], ordinary non-metrical language.

Pros'e-cute [L. *prō*, forward, *sequī* (p.p. *secūtus*), to follow], carry on, follow, take legal action against. **Prosecu'tion.**

Pros'e-lyte [Gk. *prosēlytos*; *pros*, to, *elytos*, fr. stem. *elyth*, come], new convert to a religion.

Pro'se-lyt-ize, gain converts.

Pros'o-dy [Gk. *pros*, to, *odē*, an ode], laws of versification. **Prosod'ic.**

Pros'pect [L. *prospicere* (p.p. *prospectus*); *prō*, forward, *specere*, to look], outlook, expectation.

Pro-spect', explore for metals.

Pro-spec'tive, looking forward, future.

Pro-spec'tus, account of something proposed.

Pros'per [L. *prosper*, prosperous], succeed, thrive.

Pros-per'i-ty, good fortune, success.

Pros'per-ous [L. *prosper*, prosperous; *prō*, for, *spēs*, hope], successful, thriving.

Pros'tit-ute [L. *prō*, forth, *statuere*, to place], to devote to base or unworthy uses; a woman of low fame. **Prostitu'tion.**

Pros'trate [L. *prō*, froward, *sternere* (p.p. *strātus*), to spread], lying at length; throw down, deprive of strength. **Prostra'tion.**

Pro'sy (*s=z*), dull and tedious.

Pro-tag'o-nist [Gk. *prōtos*, first, *agōnistēs*, combatant], leading character in play or story, champion of a cause.

Pro'te-an [Gk. *Prōteus*, sea-god], taking various shapes.

Pro-tect' [L. *prō*, forward, *tegere* (p.p. *tectus*), to cover], guard, shield.

Pro-tec'tion, preservation, shelter.

Pro-tect'or, one who protects, regent in charge of kingdom. **Protec'tive.**

Pro-tect'or-ate, office of protector of state, protectorship by a stronger state of territory inhabited by native tribes.

Pro'te-id (*e=ee*), substance of nature of albumen.

Pro'te-in (*e=ee*) [Gk. *proteios*, primary], first element in any compound.

Pro-test' [L. *prō*, forth, *testārī*, to witness; *testis*, a witness], declare solemnly, avow.

Pro'test, formal objection.

Prot'es-tant [see **Protest**], Christian not of the Roman Catholic or the Greek Church.

Prot-es-ta'tion, avowal, esp. of dissent.

Pro'to-col [Gk. *prōtos*, first, *colla*, glue], rough draft of a treaty, etc., formal statement.

Pro'to-plasm [Gk. *prōtos*, first, *plasma*, form], cell substance of living bodies. **Protoplas'mic.**

Pro'to-type [Gk. *prōtos*, first, *typos*, type], original or model.

Pro-tract' [L. *prō*, forth, *trahere* (p.p. *tractus*), to draw], draw out. **Protrac'tion.**

Pro-tract'or, instrument for measuring angles.

Pro-trude' [L. *prō*, forth, *trūdere* (p.p. *trūsus*), to thrust], thrust forward, stick out.

Pro-tru'sion (*si=zh*), act of thrusting forward.

Pro-tu'ber-ance [L. *prōtūberāre* (pr.p. *prōtūberans*), to bulge out; *prō*, forward, *tuber*, a swelling], swelling, knob. **Pro-tub'erant.**

Proud [O.E. *prút*, *prúd* fr. O.F. *prud*, *prod*, valiant], haughty, lordly, grand, over-grown (flesh).

Prove [L. *probāre*, to test], test, establish, verify, turn out to be.

Prov'en-der [O.F. *provendre*; Late L. *prœbenda*, provender, also a prebendary], dry food for animals.

Prov'erb [L. *prō*, forth, *verbum*, a word], short, pithy saying.

Pro-ver'bi-al, expressed in proverb, notorious.

Pro'vi-ant [see **Provender**], food supply, esp. of army.

Pro-vide' [L. *prō*, before, *vidēre* (p.p. *vīsus*), to see], supply, prepare for.

Prov'i-dence, foresight, God's care, God.

Prov'i-dent, forecasting, careful.

Provi-den'tial (*ti=sh*), referable to divine care. **Provi-den'tial-ly.**

Prov'ince [L. *prōvincia*. Etym. doubtful], portion of an empire or state, proper place.

Pro-vin'cial (*ci=sh*), pertaining to a province, countrified. **Provincial'ity.**

Pro-vin'cial-ism, provincial manner, word or phrase peculiar to province.

Pro-vi'sion (*si=zh*), preparation, (*pl.*) a stock of food.

Pro-vi'sion-al, partial or temporary.

Pro-vi'so [see **Provide**], conditional clause. **Provis'ory.**

Pro-vo-ca'tion, cause of anger.

Pro-voc'a-tive, causing feeling, esp. anger.

Pro-voke' [L. *prō*, forth, *vocāre* (p.p. *vocātus*), to call], call forth, irritate.

Prov'ost [L. *prœpositus*, a prefect; *prœ*, before, and *positus*, p.p. of *pōnere*, to place], chief magistrate in Scotland, president of certain colleges, chief dignitary of a cathedral or collegiate church.

Prow [L. and Gk. *prōra*, a prow; *prō*, before], fore part of a vessel. [skill.

Prow'ess [O.F. *prou*, valiant], bravery and

Prowl [etym. doubtful], rove about stealthily.

Prox'im-ate [L. *proximus*, nearest], nearest.

Prox-im'i-ty, immediate nearness.

Prox'i-mo (for L. *proximō mense*=in next month), of next month.

Prox'y [earlier *procuracy*; see **Procure**], substitute, agency for another.

Prude [O.F. *prou*, earlier *prod*, excellent], one who affects great modesty. **Prud'ish.**

Pru'dence [L. *prudēns* (*prudent-is*), short for *prōvidēns*, foreseeing; *prō*, forward, *vidēre*, to see], practical wisdom, discretion.

Pru'dent, wise and cautious. [dence.

Pru-den'tial (*ti=sh*), proceeding from pru-

Prune [?], cut off, trim.

Prune [F. fr. L. *prunum*; Gk. *prou(m)non*, a plum], dried plum.

Pru-nel'la [F. *prunelle*, a sloe], coarse woollen stuff.

Prur'i-ent [L. *prurīre* (pr.p. *pruriens*), to itch], inclined to lewd thoughts and sights.

Pry [etym. doubtful], peep narrowly, inspect closely.

Psalm (*al=ah*) [Gk. *psalmos*, song sung to the harp ; *psallein*, to twang a harp], sacred song or hymn.

Psalm'o-dy or **Psal'mo-dy** [Psalm and Gk. *ōdē*, a song], practice of singing psalms, psalms collectively.

Psal'ter (*a=aw*) [Gk. *psaltērion*, a kind of harp], Book of Psalms.

Psal'ter-y (*a=aw*) [see **Psalter**], ancient and mediæval stringed instrument played by plucking.

Pseu'do-nym [Gk. *pseudos*, false, *onoma*, name], pen name. **Pseudon'ymous.**

Psy'chic, Psy'chic-al (*ch=k*) [Gk. *psychē*, soul, life, breath], pertaining to the soul or mind.

Psy-chi'a-try (*ī*) [Gk. *psychē*, soul, *iatros*, physician], treatment of mental disease.

Psy-chol'o-gy (*ch=k*) [Gk. *psychē*, life, soul, *logos*, a discourse], science of mind.

Ptar'mi-gan [Gael. *tarmachan*. Etym. doubtful], kind of grouse.

Pto-maine [Gk. *ptōma*, corpse], bodies usually poisonous in putrefying matter.

Pu'ber-ty [L. *pūbertās*], age of maturity.

Pub'lic [L. *publicus*, earlier *poplicus*, public ; *populus*, people], pertaining to the people, general, open : people indefinitely.

Pub'li-can [see **Public**], keeper of a public-house, (*Rom. hist.*) a tax-farmer, tax-gatherer.

Pub-li-ca'tion [see **Publish**], making known, act of offering a book, etc., to the public by sale, that which is published.

Pub-li'ci-ty [see **Public**], state of being widely known.

Pub'li-cist [F. *publiciste* ; see **Public**], writer on international law or current topics.

Pub'lish [L. *publicare* (p.p. *publicātus*), to publish ; *publicus*, public], make public, print and issue from the press.   [brown.

Puce [F. *puce*, flea], flea-colour, purplish-

Puck'er [perh. cogn. with **Poke** 1], gather into folds or wrinkles.

Pud'ding (*u=oo*) [M.E. *poding* ; perh. conn. with F. *boudin*], kind of food.

Pud'dle [M.E. *podel* ; perh. dim. of O.E. *pudd*, a ditch], muddy pool ; convert cast iron into wrought iron, make watertight with clay.

Pud'gy [?], short and fat.

Pu'er-ile [L. *puer*, boy], boyish, childish. **Pueril'ity.**

Pu-er'per-al [L. *puer*, boy, *parus*, bearing], due to child-birth.

Puff [E. imit.], whiff, a light pastry ; blow in whiffs, swell with air, praise unduly.

Puf'fin [?], kind of sea bird.   [nose.

Pug [?], kind of dog with short head and

Pu'gil-ism [L. *pugil*, a boxer, allied to *pugnus*, the fist], boxing. **Pu'gilist.**

Pug-na'cious (*ci=sh*) [L. *pugnax* (*pugnāc-is*), combative ; *pugnāre*, to fight], quarrelsome, fighting. **Pugnac'ity.**

Puís-ne (*pū-nĭ*) [O.F. *puis*, after ; *né*, born ; L. *post nātus*, born after], law term for inferior in rank.

Pu'is-sant, Pu-is'sant (or *puiss=pwiss*) [F. *puissant* ; It. *possente*, powerful ; L. *posse*, to be able], powerful, mighty. **Puiss'ance.**

Pu'ling [F. *piauler*, to whimper ; imit.], whining, whimpering.   [tug.

Pull (*u=oo*) [O.E. *pullian*], draw, pluck ; a

Pull'et (*u=oo*) [F. *poulet*, dim. of *poule*, hen ; L. *pullus* (fem. *pulla*), young animal], young hen.

Pul'ley (*u=oo*) [Gk. *polidion*, dim. of *pōlos*, a pivot], grooved wheel turned in a block by a cord.

Pull'man [from designer named *Pullman*], railway saloon-carriage.

Pul'mo-na-ry [L. *pulmo* (*pulmōn-is*), lung], pertaining to the lungs.

Pulp [L. *pulpa*, pulp], soft, moist matter ; reduce to pulp.

Pul'pit (*u=oo*) [L. *pulpitum*, scaffold, stage], raised desk or platform.

Pul'sate [L. *pulsāre* (p.p. *pulsātūs*), freq. of *pellere*, to drive], throb. **Pulsa'tion.**

Pulse [L. *puls* (*pult-is*), pap of meal, etc.], seeds of pod-plants.

Pulse [L. *pellere* (p.p. *pulsus*), to drive], measured or regular beat ; to pulsate.

Pul'ver-ize [L. *pulvus* (*pulver-is*), dust], reduce to fine powder.   [animal.

Pu'ma [Peruv. *puma*], American wild

Pum'ice (*ĭ*) [O.E. *pumic-stán*, pumice-stone ; L. *pūmex* (*pūmic-is*), pumice], spongy lava.

Pump [F. *pompe* ; Ger. *pumpe* ; of imit. origin], machine for raising fluids ; raise with a pump.

Pump [?], thin-soled shoe worn with evening dress.

Pump'kin [earlier *pumpion* ; L. *pepo* (*pepōn-is*) ; Gk. *pepōn*, large melon], trailing plant and its fruit.

Pun [?], play upon words ; make puns. **Pun'ster.**

Punch [Hind. *panch*, five, from number of ingredients], alcoholic drink diluted and flavoured.

Punch [short for **Punchinello**], buffoon of a puppet-show.

Punch [L. *pungere* (p.p. *punctus*), to prick], tool for stamping or making holes ; give a blow, make holes with a tool.

Pun'cheon [L. *punctio* (*punctiōn-is*), a pricking], large cask for liquids.

Pun-chi-nel'lo [It. *pulcinello*, buffoon, dim. of *pulcino*, young chicken], buffoon, originally in a puppet show.

Punc-til'io (*i=y*) [It. *puntiglio*, dim. of *punto*, point], nice point of honour, etc. [conduct.

Punc-til'ious, attentive to nice points in

Punc'tu-al [L. *punctum*, a point], up to time, prompt. **Punctual'ity.**   [points.

Punc'tu-ate [L. *punctum*, a point], mark with

Punc'ture [L. *pungere* (p.p. *punctus*), to prick], hole made by a point ; to prick.

Pun'dit [Hind. *pandit*], learned man.

Pun′gent [L. *pungēns* (*-entis*), pr.p. of *pungere*, to prick], sharp and biting. **Pun′gency**, sharpness of odour.

Pun′ish [L. *punīre*, to punish, *pœna*, punishment], inflict penalty for a fault. **Pun′ishment**. [ment.

Pu′ni-tive [see **Punish**], pertaining to punish-

Pun′kah [Hind. *pankha*, a punkha], machine for fanning a room.

Pun′ster, one given to punning.

Punt [L. *ponto*, a punt, word of Gaulish origin], oblong, flat-bottomed boat.

Pu′ny [see **Puisne**], small and weak.

Pup, Pup′py [perh. from F. *poupée*; L. *pūpa*, a doll], young dog.

Pu′pa [L. *pūpa*, girl, doll, chrysalis], insect after the larva stage, chrysalis.

Pu′pil [L. *pūpilla*, fem. of *pūpillus*, a ward], black centre of the eye; scholar under an instructor.

Pu′pil-age, Pu′pill-age, minority.

Pup′pet [F. *poupette*, doll, dim. of L. *pūpa*], doll, figure moved by a wire.

Pur′blind [earlier *pureblind*, **Pure** and **Blind**], partly blind, seeing obscurely.

Pur′chase [O.F. *purchacer* (vb.), *porchas* (n.); *pur* (F. *pour*), for, and *chacer*, to chase], buy; buying, that which is bought, leverage. **Pur′chasable**.

Pure [L. *purus*, pure], unmixed, clear, clean, innocent.

Pur-ée (*ee=ai*) [F.], soup passed through sieve.

Pur′ga-to-ry [see **Purge**], place of purification after death. **Purgator′ial**.

Purge [L. *purgāre* (p.p. *purgātus*, to purge], cleanse, clear, purify; that which purges. **Purga′tion**.

Pu′ri-fy [F. *purifier*, to purify; L. *pūrus*, pure, *facere*, to make], make pure or clean. **Purifica′tion**.

Pu′rist, one who is excessively careful in the choice of words.

Pu′ri-tan [see **Pure**], member of Protestant sect in Elizabeth′s reign, one extremely strict in religion or morals. **Pu′ritanism**, **Purita′nical**.

Pu′ri-ty, condition of being pure.

Purl [contr. of *purfle*; F. *par*, through, and *fil*, thread (L. *per* and *filum*)], inversion of stitches in knitting.

Purl, ripple and murmur.

Pur′lieu [O.F. *pouralee*; O.F. *pur* (F. *pour*), for, *alee*, a going], environs, neighbourhood.

Pur-loin′ [O.F. *purloigner*, to prolong, steal; L. *prolongāre*, prolong; *prō*, forward, *longus*, long], steal.

Pur′ple [L. *purpura*, purple], colour formed by combining crimson and blue.

Pur′port [see **Purport′**], meaning.

Pur-port′ [O.F. *purporter*, fr. *pur* (F. *pour*), for, and *porter*, to carry (L. *prō*, and *portāre*)], mean, profess.

Pur′pose [L. *prōpōnere* (p.p. *prōpositus*), to propose], view, intention; intend.

Purr [imit.], murmur of a cat.

Purse [Late L. *bursa*, a purse; Gk. *bursa*, a hide], money-bag; pucker.

Purs′lane [O.F. *porcelaine*; L. *portulāca*, purslane], herb used in salads.

Pur′ser, account-keeper in a passenger vessel.

Pur-su′ance [see **Pursue**], following out or after.

Pur-su′ant, in accordance with.

Pur-sue′ [O.F. *porsuir*, to pursue; L. *prō*, forth, *sequi*, to follow], follow, chase.

Pur-suit′, a following, chase, occupation.

Pur′sy [O.F. *polsif*, short-winded; *polser*, to breathe; see **Pulsate**], fat and short-winded.

Pur′u-lent [L. *pūs* (*pūr-is*), matter], consisting of pus.

Pur-vey′ (*-vai*) [A.F. *purveier*, to provide; see **Provide**], provide food as a business.

Pur-vey′or, one who provides victuals.

Pur′view [O.F. *porveu*, p.p. of *porvoir*, to provide], scope, range. [festering.

Pus [L. *pus*, matter], yellowish fluid from

Push [F. *pousser*, to push; L. *pulsāre*, to beat, to thrust], drive by pressure, make one′s way; a thrust, aggressive energy.

Pu-sil-lan′i-mous [L. *pusillus*, mean, *animus*, soul], cowardly. **Pusillanim′ity**.

Pus′tule [L. *pustula*, pustule; see **Pus**], pimple containing pus.

Put [O.E. *putian*, *pýtan*], to place, set.

Put, Putt (*u* pron. as in *pup*) [see **Put**], hurl, strike (golf ball) gently towards hole.

Pu′ta-tive [L. *putāre*, to suppose], supposed.

Pu-tre-fac′tion, offensive decay.

Pu′tre-fy [L. *putrefierī*; *putrus*, rotten, *facere*, to make], become putrid.

Pu-tres′cent [L. *putrescere* (pr.p. *putrescēns*, *-entis*), to grow rotten; *putrēre*, to rot], becoming rotten.

Pu′trid [L. *putridus*, rotten], rotten, foul.

Put′tee [Hind. *patti*, bandage], strip of cloth for winding spirally round the leg.

Put′ty [F. *potée*, lit. potful], thick paste of whiting and oil.

Puz′zle [?], something which perplexes; perplex, confuse, get at by patient thought.

Pyg′my, Pig′my (Gk. *pygmē*, 13¼ ins. from elbow to knuckle, also a fist], dwarf.

Py-ja′mas (*y=ī* or *ī*) [Pers. *pae*, foot *jamah*, clothing], sleeping-suit.

Pyr′a-mid [Gk. *pỹramis*, *pyramīd-os*), perh. of Egyptian origin], solid with triangular sides. **Pyram′idal**.

Pyre [Gk. *pyra*, *pyr*, fire], funeral pile.

Pyr-o-tech′nics, Pyr-o-tech′ny (*ch=k*) [Gk. *pyr*, fire, *technē*, art], art of making fireworks.

Pyr′rhic [fr. *Pyrrhus*, King of Epirus], (victory) gained at too great cost.

Py′thon [L. *pythōn*; Gk. *pythōn*, serpent slain by Apollo; Gk. *Pythō*, older name of Delphi], very large serpent.

Pyx [L. and Gk. *pyxis*, a box; Gk. *pyxos*, box wood], box which contains the communion bread in the R.C. Church, box containing specimen coins at the Mint; to test at Mint.

Q

Quack (ă) [imit.], utter the cry of a duck; duck's cry, false pretender to skill.

Quad-ran'gle * [L. *quătuor*, four, *angulus*, an angle], four-sided figure, court surrounded by buildings. **Quadran'gular.**

Quad'rant [L. *quadrāns* (-*antis*) a fourth part; *quatuor*, four], quarter of a circle, instrument for angular measurement.

Quad-rat'ic [L. *quadrāre* (p.p. *quadrātus*) to make square], pertaining to squares.

Quad-ri-lat'er-al [L. *quatuor*, four, *latus* (*later-is*), a side], four-sided; four-sided figure.

Qua-drille' [Sp. *cuadrilla*, meeting of four persons; *cuadra*, a square], square dance.

Quad-roon' [Sp. *cuarto* ; L. *quartus*, a fourth], person of quarter-negro blood.

Quad'ru-ped [L. *quadrupedus*, four-footed; *quadru-*, four times ; *pēs* (*pĕd-is*), foot], four-footed animal.

Quad'ru-ple [L. *quadruplus*, fr. *quatuor*, four, *plicāre*, to fold], fourfold. **Quadru'plicate.**

Quaff (ā) [?], drink in large draughts.

Quag'ga (ă) [Kaffir], striped S. African wild ass.

Quag'mire (ă) [perh. *quake-mire*], bog.

Quail [?], cower.

Quail [O.F. *quaille*, perh. imit.], bird of the partridge family.

Quaint [O.F. *cointe* ; L. *cognoscere* (p.p. *cognitus*), to know], odd and antique.

Quake [O.E. *cwacian*], shake, quiver.

Qua'ker [fr. **Quake**], one of the Society of Friends.

Qual-i-fi-ca'tion, that which qualifies.

Qual'i-fy [L. *qualis*, such ; *facere*, to make], to fit, to make oneself fit, modify.

Qual'i-ta-tive, depending on quality.

Qual'i-ty [L. *qualis*, of such a kind], nature, characteristic, rank.

Qualm (*al=ah*) [O.E. *cwealm*, pestilence], sick feeling, prick of conscience.

Quan-da'ry, Quan'da-ry [?], state of perplexity.

Quan'ti-ty [L. *quantus*, how much], amount, bulk, portion. **Quan'titative.**

Quar'an-tine (*ine=een*) [F. *quarantaine*, space of forty days ; F. *quarante*, L. *quadrāgintā*, forty], isolation imposed on ships, etc., from infected places ; to impose such isolation.

Quar'rel [L. *querēla*, complaint ; *querī*, to complain], disagreement, angry dispute; dispute angrily. **Quar'relsome.**

Quar'rel [Late L. *quadrellus*, fr. L. *quadrus*, square], square-headed cross-bow bolt.

Quar'ry [orig. parts of slain deer placed on hide and given to hounds ; L. *corium*, a hide], animal pursued for prey.

Quar'ry [L. *quadrāria*, quarry for squared stones ; L. *quadrāre*, to square], stone pit ; dig from a quarry. [gallon.

Quart [L. *quartus*, fourth], fourth part of a

Quar'ter [L. *quartus*, fourth], fourth part, 8 bushels, 28 lbs. ; locality, mercy ; (*pl.*) lodgings ; divide into four equal parts, lodge.

Quar'ter-deck, part of the upper deck from the aftermast to the stern.

Quar'tern [L. *quartus*, fourth], 4-lb. loaf.

Quar-tet', Quar-tette' [It. *quartetto*, dim. of *quarto* (L. *quartus*), fourth], musical composition in four parts, party of four.

Quar'to [L. (in) *quarto*, (in) a fourth part], originally a book with 4 leaves to the sheet, now a book nearly square and usually large.

Quartz [Ger. *quarz.* Etym. doubtful], rock consisting of silica.

Quash [L. *quassāre*, freq. of *quatere* (p.p. *quassus*), to shake], squash, crush, annul.

Quas'si-a (*kwäsia, kwŏsha, or kwäsha*) [fr. *Quassi*, name of a negro of Surinam], bitter tree of S. America.

Qua-ter'na-ry [L. *quaternī*, four at a time ; *quatuor*, four], consisting of four.

Quat'rain [L. *quatuor*, four], four lines rhyming alternately.

Qua'ver [fr. obs. *quave*, cogn. with **Quake**], tremble ; shake of the voice, note equal to half a crotchet.

Quay (*kee*) [M.E. and O.F. *kay*, a quay ; cf. Bret. *kae* ; W. *cae*, an enclosure ; modern F. *quai*], wharf where vessels are loaded, etc.

Quean [O.E. *cwene*, woman], jade.

Quea'sy [Icel. *ūthra-kveisa*, colic ; Norw. *kveis*, sickness after a debauch, origin doubtful], affected with nausea, overscrupulous. **Queas'iness.**

Queen [O.E. *cwēn*, a woman], female monarch, king's wife, perfect female bee, (in chess) piece with greatest freedom of movement, one of a suit of cards. [cal.

Queer [perh. G. *quer*, crosswise], odd, whimsical.

Quell [O.E. *cwellan*, to kill ; *cwelan*, to die], put down, to calm.

Quench [M.E. *cwenkan*], extinguish, allay. **Quench'able.** [corn.

Quern [O.E. *cweorn*], hand-mill for grinding

Quer'u-lous [L. *querī*, to complain], complaining, fretful. **Quer'ulousness.**

Que'ry [L. *quære*, 2nd sing. imp. of *quærere*, to seek], anything asked, or to be asked about ; ask, doubt.

Quest [L. *quærere* (p.p. *quæsitus*), to seek], search, request ; to search.

Ques'tion, an asking, enquiry ; ask.

Ques'tion-a-ble, disputable, doubtful.

Queue (*kew*) [F. *queue* ; L. *cauda*, a tail], pigtail, line of people waiting.

Quib'ble [dim. of obs. *quib*, a sarcasm ; *quib*, a form of **Quip**], a shift from the point in question, trifle in argument. [rapid.

Quick [O.E. *cwicu*], living, ready, nimble,

Quick'en, make or become alive, make faster.

Quick'sand, mass of loose wet sand that engulfs objects.

Quick'set, formed of living plants.

* After *Qu*, *a* almost always=*ŏ*.

Quick'silver, mercury. [chewing.

Quid [var. of **Cud**], piece of tobacco for

Qui-es'cent (ĭ) [L. *quiescere* (pr.p. *quiescĕns, -entis*), to be still], at rest.

Qui'et [L. *quiēs* (*quiĕt-is*), rest], free from noise, still; stillness, peace; to calm.

Qui'e-tude, rest, calmness.

Qui-e'tus (ĭ), discharge, acquittance.

Quill [?], large feather of a wing, pen made from a feather stem, one of a porcupine's spines, fold or plait of a ruff; plait in quills.

Quilt [L. *culcita*, a cushion], bedcover, esp. when quilted; join layers by cross lines of stitching.

Quince [orig. pl. of *quine, coyn*, a quince; Gk. *Cydonion* (melon), a quince, lit. Cydonian apple], acid fruit of the apple kind.

Quin-ine' (*ine=een*) or **Qui-nine'** [Sp. *quina*, Peruv. *kina*, bark], extract from cinchona bark.

Quin'sy [Gk. *cynagchē*; *cyōn*, a dog, and *agchein*, to throttle], inflammation of the tonsils.

Quin'tain [perh. L. *quintāna*, a quintain, camp-market; *quintus*, fifth], post with arms or sandbag for tilting at.

Quin-tes'sence [M.L. *quinta essentia*, fifth essence], concentrated essence.

Quin-tet', Quin-tette' [F. *quintette*, fr. It. *quintetto*; L. *quintus*, fifth + dim. suf. *-etto*], a musical composition in five parts, a set of five singers or players. [five-fold.

Quin'tu-ple [L. *quintus*, fifth, and *-plus*, -fold],

Quip [formerly *quippy*; L. *quippe*, forsooth], smart jest, taunt.

Quire [L. *quaternī*, four at a time; *quatuor*, four], twenty-four sheets of paper.

Quire [see **Choir**], band of singers.

Quirk [?], sudden turn, quibble.

Quit [O.F. *quite*, quit; L. *quiētus*, quiet], released, free; to free, acquit, leave.

Quite [see **Quit**], entirely.

Quiv'er [perh. imit.], tremble; tremor.

Quiv'er [O.F. *cuivre*, O.H.G. *kohhar* (Ger. *köcher*), quiver], case for arrows.

Quix-ot'ic [fr. Don *Quixote*, hero of Sp. novel by Cervantes], absurdly chivalrous.

Quiz [?], make sport of as by obscure questions; one who quizzes. [stone.

Quoin (*qu=k*) [var. of **Coin**], wedge, corner-

Quoit (*qu=k*) [?], flat ring used in a game.

Quon'dam [L. *quondam*, formerly], former.

Quo'rum [L. *quōrum*, of whom, gen. pl. of *quī*, who], fixed number entitled to act for certain purposes.

Quo'ta [L. *quota*, fem. of *quotus*, how great; *quot*, how many], proportional share.

Quo-ta'tion, that which is quoted.

Quote [Late L. *quotāre*, to quote; see **Quota**], cite as a passage from some author, name the current price of. **Quot'able.**

Quoth [part of obs. *quethe*, to say; O.E. *cwethan*], said, spoke.

Quo-tid'ian [L. *quotus*, how many, *dies*, a day], returning daily, commonplace.

Quo'tient (*ti=sh*) [L. *quotiēns*, how many times; *quot*, how many], number resulting from division.

R

Rab'bet [O.F. *rabat*, recess; L. *re*, down, *ad*, to, *batuere*, beat], groove cut for a panel, door, etc.; to cut a rabbet, join by a rabbet.

Rab'bi, Rab'bin [Heb. *rabbī*, my master; *rabh*, master], Jewish master of the law.

Rab'bit [cogn. w. M.Du. *robbe*, a rabbit], burrowing, gnawing animal. (*Welsh rabbit* (explained as=*rarebit*), a dish of toasted cheese.)

Rab'ble [?], noisy crowd.

Rab'id [L. *rabidus*, mad; *rabere*, to rave], furious, extreme, affected with rabies.

Ra'bi-es, Rab'i-es [L. *rabere*, to rave], hydrophobia, canine madness.

Rac-(c)oon' [Algonquin name], small animal of the bear family. [family.

Race[1] [It. *razza*. Etym. doubtful], lineage,

Race[2] [O.N. *rás*, a running, race], trial of speed, strong current; run swiftly, contend in a race. **Ra'cer.** [ginger).

Race[3] [O.F. *raïs*, L. *rādix*, root], root (of

Ra-ceme' [L. *racēmus*, a cluster], long flower cluster. [family.

Ra'cial (*ci=sh*), pertaining to a race or

Rack[1] [perh. var. of **Wrack**], destruction; thin, flying clouds.

Rack[2] [perh. M.Du. *recken*, stretch], instrument of torture; to torture, injure by strain, strain, oppress with excessive rent.

Rack[3] [perh. as **Rack**[2]], grating above a manger, framework for keeping things on or in.

Rack'et,[1] **Racqu'et** (*qu=k*) [F. *raquette*. Etym. doubtful], tennis bat.

Rack'et[2] [perh. imit.], din.

Ra-cont-eur' [F.], skilful teller of anecdotes.

Ra'cy [see **Race**[1]], fresh and lively.

Ra'di-ant [L. *radiāre* (pr.p. *radiāns, -antis*), to radiate; *radius*, ray], emitting rays, vividly bright.

Ra'di-ate [L. *radiāre* (p.p. *radiātus*), to radiate; *radius*, ray], emit or issue in rays. **Radia'tion.**

Ra'di-a-tor, apparatus for radiating heat.

Rad'i-cal [L. *rādix* (*rādic-is*), a root], proceeding from the root, thorough; supporter of radical changes.

Rad'ish [L. *rādix*, a root], root used in salads.

Ra'di-um [L. *radiāre*, to radiate], a metal obtained from pitch-blende with the power of radiating energy.

Ra'di-us [L. *radius*, a ray], line from the centre to the circumference of a circle, thick short bone of fore-arm.

Raf'fi-a, Raph'i-a [Malagasy], kind of palm, fibre from its leaves.

Raff'ish [see **Riff-raff**], dissipated, disreputable.

Raf´fle [M.E. *rafle*, game at dice. Etym. doubtful], kind of lottery; to sell by means of lottery.

Raft [O.N. *raptr*, rafter; allied to *ráf*, roof], float of logs or timber.

Raft´er [extension of **Raft**], sloping timber of a roof.

Rag [Norw. and Swed. *ragg*, rough hair; O.N. *rǫgg*, tuft of fur], piece of torn cloth; play rough jokes on.

Rag-a-muf´fin [perh. fr. **Rag**], mean wretch, one in rags.

Rage [L. *rabiēs*, rage; *rabere*, to rave], anger, fury; to storm.

Ra-gout´ (*ou=oo*) [F. *ragoût*; F. *re-*, again, *à*, to, *goûter*, to taste; L. *re-*, *ad*, and *gustāre*], highly seasoned stewed meat and vegetables. [rhythm.

Rag´time, kind of music with inverted

Raid [northern form of O.E. *rád*, road], hostile incursion; make a raid upon.

Rail¹ [L. *rēgula*, rail, rule], bar of timber or metal.

Rail² [O.F. *raalle* (from its cry)], kind of bird.

Rail³ [F. *railler*. Etym. doubtful], reproach insolently, scold.

Rail´ler-y [F. *raillerie*; see **Rail³**], banter, jesting language.

Rail´road, Rail´way, road with rails as tracks for wheels of vehicles. [clothes.

Rai´ment [short for *arraiment*; see **Array**],

Rain [Com. Teut.; O.E. *regn, rén*], water in drops from the clouds; pour in drops. **Rain´y.**

Rain´bow, coloured arch in the sky.

Raise (*s=z*) [O.N. *reisa*, make to rise; *risa*, to rise], cause to rise, lift.

Rai´sin (*s=z*) [O.F. *raizin*, L. *racēmus*, a cluster], dried grape.

Ra´jah or **Ra´ja** (*Rahja*) [Hind. *rājā*; Skr. *rājan*, a king], Hindu king, prince, chief, or great landowner.

Rake [O.E. *raca*], toothed tool; scratch or collect with a rake.

Rake [contracted from archaic *rakehell*, **Rake** and **Hell**], worthless man.

Ra´kish, dashing and saucy.

Ral´ly [F. *rallier*; L. *re-*, again, and F. *allier*, to ally], gather again, regain strength; reunion.

Ral´ly [see **Rail³**], to banter.

Ram [O.E., Du., and O.H.G.], male sheep, engine of war for battering; to butt, force in.

Ram´ble [?], rove, wander; a stroll, aimless walking about.

Ram´e-kin, Ram´e-quin (*qu=k*) [?], breadcrumb, cheese, egg, etc., baked in small mould.

Ram´i-fy [L. *ramus*, a branch; *facere*, to make], divide into branches. **Ram´ifica-tion.**

Ram-page´ [?], rush about, storm. **Ram-pag´eous.**

Ramp´ant [F. *ramper*, to clamber; *rampant*, rearing. Etym. doubtful], standing on hind legs, aggressive.

Ram´part [F. *rampart*, a rampart; L. *re-*, again, *ante*, before, *parāre*, to prepare] defence, broad-topped mound for defence.

Ram´rod, rod used in ramming down the charge in a firearm.

Ram´shac-kle [perh. obs. *ransackle*; see **Ransack**], falling to pieces.

Ranch [Sp. *rancho*, mess, persons eating together], grazing farm in America; conduct a ranch.

Ran´cid [L. *rancidus*, stinking], tasting like old oil. **Rancid´ity.**

Ran´cor-ous, full of rancour, malignant.

Ran´cour [L. *rancor*, spite; orig. rancidness], ill-will, spite.

Ran´dom [O.F. *randon*, the force of a great stream; *randir*, to run swiftly], indefinite course; haphazard.

Range [O.F. *ranger*, to range; *reng* (F. *rang*), rank; see **Rank²**], set in a row or in order, rove, vary between limits; a row, extent, built-in cooking stove, shooting-place.

Ran´ger, keeper of a park or forest.

Rank¹ [O.E. *ranc*], luxuriant in growth, strong-tasted, extreme.

Rank² [O.F. *reng* (F. *rang*), a row; O.H.G. *hrinc*, a ring; see **Ring²**], a row, row of soldiers side by side, grade, high degree; to range, belong to a class.

Ran´kle [O.F. *draoncler, rancler*, fester; Late L. *dracunculus*, dim. of *draco*, a dragon], cause a sore, fester, give constant pain.

Ran´sack [O.N. *rann*, a house, *sækja*, to seek], search thoroughly.

Ran´som [O.F. *raenson*, later *rançon*; L. *redemptio*, a buying back; see **Redeem**], release for payment, price of release; buy the release of another.

Rant [M.Du. *randten*, to rave], declaim noisily; noisy, empty, high-sounding talk.

Ran-un´cu-lus [L. *rānunculus*, orig. dim. of *rāna*, a frog], plant of the crowfoot order.

Rap [prob. imit.], strike quickly; a knock.

Ra-pa´cious (*ci=sh*) [L. *rapax* (*rapāc-is*), rapacious; *rapere*, to seize], grasping, greedy.

Rape [L. *rāpum*, a turnip], plant with oil-producing seeds.

Rap´id [L. *rapidus*, rapid; *rapere*, to seize], fast; (*pl.*) steep part of a river where the current is swift.

Ra´pi-er [F. *rapière*. Etym. doubtful], edgeless finely-pointed sword. [plunder.

Rap´ine [L. *rapīna*, rapine; *rapere*, to seize],

Rap-par-ee´ [Ir. *rapaire*, short pike], wild Irish robber.

Rap-pee´ [F. (*tabac*, tobacco), *râpé*, rasped; see **Rasp**], coarse kind of snuff.

Rapt [L. *rapere* (p.p. *raptus*), to seize], snatched away, wholly absorbed.

Rap´ture, extreme joy or pleasure. **Rap´-turous.**

Rare [L. *rārus*, rare], scarce, unusual, thin.

Rare´bit. [See **Rabbit.**]

Rar´e-fy [L. *rārefacere*; *rārus*, rare, *facere*, to make], make or become less dense. **Rarefac´tion.**

Rar'i-ty, thinness, rareness, rare thing.

Ras'cal [A.F. *raskayle*, rabble. Etym. doubtful], mean, trickish fellow, rogue. **Ras-cal'ity.**

Rase, Raze [L. *rādere* (p.p. *rāsus*), to scrape, demolish], erase, level with the ground.

Rash [O.F. *rache*, scurf; *cf.* L. *rādere*, to scrape], skin eruption. [hasty.

Rash [cf. Du. and Ger. *rasch*, quick], over-

Rash'er [perh. fr. obs. *rash*, to slice], thin slice of bacon.

Rasp [O.F. *rasper*, to rasp; *cf.* O.H.G. *raspôn*, to rasp, *hrespan*, to pluck], coarse file; rub with a coarse file, grate harshly.

Rasp'ber-ry [formerly *raspis*, *raspes*; *cf.* M.It. *raspo*, a rasp, also a raspberry], thimble-shaped fruit.

Rat [O.E. *ræt*; etym. doubtful], one of a kind of gnawing animal; hunt rats, desert one's party. [rates.

Ra'ta-ble [see Rate [1]], liable to payment of

Ra-ta-fi'-a (*i*=*ee*) [F. *ratafia*; etym. doubtful], liqueur flavoured with kernels.

Ratch'et, Ratch [F. *rochet*, a lance-head], set of teeth on a bar or wheel allowing motion in one direction, wheel with such teeth.

Rate [1] [L. *rērī* (p.p. *ratus*), to think, reckon], value, assess for rates; proportion, charge, (*pl.*) local taxes.

Rate [2] [?], scold angrily.

Rathe (*pron.* to rhyme with Bathe), Rath [O.E. *hrathe*, *hraed*, quick], early, soon.

Rath'er [comp. of Rathe].

Rat'i-fy [F. *ratifier*, to ratify; Rate [1] and L. *facere*, to make], approve and sanction. **Rat'ification.**

Ra'ti-o (*t*=*sh*) [L. *ratio*, calculation; see Rate [1]], fixed relation of number.

Ra-tio-cin-a'tion (*t*=*sh*) [L. *ratiocinārī* (p.p. *ratiocinātus*), to reason formally; see Rate [1]], deductive reasoning.

Ra'tion (*ai* or *ă*) [L. *ratio* (*ration-is*), calculation], fixed daily allowance of food; to limit food, etc.

Ra'tion-al (*Răsh*), reasoning, sensible, wise.

Ra-tion-a'le (-*ail-ĕ*), reasoned exposition.

Ra'tion-al-ism, treating reason as the only authority in religion or the basis of certainty in all investigations.

Rat'lines, Rat'lins [formerly *raddelines*; perh. same word as prov. E. *raddlings*, long pieces of underwood twisted between upright stakes], small ropes fastened across the shrouds of a ship.

Rats'bane, rat poison, white arsenic.

Rat(t)an' [Malay *rōtan*, the rattan-cane], walking-stick made from the stem of a kind of palm, the Malay palm itself.

Rat'tle [M.E. *ratelen*, prob. imit.], to clatter; clattering sound, baby's toy.

Rat'tle-head'ed, empty-headed.

Rat'tle-snake, snake with a rattle in the tail.

Rau'cous [L. *raucus*, hoarse], hoarse, harsh.

Rav'age [L. *rapere*, to seize], lay waste.

Rave [perh. O.F. *raver*, to dream], be delirious, talk wildly. [tangle.

Rav'el [Du. *ravelen*, to ravel], untwist, en-

Rave'lin [It. *ravellino*, a ravelin; etym. doubtful], outwork of a fortification.

Ra'ven [O.E. *hræfn*; Com. Teut.], kind of crow.

Rav'en [F. *raviner*, to ravage; see Rapine], to prey, be greedy.

Rav'en-ous, devouring greedily, very hungry.

Ra-vine' (*ine*=*een*) [F. *ravine*, a ravine, a great flood; see Raven (vb.)], gorge, mountain cleft.

Rav'ish [L. *rapere*, to seize], snatch by force, to delight. **Rav'ishment.**

Raw [O.E. *hréau*; Com. Teut.], not cooked, unwrought, deprived of skin, chilly, inexperienced. [radius.

Ray [L. *radius*, a ray], line of light or heat

Ray [L. *rāia*, a ray], large flat sea-fish.

Ra'zor [O.F. *rasor*, a razor; see Rase], knife used in shaving.

Ra'zor-backed, (whale) having a dorsal fin, (hill) ridged like back of razor.

Reach [O.E. *rēcan*], stretch to, extend, gain; a stretch, power of reaching.

Re-act' [L. *re-*, back, and Act], act upon each other, act in opposition. [dency.

Re-ac'tion, responsive action, retrograde ten-

Re-ac'tion-ar-y, conservative, unduly fond of the old and out-of-date.

Read [O.E. *rǣdan*; Com. Teut.], take in the sense of written or printed characters, explain. **Read'able.**

Read'y [M.E. *rædig*, perh. fr. O.E. *grǣde*], prepared, willing, easy. **Read'iness.**

Re'al [Late L. *reālis*, real; L. *rēs*, a thing], actual, true, (property) consisting of land and houses.

Re'al (*e*=*ee* or *ai*) [Sp. *real*; L. *rēgālis*, royal], small Spanish coin.

Re'al-ism, truth to nature, insistence on detail in art and literature. **Re'alist.**

Re-al-is'tic, lifelike.

Re-al'i-ty, actual being, fact.

Re'al-ize, make real, convert into money, accomplish, understand clearly. **Re-al-i-za'-tion.**

Realm [O.F. *reaume*, a realm; L. *rēgālis*, royal], kingdom.

Ream [O.F. *remme*, Sp. *resma*, a ream; Arab. *risma*), a bundle], twenty quires or 480 sheets of paper.

Reap [O.F. *reopan*, *rihan*], cut corn.

Rear [O.F. *riere*, L. *retro*, backward], back part, hindmost. [legs.

Rear [O.E. *rǣran*], raise, rise on the hind

Rea'son (*s*=*z*) [O.F. *raisun*, L. *ratio*, reason; L. *rērī* (p.p. *ratus*), to think], motive or cause, faculty by which we distinguish right from wrong, etc.; discuss by argument.

Rea'son-a-ble, rational, moderate.

Re-as-sure' [L. *re-*, again, and Assure], restore confidence to. **Reassur'ance.**

Re'-au-mur (*au*=*ō*), name of French physicist who introduced thermometer, with freezing-point 0° and boiling-point 80°.

Re-bate' [O.F. *rabattre*, to rebate; *re-*, down, and Abate], deduct; a discount.

Reb'el [L. *re-*, against, *bellum*, war], one who resists authority.

Re-bel', resist authority. [**Rebel'lious.**

Re-bel'lion, open resistance to authority.

Re-bound' [L. *re-*, back, and **Bound** [2]], spring back; springing back by elastic force.

Re-buff' [It. *rebuffo*, check, *ribuffare*, to check; *ri-* (L. *re-*), back, *buffo*, puff], sudden check; to check.

Re-buke' [O.F. *re-*, down, *bucher*, beat], reprove, chide; reproof.

Re'bus [perh. L. *rēbus*, by things; abl. pl. of *rēs*, a thing], pictorial riddle.

Re-but' [L. *re-*, back, and **Butt** [3]], drive back, repulse. **Rebut'ment.**

Re-cal'ci-trant [L. *re-*, back; *calcitrāre* (pr.p. *calcitrans*, *-antis*), strike with the heel; *calx* (*calc-is*), heel], kicking back, refractory. **Recal'citrance.**

Re-call' [L. *re-*, back, and **Call**], call back, withdraw, call to mind; a calling back.

Re-cant' [L. *re-*, back, *cantāre*, to sing], take back openly, retract. **Recanta'tion.**

Re-ca-pit'u-late [L. *re-*, again, and **Capitulate**], repeat briefly. **Recapitula'tion.**

Re-cast' [L. *re-*, again, and **Cast**], reconstruct.

Re-cede' [L. *re-*, back, *cēdere* (sup. *cessum*), to go], move back, withdraw.

Re-ceipt' [see **Receive**], reception, acknowledgment of money paid; put a receipt on; (archaic) recipe.

Re-ceive' [L. *recipere* (p.p. *receptus*), to receive; *re-*, back, *capere*, to take], take, take in, accept.

Re-cen'sion [L. *re-*, again, *censēre*, to give an opinion], critical revision.

Re'cent [L. *recens* (*recent-is*), recent], lately come, new, modern.

Re-cep'ta-cle [L. *receptāculum*; see **Receive**], that which receives or contains.

Re-cep'tion, receiving or being received, formal receiving of guests.

Re-cep'tive, able or inclined to take in. **Receptiv'ity.**

Re-cess' [see **Recede**], niche in a room, secluded spot, suspension of business.

Re-ces'sion, act of receding.

Re-ces'sion-al, hymn sung during withdrawal of clergy and choir after service.

Rec'i-pe (*c=s*) [L. *recipe*, 2nd sing. imperative of *recipere*; see **Receive**], prescription of ingredients.

Re-cip'i-ent [L. *recipiens* (*-entis*), pr.p. of *recipere*, to receive], one who receives.

Re-cip'ro-cal [L. *reciprocus*, reciprocal; perh. fr. *re-*, back, and *pro-*, forward], mutual, interchanging. [interchange.

Re-cip'ro-cate, move backward and forward.

Rec-i-proc'i-ty (*ŏ*, *c=s*), mutual give and take, interchange of privileges.

Re-ci'tal (*ī*), account, rehearsal, narration, musical performance by one person or of one composer's works.

Rec-i-ta'tion (*c=s*), act of reciting.

Re-cit-at-ive' (*ive=eev*) [It. *recitativo*; see **Recite**], kind of musical recitation in opera and oratorio.

Re-cite' [L. *re-*, again, *citāre* (p.p. *citātus*), to quote, cite], repeat aloud, tell over.

Reck [O.E. *reccan*; Com. Teut.], care for regard.

Reck'less, heedless, careless.

Reck'on [O.E. (*ge*)*recenian*], make a calculation, estimate.

Reck'on-er, book of money tables, etc.

Re-claim' [L. *re-*, back, *clamāre*, to call], claim back, reform, prepare for cultivation.

Rec-la-ma'tion, recovery.

Re-cline' [L. *re-*, back, *clināre*, to bend], lean back, lie down.

Re-cluse' (*s* sharp) [F. *reclus* (fem. *-use*), p.p. of *reclure*, to shut up; L. *re-*, back, *claudere* to shut], one who lives secluded, a hermit.

Rec-og-ni'tion, acknowledgment, notice.

Re-cog'ni-zance, judicial bond to keep some condition.

Rec'og-nize, Rec'og-nise [O.F. *reconuiss-*, part. stem of *reconoistre*, to know again; L. *re-*, again, *cognoscere*, to know], know again, acknowledge.

Re-coil' [L. *re-*, back, *cūlus*, the hinder part], roll or spring back; rebound.

Rec-ol-lect' [L. *re-*, again, *colligere* (p.p. *collectus*), to collect], remember. **Recollec'tion.**

Rec-om-mend' [L. *re-* again, *commendāre*, to entrust], attract favour to, commit, advise.

Rec-om-men-da'tion, favourable mention.

Rec'om-pense [L. *re-*, again, *compensāre*, to compensate; see **Compensate**], reward, pay for; a reward, amends.

Rec'on-cile [L. *re-*, again, *conciliāre*, to conciliate], restore to friendship, make consistent.

Rec-on-cil-i-a'tion, renewal of friendship.

Rec'on-dite, Rec-on'dite [L. *re-*, back; *condere* (p.p. *conditus*) to hide], secret, abstruse.

Re-con'nais-sance [see **Recognize**], preliminary survey. [survey.

Re-con-noi'tre [see **Recognize**], make a

Re-cord' [L. *recordāre*, to record; *re-*, again, *cor* (*cord-is*), the heart], make note of, register.

Rec'ord [see **Record** (vb.)], written memorial, best performance of the kind.

Re-cord'er, one who records, judge of a city or borough court of quarter sessions.

Re-count' [L. *re-*, again; O.F. *conter*, to compute], count again, tell over.

Re-coup' (*ou=oo*) [L. *re-*, again; F. *couper*, to cut; F. *coup*, Late L. *colpus*, a blow], recompense for loss, get an equivalent for loss, etc.

Re-course' (*ō*) [L. *re-*, back, *cursus*, course], resort for aid.

Re-cov'er (*o=ŭ*) [L. *re-*, again, and **Cover**], cover again.

Re-cov'er [L. *recuperāre*, to recuperate], win back, cure, regain health.

Re-cov'er-y, restoration.

Rec're-ant [O.F. *recreant*, pr.p. of *recroire*, to yield in trial by combat; L. *re-*, again, *crēdere*, to believe], unfaithful, cowardly; an apostate.

Rec're-ate [L. *re-*, again, and *creāre* (p.p. *creātus*) to create], refresh, revive.

Rec-re-a'tion, amusement, pastime.

Rec're-a-tive, refreshing.

Re-crim'in-ate [L. *re-*, again, *crīminārī* (p.p. *crīminātus*), accuse of crime], accuse in return. **Recrimina'tion**.

Re-cru-des'cence [L. *re-*, again, *crūdescere* (pr.p. *crūdescens*, *-entis*), to break out; *crūdus*, raw], renewed outbreak.

Re-cruit' [F. *recruter*, to levy troops; L. *re-*, again, *crescere*, to grow], enlist new soldiers, recover health; newly enlisted soldier.

Rec'tan-gle [L. *rectus*, right, *angulus*, angle], right-angled parallelogram. **Rectan'gular**.

Rec'ti-fy [L. *rectus*, right, *facere*, to make], make or set right, purify, or refine. **Rectifica'tion**.

Rec-ti-lin'e-al, Rec-ti-lin'e-ar [L. *rectus*, straight, *linea*, a line], consisting of a straight line or lines.

Rec'ti-tude [L. *rectus*, straight, right], uprightness, honesty.

Rec'tor [L. *rector*, a ruler; *regere* (p.p. *rectus*), to rule], parson of a parish, head of certain colleges and schools, chief elective officer of some universities. **Rector'ial**.

Rec'to-ry, rector's house.

Re-cum'bent [L. *recumbere* (pr.p. *recumbens*, *-entis*), to recline; *re-*, back, *cubāre*, lie down], reclining, lying down. **Recum'bency**.

Re-cu'per-ate [L. *recuperāre* (p.p. *recuperātus*), to recuperate], recover, esp. health.

Re-cur' [L. *re-*, back, *currere*, to run], come back, happen or appear again. **Recur'rence**.

Rec'u-sant [F. *récusant*, pr.p. of *récuser*, to reject; L. *recusāre*, to reject, oppose; *re-*, back, *causa*, a cause], obstinate in refusal; one who refused to go to the established church.

Red [O.E. *réad*; Com. Teut.], a colour like blood. **Redd'en**.

Re-dact' [L. *re-*, back; *agere* (p.p. *actus*), to do], reduce to literary form, edit. **Redac'tion**.

Re-deem' [L. *redimere* (p.p. *redemptus*), to redeem; *re-*, back, *emere*, to buy], buy back, atone for, fulfil (promise).

Re-demp'tion, repurchase, ransom.

Re-din'te-grate [L. *redintegrāre* (p.p. *redintegrātus*), to restore to wholeness; *re-*, again, *integer*, whole], make whole again.

Red'o-lent [L. *redolēre* (pr.p. *redolens*, *-entis*), to emit odour; *re-*, again, and *olēre*, to be odorous], odorous, sweet-smelling.

Re-dou'ble [L. *re-*, again, and **Double**], increase, make or grow twice as much.

Re-doubt' [F. *redoute*; L. *re-*, back, *dūcere* (p.p. *ductus*), to lead], small outwork.

Re-doubt'a-ble [L. *re-*, back, *dubitāre*, to doubt], formidable, valiant.

Re-dound' [L. *redundāre*, to overflow; *re-*, back, *unda*, a wave], contribute to.

Re-dress' [L. *re-*, again; F. *dresser*, to erect], set right; remedy.

Re-duce' [L. *re-*, back, *dūcere* (p.p. *ductus*), to lead], bring down, diminish, capture.

Re-duc'tion, lessening, conversion to a certain state or form (in Chemistry, Arithmetic, etc.).

Re-dun'dant [L. *redundāre* (pr.p. *redundans*, *-antis*); see **Redound**], excessive, superfluous. **Re-dun'dancy**.

Re-du'pli-cate [L. *re-*, again, *duo*, two, *plicāre*, to fold], redouble, repeat. **Reduplica'tion**.

Reed [O.E. *hréod*, Com. W. Germanic], hollow tall grass, rustic pipe, sounding part of some instruments. **Reed'y**.

Reef [perh. fr. Du. *rif*, a reef; *cf.* **Rive**], chain of rocks at or near surface of water.

Reef [O.N. *rif*, a reef in a sail], portion of a sail that can be taken in and rolled up; roll or fold part of a sail.

Reek [O.E. *réc*, Com. Teut.], steam, smoke (Scot.), rank smell; to steam.

Reel [Gael. *righil*, a reel], Scottish dance.

Reel [O.E. *hréol*], spool on which yarn is wound; wind upon a reel, to stagger.

Reeve [O.E. *geréfa*, etym. dub.], (formerly) bailiff, steward.

Re-fec'tion [L. *reficere* (p.p. *refectus*), to make again], repast, refreshment.

Re-fec'to-ry [M.L. *refectorium*; see **Refection**], room where meals are taken in monasteries, etc.

Re-fer' [L. *re-*, back, *ferre*, to carry], trace back, assign to, to appeal, have relation.

Ref-er-ee', one to whom something is referred, umpire.

Ref'er-ence, act of referring, allusion, regard.

Re-fer-en'dum, referring political questions to a direct general vote.

Re-fine' [L. *re-*, again; Late L. *fīnus*, fine], to purify, polish, become pure. **Refine'ment**.

Re-flect' [L. *re-*, back, *flectere* (p.p. *flexus*), to bend], throw back as light, etc., to mirror, think, reproach. **Reflec'tion**.

Re-flect'or, surface that reflects rays.

Re'flex, directed back, involuntary (of muscular activities); reflected image.

Re-flex-ive (word), expressing an agent's action upon himself.

Ref'lu-ent [L. *re-*, back, *fluere* (pr.p. *fluens*, *-entis*), to flow], flowing back.

Re'flux [L. *refluxus*, p.p. of *refluere*, to flow back], flowing back.

Re-form' [L. *re-*, again, *forma*, shape, form], restore, improve; amendment.

Ref-or-ma'tion, change for the better, thorough amendment.

Re-form'a-to-ry, institution for the reforming of offenders.

Re-fract' [L. *re-*, back, *frangere* (p.p. *fractus*), to break], bend sharply from its course. **Refrac'tion**.

Re-frac'to-ry, obstinate, unmanageable.

Re-frain' [L. *refrenāre*, to repress; *re-*, back, *frēnum*, a curb], hold back, abstain.

Re-frain' [L. *refringere*, to break back ; *re-*, back, and *frangere*, to break], phrase repeated at the end of each verse.

Re-fresh' [L. *re-*, again ; O.F. *freis*, fem. *fresche*, fresh], renew, revive, enliven.

Re-fresh'ment, new life, that which refreshes, esp. food and drink.

Re-fri'ger-ate (ā) [L. *re-*, again, *frigerāre* (p.p. *frigerātus*), to cool, *frigus*, cold], cause to become cool, freeze.

Re-fri'ger-a-tor, apparatus for cooling or freezing.

Ref'uge [L. *re-*, back, *fugere*, to flee], shelter.

Ref-u-gee', one who flees for safety to a foreign land.

Re-ful'gent [L. *re-*, back, *fulgens (-entis)*, pr.p. of *fulgēre*, to shine], casting a bright light. Reful'gence. [repay.

Re-fund' [L. *re-*, back, *fundere*, to pour], Re-fu'sal, act of refusing, option to take or leave.

Re-fuse' (*s=z*) [L. *refundere* (p.p. *refusus*), to pour back, to restore, to reject], deny as a request, reject.

Ref'use (*s* sharp), waste matter, dregs.

Ref-u-ta'tion, act or process of disproving.

Re-fute' [L. *refutāre* ; *re-*, back, *futāre*, perh. from same root as *fundere*, to pour], disprove.

Re-gain' [L. *re-*, again ; F. *gagner*, to gain], get again, recover, get back to.

Re'gal [L. *rēgālis*, royal ; *rex* (*rēg-is*), a king], royal, kingly.

Re-gale' [F. *régaler* ; etym. doubtful], refresh, feast. Regale'ment.

Re-ga'li-a [L. neut. pl. of *rēgālis*, regal], symbols or emblems of royalty.

Re-gard' [L. *re-*, back ; F. *garder*, to guard], look at, consider, care for ; a look, respect, care, (pl.) expression of goodwill.

Re-gat'ta [It. *regatta*, orig. a strife ; etym. doubtful], series of yacht or boat races.

Re-gen'er-ate [L. *re-*, again, *generāre*, to generate], give new, esp. higher, life to.

Re'gent [L. *regere* (pr.p. *regens, -entis*) to rule], ruler in the minority, etc., of a sovereign. Re'gency.

Re'gi-cide (*rē-*) [L. *rex* (*rēg-is*), king, *cædere*, to kill], king murder, murderer of a king.

Re-gime' (*rē-zheem'*) [L. *regimen*, guidance ; *regere*, to rule], mode or system of rule or management.

Re'gi-men (*rē*) [L. *regimen*, guidance ; *regere*, to rule], government, systematic diet.

Re'gi-ment (*rē*) [Late L. *regimentum* ; L. *regere*, to rule], organized body of soldiers.

Re-gi-men'tals, military dress.

Re'gion (*gi=j*) [L. *regio* (*region-is*), territory ; *regere*, to rule], portion of space or territory more or less definite.

Re'gion-al, pertaining to a region, sectional.

Re'gis-ter (*rē*) [M.L. *regestrum* ; *regestum*, book of records ; L. *re-*, back, *gerere* (p.p. *gestus*), to carry], record, list of names, sliding plate in a stove, compass of a voice ; record formally, insure (a letter, etc.).

Re'gis-trar (*ē*), keeper of records. Registra'tion.

Re'gis-try (*ē*), place where a register is kept.

Reg'nant [L. *regnāre* (pr.p. *regnans, -antis*), to reign], ruling.

Re'gress, withdrawal.

Re-gress' [L. *regredī* (p.p. *regressus*), to go back ; *re-*, back, *gradī*, to go], go back, return. Regres'sion.

Re-gret' [O.F. *regrater, regreter*, to regret; etym. doubtful], sorrow for the past ; look back with sorrow. Regrett'able, Regrett'-ably.

Reg'u-lar [L. *rēgula*, a rule ; *regere*, to rule], according to rule, orderly ; soldier of a standing army. Regular'ity.

Reg'u-late, adjust by rule, order. Reg'ulator.

Re-ha-bil'i-tate [L. *re-*, again, *habilitāre* (p.p. *habilitātus*), to make fit], restore to former rank, position, or reputation.

Re-hears'al, recital, preparatory practice.

Re-hearse' [L. *re-*, again, and O.F. *hercer*, to harrow, *herse*, a harrow], say over, recount in order, recite for practice.

Reign [L. *regnum*, kingdom ; *regere*, to rule], royal authority, period of a sovereign's rule ; exercise sovereign power, prevail.

Re-im-burse' [L. *re-*, again, and obs. E. *imburse*, put in a purse ; L. *in*, in, *bursa*, purse], refund, pay back to. Reimburse'-ment.

Rein [O.F. *resne* ; cf. It. *redina*, a rein ; perh. fr. L. *retinēre*, to hold back ; see **Retain**], strap on a bridle, restraint ; control with the reins, check.

Rein'deer [O.N. *hreindyri* ; *hreinn*, reindeer, *dyr*, deer], deer of sub-arctic regions.

Re-in-force' [L. *re-*, again, *in*, in, *fortis*, strong], add new strength to. Reinforce'-ment.

Re-in-state' [L. *re-*, again, and obs. E. *instate*], restore to a former state.

Re-it'er-ate [L. *re-*, again ; *iterāre* (p.p. *iterātus*), to repeat ; *iterum*, again], repeat again and again. Reitera'tion.

Re-ject' [L. *rejicere* (p.p. *rejectus*) ; *re-*, back, *jacere*, to throw], cast from one, refuse. Rejec'tion.

Re-joice' [O.F. *rejoir* (pr.p. *rejoissant*), to rejoice], feel joy, triumph.

Re-join' [L. *re-*, again, *jungere*, to join], join again, state in reply.

Re-join'der, answer to a reply, a reply.

Re-ju've-nate [L. *re-*, again, *juvenis*, young], make young again. Rejuvena'tion.

Re-juv-en-esce' [L. *re-*, again, *juvenis*, young], to become young again. Rejuves'cence.

Re-lapse' [L. *re-*, again, *lapsus*, slipped], slide or fall back ; a falling back.

Re-late' [L. *re-*, again, and *lātus*, p.p. of *ferre*, to carry], connect, have reference to, tell.

Re-la'tion, act of telling, account, reference, kinship, kinsman.

Rel'a-tive, connected with, not absolute ; kinsman or kinswoman. Relativ'ity.

Re-lax' [L. *re-*, again, *laxus*, slack], slacken.

Re'lax-a'tion (*rē*), slackening, amusement.

Re-lay' [O.F. *relais*, a relay; *relayer*, to provide anew; etym. doubtful], provision, as of horses for successive use; relief-gang.

Re-lease' (*s* sharp) [O.F. *relesser*; L. *relaxāre*, to relax], let go, free; liberation from care, pain, etc.

Rel'e-gate [L. *re-*, back, *lēgāre* (p.p. *lēgātus*), to send], remove, usually to an inferior position. **Relega'tion.**

Re-lent' [L. *re-*, back, *lentus*, slow, soft], become less hard. **Relent'less.**

Rel'e-vant [L. *relevans* (-*antis*), pr.p. of *relevāre*, to raise again; see **Relieve**], bearing upon, applicable. **Re'levance, Re'levancy.**

Re-li'a-ble, worthy of dependence.

Re-li'ance, dependence, ground of trust.

Rel'ic [L. *relinquere* (p.p. *relictus*), to leave behind], that which remains, a memorial.

Rel'ict [L. *relicta*, fem. of p.p. of *relinquere*, to leave behind], widow.

Re-lief, succour, ease, projection of design in moulding, prominence.

Re-lieve' [L. *re-*, again, *levāre*, to raise], set off by contrast, give aid or ease to.

Re-li'gion (-*li*-) [L. *religio*; perh. connected with *ligāre*, to bind], system of faith and worship. **Reli'gious.**

Re-lin'quish [L. *relinquere*, to relinquish; *re-*, back, *linquere*, to leave], resign, give up. **Relin'quishment.**

Rel'i-qua-ry, small box for relics.

Rel'ish [M.E. and O.F. *reles*, an after-taste; see **Release**], eat with pleasure, enjoy; flavour, good appetite.

Re-luc'tant [L. *re-*, back, *luctans* (-*antis*), pr.p. of *luctāri*, to struggle], striving against, unwilling. **Reluc'tance.**

Re-ly' [O.F. *relier*, bind together; L. *re-*, back, *ligāre*, to bind], depend (upon), trust.

Re-main' [L. *re-*, back, *manēre*, to stay], stay behind, continue.

Re-main'der, anything that is left, rest.

Re-mand' [L. *re-*, back, *mandāre*, to send], send back, esp. to prison until further evidence is obtained.

Re-mark' [F. *remarquer*, to remark], to mark anew, notice, say; a notice, comment.

Re-mark'a-ble, noticeable, wonderful.

Re-me'di-al, affording a remedy.

Rem'e-dy [L. *remedium*, a remedy; *re-*, again, *medēri*, to cure], cure; to cure, correct.

Re-mem'ber [L. *re-*, again, *memorāre*, call to mind; *memor*, mindful], keep in or recall to mind. [tion.

Re-mem'brance, bringing to mind, recollec-

Re-mind' [L. *re-*, again; O.E. *gemynd*, memory], bring to the remembrance of.

Rem-i-nis'cence [L. *reminisci*, to remember; *re-*, again, and *meminī*, to remember], remembering, (pl.) narration of remembered experience. **Reminis'cent.**

Re-miss' slack, negligent, careless.

Re-mis'sion (*ssi*=*sh*), abatement, pardon.

Re-mit' [L. *re-*, back, *mittere* (p.p. *missus*), to send], send, abate, forgive.

Re-mit'tance, sum remitted.

Rem'nant [short for *remenant*, fr. O.F. *remenant*, remaining], remaining portion, scrap.

Re-mon'strance, protest.

Re-mon'strate [L. *re-*, again, *monstrāre* (p.p. *monstrātus*), to show], urge reasons in opposition.

Re-morse' [L. *re-*, again, *mordēre* (p.p. *morsus*), to bite], self-accusing regret.

Re-mote' [L. *remōtus*, removed], far away, distant.

Re-mov'al (*o*=*oo*), act of removing.

Re-move' (*o*=*oo*) [L. *re-*, again, *movēre*, to move], move away, take away; step in a scale of gradation. **Remov'able.**

Re-mu'ner-ate [L. *re-*, again, *mūnerārī*, to give something; *mūnus* (*mūner-is*), a reward], to reward, pay. **Remunera'tion.**

Re-nas'cence, Re-nais'sance [L. *re-*, again, *nascī*, to be born], revival of learning, art, etc. **Renas'cent.**

Ren-con'tre (pron. as F.), **Ren-coun'ter** [L. *re-*, again, *in*, in, *contra*, against], sudden meeting, unexpected fight.

Rend [O.E. *rendan*], tear.

Ren'der [O.F. *rendre*, to render; L. *re-*, back, *dare*, to give], pay back, yield, translate.

Ren'der-ing, version, translation.

Ren'dez-vous (*ou*=*oo*) [F. *rendez-vous*, betake yourselves, imperative of *rendre*], meeting-place; to meet by arrangement.

Ren-di'tion [F. *rendre*, to render], surrender, translation.

Ren'e-gade [Sp. *renegado*, orig. p.p. of *renegar*, to forsake the faith; L. *re-*, again; *negāre*, to deny], traitor.

Re-new' [L. *re-*, again, and **New**], restore, make as good as new.

Re-new'al, making again, restoration.

Ren'net [fr. *renne*, obs. form of **Run**], preparation for curdling milk.

Ren'net [F. *reinette*; perh. fr. *reine*, queen], kind of apple.

Re-nounce' [L. *re-*, back, *nuntiāre* (p.p. *nuntiātus*), to bring news; *nuntius*, a messenger], cast off, disown.

Ren'o-vate [L. *re-*, again, *novāre* (p.p. *novātus*), to make new; *novus*, new], restore to freshness, renew. **Renova'tion.**

Re-nown' [L. *re-*, again, and *nōmināre*, to name; *nōmen*, a name], fame.

Rent [obs. form of **Rend**], a break, tear.

Rent [O.F. *rente*; L. *reddere* (p.p. *redditus*), to render], payment for use of house, land, etc.; let for rent, hold as tenant.

Rent'al, sum total of rents.

Re-nun-ci-a'tion [see **Renounce**], disavowal, abandonment.

Re-pair' [L. *re-*, again, *parāre* (p.p. *parātus*), to make ready], mend; restoration, condition with respect to soundness. **Rep'arable.**

Re-pair' [L. *repatriāre*, to go back to one's country; *re-*, back, and *patria*, native land], go back (to), resort.

Rep-a-ra'tion, restoration, amends.

Rep-ar-tee′ [F. *repartie*, orig. fem. p.p. of *repartir*, to redivide, reply; L. *re-*, again, *partīre*, to divide], smart, witty reply.

Re-past′ [L. *re-*, again, *pastus*, food; *pascere*, to feed], a meal.

Re-pa′tri-ate [L. *re-*, again, *patriāre*, fr. *patria*, fatherland], to restore or return to native land. **Repatria′tion.**

Re-peal′ [L. *re-*, again, *appellāre*, to call upon], revoke, annul; act of repealing.

Re-peat′ [L. *re-*, again, *petere*, to seek], to do, or say over again.

Re-peat′er, a fire-arm that fires several shots without reloading, kind of watch, recurring decimal.

Re-pel′ [L. *re-*, back, *pellere*, to drive], drive back, reject. [repel.

Re-pel′lent, very distasteful, tending to

Re-pent′ [L. *re-*, again, *pœnitēre*, make sorry], be sorry for wrong-doing.

Re-pent′ance, sorrow for sin or for what one has done.

Rep′er-toire (*toire=twahr*) [F. *répertoire*, see Repertory], stock of plays, songs, etc.

Rep′er-to-ry [L. *repertōrium*, repertory; *reperīre*, find out; *re-*, again, and *parere*, to produce], store, esp. of facts, treasury.

Rep-e-ti′tion, act of repeating.

Re-pine′ [L. *re-*, again; O.E. *pin*, pain], murmur, feel discontent.

Re-place′ [L. *re-*, back, and Place], put back in place, take or fill the place of.

Re-plen′ish [L. *re-*, again; Late L. *plēnēre*, to fill; L. *plēnus*, full], fill again, stock anew. **Replen′ishment.**

Re-plete′ [L. *re-*, again, *plēre* (p.p. *plētus*), to fill], full to excess. **Reple′tion.**

Rep′li-ca [It. *replica*, a replica; L. *replicāre*, to reply], artist's copy of a work of his own, exact copy.

Re′pli-cate, tone one or more octaves above or below a given note.

Re-ply′ [L. *re-*, back, *plicāre*, to fold], answer; an answer.

Re-port′ [L. *re-*, back, *portāre*, to carry], bring back an account, relate, take notes for the press; relation, repute, hearsay, resounding noise. **Repor′ter.**

Re-pose′ (*s=z*) [L. *re-*, again, *pausāre*, to pause], to rest; rest, quiet. **Repose′ful.**

Re-pose′ [L. *re-*, back, *pōnere* (p.p. *positus*), to place], to put (trust) in.

Re-pos′i-to-ry, place where things are stored.

Rep-re-hend′ [L. *re-*, back, *prehendere* (p.p. *prehensus*), to seize], reprove, find fault with. **Re-prehen′sion.**

Rep-re-hen′si-ble, deserving reproof.

Rep-re-sent′ [L. *re-*, again, *præsentāre* (p.p. *præsentātus*), to present], portray, stand in the place of, show.

Rep-re-sen-ta′tion, likeness, description.

Rep-re-sent′a-tive, fitted or elected to represent, typical; substitute.

Re-press′ (L. *re-*, back, and Press], press back or down, check.

Re-prieve′ [F. *repris*, p.p. of *reprendre*, fr. L. *re-*, again; F. *prendre*, to take], delay

the punishment of; pardon or lessening of sentence, respite.

Rep′ri-mand [L. *reprimere*, to repress], reprove sharply; severe reproof.

Re-pri′sal (*s=z*) [O.F. *reprisaille*, a reprisal; L. *reprehendere*, to seize again], act of taking from an enemy in retaliation, act of retaliation.

Re-proach′ [F. *reprocher* (vb.); perh. L. *reprobāre*, to reject on trial], blame because of fault; shame, blame.

Rep′ro-bate [L. *reprobāre* (p.p. *reprobātus*), reject on trial; *re-*, back, *probāre*, to test], wicked; one who is given up to wickedness; condemn.

Rep-ro-ba′tion, strong disapproval.

Re-pro-duce′ [L. *re-*, again, and **Produce**], bring forward again, portray, bring forth new beings (animals, plants). **Reproduc′tion.**

Re-proof′, blame, rebuke.

Re-prove′ (*ove=oov*) [L. *reprobāre*, to reprove; *re-*, back, *probāre*, to test], chide, rebuke.

Rep′tile [L. *reptilis*, creeping; *rēpere* (p.p. *reptus*), to creep], crawling animal. **Reptil′ian.**

Re-pub′lic [L. *rēspublica*; *rēs*, a concern, *publica*, fem. of *publicus*, public], state, esp. one under an elective head. **Re-pub′lican.**

Re-pu′di-ate [L. *repudiāre* (p.p. *repudiātus*), to repudiate; *re-*, back, *pudēre*, to be ashamed], cast off, disclaim. **Repudia′-tion.**

Re-pug′nant [L. *re-*, back, *pugnāre*, to fight], hostile, offensive. **Repug′nance.**

Re-pulse′ [L. *re-*, back, *pellere* (p.p. *pulsus*), to drive], drive back; refusal, defeat.

Re-pul′sion (*si=sh*), rejection, strong dislike.

Re-pul′sive, offensive.

Rep′u-ta-ble, respectable.

Rep-u-ta′tion, credit, supposed character.

Re-pute′ [L. *re-*, again, *putāre* (p.p. *putātus*), to think], hold, think; reputation.

Re-quest′ [see **Require**], asking; to ask.

Re′qui-em (*rē* or *rĕ*) [L. *requiem*, acc. of *requiēs*, rest (first word of the mass for the dead)], solemn service for the dead.

Re-quire′ [L. *requīrere* (p.p. *requīsitus*); *re-*, back, and *quærere*, to seek], demand, need.

Req′ui-site, necessary; something necessary.

Req-ui-si′tion, formal demand.

Re-qui′tal, return (good or bad).

Re-quite′ [L. *re-*, again, and **Quit**], make return (for).

Rere′dos [A.F. *reredos*, *rere*, rear, *dos* (L. *dorsum*), back], wall or screen behind an altar.

Re-scind′ (*ĭ*) [L. *re-*, back, *scindere*, to cut], cut off, annul.

Re′script [L. *re-*, back, *scrībere* (p.p. *scriptus*), to write], edict or decree, a rewriting, palimpsest.

Res′cue [O.F. *rescoure*, to rescue; L. *re-*, again, *ex*, away, *quatere*, to shake], save, free; act of saving from danger, etc.

Re-search' [obs. F. recerche (F. recherche); L. re-, again, and **Search**], search for a special purpose. [ness.

Re-sem'blance (s=z) [see **Resemble**], like-

Re-sem'ble (s=z) [L. re-, again, simulāre, to make like ; similis, like], be like.

Re-sent' (s=z) [L. re-, again, sentīre, to feel], take ill, show displeasure. **Resent'ment.**

Res-er-va'tion, a keeping back, something held back, land reserved for American Indian tribes, etc.

Re-serve' (s=z) [L. re-, back, servāre, to keep], keep back, hold over; restraint, store for future use.

Res'er-voir (voir=vwahr) [F. réservoir ; Late L. reservāre, to reserve], place for storing water.

Re-set' [O.F. receter ; L. recipere, to receive], receive (stolen goods). **Reset'ter.**

Re-side' (s=z) [L. residēre, to remain behind; re-, back, sedēre, to sit], dwell.

Res'i-dence, dwelling, stay.

Res-i-den'tial (ti=sh), pertaining to residents.

Re-sid'u-al, Re-sid'u-a-ry, remaining.

Res'i-due [L. residuum, remainder ; re-, back, sedēre, to sit], that which remains over. **Resid'uum.**

Re-sign' (sign=zine) [L. re-, back, signāre, to sign], give up, yield.

Res-ig-na'tion, giving up, submission.

Re-sile' [L. re-, back, salīre, to jump], start back, recoil. **Resil'ience.**

Res'in (s=z) [L. rēsīna; cogn. with Gk. rētinē, resin], ooze from certain trees, esp. pines. **Res'inous.**

Re-sist' (-zist') [L. re-, against, sistere, to stand], withstand, check.

Re-sist'ance (-zist'-), opposition.

Res'o-lute [see **Resolve**], determined, firm.

Res-o-lu'tion, decision, analysis.

Re-solve' (s=z) [L. re-, back, solvere (p.p. solūtus), to loosen], analyse, melt, decide ; fixed purpose.

Res'o-nant [L. re-, back, sonāre (pr.p. sonans, -antis), to sound], capable of returning sound. **Res'onance.**

Re-sort' (s=z) [O.F. re-, again, sortir, to go out ; etym. dub.], betake one's self ; a haunt, resource, recourse.

Re-sound' (s=z) [L. re-, again, and **Sound**], ring or re-echo with sound.

Re-source' (ō) [O.F. re(s)sourdre. to rise again], expedient, (pl.) available means. **Resource'ful.**

Re-spect' [L. respicere (p.p. respectus), look back upon ; re-, back, specere, look at], regard, honour ; particular, esteem, regard. **Respect'ful.**

Re-spect'a-ble, worthy of respect, of fair standing, fairly good. **Respectabil'ity.**

Re-spec'tive, proper to each, relative.

Re-spec'tive-ly, as each belongs to each.

Res-pir-a'tion, breathing.

Res'-pir-a-tor, appliance of gauze or wire for covering the mouth.

Re-spire' [L. respirāre; re-, back, and spirāre, to breathe], breathe. **Respira'tion.**

Res'pite [O.F. respit, respite ; L. respectus, respect], delay, a pause.

Re-splen'dent [L. re-, again, splendēre (pr.p. splendens, -entis), to shine], very bright.

Re-spond' [L. re-, back, spondēre (p.p. sponsus), to answer], to reply, perform answering action.

Re-spond'ent, answering ; defendant.

Re-sponse', answer, reply.

Re-spon'si-ble, accountable, answerable. **Responsibil'ity.**

Re-spon sions, first of three examinations for Oxford B.A. degree.

Re-spon'sive, ready to respond.

Rest[1] [O.E. rœst; cf. Ger. rast, Du. rust], state of quiet, a pause ; to lie, rely.

Rest[2] [F. rester (vb.); L. restāre; re-, back, and stāre, to stand], remain over ; remainder.

Rest[3] [for **Arrest**], socket for tilter's spear.

Res'tau-rant (au=ō, or pron. word as F.) [F. restaurant, pr.p. of restaurer, to refresh], place where meals may be had.

Rest-har-row [Rest[3] and **Harrow**], a shrub with tough roots.

Res-ti-tu'tion [L. re-, again, statuere, to set up], restoration, amends.

Rest'ive [O.F. restif, restive ; F. rester, to remain], resisting control, obstinate.

Res-to-ra'tion, recovery, replacement.

Re-stor'a-tive, something which serves to restore (health, etc.).

Re-store' [L. re-, again, staurāre (p.p. staurātus), to set up], recover, renew, give back.

Re-strain' [L. re-, back, stringere, to bind], hold back, imprison.

Re-straint', repression, check.

Re-strict' [L. restringere (p.p. restrictus), to restrain], to limit, curb. **Restric'tion.**

Re-sult' (s=z) [L. resultāre; re-, back, salīre, to leap], arise as a consequence; consequence, effect.

Re-sult'ant, following as a consequence; combined effect.

Re-sume' [L. re-, again, sūmere (p.p. sumptus), to take], take back, begin again.

Ré'su-mé [F. pp. of résumer, to resume], summary.

Re-sump'tion, act of resuming.

Res-ur-rec'tion [L. resurgere (p.p. resurrectus), to rise again ; re-, again, surgere, to rise], a rising, esp. from the dead.

Re-sus'ci-tate [L. resuscitāre (p.p. resuscitātus); re-, again, sub-, from below, citāre, to rouse], revive. **Resuscita'tion.**

Re-tail [O.F. retail, a shred ; retaillier, to cut small ; see **Tailor**], sell in small quantities, give details of.

Re-tain' [L. retinēre (p.p. retentus); re-, back, tenēre, to hold], continue to hold, engage the services of.

Re-tain'er, attendant, fee paid to a barrister for right to his services.

Re-tal'i-ate [L. retaliāre (p.p. retaliātus) ; re-, again, tālis, such], return like for like. **Retalia'tion.**

Re-tard' [L. *re-*, again, *tardāre*, make slow; *tardus*, slow], keep back, delay. **Retarda'tion.**

Retch [O E. *hrǣcan*, to spit, *hráca*, a spittle], strain as in vomiting.

Re-ten'tion [see Retain], act of withholding.

Re-ten'tive, having power to retain.

Ret'i-cent [L. *reticēre* (pr.p. *reticens*, *-entis*), to be very silent; *re-*, back, *tacēre*, to be silent], inclined to keep silent. **Ret'icence.**

Re-tic'-u-late [L. *rēticulum*, double dim. of *rēte*, a net], divide into a network.

Re-tic-u-la'tion, network.

Ret'i-cule [L. *rēticulum*, double dim. of *rēte*, a net], small handbag.

Ret'i-na [M.L. *rētina*; perh. fr. *rēte*, a net], lining membrane of the back part of the eye.

Ret'i-nue [O.F. *retenue*, orig. fem. p.p. of *retenir*, to retain], body of retainers.

Re-tire' [F. *retirer*; L. *re-*, back; F. *tirer*, to pull], withdraw. **Retire'ment.**

Re-tort' [L. *re-*, back, *torquēre* (p.p. *tortus*), to twist], return as an argument, etc.; witty or severe reply, vessel for distilling or decomposing by heat.

Re-trace' [L. *re-*, back, and **Trace**], trace back.

Re-tract' [L. *re-*, back, *trahere* (p.p. *tractus*), to draw], draw back, withdraw. **Retrac'tion.**

Re-treat' [L. *re-*, back, *trahere*, to draw], retirement, departure, shelter; withdraw.

Re-trench' [obs. F. *retrencher*; L. *re-*, back; F. *trencher*, to cut], cut down, lessen.

Ret-ri-bu'tion [L. *re-*, back, *tribuere* (p.p. *tribūtus*), to pay], repayment, punishment.

Re-trieve' [L. *re-*, again; O.F. *trover*, to find], regain, repair. **Retriev'al.**

Re-triev'er, dog which finds and brings killed or wounded game.

Ret'ro-cede [L. *retrō*, backwards, *cēdere*, to go], move back. **Retroces'sion.**

Ret-ro-cede' [F. *rétrocéder*; L. *retrō*, backwards, *cēdere*, to go], cede (territory) back again.

Ret'ro-grade [L. *retrō*, backwards, *grādī* (p.p. *gressus*), to go], tending backward; move backward.

Re-tro-gres'sion, act of going backward. **Retrogres'sive.**

Ret'ro-spect [L. *retrō*, backward, *specere* (*spicere*), to look], a survey of the past; look backward.

Re-turn' [O.F. *retorner*; L. *re-*, back; F. *tourner*, to turn], turn, go, or give back, elect, report; act of returning, that which is returned, election, official report.

Re-un'ion (*re-yoon'yŭn*) [L. *re-*, again, and **Union**], state of being reunited, social gathering.

Re-veal' [L. *revēlāre* (p.p. *revēlātus*), to reveal; *re-*, back, *vēlum*, a veil], disclose.

Re-veil'le (*veille=vēlĕ* or *vailyĕ*) [F. *réveillez*, wake ye; L. *re-*, again, and *vigilāre*, to watch], waking signal in the morning.

Rev'el [O.F. *reveler*, to riot; L. *rebellāre*, to rebel], riotous merrymaking; to delight (in), indulge without restraint.

Rev-el-a'tion, act of disclosing, knowledge disclosed, last book of the Bible.

Rev'el-ry, noisy festivity.

Re-venge' [L. *re-*, again, *vindicāre*, to vindicate], return evil for evil; returning of evil for evil.

Rev'e-nue [O.F. *revenir* (p.p. *revenu*), to return; L. *re-*, back, *venīre*, to come], income of a state or person.

Re-ver'ber-ate [L. *re-*, back, *verberāre*, to beat], resound, re-echo. **Reverbera'tion.**

Re-vere' [L. *re-*, again, *verērī*, to fear], regard with deep respect.

Rev'er-ence, deep respect and esteem.

Rev'er-end, worthy of reverence, title given to a clergyman. [reverence.

Rev'er-ent, Rev'er-en'tial (*ti=sh*), expressing

Rev'er-ie [O.F. *rever*, *resver*, to dream. Etym. doubtful], fit of musing, daydreaming.

Re-ver'sal, act of reversing, overthrowing.

Re-verse' [L. *re-*, back, *vertere* (p.p. *versus*), to turn], turned backward, contrary; complete change, defeat, back or under surface; overturn, turn in opposite direction. **Rever'sible.**

Re-ver'sion, right of succession to property or office, return to a previous state.

Re-vert', to return, come back. **Revert'ible.**

Re-view' [L. *re-*, again, *vidēre*, to see], look back, inspect, write a review of; a looking back, criticism, periodical, inspection.

Re-vile' [L. *re-*, again, *vīlis*, vile], abuse.

Re-vi'sal (*s=z*), **Re-vis'ion** (*s=zh*), re-examination.

Re-vise' (*s=z*) [F. *reviser*, to revise; L. *re-*, again, *vidēre* (p.p. *vīsus*), to see], re-examine, to look over and amend

Re-vi'val, state of being revived, renewed attention to something.

Re-vive' [L. *re-*, again, *vivere*, to live], return to life or vigour; restore to life or vigour.

Re-viv'i-fy [L. *re-*, again, and **Vivify**], cause to revive.

Rev-o-ca'tion [see Revoke], recall, repeal.

Re-voke' [L. *re-*, back, *vocāre* (p.p. *vocātus*), to call], repeal, cancel, to fail to follow suit in card playing.

Re-volt' [F. *révolte*, revolt; see **Revolve**], turn away, esp. with abhorrence, to rebel; rebellion.

Rev-o-lu'tion [see Revolve], motion round a centre, a total change, esp. of government. **Re-volu'tionary.**

Re-volve' [L. *re-*, back, *volvere* (p.p. *volūtus*), to roll], turn round, ponder.

Re-volv'er, pistol with revolving cartridge-chambers.

Re-vul'sion [L. *re-*, back, *vellere* (p.p. *vulsus*), to pull], sudden reaction.

Re-ward' (*a=aw*) [O.N.F. *rewarder*; O.F. *regarder*. Doublet of **Regard**], return, recompense; to recompense, to pay.

Rhap′so-dize, talk or write with high-flown enthusiasm.

Rhap′so-dy [Gk. *rhapsōidia*, rhapsody; *rhaptein*, to stitch together, *ōidē*, an ode], high-flown enthusiastic statement or composition. **Rhapsod′ical**.

Rhet′o-ric [Gk. *rhētoricos (technē)*, art of rhetoric; *rhētōr*, an orator], art of impressive speaking.   [writer.

Rhet-o-ri′cian (*ci = sh*), rhetorical speaker or

Rheum (*eu = oo*) [Gk. *rheuma (rheumat-os)*, rheum, *rheein*, to flow], mucous discharge.

Rheu-ma′tic [see **Rheum**], pertaining to rheumatism.

Rheu′ma-tism [see **Rheum**], disease of the joints and muscles.

Rhi-noc′e-ros (*c = s*) [Gk. *rhis (rhin-os)*, nose, *ceras*, horn], thick-skinned animal with one or two horns on the nose.

Rho′do-den′dron [Gk. *rhodon*, a rose, *dendron*, a tree], shrub with large flowers.

Rhomb, Rhom′bus [Gk. *rhombos*, a rhombus, *rhembein*, to revolve], equilateral four-sided figure having only the opposite angles equal.

Rhom′boid [Gk. *rhomboeidēs*], four-sided equiangular figure having only the opposite sides equal.

Rhu′barb [M.L. *rhabarbarum*, foreign rha, or rhubarb; Gk. *rhā*, rhubarb, perh. fr. the river Rha or Volga], large plant with fleshy leaf-stalks, a drug.

Rhyme [spelt *rhyme* by confusion with **Rhythm**; see **Rime** 2], recurrence of words ending in similar sounds at intervals in verse; to make rhymes, to end in rhymes. **Rhyme′ster**.

Rhythm [Gk. *rhythmos*, rhythm, *rheein*, to flow], measured movement. **Rhyth′mical**.

Rib [O.E. *rib, ribb*, Com. Teut.], one of the curved bones springing in pairs from the spine, curved bar from the keel of a ship.

Rib′ald [O.F. *ribaut, ribauld*, a menial], low and scurrilous.

Rib′ald-ry, low, vulgar language.

Rib′and, Rib′bon [O.E. *riban, ruban*, riband. Etym. doubtful], narrow woven fabric, usually of silk.

Rice [L. and Gk. *oryza*; cf. Arab. *aruz(z)*, rice], a grain growing in warm climates.

Rich [O.E. *rice*, Com. Teut. Perh. fr. L. *rex*, a king], well supplied, wealthy, costly, highly flavoured.

Rick [O.E. *hrēac*; cf. Du. rook; Norw. *rauk*], stack of grain, hay, etc.

Rick′ets [Etym. doubtful], disease of children affecting the bones.

Rick′et-y, shaky.

Ric′o-chet (*chet = shai* or *shĕt*) [F. *ricochet*. Etym. doubtful], rebound of bullet, etc., skipping on water of flat stone; skip or bound along.   [clear.

Rid [O.N. *rythja*, to clear], to free, to clear; **Rid′dance**, freeing, deliverance.

Rid′dle [O.E. *hriddel*, earlier *hridder*, fr. *hrid-*, stem of verb to shake], coarse sieve; pass through a riddle, pierce with holes.

Rid′dle [O.E. *rǣdels*, fr. *rǣdan*, to consider], puzzling question; speak in riddles, explain riddles.

Ride [O.E. *ridan*, Com. Teut.], go on horseback, etc., or in a vehicle, float; excursion on horseback, riding path.

Ri′der, one who rides, clause added to a bill in course of discussion.

Ridge [O.E. *hrycg*, Com. Teut.], summit between slopes.

Rid′i-cule [L. *ridēre*, to laugh], mockery; laugh at.

Ri-dic′u-lous, laughable, droll.

Ri′ding [for *thriding*, third part], a division, esp. one of three administrative divisions of Yorks.   [abounding.

Rife [O.N. *rīfr*, abundant], prevailing,

Riff′raff [earlier *riff* and *raff*; O.F. *rif et raf*, every bit], refuse, sweepings; the rabble.

Ri′fle [O.F. *rifler*, to scratch], search and rob.

Ri′fle [short for *rifled gun*, fr. *rifle*, to form grooves; O.F. *rifler*, to scratch], gun whose barrel is grooved with spirals, one of these grooves; to form grooves in the barrel of a gun.

Rift [Dan. and Norw. *rift*; cf. Norw. *riva*, Dan. *rive*, to tear], split, cleft.

Rig [Etym. dub., cf. Norw. *rigga*, to bind up, rig], fit with tackling, to dress; dress.

Rig′ging, ropes, chains, etc., of a ship.

Right [O.E. *riht*, Com. Teut.], straight, just, fit, correct, on the side farther from the heart; immediately, truly; straight course, justice; do justice, become upright again.

Right′eous (*eo = y* or *sh*) [O.E. *rihtwis*; *riht*, right, *wis*, wise], just, free from sin.

Rig′id (*g = j*) [L. *rigidus*, stiff], stiff, strict, precise.

Ri-gid′i-ty, stiffness.

Rig′ma-role [Prob. corruption of obs. *ragman roll*, a document with many signatures], foolish talk.   [shuddering.

Rig′or [L. *rigēre*, to be stiff], convulsive

Rig′or-ous, severe.   [severity.

Rig′our [L. *rigēre*, to be stiff], strictness,

Rill [cf. Du. *ril*, Ger. *rille*], small stream.

Rim [O.E. *rima*; cf. O.N. *rime*, a ridge], border, edge.

Rime 1 [O.E. and O.N. *hrīm*], white frost.

Rime 2 [O.F. *rime*; prob. fr. L. *rhythmus*, rhythm], rhyme.

Rind (*i* long) [O.E. *rind*], peel, shell.

Rin′der-pest [Ger. *rinder* (pl. of *rind*, ox) and Pest], disease of cattle.

Ring 1 [O.E. *hringan*; Com. Teut., cf. O.N. *hringja*, Ger. *ringen*, perh. imit.], to sound as a bell; sound as of a bell.

Ring 2 [O.E. *hring*; Com. Teut., cf. O.N. *hringr*, Du. and Ger. *ring*], circle, circular hoop; combination of traders, etc.

Ring′lead-er, leader, esp. in evil.

Ring′let [dim. of **Ring** 2], curl.

Rink [perh. O.F. *renc*, rank], sheet of ice for curling or skating, place for roller-skating.

Rinse [F. *rincer*; orig. unknown], wash out.

Ri′ot [O.F. *riote*; cf. It. *riotta*. Etym. doubtful], uproar, tumult; engage in riot.

Rip [cf. Fris. *rippe*, to rip or tear], tear or cut open or off.

Rip-a′ri-an [L. *ripa*, a bank], pertaining to river banks.

Ripe [O.E. *rípe*; cf. Du. *rijp*, Ger. *reif*], ready for reaping, mature.

Ri-poste′ [F. fr. It. *risposta*, response], quick return-thrust in fencing, counterstroke.

Rip′ple [?], dimple as running water, sound like a brook; wavy appearance, a sound as of little waves.

Rip′ple [Of obscure origin; cf. Du. *repel*, Ger. *riffel*], iron comb used to clear seeds from flax; treat with a ripple.

Rise (s=z) [O.E. *risan*; Com. Teut.], move upward, get up, occur, come into existence; a going or getting up, beginning, ascent.

Ris′i-ble (s=z) [L. *ridére* (p.p. *risus*), to laugh], having power to laugh, laughable. **Risibil′ity.**

Risk [It. *risco*, risk; perh. L. *resecāre*, to cut off short; *re-*, back, and *secāre*, to cut], chance of loss, danger; chance loss, endanger. **Risk′y, Risk′iness.**

Ris′sole [F. *rissole*; perh. L. *russeolus*, reddish], fried cake of minced meat, etc.

Rite [L. *rītus*, a rite], formal act of religion.

Rit′u-al, pertaining to rites; prescribed form of divine service, book of rites. **Rit′ualism.**

Ri′val [L. *rivus*, a stream], competitor; competing; strive to equal or excel. **Ri′valry.**

Rive [O.E. *rífa*; cf. Dan. *rive*; Swed. *rifva*, to rive], rend, split. **Riv′en.**

Riv′er [O.F. *rivere*, river; Late L. *rīpāria*, shore, river; L. *rīpa*, shore], large stream.

Riv′et [O.F. *river*, to clinch; etym. doubtful], pin or bolt whose headless end is beaten out after insertion; fasten with rivets; fix the attention. **Riv′eter.**

Riv′u-let [see River], small stream.

Roach [O.F. *roche*; etym. doubtful], small freshwater fish.

Road [O.E. *rád*, fr. *rídan*, to ride], highway, a public passage, place where ships ride at anchor. **Road′stead.**

Roam [?], wander, rove.

Roan [O.F. *roan*; cf. It. and Sp. *roano*, a roan horse; etym. doubtful], chestnut, brown, or black interspersed with gray or white.

Roan [perh. from *Rouen*], kind of sheepskin leather.

Roar [O.E. *rárian*, prob. imit.], make a full, loud sound; deep loud cry, loud confused sound.

Roast [O.F. *rost* (n.), *rostir* (vb.), roast; perh. O.H.G. *rôsten*, to roast; *rôst*, gridiron], cook before the fire or in an oven; meat roasted or for roasting.

Rob [O.F. *robber*, *rober*, to disrobe, plunder], despoil (of), plunder.

Rob′ber, thief, plunderer. **Rob′bery.**

Robe [O.F. *robe*, orig. meaning *booty*], outer dress, flowing gown invest with a robe, to dress.

Rob′in [O.F. *Robin*, pet name for *Robert*], small bird with a red breast.

Ro-bust′ [L. *robustus*, fr. *robur*, strength], strong, vigorous. **Robust′ness.**

Rock [1] [O.F. *roke*; etym. doubtful], large mass of stone or crag. **Rock′ery.**

Rock [2] [O.F. *roccian*; cf. Ger. *rücken*, to tug], sway, cause to sway.

Rock [3] [cf. O.N. *rokkr*; Swed. *rock*; Dan. *rok*, a distaff], distaff.

Rock′er, curving piece of wood on which a cradle, etc., rocks.

Rock′et [It. *rocchetta*, bobbin to wind silk on, rocket; see **Rock** [3]], projectile firework.

Rock′y, abounding in rocks.

Ro-co′co [F.; etym. doubtful], with much conventional decoration, in the style of the time of Louis XIV.

Rod [O.E. *rodd*; cf. O.N. *rudda*, a club], straight stick, measure of $5\frac{1}{2}$ yds.

Ro′dent [L. *rōdens* (*-entis*), pr.p. of *rōdere*, to gnaw], gnawing; gnawing animal.

Rod-o-mon-tade′ [fr. *Rodomonte*, character in "Orlando Furioso"], boastful talk.

Roe [O.E. *ráha*; Com. Teut.], small deer.

Roe [M.Du., M.H.G. *roge*], spawn of fishes.

Rogue [?], vagrant, knave.

Rogu′er-y, knavish tricks.

Rogu′ish, knavish, mischievous.

Roi′ster [F. *rustre*, L. *rusticus*], revel uproariously. **Roi′sterer.**

Rôle [F. *rôle*; O.F. *roller*, to roll], part or character.

Roll (ō) [O.F. *roller* (vb.), *rolle* (n.), roll; L. *rotula*, dim. of *rota*, a wheel], turn over and over, inwrap, press with a roller, rumble; act of rolling, that which is rolled up, list, small, separately baked piece of bread.

Roll′er, cylinder, swelling wave.

Rol′lick [?], be jovial and boisterous.

Rō′ly-pō′ly [perh. from Roll], boiled pudding of paste and jam in a roll.

Ro′man [L. *Rōmānus*, fr. *Rōma*, Rome], connected with Rome or the Church of Rome; ordinary upright type.

Ro-mance′ [O.F. *romanz*, a romance; *parler romanz*, to speak Romance, *i.e.* every-day Latin; L. *Rōmānus*, Roman; *Rōma*, Rome], (languages) derived from Latin; mediæval tale of chivalry, wonderful tale; indulge in extravagant stories.

Ro-man′tic [see **Romance**], fanciful, extravagant. **Roman′ticism.** [ture.

Ro-man-esq′ue, romantic; kind of architec-

Rom′any [Gipsy, *Romani*, fem. and pl. of *Romano*, adj. fr. *Rom*, gipsy], a gipsy, the gipsies, gipsy language.

Romp [perh. O.F. *ramper*, to clamber; etym. doubtful], play boisterously; rough frolic.

Ron′deau, Ron′del [F., later form *rondel*, later *rondeau*], short poem with only two rhymes and the opening words used twice as a refrain.

Ron′do [It.], musical composition in which the leading theme recurs.

Rood [O.E. *ród*, a cross; cogn. with **Rod**], cross, measure of $\frac{1}{4}$ acre.

Roof [O.E. *hróf*; cf. O.Icel. *rhóf*], cover of a building; cover with a roof. [smaller.

Rook [O.E. *hróc*], bird like the crow, but

Rook [O.F. *roc*; Pers. *rukh*], castle (chess).

Room [O.E. *rúm*; Com. Teut., cf. Ger. *raum*], space, an apartment.

Room'y, spacious, large.

Roost [O.E. *hróst*; cf. M.Du. *roest*], a perch; to perch. **Roost'er**.

Root [O.E., O.N. *rót*; cf. Swed. *rot*; Dan. *rod*, a root], part of a plant which grows downwards, source; plant deeply, pull or dig (out).

Root, Rout (*rowt*) [O.E. *wrótan*, fr. prec.], grub up (as swine).

Rope [O.E. *ráp*; Com. Teut.], large, stout cord; tie with rope or cord.

Rope'walk, long, low building where ropes are made.

Ro'sa-ry (*s=z*) [L. *rosārium*, rose-garden: Late L. sense, wreath], set of prayers, string of beads for counting prayers.

Rose (*s=z*) [L. *rosa*, perh. from Gk. *rhodon*, a rose], shrub and its flower, rich red colour, disease of skin, perforated cap of spout of watering pot.

Ro'se-ate, tinged with rose-colour.

Rose-ma'ry [L. *rōsmarīnus*; *rōs*, dew, *marīnus*, marine], aromatic shrub.

Ro'ser-y (*s=z*), rose-garden.

Ro-sette' [F. *rosette*, dim. of **Rose**], ornament in the form of a rose.

Rose'wood, dark cabinet wood named from its fragrance.

Ros'in (*s=z*) [changed from **Resin**], amber-coloured resin; smear or rub with resin.

Ros'ter [Du. *rooster*, list], list showing turns for duty of individuals in military force.

Ros'trum [L. *rostrum*, a beak (pl. *rostra*, pulpit for speakers in the forum, adorned with beaks of ships)], platform for public speaking.

Ro'sy, like a rose, blooming, red.

Rot [O.E. *rotian*; Com. Teut.], to decay; decay, putrefaction.

Ro'ta-ry [L. *rota*, a wheel], turning as a wheel; kind of club. **Rota'rian**.

Ro-tate' [L. *rota*, a wheel], turn as a wheel, arrange in turn. **Rota'tion**.

Rote [O.F. *rote*; lit. a beaten track; etym. doubtful; see **Route**], mere repetition.

Rot'ten [O.N. *rotinn*; cf. Swed. *rutten*], decayed. **Rot'tenness**.

Ro'tor [L. *rota*, a wheel], a metal tower revolved by the wind.

Ro-tun'da [earlier *rotonda*; It. fem. of *rotondo*, round], round building.

Ro-tund'i-ty [L. *rotundus*, round], roundness.

Rouge (*roozh*) [F. *rouge*; L. *rubeus*, red], red powder for colouring the cheeks; apply or use such.

Rough (*gh=ff*) [O.E. *rúh*; cf. Du. *ruig*; Ger. *rauh*], uneven, uncut, boisterous, rude.

Roul-ette' (*roo-let'*) [F. *roulette*, double dim. of *roue*, a wheel; L. *rota*, a wheel], a game of chance played on a table with a rotating wheel.

Round [L. *rotundus*, round], circular, spherical, not minutely accurate, sonorous, plain; circular series or course, step of a ladder, vocal composition like a catch, charge for firearm; about; make or go round.

Round'a-bout, indirect; merry-go-round.

Round'e-lay [F. *rondelet*, little song, and **Lay**], short, simple song with refrain.

Rouse (*s=z*) [?], wake from sleep, stir.

Rout [O.F. *route*, a rout, a way; L. *rupta*, fem. p.p. of *rumpere*, to break], disturbance, mob, defeat and flight; defeat and put to flight.

Rout [var. of **Root**], force or fetch (out).

Route (*ou=oo*) [F. *route*], way to be passed, course.

Rou-tine' (*roo-teen'*) [F. *routine*, dim. of *route*, a way], round of duties, etc.

Rove [?], wander.

Rove [?], long band of cotton, etc., drawn out and slightly twisted.

Row [?], (colloq.) brawl.

Row [1] [O.E. *ráw*; cf. Ger. *reihe*], number of persons or things set in a line.

Row [2] [O.E. *rówan*; cf. O.N. *róa*, to row; cogn. with L. *remus*, an oar], propel with or use oars.

Rowan (*ro'an* or *row'an*) [Swed. *rön*; Icel. *reynir*, a rowan], mountain ash; its berry.

Row'dy [?], rough and noisy; rowdy person. **Row'dyism**.

Row'el [Late L. *rotella*, dim. of *rota*, a wheel], wheel of a spur.

Row'lock [O.E. *árloc*; **Oar** and **Lock** [2]], support for an oar.

Roy'al [O.F. *roial*; L. *rēgālis*; doublet **Regal**], kingly, suitable for a king or queen. **Roy'alist**.

Roy'al-ty, sovereignty, sum paid to a land-owner for permission to work a mine, percentage paid to author on sales of books, etc.

Rub [M.E., L.G. *rubben*; of obscure origin], move along a surface with pressure, fret; act of rubbing, friction, inequality that deflects a bowl, impediment.

Rub'ber, one who or that which rubs, caoutchouc.

Rub'ber [?], contest of three games.

Rub'bish [perh. corrupt form of old pl. of **Rubble**], waste matter, trash.

Rub'ble [?], rough stones used in masonry.

Ru'bi-cund [L. *rubicundus*; *rubēre*, to be red], ruddy, red.

Ru'bric [L. *rubrica*; *ruber*, red], direction for conduct of divine service, heading in special lettering.

Ru'by [O.F. *rubi*, *rubis*, ruby; L. *rubeus*, red], red precious stone.

Ruche (*roosh*) [F.], frill of lace, etc.

Ruck [of Scand. origin; perh. fr. Norw. *ruka*, cogn. with **Rick**], crowd, general run.

Ruck [O.N. *hrukka*, to crease], a crease or wrinkle; to crease.

Ruck'le [of Scand. origin], to make a rattling sound in the throat.

Ruck'sack (*rōŏk*) [Ger. *rucksack*, lit. a back-sack], a bag slung over the shoulders for carrying walker's necessaries.

Rud'der [O.E. *róther*, from **Row**²], appliance for steering. [reddish.

Rud'dy [O.E. *rudig*, cogn. with **Red**], red or

Rude [L. *rudis*, rude], rough, uncivil, in natural state. **Rude'ness**.

Ru'di-ment [L. *rudimentum*; *rudis*, rude], (pl.) first principles, imperfect beginnings. **Rudimen'tary**. [herb.

Rue ¹ [F. *rue*; L. *rūta*; Gk. *rhutē*, rue], bitter

Rue ² [O.E. *hréowan*; cf. Du. *rouwen*, Ger. *reuen*], repent of, wish undone; regret, pity.

Rue'ful, mournful.

Ruff [perh. shortened from **Ruffle**], plaited or crimped collar.

Ruf'fi-an [O.F. *rufyen*, ruffian; cf. Port. and Sp. *rufian*; etym. dub.], brutal, coarse man. [etc.

Ruf'fle [?], disturb smoothness; frill of lace,

Rug [Cf. Swed. *rugg*, ruffled hair], thick covering for a floor, etc.

Rug'ged [Cf. M.Swed. *ruggig*, rough, hairy; cogn. with **Rug**], rough.

Ru'in [L. *ruīna*, ruin; *ruere*, to rush, fall], destruction, that which is fallen; destroy, bring to poverty. **Ru'inous**.

Ru-in-a'tion, state of ruin.

Rule [L. *rēgula*, a rule; *regere*, to rule], governing direction, order, normal state of things, ruler or measurer; govern, draw lines guided by a ruler.

Ru'ler, one who rules, strip of wood used in ruling paper.

Rum [perh. short for earlier *rumbullion*, *rumbustion*; etym. doubtful], liquor distilled from sugar-cane.

Rum [?] (slang), odd, queer.

Rum'ble [M.E. *romblen*; cf. Du. *rommelen*, Ger. *rummeln*; prob. imit.], make a continuous heavy sound; rumbling noise, extra seat at back of carriage.

Ru'min-ate [L. *rūmināri* (p.p. *rūminātus*), to ruminate; *rūmen*, the throat], chew the cud, ponder. **Rumina'tion. Ru'minant**.

Rum'mage [fr. older F. *arrumage*, now *arrimage*, a search], search by turning over; thorough search.

Rum'mer [Du. *romer*, a wine-glass], large drinking-glass.

Ru'mour [L. *rūmor*, rumour], popular report; tell from one to another.

Rump [Prob. Scand. orig.], tail end.

Rum'ple [Cf. M.Du. *rompelen*], make uneven, wrinkle.

Run [M.E. *rinne*(*n*), *renne*(*n*), prob. from O.N. *rinna*, to run], move swiftly, flow, have a course; act of running, a course, urgent demand, range of pasture.

Run'a-gate [M.E. *renegat*, fr. **Run** and *agate*, away; see **Renegade**], (arch.) vagabond.

Rune [O.N. and Icel. *rún*, cogn. with O.E. *rún*, whisper, mystery], character of the old alphabet of the Northmen.

Rung [O.E. *hrung*; cf. Du. *rong*, Ger. *runge*], step of a ladder, spoke, cross-bar.

Ru'nic, pertaining to runes.

Run'nel [O.E. *rynele*, cogn. with **Run**], small brook.

Run'ner, one who runs, trailing plant, one of the pieces on which a sledge slides.

Ru-pee' [Hind. *rūpiyah*; Skr. *rūpya*, wrought silver], silver coin and monetary unit of India.

Rup'ture [L. *rumpere* (p.p. *ruptus*), to break], a bursting, breach of friendly relations; to burst, break.

Ru'ral [L. *rūrālis*; *rūs* (*rūr-is*), the country], pertaining to the country.

Ruse (*s=z*) [O.F. *ruse*; *ruser*, to drive back], trick.

Rush [O.E. *risc*; cf. M. Du. *risch*, Ger. *rusch*], marsh plant.

Rush [A. F. *russher*, fr. O.F. *re*(*h*)*usser*], violent course of running; move forward with force, take by sudden attack.

Rusk [Sp. *rosca*, roll of bread], light bread crisped in an oven.

Rus'set [O.F. *rousset*, fr. *rous*, red; L. *russus*, red], reddish-brown.

Rust [O.E. *rúst*, cogn. with **Red**], red crust on iron, mould on plants; contract rust. **Rust'y**.

Rus'tic [L. *rusticus*; *rūs*, the country], rural, countrified, simple; simple country person. **Rustic'ity**.

Rus'ti-cate, reside in the country, send away from a university for a time. **Rustica'tion**.

Rus'tle [imit., cf. Du. *ridselen*], make sounds like the moving of silk; sound of rustling.

Rut [?], track worn by a wheel.

Ruth [see **Rue**²], pity.

Ruth'less (*u=oo*), pitiless.

Rye [O.E. *ryge*; cf. O.N. *rugr*], kind of grain.

Ry'ot [Hind. *raiyat*], Indian peasant.

S

Sab-ba-ta'ri-an, strict Sabbath-keeper.

Sab'bath [Heb. *shabbāth*, Sabbath; *shābath*, to rest], season or day of rest. **Sabbat'ical**.

Sa'ble [O.F. *sable*, sable-fur, prob. of Slavonic orig.; cf. Polish and Czech *sobol*, the sable. As black sable was best liked, the word *sable* also means "black"], animal of the weasel kind, also its fur, (pl.) mourning dress; dark.

Sa-bot' [F.; etym. doubtful], wooden shoe.

Sa'bre [F. *sabre*; Ger. *sabel*, sabre], cavalry sword with curved blade. [term].

Sac [L. *saccus*, a sack], small bag (scientific.

Sac'cha-rine (*ch=k*) [Gk. *saccharon*, sugar], pertaining to sugar, sweet.

Sa-cer-do'tal [L. *sacerdōs* (*sacerdōt-is*), a priest; *sacer*, holy; *dare*, to give], priestly.

Sach'et (*chet=shai*) [F. *sachet*, dim. of *sac*; L. *saccus*, a bag], small perfumed bag.

Sack [O.E. *sacc*; L. *saccus*; Gk. *saccos*; Heb. *saq*, a sack], large bag.

Sack [formerly *seck*, *wyne seck*; F. *vin sec*, dry wine, sack], a white wine.

Sack [perh. L. *saccāre*, put in a sack], pillage ; to plunder.

Sack'but [F. *saquebute* ; etym. doubtful], obsolete bass trumpet with slide for altering pitch.

Sac'ra·ment [L. *sacer*, sacred], religious rite, as the Lord's Supper and Baptism. **Sacramen'tal.**

Sa'cred [p.p. of obs. *sacre*, to render holy ; L. *sacer*, holy], holy, set apart.

Sac'ri·fice [L. *sacer*, holy, *facere*, to make], offering, esp. to a god ; offer up, give up for a purpose. **Sac'rificial.**

Sac'ri·lege [L. *sacer*, holy, *legere*, to gather], profaning of sacred things. **Sacrileg'ious.**

Sac'rist, Sac'ris·tan [L. *sacrista*, a sacristan ; *sacer*, sacred], official having charge of sacred vestments and utensils.

Sac'ris·ty [L. *sacer*, sacred], vestry.

Sac'ro·sanct [L. *sacrum* (abl. *sacro*), sacred, *sanctus*, saint], inviolable, secured by religious sanction against outrage.

Sad [O.E. *saed* ; Com. Teut. ; cogn. with L. *satis*, enough], mournful, dull, doughy.

Sad'den, make or become sad.

Sad'dle [O.E. *sadol* ; Com. Teut.], rider's seat, special joint of mutton or venison ; put a saddle on.

Sad'dler, one who makes saddles.

Sad'du·cee [L.L. *Sadducœus*, fr. late Heb. *Cadduqi*], member of Jewish sect of the time of Christ that denied resurrection of the dead, existence of spirits, and the obligation of the traditional law.

Safe [F. *sauf* ; L. *salvus*, safe], secure, unharmed ; fireproof box for valuables, cool receptacle for meat.

Safe'guard, defence ; protect.

Safe'ty, freedom from danger.

Saf'fron [F. *safran* ; Arab. *za'farān*], kind of crocus, also its dried stigmas, deep orange yellow.

Sag [M.E. *saggen* ; cf. Du. *zakken*], sink in the middle, droop.

Sa'ga [O.N. and Icel. *saga* ; *segja*, to say], Scandinavian legend.

Sa·ga'cious (*aci=aish*) [L. *sagax* (*sagāc-is*) ; *sāgīre*, to discern acutely], shrewd, wise.

Sa·ga'ci·ty, soundness of judgment.

Sage [F. *sage*, wise ; L. *sapere*, to know], wise ; wise man.

Sage [M.E. and F. *sauge* ; L. *salvia*, sage ; L. *salvāre*, to heal], aromatic herb.

Sa'go [Malay *sāgū*, sago], food starch from the pith of certain palms.

Sail [O.E. *seg(e)l*, Com. Teut.], sheet of canvas to catch the wind, fleet of sailing-vessels, journey by water ; travel by water, begin a voyage.

Sail'or, seaman.

Sain'foin [F. *sain*, healthy, *foin*, hay], herb used as fodder.

Saint [O.F. *saint* ; L. *sanctus*, holy], holy person, one who is canonized.

Sake [O.E. *sacu*, a quarrel, sake ; cf. Du. *zaak*, a lawsuit, thing ; Ger. *sache*, affair], out of consideration or regard for.

Sa·laam', Sa·lam' [Arab. *salām*, saluting], in the East a ceremonious salutation ; make a salaam (to).

Sal'ad [O.It. *salata*, a salad ; L. *sāl*, salt], preparation of raw herbs.

Sal·a·man'der [L. and Gk. *salamandra*, a kind of lizard], newt-like animal supposed to live in fire, spirit living in fire.

Sal'a·ry [L. *salārium*, orig. money given to soldiers to buy salt ; *sāl*, salt], fixed payment for service.

Sale [O.E. *sala*, prob. fr. O.N. *sala* ; cogn. with **Sell**], act of selling, market, auction.

Sal'ic, Sal'ique [F. *salique*, fr. *Salii*, tribe of the Franks], (law) excluding females from throne.

Sa'li·ent [L. *salīre* (pr.p. *saliens*, *-entis*), to leap], leaping, projecting, prominent.

Sa'line (*sai'līne* or *sā-līne'*) [L. *salīnus*, saline, *sāl*, salt], consisting of or containing salt.

Sa·li'va [L. *saliva*, spittle], digestive fluid from glands.

Sal'low [O.E. *salo* ; cf M. Du. *salu*, discoloured], of a dull yellowish colour.

Sal'low [O.E. *sealh*], willow.

Sal'ly [L. *salīre*, to leap], rush out ; rush of troops from a besieged place, dart of wit, etc.

Sal·ma·gun'di [F. *salmigondis* ; etym. dub.], dish of seasoned chopped meat, anchovies, etc.

Salm'on (*ŏ*) [A.F. *samoun* ; L. *salmo*, salmon ; perh. from L. *salīre*, to leap], large food fish.

Sa·loon' [F. *salon*, a reception room ; *salle*, a room ; O.H.G. *sal*, a hall, a room], large public room, also in ship, train.

Salt [O.E. *sealt* ; Com. Teut. ; cogn. with L. *sāl*], substance found in earth and water, esp. sea-water, kind of chemical compound ; season or preserve with salt ; impregnated or preserved with salt.

Salt'cell·ar [Salt and obs. *saler*, fr. O.F. *salier* ; L. *salārium*, salt-holder], small salt-holder.

Salt·pe'tre [Late L. *salpetra* ; L. *sāl*, salt, and Gk. *petra*, rock], crystalline salty substance, nitre.

Sa·lu'bri·ous [L. *salubris*, healthy, *salus*, health], healthy. **Salu'brity.**

Sal'u·ta·ry [L. *salus* (*salūt-is*), health], wholesome, beneficial.

Sal·u·ta'tion, form of address at meeting or parting, gesture or message of greeting.

Sa·lute' [L. *salus* (*salūt-is*), health], greet, kiss ; ceremony of respect, complimentary firing of cannon, etc.

Sal'vage [O.F. *salvage*, lit. a saving ; L. *salvāre*, to save], compensation to persons who help to save ship or cargo, property saved from wreck, etc. **Sal'vor.**

Sal·va'tion [L. *salvus*, safe], saving of the soul, deliverance from danger, etc.

Salve [O.E. *sealf* ; cf. Du. *zalf* ; Ger. *salbe*], healing ointment ; gloss over.

Sal'ver [Sp. *salva*, a salver, a tasting of food or drink before serving ; *salvar*, to save], tray.

Sal'vo [It. *salva*, salutation, perh. from L. *salvē*, hail!], discharge of firearms as salute.

Same [O.N. *same* ; cf. Du. and Swed. *samme*, the same], unchanging, not different, of the like kind.

Same'ness, lack of variety.

Sam'ite (*ă*) [O.F. *samit*], rich silk dress-fabric interwoven with gold.

Sa'mo-var [Russ. *samovaru*, self-boiler], Russian tea-urn.

Sam'phire [earlier *sampere* ; F. (herbe de) *Saint Pierre*, Saint Peter], cliff plant whose leaves are used in pickles.

Sam'ple [from obs. *essample*, var. of **Example**], specimen ; test samples.

Sam'pler [as **Sample**], piece of worsted work containing letters, etc.

San-a-to'ri-um [see below], place or establishment for the treatment of invalids.

San'a-to-ry [L. *sānātor*, a healer, *sānāre*, to heal], conducive to health, curative.

Sanc'ti-fy [L. *sanctus*, holy, *facere*, to make], make sacred or holy. **Sanc'ti-fica'tion.**

Sanc-ti-mo'ni-ous [L. *sanctimōnia*, holiness ; *sanctus*, holy], hypocritically pious. **Sanc'timony.**

Sanc'tion [L. *sancīre* (p.p. *sanctus*), to make holy], confirmation, approval ; confirm, approve. [holiness.]

Sanc'ti-tude, Sanc'ti-ty [L. *sanctus*, holy].

Sanc'tu-a-ry [L. *sanctus*, holy], holy place, place of worship, refuge.

Sanc'tum [L. neut. of *sanctus*, holy], sacred place, shrine, private place of retreat.

Sand [O.E., Com. Teut.], fine particles of stone, (pl.) stretches of sand.

San'dal [Gk. *sandalion* ; etym. dub., a sandal], sole strapped on as a shoe.

San'dal-wood [Arab. *candal* ; Skr. *chandana*], compact fragrant wood.

Sand'wich [from an Earl of *Sandwich*, who had sandwiches brought to him while gambling], slices of bread with meat, etc., between ; insert between layers.

Sand'y, full of, covered with, or like sand.

Sane [L. *sānus*, healthy], mentally sound.

San'gar (*sang'gar*) [Hind. *sunga*, a sangar], stone breastwork.

San'gui-na-ry [L. *sanguis* (*sanguin-is*), blood], bloody, bloodthirsty.

San'guine [L. *sanguis* (*sanguin-is*), blood], blood-red, hopeful.

San'he-drim, San'he-drin [Late Heb. *sanhedrin* ; Gk. *sunedrion*, "a sitting together"], supreme council and highest court of justice at ancient Jerusalem.

San'i-ta-ry [L. *sānus*, healthy], pertaining to health.

San-i-ta'tion, use of sanitary measures.

San'i-ty [L. *sānitas* (*sānitāt-is*), health ; *sānus*, healthy, whole], soundness of mind.

San'ta Claus [U.S.A., fr. Du. *Sint Klaas*, St. Nicholas], personage who fills stockings at Christmas.

Sap [O.E. *sæp*, Com. W. Germanic], juice of plants.

Sap [F. *saper* ; F. *sappe*, or It. *zappa*, spade], digging underground trenches to approach a besieged place, undermine, weaken ; an underground trench.

Sap'i-ence [L. *sapere*, to know], wisdom, fancied wisdom. **Sa'pient.**

Sap'ling [see **Sap** 1], young tree.

Sap-o-na'ceous (*ce=sh*) [L. *sāpo* (*sāpōn-is*), soap], soapy.

Sap'per [see **Sap** 2], military engineer.

Sap'phire [O.F. *safir* ; Gk. *sappheiros*, a sapphire], blue precious stone.

Sa'ra-cen [L.L. *Saracēnus*], Arab or Moslem of time of the Crusades.

Sar'casm [Gk. *sarcasmos*, a sneer ; *sarcazein*, to tear flesh, to sneer], cutting expression, biting wit.

Sar-cas'tic, sneering, bitingly witty.

Sarce'net, Sars'enet [A.F. *sarzinett*, cloth made by the Saracens ; L. *Saracēnus*, Saracen], fine thin silk.

Sar-coph'a-gus [Gk. *sarx*, flesh, *phagein*, to eat], stone coffin.

Sar'dine (*ine=een*) [Gk. *sardē* ; prob. from *Sardinia*], small fish preserved in oil.

Sar-don'ic [L. *Sardonicus, Sardonius* ; Gk. *Sardonios* ; etym. uncert.], bitterly scornful.

Sar-gas'so [Port. *sargaço*], a floating seaweed found in the Gulf Stream.

Sar-sa-par-il'la [Sp. *zarzaparilla*, from *zarza*, bramble, and perh. dim. of *parra*, vine], dried roots of a kind of smilax.

Sar-to'ri-al [L. *sartor*, a tailor], pertaining to a tailor or his work. [frame.]

Sash [F. *châssis* ; L. *capsa*, a case], window-

Sash [Arab. *shāsh*, muslin], scarf for waist or shoulder.

Sas'sen-ach [Gael. and Ir. for *Saxon*], the Highlander's name for a Lowlander or any other of non-Celtic race.

Sa-tan'ic [Heb. *sātān*, adversary], like Satan, diabolical.

Satch'el [L. *saccellus*, dim. of *saccus*, a sack], hand-bag.

Sate [earlier *sade* ; O.E. *sadian* ; assim. to L. *satis*, enough], satiate, glut. [cloth.]

Sat-een' [from **Satin**], glossy cotton or woollen

Sat'el-lite [L. *satelles* (*satellitis*), an attendant], attendant, secondary planet.

Sa'ti-ate (*t=sh*) [L. *satis*, enough], overfill, cloy.

Sa-ti-a'tion (*t=sh*), **Sa-ti'e-ty**, gratification beyond desire.

Sat'in [F. *satin*, prob. fr. L. *sēta*, silk], glossy silk cloth. **Sat'inette.**

Sat'ire [L. *satira*, *satura*, a kind of poetry, orig. a medley ; fr. *lanx satura*, full dish], composition in prose or verse holding up vice or folly or individuals to ridicule, use of ridicule to discourage vice or folly.

Sat-ir'ic-al, cutting, sarcastic. **Sat'irist.**

Sat'ir-ize, attack with satire.

Sat'is-fac'tion, content, amends.

Sat'is-fy [L. *satis*, enough, *facere* (p.p. *factus*), to make], gratify fully, content, convince, solve (doubt).

Sa′trap (*Sa=Sai*), **Sat′rap** [L. and Gk. *satrapēs* ; O. Pers. *khsatra-pāvā*, guardian of a province], ancient Persian provincial governor. [Satura′tion.

Sat′u-rate [L. *satur*, full], fill fully, soak.

Sat′ur-day [O.E. *Sœtern(es) dœg*, transl. of L. *Sāturnī diēs*, day of Saturn], seventh day of the week.

Sat′ur-nine [O.F. *saturnin* ; L. *Sāturnus*, Saturn], gloomy.

Sat′yr [Gk. *satyros*, a satyr], woodland deity (part man part beast) of the Greeks.

Sauce [L. *salsa*, a salted thing ; *sāl*, salt], preparation used as a relish, impertinence.

Sau′cer [O.F. *saussier* (fr. **Sauce**)], small concave plate under a cup.

Sau′cy, pert, impudent. **Sauc′iness.**

Saun′ter [?], walk about idly.

Sau′ri-an [Gk. *sauros*, lizard], one of the lizard tribe.

Sau′sage [Late L. *salsīcia* ; L. *salsus*, salted ; *sāl*, salt], minced meat in a skin.

Sav′age [L. *silvāticus*, belonging to a wood ; *silva*, a wood], wild, uncivilized, brutal ; uncivilized human being. **Sav′agery.**

Sa-van′na*h* [Sp. *zavana* ; perh. of Carib. origin], plain, usually a treeless plain, in tropical America.

Save [F. *sauver* ; L. *salvāre* (p.p. *salvātus*), to save], make safe, rescue, lay up, prevent ; except.

Sav′e-loy [O.F. *cervelat* ; It. *cervellata*, a sausage (containing brains) ; It. *cervello*, L. *cerebellum*, dim. of *cerebrum*, brain], seasoned cooked and dried sausage.

Sa′ving, thrifty ; except ; (n. pl.) sums laid by.

Sa′viour, deliverer, Jesus Christ.

Sa′vo-ry [prob. cogn. with **Savour**], herb of the mint family.

Sa′vour [L. *sapor*, taste], taste and odour ; partake of the quality (of).

Sa′vour-y, having an appetizing taste; dish served at beginning or end of dinner.

Sa-voy′ [fr. *Savoie* in France], kind of cabbage.

Saw [1] [O.E. *sagu* ; cogn. with L. *secāre*, to cut], cutting instrument with a toothed edge ; cut with a saw.

Saw [2] [O.E. *sagu*, fr. *secgan*, to say], proverbial saying.

Saw′dust, wood-dust produced by sawing.

Saw′yer, one employed in sawing.

Sax′i-frage [L. *saxum*, stone, *frangere*, to break], rock plant.

Sax′ophone [*Sax*, the inventor, Gr. *phone*, voice], keyed brass reed instrument.

Say (O.E. *secgan* ; Com. Teut., Ger. *sagen*], to speak ; what one has to say, share in a decision.

Scab [cf. Swed. *skabb* ; Dan. *skab*, scab], crust on a sore, disease of sheep. **Scab′by.**

Scab′bard [A.F. *escaubers* (pl.) ; see **Scale** [2] and **Hauberk**], sheath.

Scaf′fold [O.F. *schaffaut*, *eschaffaut* ; *cf.* It. *catafalco*, a stage, scaffold. Etym. doubtful], temporary structure of timber, stage for execution.

Scaf′fold-ing, supporting framework.

Scald (*a=aw*) [L.L. *excaldāre*, to scald ; *ex*, out, *calidus*, hot], burn with hot liquid, expose to a boiling heat ; burn from hot liquid or steam.

Scald (*a=aw*) [O.N. *skald*], ancient Scandinavian bard.

Scale [1] [O.N. *skál*, a bowl ; cogn. with **Scale** [2]], dish of a balance, (pl.) a balance ; to weigh, have weight of.

Scale [2] [O.F. *escale* ; O.H.G. *scala*, a scale], thin bony plate on the skin of a fish or a lizard ; clear of scales.

Scale [3] [L. *scala*, a ladder], anything graduated, series of musical tones ; climb.

Sca-lene′ [Gk. *scalēnos*, scalene, uneven], having three unequal sides and angles.

Scal′lop [O.F. *escalope* ; M. Du. *schelpe*, a shell], fan-shaped bivalve, curving on the edge ; cut into scallops.

Scalp [Northern M.E. *scalp* ; app. of Scand. orig ; cf. O.N. *skálpr*], outer covering of the skull ; deprive of the scalp.

Scal′pel [L. *scalpellum*, dim. of *scalprum*, a knife ; *scalpere*, to cut], dissecting knife.

Sca′ly, covered with scales.

Scamp [formerly, a fugitive ; perh. O.N.F. *escamper*, to flee ; L. *ex*, out of, *campus*, battlefield], rascal. [negligently.

Scamp [perh. var. of **Scant**], do (work)

Scamp′er [perh. O.N.F. *escamper*, to flee], run with speed ; hasty run.

Scan [L. *scandere*, to climb], read verse marking the poetic feet, look closely at.

Scan′dal [Gk. *scandalon*, a snare, stumbling-block], malicious talk, disgrace. **Scan-dalous.**

Scan′dal-ize, offend, shock.

Scan′sion, act of scanning verse.

Scant, Scant′y [O.N. *skamt*, short], scarcely sufficient ; keep poorly supplied.

Scant′ling [O.F. *escantillon*, sample ; etym. uncert.], small quantity, allotted portion, prescribed measurement in building, etc.

Scape [L. *scapus*], a radical stem bearing flowers and no leaves, as in the primrose.

Scape′goat [*scape* short for **Escape**, and **Goat**], one who bears blame for others.

Scape′grace [*scape*, short for **Escape** and **Grace**], graceless, reckless person.

Scap′u-lar [L. *scapulæ*, shoulder-blades], of or for the shoulder-blades.

Scar [Gk. *eschara*, hearth, scar of a burn], mark left by a wound ; leave mark of a wound.

Scar′ab [L. *scarabœus*], sacred beetle of Egypt, gem cut to the shape of this.

Scarce (*a=ai*) [O.N.F. *escars*, scarce ; Late L. *scarpsus*, for L. *excerptus*, selected ; see **Excerpt**], rare, not plentiful.

Scarce′ly, hardly, with difficulty.

Scarce′ness, Scar′ci-ty (*a=ai*), rarity, want.

Scare [obs. *skerre*, timid ; O.N. *skirra* timid], frighten ; fright.

Scarf [Du. *scherf*, a shred ; *cf.* Ger. *scherbe* ; perh. fr. O.N.F. *escarpe*, a pilgrim's scrip hung from the neck], covering for neck and shoulders.

G

Scar′i-fy [L.L. *scarificāre*, to scarify; Gk. *scariphaomai*, I scratch; *scariphos*, a style], scratch or cut the skin of.

Scar-ia-ti′na (*i=ee*) [It. *scarlattina*; *scarlatto*, scarlet], form of scarlet fever.

Scar′let [Pers. *saqalāt*, *siqalāt*, scarlet cloth], deep bright red.

Scarp [It. *scarpa*, a scarp; cf. M.H.G. *scharpf*, sharp], steep slope as part of a fortification.

Scath, Scathe [O.N. *skathe*; cf. Swed. *skada*; Dan. *skade*, harm], harm; injure. **Scathe′less.**

Scat′ter [Northern form of **Shatter**], strew about, disperse.

Scav′en-ger [formerly *scavager*; O.F. *es-cauver*, to inspect], street cleaner.

Scene [Gk. *scēnē*, tent, stage, scene], place of occurrence, stage view, part of a play, theatrical display, heated conversation.

Sce′ne-ry, landscape, the paintings, etc., used on a stage.

Scen′ic, pertaining to scenery.

Scent [formerly *sent*; L. *sentīre*, to feel, perceive], to smell; odour, odour left in the track of an animal, sense of smell.

Scep′tic (*sc=sk*) [Gk. *scepsis*, inquiry; *scepticos*, thoughtful, inquiring], doubter, one who doubts whether knowledge of reality is possible.

Scep′ti-cal, doubting, slow to believe.

Scep′ti-cism, doubting attitude of mind.

Scep′tre [Gk. *scēptron*, a prop, a sceptre], staff borne by a sovereign.

Sched′ule [L. *schedula*, dim. of *scheda*, a strip of papyrus; Late Gk. *schedē*, a tablet], formal list or inventory, appendix to Act of Parliament or deed; to enter in a schedule.

Scheme (*ch=k*) [formerly *schema*; L. and Gk. *schēma*, shape], plot, plan; to plan **Schema′tic.**

Scher′zo (*skairt′sō*) [It. from Ger. *scherz*, jest], a lively movement in music usu. following a slow one.

Schism [Gk. *schisma*, schism; *schizein*, to cleave], division, breach of unity. **Schis-ma′tic.**

Schist [Gk. *schistos*, easily cleft; *schizein*, to cleave], rock easily divided into slabs. **Schis′tose.**

Schol′ar (*ch=k*) [O.E. *scolere*; L.L. *scholāris*, scholar], school-child, learned person.

Schol′ar-ship, learning, a foundation for the maintenance of a student.

Scho-las′tic, scholarlike, pedantic, pertaining to schools. **Scholas′ticism.**

Scho′li-ast (*ch=k*), writer of marginal notes on the classics.

School (*ch=k*) [O.E. *scōl*; L. *schola*, school; Gk. *scholē*, rest, leisure, a school], place for instruction, body of scholars, group devoted to a principle, etc.; to train. [shoal.

School [Du. *school*; doublet of **Shoal**],

Schoon′er (*ch=k*) [orig. *scooner*, perh. fr. Scot. *scun*, *scoon*, to glide swiftly], small vessel rigged fore and aft.

Schot′tische (*shot′tish* or *shotteesh′*) [Ger. *schottisch*, Scottish], kind of dance.

Sci-at′ic [L. *sciaticus*; Gk. *ischiadicos*, subject to loin pain; *is-chion*, socket of thigh-bone], pertaining to the hip-joint.

Sci-at′i-ca, neuralgia in the thigh.

Sci′ence [L. *scientia*, knowledge; *scīre*, to know], systematized knowledge, branch of systematized knowledge.

Sci-en-tif′ic [Science and L. *facere*, to make], pertaining to or agreeing with science.

Scim′e-tar, Scim′i-tar [It. *scimitarra*; perh. fr. Pers. *shamshīr*, a scimitar], Eastern curved sword.

Scin′til-late [L. *scintilla*, a spark], send out sparks. **Scintilla′tion.**

Sci′o-list [L.L. *sciolus*, a smatterer: *scīre*, to know], smatterer.

Sci′on [O.F. *cion*, a scion, a shoot; etym. doubtful], shoot or sprout, descendant.

Scir′r′us (*sci=si* or *ski*) [Gk. *sciros*, hard], hard swelling.

Scis′sion [L. *scindere* (p.p. *scissus*), to cut], act of cutting.

Scis′sors [O.F. *cisoires*; *cisel*, (pl.) *ciseaux*, a chisel], two small blades on a central pin.

Scoff [M.E. *scof*, *skof*; etym. doubtful], a sneer; to mock, sneer.

Scold [cf. Du. *schelden*; Ger. *schelten*; perh. O.N. *skald*, poet (one who writes lampoons?)], rebuke noisily; scolding person.

Scol′lop, see **Scallop.**

Sconce [L. *absconsa*, var. of *abscondita*, fem. p.p. of *abscondere*, to hide], fort; (colloq.) top of head, candle-socket, projecting candle-stick.

Scone (*ŏ*) [Sc. perh. from M. Du. *schoonbrot*, fine bread], soft cake of flour or meal usually cooked on a griddle.

Scoop [M.L.G. *schōpe*; Swed. *skopa*, a scoop], ladle, deep shovel; to ladle out, dig out.

Scope [Gk. *scopos*, mark to shoot at, watcher; *scopein*, to look], range of view or action.

Scor-bu′tic [L. *scorbūtus*, scurvy], afflicted with scurvy.

Scorch [L. *ex*, off, *cortex* (*cortic-is*), bark], burn on the surface, parch, go very quickly (slang, used of cyclists and motorists).

Score [O.N. *skor*, a cut, twenty], scratched line, account, twenty, number of points gained, musical parts written one above another; to notch, mark, make points, succeed.

Sco′ri-a [L. and Gk. *scōria*, refuse], slag, rough sponge-like masses of cooled lava.

Scorn [O.F. *escorner*, to scorn, orig. to dishorn; prob. of Teut. origin], lofty contempt; despise, disdain. **Scorn′ful.**

Scor′pi-on [L. *scorpio*, a scorpion], animal with lobster-like claws and jointed tail with sting at the end.

Scotch [perh. var. of **Score**], gash.

Scot′ti-cism, idiom peculiar to the Scots.

Scot′-free [O.E. *sc(e)ot*, fr. O.N. *skot*, a payment, and **Free**], untaxed, unhurt.

Scoun′drel [orig. obscure], rascal.

Scour[1] [L. *ex*, very, *curāre*, to take care of], clean or brighten by rubbing, clear out (a channel, etc.).

Scour[2] [orig. obscure], run swiftly, esp. in search.

Scourge [M. It. *scoriāre*, to whip; L. *excoriāre*, to flay], a whip; to lash.

Scout [O.F. *escouter*, to listen], one sent out to observe and bring in tidings; act as a scout.

Scout [cf. O.N. *skúta*, a taunt; *skióta*, to shoot], reject with contempt.

Scowl [Prob. Scand.; cf. Dan. *skule*, to scowl], look sullen; a frown.

Scrag'gy [Fr. obs. *crag*, neck; cf. Du. *kraag*; Ger. *kragen*], lean and bony. **Scragg'iness.**

Scram'ble [orig. obscure; perh. var. of *scrabble*, a freq. of **Scrape**], clamber on all-fours, struggle with others (for); act of scrambling.

Scrap [O.N. *skrap*, scraps, lit. scrapings], fragment. **Scrap'py.**

Scrape [O.E. *scrapian*; O.N. *skrapa*, to scrape], grate harshly over, gather in small portions; act of scraping, a fix.

Scratch [etym. dub.; perh. a confusion of obs. *Scrat* and *Cratch*], mark with something sharp, withdraw from a competition; slight wound, one with the heaviest handicap; collected haphazard.

Scrawl [perh. contraction of *scrabble*, to scrawl], write carelessly; inelegant writing.

Scream [Early M.E. *scrœmen*, *screamen*], utter a sharp cry; shrill cry.

Screech [modification of imitative *Scritch*], scream harshly; harsh shrill cry.

Screed [var. of **Shred**], piece torn off, long tiresome utterance.

Screen [M.E. *skre(e)ne*; etym. doubtful; conn. with O.F. *escren*, a screen], something which conceals or protects; protect, shelter or hide.

Screw [O.F. *escro(u)e*, screw. Etym. doubtful], spirally grooved nail or cylinder, ship's propeller, miserly person, unsound horse; turn as a screw, twist, oppress.

Scrib'ble [L. *scrībere*, to write], write without care or grace.

Scribe [L. *scrībere*, to write], writer, Jewish doctor of the law. [*sterers.*

Scrim [?], cloth used for lining by uphol-

Scrim'mage [var. of **Skirmish**], confused fight.

Scrimp [etym. doubtful; cf. Sw., Dan. *skrumpen*, shrivelled; remotely allied to O.E. *scrimman*, to be paralysed], scanty; allow too little.

Scrip [O.F. *escrepe*, wallet, purse; etym. doubtful], small bag, pilgrim's wallet.

Scrip [short for **Script**], certificate of stock.

Script [O.F. *escript*; L. *scrībere* (p.p. *scriptus*), to write], written characters.

Scrip'ture [L. *scrībere* (p.p. *scriptus*), to write], the Bible. **Scrip'tural.**

Scriv'en-er [O.F. *escrivain*, L.L. *scrībānus*, scrivener], professional writer, notary.

Scrof'u-la [L. *scrōfula*, a scrofulous swelling, orig. a little pig; *scrōfa*, a sow], disease affecting glands of the neck. **Scrof'ulous.**

Scroll [earlier form *Scrow*; A.F. *escrowe*, a scroll; cf. M. Du. *schrōde*, a strip], roll of paper or parchment, ornament like this.

Scrub [var. of **Shrub**], brushwood, stunted tree, breed of small cattle, insignificant person.

Scrub [Dan. *skrubbe*, brushwood; etym. doubtful], rub hard, scour; a scrubbing.

Scruff [var. of **Scuff**; etym. doubtful], nape (colloquial).

Scrunch, see **Crunch**.

Scru'ple [L. *scrūpulus*, dim. of *scrūpus*, a small pebble], 20 grains, doubt; hesitate for conscientious reasons.

Scru'pu-lous, exact, conscientious.

Scru'tin-eer [see **Scrutiny**], examiner of ballot-papers.

Scru'ti-nize, regard narrowly.

Scru'ti-ny [L. *scrūtārī*, to search; *scrūta* (pl.), broken pieces], close examination.

Scud [?], loose, flying clouds or spray; move swiftly.

Scuf'fle [Swed. *skuffa*, to push], struggle confusedly; rough struggle.

Scull [?], short oar, oar at the stern.

Scul'ler-y [O.F. *escuelerie*, office of keeping the dishes; *escuelle*, a dish], back kitchen.

Scul'lion [perh. alteration of F. *souillon*, a scullion], servant who cleans pots, etc.

Sculp'tor, one who carves works of art.

Sculp'ture [L. *sculpere* (p.p. *sculptus*), to cut], art of carving in stone, etc., piece of sculpture.

Scum [Dan. and Swed. *skum*, froth], surface froth or impurity.

Scup'per [Perh. fr. O.F. *escope*; Swed. *scopa*, to scoop; etym. uncert.], hole in a ship level with deck for letting off water.

Scurf [O.E. *scurf*; cf. Swed. *skorf*; Dan. *skurv*, scurf], dry scales on the skin.

Scur'rile, **Scur'ri-lous** [L. *scurrīlis*; *scurra*, a buffoon], coarse (language, etc.).

Scur'ry [see **Scour**[2]], run in a hurry.

Scur'vily, shabbily, meanly.

Scur'vy [see **Scurf**], disease due to excessively salted food.

Scut [Etym. dub.], short erect tail.

Scut'age (*u=oo*) [L. *scutagium*, fr. *scutum*, shield], shield-money paid to king in lieu of personal service.

Scutch'eon (*eon=n*), short for **Escutcheon.**

Scut'tle [O.E. *scutel*, a dish; L. *scutella*, a small tray; *scutra*, a tray], coal-box.

Scut'tle [freq. of **Scud**], bustle, hurry along.

Scut'tle [O.F. *escoutille*; Sp. *escotilla*, hatchway], opening with lid in ship's deck, etc.; make holes in the bottom of a ship.

Scythe [O.E. *sithe*], instrument for mowing.

Sea [O.E. *sǣ*; cf. Du. *zee*; Ger. *see*], whole body of salt water, body of water less than an ocean, inland body of water, esp. if salt, rough weather.

Sea'board, **Sea-coast'**, land next the sea.

Sea'far-ing, employed as a sailor

Seal [O.F. *seel*; L. *sigillum*, a seal; dim. of *signum*, a mark], stamp for making an impression, the impression made; set a a seal to, shut close.

Seal [O.E. *seolh*; cf. O.N. *selr*], sea-animal that feeds on fish.

Seam [O.E. *séam*, cogn. with Sew], line of junction of two edges sewn together, joint, thin layer.

Seam'stress, **Semp'stress**, needlewoman.

Sear [O.E. *séar*], burn to dryness, wither; withered.

Search [L. *circāre*, to go round; *circus*, a ring], seek, look through; act of searching or seeking.

Sea'son (*son=zon*) [O.F. *seson, seison*, season; Late L. *satio*, sowing-time], division of the year, suitable time, time; bring into condition by exposure, time, etc.; to spice.

Sea'son-a-ble, timely.

Sea'son-ing, salt, spices, etc.

Seat [O.N. *sæti*; cogn. with Sit], something to sit on, abode; to place on a seat, afford seats for.

Sea'-ur'chin, spiny sea-animal.

Se'cant [L. *secāre* (pr.p. *secans, -antis*), to cut], cutting, term in mathematics.

Se-cede' [L. *sē-*, aside, *cēdere* (p.p. *cessus*), to go], withdraw from. **Seced'er.**

Se-ces'sion, withdrawal.

Se-clude' [L. *sē-*, apart, *claudere* (p.p. *clausus*), to shut], withdraw into or place in solitude.

Se-clu'sion, retirement.

Sec'ond [L. *secundus*, second; *sequi*, to follow], next to first, another, one next first, backer, sixtieth part of a minute; to support. [advanced.

Sec'ond-a-ry, of second place, (education)

Se'cre-cy, privacy, keeping of secrets.

Se'cret [L. *sē-*, apart, *cernere* (p.p. *crētus*), to separate], hidden; something concealed.

Sec-re-ta'ri-al, pertaining to a secretary.

Sec're-ta-ry [Late L. *sēcrētārius*, a confidential officer; L. *sēcrētus*, secret], one who attends to correspondence, minister of state.

Se-crete', hide, produce by secretion.

Se-cre'tion, concealment, the process of separating substance from blood or sap, also one of the substances.

Se-cre'tive, **Se'cret-ive**, tending to secrete or to keep secret.

Sect [L. *secta*, a set of people, a suit; perh. fr. *sequi* (p.p. *secūtus*), to follow], body of persons attached to the same opinion.

Sec-ta'ri-an, pertaining to a sect, too much attached to a sect. **Secta'rianism.**

Sec'tion [L. *secāre* (p.p. *sectus*), to cut], separation by cutting, a distinct part. **Sec'tional.**

Sec'tor, part of a circle between radii.

Sec'u-lar [L. *sæculum*, a generation, an age], pertaining to worldly things, lasting for, occurring once in, an age. **Sec'ularism.**

Se-cure' [L. *sē-*, apart, *cūra*, care], sure, safe; make safe, get possession of.

Se-cu'ri-ty, freedom from care, safety.

Se-dan' [fr. *Sedan* in France], portable chair on poles.

Se-date' [L. *sēdāre* (p.p. *sēdātus*), to settle; *sedēre*, to sit], calm, composed.

Sed'a-tive, soothing remedy.

Sed'en-ta-ry [L. *sedēre* (pr.p. *sedens, -entis*), to sit], requiring much sitting.

Sed-e'runt [L.=they have sat down], sitting or duration of meeting of a board or committee. [plant.

Sedge [O.E. *secg*; cogn. with Saw [1], marsh

Sed'i-ment [L. *sedimentum*, sediment; *sedēre*, to sit], dregs, deposit.

Se-di'tion (*ĭ*) [L. *sed-* (*sē-*), apart, *īre* (p.p. *it-us*), to go], agitation against the law, conduct tending to rebellion. **Sedi'tious.**

Se-duce' [L. *sē-*, aside, *dūcere* (p.p. *ductus*), to lead], lead astray.

Se-duc'tive, tempting. **Seduc'tion.**

Sed'u-lous [L. *sēdulus*, careful; cf. L. *sēdulo*, sincerely], steadily industrious.

See [O.E. *séon*; cf. Ger. *sehen*], perceive by the eye, understand.

See [L. *sēdes*, a seat], seat or jurisdiction of an archbishop or a bishop.

Seed [O.E. *sǣd*; cogn. with Sow], that from which a plant grows, origin, offspring. **Seed'ling.**

Seed'y, full of seeds, shabby, worn-out.

Seek [O.E. *sécan*; Com. Teut.], try to find, look for.

Seem [O.E. *séman*, to make agree; cogn. with Same], look, appear.

Seem'ly [O.N. *sœmiligr*, seemly; fr. *sœmr*, becoming], suitable, becoming.

Seer, person with unusual insight, esp. as regards the future, prophet.

See'saw [redupl. of Saw], plank balanced to move up and down; move up and down.

Seethe [O.E. *séothan*], boil, surge or foam up, to be in a state of inward turmoil.

Seg'ment [L. *segmentum*; *secāre*, to cut], part cut off, section.

Seg're-gate [L. *sē-*, apart, *grex* (*greg-is*), a flock], set apart. **Segrega'tion.**

Seig-neur' (*sain-yer'*), **Seig'nior** (*seen'yor*), [O.F. fr. L.; see Senior], lord of manor, landholder. **Seignior'ial.**

Seine (*sain*) [O.E. *segne*; L. *sagēna*; Gk. *sagēnē*, a seine], fishing-net made to hang vertically.

Seis-mol'o-gy (*seis=sīz*) [Gk. *seismos*, an earthquake; *logos* discourse], science of earthquakes.

Seize [O.F. *seisir*; Late L. *sacīre*, take possession of], lay hold of.

Sei'zure (*z=zh*), act of seizing; *med.* shock.

Sel'dom [O.E. *seldan, seldon, seldum* (dative pl. of *seld*, rare)], rarely, not often.

Se-lect' [L. *sē-*, apart, and *legere* (p.p. *lectus*), to choose], picked out, of special value; choose from a number.

Se-lec'tion, choice, things chosen.

Self [O.E. *self*; Com. Teut.], one's own person, one's own. As a prefix *self* expresses reflexive action.

Self-de-ni'al, forbearance from gratifying self.

Self-ev'i-dent, evident without proof.

Self-im-por'tant, conceited, pompous.

Self'ish, caring unduly for one's self.

Self-pos-sessed', calm and cool. [goodness.

Self-right'eous, pleased with one's own

Self-will', obstinacy.

Sell [O.E. *sellan*, to hand over; Com. Teut.], give for money. Sell'er.

Sel'vage, Sel'vedge (M. Du. *self*, self, *egge*, edge], edge of cloth woven firmly.

Sem'a-phore [Gk. *sēma*, a sign; *pherein*, to bear], signalling apparatus.

Sem'blance [F. *sembler*, to seem; L. *simulāre*, to simulate], likeness, show.

Sem'i-breve [L. *sēmi-*, half, *brevis*, short], a note in music having half the length of a breve, longest note in ordinary use.

Sem'i-cir-cle [L. *sēmi-*, half, and Circle], half of a circle. Semi-cir'cular.

Sem'i-co'lon [L. *sēmi-*, half, and Colon], punctuation mark [;].

Sem'in-al [L. *seminalis*, fr. *sēmen*, seed], germinal, bringing forth fruits.

Sem'i-na-ry [L. *sēminārium*, a seed-plot; *sēmen*, a seed], place of education.

Sem'i-qua'ver [L. *sēmi-*, half, and Quaver], note in music having half the length of a quaver.

Sem'i-tone [L. *sēmi-*, half, and Tone], an interval approximately equal to half a tone (music).

Sem-o-li'na [It. *semolino*, dim. of *semola*, bran; L. *simila*, fine flour], hard grains left after sifting flour.

Sem'pi-ter'nal [L. *semper*, always; *æternus*, eternal], without end.

Semp'stress [as Seamstress], seamstress.

Sen'ate [L. *senātus*, senate; *senex*, old], legislative body, state council.

Sen'a-tor, member of a senate. Senator'ial.

Send [O.E. *sendan*], bid go, cause to go, grant.

Sen'esch-al [O.F. *seneschal*, orig. "old servant"; cogn. with L. *senex*, old], steward.

Se'nile [L. *senīlis*, senile; *senex*, old], pertaining to old age. Senil'ity.

Se'nior [L. *senior*, comp. of *senex*, old], elder, superior; one who is older than another. Senior'ity.

Sen'na [Mod. L. *senna*, *sena*; Arab. *sanā*, senna], medicinal leaves of a plant.

Sen-sa'tion [see Sense], impression through the senses, excitement, exciting event. Sensa'tional.

Sense [L. *sentīre* (p.p. *sensus*), to feel], faculty of perceiving by certain organs, understanding, meaning, what is reasonable.

Sen-si-bil'i-ty [L. *sensus*, felt], capacity to feel, delicacy of feeling.

Sen'si-ble [L. *sensus*, felt], perceptible, perceiving, possessed of sound judgment, reasonable. [affected.

Sen'si-tive [see Sense], quick to feel or be

Sen'si-tize [see Sense], make sensitive.

Sen'so-ry [see Sense], pertaining to sensation.

Sen'su-al [see Sense], pertaining to or derived from sense and appetite. Sen'suality.

Sen'su-ous [see Sense], pertaining to or pleasing to the senses. Sen'suousness.

Sen'tence [L. *sentīre*, to feel], judgment, combination of words containing sense in complete form; pronounce judgment upon. [formal.

Sen-ten'tious (*ti=sh*), pithy, affectedly

Sen'tient (*ti=sh*) [L. *sentiens* (*-entis*), pr.p. of *sentīre*, to feel], having sense-perception.

Sen'ti-ment [L. *sentīre*, to feel], opinion, tenderness of feeling, an emotion, emotional view.

Sen-ti-ment'al [see Sentiment], possessing too much sentiment, mawkishly tender.

Sen'ti-nel [F. *sentinelle*], soldier on guard.

Sent'ry [perh. shortened form of *centrinel*, *centronel*, var. of Sentinel], soldier on guard.

Sep'al [Assim. of L. *separ*, separate, to termination of Petal], calyx-leaf.

Sep'a-rate [L. *sē-*, apart, *parāre* (p.p. *parātus*), to get ready], divide, set apart; distinct.

Sep-a-ra'tion, act of separating, disunion.

Se'pi-a [L. and Gk. *sēpia*, sepia], cuttlefish, brown pigment from its secretion.

So'poy [Hind. *sipāhī*; Pers. *sipāhī*, a soldier], Indian soldier serving in British Army.

Sep-tem'ber [L. *septem*, seven], the ninth month (Rom. seventh).

Sep-ten'ni-al [L. *septem*, seven, and *annus*, a year], lasting seven years, once in seven years.

Sep'tic [Gk. *sēpein*, to make putrid], having power to promote putrefaction.

Sep'tu-ple [L. *septem*, seven, and *-plus* (allied to *plēnus*, full], sevenfold.

Sep'ul-chre (*ch=k*) [O.F. *sepulcre*; L. *sepulcrum*, fr. *sepelīre* (p.p. *sepultus*), to bury], a grave, tomb.

Se-pul'chral, pertaining to burial, hollow.

Sep'ul-ture [L. *sepelīre* (p.p. *sepultus*), to bury], burial.

Se'quel [L. *sequī*, to follow], that which follows, continuation.

Se'quence [L. *sequī*, to follow], succession, order of following.

Se-ques'ter, Se-ques'trate [L. *sequester*, a trustee; perh. fr. *sequī*, to follow], seize and hold till claims are paid. Sequestra'tion.

Se-ques'tered, secluded.

Se'quin [It. *zecchino*, fr. *zecca*, the mint; Arab. *sikka*, a die], old gold coin of Italy and Turkey, coinlike ornament.

Ser-ag'lio (*sĕr-ahl'yō*) [It. *serraglio*, an enclosure; L. *sera*, a bolt], walled palace, esp. of Sultan, containing harem.

Ser'aph [Heb. *serāphīm*, seraphs, exalted ones; cf. Arab. *sharīf*, high], one of a class of angels (*pl.* -im, -s). Sera'phic.

Sere, Sear [O.E. *sēar*], withered.

Ser-e-nade' [It. *serenata*, fr. L. *serēnus*, clear, bright], music at night in the open air, esp. under a lady's window; perform a serenade.

Se-rene' [L. *serēnus*, bright, clear], calm. Seren'ity.

Serf [L. *servus*, a slave], worker whose service is attached to the soil. **Serf′dom.**

Serge [O.F. *serge*; L. *sericus*, silken; Gk. *Sēres*, the Chinese], woollen twilled stuff.

Ser′geant, Ser′jeant (*sar′jent*) [O.F. *sergent, serjant*; Late L. *serviens* (*servient-is*), an officer; orig. pr.p. of *servīre*, to serve], formerly lawyer of high rank (in this sense now always *serjeant*), non-commissioned officer.

Se′ri-al, pertaining to a series; story published in parts.

Ser-i-a′tim (*ē* or *ee*) [M.L. *seriatus*, in order, fr. *seriēs*, a row], point by point.

Ser-i-cul′ture, Ser′i-ci-cul-ture [L. *sēricum*, silk; *cultūra*, culture], breeding of silkworms.

Se′ries [L. *seriēs*, a row; *serere*, to join], succession of things.

Se′ri-ous [L. *sērius*, serious], grave, weighty.

Ser′io-com′ic, combining the serious and the comic.

Ser′mon [L. *sermo* (*sermōn-is*), a speech], discourse, esp. on Scripture. **Ser′monize.**

Ser′pent [L. *serpens* (*-entis*), serpent; *serpere*, to creep], reptile without limbs.

Ser′pent-ine, like a serpent; to move like a serpent, to wind.

Ser′rate, Ser-ra′ted [L. *serrātus*, notched; *serra*, a saw], notched.

Ser′ried [F. *serrer*, to press close; L.L. *serāre*, to bolt], in close order, compact.

Se′rum [L. *serum*, whey, serum], watery part of blood.

Ser′vant [O.F. *servir* (pr.p. *servant*), to serve], one who serves.

Serve [L. *servīre*, to serve; *servus*, a slave], work for, be a hired assistant, help, supply the wants of.

Serv′ice (*ice*=*iss*), act of serving, occupation of a hired servant, branch of public employment, esp. military or naval duty, liturgy, set of plates, etc.

Serv′ice [M.E. *serve*, O.E. *syrfe*; L. *sorbus*, service-tree], European tree, bearing small round or pear-shaped fruit edible when over-ripe.

Serv′ice-a-ble, doing service, useful.

Ser-vi-et′te [F.], table napkin.

Serv′ile [L. *servilis*, fr. *servus*, a slave], befitting a slave, cringing. **Servil′ity.**

Serv′i-tor, servant, attendant.

Serv′i-tude, slavery, bondage.

Ses′a-me [Gk. *sēsamē*], Eastern herbaceous plant, also its seeds, mysterious password in Arabian Nights tale.

Ses′sion [L. *sedēre* (sup. *sessum*), to sit], sitting of a court, etc., period during which Parliament sits, schools, colleges are open.

Set[1] [O.E. *settan*; Com. Teut., causal of *sittan*, to sit], place, fix, indicate the position of game, sink out of sight (of the sun), (with *out*) start; rigid; turn, descent.

Set[2] [Late L. *secta*, set of people], group.

Set-tee′ [var. of Settle[1]], long seat with a back.

Set′ter, dog which sets game.

Set′tle[1] [O.E. *setl*, cogn. with Sit and Set[1]], bench with a high back.

Set′tle[2] [O.E. *setlan* (see Settle[1]), to settle, and perh. *sahtlian*, to reconcile], establish, compose, decide, come to rest.

Set′tle-ment, act of settling, occupation by colonists, irrevocable deed disposing of property. **Sett′ler.**

Sev′en [O.E. *seofon*], one more than six.

Sev-en-teen′ [Seven and Ten], number made up of seven added to ten. [ten.

Sev′en-ty [Seven and suf.-*ty*, tens], seven times

Sev′er [O.F. *sevrer*; L. *sēparāre*, to separate], divide, part.

Sev′er-al [A.F. *several*; Med. L. *separalis*, fr. L. *sēparāre*; see Separate], not many but more than two, separate. **Sev′erally.**

Sev′er-ance, separation.

Se-vere′ [L. *sevērus*, grave], strict, stern.

Se-ver′i-ty, harshness, gravity.

Sew (*ew*=*ō*) [O.E. *siwian*; Com. Teut.], unite by stitches.

Sew′er (*ew*=*ū*) [O.F. *seuviere*, a sluice; L. *ex*, out, *aqua*, water], underground drain.

Sex [F. *sexe*; L. *sexus*, sex], condition of being male or female, males or females collectively.

Sex′tain [L. *sextus*, sixth], stanza of six lines.

Sex′tant [L. *sextans* (*-antis*), a sixth part of an as (a coin); *sex*, six], sixth part of a circle, instrument for measuring the angular distance of objects.

Sex′ton [M.E. *sekesteyn*, corruption of *Sacristan*], parochial officer who performs duties pertaining to a church.

Sex′tu-ple [L. *sextus*, sixth; suf. -*ple*, ult. fr. *plicāre*, to fold], sixfold.

Sex′u-al, based upon sex. [Shab′biness.

Shab′by [O.E. *sceabb*, a scab], worn, mean.

Shac′kle [O.E. *sceacul*, a loose fetter; see Shake], a fetter; to fetter, chain.

Shade [O.E. *scœd, sceadu*; cogn. with Sky], place not exposed to light, screen, ghost, degree of colour; to screen, mark with gradation of colour.

Shad′ow [O.E. *sceadu*; see Shade], figure projected by a body intercepting light, indistinct image; set (forth) dimly, darken, follow closely.

Shad′ow-y, dim.

Sha′dy, affording shade, of doubtful honesty.

Shaft [O.E. *sceaft*; Com. Teut., a spear-shaft], arrow, column, pole, well-like opening in the ground.

Shag [O.E. *sceacga*; cf. O.N. *skegg*, a beard], rough growth of hair, coarse kind of cut tobacco, cloth with long nap.

Shag′gy, rough with long hair or wool.

Sha-green′ [var. of Chagrin], leather made from skin of sharks, etc.; rough-grained leather made from skin of horses, etc.

Shah [Pers. *shāh*, a king], supreme ruler of Persia.

Shake [O.E. *sceacan*; cf. O.N. and Swed. *skaka*, to shake], move rapidly one way and the other, move from firmness; trembling, act of shaking, a trill (music).

Shak'o [Hung. *csákó*, a cap], kind of military cap.

Sha'ky, trembling.

Shale [O.E. *scealu*; cogn. with O.N. *skál*], fine-grained rock that splits into plates.

Shal-lot', Shal-ot' [L. *ascalōnia*, a shallot; *Ascalōnius*, belonging to *Ascalon*], kind of onion native in Syria.

Shal'low [M.E. *schalowe*; prob. cogn. with **Shoal**], not deep; a shallow place.

Sham [perh. var. of **Shame**], imposture, humbug; feign.

Sham'ble [O. Du. *schampelen*, to stumble; O.F. *escamper*; L. *ex*, out, *campus*, a field; cf. **Scamper**], shuffle along.

Sham'bles [pl. of obs. *shamble*, a butcher's stall; O.E. *scamel*; L. *scamellum*, a stool], slaughter-house.

Shame [O.E. *sc(e)amu*; Com. Teut.], sensation caused by disgrace, etc., disgrace; make ashamed. **Shame'faced.**

Sham'my, Sham'oy [orig. *Chamois* leather], soft leather.

Sham-poo' [Hind. *chāmpnā*, press, shampoo], lather, wash or rub the hair, massage.

Sham'rock [Ir. *seamrog*, trefoil], trefoil plant.

Shank [O.E. *sc(e)anca*; cogn. with **Shake**], leg, shin, a stem.

Shan'ty [?], hut.

Shape [O.E. *scieppan*, to shape; Com. Teut.], to form; form, figure, mould.

Shape'ly, well-formed.

Shard, Sherd [O E. *sceard*, a fragment], fragment, wing-case of a beetle.

Share [O.E. *scear*, a ploughshare; *sceran*, to shear], cutting part of a plough.

Share [O.E. *scearu*, a share; *sceran*, to shear], portion; divide, take part in.

Shark [perh. fr. L. *carcharus*; Gk. *charcharias*, a kind of shark, fr. *charcharos*, jagged (fr. its teeth)], large fish dangerous to man; a swindler.

Sharp [OE. *scearp*; Com. Teut.], having a thin edge or fine point; sign in music ♯. **Sharp'en.** [pieces.

Shat'ter [var. of **Scatter**], break into many

Shave [O.E. *sc(e)afan*; Com. Teut.], cut off hair with a razor; narrow escape.

Sha'ving, thin slice of wood, etc., pared off.

Shawl [Pers. *shāl*, a shawl], loose shoulder-covering.

Sheaf [O.E. *scēaf*; Com. Teut.], bundle, esp. of corn-stalks.

Shear [O.E. *sceran*; Com. Teut.], cut or clip; (n. pl.) two-bladed cutting instrument.

Sheath [O.E. *scǣth*; cogn. with **Shed** [2]], case for a sharp instrument.

Sheathe, put into a sheath.

Shed [1] [var. of **Shade**], slight building.

Shed [2] [O.E. *sc(e)ādan*, to part; Com. Teut.], pour forth, give off; a parting.

She-been' [Ir. *shebeen*, a pot-house], unlicensed house selling alcoholic drink; to sell drink without a licence. **Shebeen'ing.**

Sheen [fr. obs. *sheen*, beautiful; fr. O.E. *sciene*, Ger. *schön* (meaning, but not etym., conn. with **Shine**)], brightness, glitter.

Sheep [O.E. *scēap*; cf. Du. *schaap*; Ger. *schaf*], woolly ruminant animal.

Sheep'ish, bashful.

Sheer [O.N. *skœrr*, bright; *skina*, to shine], unmixed, downright.

Sheer [prob. a use of **Shear**], abrupt change in a ship's course; turn aside, swerve.

Sheet [O.E. *sciete*, *scȳte*, linen cloth, and *scēat*, a corner, all cogn. with **Shoot**], large, broad piece of anything thin, expanse; rope which fastens a sail.

Sheik, Sheikh (*ei=ee* or *ai*) [Arab. *shaikh*, an elder, chief], Arab chief.

Shek'el [Heb. *shegel*, a shekel; *shāqal*, to weigh], ancient Babylonian and Jewish weight and coin.

Shel'drake [**Shield** and **Drake**], kind of spotted wild drake.

Shelf [prob. fr. (M.)L.G. *schelf*, shelf], flat tablet or ledge.

Shell [O.E. *sciell*, *scill*; cogn. with **Scale** [2]], hard covering, hollow projectile; strip off or take out of the shell, throw shells or bombs into. **Shell-shock.**

Shelter [perh. from **Shield** + *-ture*], protection, refuge; give or take shelter.

Shelve [see **Shelf**], furnish with shelves, to set aside, defer.

Shelve [?], to slope gradually.

Shep'herd, one who tends sheep.

Sher'bet [Arab. *sharbat*, beverage, syrup], drink of fruit-juice and sweetened water.

Sher'iff [O.E. *scír-gerēfa*; *scír*, a shire, *gerēfa*, an officer], county, city, and borough officer with duties now mainly nominal, (in Scotland) a local judge.

Sher'ry [formerly *sherris*; fr. *Xeres*, a town in Spain], a white Spanish wine.

Shew, same as **Show**.

Shib'bo-leth [Heb.], a test-word used by a sect, etc., old-fashioned doctrine.

Shield [O.E. *sceld*; Com. Teut.], broad piece of defensive armour, protection; to protect.

Shift [O.E. *sciftan*, to divide; cf. Du. *schiften*, O.N. *skipta*, to divide], to change; change, relay of workmen, also their time of working, undergarment, trick.

Shift'less, destitute of expedients, lazy.

Shift'y, ready with expedients. **Shif'tiness.**

Shil-la'lah, Shil-le'lah, Shil-le'lagh (*e=ai*) [fr. *Shillelagh* in Ireland], Irishman's cudgel.

Shil'ling [O.E. *scilling*; Com. Teut.], silver coin equal to 12 pence.

Shilly-shally [orig. *Shill I*, *shall I*, altered form of *Shall I*, *shall I*], to be undecided, vacillate.

Shim'mer [O.E. *scymrian*, fr. *sciman*, to shine; cf. Ger. *schimmern*], to gleam tremulous light.

Shin [O.E. *scinu*; West Fris. *skine*; (M.)L.G. *schēne*; O.H.G. *scina*; perh. cogn. with **Skin**], front leg below the knee.

Shine [O.E. *scinan*; Com. Teut.; cf. Ger. *scheinen*], give light, be bright. **Shi'ny.**

Shin'gle [perh. fr. Norw. *singl*, coarse gravel], loose pebbles.

Shin'gle [L. *scindula*, later form of *scandula*, a shingle], flat piece of wood used in roofing.

Shin'gle [?], mode of dressing short hair.

Shin'gles [L. *cingula*, a belt; *cingere*, to gird], a skin disease.

Shin'ty [?], Scottish game like hockey.

Ship [O.E. *scip*; Com. Teut.], sea-going vessel; send by sea, take aboard, embark.

Ship'ping, all the ships of a place.

Ship'shape, orderly.

Shire [O.E. *scír*, business, province], county.

Shirk [prob. var. of **Shark**], evade, neglect.

Shirt [O.E. *scyrte*; doublet of **Skirt**], man's under-garment.

Shiv'er [dim. of obs. *shive*, a slice], splinter; shatter.

Shiv'er [M.E. *chiveren*], tremble as from cold.

Shoal [var. of **Shallow**], shallow, sandbank.

Shoal [O.E. *scolu*, a troop], multitude of fishes, crowd.

Shock [F. *choc*], sudden violent onset; stun, strike with horror.

Shock [cf. O. Du. *schocke*; Swed. *skock*, a heap; prob. cogn. with **Shake**], group of sheaves set on end.

Shock [perh. var. of **Shag**], mass of hair.

Shock'ing, extremely offensive.

Shod'dy [etym. doubtful], fabric made of woollen cuttings; worthless.

Shoe (*oe*=*oo*) [O.E. *scóh*; Com. Teut.], covering for the foot; furnish with shoes.

Shoot [O.E. *scéotan*, to shoot (intrs.); Com. Teut.; cf. Ger. *schiessen*], let fly, discharge a missile, pass rapidly through, over, or under, sprout; a rapid, young branch.

Shop [O.E. *sceoppa*, a stall, booth], place for retail selling, building where artisans work; buy in shops.

Shop'lift'ing, theft from a shop. [lake.

Shore [M.E. *schore*], land adjoining sea or

Shore [M.E. *schore*; cf. O.N. *skortha*; M. Du. *schóre*, a prop], prop; to prop or support.

Short [O.E. *sceort*], not long in space or time, scanty; (n. pl.) short breeches. **Short'en.**

Short'age, amount of deficiency.

Short'hand, short method of writing.

Short'ly, in few words, before long.

Shot [O.E. *gesceot* (p.p.s.), fr. *scéotgn*, to shoot], variegated; projectile from a fire-arm, flight of a missile, marksman.

Shoul'der (*ou*=*ō*) [O.E. *sculder*; cf. Ger. *schulter*], region of the joint which connects arm and body; jostle.

Shout [?], call out; loud cry.

Shove (*ove*=*ŭv*) [O.E. *scúfan*; cf. Du. *schuiven*; Ger. *schieben*], push.

Shov'el (*o*=*ŭ*) [O.E. *scofl*; see **Shove**], scoop with a handle; take up with a shovel.

Show [O.E. *scéawian*, to see, to cause to see], to exhibit, make clear; exhibition, appearance, display.

Show'er [O.E. *scúr*; cf. Du. *schoer*; O.N. *skúr*], short fall of rain, snow, or hail; to fall or pour in a shower.

Show'y, making a show, gaudy.

Shrap'nel [fr. General *Shrapnel*], kind of explosive shell.

Shred [O.E. *scréade*, cogn. with **Shroud**], strip torn off, fragment; cut or tear into small pieces.

Shrew (*ew*=*oo*) [O.E. *scréawa*, a shrew-mouse], a scold, mouse-like animal. **Shrew'ish.**

Shrewd (*ew*=*oo*) [M.E. *schrewed*, p.p. of *schrewen*, to curse], sharp-witted, keen.

Shriek [var. of **Screech**], to scream; piercing scream.

Shrift [O.E. *scrift*, confession; prob. L. *scribere*, to write], confession and absolution.

Shrike [O.E. *scríc*, *scréc*; cogn. with **Shriek**], butcher-bird.

Shrill [M.E. *shrille*; cf. Scot. *skirl*, a shrill sound; L. Ger. *schrell*, shrill], sharp and piercing in tone.

Shrimp [prob. cogn. with M.H.G. *schrimpen*, to shrivel up], small shellfish.

Shrine [L. *scrinium*, a chest], case for relics, holy place.

Shrink [O.E. *scrincan*; cf. M. Du. *schrinken*], to contract, recoil, flinch from. **Shrink'age.**

Shrive [O.E. *scrifan*, to shrive; prob. L. *scribere*, to write], hear confession and give absolution.

Shriv'el [etym. dub.; cf. Swed. dial. *skryvla*, to shrivel], draw or be drawn into wrinkles, wither.

Shroud [O.E. *scrúd*, a garment], dress for the dead; (pl.) set of ropes from mast to ship's side; to dress for the grave, hide, veil.

Shrove'tide [see **Shrive** and **Tide**], the Sunday before Lent and two following days.

Shrub [O.E. *scrybb*], small woody plant.

Shrub [Arab. *shurb*, a drink, cogn. with **Sherbet**], mixture of rum, sugar, and lemon juice.

Shrub'ber-y, ground covered with shrubs.

Shrug [cogn. with **Shrink**; etym. dub.], draw up the shoulders; drawing up of the shoulders.

Shud'der [M.E. *schoderen*; cogn. with M.L.G. *schöderen*; M. Du. *schúderen*], shake with fear or dislike; act of shaking as with fear.

Shuf'fle [var. of **Scuffle**], move in a slovenly way, evade questions, mix (cards); slovenly motion, evasion. **Shuf'fler.**

Shun [O.E. *scunian*; Etym. dub.], avoid.

Shunt [?], turn off to one side. [close.

Shut [O.E. *scyttan*; cogn. with **Shoot**], to shut'ter, movable cover for a window.

Shut'tle [O.E. *scyt(t)el*, a bolt; see **Shut**], instrument used in weaving by which the weft-thread is carried between the threads of the warp.

Shy [O.E. *scéoh*, corresp. to M.H.G. *schiech*], bashful; start through fright; a start aside.

Shy [?], fling; a throw.

Sib'i-lant [L. *sibiláre* (pr.p. *sibilans*, *-antis*), to hiss. Imit.], hissing. **Sib'ilance.**

Sib'yl [L. and Gk. *Sibylla*], inspired prophetess. **Sib'ylline.**

Sick [O.E. *séoc*; Com. Teut.], ill, affected with nausea.

Sic'kle [L. *secula*, a sickle; *secāre*, to cut], reaping-hook.

Sick'ly, ailing, feeble, faint.

Side [O.E. *side*; Com. Teut.], surface of a solid, right or left part of body, party; take part (with).

Side'board, piece of dining-room furniture.

Side'long, oblique, not direct.

Si-de're-al (ĭ) [L. *sīdus* (*sīder-is*), a star], relating to the stars.

Side'ways, Side'wise, to one side.

Si'ding, side-track.

Si'dle (ĭ) [obs. *sideling*, sidelong], move sideways or stealthily.

Siege [O.F. *siege*, a seat, ult. fr. L. *sedes*, a seat], continued attempt to take possession, esp. of a city by an army.

Si-en'na [short for It. *terra di Sienna*, earth of Sienna], reddish-brown earth used as pigment in oil- and water-colour painting.

Si-er'ra [Sp. *sierra*; L. *serra*, a saw], chain of mountains.

Si-es'ta [Sp. *siesta*; L. *sexta* (hora), sixth hour, noon], midday nap.

Sieve [O.E. *sife*; cf. Ger. *sieb*], perforated utensil for sifting.

Sift [O.E. *siftan*, fr. *sife*, a sieve], separate fine from coarse with a sieve, examine minutely.

Sigh [O.E. *sican*; cf. Dan. *sukke*, prob. imit.], take a deep audible breath; act of sighing

Sight (*igh*=ī) [O.E. *gesihth*; cf. Ger. *sicht*], sense of seeing, view, spectacle; get sight of.

Sight'ly (*igh*=ī), pleasing to the sight.

Sign (*ig*=ī) [L. *signum*, a mark], token, mark, omen, gesture, division of the Zodiac; make a sign, write one's name.

Sig'nal [L. *signum*, a sign], sign to convey a message; communicate by signals; outstanding.   **Sig'nally.**

Sig'nal-ize, distinguish.

Sig'na-to-ry [L. *signāre* (p.p. *signātus*), to mark; *signum*, a mark], signing; one who signs.

Sig'na-ture, name signed, key and rhythm sign in music.

Sig'net [F. *signet*, dim. of *signe*; L. *signum*, a mark], small seal.

Sig-nif'i-cance, special importance, expressiveness.

Sig-nif'i-cant, expressive, important.

Sig-ni-fi-ca'tion, meaning.

Sig'ni-fy [L. *signum*, a sign, *facere*, to make], show by a sign, mean.   **Signif'icative.**

Si'lence [L. *silēre* (pr.p. *silens*, *-entis*), to be silent], cessation from speech, complete stillness; make silent, overcome an argument.

Si'lent, perfectly quiet, not talkative.

Sil-hou-ette' [fr. E. de *Silhouette*, a French minister of finance], profile portrait in black; to throw up the outline of.

Sil'i-ca [L. *silex* (*silic-is*), flint], main substance of quartz, flint, etc.   **Sili'cious.**

G *

Silk [O.E. *sioloc, seoloc*; O.N. *silki*; prob. fr. L. *sēricus*, silk; L. *sēres*, the people (perh. the Chinese), from whom silk first came], silkworm thread, also cloth from it.

Sill [O.E. *syll(e)*; cf. O.N. *syll, svill*, Dan. *syld*], wood or stone at the foot of a door or window.

Sil'ly [O.E. *sœlig*; cf. O.H.G. *sâlig*, happy], foolish.

Si'lo [Sp. *silo*; L. *sīrus*; Gk. *siros*], pit for storing fodder.

Silt [Dan. and Norw. *sylt*, salt-marsh], sediment deposited by water; choke or become choked with silt.

Sil'van, Syl'van [L. *silva*, a wood], pertaining to woods.

Sil'ver [O.E. *siolfor, seolfor*], silver. Etym. doubtful], white precious metal.

Sil'ver-smith, worker in silver.

Sim'i-an [L. *simia*, an ape], pertaining to apes, apelike.

Sim'i-lar [L. *similis*, like], like, of the same kind, resembling.

Sim-i-lar'i-ty, likeness.

Sim'i-le [L. neut. of *similis*, like], comparison used to heighten effect.

Sim-il'i-tude, likeness, a simile.

Sim'mer [later form of obs. *simper*], boil gently, to be just below boiling-point.

Sim'nel [O.F. *simenel*; prob. imitative; L. *simila*, fine flour], kind of rich cake eaten on Mid-Lent Sunday.

Sim'o-ny (ĭ or ī) [Late L. *simōnia*; fr. *Simon Magus* (Acts. viii. 18)], buying or selling of ecclesiastical preferments.

Sim-oom' (ĭ) [Arab. *semūm*, simoom; fr. root *samm*, poison], hot desert wind.

Sim'per [cf. Norw. *semper*, elegant; origin difficult to trace], smile affectedly; a smirk.

Sim'ple [L. *simplex* (*simplic-is*), onefold], unmingled, plain, artless; medicinal plant.

Sim'ple-ton, one of weak intellect.

Sim-plic'i-ty, plainness.

Sim'pli-fy, make simple or simpler.   **Sim'-plifica'tion.**

Sim-u-la'crum (*a*=*aī*) (*pl.* -cra) [as **Simulate**], deceptive substitute.

Sim'u-late [L. *similis*, like], assume, pretend.

Sim-ul-ta'ne-ous [L. *simul*, at the same time], happening at the same time.

Sin [O.E. *synn*; cf. Ger. *sünde*], transgression of God's law; do wrong.

Since [O.E. *siththon*, for *sith thon*, after that], from the time of; ago; because.

Sin-cere' [L. *sincērus*, sincere. Etym. doubtful], honest, real.

Sin-cer'i-ty, honesty of mind or intention.

Sine [L. *sinus*, a curve], in trigonometry, the ratio of the side of a right-angled triangle opposite the given angle to the hypotenuse.

Si'ne-cure (ĭ or ī) [L. *sine*, without, *curā*, care (of souls)], office with few or no duties.

Sin'ew [O.E. *sinu*], white tissue joining muscle to bone.

Sing [O.E. *singan*; Com. Teut.], utter musical vocal sounds, celebrate in song or verse.

Singe [O.E. *sencgan*; cogn. with M. Du. *zengen*], burn slightly, esp. on the surface.

Sin'gle [L. *singulus*, single; *singuli* (pl.), one by one], one only, unmarried, sincere; to select; (n. pl.) game at tennis between two. **Sin'gleness**, **Sin'gly**.

Sing'song, monotonous; impromptu concert.

Sin'gu-lar [L. *singuli*, one by one], single,

Sin-gu-lar'i ty, peculiarity. [unusual.

Sin'is-ter [L. *sinister*, on the left hand], on left side of shield, etc., from bearer's point of view (*heraldry*), dark, portending disaster.

Sink [O.E. *sincan*; Com. Teut.], enter deeply, fall lower, bring low; box with a drain.

Sink'er, a weight that causes sinking.

Sin'ner, one who has sinned.

Sin-u-os'i-ty, state of being sinuous, bend.

Sin'u-ous [L. *sinus*, a bend], bending in and out.

Sip [?, prob. conn. with **Sup**], drink in small quantities; taking of a liquid with the lips, a small mouthful.

Si'phon (*i*) [L. *sipho*; Gk. *siphōn*, a tube], bent tube, bottle of lemonade, etc., in which liquid is forced out by pressure through a tube.

Sip'pet [dim. of **Sip**], small piece of bread soaked in liquid, one of the small pieces of toast served with some dishes.

Sir [short for **Sire**], title for a knight or a baronet, respectful form of address to a man.

Sir'dar [Pers. *sardār*, a chief; *sar*, head, and *-dar*, holding], (in India, etc.) military chief, commander-in-chief of the Egyptian army.

Sire [O.F. *sire*; L. *senior*, older], form of address to a king, father.

Si'ren [L. *sīrēn*; Gk. *seirēn*, a siren], monster, half 'oman, half bird, who lured by song, instrument used in fog-signalling.

Sir'loin [O.F. *surlonge*; F. *sur*, upon, *longe*, loin], upper part of loin of beef.

Si-roc'co [It. *sirocco*; Arab. *sharq*, east], hot south wind in Southern Europe.

Sis'kin [M.L.G. *ziseke*; Polish *czyzik*, a siskin], yellowish-green finch.

Sis'ter [Com. Teut.; cogn. with L. *soror*], daughter of same parents as another person, member of a sisterhood.

Sis'ter-hood, relation between sisters, society of women living together under monastic vows or devoted to charitable work.

Sis'ter-in-law, a sister of one's husband or wife, wife of one's brother.

Sit [O.E. *sittan*; Com. Teut.; cogn. with L. *sedēre*], rest on haunches, occupy a seat, hold office of judge, Member of Parliament, etc., take up position for portrait, incubate, sit upon (a horse).

Site [L. *situs*, a site], ground occupied by or suitable for a town or building.

Sit'u-ate [Late L. *situāre* (p.p. *situātus*), to situate; L. *situs*, site, place], to place.

Sit-u-a'tion, position, place, case.

Six [O.E. *six*; Com. Teut.; cogn. with L. *sex*], one more than five.

Six-teen' [**Six** and **Ten**], the number made up of six added to ten.

Six'ty [**Six**, and *-ty*, tens], six times ten.

Si'zar (*i*) [see **Size** [2]], student of Cambridge or Dublin who pays reduced or no fees.

Size [1] [It. *sisa*, *assisa*, painter's glue; etym. dub.], thin glue.

Size [2] [short for **Assize**], bigness, bulk, allowance of food. **Size'able**, **Siz'able**.

Sjam'bok (*zhambok*) [S. Afr. Dutch], whip of rhinoceros hide.

Skate [O.N. *skata*, a skate], flat fish.

Skate [orig. in pl. *schates*; Du. *schaatsen*, skates, pl. of *schaats*], one of a pair of steel blades attachable to boots for gliding over ice; move on skates.

Skein (*ei=ā*) [O.F. *escaigne*, a skein; of obscure orig.], bundle of coiled thread or yarn.

Skel'e-ton [Gk. *skeletōn*, orig. neut. of *skeletos*, dried; *skellein*, to dry], bony framework of an animal, framework.

Skep [O.N. *skeppa*, a basket], wicker basket, straw or wicker beehive.

Sker'ry [O.N. *sker*], rugged rock or chain of rocks covered at times by the sea, a reef.

Sketch [Du. *schets*; It. *schizzo*, a sketch; Gk. *schedios*, off-hand], rough drawing, short description; make a rough draft, outline.

Skew'er (*ew=ū*) [var. of dial. **Skiver**, of unknown origin], pin for fastening meat, etc.

Ski (*shee*) [Norw. fr. O.N. *skith*, snowshoe], wooden runner for travelling over snow in Norway, etc.

Skid [orig. unknown; perh. conn. with O.N. *skith*, billet of wood], drag for a waggon; cause to move on skids, slip sideways, (of a wheel) slip without turning.

Skiff [F. *esquif*, a skiff; O.H.G. *scif*, ship], small, light boat.

Skil'ful, clever.

Skill [O.N. *skil*, a distinction, *skilja*, to separate], ability to see and do, cleverness.

Skil'let [?], small metal cooking vessel with a long handle and usu. legs.

Skim [perh. fr. O.F. *escumer*; cogn. with **Scum**], pass over lightly, take off the surface.

Skimp [cf. Icel. *skemma*, to shorten], to supply meagrely. **Skimp'y**.

Skin [O.N. *skinn*, skin], outer cover of the flesh, husk; to strip off skin.

Skin'flint, miser.

Skip [M. Swed. *skuppa*, *skoppa*, to leap], leap lightly, pass over; light leap.

Skip'per [M. Du. *schipper*, fr. *schif*, a ship], master of a ship.

Skir'mish [O.F. *eskirmir* (pr.p. *eskirmissant*), to fight, fence; O.H.G. *scirman*, to defend], fight in small parties; slight fight.

Skirt [O.N. *skyrta*, a shirt; doublet of **Shirt**], loose lower part of a dress, edge; to border.

Skit [perh. fr. O.N. *skytja*; Etym. dub., cf. Swed. *skjóta*, to shoot], short satire.

Skit′tish, freakish, fickle.

Skit′tles [?] nine-pins. [gull.

Sku′a [O.N. *skúfr*; Icel. *skúmur*], brown

Skulk [Dan. *skulke*; cf. Swed. *skolka*, play the truant], get out of the way like a sneak, lurk.

Skull [early *scolle*; etym. difficult to trace], skeleton of the head.

Skunk [Algonquin *segankw*, *segongw*, a skunk], N. American animal of the weasel kind that emits a fetid fluid.

Sky [O.N. *ský*, a cloud], the apparent great dome over our heads, the heavens.

Sky′light, roof-window.

Slab [O.F. *esclabe*, etym. dub.], thickish flat piece, esp. of stone.

Slack[1] [O.E. *sleac*; Com. Teut.; cogn. with Lax], loose; break up (lime) with water.

Slack[2] [of doubtful orig.; cf. older Flem. *slecke*, Du. *slak*, Ger. *schlacke*, slag], small coal.

Slag [M.L.G. *slagge*, slag], dross of metal.

Slake [O.E. *sleacian*, *slacian*, fr. *sleac*, slack], quench (thirst), slack (lime).

Slam [cf. Sw. and Norw. *slamra*, to slam; imit.], shut with force.

Slan′der [O.F. *esclandre* (n.); L. *scandalum*, scandal], false utterance meant to injure; injure by false statements. **Slan′derous**.

Slang [orig. uncertain], colloquial form of expression; scold vigorously. **Slang′y**.

Slant [Norw. *slenta*, to slip, glance aside], to slope; a slope. **Slant′wise**.

Slap [L.G. *slapp*; imit.], blow with the open hand; strike with the open hand.

Slap′dash′, in a bold, careless way.

Slash [fr. O.F. *esclachier*, to break in pieces], cut in long slits; long cut.

Slate [O.F. *esclat*, splinter, slate], rock which splits into plates, slab of it; cove with slates. [severely.

Slate [O.E. *slétan*, to tear], scold, criticize

Slat′tern [fr. obs. *slatter*, to splash, throw about; cf. O.N. *sletta*, to fling about], untidy woman.

Slaugh′ter [O.N. *slátr*, meat], extensive or violent killing; kill, butcher.

Slave [Late L. *sclavus*, a Slavonian captive, a slave], person who is the legal property of another; to drudge.

Sla′ver, ship or person engaged in slave-trade.

Sla′ver [Icel. *slafra*, to slaver], let saliva run from the mouth.

Sla′ver-y, condition of a slave, great drudgery.

Sla′vish, befitting a slave.

Slay [O.E. *sléan*; Com. Teut.], kill.

Sled, Sledge [M. Du. *sleedse*, *slede*; O.N. *slethi*; cogn. with Slide], vehicle on runners.

Sledge [O.E. *slecg*, fr. *sléan*, to slay], a blacksmith's heavy hammer. **Sledge′hammer**.

Sleek [var. of M.E. *slike*; cf. O.N. *slíkr*, Ger. *schlick*, grease], smooth and glossy.

Sleep [O.E. *slép*; cogn. with L. Ger *slap*, loose], natural state of unconsciousness; to be in this state. **Sleep′iness**.

Sleep′er, one who sleeps, piece of timber between rails, a railway sleeping-car.

Sleet [prob. fr. O.E. *slét*, hail; Ger. *schlosse*, a hailstone], hail or snow mixed with rain.

Sleeve [O.E. *slíf*; cogn. with Slip], part of dress covering the arm.

Sleigh (*ei*=*ai*) [Du. *slee*, short for *slede*, a sledge; see Sled], carriage on runners.

Sleight (*eigh*=ī) [O.N. *slœgth*, cunning, *slœgr*, sly], artful trick, skill.

Slen′der [perh. fr. O.F. *esclendre*; etym. difficult to trace], slim, not strong.

Sleuth′hound [Sleuth, var. of Slot[2]], bloodhound.

Slice [O.F. *esclice*, a splinter; O.H.G. *slīzan*, to slit, to shiver], thin piece cut off; cut into thin broad pieces.

Slide [O.E. *slīdan*, to slide, and *slíde*, a slip], move along smoothly and continuously; track on ice, act of sliding, something which slides.

Slight [M. Du. *slicht*, plain], not decidedly marked, slender; disregard; mark of neglect or contempt.

Slim [orig. meaning "oblique"; M. Du. *slim*, awry, crafty], weak, slight, crafty.

Slime [O.E. *slim*; Com. Teut.], soft, sticky substance, soft mud.

Sli′my, pertaining to or like slime.

Sling [Etym. difficult to trace; cf. M.L.G. *slinge*], instrument for throwing stones, support for injured arm; hurl, hang so as to swing.

Slink [O.E. *slincan*], steal away.

Slip [perh. fr. M.L.G. *slippen*], move smoothly, lose one's footing, err slightly; slight error, a cutting strip, cover easily slipped on.

Slip′per [fr. Slip], light shoe. [unreliable.

Slip′per-y, causing slips by smoothness,

Slip′shod, down at heel, careless.

Slit [prob. conn. with O.E. *slītan*; cogn. with Slice], cut lengthwise; long opening.

Sli′ver (ĭ or ī) [obs. *slive*, to splinter, fr. O.E. *slīfan*, to splinter], splinter, strand of flax, cotton, etc.

Slob′ber, Slab′ber [cf. Du. *slobber*, to slaver], to run at the mouth, botch, do badly.

Sloe [O.E. *slá(h)*; cf. Du. *slee*], blackthorn, its fruit.

Slog [perh. cogn. with Slay], hit wildly.

Slo′gan [Gael. *sluagh-ghairm*, slogan; *sluagh*, host, *gairm*, outcry], war-cry of a Highland clan.

Sloid, Sloyd [Swed. *slöjd*, skill], system of manual training, esp. by wood-carving.

Sloop [Du. *sloep*; Low G. *slûp*, a sloop], small one-masted vessel.

Slop,[1] [O.E. -*sloppe*, liquid droppings], (n. pl.) weak liquid food, rinsings; to spill.

Slop[2] (pl.) [O.N. *sloppr*, a loose gown], ready-made clothes.

Slope [O.E. *slopen*, p.p. of *slúpan*, to slip], oblique direction, slanting surface; to slant.

Slop′py [see Slop[1]], wet, plashy.

Slot[1] [perh. O.F. *esclot*], narrow opening.

Slot² [O.F. *esclot*; O.N. *slóth*, a track], track of a deer.

Sloth (*ŏ*) [fr. **Slow**], laziness, tree-animal.

Slouch [perh. fr. Icel. *slókr*, lazy fellow; etym. uncert.], ungainly walk; walk with a slouch.

Slough (*ou* like *ow* in cow) [O.E. *slóh*; etym. dub.], hole full of mire.

Slough (*ough=uff*) [M.E. type *sloh*, of doubtful orig., perh. conn. with L.G. *sluwe*, *slu*, husk, peel], cast-off skin of a reptile; cast off, shed in the form of dead matter.

Slov'en (*o=ŭ*) [perh. fr. Du. *slof*, *sloef*, a sloven], person careless in dress or work, etc.

Slow [O.E. *slaw*; Com. Teut.], not quick, behind in time; slacken speed.

Slow-worm (*or=ŭr*) [O.E. *slá-wyrm*], harmless reptile, blind-worm.

Slug [perh. of Scand. origin; cf. Norw. *slugg*, large, heavy body], snail-like animal with no shell.

Slug [perh. of same origin as prec.], bullet of irregular shape.

Slug'gard [Swed. dial. *slogga*, be sluggish; *sloka*, to droop], lazy slow person.

Slug'gish, lazy and slow.

Sluice [Late L. *exclūsa*, a floodgate; L. *exclūdere* (p.p. *exclūsus*), shut out], structure with sliding gate for controlling flow of water, floodgate; wet copiously.

Slum [cf. prov. E. *slump*, muddy place], foul street; to visit slums.

Slum'ber [M.E. *slumeren*, fr. *slumen*], to sleep, usu. lightly; sleep. **Slum'brous.**

Slump [imit. of noise made by falling into water], sink through, to fall rapidly; rapid fall in value.

Slur [cf. Du. *sleuren*, to trail], to soil, pass over lightly; a stain, slight mark connecting notes (music).

Slush [cf. Norw. *slusk*, mud], half-melted, muddy snow.

Slut [Swed. dial. *slåta*; cf. Ger. dial. *schlutt*; Norw. *slott*, an idler], slovenly woman.

Slut'tish, untidy.

Sly [O.N. *slœgr*, sly], knowing, cunning. **Sly'ly.**

Smack [prob. fr. Du. *smak*], small decked sailing vessel.

Smack [Com. Du. *smæc*; cf. Ger. *geschmack*, fr. *schmecken*, to taste], taste, slight flavour; taste slightly of.

Smack [prob. imit., corresp. to M. Du., M.L.G.*smacken*], kiss, sharp blow; to kiss noisily, crack (a whip), slap.

Small (*a=aw*) [O.E. *smæl*; Com. Teut.], little, petty.

Small'pox, eruptive disease.

Smart [O.E. *smeortan*; cf. Ger. *schmerzen*], feel sharp pain; sharp pain; sharp, showy, clever, fashionable. **Smar'ten.**

Smash [prob. imit.; cf. Norw. dial. *smaska*, to crush], a dashing to pieces; shatter, fly in pieces.

Smat'ter-ing [origin unknown; cf. Swed. *smattra*, to clatter], slight surface knowledge. **Smatt'erer.**

Smear [O.E. *smeru*, fat], to daub, rub with grease, etc.; a daub.

Smell [M.E. *smel*, smell, *smellen*, to smell], perceive by the nose, scent; sensation through the nose, odour. [kind.

Smelt [O.E. *smelt*], small fish of the salmon

Smelt [Dan. *smelte*; cf. M. Du. *smalt*, grease; O.H.G. *smalz*, fat], melt ore.

Smi'lax [Gk. *smilax*, bindweed], delicate trailing plant.

Smile [Swed. *smila*; cf. Dan. *smile*, to smile], relax features into pleased expression; act of smiling, smiling expression.

Smirch [app. fr. O.F. *esmorcher*, to torture with hot irons], to soil; a stain.

Smirk [O.E. *smercian*], smile affectedly; forced smile.

Smite [O.E. *smitan*; cf. Du. *smijten*; Ger. *schmeissen*], strike a blow.

Smith [O.E. *smith*; Com. Teut.; cf. Du. *smid*; Ger. *schmied*], one who works in metals.

Smith'y, workshop of a blacksmith.

Smock [O.E. *smoc*; prob. conn. with O.E. *smigan*, to creep into], chemise, shirt.

Smock-'frock', outer garment worn by labourers.

Smoke [O.E. *smoca*; cf. *smēocan*, to smoke], vapour from burning; emit smoke, apply smoke to, inhale and expel the smoke of tobacco, to cure or preserve by exposure to smoke, use in smoking.

Smo'ky, emitting or filled with smoke.

Smolt [?], young river-salmon.

Smooth [O.E. *smēthe*], even; make even.

Smoth'er (*o=ŭ*) [M.E. *smorther*; fr. O.E. *smorian*, to stifle; cogn. with **Smoke**], cover so closely as to prevent breathing, suffocate with smoke, suppress.

Smoul'der (*ŏ*) [perh. conn. with L.G. *smölen*, Du. *smeulen*], burn without flame.

Smudge [etym. dub.], a stain; to smear.

Smug [etym. doubtful], smooth and prim.

Smug'gle [L. Ger. *smuggeln*; cf. Du. *smokkelen*], import or export without paying legal duties, pass by stealth. **Smug'gler.**

Smut [Swed. *smuts*, dirt], soot or coal-dust, spot made by soot, etc.; to blacken.

Smut'ty, soiled with smut.

Snack [perh. fr. **Snatch**; etym. doubtful], light or hurried meal.

Snaf'fle [Du. *snavel*, horse's muzzle; cf. M. Du. *snavel*; M.H.G. *snabel*, bill, snout; etym. uncert.], bridle with slender mouthpiece without curb; to put snaffle on.

Snag [prob. Scand.; cf. Norw. *snage*, projection of land], stump of a branch, stump or rock in river-bed.

Snail [O.E. *snœgl*], slimy mollusc.

Snake [O.E. *snaca*, a snake], long, limbless reptile.

Snap [M. Du. *snappen*, to snap], break short, try to bite; sudden break, sudden bite, sharp noise, small catch.

Snap'pish, temper.

Snare [O.N. *snara*, cord; cf. Du. *snaar*, string; cogn. with L. *nēre*, to spin], noose or other trap; catch in a snare.

Snarl [freq. of earlier *snar*, *snarre*, to show teeth like a dog; cogn. with **Sneer**], to growl, grumble; a growl. [entangled.
Snarl [freq. of **Snare**], knot; become
Snatch [etym. doubtful; perh. related to **Snack**], seize abruptly; the act of catching at, fragment.
Sneak [of obscure orig.; O.E. *snican*, to creep], come or go meanly; underhand person.
Sneer [prob. imit.; to snort as a horse], speak contemptuously; contemptuous smile or remark.
Sneeze [M.E. *snesen*, var. of *fnesen*; cogn. with E. *fnœst*, a blast], eject air convulsively; sound of sneezing.
Sniff [imit.], draw air up the nose; that which is taken by sniffing.
Snig'ger [imit.], laugh with catches of the breath. [a clip.
Snip [Du. *snippen*, to snip], cut with shears;
Snipe [of obscure orig., prob. Scand.], wading-bird with long beak.
Snip'pet [dim. of **Snip**], small piece.
Sniv'el [O.E. *snyflan*, fr. *snofl*, mucus; cogn. with **Snuff** [2]], run at the nose, cry.
Snob [orig. slang; of obscure origin], one who esteems others according to social position or wealth. **Snobb'ish, Snobb'ery.**
Snooze [slang word of obscure orig.], doze, sleep; a nap.
Snore [prob. imit.; cf. **Snort**], breathe noisily in sleep; harsh sound made in sleep.
Snort [prob. imit.], force air noisily through the nose; sound made by snorting.
Snout [M.E. and M.D. *snūte*], nose (and mouth) of a beast, fish, etc.
Snow [O.E. *snāw*; Com. Teut.], vapour frozen into white flakes; fall as snow.
Snub [Dan. *snubbe*; Swed. and O.N. *snubba*, to snub], to check, slight intentionally; a check; short and stumpy. [of a candle.
Snuff [1] [?], charred candle-wick; crop the snuff
Snuff [2] [M.Du. *snuffen*, to clear the nose; *snuf*, scent], powdered tobacco; use snuff, inhale (smell).
Snuff'ers [see **Snuff** [1]], candle-scissors.
Snuf'fle [see **Snuff** [2]], speak through the nose.
Snug [etym. dub.], cosy, comfortable. **Snug'gle.**
Snug'ger-y, snug place, esp. private room.
So [O.E. *swā*; Com. Teut.], thus, similarly, to a degree, on condition that.
Soak [O.E. *socian*, fr. *sūcan*, to suck], wet thoroughly. **Soak'ing.**
Soap [O.E. *sāpe*; cf. Du. *zeep*; Ger. *seife*], substance of oils and fats with alkali used in washing; to rub soap on. **Soap'y.**
Soar [Late L. *exaurāre*, expose to air; L. *ex*, out, *aura*, a breeze], fly high.
Sob [prob. imit.], weep convulsively; sound of sobbing. **Sob'bingly.**
So'ber [L. *sōbrius*, perh. fr. *sē-*, apart, and *ēbrius*, drunken], grave, temperate, not intoxicated; make serious.
So-bri'e-ty, temperance, seriousness.
So'bri-quet (*uet=ai*), **Sou'bri-quet** (*ou=oo*) [F. *sobriquet*. Etym. doubtful], nickname.

So'cia-ble (*ci=sh*) [L. *socius*, companion], inclined to society, friendly. **Sociabil'ity.**
So'cial (*ci=sh*) [L. *socius*, companion], relating to society, living in companies, friendly, festive. **Social'ity.**
So'cial-ism (*ci=sh*), theory of social reconstruction aiming at community of interests. **So'cialist, Socialist'ic.**
So-ci'e-ty [L. *socius*, companion], companionship, number of persons united for a purpose, those who take the lead in social life.
So-cin'ian [fr. *Socinus*, theologian of 16th cent.], one who denies the Trinity, like the Unitarian of to-day.
So-ci-ol'o-gy [see **Sociable**; Gk. *logos*, discourse], science of human society, its laws, etc. **Sociolog'ical.**
Sock [O.E. *socc*; L. *soccus*, a light shoe, sock], stocking with a short leg, ancient comic actor's light shoe.
Sock'et [A.F. *soket*, dim. of *soc*, a ploughshare], hollow into which something is fitted.
Sod [?], soil containing roots, piece of turf.
So'da [origin unknown; M.L. *soda*, solid], alkali from decomposing salt, etc.
So-da'li-ty [L. *sodalis*, fellow], a brotherhood or fellowship.
Sod'den [p.p. of **Seethe**], heavy with moisture.
So'fa [Arab. *soffah*, a bench], long cushioned seat with back and ends.
Soft [O.E. *sōfte*, var. of *sēfte*], yielding, not firm or rough, low-toned.
Soil [L. *solum*, ground], earth.
Soil [A.F. *soyler*; O.F. *soillier*, fr. *soil*, mire, perh. from L. *suillus*, of swine, fr. *sūs*, a pig. Doublet of **Sully**], make dirty, stain.
Soi-rée' (*swa-rai'*) [F. *soirée*, evening, evening party], evening party, social gathering.
So'journ (*ŏ*) [O.F. *sojourner*, to sojourn; L. *sub*, under, *diurnāre*, to stay; *diurnus*, daily], dwell for a time; temporary stay. **So'journer.**
Sol'ace [O.F. *solas*, solace; L. *sōlāri* (p.p. *sōlātus*), to console], comfort; to comfort.
So'lan-goose [O.N. and Icel. *súla*, gannet; O.N. *and*, duck; see **Goose**], gannet, sea-bird, rambling goose. [sun.
So'lar [L. *sōl*, the sun], of or pertaining to the
Sol-a'tium (*sōlaishum*) (*pl.* -tia) [L.=solace], thing given as consolation or compensation.
Sol'der (*ŏ*) [L. *solidāre*, to make firm; *solidus*, firm], metallic cement; to unite with metallic cement.
Sol'dier (*sōljer*) [Late L. *soldārius*, one who fights for pay; L. *soldum*, pay; *solidus*, solid], man in military service.
Sole [L. *solea*, the sole-fish], flat fish.
Sole [L. *solea*, sole of a foot, or of a shoe; *solum*, ground], under surface of foot or shoe; put on a sole.
Sole [L. *sōlus*, alone], only.
Sol'e-cism (*ŏ*) [Gk. *soloicismos*; *soloicos*, speaking badly like a dweller in *Soloi* in Cilicia], deviation from the grammar of a language or from social usages.

Sol'emn [L. *solemnis*, customary, festive], sacred, serious. **Solem'nity.**

Sol'em-nize, perform with ceremony, make solemn. **Solemniza'tion.**

Sol-fa [fr. the syllables *sol* and *fa* of the scale], syllables sung to the respective notes of the major scale.

Sol-feg'gio (*feggio=fedjo*) [It. *sol, fa,* and suf. *-eggio*], system or exercise in which sol-fa syllables are used.

So-li'cit (*li*) [L. *sollicitus,* anxious, perh. fr. *sollus,* whole, and *citus,* aroused], beseech, ask. **Solicita'tion.**

So-li'ci-tor, one legally qualified to advise clients and to prepare causes for barristers.

So-li'cit-ous, anxious.

So-li'cit-ude, anxiety.

Sol'id [L. *solidus,* firm], firm, hard ; substance not fluid.

Sol-i-dar'i-ty, unity of interests.

So-lid'i-fy [L. *solidus,* firm ; *facere,* to make], render or become solid.

So-lid'i-ty, state of being solid, volume.

So-lil'o-quize, talk to oneself.

So-lil'o-quy [L. *sōlus,* alone ; *loqui,* to speak], a discourse or speech to oneself.

Sol'i-taire [F. *solitaire,* solitary], gem set by itself, a game which can be played by one person.

Sol'i-ta-ry [L. *sōlus,* alone], alone, lonely.

Sol'i-tude [L. *sōlus,* alone], lonely life, loneliness.

So'lo [It. *solo* ; L. *sōlus,* alone], performance by one, kind of card-game. **Sol'oist.**

Sol'stice (*ice=iss*) [L. *sōl,* the sun; *sistere,* to make to stand; *stāre,* to stand], time when the sun reaches one of two points in the ecliptic farthest from the equator, one of these points. **Solsti'tial.**

Sol'u-ble [see Solve], capable of being dissolved in fluid, that can be solved. **Sol'ubil'ity.**

So-lu'tion [see Solve], dissolving, product of a dissolved solid in liquid, explanation.

Solve [L. *solvere* (p.p. *solūtus*), to loosen], explain, clear up. **Solvabil'ity.**

Sol'vent [L. *solvens (-entis),* pr.p. of *solvere,* to loosen], able to pay all debts : fluid that dissolves something. **Sol'vency.**

Som'bre [F. *sombre,* gloomy ; perh. fr. L. *ex,* out, *umbra,* shade], dull, somewhat dark.

Som-brer'o (*e=ai*) [Span. *sombrero,* fr. *sombra,* shade ; see **Sombre**], broad-brimmed (usually) felt hat.

Some (*sŭm*) [O.E. *sum* ; Com. Teut.], unspecified persons or things, indefinite quantity **or** number; unspecified (person or thing); approximately.

Som'er-sault, Som'er-set (*o=ŭ*) [L. *suprā,* over, *sa'tus,* a leap ; *salīre,* to leap], leap turning heels over head.

Some'what, something ; more or less.

Som-nam'bu-list [L. *somnus,* sleep ; *ambulāre,* to walk], sleep-walker.

Som'no-lence, Som'no-len-cy [L. *somnus,* sleep], sleepiness.

Som'no-lent [L. *somnus,* sleep], sleepy, drowsy.

Son (*o=ŭ*) [O.E. *sunu* ; Com Teut. ; cf. Ger. *sohn*], male child.

So-na'ta [It. *sonata,* fr. L. *sonāre,* to sound], piece of music in several movements.

So-na-ti'na [It., dim. of *sonata*], short simple form of sonata.

Song [O.E. *sang,* fr. root of *singan,* to sing], vocal music, short poem set to music, poetry.

Song'ster, fem. **Song'stress,** singer.

Son'-in-law, daughter's husband.

Son'net [It. *sonetto,* dim. of *suono* ; L. *sonus,* sound], rhymed poem of fourteen lines. **Sonneteer'.**

So-no'rous [L. *sonāre,* to sound], high-sounding. **Sonor'ity.**

Soon [O.E. *sōna* ; cf. O.H.G. *sān*], before long, shortly.

Soot [O.E. and O.N. *sōt* ; perh. cogn. with **Sit**], fine black powder from smoke.

Sooth [O.E. *sōth*], truth.

Soothe [O.E. *gesōthian,* fr. *sōth,* sooth], soften, calm, mitigate.

Sooth'say'er, one who foretells events.

Soot'y, soiled by soot, like soot.

Sop [O.E. *sopp* ; cogn. with *súpan,* to sup], food dipped in liquid, a bribe.

Soph'ist (*ŏ*) [Gk. *sophistēs,* a sophist; *sophizein,* to instruct], paid teacher of philosophy and rhetoric in ancient Greece, one who uses arguments apparently but not really sound. [*ing.*

So-phis'tic-al, not sound or simple in reason-

Soph-is'ti-cate, render artificial, spoil, use sophistry. **Sophistica'tion.**

Soph'is-try, insincere argument.

Sop-o-rif'ic [L. *sopor,* sleep ; *facere,* to make], causing sleep ; that which induces sleep.

So-pra'no (*a=ah*) [It. *soprano,* soprano ; Late L. *superānus,* chief], highest voice.

Sor'cer-er, fem. **Sor'cer-ess** [L. *sors* (*sort-is*), lot, fate], magician.

Sor'cer-y, magic, witchcraft. [*niggardly.*

Sor'did [L. *sordidus,* dirty], base, mean,

Sore [O.E. *sár* ; Com. Teut.], painful, distressing ; painful or diseased place.

Sor'rel [O.F. *sorel,* dim. of *sor,* sorrel (horse)], yellowish or reddish brown colour.

Sor'rel [O.F. *surele, sarele,* sorrel], plant with sour juice.

Sor'row [O.E. and O.N. *sorg* ; Com. Teut.], grief ; feel sorrow. **Sorrowful.**

Sor'ry [O.E. *sárig*], grieved, regretful, wretched. **Sor'riness.**

Sort [L. *sors* (*sort-is*), lot], character, kind ; separate and arrange, classify.

Sor'tie (*ie=ee*) [F. *sortie* ; orig. fem. of p.p. of *sortir,* to go out], sally.

Sot [Late L. *sottus,* a sot. Etym. doubtful], drunkard.

Sot'tish [see **Sot**], like a sot, stupid.

Sou (*ou=oo*) [F. *sou*], small French coin.

Sou'chong (*ou=oo* ; *ch=sh*) [Chin. *siu, siao,* small, *chung,* sort], black tea made from young leaves.

Sough (*suf*, *sow* (rhyming with **Cow**) or *sooch* with guttural *ch*) [O.E., *swōgan*, to resound, prob. imit.], moaning sound as of wind in trees.

Soul (*ou=ō*) [O.E. *sáw(e)l*, *sáwol*, *sáwul*; Com. Teut.], spiritual part of man. **Soul'ful.**

Sound [1] [O.E. *gesund*], whole, healthy, reliable, deep (of sleep).

Sound [2] [O.E., O.N. *sund*, strait; cogn. with **Swim**], narrow sea.

Sound [3] [F. *son*; L. *sonus*, sound], sensation of hearing, what is or may be heard; utter a sound, cause to sound.

Sound [4] [O.F. *sonder*, to sound; prob. fr. **Sound** [2]], measure depth.

Soup (*ou=oo*) [F. *soupe*; cogn. with **Sup**], liquid food made from meat, etc.

Sour [O.E. *súr*; Com. Teut.], acid, sharp; turn sour.

Source (*ou=ō*) [O.F. *sors*, a source; L. *surgere*, to rise], beginning of a stream, origin.

Souse [O.F. *sous*, *souce*, sauce], pickle made with salt; to plunge.

South [O.E. *súth*; Com. Teut], opposite north, direction in which the sun appears at noon to people north of Tropic of Cancer; (of a wind) coming from the south.

South'ern, of or pertaining to the south.

South'ward(s), towards the south.

South-west'er, waterproof hat with broad brim behind.

Sou-ve-nir' (*soo-ven-eer'*) [F. *souvenir*, to remember; L. *subvenire*, occur to one's mind; *sub-*, under, and *venire*, to come], memento, keepsake.

Sov'er-eign [O.F. *soverain*, *souverein*; Late L. *superānus*, chief; L. *super*, above], supreme; monarch, coin worth 20 shillings.

Sow [O.E. *sáwan*; Com. Teut.], scatter seed. **Sow'er.**

Sow [O.E. *sugu*, *sú*, a sow, fr. root *su-*, to produce (of doubtful origin)], female swine.

Spa [from *Spa* in Belgium], spring of mineral water, place possessing this.

Space [L. *spatium*, space], room, interval between objects, period of time; set at intervals. [ness.

Spa'cious (*ci=sh*), vast, roomy. **Spa'cious-**

Spade [1] [O.E. *spadu*, fr. or cogn. with Gk. *spathē*, a broad blade], tool for digging.

Spade [2] [Span. *espada*, sword; cogn. with **Spade** [1]], playing card with black spade-shaped figure(s), (in pl.) suit of these cards.

Spagh-et'ti (*g* hard) [It.], kind of macaroni.

Span [O.E. *spannan*, to span; cf. Du. and Ger. *spannen*], distance between tips of thumb and little finger of extended hand, nine inches, small space, full extent (of arch, etc.), pair of animals driven together; stretch over as an arch, to yoke.

Span'gle [prob. fr. M. Du. *spang*, clasp, buckle], glittering ornament.

Span'iel [O.F. *espaigneul*, spaniel, Spanish dog; Sp. *España*, Spain], dog with drooping ears.

Spank [?], slap, move quickly. **Spank'ing.**

Span'ner [see **Span**], implement for turning nut of screw.

Spar [1] [M.L.G. *spar*, *sper*, allied to O.E. *spæren*, gypsum], bright crystalline mineral.

Spar [2] [cf. M. Du., M.L.G. *sparre*; O.N. *sparri*], long piece of timber, ship's mast, yard.

Spar [3] [?], fight as cocks, dispute.

Spar'a-ble [corruption of *sparrow-bill*], headless nail for soles and heels of boots.

Spare [O.E. *sparian*, to spare], save, set aside, show mercy to; scanty, lean, held in reserve.

Spark [1] [O.E. *spearca*; cf. M. Du. *sparcke*; O.N. *spraka*, to crackle, perh. imit. of crackling of burning wood], particle of fire; emit sparks.

Spark [2] [prob. figurative use of prec.], gay young fellow. [glitter.

Spark'le [freq. of **Spark** [1]], emit sparks,

Spar'row [O.E. *spearwa*], small bird.

Sparse [L. *spargere* (p.p. *sparsus*), to scatter], thinly scattered.

Spar'tan [L. *Sparta*; Gk. *Spartē*], native of Sparta; like the Spartans, who were noted for endurance and frugality.

Spasm [Gk. *spasmos*, a spasm; *spaein*, to draw], sudden muscular contraction.

Spas-mod'ic, by fits and starts.

Spat [for *spatter-dash*], short cloth gaiter.

Spate [etym. doubtful], river-flood.

Spa'tial (*ti=sh*), of space.

Spat'ter [freq. of stem found in Du. *spatten* to burst], sprinkle with mud or liquid.

Spat'u-la [L. *spatula*, var. of *spathula*, dim. of *spatha*, a broad blade], broad-bladed instrument used for stirring mixtures, spreading ointments, etc.

Spav'in [O.F. *espavain*], disease of horses.

Spawn [L. *expandere*, to spread out], eggs of fishes, frogs, etc.; deposit (eggs) as fishes.

Speak [O.E. *sp(r)ecan*; cf. Du. *spreken*; Ger. *sprechen*], utter words, converse, deliver a speech, communicate with (a ship).

Speak'er, one who speaks, presiding member of the House of Commons, etc.

Spear [O.E. *spere*; cf. Du. and Ger. *speer*; perh. cogn. with **Spar** [2]], pointed weapon for thrusting or throwing; pierce with a spear.

Spear'mint, aromatic plant.

Spe'cial (*ci=sh*) [short for **Especial**], particular, distinctive.

Spe'cial-ist [*ci=sh*], one who takes up a particular branch of a science, etc.

Spe-ci-al'i-ty, **Spe'cial-ty** (*ci=sh*), special quality or object. **Spe'cialize.**

Spe'cie (*spee'-shi-ee* or *spee'-shee*) [L. abl. of *speciēs*, kind; *in specie*, in kind], coin.

Spe'cies (*spe'-shi-eez* or *spe'-sheez*) (pl. **Species**) [L. *speciēs*], a kind, a class.

Spe-cif'ic [see **Specify**], definite; definite cure.

Spec-i-fi-ca'tion, definite or detailed description.

Spe'ci-fy [O.F. *specifier*, to specify; L. *speciēs*, kind, *facere*, to make], name definitely or expressly.

Spec'i-men [L. *specimen*, a specimen; *specere*, to look], sample.

Spe'cious [L. *speciēs*, kind, appearance], pleasing in appearance, plausible.

Speck [O.E. *specca*], spot, stain.

Speck'led [*speckle*, dim. of Speck], marked with small spots.

Spec'ta-cle [L. *spectāculum*, a spectacle; *spectāre*, freq. of *specere*, to look], show, (pl.) lenses to assist the sight.

Spec-tac'u-lar, of the nature of a show.

Spec-ta'tor [L. *spectāre*, to see], looker-on.

Spec'tre [L. *spectrum*, a vision; *specere*, to look, see], ghost. Spec'tral.

Spec'tro-scope [L. *spectrum*, a vision; Gk. *scopein*, to look], instrument for producing and examining the spectra of rays of light.

Spec'trum (pl. Spectra) [L. *spectrum*, a vision], an image seen with closed eyes, coloured band into which a beam of light may be decomposed.

Spec'u-late [L. *speculārī* (p.p. *speculātus*), to behold, *specula*, a watch-tower, *specere*, to look], form a theory, buy riskily. [sale.

Spec-u-la'tion, theory, risky purchase or

Speech [O.E. *sp(r)œc*], talk, language, an address. Speech'ify.

Speed [O.E. *spēd*; cf. O.H.G. *spuon*, to prosper], swiftness, rate of motion; succeed, move quickly, further, say good-bye to.

Speed-om'eter [Gk. *metrein*, to measure], speed-indicator, esp. on a motor vehicle.

Speed'y, rapid.

Spell [O.E. *spel*, *spel(l)*, a saying, story], a set of words supposed to have magical power, a charm, turn at work, short period.

Spell [O.F. *espeller*], name in order the letters of a word, read letter by letter, make out by study, signify.

Spelt'er [corresp. to O.F. *espeautre*; Low Ger. *spialter*, pewter], zinc.

Spen'cer [fr. an Earl of *Spencer*], short jacket.

Spend [L. *expendere*, to lay out; disburse], put out money, waste, employ (time).

Spend'thrift, wasteful spender.

Sperm [L. and Gk. *sperma*, seed; Gk. *speirein*, to sow], male generative fluid, spermaceti.

Sper-ma-ce'ti [L. *sperma*, sperm; *cētus*, a whale], waxy matter obtained from the sperm whale.

Spew [O.E. *spēowan*, *spīwan*], vomit.

Sphag'num [Gk. *sphagnos*, a kind of moss], moss used for surgical dressings.

Sphere [Gk. *sphaira*, a ball], ball, range of action. Spher'oid.

Spher'ic-al, of or like a sphere.

Sphinx [Gk. *sphigx*, sphinx; *sphiggein*, to strangle], in Greek mythology a monster with woman's head and lion's body, stone image near pyramids of Egypt.

Spice [O.F. *espice*; L. *speciēs*, kind (in Late L. also means " spice ")], flavouring substance, slight trace; to flavour with spice.

Spick and Span [earlier *spike-and-span-new*], wholly new, as trim as when new.

Spic'y, containing spice, fragrant, pungent.

Spi'der [O.E. *spīthre*, *spinthre*, fr. *spinnan*, to spin], web-spinning animal.

Spig'ot [O. Port. *espiga*, ear of corn, dim. fr. L. *spīca*, ear of corn, point], peg to stop the vent of a cask.

Spike [Swed. and Norw. *spik*, a nail], large nail, sharp-pointed piece of metal or wood.

Spike [L. *spīca*, ear of corn, point], ear of corn.

Spike'nard [L. *spīca nard*; Gk. *nardou stachus*, spike of nard], costly aromatic ointment.

Spill [O.E. *spillan*; M. Du., M.L.G. *spillen*, to destroy], drop (liquid) out of a vessel, run over, fall out, shed (blood); a fall from a horse.

Spill [Du. *spil*; M. Du. and M.L.G. *spille*], strip of wood, or spiral twist of paper for lighting gas, etc.

Spin [O.E. *spinnan*; perh. cogn. with Span], draw out and twist into thread, to whirl.

Spin'ach, Spin'age [Sp. *espinaca*; etym. doubtful], pot herb.

Spi'nal [see Spine], relating to the spine.

Spin'dle [O.E. *spinel*, fr. *spinnan*, to spin], pin on which thread is twisted in a spinning-wheel, or on which a bobbin is held in a spinning-machine.

Spin'drift [var. of *spoondrift*], blown spray.

Spine [O.F. *espine*; L. *spīna*, thorn, backbone], thorn, backbone.

Spin'et [M.F. *espinette*; It. *spinetta*], old-fashioned musical instrument.

Spin'na-ker [perh. formed from *spinx*, a mispronunciation of *Sphinx*, the name of the first yacht to carry the sail], large three-cornered sail carried by racing-yachts.

Spin'ner-et [see Spin], organ on the under side of spiders, silkworms, etc.

Spin'ny, Spin'ney [O.F. *espinei*, a thorny place, fr. *espine*], small grove.

Spin'ster [fr. Spin], unmarried woman.

Spi'ny, thorny, full of spines.

Spi'ra-cle [L. *spirāre*, to breathe], breathing-hole in animals.

Spir-aе'a (*ae=ee*) [Gk *speiraia*, meadow-sweet] perennial herb with small white or pink flowers.

Spi'ral [L. *spīralis*; see Spire [2]], winding like a screw.

Spire [1] [O.E. *spīr*; cf. Du. *spier*; Ger. *spiere*, a spar], tapering portion of a steeple, any tapering body.

Spire [2] [L. *spīra*; Gk. *speira*, a coil], coil, a single twist.

Spir'it [L. *spiritus*, breath, *spirāre*, to breathe], life distinct from matter, soul, ghost, liveliness, energy; (pl.) mental state, liquid produced by distillation.

Spir'it-ed, full of spirit, animated.

Spir'it-u-al, not material, holy, ecclesiastical. Spiritua'lity.

Spir'it-u-al-ism, belief in communion between the living and the dead.

Spir'it-u-ous, containing alcohol.

Spirt [see Spurt].

Spit [O.E. *spitu*; cf. Du. *spit*; Ger. *spiess*], prong for holding meat while roasting, point of land.

Spit [O.E. *spittan*, *spǽtan*, to spit], saliva; eject saliva from the mouth. **Spittoon'**.

Spite [short for Despite], active ill-will; thwart.

Spit'tle [O.E. *spátl*], thick moist matter in the mouth, saliva.

Splash [coined by prefixing *s* to Plash], dash about (water, etc.); dash of water, etc.

Splash'board, board in front of a vehicle.

Splat'ter [var. of Spatter], make continuous splashing.

Splay [short for Display], turned outward, flat; slanting surface (in architecture); to make with a slope.

Spleen [L. *splēn*; Gk. *splen*, the spleen], gland in the body, ill-humour. [showy.

Splen'did [L. *splendēre*, to shine], very bright.

Splen'dour [L. *splendēre*, to shine], great brightness, magnificence.

Splen-et'ic [Late L. *spleneticus*; as Spleen], affected with spleen, peevish.

Splice [M. Du. *splissen*, to splice; Du. *splijten*, to split], unite by interweaving or interlapping.

Splint, Splin'ter [Swed. *splint*, a spike; cf. Dan. *splint*, a splinter], piece split off, (pl.) contrivances for keeping a broken limb in position; split into thin pieces.

Split [M. Du. *splitten*, to split; etym. dub.], divide lengthwise; crack or rent.

Splotch [etym. dub.], smear, blot, stain.

Splut'ter [imit., var. of Sputter], sputter.

Spoil [L. *spoliāre*, to strip; L. *spolium*, skin stripped off, booty], to plunder, mar, destroy, go bad; plunder.

Spoke [O.E. *spáca*; cf. Du. *speek*], ray of a wheel, rung of ladder, each handle of steering-wheel.

Spokes'man, man who speaks for others.

Spo-li-a'tion [see Spoil], plunder, deprivation.

Spon'dee [Gk. *spondeios*, a spondee; *spondai*, solemn treaty; *spondē*, libation to the gods; *spendein*, to pour out], metrical foot of two long syllables. **Sponda'ic**.

Sponge (*o=ŭ*) [O.E. *sponge*; Gk. *spoggia*, a sponge, var. of *spoggos*, fungus], porous animal substance; use a sponge to, get by mean arts. **Spong'er**.

Spon'gy (*o=ŭ*), soft like sponge

Spon'sor [L. *spondēre* (p.p. *sponsus*), to promise], surety, godfather or godmother.

Spon-ta'ne-ous [L. *spontāneus*, willing; *sponte*, of one's own accord], voluntary, unforced. **Spontane'ity**.

Spook [Du. *spook*], ghost.

Spool [M. Du. *spoele*], reel for thread, etc.

Spoon [O.E. *spón*; Com. Teut.], utensil, oval bowl with a handle to convey liquid food to the mouth; use a spoon.

Spoon'er-ism [fr. Rev. W. A. *Spooner*], accidental transposition of initial letters, *e.g.* half-warmed *fish* for half-formed *wish*.

Spoor [Du. *spoor*], an animal's track or scent; follow by spoor.

Spo-rad'ic [Gk. *sporadicos*, scattered; *speirein*, to scatter], occurring here and there.

Spore [Gk. *spora*, sowing, seed; *speirein*, to sow], small grain or germ.

Spor'ran [Gael. *sporan*, a purse, a sporran], pouch in front of a kilt.

Sport [short for Disport], amusement, outdoor pastime; play, wear in public.

Sport'ive, playful.

Sports'man, one who hunts, fishes, etc.

Spot [M.E. and O. Fris. *spot*; cf. M. Du. *spotten*, to spot], stain, speck, place; cover with spots, detect. **Spot'ty**.

Spouse (*s=z*) [L. *sponsa*, betrothed woman; *spondēre* (p.p. *sponsus*), to promise], husband or wife.

Spout [M.E. *spouten*; cf. Du. *spuiten*], throw out as water through a pipe; discharging-pipe.

Sprain [perh.fr. O.F. *espreindre*, to press out; etym. dub.], wrench ankle, wrist, etc.; lameness caused by spraining.

Sprat [O.E. *sprott*; cf. O.E. *sprot*, a twig; cogn. with Sprout], small fish.

Sprawl [O.E. *spreawlian*; cf. N. Fris. *spraweli*], spread the limbs carelessly.

Spray [?], sprig of flowers or leaves.

Spray [M. Du. *spragen*; M.L.G. *sprœjen*, to sprinkle], water flying in small drops; throw spray on.

Spread [O.E. *sprédan*; cf. Du. *spreiden*; Ger. *spreiten*], extend the surface of, to unfold, to scatter. [bout.

Spree [perh. allied to Spry], frolic, drinking

Sprig [?], small shoot or twig.

Spright'ly [see Sprite], lively.

Spring [O.E. *springan*, *sprincan*; cf. Du. and Ger. *springen*; O.N. *springa*, to burst], leap, fly back when bent, arise; leap, flying back, elastic contrivance usu. of metal, source esp. of a stream, season before summer.

Spring'bok [S. Af. Du. *springen*, to spring; *bok*, goat], South African gazelle.

Springe (*g=j*) [see Spring], snare with a spring-noose.

Spring'-tide, high tide soon after new and full moon, (poetical) spring-time.

Spring'y, elastic.

Sprin'kle [formerly *sprenkle*; perh. Du. *sprenkelen*, to sprinkle], scatter in small drops or particles.

Sprint [O.N. *spretta*, to start], short race at full speed; run at full speed.

Sprit [O.E. *spréot*, a pole; cogn. with Sprout], spar set diagonally to extend fore and aft sail.

Sprite [L. *spīritus*, a spirit], fairy, elf.

Sprocket [?], tooth of a cog-wheel.

Sprout [O.E. *sprútan*; cf. Du. *spruiten*; cogn. with Sprat], shoot forth; shoot of a plant.

Spruce [O.F. *Pruce*, Prussia], kind of fir.

Spruce [prob. O.F. *Pruce*, Prussia, with reference to Prussian leather jerkin], neat.

Spry [?], nimble.

Spud [?], kind of small spade for digging up roots.

Spue [see **Spew**].

Spume [L. *spūma*, foam], foam ; to foam.

Spunk [orig. obscure ; prob. conn. with **Funk**], pluck, courage, mettle.

Spur [O.E. *spura*, *spora* ; Com. Teut.], pricking instrument fixed to a rider's heel, hard projection on cock's leg, incentive, projecting mountain range ; incite, ride hard.

Spurge [L. *expurgāre*, to clear away], plant with acrid juice.

Spu′ri-ous [L. *spurius*, false], not genuine.

Spurn [O.E. *spurnan*, *spornan* ; cf. O.N. *sporna* ; cogn. with **Spur**], kick aside, treat with scorn.

Spurt [?], gush suddenly, make sudden effort ; jet, short violent effort.

Sput′ter [freq. of **Spout**], emit with a spitting sound, utter words hurriedly and confusedly.

Spu′tum [p.p. of L. *spuere*, to spit], spittle.

Spy [short for **Espy**], gain sight of, search closely ; one who watches secretly.

Squab′ble (*a=ŏ*) [Swed. dial. *skvabbel*, a dispute ; prob. imit.], to quarrel noisily ; a brawl.

Squad (*a=ŏ*) [It. *squadra*, a square], small party, esp. for drill.

Squad′ron (*a=ŏ*) [It. *squadrone*, aug. of *squadra*, a square], a body of cavalry, detachment of a fleet.

Squal′id (*a=ŏ*) [L. *squālidus*, dirty ; *squālēre*, to be dirty], dirty through neglect, mean. **Squalid′ity.**

Squall (*a=ŏ*) [perh. fr. Swed. *sqvala*, to gush out. Etym. doubtful], violent gust of wind, loud scream ; cry violently. **Squal′ly.** [ness.

Squa′lor (*a=ŏ*) [L. *squalēre*, to be dirty], foul-

Squan′der (*a=ŏ*) [?], spend wastefully.

Square [O.F. *esquare* ; L. *ex-*, out, *quadrus*, 4-cornered], equal-sided rectangle, 4-sided area, L-shaped or T-shaped instrument, product of a number multiplied by itself ; having 4 sides and 4 right angles, fair, honest ; multiply (number) by itself, adjust.

Squash [O.F. *esquasser*, to crush ; L. *exquassāre*], crush ; a crowd.

Squash [Amer.-Ind. *asqutasquash*], pumpkin.

Squat [O.F. *esquatir*, to flatten ; O.F. *es-* (L. *ex-*), extremely, and *quatir*, to beat down], sit on the heels or hams ; short and thick. [title.

Squat′ter [see **Squat**], settler on land without

Squaw [Amer.-Ind. *squa*, a squaw], American-Indian woman.

Squawk [imit.], utter harsh cry ; harsh cry.

Squeak [prob. imit. ; cf. Swed. *sqväka*], utter a sharp shrill cry ; sharp shrill sound.

Squeal [imit. ; cf. M. Swed. *sqwæla*, to squeal], utter a prolonged shrill cry ; prolonged shrill cry.

Squeam′ish [earlier *squeamous*. Etym. doubtful], easily disgusted, sickish, over-scrupulous.

Squee′gee [etym. doubtful ; cf. **Squeeze**], rubber-edged brush for wet deck or road.

Squeeze [E., perh. strengthened form of obs. *quease*], press ; pressure.

Squelch [cf. dial. *quelch*, a blow], crush ; sound made by crushing.

Squib [prob. imit.], small firework, short witty essay.

Squill [L. *squilla* ; Gk. *skilla*, a squill], plant used in medicine.

Squint [cf. Du. *shuinte*, to slant], look obliquely, to have the eyes looking in different directions ; looking obliquely.

Squire [as **Esquire**], chief landed proprietor in a district, attendant on a knight (middle ages) ; to escort (a lady).

Squirm [prob. imit.], wriggle.

Squir′rel [Gk. *skiouros*, squirrel, perh. fr. *skia*, shadow, and *oura*, tail], gnawing animal with a bushy tail.

Squirt [orig. uncertain ; cf. Low G. *swirtjen*, fr. *swiren*, to whirl], eject a jet of water, etc. ; instrument for squirting.

Stab [prob. Swed. dial. *stabbe*, a thick stick ; O.N. *stabbi*, a stump], pierce with a knife, etc. ; a thrust with a knife, etc., wound therefrom.

Sta′ble [L. *stabilis*, firm], fixed, firm. **Stabil′ity.**

Sta′ble [L. *stabulum*, a stall ; O.E. *estable*, a stable ; L. *stāre*, to stand], house for horses ; to put in a stable. **Stab′ling.**

Stack [O.N. *stakkr*, haystack], large pile of grain, hay, etc., number of chimneys standing together, a tall chimney ; lay in a pile.

Sta′di-um [L. *stadium* ; Gk. *stadion*], Gk. measure of about 202 yds., course for foot-race.

Staff [O.E. *stœf* ; Com. Teut. ; (pl.) **Staffs**, (mus.) **Staves**], stick, pole, five lines used in writing music, body of assistants.

Stag [prob. fr. O.E. *staega* ; O.N. *steggr*, *steggi*, a male animal (he-bird, drake, tom-cat, etc.], male of a deer.

Stage [O.F. *estage*, stage, dwelling-place ; Late L. *staticum*, dwelling-place ; L. *stāre* (sup. *statum*), to stand], raised platform, dramatic art, scene of activity, degree of progress, stopping-place, road between two stopping-places ; put a play on the stage.

Stag′ger [O.N. *stakra*, freq. of *staka*, to push], sway from side to side as if about to fall ; reeling motion. **Stagg′erer.**

Stag′nant [L. *stagnans* (*-antis*), pr.p. of *stagnāre*, to stagnate], not flowing, dull.

Stag′nate [L. *stagnāre* (p.p. *stagnatus*), to stagnate ; *stagnum*, a pool], cease to flow, become dull. **Stagna′tion.**

Sta′gy, theatrical in manner. [steady.

Staid [formerly *stayed*, p.p. of **Stay**], sober,

Stain [O.F. *desteindre* ; L. *dis*, apart ; *tingere*, to dye], discolour, dye ; discoloration, blemish.

Stair [O.E. *stœger* ; cf. Du. *steiger* ; Ger. *steg*, a path], series of steps, one of the steps.

Stair′case, stairs with their framework.

Stake[1] [O.E. *staca*; cf. M. Du. *stake*; O.N. *stjaki*; cogn. with **Stack**], pointed stick, post; fix with stakes, mark (out) with stakes.

Stake[2] [?], money wagered, pledge; to wager.

Sta-lac'tite [Gk. *stalactos*, trickling, *stalassein*, to drip], hanging cone of carbonate of lime.

Sta-lag'mite [Gk. *stalagmos*, dripping, *stalassein*, to drip], deposit of lime on the floor.

Stale [etym. difficult to trace; prob. from Teut. root *sta*, to stand], tasteless from age, not new.

Stale'mate [Stale and Mate. See **Checkmate**], position of king in chess which results in a drawn game.

Stalk (*al=aw*) [M.E. *stalke*, dim. of O.E. *stœla*, a stalk], stem, tall chimney.

Stalk [O.E. *stealcan*, to walk warily, perh. fr. *stealc*, high], proceed under cover, walk with stately steps.

Stall (*a=aw*) [O.E. *steal(l)*; Com. Teut.], stable, division in a stable, table on which things are placed for sale, fixed seat in the choir, seat in a theatre; put in a stall.

Stal'lion (*ă*) [O.F. *estalon*, a stallion; O.H.G. *stal*, a stall], male horse.

Stal'wart (*a=aw*) [earlier *stalworth*; O.E. *stael*, place, *vierthe*, worth], bold and strong.

Sta'men [L. *stāmen*, thread, warp; *stāre*, to stand], pollen-bearing part of a plant.

Stam'i-na [L. pl. of *stāmen*, thread], staying-power, vigour.

Stam'mer [O.E. *stamerian*; cogn. with **Stumble**], speak haltingly; this habit of speech. **Stam'merer**.

Stamp [Early M.E. *stampen*; cf. Du. *stampen*; Ger. *stampfen*], bring down one's foot, crush, impress with a mark, put a stamp on; act of stamping, that which stamps, thing stamped, official mark, kind, sort.

Stam-pede' [Sp. *estampido*, a crash, *estampar*, to stamp], wild, frightened running away.

Stanch, Staunch [O.F. *estanchier*, to stanch; L. *stagnāre*, to stagnate], stop the flowing of blood.

Stan'chion [O.F. *estanchon*, dim. of *estance*, a situation, a stanchion; Late L. *stantia*, an abode], prop of timber or iron.

Stand [O.E. *standan*, *stondan*; Com. Teut., cogn. with L. *stăre*], be erect on the feet, stop, endure, hold good, be equivalent; act of standing, a stop, station, something on which things may be placed, raised structure for spectators.

Stand'ard [O.F. *estandard*, fr. O.H.G. *standan*, to stand, and O.F. *estendard*, fr. L. *extendere*, to extend], distinctive flag, thing serving as a basis of comparison; being or according with a standard of comparison. **Stand'ardize**.

Stand'ing, continuance, position.

Stan'na-ry [Late L. *stannāria*, from L. *stannum*, tin], tin-mine, tin-mining district.

Stan'za [It. *stanza*, fr. L. *stāre* (pr.p. *stans*, *stantis*), to stand], group of lines of verse.

Sta'ple [O.F. *estaple* market; Low G. *stapel*, a heap], principal article of commerce, fibre of wool, etc.; chief.

Sta'ple [O.E. *stapol*; cf. Du *stapel*; Dan. *stabel*, a pile], bent loop of iron with pointed ends.

Star [O.E. *steorra*; cf. Du. *ster*; Ger. *stern*], heavenly body, object with radiating points. **Star'ry**.

Star'board [O.E. *stéorbord*; *stéor*, a rudder, *bord*, board], right-hand side of a ship.

Starch [O.E. *stercan*, to strengthen; cogn. with **Stark**], stiffening substance; stiffen with starch.

Stare [O.E. *starian*, to stare; *stær*, stiff], look fixedly; fixed look. [wholly.

Stark [O.E. *stearc*, strong], stiff, strong;

Star'ling [O.E. and Dan. *staer*, a starling, and noun suf. *-ling*], bird with dark plumage shot with purple, green, and blue.

Start [M.E. *sterten*; cogn. with Du. *storten*; Ger. *stürzen*, to hurl], move suddenly from surprise, etc., begin; sudden motion, a beginning.

Start'le [freq. of Start], give shock to.

Starve [O.E. *steorfan*, to die], perish from cold or hunger, lack food; deprive of food, destroy by want. **Starva'tion**.

Starve'ling, starving person.

State [L. *stāre* (sup. *statum*), to stand], condition, pomp, nation; to express in words.

State'ly [see State], dignified, lofty.

State'ment, expression in words, account.

State'room, room for ceremonial occasions; private saloon in steamer or train.

States'man, one versed in state affairs.

Stat'ic, Stat'ic-al [Gk. *staticos*, at a standstill; *statos*, placed, standing], pertaining to bodies at rest or forces in equilibrium.

Sta'tion [L. *stāre* (sup. *statum*), to stand], standing-place, railway stopping-place, position, military post; assign a position to.

Sta'tion-a-ry, not moving, fixed.

Sta'tion-er [earlier, a bookseller; L. *stātiōnārius*, stationary, in M.L. a bookseller], one who sells writing materials, etc.

Sta'tion-er-y, things sold by stationers.

Stat'ist [fr. State], one who deals with statistics. [ti'cian.

Sta-tis'tics, classified numerical facts. **Statis-**

Stat'u-a-ry [see Statue], sculptor, statues.

Stat'ue [L. *statua*, a standing image; *stāre*, to stand], sculptured or cast figure.

Stat'u-esque', having the dignity of a statue. **Statuet'te**, small statue.

Stat'ure [L. *stāre* (sup. *statum*), to stand], height of a person.

Sta'tus [L. *stāre* (sup. *statum*), to stand], position in society, a profession, etc.

Stat'ute [L. *statuere* (p.p. *statūtus*), to place, causal of *stāre*, to stand], law passed by a legislature. **Stat'utory**.

Staunch, Stanch [O.F. *estanche*], trustworthy, loyal.

Stave [var. of **Staff**], side-timber of a cask, verse; to break in the timbers of, ward off, delay, break hole (in cask, boat).

Stay [O.F. *estayer*, to prop ; M. Du. *stade*, *staeye*, a prop], stop, prop, delay ; a prop, (pl.) a corset.

Stay [O.E. *stœg* ; perh. fr. O.F. *estaye*], rope supporting spar or mast.

Stead [O.E. and Du. *stede*, a place, cogn. with **Stand**, as in **Bedstead**], place, room.

Stead'fast, firm, resolute.

Stead'ing, the barns, stables, etc., of a farm.

Stead'y, firm, constant ; make or become steady.

Steak (*ea=ai*) [O.N. *steikja*, to roast on a spit], slice of beef, etc., cut for broiling, etc.

Steal [O.E. *stelan* ; cf. Du. *stelen* ; Ger. *stehlen*], take wrongfully or by surprise, move silently.

Stealth, secret procedure. **Stealth'y.**

Steam [O.E. *stéam* ; cf. Du. *stoom*], water in the state of vapour ; give out steam, apply steam to, move under steam-power.

Steam'er, ship propelled by steam, vessel in which articles are steamed.

Ste'a-rin [Gk. *stear*, fat], chief constituent of tallow and suet. [horse.

Steed [O.E. *stéda*], spirited horse, esp. war-

Steel [O.E. *style* ; cf. Du. *staal* ; Ger. *stahl*], alloy of iron and carbon, sharpening implement ; harden.

Steel'yard [fr. the London *Steelyard*, where the Hanse merchants used to meet], kind of balance with unequal arms.

Steep [O.N. *steypa*, pour out liquids], soak in liquid.

Steep [O.E. *stéap*, cogn. with prec.], having a decided slope ; slope, precipice.

Stee'ple [O.E. *stýpel*, cogn. with prec.], tower and spire together.

Stee'ple-chase, horse-race across country, over hedges, ditches, etc. (perh. orig. with a steeple as goal).

Steer [O.E. *stéor* ; cf. Du. and Ger. *stier*, a bull], young male of the ox kind.

Steer [O.E. *stéoran*, fr. *stéor*, a rudder], guide a vessel, motor-vehicle, etc., direct one's course. **Steers'man.**

Steer'age, part of a ship allotted to passengers paying least, effect of helm on ship.

Stel'lar [L. *stélla*, a star], relating to stars.

Stem [O.E. *stefn*, *stemn* ; cf. O.N. *stafn*, *stamn*, stem of a ship], main body, stalk, part of word to which case-endings are added, upright front part of a ship.

Stem [cf. O.N. *stemma*, to stem ; Dan. *stemme* ; Ger. *stemmen*], check. [smell.

Stench [O.E. *stenc*, cogn. with **Stink**], evil

Sten'cil [perh. O.F. *estenceler*, to sparkle, cover with stars, *estencele*, a spark], thin plate with pattern cut out, used in marking, painting, etc., the pattern so made.

Sten-og'ra-phy [Gk. *stenos*, narrow, *graphein*, to write], shorthand. **Stenograph'ic.**

Sten-to'ri-an [Gk. *Stentor*, a herald in the Trojan war], extremely loud. **Sten'tor.**

Step [O.E. *steppan*, cogn. with **Stamp**], set down the foot ; pace, footprint, surface to place the foot on in ascending and descending, socket for mast.

Step'child [O.E. *stéopcild* ; *stéop*, orphaned, *cild*, child], one's wife's or husband's child by a previous marriage.

Steppe [Russ. *stepe*, a steppe], treeless plain in Russia.

Ste're-o-scope [Gk. *stereos*, solid, *scopein*, to look], instrument for giving to pictures the effect of solid forms. **Ste'reoscopic.**

Ste're-o-type [Gk. *stereos*, solid, *typos*, type], printing-plate cast from a mould made from an assemblage of type ; prepare for printing in stereotype, fix.

Ster'ile [L. *sterilis*, barren], unfruitful, free from living germs, esp. of disease.

Ster'il-ize, destroy germs. **Steril'ity.**

Ster'ling [M.E. ; of uncertain origin], of standard value, genuine.

Stern [O.E. *styrne*], severe, rigid.

Stern [O.N. *stjórn*, a steering helm], back part of a vessel.

Stern-u-ta'tion [L. *sternutáre* (sup. *sternutátum*), to sneeze], act of sneezing. [ing.

Ster'to-rous [L. *stertere*, to snore], like snor-

Steth'o-scope [Gk. *stethos*, chest, *scopein*, to see], instrument for examining the organs of the chest.

Ste've-dore [Sp. *estivador*, wool-packer ; L. *stípáre*, to press together], one who loads and unloads ships.

Stew [O.F. *estuve*, a stew, stove ; O.H.G. *stupa*, hot room for a bath], boil slowly in little water ; dish prepared by stewing, an agitated state.

Stew'ard [O.E. *stigweard*, fr. *stigu*, sty, and *weard* ; lit. a "sty ward"], manager of an estate, etc., one who provides for the table of a club, ship, etc., passengers' attendant on a ship. **Stew'ardess.**

Stick [O.E. *sticca*, a stick, *stician*, to stick ; cf. Ger. *stechen*], slender piece of wood ; pierce, adhere, be stayed, hesitate.

Stic'kle [fr. obs. *stickle*, to umpire, prob. fr. O.E. *stihtan*, to found], to contend about trifles. **Stick'ler.**

Stic'kle-back [O.E. *sticel*, a prickle, and **Back**], small fish with sharp spines on the back.

Stick'y, adhesive, gluey.

Stiff [O.E. *stif*, stiff], not easily bent, firm.

Sti'fle [O.N. *stifla*, to dam up, to choke], smother.

Stig'ma [Gk. *stigma* (*stigmat-os*), a mark, brand], mark of disgrace, top of pistil of flower. **Stigma'tic.**

Stig'ma-tize, describe opprobriously (as).

Stile [O.E. *stigel*, fr. *stigan*, to climb], steps over a fence or wall.

Sti-let'to [It. dim. of *stilo*, a dagger ; L. *stilus*, an iron pin], small dagger.

Still [O.E. *stille*], motionless, quiet ; to calm ; to this time, yet ; nevertheless. **Stil'ly.**

Still [L. *stilláre* (p.p. *stillátus*), to drip], distilling vessel. [storeroom.

Still'room, room for distilling, house-keeper's

Stilt [Swed. *stylta* ; Dan. *stylte*, a stilt], pole with a rest for the foot, usually in pairs.

Stilt'ed, as if on stilts, pompous.

Stim'u-lant [L. *stimulans* (*-antis*), pr.p. of *stimulāre*, to stimulate], that which stimulates, esp. alcoholic drink.

Stim'u-late [L. *stimulāre* (p.p. *stimulātus*), to prick forward], excite, spur on.

Stim'u-lus [L. *stimulus*, a goad], something that rouses.

Sting [O.E. *stingan*; cf. O.N. *stinga*], sharp organ connected with a poison gland; wound with a sting. **Sting'ingly**.

Stin'gi-ness (*g=j*), miserliness.

Stin'gy (*g=j*) [from obs. *stingy* (*g* hard), nipping; fr. **Sting**], mean and hard.

Stink [O.E. *stincan*; cf. Du. and Ger. *stinken*], emit a bad smell; bad smell.

Stint [O.E. *styntan*, fr. *stunt*, dull; cf. O.N. *stuttr*, short], keep on short allowance; fixed amount.

Sti'pend [L. *stipendium* (for *stip-pendium*), tax, tribute; L. *stips*, small coin, *pendere*, to weigh, hence to pay], settled pay.

Sti-pen'di-ar-y, one who receives a stipend, paid police magistrate.

Stip'ple [Du. *stippelen*, to dot over; *stippel*, a speck, dim. of *stip*, a point], engrave by dots.

Stip'u-late [L. *stipulāri* (p.p. *stipulātus*), to stipulate; O.L. *stipulus*, firm], make conditions. **Stip'ulation**.

Stir [O.E. *styrian*; cf. Du. *storen*; Ger. *stören*], move, rouse; a bustle.

Stir'ring, active, exciting.

Stir'rup [O.E. *stiráp*, *stigráp*, orig. a looped rope; *stigan*, to climb, *ráp*, a rope], foot-rest for a rider.

Stitch [O.E. *stice*, pricking, *stician*, to pierce], pass of a needle, turn in knitting, local sharp pain; sew.

Stith'y [obs. *stith*, an anvil; O.N. *stethi*, an anvil], anvil, smithy.

Sti'ver [Du. *stuiver*], small Dutch coin.

Stoat [M.E. *stot*, a stoat or any male animal; cogn. with O.N. *stútr*, a bull], ermine, esp. in its summer coat.

Stock [O.E. *stocc*; cf. Du. *stok*; Ger. *stock*], trunk, post, part in which other parts are inserted, family, fund, store, liquor for soup, animals raised on a farm, flower; lay up; often repeated.

Stock-ade' [Sp. *estacada*, a fence, *estaca*, a stake], inclosure or defence of stakes.

Stock'fish, salted and dried fish.

Stock'ing [dim. of *stock*, used as short for *nether-stock*; the *upper-stock* was above the knee], covering for the foot and leg.

Stocks, timber frame with holes for feet at one time used for petty offenders, timbers on which a ship rests while building.

Stod'gy [?], heavy, indigestible.

Sto'ic [L. *Stoicus*; Gk. *Stōicos*, a Stoic, lit. belonging to the colonnade because Zeno taught under a colonnade at Athens; Gk. *stōa*, a colonnade], philosopher of the school of Zeno, one who cultivates indifference to pleasure and pain.

Sto'ic-al indifferent to pleasure or pain.

Sto'i-cism, indifference to pleasure or pain.

Stoke [fr. **Stoker**], tend a furnace.

Sto'ker [Du. *stoker*, kindler, cogn. with Du. *stok*, a stick], one who tends a fire.

Stole [L. *stola*, Gk. *stolē*, a robe], shoulder-band worn by clergymen.

Stol'id [L. *stolidus*, stolid], hard to stir, dull. **Stolid'ity**.

Stom'ach (*o=ŭ, ch=k*) [Gk. *stomachos*, dim. of *stoma*, mouth], principal digestive organ, appetite; to put up with. **Stoma'chic**.

Stom'ach-er (*o=ŭ, ch=k*), front-piece in ancient dress.

Stone [O.E. *stán*; cf. Du. *steen*; Ger. *stein*], piece of rock, kernel-case, gem, 14 lbs.; throw stones at, take stones out of.

Sto'ny, full of stones, like stone.

Stool [O.E. *stól*; cf. Du. *stoel*; Ger. *stuhl*], backless seat, foot-rest.

Stoop [O.E. *stúpian*; cf. M. Du. *stuypen*; O.N. *stúpa*; cogn. with **Steep**], bend forward or down; a bend forward.

Stop [O.E. *stoppian*; Late L. *stuppāre*, to stop; L. *stuppa*, oakum, tow], close as a hole, stand still, cause to stand still; pause, check, set of organ pipes.

Stop'page, act of stopping, state of being stopped.

Stop'per, **Stop'ple**, plug for a bottle, etc.

Stor'age, act of storing, place for storing.

Store [L. *instaurāre*, to provide necessaries], quantity, place of deposit, shop, (pl.) supplies; lay away, stock, furnish.

Sto'rey, **Sto'ry** [L. *instaurāre*, to build], floor of a building on one level.

Stork [O.E. *storc*; cf. Du. *stork*; Ger. *storch*], kind of wading-bird.

Storm [O.E. *storm*; cf. Du., Swed., and Dan. *storm*; Ger. *sturm*; cogn. with **Stir**], violent disturbance of the atmosphere, etc., attack on a fort; rage, assault.

Sto'ry [O.F. *estoire*; L. *historia*, a history, tale], tale. **Stor'ied**.

Stoup (*ou=oo*) [O.N. *staup*, cf. O.E. *stéap*], flagon; holy-water basin.

Stout [O.F. *estout*; perh. fr. L. *stultus*, foolish], strong, bulky; malt liquor.

Stove [O.E. *stofa*, heated room], apparatus in which fire is made.

Stow [O.E. *stówigan*, fr. *stów*, a place], pack, put in a suitable place.

Stow'a-way, one who conceals himself on board ship, to steal a free passage.

Strad'dle [formerly *striddle*; freq. of **Stride**], part the legs wide.

Strag'gle [perh. freq. of M.E. *stráken*, to roam], spread widely apart, stray.

Straight [O.E. *streht*, p.p. of *streccan*, to stretch], direct, not bent, honest.

Straight-en, make straight.

Straight-for'ward, honest, frank.

Straight'way [**Straight** and **Way**], without delay.

Strain [O.F. *estreindre*; L. *stringere*, to draw tight], stretch tightly, sprain, wrest meaning of, filter; extreme effort.

Strain [O.E. *stréon*, gain, product, progeny], musical period, tone, stock.

Strait [L. *strictus*, p.p. of *stringere*, to draw tight], narrow ; narrow passage, difficulty.

Strait'en, hamper.

Strand [O.N.F. *estran* ; O.H.G. *streno*, a cord], string or wire of a rope.

Strand [O.E. *strand*], shore ; run aground.

Strange [L. *extrāneus*, foreign, on the outside ; *extra*, without], foreign, new, odd, shy.

Stran'ger, foreigner, one who is unknown.

Stran'gle [Gk. *straggalizein*, to strangle ; *straggalē*, a halter], kill by squeezing the throat.

Stran-gu-la'tion, act of strangling, constriction.

Strap [O.E. *stropp*, fr. L. *struppus*, a strap], strip of leather ; fasten or beat with a strap.

Strap'ping, tall and strong.

Strat'a-gem [Gk. *stratēgēma*, a stratagem ; *stratēgos*, general, leader], artifice, secret plot. [strategy.

Strat-eg'ic (*ee* or *ē*), serving the ends of **Strat'e-gy**, generalship. **Strat'egist**.

Strath [Gael. *srath*; perh. cogn. with *Stratum*], broad valley.

Strath-spey (*ey=ā*) [Strath and name of river *Spey*], Scottish dance resembling a reel.

Strat'i-fied [L. *strātum*, a layer ; *facere*, to make], arranged in layers.

Stra'tum, (*pl.*) **Stra'ta** [L. *strātum*, a layer], layer or set of layers. [grain.

Straw [O.E. *streaw*], stalk, dry cut stalks of

Straw'ber-ry [Straw (because of runners) and Berry], plant and its pulpy fruit.

Stray [O.F. *estraier*, to stray ; L. *strāta*, a street], wander, lose one's way ; animal that has strayed ; strayed, occurring now and then.

Streak [O.E. *strica*, cogn. with **Strike**], long mark ; make streaks. **Streak'y**.

Stream [O.E. *stréam*, cf. Ger. *strom*], body of running water, a flow ; to flow.

Stream'let, little stream.

Stream'er, very long narrow flag, shooting stream of light.

Street [L. *strāta* (*via*), paved (way) ; *sternere* (p.p. *strātus*), to strew, pave], road and its houses in a town or village, the road only.

Strength [O.E. *strengthu*, fr. *strang*, strong], quality or state of being strong.

Stren'u-ous [L. *strenuus*, strenuous ; Gk. *strenēs*, strong], strong and earnest.

Stress [O.F. *estrecier*, to straiten, contract ; fr. L. *strictus*, tightened], pressure, strain.

Stretch [O.E. *streccan*], draw out, reach out ; extension, reach, effort.

Stretch'er, frame for carrying wounded or dead persons.

Strew (*ew=oo*) [O.E. *streawian*, fr. *streaw*, straw], scatter.

Stri'a-ted [L. *stria*, a streak], marked with small parallel channels.

Strick'en (p.p. of **Strike**), afflicted, weakened.

Strict [L. *stringere* (p.p. *strictus*), to tighten], exact, severe

Strict'ure, unfavourable criticism, morbid contraction.

Stride [O.E. *strīdan*], walk with long steps, stand with legs apart ; long step.

Stri'dent [L. *strīdere* (pr.p. *stridēns*, *-entis*), creak], grating, harsh. [contest.

Strife [O.F. *estrif* ; O.N. *strith*, strife], quarrel,

Strike [O.E. *strican*, to go], hit, impress, occur to, ignite (match), stamp (coin), lower (sail, etc.), quit work in a trade dispute ; act of quitting work.

Stri'king, very noticeable, impressive.

String [O.E. *streng*, cogn. with **Strong**], twine, cord of a musical instrument, series ; thread on a string, supply with a string.

Strin'gent [L. *stringere* (pr.p. *stringēns*, *-entis*), to tighten], strict, binding strongly. **Strin'gency**.

String'y, ropy, fibrous.

Strip [O.E. *strýpan*], deprive (of), peel, undress ; narrow piece.

Stripe [M. Du. *strijpe*, a stripe in cloth], narrow marking, lash-stroke.

Strip'ling [dim. of *Strip*], lad. [contend.

Strive [O.F. *estriver*, to strive], try hard,

Stroke [O.E. *strāc*, fr. *strican*, to strike], blow, shock.

Stroke [O.E. *strācian*, fr. *strāc*, a stroke], pass the hand gently in one direction.

Stroll (*ō*) [?], walk leisurely ; a saunter.

Strong [O.E. *strang*], firm, healthy, not easily overcome, powerfully affecting senses, forming inflections by internal vowel-change.

Strop [as **Strap**], strip of leather or implement for sharpening razors.

Stro'phe [Gk. *strophē*, a turning ; *strephein*, to turn], metrical series of lines forming a division of a lyric poem, lines recited during turn made in dancing by ancient Greek chorus.

Struc'ture [L. *struere* (p.p. *structus*), to build], a building, manner of building, manner of construction. **Struc'tural**.

Strug'gle [M.E. *strogelen*], strive hard, make violent effort, contend, wrestle ; hard contest, violent effort.

Strum [imit. var. of **Thrum** 2], play unskilfully on a stringed instrument.

Strut 1 [Dan. *strutte*, to strut], walk pompously or with affected gait. [rafter.

Strut 2 [cogn. with **Strut** 1], support for a

Strych'ni-a, Strych'nine (*ch=k*) [Gk. *strychnos*, night-shade], deadly poison.

Stub [O.E. *stybb*, cf. O.N. *stubbi*], stump ; clear (land) of stubs. **Stub'by**.

Stub'ble [Late L. *stupula*, var. of L. *stipula*, stubble], stumps of grain after harvest.

Stub'born [M.E. *stoburn*, *stiborn*, prob. fr. O.E. *stybb*, a stub], obstinate. **Stub'born-ness**.

Stuc'co [It. *stucco* ; O.H.G. *stucchi*, a crust], fine plaster used for decoration.

Stud [O.E. *stód*, cogn. with **Stand**], collection of horses.

Stud [O.E. *studu*, a post], two-headed button, boss ; adorn with knobs, set thickly

Stu′dent [L. *studēre* (pr.p. *studēns, -entis*), to study], one who studies, learner.

Stu′di-o [It. *studio*, a studio; L. *studium*, study], artist's working-room.

Stu′di-ous, given to study, painstaking.

Stud′y [L. *studium*, zeal, study], application of mind, subject studied, room for study; apply the mind. [to cram.

Stuff [L. *stupa, stuppa*, tow], material, trash;

Stuff′y, ill-ventilated, close.

Stul′ti-fy [L. *stultus*, foolish; *facere*, to make], reduce to absurdity, show in ridiculous light, make ineffective. **Stulti-fica′tion.**

Stum′ble [M.E. *stomblen, stomelen, stumlen*, a doublet of **Stammer**], trip; act of tripping, blunder.

Stump [O.N. *stumpr*, cogn. with **Stub**], remnant of a cut tree or limb, rod of a wicket; walk clumsily, go round making speeches, put out of play.

Stump′y, short and thick.

Stun [O.E. *stunian*, to resound], knock senseless, bewilder.

Stunt [O.E. *stunt*, dull; cf. O.N. *stuttr*, short], check growth.

Stu′pe-fy [L. *stupēre*, to be stupid; *facere*, to make], make stupid or dull. **Stupe-fac′tion.**

Stu-pen′dous [L. *stupēre*, to be amazed], amazing, esp. from size.

Stu′pid [L. *stupidus*, stupid; *stupēre*, to be amazed], dull, not clever. **Stupid′ity.**

Stu′por [L. *stupēre*, to be amazed], dazed state, helpless surprise.

Stur′dy [O.F. *estourdi*], amazed, heedless. Etym. doubtful], strongly built, robust.

Stur′geon [O.H.G. *sturjo*, sturgeon], large food-fish resembling the shark.

Stut′ter [freq. of obs. *stut*, to stutter; cf. Du. *stotteren*; Ger. *stottern*], to stammer; a stammer.

Sty [O.E. *stigu*, prob. fr. *stigan*, to climb], place for pigs.

Sty, Stye [O.E. *stigend*, lit. "rising"; *stigan*, to rise], swelling on the eyelid.

Styg′ian [Gk. *Styx (Stygos)*, the Styx], murky, gloomy, as in Hades.

Style[1] [O.F. *stile, style*; L. *stilus*, iron pin for writing, way of writing], engraver's tool, manner, superior manner, diction, designation; to name.

Style[2] [Gk. *stylos*, a pillar], pin of a dial, part of a flower. [style.

Styl′ist, person who has or aims at a good

Styl′ish, having style, highly fashionable.

Styl′o-graph [**Style**[1] and Gk. *graphein*, to write], fountain pen with point instead of split nib. **Stylograph′ic.**

Styp′tic [Gk. *stypticos*, astringent; *styptein*, to contract], stopping bleeding.

Styx, one of the mythical rivers of Hades, the Greek abode of the dead.

Sua′sion (*u=w*) [L. *suādēre* (p.p. *suāsus*), to urge], persuasion.

Suave (*u=w*) [L. *suāvis*, sweet], sweet, pleasant, bland.

Suav′i-ty (*u=w*), softness, pleasantness.

Sub-ah-dar′ (*u=oo*) [Hind. *subah*, a province, *-dar*, *-keeping*], chief native officer of sepoys.

Sub′al-tern [M.L. *subalternus*, subordinate; L. *sub-*, under, *alter*, another], officer below a captain; inferior.

Sub′cu-ta′ne-ous [L. *sub*, under, *cutis*, skin], under the skin.

Sub′di-vide [L. *sub*, under, *dīvidere*, to divide], divide parts.

Sub′di-vi′sion, part of a part.

Sub-due′ [L. *subdere*, to subdue], bring under, overcome, soften. **Subdu′al.**

Sub′ject, owing obedience, exposed; one who is ruled, matter dealt with.

Sub-ject′ [L. *subjicere* (p.p. *subjectus*); *sub*, under, *jacere*, to throw], bring under control, make liable.

Sub-jec′tion, act of subjecting.

Sub-jec′tive, derived from one's own consciousness, imaginary. Cf. **Objective.**

Sub-join′ [L. *subjungere* (p.p. *subjunctus*); *sub*, under, *jungere*, to join], add at the end.

Sub′ju-gate [L. *subjugāre* (p.p. *subjugātus*); *sub*, under, *jugum*, a yoke], bring under control. **Subjuga′tion.**

Sub-junc′tive [see **Subjoin**], sometimes used in subordinate clauses.

Sub′lim-ate [L. *sublimāre* (p.p. *sublimātus*), to sublimate; see **Sublime**], convert solid to vapour by heat and reconvert to solid by cold, purify; substance prepared thus. **Sublima′tion.**

Sub-lime′ [L. *sublimis*; perh. fr. *sub*, under, and *limen*, lintel], exalted, noble. **Sublim′ity.**

Sub-lu′na-ry [L. *sub*, under, *luna*, moon], on the earth.

Sub-ma-rine′ (*ine=een*) [L. *sub*, under, *marinus*, marine], under the sea.

Sub′ma-rine, craft sailing under water.

Sub-merge′ [L. *sub*, under, *mergere* (p.p. *mersus*), to dip], to put under water, to sink. **Submer′sible.** [under.

Sub-mer′gence, Sub-mer′sion, a plunging

Sub-mis′sion, act of submitting, meekness.

Sub-mis′sive, yielding, humble.

Sub-mit′ [L. *sub*, under, and *mittere* (p.p. *missus*), to put], yield, surrender, urge, present for consideration.

Sub-or′di-nate [L. *sub*, under, and *ordināre*, to rank; *ordo (ordin-is)*, order], inferior; one below another in rank, etc.; place in a lower order.

Sub-or′di-na′tion [see **Subordinate**], subjection, inferiority.

Sub-orn′ [L. *sub*, under, *ornāre*, to equip], cause to commit perjury or other unlawful act.

Sub-pœ′na (*œ=ee*) [L. *sub*, under, *pœna*, penalty], writ summoning a witness; summon a witness.

Sub-scribe′ [L. *sub*, under, *scrībere* (p.p. *scriptus*), to write], sign, promise by signing

Sub-scrip'tion, signature, sum subscribed.

Sub'se-quent [L. *sub*, under, *sequi* (pr.p. *sequens*, *-entis*), to follow], following in time, later. **Sub'sequence.**

Sub-serve' [L. *sub*, under, *servire*, to serve], serve as a means to. **Subser'vience.**

Sub-serv'i-ent, serving to an end, truckling.

Sub-side' [L. *sub*, under, *sidere*, to settle], sink. [siding.

Sub'sid-ence, **Sub-sid'ence**, process of sub-

Sub-sid'i-a-ry, furnishing aid, supplementary.

Sub'si-dize, aid with public money.

Sub'si-dy [L. *subsidium*, reserve troops, assistance; *sub*, under, *sedere*, to sit], money grant.

Sub-sist' [L. *sub*, under, *sistere*, to stand, to place], exist, keep oneself in life.

Sub-sist ence, livelihood.

Sub'stance [L. *sub*, under, *stare* (pr.p. *stans*, *stantis*), stand], body, reality, material, meaning.

Sub-stan'tial (*ti=sh*), real, having good substance.

Sub-stan'ti-ate (*t=sh*), verify, prove. **Sub-stantia'tion.**

Sub'stan-tive, having a separate existence; old name for noun. **Substanti'val.**

Sub'sti-tute [L. *substituere* (p.p. *substitutus*), to substitute; *sub*, under, *statuere*, to put, place], one in the place of another; put in the place of another. **Sub-stitu'-tion.**

Sub-tend' [L. *sub*, under, and *tendere*, to stretch], be opposite to.

Sub'ter-fuge [L. *subter*, secretly, *fugere*, to flee], evasion, shift.

Sub-ter-ra'ne-an [L. *sub*, under, *terra*, the earth], below the ground.

Sub'tile [L. *subtilis*, fine, thin; *sub*, under, *tela*, a web], thin, fine (archaic word).

Subt'le [earlier *subtile*], fine, sly, cunning.

Sub-tract' [L. *sub*, under, *trahere* (p.p. *tractus*), to draw], withdraw, take away. **Subtrac'tion.**

Sub'tra-hend [see Subtract], sum or number to be taken away.

Sub'urb [L. *sub*, near, *urbs*, a city], outlying part of a city or town. **Subur'ban.**

Sub-ven'tion [L. *sub*, under, *venire* (sup. *ventum*), to come], grant of money in aid.

Sub-ver'sion, an overturning. **Subver'sive.**

Sub-vert' [L. *sub*, under, *vertere* (p.p. *versus*), to turn], overturn.

Sub'way [L. *sub*, under, and Way], underground passage.

Suc-ceed' [L. *succedere* (p.p. *successus*), to succeed; *sub*, near, *cedere*, to go], follow, prosper.

Suc-cess', favourable issue, good fortune, thing or person that turns out well.

Suc-ces'sion, a following in order, series.

Suc-ces'sive, following in a line or series.

Suc-ces'sor, one who follows another.

Suc-cinct' [L. *succinctus*, p.p. of *succingere*, to gird up; *sub*, under, *cingere*, to gird], brief, concise.

Suc'co-ry [corruption of Chicory (q.v.)].

Suc'cour [L. *succursus*, succour; *sub*, near, *currere*, to run], to help; aid, relief.

Suc'cu-lent [L. *succus*, juice], juicy. **Suc'culence.**

Suc-cumb' [L. *sub*, under, *cumbere*, to lie], yield, submit.

Such [O.E. *swylc*, fr. *swá*, so, *-lic*, *-like*], of a like kind, of that kind.

Suck [O.E. *súcan*], draw in with the mouth, roll about in the mouth; act of sucking, opportunity of sucking the breast.

Suck'le, give suck to.

Suck'ling, unweaned babe or animal.

Suc'tion [L. *sugere* (p.p. *suctus*), to suck], act of sucking, production of partial vacuum by removing air.

Su'da-to-ry [L. *sudare*, to sweat], promoting perspiration; hot-air bath.

Sud'den [L. *subitaneus*, sudden; *sub*, under, *ire* (sup. *itum*), to go], unexpected, abrupt, quick. **Sud'denness.**

Su-dor-if'ic [L. *sudor*, sweat; *facere*, to make], causing sweat. [water.

Suds [O.E. *séothan*, to seethe], froth of soapy

Sue [L. *sequi*, to follow], follow up, prosecute in law-court, woo.

Su'et [O.F. *seu*; L. *sebum*, tallow], hard fat of oxen and sheep.

Suf'fer [L. *sufferre*, to suffer; *sub*, under, *ferre*, to carry], bear, feel pain.

Suf'fer-ance, toleration, tacit consent.

Suf-fice' (*i*) [L. *sub*, under, *facere*, to make], be enough.

Suf-fi'cien-cy (*tci=tsh*) [L.L. *sufficientia*; see Suffice], adequate amount.

Suf-fi'cient (*ici=tsh*), enough.

Suf'fix [L. *sub*, under, *figere* (p.p. *fixus*), to fix], letter or syllable added to the end of a word.

Suf'fo-cate [L. *suffocare* (p.p. *suffocatus*); *sub*, under, *fauces*, the throat], choke by stopping breathing. **Suffoca'tion.**

Suf'fra-gan [L. *suffragium*, a vote], assistant bishop, bishop in relation to his arch-bishop.

Suf'frage [L. *suffragium*, a vote], vote, right of voting.

Suf'fra-gist, one strongly in favour of an extension of voting.

Suf-fuse' (*s=z*) [L. *sub*, under, *fundere* (p.p. *fusus*), to pour], overspread as with fluid. [suffused.

Suf-fu'sion, a suffusing, that which is

Su'gar (*s=sh*) [Arab. *sakkar*; Pers. *shakar*, sugar], sweet crystalline substance. **Su'gary.**

Sug-gest' [L. *sub*, under, *gerere* (p.p. *gestus*), to bring], cause to be thought of, hint.

Sug-ges'tion, presentation of an idea, a hint.

Sug-ges'tive, containing suggestion.

Su'i-cide [L. *sui*, of himself, *cædere*, to kill], self-murder, one who kills himself. **Suicid'al.**

Suit [O.F. *suite*, a following; L. *sequi*, to follow], suing, legal prosecution, a set; make or be fitting.

Suit'a-ble, fitting, appropriate.

Suite (*ui=wee*) [F. *suite* (as Suit)], company of attendants, set of things belonging together.

Suit′or, one who sues, petitioner, wooer.

Sulk [back formation from **Sulky**], be silently sullen.

Sul′ky [O.E. *solcen* slothful], sullen, silent from ill-humour.

Sul′len [M.E. and O.F. *solain*, lonely; L. *sōlus*, alone], gloomy-tempered, passively resentful. **Sul′lenness.**

Sul′ly [O.E. *sylian*, fr. *sol*, mire], to soil, darken.

Sul′phur [L. *sulphur*, sulphur], yellow non-metallic element.   [tion.

Sul-phur-et′ted, having sulphur in combina-

Sul-phu′ric acid, strong acid sometimes called vitriol or oil of vitriol.

Sul-phur′eous, Sul′phu-rous, containing sulphur. **Sulphurous acid,** the acid forming the fumes of burning sulphur.

Sul′tan [Arab. *sultān*, victorious, also a ruler], ruler of a Mohammedan state.

Sul-ta′na [It. *sultana*, fem. of *sultano*, sultan], wife, mother, or daughter of a sultan, kind of raisin grown at Smyrna.

Sul′try [formerly *sweltry*; O.E. *sweltan*, to die], hot and oppressive. **Sul′triness.**

Sum [L. *summa*, sum (orig. fem. of *summus*, highest)], amount, quantity of money, problem to be solved; add.

Su′mac(h) [Sp. *zumaque*; Arab. *summāq*, sumach], leaves used in tanning.

Sum′ma-ry [L. *summa*, sum], brief account; brief.

Sum′ma-rize, sum up, state briefly.

Sum-ma′tion [L. *summāre* (p.p. *summātus*), to sum], finding of total.

Sum′mer [O.E. *sumor*], warmest season; spend the summer.

Sum′mer-sault, Sum′mer-set [see **Som′er-sault**].

Sum′mit [L. *summus*, highest], top.

Sum′mon [O.F. *somoner*; L. *sub*, under, privately, *monēre*, to warn], call, bid, cite.

Sum′mons [O.F. *semonse*, orig. fem. p.p. of *semondre*, to summon], urgent call; serve with summons.

Sump′ter [Gk. *sagma*, pack-saddle], packhorse or driver.

Sump′tu-a-ry [L. *sumptus*, expense], limiting expense.   [luxurious.

Sump′tu-ous [L. *sumptus*, expense], costly,

Sun [O.E. *sunne*; cf. Du. *zon*; Ger. *sonne*], source of light and heat; expose to the sun.

Sun′day [O.E. *sunnan dæg*, day of the sun].

Sun′der [O.E. *sundrian*, fr. *sundor*, asunder], to part, separate.   [various.

Sun′dry [O.E. *syndrig*. See **Sunder**], several,

Sun′ny, pertaining to the sun, bright.

Sun′rise, time when the sun appears above the horizon.

Sun′set, time when the sun goes down.

Sun′stroke, prostration from exposure to the sun.

Sup [O.E. *sūpan*], take by spoonfuls, take supper; mouthful of liquid.

Su′per-a-bun′dance [L. *super*, beyond, and **Abundance**], excess.

Su′per-an′nu-ate [formerly *superannate*; L. *super*, beyond, *annus*, a year], dismiss or pension off as too old. **Superannua′tion.**

Su-perb′ [L. *superbus*, proud], grand, magnificent.

Su′per-car′go [L. *super*, above, and **Cargo**], officer in a merchant ship who manages the sales.

Su-per-cil′i-ous [L. *supercilium*, eyebrow; *super*, above, *cilium*, eyelid], lofty with pride, disdainful.

Su-per-er-o-ga′tion [L. *superērogāre* (p.p. *superērogātus*), pay out in excess; *super*, beyond, *ē* (*ex*), out, *rogāre*, to ask], doing of more than is required.

Su-per-fi′cial (*ici=ish*), on the surface.

Su-per-fi′cies [L. *super*, above, *faciēs*, face], surface.

Su′per-fine [L. *super*, beyond, and **Fine**], very fine, too fine.

Su-per′flu-ous [L. *super*, over, *fluere*, to flow], more than is wanted, needless.

Su-per-hu′man [L. *super*, above, *humānus*, human], above what is human.

Su-per-in-tend′ [L. *super*, above, *intendere*, apply the mind to], oversee with authority. **Superintend′ence.**

Su-per-in-tend′ent, overseer, manager.

Su-pe′ri-or [L. *superior*, comp. of *superus*, high; *super*, above], higher, better, consciously better; one who surpasses another, head of a monastery.   [vantage.

Su-pe-ri-or′i-ty, higher position, etc., advantage.

Su-per′la-tive [L. *super*, beyond, *lātus*, p.p. of *ferre*, to bear], in the highest degree.

Su′per-man [L. *super*, beyond, and **Man**], ideal man, overman of Nietzsche's philosophy.   [lofty.

Su-per′nal [L. *supernus*, upper], heavenly,

Su-per-nat′u-ral [L. *super*, beyond, *nātūra*, nature], beyond nature, miraculous.

Su-per-nu′mer-a-ry [L. *super*, beyond, *numerus*, number], beyond the number stated; extra person engaged.

Su-per-scribe′ [L. *super*, above; *scrībere* (p.p. *scriptus*), to write], write above or upon.

Su-per-scrip′tion, a writing above or upon.

Su-per-sede′ [L. *super*, beyond, *sedēre* (sup. *sessum*), to sit], replace, displace.

Su-per-ses′sion [see **Supersede**], replacement by another.

Su-per-sti′tion [L. *superstitio*; *super*, above, *stare* (sup. *statum*), to stand], irrational fear of, or reverence for, the unknown. **Supersti′tious.**

Su-per-vene′ [L. *super*, over, and *venīre*, to come], come as something additional or as an interruption. **Superven′tion.**

Su-per-vise′ [L. *super*, over, *vidēre* (p.p.*vīsus*), to see], oversee, superintend.

Su-per-vi′sion, superintendence, charge.

Su-per-vi′sor, overseer.

Su′pine [L. *supīnus*; fr. root of *super*, above], (verbal noun), lying on the back, listless.

Sup'per [O.F. *soper*, to sup], evening meal.

Sup-plant' [L. *supplantāre*; *sub*, under, *planta*, sole of foot], to displace.

Sup'ple [L. *supplex*, supple; *sub*, under, *plicāre*, to fold], pliant, bending.

Sup'ple-ment [L. *supplēmentum*, a filling up; *sub*, under, up, *plēre*, to fill], that which serves to complete or make perfect.

Sup-ple-ment', add something to. [thing.

Sup-ple-men'ta-ry, added to supply some-

Sup'pli-ant or **Sup'pli-cant** [F. *suppliant*, pr.p. of *supplier*; L. *supplicāre*, to beseech], entreating; one who entreats.

Sup'pli-cate [L. *supplicāre* (p.p. *supplicātus*), to beseech; *supplex* (*supplic-is*), bending under], make humble petition to or for.

Sup-pli-ca'tion, humble prayer.

Sup-ply' [L. *supplēre*, to fill up; *sub*, under, *plēre*, to fill], fill up, provide; that which supplies a want, stock.

Sup-port' [L. *supportāre*; *sub*, under, *portāre*, to carry], hold up, endure, aid; means of living, prop, aid. **Suppor'table**.

Sup-pose' [L. *suppōnere* (p.p. *suppositus*), to substitute for; *sub*, under, *pōnere*, to place], assume to be true, believe. **Suppos'edly**.

Sup-po-si'tion, that which is supposed.

Sup-po-si-ti'tious, substituted for the real, spurious.

Sup-press' [L. *supprimere* (p.p. *suppressus*), to suppress; *sub*, under, *premere*, to press], put down, stop, conceal, restrain.

Sup'pu-rate [L. *suppūrāre* (p.p. *suppūrātus*), to suppurate; *sub*, under, *pūs* (*pūr-is*), matter], form pus, fester. **Suppura'tion**.

Su-prem'a-cy, highest authority.

Su-preme' [L. *suprēmus*, highest, superl. of *superus*, high], highest, greatest.

Su'rah [perh. from *Surat* in India], kind of soft twilled silk.

Sur-cease' [O.F. *surseoir* (p.p. *sursis*), to delay; L. *super*, over, *sedēre*, sit], cease; cessation.

Sur-charge' [F. *sur*, over, *charger*, to load], overcharge, amount in official account not allowed by auditor and having to be refunded by person responsible, too great a load; overload, exact additional charge.

Surd [L. *surdus*, deaf], quantity which cannot be expressed by rational numbers.

Sure (*s*=*sh*) [O.F. *sur*, L. *sēcūrus*, free from care], certain, safe, positive.

Sure'ty (*s*=*sh*), security, person answerable for another.

Surf [earlier *suffe*; perh. var. of *Sough*], sea breaking on shore.

Sur'face [L. *super*, above, *faciēs*, the face], outside, that which has length and breadth but no thickness.

Sur'feit [O.F. *sorfait*, orig. p.p. of *sorfaire*, to augment; L. *super*, above, *facere*, to make], excess, esp. in eating and drinking; indulge to excess. [billow.

Surge [L. *surgere*, to rise], billow; move as a

Sur'geon [short for *Chirurgeon*], doctor who performs operations.

Sur'ge-ry [Gk. *cheirourgia*, surgery; *cheir*, the hand, *ergein*, to work], surgical work, surgeon's room.

Sur'gi-cal, pertaining to surgery.

Sur'ly [prob. fr. *Sour*], gloomy and ill-natured, rude. **Sur'liness**.

Sur-mise' (*s*=*z*) [O.F. *surmise*, orig. fem. p.p. of *surmettre*, put upon; L. *super*, above, *mittere*, to put], guess; to guess, infer.

Sur-mount' [F. *sur* (L. *super*), over, *monter*, to mount], overcome, be on top of, get over. **Surmount'able**.

Sur'name [F. *sur* (L. *super*), over, and **Name**], added name, family name.

Sur-pass' [F. *sur* (L. *super*), beyond, *passer*, to pass], go beyond, excel.

Sur'plice (*ice*=*iss*) [Late L. *superpelliceum*; L. *super*, over, *pellicius*, made of skins], clergyman's or chorister's white over-dress.

Sur'plus [L. *super*, over, *plus*, more], what remains over. **Sur'plusage**.

Sur-prise' (*s*=*z*) [O.F. *surprise*, orig. fem. p.p. of *surprendre*, to surprise; L. *super*, upon, *prehendere*, to seize], act of taking unexpectedly, astonishment, that which causes astonishment; take unawares.

Sur-ren'der [O.F. *surrendre*, to surrender; L. *super*, over, *reddere*, to restore], yield; a yielding.

Sur-rep-ti'tious [L. *surripere* (p.p. *surreptus*), to pilfer; *sub*, under, *rapere*, to seize], underhand, stealthy.

Sur-round' [orig. *suround*, meaning to overflow; O.F. *suronder*, L. *superundāre*, to overflow; *super*, over, and *undāre*, to flow], come or be all round, enclose.

Sur'tax [F. *sur* (L. *super*), over, and **Tax**], additional tax; impose such.

Sur-veil'lance (*sur-vail'yans*) [F. *surveiller*, to superintend; L. *super*, over, *vigilāre*, to watch], watch, supervision.

Sur-vey' [O.F. *sourveior*; L. *super*, over, *vidēre*, to see], take a view of, measure and examine (land), description.

Sur'vey, general view, examination.

Sur-vey'or, overseer, one who surveys or measures land.

Sur-vi'val, remaining person or thing from earlier time.

Sur-vive' [L. *super*, beyond, *vīvere*, to live], outlive, remain alive.

Sur-vi'vor, one who survives.

Sus-cep'ti-ble, **Sus-cep'tive** [L. *suscipere* (p.p. *susceptus*), to undergo; *sub*, under, *capere*, to take], capable of impression, liable. **Susceptibil'ity**.

Sus-pect' [L. *suspicere* (p.p. *suspectus*), to suspect; *sub*, under, *specere*, to look], imagine to exist, to distrust; one suspected of crime.

Sus-pend' [L. *sub*, under, *pendere* (sup. *pensum*), to hang], hang, delay, cause to withdraw for a time.

Sus-pend'ers, braces, elastics attached to tops of stockings.

Sus-pense', anxious uncertainty, a stop.

Sus-pen'sion, a withholding, a stop.

Sus-pen′sion-bridge, bridge hung without central piers.

Sus-pi′cion, distrust and doubt, slight or uncertain belief.

Sus-pi′cious [L. *suspiciōsus*; see **Suspect**], full of suspicion, distrustful.

Sus-pire′ [O.F. *souspirer*; L. *suspirare,* to sigh], (poet.) to sigh.

Sus-tain′ [L. *sub,* under, *tenēre,* to hold], uphold, support.

Sus′te-nance, support, food.

Sus-ten-ta′tion, support, upkeep.

Sut′ler [Du. *zoetelaar,* scullion, sutler], one who follows an army and sells provisions to troops.

Sut-tee′ [Skrt. *satī,* a virtuous wife], burning of a Hindu widow on a funeral pile, the widow so burned.

Su′ture [L. *suere* (p.p. *sūtus*), to sew], a sewing together (in surgery), seamlike joining of bones (as in skull).

Su′ze-rain [L. *sursum,* upward ; *sub,* under, *versus,* turned], a superior (of a prince, etc.). **Su′zerainty.**

Swab [Back formation, fr. *swabber,* Du. *zwabber,* drudge of a ship], mop for cleaning decks, etc. ; clean with a swab.

Swad′dle [O.E. *swethel,* swaddling-band ; cogn. with **Swathe**], swathe in bandages.

Swag′ger [fr. obs. *swag,* to sway], walk with a grand air, brag.

Swain [O.N. *sveinn,* a boy ; cf. O.E. *swán*], a rustic, lover.

Swal′low (*a=ŏ*) [O.E. *swalewe*; cf. Du. *zwaluw*], long-winged migratory bird.

Swal′low [M.E. *swolwen, swelwen*; O.E. *swelgan*], cause or allow to pass down the throat.

Swamp (*a=ŏ*) [cf. O.E. *swamm,* fungus, and dial. E. *sump,* puddle], wet spongy land ; become filled with water, sink.

Swan (*a=ŏ*) [O.E. *swan*; cf. Ger. *schwan*], long-necked water-bird. [ground.

Sward (*a=aw*) [O.E. *sweard,* skin], lawn-like

Swarm (*a=aw*) [O.E. *swearm*; cf. Du. *zwerm*; Ger. *schwarm*], large number of bees, etc., a throng ; move in a swarm, to throng.

Swarm [?], climb by using hands and knees.

Swarth′y (*a=aw*) [obs. *swarth,* fr. O.E. *sweart,* dark-hued], dark-complexioned.

Swash [imit.], (arch.) strike violently, wash about, make sound of anything washing about.

Swash-buck′ler (*a=ŏ*), bully, lit. one who flourishes a shield.

Swath (*a=aw*) [O.E. *swœth, swathu,* a track ; cogn. with Low Ger. *swade,* a scythe], line of cut grass or corn.

Swathe [M.E. *swathen* ; O.E. *swathu,* a track], enclose in wraps or cloths.

Sway [M.E. *sweiyen*; cf. Swed. *svaja,* to jerk], swing, wave, rule, influence ; swinging motion, rule.

Swear (*ea=ai*) [O.E. *swerian,* to speak, to swear], take an oath, cause to take oath, promise on oath, declare earnestly, use profane oaths.

Sweat [O.E. *swát,* sweat (noun)], emit moisture from the pores, to toil, to employ at starvation wages ; moisture on the skin.

Sweat′er, one who sweats, thick woollen jersey.

Sweep [M.E. *swepen,* fr. O.E. *swápan,* to swoop], brush with a broom, glide swiftly, stretch in a curve ; range of a stroke, long oar, one who sweeps, esp. chimneys.

Sweet [O.E. *swéte* ; cf. Du. *zoet* ; Ger. *süss*], tasting like sugar, pleasant, fresh ; sweetmeat, (pl.) sweet dishes, delights.

Sweet′meat, confection.

Swell [O.E. *swellan* ; cf. Ger. *schwellen*], increase in size or volume, bulge ; increase, flow of the sea, person of distinction or exceptionally well-dressed.

Swel′ter [O.E. *sweltan,* to die], be faint or moist with heat.

Swerve [O.E. *sweorfan,* to rub ; cf. O.N. *swerfa,* to file], go off a regular line.

Swift [O.E. *swift,* to move quickly], quick, rapid ; kind of bird.

Swill [O.E. *swilian,* to wash], rinse, drink greedily ; pigs' liquid food.

Swim [O.E. *swimman*], move in water by strokes ; act of swimming.

Swim [O.E. *swima,* a swoon], be dizzy.

Swim′ming-ly, with ease.

Swin′dle [fr. **Swindler**], cheat deliberately ; fraudulent scheme.

Swin′dler [Ger. *schwindler,* visionary projector, swindler, *schwindeln,* to be dizzy], one who cheats.

Swine [O.E. *swin*; cf. Ger. *schwein,* pig], pigs.

Swing [O.E. *swingan*], move to and fro, whirl, hang so as to be free to swing, swaying motion, swinging seat.

Swinge (*ge=j*) [O.E. *swengan,* causative of *swingan,* to swing], (archaic) beat, whip.

Swinge′ing, huge.

Swi′nish [see **Swine**], piggish, gross.

Swink [O.E. *swincan*], (archaic) toil.

Swipe [O.E. *swipian,* to beat], hit cricketball, etc., with sweeping stroke.

Swirl [Norw. *svirla,* to whirl round, freq. of *sverra,* to hum, whirl], whirl ; eddy.

Swish [imit.], cut the air with a cane, etc.

Switch [M.Du. *swick,* a whip], flexible twig, tress of dead hair, movable part of a rail, device for shifting an electric current ; whip, transfer by a switch.

Swiv′el [O.E. *swifan,* to move quickly], ring that turns round on a pin.

Swoon [M.E. *swounen* ; O.E. *swógan,* to sough], to faint ; fainting fit.

Swoop [O.E. *swápan,* to rush], come down as a hawk ; act of swooping.

Sword (*ŏ* or *ō*) [O.E. *sweord* ; cf. Ger. *schwert*], long weapon with a cutting blade.

Syb′ar-ite [Gk. *Sybarītēs,* inhabitant of *Sybaris*], luxurious and effeminate person.

Syc′a-more [earlier *sycomore,* Gk. *sycomoros,* a sycamore ; *sycon,* fig, *moron,* mulberry], large timber-tree, fig-tree of Syria and Egypt.

Syc'o-phant [Gk. *sycophantēs*, informer; perh. fr. Gk. *sycon*, fig, and *phainein*, to show], mean flatterer. **Sycophan'tic, Sy'cophancy.**

Syl-lab'ic, uttered in syllables.

Syl'la-ble [Gk. *syllabē*, syllable; *syn-*, together, *lambanein*, to take], word or part of a word that can be pronounced by itself but cannot be broken up into similar parts; pronounce by syllables. [gramme.

Syl'la-bus (as **Syllable**), an abstract, pro-

Syl'lo-gism [O.F. *silogime*; L. *syllogismus*; Gk. *syllogismos*; Gk. *syl-* (*syn-*), together, *logizesthai*, to reason; *logos*, discourse, reasoning], a form of reasoning from premises.

Sylph [F. *sylphe*; perh. Gk. *silphē*, kind of beetle], fairy, slender, graceful woman.

Syl'van, Sil'van [L. *silva*, a wood], pertaining to a wood.

Sym'bol [Gk. *symbolon*, a token; *syn-*, together, *ballein*, to throw], visible sign of an idea, character. **Symbol'ical, Sym'bolism.**

Sym-met'ric, Sym-met'ric-al, with correspondence of arrangement.

Sym'me-try [Gk. *symmetria*; *syn-*, with, *metron*, a measure], due proportion of parts, balance or correspondence of parts.

Sym-path-et'ic, full of, expressing sympathy.

Sym'pa-thize, feel or express pity for.

Sym'pa-thy [Gk. *sympatheia*; *syn-*, with, *pathein*, to suffer], fellow-feeling, pity.

Sym'pho-ny [Gk. *symphōnia*; *syn-*, together, *phōnē*, sound], harmony, an orchestral composition. **Symphon'ic, Sympho'nious.**

Sym-po'si-um (ŏ, *s=z*) [Gk. *symposion*; *syn-*, together, *posis*, a drinking], drinking-party, contributions from several authors on one subject.

Symp'tom [Gk. *symptōma*, casualty, symptom; *syn-*, together, *piptein*, to fall], sign of the existence of something. **Symptoma'tic.**

Syn'a-gogue [Gk. *synagōgē*; *syn-*, together, *agein*, to bring], Jewish place of worship, Jewish congregation.

Syn'chron-ism [Gk. *syn-*, together, *chronos*, time], occurrence at one time. **Syn'chronize, Syn'chronous.**

Syn'co-pate, shorten by taking from the middle of a word, invert rhythm.

Syn'co-pe [L. *syncopē*, Gk. *sygcopē*, syncope; Gk. *syn-*, together, *coptein*, to cut], syncopated spelling, a fainting.

Syn'dic [Gk. *syndicos*; *syn*, together, *dicē*, justice], official of kind differing in different countries and at different times. [etc.

Syn'di-cate, association of commercial firms,

Syn-ec'do-che (*ch=k*) [Gk. *synecdochē*; *syn*, together, *ecdechesthai*, to take], figure of speech by which a part represents the whole, or a whole the part.

Syn'od [Gk. *synodos*; *syn*, together, *hodos*, a way], church court. **Syn'odal, Synod'ical.**

Syn'o-nym [Gk. *synōnymos*, of like meaning; *syn-*, together, *onyma*, a name], word having the same meaning as another.

Syn-on'y-mous [see **Synonym**], having the same meaning.

Syn-op'sis [Gk. *synopsis*; *syn-*, together, *opsis*, sight], general view, an abstract, summary. **Synop'tical.**

Syn'tax (Gk. *syntaxis*; *syn-*, with, *tasso*, order], arrangement of words in speech or writing, sentence-construction. **Syntac'tical.**

Syn'thes-is (*pl.* **Syntheses**), putting together.

Syn-thet'ic [Gk. *syn-*, with, *tithēnai*, to put], built up of separate elements into a whole.

Syr-in'ga [fr. **Syringe**], flowering shrub.

Syr'inge [L. *syrinx*, Gk. *syrigx*, a reed, pipe], tube and piston for injecting liquid; inject by a syringe.

Syr'up, Sir'up [Arab. *sharāb*, beverage], sweet, thick fluid.

Sys'tem [Gk. *systēma*; *syn-*, together, *+ste*, root of *stenai*, to stand], set of connected things or parts, plan.

Sys-tem-a'tic, System-at'ic-al, planned.

Sys'tem-a-tize, arrange methodically.

T

Taal [Du. *taal*, language], Cape Dutch speech.

Tab [perh. cogn. with **Tape**], small flap, luggage label.

Tab'ard [O.F. *tabart*; etym. unknown], herald's cloak.

Tab'by [F. *tabis*, Sp. *tabi*, Arab. *'utābi*, watered silk], watered silk, mottled or streaked cat, esp. female.

Tab'er-na-cle [L. *tabernāculum*, a tent, *taberna*, a hut], slightly built or movable dwelling.

Ta'ble [L. *tabula*, a board, table], slab, article of furniture with a flat top, list.

Tab'leau (*eau=ō*) [F. *tableau*, picture], silent dramatic group.

Ta'ble-land, high, level area.

Tab'let [M.L. *tabuleta*, dim. of L. *tabula*, a table], small slab, thin sheet of ivory, wood, etc., for writing; kind of confection.

Tab'loid, drug compressed into form of small disk or pellet.

Ta-boo', Ta-bu' [Polyn. *tabu*], a forbidding of approach to or contact with a person or thing; prohibited, sacred; forbid.

Ta'bor [Arab. *tambūr*, lute, drum], small drum.

Tab'u-lar [see **Table**], arranged in tables, broad and flat.

Tab'u-late (see **Table**), form into a table or tables.

Ta'cit [L. *tacitus*, silent, *tacēre*, to be silent], silent, unexpressed but implied.

Ta'ci-turn [L. *taciturnus*, taciturn, *tacitus*, silent], silent, reserved. **Tacitur'nity.**

Tack [doublet of archaic *tache*, clasp, hook; O.F. *tache*, nail], small nail, rope for securing a corner of a sail, also the corner, course of a ship in relation to wind, change of course; fasten by tacks, change a ship's course.

Tack′le [M.E. *takel*, tackle ; O.N. *taka*, to seize], apparatus, esp. for lifting weights, managing sails, etc. ; grapple with.

Tact [L. *tangere* (p.p. *tactus*), to touch], intuitive perception of the right thing to do. [manager.

Tac-ti′cian (*ci*=*sh*) [see **Tactics**], skilful

Tac′tics [Gk. *tactica*, matters pertaining to arrangement, *tassein*, to arrange], art of disposing forces, plan of action.

Tad′pole [M.E. *tadpolle*, tadpole, *i.e.* **Toad** and **Poll** (head)], young of a frog, etc.

Taf′fe-ta [It. *taffetà* ; Pers. *tāftah*, twisted ; *tāftan*, to twist], silken or linen fabric.

Taff′rail [Du. *tafereel*, dim. of *tafel*, table], upper part of a ship's stern.

Tag [perh. Swed. *tagg*, a prickle, tooth], appendage, metal point at the end of a lace, hackneyed quotation ; to tack.

Tail [O.E. *tæg(e)l* ; cf. O.N. *tagl* ; Swed. *tagel*], hindmost part, appendage.

Tail [O.F. *taille*, a cutting ; see **Tally**], estate limited to certain heirs.

Tail′or [F. *tailler* ; Late L. *tăleāre*, to cut], maker of clothes, esp. men's. **Tail′oress**.

Taint [F. *teint*, n.and p.p. of *teindre*, to tinge ; L. *tingere*, to tinge], infect, to stain ; a stain, corrupt condition.

Take [O.N. *taka*, to take], lay hold of, accept, gain, understand, jump over, consider, conduct, convey, be effective ; a catch.

Talc [F. *talc*, Arab. *talq*, talc], soft, smooth mineral (silicate of magnesium), also mica.

Tale [O.E. *talu*, a number, a story ; cogn. with **Tell**], story, a number.

Tal′ent [Gk. *talanton*, a balance], special gift, faculty, ancient weight and denomination of money.

Ta′les (*tail′ees*) [L. *tales* (*de circumstantibus*), such (of those standing round) ; L. *talis*, such], jurors added to supply deficiency.

Tal′is-man [Arab. *tilsamān* (pl. of *tilsam*, a talisman] ; Late Gk. *telesma*, mystery], magical charm. **Talisman′ic**.

Talk (*al*=*aw*) [M.E. *talken* ; cogn. with **Tale**], converse, speak, discuss ; conversation, rumour.

Talk′a-tive (*al*=*aw*), given to talking.

Tall (*a*=*aw*) [perh. Celtic, or O.E. *getæl*, swift ; cf. W. and Corn. *tal*, high], of more than common height.

Tal′low [M.E. and M. Du. *talgh* ; cf. Ger., Dan., Swed., *talg*], hard fat refined.

Tal′ly [F. *taille*, a notch, *tailler*, to cut ; Late L. *tăleāre*, to cut, *tălea*, a slip of wood], account kept by notches on wood, counterpart ; correspond.

Tal′on [Late L. *tālo* (*tālon-is*) ; L. *tālus*, ankle], claw of a bird of prey.

Tam′a-rind [Sp. *tamarindo*, fr. Arab. *tamr*, a ripe date, *Hind*, India], a tropical tree, its fruit.

Tam′a-risk [L. *tamariscus* ; etym. doubtful], evergreen shrub.

Tam′bour [F. *tambour*, a drum ; Arab. *tunbur*, drum (prob. imit.)], drum, embroidery frame.

Tam-bour-ine′ (*ine*=*een*) [F. *tambourin*, dim. of *tambour*, a drum], small one-sided drum with bells.

Tame [O.E. *tam* ; cf. Du., Swed., Dan., *tam* ; Ger. *zahm*], not wild, spiritless ; make tame.

Tam′man-y [*Tammany* Hall, New York, is central office of U.S. Democratic Party], political corruption. [alter.

Tam′per [var. of **Temper**], meddle so as to

Tam′pi-on [O.F. *tampon*, bung], wooden stopper for gun muzzle.

Tan [F. *tan* ; Med.L. *tannum*], bruised bark, yellowish-brown colour ; turn skins into leather with tan, etc., brown by exposure to the sun.

Tan′dem [L. *tandem*, at length (orig. facetious use)], vehicle with two horses, one behind the other, bicycle for two riders.

Tang [1] [M.E. *tang*, a sting ; cogn. with **Tang** [2]], strong taste.

Tang [2] [O.N. and Norw. *tange*, part of knife that goes into the handle], point, projection, esp. part inserted in handle.

Tang [3] [imit.], make twanging sound.

Tang [4] [see **Tangle**], kinds of seaweed.

Tan′gent [L. *tangere*, to touch], straight line touching but not cutting a curve. **Tangen′tial**.

Tan′gi-ble [L. *tangere*, to touch], perceptible to touch, real. **Tan′gibil′ity**.

Tan′gle [Dan. *tang*, seaweed ; cf. O.N. *thang*, seaweed], unite confusedly ; confused knot, large seaweed.

Tank [Port. *tanque* ; L. *stagnum*, a pool], large vessel for liquid, gas, etc. (*milit.*) motor vehicle with guns.

Tank′ard [cf. F. *tanquart* ; M. Du. *tanckært* ; etym. doubtful], large drinking-vessel.

Tan′ner, one who tans hides for leather.

Tan′nin [F. *tanin* ; see **Tan**], acid got from oak-bark, etc.

Tan′sy [Late L. and Gk. *athanasia*, immortality ; Gk. *a-*, not, *thanatos*, death], aromatic herb.

Tan′ta-lize [Gk. *Tantalos*, character in mythology, who was condemned to stand up to chin in water, which receded when he tried to drink], tease with hopes of good that keeps beyond reach. **Tantaliza′tion**.

Tan′ta-mount [F. *tant* ; L. *tantus*, so much, and **Amount**], equal in value or effect.

Tan′trum [?], display of temper.

Tap [1] [F. *tapper*, to tap ; Low G. *tappen*, to grope], strike lightly ; gentle stroke.

Tap [2] [O.E. *tæppa* ; cf. Du. *tap* ; O.N. *tappi*], hole or pipe through which liquor is drawn ; draw liquid from, insert a tap. [linen.

Tape [O.E. *tæppe*], narrow band of cotton or

Ta′per [O.E. *taper* ; cf. Ir. *tapar* ; W. *tampr*], small wax candle ; become small towards one end.

Tap′es-try [F. *tapisserie*, tapestry ; *tapis*, carpet], textile with pictorial designs.

Tap-i-o′ca [Braz. *tapioka* ; *tipioca*, juice of cassava ; *tipi*, dregs, *ōk*, to squeeze], starchy, granular food-stuff.

Ta'pir [Braz. *tapīra*, a tapir], hoofed animal with long muzzle.

Tap'ster [see Tap²], man employed to draw and serve liquor.

Tar [O.E. *teoru*; cogn. with **Tree**], thick liquid from wood and coal; smear with tar.

Tar-an-tel'la, Tar-an-telle' [It. *Taranto*, in Italy], a quick whirling Italian dance.

Tar'dy [L. *tardus*, slow], slow, late, reluctant.

Tare [Arab. *tarhah*, what is thrown away], allowance made from gross weight of goods for enclosing case.

Tare [M.E. *tare* (-*fytche*), wheat-vetch; cf. Du. *tarwe*, wheat], kind of weed, vetch.

Tar'get [O.N. *targa*, a target], small shield, mark to shoot at.

Tar'iff [Sp. *tarifa*, list of prices; Arab. *ta'rīf*, notification], scheme of duties on goods.

Tar'la-tan [F. *tarlatane*; etym. doubtful], thin cotton dress-material.

Tarn [O.N. *tjörn*, tarn, pool], mountain lake.

Tar'nish [F. *ternir* (pr.p. *ternissant*), to dim, perh. fr. O.H.G. *tarni*, secret], lessen or lose lustre; stain.

Tar-pau'lin [Tar and *palling*, covering. See Pall], tarred canvas or other waterproof.

Tar'ry, covered with or like tar.

Ta'rry (*ă*) [orig. obscure], stay behind, delay.

Tart [E.], sharp, sour. [fruit-pie.

Tart [F. *tarte*, an open tart; Med. L. *tarta*],

Tar'tan [?], woollen fabric with crossing stripes, pattern on the fabric.

Tar'tar [Late L. *tartarum*; Arab. *durd*, dregs], deposit from wine, incrustation on the teeth.

Task [Late L. *tasca*, a task; L. *taxāre*, to tax], set piece of work; impose a task on, to strain.

Tas'sel [perh. L. *taxillus*, small die, dim. of *tālus*, knuckle-bone, die made of knuckle-bone], tuft of loose threads or cords.

Taste [O.F. *taster*, to feel, taste; L. *taxāre*, intensive form of *tangere*, to touch], try by eating or drinking a little, have a flavour; sensation in the mouth, liking, power of perceiving excellence, style.

Tast'y, of pleasant flavour. [rags.

Tat'ter [cf. O.N. *tötrar*, rags], rag; tear to

Tat'ting [?], kind of knotted thread-work.

Tat'tle [E., imit.], talk idly; idle talk.

Tat-too' [Du. *taptoe*; *tap*, tap, *toe*, to shut (referring to closing of public house)], beat of drums or bugle-call recalling soldiers to quarters.

Tat-too' [Tahitian, *tatau*, tattoo], prick colour-marks into the skin.

Taunt [prob. fr. F. *tant pour tant*, so much for so much; L. *tantum*, so much], jeer at; insulting reproach. [tight.

Taut [M.E. *togt*, prob. p.p. of *togen*, to pull],

Tau-tol'o-gy [Gk. *tautologia*; *to auto*, the same, *logos*, discourse], repetition of the same meaning in different words. **Tauto-log'ical.**

Tav'ern [L. *taberna*, a hut], public-house.

Taw [O.E. *tawian*, to prepare], make leather by soaking skins in alum, etc.

Taw [perh. Gk. letter T (*taū*)], game at marbles, line from which marbles are played, marble to play with.

Taw'dry [orig. bought at St *Audry's* fair in Isle of Ely], cheap and showy. **Taw'dri-ness.**

Taw'ny [A.F. *taune*; O.F. *tané*; fr. *tan*, tan], dull yellowish brown.

Tax [L. *taxāre*, to tax], government charge on persons, property, etc., demand; impose taxes, to strain, to charge (with). **Tax'able.**

Tax'i-cab [F. *taxe*, tariff, and **Cab**], cab in which fare is indicated by taximeter.

Tax'i-der-my [Gk. *taxis*, arrangement, *derma*, skin], preparing and mounting skins of animals. **Tax'idermist.**

Tax-im'e-ter [F. *taxe*, tariff, and **Metre**], indicator of distance travelled and fare due.

Tea [Chin. *tē*, *ch'a*, *ts'a*], prepared leaves of a shrub, infusion of these leaves, meal including tea.

Teach [O.E. *tæcan*], impart knowledge. **Teach'able.** [wood.

Teak [Malayalam *tekka*], tree with strong

Teal [M.E. *tele*, etym. dub.], small wild duck.

Team [O.E. *téam*, a family, a set; cf. Ger. *zaum*, a bridle], beasts of burden harnessed together, set of players on a side.

Team'ster, driver of a team. [eye.

Tear [O.E. *tēar*, *tér*], drop of fluid from the

Tear (*ea=ai*) [O.E. *teran*; cf. Ger. *zehren*), pull apart, rend, to become torn; a rent.

Tease (*s=z*) [O.E. *tæsan*, to pluck], vex and irritate, pull apart fibres.

Teat [O.F. *tete*; F. *tette*; Low G. *titte*, a teat], nipple of a female.

Tech'nic-al (*ch=k*) [Gk. *technē*, art], pertaining to an art, science, or handicraft. **Technical'ity.**

Tech-niq'ue (*i=ee*), **Tech'nics** [Gk. *technē*, art], artistic execution.

Tech-nol'o-gy [Gk. *technē*, art; *logos*, discourse], industrial science, study of the development of industrial science among races. **Technolog'ical.**

Te'chy, Tet'chy [O.F. *tache*, blemish; prob. of Celtic origin], peevish, touchy.

Ted [Icel. *tedhja*, to spread manure], spread or turn (hay) for drying.

Te'di-ous, tiresome from slowness or continuance.

Te'di-um [L. *tædium*, tedium; *tædet=*it wearies], wearisomeness.

Tee [perh. ult. fr. O.N. *tja*, to point out], mark aimed at in quoits, etc., small heap of earth from which to strike the ball in golf; to place on a tee.

Teem [O.E. *týman*], abound, be full, swarm.

Teem [O.N. *tœma*, to empty], pour from a melting-pot. [gums.

Teethe [see **Tooth**], have teeth cutting the

Tee-to'tal [emphasized form of **Total**], abstaining from intoxicants. **Teeto'taller.**

Tee-to'tum [letter T and L. *tōtum*, the whole], spinning toy.

Teg'u-ment [L. *tegumentum* ; *tegere*, to cover], covering.

Tel'e-gram [Gk. *tēle-*, far, *gramma*, letter of the alphabet], message by telegraph.

Tel'e-graph [Gk. *tēle-*, far, *graphos*, written], electrical apparatus for distant communication by signs ; communicate by telegraph. **Telegraph'ic.**

Te-lep'a-thy [Gk. *tēle-*, far, *patheia*, feeling], influence of one mind on another at a distance. **Telepath'ic.**

Tel'e-phone [Gk. *tēle-*, far, *phōnē*, sound], instrument for reproducing speech at a distance ; communicate by telephone. **Telephon'ic.**

Tel'e-scope [Gk. *tēle-*, far, *scopein*, to look], instrument for far-seeing. **Telescop'ic.**

Tel'e-vi'sion [Gk. *tēle-*, far, and **Vision**], the transmission and reproduction of scenes and objects instantaneously enabling one actually to witness a thing taking place at a distance.

Tell [O.E. *tellan*. See **Tale**], to number, narrate, impart, discern, order.

Tell'er, bank official who receives and pays out money, counter of votes.

Tel-lu'ri-an [L. *tellus* (*tellūr-is*), the earth], pertaining to the earth.

Te-mer'i-ty [L. *temeritas* ; *temere*, rashly], rashness, boldness.

Tem'per [L. *temperāre* (p.p. *temperātus*), to temper ; *tempus* (*tempor-is*), time], prepare by combining, bring to proper hardness, soften ; disposition, calmness, condition of metal as to hardness.

Tem'per-a-ment [L. *temperamentum* ; *temperāre*, to temper], peculiar character of a person. **Temperamen'tal.**

Tem'per-ance, moderation, esp. in drinking.

Tem'per-ate, moderate, not too much.

Tem'per-a-ture, degree of heat or cold.

Tem'pest [L. *tempestas*, season, weather, tempest ; *tempus*, time], furious storm.

Tem-pest'u-ous, very stormy.   [worship.

Tem'ple [L. *templum*, a temple], place of

Tem'ple [O.F. *temple* ; L. *tempora* (pl.), the temples], side of the head between forehead and ear.

Tem'po-ral [L. *tempus* (*tempor-is*), time], pertaining to time, secular ; of the temples.

Tem-por-al'i-ty, Tem'por-al-ty, property of religious corporation.

Tem'po-ra-ry [L. *tempus* (*tempor-is*), time], for a time only.

Tem'po-rize, comply for the time.

Tempt [L. *tentāre*, *temptāre*, to test, freq. of *tenēre*, to hold], lead into evil (arch.), test.

Temp-ta'tion, act of tempting.

Ten [O.E. *tien* ; Ang. *tén*], one more than nine.

Ten'a-ble [L. *tenēre*, to hold], that can be held.

Te-na'cious (*ci=sh*) [L. *tenax* (*tenāc-is*), tenacious ; *tenēre*, to hold], holding fast, stubborn. **Tena'city.**

Ten'ant [F. *tenant*, pr.p. of *tenir*, to hold ; L. *tenēre*], occupant under a landlord. **Ten'ancy.**

Ten'ant-ry, body of tenants.

Tend [short for **Attend**], look after.

Tend [F. *tendre*, L. *tendere*, to stretch], move towards, incline.

Tend'en-cy, inclination, drift.

Tend'er [see **Tend**], vessel which attends other vessels, carriage with fuel and water attached to a locomotive.

Ten'der [see **Tend**], an offer ; to offer.

Ten'der [O.F. *tendre*, L. *tener*, tender], delicate, soft, kind.

Tend'on [M.L. *tendo* (*tendin-is*), a tendon; *tendere*, to stretch], sinew.

Ten'dril [L. *tendere* ; F. *tendre* ; etym. doubtful ; see **Tender**], leafless portion of a plant attaching itself to other bodies.

Ten'e-ment [L. *tenēre*, to hold], land held by an owner, an abode, a building divided into separate dwellings.

Ten'et, Te'net [L. *tenet*=he holds ; *tenēre*, to hold], opinion, doctrine.

Ten'nis [perh. F. *tenez* ! hold, take this, play! *tenir*, to hold], game with ball and rackets.

Ten'or [L. *tenor*, a holding on ; *tenēre*, to hold], course, general drift, high male voice.

Tense [L. *tempus*, time], verb-form denoting time.

Tense [L. *tendere* (p.p. *tensus*), to stretch], tightly stretched, rigid.

Ten'sile [L. *tensus*, stretched], capable of being stretched.

Ten'sion [L. *tensus*, stretched], state of being stretched, mental strain.

Tent [L. *tendere*, to stretch], portable shelter of canvas, etc., stretched on poles.

Tent [L. *tentāre*, to try, to probe], roll of lint used to keep a wound open.

Ten'ta-cle [Mod. L. *tentāculum* ; L. *tentāre*, to feel], a feeler. **Tenta'cular.**

Ten'ta-tive [L. *tentāre*, to try], experimental.

Ten'ter [L. *tentus*, stretched], frame for stretching cloth.

Ten'ter-hooks, hooks that hold the cloth. *On tenterhooks*, in a state of mental torment or suspense.

Ten'ter [see **Tend**], one who tends machines in a factory.   [uous.

Te-nu'i-ty [L. *tenuis*, thin], thinness. **Ten'-**

Ten'ure [L. *tenēre*, to hold], right or manner of holding.

Te-o-call'i [Mex. *teotl*, God, *calli*, house], Mexican temple.   [Tepid'ity.

Tep'id [L. *tepidus*, warm], lukewarm.

Ter'e-binth [Gk. *terebinthos*, turpentine-tree], turpentine-tree.

Ter-gi-ver-sa'tion [L. *tergum*, the back, *versāri*, freq. of *vertere*, to turn], desertion of principle.

Term [L. *terminus*, limit], bound, limited time, date on which rent is paid, etc., word or expression ; to name.

Ter'ma-gant [O.F. *Tervagant*, It. *Trivigante*, a supposed Saracen idol], fierce, violent woman.

Ter'mi-nal [L. *terminus*, a boundary], pertaining to the end ; an end part.

Ter'mi-nate [L. *terminus*, a boundary], to limit, end. **Ter'minable.**

Ter-mi-na′tion, end, ending.

Ter-min-ol′o-gy [L. *terminus*, end, Gk. *logos*, discourse], terms used in a science, etc. **Terminolog′ical.** [line, etc.).

Ter′mi-nus [L. *terminus*, end], end (of a railway

Ter′mite [L. *termes* (*termit-is*), wood-worm ; *terere*, to rub], white ant.

Tern [Dan. *terne*], kind of sea-bird.

Tar′na-ry [L. *terni*, by threes ; *tres*, three], proceeding by threes.

Ter′psi-chor-e′an, [Gk. *Terpsichore*, Muse of dancing], relating to dancing.

Ter′race [It. *terraccia* ; It. and L. *terra*, earth], raised level space, street.

Ter′ra-cot′ta [It. *terra cotta*, baked earth ; L. *terra*, earth ; *cocta*, fem. p.p. *coquere*, to cook], kind of hard pottery, brownish-red colour. [tortoise.

Ter′ra-pin [prob. Amer.-Ind.], fresh-water

Ter-ra′que-ous [L. *terra*, earth, *aqua*, water], formed of land and water.

Ter-res′tri-al [L. *terra*, earth], earthly.

Ter′ri-ble, Ter′rif′ic [L. *terrere*, to frighten], causing terror.

Ter′ri-er [Late L. *terrarius*, belonging to earth ; *terra*, earth], small dog.

Ter′ri-fy [L. *terrere*, to frighten, *facere*, to make], frighten.

Ter-ri-to′ri-al, pertaining to territory ; member of the territorial army.

Ter′ri-to-ry [L. *territorium*, territory ; *terra*, earth], large extent of land. [fear.

Ter′ror [L. *terrere*, to frighten], extreme

Ter′ror-ize, force or rule by terror.

Terse [L. *tergere* (p.p. *tersus*), to wipe, polish], neat and concise. [third order.

Ter′tia-ry (*ti*=*sh*) [L. *tertius*, third], of the

Tes′sell-at-ed [L. *tessella*, a small cube, dim. of *tessera*, a die], laid with checkered work.

Test [L. *testum*, an earthen pot, esp. (M.L.) one for trying metals in], means of trial, standard ; put to the proof.

Tes′ta-ment [L. *testamentum*, a will ; *testari*, to witness], will, each of the two main divisions of the Bible. **Testamen′tary.**

Tes-ta′tor, *fem.* Testa′trix [L. *testari*, to witness, *testis*, a witness], maker of a will.

Test′er [O.F. *teste*, a head ; L. *testa*, a tile], flat canopy, esp. over four-poster bed.

Tes′ti-fy [L. *testis*, a witness, *facere*, to make], bear witness.

Tes-ti-mo′ni-al, certificate of character, gift in token of esteem.

Tes′ti-mo-ny [L. *testimonium* ; *testis*, a witness], witness, evidence.

Tes′ty [O.F. *testu*, testy ; O.F. *teste*, the head], fretful, easily irritated.

Tet′an-us [Gk. *tetanos*, fr. *teinein*, to stretch], disease marked by spasm and rigidity of many or all voluntary muscles, esp. by lockjaw. **Tetan′ic.**

Tet′chy [see Techy], peevish, fretful.

Teth′er [prob. O.N. *tjóthr*], rope confining a grazing animal, scope ; tie with a tether.

Tet′ra-gon [Gk. *tetragonos*, four-cornered ; *tetra-*, comb. form of *tettares*, four, *gonia*, an angle], figure with four angles.

Tet-ra-he′dron [Gk. *tetra-*, four, *hedra*, a base], triangular pyramid.

Te′trarch [Gk. *tetrarches* ; *tetra-*, four, *archein*, to rule], Roman governor of the fourth part of a province.

Text [L. *texere* (p.p. *textus*), to weave], words of an author, passage of Scripture, large handwriting.

Tex′tile [L. *textus*, woven], of weaving ; woven fabric.

Tex′tu-al [L. *textus*, woven], pertaining to the text. **Text′ualist**, one adhering to the letter of the text.

Tex′ture [L. *textus*, woven], connection of interwoven threads, tissue.

Thane [O.E. *theg(e)n*, a soldier, a thane], (in old English hist.), one of a class between hereditary nobles and ordinary freemen.

Thank [O.E. *thancian* ; cf. Ger. *danken*], express gratitude ; (n. pl.) expression of gratitude. **Thank′ful.**

That [O.E. *thæt*, orig. the neuter of the definite article. See **The**], the person or thing pointed to or understood, so, who, which, conjunction introducing subordinate clause.

Thatch [O.E. *thæc* ; cf. Dan. *dak* ; Ger. *dach*], roof of straw or rushes ; cover with thatch.

Thau′ma-tur-gy [Gk. *thauma* (*thaumat-os*), a wonder ; *ergon*, a work], magic.

Thaw [O.E. *thawian* ; cf. Du. *dooijen* ; Ger. *tauen*], melt ; melting of ice, etc.

The [O.E. *the* or *se* (masc.), *theo* or *seo* (fem.), *thæt* (neut.)], the definite article ; (adv.) in that degree.

The′a-tre (*re*=*er*) [Gk. *theatron*, a place for shows; *thea*, a spectacle], playhouse, drama, scene (of war, etc.), hall with seats in tiers and a platform.

The-at′ric-al, of or suited to the theatre.

Theft [O.E. *theofth* ; see **Thief**], act of stealing.

Their [O.N. *their(r)a*, gen. pl. of *sá*, *sú*, that, they], possessive adj. corresponding to they.

The′ism [Gk. *theos*, god], doctrine that there is a supernaturally revealed God. **The′ist.**

Theme [Gk. *thema*, a theme ; *tithenai*, to place], subject on which one speaks or writes.

Then [O.E. *thænne* ; cf. Du. *dan* ; Ger. *denn*], at that time, after that, therefore, that being so ; existing.

Thence [M.E. *thenne* ; O.E. *thanon*, and old gen. ending, -*es*], from there, for that reason.

The-oc′ra-cy [Gk. *theos*, god ; *cratia*, government], government by God through priests, state so governed. **Theocrat′ic.**

The-od′o-lite [?], surveying instrument for measuring angles.

The-og′-o-ny [Gk. *theos*, god, *gonia*, origin], birth and genealogy of the gods.

The-ol′o-gy [Gk. *theos*, god, *logos*, discourse], science of religion. **Theolog′ical.**

The′o-rem [Gk. *theorema*, a spectacle, *theorein*, to behold], proposition to be proved. **The′orist.**

The-o-ret'i-cal, pertaining to theory, not practical.

The'o-rize, form theories.

The'o-ry [Gk. *theōria*, a theory; *theōrein*, to behold; *theōros*, a spectator], exposition of the principles of a science, speculative view.

The-os'o-phy [Gk. *theos*, God, *sophia*, wisdom], a philosophy which attributes immediate divine revelation to specially gifted people. Theos'ophist.

Ther-a-peu'tics [Gk. *therapeuticos*, tending; *therapeuein*, to wait on, cure; *therapōn*, a servant], science of remedies.

There [O.E. *thér*, *thér*; cf. Du. *daar*; Ger. *da*], in, to or at that place; also an expletive or introductory word.

There'fore, for that or this reason.

Ther'mal [Gk. *thermē*, heat], hot, warm.

Ther-mom'e-ter [Gk. *thermē*, heat; *metron*, a measure], instrument for measuring temperature. Thermomet'rical.

The-sau'rus [Gk. *thesauros*, treasure], lexicon, cyclopædia.

The'sis (pl. Theses) [Gk. *thesis*, a thing laid down, proposition; *tithenai*, to place], proposition, essay on a subject.

Thews [O.E. *théaw*, habit, (pl.) manners], muscles or strength.

Thick [O.E. *thiece*; cf. Du. *dik*; Ger. *dick*], deep between opposite surfaces, crowded, numerous, viscid, muddy, muffled.

Thicket [O.E. *thiccet*; see Thick], wood or shrubs closely set.

Thief [O.E. *théof*; cf. Du. *dief*; Ger. *dieb*], one who steals. Thiev'ish.

Thieve [O.E. *gethéofian*. See Thief], steal, practise theft.

Thigh' [O.E. *théoth*; cf. Du. *dij(e)*; O.H.G. *dioh*], part of leg between thigh and knee.

Thim'ble [O.E. *thýmel*, a thimble; *thúma*, thumb], metal cap for the finger for sewing.

Thin [O.E. *thynne*; cf. Du. *dun*; Ger. *dünn*], slim, lean, not crowded, fine; make less crowded. Thin'ness.

Thing [O.E. *thing*; cf. Du. and Ger. *ding*; O.N. *thing*], whatever may be an object of thought, generally inanimate object, deed; parliament in Scand. countries.

Think [O.E. *thenc(e)an*; cf. O.N. *thekkja*; Ger. *denken*], employ the mind, believe.

Third [formerly *thrid*; O.E. *thridda*], last of three, one of three equal divisions of a whole.

Thirst [O.E. *thurst*; cf. Du. *dorst*; Ger. *durst*], desire for drink; to desire drink.

Thir-teen' [O.E. *thréoténe*, *thréotýne*. See Three and Ten], three and ten.

Thir'ty [O.E. *thritig*, *thrittig*, fr. *thri*, three, *-tig*, ten], three times ten.

This [O.E. *thes* (masc.), *théos* (fem.), *this* (neut.), prob. from root of *thaet*. See The], the person or thing close at hand or understood.

This'tle [O.E. *thistel*; cf. Du. and Ger. *distel*; O.N. *thistill*], prickly plant. This'ly.

Thith'er [O.E. *thider*], to that place.

Thong [O.E. *thwang*; cf. O.N. *thoengr*; cogn. with Twinge], leather strap.

Tho'rax [L. and Gk. *thōrax*], chest.

Thorn [O.E. and O.N. *thorn*; cf. Du. *doorn*; Ger. *dorn*], prickle, plant bearing prickles.

Thor'ough (*thŭr*) [var. of Through], complete, perfect.

Thor'ough-fare, unobstructed road.

Though [O.E. *théah*, *théh*; M.E. *thogh*; cf. O.N. *thó*; Du. and Ger. *doch*], notwithstanding, supposing that, however.

Thought (*ough*=*aw*) [O.E. (*ge*)*thóht*. See Think], act of thinking, concern.

Thou'sand (*s*=*z*) [O.E. *thusénd*; cf. Du. *duizend*, Ger. *tausend*], ten hundred.

Thral'dom, bondage.

Thrall (*a*=*aw*) [O.E. *thrǽl*; cf. O.N. *thrǽll*, Dan. *trœl*, cogn. with O.E. *thrégan*, to run], slave, bondman; enslave.

Thrash, Thresh [O.E. *therscan*; Com. Teut.; cf. O.N. *threshja*, Du. *dorschen*, Ger. *dreschen*], beat out grain from, beat soundly.

Thread [O.E. *thrǽd*, fr. *thráwan*, to twist, hurl], small twist of fibre, spiral ridge of screw; pass thread through, make way through.

Thread'bare, having the nap worn off.

Threat [O.E. *thréat*, a crowd, calamity, fr. (*á*)*thréotan*, to afflict], expression of purpose of ill.

Threat'en [M.E. *thretenen*. See Threat], use a threat or threats, presage, appear likely to.

Three [O.E. *thri*, *thréo*, *thrío*; cf. Du. *drie*, Ger. *drei*], one more than two.

Thren'o-dy [Gk. *thrēnōidia*, a lamenting; *thrēnos*, a wailing, *ōidē*, an ode], song of lamentation.

Thresh'old [O.E. *therscwald*, *therscold*; *therscan*, to thresh, *wald*, floor], sill of a door.

Thrice [M.E. *thriës*, *thryěs*, fr. earlier *thriě*, *thryě*, O.E. *thri*, three, and *s* of advbl. gen.], three times.

Thrift [O.N. *thrift*; *thrifa*, to grasp], good management, frugality. Thrift'y.

Thrill [O.E. *thyrlian*, fr. *thurh*, through], pierce with emotion; a quiver, tremulous excitement.

Thrive [O.N. *thrifa*, to grasp, to thrive], prosper, develop well.

Throat [O.E. *throte*; cf. O.H.G. *drozza*, Ger. *drossel*], front of the neck, gullet or wind-pipe.

Throb [E., prob. imit.], beat with unusual rapidity; pulsation.

Throe [M.E. *throwe*, a throe; orig. obscure], violent pang.

Throne [Gk. *thronos*, a seat], king's chair of state; to place on a throne.

Throng [O.E. (*ge*)*thrang*, fr. *thringan*, to crowd], crowd; to crowd or press.

Thros'tle [O.E. *throstle*; cogn. with Thrush], song-thrush, spinning machine.

Throt'tle [dim. of Throat], choke, strangle; valve, throat.

Through [O.E. *thurh*; cf. Du. *door*, Ger. *durch*], from end to end, by means of.

Through-out', in every part, right through.

Throw [O.E. *thráwan*, to twist, hurl; cf. Ger. *drehen*, Du. *draaijen*], fling, to cast; a cast, distance which anything is thrown.

Thrum [O.E. *thrum*; cf. O.N. *thrŏmr*, an edge, Ger. *trumm*], strong linen thread, fringe of threads left on loom when web has been cut.

Thrum [Imitative. See **Strum**], play unskilfully, tap idly.

Thrush [O.E. *thrýsce*; cogn. with **Throstle**], singing-bird.

Thrush [?], disease of mouth.

Thrust [O.N. *thrýsta*, to thrust], drive with force; violent push or driving.

Thud [appar. imit.; cogn. with O.E. *thyddan*, to strike], dull sound of a blow or fall.

Thug [Hind. *thag*, *thug*], formerly a professional assassin in India, cut-throat. **Thu'ggee**, practice of the thugs.

Thumb [O.E. *thúma*; cf. Du. *duim*, Ger. *daumen*], short, thick inner finger; handle awkwardly, soil with the thumbs.

Thump [imit.], dull, heavy blow; strike with a heavy blow.

Thun'der [O.E. *thunor*; M.E. *thoner*, etc.; cf. Ger. *donner*, O.N. *thorr*, Thor], loud noise after lightning; m»ke a loud heavy noise. **Thun'derous**.

Thun'der-struck, amazed.

Thurs'day [O.E. *thunres dæg*, Thunor or Thor's day], fifth day of the week.

Thus [O.E. *thus*; cf. Du. *dus*, prob. cogn. with **That**], in this way, therefore.

Thwack [var. of **Whack**], heavy blow.

Thwart [M.E. *thwart*; cf. O.N. *thverr*, perverse; Dan. *tvœrt*, transverse], cross (in a purpose); cross seat of a boat.

Thyme [Gk. *thumon*, fr. *thuein*, to burn incense], fragrant shrub.

Thy'roid [Gk. *thyreoeidēs*; *thyreos*, a shield; *eidos*, form], shield-shaped (gland of the throat).

Ti-a'ra [L. and Gk. *tiăra*; prob. of Pers. origin], triple crown of the pope, ornamental coronet, kind of Persian turban.

Tib'i-a [L. *tibia*], shin-bone.

Tic [F. *tic*, a twitching], neuralgia of the face.

Tick [L. *tēca*, *thēca*, Gk. *thēkē*, a case], cover of bedding. **Tick'ing**

Tick [poss. shortened fr. *teke*, corresp. to M.L.G. *tēke* (orig. obscure)], mite on hair or fur.

Tick [imit.], sound of a clock, beat as a clock.

Tick [perh. imit.; cf. Du. *tik* and *tikken*, to touch lightly], mark set against items on a list; check by marks.

Tick'et [O.F. *estiquet*, Ger. *stecken*, to stick], card entitling holder to admission, conveyance, etc.

Tic'kle [M.E. *tik(e)len* (orig. obscure); cogn. with **Tick**], touch lightly so as to produce a kind of spasm and laughter.

Tick'lish, easily tickled, somewhat difficult.

Ti'dal, pertaining to tides.

Tide [O.E. *tid*, time; cf. Du. *tijd*, Ger. *zeit*, O.N. *títh*], time, alternate rise and fall of the sea; drift with the tide, get (over).

Ti'dings [O.N. *tithindi*, tidings], news.

Ti'dy [O.E. *tíd*, time], orderly, neat; put in order.

Tie [O.E. *tígan*, fr. *téag*, *téah*, a rope, fr. *téu(ha)n*, to pull], knot, thing that unites, equality in a contest; bind.

Tier (*ie=ee*) [formerly *tire*; F. *tirer*, to draw; O.F. *tire*, perh. Teut. orig.], row, esp. raised row of several.

Tierce [O.F. *tierz*, *tierce*; L. *tertius*, third], third of a pipe (42 gals.), church office of third hour, third position for guard in fencing, sequence of three cards.

Tiff [Of obscure origin], fit of peevishness, draught of liquor.

Tif'fin [Anglo-Indian], lunch.

Ti'ger (*g* hard) [L. and Gk. *tigris*, a tiger], wild animal of the cat kind. **Ti'gerish**, **Ti'grish**.

Tight [O.N. *théttr*, tight, esp. water-tight], firmly held together.

Tike [O.N. and Norw. *tik*, a tike], cur.

Tile [L. *tēgula*, a tile; *tegere*, to cover], slab of baked clay; to cover with tiles.

Till [poss. M.E. *tillen*, to pull; O.E. (*for*)*tyllan*, to pull], money-drawer.

Till [O.E. *tilian*, *teolian*, to strive for, to till; *til*, good(ness)], cultivate.

Till [O. Northumb. *til*; O.N. *til* (prep. and conj.), from *til*, a purpose], up to, until.

Till'age, **Tilth** [see **Till**], cultivation (of soil)

Till'er [O.E. *tilian*, to till], one who tills.

Till'er [see **Till**], lever for a rudder.

Tilt [O.E. *teld*, a tent], canvas covering.

Tilt [M.E. *tilten*; O.E. *tealt*, unsteady; cf. O.N. *tŏlta*, to amble], tournament, raise one end, ride and thrust with a lance.

Tim'ber [O.E. *timber*; cf. Du. *timmer*, Ger. *zimmer*, a room, timber], wood suitable for building, etc.

Tim'bre (*re=er*) or as in F. [F. *timbre*, a clock-bell; L. *tympanum*, a drum], quality of tone.

Time [O.E. *tima*; cf. O.N. *tími*, Dan. *time*, cogn. with **Tide**], duration, a point or period of duration, occasion; record the time, choose time of.

Time'ly, occurring in good time.

Time'piece, clock to measure time.

Time'serv-er, one who basely adapts his opinions to the times.

Tim'id [L. *timidus*, timid, *timēre*, to fear], easily frightened. **Timid'ity**.

Tim'or-ous [L. *timor*, fear, *timēre*, to fear], fearful of danger. **Tim'orousness**.

Tin [O.E., O.N., Du., Dan. *tin*; cf. Ger. *zinn*], a white metal, vessel for tin; cover with tin, pack in tins.

Tinc'ture [L. *tingere* (p.p. *tinctus*), to dye], solution of a vegetable or animal drug, slight flavour.

Tin'der [O.E. *tynder*, fr *tindan*, to kindle], scorched linen, etc., used for kindling.

Tine [O.E. *tind*; cf. O.N. *tindr*, Swed. *tinne*], prong as of an antler.

Tinge [L. *tingere* (p.p. *tinctus*), to dye], colour slightly; slight colour. [thrills.

Tin′gle [Var. of Tinkle], feel a succession of

Tink′er [orig. uncertain], mender of metal ware; mend roughly.

Tin′kle [freq. of M.E. *tinken*, to ring; imit.], give forth small, sharp sounds.

Tin′sel [O.F. *estincelle*; *scintilla*, a spark], glittering metallic sheets.

Tint [formerly tinct; L. *tingere* (p.p. *tinctus*), to dye], slight colouring; to colour.

Tin-tin-nab-ul-a′tion [L. *tintinnabulum*, a bell], tinkling of bells.

Ti′ny [?], very small.

Tip[1] [E.], small end; cover the end of.

Tip[2] [M.E., Du., Dan. *tip*; of obscure origin], tilt; small present of money, secret information.

Tip′pet [Orig. uncertain; perh. fr. L. *tapēte*, cloth], cape.

Tip′ple [Orig. uncertain; see Tip[2]], take strong drink habitually.

Tip′ster, one who gives tips about races, etc.

Tip′sy [see Tip[2]], rendered foolish by strong drink.

Ti-rade′ [F. *tirade*; It. *tirata*, a drawing, pulling; It. and Late L. *tirāre*, to pull], long speech full of condemnation.

Tire[1] [short for Attire], head-dress; to attire.

Tire[2], **Tyre** [perh. as Tire[1]], band round the rim of a wheel. [weary.

Tire[3] [O.E. *tiorian*, *téorian*; etym. dub.],

Tire′some, wearisome.

Ti′ro, Ty′ro [L. *tiro*; *tiro* is the better spelling], beginner in learning.

Tis′sue [O.F. *tissu*, woven thing, also woven, p.p. of O.F. *tistre*, to weave; L. *texere*, to weave], woven fabric, substance of an organ. Tis′sue-pa′per.

Tit [Icel. *tittr*, a bird, orig. a small thing], small bird.

Ti-tan′ic [L. and Gk. *Titan*, one of a family of mythical giants], enormous in strength or size.

Tit′bit [see Tit], choice morsel.

Tithe [O.E. *téotha*, cogn. with Ten], tax (originally of one-tenth).

Tit′il-late [L. *titillāre* (p.p. *titillātus*), to tickle], tickle, excite pleasantly.

Tit′i-vate, Titt′i-vate [?], adorn, smarten oneself.

Ti′tle [L. *titulus*, a title], distinguishing name, claim, name of book, heading.

Tit′mouse [now commonly shortened to Tit, *q.v.*; M.E. *titmóse*; O.E. *máse*, a name for several small birds], a tit.

Tit′ter [imit.], laugh or giggle with restraint; restrained laugh.

Tit′tle [L. *titulus*, a title; Late L. *titulus*, a mark over a word], very small part.

Tit′u-lar, existing in title or name only.

To [O.E. *tó*; cf. Du. *toe*, Ger. *zu*], in the direction of, (adv.) to the required position, so far as.

Toad [O.E. *tádige*; etym. dub.], frog-like animal with rough skin.

Toad′stool, umbrella-shaped fungus.

Toad′y [shortened fr. *toad-eater*, formerly an assistant to a mountebank], mean flatterer. Toad′yism.

Toast [L. *torrēre* (p.p. *tostus*), to parch], brown by the fire, warm thoroughly; bread toasted.

Toast [from spiced toast often put in drink], drink the health of; person or sentiment named before drinking.

To-bac′co [Sp. and Haytian *tabaco*], plant used for smoking.

To-bog′gan [Amer.-Ind. *odaban-ak*, a sledge], sled used for going downhill.

Toc′sin [F. *tocsin*; O.F. *toquer*, to strike, *sing*, a bell; fr. Late L. *signum*, a bell], alarm-bell.

To-day′ [O.E. *tó dæg*, on (this) day], the present day.

Tod′dle [perh. a form of Totter], walk with short, tottering steps.

Tod′dy [Hind. *tārī*, *tādī*; Hind. and Pers. *tār*, a palm-tree], fermented palm juice, sweetened spirits and hot water.

To-do, see Ado.

Toe [O.E. and O.N. *tá*; cf. Du. *teen*, Ger. *zehe*], one of the members at the extremity of the foot; reach with the toes.

Tof′fee, Tof′fy [of uncertain origin], sweetmeat containing butter and sugar.

Toft [O.N. *topt*], homestead, hillock.

To′ga [L. *toga*; cogn. with *tegere*, to cover], ancient Roman's outer garment.

To-geth′er [O.E. *tógedere*; *tó*, to, *gador*, together], in company.

Toil [O.F. *toillier*, to mix; L. *tudiculāre*, to stir up; *tudicula*, machine for bruising olives; *tudes*, a mallet], oppressive work; to labour.

Toi′let [F. *toilette*, orig. clothes-bag; *toile*, cloth], process of dressing, costume.

Toils [F. *toile*, cloth; L. *tēla*, a web], net, snare.

To-kay′ [fr. town of *Tokay*], wine from Tokay in Hungary.

To′ken [O.E. *tác(e)n*; cf. Du. *teeken*, Ger. *zeichen*; cogn. with Teach], a sign.

Tol′er-ance, Tol-er-a′tion, forbearance, endurance.

Tol′er-ate [L. *tolerāre* (p.p. *tolerātus*), to tolerate; allied to *tollere*, to lift], put up with.

Toll [M.E. *tollen*, to draw, etym. dub.], sound as a bell.

Toll [O.E. *toll, toln*; perh. fr. L. *telōnium*; Gk. *telōnion*, a toll-house, or cogn. with Tale], tax paid, esp. for use of roads.

Tom′a-hawk [Renâpe (N. Amer. Indian of Virginia), *tāmāhāk*; Delaware, *tamoihecan*], American-Indian war-axe.

To-ma′to (*ma*==*mah*) [Sp. *tomate*; Mex. *tomatl*], plant with red or yellow fruit; (pl.) Tomatoes.

Tomb (*toom*) [Gk. *tymba, tymbos*, a tomb], stone over a grave, the grave.

Tome [L. *tomus*; Gk. *tomos*; Gk. *temnein*, to cut], large volume.

To-mor'row, day after to-day. [mouse.

Tom'tit [see **Tit** and **Titmouse**], blue tit-

Tom'tom [Hind. *tamtam*; imit.], native Indian drum.

Ton (*o*=*ŭ*) [same as **Tun**. O.E. *tunne*, large cask], weight of twenty hundred-weight.

Tone [Gk. *tonos*, a tone; *teinein*, to stretch], interval between two musical sounds, prevailing character; give a tone to, harmonize.

Tongs [O.E. *tange* (sing.); cf. Du. and Dan. *tang*, Ger. *zange*], two-limbed grasping instrument.

Tongue (*o*=*ŭ*) [O.E. *tunge*; cf. O.N. and Swed. *tunga*, Du. *tong*, Ger. *zunge*], muscular organ in the mouth, language.

Ton'ic [lit. giving tone; Gk. *tonicos*; *tonos*, a tone], medicine that increases the strength, first tone of a scale.

To-night', on this night. [per ton.

Ton'nage, weight of goods carried, charge

Ton-neau' (*ton-nō'*) [F. *tonneau*, a cask], back part of motor car.

Ton'sil [L. *tonsilla*, a sharp stake, *tonsillæ*, tonsils], one of two organs in the throat. **Tonsilli'tis.**

Ton-so'ri-al, of a barber.

Ton'sure [L. *tonsure* (p.p. *tonsus*), to clip], the shaven crown of priests.

Ton'tine (*ine*=*een*) [named fr. the Italian, L. *Tonti*], annuity shared by subscribers, growing larger to survivors as other subscribers die.

Tool [O.E. *tól*; cf. O.N. *tól*, O.E. *tawian*, to prepare], an instrument; ornament the binding of a book.

Toot [Swed. and Norw. *tuta*; cf. M. Du. *tuyten*; Dan. *tude*; O.N. *thjóta*; imit.], sound a horn.

Tooth [O.E. *tóth*; Com. Teut.; cogn. with L. *dens*, *dentis*], bony growth in the jaw, tooth-shaped projection.

Top [O.E., common W. Germanic and Norse], highest part; to surpass, take top off.

Top [Late O.E.; orig. obscure], toy for spinning.

To'paz [Gk. *topazos*, *topazion*, a topaz], gem, generally yellowish.

To'per [F. *tóper*, cover a stake in dice-playing; *tôpe!* agreed ! I pledge you], hard drinker.

Top-gal'lant, above the topmast.

Top'ic [L. and Gk. *topica* (pl.), title of a treatise by Aristotle; Gk. *topos*, a place], subject of discourse or talk.

Top'ic-al [see **Topic**], of topics, dealing with local or current topics.

Top'mast, second part of mast from the deck.

Top-og'ra-phy [Gk. *topos*, a place; *graphia*, description], detailed description of a town or district. **Topograph'ical.**

Top'ple [O.E. *top*, the top], totter and fall.

Top'sy-tur'vy [formerly *topsy-tervy* (prob. *top so tervy*, prob. cogn. with O.E. *tearflian*, roll over)], upside down.

Toque (*oque*=*ōk*) [F. *toque*], small bonnet.

Tor [W. *tor*, a knob], rocky peak, esp. on Dartmoor.

Torch [L. *torquēre* (p.p. *tortus*), to twist], piece of resinous wood, etc., for carrying lighted. [fighter.

Tor-e-a-dor' [Sp. *toro*, L. *taurus*, a bull], bull-

Tor'ment [L. *tormentum*, an engine for hurling stones, rack; *torquēre*, to twist], extreme pain, that which gives pain.

Tor-ment', put to pain, vex.

Tor-na'do [Sp. *tronada*, a thunder-storm, *tronar*, to thunder; L. *tonāre*, to thunder], violent whirling wind.

Tor-pe'do [L. *torpēdo*, a cramp-fish (which numbs); *torpēre*, to be numb], fish which emits electric discharges, machine for blowing up ships, explosive cartridge.

Tor'pid [L. *torpidus*; *torpēre*, to be numb], numb, sluggish. **Torpid'ity.**

Tor'por [L. *torpor*; *torpēre*, to be numb], inactivity, numbness.

Tor'rent [L. *torrēns*, raging, boiling, pr.p. of *torrēre*, to heat], violent stream.

Tor-ren'tial, pertaining to or like a torrent.

Tor'rid [L. *torridus*, scorched; L. *torrēre*, to scorch], scorched, violently hot.

Tor'sion [L. *torsio*; *torquēre* (p.p. *tortus*), to twist], twisting.

Tor'so [It. *torso*, stump, stalk; L. *thyrsus*, Gk. *thyrsos*, a stalk, the Bacchic wand], trunk of a human body or statue.

Tor'toise (*oise*=*ŭs*) [Late L. *tortūca*, a tortoise; L. *torquēre* (p.p. *tortus*), to twist], reptile encased in two shells.

Tor'tu-ous [L. *tortuōsus*; *torquēre*, to twist], twisted, winding.

Tor'ture [L. *torquēre* (p.p. *tortus*), to twist], agony; pain extremely.

To'ry [Ir. *toiridhe*, *toruighe*, pursuer, searcher, plunderer], extreme Conservative, member of party that opposed the Revolution of 1688, orig. Irish robber.

Toss [cf. Norw. *tossa*, to scatter, spread out], throw, throw up, fling oneself; a throw.

Tot [O.N. *tottr*, nickname of a dwarfish person], tiny child.

Tot [short for **Total**], addition sum, total of an addition; add.

To'tal [L. *tōtus*, whole], whole; the whole.

To'tem [Algonkin *totem*], hereditary emblem, esp. animal of N. Amer. Ind. clan or group.

Tot'ter [form of a freq. fr. stem, *tot*-, expressing instability], shake, walk unsteadily.

Tou-can', **Tou'can** [Braz. *tucano*], American bird with huge beak.

Touch [F. *toucher*, to touch; cf. Ger. *zucken*, to twitch], come in contact with, handle, move feelings of; sense of feeling, contact, stroke.

Touch'ing, affecting, pathetic.

Touch'hole, small hole in cannon by which it is fired.

Touch'stone, stone used for testing alloys of gold; standard, criterion. [tinder.

Touch'wood, decayed wood, etc., used as

Touch'y [corrupt. of **Techy**], apt to take offence.

Tough (*gh=f*) [O.E. *tóh*; cf. Du. *taai*; Ger. *zäh(e)*; cogn. with **Tooth**], flexible, but not easily broken or separated, stubborn, difficult.

Tou-pee' [F. *toupet*, dim. of *toupe*, a tuft], small tuft of artificial hair.

Tour (*ou=oo*) [F. *tour*, lit. a turn; *tourner*, to turn], journey from place to place.

Tour'ist (*ou=oo*), one who makes a tour.

Tour'na-ment, Tour'ney (*ou=oo*) [O.F. *tornoiement*; *torner*, to turn], mock fight in which many are engaged, contest where many are engaged.

Tous'le (*ou=ow, sle=zl*) [fr. obs. or dial. *touse*], pull about, make untidy.

Tou'sy [see **Tousle**], unkempt, shaggy.

Tout [prob. fr. O.E. *tútian, tótian*], solicit custom; one who touts.

Tow (as in Toe) [orig. doubtful, perh. conn. with O.N. *tó*, a tuft of wool], coarse, broken hemp.

Tow (as in Toe) [O.E. *togian*; cf. O.N. *toga*, to pull], drag by a rope; state of being towed.

To'ward, To'wards [O.E. *tóweard*, fr. **To** and *ward*], in the direction of, in relation to, for, near.

Tow'el [F. *touaille*; O.H.G. *dwahilla*, towel; O.H.G. *thwéan*, to wash], cloth for wiping.

Tow'er [L. *turris*, Gk. *tursis, turris*, a tower], tall structure, often forming part of a large building, fortress; be very high.

Town [O.E. *tún*; cf. Dan. *tuin*; O.N. *tún*; Ger. *zaun*, a hedge], collection of houses larger than a village.

Tox'ic [Gk. *toxicon*, poison for arrows, *toxa*, bow and arrows], poisonous.

Tox'in, any poisonous ptomaine.

Toy [Du. *tuig*, tools, trash; *speeltuig*, plaything, toy], plaything; to play.

Trace [L. *trahere* (p.p. *tractus*), to draw], mark left; mark out, to track. **Trace'able.**

Trace [O.F. *traiz*, later *traicts* (pl. of *traict*); see **Trait**], in pl. side-straps of a harness.

Tra'cer-y, ornamental stone-work at the head of Gothic windows.

Trach-e'a, Tra'che-a (*ch=k*) [L. *trāchēa*, Gk. *tracheia*, lit. the rough], wind-pipe.

Track [Du. *trek*, a draught; *trekken*, to pull], mark left by a passer-by, trace, pathway; follow traces.

Tract [L. *tractus*, a region; *trahere* (p.p. *tractus*), to draw], region of indefinite extent.

Tract [short for **Tractate**, now little used; L. *tractāre* (p.p. *tractātus*), to handle, freq. of *trahere* (p.p. *tractus*), to draw], short written discourse.

Tract'a-ble, easily led or managed.

Trac'tate, treatise.

Trac'tion [L. *trahere* (p.p. *tractus*), to draw], act of drawing.

Trade [old meaning, path; see **Tread**], exchange of goods, occupation; buy and sell.

Tra-di'tion [L. *trādere* (p.p. *trāditus*), to deliver; *trans*, across, *dare*, to give], opinion, belief or custom passed on orally. **Tradi'tional, Tradi'tionary.**

Tra-duce' [L. *trans*, across, *dūcere*, to lead], to slander.

Traf'fic [F. *trafiquer*; It. *trafficare*; etym. doubtful], to trade; trade, coming and going of persons or goods by road, etc.

Tra-ge'di-an, actor in tragedy.

Tra'ge-dy [Gk. *tragōidia*, tragedy; *tragōidos*, lit. goat-singer; *tragos*, a goat, *-ōidos*, a singer (history doubtful)], noble drama with unhappy end, a calamity.

Trag'ic, Trag'ic-al [Gk. *tragicos*, tragic; *tragos*, a goat], pertaining to tragedy.

Trail [L. *trāgula*, a drag-net, sledge; *trahere*, to draw], draw along, to track; a track, something hanging loose behind.

Train [F. *trainer*, to trail; L. *trahere*, to draw], teach by practice, prepare by exercise, etc., direct (fire-arm); that which is in the rear, line of railway carriages, trailing part of a robe.

Train-oil [formerly *trane-oyle* or *trane*; M. Du. *traen*, a tear, train-oil], oil got from blubber of whale.

Trait [F. *trait*, n. and p.p. of *traire*, to draw; L. *trahere*, to draw], stroke, feature.

Trai'tor [L. *trādere*, to betray], one who betrays. **Trai'torous.**

Tra-jec'to-ry [L. *trajicere* (p.p. *trajectus*), to throw across; *trans*, across, *jacere*, to throw], curve described by a projectile in its flight.

Tram [prob. fr. L.G. *traam*, balk, beam; E. Fris. *trame, tram*, beam, or step of ladder], wagon in coal-pit, car on tramway, metal rails for tram.

Tram'mel [F. *tramail*, a trammel; Late L. *tramaculum*, kind of fishing-net; prob. from L. *tri-*, triple, and *macula*, a mesh], net, a shackle; to shackle, confine.

Tramp [M.E. and Ger. *trampen*; cf. Dan. *trampe*; Swed. *trampa*], go on foot, walk heavily; journey on foot, sound of steps, vagabond, cargo-ship, not of regular line.

Tram'ple [freq. of **Tramp**], tread under foot.

Tram'way [see **Tram**], street-railway.

Trance [L. *transire*, pass away, die; *trans*, across, *īre*, to go], sleep resembling death, state of extreme exaltation.

Tran'quil [L. *tranquillus*, tranquil], quiet, calm. **Tran'quillize.**

Tran-quil'li-ty, calmness.

Trans-act' [L. *transigere* (p.p. *transactus*), to transact; *trans*, across, and *agere*, to do], carry through, complete (business).

Trans-ac'tion, performance, a proceeding.

Trans-ac'tor, one who transacts.

Tran-scend' [L. *transcendere*; *trans*, beyond, *scandere*, to climb], rise above, surpass. **Transcend'ence, -ency.**

Tran-scend'ent, excelling, surpassing.

Tran-scen-den'tal, surpassing others, vague and abstruse, beyond sense experience.

Tran-scribe' [L. *trans*, across, *scrībere* (p.p. *scriptus*), to write], copy in writing.

Tran'script [see Transcribe], written copy.

Tran-scrip'tion, act of copying, a copy.

Tran'sept [L. *trans*, across, *septum*, enclosure], transverse portion of a cross-shaped church.

Trans-fer' [L. *trans*, across, *ferre* (p.p. *lātus*), to carry], convey from one to another.

Trans'fer, conveyance of property, etc.

Trans'fer-ence, conveyance, passage.

Trans-fig-u-ra'tion, change of appearance.

Trans-fig'ure (*gure*=*ger*) [L. *trans*, across, *figūra*, a figure], change in form or appearance.

Trans-fix' [L. *trans*, across, *fingere* (p.p. *fixus*), to fix], pierce through.

Trans-form' [L. *trans*, across, *forma*, shape], change the form, appearance, or character.

Trans-for-ma'tion, change of appearance, form, or substance.

Trans-fuse' (*s*=*z*) [L. *trans*, across, *fundere* (p.p. *fūsus*), to pour], transfer by pouring. **Transfu'sion**.

Trans-gress' [L. *transgredī* (p.p. *transgressus*); *trans*, beyond; *gradī*, to walk], break (law, etc.), exceed the limits.

Trans-gres'sion, infringement of law, sin.

Tran'si-ent (*s*=*z*) [L. *trans*, across; *īre* (sup. *ĭtum*), to go], passing, not lasting.

Trans'it [L. *transīre* (p.p. *transĭtus*), to go across], passage through or over.

Tran-si'tion (*ti*=*zh*), passage, change from one state to another. **Transi'tional**.

Tran'si-tive, passing over to an object.

Tran'si-to-ry, short-lived.

Trans-late' [L. *trans*, across, *ferre* (p.p. *lātus*), to bear], to change from one place or language to another.

Trans-la'tion, removal, a rendering in another language.

Trans-lu'cent [L. *trans*, beyond, *lūcēre* (p.p. *lūcēns*, -*entis*), to shine], admitting light.

Trans-ma-rine' (*ine*=*een*) [L. *trans*, across, *marīnus*, marine], beyond the sea.

Trans'mi-grate [L. *trans*, across, *migrāre* (p.p. *migrātus*), to wander; *meāre*, to go, *ager*, a field], pass from one country or body to another.

Trans-mis'sion (*ss*=*sh*) [L. *trans*, across, *missus*, sent], act of transmitting.

Trans-mit' [L. *trans*, across, *mittere*, to send], cause to pass over or through, send.

Trans-mog'ri-fy [coined word], transform (used humorously). **Transmog'rification**.

Trans-mu-ta'tion [L. *trans*, across, *mutātus*, changed], change into another form or substance. **Transmute'**.

Tran'som [L. *transtrum*; *trans*, across, and suf. -*trum*, signifying agent], crossbeam.

Trans-pa'rence, Trans-pa'ren-cy, quality of being transparent.

Trans-pa'rent [L. *trans*, through, *parēns* (-*entis*), pr.p. of *pārēre*, to appear], that can be seen through, admitting light, frank, obvious.

Tran-spire' [L. *trans*, through, *spīrāre*, to breathe], pass off in vapour through skin, etc., come to be known.

Trans-plant' [L. *trans*, across, *plantāre*, to plant], remove and plant in another place. **Transplanta'tion**.

Trans-port' [L. *trans*, across, *portāre*, to carry], convey from one place to another, carry away with strong feeling.

Trans'port, conveyance, vehement emotion.

Trans-por-ta'tion, removal of offenders beyond seas.

Trans-pose' (*s*=*z*) [L. *trans*, across, F. *poser*, to put], cause to change places, change the key in music. **Transposi'tion**.

Trans-ship' [L. *trans*, across, and Ship], transfer from one ship to another.

Tran-sub-stan-ti-a'tion (*ti*=*shi*) [Late L. *transubstantiātiō*; L. *trans*, across, *substantia*, substance], change of sacramental bread and wine into the body and blood of Christ.

Trans-verse' [L. *trans*, across, *vertere* (p.p. *versus*), to turn], lying or being across.

Trap[1] [O.E. *treppe*; cf. M. Du. *trappe*, a trap; Swed. *trappa*, a stair; Ger. *treppe*, a flight of steps], contrivance for catching unawares, bend in a pipe to prevent return flow of gas by liquid, movable step-ladder, wheeled vehicle.

Trap[2] [Swed. *trappa*, a stair; *trapp*, trap-rock], dark igneous rock.

Trap[3] [F. *drap*, cloth; *draper*, to clothe], furnish with trappings, adorn.

Tra-pan' [see Trepan[2]].

Trap-door, lifting or sliding door.

Tra-peze' [F. *trapèze*; see Trapezium], suspended swinging bar used for acrobatic and gymnastic performances.

Tra-pe'zi-um [Gk. *trapezion*, a table, a trapezium; *tra*- (*tetra*), four, *peza*, *pous*, a foot], four-sided plane figure of which only two sides are parallel.

Trap'e-zoid [Gk. *trapezoeidēs*], four-sided plane figure of which no two sides are parallel.

Trap'per, one who traps animals.

Trap'pings [see Trap[3]], ornaments to be put on horses, ornamental accessories of office.

Trash [perh. Icel. *tros*, rubbish, fallen twigs; Swed. *krasa*, to bruise; Dan. *krase*, to crash], worthless stuff, rubbish. **Trash'y**.

Trav'ail [O.F. *travail*, toil], labour with pain, severe toil.

Trav'el [var. of Travail], make a journey, proceed; journeying.

Trav'el-ler, one who travels.

Trav'erse [O.F. *traverse*, fem. of *travers*, crosswise; L. *trans*, across, *versus*, turned], to cross; laid across; cross-piece of a structure.

Trav'er-tine [It. *travertino*; L. *tiburtinus* (*lapis*, stone), of *Tibur*, the modern Tivoli], kind of limestone.

Trav'es-ty [L. *trans*, implying change, *vestīre*, to clothe; *vestis*, a garment], burlesque imitation; represent so as to render ridiculous.

Trawl [of obscure origin], fish with a trawl-net; net for dragging along the sea-bottom.

Trawl′er, person who trawls, trawl-boat.

Tray [O.E. *trieg*, *trig*], flat broad vessel on which dishes, etc., are carried.

Treach′er-ous [O.F. *trechier*, to beguile ; L. *tricārī*, to make difficulties], faithless, not to be relied on.

Treach′er-y [L. *trīcārī*, to make difficulties], breach of faith, treason.

Trea′cle [Gk. *thēriacē*, an antidote ; *thērion*, *thēr*, a wild beast], syrup obtained in refining sugar.

Tread [O.E. *tredan* ; Com. Teut.], to step ; a step.

Tread′le, Tred′dle [O.E. *tredel*, step], lever of a machine moved by the foot.

Trea′son [L. *trāditio*, treason ; *trādere*, to deliver over], disloyalty, treachery. **Trea′sonable.**

Treas′ure (*s=z*) [Gk. *thēsauros*, treasure], reserve stock of money, something valuable ; lay up, value greatly.

Treas′ure-trove [A.F. *tresor trové*], gold, etc., of unknown ownership found hidden away.

Treas′ur-er, one who has charge of funds.

Treas′ur-y, place or building where treasure is kept, department which has charge of the finance.

Treat [L. *tractāre*, to handle, freq. of *trahere*, to draw], act towards, handle, entertain with food, etc., discuss terms ; entertainment.

Trea′tise [A.F. *tretiz* ; O.F. *traitier* ; F. *traiter* ; L. *tractāre*, to handle], composition on a definite subject.

Treat′ment, manner of dealing with.

Trea′ty [O.F. *traité*, a treaty, p.p. of *traiter*, to treat], agreement between nations, etc.

Treb′le [L. *triplus*, threefold], threefold ; soprano, the highest part in a harmonized musical composition ; make threefold.

Tree [O.E. *tréo*], large woody plant.

Tre′foil [L. *trifolium* ; *tri-*, allied to *tres*, three, *folium*, a leaf], clover, plant with clover-like leaves.

Trek [Du. *trek*, a trek ; *trekken*, to trek], a journey by ox-wagon ; travel by ox-wagon, migrate.

Trel′lis [O.F. *treliz*, a trellis ; L. *tri-*, three, *licium*, a thread], frame of cross-bars.

Trem′ble [Late L. *tremulāre*, to tremble ; *tremere*, to fear], shake from fear, etc.

Tre-men′dous [L. *tremendus*, lit. to be feared ; *tremere*, to tremble], terrible, overpowering.

Trĕm′o-lo [It. fr. L. *tremere*, to tremble], intentionally tremulous effect in music.

Trem′or [L. *tremere*, to tremble], a trembling.

Trem′u-lous, shaking, quivering.

Trench [O.F. *trencher* ; Late L. *trincāre*, to cut], to cut, esp. a ditch, encroach ; a ditch.

Trench′ant [O.F. *trenchant*, pr.p. of *trencher*, to cut], cutting, sharp.

Trench′er [O.F. *trenchvir* ; *trencher*, to cut], wooden platter, cap with a stiff square top.

Trend [M.E. *trenden*], have a particular direction ; general direction, tendency.

Tre-pan′[1] [Gk. *trypanon*, a trepan, a borer; *trypan*, to bore], surgical saw for the skull ; operate with the trepan. **Tre-pan′ning.**

Tre-pan′[2] [etym. uncert. ; perh. orig. rogues' slang ; F. *trappe*, a trap], ensnare.

Tre-pang′ [Malay *trīpang*], sea-slug used in China for soup.

Trep-i-da′tion [L. *trepidāre* (p.p. *trepidātus*), to tremble, *trepidus*, trembling], fear and trembling.

Tres′pass [O.F. *tres-* (L. *trans*), across, *passer*, to pass], intrude, offend ; unwarranted intrusion, sin.

Tress [O.F. *tresce*, a plait or braid of hair; Late L. *tricia*], long lock or plait of hair.

Tres′tle [L. *transtellum*, dim. of *transtrum*, a cross-beam], supporting framework.

Tret [perh. O.F. *traite*, transportation ; (as **Trait**)], allowance for waste in transport.

Trews [var. of **Trousers**], Highlander's tartan trousers.

Tri′ad [Gk. *trias* (*triad-os*), triad ; *treis*, three], group of three.

Tri′al [see **Try**], process of trying or testing, examination by a judge, affliction.

Tri-an′gle [L. *triangulus*, three-cornered ; *tri-*, thrice, *angulus*, a corner], three-sided figure.

Tri-an′gu-lar, three-cornered. **Trian′gulate.**

Tri′bal, pertaining to a tribe or tribes.

Tribe [Late L. *tribus*, a tribe], group of families under chiefs.

Tri′brach [Gk. *tri-*, thrice, *brachus*, short], metrical foot of three short syllables, ⌣ ⌣ ⌣.

Trib-u-la′tion [L. *tribulāre* (p.p. *tribulātus*), to rub out corn, to afflict], severe trial.

Trib-u′nal, seat of a judge, court of justice.

Trib′une [L. *tribūnus*, chief officer of a tribe ; *tribūnāle*, judgment seat], ancient Roman officer chosen by the people, platform, bishop's throne.

Trib′u-ta-ry, paying tribute, subject ; river flowing into a larger one.

Trib′ute [L. *tribuere* (p.p. *tribūtus*), to give, pay], payment in acknowledgment of submission, personal contribution.

Trice[1] [M. Du. *trisen* ; M.L.G. *trissen* ; Ger. *triezen*, to hoist], haul up, hoist, tie.

Trice[2] [perh. from **Trice**[1]], very short time.

Trick [Picard and Norman form of *triche*, deceit], sly act, practical joke, mannerism, cards played in a round ; to cheat, to dress.

Trick′er-y, fraud, deception.

Trick′le [perh. M.E. *triklen*, for *striklen*, to trickle, freq. of *striken*, to flow ; etym. uncert.], run in drops or in a small stream.

Trick′ster, one who tricks.

Trick′sy, playful.

Tri′col-our [F. *tricolore* ; L. *tri-*, three, *color*, colour], flag of three colours, esp. French flag.

Tri′cy-cle [Gk. *tri-*, three, *cyclos*, a circle], three-wheeled cycle.

Tri′dent [L. *tridens* (*-entis*), *tri-*, three, *dens*, a tooth, prong], three-pronged spear.

Tri-en′nial [L. *triennium*, period of three years ; *tri-*, three, *annus*, a year], lasting three years, happening every three years.

Tri′fle [O.F. *trufle*, mockery, var. of *truffe*, a jest ; etym. uncert.], thing of little value, light dish ; act or talk frivolously.

Tri′fling, of small value, paltry.

Trig′ger [formerly *tricker* ; Du. *trekker*, trigger ; *trekken*, to pull], catch which on being pressed releases hammer of a gun-lock.

Trig-o-nom′e-try [Gk. *trigōnon*, a triangle, *metron*, a measure], branch of mathematics which treats of the relations of sides and angles of triangles. **Trigonomet′rical.**

Trill [It. *trillare* (vb.); *trillo* (n.) ; imit.], quaver ; shake or quaver.

Tril′lion (*trĭlyŭn*) [Gk. *tri-*, thrice, and **Million**], a million million million. (In France and U.S.A., a million million.)

Tril′og-y [Gk. *tri-*, thrice, *logos*, discourse], set of three literary compositions, each complete in itself, but with one common theme.

Trim [O.E. *trymian*, make firm, fr. *trum*, strong], make ready for sailing, clip, adjust, adorn (dress) ; dress, condition ; in good order, neat.

Tri′me-ter [Gk. *tri-*, and *metron*, measure], a verse of three measures.

Trim′mer, one who trims, time-server.

Trim′ming, ornamentation of ribbon, etc.

Trin′i-ty [L. *trinus*, (pl.) *trini*, by threes], union of three in one. **Trinitar′ian.**

Trin′ket [M.E. *trenket*, a knife ; O.N.F. *trenquer*, to cut], small ornament.

Tri′o (*tree′-o* or *tri-o*) [It. *trio*, L. *tres*, three], set of three, musical composition for three parts.

Tri′o-let [F.], 8-lined poem, rhymed, in which 1st and 2nd lines recur twice.

Trip [O.F. *treper*, *trip(p)er*], move with light steps, make a false step, cause to stumble ; journey, nimble step, a stumble. **Tripp′-ingly.**

Tri-par′tite, Trip′ar-tite [L. *tri-*, three, *partiri* (p.p. *partitus*), to divide], divided into three parts.

Tripe [F. *tripe* ; etym. doubtful], large stomach of cattle or sheep cut up and used as food.

Trip′le [L. *triplus*, triple ; L. *tri-* (*tres*), three, and *-plus*, allied to *plenus*, full], threefold ; to treble.

Trip′let, set of three, three notes performed in the time of two, three lines rhyming together.

Tri′pod [Gk. *tripous* (*tripod-os*), a tripod ; *tri-*, three, *pous*, foot], stool, etc., on three feet.

Tri′pos [formerly *tripus*, fr. tripod on which M.A. sat to deliver a speech], honours examination (Cam. Univ.).

Tri′reme [L. *tri-* (*tres*), three, *rēmus*, an oar], ancient galley having three ranks of rowers.

Tri-sect′ [Gk. *tri-*, thrice ; L. *secare* (p.p. *sectus*), to cut], divide into three equal parts. **Trisec′tion.**

Tri-syl′la-ble [Gk. *tri-*, thrice, and **Syllable**], word, or metric foot, of three syllables. **Trisylla′bic.**

Trite [L. *terere* (p.p. *trītus*), to rub, wear away], worn out, stale. **Trite′ness.**

Tri′ton [L. and Gk. *Trītōn*], a sea-god.

Trit′u-rate [L. *triturāre* (p.p. *triturātus*), to rub down ; *trītus*, rubbed], to rub, grind.

Tri′umph [Gk. *thriambos*, a hymn to Bacchus], celebrate victory, rejoice over success ; Roman procession in honour of victory, great success.

Tri-umph′al, celebrating triumph.

Tri-umph′ant, rejoicing for success.

Tri-um′vi-rate [L. *trium*, gen. of *tres*, three, *vir*, a man], union of three in office.

Tri′une [L. *tri-* (*tres*), three, *unus*, one], three in one.

Triv′et [L. *tripēs*, three-footed ; *tri-* (*tres*), three, *pes* (*ped-is*), a foot], tripod or bracket to hold a kettle, etc.

Triv′i-al [L. *trivia*, cross-road ; *tri-* (*tres*), three, *via*, a way], trifling, petty. **Trivi-al′ity.**

Tro′chee (*ch=k*) [Gk. *trochaios*, running, a trochee ; *trechein*, to run], metrical foot consisting of a long syllable followed by a short one. **Trocha′ic.**

Trog′lo-dyte [Gk. *troglē*, cave, *duein*, to enter], cave-dweller of prehistoric W. Europe.

Troll[1] [perh. fr. O.F. *trauler*, to run, to draw to and fro ; Ger. *trollen*, to roll, to troll ; etym. uncert.], sing carelessly.

Troll[2] [O.N. and Swed. *troll* ; Dan. *trold*, a troll], giant, friendly but tricky dwarf.

Trol′ley, Trol′ly [prob. fr. **Troll**[1]], truck that can be tilted, small wheel at the end of a metallic rod on an electric car to connect with an overhead wire.

Trom′bone [It. *trombone* ; aug. form of *tromba*, a trumpet], brass wind-instrument.

Troop [F. *troupe* ; O.F. *trope*, a troup ; etym. doubtful], company, a body of soldiers, (pl.) soldiers ; move in a troop.

Troop′er, cavalryman.

Trope [Gk. *tropos*, a turn], figure of speech.

Tro′phy [Gk. *tropaion*, a trophy ; *tropē*, rout, *trepein*, to turn], memorial of victory.

Trop′ic, one of the two parallels of latitude about 23° 28′ N. and S. of the Equator respectively ; (pl.) region between these.

Trop′ic-al [Gk. *tropicos*, relating to a turning ; *tropos*, a turn], within or pertaining to the tropics, figurative (from **Trope**).

Trot [O.F. *troter*, *trotier*, to trot ; Low L. *tolūtārius*, going at a trot ; L. *tollere*, to lift], pace of a horse in which the feet are lifted in diagonal pairs ; go at a trot.

Troth [var. of **Truth**], truth, faith.

Trou-ba-dour′ (*ou* (both) *=oo*) [Prov. *trobador*, a troubadour ; *trobar*, to find ; Late L. *tropāre*, to versify], formerly a lyric poet of Provence.

Trou′ble [L. *turbula*, dim. of *turba*, a crowd], to distress, annoy ; affliction, inconvenience.

Troub'le-some (*some*=*sum*), causing trouble.

Troub'lous, full of trouble.

Trough (*gh*=*f*) [O.E. *trog*; Com. Teut.], long vessel for water, long narrow depression, hollow between two waves.

Trounce [O.F. *trons*, a truncheon], beat severely.

Trou'sers [earlier *trouses*, *trowses*; F. *trousses*, breeches], two-legged garment.

Trous-seau' (*trooso'*) [F. *trousseau*, dim. of *trousse*, a bundle], bride's outfit.

Trout [L. *tructa*, a trout; Gk. *trōktēs*, a nibbler; *trōgein*, to bite], fresh-water fish.

Trow, Trow [O.E. *trúwian*, *tréowan*], believe, think.

Trow'el [Late L. *truella*, dim. of L. *trua*, a ladle], mason's flat-bladed tool, gardener's scoop.

Troy [prob. fr. *Troyes*, in France], system of weights for gold and silver.

Tru'ant [F. *truand*, a beggar; Gael. and Ir. *truaghan*, a wretch], one who stays away from work; wandering. **Tru'ancy.**

Truce [O.E. *tréow*, compact], temporary peace.

Truck [F. *troquer*; M.L. *trocāre*; etym. uncert.], barter; to exchange, trade.

Truck [Gk. *trochos*, a runner, *trechein*, to run], low wheeled vehicle, open railway wagon.

Truck'le [L. *trochlea*, a pulley], cringe.

Truc'u-lent [L. *truculentus*, cruel; *trux* (*truc-is*), fierce], fierce, savage.

Trudge [perh. fr. F. *trucher*, to beg; etym. doubtful], walk along, esp. wearily.

True [O.E. *tréowe*], according to fact, real, faithful.

Truf'fle [F. *truffe*; perh. L. *tūbera*, pl. of *tūber*, a tuber], edible underground fungus.

Tru'ism, self-evident truth.

Tru'ly, truthfully, sincerely.

Trump [O.F. *trampe*, O.H.G. *trumpa*, Slovenian *tromba*, Russ. *truba*, a trumpet], trumpet; make up, fabricate.

Trump [F. *triomphe*; see **Triumph**], card which takes any of the other suits; take with a trump card.

Trump'er-y [F. *tromperie*; *tromper*, to deceive, orig. to sound a horn], trash; worthless.

Trump'et [F. *trompette*, dim. of *trompe*, a horn], wind instrument; proclaim as by sound of trumpet.

Trun'cate [L. *truncāre* (p.p. *truncātus*), to cut off], cut the top or end from.

Trun'cheon (*ch*=*sh*) [O.N.F. *tronchon*; O.F. *tronson*, a thick stick; *tronc*, a trunk], short thick staff, baton.

Trun'dle [L.G. *tröndeln*, to trundle], small wheel, truck; to roll.

Trunk [L. *truncus*, a trunk], main part of the body, etc., elephant's long flexible snout, box with a hinged lid.

Trun'nion (*trănyŭn*) [F. *trognon*, a stump], projecting stump on each side of a cannon.

Truss [F. *trousse*; O.F. *trusse*; etym. doubtful], bundle, kind of surgical bandage; bind close, to skewer.

H *

Trust [O.N. *traust*; Swed. and Dan. *tröst*, consolation], firm belief, credit given, estate held for use of another; rely on, have confidence in.   [another.

Trus-tee', one who holds property in trust for

Trust'y, deserving confidence, strong.

Truth [O.E. *trēwth*, *trēowth*], that which is true, reality. **Truth'ful.**

Try [F. *trier*, to sift; Late L. *trītāre*, to pound small], to test, to attempt, investigate judicially; an attempt.

Try'ing, striving, testing severely.

Tryst [O.F. *trist(r)e*; prob. cogn. with **Trust**], appointed meeting; to set time and place for a meeting, engage to meet.

Tsar. See **Czar.**   [fly.

Tset'se [S.Afr. *tsetse*], noxious South African

Tub [M. Du. *tobbe*, a tub; etym. doubtful], open vessel of wooden staves.

Tube [L. *tubus*, a tube; cogn. with *tūba*, a trumpet], long hollow cylinder.

Tu'ber [L. *tūber*, a hump], thick part of an underground stem, like the potato.

Tu'ber-cle [L. *tuberculum*, dim. of *tuber*, a swelling], knob-like projection, small granular tumour. **Tuber'cular.**

Tu-ber'cu-lo'sis, consumption and allied diseases.

Tu'ber-ose [L. *tūberōsus*, covered with tubers], a flower; covered with tubercles.

Tu'ber-ous [L. *tūberōsus*; see **Tuber**], knobbed.   [shaped.

Tu'bu-lar [L. *tubulus*, a small tube], tube-

Tuck [Low G. *tukken*, to pull up, tuck], fold under, gather into flat folds; flat fold.

Tuck [O.N.F. *toquer*, var. of F. *toucher*, to touch], beat of drum.

Tues'day [O.E. *Tíwes dæg*, the day of *Tiw*, god of war], third day of the week.

Tu'fa, Tuff [It. *tufo*, *tufa*, L. *tophus*, soft sandy stone], rock of cellular texture.

Tuft [F. *touffe*; cf. O.H.G. *zopf*, a tuft], bunch of grass or feathers or the like joined together at the base.

Tug [O.N. *tog*, a rope], pull strongly; strong pull, small steamboat to tow vessels.

Tu-i'tion [L. *tuērī* (p.p. *tuitus*), to protect], teaching.

Tu'lip [It. *tulipano*, a tulip; Turk. *tulbend*, a turban], plant growing from a bulb.

Tulle (*u*=*ōō*) [F. fr. town of *Tulle* in France], fine silk net.

Tum'ble [M.E. *tumblen*; O.E. *tumbian*], to roll, fall, perform acrobatic feats, rumple; a fall.

Tum'bler, acrobat, pigeon that turns somersaults, stemless drinking-glass.

Tum'brel, Tum'bril [O.F. *tomberel*, fr. *tomber*, to fall; of Teut. orig., cf. **Tumble**], two-wheeled cart used to carry victims to execution in French Revolution.

Tu'mid [L. *tumēre*, to swell], swollen, inflated.

Tu'mour [L. *tumēre*, to swell], growth in the body.

Tu'mult [L. *tumultus*, a tumult; *tumēre*, to swell], uproar of a multitude, commotion.

Tu-mul'tu-ous, disorderly, agitated.

Tu'mu-lus [L. *tumĕre*, to swell], sepulchral mound. **Tu'mular.**

Tun [O.E. *tunne*, barrel; cf. Du. *ton*; O.N. *tunna*; cogn. with **Ton**], large cask.

Tune O.F. *tun*, F. *ton*, a tune; L. *tonus*, a tone], melody, air, right intonation, mood; put (an instrument) in tune. **Tune'ful.**

Tung'sten [Swed. *tung*, heavy, *sten*, stone], a heavy metal.

Tu'nic [L. *tunica*, a tunic], body garment.

Tun'nel [O.F. *tonnel*, dim. of *tonne*, a tun], underground passage; to make a tunnel.

Tun'ny [L. *thunnus*, Gk. *thunnos*, a tunny], large sea-fish.

Tup [cf. Swed. and Norw. *typp*, a cock], a ram.

Tur'ban [Turk. *tulbend, dulbend*; Pers. *dulband*], cap with scarf wound round it.

Tur'bid [L. *turbāre*, to disturb; *turba*, a crowd], muddy, disturbed, disordered.

Tur'bine [L. *turbo* (*turbin-is*), a wheel, a top, a whirlwind; *turbāre*, to disturb], wheel driven by jets of water, air, or steam, form of steam-engine.

Tur'bot [Late L. *turbo*, a turbot; L. *turbo*, a spindle], large flat fish.

Tur'bu-lent [L. *turbulentus*, turbulent; L. *turbāre*, to disturb], disturbed, riotous. **Tur'bulence.**

Tu-reen' [earlier *terrene*; F. *terrine*, an earthen pan; L. *terra*, the earth], deep vessel for soup.

Turf [O.E.; Com. Teut.], surface earth filled with roots of grass, sod, racecourse.

Tur'gid [L. *turgidus*; *turgēre*, to swell], swollen, bombastic.

Tur'key [F. *Turquie*, Turkey], large fowl.

Tur'mer-ic [F. *terre-mérite*, perh. corruption of Arab. *kurkum*, saffron], E. Ind. plant of ginger family.

Tur'moil [? perh. fr. **Turn** and **Moil**], disquiet, confused agitation.

Turn [L. *tornāre*, turn in a lathe, *tornus*, a lathe; Gk. *tornos*, a tool to draw circles with], move round, to change, form on a lathe; movement round, change, short walk, etc., succession, due chance, occasional act.

Tur'nip [L. *nāpus*, kind of turnip; orig. of *tur-*, unknown], plant with a round root.

Turn'key, prison warder.

Turn'pike, toll-gate; a high-road.

Tur'pen-tine [Gk. *terebinthos*, the terebinth tree], resinous oily fluid.

Tur'pi-tude [L. *turpis*, base], baseness.

Tur'quoise [F. *turquoise*, orig. fem. of *turquois*, Turkish], blue precious stone.

Tur'ret [F. *tourette*, dim. of *tour*, tower], small tower. **Tur'reted.**

Tur'tle [Sp. *tortuga*, sea-turtle], sea-tortoise.

Turt'le [L. *turtur*; imit.], kind of dove.

Tusk [O.E. *tux*], long, protruding tooth.

Tus'sle [see **Tousle**], a scuffle; to struggle.

Tus'sock [perh. an altered form of **Tusk**], tuft (of grass, etc.).

Tu'te-lage [L. *tūtēla*, protection; *tuērī*, to guard], guardianship, period of being under guardianship.

Tu'te-la-ry, guardian.

Tu'tor [L. *tūtor*, a guardian; L. *tuērī* (p.p. *tuitus*), to guard, protect], guardian, private teacher, college official who instructs students. **Tutor'ial.**

Twad'dle [orig. *twattle*, var. of **Tattle**], silly talk.

Twain [O.E. *twegen*, two], two, two parts.

Twang [var. of **Tang**³], strike a stringed instrument; harsh quick sound, nasal sound.

Tweak [M.E. *twikken*; O.E. *twiccian*], to pull with a jerk; a twitch.

Tweed [from an accidental misreading of *tweel*, through association with R. *Tweed*; Sc. form of *twill*], woollen fabric.

Twee'zers [formerly *tweezes*; *tweese*, a surgeon's case of instruments; M.F. *estui*, a sheath, case], very small tongs or pincers.

Twelfth [O.E. *twelfta*], next after eleventh.

Twelfth-day, the twelfth day after Christmas, the Epiphany.

Twelfth-night, the eve of the Epiphany.

Twelve [O.E. *twelf*; Com. Teut.], one more than eleven.

Twen'ty [O.E. *twentig*], twice ten.

Twice [O.E. *twiges*], two times. [twirl.

Twid'dle [Norw. *tvidla*, var. of *tvirla*, to twirl],

Twig [O.E. *twigge*], small branch.

Twi'light [O.E. *twi-*, double; *léoht*, light], faint light before sunrise and after sunset.

Twill [O.E. *twilic*; cogn. with Ger. *zwillich*, two-threaded], ribbed fabric.

Twin [O.E. *twinn*], one of two at a birth; forming one of a pair. [wind.

Twine [O.E. *twin*], small cord, twist; to

Twinge [O.E. *twengan*], darting local pain; to twitch. [a gleam.

Twin'kle [O.E. *twinclian*], to wink, sparkle;

Twirl [freq. of O.E. *thweran*, to turn, move round quickly; rapid circular movement, a twist.

Twist [O.E.], wind as one thread about another; act of twisting, that which is formed by twisting.

Twit [O.E. *ætwitan*], to reproach, to taunt.

Twitch [M.E. *twicchen*], pull with a jerk; a jerking pull.

Twit'ter [M.E. *twiteren*, imit.], make sounds like a swallow; succession of tremulous sounds. [one.

Two (*wo=oo*) [O.E. *twegen*], one more than

Tym'pa-num [Gk. *tympanon*, a drum], eardrum.

Type [Gk. *typos*, a blow, mark of a blow, type; *typtein*, to strike], stamp, the representative, raised letter, etc., used in printing.

Type'wri-ter, machine for writing by type.

Ty'phoid [Gk. *typhos*, stupor, and *-oid*, fr. *eidos*, resemblance], kind of low fever.

Ty-phoon' [Arab. *tūfān*, a hurricane; Gk. *typhōn, typhōs*, a whirlwind], violent whirlwind.

Ty'phus [Gk. *typhos*, smoke, mist, stupor], dangerous contagious fever.

Typ'ic-al, serving as a type.

Typ'i-fy, represent by a type, be a type of.

Ty'pist, one who works a typewriter.

Typ-og'ra-pher [Gk. *typos*, type, *graphia*, description], printer. **Typograph'ical.**

Ty-ran'nic-al, acting as a tyrant.

Tyr'an-nize, act the tyrant.

Tyr'an-ny, tyrant's rule, cruel rule.

Ty'rant [Gk. *tyrannos*, sovereign, master], oppressive ruler, cruel master.

Ty'ro. [See Ti'ro.]

U

U-biq'ui-tous, in all places at one time.

U-biq'ui-ty [L. *ubique*, everywhere; *ubi*, where, *-que*, allied to *quis*, who], omnipresence.

Ud'der [O.E. *úder*], milk gland of cows.

U-do'meter [L. *udus*, damp, and **Meter**], rain-gauge.

Ug'li-ness, quality of being ugly.

Ug'ly [O.N. *uggligr*, dreadful; *uggr*, fear], offensive to the sight, ill-omened.

Uh'lan [Ger. *uhlan*; Pol. *ulan*, a lancer; Turk. *oghlān*, a youth], cavalryman armed with a lance in Prussian and some other armies.

U-kase' [Russ. *ukaz'*, an edict], decree of the Russian Government.

Ul'cer [L. *ulcus* (*ulcer-is*), a sore; Gk. *helcos*, a wound, sore], sore discharging pus. **Ul'cerate, Ul'cerous.**

Ul'ster [from prov. of *Ulster* in Ireland], long loose overcoat.

Ul-te'ri-or [L. *ulterior*, comp. of O.L. *ulter*, on the other side], situated beyond, in the background.

Ul'ti-mate [L. *ultimāre* (p.p. *ultimātus*), come to an end; *ultimus*, last], last, final.

Ul-ti-ma'tum (*a=ai*) (pl. *-ta, -tums*), final proposal.

Ul'ti-mo [L. abl. of *ultimus*] (usu. abbr. *ult.*), of last month.

Ul-tra-ma-rine' [*ine=een'*] [L. *ultra-*, beyond, *marinus*, marine], beyond the sea; a blue pigment.

Ul-tra-mon'tane, beyond (south of) the Alps [L. *ultra-*, beyond; *mons* (*mont-is*), mountain], name applied to a party in R.C. Church.

U'lu-late [L. *ululāre* (p.p. *ululātus*), to howl], to howl, wail. **Ulula'tion.**

Um'bel [L. *umbella*, a parasol, dim. of *umbra*, a shade], flower cluster with stalks from a common centre. [paint.

Um'ber [L. *umbra*, a shade], brown or reddish

Um'brage [L. *umbra*, a shade], shade, offence.

Um-bra'geous, shady, giving shade.

Um-brel'la [It. *ombrella*, dim. of It. *ombra* (L. *umbra*), a shade], portable rain-screen.

Um'pire [formerly *numpire*; M.E. *nompere*, O.E. *nomper*, peerless; L. *non*, not, *par*, equal], judge, referee.

Un- is an English prefix of negation which is used to form nouns, adjectives, and adverbs, when it means *not*, *absence of*. Most of

these are not given in the dictionary except here. Among these are: **Un-a'ble, Un-ac-cept'a-ble, Un-ac-cus'tomed, Un-ac-know'ledged, Un-ac-quaint'ed, Un-a-dorned', Un-ad-vi'sed-ly, Un-af-fect'ed, Un-aid'ed, Un-al-loyed', Un-alt'er-a-ble, Un-a'mi-a-ble, Un-an'-swer-a-ble, Un-ap-pre'ci-a-ted, Un-ap-proach'a-ble, Un-armed', Un-asked', Un-a-spir'ing, Un-as-sail'a-ble, Un-as-sum'ing, Un-at-tend'-ed, Un-at-tract'ive, Un-au'thor-ized, Un-a-vail'a-ble, Un-a-vail'ing, Un-a-ware', Un-bear'a-ble, Un-be-fit'ting, Un-be-lief', Un-be-liev'er, Un-bi'as(s)ed, Un-bid'den, Un-blush'ing, Un-bound'ed, Un-called', Un-can-on'ic-al, Un-ceas'ing, Un-cer'tain, Un-cer'tain-ty, Un-chal'lenged, Un-change'a-ble, Un-char'it-a-ble, Un-chast'-ened, Un-chris'tian, Un-civ'il, Un-ci'vil-ized, Un-clean', Un-come'ly, Un-com'fort-a-ble, Un-com'mon, Un'com-mu'ni-ca-tive, Un-com'-pro-mi'sing, Un-con-cern', Un-con-di'tion-al, Un-con-fined', Un-con-firmed', Un-con-nect'ed, Un-con-ge'ni-al, Un-con'scious, Un-cul'ti-va-ted, Un-cut', Un-da'ted, Un-daunt'ed, Un-de-fined', Un-de-mon'stra-tive, Un-de-ni'a-ble, Un-dis-guised', Un-dis-pu'ted, Un-dis-tin'guished, Un-dis-turbed', Un-di-vi'ded, Un-doubt'ed, Un-dressed', Un-du'ly, Un-du'ti-ful, Un-dy'ing, Un-earned', Un-earth'ly, Un-ea'sy, Un-ed'u-cat-ed, Un-e-mo'tion-al, Un-em-ployed', Un-end'ing, Un-en-du'ra-ble, Un-en-light'ened, Un-en'ter-pri'-sing, Un-en'vi-a-ble, Un-e'qual, Un-e'qualled, Un-e-quiv'o-cal, Un-err'ing, Un-es-sen'tial, Un-e'ven, Un-ex-am'pled, Un-ex-celled', Un-ex-cep'tion-a-ble, Un-ex-pect'ed, Un-ex-plored', Un-fad'ing, Un-feel'ing, Un-fair', Un-faith'ful, Un-fam-il'iar, Un-fash'ion-a-ble, Un-fath'om-a-ble, Un-fa'vour-a-ble, Un-feel'ing, Un-feigned', Un-fer-ment'ed, Un-fil'i-al, Un-fin'ished, Un-fit', Un-flinch'ing, Un'fore-seen', Un'-for-giv'ing, Un-formed', Un-for'tu-nate, Un-found'ed, Un-fre-quent'ed, Un-friend'-ly, Un-fruit'ful, Un-fur'nished, Un-gal'-lant, Un-gen'er-ous, Un-gen'tle-man-ly, Un-glazed', Un-god'ly, Un-gov'ern-a-ble, Un-grace'ful, Un-gra'cious, Un-gram-ma'tic-al, Un-grate'ful, Un-ground'ed, Un-grudg'ing, Un-guard'ed, Un-hal'lowed, Un-hap'py, Un-harmed', Un-health'y, Un-heard', Un-heed'ing, Un-hes'it-a-ting, Un-ho'ly, Un-hoped', Un-i-mag'in-a-ble, Un-im-paired', Un-im-pas'sioned, Un-im-peach'a-ble, Un-im-port'ant, Un-in-hab'it-ed, Un-in'jured, Un-in-tel'li-gent, Un-in-tel'li-gi-ble, Un-in-ten'tion-al, Un-in'ter-est-ing, Un-in-ter-rupt'ed, Un-in-vit'ing, Un-just', Un-jus-ti-fi'a-ble, Un-kind', Un-known', Un-li'censed, Un-like', Un-lim'it-ed, Un-love'ly, Un-luck'y, Un-man'ly, Un-man'ner-ly, Un-mean'ing, Un-men'tion-a-ble, Un-mer'ci-ful, Un-mer'-it-ed, Un-mind'ful, Un-mis-ta'ka-ble** or **Un-mis-take'a-ble, Un-mit'i-ga-ted, Un-**

U

mixed', Un-mu'si-cal, Un-name'a-ble, Un-nat'u-ral, Un-nav'i-ga-ble, Un-ne'ces-sa-ry, Un-nei*gh*'bour-ly, Un-no'ticed, Un-ob-jec'tion-a-ble, Un-ob-serv'ant, Un-ob-trus'ive, Un-oc'cu-pied, Un-of-fend'ing, Un-of-fi'cial, Un-op-posed', Un-or'tho-dox, Un-os-ten-ta'tious, Un-paid', Un-pal'-at-a-ble, Un-par'don-a-ble, Un-par-lia-men'ta-ry, Un-pa-tri-ot'ic, Un-pleas'ant, Un-po-et'ic, Un-pol'ished, Un-pop'u-lar, Un-prac'tic-al, Un-pre'ju-diced, Un-pre-med'it-a-ted, Un-pre-pared', Un-pre-tend'-ing, Un-prin'ci-pled, Un-pro-duct'ive, Un-pro-fes'sion-al, Un-prof'it-a-ble, Un-prom'is-ing, Un-proved', Un-pub'lished, Un-punct'u-al, Un-qua'li-fied, Un-ques'-tion-a-ble, Un-rea'dy, Un-re'al, Un-re-al'i-ty, Un-rea'son-a-ble, Un-re-cord'-ed, Un-re-deemed', Un-re-fined', Un-re-gen'er-ate, Un-reg'is-tered, Un-re-la'ted, Un-re-lent'ing, Un-re-li'a-ble, Un-re-lieved', Un-re-mit'ting, Un-rep-re-sent'-ed, Un-re-quit'ed, Un-re-served', Un-re-strained', Un-right'eous, Un-ripe', Un-ri'valled, Un-ro-man'tic, Un-ruf'fled, Un-safe', Un-said', Un-sat-is-fac'to-ry, Un-sa'voury, Un-scrip'tu-ral, Un-scru'-pu-lous, Un-sea'son-a-ble, Un-seem'-ly, Un-seen', Un-self'ish, Un-ser'vice-a-ble, Un-set'tled, Un-sha'ken, Un-shape'ly, Un-shrink'ing, Un-sight'ly, Un-skil'ful, Un-so'ci-a-ble, Un-soiled', Un-so-li'cit-ed, Un-so-phis'ti-ca-ted, Un-sou*ght* (*ou=aw*), Un-sound', Un-spar'ing, Un-speak'a-ble, Un-spok'en, Un-spot'ted, Un-sta'ble, Un-stamped', Un-stead'y, Un-stint'ed, Un-strung', Un-stud'ied, Un-sub-stan'tial, Un-suc-cess'ful, Un-suit'a-ble, Un-sul'lied, Un-sung', Un-sur-passed', Un-sus-cep'ti-ble, Un-sus-pect'ing, Un-swerv'ing, Un-taint'ed, Un-ta'ma-ble or Un-tame'a-ble, Un-tast'ed, Un-tau*ght*', Un-ten'a-ble, Un-thank'ful, Un-think'ing, Un-thrift'y, Un-ti'dy, Un-time'ly, Un-ti'tled, Un-touched', Un-trod', Un-trod'den, Un-trou'bled, Un-true', Un-truth', Un-used', Un-u'su-al, Un-ut'ter-a-ble, Un-var'-nished, Un-va'ry-ing, Un-war'rant-ed, Un-wa'ry, Un-wa'vering, Un-wear'ied, Un-wel'come, Un-well', Un-*wh*ole'some, Un-wield'y, Un-will'ing, Un-wise', Un-wit'ting, Un-wo'man-ly, Un-won'ted, Un-world'ly, Un-wor'thy, Un-*wr*it'ten, Un-*wr*ought', Un-yield'ing.

Un- as a prefix to simple verbs frequently gives them a contrary sense. Among verbs thus formed are: Un-bar', Un-bolt', Un-bur'den or Un-bur'then, Un-close', Un-clothe', Un-cork', Un-cov'er, Un-do', Un-dress', Un-earth', Un-fast'en, Un-fit', Un-furl', Un-gird', Un-hinge', Un-horse', Un-lace', Un-lade', Un-learn', Un-load', Un-lock', Un-moor', Un-nerve', Un-pack', Un-pin', Un-rav'el, Un-rid'dle, Un-robe', Un-roll', Un-say', Un-set'tle, Un-sheathe', Un-swathe', Un-tie', Un-twist', Un-veil', Un-*wr*ap', Un-yoke'.

U-na-nim'i-ty, state of being unanimous.

U-nan'i-mous [L. *unus*, one, *animus*, mind], of one mind.   [unexpectedly.

Un-a-wares' [*un-*, not, and **Aware**], suddenly,

Un-bend' [*un-*, expressing reversal, and **Bend**], loosen, relax.

Un-bos'om (*os=ooz*) [*un-*, with contrary sense, and **Bosom**], disclose freely.

Un'ci-al [L. *uncialis*, inch-high, *uncia*, inch], written in large unjoined characters like early MSS., large size, capital.

Un'cle [L. *avunculus*, a mother's brother, dim. of *avus*, a grandfather], parent's brother, aunt's husband.

Un-con'scion-a-ble (*sci=sh*), [*un-*, not, **Con-science** and **Able**], quite unreasonable.

Un-couth' (*ou=oo*) [O.E. *uncúth*; *un-*, not, *cúth*, p.p. of *cunnan*, to know], odd, awkward, ungainly.

Unc'tion [L. *ung(u)ere* (p.p. *unctus*), to anoint], act of anointing, anything soothing, religious fervour, gush.

Unc'tu-ous, oily, bland.

Un'der [O.E. *under*], below, beneath, included in, in the time of.

Un-der-bred' [see **Under** and **Breed**], not thoroughly bred, ill-mannered.

Un-der-do', cook insufficiently.

Un-der-go', pass through, endure.

Un-der-grad'u-ate, student who has not taken his first degree.

Un'der-growth, shrubs or small trees growing among large ones.

Un-der-hand', secret, done with the hand held under the ball and lower than the shoulder or elbow.

Un'der-ling [**Under** and suf. *-ling*], one in an inferior position.

Un-der-neath' [**Under** and O.E. *neothan*, nether], beneath, below.

Un-der-rate', rate too low.   [beneath.

Un-der-shot', (wheel) moved by water passing

Un-der-stand', have knowledge of, infer, take for granted.

Un-der-stand'ing, power to understand, intelligence, agreement.

Un'der-stud'y, one who studies so as to be ready to take the part of another.

Un-der-take', take upon oneself.

Un'der-ta-ker, one who manages funerals.

Un'der-ta-king, project engaged in, a promise.

Un'der-tone, low tone.

Un'der-*wr*i-ter, insurer, esp. of shipping.

Un-due' [*un-*, not; O.F. *deü*, p.p. of *devoir*, to owe], not due, excessive.

Un'du-late [L. *undulāre* (p.p. *undulātus*), to undulate; *unda*, a wave], have an appearance as of waves.

Un-du-la'tion, wavy appearance.

Un'du-la-to-ry, wavy.

Un-gain'ly [*un-*, not, O.N. *gegn*, ready, serviceable], clumsy, ill-shaped.

Un'guent [L. *unguere* (pr.p. *unguens, -entis*), to anoint], ointment.

Un-hand' [*un-*, expressing contrary sense and **Hand**], take hands off.

U'ni-corn [L. *unus*, one, *cornū*, a horn], fabulous animal with one horn.

U-ni-fi-ca'tion, act of making into one.

U'ni-form [L. *unus*, one, *forma*, form], not varying; distinctive dress worn by members of the same body. **Un'iformly.**

U-ni-form'i-ty, sameness, consistency.

U'ni-fy [M.L. *ūnificāre* (p.p. *ūnificātus*) ; *unus*, one, *facere*, to make], make into one, reduce to unity.

U'ni-on (*yoon'yŭn*) [L. *ūnio* (*ūniōn-is*) ; union ; *ūnus*, one], act of uniting, combination. **U'nionist.**

U-nique' (*ique=eek*) [L. *ūnicus*, single ; *ūnus*, one], single in kind or excellence. **Unique'ness.**

U'ni-son [L. *ūnus*, one, *sonus*, sound], unity of pitch, agreement.

U'nit [shortened from **Unity**], single thing or person, one, group regarded as an individual.

U'nit-a-ry, of a unit.

U-nite' [L. *ūnīre* (p.p. *ūnītus*), to unite ; *ūnus*, one], join in one.

U'ni-ty, oneness, the number one.

U'ni-ver'sal, general, including all.

U'ni-verse [L. *ūnus*, one, *vertere* (p.p. *versus*), to turn], all existing things as a whole.

U-ni-ver'si-ty [L. *universitas*, whole, universe], high educational institution.

Un-kempt' [*un-*, not, O.E. *cemban*, to comb], not combed.

Un-less' [formerly *on les*, *on lesse* ; **On** and **Less**], if it be not, except.

Un-man' [*un-*, expressing reversal, and **Man**], dishearten, make womanish.

Un-pre'ce-dent'ed [*un-*, not ; L. *pre-*, before, *cedere*, to go], not preceded by a like case.

Un-ru'ly [*un-*, not, and **Rule**], disorderly.

Un-seat' [*un-*, expressing a contrary sense, and **Seat**], throw from one's seat, deprive of a seat in parliament.

Un-til' [altered from **Unto**], as far as, so that at length, before (with neg.).

Un'to [M.E. *unto*, for *undto*, from Goth. *und*, unto, and **To**], even to.

Un-to'ward [*un-*, not, O.E. *tóweard*, about to come], perverse, inconvenient, unlucky.

Up [O.E. *úp*(*p*)], to or in a higher place, value, etc., wholly.   [Java.

U'pas [Malay. *úpas*, poison], poison-tree of

Up-braid' [O.E. *úp*, up, *bregdan*, to braid, weave, lay hold of], to reproach.

Up'bring-ing, training, education.

Up-heav'al, act of upheaving, a lifting of part of the earth's crust.

Up-heave', lift from below.

Up-hold', hold up, to support. **Uphold'er.**

Up-hol'ster-er [earlier *upholster*, *upholdster* ; fr. **Up** and **Hold**], one whose trade it is to furnish rooms. (*Verb*) **Uphol'ster.**   [etc.

Up-hol'ster-y, hangings, carpets, coverings,

Up'land, high land.

Up-lift', raise.

Up'lift, feeling of exaltation.

Up'most, highest, on the top.

Up'per [comp. of **Up**], higher.

Up'pish [from **Up** and suf. *-ish*], proud.

Up'right, erect, righteous.

Up'roar [Du. *oproer* ; *op*, up, *roeren*, to excite], noisy confusion. **Uproar'ious.**

Up-root', tear up by the roots.

Up-set', overturn, disturb.

Up'set, lowest selling (price), reserve (price).

Up'shot, result, end.

Up-stairs', on or toward an upper storey.

Up'start, one who has risen suddenly.

Up'ward, **Up'wards** [**Up** and suf. *-ward*], from lower to higher.

Ur'ban [L. *urbānus*, belonging to a city ; *urbs* (*urb-is*), a city], pertaining to a city or town.

Ur-bane' [as **Urban**], courteous.

Ur-ban'i-ty, courtesy.

Ur'chin [L. *ēricius*, a hedgehog], hedgehog, little boy.

Urge [L. *urgēre*, to urge], press, insist upon.

Ur'gen-cy, pressure.

Ur'gent, pressing.   [body.

Urn [L. *urna*, an urn], vase with a rounded

Ur'sine [L. *ursus*, a bear], pertaining to or like a bear.

U'sage (*s=z*), custom, treatment.

Use [L. *ūtī* (p.p. *ūsus*), to use], using, employment, need, usage.

Use (*s=z*), employ, treat.

Use'ful, of use, serviceable.

Use'less [O.E. *léas*, free from], of no use.

Ush'er [L. *ostiārius*, a door-keeper, *ostium*, a door], officer or servant acting as doorkeeper or walking before persons of rank, assistant schoolmaster ; introduce or escort.

Us-que-baugh' (*augh=aw*) [Ir. *uisge beatha*, water of life], whisky.

U'su-al (*s=z*), customary, common.

Us'u-fruct [L. *usus*, use, *fructus*, fruit], use of property without the right to dispose of it. **Usufruct'uary.**

U'su-rer, one who exacts usury.

U-su'ri-ous (*s=z*), partaking of usury.

U-surp' [L. *ūsurpāre*, to employ, also to usurp. Etym. doubtful], seize and hold wrongfully. **Usurpa'tion.**

U'su-ry [L. *ūsūra*, use, enjoyment, usury], excessive interest, interest charged to a borrower, the exaction of this.

U-ten'sil [L. *ūtensilis*, fit for use ; *ūtī* (pr.p. *ūtens*, *-entis*), to use], instrument or tool, esp. for kitchen use.

U-til-i-ta'ri-an, pertaining to utility ; one whose ideal is the greatest good of the greatest number of people.

U-til'i-ty [L. *ūtilis*, useful, *ūtī*, to use], usefulness.

U'til-ize, make use of. **Utiliza'tion.**

Ut'most [O.E. *ūtemest* ; double superl. of *út*, out], extreme, last.

U-to'pi-an [lit. *nowhere* ; Gk. *ou*, not, *topos*, a place], ideal but unpractical.   [plete.

Ut'ter[1] [O.E. *uttera*, comp. of *út*, out], com-

Ut'ter[2] [M.E. *uttren* ; O.E. *útian*, to utter ; *út*, out], give forth, express audibly.

Ut'ter-ance [see **Utter**[2]], an uttering, power of speech.

U'vu-la [Late L. *ûvula*, dim. of L. *ûva*, a grape], fleshy part which hangs at the back of the palate.

Ux-o'ri-ous [L. *uxor* (*uxŏr-is*), a wife], excessively fond of one's wife.

V

Va'can-cy, emptiness, gap, unoccupied post.

Va'cant [O.F. *vacant*; see **Vacate**], empty.

Va-cate' [L. *vacāre* (p.p. *vacātus*), to be empty], leave empty, quit occupation of.

Va-ca'tion, act of vacating, period of cessation from work, holidays.

Vac'ci-nate, inoculate with vaccine to secure immunity from smallpox. **Vac'cina'tion**.

Vac'cine [L. *vaccīnus*, belonging to cows; *vacca*, a cow], pertaining to cows; virus of cowpox.

Va'cil-late [L. *vacillāre* (p.p. *vacillātus*), to vacillate], waver. **Vacilla'tion**.

Vac'u-ous [L. *vacuus*, empty], empty. **Vacu'ity**.

Vac'u-um, empty space.

Vag'a-bond [L. *vagābundus*, strolling about; *vagāri*, to wander], wanderer, tramp, rascal.

Va-ga'ry [L. *vagāri*, to wander], wild freak, whim.

Va'grant [earlier *vagaraunt*; A.F. *wakerant*; cogn. with **Walk**], wandering; a tramp. **Va'grancy**.

Vague [L. *vagus*, wandering, *vagāri*, to wander], indefinite, hazy. **Vague'ness**.

Vain [L. *vānus*, empty, vain], worthless, ineffectual, conceited.

Val'ance, **Val'ence** [prob. fr. *Valence*, in France], hanging drapery of a bed, etc.

Vale [F. *val*, L. *vallis*, a valley], valley.

Val-e-dic'tion [L. *valē*, farewell, and *dicere* (p.p. *dictus*), to say], a farewell.

Val-e-dic'to-ry [see **Valediction**], in farewell.

Val'en-tine [from St *Valentine's* Day, Feb. 14], love-missive sent on St Valentine's Day.

Val'et (*val'ĕt* or *val'at*) [F. *valet*, a groom; var. of **Varlet**], attendant man-servant.

Val-e-tu'di-na'ri-an [L. *valētūdo* (*valētūdi-nis*), health; *valēre*, to be strong], invalid.

Val-hal'la [O.N. *valhöll*, gen. *-hallar*, hall of the slain], Norse heaven.

Val'iant (*i=y*) [O.F. *vailant*, pr.p. of *valoir*, to be worth; L. *valēre*, to be strong], brave.

Val'id [L. *validus*, strong; *valēre*, to be strong], of force, sound. **Valid'ity**.

Va-lise' (*va-leez'*) [F. *valise*; It. *valigia*. Etym. unknown], travelling-bag.

Val'ley [O.F. *valee*; L. *vallis*, a valley] low tract between hills.

Val'or-ous, brave.

Val'our [L. *valor* (*valŏr-is*), worth; *valēre*, to be strong, be worth], personal courage.

Val'u-a-ble, of great value, precious; (n. pl.) things of value.

Val-u-a'tion, setting a price, estimate of value.

Val'ue [O.F. *value* (fem. of p.p. of *valoir*, to be worth); L. *valēre*, to be worth], worth, esteem; to rate, prize highly.

Valve [L. *valva*, leaf of a folding-door; cogn. with *volvere*, to roll], (rare) leaf of a folding-door, movable lid for controlling passage of fluid.

Val'vu-lar, pertaining to a valve or valves.

Vamp [M.E. *vaumpay*; M.F. *avant-pied*; *avant*, before, and *pied*, foot], upper front part of a boot; to patch, improvise an accompaniment.

Vam'pire [Ger. *vampyr*; Serb. *vampir*; prob. of Turkish orig.], blood-sucking ghost, blood-sucking bat.

Van[1] [short for **Van-guard**; O.F. *avant-warde*, *avant*, before, *warde*, guard], front or front part of army or fleet.

Van[2] [L. *vannus*, a fan], winnowing-machine.

Van[3] [short for **Caravan**], waggon, usually covered.

Van'dal [L. *Vandalus*, German race which ravaged Gaul, etc., fr. Teut. root], one who mischievously destroys works of art. **Van'dalism**.

Van-dyke' [from *Van Dyck*, Flemish painter], picture by Vandyke, border with large points, one of the points; to cut cloth in this manner.

Vane [O.E. *fana*, small flag], weather-cock, blade of a wind-mill.

Van'guard [see **Van**[1]], front troops of an army.

Va-nil'la [Sp. *vainilla*, a pod, dim. of *vaina*, a sheath; L. *vagina*, sheath pod], kind of orchid, flavouring got from the bean of the plant.

Van'ish [O.F. *esvanir*; L. *ex-*, out, *vanescere*, to vanish; *vānus*, empty], go out of sight.

Van'i-ty [L. *vānus*, empty], empty pride.

Van'quish [O.F. *veinquir*, L. *vincere*, to conquer], to defeat.

Van'tage [short for M.E. *avantage*, advantage], advantage.

Vap'id [L. *vapidus*, stale, flat], spiritless, insipid, flat. **Vapid'ity**.

Va'por-ous, having the form of vapour.

Va'pour [L. *vapor*, vapour], moisture in the air; to boast. **Va'porize**.

Va'ri-a-ble, changeable.

Va'ri-ance, quarrel.

Va'ri-ant, thing differing in details from something essentially the same.

Va-ri-a'tion, partial change or difference.

Var'i-cose [L. *vār. (varic-is*), a dilated vein; *vārus*, crooked], irregularly swollen (esp. of veins).

Va'ri-e-ga-ted [L. *varius*, variegated, various, *agere*, to drive, make], having patches of different colours.

Va-ri'e-ty, diversity, collection of different things, a sort or kind.

Va'ri-ous [L. *varius*, variegated, various], different, diverse, several.

Var'let [M.F. *varlet*; older *vaslet*, dim. of O.F. *vasal*, a vassal], rascal, servant.

Var'nish [O.F. *vernis* (n.); etym. doubtful], solution of a resinous material, gloss ; lay varnish on.

Va'ry [L. *variāre*, to vary], to change, be different in kind, etc.

Vas'cu-lar [L. *vasculum*, dim. of *vās*, a vessel], of or containing vessels for conveying blood, etc.

Vase (*s=z*) [L. *vāsum*, var. of *vās*, a vessel], ornamental hollow vessel.

Vas'e-line (or *-een*) [Ger. *wasser*, water, and Gk. *elaion*, oil], ointment from petroleum.

Vas'sal [M.L. *vassallus*, *vassus*, Bret. *goaz*, a servant], feudal tenant, retainer. **Vas'-salage.**

Vast [L. *vastus*, vast], of great extent.

Vat [O.E. *fæt*], large tub.

Vat'i-can [L. (*Mons*) *Vaticānus*, name of hill in Rome], palace and official residence of the Pope.

Va-ti-ci-na'tion [L. *vāticinārī* (p.p. *vāticinātus*), to prophesy ; *vātes*, a prophet ; *canere*, to sing], prophecy.

Vaude'ville (*vōdvil*) [fr. *Vau de Vire*, valley of the Vire, in Normandy], variety entertainment.

Vault[1] [O.F. *voute* ; L. *volvere* (p.p. *volūtus*), to roll], arched roof or chamber, cellar ; cover with a vault.

Vault[2] [M.F. *volter*, to vault, *volte*, a turn round ; same as **Vault**[1]], to leap, esp. with hand resting on something ; a leap.

Vaunt [F. *vanter* ; Late L. *vānitāre*, to speak vanity ; L. *vānus*, vain], to boast; a boast.

Veal [O.F. *veĕl* ; L. *vitellus*, dim. of *vitulus*, a calf], calf's flesh as food.

Veer [F. *virer* ; Late L. *virāre*, to turn round. Etym. doubtful], change direction, to turn, change one's mind, slacken, let out.

Ve'ge-ta-ble (*vĕ-*) [L. *vegetābilis*, full of life ; *vegetāre*, to quicken], pertaining to plants ; a plant, food-plant.

Ve'ge-tal, of the nature of a vegetable.

Ve'ge-ta'ri-an, one who lives on vegetable food.

Ve'ge-tate [L. *vegetāre* (p.p. *vegetātus*), to enliven ; *vegetus*, lively, *vegēre*, to arouse], grow as plants do, do nothing but eat and grow.   [general.

Ve-ge-ta'tion, vegetable growth, plants in

Ve'he-mence, great force, strong feeling.

Ve'he-ment [L. *vehemens (-entis)* ; perh. *vē-*, apart from, and *mens (ment-is)*, mind], violent, intense, impetuous, passionate.

Ve'hi-cle [L. *vehiculum* ; *vehere*, to carry], a carriage, means of conveyance. **Vehi'-cular.**

Veil (*ei=ai*), **Vail** [O.F. *veile*, a veil ; L. *vēlum*, a sail, a veil], cover for the face, curtain ; to cover with a veil, hide.

Vein (*ei=ai*) [L. *vēna*, a vein], vessel which carries blood to the heart, fissure containing ore, disposition, mood.

Veld (*d* as *t*), **Veldt** [Du. *veld*, field], grass country of S. Africa.

Vel'lum [O.F. *velin*, vellum ; L. *vitulīnus*, of a calf], fine parchment.

Ve-loc'i-pede (*c* soft) [L. *vēlōx (vēlōc-is)*, swift ; *pēs (ped-is)*, a foot], a cycle.

Ve-lo'ci-ty (*ō*) [L. *vēlōx (vēlōc-is)*, swift], swiftness, speed.

Ve-lours' (*ou=oo*) [F.*velours*, velvet], woollen fabric with velvet pile.

Vel'vet [Low L. *velluētum*, velvet ; L. *villus*, shaggy hair], silk fabric with close nap. **Vel'veteen.**

Ve'nal [L. *vēnus*, sale], ready to accept bribes. **Venal'ity.**

Vend [L. *vendere*, to sell], sell. **Vend'er, Vend'or,** seller.

Ven-det'ta [It. *vendetta*, L. *vindicta*, vengeance ; *vindicāre*, to avenge], blood-feud (in Italy).

Vend'i-ble, saleable.

Ve-neer' [Ger. *furniren*, F. *fournir*, to furnish], overlay with a thin coating of fine wood ; thin coating.   [worthy.

Ven'er-a-ble, deserving reverence, old and

Ven'er-ate [L. *venerārī* (p.p. *venerātus*), to venerate ; cogn. with *venus (vener-is)*, love], to honour with respect.

Ven-er-a'tion, respect with awe.

Ven'e-ry [L. *vēnārī*, to hunt], hunting.

Venge'ance [F. *venger*, L. *vindicare*, to avenge], punishment inflicted for wrong to oneself or another one is interested in.

Ve'ni-al [L. *venia*, pardon], pardonable.

Ven'i-son or **Ven'i-son** [L. *vēnātio*, the chase, game ; *vēnārī*, to hunt], deer-flesh.

Ven'om [L. *venēnum*, poison], poison, spite. **Ven'omous.**   [or veins.

Ve'nous [L. *vēna*, a vein], pertaining to a vein

Vent [M.F. *fente*, a rift ; L. *findere*, to cleave], opening for air or fluid to escape, utterance ; give outlet to.

Ven'ti-late [L. *ventilāre* (p.p. *ventilātus*), to blow ; *ventus*, wind], to air, make public. **Ventila'tion.**

Ven'ti-la-tor, contrivance for ventilating.

Ven'tral [L. *venter*, the belly], abdominal.

Ven'tri-cle [L. *ventriculus*, dim. of *venter*, the belly], cavity of an organ, esp. one of two cavities of the heart.

Ven-tril'o-quism [L. *ventriloquus*, speaking from the belly ; *venter*, belly, *loqui*, to speak], art of speaking so that the sound does not seem to come from the speaker. **Ventril'oquist.**

Ven'ture [shortened from M.E. *aventure*, adventure], dare, to risk ; a risk.

Ven'ture-some, Ven'tu-rous, bold, daring.

Ven'ue [F. *venue*, a coming ; F. *venir*, L. *venīre*, to come], place where an action is laid.

Ve-ra'cious (*aci=aish*) [L. *vērāx (vērāc-is)*, true; *vērus*, true], truthful, true. **Vera'city.**

Ve-ran'da(h) [Port. *varanda*, perh. fr. *vara*, a rod ; etym. doubtful], open portico or roofed gallery extending along front or side of a building.

Verb [L. *verbum*, a word], part of speech expressing being, action, or suffering.

Ver'bal [L. *verbum*, a word], expressed in words, oral, pertaining to a verb.

Ver-ba′tim, word for word.

Ver-be′-na [L. *verbēna*, sacred bough], a plant with fragrant leaves.

Ver′bi-age, wordiness.

Ver-bos′i-ty, wordiness. **Verbose′**.

Ver′dant [L. *viridis*, green], green, fresh. **Ver′dancy**.

Ver′dict [L. *vērē dictum*, truly said], judgment, decision of a jury.

Ver′di-gris [M.F. *verd de grice*; O.F. *vert de Grece*, green of Greece], green rust on copper.

Ver′dure [O.F. *verd*, L. *viridis*, green], greenness, green vegetation.

Verge [L. *virga*, a twig, rod], border, edge, wand carried before a bishop, etc.

Verge [L. *vergere*, to bend, incline], border on.

Ver′ger, one who carries a verge, an official who looks after a church interior.

Ver-i-fi-ca′tion, confirmation.

Ver′i-fy [M.L. *vērĭficāre* (p.p. *vērĭficātus*), to verify; *vērus*, true, *facere*, to make], prove to be true, confirm. **Verifi′able**.

Ver′i-ly [L. *vērus*, true], truly.

Ver-i-si-mil′i-tude [L. *verus*, true, *similis*, like], likelihood.

Ver′i-ty [L. *vērus*, true], truth. **Ver′itable**.

Ver′juice [O.F. *verjus*; fr. *verd*, L. *viridis*, green, and L. *jus*, juice], juice of sour apples, sour grapes, etc.

Ver-mi-cel′li (*c*=*ch* or *s*) [It. pl. of *vermicello*, dim. of *verme*, L. *vermis*, a worm], paste like macaroni made in long slender threads.

Ver-mic′u-lar [L. *vermiculus*, dim. of *vermis*, worm], like a worm.

Ver-mil′ion [F. *vermillon*, a little worm, cochineal insect; L. *vermiculus*, dim. of *vermis*, a worm], bright red pigment.

Ver′min [L. *vermis*, a worm], noxious animals. **Ver′minous**.

Ver′mouth, Ver′muth (*ou*, *u*=*oo*) [Ger. *wermuth*, wormwood], strong alcoholic liquor flavoured with wormwood.

Ver-nac′u-lar [L. *vernāculus*, native, *verna*, a home-born slave], of one′s own country; one′s native language.

Ver′nal [L. *vernālis*; *vēr*, spring], pertaining to spring.

Ver′sa-tile [L. *vertere* (p.p. *versus*), to turn], turning easily from one thing to another. **Versatil′ity**.

Verse [L. *vertere* (p.p.*versus*), to turn], poetry, a metrical line of poetry or a group of such lines, poetry in general, section of chapter of the Bible.

Versed [L. *versārī* (p.p *versātus*), freq. of *vertere*, to turn], practised, skilled.

Ver′si-fy [F. *versifier*; L. *versus*, turned, *facere*, to make], turn into verse, make verse. **Versifica′tion**.

Ver′sion [L. *vertere* (p.p. *versus*), to turn], rendering, translation, account.

Ver′te-bra (pl. -bræ) [L. *vertebra*, a joint; *vertere*, to turn], joint of the spine.

Ver′te-brate, having a spine.

Ver′tex [L. *vertex* (*vertic-is*), top; *vertere*, to turn], highest point.

Ver′ti-cal [L. *verticālis*, vertical, *vertex*, top], directly overhead, upright.

Ver′ti-go (or Ver-ti′go) [L. *vertigo* (*vertigin-is*), giddiness; *vertere*, to turn], dizziness. **Vertig′inous**.

Verve [F. *verve*; etym. doubtful], spirit, energy.

Ver′y [O.F. *verai*, L. *vērus*, true], true; in a high degree.

Ves′i-cle [L. *vēsĭcula*, dim. of *vēsĭca*, a bladder], small cavity or cell in a body.

Ves′per [L. *vesper*, evening star], evening star, evening.

Ves′pers, evensong, evening worship.

Ves′sel [L. *vascellum*, dim. of *vās*, a vase], hollow receptacle, ship, duct or canal holding or conveying blood, etc.

Vest [L. *vestis*, a garment, *vestīre*, to clothe], waistcoat; clothe, put in possession.

Ves′ta [L. *Vesta*, Gk. *Hestia*, goddess of the hearth], wax match.

Ves′tal, pertaining to Vesta, pure; vestal virgin.

Ves′ti-bule [L. *vestibulum*; etym. doubtful], porch, entrance-hall.   [trace.

Ves′tige [L. *vestigium*, footstep], particle,

Vest′ment [L. *vestis*, a garment], royal or priestly garment.

Ves′try [L. *vestiārium*, wardrobe; *vestis*, garment], room attached to a church where vestments are kept, also where meetings are held, meeting of ratepayers of a parish, board elected by them.

Ves′ture [L. *vestīre*, to clothe], dress.

Vetch [O.F. *veche*; L. *vicia*, a vetch], plant of the bean kind.

Vet′er-an [L. *veterānus*; *vetus* (*veter-is*), old], of long experience; old soldier, man of long experience.

Vet′er-i-na-ry [L. *veterinārius*, of beasts of burden, perh. fr. *vetus* (*veter-is*), old], of or for treatment of diseases of animals.

Ve′to [L. *veto*, I forbid], forbidding, right of rejecting; prohibit, refuse assent to.

Vex [L. *vexāre* (p.p.s *vexātus*), to vex], to trouble, annoy; (Scots) to grieve.

Vex-a′tion, trouble, annoyance.

Vex-a′tious, annoying, disturbing.

Vi′a-duct [L. *via ducta*, led way; *via*, a way, *ducere* (p.p. *ductus*), to lead], long bridge carrying road or railway over a valley or dip in ground.

Vi′al, see Phial [Gk. *phiale*, a shallow bowl], small bottle.

Vi′ands [L. *vīvenda*, neut. pl. fr. gerundive of *vivere*, to live], food.

Vi-bra′tion, motion to and fro.

Vi′brate [L. *vibrāre* (p.p.s *vibrātus*), to swing], move to and fro, swing, quiver, resound.

Vic′ar [L. *vicārius*, a deputy, deputed], in England a parish priest with some one over him who receives most of the tithes, delegate for another.

Vic′ar-age, benefice or house of a vicar.

Vi-ca′ri-ous, acting or suffering for another.

Vice [F. *vice*, L. *vitium*, vice], fault, wickedness.

Vice [F. *vis*, a vice; L. *vītis*, a vine], instrument for gripping an article that is being worked upon.

Vice-ge'rent [L. *vice*, in place of, *gerere* (pr.p. *gerens*, *-entis*), to carry on rule], substitute for a superior.

Vice'roy [L. *vice*, in place of; O.F. *roy* (L. *rex*), king], one who governs as a delegate for the sovereign.

Vi'cin-age (*vi-*) [L. *vicinus*, near; *vicus*, a village], neighbourhood. **Vicin'ity.**

Vi'cious (*ci*=*sh*) [L. *vitium*, vice], wicked, given to evil practices.

Vi-cis'si-tude [L. *vicissim*, by turns], change.

Vic'tim [L. *victima*, a victim; perh. cogn. with Goth. *weihan*, to consecrate], a living being sacrificed, one who suffers through cruel treatment or dangerous undertaking.

Vic'tim-ize, make a victim of, cheat.

Vic'tor [L. *vincere* (p.p. *victus*), to conquer], conqueror.

Vic-to'ri-a [from Queen *Victoria*], low four-wheeled carriage for two.

Vic-to'ri-ous, conquering.

Vic'to-ry, defeat of an enemy.

Vict'ual [L. *victuālia*, provisions; L. *vivere* (p.p. *victus*), to live], supply with provisions; (n. pl.) food.

Vict'ual-ler, tavern-keeper, provision-ship.

Vie [M.E. *vien*, short for *envien*, to vie; O.F. *envier*, to invite], strive for superiority.

View [O.F. *veue*, fem. p.p. of *veoir*, to see; L. *vidēre*, to see], sight, inspection, scene, picture of a scene, opinion; look at.

Vi'gil (*vi-*) [L. *vigil*, awake; *vigēre*, to be lively], watch, eve of a festival.

Vi'gi-lance, watchfulness.

Vign-ette (*veen-yet'*) [dim. of F. *vigne*, vine], ornament of leaves and tendrils in architecture or round printed capitals, small engraving, esp. on title-page or at beginning of chapter of book.

Vig'o-rous, strong, robust.

Vig'our [L. *vigor*, vigour; *vigēre*, to be lively], active strength, energy.

Vik'ing, **Vi'king** [O.N. *vikingr*, a pirate, lit. a warrior; *vig*, war], Northern sea-robber.

Vile [L. *vilis*, vile], low, base, sinful.

Vil'i-fy [L. *vilis*, vile, *facere*, to make], speak ill of, defame.

Vil'la [L. *villa*, a farm-house], country or suburban residence.

Vil'lage [O.F. *village*; L. *villāticus*, belonging to a farm-house], group of houses smaller than a town.

Vil'lain [A.F. *vilein*, a bondman; Late L. *villānus*, a farm-servant], rascal.

Vil'lain-ous, rascally, wicked.

Vil'lain-y, extreme wickedness.

Vim [L. *vis*, acc. *vim*, strength], vigour.

Vin'di-cate [L. *vindicāre* (p.p. *vindicātus*), to lay claim to; *vindex*, a claimant], maintain cause of, defend, justify. **Vin'dicator.**

Vin-dic'tive [shortened fr. *vindicative*; L. *vindicta*, vengeance; *vindicāre*, to avenge], revengeful.

Vine [L. *vīnea*, a vineyard; *vīnum*, wine], climbing plant which bears grapes.

Vin'e-gar [F. *vinaigre*; *vin* (L. *vinum*), wine, and *aigre* (L. *acer*), sour, sharp], sour liquid got from wine, cider, etc.

Vi'ner-y [see Vine], hothouse for vines.

Vine'yard [O.E. *wingeard*], plantation of vines.

Vi'nous [L. *vinum*, wine], of, like, or due to wine.

Vint'age [F. *vendange*; L. *vindēmia*, vintage; L. *vinum*, wine, *dēmere*, to take away], time of grape-gathering, season's produce of grapes or wine.

Vint'ner [L. *vinētum*, a vineyard; *vinum*, wine], wine-seller.

Vi'ol [Late L. *vitula*, a viol; etym. doubtful], stringed musical instrument, predecessor of violin.

Vi-o'la [It. *viola*], large kind of violin.

Vi'o-late [L. *violāre* (p.p. *violātus*), to violate; *vis*, force], to abuse, profane, transgress. **Viola'tion.**

Vi'o-lence, violent conduct, unjust force.

Vi'o-lent [L. *violentus*, violent; *vis*, force], forcible and fierce.

Vi'o-let [M.F. *violet*, dim. of *viole* (L. *viola*), a violet], small flower of various colours; bluish purple.

Vi-o-lin' [It. *violino*, dim. of *viola*, a viol], four-stringed instrument, fiddle.

Vi-o-lon-cel'lo (*c*=*tch*) [It. dim. of *violone*, a bass-viol], long-stringed bass violin.

Vi'per [L. *vipera*, a viper], kind of venomous snake. **Vi'perous.**

Vi-ra'go (*a*=*ai*) [L. *virāgo*, a manlike woman; *vir*, a man], turbulent woman.

Vir'gin [L. *virgo* (*virgin-is*), a virgin], maid. **Virgin'ity.**

Vir'gin-al, **Vir'gin-als** [fr. Virgin], square legless musical instrument of the 16th and 17th centuries.

Vi-rid'i-ty [L. *viridis*, green], greenness.

Vir'ile [L. *virilis*, virile; *vir*, a man], having masculine vigour.

Vir-il'it-y, manhood, manliness.

Vir-tu (*u*=*oo*) [It. *virtù*, doublet of Virtue], love of the fine arts, (*articles of virtu*, things that are valuable because of workmanship, antiquity, rarity, etc.).

Vir'tu-al [M.L. *virtuālis*; see Virtue], in effect though not in name.

Vir'tue [L. *virtus*, manly excellence; *vir*, a man], inherent power, merit, moral excellence.

Vir-tuo'so (*pl.*) **-si** (*i*=*ee*) [It.], one with special knowledge of the fine arts, one skilled in playing or singing. **Virtuos'ity.**

Vir'tu-ous, having moral excellence.

Vir'u-lent [L. *virulentus*, virulent; L. *virus*, poison], poisonous, bitter in enmity. **Vir'ulence.** [venom.

Vi'rus [L.], contagious poisonous matter.

Vis'age (*s*=*z*) [L. *visus*, sight, look; *vidēre*, to see], face.

Vis'cer-a [L. *viscera* (pl.)], entrails.

Vis'cid, **Vis'cous** [L. *viscum*, mistletoe; Gk. *ixos*, mistletoe], sticky. **Viscos'ity.**

Vis'count [L. *vice*, in place of ; *comes*, a count], nobleman below an earl.

Vi-sé (*vee'zai*) [p.p. of F. *viser*, fr. L. *videre*, to see], endorsement on passport, etc., showing that it has been found correct ; p.p. **Viséd** or **Visé'd.**

Vis'i-ble (*s=z*) [L. *vidēre* (p.p. *visus*), to see], that can be seen. **Visibil'ity.**

Vi'sion (*si=zh*) [L. *vidēre* (p.p. *visus*), to see], sight, that which is seen, esp. in a dream.

Vi'sion-a-ry, fanciful ; one who sees visions.

Vis'it [*s=z*] [L. *visitāre*, freq. of *visere*, to behold, fr. *visus*, p.p. of *vidēre*, to see], go to see, call, afflict ; act of going to see.

Vis'it-ant, Vis'it-or, one who visits.

Vis-it-a'tion, official visit, divine dispensation.

Vi'sor [O.F. *visiere*, visor ; *vis*, the face], front upper part of a helmet, mask.

Vis'ta (It. *vista*, lit. a view, also fem. p.p. of *videre*, to see ; L. *vidēre*], view through an avenue or the like, mental prospect or retrospect.

Vis'u-al [L. *visus*, sight, also p.p. of *vidēre*, to see], pertaining to sight.

Vis'u-a-lize, make visible to sight, call up mental picture of.

Vi'tal [L. *vitālis*, vital ; *vīta*, life], relating to life, essential.

Vi-tal'i-ty, principle of life, vital force.

Vi'tal-ize, give life to.

Vi'tals, organs necessary for life.

Vit'a-min(e) [L. *vita*, life], life-giving element in food.

Vi'ti-ate (*viti=vishi*) [L. *vitiāre* (p.p. *vitiātus*), to vitiate ; *vitium*, vice], impair, corrupt.

Vit'i-cul-ture [L. *vitis*, a vine ; *cultura*, culture], cultivation of the vine.

Vit're-ous [L. *vitrum*, glass], consisting of or like glass. **Vitreos'ity.**

Vit'ri-ol [L. *vitreolus*, glassy, *vitrum*, glass], sulphuric acid, bitter speech. **Vitriol'ic.**

Vi-tu'per-ate (*i*) [L. *vituperāre* (p.p. *vituperātus*), to blame ; *vitium*, vice, *parāre*, to prepare], blame loudly, scold. **Vitupera'tive.**

Vi-tu-per-a'tion, abuse.

Vi-va'cious (*vi*) [L. *vīvāx* (*vīvāc-is*), tenacious of life ; *vivere*, to live], lively, sprightly.

Vi-va'ci-ty, liveliness.

Viv'id [L. *vividus*, lively ; *vivere*, to live], intensely bright, lively.

Viv'i-fy [F. *vivifier* ; L. *vivus*, living, *facere*, to make], give life to.

Vi-vi'par-ous [L. *vivus*, living, *parēre*, to bring forth], bringing forth young alive (not hatching by means of egg).

Viv-i-sec'tion [L. *vivus*, living, *sectio* (*section-is*), a cutting], dissection of living animals.

Vix'en [O.E. *fyxen*], female fox, ill-tempered woman.

Viz-ier' (*ie=ee*) [Arab. *wazīr*, a councillor, orig. a porter ; *wazara*, to bear a burden], high official in Mohammedan states.

Vo'ca-ble [F. *vocable*, L. *vocābulum* ; L. *vocāre*, to call, *vōx* (*vōc-is*), voice], a word (esp. with reference to form).

Vo-cab'u-la-ry [see **Vocable**], alphabetical list of words, stock of words.

Vo'cal [L. *vōcālis*, vocal ; *vōx* (*vōc-is*), voice], relating to the voice or speech.

Vo'cal-ist, singer. [sounds.

Vo'cal-ize, form into voice, sing to the vowel

Vo-ca'tion [L. *vocāre* (p.p. *vocātus*), to call], divine summons, calling, business. **Voca'tional.**

Voc'a-tive [L. *vocāre*, to call], case used in address.

Vo-cif'er-ate [L. *vōciferārī* (p.p. *vōciferātus*); *vōx* (*vōc-is*), voice, *ferre*, to carry], exclaim, shout. **Vocifera'tion.**

Vo-cif'er-ous, noisy, clamorous.

Vod'ka [Russ. *vodka*], intoxicating liquor distilled from rye.

Vogue [F. *vogue*, fashion, orig. sway ; It. *vogare*, to row in a galley ; M.H.G. *wāgen*, to fluctuate], prevailing fashion.

Voice [L. *vōx* (*vōc-is*), voice], sound uttered by the mouth, a vote, form of a verb which shows the relation between subject and action ; give utterance to.

Void [O.F. *voide*. Etym. doubtful], empty, null, invalid ; empty space ; render invalid.

Vol'a-tile [L. *volāre* (p.p. *volātus*), to fly], subject to evaporation, light-hearted, airy, fickle. **Volatil'ity.**

Vol-can'ic, pertaining to volcanoes.

Vol-ca'no [It. *volcano* ; L. *Volcānus*, *Vulcānus*, Vulcan, the god of fire], mountain from which molten rock, steam, and gases issue.

Vole [shortened from *vole-mouse* ; Norw. *voll*, field], a mouse-like rodent.

Vo-li'tion (*i*) [M.L. *volitio*, volition ; L. *volo*, I wish], exercise of will, choice.

Vol'ley [L. *volāre*, to fly], discharge of missiles; discharge in a volley.

Volt [from A. *Volta*, an Italian physicist], unit of electromotive force. **Volt'age.**

Vol'u-ble [L. *volābilis*, voluble ; *volvere*, to roll], of rapid and fluent speech. **Volubil'ity.**

Vol'ume [L. *volūmen* (*volūmin-is*), a roll, scroll ; L. *volvere*, to roll], book or part of a book bound in one cover, bulk.

Vo-lu'mi-nous, consisting of many volumes, producing many books, bulky.

Vol'un-ta-ry [L. *voluntās*, free will ; *velle* (pr.p. *volens*, *-entis*), to will, wish], done of one's free will ; organ solo in church.

Vol-un-teer', one who serves of his own free will ; to offer service.

Vo-lup'tu-ous [L. *voluptās*, pleasure], luxurious, sensual.

Vom'it [L. *vomere* (p.p. *vomitus*), to vomit], eject from the stomach by the mouth ; that which is vomited, an emetic.

Vo-ra'cious (*ci=sh*) [L. *vorax* (*vorāc-is*), greedy ; *vorāre*, to devour], greedy in eating.

Vor-a'ci-ty, greed in eating.

Vor'tex; (pl.) **Vor'tices, Vor'texes** [L. *vortex*, *vertex*, a whirlpool], whirling gas or liquid, whirlpool.

Vor-tig'in-ous [L. *vertigo*, var. of vertigo], whirling.

Vo'ta-ry [L. *vovēre* (p.p. *vōtus*), to vow], worshipper, one devoted. **Vot'aress.**

Vote [L. *vōtum*, a wish; *vovēre* (p.p. *vōtus*), to vow, formal expression of choice or opinion by ballot, etc.; give a vote, choose or grant by suffrage.

Vo'tive, given, etc., in fulfilment of a vow.

Vouch [O.F. *vochier*; L. *vocāre*, to call, summon], confirm, be surety.

Vouch'er, one who or anything (esp. a document) which proves the correctness of a transaction.

Vouch-safe' [see **Vouch** and **Safe**], condescend to grant.

Vow [O.F. *veu, vou*; L. *vōtum*, a vow], solemn promise; assert solemnly.

Vow'el [L. *vocālis* (*littera*), vocāl (letter)], letter which represents an open sound, an open sound.

Voy'age [L. *viāticum*, provisions for a journey; *via*, a way], sea journey.

Vul'can-ite [L. *Vulcanus*, god of fire], rubber hardened with sulphur.

Vul'gar [L. *vulgāris*, relating to the common people; *vulgus*, the common people], common, coarse, in general use. **Vul'garize.**

Vul-gar'-i-ty, coarseness, low manners.

Vul'gate [L. (*editio*) *vulgata*, fem. p.p. of *vulgare*, to make public], Latin version of the Bible prepared by Jerome in the 4th century.

Vul'ner-a-ble [L. *vulnerāre*, to wound; *vulnus* (*vulner-is*) a wound], capable of being wounded. **Vulnerabil'ity.**

Vul'pine [L. *vulpīnus*; *vulpes*, a fox], foxy, cunning.

Vul'ture [L. *vultur*, a vulture, *vellere*, to pluck], carrion-eating bird.

Vy'ing, pr.p. of **Vie** (q.v.).

W

Wad (*a=ŏ*) [Swed. *vadd*, wadding], little mass of soft material; to form into a wad, to line with wadding, to put a wad into. [padding.

Wad'ding (*a=ŏ*), soft material used for

Wad'dle (*a=ŏ*) [freq. of **Wade**], rock in walking.

Wade [O.E. *wadan*; cogn. w. L. *vādere*, to go], walk as through water.

Wa'der, one who wades, wading bird, (pl.) high waterproof boots. [dry.

Wad'i (*a=ŏ*) Arab. *wādī*], watercourse often

Wa'fer [O.F. *waufre*, Low Ger. *wafel*, Ger. *waffel*, a wafer], thin cake, disc used for sealing.

Waft [for *waff*, var. of **Wave**], impel through air or water; sweep of a wing, whiff, a waving.

Wag¹ [M. Swed. *wagga*, to wag, to sway], move or be shaken to and fro; a shake.

Wag² [for *wag-halter*, gallows-bird], a wit.

Wage [O.F. *wage*, later *gage*, a gage, wage], (generally pl.) regular payment for work done. [on.

Wage [O.F. *wagier, waigier*, to pledge], carry

Wa'ger [O.F. *wageure*; Low L. *wadiātūra*, a wager, *wadiāre*, to pledge], a bet; to stake.

Wag'gish, roguish in merriment. **Wag'gery.**

Wag'gle [freq. of **Wag¹**], wag frequently.

Wag'gon, Wag'on [Du. *wagen*, a waggon], four-wheeled vehicle for loads. **Wag'-(g)oner.**

Wag(g)-on-ette' [dim. of **Wagon**], carriage with seats along the sides.

Waif [Icel. *veif*, a thing flapping about], ownerless object, homeless person, esp. child.

Wail [O.N. *vœla*, to wail, *vœ!* woe!], make a mournful outcry; plaintive cry.

Wain [O.E. *wœgn*; cogn. with L. *vehere*, to carry], waggon.

Wain'scot [Du. *wagenschot*; M. Du. *waeghe*, a wave, *schot*, a partition], wooden lining of room walls; line with wainscot.

Waist [M.E. *waest*, strength; see **Wax²**], part of the body immediately below the ribs, middle part of a ship.

Waist'coat, man's vest.

Wait [O.F. *waiter*, to watch; O.H.G. *wahta*, a watchman], to stay, attend at table; watch.

Wait'er (fem. **Wait'ress**), attendant at table in hotels, etc., a tray.

Waits [O.F. *waite*, a watchman], a band of carol-singers.

Waive [O.F. *guesver*, to waive; prob. fr. Icel. *veifa*, to vibrate], give up claim to, put aside.

Wake [partly fr. O.E. *wacan*, to arise, and partly fr. O.E. *wacian*, to watch], watch by a corpse; be awake, rouse, watch (a corpse].

Wake [Icel. *vök*, opening in ice; *vökr*, wet], track of a ship.

Wa'ken [O.E. *wœcnan*], cease to sleep, rouse.

Wale, Weal [O.E. *walu*, a weal; cogn. with L. *volvere*, to roll], ridge raised on flesh by stroke of a rod, etc.; orig. sense *rod*.

Walk (*wawk*) [O.E. *wealcan*, to roll, rove], move on by steps, cause to walk; act of walking, manner of walking, manner of life, path.

Wall (*a=aw*) [L. *vallum*, a rampart, orig. row of stakes], long structure of stones, etc.

Wall-eyed [Icel. *vald-eythr*, wall-eyed, fr. *vagl*, a beam, and *eythr*, eyed; *auga*, eye], with eyes showing abnormal amount of white.

Wal'let (*a=ŏ*) [?], bag or sack, leather case.

Wal'lop (*a=ŏ*) [?], thrash.

Wal'low (*a=ŏ*) [O.E. *wealwian*, to roll; cogn. with L. *volvere*], roll in mire, etc.

Wal'nut (*a=aw*) [O.E. *wealh*, foreign; Gaulish, *hnutu*, nut], tree, also its edible nut.

Wal'rus (*a=aw*) [Du. *walrus*; Icel. *hross-hvalr*, horse-whale], large tusked arctic animal.

Waltz (*wawlss*) [Ger. *walzer*, a waltz, *walzen*, to roll], whirling dance; dance a waltz.

Wam′pum (*a=ŏ*) [Amer.-Ind. *wampum*; *wompi*, white], shell beads used for money or decoration.

Wan [O.E. *wann*], pale, exhausted-looking.

Wand (*a=ŏ*) [O.N. *vöndr*, a switch], slender rod.

Wan′der (*a=ŏ*) [O.E. *wandrian*], go from place to place, ramble, rave.

Wane [O.E. *wanian*], decrease, diminish.

Want (*a=aw*) O.N. *vant*, neut. of *vanr*, lacking], lack, need, scarcity; be without, feel need of.

Wan′ton (*a=ŏ*) [M.E. *wantoun*, *wantowen*, *wan-*=pref. *un-*, *-towen*, fr. O.E. *togen*, p.p. of *téon*, to draw, educate], reckless, heedless, playful; to frolic.

Wap′en-take [O.N. *vápnatak*; *vápn*, a weapon, *taka*, to touch], division of some counties.

War (*a=aw*) [O.F. *werre*, F. *guerre*, war; O.H.G. *werra*, broil], conflict (usually between nations); make war. **War′like.**

War′ble (*a=aw*) [O.F. *werbler*, to warble; M.H.G. *werbelen*, old form of Ger. *wirbeln*, to whirl], sing in a trilling manner.

Ward (*a=aw*) [O.E. *weard*, a guard], to guard, turn aside; protection, child under a guardian, division of a city, division of a hospital, defensive motion in fencing.

Ward′en (*a=aw*) [A.F. *wardein*, Low L. *gardiānus*, a guardian], guardian, head official.

Ward′er (*a=aw*), a keeper, a staff of authority.

Ward′robe (*a=aw*) [O.F. *warderobe*, later *garderobe*, a place for keeping robes], a cabinet for clothes, stock of clothes.

Ware[1] [O.E. *waru*], (pl.) merchandise; (coll.) manufactured articles, esp. pottery.

Ware[2] [O.E. *wœr*, heedful], aware, look out for.

Ware′house, storehouse for goods, large shop.

War′fare (*a=aw*), state of war.

War′lock (*a=ŏ*) [O.E. *wœrloga*, traitor; *wœr*, truth, *loga*, a liar], wizard.

Warm (*a=aw* [O.E. *wearm*], hottish, excited; make or become warm.

Warmth (*a=aw*), gentle heat, zeal, fervour.

Warn (*a=aw*) [O.E. *w(e)arnian*], give notice, to caution.

Warn′ing (*a=aw*), previous notice, a caution.

Warp (*a=aw*) [O.E. *wearp*, fr. *weorpan*, to throw; cogn. w. O.N. *varpa*], twist out of shape, pervert, move a ship by means of a rope attached to a fixed point; threads stretched lengthwise in a loom.

War′rant (*a=ŏ*) [O.F. *warant*, *garant*, a warrant; Ger. *gewähren*, to certify, warrant], thing giving authority, assurance; serve as warrant for, justify. **War′ranty.**

War′ren (*a=aw*) [O.F. *warenne*; Low L. *varenna*, a game-preserve], ground for breeding rabbits, or where rabbits abound.

War′ri-or(*a=aw*) [see **War**], one experienced in war.

Wart (*a=ŏ*) [O.E. *wearte*], small hard growth on the skin.

Wa′ry [see **Ware**[2]], cautious. **Wa′rily.**

Wash (*a=ŏ*) [O.E. *wœscan*], cleanse with water, etc., carry along by or as by water, tint lightly; act of washing, clothes washed at once, motion of water, liquid food for pigs, lotion, thin coating. [etc.

Wash′er (*a=ŏ*), flat ring of metal, rubber.

Wash′y (*a=ŏ*), watery, weak. [**Wasp′ish.**

Wasp (*a=ŏ*) [O.E. *wœps*], stinging insect.

Was′sail (*as*=*ŏs* or *ăs*) [O.E. *wes hál*, lit. "be whole"], drinking-festival.

Wast′age, amount wasted. **Waste′ful.**

Waste [O.F. *vast*, waste; M.H.G. *vaste*, a waste; L. *vastus*, waste, vast], uncultivated, refuse; to ruin, wear away, spend uselessly; desert, useless spending, refuse.

Wast′rel (*a=ai*), thing spoilt in the making, good-for-nothing person.

Watch (*a=ŏ*) [O.E. *wœcce*, a watch, *wacian*, to watch], wakeful attention, division of the night, part of crew on duty together, small timepiece; (rare) wake, give heed to. **Watch′fulness.**

Watch′word (*a=ŏ*), password, motto.

Wa′ter (*a=aw*) [O.E. *wœter*], liquid composed of hydrogen and oxygen, lustre of a diamond; shed, sprinkle, or supply with water.

Wa′ter-fall′, stream descending over precipice or steep slope. [spa.

Wa′ter-ing-place′, frequented seaside place.

Wa′ter-logged, so filled or saturated with water as barely to float.

Wa′ter-mark, limit of high or low water, faint design in some paper.

Wa′ter-proof, not letting water through; a rain-coat. [basins.

Wa′ter-shed, line of separation between river-

Wa′ter-spout, whirling column of water.

Wat′tle (*a=ŏ*) [O.E. *watel*, a hurdle], twig or flexible rod, an Australian tree, fleshy appendage under a bird's throat.

Wave [O.E. *wafian*, to wave the hand], move as a field of corn in wind, flutter, beckon, shape like an undulating surface; advancing swell of the sea, waving motion.

Wa′ver [O.E. *wœfre*, restless], reel, totter, hesitate.

Wa′vy, showing contrary curves.

Wax[1] [O.E. *weax*], sticky substance produced by bees; apply wax to. **Wax′en.**

Wax[2] [O.E. *wexzan*], grow bigger, become.

Wax′work, figure or figures in wax.

Way [O.E. *weg*], that along which one passes, road, manner.

Way′fa-rer, traveller (esp. on foot).

Way-lay′, lie in wait for.

Way′ward [for *awayward*; see **Away**], unaccountable, wilful.

Weak [back-formation from *weaken*; O.E. *wac*, weak], lacking strength, feeble, inflected by addition of syllables.

Weak′en [O.E. *wœcan*], make or become weak.

Weak′ling, feeble creature.

Weak′ly, with little strength, feeble.

Weal[1] [O.E. *wela*], well-being, happiness

Weal[2] [see **Wale**].

Wealth [Weal[1] and **th**], riches, abundance. **Wealth'iness.**

Wean [O.E. *wenian*, to accustom, *áwenian*, accustom to do without], accustom to food other than the mother's milk.

Wean'ling, new-weaned child, etc.

Weap'on [O.E. *wǽpen*], something to fight or defend oneself with.

Wear (*wair*) [O.E. *werian*], be dressed in, last, waste by rubbing, etc.; dress, loss by wearing.

Wear (*wair*) [var. of **Veer**], bring (ship) about by putting down of helm, tack.

Wea'ri-ness, tiredness, fatigue. **Wear'isome.**

Wea'ry [O.E. *wérig*], tired, tiresome; to tire.

Wea'sel (*s=z*) [O.E. *wesle*], slender blood-thirsty animal.

Weath'er [O.E. *weder*], state of atmosphere with respect to heat and cold, rain and dryness, etc.; affect by weather, come through, get to windward of.

Weath'er-cock, vane. [fabric.

Weave [O.E. *wefan*], interlace thread into a

Web [O.E. *webb*], woven piece, product of a spinning creature, membrane uniting toes (esp. of swimming-birds). **Webbed.**

Wed [O.E. *weddian*, to pledge, to betroth], marry.

Wed'ding, marriage ceremony and festivity.

Wedge [O.E. *wecg*], piece of hard material with a thin edge; cleave with a wedge, press closely as with a wedge.

Wed'lock [O.E. *wedlác*, lit. a pledge; *wed*, *wedd*, a pledge, *lác*, a sport, a gift], state of marriage.

Wednes'day (*wĕnz-dai*) [O.E. *wódnes daeg*, day of Woden or Odin], fourth day of the week.

Weed [O.E. *wéod*; etym. dub.], wild plant regarded as troublesome; free from weeds.

Weeds [earlier sense in *sing.* garment; O.E. *wǽde*, garment], widow's mourning garb.

Week [O.E. *wice*], period of seven days.

Week'ly, occurring or done once a week.

Ween [O.E. *wénan*], suppose, think.

Weep [O.E. *wépan*], to cry aloud], shed tears, lament.

Weep'er, one who weeps, (pl.) white or black bands worn on mourning-dress.

Wee'vil [O.E. *wifel*], snout beetle.

Weft [O.E.; see **Weave**], threads that cross the warp.

Weigh (*ei=ai*) [O.E. *wegan*, to carry], swing up, to examine by balance, estimate, have weight of.

Weight [O.E. *wiht*, fr. *wegan*], heaviness, scale of heaviness, something heavy; load with weights.

Weight'y, heavy, important.

Weir, Wear (*ei=ee*; *ea=ee*) [O.E. *wer*, fr. *werian*, to defend], dam, fence of stakes in a stream to catch fish.

Weird (*ei=ee*) [O.E. *wyrd*, fate; *werthan*, to happen], pertaining to fate, unearthly.

Wel'come (*o=ŭ*) [Lit. *well come*], received gladly; hail!; glad reception; receive gladly.

Weld [Swed. *välla*, to well up], press or beat (two pieces of red-hot metal) into union.

Wel'fare, well-being, prosperity.

Wel'kin [O.E. *wolcnu*, clouds], sky.

Well [O.E. *wella*], a spring, shaft in ground down to water or oil; flow as from a well.

Well [O.E. *wel*, orig. "agreeably to a wish," cogn. with **Will**], in a good manner, fully, to a large extent; happy, advantageous, healthy.

Welsh-rab'bit [perh. corruption of *Welsh rare bit*; O.E. *wǽlisc*, foreign], dish of toasted cheese.

Welt [M.E. *welte*; cogn. with O.E. *wyltan*, to roll], strip of leather between upper leather and sole, a weal; sew a welt on, to whip.

Wel'ter [M.E. *walten*; cogn. with **Wallow**], tumble about; general disorder. [skin.

Wen [O.E. *wenn*], harmless tumour of the

Wench [M.E. *wenche*, earlier *wenchel*, a child; cogn. with O.E. *wancol*, tottering], young woman.

Wend [O.E. *wendan*, to turn], go, to direct (one's steps).

Were'wolf, Wer'wolf (*o=oo*) [O.E. *wer*, a man, *wulf*, a wolf], man turned into a wolf.

West [O.E.], in the direction of sunset. **West'ern.**

West'ward, West'wards [O.E. *west* and *weard*], towards the west.

Wet [O.E. *wǽt*], soaked or covered with liquid; moisture; soak, make moist.

Weth'er [O.E. *wethr*], castrated ram.

Whack [imit.], resounding blow; give such a blow to.

Whale [O.E. *hwǽl*], large sea-animal.

Wha'ler, ship or man employed in whale-catching.

Wharf (*a=ŏ*) [O.E. *hwerf*, a dam], platform beside which ships are loaded and unloaded.

Wharf'age, fee paid for use of a wharf.

Wharf'in-ger [for *wharfager*; see **Wharf**], man who owns or has the care of a wharf.

What [O.E. *hwæt*, neut. of *hwa*, who], that which, which (in asking questions).

What'not, piece of furniture with shelves.

Wheal [Corn. *hwel*], mine, esp. tin-mine.

Wheat [O.E. *hwǽte*, wheat; cogn. with **White**], kind of corn.

Wheed'le [perh. from O.E. *wǽdlian*, to beg], flatter, coax.

Wheel [O.E. *hwéol*], circular revolving frame; convey on wheels, turn.

Wheeze [O.E. *hwǽsan*], breathe hard with a whistling sound; sound of wheezing. **Whee'zy.**

Whelk [O.E. *wiloc*], spiral-shelled mollusc.

Whelp [O.E. *hwelp*], cub, puppy.

When [O.E. *hwænne*], at which or what time.

Whence [M.E. *whennes*, fr. O.E. *hwanan*], from which or what place.

Where (*e=ai*) [O.E. *hwár*], at or in which or what place. [is.

Where'a-bouts, place where a person or thing

Where-by', by which.

Where'fore, for which, or what, reason.

Where'with-al, with which ; the necessary means.

Wher'ry [?], passenger barge on rivers.

Whet [O.E. *hwettan*, fr. *hwæt*, bold, keen], make sharp, keen, or eager ; that which makes the appetite keen.

Wheth'er [O.E. *hwæther*], which of two ; if.

Whet'stone, stone for tool-sharpening.

Whew, sound expressing astonishment.

Whey (*cy=ai*) [O.E. *hwǽg*, whey], thin part of milk.

Whiff [imit.], quick puff ; to puff.

Whig [short for *Whiggamore* ; perh. fr. Sc. *whig*, to jog], one of party opposed to Tories.

While [O.E. *hwíl*], space of time ; pass pleasantly ; during the time that, whereas. Whilst.

Whim [O.N. *hvima*, to wander with the eyes], freak, fancy.

Whim'per [for *whimmer* ; perh. cogn. with Whine], whine softly ; low broken cry.

Whim'si-cal, fantastic, fanciful. Whimsi-cal'ity.

Whim'sy [Norw. *kvimsa*, to skip], queer notion, whim.

Whin [W. *chwyn*, a weed], gorse, furze.

Whin [?], kind of stone.

Whine [O.E. *hwínan*], utter a plaintive cry, complain ; complaining tone.

Whing'er [?], short sword, dirk. [joyfully.

Whin'ny [freq. of Whine], neigh softly or

Whip [M.E. *wippen*, to jump up and down suddenly], lash, thrash lightly, whisk ; a lash, parliamentary official who secures attendance of members of his party, etc., his summons.

Whip'pet [?], kind of racing-dog.

Whir(r) [init. ; perh. Dan. *hvirre*, to whirl], make a sound of quick whirling.

Whirl [O.N. and Swed. *hvirfla* ; Ger. *wirbeln*, to whirl], turn round rapidly ; turning rapidly.

Whirl'i-gig, whirling frame with seats, spinning toy.

Whirl'pool, circular current in water.

Whirl'wind, mass of whirling air.

Whisk [Dan. *viske* ; Swed. *viska*, to wipe], quick sweeping motion, small besom, egg-beater ; brush or agitate lightly.

Whisk'er [see Whisk], hair on a man's cheek.

Whis'key, Whis'ky [Ir. *uisge*, water ; W. *wysg*, a stream], liquor distilled from barley, etc.

Whis'per [O. Northumb. *hwisprian* ; imit.], speak under the breath ; low soft speech, rustling sound.

Whist [akin to Hist, interj. enjoining silence], game at cards.

Whis'tle [O.E. *hwistlian* ; imit.], make a piping sound ; shrill piping sound, instrument for producing such sound.

Whit [O.E. *wiht*, a creature, a thing], particle.

White [O.E. *hwít*], of the colour of snow, without colour. Whit'en.

White'bait, small fish, prob. fry of herring and sprats.

White'wash, lime and water ; whiten with whitewash, clear a reputation. [place.

Whith'er [O.E. *hwider*], to what or which

Whi'ting [see White], prepared chalk, a food-fish.

Whi'tish, nearly white.

Whit'low [corruption of *quickflaw*], inflammation of the finger.

Whit'tle [from obs. noun *whittle*, a knife], pare or cut with a knife.

Whiz(z) [cogn. with Hiss ; imit.], hum and hiss ; humming hissing sound.

Who (*o=oo*) [O.E. *hwá*], a rel. and interrog. pronoun referring to a person or persons ; which one ?

Who-ev'er (*o=oo*), any person who.

Whole [O.E. *hál*, whole ; cogn. with Heal], all, entire, healthy ; entire thing.

Whole-sale', sale of goods in large quantity ; on a large scale.

Whole'some, promoting health, sound.

Whol'ly, completely.

Whoop [formerly *hoop* ; see Hoop²], shout, hoot as an owl, to cough with a back-draw ; a cry in pursuit, a hoot, a sound in drawing breath.

Whorl [contr. of M.E. *whorvil*, from O.E. *hweorfan*, to turn], ring of flowers, etc., round a stem, spiral turn.

Whor'tle-ber-ry [O.E. *heorotberige*, hart-berry], fruit of a small shrub, bilberry.

Who'so, Who-so-ev'er, whoever.

Wick [O.E. *weoce*], fibres or tape in lamp or candle.

Wick'ed [from obs. *wikke*, evil ; cogn. with Weak], bad, sinful.

Wick'er [M.E. *wiker*, pliant twig ; O.E. *wícan*, to bend], made of pliant twigs.

Wick'et [F. *guichet* ; perh. O.H.G. *wisken*, to whisk], small gate, in cricket three erect stumps with two bails on top.

Wide [O.E. *wíd*], broad, spacious across, far.

Wid'geon [O.F. *vigeon* ; prob. fr. L. *vipio*, kind of small crane], kind of wild duck.

Wid'ow [O.E *widwe* ; cogn. with L. *viduus*, bereft], woman whose husband is dead.

Wid'ow-er, man whose wife is dead.

Width, extent from side to side.

Wield [O.E. *gewyldan*, to rule], to sway, handle with power.

Wife [O.E. *wíf*, a woman], married woman, (rare) woman.

Wig [short for Periwig], artificial covering of hair for the head.

Wight [O.E. *wiht*, a creature], human being.

Wig'wam [Amer. Ind. *wigwam* ; Algonquin, *wikiwam*, a house], tent or hut of a North American Indian.

Wild (*i*) [O.E. *wilde*], in a state of nature, not tamed, desert, tempestuous ; a waste.

Wil'der-ness [obs. *wildern*, a desert ; O.E. *wilder*, a wild animal], desert, uninhabited region.

Wile [O.E. *wil*, perh. fr. O.F. *guile*, a wile], sly trick ; deceive, (used incorrectly) to while. Wi'ly, Wi'liness.

Wil'ful, self-willed, intentional.

Will [O.E. *willa* (n.); *willan* (v.)], faculty by which a person decides or chooses, a wish, testament; determine, wish, bequeath.

Will'ing, desirous, ready, consenting. **Will'ingness**.

Will'-o'-the-wisp' [*Will*, short for *William*, and **Wisp**], light on marshy ground.

Wil'low [O.E. *welig*], tree with pliant branches.

Wil'low-y, pliant, graceful.

Will'y-nill'y [=*will he, will he not*], whether one wishes to do a thing or not.

Wilt [?], wither, droop.

Wim'ple [O.E. *winpel*; perh. fr. **Wind**,[2] and O.E. *pœll, pell*, a covering), cover for neck and chin worn by nuns; lie in folds, ripple.

Win [O.E. *winnan*], to gain, earn, gain a victory.

Wince [A.F. *wencir*; O.F. *guenchir*], shrink, start back.

Win'cey [perh. corrupt. of *linsey-woolsey*], cloth of cotton warp and woollen weft.

Winch [O.E. *wince*], crank with a handle.

Wind[1] (*i*) [O.E. *windan*], to coil, go in a circular or curved course, turn repeatedly.

Wind[2] (*i*) [O.E.], air in motion; exhaust the breath, renew it by rest, sound by blowing.

Wind'fall, unexpected gain.

Wind'ing (*i*), a turn, curve.

Wind'lass (*i*) [O.N. *vindiláss*; fr. *vindill*, a winder, and *áss*, a beam], machine for hoisting.

Win'dle-straw (*i*) [**Wind** (vb.), and **Straw**], stalk of various grasses.

Win'dow [O.N. *vindauga*, lit. " wind-eye "], opening in a wall or roof, usually filled with glass.

Wind'pipe, passage for the breath.

Wind'y, exposed to wind, wordy.

Wine [L. *vinum*, wine], liquor prepared from grapes.

Wine'bib-ber [L. *vinum*, wine; *bibere*, to drink], drinker of much wine.

Wing [Norw. *vengja*; cf. Dan. and Swed. *vinge*, a wing], organ of flight, flight, projecting part of building, etc.; to fly, wound in wing or arm.

Wink [O.E. *wincian*], shut and open the eyes, shut one eye quickly, (with *at*) pretend not to notice; act of winking.

Win'kle [O.E. *wincla*], kind of shell-fish.

Win'ning, Win'some, charming.

Win'now [O.E. *windwian*, to winnow; *wind* (n.), wind], separate as chaff from grain.

Win'ter [O.E.], cold season; spend the winter, keep or feed during the winter.

Win'try, suitable to or like winter, cold.

Wipe [O.E. *wipian*], clean or dry by rubbing.

Wire [O.E. *wir*, a wire; cf. Swed. *vira*, to twist], thread or slender rod of metal; put wire through, to telegraph.

Wire'less, without wires; telegraphy without wires.

Wire'pul-ler, intriguer.

Wi'ry, drawn out like wire, tough. **Wir'i-ly**, **Wir'i-ness**.

Wis'dom (*s=z*) [O.E. *wisdóm*], quality of being wise, knowledge of the best means for the best ends, wise sayings.

Wise (*s=z*) [O.E. *wis*], having knowledge, prudent, judging soundly.

Wise [O.E. *wise*, way], way, manner.

Wise'a-cre (*wiz-aik-er*) [M. Du. *wijs-segger*, fr. Ger. *weissager*, a foreteller, lit. wise sayer; cogn. with O.E. *witiga*, prophet], would-be-wise person.

Wish [O.E. *wyscan*], to desire, long; a desire.

Wish'y-wash'y [redup. of **Washy**], weak and thin.

Wisp [earlier *wips*; cogn. with **Wipe**], small bundle as of straw.

Wis-ta'ri-a [fr. C. *Wistar*, an American], a climbing-plant.

Wist'ful [perh. from **Whist**, with added meaning of *wishful*], longing, pensive.

Wit [O.E. *witan*, to know], sense, clever and apt language, witty person; know; *to wit*, that is to say.

Witch [O.E. *wicce*], woman with magical power, ugly old woman, very attractive woman.

Witch'craft, practices of witches.

Witch'er-y, enchantment.

Witch'ing, enchanting.

With [O.E., shortened fr. *witner*, against], by, in opposition to, in company of, in relation to, possessing, through.

With-al' [arch.], with, at the same time, also.

With-draw', take back, retire.

With-draw'al, taking back, retiring.

Withe (*i*; *e=i* or silent), **With'y** [O.E. *withig*], willow twig.

With'er [M.E. *widren*, to expose to weather], fade, dry up.

With'ers [O.E. *wither*, against], ridge between a horse's shoulder-bones.

With-hold', hold back.

With-in', inside, not beyond.

With-stand', stand against, resist.

Wit'ness [O.E. *witnes*], evidence, onlooker, one who testifies; see, sign as witness, state facts, prove.

Wit'ti-cism [for *wittyism*], witty (or would-be witty) saying.

Wit'ting-ly [from **Wit**], knowingly.

Wit'ty, having wit, keen and amusing.

Wive, take a wife.

Wiz'ard [**Wise** and suf. *-ard*], magician. **Wiz'ardry**.

Wiz'ened [O.E. *wisnian*], dried, shrunken.

Woad [O.E. *wád*], plant yielding blue dye.

Wob'ble, Wab'ble [freq. of obs. *wap*, to flutter], move unsteadily.

Woe [O.E. *wá*], grief, misery.

Woe'be-gone [**Woe** and **Begone**, p.p. of O.E. *begán*, to surround], sorrowful.

Woe'ful, Wo'ful, sorrowful, wretched.

Wold [O.E. *weald, wald*, a forest], uncultivated plain or low hill.

Wolf (*o=oo*) [O.E. *wulf*], wild animal of the dog kind. **Wolf'ish**.

Wom'an (*o=oo*) [O.E. *wifman*, lit. *wife*-man], grown-up human female.

Wom'an-hood (o=oo), the state of being a woman.

Wom'an-ish (of a man), like a woman.

Wom'an-ly, befitting a woman.

Womb (woom) [O.E. wamb], place where anything is generated or produced.

Wom'bat [corrupt. of Austrl. womback], kind of pouched animal.

Won'der (o=ŭ) [O.E. wundor, portent], surprise, miracle; be surprised, query in the mind. Won'derment.

Won'der-ful, surprising, strange.

Won'drous [formerly wonders], wonderful.

Wont (o=ō or ŭ) [M.E. woned, pp. of wonien, to dwell], custom, accustomed.

Won'ted, accustomed, usual.

Woo [O.E. wogian, of obscure origin], to court, make love to.

Wood [O.E. wudu], large collection of trees, substance between a tree's pith and bark.

Wood'bine [Wood and Bine, dial. form of Bind], honeysuckle.   [from it.

Wood'cut, engraving on wood, also a print

Wood'en, made of or like wood.   [trees.

Wood'peck-er, bird which pecks holes in

Wood'ruff, Wood'roof [O.E. wuderófe; perh. allied to O.E. róf, strong], kinds of plant, some of them aromatic.   [wood.

Wood'y [see Woo], well wooded, consisting of

Woo'er, suitor.   [cloth.

Woof [M.E. oof], weft or cross-threads of

Wool [O.E. wull], hair of sheep, etc.

Wool'-gath'er-ing, absent-minded; inattention.

Wool'len, made of wool; cloth of wool.

Wool'ly, consisting of or like wool.

Wool'sack, Lord Chancellor's seat in the House of Lords.

Word (o=ŭ) [O.E., cogn. with L. verbum], sound or combination of sounds conveying an idea, tidings, promise; express in words.

Word'y, in words, using many words.

Work (o=ŭ) [O.E. weorc], effort directed to an end, labour; put forth effort, to labour, ferment. Work'able.

Work'a-day, used on workdays, ordinary.

Work'box, box for sewing implements.

Work'house, house for paupers.   [operation.

Work'ing, engaged in manual labour;

Work'man-ship, art or skill of a workman.

World (o=ŭ) [O.E. weoruld, world; wer, a man, eld, age], earth, universe, heavenly body like the earth, mankind, a class of men.

World'ling, one devoted to worldly pursuits.

World'ly, devoted to the pleasures and pursuits of this life. World'liness.

Worm (o=ŭ) [O.E. wyrm; cogn. with L. vermis], small creeping animal; work gradually and secretly.

Worm'wood [O.E. wermód, orig. unknown], plant with a bitter taste.

Wor'ry (o=ŭ) [O.E. wyrgen, to strangle], to harass, tear with the teeth; vexation, fret.

Worse (o=ŭ) [O.E. wyrs (adv.), wyrsa (adj.)], comparative of bad, evil, ill.

Wor'ship (o=ŭ) [O.E. weorthscipe, see Worth], title of honour, religious reverence, adoration; adore.

Wor'ship-per, one who worships.

Worst (o=ŭ), bad in the highest degree; to defeat.

Worst'ed (woor'sted or woo'sted) [fr. Worsted, in Norfolk], well-twisted woollen yarn.

Worth (o=ŭ) [O.E. wyrthe; cogn. with L. vereri, respect], of value; value.

Wor'thy, having merit, deserving.

Wound (ou=oo) [O.E. wund], a hurt; inflict a wound.   [seaweed.

Wrack [O.E. wrœc, expulsion], wreck, coarse

Wraith [?], person's ghost seen before or after death.

Wran'gle (freq. of Wring], quarrel noisily.

Wrangl'er, one who wrangles, one in first class of mathematical honours at Cambridge University.

Wrap [M.E. wrappen], cover by winding or folding; (n. pl.) shawls, rugs, etc.

Wrap'per, loose outer garment, paper enclosing newspaper, etc.

Wrath (a=aw) [O.E. wrœththu, fr. wráth], violent anger.

Wreak [O.E. wrecan, to avenge, orig. to drive], inflict, esp. vengeance or wrath.

Wreath [O.E. wrœth], something intertwined, garland.

Wreathe, entwine, encircle.

Wreck [formerly wrack; O.E. wrœc, expulsion], ruin, ruins of a ship; bring ruin upon, destroy.

Wreck'age, wrecked material.

Wreck'er, one who causes wrecks or plunders from them, one who recovers wrecked vessel or cargo.

Wren [O.E. wrenna], small singing-bird.

Wrench [O.E. wrenc], violent twist or pull, tool; pull with a twist.

Wrest [O.E. wrœstan], twist or force away; key for tuning a harp, etc.

Wres'tle [see Wrest], contend by grappling; a struggle.   [knave.

Wretch [O.E. wrecca], miserable person,

Wretch'ed, miserable, inferior, contemptible.

Wrig'gle (freq. of wrig, to move about], twist like a worm; wormlike twist.

Wright [O.E. wyrhta, a worker, wyrht, work; wyrcan, to work], workman, esp. in wood.

Wring [O.E. wringan], twist and squeeze, pain, extort.

Wring'er, machine for pressing water from clothes.

Wrin'kle [M.E. wrinkel; cf. M. Du. wrinckel], slight fold; to crease.

Wrist [O.E. wrist, orig. handwrist; writhan to twist about; joint between hand and arm.   [wrist

Wrist'let, band on wrist, watch carried on

Writ [O.E. gewrit, a writing], writing, form of written command.   [etc.

Write [O.E. writan], make letters with a pen,

Writhe [O.E. writhan], to twist, distort.

Wri'ting, formation of letters on paper, etc. anything written or printed.

Wrong [O.E. *wrang*; Icel. *rangr*, awry; Dan. *vrang*, wrong], not right, incorrect; error, injury; treat unjustly.

Wroth (*ŏ*) [O.E. *wráth*], wrathful, angry.

Wry [M.E. *wrien*, to twist; O.E. *wrigian*, to turn], twisted.

X

Xy'lo-graph (*x=z*) [Gk. *xylon*, wood; *graphein*, to write], wood-engraving.

Xy'lo-nite (*x=z*) [Gk. *xylon*, wood], celluloid.

X-rays [letter X; see **Ray**], rays penetrating many things which cannot be penetrated by ordinary light.

Y

Yacht (*yŏt*) [Du. *jagt*; M.Du. *jacht*, a yacht, a hunting; Du. and Ger. *jagen*, to hunt], private pleasure vessel.

Ya-hoo' [word coined by Swift], brute in human shape.

Yak [Tibetan *gyak*], humped Tibetan ox.

Yam [Port. *inhame*, a yam], tropical plant with fleshy roots.

Yan'kee [?], inhabitant of New England, inhabitant of the United States. **Yan'keedom.**

Yap [imit.], to bark, yelp.

Yard [O.E. *gyrd*, a stick], unit of long measure, 3 feet, spar to support a sail.

Yard [doublet of **Garden**; O.E. *geard*, an enclosure], enclosed ground.

Yard'arm, either half of a sail-yard.

Yarn [O.E. *gearn*, thread], spun fibre, a story, esp. a sailor's.

Yar'row [O.E. *gœrwe*, yarrow], aromatic plant, milfoil.

Yaw [O.N. *jaga*, to move to and fro, orig. to hunt], keep deviating from a (ship's) course.

Yawl [Du. *jol*, a yawl], ship's boat, kind of small yacht.

Yawn [O.E. *geonian*, *gánian*], to gape, open mouth wide through drowsiness or boredom; involuntary gape.

Yea (*yai*) [O.E. *géa*], yes.

Yean [O.E. *éanian*], bring forth young (kid or lamb). **Yean'ling.**

Year [O.E. *gé(a)r*], period of twelve months. **Year'ling**, animal in its second year. **Year'ly**, once a year, from year to year.

Yearn [O.E. *giernan*; cogn. with Gk. *khairein*, to rejoice], feel desire or tenderness, to long.

Yeast [O.E. *gist*], barm, substance causing fermentation. **Yeast'y**, frothy.   [scream.

Yell [O.E. *gellan*], scream as with agony; loud

Yel'low [O.E. *geolu*, yellow, allied to **Gall**[1]], colour like gold.

Yelp [O.E. *gielpan*], bark shrilly; shrill bark.

Yeo'man [M.E. *yoman*, *yeman*; perh. fr. O.E. *gá*, village], small landowner, member of the yeomanry force.

Yeo'man-ry, volunteer cavalry.

Yes [O.E. *gise*, *gese*, perh. fr. *géa swá*, yea so], a word of affirmation.

Yes'ter-day [O.E. *geostra-*, *yester-*, *dæg*, day, yesterday], the day last past.

Yet [O.E. *git*], still, so far, nevertheless, moreover.

Yew [O.E. *iw*], evergreen tree.

Yid'dish [Ger. *jüdisch*, Jewish], mixture of Hebrew and German used by Jews.

Yield [O.E. *gieldan*, to pay], to produce, give up, give way; amount produced.

Yo'del [Ger. dial. *jodeln*], sing with rapid change from natural to falsetto voice.

Yoke [O.E. *geoc*], neck-frame for draught animals, bondage; put a yoke on, to couple.

Yolk (*ol=ō*) [O.E. *geolca*, yellow], yellow part of an egg.

Yon, Yon'der [O.E. *geon*], over there.

Yore [O.E. *geára*, lit. of years], time long past, days of old.

Young [O.E. *geong*], in an early period of growth, not old; offspring, young people. **Young'ster**, child.

Youth (*ou=oo*) [O.E. *geoguth*], state or time of being young, young man, young people. **Youth'ful**, pertaining to, or suitable to, youth.

Yule [O.E. *geól*, the feast; etym. doubtful], Christmas.

Z

Za'ny [Ital. *Zanni*, abbr. of *Giovanni*, John], buffoon.

Za-re'ba [Arab. *zaríba(t)*, a fold, a pen], stockade (Egypt and Sudan).

Zeal [L. *zēlus*, Gk. *zēlos*, zeal], fervour, eagerness.

Zeal'ot, one who is over-zealous, fanatic.

Zeal'ous, filled with zeal, ardent.

Ze'bra [Port. fr. W. Afr. *zebra*], striped animal allied to the horse.

Ze'bu [F. *zébu*; Tibetan *mdzopo*], humped East Indian ox.

Zemst'vo [Russ.], formerly an elective assembly regulating affairs of district in Russia.

Ze-na'na [Hind. *zenāna*, Pers. *zenān*, pl. of *zen*, a woman], women's apartments (India).

Zen'ith [Arab. *semt*, way, *er-ras*, of the head], point of the heavens directly overhead, height of success.

Zeph'yr [Gk. *zephyros*, the west wind], west wind, soft wind.

Zep'pelin (*z=ts*) [fr. Count *Zeppelin*, German inventor], airship.

Ze'ro [It. *zero*, short for *zefiro*; Arab. *sifr*, a cipher], nothing, lowest point.

Zest [M.F. *zest*, skin of walnut-kernel; Gk. *schistos*, cleft, *schizein*, to cleave], relish.

Zig'zag [Ger. *zickzack*, redup. of *zacke*, a tooth, prong], having straight lines and sharp turns.

Zinc (*c* = *k*) [etym. doubtful; cf. F. *zinc*, Ger. *zink*], bluish-white metal.

Zin'ga-ro (pl. -ri) [It.], gipsy.

Zi'on-ist, one who advocates the settlement of Jews in Palestine (Zion = Jerusalem).

Zith'er [Ger. *zither*], stringed instrument with flat sounding-board.

Zo'di-ac (*c* = *k*) [Gk. *zōdiacos*, zodiac; *zōdiacos*, belonging to animals; *zōdion*, dim. of *zōion*, an animal], imaginary belt in the heavens with the ecliptic in the middle. Zodi'acal.

Zone [Gk. *zōnē*, a girdle], belt, division of the earth bounded by circles parallel to the equator.

Zo-o-lo'gic-al [-*lō-ĵic*-], pertaining to zoology.

Zo-ol'o-gy [Gk. *zōion*, an animal; *logos*, discourse], science of animal life.

Zo'o-phyte [Gk. *zōos*, living; *phyton*, a plant], plant-like animal.

Zou'ave (*ou* = *oo*) [F. *Zouave*; N. Afr. *Zouaova*, name of a tribe in Algeria], one of a French light-infantry corps.

Zy-mot'ic [Gk. *zymōsis*, fermentation; *zymē*, leaven], of fermentation, applied to diseases produced by germs, etc.

SOME CURRENT WORDS AND PHRASES

Accu'mulator (*u* = *ū*), apparatus for storing electricity.

Airgraph, letter photographed to reduce size and the photo conveyed by air.

Air Mail, letters, etc., carried by aircraft.

Airport, an aerodrome or station equipped for regular flying.

Anti-Semitism, opposition to Jews.

Anzac (initials of "Australian and New Zealand Army Corps"), an Australian or New Zealand soldier, the part of Gallipoli which these troops occupied in 1915.

Assembling-Shop, the department in a factory where the various parts of a thing to be made are brought together.

Atmosphe'rics, noises produced in a wireless set by electricity in the air.

Atomic Energy, power released by the "splitting" of the atom. This was used in the Second World War to produce a bomb of tremendous destructive capacity.

Audi'tion, a trial by hearing of speakers, vocalists or instrumentalists.

Bears and Bulls: a bear is one who sells stock expecting a fall in the price, a bull one who buys expecting a rise.

Belisha Crossings, official crossing places for pedestrians on busy streets, instituted by Mr Hore-Belisha, sometime Minister of Transport.

Best Seller, a term applied to books (and sometimes authors) having a large sale.

Blind-alley (originally applied to a street with no exit at one end), used of an occupation for a young person not leading to a regular means of livelihood later on.

Block System, a system on railways by which no two trains should be on a section or block of a line at one time.

Blue Books, Parliamentary or Privy Council reports, so called from their blue paper covers.

Board of Trade Units, standard electrical units in which is measured the amount of electricity a consumer has used.

Bolshevism, adaptation of Russian word meaning *the majority*. A communistic form of government that aims at the attainment of equality.

Borstal System, a system of imprisonment for young criminals, an important feature of which is the indeterminate sentence, the duration of confinement depending on conduct. On discharge such criminals are assisted by a Borstal Association. So called from *Borstal*, a suburb of Rochester.

Broadcasting, spreading abroad from a wireless transmitting station news, musical programmes, speeches, etc., to the receiving sets of listeners.

Buzzer, an electric apparatus for making a loud, buzzing noise, for example, an alarm.

By-Pass, a by-road or loop constructed for the relief of traffic by avoiding a town or village, or any congested point.

Car'tel, union of manufacturers to regulate prices, output, etc.; especially in Germany and Austria.

Cha'ssis (*ch* = *sh*), base frame of a motor vehicle or aeroplane with mechanism, as distinguished from the body or upper part.

Clearing House, an institution established by the banks for the exchange of bills and cheques and the settling of balances due to or from each. The Railway Companies also have their Clearing House.

Comb-out, the process of clearing out, e.g. employees, underworld.

Communiqué, an official despatch.

Com'plex, used colloquially to mean any idea which fills the mind: e.g. *inferiority complex*, a persistent lack of self-confidence.

Concentration-camp, a camp into which persons suspected of activities against the state are collected.

Contemptibles, Old, the soldiers of the British Expeditionary Force in the early months of the war of 1914-18. The Kaiser was erroneously said to have spoken of Sir John French's "Contemptible Little Army."

Dáil, or Dáil E'ireann (*dawil eeren*), parliament of Irish Free State (Eire).

Dehydrate, to extract water from. A process used largely in the Second World War to save shipping space in transporting food.

Dictaphone, a machine that records speech which can afterwards be reproduced.

Dictator, the ruler of a state whose word is law; one who rules absolutely.

Dora (colloquialism), Defence of the Realm Act, a war measure of 1914.

Drowned Valley, a valley which has sunk beneath sea-level.

Earth, to connect with the earth (wireless term).

Excess Profits, profits made in excess of a certain limit, on which a higher scale of income-tax is imposed.

Fascisti, party in Italy opposed to Socialism.

Fifty-fifty, dividing a hundred or a whole into two equally—"going halves."

Flex, flexible insulated wire for carrying electricity.

Flying-Boat, a huge multi-engined aeroplane, with a boat-shaped hull designed to take off from and land on the water. They are used mainly to carry mails and passengers on long-distance routes.

Fool-proof, proof against being put out of order by ignorant or careless handling.

Fuselage, the body of an aeroplane.

Glider, flying-machine without an engine.

Graft, direct bribes taken by one holding an official position, or profits wrongfully made by virtue of that position.

Grid (common meaning), a network of wires, pipes, etc., for the distribution of electric current, water, etc., over a definite area.

Ground Speed, speed of an aeroplane relative to the earth—less than the *Air Speed*, at which it would travel if there were no wind affecting it.

Hansard, a printed official report of the doings of the British Parliament. Named from the publishers.

Helicopter, an aircraft kept in the air by revolving wings. It can rise directly off, and descend vertically to, the ground, and can reduce speed in travelling to a few miles per hour, or halt in mid-air.

Highbrow, a superior, intellectual person.

Hike (American), a long tramp for pleasure.

Hobson's Choice, the thing offered or nothing. *Hobson* is said to have let out horses for hire at Cambridge and to have made his customers take in turn the horse next the stable door.

Internal Combustion, (see **Combustion**), in the engines or motors of aircraft, motorcars, etc., the principle by which a mixture of petrol, or other gas, and air is exploded in the cylinder by means of an electric spark in such a way that the explosive force acts directly on the piston. In engines where coal or oil is the fuel, combustion is *outside* the cylinder.

Jamboree, an assembly, especially of Boy Scouts.

Jet-propulsion, the use of air, first compressed and then heated to make it expand, for the purpose of driving or propelling machines.

Joy-ride, pleasure trip in car, aeroplane, etc., sometimes without permission of owner.

Joy-stick (colloq.), control-lever by means of which aeroplane is steered.

King's Evidence, witness for the Crown by an accomplice.

Kultur (pron. *Kooltoor*), German education which aimed at supremacy of the state in Germany and of Germany in the world.

Labour Exchange, a State agency for bringing together employers requiring labour and workpeople desiring work, and where unemployment benefit is paid out.

League of Nations, compact or agreement among nations established in 1919 for prevention of war. Dissolved in 1946. See **United Nations Organisation**.

Listening-in, listening to messages, speeches, music, etc., broadcast by wireless.

Lloyd's, an association in London for collecting shipping intelligence, registering and insuring vessels, etc.

Looping the loop, an air feat, the aeronaut causing the machine to execute a complete circle or back-somersault.

Machine-gun (Hotchkiss, Lewis, Bren, etc.), one so constituted that a large number of shots can be fired automatically and swiftly.

Mechanization, as applied to the army, the substitution of motor for horse transport, tanks for man-power, etc.

Mi'crophone ($\bar{\imath}$), instrument for increasing sound; part of broadcasting apparatus.

Monroe Doctrine, a policy declared in 1823 by President *Monroe*, U.S.A., of which the main feature was that no further interference (e.g. colonisation) by European powers on the American continent would be tolerated.

Multilateral School, a secondary school providing all types of courses for all children in a given area.

Multiple store (as chain-store in America), one of several shops of the same kind belonging to the same firm, opened in different localities.

Na'zi ($z = ts$), member of the German National-Socialist party. (Abbreviation of *Nationalsozialist*.)

Nose Dive, the dive, nose first, of an aeroplane towards the earth.

O'scillate, to transmit—through faulty operation of a wireless set—waves which cause disturbances in other sets.

Pa'ci-fist, Pa'cif'i-cist, one who refuses to fight, believing that war is evil.

Postal Union, a union of the chief countries to regulate international postal matters.

Profiteer', to exact excessive profit, especially in a time of national emergency ; one who exacts excessive profit.

Py'lon (ī), (1) a structure to support cables carrying electric power ; (2) a mark set up to guide aeroplanes.

Radiogram, a wireless message sent usually from a ship to a receiving office on land, and thence transmitted to the recipient by telegraph. A radiogram may also be sent to a ship from a wireless station.

Radiolocation, method of detecting the presence and position of aircraft.

Revue, a light, musical comedy.

Röntgen Rays (X-Rays), rays which are due to an electric current through a vacuum tube and which penetrate some opaque substances.

Sabotage, the wilful destruction of machinery, etc., or delaying production by deliberately slow work.

Seaplane, or Hydroplane, an aeroplane made to " take off " from, or to alight upon, water.

Soviet (a Russian word meaning *council*), a local governing body elected by workers ; an all-Russian congress of delegates from local councils.

Speeding-up, getting work done at a quicker rate than formerly.

Standing Orders, settled regulations for the conducting of business.

Stra'tosphere ($a = ai$), the layer of atmospheric air above a height of about seven miles from the earth. In this layer the temperature remains constant.

Sur-Tax, an increased tax (on a graduated scale) levied on incomes over a certain sum per annum.

Swas'tika (*swāstikā*) (from words meaning *well-being*), primitive symbol or ornament, used by the Nazis (*q.v.*) as their party badge.

Tanker, a steamship constructed to carry mineral oil in bulk.

Therm (in measuring gas consumption), a unit equal to 100,000 British Thermal Units. A thermal unit is the amount of heat required to raise one pound of water one degree F.

The Three Estates, in Britain the episcopal peers, the secular peers, and the Commons. (Sometimes erroneously applied to King, Lords, and Commons.)

Toc H, an association of ex-servicemen to foster the sense of comradeship which grew up during the war of 1914–18. (Toc H is the telephonist's expression for T.H., the initials of Talbot House, a rest-house for soldiers during the war, at a town in Belgium.)

Trailer (American), (1) portions of a film shown in advance by way of advertisement ; (2) supplementary vehicle drawn usually by a motor-car.

Transform'er, an instrument which receives electrical power in one form and gives it out in another : e.g. reduces the voltage of electricity to make it suitable for heating and lighting.

Truck System, the system of paying wages in goods instead of money.

Tube, a common name applied to the narrow-gauge electric underground railways in London and other large towns. The tracks are laid in circular tubes.

U Boat (Ger. *Untersee Boot*, under-water boat), a German submarine.

Ultra-Violet Rays, invisible, but very powerful rays, lying beyond the violet end of the solar spectrum. They are much used in the treatment of certain diseases, and in photography.

United Nations Organisation (U.N.O.), an association of nations formed in 1945 to promote the security, justice, welfare, and human rights of all peoples. This replaced the League of Nations, *q.v.*

Vita glass (ī), trade name for a kind of glass which admits the ultra-violet rays in sunlight.

Wireless, without wires—a message without wires—a wireless telegram—a wireless set. See Radiogram.

ADDITIONAL

Basic English, simplified form of English with very small vocabulary.

Commando, member of armed forces trained for specially hazardous service.

Ersatz, artificial substitute or imitation of an article usually made from a natural product.

Esperanto, a language intended for universal use, invented by a Polish physician.

Fifth Column, used of any activity, particularly among the civil population, which has the object of helping an enemy.

Pakistan, British Dominion formed in 1947 from Moslem areas of India.

Plastics, natural and synthetic materials that can be moulded into permanent shape by heating and/or pressure (e.g. bakelite).

Quisling, a traitor (from the name of a Norwegian who helped Germany to gain control of Norway in 1940).

Ribbon Development, the building of houses, etc. along main roads.

Totalitarian, used of a dictatorial form of government by one party, no rival parties being permitted.

CLASSICAL AND FOREIGN WORDS AND PHRASES

Occurring frequently in English books and conversation

Abbreviations: L., *Latin*; F., *French*; It., *Italian*; Ger., *German*; P., *Portuguese*; Gk., *Greek*.

NOTES AS TO PRONUNCIATION

1. In using **Latin** and **Greek** phrases it is customary to pronounce as in English, except that *every* letter is sounded.

2. In **French**, a=*ā (father)* or *ă (bat)*; au=*ō*; e without accent is hardly pronounced at the end of a syllable; é=*ai (bait)*; è, ê, or ai=*e* in *get*, but longer; i=*ee* or *ĭ (bit)*; ou=*oo*; oi=*wa*; u=a sound between *oo* and *ĭ (bit)*; eu=a sound between *ai* and *oo*; ch=sh; j, and g before *e* or *i*=*zh*; s, t, x, and z (preceded by *e*) at the end of a syllable are usually silent; single n has a nasal sound, somewhat like a faintly sounded *ng*.

3. In **German**, a=*ă (bat)* or *ā (father)*; ä=*ai*; ai=*i (tied)*; au=*ow*; äu=*oi*; e=*ai (bait)* or *ĕ (bet)*; ei=*ī (bite)*; eu=*oi*; i=*ee* or *ĭ (bit)*; ie=*ee*; ö=*u* in *murder*; u=*oo*; ü=sound between *oo* and *ĭ (bit)*; ch=*ch* in *loch*; g is always hard; j=*y (yes)*; s often=*z*; v=*f*; w=*v*; z=*ts*.

4. In **Italian**, a=*ă (bat)* or *ā (father)*; ae=*i (tied)*; e=*aī (bait)* or *ĕ (bet)*; i=*ee* or *ĭ (bit)*; u=*oo*; c before *e* or *i*=*ch*; ch=*k*; z=*dz*; final e is sounded.

À bas   Auf Wiedersehen

À bas (F.), down with.
Ab initio (L.), from the beginning.
Abonnement (F.), subscription.
Ab ovo (L.), from the beginning (lit. the egg).
Abrégé (F.), abridgment.
Absit omen (L.), may there be no ill omen.
Ab urbe condita (L.), from the founding of the city (Rome).
Ad aperturam (L.), wherever the book opens.
Ad finem (L.), to the end.
Ad infinitum (L.), to infinity. [restriction.
À discrétion (F.), at discretion, without
Ad hoc (L.), for that purpose.
Ad majorem Dei gloriam (L.), for the greater glory of God—the Jesuits' motto.
Ad nauseam (L.), to the point of disgust.
À outrance (F.), to the death.
Ad referendum (L.), for further consideration.
Ad valōrem (L.), according to value.
Ad vitam aut culpam (L.), for life or till fault.
Advocatus diaboli (L.), devil's advocate, adverse critic.
Affaire d'honneur (F.), an affair of honour, a duel.
Affaire de cœur (F.), an affair of the heart, a love affair.
A fortiori (L.), with stronger reason.
Aide-de-camp (F.), officer who helps a general by carrying orders, etc.
À la bonne heure (F.), very well (lit. "in good time").
À la carte (F.), from the bill of fare.
À la mode (F.), in fashion.

Al fresco (It.), in the open air.
Alma mater (L.), fostering mother (applied by students to their university).
Alter ego (L.), one's other self (applied to a very close friend or companion).
Alto relievo (It.), high relief.
Alumnus (L.), pupil of a school or university.
Amende honorable (F.), reparation.
Amor patriæ (L.), love of country.
Amour propre (F.), self-love.
Ancien régime (F.), former order of things.
Anglicè (L.), in English.
Anno Domini (L.), in the year of our Lord.
Anno urbis conditæ, A.U.C. (L.), in the year the city (Rome) was built (753 B.C.).
Annus mirabilis (L.), the wonderful year.
Ante meridiem (L.), before noon.
A posteriori (L.), (reasoning) after the event.
A priori (L.), (reasoning) before the event.
À propos (F.), to the point.
Aqua vitæ (L.), brandy, spirit (lit. "water of life." Cf. Eau de vie).
Argumentum ad hominem (L.), argument appealing to a particular man, but not necessarily general.
Arpeggio (It.), striking of notes of a chord in rapid succession.
Arrière pensée (F.), a mental reservation.
Atelier (F.), studio, workshop.
Au fait (F.), well instructed, up to the mark.
Au fond (F.), to the bottom.
Au grand sérieux (F.), seriously.
Au revoir (F.), good-bye, until we meet again.
Auf Wiedersehen (Ger.), good-bye, until we meet again.

245

Auto da fé (Port.), act of faith, public burning of victims of the Inquisition.

Avant-coureur (F.), fore-runner.

Beau idéal (F.), ideal of perfection.

Beau monde (F.), the fashionable world.

Bel esprit (F.), a brilliant mind.

Belles-lettres (F.), literature.

Bête noire (F.), an object of special aversion.

Billet doux (F.), a love-letter.

Bizarre (F.), odd, fantastic.

Blasé (F.), fatigued with pleasure.

Bona fide (L.), in good faith.

Bon gré, mal gré (F.), willing or unwilling.

Bonhomie (F.), good nature.

Bon ton (F.), good breeding, fashion.

Bordereau (F.), a memorandum.

Bric-à-brac (F.), ornamental odds-and-ends.

Bundesrat (Ger.), the Federal Council of the German States.

Cacoëthes loquendi (L.), a mania for speaking.

Cacoëthes scribendi (L.), a mania for writing.

Cæteris paribus (L.), other things being equal.

Carpe diem (L.), enjoy the (present) day.

Carte blanche (F.), full power, free permission.

Casus belli (L.), occasion for war.

Ça va sans dire (F.), that goes without saying, that is a matter of course.

Cave canem (L.), beware of the dog.

Chacun à son gout (F.), every one to his taste.

Char-à-banc (F.), carriage with benches.

Chargé d'affaires (F.), deputy ambassador.

Châteaux en Espagne (F.), castles in the air.

Chef-d'œuvre (F.), a masterpiece.

Chevalier d'industrie (F.), a swindler. [shade.

Chiaroscuro (It.), distribution of light and

Cicerone (It.), a guide.

Ci-devant (F.), former.

Comme il faut (F.), as it should be.

Compos mentis (L.), of a sound mind.

Con amore (It.), with love, eagerly.

Concierge (F.), door-keeper.

Congé (F.), leave.

Contretemps (F.), an untoward event.

Conversazione (It.), official reception.

Corpus delicti (L.), substance of the offence.

Corrigenda (L.), corrections to be made.

Couleur de rose (F.), rose-colour.

Coup d'état (F. *coo-dai-ta*), a stroke of policy.

Coup de grâce (F. *coo-dé-grass*), a finishing stroke.

Coup de main (F.), a bold stroke.

Crèche (F.), public nursery for infants.

Cui bono ? (L.), for whose good is it ?

Cum grano salis (L.), with a grain of salt, with reservation.

Currente calamo (L.), with a rapid pen, as one writes.

Da capo (It.), repeat from the beginning.

Dalai Lama, the head of the Buddhists in Tibot.

Data (L.), things given.

Début (F.), first public appearance.

De facto (L.), in fact, actual.

Dei gratia (L.), by the grace of God.

Dénouement (F.), final solution, unravelling of plot in story or drama.

De novo (L.), anew.

Deo gratias (L.), thanks to God.

Deo volente (L.), God willing.

De profundis (L.), from the depths.

Desideratum [L.], a thing desired.

De trop (F. *dě trō*), too much, too many, superfluous.

Deus ex machina (L.), literally, a god from the machinery (in a theatre), providential interposition, one whose unexpected interference solves a difficulty. [fact.

Dichtung und Wahrheit [Ger.], fiction and

Dictum (L.), a saying, a decision.

Dies iræ (L.), day of wrath, the day of judgment.

Dieu et mon droit (F.), God and my right.

Disjecta membra (L.), scattered limbs or remains.

Distingué (F.), of distinguished appearance.

Distrait (F.), absent-minded.

Diva (It.), a celebrated lady singer.

Dolce far niente (It.), pleasant idleness.

Double entente (F.), a double meaning.

Douceur (F.), gratuity, bribe.

Dramatis personæ (L.), characters in a drama.

Dulce domum (L.), sweet home.

Eau de vie (F.), "water of life," brandy.

Ecce Homo (L.), Behold the man !

Éclat (F.), distinction, glory.

Édition de luxe (F.), a very fine edition.

Élan (F.), dash. [abundance.

Embarras de richesse (F.), perplexing

Emeritus (L.), retired from office.

En famille (F.), with one's family.

Enfants perdus (F.), a forlorn hope, lit. "lost children."

Enfant terrible (F.), a child that annoys by untimely remarks.

En fête (F.), on holiday.

En masse (F.), in a body.

En passant (F.), in passing.

En rapport (F.), in sympathy.

En route (F.), on the way.

En suite (F.), in a set.

Entente cordiale (F.), friendly understanding between two nations.

Entre nous (F.), between ourselves.

Ergo (L.), therefore.

Erratum, pl. Errata (L.), an error.

Esprit de corps (F.), regard for the interests of a body one belongs to.

Et cetera (L.), and the other things, and so on.

Eureka (Gk.), I have found it. [authority.

Ex cathedra (L.), from the chair, with

Excelsior (L.), higher.

Exempli gratia (L.), for example.

Exeunt omnes [L.], all go out.

Exit (L.), goes out.

Ex libris (L.), from the books of ——.

Ex officio (L.), by virtue of his office.

Ex parte (L.), on one side.

Ex post facto (L.), after the deed is done.

Extempore (L.), unpremeditated.
Extra muros (L.), beyond the walls.

Facile princeps (L.), easily first.
Facilis descensus Averni (L.), the descent to Avernus is easy.
Fait accompli (F.), thing already done.
Faux pas (F.), false step, a mistake.
Felo de se (L.), suicide.
Festina lente (L.), hasten slowly.
Fête champêtre (F.), a rural festival.
Feu de joie (F.), gun-firing as a sign of joy.
Feuilleton (F.), part of a newspaper devoted to light literature.
Fiat justitia, ruat cœlum (L.), let justice be done though the heavens fall.
Fiat lux (L.), let there be light.
Fidei defensor (L.), defender of the faith.
Fin de siecle (F.), end of the 19th century; decadent.
Finis (L.), the end.
Flagrante bello (L.), during hostilities.

Garçon (F.), waiter.   [joyful.
Gaudeamus igitur (L.), let us therefore be
Genius loci (L.), the spirit of the place.
Gloria in excelsis (L.), Glory to God in the Highest.
Guerre à outrance (F.), war to the uttermost.

Ha'ra-ki'ri (Japanese), method of suicide adopted by nobles in Japan.
Hauteur (F.), haughtiness.
Hic jacet (L.), here lies.
Honi soit qui mal y pense (F.), evil to him who evil thinks.
Horribile dictu (L.), horrible to tell.
Hors de combat (F.), out of condition to fight.   [relish.
Hors d'œuvre (F.), an extra dish served as a
Hortus siccus (L.), a collection of dried plants.
Hôtel de ville (F.), a town hall.
Hôtel-Dieu (F.), a hospital in Paris.

Ibidem (L.), in the same place.
Ich dien (Ger.), I serve.
Id est (L.), that is.
Ignis fatuus (L.), a will-o'-the-wisp.
Impedimenta (L.), baggage.   [sanction.
Imprimatur (L.), official licence to print,
Imprimis (L.), in the first place.
In camerâ (L.L.), in (a judge's) private room.
In extremis (L.), at the point of death.
In forma pauperis (L.), as a poor man.
Infra dignitatem (L.), below one's dignity.
In loco parentis (L.), in the place of a parent.
In medias res (L.), into the midst of things.
In memoriam (L.), in memory.
In nomine (L.), in the name of.
In perpetuam (L.), for ever.
In posse (L.), in possible existence.
In propria persona (L.), in one's own person.
In re (L.), in the matter of.
In statu quo (L.), in the existing state.
Inter alia (L.), among other things.
In toto (L.), entirely.   [statement.
Ipse dixit (L.), he himself said it, a dogmatic

Je ne sais quoi (F.), I know not what.
Jeu d'esprit (F.), a witticism.

Laissez faire (F.), let alone.
Lapsus linguæ (L.), a slip of the tongue.
Lares et penates (L.), household gods.
Le beau monde (F.), the fashionable world.
Lèse-majesté (F.), high treason.
Lettre de cachet (F.), a sealed letter, a royal warrant.   [law.
Lex non scripta (L.), unwritten or common
Liaison (F.), union.
Lingerie (F.), (supply of) linen articles.
Lingua Franca (L.), a mixed language spoken by Europeans in the East.
Locum tenens (L.), a substitute.
Locus standi (L.), recognised position.
Lusus naturæ (L.), a freak of nature.

Magnum opus (L.), a great work.
Mal à propos (F.), ill-timed.
Mal de mer (F.), sea-sickness.
Mariage de convenance (F.), a marriage of convenience.   [shyness.
Mauvaise honte (F.), false modesty, awkward
Mauvais sujet (F.), "a bad subject," a worthless fellow.
Mea culpa (L.), through my fault.
Memento mori (L.), a reminder of death.
Memorabilia (L.), things to be remembered.
Mens sana in corpore sano (L.), a sound mind in a sound body.
Mésalliance (F.), unsuitable marriage.
Meum et tuum (L.), mine and thine.
Mirabile dictu (L.), wonderful to say.
Mise en scène (F.), a getting up for the stage, stage effect.
Modus operandi (L.), manner of operation.
Mors janua vitæ (L.), death is the gate of life.
Multum in parvo (L.), much in little.   [tions.
Mutatis mutandis (L.), with necessary altera-

Née (F.), born (used before the maiden surname, but not Christian name, of a married lady).
Négligé (F.), loose or unceremonious dress.
Nemine contradicente (L.), without opposition.
Nemo me impune lacessit (L.), no one assails me with impunity.
Ne plus ultra (L.), nothing further.
Nil admirari (L.), to wonder at nothing.
Nil desperandum (L.), nothing to despair about.
N'importe (F.), it doesn't matter.
Nisi Dominus frustra (L.), unless God (be with us, all is) vain.   [obligations.
Noblesse oblige (F.), nobility brings with it
Nolens volens (L.), willing or unwilling.
Noli me tangere (L.), do not touch me.
Nom de guerre (F.), an assumed name.
Non compos mentis (L.), of unsound mind.
Non sequitur (L.), it does not follow.
Nota bene (L.), mark well.   [rich.
Nouveau riche (F.), person newly become
Nuance (F.), very slight difference in meaning, etc.

Nulli secundus (L.), second to none.
Nunc aut nunquam (L.), now or never.

Obiter dictum (L.), a thing said by the way.
On dit (F.), people say, it is said.
Onus probandi (L.), the burden of proving.
Optimates (L.), people of the first rank.
O tempora! O mores! (L.), O the times! O the manners!
Otium cum dignitate (L.), ease with dignity.
Outré (F.), carried to excess, eccentric.

Par excellence (F.), pre-eminently.
Par exemple (F.), for example.
Pari passu (L.), with equal pace.
Parole d'honneur (F.), word of honour.
Partie carrée (F.), a party of four persons.
Passé (F.), past the prime of life.
Passe-Partout (F.), border on a picture.
Paterfamilias (L.), the father of a family.
Paternoster (L.), " Our Father " (the Lord's Prayer).
Pax vobiscum (L.), peace be with you.
Peccavi (L.), I have sinned.
Per contra (L.), on the other side.
Per diem (L.), by the day.   [wrong.
Per fas et nefas (L.), through right and
Per se (L.), by itself, himself, etc.
Petit-maître (F.), a fop.
Pièce de résistance (F.), principal dish.
Pied-à-terre (F.), resting-place, temporary lodging.
Pinxit (L.), —— painted (this picture).
Poeta nascitur, non fit (L.), a poet is born, not made.   [I. 5).
Pons asinorum (L.), the asses' bridge (Euclid
Poste restante (F.), department in the post-office where letters remain till called for.
Post mortem (L.), after death.
Pour passer le temps (F.), to pass the time.
Pour prendre congé (F.), to take leave.
Preux chevalier (F.), a gallant knight.
Prima donna (It.), chief female singer.
Primâ facie (L.), at first sight.
Primus inter pares (L.), first among his equals.
Pro bono publico (L.), for the public good.
Pro patria (L.), for one's country.
Pro re nata (L.), for occasion as it arises.
Pros and cons [*con* for *contra*, against], (L.), arguments for and against.
Protégé, *fem.* **Protégée** (F.), one to whom another is protector or patron.
Pro tempore (L.), for the time being.

Quantum sufficit, shortened to **Quant. suff.** (L.), as much as suffices.
Quasi (L.), as if, in a manner.
Quid nunc (L.), what now ? a gossip.
Quid pro quo (L.), a return for a favour.
Qui va là ? (F.), who goes there ?
Qui vive ? (F.), who goes there ? On the qui vive, on the alert.
Quod erat demonstrandum (Q.E.D.) (L.), which was to be proved.
Quod erat faciendum (L.), which was to be done.
Quondam (L.), former.

Raison d'être (F.), reason for existence.
Rara avis (L.), a rare bird, a rarity.
Re (L.), in the matter of.
Réchauffé (F.), a warmed-up dish, stale.
Recherché (F.), sought after, refined, particularly nice.
Reductio ad absurdum (L.), a reducing to the absurd.
Reichstag (Ger.), the parliament of the German Empire.
Renaissance (F.), revival (as of letters).
Répondez, s'il vous plaît—R.S.V.P. (F.), reply, if you please.
Requiescat in pace (L.), may he (or she) rest in peace.
Résumé (F.), an abstract or summary.
Resurgam (L.), I shall rise again.
Revenons à nos moutons (F.), let us return to our sheep ; let us return to our subject.
Rôle (F.), an actor's part, one's function.
Roué (F.), a debauched man.

Sanctum sanctorum (L.), holy of holies, a place of refuge.
Sang froid (F.), cold blood, coolness.
Sans peur et sans reproche (F.), without fear and without reproach.
Sans souci (F.), without care.
Sartor resartus (L.), the tailor retailored.
Sauve qui peut (F.), save himself who can.
Savoir-faire (F.), knowledge of what to do, tact.
Schadenfreude (Ger.), joy in the misfortunes of others
Semper fidelis (L.), always faithful.
Semper idem (L.), always the same.
Seriatim (L.), in regular order.
Sic (L.), thus (often used to call attention to a quoted inaccuracy or absurdity).
Sic itur ad astra (L.), thus do we travel to the stars (or immortality).
Sic transit gloria mundi (L.), so passes the glory of the world. •   [adjourned.
Sine die (L.), without date, indefinitely
Sine qua non (L.), an indispensable condition.
Soi-disant (F.), self-styled.
Sotto voce (It.), in an undertone.   [tity.
Soupçon (F.), suspicion, a very small quan-
Status quo (L.), " the state in which," the existing state of affairs.
Stet (L.), let it stand.
Sturm und Drang (Ger.), storm and stress.
Suaviter in modo, fortiter in re (L.), gently in manner, resolutely in deed.
Sub judice (L.), under consideration.
Sub pœna (L.), under a penalty.
Sub rosa (L.), " under the rose," secretly.
Sui generis (L.), of its own kind, unique.
Summum bonum (L.), the chief good.

Tableau vivant (F.), a living picture, a group of figures to represent a scene.   [price.
Table-d'hôte (F.), restaurant meal at fixed
Tabula rasa (L.), a blank tablet.
Tempora mutantur (L.),the times are changed.
Tempus fugit (L.), time flies.
Terra firma (L.), solid earth, dry land.

Terra incognita (L.), an unknown country.
Tertium quid (L.), a third something.
Tête-à-tête (F.), a conversation between two.
Tour de force (F.), feat of strength or skill.
Tout ensemble (F.), the whole taken together.
Tu quoque (L.), "thou also," "so are you," an argument which in effect says, " You are as bad as I am."

Ubi supra (L.), where above-mentioned.
Ultimatum (L.), a final proposal, a peremptory demand, the refusal of which is to be followed by war.
Ultra vires (L.), beyond one's powers.
Ut infra (L.), as below.
Ut supra (L.), as above.

Vade mecum (L.), " go with me," something carried constantly.
Væ victis (L.), woe to the vanquished.
Vale (L.), farewell.

Veni, vidi, vici (L.), I came, I saw, I conquered.
Verbum sat sapienti, shortened to **Verb. sap.** (L.), a word is enough for a wise man
Versus (L.), against.
Via (L.), by way of.
Via media (L.), a middle course.
Vice (L.), in the place of.
Vice versa (L.), the other way about.
Vide (L.), see.
Videlicet (L.), namely (usually contracted to viz.).
Vis-à-vis (F.), opposite, facing.
Vis inertiæ (L.), the power of resisting change.
Viva voce (L.), by word of mouth.
Voilà (F.), behold !
Volente Deo (L.), God willing.
Vox populi, vox Dei (L.), the voice of the people is the voice of God.

Zeitgeist (Ger.), the spirit of the time.

CLASSICAL NAMES

GODS AND GODDESSES (GREEK AND ROMAN)

Æs-cu-la′pi-us, the god of medicine.
A-pol′lo, Phœ′bus A-pol′lo, the sun-god.
Au-ro′ra (R.), **E′os** (Gk.), dawn goddess.
Bacc′hus (R.), **Di-ony′sos** (Gk.), wine god.
Bel-lo′na (R.), goddess of war.
Ce′res (R.), **De-me′ter** (Gk.), the goddess of agriculture.
Cu′pid (R.), **E′ros** (Gk.), the god of love.
Cyb′el-e, the earth goddess.
Di-a′na (R.), **Ar′te-mis** (Gk.), the goddess of hunting.
Flo′ra, the goddess of flowers.
He′be, the goddess of youth.
Hy-gei′a, the goddess of health.
Hy′men, the god of marriage.
Ja′nus (R.), a god whose temple was open in time of war.

Ju′no (R.), **He′ra** (Gk.), the chief goddess.
Ju′pi-ter (R.), **Zeus** (Gk.), the most powerful of the gods.
Mars (R.), **A′res** (Gk.), the god of war.
Mer′cur-y (R.), **Her′mes** (Gk.), the messenger of the other gods.
Mi-ner′va (R.), **Pal′las A-the′na** (Gk.), the goddess of wisdom, arts, sciences, etc.
Mor′pheus, the god of sleep.
Nep′tune (R.), **Po-sei′don** (Gk.), sea-god.
Pan, the god of shepherds.
Plu′to, the god of the underworld.
Plu′tus, the god of wealth.
Rhe′a, the wife of Saturn.
Sat′urn, the god of agriculture.
Ve′nus (R.), **Aph-ro-di′te** (Gk.), the goddess of love and beauty.

OTHER CLASSICAL NAMES

(*Ch*, which in Greek had nearly the sound of *ch* in Scottish *loch*, is pronounced as *k* in English.)

Ach-er′on, one of the rivers of Hades ; Hades itself.
Ach-il′les, the chief hero of Homer's *Iliad.*
Ac′ti-um, a promontory in the West of Greece near which Octavian, Julius Cæsar's adopted son and successor, defeated Mark Antony and Cleopatra (31 B.C.).
Ae-ge′us, a king of Athens, after whom the Ægean Sea is named, as he drowned himself in it, supposing his son Theseus to be dead.
Æ-ne′as, the hero of Virgil's *Æneid.*
Æs′chy-lus (*ae*=*ee*), a Greek tragic poet.
Ag-a-mem′non, commander of the Greek army in the Trojan war.
A′jax, name of two Greek leaders in the Trojan war.

Al-ci-bi′a-des, an Athenian leader, and disciple of Socrates.
Alexander the Great, son of Philip, king of Macedonia, conqueror of Western Asia in the fourth century B.C.
Am′mon, ancient Egyptian god.
An-chi′ses, the father of Æneas.
An-drom′ach-e, wife of Hector of Troy.
An-drom′ed-a, an Ethiopian princess, rescued by Perseus from a sea-monster after he had slain Medusa.
A′pis, the sacred bull of the ancient Egyptians worshipped at Memphis, in Lower Egypt.
A-rach′ne, a maiden of Lydia in Asia Minor. Athena transformed her into a spider.
Ar′bel-a, an Assyrian town near which Alexander the Great defeated Darius, king of Persia (331 B.C.).

Ar-cad'i-a, a mountainous, pastoral country of ancient Greece.

Ar-e-op'a-gus, " Mars' Hill " in Athens.

Ar'go-nauts, the Greek heroes who sailed in search of the golden fleece.

Ar-is-ti'des, a very just Greek leader in fifth century B.C.

Ar-is-toph'an-es, a Greek comic poet.

Ar'is-tot-le, a great Greek philosopher.

At-a-lan'ta, a princess of Arcadia noted for her fleetness of foot.

At-lant'is, a fabled island in the Atlantic said to have sunk.

At'ro-pos, one of the three Fates, Greek Goddesses. The others were **Clo'tho** and **Lach'es-is.** Clotho spun the thread of life, Lachesis assigned it, and Atropos cut it.

A-ver'nus, a lake near Naples, supposed to be an entrance to Pluto's kingdom of Hades ; Hades itself. [wine.

Bac-chan'tes, priestesses of Bacchus, god of

Bu-ceph'a-lus, war-horse of Alexander.

By-zan'ti-um, Constantinople or Istanbul.

Cal-li'op-e, the Muse of epic poetry.

Cas-san'dra, Priam's daughter, a true prophetess of evil whom no one believed.

Cer'ber-us, the three-headed dog guarding the entrance to Hades.

Cha'ron, the ferryman of the dead over the river Styx to Hades.

Cha-ryb'dis, a whirlpool in the Strait of Messina near Sicily. **Scyl'la,** on the Italian side of the Strait, is a rock dangerous to ships.

Chi'ron, a very wise centaur. [etc.

Cir'ce, a sorceress who turned men into swine,

Cle-o-pa'tra, a beautiful queen of Egypt.

Cli'o, the Muse of history.

Clo'tho, one of the Fates. See **Atropos.**

Cly-tem-nes'tra, wife of Agamemnon.

Col'chis, a country at the eastern end of the Black Sea.

Co'mus, the god of revelry.

Cor-y-ban'tes, priests of the goddess Cybele.

Crœ'sus (*œ*=*ee*), a very rich king of Lydia, in Asia Minor.

Cy-be'le, Phrygian goddess worshipped at Rome also as Ops. [Sicily.

Cy'clops, (pl.) **Cy-clo'pes,** one-eyed giants in

Dam'o-cles, a flatterer whom Dionysius of Syracuse punished by inviting him to a banquet, where he was seated under a sword suspended by a hair.

Dan'a-e, mother of Perseus.

Del'phi, a town near Mount Parnassus, the seat of an oracle of Apollo.

De-mos'then-es, a famous Greek orator.

Di'do, queen and foundress of Carthage.

Dio'ge-nes (*ŏ*), a cynical philosopher.

Er'e-bus, a kingdom of darkness on the way to Hades.

Eu-rip'id-es, a famous Greek tragic poet.

Eu-ryd'i-ce, the wife of Orpheus.

Eu-ter'pe, the Muse of lyric poetry and music.

Gan'y-mede, a youth who was made cup-bearer to Zeus.

Ha'des, the lower world.

Hec'tor, son of Priam, greatest of the Trojan heroes.

Hec'u-ba, wife of Priam.

Hel'en, a beautiful Greek woman, the chief cause of the Trojan war.

Hel'i-con, mountains in Greece, the abode of Apollo and the Muses.

He'ra, Grecian goddess corresponding to the Juno of the Romans.

Her'cu-les, a Greek hero of great strength.

He'ro, a Thracian maiden beloved by **Le-an'der.**

He-rod'o-tus, the first Greek historian.

Hes-per'i-des, three sisters who guarded golden apples in a garden.

Hip-pol'y-te, a queen of the Amazons.

Ho'mer, the great Greek epic poet.

Hor'ace, a great Roman poet.

Il'i-on or **Il'i-um,** Troy.

Iph-i-ge-ni'a, daughter of Agamemnon, and priestess of Diana.

I'ris (the rainbow), a messenger of the gods.

Ix-i'on, a Thessalian king punished in Hades by being bound to a revolving wheel : he had dared to love Hera.

Ja'son, the leader of the Argonauts.

Lach'e-sis, one of the Fates. See **Atropos.**

La-oc'o-on, a priest who with his two sons was killed by serpents.

Le-an'der, a youth of **A-by'dos,** on the southern side of the Hellespont, which he swam every night to visit **Hero.**

Le-on'i-das, king of Sparta, who defended the Pass of **Ther-mop'y-lae** against the Persians (480 B.C.).

Leth'e, one of the rivers of Hades. [Jason.

Me-de'a, a sorceress who helped and married

Me-du'sa, one of three sisters called *Gorgons.* Her aspect turned beholders to stone.

Mel-pom'e-ne, the Muse of tragedy. [Helen.

Men-e-la'us, a king of Sparta, husband of

Mi'das, a king of Phrygia whose touch turned things into gold.

Nai'a-des (or **Nai'ads**), nymphs of springs, rivers, and lakes.

Ne-re'i-des, fifty sea-nymphs.

O-lym'pus, a mountain in Greece whose summit was the abode of the gods.

Or'pheus, a wonderful player on the lyre. He followed his wife Eurydice to Hades to bring her back.

O-si'ris, one of the gods of ancient Egypt.

Pan-do'ra, the first woman (in Greek poetry).

Par'is, the younger son of Priam. He carried off Helen. [Apollo.

Par-nas'sus, a mountain in Greece sacred to

Peg'a-sus, a winged horse in fable.

Pel-op-on-ne'sus, peninsula of S. Greece.

Pe-nel'o-pe, the wife of Ulysses.

Per'seus, the slayer of Medusa.

Pha'e-thon or **Pha'e-ton,** a son of Phœbus, the sun-god.

Phle'ge-thon, one of the rivers of Hades.

Pla'to, a Greek philosopher.

Plei'ad [Gk. *pleias,* (pl.) *pleiades*], (pl.) cluster of small stars in constellation Taurus; (sing.) brilliant group of persons or things.

Pri'am, king of Troy at the time of the Trojan war.

Pro-me'theus, a Greek hero who stole fire from heaven.

Pro-ser'pi-na, Pros'er-pine, Per-seph'on-e, daughter of Ceres and wife of Pluto.

Psy'che (*si'ki*), a nymph whom Cupid loved.

Sa'ppho, a Greek poetess who lived about 600 B.C.

Sat'yrs, demi-gods like men, with feet, legs, and horns of goats.

Scy'lla, see *Charybdis.*

Sis'y-phus, a mythical person condemned in Hades to roll uphill a stone which always came down again.

Soc'ra-tes, a Greek philosopher whose teaching Plato has preserved. He was condemned to drink the juice of the hemlock, a deadly poison.

Soph'o-cles, a Greek tragic poet. [itself.

Styx, one of the rivers of Hades ; Hades

Tan'tal-us, a king whom the poets describe as having constant thirst in the lower world. Waters always recede from his mouth before he can drink. [itself.

Tar'tar-us, a region beneath Hades ; Hades

Terp-sich'ore, the Muse of dancing.

The'seus, slayer of the Cretan monster Minotaur, afterwards king of Athens.

Ti'tans, gigantic sons of Cœlus (heaven) and Terra (earth).

Ulys'ses (**Odys'seus** in Greek), a Greek hero in the Trojan war.

Vir'gil, a Roman poet, author of the *Æneid.*

LATIN ROOTS

acuo, *I sharpen;* **acer,** *sharp;* **acus,** *a needle;* **acutus,** *sharp:* acid, acrid, eager, acute, acerbity. [edify.

aedes, *a house;* **aedifico,** *I build:* edifice,

aequus, *equal, just;* **iniquus,** *unequal:* equal, equation, adequate, iniquity.

aestimo, *I value:* esteem, estimate.

ager, *a field:* agriculture, peregrination. [Through the French: pilgrim.]

ago, *I do* (**actus,** *done*); **agito,** *I stir up:* agent, agile, act, enact, agitate.

alius, *another;* **alienus,** *belonging to another:* alien, alienate.

alter, *the other of two:* alter, alternate.

altus, *high;* F. **haut,** *high:* altitude, altar, exalt. [Through the French : haughty.]

amo, *I love* (**amātus,** *loved*); **amicus,** *a friend;* **inimicus,** *hostile:* amiable, amorous, amicable, inimical. [Through the French : enemy.]

ango, *I choke:* anger, anxiety.

angulus, *a corner:* angle, angular, triangle.

anima, *life:* animate, animal.

animus, *the mind, the soul:* equanimity, unanimous, animosity.

annus, *a year:* annual, perennial.

antiquus, *old:* antiquity, antic. [Through French : ancient.]

aperio, *I open* (**apertus,** *opened*), F. **ouvert,** *open:* aperture, aperient, April. [Through the French : overture.]

aptus, *fit:* apt, adapt, attitude.

arbitror, *I think;* **arbiter,** *a judge:* arbitrate, arbitror, arbitrary.

ardeo, *I burn* (sup. **arsum**): ardent, ardour, arson.

arma, *arms:* arms, armament, alarm.

ars (**artis**), *art:* art, artist.

asper, *rough:* asperity.

audio, *I hear* (**auditus,** *heard*): audience, auditor.

augeo, *I increase* (**auctus,** *increased*): augment, auction, author, autumn.

bellum, *war:* belligerent, bellicose, rebel.

bene, *well:* benefit, benevolent.

bibo, *I drink:* imbibe, bibulous.

bis, bi, *twice, two;* **bini,** *two by two:* biscuit (**bis** and **coctus**), combine, biped, balance (**bis** and **lanx,** *the scale of a balance*), binary.

bonus, *good:* boon, bounty. [semibreve.

brevis, *short:* brevity, brief, abridge, breve,

cado, *I fall* (sup. **casum**): case, chance, casual, accident, occasion, decay.

caedo, *I cut, I kill* (**caesus,** *cut, killed*): decide, precisely, suicide, chisel.

campus, *a plain, a battlefield;* F. **champ:** camp, campaign. [From the French : champion, scamper.]

candeo, *I am white, I shine:* candid, candidate, candle.

cano, *I sing* (**cantus,** *sung*); **carmen,** *a song;* F. **chanter,** *to sing:* cantata, cant. [Through French : chant, charm.]

capio, *I take* (**captus,** *taken*): capable, captive, accept, anticipate, occupy. [Through French : perceive, caitiff.

caput, *a head* (**capitis,** *of a head*): captain, capital, precipice, cattle, chattels. [Through French : chief, mischief.]

causa, *a cause:* cause, accuse.

caveo, *I warn* (**cautus,** *warned*): cautious.

cedo, *I go, I yield* (sup. **cessum**): cede, cession, cease, ancestor, proceed.

centum, *a hundred:* cent, century.

cerno, *I sift, I judge* (**cretus,** *sifted, judged*): concern, discernment, decree, secret, secretary.

certus, *sure:* certain, certify, ascertain.

cieo, *I call* (**citus,** *called*): recite.

circus, *a ring:* circus, circle, circuit.

civis, *a citizen:* civil, city, citizen.

clamo, *I call out* (**clamatus,** *called*): claim, clamour, proclaim, declaim.

clarus, *clear:* clear, clarion, chanticleer.

claudo, *I shut* (**clausus,** *shut*): clause, close, conclusion, include, preclude.

colo, *I cultivate* (**cultus,** *cultivated*): colony, cultivate, culture, agriculture.

coquo, *I cook* (**coctus,** *cooked*): cook, concoct, biscuit, kitchen.

cor, *a heart* (**cordis,** *of a heart*), F. **cœur,** *the heart:* cordial, according, record. [Through the French: courage.]

corpus, *a body* (**corporis,** *of a body*): corps, corpse, corporation, corporal.

credo, *I believe, I intrust* (**creditus,** *intrusted*): credit, creed, incredible.

creo, *I make out of nothing* (**creatus,** *created*): create, creature.

cresco, *I grow:* crescent, decrease.

crimen, *a crime* (**criminis,** *of a crime*): crime, criminal.

cura, *care:* cure, secure, curious, accurate. [Through French: sure.]

curro, *I run* (sup. **cursum**): current, course, occur, recur.

curvus, *crooked:* curve, curb.

damnum, *loss:* damage, condemn.

debeo, *I owe* (**debitus,** *owed*). [Through French: debt, due, duty, endeavour.]

deus, *a god,* **divinus,** *pertaining to a god:* deity, deify, divine.

dico, *I say* (**dictus,** *said*): diction, dictate, addicted, interdict, verdict, condition.

dies, *a day:* F. **jour,** *a day:* dial, diurnal. [Through French: journal, journey.]

dignus, *worthy:* dignity, dignitary, dignify, deign, dainty, indignant.

do, *I give* (**datus,** *given*): donation, condone, date, add, tradition.

doceo, *I teach* (**doctus,** *taught*): docile, doctor, doctrine, document.

dominus, *a lord:* domina, *a lady:* dominate, dominant, predominant, domain, don. [Through French: damsel, dame.]

domus, *a house:* dome, domestic.

duco, *I lead* (**ductus,** *led*): duke, introduce, education, duct, viaduct.

duo, *two* (**dubius,** *doubtful*), dual, duel, double, doubt, dubious, redoubtable, dozen (from **duo,** and **decem,** *ten*).

durus, *hard:* durable, endure, durance.

eo, *I go* (sup. **itum**): ambitious, exit.

esse, *to be* (**ens,** *a thing;* **entis,** *of a thing*): entity, absence, essential.

experior, *I try* (**expertus,** *having tried*): experiment, experience, expert.

externus, *outward, foreign:* external, extreme. [Through French: strange.]

facies, *the face:* face, superficial, fashion.

facio, *I make* (**factus,** *made*); **fio,** *I am made,* or *I become;* F. **faire,** *to make:* fact, factory, feat, effect, sufficient, affect, affectionate, perfect, manufactory, profit, difficult, traffic. [Through French: affair.] To these add the verbs ending in *fy:* glorify, etc.

fallo, *I deceive* (**falsus,** *deceived*): fail, false, infallible, fault.

fama, *fame:* fame, infamous.

familia, *a household:* family, familiar.

faveo, *I favour:* favour, favourite.

fendo, *I keep off, I strike* (**fensus,** *kept off*), defender, offensive, fender.

fera, *a wild beast;* **ferox,** *wild:* ferocious, fierce.

fero, *I bear, I carry:* ferry, confer, interfere, defer, offer, prefer.

fides, *faith:* confide, confident, fidelity. [Through French: fealty, defiance.]

fingo, *I feign* (**fictus,** *feigned*): fiction, feign, feint, figment. [definite.

finis, *the end, a boundary:* fine, final, finish,

firmus, *strong:* firm, confirm, infirmary.

fluo, *I flow* (sup. **fluxum**): fluid, fluent, influence, flux, confluence, affluence.

forma, *a shape, a form:* form, perform, reform, transform, conform.

fortis, *strong, valiant:* fort, fortress, force, effort, comfort, fortify.

frango, *I break* (**fractus,** *broken*): fragment, fragile, fraction, refract, infringe. [Through French: frail.]

frons, *the forehead, the front* (**frontis,** *of the forehead*): front, frontier.

fuga, *flight,* **fugio,** *I flee:* fugitive, refuge.

fundo, *I pour out, I melt* (**fusus,** *poured*): foundry, confound, confuse, fuse.

gaudium, *joy:* gaudy. [Through French: joy, rejoice.]

genus, *a race, a kind* (**generis,** *of a race*): generation, general, genius, genial, ingenuity, gentle. [Through French: engine.]

gero, *I bear, I carry* (**gestus,** *carried*): germ, digest, gesture, jest.

gradior, *I go* (**gressus,** *having gone*); **gradus,** *a step:* grade, degrade, retrograde, gradual, degree, progress, transgress, ingredient.

granum, *a grain of corn:* grain, garner, pomegranate, grenade (named from its likeness to a pomegranate filled with seeds), grenadier.

gratia, *favour:* grace, grateful, gratify. [Through French: agree.]

habeo, *I have* (**habitus,** *had*): habit, exhibit.

haereo, *I stick to* (sup. **haesum**): adhere, coherent, hesitate.

honor, *respect, honour:* honour, honest.

horreo, *I dread* (**horridus,** *rough, bristly*): horror, abhor, horrid, horrible.

hortus, *a garden:* horticulture.

hospes, *a host, a guest* (**hospitis,** *of a host*): host, hospitable, hospital. [Through French: hostel, hotel, ostler.]

humus, *the ground,* homo, *man:* human, humane, humble, humility.

impero, *I command* (**imperatum,** *commanded*): imperative, imperial, empire.

jacio, *I throw* (**jactus,** *thrown*): ejaculation, object. [Through French: jet.]

jungo, *I join* (**junctus,** *joined*), jugum, *a yoke:* join, joint, junction, jugular, conjugal, subjunctive, conjunction.

jus, *law, justice* (**jūris,** *of law*); **judex,** *a judge* (**judicis,** *of a judge*): justice, injure, judicial, judicious, prejudice, jury. [Through French: judge.]

labor, *toil:* labour, elaborate, laboratory.

latus, *brought* or *carried:* relate, translated, elate. [Through French: delay.]

lego, *I appoint:* legate, delegate.

lego, *I gather, I choose, I read* (**lectus,** *gathered*): legend, lecture, lesson, elect, religious, diligent, neglect, college, colleague, collect, recollect, intellect.

levo, *I raise* (**levatus,** *raised*): elevate, levity (F. **lever,** *to raise*), levy, relief.

lex, *a law* (**legis,** *of a law*): legal, legitimate, privilege. [Through French: loyal.]

liber, *free:* liberty, liberate, liberal. [Through French: deliver, livery.]

liber, *a book:* library, libel.

libra, *a balance:* equilibrium, deliberate. [Through French: level.]

liquens, *fluid:* liquor, liquid, liquidate.

litera, *a letter:* literary, literal. [Through French: letter.]

locus, *a place:* local, locality, localise. [Through French: lieutenant.]

ludo, *I play, I deceive* (**lusus,** *played*): delude, allusion, elude, collusion.

luo, *I wash* (**lutus,** *washed*): ablution, dilute. [Through French: deluge.]

lux, *light,* **lumen,** *a light:* **luceo,** *I shine:* lucid, illuminate, illustration, lustrous.

magnus, *great:* major, *greater;* **maximus,** *greatest:* magnitude, magnify, main, majority, maxim, maximum.

malus, *bad:* male, *ill:* malcontent, malicious, malignant, malefactor.

mando, *I give in charge, I command:* mandate, mandatory, command, mandamus, recommend.

maneo, *I remain* (sup. *mansum*): mansion, manse, permanent, remain, remnant.

manus, *the hand:* manuscript, emancipation. [Through French: manage, manner, maintain, legerdemain.]

mater, *a mother:* maternal, matron, matricide.

materia, *stuff, matter:* material, matter.

medeor, *I heal:* remedy, medicine.

medius, *middle:* mediate, Mediterranean, intermediate, immediately. [Through the French: mean, means.]

memor, *mindful:* memory, remember, commemorate, memorial, memorable. [Through the French: memoir].

mens, *the mind* (**mentis,** *of the mind*): mental, demented, mention.

merx, *merchandise* (**mercis,** *of merchandise*): mercantile, commerce. [Through French: mercy — originally a *reward* — merchant, mercenary.]

metior, *I measure* (**mensus,** *measured*): mete, immense, commensurate. [Through French: measure.]

minus, *less* (**minutus,** *lessened*): minute, diminish, minimise, minimum, minor.

mirus, *wonderful, strange:* miracle, admire. [Through French: marvellous.]

misceo, *I mix* (**mistus** or **mixtus,** *mixed*): mixture, miscellany.

mitto, *I send* (**missus,** *sent*); mission, missionary, message, commit, promise.

modus, *a measure:* mode, model, mould, modulate, moderate.

moneo, *I warn* (**monitus,** *warned*): monitor, summon, admonition, monster.

mons, *a mountain* (**montis,** *of a mountain*): mount, mountain, amount.

monstro, *I show, I point out:* demonstration, remonstrance.

mors, *death* (**mortis,** *of death*): mortal.

mos, *a custom* (**moris,** *of a custom*): moral, morose.

moveo, *I move* (**motus,** *moved*); move, motion, promote, moment, mob.

nascor, *I am born* (**natus,** *born*): nascent, nation, native, nature. [annex.

necto, *I bind* (**nexus,** *bound*): connect, nego, *I deny* (**negatus,** *denied*): negative. [Through French: deny.] [Through Spanish: renegade.]

niger, *black.* [Through Spanish: negro, negroid, negrito.]

noceo, *I hurt:* innocent, noxious.

nomen, *a name* (**nominis,** *of a name*): nominate, nominative, denomination. [Through the French: renown.]

nosco or **gnosco,** *I know* (**notus,** *known*): note, notice, noble, recognise, acquaintance (from **ad, con,** and **gnosco**).

novus, *new:* novel, novice, renovate.

numerus, *a number:* numerous, numerical. [Through French: number.]

nuncio, *I announce:* denounce, denunciation, pronounce, enunciation.

opus, *a work* (**operis,** *of a work*): opera, operation, operative, co-operative.

ordo, *a rank* (**ordinis,** *of a rank*): order, ordinary, ordain, co-ordinate.

orior, *I rise* (**ortus,** *having risen*); **origo,** *a beginning:* oriental, origin.

oro, *I pray:* **os,** *the mouth* (**oris,** *of the mouth*): oral, orator, adore.

panis, *bread:* pantry, company.

par, *equal:* compare. [Through French: pair, umpire, peer.]

pareo, *I appear:* appear, apparent.

paro, *I make ready* (**parātus,** *made ready*): apparatus, prepare, repair, separation, parapet (**paro** and **pectus,** *the breast,* through Italian **petto**).

pars, *a part* (**partis,** *of a part*): part, party, partisan, particular, apart.

passus, *a step:* pass, past, passenger.

pater, *a father:* paternal, patron, pattern, parricide.

patior, *I suffer* (**passus,** *having suffered*): passion, patience, passive.

pax, *peace* (**pacis,** *of peace*): pacify, pacific. [Through French: peace, pay.]

pello, *I drive* (**pulsus,** *driven*): compel, dispel, expel, repel, pulse, repulse.

pendeo, *I hang down:* dependent, suspense, perpendicular.

persŏna, *a person :* person, parson.

pes, *a foot* (**pedis,** *of a foot*): biped, quadruped, pedestrian, impede, expedition, expedient.

peto, *I seek* (**petitus,** sought): petition, competition, appetite, petulant. [depict.

pingo, *I pain.* (**pictus,** *painted*): paint, picture,

placeo, *I please* (sup. *placitum*): placid, complacency, complaisant. [Through the French : please, plea, plead.]

planus, *plain :* plane, plain, explain.

plaudo, *I clap my hands* (**plausus,** *clapped*): plaudit, applaud, applause, explode.

pleo, *I fill* (**pletus,** *filled*): complete, complement, repletion, expletive.

plico, *I fold* (**plicatus,** *folded*): complicate, complex. [Through French: apply, reply, simple, employ, plaited.] [plummet.

plumbum, *lead :* plumber, plumbago, plumb,

pœna, *punishment ;* **punio,** *I punish* (**punitus,** *punished*): penal, repent, punish, impunity. [Through French : pain, pine.]

pono, *I place* (**positus,** *placed*): post, compose, compound, position, deposit, impose, expose, opponent, propose.

populus, *the people ;* **publicus,** *concerning the people:* popular, population, people, public, publish, republic.

porto, *I bear, I carry :* portly, important, report, transport, comport, deportment.

portus, *a harbour :* port, opportunity.

posse, *to be able :* **potens,** *able, powerful ;* F. **pouvoir,** *to be able :* possible, potent. [Through French : power.]

precor, *I pray* (**precātus,** *having prayed*): precarious, deprecate, imprecation. [Through French : pray.]

prehendo, *I seize* (**prehensus,** *seized*): apprehend, comprehend. [Through French : enterprise, prison, apprentice.]

pretium, *a price:* appreciate. [Through French : price, precious, praise.]

primo, *I press* (**pressus,** *pressed*): press, impression. [Through French : print.]

primus, *first :* prime, primate. [From French (from **primus** and **capio**) prince, principal, principle.] [privateer.

privo, *I deprive:* deprive, privation, private,

probo, *I prove, I try :* probably, approbation. [Through French : prove, proof.]

prope, *near ;* **proximus,** *nearest ;* **proprius,** *one's own :* propitious, approximate. [Through French : approach, proper.]

pungo, *I prick* (**punctus,** *pricked*): pungent, puncture, punctilious, punctual. [Through French : point.]

purus, *pure:* purify, purity.

puto, *I lop, I prune, I think :* amputate, reputable, dispute, deputy. [Through French and Italian : count, account.]

quadra, *a square ;* **quartus,** *fourth :* quarter, quadrant, squadron, square.

quaero, *I seek* (**quaesitus,** *sought*): query. [Through French : question, inquiry, requisite.]

queror, *I complain :* querulous. [Through French : quarrel, cry.]

quietus, *quiet :* quiet, quiescent, requiem.

radius, *the spoke of a wheel :* radiate, radiance. [Through French : ray.]

rapio, *I seize* (**raptus,** *seized*): rapid, rapture. [Through French : ravage.]

rego, *I rule* (**rectus,** *ruled*) ; **rex,** *a king* (**regis,** *of a king*): regular, region, direct, regal. [Through French : reign, rule, royal, royalist, realm, adroit.]

reor, *I think, I judge* (**ratus,** *having thought ;* **ratio,** *reason*): rates, ratio, rations. [Through French : reason, rational.]

res, *a thing :* real, realise, reality.

rivus, *a stream :* river, rivulet, derive, rival (that is, one who lives near the same stream, hence one whose purposes do not suit ours).

rumpo, *I break* (**ruptus,** *broken*): abrupt, interruption. [Through French : rout.]

sacer, *holy :* sacred, sacrifice, execrate, sacrament, consecrate.

salio, *I leap* (sup. *saltum*): salient, resilient, salmon. [Through French : insult, result, assail, assault.]

salus, *health* (**salutis,** *of health*) ; **salvus,** *safe :* salute, salutary, salve. [Through French : safety.]

sanctus, *holy :* sanctify, sanction. [Through French : saint, saintly.]

satis, *enough ;* **satur,** *full :* satisfy, satisfaction, saturate, satiate.

scala, *a ladder :* **scando,** *I climb* (**scansus,** *climbed*): scale, ascend, condescension.

scio, *I know :* conscious, science.

scribo, *I write* (**scriptus,** *written*): ascribe, description, Scriptures, manuscript.

seco, *I cut* (**sectus,** *cut*): sect, section, insect, dissect.

sedeo, *I sit :* sedentary, residence, president, subsidiary. [Through the French : siege, besiege.]

senex, *old ;* **senior,** *older :* senator, senior. [Through French : sire, sir.]

sentio, *I feel* (**sensus,** *felt*): sense, sensible, sensation, sentence, consent, resentment.

separo, *I separate* (**separatus,** *separated*): separate. [Through French : sever, several.]

sequor, *I follow* (**secutus,** *having followed*): sequence, consequently, execution. [Through French : suit, pursue.]

servo, *I keep* (**servatus,** *kept*): observe, conservative.

servus, *a slave* or *servant :* serve, service, servant, serf, deserve, desert.

signum, *a mark ;* **sigillum,** *a seal :* sign, signal, design, seal.

silva, *a wood :* silvan, Pennsylvania. [Through French : savage.]

similis, *like :* similar, assimilate, dissimulate. [Through French : resemble.]

situs, *a place :* site, situation.

socius, *a companion :* society, associate.

solidus, *firm, solid, a piece of money :* solid, consolidate. [Through French : soldier.]

solus, *alone:* sole, solitary, desolate.

solvo, *I loosen* (**solutus,** *loosened*) : solve, dissolution, absolute.

specio, *I see, I look* (**spectus,** *seen*) : species, specimen, expect, respectability, special, aspect, spectacle, suspicion, conspicuous. [Through French : despise, despite.]

spero, *I hope* (**speratus,** *hoped*) : desperate. [Through French: despair, prosper.] [Through Spanish : desperado.]

spiro, *I breathe:* spirit, inspire, conspire, expiry, respiration.

spondeo, *I promise* (**sponsus,** *promised*) : despond, response, spouse.

sterno, *I spread* (**stratus,** *spread*) ; **stratum,** *a layer:* prostrate, street, consternation.

sto, *I stand:* circumstance, exist, state, stage, station, establish, instant, assist.

stringo, *I bind* (**strictus,** *bound*) : restriction, constrict, stringent, strict. [Through French : strait, straiten.]

struo, *I build* (**structus,** *built*) : construct, structure. [Through French : destroy.]

summus, *highest:* consummate, sum, summit.

sumo, *I take* (**sumptus,** *taken*) : assume, presumptuous, resume, consume.

surgo, *I rise* (sup. **surrectum**) : surge, insurrection, resurrection. [Through French : source, sortie.]

tango, *I touch* (**tactus,** *touched*) : tangible, contact.

tego, *I cover* (**tectus,** *covered*) : integument, protect, detect.

tempero, *I mix, I moderate:* temper, temperance, temperament.

tendo, *I stretch* (**tentus** or **tensus,** *stretched*) : tension, attend, contention, extensive.

teneo, *I hold* (**tentus,** *held*). [Through French : continuous, tenable, content, contain, continent, countenance.]

tento, *I try:* tentative. [Through French : tempt, attempt, taunt.]

terminus, *a boundary:* term, determine, terminus, termination.

terra, *the earth:* territory, Mediterranean, subterranean, inter, terrier.

terreo, *I frighten:* terrible, terrify, terrific, terror, deter, deterrent.

testis, *a witness:* test, protest.

traho, *I draw* (**tractus,** *drawn*) : attract. [Through French: trace, train, treat.]

tribuo, *I pay* (**tributus,** *paid*) : tribute, contributor, tributary, distribute.

turba, *a crowd:* disturb, perturbation. [Through French : trouble.]

unda, *a wave:* undulate, abundant, inundate.

unus, *one:* unite, unity, unify. [Through the French: union.]

utor, *I use* (**usus,** *having used*) : use, usual, utility, abuse.

valeo, *I am strong:* valour, valuable. [Through French : valiant, prevail.]

varius, *diverse, various:* vary, various, variety.

veho, *I carry* (**vectus,** *carried*) : vehicle.

venio, *I come:* event, prevent, intervene, venture, convenient.

verto, *I turn* (**versus,** *turned*) : adversary, conversation, reverse. [verify.]

verus, *true:* verity, veracious, very, verdict.

vestis, *a robe:* vest, vesture, invest.

via, *a way:* viaduct, devious. [Through French : voyage, convey.]

video, *I see* (**visus,** *seen*) : provide, vision, visit, advice, view. [Through French : visage, interview, envy.]

vinco, *I conquer* (**victus,** *conquered*) : victory, convict, convince, invincible.

vir, *a man;* **virtus,** *manliness, strength, bravery :* virile, virago, virtue.

vita, *life;* **vivo,** *I live* (sup. **victum**) : vivid, vital, victuals, survive, convivial.

volo, *I fly:* volatile, volley.

volvo, *I roll* (**volutus,** *rolled*) : revolve, revolution, convolvulus, volume. [Through French : vault.]

voveo, *I vow* (**votus,** *vowed*) : vote, devote. [Through French : vow.]

vox, *the voice* (**vocis,** *of the voice*) : vocal, vocabulary. [Through French : voice, vowel.]

GREEK ROOTS

aër, *the air:* aerial, air.

agōn, *a wrestling:* agony, antagonist.

angelos, *a messenger:* angel, evangelist.

archē, *the beginning, government:* monarch, archaic, anarchy.

arithmos, *number:* arithmetic.

atmos, *vapour:* atmosphere.

basis, *the foot, the foundation:* base.

biblos, *a book:* Bible, biblical, bibliography.

charactēr, *a mark:* character.

christos, *anointed:* Christ, Christian.

chronos, *time:* chronic, chronicle, anachronism, chronology.

clēros, *a lot:* clergy, clerk, clerical.

crinō, *I sift, I judge* (**crites,** *a judge*) : critic, criticize, criticism, hypocrite.

cyclos, *a wheel:* cycle, bicycle, cycloid.

demos, *the people:* democrat, demagogue.

eleēmosynē, *pity.* [Through Latin : alms, eleemosynary.]

ergon, *a work:* energy, metallurgy.

gē, *the earth:* geography, geology.

gonia, *a corner, an angle:* diagonal, polygon.

graphō, *I write;* **gramma,** *a letter:* telegram, photograph, grammar, geography.

hedra, *a seat:* cathedral.

hippos, *a horse:* hippopotamus, hippodrome.
hodos, *a way:* exodus, method.
holos, *the whole:* catholic, holograph (written throughout by the person who signs).
hydor, *water:* hydraulic.

idein, *to see:* idea, ideal.

micros, *little:* microscope.
monos, *alone:* monarch, monastery.
mousa, *a muse:* music, museum.

nomos, *a law:* economy, antinomian.

oicos, *a house:* economy, parish (**para,** *beside,* and **oicos**).

pathos, *suffering:* pathos, pathetic, sympathy.

phainō, *I appear:* phantom, fancy, fantastic, phenomenon.
poieō, *I make:* poem, poet.
polis, *a city:* police, politics.
poly, *much;* **polloi,** *many:* polygamy, polyanthus.

scholē, *leisure:* school, scholastic.
scopeō, *I view:* microscope, episcopal, bishop (from Greek *episcopos,* an overseer, through Old English *biscop*).
stellō, *I send:* apostle, epistle.
stratos, *an army:* strategy, stratagem.

tēlē, *afar:* telegram, telescope, telepathic.
theos, *a god:* theology, polytheism.
tomē, *a cutting, a division:* tome, atom, anatomy.
tropos, *a turning:* tropic, heliotrope.

zēlos, *ardour:* zeal, jealousy.

LATIN PREFIXES

a, ab, abs, *from, away:* a-vert, ab-hor, abs-tain.
ad (with modifications—**ac, af, ag, al, an, ap, ar, as, at, a**), *to, towards, on, at:* ad-mit, ac-cidental, af-fect, ag-grieve, al-low, an-nounce, ap-pear, ar-range, as-sist, at-tain, at-tach, a-gree.
ambi, amb, am, *both, round about:* ambi-dextrous, amb-itious, am-putate.
ante, anti, *before:* ante-cedent, ante-date, anti-cipate.
bis, bi, *twice:* bis-cuit, bi-cycle. [locution.
circum, *round, about:* circum-stance, circum-
con (with modifications—**cog, col, com, cor, co**), *with, together, altogether, completely:* con-vict, cog-nate, col-lect, com-mand, cor-rect, co-pastor.
contra, contro, counter, *against:* contra-dict, contro-vert, counter-act.
de, *down, away, from, completely:* de-scend, de-mand, de-part; *de* sometimes indicates reversal, as in de-populate.
demi, *half:* demi-god.
dis, di (with modification **dif**), *asunder, apart, completely:* dis-appointed, dis-tract, di-verge, dif-ficulty; *dis* sometimes indicates reversal, as in dis-place.
ex, e (with modification **ef**), *out of, from:* ex-perience, e-vent, ef-fort; *ex* sometimes means "thoroughly," as in ex-cruciate.
extra, *beyond:* extra-ordinary.
in, F. **en, em** (with modifications—**il, im, ir**), *in, into, upon:* in-crease, ir-trude, in-act, em-ploy, il-lumine, im-merse, im-prove, ir-radiate.
in (with modifications—**il, im, ir, en**), *not:* in-human, il-legal, im-possible, ir-regular, en-emy.
inter, O.F. **enter** (with modification—**intel**), *between, among:* inter-val, enter-tain, intel-lect.

intro, intra, *within:* intro-duce, intra-mural.
mis (L. **minus,** *less*), *wrong, badly:* mis-fortune, mis-chief.
non (with modifications—**ne, n-**), *not:* non-sense, ne-farious, n-euter.
ob, o, o(b)s (with modifications—**oc, of, op**), *against, in the way of, completely:* ob-tain, o-mit, os-tensible, oc-cur, of-ficer, op-pon-ent.
pene, *almost:* pen-ultimate.
per (with modification—**pel**), F. **par,** *through, thoroughly:* per-ceive, par-don, pel-lucid.
post, *after:* post-script. [tend.
pre (Med. L. **pre,** L. **prœ**), *before:* pre-dict, pre-**preter** (L. **prœter**), *beyond:* preter-natural.
pro (**pur, por, pol,** from F. **pour**), *for, instead of, before, forth:* pro-vide, pur-pose, por-trait, pol-lute.
re, red, *back, again:* re-spect, red-eem; *re* sometimes has frequentative force, as in re-volve, sometimes negative force, as in re-veal.
retro, *back, backwards:* retro-grade.
se, sed, *apart, away:* se-clude, sed-ition.
semi, *half:* semi-circle.
sine, *without:* sine-cure.
sub (with modifications—**suc, suf, sug, sum, sup, sur, sus, su**), *under:* sub-ject, suc-ceed, suf-fer, sug-gest, sum-mon, sup-ply, sur-render, sus-tain, su-spect; *sub* sometimes implies secrecy, as in sub-orn; nearness, as in sub-urb; aid, as in sub-sidy; substitution, as in sup-plant; almost, as in sub-tropical.
subter, *under:* subter-fuge.
super, F. **sur,** *over, above, beyond:* super-fluous, sur-face.
trans, tran, tra, *across, beyond:* trans-port, tran-scribe, tra-duce. [fashionable.
ultra, *beyond, extremely:* ultra-marine, ultra-
vice, F. **vis,** *instead of:* vice-roy, vis-count.

LATIN SUFFIXES

ac, al, an (ane), **ar, ary, ent, ic, il, ine, ite, ory,** *relating to, being :* cardiac, regal, human, humane, lunar, epistolary, fluent, civic, civil, feminine, definite, preparatory.

age, cy, ence (ance), **ice, ism, ment, mony, our, tion** (sion, ion), **ty, tude, ture,** *condition, state or quality of :* bondage, infancy, innocence, vigilance, service, heroism, government, matrimony, favour, condition, passion, union, cruelty, turpitude, rupture.

an, ary, ate, ee, eer (ier), **ess, ist, ite, ive, or, tor, trix, ant, ent,** *a doer, or one who is :* artisan, missionary, delegate, absentee, auctioneer, brigadier, seamstress, artist, favourite, captive, actor, doctor, executrix, informant, student.

ant, et, id, ive, tory, und, *having quality of :* dormant, dulcet, humid, festive, transitory, rotund.

ary, ory, *place for :* granary, dormitory.

ate, ite, esce, fy, ish, *to make :* abbreviate, expedite, effervesce, purify, finish.

cule, culum, icle, le, let, cle, el, ule, *diminutives :* animalcule, vasculum, particle, rivulet, corpuscle, satchel, globule.

endous, fic, *fit to cause :* stupendous, soporific.

escent, *increasing :* convalescent.

ess, *feminine :* poetess.

ferous, *producing :* carboniferous.

oon, *augmentative,* ball-oon, tromb-one.

ous, ose, *full of :* humorous, verbose.

GREEK PREFIXES

a, an, *not, without :* a-pathy, an-archy.

amphi, *about, on both sides :* amphi-theatre.

ana, *up, again :* ana-tomy, ana-lyse.

anti, *opposite to, against :* anti-pathy.

apo, *from, away :* apo-strophe, aph-orism.

arch, *chief :* arch-bishop.

auto, *self :* auto-matic.

cata, *down :* cata-ract, cath-edral.

di, *twice :* di-phthong.

dia, *through :* dia-meter.

ec, ex, *out of, from :* ec-stasy, ex-odus.

en, em, *in, on :* en-ergy, em-phasis.

epi, *upon :* epi-gram.

eu, *well :* eu-phemism.

hemi, *half :* hemi-sphere.

hyper, *above, too much :* hyper-critical.

hypo, *under :* hypo-crite.

meta, *beyond, change :* meta-morphosis.

para, *beside, from :* par-allel, para-sol.

peri, *round, about :* peri-meter.

poly, *many :* poly-syllable.

pro, *before :* pro-gramme.

syn (with modifications—**syl, sym, sy**), *without :* syn-agogue, syl-lable, sym-pathy, sy-stem.

GREEK SUFFIXES

isk, *a diminutive :* asterisk.

ism, sis, y, *condition, state, or art of :* atheism, analysis, anatomy.

ist, te, *one who does, or is :* atheist, athlete.

ic, ical, *relating to, being :* angelic, arithmetical.

ize, *verb ending :* baptize.

ma, *object of an action :* panorama.

ENGLISH PREFIXES

a, *on, in :* a-field, a-drift, a-side.

be, *about :* be-speak, be-take.

for, *completely, against :* for-bear, for-bid.

fore, *before :* fore-see, fore-tell.

gain, *against :* gain-say.

mis, *failure :* mis-behave, mis-hap.

n, *not :* n-ever, n-either, n-or.

out, *beyond :* out-do, out-run.

to, *the :* to-day.

un, *not :* un-happy, **for und** (Frisian), *and,* in un-to and un-til.

un, *reversal :* un-lock, un-do, un-say.

wan, *without :* wan-ton.

with, *against, back :* with-hold, with-stand.

I *

ENGLISH SUFFIXES

able, *what may be:* blamable.

ar, ard, er, ster, *one who is or does:* beggar, standard, baker, punster.

art, ard, *intensive:* braggart, laggard.

dom, ery, hood (head), lock, ness, ship, ter, *condition, state or quality of:* freedom, slavery, childhood, Godhead, wedlock, kindness, friendship, laughter.

en, *made of, like:* wooden, golden.

en, er, se, *to make:* darken, lower, cleanse.

ern, ward, *direction:* eastern, westward.

le, l, er, *frequentative, diminutive:* sparkle, drawl, batter.

fold (after adjectives of number), twofold, manifold.

ful, *full of:* truthful.

kin, ling, ock, ie, *diminutives:* lambkin, dwelling, hillock, birdie.

less, *without, free from:* faultless, careless.

ly, *like:* manly, sweetly.

ster, en, *marking feminine:* spinster, vixen.

ABBREVIATIONS AND CONTRACTIONS

A.A., Automobile Association.

@, at or to.

A.B., able-bodied seaman, also (L. *Artium Baccalaureus*) Bachelor of Arts. See **B.A.**

A.C. [L. *Ante Christum*], before Christ.

A/c. or **Acct.,** account.

A.C.P., Associate of the College of Preceptors.

A.D. (L. *anno Domini*), in the year of our Lord.

A.D.C., Aide-de-camp.

Adjt., Adjutant.

Ad lib. (L. *ad libitum*), at pleasure.

Æt. (L. *ætatis*), of age (so and so).

A.H. (L. *Anno Hegiræ*), in the year of the Hegira.

A.Inst.C.E., Associate of the Institution of Civil Engineers.

A.K.C., Associate of King's College (London).

A.M. (L. *Artium Magister*), Master of Arts. See **M.A.** Also (L. *Ante meridiem*) before noon.

Anon., anonymous.

A.R.A., Associate of the Royal Academy.

A.R.C.M., Associate of the Royal College of Music. [Organists.

A.R.C.O., Associate of the Royal College of

A.R.H.A., Associate of the Royal Hibernian Academy.

A.R.S.A., Associate of the Royal Society of Arts, Associate of the Royal Scottish Academy.

A.U.C. (L. *anno urbis conditæ* or *ab urbe condita*), in the year from the building of [the city—*i.e.* Rome.

b., born.

B.A., Bachelor of Arts.

Bart. or **Bt.,** Baronet.

B.B.C., British Broadcasting Corporation.

B.C., before Christ, British Columbia.

B.C.L., Bachelor of Civil Law.

B.Com., Bachelor of Commerce.

B.D., Bachelor of Divinity.

B.Ed., Bachelor of Education.

B.L., Bachelor of Law.

b.l., bill of lading.

B.M., Bachelor of Medicine.

B.O.A. British Optical Association.

Bot., botany, bought.

Bros., Brothers.

B.S. or **Ch.B.** (L. *Chirurgiæ Baccalaureus*), Bachelor of Surgery.

B.Sc., Bachelor of Science.

B.Th., Bachelor of Theology.

B.V., Blessed Virgin.

C., centigrade.

C.A., Chartered Accountant.

Cantab. (L. *Cantabrigiensis*), of Cambridge.

Cantuar. (L. *Cantuariensis*), of Canterbury.

Cap., Capital; also (L. *caput*), chapter.

Capt., Captain.

C.B., Companion of the Bath.

C.B.E., Commander of the Order of the British Empire.

C.C., County Councillor; Catholic clergyman.

C.D.V., Carte-de-visite.

C.E., Civil Engineer; Church of England.

Cent. (L. *centum*), a hundred.

Cf. (L. *confer*), compare.

C.G., Coast-guard.

C.H., Order of the Companions of Honour.

C.I., Imperial Order of the Crown of India.

C.I.E., Companion of the Order of the Indian Empire.

C.i.f., Cost, insurance, and freight.

Cir. (L. *circa, circum*), about.

C.J., Chief Justice.

C.M. or **Ch.M.** (L. *Chirurgiæ Magister*), Master of Surgery.

C.M.G., Companion of the Order of St. Michael and St. George.

C.O., Commanding Officer.

Co., Company or county.

C/o, care of.

C.o.d., Cash on delivery.

Col., Colonel; Colonial; Column.

Coll., college.

Con. (L. *contra*), against.

C.P., Common Pleas; Clerk of the Peace.

C.P.C., Clerk of the Privy Council.

C.P.S. (L. *Custos Privati Sigilli*), Keeper of the Privy Seal.

Cr., Credit, Creditor.
C.S. (L. *Custos Sigilli*), Keeper of the Seal ; Civil Service ; Court of Session.
C.S.I., Companion of the Star of India.
Cur., curt., current ; this month.
C.V.O., Commander of the Royal Victorian Order. [weight.
Cwt. (L. *centum* and E. *weight*), hundred-

D., 500 ; d. (L. *denarius*, pl. *denarii*), penny or pence.
D.B.E., Dame Commander of the Order of the British Empire.
D.C.L., Doctor of Civil Law.
D.C.M., Distinguished Conduct Medal.
D.D. (L. *Divinitatis Doctor*), Doctor of Divinity.
D.F., Defender of the Faith.
D.G. (L. *Deo Gratia*), By the Grace of God.
D.Lit. or Litt., Doctor of Literature.
D.L.O., Dead Letter Office.
Do. (It. ditto), the same.
Doz., dozen.
D.P.H., Diploma in Public Health.
D.Phil., Doctor of Philosophy.
Dr., Doctor, Debtor.
D.Sc., Doctor of Science.
D.S.O., Distinguished Service Order.
D.T., Doctor of Theology ; also delirium tremens.
D.V. (L. *Deo volente*), God willing.
Dwt. (L. *denarius* and E. *weight*), penny-weight.

Eblan. (L. *Eblanensis*), of Dublin.
Ebur., Ebor. (L. *Eburacum*), York ; (L. *Eburacensis*), of York.
E.C., Established Church ; East Central (London postal district).
E.E., Electrical Engineer ; Errors excepted.
E.E.T.S., Early English Text Society.
e.g. (L. *exempli gratia*), for example.
E.I., East Indies ; East Indian. [Horse.
E.M. (L. *Equitum Magister*), Master of the Esq. or Esqr., Esquire.
Etc. (L. *et cetera*), and the rest.
Et seq. or sq. or sqq. (L. *et sequentes* or *sequentia*), and the following.

F. or Fahr., Fahrenheit.
F.A.S., Fellow of the Antiquarian Society.
F.B.A. Fellow of the British Academy.
F.B.O.A. Fellow of the British Optical Fcp., foolscap. [Association.
F.C.S., Fellow of the Chemical Society.
F.D. (L. *Fidei Defensor*), Defender of the Faith.
Fec. (L. *fecit*), (he or she) made (it).
F.E.I.S., Fellow of the Educational Institute of Scotland.
F.E.S., Fellow of the Entomological Society ; Fellow of the Ethnological Society.
F.F.A., Fellow of the Faculty of Actuaries.
F.F.P.S., Fellow of the Faculty of Physicians and Surgeons.
F.G.S., Fellow of the Geological Society.
F.I.A., Fellow of the Institute of Actuaries.

F.I.C., Fellow of the Institute of Chemistry.
F.M., Field Marshal.
Fo. or Fol., folio or folios.
F.o.b., free on board.
F.P.S., Fellow of the Philological Society.
F.R.A.S., Fellow of the Royal Astronomical Society. [Physicians.
F.R.C.P., Fellow of the Royal College of
F.R.C.P.E., Fellow of the Royal College of Physicians, Edinburgh. [Surgeons.
F.R.C.S., Fellow of the Royal College of
F.R.C.S.E., Fellow of the Royal College of Surgeons, Edinburgh.
F.R.C.S.I., Fellow of the Royal College of Surgeons, Ireland.
F.R.C.S.L., Fellow of the Royal College of Surgeons, London. [Society.
F.R.G.S., Fellow of the Royal Geographical
F.R.Hist.S., Fellow of the Royal Historical Society.
F.R.I.B.A., Fellow of the Royal Institute of British Architects.
F.R.S., Fellow of the Royal Society.
F.R.S.E., Fellow of the Royal Society, Edinburgh.
F.R.S.G.S., Fellow of the Royal Scottish Geographical Society.
F.R.S.S., Fellow of the Royal Statistical Society. [Antiquaries.
F.S.A., Fellow of the Society of Arts, *or* of
F.Z.S., Fellow of the Zoological Society.

G.B., Great Britain.
G.C., George Cross.
G.C.I.E., Grand Commander of the Indian Empire.
G.C.M., greatest common measure.
G.C.M.G., Grand Cross of St Michael and St George.
G.C.S.I., Knight Grand Commander of the Star of India.
G.C.V.O., Grand Cross of the Royal Victorian Order.
G.H.Q., General Head Quarters.
G.M.T., Greenwich Mean Time.
G.O.C., General Officer Commanding.
G.P.O., General Post Office.
G.R. (L. *Georgius Rex*), King George.
G.R.I. (L. *Georgius Rex Imperator*), George, King and Emperor.

H.B.M., His Britannic Majesty.
H.H., His (or Her) Highness.
H.I.H., His (or Her) Imperial Highness.
H.M., His (or Her) Majesty.
H.M.I.(S.), His Majesty's Inspector (of Schools). [Service.
H.M.S., His Majesty's Ship, His Majesty's
H.P., horse-power.
H.R.H., His (or Her) Royal Highness.
H.S.H., His (or Her) Serene Highness.

Ib. or Ibid. (L. *ibidem*), in the same place.
I.C. or I.X., Iesus Christus—Jesus Christ. (X in Greek = guttural Ch.)
I.C.S., Indian Civil Service.
Id. (L. *idem*), the same.
i.e. (L. *id est*), that is.

I.H.S. (L. *Iesus Hominum Salvator*), Jesus the Saviour of men.
I.L.P., Independent Labour Party.
Imp. (L. *Imperator*), Emperor, Imperial.
incog. (It. *incognito*), unknown, with name concealed.
I.N.R.I. (L. *Iesus Nazarenus Rex Iudæorum*), Jesus of Nazareth, King of the Jews.
I.O.F., Independent Order of Foresters.
I.O.G.T., Independent Order of Good Templars.
I.O.O.F., Independent Order of Oddfellows.
I.O.U., I owe you.
I.S.O., Imperial Service Order.

J.C., Jesus Christ ; Justice Clerk.
J.C.D. (L. *Juris Civilis Doctor*), Doctor of Civil Law.
J.P., Justice of the Peace.
J.U.D. (L. *Juris Utriusque Doctor*), Doctor of both Laws (Canon and Civil).
Jun., Jr., Junior.

K.B., Knight of the Bath.
K.B.E., Knight Commander of the Order of the British Empire.
K.C., King's Counsel.
K.C.B., Knight Commander of the Bath.
K.C.I.E., Knight Commander of the Indian Empire.
K.C.M.G., Knight Commander of St Michael and St George.   [India.
K.C.S.I., Knight Commander of the Star of
K.G., Knight of the Garter.
Kilom., Km., kilometre.
K.M., Knight of Malta.
K.P., Knight of St Patrick.
K.T., Knight of the Thistle.
Kt., Knight.

£, l, or **L** (L. *libra*), pounds sterling.
L. or **lb.** (L. *libra*), pounds in weight.
L.A., Law Agent ; Literate in Arts.
Lat., latitude.
L.C., Lord Chancellor ; Lord Chamberlain.
L.C.C., London County Council.
L.C.M., least common multiple.
L.C.P., Licentiate of the College of Preceptors.
L.D.S., Licentiate of Dental Surgery.
L.I., Light Infantry.
Lib. (L. *liber*), book.
Lieut., Lieutenant.   [Literature.
Litt.D. (L. *Literarum Doctor*), Doctor of
L.L.A., Lady Literate in Arts.
LL.B. (L. *Legum Baccalaureus*), Bachelor of Laws.
LL.D. (L. *Legum Doctor*), Doctor of Laws.
L.M., Long Metre ; Licentiate in Midwifery.
Long., longitude.
Loq. (L. *loquitur*), he speaks.
L.R.A.M., Licentiate of the Royal Academy of Music.   [Music.
L.R.C.M., Licentiate of the Royal College of
L.R.C.P., Licentiate of the Royal College of Physicians.

L.R.C.P.E., Licentiate of the Royal College of Physicians, Edinburgh.
L.R.C.S., Licentiate of the Royal College of Surgeons.
L.R.C.S.E., Licentiate of the Royal College of Surgeons, Edinburgh.
L.R.C.V.S., Licentiate of the Royal College of Veterinary Surgeons.
L.S., Linnæan Society.
L.S.D. (L. *libræ, solidi, denarii*), pounds, shillings, pence.

M. (L. *mille*), thousand ; also (L. *meridies*), noon ; Monsieur.
M.A., Master of Arts.
M.B. (L. *Medicinæ Baccalaureus*), Bachelor of Medicine.
M.B.E., Member of the Order of the British Empire.
M.C., Master of Ceremonies ; Military Cross.
M.Com., Master of Commerce (Univ. of Birmingham).
M.Comm., Master of Commerce and Administration (Univ. of Manchester).
M.D. (L. *Medicinæ Doctor*), Doctor of Medicine.
M.E., Mechanical, Mining, or Military Engineer.
Mem., Memorandum.
Messrs or **MM.** (F. *Messieurs*), gentlemen.
M.F.H., Master of Foxhounds.
M.Inst.C.E., Member of the Institute of Civil Engineers.
M.I.E.E., Member of the Institution of Electrical Engineers.
Mlle. (F.), Mademoiselle (E. *Miss*).
M.M., Military Medal.
Mme. (F.), Madame (E. *Mrs*).
M.O.H., Medical Officer of Health.
M.P., Member of Parliament.   [Society.
M.P.S., Member of the Pharmaceutical
M.R., Master of the Rolls.
Mr, Master or Mister.
M.R.C.P., Member of the Royal College of Physicians *or* Preceptors.   [Surgeons.
M.R.C.S., Member of the Royal College of
M.R.C.V.S., Member of the Royal College of Veterinary Surgeons.   [Academy.
M.R.I.A., Member of the Royal Irish
Mrs, Mistress.
M.R.S.T., Member of the Royal Society of Teachers.
MS., manuscript ; **MSS.**, manuscripts.
Mus.B., Bachelor of Music.
Mus.D., Doctor of Music.   [Order.
M.V.O., Member of the Royal Victorian

N.B., New Brunswick ; (L. *nota bene*), note well.   [dissenting.
Nem. con. (L. *nemine contradicente*), no one
Nem. dis. (L. *nemine dissentiente*), no one dissenting.
Non-Com., non-commissioned.
Non. Con., not content ; dissenting (House of Lords).
Non seq. (L. *non sequitur*), it does not follow.
No., Nos., number, numbers (in order).

N.P., Notary Public.
N.S., new style, Nova Scotia.
N.T. New Testament.
N.Z., New Zealand.

Ob. (L. *obiit*), (he or she) died. [Empire.
O.B.E., Officer of the Order of the British
O.C., Officer in Command.
O.H.M.S., On His Majesty's Service.
O.M., Order of Merit.
O.S., old style.
O.T., Old Testament.
Oxon. (L. *Oxonia*), Oxford, also (L. *Oxoniensis*) of Oxford.
Oz., ounce *or* ounces.

Par., Paragraph. [Constable.
P.C., Privy Council *or* Councillor; Police
p.c., post-card, per cent.
Per cent. (L. *per centum*), by the hundred.
Ph.D. (L. *Philosophiæ Doctor*), Doctor of Philosophy.
Pinx. or **Pxt.** (L. *pinxit*), he (or she) painted it.
P.L.C., Poor Law Commissioners.
P.M. (L. *post meridiem*), after noon.
P.M.G., Postmaster-General.
P. & O., Peninsular and Oriental (Steam Navigation Co.).
P.O., post office, postal order.
pop., population.
P.P., Parish Priest.
pp., pages.
P.P.C. (F. *pour prendre congé*), to take leave.
P.R.A., President of the Royal Academy.
Pres., President.
Prof., Professor.
Pro tem. (L. *pro tempore*), for the time being.
Prox. (L. *proximo*), next month.
P.R.S., President of the Royal Society.
P.R.S.A., President of the Royal Scottish Academy. [Seal.
P.S. (L. *post scriptum*), written after; Privy
P.T.O., please turn over.
Pxt. (L. *pinxit*), (he or she) painted (it).

Q. or **Qu.**, Query or question.
Q.E.D. (L. *quod erat demonstrandum*), which was to be proved.
Q.E.F., which was to be done.
Q.-M., Quarter-master.
Q.-M.-G., Quarter-Master-General.
Q.S., Quarter Sessions.
q.v. (L. *quod vide*), which see.

R. (L. *rex*), king; also (L. *regina*), queen; Réaumur (thermometer). [Artillery.
R.A., Royal Academy or Academician, Royal
R.A.C., Royal Automobile Club.
R.A.F., Royal Air Force.
R.A.M., Royal Academy of Music.
R.A.M.C., Royal Army Medical Corps.
R.A.S., Royal Agricultural Society; Royal Asiatic Society; Royal Astronomical Society.
R.C.P., Royal College of Physicians.
R.C.S., Royal College of Surgeons.

R.D., Rural Dean.
R.E., Royal Engineers.
Rev., Reverend.
R.F.A., Royal Field Artillery.
R.G.S., Royal Geographical Society.
R.H.A., Royal Horse Artillery.
R.H.S., Royal Historical or Horticultural Society. [tects.
R.I.B.A., Royal Institute of British Archi-
R.I.P. (L. *requiescat in pace*), may he (or she) rest in peace.
R.M., Royal Marines, Royal Mail, Resident Magistrate.
R.M.A., Royal Military Academy.
R.M.S., Royal Mail Steamer.
R.N., Royal Navy.
R.N.R., Royal Naval Reserve.
R.S., Royal Society.
R.S.A., Royal Society of Antiquaries, Royal Scottish Academy, Royal Society of Arts.
R.S.E., Royal Society of Edinburgh.
R.S.F.S.R., Russian Soviet Federal Socialist Republic.
R.S.V.P. (F. *répondez, s'il vous plaît*), reply, if you please.
Rt. Hon., Right Honourable. [Colours.
R.W.S., Royal Society of Painters in Water-

s., shilling.
S.A., South Africa.
Sc. (L. *scilicet*), to wit, namely. [(it).
Sc. or **sculp.** (L. *sculpsit*), (he or she) engraved
Sc.B. (L. *Scientiæ Baccalaureus*), Bachelor of Science.
Sc.D. (L. *Scientiæ Doctor*), Doctor of Science.
Seq. or **Sqq.** (L. *sequentes or sequentia*), the following, the next.
S.J., Society of Jesus.
S.O.S., Wireless signal sent out by ships in last extremity of distress.
S.P.C.A., Society for the Prevention of Cruelty to Animals.
S.P.C.C., Society for the Prevention of Cruelty to Children.
S.P.C.K., Society for the Propagation of Christian Knowledge. [Gospel.
S.P.G., Society for the Propagation of the
Sp. gr., specific gravity.
S.P.Q.R. (L. *Senatus Populusque Romanus*), Senate and People of Rome.
s.s., steamship.
S.S.C., Solicitor before the Supreme Courts (Scotland).
St., Saint; Street; Stone.
Stg., sterling.
s.v. (L. *sub voce or sub verbo*), under the word or title.

T.C.D., Trinity College, Dublin.
T.T.L., to take leave.

U.K., United Kingdom.
Ult. (L. *ultimo*), last; of the last month.
U.S.A., United States of America.
U.S.N., United States Navy.
U.S.S.R., Union of Soviet Socialist Republics.

v. (L. *versus*), against; also (L. *vide*) see.

V.A., Vicar-Apostolic; Vice-Admiral; Royal Order of Victoria and Albert.

V.A.D., Voluntary Aid Detachment.

V.C., Victoria Cross.

Verb. sap. (L. *verbum satis sapienti*), a word is enough for a wise man.

V.G., Vicar-General.

Vid. (L. *vide*), see.

Viz. (L. *videlicet*), namely.

V.S., Veterinary Surgeon.

W.S. Writer to the Signet (Scotland).

X. or **Xt.**, Christ. (X in Greek stands for guttural Ch.)

Xm. or **Xmas**, Christmas.

Y.M.C.A., Young Men's Christian Association.

Y.W.C.A., Young Women's Christian Association.

Z.S., Zoological Society.

SPELLING HINTS

English spelling is so far from phonetic that hard and fast rules are out of the question. The following hints, however, may prove useful:—

1. To form the plural of nouns ending in *y* preceded by a consonant, change the *y* to *i* and add *es : lady, ladies ; duty, duties.* **(Note:** the singular of such words originally ended in *ie.*) When the *y* is preceded by a vowel, add *s : boy, boys ; day, days.*

2. Similarly form the 3rd singular of verbs ending in *y : deny, denies ; display, displays.* The past tense of such verbs is similarly formed : *deny, denied ; display, displayed.*

3. To form the plural of nouns ending in *s, x, ch, sh,* add *es : grass, grasses ; fox, foxes ; church, churches ; fish, fishes.*

4. To form the plural of nouns ending in *o* preceded by a consonant, add *es : potato, potatoes.*

Common Exceptions : *altos, cameos, cantos, grottos, pianos, mementos, tiros.*

5. To form the plural of nouns ending in *f* or *fe,* change *f* or *fe* into *ves : leaf, leaves ; knife, knives.*

Common Exceptions : *hoofs, reefs, roofs, briefs, chiefs, fifes, griefs, gulfs, proofs, safes.*

6. Drop silent *e* before a suffix beginning with a vowel : *come, coming ; cure, curable.* **(Note:** the *e* is retained to soften *c* or *g,* as in *serviceable, courageous, singeing* (pres. part. of *singe*), and in *dyeing* (pres. part. of *dye*), to distinguish it from *dying.*

7. In compound words *ll* frequently becomes *l : all, almost ; till, until ; full, fill, fulfil ; skill, full, skilful ; thrall, enthral.*

8. When a syllable is added to a word with a single final consonant, such consonant is frequently but not always doubled : *travel, travelled, traveller ; run, running, runner ; appal, appalled, appalling ; wool, woollen ; sham, shamming ; flog, flogging ; bar, barred, barring.*

Common Exceptions : *appeal, appealed ; benefit, benefited.*

9. Final *our* becomes *or* before adding *ous : humour, humorous ; valour, valorous.*

10. Diphthongs **EI, IE.**

> "When the diphthong rhymes with **key**
> The **i** must go before the **e**
> Unless the diphthong follows **c.**"

Examples : *belief, field, piece, siege, receive, deceit.*

Common Exceptions : *either, neither, plebeian, skein, seize, weir, weird.*

11. Many examples of double consonant are accounted for by the **law of assimilation,** the final consonant of a prefix becoming the same as the first consonant of the root of a word. In this connection note the various modifications of the Latin prefixes *ad, con, in, ob, sub,* and the Greek prefix *syn : accident, affect, aggrieve, allow, announce, appear, arrange, assist, attain, collect, command, correct, illumine, immerse, irradiate, occur, opponent, succeed, suffer, surrender, syllogism, symmetry.*

ENGLISH AUTHORS AND THEIR WORKS

A

Abercrombie, Lascelles (1881-1938), poet and critic: *Interludes and Poems ; Deborah ; The Epic ; Thomas Hardy.*

Addison, Joseph (1672-1719), poet and essayist : *The Campaign* (on Blenheim); *Rosamund* (opera); *Cato ; The Free-holder ;* contributed to *The Tatler* and *The Spectator.*

Ælfric (955 ?-1022), scholar: *Homilies ; Latin Grammar.* Translated parts of Old Testament. *Life of Ethelwold.*

Ainsworth, William Harrison (1805-1882), novelist : *The Tower of London ; Windsor Castle ; Old Saint Paul's.*

Akenside, Mark (1721-1770), poet : *The Pleasures of the Imagination ; Hymn to the Naiads.*

Alcott, Louisa May (1832-1888), American novelist : *Little Women ; Little Men.*

Alcuin (735-804), scholar : Letters and Latin poems.

Alfred the Great (848-900 or 901), translator: said to have begun *Old English Chronicle.* Translated—Orosius' *Histories ;* Bede's *Historia Ecclesiastica ;* Boethius ; Gregory's *Cura Pastoralis.*

Andrewes, Lancelot (1555-1626), translator and theologian : *A Manual of Private Devotions.*

Anselm (1033-1109), theologian: *Cur Deus Homo ; De Incarnatione Verbi ; Monologion,* etc.

Arbuthnot, Doctor John (1667-1735), physician and wit : *The History of John Bull ; The Art of Political Lying ; Memoirs of Martin Scriblerus.*

Armstrong, John (1709-1779), physician and poet : *The Art of Preserving Health.*

Arnold, Matthew (1822-1888), poet and critic : Poems :—*Sohrab and Rustum ; Balder Dead ; Tristram and Iseult ; The Scholar Gipsy ; Thyrsis.* Shorter poems, including : *Rugby Chapel ; Westminster Abbey ; Mycerinus ; Empedocles on Etna ; Requiescat ; The Forsaken Merman.* Prose :—*Essays in Criticism ; Celtic Literature ; On Translating Homer ; Literature and Dogma ; St. Paul and Protestantism.*

Arnold, Thomas (1795-1842), headmaster of Rugby : *History of Rome.*

Ascham, Roger (1515-1568), scholar : *The Scholemaster.*

Atterbury, Francis (1662-1732), Bishop of Rochester : Sermons, dissertations and letters.

Austen, Jane (1775-1817), novelist: *Northanger Abbey ; Pride and Prejudice ; Sense and Sensibility ; Emma ; Mansfield Park ; Persuasion.*

Aytoun, William Edmondstoune (1813-1865), poet : *Lays of the Scottish Cavaliers ; Firmilian ; Bothwell ;* joint author of the *Bon Gaultier Ballads.*

B

Bacon, Francis, Lord Verulam, Viscount St Albans (1561-1626), essayist, historian and scientist : *Essays ; The Advancement of Learning ; Novum Organum ; Reign of Henry VII. ; De Augmentis ; Sylva Sylvorum ; The New Atlantis.*

Bacon, Roger (1214 ?-1294), scientist and philosopher: *Opus Majus ; Opus Secundum ;* and *Opus Tertium ;* also *Compendium Studii Philosophiæ* and *Compendium Studii Theologicæ.*

Bagehot, Walter (1826-1877), economist and miscellaneous writer: *The English Constitution ; Physics and Politics ; Lombard Street.*

Bailey, Philip James (1816-1902), poet : *Festus.*

Baillie, Joanna (1762-1851), dramatist and poet : *Plays of the Passions ; Fugitive Verses.*

Bale, John (1495-1563), writer of miracle plays : *Kyng Johan.*

Ballantyne, Robert Michael (1825-1894), novelist : *The Young Fur Traders ; The Coral Island ; Ungava ; Martin Rattler.*

Barbour, John (1316?-1395), poet : *Brus* (historical poem) ; attributed—*Buik of Alexander, A Troye Romance,* and collection, *Legends of the Saints.*

Barclay, Alexander (1475?-1552), poet : *The Ship of Fools* (translation) ; *Eclogues.*

Barclay, Robert (1648-1690), prose writer: *Apology for the Quakers.*

Barham, Richard Harris (1788-1845), novelist and humorous poet : *Ingoldsby Legends.*

Barnes, William (1801-1886), poet : Poems in Dorset dialect.

Barnfield, Richard (1574-1627), poet : *As it Fell upon a Day.*

Barrie, Sir James Matthew (1860-1937), novelist and dramatist : Novels and Sketches—*Auld Licht Idylls ; When a Man's Single ; An Edinburgh Eleven ; A Window in Thrums ; My Lady Nicotine ; The Little Minister ; Sentimental Tommy*

Plays— *Jane Anne; Professor's Love Story; Little White Bird; Little Minister; Quality Street; The Admirable Crichton; Peter Pan; Dear Brutus; What Every Woman Knows; Mary Rose.*

Baxter, Richard (1615–1691), theologian: *The Saints' Everlasting Rest.*

Beattie, James (1735–1803), poet: *The Minstrel.*

Beaumont and Fletcher (Francis Beaumont, 1584–1616, and John Fletcher, 1579–1625), poets and playwrights; In collaboration:—*Philaster; The Maid's Tragedy; A King and No King; The Knight of the Burning Pestle; The Scornful Lady.*

Beckford, William (1760?–1844), romance writer: *Vathek.*

Beddoes, Thomas Lovell (1803–1849), poet and dramatist: *The Bride's Tragedy; Death's Jest Book; Poems.*

Bede, The Venerable (673–735), theologian and historian: Lives of St Cuthbert, and the Abbots of Jarrow and Wearmouth; Ecclesiastical History of the English People.

Behn, Mrs Aphra (1640–1689), poet, playwright and novelist: *The Rover, or the Banished Cavalier; The City Heiress; The Town Fop; The Lucky Chance; The Widow Ranter; Sir Patient Fancy.*

Bek, Thomas, of Castleford (fl. 1320): *Chronicle.*

Belloc, Hilaire (born 1870), journalist and miscellaneous writer: *Danton; Robespierre; The Path to Rome; Cautionary Tales.*

Bennett, Arnold (1867–1931), novelist and dramatist: *Anna of the Five Towns; The Old Wives' Tale; Clayhanger; Hilda Lessways; Sacred and Profane Love; Buried Alive; The Card; The Lion's Share; Milestones.*

Bentham, Jeremy (1748–1832), political writer: *A Fragment on Government; Introduction to the Principles of Morals.*

Bentley, Richard (1662–1742), critic: *Dissertation upon the Letters of Phalaris.*

Berkeley, George (1685–1753), philosopher: *Essay towards a New Theory of Vision; Principles of Human Knowledge; Hylas and Philonous; Alciphron, or the Minute Philosopher; Siris.*

Berners, Lord: see Bourchier.

Besant, Sir Walter (1836–1901), prose writer: *All Sorts and Conditions of Men.* In collaboration with James Rice (1844–82), *Ready Money Mortiboy; The Golden Butterfly.*

Binyon, Lawrence (1869–1943), poet: *The Art of Asia; English Poetry in Relation to Painting and Other Arts; The Four Years; Sakuntala.*

Black, William (1841–1898), novelist: *In Silk Attire; A Daughter of Heth; The Strange Adventures of a Phaeton; A Princess of Thule.*

Blackmore, Richard Doddridge (1825–1900), novelist: *Lorna Doone; The Maid of Sker; Cripps the Carrier; Perlycross.*

Blackstone, Sir William (1723–1780), legal writer: *Commentaries on the Laws of England.*

Blair, Robert (1699–1746), poet: *The Grave.*

Blake, William (1757–1827), poet: *Poetical Sketches; Songs of Innocence; The Book of Thel; Songs of Experience; Urizen: or The Marriage of Heaven and Hell.*

Blind Harry (Henry the Minstrel, late fifteenth century), poet: *Book of William Wallace.*

Borrow, George (1803–1881), prose writer: *The Zincali, or The Gypsies in Spain; The Bible in Spain; Lavengro; The Romany Rye; Wild Wales.*

Boswell, James (1740–1795), prose writer: *Account of Corsica; Life of Johnson; Journal of a Tour to the Hebrides.*

Boucicault Dion (1820–1890), dramatist: *The Colleen Bawn; The Shaughraun.*

Bourchier, John, Lord Berners (1467–1533), translator: *Froissart's Chronicles; Huon of Bordeaux; Golden Book of Marcus Aurelius.*

Boyle, Robert (1627–1691), prose writer: *The Sceptical Chymist; The Excellency of Theology compared with Natural Philosophy.*

Braddon, Mary Elizabeth (1837–1915), novelist: *Lady Audley's Secret; Aurora Floyd.*

Bridges, Robert (1844–1930), poet: *Prometheus the Fire Giver; Eros and Psyche; Nero; Palicio; Return of Ulysses; Christian Captives; Achilles in Scyros; Humours of the Court; Feast of Bacchus.*

Brome, Richard (d. 1652?), poet and dramatist: *A Jovial Crew.*

Brontë, Anne (1820–1849), novelist: *Agnes Grey; The Tenant of Wildfell Hall.*

Brontë, Charlotte (1816–1855), novelist: *Jane Eyre; Shirley; Villette.*

Brontë, Emily (1818–1848), novelist: *Wuthering Heights.*

Brooke, Henry (1703–1783), poet, dramatist and novelist: *Fool of Quality.*

Brooke, Rupert (1887–1915), poet: *Poems, including England.*

Brooke, Stopford (1832–1916), critic: *Golden Book of Coleridge;* Studies of Browning, Tennyson, Shelley, and of English Literature generally.

Brougham and Vaux, Henry Peter Brougham, 1st baron (1778–1868), critic: *Sketches of the Statesmen of the Time of George III.; Lives of Men of Letters and Science; Autobiography.*

Brown, John (1810–1882), prose writer: *Rab and His Friends; Pet Marjorie; Our Dogs.*

Browne, Sir Thomas (1605–1682), prose writer: *Religio Medici; Pseudodoxia Epidemica; The Garden of Cyrus; Hydriotaphia; Christian Morals; A Letter to a Friend.*

Browne 265 Campbell

Browne, William (1591–1643), poet: *Britannia's Pastorals*; *Shepherd's Pipe*.

Browning, Elizabeth Barrett (1806–1861), poet: *Essay on Mind*; translation of *Prometheus Bound*; *The Seraphim*; *Lady Geraldine's Courtship*; *Drama of Exile*; *The Poet's Vow*; *Cowper's Grave*; *Sonnets from the Portuguese*; *Casa Guidi Windows*; *Aurora Leigh*.

Browning, Robert (1812–1889), poet: *Paracelsus*; *Sordello*; *Pippa Passes*; *Strafford*; *Colombe's Birthday*; *Luria*; *Dramatic Lyrics*; *Dramatic Romances*; *Christmas Eve and Easter Day*; *Men and Women*; *Dramatis Personæ*; *The Ring and the Book*; *Balaustion's Adventure*; *Prince Hohenstiel-Schwangau*; *Fifine at the Fair*.

Bryant, William Cullen (1794–1878), American poet and journalist: *The Embargo*; *Sketches of the Times*; *The Fountain*.

Bryce, James, Viscount (1838–1922), prose writer: *The Plague of London*; *The May Queen*; *The Holy Roman Empire*; *The American Commonwealth*.

Buchan, John, Baron Tweedsmuir (1875–1940), novelist, historian, biographer: *Salute to Adventurers*; *The Thirty-nine Steps*; *Greenmantle*; *Mr Standfast*; *Midwinter*; *Oliver Cromwell*.

Buchanan, George (1506–1582), poet and scholar: *Chamæleon*; *Admonition to the Trew Lordis*; *History of Scotland*.

Buchanan, Robert (1841–1901), poet: *London Poems*.

Buckhurst, Thomas Sackville, Lord (1536–1608), dramatist: *Gorboduc* (in conjunction with Thomas Norton).

Bunyan, John (1628–1688), prose writer: *Pilgrim's Progress*; *The Holy War*; *Grace Abounding*; *Life and Death of Mr Badman*.

Burke, Edmund (1729–1797), prose writer: *Vindication of Natural Society*; *Inquiry into the Ideas of the Sublime and Beautiful*; *Observations on the Present State of the Nation*; *Thoughts on Present Discontents*; *Speech on American Taxation*; *Speech on Conciliation with America*; *Reflections on the French Revolution*; *Thoughts on French Affairs*; *Letter to a Noble Lord*; *Letter on a Regicide Peace*.

Burnet, Gilbert (1643–1715), Bishop of Salisbury: *History of the Reformation*; *History of My Own Times*.

Burnet, Thomas (about 1635–1715), theological writer: *The Sacred Theory of the Earth*.

Burney, Frances, Madam D'Arblay (1752–1840), novelist: *Evelina*; *Cecilia*; *Camilla*; *The Wanderer*; *Memoirs of Dr Burney*.

Burns, Robert (1759–1796), poet: Songs include: *Mary Morison*; *To Mary in Heaven*; *Ae Fond Kiss*; *Ye Banks and Braes*; *John Anderson, my Jo*; *Auld Lang Syne*; *Comin' Thro' the Rye*; *Bonnie Jean*; *My Nannie O*; *O Wert Thou in the Cauld Blast*. Satires: *The Holy Fair*; *Holy Willie's Prayer*; *To the Unco' Guid*. Poems on Man: *The Twa Dogs*; *A Man's a Man for a' That*. National Poems: *The Cottar's Saturday Night*; *Hallowe'en*; *The Jolly Beggars*; *Tam o' Shanter*; *Scots Wha Hae*; *The Brigs o' Ayr*. Nature Poems: *The Birks o' Aberfeldy*; *To a Mouse*; *To a Mountain Daisy*. Humorous Poems: *Address to the De'il*; *Duncan Gray's Wooing*; *Captain Grose's Peregrinations*.

Burton, Robert (1577–1640), scholar: *The Anatomy of Melancholy*.

Burton, Sir Richard (1821–1890), traveller and linguist: *Pilgrimage to El Medinah and Mecca*; *Translation of Arabian Nights*.

Bury, Richard of (1281–1345), critic: *Philobiblon*.

Butler, Joseph (1692–1752), Bishop of Bristol: *Sermons*; *The Analogy of Religion*.

Butler, Samuel (1612–1680), poet: *Hudibras*; *The Elephant and the Moon*.

Butler, Samuel (1835–1902), novelist: *Erewhon*; *Erewhon Revisited*; *The Way of All Flesh*; *Odyssey*; *Note-books*.

Byrom, John (1691–1763), poet: *Christians Awake*.

Byron, Lord (1788–1824), poet: *Hours of Idleness*; *English Bards and Scotch Reviewers*; *Childe Harold's Pilgrimage*; *The Giaour*; *The Bride of Abydos*; *The Corsair*; *Lara*; *The Siege of Corinth*; *Parisina*; *The Prisoner of Chillon*; *The Dream*; *Manfred*; *Beppo*; *Don Juan*; *The Prophecy of Dante*; *Marino Faliero*; *Sardanapalus*; *The Two Foscari*; *Cain*; *The Vision of Judgment*; *When We Two Parted*; *Maid of Athens*.

C

Caedmon (died 680), poet: Paraphrases of the early Scriptures into verse, also of the lives of Christ and His Apostles.

Caine, Sir Thomas Henry Hall (1853–1931), novelist: *The Shadow of a Crime*; *The Son of Hagar*; *The Deemster*; *The Bondman*; *The Scapegoat*; *The Manxman*; *The Christian*; *The Eternal City*; *The Prodigal Son*.

Calverley, Charles Stuart (1831–1884): Parodies; *Verses and Translations*; *Fly-leaves*.

Cambrensis, Giraldus (1147–1223), churchman and historian: *Topography of Ireland*; *History of the Conquest of Ireland*; *Description of Wales*; *Itinerary*.

Camden, William (1551–1623), historian: *Britannia*.

Campbell, Thomas (1777–1844), poet: *The Pleasures of Hope*; *Gertrude of Wyoming*. Popular shorter poems: *Ye Mariners of England*; *Hohenlinden*; *The Battle of the Baltic*; *Lord Ullin's Daughter*; *The Soldier's Dream*.

Campion, Thomas (1575 ?–1619 ?), poet and musician: Lyrics.

Carew, Thomas (1594 ?–1639), poet: *Cœlum Britannicum* (masque); *The Rapture; Disdain Returned; The Cruel Mistress; Ask me no more.*

Carlyle, Thomas (1795–1881), essayist and historian: *Life of Schiller;* translation of Goethe's *Wilhelm Meister;* Essays on German writers; Essays on Burns, Johnson, Voltaire, etc.; *Sartor Resartus; The French Revolution; Chartism; Heroes and Hero Worship; Past and Present; Cromwell's Letters and Speeches; Latter Day Pamphlets; Life of Sterling; History of Frederick the Great.*

"Carroll, Lewis" (Rev. Charles Lutwidge Dodgson, 1832–1898), romance writer: *Alice in Wonderland; Through the Looking-Glass.*

Cavendish, George (about 1500–1561): *Life of Wolsey.*

Cavendish, Henry (1731–1810), physicist: Record of research on analysis of air and on water.

Caxton, William (1422–1491), author, translator and printer: Translations of *Reynard the Foxe; The Golden Legend; Lyf of Jason.*

Channing, William Ellery (1780–1842), American critic: *Remarks on the Character and Writings of John Milton; Remarks on the Life and Character of Napoleon Bonaparte; Essay on the Character and Writings of Fénelon.*

Chapman, George (1559–1634), poet and dramatist: *All Fools; Monsieur d'Olive; Bussy d'Ambois; The Conspiracy of Byron; The Tragedy of Byron; The Revenge of Bussy d'Ambois; Ovid's Banquet of Sense;* completed Marlowe's *Hero and Leander; Iliad* (translation into verse); *Odyssey* (translation).

Chatterton, Thomas (1752–1770), poet: *The Rowley Poems; The Excelente Balade of Charitie.*

Chaucer, Geoffrey (1340–1400), poet: *The Parlement of Foules; The Hous of Fame; Troilus and Criseyde; Legende of Good Women; Canterbury Tales,* etc.

Cheke, Sir John (1514–1557), prose writer: *Hurt of Sedition.*

Chesterfield, Philip Dormer Stanhope, Earl of (1694–1773): Letters to his Son.

Chesterton, G. K. (1874–1936), essayist and novelist: *Man Alive; The Victorian Age in Literature; The Flying Inn; A Short History of England; Irish Impressions; Magic.*

Chillingworth, William (1602–1644); *The Religion of the Protestants a Safe Way to Salvation.*

Church, Richard William (1815–1890), prose writer: *The Oxford Movement.*

Churchill, Charles (1731–1764), poet: *The Rosciad; Night; The Prophecy of Famine; Epistle to Hogarth; The Ghost; Gotham.*

Cibber, Colley (1671–1757), poet: *Love's Last Shift; The Provoked Husband; The Nonjuror.*

Clarendon, Earl of: see **Hyde.**

Clemens: see **Twain.**

Cleveland, John (1613–1658), poet: *The Rebel Scot.*

Clough, Arthur Hugh (1819–1861), poet: *The Bothie of Tober-na-Vuolich; Easter Day; Say not the Struggle Naught Availeth; Where Lies the Land.*

Cobbett, William (1762–1835), miscellaneous writer: *Peter Porcupine; A History of the Reformation; Rural Rides in England; An English Grammar.* Edited the *Political Register.*

Cockburn, Henry Thomas, Lord (1779–1854), Scottish judge: *Memorials of His Time.*

Coleridge, Samuel Taylor (1772–1834), poet: *The Rime of the Ancient Mariner; Love; Christabel; Kubla Khan; The Nightingale; Hymn before Sunrise in the Vale of Chamouni; Youth and Age; The Knight's Tomb; Work without Hope; The Ballad of the Dark Ladie; The Three Graves; Biographia Literaria* (prose).

Collier, Jeremy (1650–1726), prose writer: *Short View of the Immorality and Profaneness of the English Stage.*

Collins, Anthony (1676–1729), prose writer: *Discourse on Freethinking.*

Collins, William Wilkie (1824–1889), novelist: *The Woman in White; The Moonstone.*

Collins, William (1721–1759), poet: *Persian Eclogues; On the Passions; To Evening; On Liberty; On Simplicity; On Pity; On Fear.*

Colman, George (1732–1794), dramatist: *The Clandestine Marriage* (in collaboration with Garrick).

Congreve, William (1670–1729), poet and dramatist: *The Old Bachelor; The Double Dealer; Love for Love; The Mourning Bride; The Way of the World.*

Conrad, Joseph (1857–1924), novelist: *Almayer's Folly; Under Western Eyes; Reminiscences; 'Twixt Land and Sea; Within the Tides; The Shadow Line; Chance; Victory; The Arrow of Gold; The Rescue.*

Constable, Henry (1562–1613), poet: *Diana.*

Cooper, Anthony Ashley: see **Shaftesbury.**

Cooper, James Fenimore (1789–1851), American novelist: *Precaution; The Spy; The Pioneers; The Pilot; The Last of the Mohicans; The Prairie; The Red Rover; The Pathfinder; The Deerslayer.*

Corelli, Marie (1864–1924), novelist: *A Romance of Two Worlds; Vendetta; Thelma; Ardath; The Soul of Lilith; Barabbas; The Sorrows of Satan; The Mighty Atom; The Master Christian; Temporal Power.*

Cory, William (1823–1892), poet: *Ionica.*

Coryate, Thomas (1577–1617), traveller: *Coryate's Crudities Hastily Gobbled Up.*

Coverdale, Miles (1488-1568): Translator of the Psalms in the Prayer Book.

Cowley, Abraham (1618-1667), poet and essayist: *Poetical Blossoms; Love's Riddle; The Guardian*, re-named later *The Cutter of Coleman Street; The Mistress; Davideis; Odes; Essays; Letters.*

Cowper, William (1731-1800), poet: *Olney Hymns; Truth; Progress of Error; The Task.* Short Poems: *John Gilpin*, etc. *Homer* (translation).

Crabbe, George (1754-1832), poet: *The Library; The Village; The Newspaper; The Parish Register: The Borough; Tales of the Hall.*

Craik, Mrs Dinah Maria (1826-1887), novelist: *John Halifax, Gentleman.*

Cranmer, Thomas (1489-1556), Archbishop of Canterbury: Preface to the Great Bible; Prayers for English Prayer Book.

Crashaw, Richard (1613 ?-1649), poet: *Steps to the Temple; Delights of the Muses; The Flaming Heart; Hymn to St Theresa.*

Crawford, Francis Marion (1854-1909), American novelist: *Mr Isaacs; Dr Claudius; A Roman Singer; A Cigarette-Maker's Romance; Zoroaster; Francesca da Rimini.*

Crowne, John (1640 ?-1703), dramatist: *Sir Courtly Nice; Darius.*

Cumberland, Richard (1732-1811), dramatist: *The West Indian; The Fashionable Lovers.*

Cynewulf, Northumbrian poet of the eighth century. Attributed—*Christ; Andreas; Elene, Guthlac, Juliana* (Lives of Saints). Perhaps *The Dream of the Rood*, and *Phœnix.*

D

Daniel, Samuel (1562-1619), poet: *Delia; The Complaint of Rosamond; The Civil Wars; Musophilus; A Defence of Rime; The Queene's Arcadia; Hymen's Triumph.*

Darwin, Charles Robert (1809-1882), scientist: *Journal of Researches; The Origin of Species; The Fertilization of Orchids; Climbing Plants; The Descent of Man; Expression of the Emotions; Earthworms.*

Darwin, Erasmus (1731-1802), physician and physiologist: *The Botanic Garden.*

Davenant, Sir William (1606-1668), dramatist: *Albion. The Siege of Rhodes* (first English opera); *Gondibert.*

Davidson, John (1857-1909), poet: *Fleet Street Eclogues.*

Davies, Sir John (1569-1626), poet: *Nosce Teipsum.*

Davies, William H. (1870-1940), poet: *The Soul's Destroyer; The Autobiography of a Super Tramp; Nature Poems and Others; Forty New Poems; A Poet's Pilgrimage.*

Day, John (born 1574), dramatist: *The Isle of Gulls; Law Trickes; The Parliament of Bees* (Masque).

Day, Thomas (1748-1789), novelist: *Sandford and Merton.*

Defoe, Daniel (1661 ?-1731), essayist and novelist: *Essay on Projects; The True Born Englishman; The Shortest Way with the Dissenters; Robinson Crusoe; Memoirs of a Cavalier; Captain Singleton; Moll Flanders; Colonel Jack; Raxana; Journal of the Plague; A Tour through the Whole of Britain.*

Dekker, Thomas (1570 ?-1640 ?), dramatist: *The Shoemaker's Holiday; Old Fortunatus; The Virgin Martyr* (collaboration with Massinger); *Satiro-mastix; The Belman of London; The Guls Hornboke.*

De la Mare, Walter (born 1873), poet: *Songs of Childhood; Henry Brocken; Poems; The Three Mulla Mulgars; The Return; The Listeners; Peacock Pie; Motley and other Poems; Memoirs of a Midget; The Riddle; The Veil.*

De Morgan, William (1839-1917), novelist: *Joseph Vance; Alice-for-Short.*

Denham, Sir John (1615-1669), poet: *Cooper's Hill; Elegy on Cowley.*

De Quincey, Thomas (1785-1859), essayist: *Confessions of an Opium Eater; Letters to a Young Man; On Murder Considered as One of the Fine Arts; The Revolt of the Tartars; Suspiria de Profundis; Joan of Arc; The English Mail Coach; Klosterheim; The Logic of Political Economy.*

Dibdin, Charles (1745-1814), musician, dramatist, actor, song-writer: *The Waterman; The Quaker; Jack Ratlin; The Bells of Aberdovey.*

Diceto, Ralph of (d. 1200): Chronicle.

Dickens, Charles (1812-1870), novelist: *Sketches by Boz; Pickwick Papers; Oliver Twist; Nicholas Nickleby; The Old Curiosity Shop; Barnaby Rudge; American Notes; The Christmas Carol; Martin Chuzzlewit; The Chimes; The Cricket on the Hearth; Pictures from Italy; Dombey and Son; David Copperfield; Bleak House; Hard Times; Little Dorrit; A Tale of Two Cities; The Uncommercial Traveller; Great Expectations; Our Mutual Friend; The Mystery of Edwin Drood* (unfinished).

Dillon, Wentworth, Earl of Roscommon (1634-1685), poet-critic: *Essay on Translated Verse.*

Disraeli, Benjamin, Earl of Beaconsfield (1804-1881), novelist and statesman: *Coningsby; Sybil; Tancred; Lothair; Vivian Grey; Alroy; Henrietta Temple.*

Dobell, Sydney (1824-1874), poet: *The Roman; Balder.*

Dobson, Austin (1840-1921), poet and critic: *Vignettes in Rhyme; Proverbs in Porcelain; Fielding; Richard Steele; Life of Oliver Goldsmith; Horace Walpole; Eighteenth Century Vignettes; The Story of Rosina.*

Donne, John (c. 1571-1631), poet: *The Will; Go and catch a falling star; Satires.*

Douglas, Gawain (1474?–1522), poet: *The Palace of Honour; King Hart; Æneid* (translation).

Doyle, Sir Arthur Conan (1859–1930), novelist: *Micah Clarke; The White Company; Rodney Stone; The Adventures of Sherlock Holmes; The Memoirs of Sherlock Holmes; The Hound of the Baskervilles; The Return of Sherlock Holmes.*

Doyle, Sir Francis Hastings (1810–1888), poet: *The Red Thread of Honour; The Private of the Buffs.*

Drayton, Michael (1563–1631), poet: *Harmony of the Church; Idea; Pastorals; The Barons' Wars; England's Heroical Epistles; The Owl; Polyolbion; The Battle of Agincourt; The Shepherd's Sirena; The Muses of Elysium; Nymphidia.*

Drinkwater, John (1882–1937), poet and dramatist: *Abraham Lincoln; Marie Stuart; Poems; Cophetua.*

Drummond, William, of Hawthornden (1585–1649), poet: *Poems; Flowers of Sion.*

Dryden, John (1631–1700), poet and dramatist: Poems and Odes: *Annus Mirabilis; To the Memory of Mrs Anne Killigrew; Eleanora; A Song for St Cecilia's Day; Alexander's Feast.* Satires: *Absalom and Achitophel; The Medal; MacFlecknoe.* Religious poems: *Religio Laici; The Hind and the Panther.* Translations: *Virgil; Palamon and Arcite; Cymon and Iphigenia*, etc. Plays: *The Indian Emperor; Tyrannic Love; The Mock Astrologer; The Conquest of Granada; Marriage à la Mode; All for Love; The Spanish Friar.* Prose: *Essay on Dramatic Poesy.*

Du Maurier, George (1834–1896), novelist: *Trilby; The Martian.*

Dunbar, William (1465?–1530?), poet: *The Thrissil and the Rois; The Dance of the Sevin Deidly Synnis.*

Dyer, John (1700–1758), poet: *Grongar Hill; The Ruins of Rome; The Fleece.*

Dyer, Sir Edward (1550–1607), poet: *My mind to me a kingdom is.*

E

Eadmer (d. 1124), scholar: *Vita Anselmi* and *Historia Novorum.*

Earle, John (1601–1665), prose writer: *Microcosmographie.*

Edgeworth, Maria (1767–1849), novelist: *Castle Rackrent; The Absentee; Ormond.*

"Eliot, George" (Mary Ann Evans, 1819–1880), novelist: *Scenes of Clerical Life; Adam Bede; The Mill on the Floss; Silas Marner; Romola; Felix Holt; Middlemarch; Daniel Deronda; The Spanish Gypsy; The Legend of "Jubal."*

Elliott, Ebenezer (1781–1849), poet: *The Village Patriarch; The Corn-Law Rhymes.*

Elliott, Jean (1727–1805), poet: *The Flowers of the Forest.*

Elyot, Sir Thomas (1490–1546), prose writer: *The Governour; The Castle of Health.*

Emerson, Ralph Waldo (1803–1882), American essayist: *Essays; Representative Men; English Traits; Poetry and Criticism.*

Ethelwold, Bishop of Winchester (fl. 963): English Version of Benedictine Rule.

Etherege, Sir George (1635?–1691), dramatist: *She Would if she Could; The Man of Mode.*

Evelyn, John (1620–1706), prose writer: *Diary; Sylva* (on tree planting).

F

Fabyan, Robert (d. 1513), English chronicler: *The Concordance of Histories.*

Falconer, William (1732–1769), poet: *The Shipwreck.*

Farquhar, George (1678–1707), dramatist: *Love and a Bottle; The Constant Couple; The Recruiting Officer; The Beau's Stratagem.*

Feltham, Owen (1602?–1668), prose writer: *Resolves.*

Ferguson, Sir Samuel (1810–1886), poet: *Conary; Lays of the Western Gael.*

Fergusson, Robert (1750–1774), poet: *Daft Days; Leith Races; Auld Reekie; Ode to a Gowdspink.*

Ferrier, Susan Edmonstone (1782–1854), novelist: *Marriage; The Inheritance; Destiny.*

Field, Eugene (1850–1895), American poet: *With Trumpet and Drum; A Little Book of Western Verse; The Love Affairs of a Bibliomaniac.*

Fielding, Henry (1707–1754), novelist: *Tom Thumb the Great; Joseph Andrews; A Journey from this World to the Next; Tom Jones; Amelia; The History of Jonathan Wild the Great.*

Finlay, George (1799–1875), historian: *History of Greece, from the Conquest by the Romans to 1864.*

Fitzgerald, Edward (1809–1883), scholar, translator and poet: *Euphranor; Six Dramas of Calderon* and *The Rubáiyát of Omar Khayyám* (translation).

Flecker, James Elroy (1884–1915), poet and dramatist: *The Bridge of Fire; The Golden Journey to Samarcand.* Play: *Hassan.*

Flecknoe, Richard (d. 1678), poet, dramatist and miscellaneous writer: *Miscellania, or Poems of All Sorts; Love's Dominion; The Damoiselles à la Mode* (a comedy).

Fletcher, Giles (1588?–1623), poet: *Christ's Victory and Triumph.*

Fletcher, John (1579–1625), poet: *The Faithful Shepherdess; The Humorous Lieutenant; Rule a Wife and Have a Wife; The Loyal Subject; Bonduca; Valentinian.* See **Beaumont.**

Fletcher, Phineas (1582–1650), poet: *The Purple Island.*

Florio, John (1553?–1625), man of letters: Translated Montaigne's *Essais.*

Foote, Samuel (1720—1777), dramatist: *The Mayor of Garratt.*

Ford, John (about 1586–1640), poet and dramatist: *The Witch of Edmonton* (in collaboration with Dekker and Rowley); *The Lover's Melancholy; The Broken Heart; Love's Sacrifice; Perkin Warbeck.*

Forster, John (1812–1876), prose writer: *Life of Landor; Life of Dickens.*

Fox, George (1624–1691): (Founder of "Society of Friends," or Quakers): *Journal.*

Foxe, John (1516–1587), prose writer: *The Book of Martyrs* (Protestant).

Franklin, Benjamin (1706–1790), American prose writer: Pamphlets on *Paper Currency, Population, National Wealth,* and *Free Trade; Experiments and Observations on Electricity; Political, Miscellaneous, and Philosophical Pieces.*

Frazer, Sir James George (1854–1928), anthropologist: *The Golden Bough.*

Freeman, Edward Augustus (1823–1892), historian: *History of the Norman Conquest.*

Frere, John Hookham (1769–1846), poet: *The Monks and the Giants.*

Froude, James Anthony (1818–1894), historian: *The Nemesis of Faith; Short Studies on Great Subjects; History of England from the Fall of Wolsey to the Defeat of the Spanish Armada; The English in Ireland in the Eighteenth Century; Bunyan; Life of Carlyle; Oceana; The Two Chiefs of Dunboy; Life and Letters of Erasmus.*

Fuller, Thomas (1608–1661), prose writer: *The Holy State; Good Thoughts in Bad Times; Good Thoughts in Worse Times; A Pisgah Sight of Palestine; A Church History of Britain; Mixt Contemplations in Better Times; The Worthies of England.*

G

Galsworthy, John (1867–1933), novelist and dramatist: *The Island Pharisees; The Man of Property; The White Monkey; The Patrician; Saint's Progress; The Forsyte Saga.* Plays: *Strife; Justice; The Skin Game.*

Galt, John (1779–1839), novelist: *Ayrshire Legatees; Annals of the Parish; The Provost; The Entail.*

Gardiner, Samuel Rawson (1829–1902), historian: *The Early Stuarts.*

Garnett, Richard (1835–1906), prose writer: *Life of Carlyle; History of Italian Literature.*

Garrick, David (1717–1779), actor: *The Lying Valet;* collaborated with Colman in *The Clandestine Marriage.*

Garth, Sir Samuel (1661–1719), poet: *The Dispensary.*

Gascoigne, George (1525?–1577), poet and translator: translation of Ariosto's *The Supposes* (first English prose comedy); *A Hundred Sundrie Flowres* (poems); *The Glasse of Government; The Steele Glas.*

Gaskell, Elizabeth Cleghorn (1810–1865), novelist: *Mary Barton; Cranford; Sylvia's Lovers; Cousin Phillis; Life of Charlotte Brontë.*

Gay, John (1685–1732), poet and dramatist: *The Shepherd's Week; Trivia; Fables; Acis and Galatea; The Beggar's Opera; Black-Eyed Susan; Polly.*

George, Henry (1839–1897), American prose writer: *Progress and Poverty; The Condition of Labor; Political Economy.*

Gibbon, Edward (1737–1794), prose writer: *The Decline and Fall of the Roman Empire; Memoirs; Autobiography.*

Gifford, William (1756–1826), critic: edited Ben Jonson: criticism of Keats.

Gilbert, Sir W. S. (1836–1911), poet and dramatist: *Bab Ballads; Foggerty's Fairy.* In collaboration with Sir A. S. Sullivan: *Thespis; Trial by Jury; The Sorcerer; H.M.S.Pinafore; The Pirates of Penzance; Patience; Iolanthe; Princess Ida; The Mikado; Ruddigore; The Yeomen of the Guard; The Gondoliers; Utopia Limited; The Grand Duke.*

Gissing, George (1857–1903), novelist: *Demos; Thyrza; New Grub Street; The Odd Women; The Private Papers of Henry Ryecroft; Life of Dickens.*

Gloucester, Robert of (d. 1300?): Chronicle in long-lined verse. (Authority on the Battle of Evesham.)

Glover, Richard (1712–1785), poet: *Leonidas; Boadicea; The Athenaid.*

Godwin, Mrs Mary (Wollstonecraft) (1759–1797), miscellaneous writer: *Reply to Burke's Reflections on the French Revolution; Vindication of the Rights of Women.*

Godwin, William (1756–1836), philosopher and novelist: *Political Justice; Caleb Williams; St Leon.*

Goldsmith, Oliver (1728–1774), poet and dramatist: *The Traveller; The Deserted Village; Retaliation; Essays; Vicar of Wakefield; The Good Natur'd Man; She Stoops to Conquer.*

Gosson, Stephen (1554–1624), satirist: *The School of Abuse.*

Gower, John (1325?–1408), poet: *Cinquante Balades; Mirour de l'Omme; Vox Clamantis; Confessio Amantis.*

Grahame, Kenneth (1859–1932), prose writer: *Golden Age; Wind in the Willows.*

Gray, Thomas (1716–1771), poet: *Elegy Written in a Country Churchyard; The Bard; The Progress of Poesy; On a Distant Prospect of Eton College; On Spring; To Adversity; On the Pleasures Arising from Vicissitude.*

Green, John Richard (1837–1883), historian:

The Making of England; The Conquest of England; Short History of the English People.

Green, Thomas Hill (1836–1882), philosopher: *Prolegomena to Ethics.*

Greene, Robert (1560?–1592), poet and dramatist: *Mamilia; Friar Bacon and Friar Bungay; Euphues' Censure to Philautus; Pandosto; Alphonsus, King of Aragon; Menaphon; James IV.; George-a-Greene; The Repentance of Robin Greene; A Groatsworth of Wit Bought with a Million of Repentance.*

Greville, Fulke, Lord Brooke (1554–1628): biographer of Sidney.

Grostete, Robert (d. 1253): On Theology, Aristotle, etc.

Grote, George (1794–1871), historian and politician: *History of Greece.*

Guildford, John of (prob. fl. 1225), attributed *The Owle and the Nightingale.*

H

Habington, William (1605–1654), poet: *Castara.*

Hake, Thomas Gordon (1809–1895), poet: *New Symbols.*

Hakluyt, Richard (1553?–1616), prose writer: *Voyages.*

Hales, Alexander of (d. 1245), theologian: *Summa Universa Theologiæ.*

Hales, John (1584–1656), prose writer: *Golden Remains* (Sermons).

Hall, Edward (1499?–1547), historian: Chronicle, *The Union of the Two Noble Families of Lancaster and Yorke* (used by Shakespeare).

Hall, Joseph (1574–1656), poet: *Virgidemiarum* (satires).

Hallam, Henry (1777–1859), historian: *View of the State of Europe during the Middle Ages; The Constitutional History of England; Introduction to the Literature of Europe.*

Hamilton, Sir William Rowan (1788–1856), metaphysician: *Discussions on Philosophy;* Lectures on Metaphysics and Logic.

Hardy, Thomas (1840–1928), novelist and poet: *Under the Greenwood Tree; A Pair of Blue Eyes; Far from the Madding Crowd; The Mayor of Casterbridge; Tess of the D'Urbervilles; Life's Little Ironies; Jude the Obscure; Wessex Tales; The Dynasts* (poetic drama); *Collected Poems,* including Wessex poems; *Time's Laughing Stocks; Satires of Circumstance; Moments of Vision.*

Harrison, Frederick (1831–1923), historian: *The Meaning of History; Early Victorian Literature; Oliver Cromwell.*

Harte, Francis Bret (1839–1902), American poet and novelist: *East and West Poems; M'Liss; Truthful James and Other Poems; Two Men of Sandy Bar; Tales, Poems, and Sketches; The Luck of Roaring Camp.*

Hawes, Stephen (d. 1523?), poet: *The Pastime of Pleasure; History of Grand Amour and La Belle Pucelle; Example of Virtue; Conversion of Swearers; The Temple of Glasse.*

Hawker, Robert Stephen (1804–1875), poet: *The Quest of the Sangreal;* Shorter pieces—*The Song of the Western Men; Queen Gwennyvar's Round; The Bells of Bottreaux.*

Hawthorne, Nathaniel (1804–1864), American novelist: *The Scarlet Letter; The House of the Seven Gables; Tanglewood Tales; The Blithedale Romance; A Rill from the Town Pump.*

Hazlitt, William (1778–1830), essayist and miscellaneous writer: *The Characters of Shakespeare's Plays; Lectures on the English Poets; English Comic Writers; Dramatic Literature of the Age of Elizabeth; The Spirit of the Age; Life of Napoleon.*

Hearn, Lafcadio (1850–1906), writer on Japanese subjects: *Glimpses of Unfamiliar Japan; Out of the East; Japan: an Attempt at Interpretation.*

Hemans, Mrs Felicia (1793–1835), poetess: *Verses.*

Henley, William Ernest (1849–1903), poet and critic: *London Voluntaries; Hospital Sketches.* Collaborated with **R. L. Stevenson** in plays—*Beau Austin; Deacon Brodie; Admiral Guinea; Macaire.*

Henry, O. (William Sidney Porter, 1862–1910), American story-writer: *Cabbages and Kings; The Four Million; The Trimmed Lamp; Heart of the West; The Voice of the City; Roads of Destiny; Whirligigs; Strictly Business; Sixes and Sevens; Rolling Stones.*

Henryson, Robert (1430?–1506?), poet: *The Testament of Creseid; Orpheus and Eurydice; Robyne and Makyne* (first English pastoral); *Fables.*

Herbert, George (1593–1633), poet and divine: *The Temple.*

Herchown—supposed to be **Sir Hugh of Eglintoun** (1320?–1380), poet: *Pystel of Swete Susanne* (alliterative); *The Great Gest of Arthure* (lost); *Awntyre of Gawaine* (lost); *Morte Arthure* (alliterative poem).

Herrick, Robert (1591–1674), poet and divine: *Hesperides; Noble Numbers.* Shorter poems: *Fair Daffodils; Gather ye Rosebuds while ye may; Corinna's Maying.*

Hewlett, Maurice (1861–1923), novelist and poet: *The Song of the Plough; Forest Lovers; The Spanish Jade; The Queen's Quair; The Stooping Lady.*

Heywood, John (1497?–1580?), dramatist: *The Merrie Play between Pardoner and Friar; The Curate and Neighbour Pratt; The Merrie Play between Johann the Hus-*

band, *Tib his Wife*, and *Sir John the Priest*; *Dialogue of Wit and Folly*; *The Play of the Wether*; etc.

Heywood, Thomas (1575 ?–1650), dramatist: *A Woman killed with Kindness*; *Edward IV*; *The Four Prentices of London*; *The Fair Maid of the West*.

Higden, Ralph (d. 1364), scholar of Chester: *Polychronicon*: encyclopædia of all available knowledge.

Hobbes, Thomas (1588–1679), philosopher: *De Cive*; *De Homine*; *De Corpore Politico*; *The Leviathan*.

Hogg, James (1770–1835), "The Ettrick Shepherd," poet and prose writer: *The Mountain Bard*; *The Forest Minstrel*; *The Queen's Wake*; *Madoc of the Moor*; *The Pilgrims of the Sun*; *The Border Garland*; *Kilmeny*; *The Boy's Song*.

Holcroft, Thomas (1745–1809), novelist: *Anna St Ives*; *Hugh Trevor*.

Holinshed, Raphael (d. 1580 ?): Chronicle of England and Scotland (used by Shakespeare).

Holmes, Oliver Wendell (1809–1894), American prose writer and novelist: *The Autocrat of the Breakfast Table*; *The Professor at the Breakfast Table*; *Elsie Venner*; *The Poet at the Breakfast Table*; *Poems*.

Hood, Thomas (1799–1845), poet and humorist: *The Song of the Shirt*; *The Bridge of Sighs*; *The Plea of the Midsummer Fairies*; *Fair Ines*; *I Remember*; *The Dream of Eugene Aram*.

Hooker, Richard (1554 ?–1600): prose writer: *The Laws of Ecclesiastical Polity*.

"**Hope, Anthony**" (Hawkins, Sir Anthony Hope, 1863–1933), novelist: *The Prisoner of Zenda*; *Rupert of Hentzau*.

Horne, Richard Hengist (1803–1884), poet: *Orion*.

Hovedon, Roger of (d. 1200): Chronicle.

Howe, Julia Ward (1819–1910), American poet and essayist: *Passion Flowers*; *Words for the Hour*; *From Sunset Ridge*; *The Battle Hymn of the Republic*.

Hudson, William Henry (1841–1922), naturalist and novelist: *Green Mansions*; *A Shepherd's Life*; *A Crystal Age*; *British Birds*; *Adventures among Birds*; *Far away and Long Ago*.

Hume, David (1711–1776), philosopher and historian: *Philosophical Essays*; *Enquiry into Principles of Morals*; *History of England*.

Hunt, James Henry Leigh (1784–1859), essayist and poet: *The Story of Rimini*; *Abou Ben Adhem*. Edited *The Examiner* and *The Indicator*.

Hutton, Richard Holt (1826–1907), journalist: edited the *Spectator*. *Contemporary Thought and Thinkers*.

Huxley, Thomas Henry (1825–1895), scientist: *Man's Place in Nature*; *Method and Results*; *Science and Hebrew Tradition*; *Evolution and Ethics*; *Hume*.

Hyde, Edward, Earl of Clarendon (1608–1674), prose writer: *The History of the Great Rebellion*.

I

Ingelow, Jean (1820–1897), poetess: *A Rhyming Chronicle*; *Tales of Orris*; *Stories told to a Child*; *Home Thoughts and Home Scenes*; *Off the Skelligs*; *Sarah de Berenger*; *Don John*; *The High Tide on the Coast of Lincolnshire*.

Irving, Washington (1783–1859), American essayist and historian: *The Sketch Book of Geoffrey Crayon, Gent.* (including *Rip Van Winkle*); *Bracebridge Hall*; *Tales of a Traveller*; *History of the Life and Voyages of Christopher Columbus*; *Life of Oliver Goldsmith*; *Lives of Mahomet and his Successors*; *History of New York*.

J

James I., King of Scotland (1394–1437), poet: *Kingis Quair* (King's Book); *Christ's Kirk on the Green*; *Peebles to the Play*; *Balade of Good Counsel* (doubtful authorship).

James, George P. R. (1801–1860), novelist, historian: *Richelieu*.

James, Henry (1843–1916), American novelist: *The Tragic Muse*; *What Maisie Knew*; *The Wings of the Dove*; *A Passionate Pilgrim*; *Transatlantic Sketches*; *Tales of Three Cities*; *The Bostonians*; *The Reverberator*; *A Small Boy and Others*; *Notes of a Son and Brother*; *Within the Rim*.

James, William (1842–1910), American philosopher: *Principles of Psychology*; *Talks to Teachers*; *Pragmatism—A New Name for Some Old Ways of Thinking*; *The Varieties of Religious Experience*.

Jameson, Mrs Anna (1794–1860), critic: *Characteristics of Shakespeare's Heroines*.

Jefferies, Richard (1848–1887), prose writer: *The Gamekeeper at Home*; *Wild Life in a Southern County*; *Wood Magic*; *Bevis*; *The Story of my Heart*.

Jeffrey, Francis (1773–1850), critic: Contributions to *Edinburgh Review*.

Johnson, Samuel (1709–1784), poet, dramatist, novelist, essayist, lexicographer: *London*; *The Vanity of Human Wishes*; *Irene*; *Rasselas*; *Journey to the Hebrides*; *Lives of the Poets*; *Dictionary of the English Language*; *Life of Savage*.

Jonson, Ben (1573–1637), poet and dramatist: *Every Man in his Humour*; *Volpone*; *Epicene*; *The Alchemist*; *Bartholomew Fair*; *Sejanus*; *Catiline*; *The Masque of Queens*; *Oberon*; *The Sad Shepherd*; *Epigrams*; *The Forest*; *Underwoods*; *Every Man out of his Humour*; *Cynthia's Revels*; *The Poetaster*; *The Devil is an Ass*; *The Staple*

*of News; The New Inn; Discoveries;
Eastward Ho!* (in collaboration with
Chapman and Marston).

"**Junius**": "nom de guerre" of the writer
of a series of political letters which
appeared in the *Public Advertiser*, 1769–
1772.

K

Keats, John (1795–1821), poet: *Endymion;
Hyperion; The Eve of St Agnes; Isa-
bella; Lamia.* Shorter poems: *To a
Nightingale; On a Grecian Urn; To
Autumn; On First looking into Chap-
man's Homer; When I have fears that I
may cease to be; To One who has been
Long in City pent; Bright Star! would
I were steadfast as thou art; Sleep and
Beauty; Lines on the Mermaid Tavern;
La Belle Dame sans Merci; In a Drear
Nighted December; The Eve of St Mark.*

Keble, John (1792–1866), poet and prose
writer: *Lyra Innocentium; The Christian Year.*

Kinglake, Alexander William (1809–1891),
prose writer and historian: *Eothen;
History of the War in the Crimea.*

Kingsley, Charles (1819–1875), poet and
novelist: *Sands of Dee; The Saint's
Tragedy; Andromeda; Glaucus; The
Water Babies; Yeast; Alton Locke;
Hypatia; Westward Ho!; Two Years
Ago; Hereward the Wake.*

Kingsley, Henry (1830–1876), novelist:
*Geoffrey Hamlyn; Ravenshoe; The
Hillyars and the Burtons.*

Kipling, Rudyard (1865–1936), poet and
prose writer: *Barrack-Room Ballads;
Jungle Book; Songs from Books; The
Harbour Witch; Fringes of the Fleet;
Sea Warfare; A Diversity of Creatures;
Letters of Travel.*

Knighton, Henry (d. 1366): Chronicle on
Edward III.

Knowles, James Sheridan (1784–1862):
dramatist: *William Tell; The Hunch-
back.*

Knox, John (1505?–1572), Scottish reformer
and prose writer: *Trumpet Blast against
the Monstrous Regiment of Women;
History of the Reformation in Scotland.*

Kyd, Thomas (1558–1595), dramatist: *The
Spanish Tragedy.*

L

Lamb, Charles (1775–1834), essayist: *The
Old Familiar Faces; Rosamund Gray;
John Woodvill; Tales from Shakespeare*
(in collaboration with his sister, Mary
Lamb); Specimens of the Elizabethan
Dramatists of the Age of Shakespeare, with
Short Critical Notes; *Essays of Elia.*

Landon, Letitia Elizabeth (1802–1838), poetess: *Verses.*

Landor, Walter Savage (1775–1864), poet
and prose writer: *Gebir; Chrysaor;
Idyllia Heroica; Hellenics; Rose Aylmer;
Count Julian; Fra Rupert; The Siege
of Ancona; Imaginary Conversations;
Examination of Shakespeare; Pericles and
Aspasia; Pentameron.*

Lanfranc (1009–1089), prose writer: *Treatise
of the Eucharist.*

Lang, Andrew (1844–1912), prose writer:
Joan of Arc. Writer on Scottish history,
Greek myths, anthropology, fairy tales.

Langland, William (1330?–1400?), poet:
Vision of Piers Plowman.

Latimer, Hugh (1485–1555), English reformer: Sermons.

Law, William (1686–1761), prose writer:
*The Serious Call to a Devout and Holy Life;
Letters to the Bishop of Bangor; Christian
Perfection.*

Layamon (fl. 1200), poet: Translated Wace's
Brut into English.

Lecky, William Edward Hartpole (1838–
1903), historian: *The Rise and Progress
of Rationalism in Europe; History of
European Morals from Augustus to Charlemagne; Democracy and Liberty; History
of England in the Eighteenth Century.*

Lee, Nathaniel (1653?–1692), dramatist: *The
Rival Queens; Mithridates.* Collaborated
with Dryden in *Œdipus* and *The Duke of
Guise.*

Lever, Charles James (1806–1872), novelist:
*The Adventures of Harry Lorrequer;
Charles O'Malley; Tom Burke of Ours.*

Lewes, George Henry (1817–1878), prose
writer: *Biographical History of Philosophy; Life of Goethe.*

Lewis, Matthew Gregory (1775–1818), novelist: *The Monk.*

Lindsay, Lady Anne (1750–1825), poetess:
Auld Robin Gray.

Lingard, John (1771–1851), historian: *A
History of England.*

Locke, John (1632–1704), essayist and philosopher: *Essay on Toleration; Essay
on the Human Understanding; Thoughts
concerning Education.*

Lockhart, John Gibson (1794–1854), novelist
and biographer: *Peter's Letters to his
Kinsfolk; Life of Burns; Life of Scott.*

Lodge, Thomas (1558?–1625), poet and
romance writer: *Rosalynde; Euphues'
Golden Legacy; A Defence of Stage Plays;
An Alarum against Usurers; Phillis; A
Looking-glass for London and England* (in
conjunction with Robert Greene); *A Fig
for Momus.*

London, Jack (1876–1916), American novelist: *The Song of the Wolf; The Call of
the Wild; Moon Face; Martin Eden;
South Sea Tales; Before Adam; The
Little Lady of the Big House.*

Longfellow, Henry Wadsworth (1807–1882),
American poet: *Hyperion; Voices of the*

Night; Ballads and Other Poems; Poems on Slavery; The Spanish Student; The Belfry of Bruges; Evangeline; The Golden Legend; Song of Hiawatha; Courtship of Miles Standish; Tales of a Wayside Inn; New England Tragedies; The Divine Tragedy; Three Books of Song; Aftermath; The Hanging of the Crane; The Magic of Pandora; The Skeleton in Armour.

Lovelace, Richard (1618–1658), poet: *Lucasta; On going to the Wars; To Althea from Prison.*

Lowell, James Russell (1819–1891), American poet and essayist: *Poems; The Biglow Papers; Fireside Travels; My Study Windows; Among my Books; A Moosehead Journal; Political Essays; The Old English Dramatists; Last Poems.*

Ludlow, Edmund (1617–1692), republican and regicide: *Memoirs.*

Lyall, Sir Alfred (1835–1911): Indian poems.

Lydgate, John (1370?–1451?), poet: *The Storie of Thebes; The Troye Book; The Falls of Princes; London Lickpenny.*

Lyell, Sir Charles (1797–1875), geologist and prose writer: *The Principles of Geology; The Antiquity of Man.*

Lyly, John (1553?–1606), poet: *Euphues; Campaspe; Sapho and Phaon; Endimion; Galathea; Midas; Mother Bombie; The Woman in the Moon; Love's Metamorphosis.*

Lyndesay, Sir David (1490–1555), poet: *The Dreme; The Complaint of the Papyngo; The Satire of the Three Estates; The Historie of Squire Meldrum; The Monarchie.*

Lytton, Edward Bulwer (1803–1873), novelist: *The Lady of Lyons; Richelieu; Money; Pelham; Eugene Aram; The Last Days of Pompeii; Rienzi; The Last of the Barons; Harold; The Caxtons; My Novel; Kenelm Chillingly; Ernest Maltravers; Alice; Zanoni; The Coming Race.*

M

Macaulay, Thomas Babington, Lord (1800–1859), poet, historian, and essayist: *Lays of Ancient Rome; History of England; Essays.*

M'Carthy, Justin (1830–1912), novelist and historian: *A History of our Own Times.*

M'Culloch, John Ramsay (1789–1864), economist: *Principles of Political Economy.*

MacDonald, George (1824–1905), poet and novelist: *David Elginbrod; Adela Cathcart; Robert Falconer; Gutta Percha Willie; Malcolm; The Wise Woman; The Marquis of Lossie.*

Mackenzie, Compton (born 1883), novelist: *Sinister Street.*

Mackenzie, Henry (1745–1831), essayist and novelist: *The Man of Feeling.*

Mackintosh, Sir James (1765–1832), prose writer: *Vindiciæ Gallicæ.*

"Macleod, Fiona" (William Sharp, 1856–1905), poet and critic: *The Mountain Lovers; The Sin Eater.*

Macpherson, James (1736?–1796), poet: *Fingal* and *Temora* (claimed to be translations of Gaelic poems of Ossian).

Maitland, Frederick William (1850–1906), historian: *Roman Canon Law in the Church of England; Domesday Book and Beyond; A Constitutional History of England.*

Malmesbury, William of (d. 1142), chronicler: *De gestis regum Anglorum,* and *Historia Novella.* Also a history of Glastonbury, and lives of the Saints.

Malory, Sir Thomas (fl. 1470), writer of romances: *Morte d'Arthur.*

Malthus, Thomas Robert (1766–1834), economist: *An Essay on Population; Observations on the Effect of the Corn Laws; An Inquiry into the Nature and Progress of Rent; Principles of Political Economy; Definitions in Political Economy.*

Mandeville, Bernard de (1670–1733), prose writer: *Fable of the Bees.*

Mandeville, "Sir John" (fl. 14th cent.): *The Voyaige and Travaile, which treateth of the way to Hierusalem, and of the Marvayles of Inde, with Other Islands and Countries.* Name of author almost certainly assumed. Originally written in French.

Mannyng, Robert, of Brunne (fl. 1288–1338): *Metrical Chronicle of England,* translated from French; *Handlynge of Sinne* (a series of stories from the French).

Mansel, Henry Longueville (1820–1871), metaphysician: *Philosophy of the Conditioned.*

Map, or Mapes, Walter (fl. 1200), poet and prose writer: *De Nugis Curialium* (attributed Latin original of *Lancelot du Lac*).

Marlowe, Christopher (1564–1593), poet: *Tamburlaine; Doctor Faustus; The Jew of Malta; Edward II.; Hero and Leander* (completed by Chapman).

Marprelate, Martin (pseudonym of unknown author, latter half of 16th century): *Epistle to the Terrible Priest of the Convocation House; Hay any Work for the Cooper?* (Reply to Bishop Cooper).

Marryat, Frederick (1792–1848), novelist: *Frank Mildmay; Peter Simple; Mr Midshipman Easy; Snarley-yow; Poor Jack; Masterman Ready; The Children of the New Forest; Valerie.*

Marston, John (1575?–1634), dramatist and satirist: *The Scourge of Villany; Antonio and Mellida; The Malcontent;* Collaborated with Jonson and Chapman in *Eastward Ho!*

Marvell, Andrew (1621–1678), poet: *The Rehearsal Transposed; Horatian Ode on the Return of Cromwell from Ireland;*

Thoughts in a Garden; A Drop of Dew; The Bermudas; Satires.

Masefield, John (born 1875), poet, novelist, and dramatist: Salt Water Ballads; On the Spanish Main; The Everlasting Mercy; The Widow in the Bye Street; Dauber; The Daffodil Fields. Novels: Captain Margaret; Multitude and Solitude. Play: The Tragedy of Nan.

Massinger, Philip (1583–1640), dramatist: The Virgin Martyr (with Dekker); The Unnatural Combat; The Duke of Milan; The Bondman; The Renegade; The Roman Actor; The Great Duke of Florence; A New Way to Pay Old Debts; The City Madam.

Maturin, Charles Robert (1782–1824), novelist: Melmoth the Wanderer.

Maurice, Frederick Denison (1805–1872), prose writer: The Kingdom of Christ; Prophets and Kings; The Claims of the Bible and of Science.

Meredith, George (1828–1909), poet and novelist: Modern Love; Poems and Lyrics of the Joy of Earth; Ballads and Poems of Tragic Life; A Reading of Earth; The Shaving of Shagpat; Farina; The Ordeal of Richard Feverel; Evan Harrington; Sandra Belloni; Vittoria; Rhoda Fleming; The Adventures of Harry Richmond; Beauchamp's Career; The Egoist; The Tragic Comedians; Diana of the Crossways; One of our Conquerors; Lord Ormont and His Aminta; The Amazing Marriage.

Meres, Francis (1565–1647), essayist: Palladis Tamia.

Meynell, Alice Christiana (1850–1922), poet: Preludes; Poems; Later Poems; The Rhythm of Life; The Colour of Life and Other Essays; The Children.

Mickle, William Julius (1735–1788), poet: There's nae Luck aboot the Hoose; Cumnor Hall.

Middleton, Conyers (1683–1750), prose writer: Life of Cicero.

Middleton, Thomas (1570–1627), dramatist: The Changeling; The Spanish Gipsy; Women Beware Women; A Trick to Catch the Old One; A Mad World, my Masters; A Game of Chess; The Mayor of Quinborough; The Witch.

Mill, James (1773–1836), philosopher and historian: History of India; Analysis of the Phenomena of the Human Mind.

Mill, John Stuart (1806–1873), philosopher and economist: System of Logic; Political Economy; On Liberty; Considerations on Representative Government; Utilitarianism; Auguste Comte and Positivism; Examination of Sir William Hamilton's Philosophy; The Subjection of Women.

Miller, Hugh (1802–1856), prose writer and geologist: My Schools and Schoolmasters; The Old Red Sandstone; Footprints of the Creator; The Testimony of the Rocks.

Milman, Henry Hart (1791–1868), historian: History of the Jews; History of Latin Christianity.

Milne, A. A. (born 1882), dramatist and novelist: The Dover Road; The Truth about Blayds; Success; Children's books.

Milton, John (1608–1674), poet: Hymn on the Nativity; L'Allegro; Il Penseroso; Arcades; Comus; Lycidas; Sonnets; Areopagitica; Tractate on Education; Pamphlets on Church Government; Pamphlets on Divorce; Eikonoklastes; Defensio pro Populo Anglicano; Defensio Secunda; Paradise Lost; Paradise Regained; Samson Agonistes.

Minot, Lawrence (1300 ?–1352 ?), poet: Poems on Battles of Halidon Hill, La Hogue, Calais, Neville's Cross, Winchelsea, and Guisnes.

Mitford, Mary Russell (1787–1855), poet and prose writer: Our Village; Recollections of a Literary Life.

Monmouth, Geoffrey of (1100 ?–1154): Historia Regum Britanniæ—foundation of Arthurian legend.

Montagu, Lady Mary Wortley (1690–1762): Letters.

Moore, George (1857–1933), novelist: The Brook Kerith; Ave; Salve; Vale; Abélard and Héloïse.

Moore, John (1729 or 1730–1802), novelist: Zeluco.

Moore, Thomas (1779–1852), poet and prose writer: Odes of Anacreon; Irish Melodies; Lalla Rookh; The Fudge Family in Paris; Life of R. B. Sheridan; Life of Byron; Life of Lord Edward Fitzgerald.

More, Sir Thomas (1478–1535), scholar and prose writer): Utopia; History of Richard III.

Morley, Henry (1822–1894), poet and critic: Sunrise in Italy and other Poems; Memoirs of Bartholomew Fair; English Writers; English Literature.

Morley of Blackburn, John Morley, Viscount (1838–1923), biographer and essayist: Edmund Burke; Voltaire; Rousseau; Diderot and the Encyclopædists; Life of Richard Cobden; Walpole; Studies in Literature; Machiavelli; Life of William Ewart Gladstone.

Morris, William (1834–1896), poet, prose writer, and craftsman: The Defence of Guinevere; The Earthly Paradise; The Life and Death of Jason; Sigurd the Volsung; Love is enough; Chants for Socialists; The House of the Wolfings; News from Nowhere; The Well at the World's End; The Story of the Sundering Flood.

Motherwell, William (1797–1835), poet: Jeanie Morrison; Poems, Narrative and Lyrical.

Motley, John Lothrop (1814–1877), historian: The Rise of the Dutch Republic.

N

Nairne, Lady (1766–1845), poet : *The Land o' the Leal ; Caller Herrin'.*

Napier, Sir William (1785–1860), soldier and historian : *History of the Peninsular War ; Conquest of Scinde.*

Nash, Thomas (1567–1601), novelist and prose satirist : *Jack Wilton or the Unfortunate Traveller ; Piers Pennilesse, his Supplication to the Devil ; Christ's Tears over Jerusalem ; Have with You to Saffron Walden ; Lenten Stuff ; Will Summer's Last Will and Testament ; Dido* (partly by Marlowe).

Newbolt, Sir Henry (1862–1938), poet and critic : *Poems New and Old ; Drake's Drum and Other Sea Songs ; Aladore ; The Book of the Happy Warrior ; A New Study of English Poetry ; St George's Day and Other Poems.*

Newburgh, William of (d. 1200), chronicle.

Newman, John Henry (1801–1890), poet and essayist : Many of the poems in *Lyra Apostolica ; Tracts for the Times ; Essay on Miracles ; Development of Christian Doctrine ; Loss and Gain ; University Sketches ; Callista ; Apologia pro Vita Sua ; The Dream of Gerontius ; The Grammar of Assent ;* hymn, *Lead, kindly Light.*

Newton, Sir Isaac (1642–1727), scientist : *Principia.*

"North, Christopher" : see Wilson, John.

North, Sir Thomas (1535 ?–1601 ?) : Translation of Plutarch.

Noyes, Alfred (born 1880), poet : *The Loom of Years ; Forty Singing Seamen ; Drake ; The Sea in English Poetry ; The Wine Press ; A Salute from the Fleet ; Rada ; Walking Shadows ; The Elfin Artist.*

O

Occleve, Thomas (fl. 15th cent.), prose writer : *The Gouvernail of Princes ; La Male Règle de Thomas Occleve.*

Oldham, John (1653–1683), poet : *Satires on the Jesuits.*

Oliphant, Mrs Margaret (1828–1897), novelist : *Chronicles of Carlingford ; House of Blackwood.*

Orm : a monk (fl. 1200) : *Ormulum :* paraphrases of the Gospels into verse.

O'Shaughnessy, Arthur (1844–1881), poet : *An Epic of Women ; Lays of France ; Songs of a Worker ; Music and Moonlight.*

Ossian (Ossin or Oisin), legendary Irish 3rd century hero of Celtic literature : see James Macpherson.

Otway, Thomas (1651 or 1652–1685), dramatist and poet : *Alcibiades ; Don Carlos ; The Orphan ; Caius Marius ; Venice Preserved.*

"Ouida" (Louise de la Ramée, 1840 ?–1908), novelist : *Strathmore ; Under Two Flags ; Two Little Wooden Shoes ; Moths ; Puck.*

Overbury, Sir Thomas (1581–1613), prose writer : *Sir Thomas Overbury his Observations in his Travailes.*

P

Paine, Thomas (1737–1809), prose writer : *The Rights of Man ; The Age of Reason.*

Paley, William (1743–1805), prose writer : *Evidences of Christianity ; Horæ Paulinæ ; Natural Theology.*

Palgrave, Francis Turner (1824–1897), critic and editor of *The Golden Treasury of English Songs and Lyrics.*

Paris, Matthew (d. 1259) : *Chronica Majora.*

Park, Mungo (1771–1806), traveller : *Travels in the Interior of Africa.*

Parker, Sir Gilbert (1862–1932), novelist : *Pierre and his People ; The Seats of the Mighty ; The Battle of the Strong ; Northern Lights.*

Parnell, Thomas (1679–1718), poet : *Night Piece on Death ; Hymn to Contentment ; The Hermit.*

Pater, Walter (1839–1894), essayist and critic : *Studies in the History of the Renaissance ; Marius the Epicurean ; Imaginary Portraits ; Appreciations ; Plato and Platonism ; Greek Studies ; Gaston de Latour* (unfinished).

Patmore, Coventry (1823–1896), poet : *The Angel in the House ; The Unknown Eros.*

Pattison, Mark (1813–1884), scholar and prose writer : *Casaubon ; Milton ; Autobiography.*

Paulding, James Kirke (1779–1860), American miscellaneous writer : *The Diverting History of John Bull and Brother Jonathan ; The Lay of the Scottish Fiddle* (parody) : *A Sketch of Old England by a New England Man ; Koningsmarke, the Long Finne* (including *Peter Piper picked a peck of pickled peppers) ; The Merry Tales of the Three Wise Men of Gotham ; A Life of Washington ; The Book of St Nicholas.*

Payn, James (1830–1898), novelist : *Lost Sir Massingberd ; By Proxy.*

Peacock, Thomas Love (1785–1866), novelist : *Headlong Hall ; Melincourt ; Nightmare Abbey ; Maid Marian ; The Misfortunes of Elphin ; Crotchet Castle ; Gryll Grange.*

Peele, George (1558 ?–1597 ?), dramatist : *The Arraignment of Paris ; Edward I. ; The Old Wives' Tale ; David and Bethsabe ; Battle of Alcazar.*

Pepys, Samuel (1633–1703) : *Diary.*

Petrie, Sir William Matthew Flinders (born 1853), Egyptologist : *History of Egypt.*

Philips, Ambrose (1675 ?–1749), poet and

dramatist: *Pastorals; The Distrest Mother.*

Phillips, Stephen (1868–1915), poet: *Paolo and Francesca; Herod; Ulysses.*

Pinero, Sir Arthur Wing (1855–1934), dramatist: *The Second Mrs Tanqueray; The Profligate; Lady Bountiful; The Times; The Magistrate; The Hobby Horse; The Cabinet Minister; Sweet Lavender; The Schoolmistress; The Weaker Sex; The Amazons; The Notorious Mrs Ebbsmith; The Benefit of the Doubt; Dandy Dick.*

Poe, Edgar Allan (1809–1849), American poet and story writer: *Tamerlane and Other Poems; Tales of the Grotesque and the Arabesque; The Raven and Other Poems; Tales; Eureka.*

Poore, Richard, Bishop of Salisbury: said to have written, 1237, *The Ancren Riwle* (Rule of Nuns), but this very uncertain.

Pope, Alexander (1688–1744), poet: *Pastorals; Essay on Criticism; The Rape of the Lock; Homer; Eloisa to Abelard; Elegy on an Unfortunate Lady; The Dunciad; Essay on Man; Of the Knowledge and Characters of Men; Of the Characters of Women; Of the Use of Riches; On Collecting Antiquities; Epistle to Arbuthnot; Letters; Treatise on Bathos.*

Praed, Winthrop Mackworth (1802–1839), poet: *The Vicar; Arminius; My Pretty Josephine; The Red Fisherman; The Season; The Letter of Advice; A Letter from Teignmouth.*

Prescott, William Hickling (1796–1859), historian: *Ferdinand and Isabella; Conquest of Mexico; Conquest of Peru.*

Price, Richard (1723–1791), prose writer: *On the Love of Country.*

Priestley, Joseph (1733–1804), chemist and political writer: *Letters to Burke.*

Prior, Matthew (1664–1721), poet: *Alma; Solomon; Henry and Emma; Her English Padlock; Answer to Chloe Jealous; A Better Answer; Child of Quality.*

Proctor, Bryan Waller ("Barry Cornwall," 1787–1874), poet: *English Songs.*

Purchas, Samuel (1575?–1626), prose writer: *Purchas, His Pilgrimes.*

Puttenham, George (1530?–1590): *The Art of English Poesie* (attributed, but perhaps by his brother Richard).

Q

Quarles, Francis (1592–1644), poet: *Emblems Divine and Moral.*

Quiller-Couch, Sir Arthur Thomas (1863–1944), poet and novelist: *Dead Man's Rock; Troy Town; The Splendid Spur; The Blue Pavilions; The Ship of Stars; Hetty Wesley; The Adventures of Harry Revel; Green Bays; Poems and Ballads.*

Quincey, Thomas de: see under D.

R

Radcliffe, Mrs Ann (1764–1823), novelist: *The Castle of Athlin and Dunbayne; A Sicilian Romance; The Romance of the Forest; The Mysteries of Udolpho; The Italian.*

Raleigh, Sir Walter (1552?–1618), poet and prose writer: *Lyrics; Discovery of the Empire of Guiana; A History of the World.*

Ramsay, Allan (1686–1758), poet: *The Evergreen; The Tea-Table Miscellany; The Gentle Shepherd.*

Randolph, Thomas (1605–1635), dramatist: *The Muses' Looking Glass.*

Ray, John (1627–1705), naturalist and prose writer: *The Wisdom of God in the Creation.*

Reade, Charles (1814–1884), novelist: *Peg Woffington; Christie Johnstone; It is Never too Late to Mend; The Cloister and the Hearth; Hard Cash; Griffith Gaunt; Put Yourself in his Place.*

Reeve, Clara (1729–1807), novelist: *The Old English Baron.*

Reid, Thomas (1710–1796), philosopher: *Principles of Commonsense.*

Reynolds, Sir Joshua (1723–1792), artist and prose writer: *Discourses* (to the Royal Academy.)

Ricardo, David (1772–1823), economist: *The High Price of Bullion a Proof of the Depreciation of Bank Notes; Essay on the Influence of a Low Price of Corn on the Profits of Stock; Proposals for an Economical and Secure Currency; Principles of Political Economy and Taxation.*

Rice, James (1844–1882), novelist: In collaboration with Sir Walter Besant (1836–1901), wrote *Ready Money Mortiboy; The Golden Butterfly;* etc.

Richardson, Samuel (1689–1761), novelist: *Pamela; Clarissa Harlowe; Sir Charles Grandison.*

Robertson, William (1721–1793), historian: *History of Scotland; History of the Emperor Charles V.; History of America.*

Robins, Elizabeth ("C. E. Raimond," born 1865), American novelist: *The Magnetic North; Camilla.*

Rochester, Earl of: see Wilmot.

Rogers, Samuel (1763–1855), poet: *The Pleasures of Memory; Jacqueline; Italy.*

Rolle, Richard (1290?–1349), poet: *The Pricke of Conscience.*

Roscoe, William (1753–1831), scholar and historian: *Life of Lorenzo de' Medici; Life of Leo X.*

Roscommon, Earl of: see Dillon.

Ross, Alexander (1699–1784), poet: *Helenore.*

Rossetti, Christina Georgina (1830–1894), poetess: *Goblin Market and other Poems; The Prince's Progress and other Poems; A Pageant and other Poems.*

Rossetti, Dante Gabriel (1828–1882), artist

and poet: *The Blessed Damozel; Love's Nocturn; The Staff and Scrip; The Stream's Secret; The House of Life* (sonnets); *Rose Mary; Sister Helen; Jenny; The White Ship; The King's Tragedy; Dante and his Circle.*

Rowe, Nicholas (1674–1718), poet-laureate and dramatist: *Tamerlane; Jane Shore; Lady Jane Grey; The Despairing Shepherd.*

Rowley, William (1585?–1642?), dramatist: *A New Wonder; A Match at Midnight.*

Ruskin, John (1819–1900), essayist and art critic: *Modern Painters; The Seven Lamps of Architecture; The Stones of Venice; Elements of Drawing; The Political Economy of Art.*

"Rutherford, Mark" (William Hale White, 1831–1913), novelist: *The Autobiography of Mark Rutherford; Mark Rutherford's Deliverance; The Revolution in Tanner's Lane; Catherine Furze.*

Rutherford, Samuel (1600?–1661), divine: *A Free Disputation against Pretended Liberty of Conscience.*

Rymer, Thomas (1641–1713), historian: *Foedera; Tragedies of the Last Age.*

S

Sackville, Charles, Earl of Dorset (1638–1706), poet: *To all you ladies now on land; Phyllis, for Shame,* and other lyrics.

Saintsbury, George Edward Bateman (1845–1933), critic and miscellaneous writer: *Primer of French Literature; Dryden; Short History of French Literature; History of Elizabethan Literature; Essays in English Literature; Essays on French Novelists; History of Nineteenth Century Literature; The Flourishing of Romance and the Rise of Allegory; Short History of English Literature; History of Criticism; History of Prosody.*

Sala, George Augustus (1828–1895), novelist and essayist: *The Seven Sons of Mammon; The Two Prima Donnas; William Hogarth; Paris herself again; Wat Tyler, M.P.* (burlesque).

Salisbury, John of (1115–1180,) prose writer: *Polycratus; Metalogicus; Historia Pontificalis; Life of Becket.*

Scott, Sir Walter (1771–1832), poet and novelist: Poems—*Tales of Wonder; The Eve of St John; The Minstrelsy of the Scottish Border; The Lay of the Last Minstrel; Marmion; The Lady of the Lake; The Vision of Don Roderick; Rokeby; The Lord of the Isles; The Bride of Triermain; Harold the Dauntless.* Novels—*Waverley, Guy Mannering; The Antiquary; The Black Dwarf; Old Mortality; Rob Roy; The Heart of Midlothian; The Bride of Lammermoor; The Legend of Montrose; Ivanhoe; The Monastery; The Abbot; Kenilworth; The Pirate; The Fortunes of Nigel; Peveril of the Peak; Quentin Durward; St Ronan's Well; Redgauntlet; The Betrothed; The Talisman; Woodstock; The Fair Maid of Perth; Anne of Geierstein; Count Robert of Paris; Castle Dangerous.* History: *Tales of a Grandfather; Life of Napoleon.*

Sedley, Sir Charles (1639?–1701), poet and dramatist: *The Mulberry Tree* (play); *Love still has something of the sea; Phillis is my only joy; The Knotting Song* (poems).

Seeley, Sir John Robert (1834–1895), historian and essayist: *Ecce Homo; Natural Religion; The Expansion of England; The Growth of British Policy.*

Selden, John (1584–1654), prose writer: *Table Talk.*

Service, Robert W. (born 1876), poet and prose writer: *Songs of a Sourdough; Rhymes of a Rolling Stone; Rhymes of a Red Cross Man; The Trail of '98; The Pretender.*

Shadwell, Thomas (1640 or 1642–1692), dramatist: *The Sullen Lovers; Royal Shepherdess; Epsom Wells.*

Shaftesbury, Anthony Ashley Cooper, 3rd Earl of (1671–1713), philosopher: *Characteristics of Men, Matters, Opinions, Times.*

Shakespeare, William (1564–1616), poet and dramatist: Comedies—*Comedy of Errors; Taming of the Shrew; Love's Labour's Lost; Midsummer Night's Dream; Two Gentlemen of Verona; Merchant of Venice; Much Ado about Nothing; Merry Wives of Windsor; As You Like It; Twelfth Night; All's Well that Ends Well; Measure for Measure; Pericles; Cymbeline; Winter's Tale; The Tempest; Two Noble Kinsmen.* Historical plays—*Henry VI.,* 2nd and 3rd parts; *Henry VI.,* 1st part; *Richard III.; King John; Richard II.; Henry IV.,* 1st part; *Henry IV.,* 2nd part; *Henry V.; Henry VIII.* Tragedies—*Titus Andronicus; Romeo and Juliet; Julius Cæsar; Hamlet; Troilus and Cressida; Othello; Macbeth; King Lear; Antony and Cleopatra; Coriolanus; Timon of Athens.* Poems—*Venus and Adonis; The Rape of Lucrece; Passionate Pilgrim; The Phœnix and the Turtle; Sonnets.*

Shaw, George Bernard (born 1856), critic and dramatist: *John Bull's Other Island; The Doctor's Dilemma; Major Barbara; Man and Superman; You Never Can Tell; Fanny's First Play; Overruled; Androcles and the Lion; Pygmalion; Back to Methuselah; Saint Joan.*

Shelley, Percy Bysshe (1792–1822), poet: *Queen Mab; Alastor; The Revolt of Islam; Prometheus Unbound; The Cenci; Ode on the West Wind; To a Skylark; The Cloud; Stanzas written in Dejection near Naples; Lines written among the Euganean Hills.*

Shenstone, William (1714–1763), poet: *The Pastoral Ballad; The Dying Kid; The Schoolmistress.*

Sheridan, Richard Brinsley (1751–1816), dramatist: *The Rivals; The Duenna; A Trip to Scarborough; The School for Scandal; The Critic; Pizarro.*

Shirley, James (1596–1666), poet and dramatist: *Love Tricks; The Witty Fair One; The Traitor; Hyde Park; The Lady of Pleasure; The Young Admiral; The Cardinal; The Triumph of Peace; The Contention of Ajax and Ulysses*, containing the lyric, "The Glories of our Blood and State."

Shorthouse, John Henry (1834–1903), novelist: *John Inglesant.*

Sidgwick, Henry (1838–1900), prose writer: *Political Economy; Ethics.*

Sidney, Sir Philip (1554–1586), poet and prose writer: *Arcadia; Apologie for Poetrie; Astrophel and Stella.*

Skeat, Walter William (1835–1912), scholar and philologist: *Etymological Dictionary.*

Skelton, John (1460?–1529), poet: *Magnificence*, a morality play; *Colin Clout; Why Come ye not to Court?*

Skinner, John (1721–1807), poet: *Tullochgorum; The Ewie wi' the Crookit Horn.*

Smart, Christopher (1722–1771), poet: *Song to David;* Hymns and Metrical Versions of the Psalms of David.

Smiles, Samuel (1812–1904), prose writer: *Lives of the Engineers; Self-Help; Thrift.*

Smith, Adam (1723–1790), economist: *The Theory of Moral Sentiments; The Wealth of Nations.*

Smith, Alexander (1830–1867), poet and essayist: *A Life Drama; Dreamthorpe.*

Smith, Horace (1779–1849), poet and novelist: *Rejected Addresses* (parody), written in collaboration with brother James. Novels—*Brambletye House, Tor Hill*, etc.

Smith, Sydney (1771–1845), prose writer: *Letters of Peter Plymley.*

Smollett, Tobias George (1721–1771), novelist: *Roderick Random; Peregrine Pickle; Ferdinand, Count Fathom; Sir Lancelot Greaves; Humphrey Clinker;* Translation of *Don Quixote; A History of England.*

Somerville, William (1675–1742), poet: *The Chase.*

Southerne, Thomas (1660–1746), dramatist: *The Fatal Marriage; Oronooko.*

Southey, Robert (1774–1843), poet and prose writer: *Wat Tyler; The Fall of Robespierre; Joan of Arc; Thalaba; Madoc; The Curse of Kehama; Don Roderick; Life of Nelson; Life of Wesley; History of Brazil.*

Southwell, Robert (1561?–1595), poet: *St Peter's Complaint.*

Spencer, Herbert (1820–1903), philosopher: *First Principles; Principles of Biology; Principles of Psychology; Principles of Sociology; Data of Ethics.*

Spenser, Edmund (1552?–1599), poet and prose writer: *Shepheardes Calendar; Astrophel; Fairie Queene; Complaints; The Ruines of Time; The Teares of the Muses; Virgil's Gnat; Mother Hubberd's Tale; Muiopotmos; Daphnaida; Amorette; Epithalamium; Colin Clout's Come Home Again; Hymns; Prothalamium; View of the Present State of Ireland.*

Sprat, Thomas (1635–1713), prose writer: *History of the Royal Society.*

Stanhope, Philip Henry Stanhope, 5th Earl (1805–1875), historian: *The Court of Spain under Charles II.; A Life of the Great Condé; Memoirs of Sir Robert Peel; A Life of William Pitt.*

Stanley, Arthur Penrhyn (1815–1881), historian: *The History of the Jewish Church.*

Steele, Sir Richard (1672–1729), essayist and dramatist: *The Christian Hero; Grief à la Mode; The Lying Lover; The Tender Husband; The Conscious Lovers.* Brought out *The Tatler.* Contributed 236 papers to *The Spectator.*

Stephen, Sir Leslie (1832–1904), critic and biographer: Monographs on Swift and Johnson. *Hours in a Library; English Thought in the Eighteenth Century; An Agnostic's Apology.* Editor of *Dictionary of National Biography.*

Sterne, Lawrence (1713–1768), novelist: *Tristram Shandy; A Sentimental Journey through France and Italy.*

Stevenson, Robert Louis (1850–1894), poet, novelist and essayist: Poems—*A Child's Garden of Verses; Underwoods; Ballads.* Novels—*Treasure Island; Prince Otto; Dr Jekyll and Mr Hyde; Kidnapped; Master of Ballantrae; The Wrecker; Catriona; Weir of Hermiston* (unfinished); *St. Ives* (unfinished). Essays, Sketches, etc.—*An Inland Voyage; Travels with a Donkey in the Cevennes; Virginibus Puerisque; Familiar Studies of Men and Books; New Arabian Nights; The Silverado Squatters; Pulvis et Umbra; Island Nights' Entertainments; Vailima Letters* (posthumous).

In collaboration with his step-son, Mr Lloyd Osbourne: *The Wrong Box; The Wrecker; The Ebb-Tide.*

Stewart, Dugald (1753–1828), philosopher: *Elements of the Philosophy of the Human Mind;* Philosophical Essays; Lectures on Political Economy.

Still, John (1543–1608), dramatist: Supposed author of *Gammer Gurton's Needle.*

St John, Henry, Viscount Bolingbroke (1678–1751), prose writer: *Letter to Sir W. Windham; Letters on the Study of History; The Idea of a Patriot King.*

Stoddard, Richard Henry (1825–1903), American poet: *Footprints; Poems; Adventures in Fairyland; Songs of Summer; The King's Bell; Abraham Lincoln; The Lion's Cub, with Other Verse.*

Story, William Wetmore (1819-1895), American prose writer: *A Roman Lawyer in Jerusalem; A Jewish Rabbi in Rome; The Tragedy of Nero.*

Stow, John (1525-1605) antiquary: *Survey of London; Chronicle.*

Stowe, Harriet Elizabeth Beecher (1811?-1896), American novelist: *Uncle Tom's Cabin; Dred.*

Strachey, Giles Lytton (1881-1932), essayist: *Queen Victoria; Eminent Victorians.*

Stubbs, William (1825-1901), historian: *Constitutional History of England.*

Suckling, Sir John (1609-1642), poet: *A Ballad upon a Wedding; Fragmenta Aurea* (poems).

Surrey, Henry Howard, Earl of (1517?-1547), poet: Sonnets to *Geraldine; Æneid II. and IV.* translated into blank verse.

Swift, Jonathan (1667-1745), satirical and miscellaneous writer: *The Tale of a Tub; The Battle of the Books; An Argument against Abolishing Christianity; Journal to Stella; Drapier Letters; Gulliver's Travels; A Modest Proposal.* Poems—*On the Death of Dr Swift; Cadenus and Vanessa.* Edited *The Examiner.*

Swinburne, Algernon Charles (1837-1909), poet and prose writer: *Atalanta in Calydon; Erechtheus; Hymn to Proserpine; Itylus; A Song in Time of Order; A Song in Time of Revolution; In Memory of W. S. Landor; The Garden of Proserpine; Dolores; Laus Veneris; Songs of Four Seasons; Songs before Sunrise; Tristram of Lyonnesse; Balen; Bothwell.* Translations from Villon. Prose studies on Blake, Chapman, Shakespeare, Ben Jonson, Victor Hugo. *Love's Cross Currents* (fiction).

Symonds, John Addington (1840-1893), critic: *The Renaissance in Italy.*

Synge, John Millington (1871-1909), poet and dramatist: *In the Shadow of the Glen; Riders to the Sea; The Tinker's Wedding; The Well of the Saints; The Playboy of the Western World; Deirdre of the Sorrows.*

T

Tannahill, Robert (1774-1810), poet: *The Braes of Balquhidder; Gloomy Winter's Noo Awa'; The Bonnie Woods o' Craigielea.*

Tate, Nahum (1652-1715), poet-laureate: Poems—*Memorials of the Learned; Elegies.* Plays—*Brutus of Alba; The Loyal General.*

Taylor, Bayard (1825-1878), American poet: *Ximena, or the Battle of Sierra Morena, and Other Poems; El Dorado, or Adventures in the Path of Empire; A Journey to Central Africa; The Lands of the Saracen.*

Taylor, Jeremy (1613-1667), prose writer: *The Liberty of Prophesying; Holy Living; Holy Dying; Twenty-Eight Sermons.*

Temple, Sir William (1628-1699), miscellaneous writer: *Memoirs; Essays.*

Tennant, William (1786-1848), poet: *Anster Fair.*

Tennyson, Alfred, Lord (1809-1892), poet: *Poems by Two Brothers; The Princess; Maud; Oenone; Ulysses; Tithonus; Lucretius; The Idylls of the King; Enoch Arden; Aylmer's Field; Dora; The Northern Farmer; In Memoriam.* Well-known shorter poems, such as *Crossing the Bar; Break, break, break.*

Thackeray, William Makepeace (1811-1863), novelist: *Barry Lyndon; Vanity Fair; Pendennis; Henry Esmond; The Newcomes; The Virginians; The Yellowplush Papers; The Book of Snobs; English Humorists of the Eighteenth Century; The Four Georges; The Rose and the Ring* (play).

Theobald, Lewis (1688-1744), critic: editor of Shakespeare.

Thirlwall, Connop (1797-1875), historian and theologian: *History of Greece.*

Thompson, Francis (1859-1907), poet: *Poems; Sister Songs; New Poems; The Hound of Heaven; Love in Diana's Lap.*

Thomson, James (1700-1748), poet: *The Seasons (Winter, Summer, Spring, Autumn); Liberty; The Castle of Indolence.*

Thomson, James (1834-1882), poet: *The City of Dreadful Night.*

Thoreau, Henry David (1817-1862), American prose writer: *A Week on the Concord and Merrimack Rivers; Walden.*

Thornbury, George Walter (1828-1876), poet and novelist: *Lays and Legends of the New World; Shakespeare's England; Songs of Cavaliers and Roundheads.* Novel—*The Vicar's Courtship.*

Tickell, Thomas (1686-1740), poet: *Elegy on the Death of Addison.*

Tindal, Matthew (1656-1733), prose writer: *Christianity as Old as the Creation.*

Toland, John (1670?-1722), prose writer: *Christianity Not Mysterious.*

Tourneur, Cyril (1575?-1626), dramatist: *The Atheist's Tragedy; The Revenger's Tragedy.*

Traherne, Thomas (1636?-1674), poet: *Poems; Centuries of Meditations.*

Trench, Richard Chenevix (1807-1886), scholar and poet: *The Study of Words; English Past and Present.*

Trevisa, John (1326-1412): translation into English of Higden's *Polychronicon,* and other works.

Trollope, Anthony (1815-1882), novelist: *Barchester Towers; Framley Parsonage; The Warden; Doctor Thorne; The Small House at Allington; The Last Chronicle of Barset; The Three Clerks; Orley Farm; Autobiography; Life of Thackeray.*

Turner, Sharon (1768-1847), historian: *A History of the Anglo-Saxons.*

"Twain, Mark" (Samuel Langhorne Clemens) (1835-1910), American novelist: *The Innocents Abroad; The New Pilgrim's*

*Progress; Adventures of Tom Sawyer;
A Tramp Abroad; The Adventures of
Huckleberry Finn; A Yankee at the Court
of King Arthur; Puddin'head Wilson;
Tom Sawyer Abroad; Personal Recollec-
tions of Joan of Arc; Tom Sawyer,
Detective.*

U

Udall, Nicholas (1505–1556), dramatist and
translator: *Ralph Royster Doister; translations of Erasmus, Apophthegmes and
Paraphrases.*
Ussher, James, Archbishop of Armagh (1581–
1656): *A Discourse on the Religion
anciently professed by the Irish and British;
The Principles of the Christian Religion.*

V

Vanbrugh, Sir John (1664–1726), dramatist:
*The Relapse; The Provok'd Wife; The
Confederacy.*
Vaughan, Henry (1622–1695), poet: *Silex
Scintillans; The Retreat; The World;
The Storm.*
Villiers, George, Second Duke of Buckingham
(1628–1687), dramatist: *The Rehearsal.*
Vitalis, Ordericus (1075–1142?): *Ecclesias-
tical History of England and Normandy.*

W

Wace, ? Robert (1100?–1175?), poet: *The
Roman de Brut; Roman de Rou.*
Walker, John (1732–1807), lexicographer:
*A Dictionary of the English Language;
Elements of Elocution; A Rhyming
Dictionary.*
Wallace, Alfred Russell (1822–1913), prose
writer: *The Malay Archipelago.*
Waller, Edmund (1606–1687), poet: *Collec-
tion of poems including Go Lovely Rose
and On a Girdle.*
Walpole, Horace (1717–1797), essayist: *Cor-
respondence (with Sir Horace Mann);
Memoirs; The Castle of Otranto.*
Walpole, Sir Hugh (1884–1941), novelist:
The Wooden Horse; The Cathedral.
Walton, Izaak (1593–1683), prose writer:
*Biographies of Donne, Herbert, Hooker,
and Wotton. The Compleat Angler.*
Warburton, William (1698–1779), translator
and prose writer: *The Divine Legation of
Moses Demonstrated.* Edited Shakespeare's
works.
Warner, William (1558–1609), poet:
Albion's England (rhymed chronicle).
Warton, Joseph (1722–1800), poet and critic:
Essay on the Writings of Pope.
Warton, Thomas (1728–1790), poet and
critic: *Observations on the Faerie Queene;
History of English Poetry.*

Watson, Thomas (d. 1592), poet: *Hecatom-
pathia, or Passionate Century of Love;
Teares of Fancie.*
Watson, Sir William (1858–1935), poet: *The
Prince's Quest; Epigrams of Art, Life and
Nature; Wordsworth's Grave and Other
Poems; Odes and Other Poems.*
Watts-Dunton, Theodore (1832–1914), poet:
The Coming of Love; Sonnets.
Webbe, William (born 1550), critic: *Dis-
course of English Poetry.*
Webster, John (1580?–1625?), dramatist:
*The White Devil; The Duchess of Malfi;
The Devil's Law Case; Appius and
Virginia.*
Wells, Herbert George (1866–1946), novelist:
Novels—*The Time Machine; The Wheels
of Chance; The War of the Worlds; Love
and Mr Lewisham; Kipps; Tono
Bungay; The New Machiavelli; Marriage;
The Passionate Friends; The Wife of Sir
Isaac Harmon; The Research Magnificent;
Mr Britling Sees it Through; The Soul
of a Bishop; Joan and Peter.* Other
works—*Discovery of the Future; Mankind
in the Making; A Modern Utopia; New
Worlds for Old; The Undying Fire; God,
the Invisible King; The Salvaging of
Civilisation; Outline of History.*
Wendover, Roger of (d. 1236), chronicler:
Flores Historiarum.
Wesley, Charles (1707–1788): *Hymns.*
White, Gilbert (1720–1793), naturalist:
Natural History of Selborne.
Whittier, John Greenleaf (1807–1892),
American poet: *Legends of New England;
Moll Pitcher; Poems: Lays of my Home;
Voices of Freedom; Songs of Labor; Old
Portraits and Modern Sketches; In War
Time; National Lyrics; Ballads of New
England; Poems of Nature; Saint
Gregory's Guest.*
Whyte-Melville, George John (1821–1878),
novelist: *Holmby House; The Gladiators.*
Wilde, Oscar (1856–1900), poet and drama-
tist: *Lady Windermere's Fan; A Woman
of No Importance; The Importance of
being Earnest; The Ideal Husband;
Dorian Gray* (novel).
" William (of Palerne "), title of poem by a
poet who calls himself " William."
Wilmot, John, Earl of Rochester (1647–1680),
poet: *Lyrics and criticism; Valentinian.*
Wilson, John (1785–1854) (" Christopher
North "), poet: *Part author of Noctes
Ambrosianæ; Poems and dramatic works.*
Wilson, Thomas (1530–1581), critic: *Arte of
Rhetorique; Arte of Logique; Discourses
on Usurye.*
Wilson, Woodrow (1856–1924), American
political philosopher: *The State: Ele-
ments of Historical and Practical Politics;
Sketch of Institutional History and Ad-
ministration; The State and Federal
Government of the United States; History
of the American People; Constitutional
Government of the United States.*

Wither, George (1588–1667), poet: *Juvenilia; Epithalamia; Abuses Stript and Whipt; Fidelia; The Mistress of Philarete; Hymns and Songs of the Church; Emblems; Hallelujah.*

Wolcot, John (1738–1819), poet: *The Lousiad* (satires against George III.).

Wood, Mrs Henry (1814–1887), novelist: *East Lynne; The Channings; Mrs Haliburton's Troubles; Roland Yorke.*

Wordsworth, William (1770–1850), poet: *First Poems; The Borderers; Lyrical Ballads; Pastorals; The Leechgatherer; The Prelude; The White Doe of Rylstone; Laodamia and Dion; The Excursion; Peter Bell; The Duddon Sonnets; Ecclesiastical Sonnets.* Preface to Second Edition of Lyrical Ballads.

Wotton, Sir Henry (1568–1639), poet: *How happy is he born and taught; You meaner beauties of the night.* Also works on History, Education and Architecture.

Wulfstan (Archbishop of York, 1002–1023), prose writer: *Address to the English.*

Wyatt, Sir Thomas (1503–1542), poet: Love poems and satires.

Wycherley, William (1640 ?–1716), dramatist and poet: *Love in a Wood; The Gentleman Dancing Master; The Plain Dealer; The Country Wife.*

Wycliffe, John (1320 ?–1384), reformer and prose writer: Translation of the Bible into English.

Wyntoun, Andrew of (1350 ?–1420 ?): Original Chronicle to 1406.

Y

Yeats, William Butler (1865–1939), poet: *Responsibilities; Reveries over Childhood and Youth; The Wild Swans at Coole; Michael Robartes and the Dancer; At the Hawk's Well; Two Plays for Dancers.*

Yonge, Charlotte Mary (1823–1901), novelist: *The Heir of Redclyffe; The Daisy Chain; The Chaplet of Pearls.*

Young, Arthur (1741–1820), prose writer: *Travels in France during 1787, 1788, and 1789; Tour in Ireland.*

Young, Edward (1683–1765), poet: *Night Thoughts.*

Z

Zangwill, Izrael (1864–1926) , novelist, dramatist, and miscellaneous writer: *The Children of the Ghetto; The Voice of Jerusalem.* Plays—*Merely Mary Ann; The Melting Pot.*

GREAT ARTISTS

A

Abbey, Edwin Austin (1852–1911), America: Illustrations of *She Stoops to Conquer,* and of comedies of Shakespeare—*The Jongleur; Beatrice; Richard Duke of Gloucester and the Lady Anne.*

Abbott, Francis Lemuel (1760–1803), England: *Horatio, Viscount Nelson.*

Adam, Robert (1728–1792), Scotland: architect to king; Adelphi buildings; Edinburgh, Register House, part of University; Glasgow Infirmary. Partner brother James.

Alma-Tadema, Sir Lawrence (1836–1912), Holland: *The Education of the Children of Clovis; Fredegonda; An Egyptian at his Doorway; The Pyrrhic Dance; Hadrian in Britain; Goldfish.*

Angelico, Fra (Fra Giovanni da Fiesole) (1387–1445 ?), Florence: *The Annunciation; The Adoration of the Magi; Flight into Egypt; Christ Washing Peter's Feet; Christ before Caiaphas; St Peter and the High Priest's Servant; The Deposition from the Cross; The Entry into Jerusalem; Instruments of the Passion; The Last Supper; An Angel with a Lute; The Last Judgment.*

Apelles (flourished 4th century B.C.), greatest Grecian painter.

Apollodorus (flourished 408 B.C.), Athens: *Odysseus; A Priest in Prayer; An Ajax Struck by Lightning* (all lost).

B

Bakhuysen, Ludolf (1631–1708), Flanders: *Sea-scapes.*

Baldovinetti, Alesso (1427–1499), Florence: *The Annunciation;* Altar-piece of the *Virgin and Child and Six Saints.*

Barbari, Jacopo de' (1450 ?–1515 ?), Venice: *Portrait of a Gentleman.*

Barbieri, Giovanni Francesco (Guercino) (1591–1666), Italy: *St Petronilla; Aurora; St William of Aquitaine; Dido; Angels Weeping; St Peter Raising Tabitha.*

Bartoli, Domenico (1400 ?–1449 ?), Siena: *Madonna Orans.*

Bartolommeo, Fra (1475–1517), Florence: *Last Judgment; St Mark; St Sebastian; St Paul; Pietà; Savonarola.*

Bartolozzi, Francesco (1725–1815), Florence; engraver: Plates in Boydell's *Shakespeare Gallery.*

Bassano, Jacopo da Ponte (1510–1592), Italy: Altar-piece of the *Nativity;*

pictures of peasants and villagers, cattle and landscapes.

Baudry, Paul Jacques Aimé (1828–1886), France : *Zenobia Found on the Banks of the Araxes; The Martyrdom of a Vestal Virgin; The Child; The Pearl and the Wave; Charlotte Corday after the Murder of Marat.*

Beardsley, Aubrey (1872–1898), England : Black and white illustrations; Sir Thomas Malory's *Morte d'Arthur; Salome; The Rape of the Lock.*

Beauneveu, André (15th century), France : *King Richard II.*

Bellini, Gentile (1429 ?–1507), Venice : *Madonna; Reception of an Ambassador at Constantinople; The Sultan Mahommed II.;* water-colour portrait of *A Scribe;* pen and ink drawings of Turkish types ; *Procession of a Relic of the True Cross through St Mark's Place.*

Bellini, Giovanni (1430 ?–1516), Venice : *The Madonna of the Trees; The Dead Christ; The Infant Bacchus; Portrait of a Baby; The Doge Leonardo Loredano.*

Bellini, Jacopo (1400 ?–1470 ?), Venice : *Christ Crucified; Madonnas;* attributed to him—*A Warrior Saint on Horseback; Crucifixion; Adoration of the Magi.*

Berchem, Claes Pietersz (1620–1683), Holland : *Landscapes.*

Bewick, Thomas (1753–1828), England ; wood-engraver : *Select Fables; Quadrupeds; British Birds.*

Böcklin, Arnold (1827–1901), Switzerland : *Great Park; The Walk to Emmaus; Triton and Nereid.*

Bologna, Giovanni da (1524–1608), Flanders, sculptor : *Mercury Poised on one Foot; The Rape of the Sabines;* fountain at Bologna ; two fountains in the Boboli gardens ; equestrian statue of *Cosimo de' Medici.*

Bonfigli, Benedetto (15th century), Perugia : Series of frescoes of the life of *St Louis of Toulouse.*

Bonheur, Maria Rosa (1822–1899), France : *The Horse Fair; Le Labourage Nivernais; La Fenaison; Ploughing.*

Bordone, Paris (1500–1570), Venice : *Fisherman and Doge; Daphnis and Chloe; Portrait of a Lady; Holy Family; Madonna; The Chess Players; Baptism of Christ.*

Botticelli, Sandro Filipepi (1444–1510), Florence : *The Magnificat; Primavera (Spring); Adoration of the Magi; The Virgin and Child; The Birth of Venus; The Vision of St Augustine; The Virgin Mother; Giovanni Tornabuoni and the Graces; P. Lorenzo de' Medici; L'Abbondanza.*

Boucher, François (1703–1770), France : *Madame de Pompadour; Rinaldo and Armida; Sunrise; Sunset.*

Bouguerau, Adolphe William (1825–1905), France : *The Martyr's Triumph; The Triumph of Venus; Charity; Prayer; The Invocation; Sappho; The Golden Age.*

Brangwyn, Frank (born 1867), Belgium : *Modern Commerce; Trade on the Beach; St Simeon Stylites; · Sweetmeat Seller; Turkish Boatmen; The Scoffers.*

Breton, Jules Aldolphe Aimé Louis (1827–1906), France : *Return of the Harvesters; Little Gleaner; The Day after St Sebastian's Day; Women Weeding; The Song of the Lark; Twilight Glory.*

Breughel, Jan (1568–1625), Flanders : Paintings of flowers and fruits, landscapes and sea-pieces.

Breughel, Pieter the Elder (1525 ?–1569), Flanders : Humorous pictures.

Breughel, Pieter the Younger (1564–1637), Flanders : *Christ Bearing the Cross.*

Bril, Paul (1554–1626), Flanders : *Martyrdom of S. Clement;* landscapes.

Bronzino, Angelo Allori (1502–1572), Florence : *Lucrezia Panciatichi; Venus and Cupid; Dante; Petrarch; Boccaccio.*

Brouwer, Adrian (1605 or 1606–1638), Holland : *The Gamblers.*

Brown, Ford Madox (1821–1893), England : *Christ Washing S. Peter's Feet; Job on the Ash-heap; Chaucer at the Court of Edward III.; The Last of England; Jacob and Joseph's Coat; Elijah and the Widow's Son; The Entombment.*

Brunelleschi, Filippo (1377–1446), Florence : Finished the *Cathedral at Florence;* designed the *Pitti Palace.*

Buonarroti : see **Michelangelo.**

Burgkmair, Hans (1473–1531), Germany : 700 woodcuts ; series of 135 prints of *Triumphs of Emperor Maximilian;* frescoes.

Burne-Jones, Sir Edward, Bart. (1833–1898), England : *Love among the Ruins; Briar Rose* (series) ; *The Golden Stairs; Pygmalion* (series) ; *The Mirror of Venus; Chant d'Amour; Pygmalion and the Image* (series of four) ; *Wheel of Fortune; King Cophetua and the Beggar Maid; The Story of Perseus* (series) ; *Arthur in Avalon.*

C

Cabanel, Alexandre (1823–1889), France : *Birth of Venus.*

Cameron, Sir D. Y. (1865–1945), Scotland : *Ben Ledi; The Ochils.*

Canaletto (or Antonio Canale) (1697–1768), Venice : *A View Looking towards Murano; View on the Grand Canal, Venice; Regatta on the Grand Canal.*

Cappelle, Van de (1624–1679), Holland : *A Calm.*

Caravaggio, Michelangelo Amerighi da (1569–1609), Italy : *Entombment of Christ; St Sebastian; Alof de Vignacourt and his Page; Supper at Emmaus.*

Caravaggio, Polidoro Caldara da (1495 ?–1543), Italy : *Crucifixion; Christ Bearing the Cross.*

Carpaccio, Vittore (1465 ?–1522 ?), Venice: *The Vision of S. Ursula; Life of the Virgin; Life of St Stephen; Dead Christ.*

Carracci, Ludovico, Agostino and **Annibale** (uncle and two nephews) (born 1555, 1557, 1560 respectively), Bologna:
  (1) **Ludovico:** *Madonna Standing on the Moon; John the Baptist; St Jerome; St Benedict; Limbo of the Fathers.*
  (2) **Agostino:** *Communion of St Jerome; Celestial, Terrestrial, and Venal Love.*
  (3) **Annibale:** *Dead Christ in the Lap of the Madonna; St Roch Distributing Alms.*

Castagno, Andrea del (1390–1457), Florence: *Nicola di Tolentino.*

Catena, Vicenzo di Biagio (1470 ?–1531 ?): *The Martyrdom of S. Christina.*

Cavallini, Pietro (1279 ?–1364), Rome: *Last Judgment; fresco of the Crucifixion.* Surmised to have executed the mosaics of Edward the Confessor in Westminster Abbey.

Cellini, Benvenuto (1500–1571), Florence: metal worker and sculptor: *Perseus holding the Head of Medusa.*

Cezanne, Paul (1839–1906), France: *The Bathers;* still life and landscapes.

Chantrey, Sir Francis Legatt (1781–1841), England; sculptor: *Sleeping Children.*

Chardin, Jean Siméon (1699–1779), France: *The Cook; The Admonition.*

Chodowiecki, Daniel Nicolas (1726–1801), Poland: Miniatures of *The History of the Life of Jesus Christ; Jean Calais and his Family.*

Cimabue, Giovanni (1240 ?–1302 ?), Florence: *Madonna and Child with Angels; St Francis; Saviour Enthroned and some Angels; Four Evangelists with Angels;* Mosaic of *Christ in Glory between the Virgin and John the Evangelist.*

Claude, Gellée (1600–1682), France: *Landscape with Rest on the Flight; Marriage of Isaac and Rebecca; Embarkation of the Queen of Sheba.*

Clausen, Sir George (1852–1944), England: *Girl at the Gate; Showers.*

Clouet, François (1510–1572), France: *Elizabeth of Austria; Mary, Queen of Scots; Charles IX.; Marguerite of France;* attributed to him—*Francis I.; Catherine de' Medici.*

Cole, George Vicat (1833–1893), England: *The Pool of London.*

Conegliano, Cima da (1489–1517), Venice: Altar-piece in Cathedral of Conegliano, *The Presentation in the Temple.*

Constable, John (1776–1837), England: *The Cornfield; Flatford Mill; The White Horse; The Haywain; A View on the Stour; Salisbury Cathedral from the Bishop's Garden; Hadleigh Castle; Salisbury Cathedral from the Meadows; The Cenotaph; Arundel Mill and Castle.*

Constant, Jean Joseph Benjamin (1845–1902), France: *Hamlet et le Roi; Trop Tard; Samson et Dalila; Queen Victoria.*

Cope, Sir Arthur Stockdale (1857–1940), England: Portraits.

Cornelius, Peter von (1783–1867), Germany: Designs from *Faust;* Frescoes of *Last Judgment; The Creator; The Nativity; The Crucifixion;* Series of Cartoons from *The Apocalypse.*

Corot, Jean-Baptiste Camille (1796–1875), France: *Souvenir de Morte Fontaine; Woodgatherers; Une Matinée; Macbeth; Le Lac; L'Arbre Brisé; Pastorale Souvenir d'Italie; Bibles; Spring; Lady in Blue.*

Correggio, Antonio Allegri (1494–1534), Italy: *The Education of Cupid; The Holy Night; Arrest of Christ;* Triple Altar-piece: *Repose in Egypt, with Sts. Bartholomew* and *John; Ecce Homo; St Jerome.*

Cossa, Francesco del (1435–1477 ?), Ferrara: *Allegory of Harvest.*

Costa, Lorenzo (1460–1535), Ferrara: *Madonna and Child with the Bentivoglia Family; Madonna and Child Enthroned.*

Cox, David (1783–1859), England: Landscapes; *Going to the Mill; Old Mill at Bettws-y-Coed; Outskirts of a Wood with Gypsies; Peace and War.*

Cranach, Lucas (1472–1553), Germany: *The Rest on the Flight.*

Credi, Lorenzo di (1459–1537), Florence: *The Annunciation; Study of a Baby's Arm; Virgin and Child with Saints; Madonna; Virgin and Child.*

Crivelli, Carlo (1430 ?–1493), Venice: *The Annunciation; Beato Ferretti; Madonna and Saints; Dead Christ.*

Crome, John (1769–1821), England: *The Portingland Oak; Mousehold Heath, near Norwich; Clump of Trees, Hautbois Common; The Willow; Coast Scene near Yarmouth; Bruges on the Ostend River; Slate Quarries; Fishmarket at Boulogne.*

Cruikshank, George (1792–1878), England: engraver, black and white artist: *The Political House that Jack Built; The Humorist; Life in Paris; Life in London; The Life of Sir John Falstaff.*

Cuyp, Albert (1620–1691), Holland: *Hilly Landscape in Morning Light; Night on the Banks of a River; Orpheus Charming the Beasts; Philip Baptizing the Eunuch; Meuse and Rhine Landscapes; Riders with the Boy and Herdsman; The Huntsman; Piper with Cows.*

D

Daubigny, Charles François (1817–1878), France: *Lock at Optevoz; Moonlight; Springtime; Borde de la Cure, Morvan; Return of the Flock—Moonlight.*

David, Gerard (1450 ?–1523), Holland: *St John*; *St Jerome*; *Pieta*; *Descent from the Cross*; *Marriage of St Catherine*; *Madonna Enthroned and Saints*; *Annunciation*; *Madonna with Angels and Saints*; *The Judgment of Cambyses*; *Transfiguration*.

David, Jacques Louis (1748–1825), France: *The Grief of Andromache*; *The Oath of the Horatii*; *The Death of Socrates*; *Love of Paris and Helen*; *Brutus*; *The Oath of the Tennis Court*; *Marat Assassinated*; *The Coronation* (of Josephine); *Distribution of the Eagles*; *Madame Récamier*.

David, Pierre Jean (1789–1856), France: statue of *Barra the Drummer Boy*; monument to *Bozzaris*; *Reviving Greece*; monument to *General Gobert* in Père Lachaise; Marble *Philopoemen*.

Da Vinci, Leonardo, see Vinci.

Delacroix, Ferdinand Victor Eugène (1798–1863), France: *Dante and Virgil*; *Massacre of Chios*; *Marino Faliero decapitated on the Giant's Staircase of the Ducal Palace*; *Sardanapalus*; *Taking of Constantinople by the Christians*.

Delaroche, Hippolyte (1797–1856), France: *The King in the Guard Room*; *Strafford led to Execution*; *Richelieu in his Barge and Cinq Mars on his Way to Execution*; *Young Female Martyr floating Dead on the Tiber*; *Assassination of the Duc de Guise at Blois*; *Head of an Angel*; *Napoleon at St Helena*; *Marie Antoinette leaving the Convention*.

Della Robbia, Andrea (1435–1525), Florence; sculpture: enamelled clay reliefs.

Della Robbia, Giovanni (1469–1529 ?), Florence; sculpture: enamelled clay reliefs.

Della Robbia, Girolamo (1488–1566), Florence: sculpture and architecture: built the Château de Madrid in the Bois de Boulogne.

Della Robbia, Luca (1399–1482), Florence: sculpture: singing gallery in cathedral at Florence; bronze reliefs on sacristy door in cathedral at Florence.

(The Della Robbia family developed the enamelling of clay to a high degree. It is known as the *Robbia* ware.)

Detaille, Jean Baptiste Edouard (1848–1912), France: *A Halt*; *The Conquerors*; *The Retreat*; *Hail to the Wounded*; *Bonaparte in Egypt*.

Diaz, Narcisse Virgilio (1808–1876), France: *La Fée aux Perles*; *Sunset in the Forest*; *The Storm*; *The Forest of Fontainebleau*.

Dicksee, Sir Francis Bernard (Frank) (1853–1928), England: *La Belle Dame Sans Merci*; portraits.

Domenichino, Zampieri (1581–1641), Bologna: *Communion of St Jerome*; *Adam and Eve*; *Scourging of St Andrew*; *Martyrdom of St Agnes*; *Death of Adonis*; *Diana and her Nymphs*.

Donatello, Donato di Betto Bardi (1386 ?–1466), Florence: statues of the Prophets—

David; *St John the Evangelist*; *St Peter*; *St George*; *St Mark*; *Abraham*; *St John the Baptist*. Reliefs — *Herod's Feast*; *Ascension*; *Miracles of St Anthony*.

Dou, Gerard (1613–1675), Holland: *The Herring Seller*; *The Poulterer's Shop*; *Dropsical Woman*.

Dupré, Jules (1812–1889), France: landscapes—*Morning*; *Evening*; *Crossing the Bridge*.

Dürer, Albrecht (1471–1528), Germany: *The Virgin and Child with a Pear*; *Christ Crucified*; *The Adoration of the Magi*; *The Praying Hands*; *Adam and Eve*; *Orpheus*; *Feast of the Rosaries*.

E

Eastlake, Sir Charles Lock (1793–1865), England: *Pilgrims in Sight of Jerusalem*; *Hagar and Ishmael*.

Eeckhout, Gerbrandt van den (1621–1674), Holland: *Portrait of Dappers*; *Gambling Soldiers*; *Soldiers' Merrymaking*; *Sportsman with Hounds*; *Group of Children with Goats*; *Christ in the Temple*.

Etty, William (1787–1849), England: *Coral-finders*; *Cleopatra's Arrival in Cilicia*; *Combat*; *Judith and Holofernes*.

Eyck, Hubert van (1366 ?–1426), Holland: *Worship of the Lamb*; *Maries at the Sepulchre*; *The Vision of St Francis of Assisi*.

Eyck, Jan van (1385 ?–1440), Holland: *G. Arnolfini of Lucca and his Wife*; *Travelling Altarpieces of Charles V.*; *Leal Souvenir*; *Portrait of a Man with a Turban*; *Man with the Pinks*.

F

Farquharson, Joseph (d. 1935), Scotland: *Glory of Departing Day*; *First of Winter's Snow.*

Fildes, Sir Luke (1844–1927), England: *The Casual Ward*; *The Doctor*; portraits.

Flaxman, John (1755–1826), England: statues of *St Michael*; *Nelson*; *Howe*; bas-reliefs of *Apollo*; *Marpessa*; *Pandora conveyed to Earth by Mercury.*

Floris, Frans (de Vriendt) (1520 ?–1570), Flanders: *Mars and Venus ensnared by Vulcan*; *Last Judgment.*

Forli, Melozzo da (1438–1494), Italy: *The Archangel Gabriel.*

Fragonard, Jean-Honoré (1732–1806), France: *Jeroboam Sacrificing to the Idols*; *Christ Washing the Feet of the Apostles*; *Corésus et Callirhoé*; *The Love Vow*; *The Bolt*; *The Tumble*; *The Swing*; *Billet Doux*; *The Fountain of Love*; *The Schoolmistress*; *A Lady Carving her Name on a Tree.*

Frampton, Sir George (1860–1928), England, Sculptor: *Peter Pan*; *La Belle Dame Sans Merci.*

Francesco, Piero della (16th century), Italy: *Madonna, Child, and Angels; The Dream of Constantine; Portrait of an Unknown Lady* (attributed).

Francia, Franc (1450–1517), Bologna: *The Entombment.*

Frith, William Powell (1819–1909), England: *The Derby Day; The Railway Station.*

Furse, Charles Wellington (1868–1904), England: *Diana of the Uplands; Cain; Lord Roberts; The Return from the Ride; Cubbing with the York and Ainsty; The Lilac Gown; Mr and Mrs Oliver Fishing; Lord Charles Beresford.*

Fyt, Johannes (1609–1661), Flanders: *Silenus amongst Fruit and Flowers; Diana and her Nymphs with the Produce of the Chase; Dead Game and Fruit in front of a Triumphal Arch.* (Schut and Willeborts painted the figures in this, and Quellyn the architectural backgrounds.)

G

Gaddi, Agnolo (1350 ?–1396), Florence: *Resurrection of Lazarus;* frescoes of legends of the Virgin and her Sacred Girdle; eight frescoes of the Legend of the Cross.

Gaddi, Gaddo (1260 ?–1333 ?), Florence: frescoes in Upper Church of Assisi of incidents in life of St Francis; mosaics in portico of basilica of S. Maria Maggiore, depicting legend of foundation of the Church.

Gaddi, Taddeo (1300–1366), Florence: fresco of *The Virgin and Child between Four Prophets;* altarpiece; *Virgin and Child.* Triptych— *Virgin Enthroned along with Four Saints; Baptism of Jesus; Deposition from the Cross.*

Gainsborough, Thomas (1727–1788), England: *The Painter's Daughters; The Duchess of Devonshire; Gainsborough Dupont; Miss Hippesley; The Honourable Mrs Graham; The Parish Clerk; Mrs Billington; Mrs Siddons; The Blue Boy; The Market Cart; William Pitt.*

Gellée, Claude (1600–1682), France: *Landscape with Rest on the Flight.*

Gerard, François, Baron (1770–1837), France: *The Tenth of August; Bélisaire; Psyché et l'Amour; Bataille d'Austerlitz; L'Entrée d'Henri IV.;* portraits of famous people.

Ghirlandajo, Dom del (1449–1494), Florence: *An Old Man and his Grandson; The Vision of Santa Fina.*

Gilbert, Sir John (1817–1897), England: *Holbein painting the Portrait of Anne Boleyn; Touchstone and the Shepherd; Rembrandt; Naseby; The Trumpeter; Richard II. resigning his Crown; The Turkish Water Carrier.*

Giorgione, Georgio Barbarelli (1477–1511), Venice: *The Madonna Enthroned; Concert Champêtre; Figures in a Landscape; The Sleeping Venus;* attributed— *Judith; Portrait of a Man.*

Giotto, di Bondone (1267 ?–1337), Florence: *St Francis and the Birds; Marriage of St Francis to Poverty; Allegory of Chastity; Allegory of Obedience; Vision of St Francis in Glory; High Altarpiece for St Peter's; Mosaic of Christ saving St Peter from the Waves* (celebrated *Navicella*); series of Frescoes entirely covering internal walls of chapel of the Virgin of the Annunciation (Padua).

Goes, Hugo van der (1435?–1482), Flanders: triptych of life-sized figures (Uffizi); *S. Victor and a Donar* (attributed).

Gogh, Vincent van (1853–1890), Holland: *L'Arlésienne; Sunflowers; View of Arles.*

Goya y Lucientes, Francisco José de (1746–1828), Spain: *The Duke of Wellington; Charles II.; Charles IV.; Ferdinand VII.; King Joseph; Duchess of Alva; Al Fresco Breakfast; Curate Feeding the Devil's Lamp; Los Caprichos; Los Proverbios; Los Destrastres de la Guerra.*

Goyen, Jan van, Josephszoon (1596–1656), Holland: *View of the Hague; Winter Skating Scenes; Embarkation of Charles II.* (attributed).

Gozzoli, Benozzo (1420–1498), Florence: *Virgin and Child with Saints; St Thomas Receiving the Girdle of the Virgin; The Glory of St Thomas Aquinas.*

Greuze, Jean Baptiste (1725–1805), France: *A Girl with a Dove; Sophie Arnould; The Milkmaid; La Jeune Fille qui pleure son Oiseau Mort; La Bonne Mère; Le Mauvais Fils puni; La Malédiction Paternelle; Petite Fille au Chien Noir.*

Grunewald, Mathias (1475–1530): *St Maurice and Mary Magdalen between Four Saints;* altarpieces.

H

Hals, Franz (1580 or 1581–1666), Holland: *W. van Heythuysen; A Family Group; The Laughing Cavalier; Hille Bobbe, the Witch of Haarlem.*

Heda, William Classz (1594 ?–1670 ?), Holland: *Luncheon.*

Heem, Johannes de (1606–1683 or 1684), Holland: pictures of still life: tankard, bottle, silver cup, and lemon on marble table; creepers, gourds, blackberries, twigs of orange, myrtle, and peach with butterflies, moths, and beetles; also, wreathed *Madonna.*

Heemskerk, Marten van (1498–1574), Holland: *Adam and Eve; St Luke Painting the Likeness of the Virgin and Child; Ecce Homo; Crucifixion; Judgment of Momus; Golgotha; Flight into Egypt; Christ on the Mount; Triumph of Silenus; Last Judgment.*

Helst, Bartholomeus van der (1613 ?–1670),
Holland: *Burgomaster Bicker; Andreas
Bicker the Younger; Peace of Münster.*

Herkomer, Sir Hubert von (1849–1914),
Bavaria: *The Last Muster; Found;
The Chapel of the Charterhouse.*

Heyden, Jan van der (1637–1712), Holland:
pictures of Dutch houses and *Cologne
Cathedral.*

Hobbema, Meyndert (1638–1709), Holland:
*The Avenue, Middelharnis; Ruins of
Breberode Castle; A Wooded Landscape;
A Forest.*

Hogarth, William (1697–1764), England:
engravings: *The Harlot's Progress* (6
plates); *The Rake's Progress* (8 plates);
*Mariage à la Mode; Four Times of the
Day; Strolling Actresses dressing in a
Barn.* Oil-paintings: originals of the
above: *Garrick as Richard III.; Por-
trait of the Artist with his Dog Trump;
Sigismunda; Lavinia Fenton; Shrimp
Girl; Gate of Calais; Captain Corain;
The Lady's Last Stake; Paul before
Felix; Moses Brought to Pharaoh's
Daughter.*

Holbein, Hans, the Elder (1460 ?–1524),
German: *Two Madonnas* in Moritz
Chapel; *Basilica of St Paul;* series of
Passion pictures; *Martyrdom of St
Sebastian.*

Holbein, Hans, the Younger (1497–1543),
German: *King Henry VIII.; The
Duchess of Milan; Georg Gisze; Portrait
of Morette; Earl de la Warr;* series of
Passion pictures: *Jacob Meyer and his
Wife; Madonna and St Pantalus; Kaiser
Henry with the Empress Kunigunde;
Erasmus; Sir Thomas More; Warham;
Wyatt; Thomas Cromwell; Rehoboam
receiving the Israelite Envoys; The Am-
bassadors; Triumphs of Wealth and
Poverty; Jane Seymour; Christine of
Denmark; Prince Edward.*

Hondekoeter, Melchior de (1636–1695),
Holland: *Jackdaw Deprived of his
Borrowed Plumes.*

Honthorst, Gerard van (1590–1656), Holland:
*Duke of Buckingham and Family; King
and Queen of Bohemia; Marie de Medici;
Princes Charles Louis, and Rupert; Lord
Craven; Lute Player; Allegory of Charles I.
and his Queen as Apollo and Diana.*

Hooch, Pieter de (1630–1677), Holland: *A
Dutch Interior with Soldiers; Court of a
Dutch House; A Woman Peeling Apples;
The Card Players; Mug of Beer; Music
Party; Mother Seated near a Cradle;
Smoking Party.*

Hoppner, John (1759–1810), England: *The
Countess of Oxford; The Sackville
Children; Lady C. Campbell as Aurora;
The Jessamy Bride; King Lear; Prince
of Wales; Duke and Duchess of York;
Lord Rodney; Lord Nelson; Sir Walter
Scott; Wellington; Frere; Sir George
Beaumont.*

Hunt, William Holman (1827–1910), England: *Valentine rescuing Sylvia from
Proteus; The Hireling Shepherd; Claudio
and Isabella; The Strayed Sheep; The
Light of the World; The Awakened Conscience; The Scapegoat; The Finding of
Our Saviour in the Temple; The Shadow
of Death; The Triumph of the Innocents.*

Huysum, Jan van (1682–1749), Holland:
pictures of fruit and flowers.

I

Ingres, Jean Auguste Dominique (1780–1867),
France: *Ambassadors of Agamemnon in
the Tent of Achilles; Girl after Bathing;
Portrait of the First Consul; Portrait of
the Emperor; Œdipus and the Sphinx;
Venus Anadyomene; M. Bochet; Mme
la Comtesse de Tournon; Francesca di
Rimini; Vœu de Louis XIII.; Jeanne
d'Arc.*

Israëls, Josef (1824–1911), Holland: *The
Zandvoort Fisherman; The Silent House;
Village Poor; Shipwrecked; The Cradle;
The Widower; When We Grow Old; Alone
in the World; A Frugal Meal; Toilers of
the Sea; David Singing before Saul.*

J

Janssen, Cornelius (1593–1664 ?), Flanders:
Milton.

John, Augustus Edwyn (born 1879), England:
*The Way down to the Sea; The Smiling
Woman; Peasant Industry; Robin;
Rachael; Canadians Opposite Lens;
Portraits of Ministers at the Peace Con-
ference.*

Jones, Inigo (1573–1652), England: said to
have designed the royal palaces of *Rosen-
borg* and *Frederiksborg* for the King of
Denmark. Design for palace of *Whitehall.*

Jordaens, Jacob (1593–1678), Flanders:
portrait painter.

K

Kauffman, (Maria Anna) Angelica (1741–
1807), Switzerland: *Portrait of Garrick;
Portrait of Sir Joshua Reynolds; Leonardo expiring in the Arms of Francis the
First; Lady Hamilton.*

Kaulbach, Wilhelm von (1805–1874), Germany: *Destruction of Jerusalem; Battle
of the Huns; Tower of Babel; Age of
Homer; Crusades; The Reformation.*

Kneller, Sir Godfrey (1646–1723), Germany:
*Charles II.; Louis XIV.; Forty-three
Celebrities of the Kit-Cat Club; Ten
Beauties of the Court of William III.;
Converted Chinese.*

Koninck, Philips de (1619–1688), Holland:
*Vue de l'Embouchure d'une Rivière ;
Paysage ;* portraits.

L

Lancret, Nicolas (1690–1743), France : *The
Music Lesson ; Spring ; Innocence ;
Summer.*

Landseer, Sir Edwin Henry (1802–1873),
England : *Fighting Dogs Getting Wind ; High
Life ; Low Life ; The Cavalier's Pets ; The
Old Shepherd's Chief Mourner ; Dignity
and Impudence ; The Sanctuary ; The Twa
Dogs ; Man Proposes, God Disposes.*

Lavery, Sir John (1857–1941), Ireland :
Wounded Soldiers, London Hospital, 1915 ;
portraits.

Lawrence, Sir Thomas (1769–1830), England :
*Georgina Lennox ; William Wilberforce ;
Master Lambton ; Satan.*

Leader, Benjamin Williams (1831–1922),
England : *The Valley of the Llugwy.*

Le Brun, Charles Vigée (1619–1690), France :
Marie Antoinette ; The Boy in Red.

Leighton, Frederick Leighton, Baron (1830–
1896), England : *Dante in Exile ; Wedded ;
Hercules Wrestling with Death for the
Body of Alcestis ; Clytemnestra ; Captive
Andromache ; Perseus and Andromeda ;
Electra at the Tomb of Agamemnon ; The
Daphnephoria ; The Bath of Psyche.*
Sculpture — *Athlete Struggling with a
Python.*

Lely, Sir Peter (1618–1680), Germany ; came
to England, 1641 : *Charles I. ; Oliver
Cromwell ; The Beauties* (collection of
portraits of ladies of Charles II.'s Court) ;
Susannah and the Elders.

Leonardo da Vinci, see Vinci.

Liotard, Jean Étienne (1702–1789), Switzerland : portraits of Royalty ; pastel
drawings ; *La Liseuse ; The Chocolate
Girl ; La Belle Lyonnaise.*

Lippi, Fra Filippo (1406–1469), Florence :
The Holy Family ; The Virgin.

Longhi, Pietro (1702–1762), Venice : *Daniele
Dolfino ; The Seven Sacraments ; Templa-
tion of St Anthony ; Circus ; Gambling
Scene ; Exhibition of a Rhinoceros in an
Arena ; Domestic Group ; The Fortune
Teller.*

Lorenzo, Fiorenzo di (1440 ?–1522), Italy :
*Madonna and Saints ; Nativity ; Adora-
tion of the Magi ; Adoration of the Shepherds.*

Lotto, Lorenzo (1480 ?–1556 ?), Venice : *St
Jerome ; Assumption of the Virgin ;
Entombment ; Transfiguration ; St James ;
St Vincent ; Bride and Bridegroom ;
Triumph of Chastity ; Christ and the
Adulteress ; Crucifixion ; Madonna and
Saints.*

Luini, Bernardino (1475–1533), Milan : *Head
of the Virgin Mary ; The Holy Family ;
The Madonna of the Rose Bower ; A*

Kneeling Angel (facing right); *A Kneeling
Angel* (facing left).

Lysippus (fl. 336–270 B.C.), Greece:
statues of *Alexander the Great,* and of
athletes.

M

Mabuse, Jan Gossart (1470 ?–1532 ?),
Flanders : *The Adoration of the Kings ;
Neptune and Amphitrite ; The Madonna ;
Iean Carondelet ; Adam and Eve ;
Portrait of Children of Christian II. of
Denmark.*

MacCulloch, Horatio (1805–1867), Scotland :
Kilchurn Castle and other Scottish landscapes.

Maclise, Daniel (1806–1870), Ireland : *The
Meeting of Wellington and Blücher ; The
Death of Nelson.*

Maes, Nicholas (1632–1693), Holland : *The
Cradle ; The Dutch Housewife ; The Idle
Servant ; The Card Players ; The Listen-
ing Girl.*

Manet, Edouard (1832–1883), France : (Im-
pressionist) : *A Nymph Surprised ; The
Angels at the Tomb ; The Dead Man ;
Olympia ; The Balcony ; The Execution
of the Emperor Maximilian ; The Garden ;
Hamlet.*

Mantegna, Andrea (1431–1506), Italy :
*Madonna, Child and Cherubim ; St
George ; St Euphemia ; Parnassus ;
Minerva Triumphing over the Vices ; The
Agony in the Garden ; Vestals ; The
Triumph of Scipio.*

Maris, Jacob (1837–1899), Holland : *Grey
Tower, Old Amsterdam ; Landscape near
Dordrecht ; Seaweed Carts, Scheveningen;
A Village Scene.*

Martini, Simone (Simon di Martino, Simon
Memmi) (1283–1344), Siena : *Madonna
Enthroned with the Infant ; Christ found
by His Parents in the Temple.*

"Masaccio" (Tommaso Guidi) (1401–1428),
Italy : Frescoes, including scenes from the
life of St Peter.

Mason, George Hemming (1818–1872),
England : *Ploughing in the Campagna ;
In the Salt Marshes, Campagna ; Evening
Hymn ; Girls Dancing by the Sea ;
Harvest Moon.*

Maurier, Georges Louis Palmella Busson du
(1834–1896), France : Society pictures,
black and white.

Mauve, Anton (1838–1888), Holland : *Milk-
ing Time ; A Fishing Boat Putting to Sea ;
A Flock of Sheep ; The Sand Cart ;
Watering Horses.*

May, Philip William (1865–1903), England :
Caricaturist : Studies of the guttersnipe
and coster girl.

Meer, Jan Van der, of Delft (1632–1675),
Holland : *Christ with Martha and Mary ;
Woman and Soldier ; Reading Girl ; The
Milk Woman ; The Letter ; Diana and*

the Nymphs; The Coquette; Woman Reading; Lady at a Casement; Music Master and Pupil; The Lace-Maker.

Meissonier, Jean Louis Ernest (1815–1891), France: *A Musketeer; The Bravos; La Rixe; Game of Chess; Young Man of the Time of the Regency; Retreat from Moscow; The Quarrel; Cuirassiers; The Emperor at Solferino.*

Memlinc, Hans (1430?–1494), Germany: *The Duke of Cleves; Sir John Donne; The Seven Griefs of Mary; Last Judgment; Madonna and Saints; Virgin and Child; Sybil Zambetha; The Seven Joys of Mary; Crucifixion; Newenhoven Madonna.*

Mengs, Antony Raphael (1728–1779), Bohemia: *Cupid Sharpening his Arrow; Ascension; Perseus and Andromeda; Holy Family.*

Messina, Antonello da (1430?–1479), Italy: *The Crucifixion.*

Metsu, Gabriel (1630?–1667), Holland: *Lazarus; Woman Taken in Adultery; Departure of Hagar; The Widow's Mite; Women at a Fishmonger's Shop; Market Place of Amsterdam; The Tavern; Tabby Cat; Sleeping Sportsman.*

Metsys (Matsys), Quentin (1466?–1530), Flanders: *The Magdalen; Le Banquier et sa Femme; Virgin and Christ; Mater Dolorosa.*

Michelangelo (Buonarroti) (1475–1564), Florence; Sculpture: *David; Head of a Faun; Moses; Two Slaves; The Medici Monument; Victory; Leah and Rachel; Dome of St Peter's.* Painting: *Holy Family; Frescoes in the Sixtine Chapel, from the Creation to the Flood; Last Judgment.*

Miereveld, Michiel Janez Van (1567–1641), Holland: *A Child with a Parrot; Christ and the Samaritan; Judith and Holofernes; William of Orange; Count Palatine Frederick V.; The King of Bohemia; Louise de Coligny.*

Millais, Sir John Everett (1829–1896), England: *The Boyhood of Raleigh; Souvenir of Velasquez; The Huguenot; Christ in the House of His Parents; Ophelia; The Carpenter's Shop; Autumn Leaves; The Eve of St Agnes; Vanessa; Cherry Ripe; Bubbles; The North-West Passage.*

Millet, Jean François (1814–1875), France: *The Angelus; Sailors Mending a Sail; Milkwoman; Lesson in Riding; The Winnower; Girls Sewing; The Reapers; The Gleaners; Man with a Hoe; Washerwoman at her Tub.*

" Moretto, Il " (Alessandro Bonvicino) (1498–1554), Italy: *Five Virgin Martyrs; Assumption of the Madonna; St Joseph; St Nicholas of Bari; St Justina; Adoration of the Shepherds.*

Morland, George (1763–1804), England: *The Idle and the Industrious Mechanic; The Idle Laundress and the Industrious Cottager; Inside of a Stable.*

Morland, Henry Robert (1730?–1797), England: *The Laundry Maid.*

Moro, Antonio (1512?–1575) (sometimes known as Sir Anthony More), Verona: *Queen Mary of England; Philip II. of Spain.*

Moroni, Giambattista (1510?–1578), Italy: *The Tailor; Nobleman Pointing to a Flame; Canon Ludovico; Titian's Schoolmaster* (the Jesuit, Ercole Tasso); *Coronation of the Virgin.*

Munkacsy, Michael Von (1845–1900), Hungary: *Milton Dictating 'Paradise Lost' to his Daughters; Christ before Pilate; Golgotha; The Death of Mozart; Arpad, Chief of the Magyars, taking possession of Hungary; Ecce Homo.*

Murillo, Bartolomé Estéban (1617–1682), Spain: *S. Anthony of Padua; Flight into Egypt; Nativity of the Virgin; Virgin of the Conception; Faith; Moses Striking the Rock; Return of the Prodigal; Abraham Receiving the Three Angels; Charity of San Juan de Dios; St Elizabeth of Hungary; Charity of St Thomas of Villanueva.*

Murray, Sir David (1849–1934), Scotland: *London Bridge; The River Road; The White Heat.*

N

Nasmyth, Alexander (1758–1840), Scotland *Portrait of Robert Burns; Landscapes.*

Nattier, Jean Marc (1685–1766), France: *Madame Sophie de France; Battle of Pultawa; Petrification of Phineus; Magdalen; La Camargo; Mme de Pompadour; Louis XV.; Le Silence; Le Point du Jour.*

Neer, Ærnout Van der (1603–1677), Holland: *Winter Landscape; Moonlight Scene.*

Neer, Eglon Van der (1643–1703), Holland: *Lady with the Book; Cleopatra; Tobit and the Angel; Esther and Ahasuerus.*

Neuville, Alphonse Marie de (1836–1885), France: *The Fifth Battalion of Chasseurs at the Gervais Battery; The Attack in the Streets of Magenta by Zouaves and the Light Horse; The Last Cartridges.*

O

Orcagna, Andrea (1316?–1368?), Florence: Frescoes on three walls of the Strozzi Chapel; *Last Judgment; St Zenobio Enthroned;* Marble tabernacle in Chapel of Or San Michele in Florence of combined reliefs, statuettes and mosaic.

Orchardson, Sir William Quiller (1835–1910), Scotland: *The Challenge; Christopher Sly; Queen of the Swords; Conditional Neutrality; Hard Hit; On Board the Bellerophon; Voltaire; Mariage de Convenance; A Tender Chord.*

Orpen, Sir William (1878–1931), Ireland:
*Hon. Percy Wyndham; Myself and Venus;
The Countess of Crawford and Balcarres;
The Passing of his Lordship; A Western
Wedding; Lady Bonham Carter; M.
Clemenceau; The Chef.*

Ostade, Adrian Van (1610–1685), Holland:
*The Bagpiper; Rustics in a Tavern;
Village School; Tavern Courtyard; The
Village Street; The Skittle Players.*

Ostade, Isaac Van (1621–1649), Holland:
*Laughing Boor with a Pot of Beer; Boor
Stealing a Kiss from a Woman.*

Overbeek, Johann Friedrich (1789–1869),
Germany: *Seven Years of Famine; Joseph
Sold by his Brethren; Vision of St Francis;
Christ's Entry into Jerusalem; The
Triumph of Religion in the Arts.*

P

Parmigiano, Francesco (1504–1540), Italy:
*Vision of St Jerome; Madonna and Child
with Margaret and other Saints; Cupid
Making a Bow; Amerigo Vespucci.*

Parsons, Alfred (1847–1920), England:
When Nature Painted All Things Gay; illus-
trations of *She Stoops to Conquer,* Herrick's
Poems; and *The Danube, from the Black
Forest to the Black Sea.*

Patinir, Joachim de (d. 1524 ?), Flanders:
The Baptism in Jordan.

Paton, Sir Joseph Noel (1821–1901), Scotland:
*Quarrel of Oberon and Titania; Recon-
ciliation of Oberon and Titania; Christ
Bearing the Cross; The Pursuit of Pleasure.*

Perugino, Pietro (1446–1524), Perugia: *The
Crucifixion; The Archangel Michael; The
Madonna Adoring; The Archangel Raphael
and Tobias; Delivery of the Keys to St
Peter; Gethsemane.*

Pesellino, Francesco (di Stefano) (1422–1457),
Florence: *Madonna, Child, and Saints.*

Peters, Rev. Matthew William (———1814),
England: *A Boy and a Girl.*

Pheidias (about 500–432 B.C.), Greece:
Sculptures of *The Parthenon and the
Propylæa; Zeus; Athene; Aphrodite.*

Pinturicchio, Bernardino di Biaggio (1454–
1513), Siena: *A Young Knight Kneeling;
A Knight of Rhodes; Christ Disputing
with the Doctors; Life of Pius II.; Christ
Bearing the Cross.*

Pisanello, Vittore Pisano (1380 ?–1456),
Verona: *The Vision of St Eustace.*

Pisano, Niccola (1206 ?–1278), Italy: Relief
of *Deposition from the Cross.* Pulpit at
Siena overloaded with reliefs and statuettes
including panel-reliefs of *The Nativity;
The Adoration of the Magi; The Presenta-
tion in the Temple; The Crucifixion; The
Doom; The Arca di San Domenico;
Fountain at Perugia.* Architect of the
Cathedral at Pistoia, and other Buildings.

Pollaiuolo, Antonio (1429–1498), Florence:

Martyrdom of St Sebastian; sculpture and
medals.

Polycletus (5th century B.C.), Greek sculptor.

Potter, Paul (1625–1654), Holland: *Young
Bull; The Dairy Farm.*

Poussin, Nicolas (1594–1665), France: *Death
of Germanicus; Triumphs of Flora;
Massacre of the Innocents; Seven Sacra-
ments* (series); *Last Supper; Labours of
Hercules* (series); *Triumph of Truth;
Diogenes Throwing away his Scoop;
Vision of St Paul; Holy Family;
Triumph of Pan; Sacrifice of Abraham.*

Poynter, Sir Edward John (1836–1919), England: *Faithful unto Death; The Catapult.*

Praxiteles (about 400–320 B.C.), Greece:
Sculptured group, *Hermes Carrying the Boy
Dionysus; Apollo; Aphrodite.*

Predis, Ambrogio di (15th–16th centuries),
Italy: *Beatrice d'Este.*

Puvis de Chavannes, Pierre Cecile (1824–
1898), France: *La Paix; La Guerre;
Le Travail; Le Repos; Automne; La
Nuit; La Vigilance; Marseille, Port de
l'Orient; Charles Martel; Scènes de la
Vie de Ste Geneviève; Pro Patria Ludus;
Vision Antique; Inspiration Chrétienne.*

Q

Quesnel, François (1544 ?–1619), France:
Lady of the Court of Mary Queen of Scots.

R

Raeburn, Sir Henry (1756–1823), Scotland:
*A Boy with a Rabbit; Mrs Scott Moncrieff;
The Leslie Boy; Mrs Lauzun; Sir
Walter Scott.*

Ramsay, Allan (1713–1784), Scotland: *Duke
of Argyll; Lady Mary Coke; Mrs Allan
Ramsay.*

Raphael, Sanzio (1483–1520), Italy: *The
Madonna in the Meadow; The Crucifixion;
Madonna della Colonna; Madonna della
Tenda; St George with the Garter; The
Sistine Madonna; Madonna and Child;
Madonna Granduca; Maddalena Strozzi;
Madonna della Sedia; The Transfigura-
tion.*

Rembrandt van Ryn Harmensz (1606–1669),
Holland: *The Old Soldier; Samson in
Prison; Presentation in the Temple;
Simeon in the Temple; Marriage of
Samson; Flight of the Angel; Night
Watch; Good Samaritan; Winter Scene;
Repose of the Holy Family; John the
Baptist Preaching in the Wilderness;
Jacob Blessing the Sons of Joseph; Lesson
in Anatomy; Jewish Bride;* many Por-
traits.

Reni, Guido (1575–1642), Bologna: *The
Youth of the Virgin.*

K *

Rethel, Alfred (1816–1859), Germany: *The Crossing of the Alps by Hannibal* (series); *Charlemagne frescoes; Nemesis Pursuing a Murderer; Death the Avenger; Death the Friend; Dance of Death; St Boniface.*

Reynolds, Sir Joshua (1723–1792), England: *The Holy Family; Viscount Althorp; Giorgiana, Countess Spencer, and Daughter; Lavinia Bingham, afterwards Countess Spencer; The Age of Innocence; Miss Ridge; The Young Shepherd; The Fortune Teller; Miss Bowles; Mrs Richard Hoare with her Infant Son.*

Ribera, Giuseppe (1588–1656), Spain: *Jacob's Ladder; Martyrdom of St Bartholomew; Descent from the Cross; St Januarius Emerging from the Furnace; Adoration of the Shepherds.*

Richmond, George (1809–1896), England: *Elizabeth Fry.*

Roberti, Ercole de (1450 ?–1496), Italy: *The Israelites Gathering Manna.*

Romney, George (1734–1802), England: *Lady Hamilton with a Goat; Serena Reading; Mrs Taylor; Madame de Genlis; Mrs Robinson (Perdita); Lady Hamilton; Mirth and Melancholy; The Infant Shakespeare.*

Rosa, Salvator (1615–1673), Naples: *Battle-piece; Pythagoras and the Fishermen; The Oath of Catiline; Saul and the Witch of Endor.*

Rosselli, Cosimo (1439–1507), Florence: *Picture of procession which includes Pico of Mirandola; Saints Barbara, Matthew and the Baptist: Massacre of the Innocents.*

Rossellino, Antonio (1427–1479): *Sculptured tomb of Cardinal Prince of Portugal; Medallion relief of Virgin Adoring.*

Rossellino, Bernardo (1409–1464): *Reliefs of St Stephen and the Assumption; Portrait in relief of the physician Giovanni da S. Miniato.*

Rossetti, Dante Gabriel (1828–1882), England: *The Girlhood of Mary Virgin; Ecce Ancilla Domini; The Laboratory; Giotto Painting Dante's Portrait; The Bride; The Beloved; Beata Beatrix; Proserpina in Hades; Dante's Dream.*

Rousseau, Pierre Étienne Théodore (1812–1867), France: *La Descente des Vaches; The Chestnut Avenue; The Marsh in the Landes; Hoar Frost; The Edge of the Forest; A Glade in the Forest of Fontainebleau.*

Rubens, Sir Peter Paul (1577–1640), Germany: *Fruitfulness; The Painter's Sons; Heraclitus; Democritus; Baptism of our Lord; The Circumcision; Virgin in a Glory of Angels; Raising of the Cross; Descent from the Cross;* Series of 24 pictures illustrating the *life of Marie de Medici; Triumph of Henry IV.; Assumption of the Virgin; Massacre of the Innocents; The Blessings of Peace; Helena Fourment; Martyrdom of St Peter; Martyrdom of St Thomas; Judgment of Paris.*

Ruysdael, Jacob van (1628 or 1629–1682), Holland: *The Chace; The Oaks; The Shore at Scheveningen; The Waterfall.*

S

Sacchi, Andrea (1600 ?–1661), Italy: *St Romuald Relating his Vision to Five Monks of his Order; Miracle of St Gregory; Death of St Anna.*

Sargent, John Singer (1856–1925), America: *Carmencita; Coventry Patmore; Carnation, Lily, Lily, Rose.*

Sarto, Andrea del (1487–1531), Florence: *Madonna del Sacco.*

Scheffer, Ary (1795–1858), Holland: *Margaret at her Wheel; Margaret at the Well; Francesca da Rimini.*

Schongauer, Martin (1445 ?–1491), Germany: *Altar-piece in Church of St Martin at Colmar; David with Goliath's Head; The Wise and Foolish Virgins.*

Scopas (about 400–320 B.C.), Greece; sculptor and architect: *Heads of Hercules, Atalanta and two Warriors* (helmeted).

Signorelli, Luca (1442 ?–1524), Italy: *School of Pan;* Frescoes such as *Acts of Moses, Moses and Zipporah, Paradise, Eternal Destiny of Man, Hell; Baptism of Christ.*

Snyders, Franz (1579–1657), Holland: *Stag Hunt;* pictures of flowers, fruit and animals.

Solomon, Solomon Joseph (1860–1927), England: *Samson and Delilah;* Portraits.

Steen, Jan (1626–1679), Holland: *Youth or Age?*

Stevens, Alfred (1818–1875), England; sculptor: *Wellington Monument,* intended for St Paul's Cathedral.

Stone, Marcus (1840–1921), England: Illustrated books by Charles Dickens, Anthony Trollope, etc.

Stuart, Gilbert (1755–1828): *George Washington.*

Suardi, Bartolommeo (1455 ?–1526 ?), Lombardy: *The Youthful Sforza Reading Cicero.*

Suttermans, Justus (1597–1681), Flanders: *A Prince of Denmark.*

T

Teniers, David (1582–1649), Flanders: *Works of Charity; Vertumnue and Pomona; Juno, Jupiter, and Io; Playing at Bowls; Conversation; Rocky Landscape; The Temptation of St Anthony.*

Teniers, David, the Younger (1610–1690), Flanders: *The Prodigal Son; Topers; The Five Senses; Meeting of the Civic Guards; The Village Fête.*

Teniers, David, son of David the Younger (d. 1685), Flanders: *St Dominic Kneeling before the Blessed Virgin.*

Tenniel, Sir John (1820–1914), England: *An Allegory of Justice; Dropping the Pilot* (Punch); Illustrations of *Æsop's Fables; Lalla Rookh; Alice in Wonderland; The Arabian Nights,* etc.

Terborch, Gerard (1617–1681), Holland: *Helena van der Schalke; The Letter; The Concert; The Glass of Lemonade; Ratification of the Treaty of Peace.*

Thornycroft, Sir William Hamo (1850–1925), England; sculptor: *Warrior Bearing a Wounded Youth from the Field of Battle; Lot's Wife; Artemis; Teucer; Dean Colet; King Alfred; Gladstone Monument; The Kiss.*

Thorwaldsen, Bertel (1770–1844), Denmark; sculptor: *Christ and the Twelve Apostles; Dying Lion; The Three Graces; Night; Morning.*

Tiepolo, Giovanni Battista (1692–1769), Venice: *Deposition from the Cross; Esther at the Throne of Ahasuerus; Marriage of Marie de Medici; Christ and the Adulteress.*

Tintoretto, Jacopo Robusti (1518–1594), Venice: *Adam and Eve; Death of Abel; Worship of the Golden Calf; Presentation of the Virgin in the Temple; Last Judgment; Miracle of the Slave; Crucifixion; Paradise.*

Titian, Tiziano Vecellio (1477–1576), Venice: *Christ Carrying the Cross; Sacred and Profane Love; The Tribute Money; The Three Ages; Worship of Venus; Assumption of the Virgin; Bacchus and Ariadne; Entombment of Christ; The Magdalene; St Peter Martyr;* many Portraits.

Tuke, Henry Scott (1858–1929), England: *Bathers; Pully-Hauly.*

Turner, Joseph Mallord William (1775–1851), England: *View of the Archbishop's Palace, Lambeth; Canterbury Cathedral; Malvern Abbey; Tintern Abbey; Lincoln Cathedral; Peterborough Cathedral; Shipwreck; Fishing Boats in a Squall; Sun Rising through Vapour; Ulysses; Childe Harold's Pilgrimage; The Golden Bough; The Fighting Temeraire; Bridge of Sighs; Peace; Burial at Sea.*

V

Vandyke (or Van Dyck), Sir Anthony (1599–1641), Flanders: *William of Orange and Mary Stuart as Children; The Lamentation over Christ; Vandyke with a Sunflower; The Virgin, Child and St Catherine; The Marchesa Balbi; Rinaldo and Armida; Queen Henrietta Maria; The Balbi Children; Mrs Kirke; Portrait of Francesco Moncada; Elizabeth and Phila-*

delphia Wharton; Philip, Lord Wharton; Portrait of Himself as a Young Man; Prince Carl Louis of Bavaria; The Crucifixion; Prince Ruprecht, Bavaria; The Holy Family; Maria Louisa de Tassis; Charles I. with his Equerry.

Vanloo, Charles Andrew (1705–1765), France: *Marriage of the Virgin.*

Vanloo, John Baptist (1684–1745), France: *Scourging of Christ; Colley Cibber; Owen McSwiney; Sir Robert Walpole.*

Vasari, Giorgio (1512–1574), Italy; painter, architect and art-historian: Wrote *Lives* of famous artists.

Vedder, Elihu (1836–1923), America: *Lair of the Sea Serpent; Young Marsyas; Genii and Fisherman.*

Velasquez, Diego Rodriguez de Silva y (1599–1660), Spain: *The Infanta Margarita Teresa* (in red); *The Infanta in Green; Crucifixion; Christ at the Column; Breakfast; Musicians; Portrait of His Wife; The Water Carrier; St John in the Desert; The Topers; The Forge of Vulcan; Joseph's Coat; Don Baltazar Carlos;* full-length and equestrian portraits of Olivares; *Captain Bartolommæus Borro; Venus and Cupid.*

Velde, Adrian Van de (1635 or 1636–1672), Holland: *Descent from the Cross;* Landscapes of pasture-land, and winter scenes with skaters.

Velde, William Van de (1633–1707), Holland: View off coast of Holland with Dutch shipping.

Vernet, Claude-Joseph (1714–1789), France: Views of seaports, storms, calms, and moonlight scenes. (Two brothers also achieved fame as artists.)

Veronese, Paul (1528–1588), Verona: *S. Helena's Vision of the True Cross; Marriage in Cana; Feast in the House of Levi.*

Verrocchio, Andrea del (1435–1488), Florence: *Baptism of Christ; Tobias and the Angel* (attributed); Marble Medallion of the Madonna; Sculptured Tomb of Giovanni and Piero di Medici; Bronze Statue of David; *The Unbelief of St Thomas* (bronze group); Bronze Equestrian Statue of Bartolommeo Colleoni.

Vierge, Daniel (1851–1904), Spain: *The Shooting in the Rue de la Paix; The Loan; Christmas in Spain; The Republican Meeting in Trafalgar Square; Brigandage in Sicily; The Bull Fight.*

Vinci, Leonardo Da (1452–1519), Italy: *Mona Lisa; The Last Supper.* (Attributed to him)—*The Head of Christ; Ginevra Benci; The Annunciation; Two Angels; Madonna Litta; The Virgin of the Rocks; St John.*

Vivarini, Antonio (fl. 1449–1470), Venice: *Virgin Enthroned with the Four Doctors of the Church; Coronation of the Virgin; Sts Peter and Jerome.*

Vivarini, Bartolommeo (fl. 1450–1499),

Venice: Altar-piece in nine divisions, of St Augustine and other Saints.

Vivarini, Luigi (1446 ?–1502 ?), Venice: *Scuola di S. Girolamo;* Portraits.

W

Walker, Frederick (1840–1875), England: *Spring; Philip in Church; The Old Gate; The Bathers; The Vagrants; The Plough;* Poster for Wilkie Collins' *Woman in White.*

Watt, Fiddes (born 1873), Scotland: Portraits.

Watteau, Antoine (1684–1721), France: *Leçon d'Amour; The Camp Fire; The Embarkment for Cythera; The Seasons; Fête Champêtre; Rustic Amusements; Return from the Chase; The Music Party; A Lady at her Toilet; Harlequin and Columbine; Antiope; Indifference; La Finette; The False Step.*

Watts, George Frederick (1817–1904), England: *Sir Galahad; St George Overcomes the Dragon; Mammon; Jonah; Court of Death; Love and Death; Love Triumphant; The Dweller in the Innermost.*

Webster, Thomas (1800–1886), England: *Mrs Robinson and Family; Going into School, or The Truant; The Dame's School.*

Weenix, Jan (1640–1719), Holland: Hunting Scenes; *Dead Game and a Dog.*

Weenix, Jan Baptist (1621–1660), Holland: *Jacob and Esau; Hunting Scene;* Landscapes, ruins, seaports, dead game.

West, Benjamin (1738–1820), England (born in Pennsylvania): *Death of Wolfe.*

Weyden, Roger Van der (1399 ?–1464), France: *S. Luke Drawing the Virgin;* Triptychs of the *God of Pity,* of the *Magi,* and of the *Crucifixion; The Joys and Sorrows of Mary; The Life of John the Baptist; Annunciation; Adoration; Presentation.*

Whistler, James Abbott McNeill (1834–1903), America: *Thomas Carlyle; Portrait of the Artist's Mother; Nocturne; Zaandam; Sarasate; Lady Archibald Campbell; Little Rose of Lyme Regis; The Music Room; White Girl; Connie Gilchrist.*

Wilkie, Sir David (1785–1841), Scotland: *Ceres in Search of Proserpine; Diana and Calisto; Village Politicians; Pitlessie Fair; Blind Fiddler; Alfred in the Neatherd's Cottage; Village Festival; Letter of Introduction; Chelsea Pensioners Reading the Gazette of the Battle of Waterloo; Bride's Toilet; Preaching of John Knox before the Lords of the Congregation.*

Wilson, Richard (1714–1782), England: *A Landscape; Niobe.*

Wouwerman, Philips (1619–1668), Holland: Cavalry battle-pieces; hunting and hawking parties.

Wyllie, William Lionel (born 1851), England: *Spanish Armada: The Pool of London.*

Z

Zeuxis (d. 396 B.C.), Greece: *Penelope; Helen.*

GREAT COMPOSERS

A

Arcadelt, Jacob (1514 ?–1560 ?), Netherlands: *Ave Maria;* Madrigals.

Arne, Thomas Augustine (1710–1778), England: Operas—*Rosamond, Eliza,* etc.; *The Masque of Alfred* (containing *Rule Britannia);* Oratorios; Songs — *Where the Bee Sucks,* etc.

Auber, Daniel François Esprit (1782–1871), France: Operas—*La Bergère Châtelaine, La Muette de Portici (Masaniello), Fra Diavolo, Le Domino Noir,* etc.; Concertos; Masses, etc.

B

Bach, Johann Sebastian (1685–1750), Germany: Church Music; Church Cantatas (short oratorios); Wedding Cantatas; Masses and choruses; Instrumental Music; Sonatas; Preludes; Fugues; Duets; Overtures; also Vocal Music.

Bach, Karl Philipp Emanuel (1714–1788), Germany: Sonatas and concerted pieces; *The Magnificat;* Cantatas; Songs; Oratorios; Litanies.

Balfe, Michael William (1808–1870), Ireland: Operas—*Siege of Rochelle, The Maid of Artois, Catherine Grey, Joan of Arc, Falstaff, Amelia,* or *The Love Test, Keolanthe, The Bohemian Girl, The Daughter of St Mark, The Enchantress, The Sicilian Bride, The Rose of Castile, Satanella, Bianca, The Puritan's Daughter, The Armourer of Nantes, Blanche de Nevers,* and others; perhaps best known song *Killarney.*

Beethoven, Ludwig Van (1770–1827), Germany: Sonatas for pianoforte, violin or 'cello; pianoforte and string Trios and Quartets; Concertos; Quintets; *Leonore* (opera); Symphonies: *Eroica Symphony;* Sonatas—*The Kreutzer* and *Les Adieux,*

l'absence et le retour; Overture—*Egmont;*
Prometheus (ballet); Scottish Songs.

Bellini, Vincenzo (1802–1835), Sicily:
Operas—*Il Pirata, La Sonnambula,*
Norma, I Puritani, etc.

Benedict, Sir Julius (1804–1885), Germany
(settled in England): Operas—*Gipsy's*
Warning, Brides of Venice, Crusaders,
Lily of Killarney, and others; Oratorio—
St Peter; Cantatas and Symphonies.

Bennett, Sir William Sterndale (1816–1875),
England: Cantatas—*The May Queen,*
The Woman of Samaria; Songs, etc.

Berlioz, Hector (1803–1869), France: Sym-
phonies—*Episode de la Vie d'un Artiste,*
Le Retour à la Vie, Harold en Italie,
Funèbre et Triomphale, Roméo et Juliette;
Opera—*Benvenuto Cellini; Requiem; Te*
Deum; Oratorio—*L'Enfance du Christ;*
Cantata—*La Damnation de Faust;*
Other Works—*Béatrice et Benedict, Les*
Troyens.

Bizet, Georges (1838–1875), France: Cantata
—*Cloris et Clotilde;* Operetta—*Docteur*
Miracle; Operas—*Les Pêcheurs de Perles,*
La Jolie Fille de Perth, Carmen, Djamileh,
L'Arlésienne.

Blow, John (1648–1708), England: Writer of
Hymns and Anthems.

Brahms, Johannes (1833–1897), Germany:
German Requiem; Triumphslied; Sym-
phonies; Serenades; Concertos; Over-
tures; Sonatas; Ballads; Rhapsodies;
Chorale-prelude and Fugue; Hungarian
Dances.

Buck, Dudley (1839–1909), United States:
Cantatas—*Golden Legend, Light of Asia;*
Operas—*Serapis,* and *Deseret;* Symphonic
Overture—*Marmion.*

Byrd, William (1543–1623), England: Writer
of Songs, Madrigals, and Virginal Music.

C

Cavaliere, Emilio del (1550–1602), Italy: *La*
Rappresentazione di Anima e di Corpo
(Oratorio).

Chabrier, Alexis Emmanuel (1841–1894),
France: Operas—*L'Etoile, Gwendoline,*
Le Roi Malgré Lui, Briséis; Rhapsody
España, and Piano Pieces.

Charpentier, Gustave (born 1860), France:
Impressions Fausses, Impressions d'Italie,
La Vie du Poète, Chant d'Apothéose pour
le Centenaire de Victor Hugo; Operas—
Louise, and *Julien.*

Cherubini, Maria Luigi Carlo Zenobio
Salvatore (1760–1842), Italy: Operas—*Il*
Quinto Fabio, Démophon, Lodoiska, Elise,
Médée, Les Deux Journées, Anacreon, and
others; Mass Requiems, and Quartets.

Chopin, Frédéric François (1809–1849),
Poland: *Polish Fantasia; Krakowiak*
(concerto-rondo); Polonaises; Mazurkas;
Sonata—*Allegro de Concert;* Preludes;

Ballades; Scherzos; Waltzes; Songs;
Nocturnes; and a Funeral March.

Cimarosa, Domenico (1749–1801), Italy:
Comic Operas—*Le Stravaganze del Conte,*
Le Pazzie di Stellidanza e di Zoroastro,
L'Italiana in Londra, Il Matrimonio
Segreto, etc.; Operas—*Assalone, La*
Giuditta, Il Sacrificio d'Abramo, etc.

Coleridge-Taylor, Samuel (1875–1912),
England: Choral and Orchestral Work;
Hiawatha; Orchestral Ballad in A
Minor; Negro Melodies (Piano).

Couperin, François (1668-1733), France:
Suites of Dance Music.

Cowen, Sir Frederic Hymen (1852–1935),
English: Operas—*Pauline, Thorgrim,*
Signa, Harold; Oratorios—*The Deluge,*
St Ursula, Ruth, Song of Thanksgiving,
The Transfiguration; Cantatas — *The*
Rose Maiden, The Corsair.

D

Debussy, Claude Achille (1862–1918), France:
Cantata—*L'Enfant Prodigue; Printemps;*
La Damoiselle Elue; Prélude à l'après-
midi d'un Faune; Pelléas et Mélisande;
Trois Nocturnes; Fêtes Galantes; La
Mer, etc.

Delibes, Clément Philibert Léo (1836–1891),
France: Comic Opera—*Le Roi l'a Dit,*
and others; Ballet Music.

Delius, Frederick (1862–1934), England:
Choral and orchestral work; *The Mass*
of Life; On Hearing the First Cuckoo, etc.

Donizetti, Gaetano (1797–1848), Italy:
Operas—*Anna Bolena, Lucia di Lammer-*
moor, La Fille du Régiment, Lucrezia
Borgia, La Favorita, etc.

Dussek, Johann Ludwig (1761-1812),
Bohemia: *Elégie Harmonique.*

Dvorak, Anton (1841–1904), Bohemia:
Stabat Mater; Cantata—*Spectre's Bride;*
Symphony in D; Operas; Gipsy Songs;
Bohemian Dances, etc.

E

Elgar, Sir Edward (1857–1934), England:
Oratorios—*The Dream of Gerontius, and*
The Apostles; the *Froissart;* Overture—
Scenes from the Saga of King Olaf; Song-
cycle of *Sea Pictures; Land of Hope and*
Glory; First Symphony—*Falstaff;* 2nd
Symphony in E flat; Carillons.

F

Farrant, Richard (1530–1585), England:
Church Music; Anthems—*Lord, for Thy*
tender mercy's sake, etc.

Field, John (1782–1837), Ireland: Nocturnes.

Flotow, Friedrich, Freiher von (1812–1883),
Germany: Operas—*Le Naufrage de la*

Méduse, Stradella, Martha, Indra, La Veuve Grapin, L'Ombre, etc.

G

Gade, Niels Wilhelm (1817-1890), Denmark: *Echoes of Ossian; The Erl King's Daughter;* Symphonies, etc.

Gluck, Christoph Willibald (1714–1787), Germany: Operas—*Orfeo ed Euridice, Alceste, Paris and Helena, Iphigénie en Aulide, Armide, Iphigénie en Tauride,* and others.

Gounod, Charles François (1818–1893), France: *Masse Solennelle;* Operas—*Sapho, La Nonne Sanglante, Le Médecin Malgré Lui, Faust, Reine de Saba, Irene, La Colombe, Maid of Athens, Roméo et Juliette;* Mass of *St Cecilia; The Redemption; Mors et Vita;* Sacred Songs, etc.

Grieg, Edvard Hagerup (1843–1907), Norway: Music to Ibsen's *Peer Gynt; Aus Holbergs Zeit; Ich liebe dich; Solveig's Lied; Ein Schwan;* First and Second violin concertos; Numerous pianoforte pieces.

H

Handel, George Frederick (1685–1759), Germany: Operas — *Almira, Nero, Florinda, Daphne, Rodrigo, Agrippina, Rinaldi,* and many others; Oratorios—*Saul, Israel in Egypt, Ode for St Cecilia's Day, L' Allegro, Messiah, Samson, Judas Maccabæus, Joshua, Solomon,* etc.; among other music — *Birthday Ode, Utrecht Te Deum, Dettingen Te Deum, Chandos Anthems, Esther, Acis and Galatea.*

Haydn, Franz Joseph (1732–1809), Austria: Masses and other Church Music; Oratorios — *Tobias, The Creation, The Seasons,* and others; Quartets; Symphonies; *Le Midi,* etc.; Sonatas; Operas, etc.

Herold, Louis Joseph Ferdinand (1791–1833), France; Operas—*Les Rosières, Marie, Zampa, Le Pré aux Clercs,* etc.

Hiller, Ferdinand (1811–1885), Germany: Oratorios—*Die Zerstörung von Jerusalem;* and miscellaneous works.

Hiller, Johann Adam (1728–1804), Germany: Operettas—*The Jolly Cobbler, Love in the Country, The Village Barber,* etc.

Himmel, Frederick Henry (1765–1814), Prussia: Opera—*Il Primo Navigatore;* Operetta—*Fanchon;* Oratorio—*Isaaco;* Te Deum: Cantatas.

Holst, Gustav (1874-1934), England: *The Planets, Hymn of Jesus,* etc.

Hummel, Johann Nepomuk (1778-1837), Austria: Compositions for the Pianoforte; Concerti in A and B Minor; Sonata in F sharp Minor, etc.; Chamber Music; Grand Masses; Operas.

L

Leoncavallo, Reggiero (1858–1919), Italy: Operas—*Pagliacci, La Bohème,* etc.

Liszt, Franz (1811–1886), Hungary: Oratorios—*Christus, Die Legende von der Heiligen Elizabeth;* Masses; Requiem; Cantatas; Symphonies; Concertos; etc.

Lully, Jean-Baptiste (? 1633–1687), Italy; Operas—*Thésée, Armide,* etc.; Miserere.

M

Mascagni, Pietro (1863–1945), Italy: *Cavalleria Rusticana* and other works.

Massenet, Jules (1842–1912), France: Operas—*Don César de Bazan, Les Erinnyes, Roi de Lahore, Hérodiade, Manon Lescaut, Esclarmonde, Panurge;* Pianoforte and orchestral pieces.

Mendelssohn-Bartholdy, Jakob Ludwig Felix (1809–1847), Germany: Opera—*Camacho's Wedding;* Incidental Music to Shakespeare's *Midsummer-Night's Dream;* Concerto in E; *The Isles of Fingal;* Concerto in G Minor; Oratorios—*St Paul, Elijah;* Overtures—*Melusine, Antigone, Œdipus Coloneus, Athalie;* Scotch Symphony; Songs without Words; *Spring Song;* and many other works.

Meyerbeer, Giacomo (1791–1864), Germany: Operas—*Il Crociato, Robert le Diable, Les Huguenots, Ein Feldlager in Schlesien, Le Prophète, L'Etoile du Nord, Le Pardon de Ploermel (Dinorah), L'Africaine.*

Monteverde, Claudio (1568–1643), Italy: Madrigals; Operas — *Arianna, Orfeo, Proserpina Rapita.*

Mozart, Wolfgang Amadeus (1756–1791), Austria: Operas—*Marriage of Figaro, Don Giovanni, The Magic Flute,* and others; Many Masses: *Requiem Mass; Ave Verum;* Cantatas; Symphonies; Fantasias; Serenades, and other miscellaneous works.

Mussorgsky, Modeste (1839-1881), Russia: *Pictures at an Exhibition, Night on a Bare Mountain;* Opera—*Boris Godunov.*

O

Offenbach, Jacques (1819–1880), Germany (settled in France): Opera bouffe and operetta: *Le Mariage aux Lanternes, La Fille d'Elezondo, Orphée aux Enfers, La Belle Hélène, Barbe-Bleue, La Grande Duchesse, Madame Favart,* etc.

P

Palestrina, Giovanni Pierluigi di (1524–1594), Italy: Reformer of Church Music; *Mass of Pope Marcellus,* and others.

Pergolese, Giovanni Battista (1710–1736), Italy: Oratorio — *San Guglielmo*; Operetta: *La Serva Padrona*; Cantata— *Orfeo*; *Stabat Mater.*

Peri, Jacopo (1561–1630 ?), Italy: *Dafne* (lost); *L'Euridice.*

Puccini, Giacomo (1858 - 1924), Italy: Operas—*La Bohème, Tosca, Madame Butterfly*, and others.

Purcell, Henry (1658–1695), England: Opera— *Dido and Æneas*; Music and songs for *The Tempest*, Dryden's *King Arthur* and *Indian Queen*, D'Urfey's *Don Quixote*, and others; Cantatas; Glees; Catches, etc. Best known by his Church music.

R

Rachmaninoff, Sergei Vasilievich (1873–1943), Russia: *Alcka*; *The Rock*; Trio on the Death of Tschaïkowsky; *The Miser Knight*; *Francesca da Rimini*; *The Island of Death*; Sonata in D Minor; *The Bells*; *Spring*; Prelude.

Rimsky-Korsakof, Nicholas (1844–1908), Russia: *Fireworks*; *The Nightingale*; *Scheherazade*; *Le Coq d'or.*

Rossini, Gioacchino Antonio (1792–1868), Italy: Operas—*La Pietra del Paragone, Tancredi, Barbiere di Siviglia, Otello, Cenerentola, La Gazza Ladra, La Donna del Lago, Guillaume Tell*; *Stabat Mater.*

Rubenstein, Anton Grigorovich (1829–1894), Russia: *Dmitri Donskoï*; *Tom der Narr*; *Feramors* (*Lalla Roukh*); *Nero.*

S

Saint-Saëns, Charles Camille (1835–1921), France: Operas—*Henry VIII., Proserpine, Ascanio*, and others; Sacred Drama —*Samson et Dalila.*

Scarlatti, Alessandro (1659–1725), Sicily: Operas—*Telmaco, Marco Attilio Regolo, Griselda*; Masses and other Church Music.

Schubert, Franz Peter (1797–1828), Austria: Operas—*Zauberharfe, Alfonso and Estrella, Fierabras*, etc.; Masses in F and E flat; Songs—*The Erl King, Schäfers Klagelied, Hark! Hark! the Lark*, and many others; Symphonies; Sonatas.

Schumann, Robert Alexander (1810–1856), Germany: *Papillons Fantasias*; First Symphony in B flat, and others; *Paradise and the Peri*; Opera—*Genoveva*; Music to *Manfred* and Scenes from Goethe's *Faust*; Overtures to *Julius Caesar, Hermann and Dorothea*, etc.; Songs; Quartets; Trios; and Pianoforte pieces.

Sibelius, Jean (born 1865), Finland: *Finlandia*; *The Swan of Tuonela*; Seven Symphonies.

Spohr, Ludwig (1784–1859), Germany: Operas—*Faust, Jessonda, Zemira und Azor*; Oratorios—*Die Letzten Dinge* (*Last Judgment*), *Der Fall Babylons*, and others; *Die Weihe der Töne* and other symphonies; Concertos; Sonatas; Fantasias; Rondos, etc.

Strauss, Richard (born 1864), Germany: *Macbeth*; *Don Juan*; *Guntram*; *Elektra*; *Salome.*

Sullivan, Arthur Seymour (1842–1900), England: Comic Operas (in conjunction with W. S. Gilbert)—*Sorcerer, H.M.S Pinafore, Pirates of Penzance, Patience, Iolanthe, Princess Ida, Mikado, Ruddigore, Yeomen of the Guard*, and others; Cantata—*Kenilworth*; Overtures—*In Memoriam, Marmion, Di Ballo*; Oratorios —*The Prodigal Son, Light of the World*; also *The Martyr of Antioch* and *The Golden Legend*; Song—*The Lost Chord*; Anthems, etc.

T

Tallis, Thomas (about 1510–1585), England: "Father" of English Church Music; Anthems, Te Deums, Responses, Motets.

Thomas, Ambroise (1811–1896), France: Operas—*La Double Echelle, Mina, Betty, Le Caïd*; Cantatas; Part Songs, etc.

Tschaïkowsky, Peter Ilich (1840–1893), Russia: *Winter Day-Dreams*; Overture —*Romeo and Juliet*; *The Little Shoes*; Second Symphony; *Tempest Fantasia*; Concerto in B Flat Minor; *The Oprischnik*; Polish Symphony; *Capriccio*; *1812 Overture*; *Maid of Orleans*; *Manfred*; *Hamlet*; *Mazeppa*; *Charodaïka*; *Queen of Spades*; *Sleeping Beauty*; *Casse-noisette*; *Pathetic Symphony.*

V

Vaughan Williams, Ralph (born 1872), England: Choral Works—*Towards the Unknown Region, Sancta Civitas*; Mass in G Minor; Symphonies—*Sea, London*; Opera—*Hugh the Drover*; Songs.

Verdi, Giuseppe Fortunino Francesco (1813–1901), Italy: Operas—*Ernani, Rigoletto, Il Trovatore, La Traviata, Les Vêpres Siciliennes, Simon Boccanegra, Un Ballo in Maschera, La Forza del' Destino, Don Carlos, Aïda, Falstaff*; Requiem Mass.

W

Wagner, Wilhelm Richard (1813–1883), Saxony: Operas—*Rienzi, Flying Dutchman, Tannhäuser, Lohengrin, Rheingold, Die Walküre, Tristan und Isolde, Die Meistersinger* (comic), *Siegfried, Götterdämmerung, Parsifal*. The *Nibelungen Ring* Trilogy consists of *Rheingold* (Introduction), *Walküre, Siegfried*, and *Götterdämmerung.*

Wallace, William Vincent (1814–1865), Ireland (Scottish parents): Operas— *Maritana, Matilda of Hungary, Lurline, The Amber Witch, Love's Triumph, The Desert Flower.*

Weber, Carl Maria Friedrich Ernest von (1786–1826), Germany (Austrian parent-age): *Peter Schmoll und seine Nachbarn ; Der Beherrscher der Geister ; Abu Hassen ; Kampf und Sieg ; Euryanthe ; Oberon ; Preciosa ; Der Freischütz ; Concertstück in F Minor ;* Masses ; Symphonies ; Cantatas, etc.

GREAT SCIENTISTS

A

Agassiz, Jean Louis Rodolphe (1807–1873), United States (born in Switzerland). Naturalist: upheld the "Centres of Creation" theory—Anti-Darwinian.

Ampère, André Marie (1775–1836), France. Physicist and Mathematician: noted for his investigations in Electricity and Magnetism and Electro-Dynamics.

Arago, François Jean Dominique (1786–1853), France. Astronomer and Physicist: discovered the phenomenon of rotatory magnetism.

Archimedes (287–212 B.C.), Syracuse. Mathematician and Inventor: laid down theorems on the measurement of curved surfaces and solids. Investigated Mechanics and Hydrostatics. Invented the Archimedes Screw.

Avogadro, Amadeo (1776–1856), Italy. Physicist: formulated what is known as Avogadro's Hypothesis in connection with the Atomic Theory.

B

Black, Joseph (1728–1799), Scotland. Chemist: pioneer in scientific method: evolved the theory of *latent heat.*

Boyle, Hon. Robert (1627–1691), Ireland. Chemist and Natural Philosopher: discovered what is known in pneumatics as Boyle's Law.

Brahé, Tycho (1546–1601), Sweden. Astronomer: measured the positions and motions of the celestial bodies.

Bunsen, Robert Wilhelm (1811–1899), Germany. Chemist and Physicist: discovered Spectrum Analysis, invented the Magnesium Light and the *Bunsen Burner.*

C

Cavendish, Hon. Henry (1731–1810), England. Natural Philosopher: pioneer in pneumatic chemistry. Discovered the composition of water.

Copernicus (Koppernigk) Nicolas (1473–1543), Prussia. Astronomer: established the fact that the sun is the centre of the planetary system.

Crookes, Sir William (1832–1919), England. Physicist and Chemist: prepared the way for Incandescent Electric Lighting and invented the Radiometer.

Curie, Pierre (1859–1906), and his wife **Marie Sklodowska** (1867–1935), France. Physicists: discoverers of Radium.

Cuvier, Georges (1769–1832), France (born in Würtemberg). Naturalist: established structural classification and systematised comparative anatomy.

D

Dalton, John (1766–1844), England. Chemist and Physicist: propounded the Atomic Theory.

Darwin, Charles Robert (1809–1882), England. Naturalist: expounded the theory of the Origin of Species by means of Natural Selection.

Davy, Sir Humphry (1778–1829), England. Chemist: discovered Sodium, Strontium, Calcium, Magnesium and other metals, and invented the *Davy* safety lamp.

Dumas, Jean Baptiste André (1800–1884), France. Chemist: contributed to the Atomic Theory. Researches in organic chemistry.

E

Edison, Thomas Alva (1847–1931), America: many inventions affecting telegraphy, telephony, the gramophone and the cinematograph.

Einstein, Albert (born 1879), Germany. Astronomer and Physicist: elaborated the Theory of Relativity, especially in relation to space, time and gravity.

Euclid (about 300 B.C.), Greece. Mathematician: probably the founder of the illustrious mathematical school at Alexandria. Wrote the *Elements.*

F

Fabre, Jean Henri (1823–1915), France. Entomologist and Physicist: noted for his study of the habits of Insects.

Fahrenheit, Gabriel Daniel (1686–1736), Germany. Natural Philosopher: noted for his improvements of the Thermometer and Barometer.

Faraday, Michael (1791–1867), England. Chemist and Natural Philosopher : noted for researches in Chemistry and Electricity.

Fourier, Jean Baptiste Joseph, Baron de (1768–1830), France. Mathematician and Scientist : mathematical exposition of the theory of heat.

Fresnel, Augustin Jean (1788–1827), France. Physicist : his optical investigations contributed to the establishment of the undulatory theory of light.

G

Galilei, Galileo (1564–1642), Italy. Scientist and Astronomer : invented refracting telescope and discovered many facts about the Sun, Moon, Planets and Stars.

Gay-Lussac, Louis Joseph (1778–1850), France. Chemist and Physicist : contributed to the Atomic Theory by formulating his *law of volumes*.

Geikie, Sir Archibald (1835–1924), Scotland. Geologist : the authority on Geology of Great Britain.

Geikie, James (1839–1915), Scotland. Geologist : wrote standard work on the *Great Ice Age in its Relation to the Antiquity of Man.*

Graham, Thomas (1805–1869), Scotland. Chemist and Physicist : formulated the Law of Diffusion of Gases.

H

Haeckel, Ernst Heinrich (1834–1919), Germany. Naturalist : established the fundamental law of Biogenesis.

Halley, Edmund (1656–1742), England. Astronomer and Mathematician : researches on the orbits of the planets and comets.

Harvey, William (1578–1657), England. Physician and Surgeon : discovered the Circulation of the Blood.

Helmholtz, Hermann von (1821–1894), Germany. Physiologist and Scientist : one of the discoverers of the Law of the Conservation of Energy.

Herschel, Sir William (1738–1822), England. Astronomer : established the system of the stars ; discovered the planet Uranus.

Hertz, Heinrich (1857–1894), Germany. Physicist : first to demonstrate the existence of electric waves.

Humboldt, Friedrich H. A., Baron von (1769–1859), Germany. Naturalist and Scientist : greatest work was the scientific result of his explorations in South America.

Huxley, Thomas Henry (1825–1895), England. Physiologist : among other noted works he wrote *The Evidence as to Man's Place in Nature.*

Huygens, Christian (1629–1693), Holland. Mathematician, Physicist, and Astronomer : propounded and developed the Wave Theory of Light. Discovered Polarisation.

J

Jenner, Edward (1749–1823), England. Physician : discovered the virtue of Vaccination.

Joule, James Prescott (1818–1889), England. Physicist : researches in thermo-dynamics. Determined the mechanical equivalent of heat. Experimental founder of the Theory of Conservation of Energy.

K

Kelvin, William Thomson, Lord (1824–1907), Scotland. Physicist : noted for his researches in Electricity and Thermo-Dynamics, and for the invention of various electrical and other instruments, notably his sounding apparatus and compass.

Kepler, Johann (1571–1630), Germany. Astronomer : discovered what are known as *Kepler's Laws*, governing the motions of the Planets.

L

Lamarck, Jean B. P. A. de Mounet, Chevalier de (1744–1829), France. Naturalist : expositor of the Theory of Evolution.

Laplace, Pierre Simon, Marquis de (1749–1827), France. Mathematician and Astronomer : established the fact that the Planetary System is stable.

Lavoisier, Antoine Laurent (1743–1794), France. Chemist : established the modern theory of combustion.

Leibnitz (Leibniz), Gottfried Wilhelm (1646–1716), Germany. Natural Philosopher : held that the essential quality of all substance is active force ; disputed with Newton the discovery of the Differential Calculus. He was pioneer in the study of Comparative Philology.

Liebig, Justus, Baron von (1803–1873), Germany. Chemist : noted for his investigations into the chemistry of Food and Agriculture.

Linnæus, Carl (1707–1778), Sweden. Botanist : established the modern Grouping of Plants.

Lister, Joseph, Lord (1827–1912), England. Surgeon : introduced the Antiseptic System of Surgery.

Lodge, Sir Oliver Joseph (1851–1940), England. Physicist : noted for researches in Lightning, Electricity and Wireless

Telegraphy, and in the motions of the Æther.

Lyell, Sir Charles (1797–1875), Scotland. Geologist : leader of the Uniformitarian School.

M

Marconi, Guglielmo (1874–1937), Italy. Physicist : conceived the idea of using Hertzian waves for telegraphy between two distant points. Pioneer of wireless telegraphy. In 1902 established a transatlantic wireless service from Glace Bay (Nova Scotia) to England.

Maxwell, James Clerk- (1831–1879), Scotland. Natural Philosopher : noted for investigations in Electricity, Magnetism, Colour, and the Kinetic Theory of Gases.

Mendel, Gregor Johann (1822-1884), Austria. Biologist : propounded the Theory of Heredity in Plants and Animals.

N

Napier, John (1550–1617), Scotland. Mathematician and Inventor : invented Logarithms.

Newton, Sir Isaac (1642–1727), England. Natural Philosopher : discovered the Law of Universal Gravitation and the Differential Calculus.

O

Oersted, Hans Christian (1777–1851), Denmark. Physicist : " The father of the science of electro-magnetism." The electric telegraph due to his discoveries.

Ohm, Georg Simon (1787–1854), Germany. Physicist : discovered what is known as *Ohm's Law*, relating to the measurement of electric resistance.

P

Pasteur, Louis (1822–1895), France. Chemist and Pathologist : noted for his bacteriological discoveries, and for his system of inoculation for hydrophobia, cholera and other diseases.

Poisson, Simeon Denis (1781–1840), France. Mathematician and Scientist : one of the chief founders of the science of mathematical physics.

Priestley, Joseph (1733–1804), England. Chemist and Physicist : discovered oxygen ; laid the foundation of pneumatic chemistry.

Ptolemy, Claudius (second century A.D.), Egypt. Most famous Geographer and Astronomer of Antiquity : his theories (many of them entirely wrong) were regarded as authoritative until the middle of the 16th century.

R

Ramsay, Sir William (1852–1916), England. Chemist and Physicist : discoverer of the rare gases of the atmosphere.

Rayleigh, John William Strutt, Baron (1842–1919), England. Physicist : noted for investigations in Sound and discovery of Argon.

Réaumur, René Antoine Ferschault de (1683-1757), France. Physicist : noted for his invention of the Réaumur Thermometer.

Röntgen, Wilhelm Conrad von (1845-1923), Germany. Physicist : discovered the X or Röntgen Rays.

Rutherford, Ernest, Lord (1871–1937), England. Physicist and Chemist : researches on radio-active substances and atomic structure.

S

Scheele, Karl Wilhelm (1742–1786), Sweden. Chemist : discovered oxygen independently of Priestley.

Simpson, Sir James Young (1811–1870), Scotland. Physician : discovered the anæsthetic powers of chloroform.

T

Torricelli, Evangelista (1608–1647), Italy. Mathematician and Physicist : invented the barometer. Laid the foundations of Hydromechanics.

W

Wallace, Alfred Russel (1822–1914), England. Naturalist : independently of Darwin, originated the theory of organic Evolution on the principle of natural selection.

Werner, Abraham Gottlob (1750–1817), Germany. Geologist : was the first to establish a Classification of Rocks.

Y

Young, Thomas (1773–1829), England. Physicist : discovered the phenomenon of Interference of Light. Advanced the undulatory theory.

GREAT EXPLORERS

A

Africanus, Leo (early 16th century). A Moor who travelled widely in Northern Africa and Asia Minor in the end of the 15th century, and who published an account of his travels.

Alvarez, Father Francisco (1465 ?–1541 ?), Portuguese. Went with an embassy to Abyssinia (1520–26) and wrote an account (the first) of the country.

Amundsen, Roald (1872–1928), Norwegian Polar explorer. Was the first to sail through the North-West Passage from Baffin Bay to the Pacific by north of Canada (1906). First to reach the South Pole (1911). Flew over the North Pole by aeroplane (1926). Died in Arctic.

Anson, George, Lord (1697–1762), English admiral. Sailed round the world (1740–44).

B

Baffin, William (1584–1622), English navigator. Voyaged to Greenland and Spitzbergen (1612–14). While in search of a North-West Passage discovered Smith Sound and explored Hudson Strait and Baffin Bay (1615).

Baker, Sir Samuel White (1821–1893), African traveller. Explored the White Nile and discovered Lake Albert.

Balboa, Vasco Nunez de (1475–1517), Spaniard. Crossed the Isthmus of Darien and discovered the Pacific Ocean. Obtained first information respecting Peru.

Banks, Sir Joseph (1744–1820). Accompanied Cook in his voyage round the world. President of the Royal Society for forty years. Did more than any other man to promote the settlement of Australia.

Barents, Willem (died 1597), Dutch Arctic explorer. Made three voyages to find a North-East Passage by north of Asia to the East, but was unable to proceed farther than the north-east of Novaya Zemlya.

Barth, Heinrich (1821–1865), German. African explorer. Travelled in Northern Africa and Asia Minor. During 1850–55 was engaged in exploration of the Sahara.

Bass, Dr George, a navy surgeon. Sailed round Tasmania in 1798, thus proving it to be an island.

Bering, Vitus (1680–1741), Dane. Explored the north-east coast of Asia and part of the western coast of Alaska. Proved the existence of open sea between Asia and North America.

Bougainville, Louis Antoine de (1729–1811), Frenchman. Made a voyage round the world (1766–69), the first undertaken by the French.

Bruce, James (1730–1794), Scotsman.

Travelled through Barbary States, Asia Minor and Abyssinia, and found the source of the Blue Nile.

Bruce, Wm. Spiers (1867–1921), Scotsman, naturalist. Took part in "Challenger" Expedition (*see* Murray, Sir John), and in expeditions to the Arctic and Antarctic regions. Headed the Scottish National Antarctic Expedition (1902–04) and discovered Coats' Land.

Burckhardt, John Lewis (1784–1817), Swiss explorer. Travelled in Asia Minor and Syria, and, disguised as an Arab, made the pilgrimage to Mecca (1814).

Burke, Robert O'Hara (1820–1861), **Wills, William John** (1834–1861). Traversed the Australian Continent from south to north (1861). Both perished on the return journey.

Burton, Sir Richard Francis (1821–1890), English traveller. Disguised as an Arab, journeyed through Arabia to Mecca (1851). In 1858, with J. H. Speke, discovered Lake Tanganyika. Afterwards travelled in Brazil, North America, Palestine and West Africa.

C

Cabot, John (1450–1498), a Venetian, settled in England. Was commissioned to find a route to Asia by the west. Discovered C. Breton Island, and coasting north discovered Newfoundland. In 1498 coasted Baffin Island, Labrador, Nova Scotia and New England. Was the first to reach the North American Continent.

Cabot, Sebastian (1476–1557), son of above. Explored the Parana River in South America (1525). Directed an expedition (1553) to find a North-East Passage to China. Reached White Sea and was the means of opening up trade with Russia.

Cameron, Verney Lovett (1844–1894), African explorer. Started (1873) from Zanzibar to help Dr Livingstone and continued his journey to Benguella. First to cross Equatorial Africa from sea to sea.

Cano, Juan Sebastian del (c. 1460–1526). Accompanied Magellan in his attempt to reach the East Indies by sailing westwards, and with Magellan's expedition completed the first circumnavigation of the globe.

Carteret, Philip (died 1796), English navigator. Undertook a voyage of exploration to the South Seas (1766–69). Discovered Pitcairn and other islands.

Cartier, Jacques (1491–1557), French navigator. Visited Newfoundland, discovered Anticosti, sailed up the St Lawrence as far as Montreal. He made the first landing on Canadian soil at Esquimaux Bay in 1534.

Cavendish, Sir Thomas (1555 ?–1592), English seaman. Led an expedition to the South Seas and circumnavigated the world (1586–88).

Champlain, Samuel de (1567–1635), French Governor of Canada. Explored the coasts of Canada, journeyed in the interior, discovered L. Champlain, and founded Quebec.

Chancellor, Richard (died 1556), English seaman. With Sir Hugh Willoughby tried to find a North-East Passage to India. Reached the White Sea and journeyed overland to Moscow.

Clapperton, Hugh (1788–1827), Scotsman, African explorer. Travelled through Central Sudan to L. Chad (1823) and Sokoto.

Columbus, Christopher (1446 ?–1506). Genoese in the service of Spain. In 1492, under the patronage of Ferdinand and Isabella, sailed westwards to find a sea route to India, and discovered the islands now known as the West Indies. Made three more voyages to the West Indies. In the last discovered Central America and Continent of South America.

Cook, James (1728–1779), English navigator. Commanded a scientific expedition (1768–71) to Pacific. Explored Pacific Ocean and disproved the existence of a great southern continent. Discovered many islands, including New Caledonia and the Sandwich Islands. Traced the coasts of the North and South Islands of New Zealand and the east coast of Australia. In another voyage (1772–75) explored the Antarctic Ocean. In his last voyage (1776) discovered many islands in the Pacific. Was killed at Hawaii.

D

Dampier, William (1652–1715), English navigator. As a buccaneer circumnavigated the world. In 1699 explored the north-west coast of Australia, New Guinea, New Britain, etc. In one of his voyages his sailing-master, Alexander Selkirk, the prototype of Robinson Crusoe, was landed on Juan Fernandez and rescued on a subsequent voyage.

Davis, John (c. 1550–1605), English navigator. Sought for a North-West Passage to Asia. Discovered Davis Strait. Acted as pilot-major to the first fleet of the East India Company (1599).

Diaz, Bartholomeu (c. 1455–1500), Portuguese navigator. Was the first to discover and sail round the Cape of Good Hope (1486).

Drake, Sir Francis (1545–1596), Elizabethan adventurer. The first Englishman to sail the Pacific Ocean and to circumnavigate the world. Failed to find a northern passage from the Pacific to the Atlantic.

Du Chaillu, Paul Belloni (1837–1903), Frenchman. African explorer. Made known the existence of the gorilla as a result of his travels in the Gabun country. Discovered the dwarf races of Central Africa.

E

Emin Pasha (Edward Schnitzer) (1840–1892), German Jew. Became Governor of Egyptian Sudan (1878). Made extensive geographical discoveries in Central Africa. Was killed in battle with the Mahdi.

Eyre, Edward John (1815–1901), Australian explorer. Tried to find an overland route from South to West Australia, and succeeded in reaching Albany. Discovered Lakes Eyre and Torrens.

F

Flinders, Matthew (1774–1814), English seaman. With Bass discovered Tasmania to be an island (1798). Explored the coasts of Australia.

Forrest, John, Baron (1847–1918). Crossed the Australian Continent from Perth to Adelaide (1870). Made another expedition into heart of Continent (1874).

Franklin, Sir John (1786–1847). Explored the northern coast of Canada (1819–22 and 1825–27). In 1845 sailed *via* Baffin Bay and Lancaster Sound to find a North-West Passage to the Pacific. Perished with whole of the expedition, which, however, had gained a point already reached from the west.

Frémont, John Charles (1813–1890), American "Pioneer." Discovered a route over Rocky Mountains to California (1844).

Frobisher, Sir Martin (1535–1594), Elizabethan adventurer and navigator. Tried to find North-West Passage to India. Annexed country round Frobisher's Bay (Baffin Island).

G

Gama, Vasco da (1469–1524), Portuguese navigator. First to find the route to India by the Cape (1497). In subsequent voyages founded Portuguese colonies on west coast of Africa and in India.

Gilbert, Sir Humphrey (1539–1583), English navigator. Annexed Newfoundland (1583).

Grant, James Augustus, C.B. (1827–1892). Explored the sources of the Nile (1860–63) along with J. H. Speke.

Greely, Adolphus Washington (1844–1935), American Arctic Explorer. Led an expedition to the head of Smith Sound (1881–84).

H

Hakluyt, Richard (1553–1616), geographer of the Elizabethan period. Published an account of English voyages and discoveries.

Hawkins, Sir Richard (1562–1622), English

navigator. Made an expedition (1593) to the South Seas.

Hudson, Henry (died 1611), English navigator. Undertook three voyages in quest of a North-East Passage to China. Discovered Hudson River and Hudson Strait and Bay.

Humboldt, Friedrich Heinrich Alexander, Baron von (1769–1859), German naturalist and scientist. Explored the course of the Orinoco and made a journey of scientific exploration in Equatorial America to the sources of the Amazon and in Mexico (1799–1804). Also travelled in Central and Western Asia (1829).

J

Jenkinson, Anthony (fl. 16th century), Englishman. Travelled through Persia (1561), Russia, Bokhara, and returned by the Caspian and Volga.

K

Kaempfen, Engelbrecht (1651–1716), German. Travelled in Persia, India, Java and Japan. Wrote a history of Japan.

Krapf, Ludwig (19th century). He and **J. Rebmann**, missionaries in Africa, discovered Kilimanjaro and Kenya (1848–49).

L

La Condamine, Charles Marie de (1701–1774), French geographer. Explored the river Amazon.

Lancaster, Sir James (died 1618). Made a voyage to the Indian Ocean (1591–94) which led to the founding of the East India Company. Afterwards promoted efforts for the discovery of a North-West Passage.

Lander, Richard (1804–1834), Englishman. Travelled in West Africa. Along with his brother discovered the mouth of the River Niger (1830).

La Pérouse, François (1741–1788 ?), French explorer. Explored the north-west coast of North America (in search of a north-west passage), north-eastern coasts of Asia, discovered La Perouse Strait, and visited many of the Pacific Islands (1785–88).

Leichardt, Ludwig (1813–1848 ?), German. Australian explorer. Travelled overland from Sydney to the Gulf of Carpentaria (1844). On another expedition to the north-west (1847) was lost.

Lemaire, James (died 1616), Dutch navigator. With Cornelius Schouten discovered the Strait of Lemaire and rounded Cape Horn.

Linschoten, Jan Hugen van (1563–1611), Dutch traveller. Visited India, Africa, China and the Malay Archipelago, and wrote descriptions of these countries.

Livingstone, David (1813–1873), Scots missionary and explorer. One of the pioneers of exploration in Central Africa. Explored the River Zambesi, and discovered the Victoria Falls, Lakes Ngami and Nyasa. Crossed South Africa from Loando (west) to Quilimane (east). Did much for the suppression of slavery.

M

M'Clintock, Sir Francis Leopold (1819–1907), Arctic explorer. Commanded several Franklin relief expeditions. Rescued M'Clure, and (1859) brought home authentic news of Franklin's death.

M'Clure, Sir Robert John le Mesurier (1807–1873). Took part in several Franklin relief expeditions. Was the first to traverse the North-West Passage from west to east (1850–54).

Mackenzie, Sir Alexander (1755–1820), Canadian explorer. Discovered and explored the Mackenzie River to its mouth in the Arctic Ocean.

Magellan, Ferdinand (1470–1521), Portuguese in service of Spain. In voyage to find a western route to the East Indies discovered the Straits of Magellan (1520). Reached the Philippines, where he was killed. His expedition was the first to circumnavigate the globe.

Mandeville, Sir John (Jehan de Mandeville) (14th century), name used by the compiler of a French book of travels. The author pretends to have travelled over most of the then known world, but much of the book is pure invention.

Murray, Sir John (1841–1914), Editor of the Reports on the "Challenger" Scientific Expedition round the world (1872–76), which he accompanied as naturalist.

N

Nachtigal, Gustav (1834–1885). German explorer of the Central Sahara and Sudan (1869–74).

Niebuhr, Carsten (1733–1815). Danish explorer of parts of Arabia, Asia Minor, Persia and India.

Nansen, Dr Fridtjof (1861–1930), Norwegian scientist and explorer. Crossed Greenland (1888) from east to west. Drifted across the Arctic Ocean in the *Fram* (1893–96).

Nordenskjöld, Nils Adolf Eric, Baron (1832–1901), Swedish explorer. Made voyages of discovery round Spitsbergen (1858–72). First to navigate the North-East Passage by the north of Europe and Asia (1878–79).

O

Orellana, Francisco de (died 1549). Spanish explorer who followed the course of the Amazon from its source to the sea (1541).

P

Park, Mungo (1771–1806), Scottish explorer. In two journeys he traced the course of the Niger for over a thousand miles and established the fact that it was distinct from the Congo.

Parry, Sir William Edward (1790–1855), English navigator. Made five voyages to the Arctic regions. Discovered many channels and islands, including Cornwallis, Bathurst and Melville Islands.

Peary, Robert Edwin (1856–1920), American Arctic explorer. Discovered Greenland to be an island. Was the first to reach the North Pole (1909).

Polo, Marco (1254–1324). Venetian who with his father and brother visited China in 1266. Marco Polo spent many years there under Kublai Khan, and travelled throughout Central Asia.

Q

Quiros, Pedro Fernandez de (died 1614), Spanish navigator. Along with Luis Vaez de Forres tried to find a continent in the Antarctic Ocean. Discovered several of the New Hebrides.

R

Raleigh, Sir Walter (1552–1618), courtier, navigator and author. Sent out an expedition (1584) which took possession of Virginia and attempted to colonise it. Sailed to Guiana (1595), explored the coasts of Trinidad and sailed up the Orinoco. In 1616 undertook an abortive voyage to Guiana in search of gold.

Ross, Sir James Clark (1800–1862), Polar explorer. Nephew of Sir John Ross. Discovered the north magnetic pole (1831). Made three voyages to the Antarctic (1839–43). Discovered Victoria Land, and the Erebus and Terror volcanoes.

Ross, Sir John (1777–1856), Arctic explorer. Discovered King William Land and Boothia Felix (1829).

S

Scoresby, William (1789–1857), English navigator. Explored the east coast of Greenland (1822).

Scott, Captain Robert Falcon (1868–1912), Antarctic explorer. In 1901 led an expedition to King Edward Land and in 1910 to McMurdo Sound. Reached the South Pole (1912).

Selous, Frederick Courteney (1851–1917), Englishman. From 1872 for over twenty years travelled South Central Africa and explored Mashonaland and Matabeleland.

Shackleton, Sir Ernest Henry (1874–1922), Polar explorer. Took part in Capt. Scott's Antarctic expedition (1901). Organised three Antarctic expeditions, one of which

reached a point 97 miles from the South Pole.

Speke, John Hanning (1827–1864), African explorer. Discovered Lake Tanganyika along with Richard Burton, and Lake Victoria, and explored the upper waters of the Nile.

Stanley, Sir Henry Morton (1841–1904), American (born in Wales). African explorer. As correspondent of *New York Herald* rescued Livingstone at Ujiji (1871), and with him explored north end of Lake Tanganyika. Explored Lakes Victoria and Albert and the Congo and journeyed through Central Africa (1874–78). Founded the Congo Free State (1879–84). Rescued Emin Pasha at L. Albert (1889).

Stefansson, Vilhjálmur (born 1879), Canadian Arctic explorer and scientist. Conducted extensive explorations in Arctic regions north of Canada and is noted for researches among the Eskimo.

Stuart, John M'Douall (1818–1866), Australian explorer. Explored round L. Torrens (1858). Crossed the Continent from south to north (1860).

Sturt, Charles (c. 1800–1869), Australian explorer. Made several journeys into the interior and through South Australia. Explored the rivers Darling and Murray.

T

Tasman, Abel Jansen (1603–1659), Dutch navigator. Discovered Tasmania and New Zealand (1642) and the Fiji and other islands in the Pacific. Explored the coast of New Guinea and the north and northwest coasts of Australia (1644). Was the first to demonstrate that Australia was an island.

Torres, Luis Vaez de, Spanish navigator of 16th–17th centuries. Discovered Torres Strait (1606), several islands of the New Hebrides and explored coasts of New Guinea.

V

Vambéry, Arminius (1832–1913), Hungarian orientalist and traveller. Disguised as a dervish travelled through Turkestan to Samarkand (1862–64).

Vancouver, George (1758–1798), English seaman. Surveyed the western coast of North America from Cape Mendocino northwards.

W

Wilkes, Charles (1798–1877), American Antarctic explorer. Was the first to sight the Antarctic continent (1840).

Willoughby, Sir Hugh (died 1554). With Richard Chancellor tried to find a northeast passage to China. Reached coast of Lapland, where he and his crew perished.

Wills, William John. *See* Burke.

PRONUNCIATION OF SOME PLACE NAMES IN THE BRITISH ISLES AND THE DOMINIONS.

(See pages iii. and iv.)

Aber-gaven'ny, Monmouthshire.
Aln'wick, Northumberland.
An'dov-er, Hampshire.
Ar-ma'gh, Northern Ireland.
Arn'hem-land, Australia.
Ar'un-del, Sussex.
Ash'by-de-la-Zou'ch (*ouch=oosh*), Leicestershire.
Ath-a-bas'ka, river, Canada.
Beaulieu (*Bū'li*), Hampshire.
Beauly (*Bū'li*), Inverness-shire.
Bech-u-an'a-land (*chu=tshōō*), South Africa.
Bel-fast' (not *Bel'*), Northern Ireland.
Bid'e-ford, Devon.
Bloem'fon-tein (*oe=oo, ei=ai*), Orange Free State.
Brech'in (*e=ee, ch* as in *loch*), Angus.
Cal'gary, Alberta.
Calne, Wiltshire.
Can'ber-ra, Australia.
Cav'an, Eire.
Chelms'ford, Essex.
Chel'tenham, Gloucestershire.
Cirencester (*Cis'is-ter*), Gloucestershire.
Clwyd (*Kloo'id*), river, Wales.
Cole-raine' (*o=ō*), Northern Ireland.
Cul-lod'en, Inverness-shire.
Den'bigh, Wales.
Dept'ford, London.
Der'by (*er=ar*), England; Western Australia.
Dol-ge'lly (*ll=l* preceded by a consonant like *h*), Merioneth.
Don-e-gal' (*a=aw*), Eire.
Drogheda (*Draw'e-da*), Eire.
Dum-fries' (*fries—frees*), Scotland.
Dun-e'din (*e=ee*), New Zealand.
Eir'e (*ei=ai*).
E'ly (*e=ee*), Cambridgeshire.
Eyre (*ey=ai*), peninsula and lake, South Australia.
Fer-man'agh, Northern Ireland.
Fre'mantle (*e=ee*), Western Australia.
Frome (*Froom*), Somersetshire.
Gal'way (*a=aw*), Eire.
Gas-pe' (*e=ai*), peninsula, Quebec.
Gee-long' (*G=J*), Victoria.
Glamis, Angus.
Glouces'ter (*o=ŏ*), England.
Green'wich (*Grin'ij*), London.
Guelph (*Gwelf*), Ontario.
Her'tford (*er=ar*), England.
Hol'y-head (*o=ŏ*), Wales.
Il-fra-com'be (*combe=coom*), Devon.
Keigh'ley (*eigh=eeth*), Yorkshire.
Kes'wick (*Kez'ik*), Cumberland.
Kin-car'dine, Scotland.
Kirkca'ldy (*Kir-kaw'di*), Fifeshire.

Kirkcu'dbright (*Kir-koo'bri*), Scotland.
Lach'lan (*ach=āk*), river, New South Wales.
Leeuwin (*Loo'in*), cape, Western Australia.
Le'icester, England.
Leigh (*Lee*), Lancashire.
Le'in-ster (*ei=ĕ*), Eire.
Leominster (*Lem'ster*), Herefordshire.
Ler'wick, Shetland.
Lev'en (*ev=eev*), Scotland.
Lewes (*Lū'is*), Sussex.
Llan-dud'no (*ll=hl, u=i*), Carnarvonshire.
Llan-ell'y (*ll=hl*), Carmarthenshire.
Loughborough (*Lŭff'bur-u*), Leicestershire.
Low'estoft (*ow=ō*), Norfolk.
Mal'vern (*a=aw*), Worcestershire.
Marlborough (*Mawl'bru*), Wiltshire.
Marylebone (*Mar'i-bon*), London.
Mer-i-on'-eth (*th* as in *the*), Wales.
Milngavie (*Mŭl-gī'*), Dumbartonshire.
Mont-re-al' (*a=aw*), Quebec.
Mor'ay (*o=ŭ*), Scotland.
Neagh (*Nai*), lough, Northern Ireland.
Newfoundland (*Nū-fun[d]-land*, accent on first or last syllable).
Nova Scotia (*Skō'sha*).
O-a-ma-ru', New Zealand.
Read'ing, Berkshire.
Rei'gate (*ei=ī*), Surrey.
Re-gin'a (*g=j, i=ī*), Saskatchewan.
Sag-ue-nay', river, Canada.
St. Just (*u=oo*), Cornwall.
Sal'is-bury (*Salis = Sa'wlz*), Wiltshire; island, Canada.
Sanqu'har (*qu=k*), Dumfriesshire.
Sas-katch'e-wan, river, Canada.
Sault Sainte Marie (*Soo* or *Sō Saint Ma-ree'*), Ontario.
Sca'fell (*a=aw*), mountain, Cumberland.
Scilly, islands, Cornwall.
Scone (*Scoon*), Perthshire.
Slough, Buckinghamshire.
So'lent (*o=ō*), strait, Hampshire.
South'wark, London.
Stel'len-bosch (*bosch=bŏs* or *bōosh*), Cape Province.
Stran-raer' (*ae=ah*), Wigtownshire.
Teignmouth (*Tin'muth* or *Tain'muth*), Devon.
Tin-tag'el (*g=j*), Cornwall.
Tor-quay' (*quay=kee*), Devon.
Uttoxeter (*Uks'e-ter*), Staffordshire.
Will'es-den, London.
Wis'bech (*Wiz'beech*), Cambridgeshire.
Worcester (*Woos'ter*), England; Cape Province.
Wymondham (*Wind'am*), Norfolk.
Yeo'vil, Somersetshire.
Youghal (*Yawl*), Eire.

FORMS OF ADDRESS

Ambassador.—His Excellency ——. Begin letters " My Lord " or " Sir " according to his rank.

Archbishop.—His Grace the Lord Archbishop of ——. Begin letters " My Lord Archbishop."

Archdeacon.—The Venerable the Archdeacon of ——. Begin letters " Venerable Sir " or " Reverend Sir."

Baron.—The Right Honourable Lord ——. Begin letters " My Lord."

Baronet.—Sir X—— Y——, Bart. Begin letters " Sir."

Bishop.—The Right Reverend the Lord Bishop of ——. Begin letters " My Lord Bishop."

Cardinal.—His Eminence Cardinal ——. Begin letters " Your Eminence " or " Most Eminent and Most Reverend Sir."

Clergyman.—Rev. B—— C——. Begin letters " Rev. Sir " or " Sir."

Dean.—The Very Rev. the Dean of ——. Begin letters " Very Rev. Sir."

Doctor (D.D., LL.D., D.Sc., M.D., etc.).— Rev. A. B——, D.D., A. B——, Esq., LL.D. (D.Sc., M.D., etc.).

Duke.—His Grace the Duke of ——. Begin letters " My Lord Duke." A duke's wife is Her Grace the **Duchess** of ——. Begin letters " Madam."

Earl.—The Right Hon. the Earl of —— or The Earl of ——. Begin letters " My Lord."

Governor of a Colony.—His Excellency (usual designation), Governor of ——. Begin according to rank.

Governor, Lieutenant.—The Honourable —— Lieutenant Governor of. Begin according to rank.

King or Queen.—The King's (or (Queen's Most Excellent Majesty. Begin letters " Sire " (or " Madam "), or " May it please Your Majesty."

Knight.—Sir S—— F—— and initials indicating order, if any, as K.C.B. Begin letters " Sir."

Lord Mayor (of London, York, or Dublin). —The Right Hon. the Lord Mayor of ——. Begin letters " My Lord."

Lord Provost.—The Right Hon. the Lord Provost of Edinburgh, or Glasgow. The Lord Provost of Aberdeen, Perth, or Dundee.

Marquis.—The Most Hon. (or Noble) the Marquis of ——. Begin letters " My Lord Marquis."

Mayor.—The Right Worshipful the Mayor of ——. Begin letters " Sir."

Moderator of General Assembly of Church of Scotland.—The Right Rev. B—— C——.

Pope.—His Holiness the Pope. Begin letters " Most Holy Father."

President of the U.S.A.—The President, White House, or His Excellency the President of the U.S.A. Begin letters " Mr President " or " Sir."

Prince or Royal Duke.—His Royal Highness the Prince of —— or His Royal Highness the Duke of ——. Begin letters " Sir."

Princess or Royal Duchess.—Her Royal Highness the Princess of —— or Her Royal Highness the Duchess of ——. Begin letters " Madam."

Privy Councillors.—Right Honourable.

Secretary of State.—The Right Hon.——, (or according to rank) His Majesty's Principal Secretary of State for —— (department). Begin letters according to his rank.

Viscount.—The Right Hon. the Lord Viscount. Begin letters " My Lord."

ROMAN NUMERALS

I, II, III, IV or IIII, V, VI, VII, VIII, IX, X, XI, XII, XIII, XIV, XV, XVI, XVII, XVIII, XIX, XX, XXI, XXII, XXIII, XXIV, XXV, XXVI, XXVII, XXVIII, XXIX, XXX=30, XL=40, L=50, LX=60, LXX=70, LXXX=80, XC=90, C=100, CX=110, CC=200, CCC=300, CCCC=400, D=500, DC=600, DCC=700, DCCC=800, DCCCC=900, M=1000, MDCCCL=1850, MCMXIV=1914, MCMXLIX=1949.

MATHEMATICAL SIGNS

+ increased by, − diminished by, × multiplied by, ÷ divided by.

~ the difference between two quantities.

= equal to.

> is greater than ; < is less than.

∵ because ; ∴ therefore.

², ³, ⁴, the second, third, and fourth powers.

√, ∛, ∜, square root, cube root, fourth root.

‖ parallel to ; ⊥ perpendicular to.

π (Greek letter *pi*), the ratio of the circumference of a circle to its diameter=3·1415926 . . .

WEIGHTS AND MEASURES

AVOIRDUPOIS WEIGHT

16 drams=1 ounce (oz.), (437½ grs.).
16 oz.   =1 pound (lb.).
14 lb.   =1 stone.

28 lb. =1 quarter.
4 qr. =1 hundredweight (cwt.).
20 cwt.=1 ton.

TROY WEIGHT

(*For Gold and Silver*)

The ounce is the unit.
For a less quantity decimal parts are employed.
For a larger, multiples of an ounce.

(*For Precious Stones*)

The metric carat of 200 millegrammes is the legal standard of weight.

APOTHECARIES' WEIGHT
(*Prior to* 1864)

20 grains =1 scruple.
3 scruples=1 drachm.

8 drachms=1 ounce (480 grs.).
12 ounces =1 lb.

(*Since* 1864)

437½ grains =1 ounce.

16 ounces =1 lb.

APOTHECARIES' FLUID MEASURE

60 minims =1 drachm.
8 drachms =1 ounce.

20 ounces =1 pint.
8 pints =1 gallon.

Large Bottles in Drug Trade

40 ounces =1 quart (or corbyn).

80 ounces =½ gallon (or Winchester quart).

Approximate Measures

1 drop   =1 minim.
1 " tea-spoon "=⅛ fluid ounce.

1 " dessert-spoon "=½ fluid ounce.
1 " table-spoon " =½ ,,   ,,

The Apothecaries' *drachm* and the Avordupois *dram* are not the same. A fluid *drachm* (54·688 grs.) is equal in weight to two Avoirdupois *drams*.
An ounce of distilled water at 62° F. is equal in weight to the Avoirdupois ounce (437½ grs.).

LONG MEASURE

12 inches=1 foot.
3 ft.   =1 yard.
5½ yd.   =1 rod, perch, or pole.

40 poles=1 furlong.
8 fur. =1 mile.
3 ml. =1 league.

SURVEYORS' MEASURE (LINEAL)

7·92 inches   =1 link.
100 links, or 22 yards=1 chain.

10 chains=1 furlong.
80   ,,   =1 mile.

NAUTICAL MEASURE

6 feet =1 fathom.
607·56 ft. =1 cable.

10 cables=1 nautical (sea) mile.
60 nautical or geographical miles= 1 degree.

A knot is a unit of speed representing "one nautical mile per hour." A ship doing so many *knots*, means going so many *miles per hour*.

SQUARE MEASURE

144 square inhes=1 sq. foot.
9 sq. ft.   =1 sq. yard.
30¼ sq. yd.   =1 sq. pole.
40 sq. pl.   =1 rood.

4 ro.=4840 sq. yd.=10 sq. chains
1 acre.
640 acres=1 sq. mile.

SURVEYORS' MEASURE (SQUARE)

144 square inches=2·2958 sq. links.	10,000 sq. links=1 sq. chain.
20·662 sq. links =1 sq. yard.	25,000 sq. ,, =1 rood.
625 sq. ,, =1 sq. pole.	100,000 sq. ,, =1 acre.

CUBIC MEASURE

1728 cubic metres=1 cub. foot.	40 cub. ft.=1 load of rough timber.
27 cub. ft. =1 cub. yard.	50 cub. ft.=1 load of squared timber.

MEASURE OF CAPACITY

4 gills =1 pint.	4 pecks=1 bushel.
2 pt. =1 quart.	8 bus. =1 quarter.
4 qt. =1 gallon.	36 bus. =1 chaldron.
2 gall. =1 peck.	

The bushel varies locally and with the article measured, and is reckoned by weight. See under *Miscellaneous Weights and Measures.*

COTTON YARN

120 yards =1 lea or skein.	18 hanks=1 spindle.
7 skeins=1 hank.	Count =number of hanks in 1 lb.

LINEN YARN

300 yards=1 cut, hank, or lea.	4 hasps=1 spindle.
2 cuts =1 heer.	Count=number of hanks in 1 lb.
6 heers =1 hasp.	

WORKED YARN

80 yards =1 wrap.	Count=number of hanks
7 wraps=1 hank.	in 1 lb.

SIZES OF BARRELS

Firkin or Quarter Barrel	=	9 gallons.	Pipe (of *Madeira* or *Cape*)	=	92 gallons.
Kilderkin, Rundlet, or ½ Barrel	=	18 ,,	,, (of *Sherry* or *Tent*)	=108 ,,	
Barrel	=	36 ,,	Butt (of *Lisbon* or *Bucellas*)	=117 ,,	
Hogshead (1½ Barrels)	=	54 ,,	Aum (of *Hock* or *Rhenish*)	=	30 ,,
Puncheon (2 Barrels)	=	72 ,,	Hogshead (of *Brandy*)	=	60 ,,
Butt of Ale (3 Barrels)	=108 ,,		,, (of *Claret*)	=	46 ,,
Anker	=	10 ,,	,, (of *Port*)	=	57 ,,
Tierce	=	42 ,,	,, (of *Sherry*)	=	54 ,,
Pipe (of *Port* or *Masdew*)	=115 ,,		,, (of *Madeira*)	=	46 ,,
,, (of *Teneriffe*)	=100 ,,		Puncheon (of *Brandy* or *Rum*)	=120 ,,	
,, (of *Marsala*)	=	93 ,,			

SHIP MEASUREMENT

Gross tonnage, the total in cubic feet of all enclosed spaces of a vessel, divided by 100.

Nett tonnage, the total in cubic feet of spaces used for cargo or passengers, divided by 100.

PAPER MEASURE

Writing Paper

24 sheets=1 quire.	20 quires= 1 ream.

Printing Paper

25 sheets=1 quire.	2 reams =1 bundle.
516 ,, =1 ream.	5 bundles =1 bale.

SIZES OF BOOKS

(8vo = Octavo; 4to = Quarto)

Foolscap 8vo	$6\frac{3}{4} \times 4\frac{1}{4}$ inches.		Crown 4to	$10 \times 7\frac{1}{2}$ inches.
Crown 8vo	$7\frac{1}{2} \times 5$,,		Demy 4to	$11\frac{1}{4} \times 8\frac{3}{4}$,,
Demy 8vo	$8\frac{3}{8} \times 5\frac{5}{8}$,,		Crown Folio	15×10 ,,
Royal 8vo	$10 \times 6\frac{1}{4}$,,		Royal Folio	$20 \times 12\frac{1}{2}$,,
Imperial 8vo	$11 \times 7\frac{1}{2}$,,			

SOME OLD MEASURES

Cubit	= 18 inches.		Roman Mile	= 1614 yards.
English Ell	= 45 ,,		Roman Pace	= 5 feet.
Scottish Ell	= 37·2 ,,		Hide	= 120 acres (average).
Hand	= 4 ,,		Virgate or Yard of Land	= $\frac{1}{4}$ of a hide.
Scottish Mile	= 1984 yards.		Carucate	= 180 to 200 acres.
Irish Mile	= 2240 ,,		Boll (generally)	= 6 bushels.

MISCELLANEOUS WEIGHTS AND MEASURES

Bag of cocoa		112 lbs.
,, coffee		140 to 168 lbs.
,, hops		280 lbs.
,, pepper (black)		316 ,,
,, ,, (white)		168 ,,
,, rice		168 ,,
,, sago		112 ,,
,, sugar		112 to 196 lbs.
Bale of cotton (Egyptian)		700 ,, 740 ,,
,, ,, (Indian)		500 ,, 600 ,,
,, ,, (United States)		400 ,, 500 ,,
Bar (mint) of gold		400 ozs. Troy.
,, ,, silver		1000 to 1100 ozs. Troy.
Barrel of anchovies		30 lbs.
,, beef		200 ,,
,, butter		4 firkins or 224 lbs.
,, flour (United States)		196 lbs.
,, gunpowder		100 ,,
,, herrings (cured), Scotland		26$\frac{3}{4}$ gallons.
,, raisins		112 lbs.
,, soft soap		256 ,,
Bushel (English) of barley		56 ,,
,, (French) ,,		52$\frac{1}{2}$,,
,, of coal		80 ,,
,, (English) of oats		39 ,,
,, (Foreign) ,,		38 and 40 lbs.
,, of rye		60 lbs.
,, (English) of wheat		60 ,,
,, (Foreign) ,,		62 ,,
Chaldron of coal		85 bushels.
Chest of cloves		200 lbs.
,, tea		84 ,,
Code of herrings		500 herrings.
Cord of wood		128 cubic feet.
Cran (mainly Scotland) of herrings		37$\frac{1}{2}$ gallons.
Firkin of soft soap		64 lbs.
Hogshead of sugar		13 to 16 cwt.
,, tobacco		12 ,, 18 ,,
Last of herrings		13,200 herrings.
,, hides		12 dozen.
,, wool		12 sacks.
Load of hay		36 trusses.
,, straw		36 ,,
Long hundred of herrings		33 warps or 132 herrings.
Matt of cloves		80 lbs.
Maze (Isle of Man and Ireland) of herrings		615 herrings.
Mease of herrings		600 ,,

Pack of soft soap	. . . .	256 lbs.
Peck of flour	. . . . . .	14 ,,
Pig of ballast	. . . . . .	56 ,,
Pocket of hops	. . . . . .	168 to 224 lbs.
Quarter (English) of wheat	. . . .	480 lbs.
Quintal (Newfoundland, etc.), of fish	. .	100 and 112 lbs.
Sack of coal	. . . . . .	224 lbs. or 2 cwt.
,, flour	. . . . . .	280 lbs.
,, potatoes	. . . . .	168 ,,
,, wool	. . . . .	364 ,,
Seam of glass	. . . . . .	120 ,,
Square of flooring	. . . . .	100 square feet
Stack of wood	. . . . . .	108 cubic feet
Stone of meat	. . . . . .	8 lbs.
Ten hundred (one thousand) herrings	. .	1320 herrings.
Ten thousand herrings	. . . .	13,200 ,,
Ton of coal	. . . . .	10 sacks or 28 bus.
,, hay	. . . . .	36 trusses.
Truss (new, *i.e.* up to 1st Sept.) of hay	. .	60 lbs.
,, (old) of hay	. . . . .	56 ,,
,, of straw	. . . . .	36 ,,
Warp of herrings	. . . . . .	4 herrings.

METRIC SYSTEM OF WEIGHTS AND MEASURES

MEASURE OF LENGTH

Myriametre	=10,000 metres	=6·2138 miles.	
Kilometre	= 1000 ,,	=0·62137 mile, or 3280 ft. 10 in.	
Hectometre	= 100 ,,	=328 ft. 1 in.	
Dekametre	= 10 ,,	=32 ft. 9·7 in.	
Metre	. . . .	=3 ft. 3·37 in.	
Decimetre	= 0·1 metre	=3·937 in.	
Centimetre	= 0·01 ,,	=0·3937 in.	
Millimetre	= 0·001 ,,	=0·03937 in.	

MEASURE OF SURFACE

Hectare	=10,000 sq. metres	=2·471 acres.
Are	= 100 ,,	=119·6 sq. yds.
Centare	= 1 ,,	=10 sq. ft. 110 sq. in.

MEASURE OF CAPACITY

		Liquid Measure.	Dry Measure.
Kilolitre or Stere	=1000 litres	=219·975 gals.	=27 bush. 2 pks.
Hectolitre	= 100 ,,	= 21·998 ,,	= 2 bush. 3 pks.
Dekalitre	= 10 ,,	= 2·200 ,,	= 1 pk. 0·8 qt.
Litre	. . . .	=1·760 pt.	
Decilitre	= 0·1 litre	=0·176 pt.	
Centilitre	= 0·01 ,,	=0·018 pt.	
Millilitre	= 0·001 ,,	=0·002 pt.	

WEIGHT

Millier or Tonneau	=1,000,000 grams	=19 cwts. 76·6 lbs.
Quintal	= 100,000 ,,	=1 cwt. 108·46 lbs.
Myriagram	= 10,000 ,,	=22·046 lbs.
Kilogram or Kilo	= 1,000 ,,	= 2·2046 lbs.
Hectogram	= 100 ,,	= 3·5274 oz.
Dekagram	= 10 ,,	= 0·3527 oz.
Gram	. . . .	= 0·0353 oz.
Decigram	= 0·1 gram	= 0·0035 oz.
Centigram	= 0·01 ,,	= 0·0004 oz.
Milligram	= 0·001 ,,	

SOME COMMON WEIGHTS AND MEASURES WITH THEIR METRIC EQUIVALENTS

1 mile =1·6093 kilometre.	1 cub. ft. =0·02832 cub. metre.
1 yard =0·9144 metre.	1 cub. in. =16·39 cub. centimetres.
1 foot =0·3048 metre.	1 bushel =36·37 litres.
1 inch =2·54 centimetres.	1 peck =9·092 litres.
1 sq. mile =259 hectares.	1 dry qt. =1·101 litre.
1 acre =0·4047 hectare.	1 gal. =4·546 litres.
1 sq. yd. =0·8361 sq. metre.	1 liquid qt.=1·136 litres.
1 sq. ft. =0·0929 sq. metre.	1 ton =1016 kilograms.
1 sq. inch=6·452 sq. centimetres.	1 lb. =0·4536 kilogram.
1 cub. yd.=0·7646 cub. metre.	1 oz. =28·35 grammes.

MONEY OF OTHER COUNTRIES AND ITS APPROXIMATE VALUE[1]

IN BRITISH DOMINIONS

	Monetary Unit	*Value*	*Value of £1 stg.*
Australia	**£ stg.**	..	**£1, 5s.**
Br. Honduras	**Dollar**	**4s. 1¼d. (par)**	..
Canada	**Dollar**	**4s. 3d.**	**19s. 4d.**
Ceylon	**Rupee**	**1s. 6d.**	**£1.**
Cyprus	**Piastre**	**1⅓d. (par)***	..
Hongkong	**Dollar**	**1s. 3d.†**	**£1, 2s. 8d.**
India	**Rupee**	**1s. 6d.**	**£1.**
Mauritius	**Rupee**	**1s. 6d. (par)**	..
Newfoundland	**Dollar**	**4s. 1¼d. (par)**	..
New Zealand	**£ stg.**	..	**£1, 4s. 9·6d.**
Palestine	**£ Palestine**	**(par)**	**£1.**
Straits Settlements	**Dollar**	**2s. 4d.**	**£1.**
Sudan	**£ Egyptian**	**£1, 0s. 6½d. (par)**	..
Union of South Africa	**£ stg.**	..	**£1, 0s. 0·3d.**

The following British Dependencies also have Imperial Sterling Coinage :—East Africa, Channel Islands, Gibraltar, St. Helena, British West Africa, British West Indies, British Guiana, Falkland Islands, Fiji Islands.

* **The par or nominal value is given where the actual or day-to-day value is not available.**

† **Varies with the price of silver.**

IN EUROPE

Belgium	**Belga**	8·1d.	**16s. 11d.**
Bulgaria	**Leva**	½d.	**12s.**
Czecho-Slovakia	**Krone**	1¾d.	**17s. 5d.**
Danzig	**Gulden**	9¼d.	**£1, 0s. 9¾d.**
Denmark	**Krone**	11d.	**£1, 4s. 8d.**
Estonia	**Kroon**	1s. 1½d.	**19s. 7d.**
Finland	**Markka**	1d.	**£1, 3s. 4d.**
France	**Franc**	1¾d.	£1, 8s. 6d.
Germany	**Reichsmark**	1s. 7d.	12s. 1½d.
Greece	**Drachma**	½d.	**£1, 9s. 2½d.**
Hungary	**Pengo**	9½d.	**18s.**
Italy	**Lira**	2½d.	**£1, 0s. 5¾d.**
Latvia	**Lat**	9½d.	**19s. 7d.**
Lithuania	**Lita**	8½d.	**11s. 11d.**

[1] The rates quoted are those obtaining before the Second World War.

	Monetary Unit	Value	Value of £1 stg.
Luxembourg	Franc	1·37d. (par)	..
Netherlands	Florin	2s. 2½d.	14s. 11¼d.
Norway	Krone	1s. 0d.	£1, 1s. 11d.
Poland	Zloty	9¼d.	12s.
Portugal	Escudo	2¼d.	£1, 0s. 0½d.
Rumania	Leu	⅛d.	16s. 5¼d.
Russia	Rouble	9d.	..
Spain	Peseta	5¾d.	£1, 13s. 4d.
Sweden	Krone	1s. 0¼d.	£1, 1s. 4½d.
Switzerland	Franc	11d.	17s. 2½d.
Turkey	Piastre	½d.	£5, 12s. 0d.
Yugoslavia	Dinar	1d.	15s. 7d.

IN OTHER COUNTRIES

Algeria	Same as France.		
Argentina	Peso	1s. 2½d.	£1, 8s. 8¾d.
Belgian Congo	Same as Belgium.		
Bolivia	Boliviano	2d.	£9, 4s. 0d.
Brazil	Milreis	2½d.	£2, 6s. 0d.
Chile	Peso	2d.	£2, 18s. 0d.
China	Dollar	1s. 2⅓d. (par) *	..
Colombia	Peso	2s. 3d.	£1, 15s. 8d.
Costa Rica	Colon	1s. 11d. (par)	..
Cuba	Peso	4s. 1⅓d. (par)	..
Ecuador	Sucré	3¼d.	£2, 18s. 3d.
Egypt	£ Egyptian	..	19s. 11¾d.
Guatemala	Quetzal	3s. 11d.	£1, 1s. 0d.
Haiti	Gourde	9⅝d. (par)	..
Iran	Rial	2·4d. (par)	..
Iraq	Dinar	£1 (par)	..
Japan	Yen	1s. 2d.	£1, 15s. 0d.
Korea	Same as Japan.		
Liberia	British and U.S. currency.		
Mexico	Peso	1s. 1¼d.	£1, 16s. 10d.
Nicaragua	Cordoba	8¾d.	£5, 11s. 0d.
Panama	Balboa	4s. 2d. (par)	..
Paraguay	Peso	4s. (par)	..
Peru	Sol	1s. 0½d.	£1, 2s. 0d.
Salvador	Colon	1s. 6⅝d.	£1, 6s. 1½d.
Siam (Thailand)	Baht	1s. 10¼d.	19s. 8d.
U.S.A.	Dollar	4s. 0¼d.	£1, 0s. 6d.
Uruguay	Peso	3s. 4d.	£1, 6s. 1½d.
Venezuela	Bolivar	1s.	15s. 9½d.

* **Varies according to price of silver.**

RAILWAY GAUGES

(The gauge is the inside measurement between the rails.)

Standard Gauge, 4 ft. 8½ in., is used mostly in Great Britain, France, Belgium, Netherlands, Denmark, Sweden, Germany, Austria, Hungary, Switzerland, Italy, European Turkey, Canada, and U.S.A.

Narrow Gauge is any gauge less than 4 ft. 8½ ins. *E.g.*, a 3 ft. 6 in. gauge is used in Queensland, Western Australia, New South Wales (also 4 ft. 8½ in.), New Zealand, South Africa, Egypt (also 4 ft. 8½ in.), Japan; a 3 ft. 5½ in. gauge is used in Asia Minor (also 4 ft. 8½ in.); a 2 ft. 6 in. and a 3 ft. 3⅜ in. gauge are used in India (also 5 ft 6 in.).

Broad Gauge is any gauge more than 4 ft. 8½ in. *E.g.*, a 5 ft. gauge is used in Russia, a 5 ft. 3 in. gauge in Ireland, Victoria, and New South Wales, and a 5 ft. 6 in. gauge in India, Ceylon, Spain, and Portugal.

FOR SUPPLEMENTARY NOTES

FOR SUPPLEMENTARY NOTES

Printed in Great Britain by T. and A. CONSTABLE LTD., Edinburgh.

30-10-I